Beyond Our Borders

Landmark in the Legal Environment

Seventh Edition

The Legal Environment Today

Business in Its Ethical, Regulatory, E-Commerce, and Global Setting

Roger LeRoy Miller
Institute for University Studies
Arlington, Texas

Frank B. Cross
Herbert D. Kelleher
Centennial Professor in Business Law
University of Texas at Austin

(John Elk III/Lonely Planet Images/Getty Images)

SOUTH-WESTERN
CENGAGE Learning·

Australia · Brazil · Japan · Korea · Mexico · Singapore · Spain · United Kingdom · United States

SOUTH-WESTERN
CENGAGE Learning·

The Legal Environment Today
Business in Its Ethical, Regulatory, E-Commerce, and Global Setting

SEVENTH EDITION

Roger LeRoy Miller
Frank B. Cross

Vice President and Editorial Director:
Jack Calhoun

Editor-in-Chief:
Rob Dewey

Senior Acquisitions Editor:
Vicky True-Baker

Senior Developmental Editor:
Jan Lamar

Executive Marketing Manager:
Lisa L. Lysne

Marketing Manager:
Laura-Aurora Stopa

Senior Marketing Communications Manager:
Sarah Greber

Production Manager:
Bill Stryker

Technology Project Manager:
Kristen Meere

Manufacturing Planner:
Kevin Kluck

Editorial Assistant:
Ben Genise

Compositor:
Parkwood Composition Service

Senior Art Director:
Michelle Kunkler

Internal Designer:
Bill Stryker

Cover Designer:
Rokusek Design

Cover Images:
© Olaru Radian-Alexandru/Shutterstock;
© R. Gino Santa Maria/Shutterstock;
© Kuzma/Shutterstock

Library of Congress Control Number: 2011940273

ISBN-13: 978-1-111-53061-7
ISBN-10: 1-111-53061-0

South-Western Cengage Learning
5191 Natorp Blvd.
Mason, OH 45040
USA

Cengage Learning products are represented in Canada by Nelson Education, Ltd.

For your course and learning solutions, visit **www.cengage.com**.

Purchase any of our products at your local college store or at our preferred online store at **www.cengagebrain.com**.

Printed in Canada
1 2 3 4 5 6 7 15 14 13 12 11

Contents in Brief

▶ *Appendices*

Contents*

*Consult the inside front and back covers of this book for easy reference to the many special features in this textbook.

Unit One

The Foundations 1

Unit Two

The Commerical Environment 205

Appendices

It is no exaggeration to say that today's legal environment is changing at a pace never before experienced. In many instances, technology is both driving and facilitating this change. The expanded use of the Internet for both business and personal transactions has led to new ways of doing business and, consequently, to a changing legal environment for the twenty-first century. Other factors that have affected the legal environment include the recent economic recession and our nation's ongoing struggle to regain financial stability, combat joblessness, and reduce the national debt. In the midst of this evolving environment, however, one thing remains certain: For those entering the business world, an awareness of the legal and regulatory environment of business is critical.

The Seventh Edition of *The Legal Environment Today: Business in Its Ethical, Regulatory, E-Commerce, and Global Setting* is designed to bring this awareness to your students. They will learn not only about the traditional legal environment but also about some of the most significant recent developments in the e-commerce environment. They will also be motivated to learn through our use of high-interest pedagogical features that explore real-life situations and legal challenges facing businesspersons and consumers. We believe that teaching the legal environment can be enjoyable and so, too, can learning about it.

What's New in the Seventh Edition

Instructors have come to rely on the coverage, accuracy, and applicability of *The Legal Environment Today.* To make sure that our text engages your students' interest, solidifies their understanding of the legal concepts presented, and provides the best teaching tools available, we now offer the following items either in the text or in conjunction with the text.

New Chapter on Mortgages and Foreclosures after the Recession

For the Seventh Edition, we have included an entirely new chapter (Chapter 13) entitled **Mortgages and Foreclosures after the Recession.** This chapter examines some of the mortgage-lending practices that contributed to the Great Recession and discusses the legal reforms enacted in response to it.

New Highlighted and Numbered Case Examples

One of the more appreciated features of *The Legal Environment Today* has always been the highlighted numbered examples in each chapter that clarify legal principles for students. Because many instructors use cases to illustrate how the law applies to business, for this edition, rather than presenting more excerpted cases in each chapter, we have expanded the in-text numbered examples to include **Case Examples.** These *Case Examples* are integrated appropriately throughout the text and present the facts, issues, and rulings from actual court cases. Students can quickly read through the *Case Examples* to see how courts apply the legal principles under discussion in the real world.

New Cases and Case Problems

The Seventh Edition of *The Legal Environment Today* is filled with new cases and problems. We have included new cases from 2010 and 2011 in every chapter. That means more than 75 percent of the cases are new to this edition. We have carefully selected the new cases using the criteria that (1) they illustrate important points of law, (2) they are of high-interest to students and instructors, and (3) they are simple enough factually for legal environment students to understand. We have made it a point to find recent cases that enhance learning. We have also eliminated cases that are too difficult procedurally or factually.

New *Linking the Law to* . . . Features

For the Seventh Edition of *The Legal Environment Today,* we have added a **special new feature entitled *Linking the Law to* . . . [Accounting, Economics, Management, Marketing, or Taxation].** This special feature appears in selected chapters to underscore how the law relates to various other disciplines in the typical business school curriculum. It not only enables instructors to meet AACSB teaching requirements but also provides vital and practical information to students on how the subjects they study are interconnected. In addition, each feature concludes with a *For Critical Analysis* question designed to encourage students to engage in critical thinking and to consider the implications of the topic under discussion. Some examples of the *Linking the Law to* . . . feature include:

- *Linking the Law to Managerial Accounting:* Managing a Company's Reputation (Chapter 2).
- *Linking the Law to Marketing:* Going Global (Chapter 7).
- *Linking the Law to Marketing:* Trademarks and Service Marks (Chapter 8).
- *Linking the Law to Management:* Quality Control (Chapter 11).
- *Linking the Law to Management:* Human Resource Management Comes to the Fore (Chapter 18).

New Coverage of Hot Topics

To pique student interest from the outset, many chapters open with the latest news surrounding the legal topics under discussion. A section of text within that chapter further explores the topic. For example, Chapter 8 discusses the patent infringement lawsuit filed by Apple, Inc., against Samsung for too closely imitating the iPhone and iPad. Chapter 13 discusses the $20 million settlement paid by Bank of America in 2011 for fraud relating to mortgage securities. The employment and labor law chapters (Chapters 17 and 18) include a discussion of the recently settled NFL lockout, as well as the United States Supreme Court's 2011 decision in a gender-discrimination case against Wal-Mart.

New *Video Questions*

In response to popular demand, we have created several new **Video Questions** for this edition. These questions refer students to the text's Web site to view a particular video clip before answering a series of questions in the book. Some of the new videos are clips from actual movies or television series, such as *Field of Dreams, Midnight Run,* and *Mary Tyler Moore.*

New *Managerial Implications*

We have devised a special new item of case pedagogy for this edition. At the end of selected cases that have particular importance for business managers, we have included a new section entitled **Managerial Implications.** These sections point out the significance of the court's ruling in the case for business owners and managers.

New *ExamPrep* Sections

In every chapter, we have added a new **ExamPrep section** that includes two **Issue Spotters.** These *Issue Spotters* facilitate student learning and review of the chapter materials. In addition, the section refers students to Appendix G for the answers to the Issue Spotters. The *Before the Test* portion of this section refers students to the text's Web site for additional study tools, such as Flashcards and Interactive Quizzes correlated to the chapter.

▶ Practical and Effective Learning Tools

Today's business leaders must often think "outside the box" when making business decisions. For this reason, we have included numerous critical-thinking elements in the Seventh Edition that are designed to challenge students' understanding of the materials beyond simple retention. In addition, we have retained and improved the many practical features of this text to help students learn how the law applies to business. (We have also added new *Linking the Law to . . .* features and the *Managerial Implications* sections, as mentioned, both of which provide practical guidance for students entering the business world.)

Critical-Thinking and Legal Reasoning Elements

Your students will hone their critical-thinking and legal reasoning skills as they work through the numerous pedagogical devices throughout this edition. Most of the features in this text (including *Beyond Our Borders, Insight into Ethics, Linking the Law to . . . ,* and *Online Developments*) conclude with a *For Critical Analysis* question.

In addition, for the Seventh Edition, we continue to offer two critical-thinking questions at the end of every case in the text (unless one question has been replaced with a special new *Managerial Implications* section, as discussed earlier). These case-ending questions include *What If the Facts Were Different?* and *Ethical, E-Commerce, Economic, Global,* and *Legal Environment Dimension* questions.

This emphasis on critical thinking is reiterated in the chapter-ending materials of selected chapters, which present special *Critical-Thinking [Managerial or Legal Environment] Questions.* **Suggested answers to these questions, as well as those in the features and following the cases, can be found in both the *Instructor's Manual* and the *Answers Manual* that accompany this text.**

Online Developments

The Seventh Edition contains many new **Online Developments** features, which examine cutting-edge cyberlaw issues coming before today's courts. Here are some examples:

- Should the Law Continue to Allow Business Process Patents? (Chapter 8).
- Economic Recession Fuels the "Amazon Tax" Debate (Chapter 15).
- Corporate Blogs and Tweets Must Comply with the Securities Exchange Act (Chapter 24).

As mentioned above, each feature concludes with a *For Critical Analysis* section that asks the student to think critically about some facet of the issues discussed in the feature.

Insight into Ethics

For the Seventh Edition, we have created many new **Insight into Ethics** features, which appear in selected chapters and examine the ethical implications of various topics. These features provide valuable insights into how the courts and the law are dealing with specific ethical issues. Each of these features ends with a critical-thinking question that explores some cultural, environmental, political, social, or technological aspect of the issue. The following are some of the topics explored in these features:

- Prosecuting White-Collar Crime with the Honest-Services Fraud Law (Chapter 6).
- How Much Information Must Employers Disclose to Prospective Employees? (Chapter 10).
- Warning Labels for Video Games (Chapter 11).
- Should Pharmaceutical Companies Be Allowed to Tweet? (Chapter 19).

Preventing Legal Disputes

We continue our emphasis on providing practical information through a special feature entitled **Preventing Legal Disputes.** These brief, integrated sections offer sensible guidance on steps that businesspersons can take in their daily transactions to avoid legal disputes and litigation in a particular area.

Management Perspective

Each **Management Perspective** feature begins with a section titled *Management Faces a Legal Issue,* which describes a practical issue facing management—such as whether employment contracts can be created and modified online. A section titled *What the Courts Say* comes next and discusses what the courts have concluded with respect to the specific issue. The feature concludes with *Implications for Managers*— a section that indicates the importance of the courts' decisions for business managers and offers some practical guidance. Some examples of these features include the following:

- E-Mailed Credit-Card Receipts (Chapter 9).
- Independent-Contractor Negligence (Chapter 16).
- The Online Creation and Modification of Employment Contracts (Chapter 17).

Beyond Our Borders

Beyond Our Borders features give students an awareness of the global legal environment by indicating how international laws or the laws of other nations deal with specific legal concepts or topics being discussed in the chapter. For example, *Beyond Our Borders* features discuss Islamic law courts (Chapter 3), sexual harassment (Chapter 18), and corporate governance (Chapter 24). Each feature concludes with a *For Critical Analysis* question.

Landmark in the Legal Environment

Landmark in the Legal Environment features discuss a landmark case, statute, or other legal development that has had a significant effect on the legal environment. Each of these features has a section titled *Application to Today's Legal Environment,* which indicates how the law discussed in the feature affects today's business world. For this edition, we have included a new *Landmark in the Legal Environment* feature in Chapter 15 that discusses the United States Supreme Court's decision in the 2010 case *Citizens United v. Federal Election Commission.*

Reviewing Features in Every Chapter

For the Seventh Edition of *The Legal Environment Today,* we continue to offer a *Reviewing* feature at the end of every chapter to help solidify students' understanding of the chapter materials. Each *Reviewing* feature presents a hypothetical scenario and then asks a series of questions that require students to identify the issues and apply the legal concepts discussed in the chapter. These features are designed to help students review the chapter topics in a simple and interesting way and see how the legal principles discussed in the chapter affect the world in which they live.

You can use these features as the basis for in-class discussion, or you can encourage students to use them for self-study prior to completing homework assignments. **Suggested answers to the questions posed in the *Reviewing* features can be found in both the *Instructor's Manual* and the *Answers Manual* that accompany this text.**

Improved Content and Features on CengageNOW for *The Legal Environment Today*

To help students learn how to identify and apply the legal principles they study in this text, we have created new content and improved the features of our Web-based product for this edition. The system provides interactive, automatically graded assignments for every chapter and unit in this text. For each of the twenty-four chapters, we have devised different categories of multiple-choice questions that stress different aspects of learning the chapter materials.

By using the optional **CengageNOW** system, students can complete the assignments from any location via the Internet and can receive instant feedback on why their answers to questions were incorrect or correct (if the instructor wishes to allow feedback). Instructors can customize the system to meet their own specifications and can track students' progress.

- **Chapter Review Questions**—The first set of ten to fifteen questions reviews the basic concepts and principles discussed in the chapter and may include questions based on the cases presented in the text.
- **Brief Hypotheticals**—The next group of seven to ten questions emphasizes spotting the issue and identifying the rule of law that applies in the context of a short factual scenario.
- **Legal Reasoning**—The third category includes five questions that require students to analyze the factual situation provided and apply the rules of law discussed in the chapter to arrive at an answer.
- **IRAC Case Analysis**—The next set of four questions requires students to perform all the basic elements of legal reasoning (identify the *issue,* determine the *rule* of law, *apply* the rule to the facts presented, and arrive at a *conclusion*). These questions are based on one of the case excerpts that appear in each chapter of the text.
- **Application and Analysis**—The final set of four questions is new and is linked to the *Reviewing* features (discussed previously) that appear in every chapter of the text. The student is required to read through the hypothetical scenario, analyze the facts presented, identify the issues in dispute, and apply the rules discussed in the chapter to answer the questions.

- **Essay Questions**—In addition to the multiple-choice questions available on CengageNOW, we now also provide essay questions that allow students to compose and submit essays online. Students' essays are automatically recorded to the gradebook, which permits instructors to quickly and easily evaluate the essays and record grades.
- **Video Questions**—CengageNOW also now includes links to the Digital Video Library for *The Legal Environment Today* so that students can access and view the video clips and answer questions related to the topics in the chapter.
- **Cumulative Questions for Each Unit**—In addition to the questions relating to each chapter, the CengageNOW system provides a set of cumulative questions, entitled "Synthesizing Legal Concepts," for each of the four units in the text.
- **Additional Advantages of CengageNOW**—Instructors can utilize the system to upload their course syllabi, create and customize homework assignments, keep track of their students' progress, communicate with their students about assignments and due dates, and create reports summarizing the data for an individual student or for the whole class.

More on the Sarbanes-Oxley Act of 2002

In a number of places in this text, we discuss the Sarbanes-Oxley Act of 2002 and the corporate scandals that led to the passage of that legislation. For example, Chapter 2 contains a section examining the requirements of the Sarbanes-Oxley Act relating to confidential reporting systems. In Chapter 24, we discuss this act in the context of securities law and present an exhibit (Exhibit 24–4) containing some of the key provisions of the act relating to corporate accountability with respect to securities transactions. We also discuss corporate governance issues in Chapter 24.

Because the act is a topic of significant concern in today's business climate, we also include **excerpts and explanatory comments on the Sarbanes-Oxley Act of 2002 as Appendix D.** Students and instructors alike will find it useful to have the provisions of the act immediately available for reference.

CourseMate

CourseMate, which can be purchased for an additional fee, brings this text's legal environment concepts to life with interactive learning, study, and exam preparation tools. Built-in engagement tracking tools allow you to assess the study activities of your students. Additionally, CourseMate includes an interactive online textbook, which contains the complete content of this printed textbook enhanced by the many advantages of a digital environment. Access to the Digital Video Library is included with CourseMate.

The Legal Environment Today on the Web

When you visit our Web site at **www.cengagebrain.com**, you will find a broad array of teaching/learning resources for this text, including the following:

- *Interactive Quizzes* for every chapter.
- *Flashcards* for every chapter.
- *Answers to Issue Spotters* for every chapter (also available in Appendix G).
- *Glossary Terms.*
- *Legal Reference Materials,* including a statutes page that offers links to the full text of selected statutes referenced in the text, a Spanish glossary, and links to other important legal resources available free on the Web.

- A link to the Digital Video Library that allows students to view the videos referenced in the *Video Questions* in selected chapters for this edition.
- *Court Case Updates* (for instructors only) that present summaries of new cases from various legal publications, are continually updated, and are specifically keyed to chapters in this text.
- PowerPoint presentations (for instructors only) that have been revised for this edition.

A Dynamic Digital Video Library

The Legal Environment Today continues to include *Video Questions* at the end of selected chapters, including several new *Video Questions,* as mentioned earlier. Each of these questions directs students to the text's Web site to view a video relevant to a topic covered in the chapter. This is followed by a series of questions based on the video. An access code for the videos can be packaged with each new copy of this textbook for no additional charge. If Digital Video Library access did not come packaged with the textbook, students who would like to purchase it can do so online at **www.cengagebrain.com**.

These videos can be used for homework assignments, discussion starters, or classroom demonstrations and are useful for generating student interest. Some of the videos are clips from actual movies, such as *The Jerk* and *Field of Dreams.* By watching a video and answering the questions, students will gain an understanding of how the legal concepts they have studied in the chapter apply to the real-life situation portrayed in the video. **Suggested answers for all of the *Video Questions* are given in both the *Instructor's Manual* and the *Answers Manual* that accompany this text.** The videos are part of our Digital Video Library, a dynamic library of more than sixty-five video clips that spark class discussion and clarify core legal principles.

Case Presentation and Special Pedagogy

In addition to the components of *The Legal Environment Today* teaching/learning package, the Seventh Edition offers an effective case presentation and a number of special pedagogical devices, including those described next.

Case Presentation and Format

For this edition, we have carefully selected 2010 and 2011 cases for each chapter that not only provide on-point illustrations of the legal principles discussed in the chapter but also are of high interest to students. The cases are numbered sequentially for easy referencing in class discussions, homework assignments, and examinations. The vast majority of cases in this text are new to the Seventh Edition.

Each case is presented in a special format, which begins with the case title and citation (including parallel citations). We often include a URL, just below the case citation, that can be used to access the case online (a footnote to the URL explains how to find the specific case at that Web site). After briefly outlining the *Background and Facts* of the dispute, we present the court's reasoning *In the Words of the Court.* To enhance student understanding, we paraphrase the court's *Decision and Remedy.* We also provide bracketed definitions for any terms in the opinion that might be difficult for students to understand. As mentioned previously, each case normally concludes with two critical-thinking questions.

We give special emphasis to *Classic Cases* by setting them off with a special heading and logo. Each of these cases also includes an *Impact of This Case on Today's Legal Environment* section that stresses the significance of that particular decision for the evolution of the law in that area.

Cases may include one or more of the following sections:

• *Company Profiles*—Certain cases include a profile describing the history of the company involved to give students an awareness of the context of the case before the court. Some profiles include the URL for the company's Web site.

• *What If the Facts Were Different?*—One case in each chapter concludes with this special section. The student is asked to decide whether a specified change in the facts of the case would alter its outcome. **Suggested answers to these questions are included in both the *Instructor's Manual* and the *Answers Manual* that accompany this text.**

• *The Ethical [E-Commerce, Global, or Legal Environment] Dimension*—As discussed previously, these special new questions ask students to explore different aspects of the issues of the case and help instructors meet core curriculum requirements for business law. **Suggested answers to these questions are included in both the *Instructor's Manual* and the *Answers Manual* that accompany this text.**

• *Impact of This Case on Today's Legal Environment*—Because many students are unclear about how some of the older cases presented in this text affect today's court rulings, we include a special section at the end of classic cases that clarifies the relevance of the particular case to modern law.

Other Pedagogical Devices within Each Chapter

• *Chapter Objectives* (a series of brief questions at the beginning of each chapter provide a framework for the student as he or she reads through the chapter).
• *Contents* (an outline of the chapter's first-level headings).
• *Margin Definitions.*
• *Margin Quotations* (many of the quotations are new to this edition).
• *Exhibits.*
• *Photographs (with critical-thinking questions) and cartoons.*

Chapter-Ending Pedagogy

• *Key Terms* (with appropriate page references).
• *Chapter Summary* (in graphic format with page references).
• *ExamPrep* (including two new *Issue Spotters* for each chapter).
• *For Review* (the questions set forth in the *Chapter Objectives* section are presented again to aid the student in reviewing the chapter).
• *Questions and Case Problems* (which include a *Question with Sample Answer* in some chapters and a *Case Problem with Sample Answer* and *A Question of Ethics* in every chapter).
• *Critical-Thinking Legal Environment [Managerial] Questions* (in selected chapters).
• *Video Questions* (in selected chapters).

Unit-Ending Pedagogy—Cumulative Business Hypothetical

At the end of each unit is a **Cumulative Business Hypothetical.** This feature presents a hypothetical business situation and then asks a series of questions related to each chapter in the preceding unit. Students must analyze the facts, identify the issues, and apply the legal principles that they have learned throughout the unit. **Suggested answers to these questions are included in both the *Instructor's Manual* and the *Answers Manual* that accompany this text.**

▶ Supplemental Teaching Materials

This edition of *The Legal Environment Today* is accompanied by a vast number of teaching and learning supplements, including those listed next. For further information on the items contained in the teaching/learning package, contact your local sales representative or visit the Web site that accompanies this text at **www.cengagebrain.com**.

Each chapter of the *Instructor's Manual* contains teaching suggestions, discussion questions, and additional information on key statutes or other legal sources that you may wish to use in your classroom. These and numerous other supplementary materials (including printed and multimedia supplements) all contribute to the goal of making *The Legal Environment Today* the most flexible teaching/learning package on the market.

Printed Supplements

- *Instructor's Manual*—Includes additional cases on point with at least one case summary per chapter, answers to all *For Critical Analysis* questions in the features and all case-ending questions, and answers for the *Video Questions* at the end of selected chapters (also available on the Instructor's Resource CD-ROM [IRCD]).
- *Study Guide.*
- A comprehensive *Test Bank* (also available on the IRCD).
- *Answers Manual*—Includes answers to the *Questions and Case Problems*, the *For Critical Analysis* questions in the features, all case-ending questions, the *Video Questions* that conclude selected chapters, a set of alternate case problems, and the unit-ending *Cumulative Business Hypotheticals* (also available on the IRCD).

Software, Video, and Multimedia Supplements

- *Instructor's Resource CD-ROM* (**IRCD**)—The IRCD includes the following supplements: *Instructor's Manual, Answers Manual, Test Bank,* Case-Problem Cases, Case Printouts, PowerPoint slides, ExamView, *Handbook of Landmark Cases and Statutes in Business Law and the Legal Environment, A Guide to Personal Law, Handbook on Critical Thinking in Business Law and the Legal Environment,* transparencies, and *Instructor's Manual* for the *Drama of the Law* video series.
- **PowerPoint slides** (available only on the IRCD).
- **WebTutor™.**
- **Case Printouts**—Provides the full opinion of all cases presented in the text and referred to in selected features (available only on the IRCD).
- **Case-Problem Cases** (available only on the IRCD).
- **Westlaw®**—Ten free hours on Westlaw are available to qualified adopters.
- **Digital Video Library**—This dynamic video library features more than sixty-five video clips that spark class discussion and clarify core legal principles. Access is available for free as an optional package item with each new text. If Digital Video Library access did not come packaged with the textbook, your students can purchase it online at **www.cengagebrain.com**.
- *CourseMate*—Brings the legal environment of business concepts to life with interactive learning, study, and exam preparation tools that support this printed

textbook. Built-in engagement tracking tools allow you to assess your students' study activities. Additionally, CourseMate includes an interactive online textbook, which contains the entire contents of this printed textbook enhanced by the many advantages of a digital environment.

▶ Acknowledgments

Numerous careful and conscientious users of *The Legal Environment Today* were kind enough to help us revise the book. In addition, Cengage Learning went out of its way to make sure that this edition came out early and in accurate form. In particular, we wish to thank Rob Dewey and Vicky True-Baker for their countless new ideas, many of which have been incorporated into the Seventh Edition. Our production manager and designer, Bill Stryker, made sure that we came out with an error-free, visually attractive edition. We will always be in his debt. We also extend special thanks to Jan Lamar, our longtime developmental editor, for her many useful suggestions and for her efforts in coordinating reviews and ensuring the timely and accurate publication of all supplemental materials. We are particularly indebted to Laura-Aurora Stopa, our marketing manager, for her support and excellent marketing advice.

We must especially thank Katherine Marie Silsbee, who provided expert research, editing, and proofing services for this project. We wish to thank William Eric Hollowell, co-author of the *Instructor's Manual, Study Guide,* and *Test Bank,* for his excellent research efforts. The copyediting services of Pat Lewis and proofreading of Beverly Peavler and Lorretta Palagi will not go unnoticed. We also thank Vickie Reierson and Roxanna Lee for their proofreading and other assistance, and Suzanne Jasin for her many special efforts on the project. We are indebted to Parkwood Composition, our compositor. Its ability to generate the pages for this text quickly and accurately made it possible for us to meet our ambitious printing schedule.

Finally, numerous thorough and meticulous users of previous editions have been gracious enough to offer us their comments and suggestions on how to improve this text. We are particularly indebted to these reviewers, whom we list below. With their help, we have been able to make this book even more useful for professors and students alike.

Acknowledgments for the Seventh Edition

Martin D. Carrigan
The University of Findlay

Wade M. Chumney
Georgia Tech

Jeanne M. Gohl-Noice
Parkland College

Ruth Ann Hall
University of Alabama

Jeanette Rogers
Jefferson State Community College

Joyce Stoneking
Orange Coast College

Whitney Johnson
Saint Cloud State University

We also wish to extend special thanks to the following individuals for their contributions to the Seventh Edition, specifically for their valuable input for new Chapter 13 and for helping revise Chapter 22:

Robert C. Bird
University of Connecticut

Dean Bredeson
University of Texas at Austin

Corey Ciocchetti
University of Denver

Thomas D. Cavenagh
North Central College
Naperville, Illinois

Joan Gabel
Florida State University

Eric D. Yordy
Northern Arizona University

Acknowledgments for Previous Editions

Muhammad Abdullah
Pfeiffer University

Jane Bennett
Orange Coast College

Brent D. Clark
Davenport University

Richard L. Coffinberger
George Mason University

Teri Elkins
University of Houston

Teresa Gillespie
Seattle Pacific University

Gary Greene
Manatee Community College

Eloise Hassell
University of North Carolina,
Greensboro

Penelope L. Herickhoff
Mankato State University

Arlene M. Hibschweiler
University at Buffalo

James F. Kelley
Santa Clara University

Susan Key
University of Alabama at Birmingham

Karrin Klotz
University of Washington

Y. S. Lee
Oakland University

William J. McDevitt
Saint Joseph's University

Tom Moore
Georgia College and State University

Michael J. O'Hara
University of Nebraska at Omaha

Mark Phelps
University of Oregon

Lemoine D. Pierce
Georgia State University

G. Keith Roberts
University of Redlands

Gary Sambol
Rutgers, the State University of
New Jersey, Camden Campus

Linda Samuels
George Mason University

Martha Wright Sartoris
North Hennepin Community College

Gwen Seaquist
Ithaca College

Craig Stilwell
Michigan State University

Dawn R. Swink
University of St. Thomas

Daphyne Thomas
James Madison University

Wayne Wells
St. Cloud State University

Carrie Vaia
North Hennepin Community College

We know that we are not perfect. If you or your students find something you don't like or want us to change, we would like to hear from you. That is how we can make *The Legal Environment Today*, Seventh Edition, an even better book in the future.

Roger LeRoy Miller
Frank B. Cross

Dedication

To Kipp Nelson,
Who has redefined the meaning of the word *generous*.
Thanks for adding so much to our community.
It's an honor to know you.

R.L.M.

To my parents and sisters.

F.B.C.

The Foundations

(John Elk III/Lonely Planet Images/Getty Images)

Chapter 1

Business and Its Legal Environment

"Laws should be like clothes. They should be made to fit the people they are meant to serve."

—Clarence Darrow, 1857–1938
(American lawyer)

Contents

- **Business Activities and the Legal Environment**
- **Sources of American Law**
- **The Common Law Tradition**
- **Classifications of Law**

Chapter Objectives

After reading this chapter, you should be able to answer the following questions:

1. **What are four primary sources of law in the United States?**
2. **What is the common law tradition?**
3. **What is a precedent? When might a court depart from precedent?**
4. **What is the difference between remedies at law and remedies in equity?**
5. **What are some important differences between civil law and criminal law?**

(John Elk III/Lonely Planet Images/Getty Images)

Clarence Darrow asserts in the chapter-opening quotation above that laws should be created to serve the public. As part of the public, you have an interest in the law. Those entering the world of business will find themselves subject to numerous laws and government regulations. A basic knowledge of these laws and regulations is beneficial—if not essential—to anyone contemplating a successful career in today's business environment, as an employee, manager, or entrepreneur.

Although the law has various definitions, they all are based on the general observation that **law** consists of *enforceable rules governing relationships among individuals and between individuals and their society*. In some societies, these enforceable rules consist of unwritten principles of behavior, while in other societies they are set forth in ancient or contemporary law codes. In the United States, our rules consist of written laws and court decisions created by modern legislative and judicial bodies. Regardless of how such rules are created, they all have one feature in common: *they establish rights, duties, and privileges that are consistent with the values and beliefs of a society or its ruling group*.

In this introductory chapter, we first look at an important question for any student reading this text: How does the legal environment affect business decision making? We next describe the basic sources of American law, the common law tradition, and

Law A body of enforceable rules governing relationships among individuals and between individuals and their society.

some basic schools of legal thought. We conclude the chapter with a discussion of some general classifications of law.

▶ Business Activities and the Legal Environment

As those entering the business world will learn, laws and government regulations affect all business activities—hiring and firing decisions, workplace safety, the manufacturing and marketing of products, and business financing, to name just a few. To make good business decisions, a basic knowledge of the laws and regulations governing these activities is essential. Moreover, in today's setting, simply being aware of what conduct can lead to legal liability is not enough. Businesspersons are also under increasing pressure to make ethical decisions and to consider the consequences of their decisions for stockholders and employees (as will be discussed in Chapter 2).

Many Different Laws May Affect a Single Business Transaction

As you will note, each chapter in this text covers a specific area of the law and shows how the legal rules in that area affect business activities. Although compartmentalizing the law in this fashion facilitates learning, it does not indicate the extent to which many different laws may apply to just one transaction. **EXAMPLE 1.1** Suppose that you are the president of NetSys, Inc., a company that creates and maintains computer network systems for other business firms. NetSys also markets software for internal computer networks. One day, Janet Hernandez, an operations officer for Southwest Distribution Corporation (SDC), contacts you by e-mail about a possible contract involving SDC's computer network. In deciding whether to enter into a contract with SDC, you need to consider, among other things, the legal requirements for an enforceable contract. Are the requirements different for a contract for services and a contract for products? What are your options if SDC **breaches** (breaks, or fails to perform) the contract? The answers to these questions are part of contract law and sales law.

Other questions might concern payment under the contract. How can you guarantee that NetSys will be paid? For example, if SDC pays with a check that is returned for insufficient funds, what are your options? Answers to these questions can be found in the laws that relate to negotiable instruments (such as checks) and creditors' rights. Also, a dispute may arise over the rights to NetSys's software, or there may be a question of liability if the software is defective. There may even be an issue as to whether you and Hernandez had the authority to make the deal in the first place. Resolutions of these questions may be found in the laws that relate to intellectual property, e-commerce, torts, product liability, agency, business organizations, or professional liability. ●

Finally, if any dispute cannot be resolved amicably, then the laws and the rules concerning courts and court procedures spell out the steps of a lawsuit. Exhibit 1–1 on the following page illustrates the various areas of the law that may influence business decision making.

Breach The failure to perform a legal obligation.

Preventing Legal Disputes

To prevent potential legal disputes, be aware of the many different laws that may apply to a single business transaction. It is equally important to understand enough about the law to know when to turn to an expert for advice. It is impossible for nonexperts to keep up with the myriad rules and regulations that govern the conduct of business in the United States. When you need to choose an attorney, try to obtain recommendations from friends, relatives, or business associates who have had longstanding relationships with their attorneys. If that fails, contact your local or state bar association, or check FindLaw's online directory (at lawyers.findlaw.com).

• *Exhibit* 1–1 **Areas of the Law That May Affect Business Decision Making**

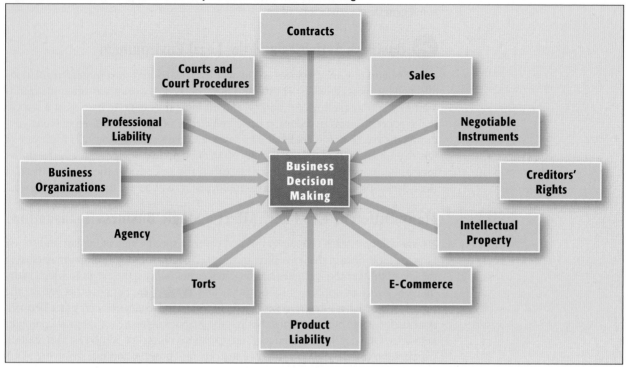

Linking the Law to Other Business School Disciplines

In all likelihood, you are taking a business law or legal environment course because you intend to enter the business world, though some of you may plan to become full-time practicing attorneys. Many of you are taking other business school courses—business communications, business statistics, economics, finance, management, marketing, and taxation, to name just a few possibilities. Most of you will take a course in accounting as well. One of our goals in this text is to show how legal concepts can be useful for managers and businesspersons, whether their activities focus on finance, marketing, or some other business discipline. To that end, several chapters conclude with a special feature called *Linking the Law to* [a specific business course].

The Role of the Law in a Small Business

Some of you may end up working in a small business or even owning and running one yourselves. The small-business owner/operator is the most general of managers. When you seek additional financing, you become a finance manager. When you "go over the books" with your bookkeeper, you become an accountant. When you decide on a new advertising campaign, you are suddenly the marketing manager. When you consider the impact that a new tax provision will have on your business, you are a tax practitioner. When you hire employees and determine their salaries and benefits, you become a human resources manager. Finally, when you try to predict market trends, interest rates, and other macroeconomic phenomena, you take on the role of a managerial economist.

Just as the various business school disciplines are linked to the law, so too are all of these different managerial roles that a small-business owner/operator must perform. Exhibit 1–2 below shows some of the legal issues that may arise as part of the management of a small business. Large businesses face most of these issues, too.

 ## Sources of American Law

There are numerous sources of American law. **Primary sources of law,** or sources that establish the law, include the following:

Primary Source of Law   A document that establishes the law on a particular issue, such as a constitution, a statute, an administrative rule, or a court decision.

Secondary Source of Law   A publication that summarizes or interprets the law, such as a legal encyclopedia, a legal treatise, or an article in a law review.

Constitutional Law   The body of law derived from the U.S. Constitution and the constitutions of the various states.

- The U.S. Constitution and the constitutions of the various states.
- Statutes, or laws, passed by Congress and by state legislatures.
- Regulations created by administrative agencies, such as the U.S. Food and Drug Administration.
- Case law (court decisions).

We describe each of these important primary sources of law in the following pages. (See the appendix at the end of this chapter for a discussion of how to find statutes, regulations, and case law.)

Secondary sources of law are books and articles that summarize and clarify the primary sources of law. Legal encyclopedias, compilations (such as *Restatements of the Law,* which summarize court decisions on a particular topic), official comments to statutes, treatises, articles in law reviews published by law schools, and articles in other legal journals are examples of secondary sources of law. Courts often refer to secondary sources of law for guidance in interpreting and applying the primary sources of law discussed here.

Constitutional Law

The federal government and the states have separate written constitutions that set forth the general organization, powers, and limits of their respective governments. **Constitutional law** is the law as expressed in these constitutions.

The U.S. Constitution is the supreme law of the land. As such, it is the basis of all law in the United States. A law in violation of the Constitution, if challenged, will be declared unconstitutional and will not be enforced no matter what its source. Because of its paramount importance in the American legal system, we discuss the U.S.

• *Exhibit* **1–2 Linking the Law to the Management of a Small Business**

Business Organization
What is the most appropriate business organizational form, and what type of personal liability does it entail?

Taxation
How will the small business be taxed, and are there ways to reduce those taxes?

Intellectual Property
Does the small business have any patents or other intellectual property that needs to be protected, and if so, what steps should the firm take?

Administrative Law
What types of government regulations apply to the business, and what must the firm do to comply with them?

Employment
Does the business need an employment manual, and does management have to explicitly inform employees of their rights?

Contracts, Sales, and Leases
Will the firm be regularly entering into contracts with others, and if so, should it hire an attorney to review those contracts?

Accounting
Do the financial statements created by an accountant need to be verified for accuracy?

Finance
What are appropriate and legal ways to raise additional capital so that the business can grow?

Constitution at length in Chapter 4 and present the complete text of the Constitution in Appendix B.

The Tenth Amendment to the U.S. Constitution reserves to the states all powers not granted to the federal government. Each state in the union has its own constitution. Unless it conflicts with the U.S. Constitution or a federal law, a state constitution is supreme within the state's borders.

Statutory Law

Statutory Law The body of law enacted by legislative bodies (as opposed to constitutional law, administrative law, or case law).

Citation A reference to a publication in which a legal authority–such as a statute or a court decision–or other source can be found.

Ordinance A regulation enacted by a city or county legislative body that becomes part of that state's statutory law.

Laws enacted by legislative bodies at any level of government, such as the statutes passed by Congress or by state legislatures, make up the body of law generally referred to as **statutory law.** When a legislature passes a statute, that statute ultimately is included in the federal code of laws or the relevant state code of laws. Whenever a particular statute is mentioned in this text, we usually provide a footnote showing its **citation** (a reference to a publication in which a legal authority—such as a statute or a court decision—or other source can be found). In the appendix following this chapter, we explain how you can use these citations to find statutory law.

Statutory law also includes local **ordinances**—statutes (laws, rules, or orders) passed by municipal or county governing units to govern matters not covered by federal or state law. Ordinances commonly have to do with city or county land use (zoning ordinances), building and safety codes, and other matters affecting only the local governing unit.

A federal statute, of course, applies to all states. A state statute, in contrast, applies only within the state's borders. State laws may vary from state to state. No federal statute may violate the U.S. Constitution, and no state statute or local ordinance may violate the U.S. Constitution or the relevant state constitution.

Uniform Law A model law created by the National Conference of Commissioners on Uniform State Laws and/or the American Law Institute for the states to consider adopting. Each state has the option of adopting or rejecting all or part of a uniform law. If a state adopts the law, it becomes statutory law in that state.

UNIFORM LAWS During the 1800s, the differences among state laws frequently created difficulties for businesspersons conducting trade and commerce among the states. To counter these problems, a group of legal scholars and lawyers formed the National Conference of Commissioners on Uniform State Laws (NCCUSL) in 1892 to draft **uniform laws** ("model statutes") for the states to consider adopting. The NCCUSL still exists today and continues to issue uniform laws: it has issued more than two hundred uniform acts since its inception.

Each state has the option of adopting or rejecting a uniform law. *Only if a state legislature adopts a uniform law does that law become part of the statutory law of that state.* Note that a state legislature may adopt all or part of a uniform law as it is written, or the legislature may rewrite the law however the legislature wishes. Hence, even though many states may have adopted a uniform law, those states' laws may not be entirely "uniform."

THE UNIFORM COMMERCIAL CODE (UCC) One of the more important uniform acts is the Uniform Commercial Code (UCC), which was created through the joint efforts of the NCCUSL and the American Law Institute.[1] The UCC was first issued in 1952 and has been adopted in all fifty states,[2] the District of Columbia, and the Virgin Islands. The UCC facilitates commerce among the states by providing a uniform, yet flexible, set of rules governing commercial transactions. Because of its importance in the area of commercial law, we cite the UCC frequently in this text. We also present excerpts of the UCC in Appendix C.

---

1. This institute was formed in the 1920s and consists of practicing attorneys, legal scholars, and judges.
2. Louisiana has adopted only Articles 1, 3, 4, 5, 7, 8, and 9.

Administrative Law

Administrative Law The body of law created by administrative agencies (in the form of rules, regulations, orders, and decisions) in order to carry out their duties and responsibilities.

Another important source of American law is **administrative law,** which consists of the rules, orders, and decisions of administrative agencies. An administrative agency is a federal, state, or local government agency established to perform a specific function. Rules issued by various administrative agencies affect almost every aspect of a business's operations, including the firm's capital structure and financing, its hiring and firing procedures, its relations with employees and unions, and the way it manufactures and markets its products. Because of its significance and influence on businesses, we discuss administrative law in great detail in Chapter 19.

Case Law and Common Law Doctrines

Case Law The rules of law announced in court decisions. Case law includes the aggregate of reported cases that interpret judicial precedents, statutes, regulations, and constitutional provisions.

The rules of law announced in court decisions constitute another basic source of American law. These rules of law include interpretations of constitutional provisions, of statutes enacted by legislatures, and of regulations created by administrative agencies. Today, this body of judge-made law is referred to as **case law.** Case law—the doctrines and principles announced in cases—governs all areas not covered by statutory law or administrative law and is part of our common law tradition. We look at the origins and characteristics of the common law tradition in some detail in the pages that follow.

The Common Law Tradition

Because of our colonial heritage, much of American law is based on the English legal system. A knowledge of this tradition is crucial to understanding our legal system today because judges in the United States still apply common law principles when deciding cases.

Early English Courts

Common Law The body of law developed from custom or judicial decisions in English and U.S. courts, not attributable to a legislature.

After the Normans conquered England in 1066, William the Conqueror and his successors began the process of unifying the country under their rule. One of the means they used to do this was the establishment of the king's courts, or *curiae regis*. Before the Norman Conquest, disputes had been settled according to the local legal customs and traditions in various regions of the country. The king's courts sought to establish a uniform set of rules for the country as a whole. What evolved in these courts was the beginning of the **common law**—a body of general rules that applied throughout the entire English realm. Eventually, the common law tradition became part of the heritage of all nations that were once British colonies, including the United States.

Precedent A court decision that furnishes an example or authority for deciding subsequent cases involving identical or similar facts.

Courts developed the common law rules from the principles underlying judges' decisions in actual legal controversies. Judges attempted to be consistent, and whenever possible, they based their decisions on the principles suggested by earlier cases. They sought to decide similar cases in a similar way and considered new cases with care, because they knew that their decisions would make new law. Each interpretation became part of the law on the subject and served as a legal **precedent**—that is, a court decision that furnished an example or authority for deciding subsequent cases involving identical or similar legal principles or facts.

In the early years of the common law, there was no single place or publication where court opinions, or written decisions, could be found. Beginning in the late thirteenth and early fourteenth centuries, however, portions of significant decisions from each year were gathered together and recorded in *Year Books*. The *Year Books* were useful references for lawyers and judges. In the sixteenth century, the *Year Books* were discontinued, and other reports of cases became available. (See the appendix to this chapter for a discussion of how cases are reported, or published, in the United States today.)

Stare Decisis

The practice of deciding new cases with reference to former decisions, or precedents, eventually became a cornerstone of the English and U.S. judicial systems. The practice forms a doctrine called **stare decisis**[3] ("to stand on decided cases").

THE IMPORTANCE OF PRECEDENTS IN JUDICIAL DECISION MAKING   Under the doctrine of *stare decisis,* once a court has set forth a principle of law as being applicable to a certain set of facts, that court and courts of lower rank must adhere to that principle and apply it in future cases involving similar fact patterns. *Stare decisis* has two aspects: first, decisions made by a higher court are binding on lower courts, and second, a court should not overturn its own precedents unless there is a strong reason to do so.

Controlling precedents in a *jurisdiction* (the area in which a court has the power to apply the law—see Chapter 3) are referred to as binding authorities. A **binding authority** is any source of law that a court must follow when deciding a case. Binding authorities include constitutions, statutes, and regulations that govern the issue being decided, as well as court decisions that are controlling precedents within the jurisdiction. United States Supreme Court case decisions, no matter how old, remain controlling until they are overruled by a subsequent decision of the Supreme Court, by a constitutional amendment, or by congressional legislation.

***STARE DECISIS* AND LEGAL STABILITY**   The doctrine of *stare decisis* helps the courts to be more efficient because if other courts have carefully reasoned through a similar case, their legal reasoning and opinions can serve as guides. *Stare decisis* also makes the law more stable and predictable. If the law on a given subject is well settled, someone bringing a case to court can usually rely on the court to make a decision based on what the law has been.

DEPARTURES FROM PRECEDENT   Although courts are obligated to follow precedents, sometimes a court will depart from the rule of precedent if it decides that a given precedent should no longer be followed. If a court decides that a precedent is simply incorrect or that technological or social changes have rendered the precedent inapplicable, the court might rule contrary to the precedent. Cases that overturn precedent often receive a great deal of publicity.

CASE EXAMPLE 1.2   In *Brown v. Board of Education of Topeka,*[4] the United States Supreme Court expressly overturned precedent when it concluded that separate educational facilities for whites and blacks, which had been upheld as constitutional in numerous previous cases,[5] were inherently unequal. The Supreme Court's departure from precedent in the *Brown* decision received a tremendous amount of publicity as people began to realize the ramifications of this change in the law. ●

Stare Decisis   A common law doctrine under which judges are obligated to follow the precedents established in prior decisions.

Binding Authority   Any source of law that a court must follow when deciding a case. Binding authorities include constitutions, statutes, and regulations that govern the issue being decided, as well as court decisions that are controlling precedents within the jurisdiction.

In a 1954 photo, a mother and daughter sit on the steps of the United States Supreme Court building after the Court's landmark ruling in Brown v. Board of Education of Topeka.

(Library of Congress)

---

3. Pronounced *stahr*-ee dih-*si*-sis.

4. 347 U.S. 483, 74 S.Ct. 686, 98 L.Ed. 873 (1954). See the appendix at the end of this chapter for an explanation of how to read legal citations.

5. See *Plessy v. Ferguson,* 163 U.S. 537, 16 S.Ct. 1138, 41 L.Ed. 256 (1896).

Persuasive Authority   Any legal authority or source of law that a court may look to for guidance but on which it need not rely in making its decision. Persuasive authorities include cases from other jurisdictions and secondary sources of law.

WHEN THERE IS NO PRECEDENT   At times, cases arise for which there are no precedents within the jurisdiction. When hearing such cases, called "cases of first impression," courts often look at precedents established in other jurisdictions for guidance. Precedents from other jurisdictions, because they are not binding on the court, are referred to as **persuasive authorities.** A court may also consider various other factors, including legal principles and policies underlying previous court decisions or existing statutes, fairness, social values and customs, public policy, and data and concepts drawn from the social sciences.

Can a court consider unpublished decisions as persuasive precedent? See this chapter's *Online Developments* feature below for a discussion of this issue.

Equitable Remedies and Courts of Equity

Remedy   The relief given to an innocent party to enforce a right or compensate for the violation of a right.

A **remedy** is the means given to a party to enforce a right or to compensate for the violation of a right. **EXAMPLE 1.3**   Shem is injured because of Rowan's wrongdoing. If

Online Developments

How the Internet Is Expanding Precedent

The notion that courts should rely on precedents to decide the outcome of similar cases has long been a cornerstone of U.S. law. Nevertheless, the availability of "unpublished opinions" over the Internet is changing what the law considers to be precedent. An *unpublished opinion* is a decision issued by an appellate (reviewing) court that is not intended for publication in a reporter (the bound books that contain court opinions).[a] Courts traditionally have not considered unpublished opinions to be "precedents," binding or persuasive, and often have not allowed attorneys to refer to (cite) these decisions in their arguments.

Increased Online Availability

The number of court decisions not published in printed books has increased dramatically in recent years. Nearly 80 percent of the decisions of the federal appellate courts are unpublished, and the number is equally high in some state court systems. Even though certain decisions are not intended for publication, they are posted ("published") almost immediately in online legal databases, such as Westlaw and Lexis. With the proliferation of free legal databases and court Web sites, the general public also has almost instant access to the unpublished decisions of most courts. This situation has caused many to question why these opinions have no precedential effect.

Should Unpublished Decisions Establish Precedent?

Prior to the Internet, not considering unpublished decisions as precedent might have been justified on the grounds of fairness. How could lawyers know about decisions if they were not printed in the

case reporters? Now that opinions are so readily available on the Web, however, this justification is no longer valid. Moreover, it now seems unfair *not* to consider these decisions as precedent because they are so publicly accessible. Some claim that unpublished decisions could make bad precedents because these decisions frequently are written by staff attorneys and law clerks, rather than by judges, so the reasoning may be inferior. If the decision is considered merely as persuasive precedent, however, then judges who disagree with the reasoning are free to reject the conclusion.

The United States Supreme Court Changed the Federal Rules on Unpublished Opinions

The United States Supreme Court made history in 2006 when it announced that it would allow lawyers to cite unpublished decisions in all federal courts. Rule 32.1 of the Federal Rules of Appellate Procedure states that federal courts may not prohibit or restrict the citation of federal judicial opinions that have been designated as "not for publication," "nonprecedential," or "not precedent."

The rule applies only to federal courts and only to unpublished opinions issued after January 1, 2007. It does not specify what weight a court must give to its own unpublished opinions or to those from another court. Basically, Rule 32.1 establishes a uniform rule for all of the federal courts that allows attorneys to cite—and judges to consider as persuasive precedent—unpublished decisions. The rule is a clear example of how technology—the availability of unpublished opinions over the Internet—has affected the law.

FOR CRITICAL ANALYSIS

Now that federal courts allow unpublished decisions to be used as persuasive precedent, should state courts follow? Why or why not?

---

a. Recently decided cases that are not yet published are also sometimes called unpublished opinions. This can be confusing because eventually they will be published in reporters and therefore will no longer be referred to as unpublished. Only those opinions that will *never* be printed in reporters are truly unpublished.

Shem files a lawsuit and is successful, a court can order Rowan to compensate Shem for the harm by paying Shem a certain amount. The compensation is Shem's remedy. •

The kinds of remedies available in the early king's courts of England were severely restricted. If one person wronged another, the king's courts could award as compensation either money or property, including land. These courts became known as *courts of law,* and the remedies were called *remedies at law.* Even though this system introduced uniformity in the settlement of disputes, when plaintiffs wanted a remedy other than economic compensation, the courts of law could do nothing, so "no remedy, no right."

REMEDIES IN EQUITY   *Equity* is a branch of law, founded on what might be described as notions of justice and fair dealing, that seeks to supply a remedy when no adequate remedy at law is available. When individuals could not obtain an adequate remedy in a court of law, they petitioned the king for relief. Most of these petitions were decided by an adviser to the king, called a *chancellor,* who had the power to grant new and unique remedies. Eventually, formal chancery courts, or *courts of equity,* were established. The remedies granted by these courts were called *remedies in equity.*

Thus, two distinct court systems were created, each having its own set of judges and its own set of remedies. **Plaintiffs** (those bringing lawsuits) had to specify whether they were bringing an "action at law" or an "action in equity," and they chose their courts accordingly. **EXAMPLE 1.4**   A plaintiff might ask a court of equity to order the **defendant** (the person against whom a lawsuit is brought) to perform within the terms of a contract. A court of law could not issue such an order because its remedies were limited to payment of money or property as compensation for damages. A court of equity, however, could issue a decree for *specific performance*—an order to perform what was promised. A court of equity could also issue an *injunction,* directing a party to do or refrain from doing a particular act. In certain cases, a court of equity could allow for the *rescission* (cancellation) of the contract, thereby returning the parties to the positions that they held prior to the contract's formation. • Equitable remedies will be discussed in Chapter 10.

THE MERGING OF LAW AND EQUITY   Today, in most states, the courts of law and equity have merged, and thus the distinction between the two courts has largely disappeared. A plaintiff may now request both legal and equitable remedies in the same action, and the trial court judge may grant either form—or both forms—of relief. The distinction between remedies at law and equity remains significant, however, because a court normally will grant an equitable remedy only when the remedy at law (monetary damages) is inadequate. To request the proper remedy, a businessperson (or her or his attorney) must know what remedies are available for the specific kinds of harms suffered. Exhibit 1–3 below summarizes the procedural differences (applicable in most states) between an action at law and an action in equity.

Plaintiff   One who initiates a lawsuit.

Defendant   One against whom a lawsuit is brought; the accused person in a criminal proceeding.

> *"Laws and institutions, like clocks, must occasionally be cleaned, wound up, and set to true time."*
>
> Henry Ward Beecher, 1813–1887
> (American clergyman and abolitionist)

• *Exhibit* **1–3 Procedural Differences between an Action at Law and an Action in Equity**

PROCEDURE	ACTION AT LAW	ACTION IN EQUITY
Initiation of lawsuit	By filing a complaint.	By filing a petition.
Decision	By jury or judge.	By judge (no jury).
Result	Judgment.	Decree.
Remedy	Monetary damages.	Injunction, specific performance, or rescission.

Equitable Principles and Maxims
General propositions or principles of law that have to do with fairness (equity).

EQUITABLE PRINCIPLES AND MAXIMS Over time, the courts have developed a number of **equitable principles and maxims** that provide guidance in deciding whether plaintiffs should be granted equitable relief. Because of their importance, both historically and in our judicial system today, these principles and maxims are set forth in this chapter's *Landmark in the Legal Environment* feature below.

Schools of Legal Thought

Jurisprudence The science or philosophy of law.

How judges apply the law to specific cases, including disputes relating to the business world, depends in part on their philosophical approaches to law. Part of the study of law, often referred to as **jurisprudence**, involves learning about different schools of legal thought and discovering how each school's approach to law can affect judicial decision making.

Natural Law The belief that government and the legal system should reflect universal moral and ethical principles that are inherent in human nature. The natural law school is the oldest and one of the more significant schools of legal thought.

THE NATURAL LAW SCHOOL Those who adhere to the **natural law** theory believe that a higher or universal law exists that applies to all human beings and that written laws should imitate these inherent principles. If a written law is unjust, then it is not a true (natural) law and need not be obeyed.

The natural law tradition is one of the oldest and more significant schools of jurisprudence. It dates back to the days of the Greek philosopher Aristotle (384–322 B.C.E.), who distinguished between natural law and the laws governing a particular nation. According to Aristotle, natural law applies universally to all humankind.

Statute of Limitations A federal or state statute setting the maximum time period during which a certain action can be brought or certain rights enforced.

The notion that people have "natural rights" stems from the natural law tradition. Those who claim that a specific foreign government is depriving certain citizens of

---

Landmark in the Legal Environment   **Equitable Principles and Maxims**

In medieval England, courts of equity were expected to use discretion in supplementing the common law. Even today, when the same court can award both legal and equitable remedies, it must exercise discretion. Students of business law should know that courts often invoke equitable principles and maxims when making their decisions. Here are some of the most significant equitable principles and maxims:

1. *Whoever seeks equity must do equity.* (Anyone who wishes to be treated fairly must treat others fairly.)
2. *Where there is equal equity, the law must prevail.* (The law will determine the outcome of a controversy in which both sides have equal merits.)
3. *One seeking the aid of an equity court must come to the court with clean hands.* (The plaintiff must have acted fairly and honestly.)
4. *Equity will not suffer a wrong to be without a remedy.* (Equitable relief will be awarded when there is a right to relief and there is no adequate remedy at law.)
5. *Equity regards substance rather than form.* (Equity is more concerned with fairness and justice than with legal technicalities.)
6. *Equity aids the vigilant, not those who rest on their rights.* (Equity will not help those who neglect their rights for an unreasonable period of time.)

The last maxim has come to be known as the *equitable doctrine of laches.* The doctrine arose to encourage people to bring lawsuits while the evidence was fresh. If they failed to do so, they would not be allowed to bring a lawsuit. What constitutes a reasonable time, of course, varies according to the circumstances of the case. Time periods for different types of cases are now usually fixed by **statutes of limitations.** After the time allowed under a statute of limitations has expired, no action can be brought, no matter how strong the case was originally.

• **Application to Today's Legal Environment** *The equitable maxims listed above underlie many of the legal rules and principles that are commonly applied by the courts today—and that you will read about in this book. For example, in Chapter 10 you will read about the* doctrine of promissory estoppel. *Under this doctrine, a person who has reasonably and substantially relied on the promise of another may be able to obtain some measure of recovery, even though no enforceable contract, or agreement, exists. The court will* estop *(bar, or impede) the one making the promise from asserting the lack of a valid contract as a defense. The rationale underlying the doctrine of promissory estoppel is similar to that expressed in the fourth and fifth maxims on the left.*

their human rights are implicitly appealing to a higher law that has universal applicability. The question of the universality of basic human rights also comes into play in the context of international business operations. For example, U.S. companies that have operations abroad often hire foreign workers as employees. Should the same laws that protect U.S. employees apply to these foreign employees? This question is rooted implicitly in a concept of universal rights that has its origins in the natural law tradition.

LEGAL POSITIVISM   In contrast, *positive,* or national, law (the written law of a given society at a particular point in time) applies only to the citizens of that nation or society. Those who adhere to **legal positivism** believe that there can be no higher law than a nation's positive law. According to the positivist school, there is no such thing as "natural rights." Rather, human rights exist solely because of laws. If the laws are not enforced, anarchy will result. Thus, whether a law is "bad" or "good" is irrelevant. The law is the law and must be obeyed until it is changed—in an orderly manner through a legitimate lawmaking process. A judge with positivist leanings probably would be more inclined to defer to an existing law than would a judge who adheres to the natural law tradition.

THE HISTORICAL SCHOOL   The **historical school** of legal thought emphasizes the evolutionary process of law by concentrating on the origin and history of the legal system. This school looks to the past to discover what the principles of contemporary law should be. The legal doctrines that have withstood the passage of time—those that have worked in the past—are deemed best suited for shaping present laws. Hence, law derives its legitimacy and authority from adhering to the standards that historical development has shown to be workable. Followers of the historical school are more likely than those of other schools to adhere strictly to decisions made in past cases.

LEGAL REALISM   In the 1920s and 1930s, a number of jurists and scholars, known as *legal realists,* rebelled against the historical approach to law. **Legal realism** is based on the idea that law is just one of many institutions in society and that it is shaped by social forces and needs. This school holds that because the law is a human enterprise, judges should take social and economic realities into account when deciding cases. Legal realists also believe that the law can never be applied with total uniformity. Given that judges are human beings with unique personalities, value systems, and intellects, different judges will obviously bring different reasoning processes to the same case.

Legal realism strongly influenced the growth of what is sometimes called the **sociological school** of jurisprudence. This school views law as a tool for promoting justice in society. In the 1960s, for example, the justices of the United States Supreme Court played a leading role in the civil rights movement by upholding long-neglected laws calling for equal treatment for all Americans, including African Americans and other minorities. Generally, jurists who adhere to the sociological school are more likely to depart from past decisions than are those jurists who adhere to the other schools of legal thought.

 ## Classifications of Law

The law may be broken down according to several classification systems. For example, one classification system divides law into **substantive law** (all laws that define, describe, regulate, and create legal rights and obligations) and **procedural law** (all

---

Legal Positivism   A school of legal thought centered on the assumption that there is no law higher than the laws created by a national government. Laws must be obeyed, even if they are unjust, to prevent anarchy.

Historical School   A school of legal thought that emphasizes the evolutionary process of law and looks to the past to discover what the principles of contemporary law should be.

Legal Realism   A school of legal thought of the 1920s and 1930s that generally advocated a less abstract and more realistic approach to the law, an approach that takes into account customary practices and the circumstances in which transactions take place. This school left a lasting imprint on American jurisprudence.

Sociological School   A school of legal thought that views the law as a tool for promoting justice in society.

Substantive Law   Law that defines, describes, regulates, and creates legal rights and obligations.

Procedural Law   Law that establishes the methods of enforcing the rights established by substantive law.

laws that establish the methods of enforcing the rights established by substantive law).

EXAMPLE 1.5 A state law that provides employees with the right to workers' compensation benefits for any on-the-job injuries they sustain is a substantive law because it creates legal rights (workers' compensation laws will be discussed in Chapter 17). Procedural laws, in contrast, establish the method by which an employee must notify the employer about an on-the-job injury, prove the injury, and periodically submit additional proof to continue receiving workers' compensation benefits. Note that a law regarding workers' compensation may contain both substantive and procedural provisions. •

Other classification systems divide law into federal law and state law or private law (dealing with relationships between persons) and public law (addressing the relationship between persons and their governments). Frequently, people use the term **cyberlaw** to refer to the emerging body of law that governs transactions conducted via the Internet. Cyberlaw is not really a classification of law, nor is it a new *type* of law. Rather, it is an informal term used to describe traditional legal principles that have been modified and adapted to fit situations that are unique to the online world. Of course, in some areas new statutes have been enacted, at both the federal and state levels, to cover specific types of problems stemming from online communications. Throughout this book, you will read about how the law is evolving to govern specific legal issues that arise in the online context.

Cyberlaw An informal term used to refer to all laws governing electronic communications and transactions, particularly those conducted via the Internet.

Civil Law and Criminal Law

Civil law spells out the rights and duties that exist between persons and between persons and their governments, and the relief available when a person's rights are violated. Typically, in a civil case, a private party sues another private party (although the government can also sue a party for a civil law violation) to make that other party comply with a duty or pay for the damage caused by the failure to comply with a duty. **EXAMPLE 1.6** If a seller fails to perform a contract with a buyer, the buyer may bring a lawsuit against the seller. The purpose of the lawsuit will be either to compel the seller to perform as promised or, more commonly, to obtain monetary damages for the seller's failure to perform. •

Much of the law that we discuss in this text is civil law. Contract law, for example, which we will discuss in Chapters 9 through 11, is civil law. The whole body of tort law (see Chapter 5) is civil law. Note that *civil law* is not the same as a *civil law system*. As you will read shortly, a **civil law system** is a legal system based on a written code of laws.

Criminal law has to do with wrongs committed against society for which society demands redress. Criminal acts are proscribed by local, state, or federal government statutes (see Chapter 6). Thus, criminal defendants are prosecuted by public officials, such as a district attorney (D.A.), on behalf of the state, not by their victims or other private parties. Whereas in a civil case the object is to obtain a remedy (such as monetary damages) to compensate the injured party, in a criminal case the object is to punish the wrongdoer in an attempt to deter others from similar actions. Penalties for violations of criminal statutes consist of fines and/or imprisonment—and, in some cases, death. We will discuss the differences between civil and criminal law in greater detail in Chapter 6.

Civil Law The branch of law dealing with the definition and enforcement of all private or public rights, as opposed to criminal matters.

Civil Law System A system of law derived from that of the Roman Empire and based on a code rather than case law; the predominant system of law in the nations of continental Europe and the nations that were once their colonies.

Criminal Law Law that defines and governs actions that constitute crimes. Generally, criminal law has to do with wrongful actions committed against society for which society demands redress.

Trials in criminal courts often concern charges of robbery and assault, as in this trial in the Clark County Regional Justice Center in Las Vegas, Nevada.

(Gary Thompson-Pool/Getty Images)

National and International Law

Although the focus of this book is U.S. business law, increasingly businesspersons in this country engage in transactions that extend beyond our national borders. In these situations, the laws of other nations or the laws governing relationships among nations may come into play. For this reason, those who pursue a career in business today should have an understanding of the global legal environment.

NATIONAL LAW   The law of a particular nation, such as the United States or Sweden, is **national law**. National law, of course, varies from country to country because each country's law reflects the interests, customs, activities, and values that are unique to that nation's culture. Even though the laws and legal systems of various countries differ substantially, broad similarities do exist, as discussed in this chapter's *Beyond Our Borders* feature below.

National Law Law that pertains to a particular nation (as opposed to international law).

Beyond Our Borders   National Law Systems

Despite their varying cultures and customs, almost all countries have laws governing torts, contracts, employment, and other areas, just as the United States does. In part, this is because two types of legal systems predominate around the globe today. One is the common law system of England and the United States, which we have discussed elsewhere. The other system is based on Roman civil law, or "code law." The term *civil law,* as used here, refers not to civil as opposed to criminal law but to codified law—an ordered grouping of legal principles enacted into law by a legislature or governing body.

In a *civil law system,* the primary source of law is a statutory code, and case precedents are not judicially binding, as they normally are in a common law system. Although judges in a civil law system commonly refer to previous decisions as sources of legal guidance, they are not bound by precedent. In other words, the doctrine of *stare decisis* does not apply.

A third, less prevalent, legal system is common in Islamic countries, where the law is often influenced by *sharia,* the religious law of Islam. *Sharia* is a comprehensive code of principles that governs both the public and private lives of Islamic persons, directing many aspects of day-to-day life, including politics, economics, banking, business law, contract law, and social issues. Although *sharia* affects the legal codes of many Muslim countries, the extent of its impact and its interpretation vary widely. In some Middle Eastern nations, aspects of *sharia* have been codified in modern legal codes and are enforced by national judicial systems.

Exhibit 1–4 below lists some countries that today follow either the common law system or the civil law system. Generally, those countries that were once colonies of Great Britain retained their English common law heritage after they achieved independence. Similarly, the civil law system, which is followed in most continental European nations, was retained

in the Latin American, African, and Asian countries that were once colonies of those nations. Japan and South Africa also have civil law systems. In the United States, the state of Louisiana, because of its historical ties to France, has, in part, a civil law system. The legal systems of Puerto Rico, Québec, and Scotland similarly include elements of the civil law system.

Realize that although national law systems share many commonalities, they also have distinct differences. Even when the basic principles are fundamentally similar (as they are in contract law, for example), significant variations exist in the practical application and effect of these laws across countries. Therefore, anyone who plans to do business in another nation would be wise to become familiar with its laws.

For Critical Analysis
Does the civil law system offer any advantages over the common law system, or vice versa? Explain.

• *Exhibit* **1–4 The Legal Systems of Selected Nations**

CIVIL LAW		COMMON LAW	
Argentina	Indonesia	Australia	Nigeria
Austria	Iran	Bangladesh	Singapore
Brazil	Italy	Canada	United Kingdom
Chile	Japan	Ghana	United States
China	Mexico	India	Zambia
Egypt	Poland	Israel	
Finland	South Korea	Jamaica	
France	Sweden	Kenya	
Germany	Tunisia	Malaysia	
Greece	Venezuela	New Zealand	

International Law   The law that governs relations among nations. National laws, customs, treaties, and international conferences and organizations are generally considered to be the most important sources of international law.

INTERNATIONAL LAW   In contrast to national law, international law applies to more than one nation. **International law** can be defined as a body of written and unwritten laws observed by independent nations and governing the acts of individuals as well as governments. International law is an intermingling of rules and constraints derived from a variety of sources, including the laws of individual nations, the customs that have evolved among nations in their relations with one another, and treaties and international organizations. In essence, international law is the result of centuries-old attempts to reconcile the traditional need of each nation to be the final authority over its own affairs with the desire of nations to benefit economically from trade and harmonious relations with one another.

The key difference between national law and international law is that government authorities can enforce national law. If a nation violates an international law, however, the most that other countries or international organizations can do (if persuasive tactics fail) is to take coercive actions against the violating nation. Coercive actions range from the severance of diplomatic relations and boycotts to, as a last resort, war. We will examine international law in Chapter 7.

Reviewing . . . Business and Its Legal Environment

Suppose that the California legislature passes a law that severely restricts carbon dioxide emissions from automobiles in that state. A group of automobile manufacturers files a suit against the state of California to prevent the enforcement of the law. The automakers claim that a federal law already sets fuel economy standards nationwide and that these standards are essentially the same as carbon dioxide emission standards. According to the automobile manufacturers, it is unfair to allow California to impose more stringent regulations than those set by the federal law. Using the information presented in the chapter, answer the following questions.

1. Who are the parties (the plaintiffs and the defendant) in this lawsuit?
2. Are the plaintiffs seeking a legal remedy or an equitable remedy?
3. What is the primary source of the law that is at issue here?
4. Read through the appendix that follows this chapter, and then answer the following question: Where would you look to find the relevant California and federal laws?

Key Terms

administrative law 7
binding authority 8
breach 3
case law 7
citation 6
civil law 13
civil law system 13
common law 7
constitutional law 5
criminal law 13
cyberlaw 13
defendant 10

equitable principles and maxims 11
historical school 12
international law 15
jurisprudence 11
law 2
legal positivism 12
legal realism 12
national law 14
natural law 11
ordinance 6
persuasive authority 9
plaintiff 10

precedent 7
primary source of law 5
procedural law 12
remedy 9
secondary source of law 5
sociological school 12
stare decisis 8
statute of limitations 11
statutory law 6
substantive law 12
uniform law 6

Chapter Summary: Business and Its Legal Environment

Sources of American Law (See pages 5–7.)	1. *Constitutional law*—The law as expressed in the U.S. Constitution and the various state constitutions. The U.S. Constitution is the supreme law of the land. State constitutions are supreme within state borders to the extent that they do not violate the U.S. Constitution or a federal law. 2. *Statutory law*—Laws or ordinances created by federal, state, and local legislatures and governing bodies. None of these laws can violate the U.S. Constitution or the relevant state constitutions. Uniform laws, when adopted by a state legislature, become statutory law in that state. 3. *Administrative law*—The rules, orders, and decisions of federal or state government administrative agencies. 4. *Case law and common law doctrines*—Judge-made law, including interpretations of constitutional provisions, of statutes enacted by legislatures, and of regulations created by administrative agencies. The common law—the doctrines and principles embodied in case law—governs all areas not covered by statutory law (or agency regulations issued to implement various statutes).
The Common Law Tradition (See pages 7–12.)	1. *Common law*—Law that originated in medieval England with the creation of the king's courts, or *curiae regis,* and the development of a body of rules that were common to (or applied throughout) the land. 2. *Stare decisis*—A doctrine under which judges "stand on decided cases"—or follow the rule of precedent—in deciding cases. *Stare decisis* is the cornerstone of the common law tradition. 3. *Remedies*—A remedy is the means by which a court enforces a right or compensates for a violation of a right. Courts typically grant legal remedies (monetary damages) but may also grant equitable remedies (specific performance, injunction, or rescission) when the legal remedy is inadequate or unavailable. 4. *Schools of legal thought*—Judges' decision making is influenced by their philosophy of law. Four important schools of legal thought, or legal philosophies, are the following: 　　a. *Natural law tradition*—One of the oldest and more significant schools of legal thought. Those who believe in natural law hold that there is a universal law applicable to all human beings and that this law is of a higher order than positive, or conventional, law. 　　b. *Legal positivism*—A school of legal thought centered on the assumption that there is no law higher than the laws created by the government. Laws must be obeyed, even if they are unjust, to prevent anarchy. 　　c. *Historical school*—A school of legal thought that stresses the evolutionary nature of law and looks to doctrines that have withstood the passage of time for guidance in shaping present laws. 　　d. *Legal realism*—A school of legal thought that generally advocates a less abstract and more realistic approach to the law that takes into account customary practices and the circumstances in which transactions take place.
Classifications of Law (See pages 12–15.)	The law may be broken down according to several classification systems, such as substantive or procedural law, federal or state law, and private or public law. Two broad classifications are civil and criminal law, and national and international law. Cyberlaw is not really a classification of law but a term that is used for the growing body of case law and statutory law that applies to Internet transactions.

ExamPrep

ISSUE SPOTTERS

1. The First Amendment to the U.S. Constitution provides protection for the free exercise of religion. A state legislature enacts a law that outlaws all religions that do not derive from the Judeo-Christian tradition. Is this law valid within that state? Why or why not?
2. Under what circumstance might a judge rely on case law to determine the intent and purpose of a statute?

—**Check your answers to these questions against the answers provided in Appendix G.**

BEFORE THE TEST

Go to **www.cengagebrain.com**, enter the ISBN number "9781111530617," and click on "Find" to locate this textbook's Web site. Then, click on "Access Now" under "Study Tools," and select "Chapter 1" at the top. There you will find an "Interactive Quiz" that you can take to assess your mastery of the concepts in this chapter, as well as "Flashcards" and a "Glossary" of important terms.

For Review

1. What are four primary sources of law in the United States?
2. What is the common law tradition?
3. What is a precedent? When might a court depart from precedent?
4. What is the difference between remedies at law and remedies in equity?
5. What are some important differences between civil law and criminal law?

Questions and Case Problems

1–1. Binding versus Persuasive Authority. A county court in Illinois is deciding a case involving an issue that has never been addressed before in that state's courts. The Iowa Supreme Court, however, recently decided a case involving a very similar fact pattern. Is the Illinois court obligated to follow the Iowa Supreme Court's decision on the issue? If the United States Supreme Court had decided a similar case, would that decision be binding on the Illinois court? Explain.

1–2. Remedies. Arthur Rabe is suing Xavier Sanchez for breaching a contract in which Sanchez promised to sell Rabe a Van Gogh painting for $150,000.

   1. In this lawsuit, who is the plaintiff, and who is the defendant?

   2. If Rabe wants Sanchez to perform the contract as promised, what remedy should Rabe seek?

   3. Suppose that Rabe wants to cancel the contract because Sanchez fraudulently misrepresented the painting as an original Van Gogh when in fact it is a copy. In this situation, what remedy should Rabe seek?

   4. Will the remedy Rabe seeks in either situation be a remedy at law or a remedy in equity?

   5. Suppose that the court finds in Rabe's favor and grants one of these remedies. Sanchez then appeals the decision to a higher court. Read through the subsection entitled "Parties to Lawsuits" in the appendix following this chapter. On appeal, which party in the *Rabe-Sanchez* case will be the appellant (or petitioner), and which party will be the appellee (or respondent)?

1–3. Legal Systems. What are the key differences between a common law system and a civil law system? Why do some countries have common law systems and others have civil law systems?

1–4. **Question with Sample Answer. Sources of Law.** This chapter discussed a number of sources of American law. Which source of law takes priority in each of the following situations, and why?

   1. A federal statute conflicts with the U.S. Constitution.

   2. A federal statute conflicts with a state constitution.

   3. A state statute conflicts with the common law of that state.

   4. A state constitutional amendment conflicts with the U.S. Constitution.

   5. A federal administrative regulation conflicts with a state constitution.

—**For a sample answer to Question 1–4, go to Appendix E at the end of this text.**

1–5. Philosophy of Law. After World War II ended in 1945, an international tribunal of judges convened at Nuremberg, Germany. The judges convicted several Nazi war criminals of "crimes against humanity." Assuming that the Nazis who were convicted had not disobeyed any law of their country and had merely been following their government's (Hitler's) orders, what law had they violated? Explain.

1–6. Reading Citations. Assume that you want to read the court's entire opinion in the case of *Pack 2000, Inc. v. Cushman,* 126 Conn.App. 339, 11 A.3d 181 (2011). Read the section entitled "Finding Case Law" in the appendix that follows this chapter, and then explain specifically where you would find the court's opinion.

1–7. *Stare Decisis.* In this chapter, we stated that the doctrine of *stare decisis* "became a cornerstone of the English and U.S. judicial systems." What does *stare decisis* mean, and why has this doctrine been so fundamental in the development of our legal tradition?

1–8. Court Opinions. Read through the subsection entitled "Decisions and Opinions" in the appendix following this chapter. What is the difference between a concurring opinion and a majority opinion? Between a concurring opinion and a dissenting opinion? Why do judges and justices write concurring and dissenting opinions, given that these opinions will not affect the outcome of the case at hand, which has already been decided by majority vote?

1–9. **A Question of Ethics. *Stare Decisis.*** On July 5, 1884, Dudley, Stephens, and Brooks—"all able-bodied English seamen"—and a teenage English boy were cast adrift in a lifeboat following a storm at sea. They had no water with them in the boat, and all they had for sustenance were two one-pound tins of turnips. On July 24, Dudley proposed that one of the four in the lifeboat be sacrificed to save the others. Stephens agreed with Dudley, but Brooks refused to consent—and the boy was never asked for his opinion. On July 25, Dudley killed the boy, and the three men then fed on the boy's body and blood. Four days later, the men were rescued by a passing vessel. They were taken to England and tried for the murder of the boy. If the men had not fed on the boy's body, they would probably have died of starvation within the four-day period. The boy, who was in a much weaker condition, would likely have died before the rest. [Regina v. Dudley and Stephens, 14 Q.B.D. (Queen's Bench Division, England) 273 (1884)]

1. The basic question in this case is whether the survivors should be subject to penalties under English criminal law, given the men's unusual circumstances. You be the judge and decide the issue. Give the reasons for your decision.

2. Should judges ever have the power to look beyond the written "letter of the law" in making their decisions? Why or why not?

1–10. **Critical-Thinking Legal Environment Question.** John's company is involved in a lawsuit with a customer, Beth. John argues that for fifty years higher courts in that state have decided cases involving circumstances similar to those of this case in a way that indicates that this case should be decided in favor of John's company. Is this a valid argument? If so, must the judge in this case rule as those other judges did? What argument could Beth use to counter John's reasoning?

The statutes, agency regulations, and case law referred to in this text establish the rights and duties of businesspersons engaged in various types of activities. The cases presented in the following chapters provide you with concise, real-life illustrations of how the courts interpret and apply these laws. Because of the importance of knowing how to find statutory, administrative, and case law, this appendix offers a brief introduction to how these laws are published and to the legal "shorthand" employed in referencing these legal sources.

Finding Statutory and Administrative Law

When Congress passes laws, they are collected in a publication titled *United States Statutes at Large*. When state legislatures pass laws, they are collected in similar state publications. Most frequently, however, laws are referred to in their codified form—that is, the form in which they appear in the federal and state codes. In these codes, laws are compiled by subject.

United States Code

The *United States Code* (U.S.C.) arranges all existing federal laws of a public and permanent nature by subject. Each of the fifty subjects into which the U.S.C. arranges the laws is given a title and a title number. For example, laws relating to commerce and trade are collected in "Title 15, Commerce and Trade." Titles are subdivided by sections. A citation to the U.S.C. includes title and section numbers. Thus, a reference to "15 U.S.C. Section 1" means that the statute can be found in Section 1 of Title 15. ("Section" may also be designated by the symbol §, and "Sections" by §§.) In addition to the print publication of the U.S.C., the federal government also provides a searchable online database of the *United States Code* at **www.gpoaccess.gov/uscode/index.html**.

Commercial publications of these laws and regulations are available and are widely used. For example, West Group publishes the *United States Code Annotated* (U.S.C.A.). The U.S.C.A. contains the complete text of laws included in the U.S.C., notes of court decisions that interpret and apply specific sections of the statutes, and the text of presidential proclamations and executive orders. The U.S.C.A. also includes research aids, such as cross-references to related statutes, historical notes, and library references. A citation to the U.S.C.A. is similar to a citation to the U.S.C.: "15 U.S.C.A. Section 1."

State Codes

State codes follow the U.S.C. pattern of arranging law by subject. The state codes may be called codes, revisions, compilations, consolidations, general statutes, or statutes, depending on the preferences of the state. In some codes, subjects are designated by number. In others, they are designated by name. For example, "13 Pennsylvania Consolidated Statutes Section 1101" means that the statute can be found in Title 13, Section 1101, of the Pennsylvania code. "California Commercial Code Section 1101" means the statute can be found in Section 1101 under the subject heading

"Commercial Code" of the California code. Abbreviations may be used. For example, "13 Pennsylvania Consolidated Statutes Section 1101" may be abbreviated "13 Pa. C.S. § 1101," and "California Commercial Code Section 1101" may be abbreviated "Cal. Com. Code § 1101."

Administrative Rules

Rules and regulations adopted by federal administrative agencies are compiled in the *Code of Federal Regulations* (C.F.R.). Like the U.S.C., the C.F.R. is divided into fifty titles. Rules within each title are assigned section numbers. A full citation to the C.F.R. includes title and section numbers. For example, a reference to "17 C.F.R. Section 230.504" means that the rule can be found in Section 230.504 of Title 17.

 Finding Case Law

Before discussing the case reporting system, we need to look briefly at the court system (which will be discussed in detail in Chapter 3). There are two types of courts in the United States: federal courts and state courts. Both the federal and state court systems consist of several levels, or tiers, of courts. *Trial courts,* in which evidence is presented and testimony is given, are on the bottom tier (which also includes lower courts handling specialized issues). Decisions from a trial court can be appealed to a higher court, which commonly would be an intermediate *court of appeals,* or an *appellate court.* Decisions from these intermediate courts of appeals may be appealed to an even higher court, such as a state supreme court or the United States Supreme Court.

State Court Decisions

Most state trial court decisions are not published. Except in New York and a few other states that publish selected opinions of their trial courts, decisions from state trial courts are merely filed in the office of the clerk of the court, where the decisions are available for public inspection. (Increasingly, they can be found online as well.) Written decisions of the appellate, or reviewing, courts, however, are published and distributed. As you will note, most of the state court cases presented in this book are from state appellate courts. The reported appellate decisions are published in volumes called *reports* or *reporters,* which are numbered consecutively. State appellate court decisions are found in the state reporters of that particular state.

REGIONAL REPORTERS   State court opinions appear in regional units of the *National Reporter System,* published by West Group. Most lawyers and libraries have the West reporters because they report cases more quickly and are distributed more widely than the state-published reports. In fact, many states have eliminated their own reporters in favor of West's National Reporter System. The National Reporter System divides the states into the following geographic areas: *Atlantic* (A., A.2d, or A.3d), *North Eastern* (N.E. or N.E.2d), *North Western* (N.W. or N.W.2d), *Pacific* (P., P.2d, or P.3d), *South Eastern* (S.E. or S.E.2d), *South Western* (S.W., S.W.2d, or S.W.3d), and *Southern* (So., So.2d, or So.3d). (The *2d* and *3d* in the abbreviations refer to *Second Series* and *Third Series,* respectively.) The states included in each of these regional divisions are indicated in Exhibit 1A–1 on the facing page, which illustrates West's National Reporter System.

• *Exhibit* **1A–1** **West's National Reporter System–Regional/Federal**

Regional Reporters	Coverage Beginning	Coverage
Atlantic Reporter (A., A.2d, or A.3d)	1885	Connecticut, Delaware, District of Columbia, Maine, Maryland, New Hampshire, New Jersey, Pennsylvania, Rhode Island, and Vermont.
North Eastern Reporter (N.E. or N.E.2d)	1885	Illinois, Indiana, Massachusetts, New York, and Ohio.
North Western Reporter (N.W. or N.W.2d)	1879	Iowa, Michigan, Minnesota, Nebraska, North Dakota, South Dakota, and Wisconsin.
Pacific Reporter (P., P.2d, or P.3d)	1883	Alaska, Arizona, California, Colorado, Hawaii, Idaho, Kansas, Montana, Nevada, New Mexico, Oklahoma, Oregon, Utah, Washington, and Wyoming.
South Eastern Reporter (S.E. or S.E.2d)	1887	Georgia, North Carolina, South Carolina, Virginia, and West Virginia.
South Western Reporter (S.W., S.W.2d, or S.W.3d)	1886	Arkansas, Kentucky, Missouri, Tennessee, and Texas.
Southern Reporter (So., So.2d, or So.3d)	1887	Alabama, Florida, Louisiana, and Mississippi.

Federal Reporters		
Federal Reporter (F., F.2d, or F.3d)	1880	U.S. Circuit Courts from 1880 to 1912; U.S. Commerce Court from 1911 to 1913; U.S. District Courts from 1880 to 1932; U.S. Court of Claims (now called U.S. Court of Federal Claims) from 1929 to 1932 and since 1960; U.S. Courts of Appeals since 1891; U.S. Court of Customs and Patent Appeals since 1929; U.S. Emergency Court of Appeals since 1943.
Federal Supplement (F.Supp. or F.Supp.2d)	1932	U.S. Court of Claims from 1932 to 1960; U.S. District Courts since 1932; U.S. Customs Court since 1956.
Federal Rules Decisions (F.R.D.)	1939	U.S. District Courts involving the Federal Rules of Civil Procedure since 1939 and Federal Rules of Criminal Procedure since 1946.
Supreme Court Reporter (S.Ct.)	1882	United States Supreme Court since the October term of 1882.
Bankruptcy Reporter (Bankr.)	1980	Bankruptcy decisions of U.S. Bankruptcy Courts, U.S. District Courts, U.S. Courts of Appeals, and the United States Supreme Court.
Military Justice Reporter (M.J.)	1978	U.S. Court of Military Appeals and Courts of Military Review for the Army, Navy, Air Force, and Coast Guard.

NATIONAL REPORTER SYSTEM MAP

CASE CITATIONS   After appellate decisions have been published, they are normally referred to (cited) by the name of the case; the volume, name, and page number of the state's official reporter (if different from West's National Reporter System); the volume, name, and page number of the *National Reporter;* and the volume, name, and page number of any other selected reporter. This information is included in the *citation.* (Citing a reporter by volume number, name, and page number, in that order, is common to all citations.) When more than one reporter is cited for the same case, each reference is called a *parallel citation.*

Note that some states have adopted a "public domain citation system" that uses a somewhat different format for the citation. For example, in Wisconsin, a Wisconsin Supreme Court decision might be designated "2011 WI 40," meaning that the decision was the fortieth issued by the Wisconsin Supreme Court in the year 2011. Parallel citations to the *Wisconsin Reports* and West's *North Western Reporter* are still included after the public domain citation.

Consider the following case citation: *Orlando v. Cole,* 76 Mass.App.Ct. 1112, 921 N.E.2d 566 (2011). We see that the opinion in this case can be found in Volume 76 of the official *Massachusetts Appeals Court Reports,* on page 1112. The parallel citation is to Volume 921 of the *North Eastern Reporter, Second Series,* page 566. In presenting appellate opinions in this text (starting in Chapter 2), in addition to the reporter, we give the name of the court hearing the case and the year of the court's decision. Sample citations to state court decisions are explained in Exhibit 1A–2 on pages 23–25.

Federal Court Decisions

Federal district (trial) court decisions are published unofficially in West's *Federal Supplement* (F.Supp. or F.Supp.2d), and opinions from the circuit courts of appeals (reviewing courts) are reported unofficially in West's *Federal Reporter* (F., F.2d, or F.3d). Cases concerning federal bankruptcy law are published unofficially in West's *Bankruptcy Reporter* (Bankr. or B.R.).

The official edition of the United States Supreme Court decisions is the *United States Reports* (U.S.), which is published by the federal government. Unofficial editions of Supreme Court cases include West's *Supreme Court Reporter* (S.Ct.) and the *Lawyers' Edition of the Supreme Court Reports* (L.Ed. or L.Ed.2d). Sample citations for federal court decisions are also listed and explained in Exhibit 1A–2.

Unpublished Opinions

Many court opinions that are not yet published or that are not intended for publication can be accessed through Westlaw® (abbreviated in citations as "WL"), an online legal database. When no citation to a published reporter is available for cases cited in this text, we give the WL citation (see Exhibit 1A–2 on page 25 for an example).

Old Case Law

On a few occasions, this text cites opinions from old, classic cases dating to the nineteenth century or earlier. Some of these are from the English courts. The citations to these cases may not conform to the descriptions given above because the reporters in which they were originally published were often known by the names of the persons who compiled the reporters.

● *Exhibit* 1A–2 **How to Read Citations**

STATE COURTS

280 Neb. 1014, 792 N.W.2d 871 (2011)[a]

> *N.W.* is the abbreviation for West's publication of state court decisions rendered in the *North Western Reporter* of the National Reporter System. *2d* indicates that this case was included in the *Second Series* of that reporter. The number 792 refers to the volume number of the reporter; the number 871 refers to the page in that volume on which this case begins.

> *Neb.* is an abbreviation for *Nebraska Reports,* Nebraska's official reports of the decisions of its highest court, the Nebraska Supreme Court.

129 Cal.App.4th 218, 120 Cal.Rptr.3d 507 (2011)

> *Cal.Rptr.* is the abbreviation for West's unofficial reports—titled *California Reporter*—of the decisions of California courts.

80 A.D.3d 476, 914 N.Y.S.2d 162 (2011)

> *N.Y.S.* is the abbreviation for West's unofficial reports—titled *New York Supplement*—of the decisions of New York courts.

> *A.D.* is the abbreviation for *Appellate Division,* which hears appeals from the New York Supreme Court—the state's general trial court. The New York Court of Appeals is the state's highest court, analogous to other states' supreme courts.

307 Ga.App. 605, 705 S.E.2d 704 (2011)

> *Ga.App.* is the abbreviation for *Georgia Appeals Reports,* Georgia's official reports of the decisions of its court of appeals.

FEDERAL COURTS

___ U.S. ___ , 131 S.Ct. 704, 178 L.Ed.2d 588 (2011)

> *L.Ed.* is an abbreviation for *Lawyers' Edition of the Supreme Court Reports,* an unofficial edition of decisions of the United States Supreme Court.

> *S.Ct.* is the abbreviation for West's unofficial reports—titled *Supreme Court Reporter*—of decisions of the United States Supreme Court.

> *U.S.* is the abbreviation for *United States Reports*, the official edition of the decisions of the United States Supreme Court. The blank lines in this citation (or any other citation) indicate that the appropriate volume of the case reporter has not yet been published and no page number is available.

a. The case names have been deleted from these citations to emphasize the publications. It should be kept in mind, however, that the name of a case is as important as the specific page numbers in the volumes in which it is found. If a citation is incorrect, the correct citation may be found in a publication's index of case names. In addition to providing a check on errors in citations, the date of a case is important because the value of a recent case as an authority is likely to be greater than that of older cases from the same court.

 ## Reading and Understanding Case Law

The cases in this text have been condensed from the full text of the courts' opinions and paraphrased by the authors. For those wishing to review court cases for future

- *Exhibit* 1A-2 **How to Read Citations, Continued**

FEDERAL COURTS (Continued)

628 F.3d 1175 (9th Cir. 2011)

> *9th Cir.* is an abbreviation denoting that this case was decided in the
> U.S. Court of Appeals for the Ninth Circuit.

761 F.Supp.2d 718 (S.D. Ohio 2011)

> *S.D. Ohio* is an abbreviation indicating that the U.S. District Court
> for the Southern District of Ohio decided this case.

ENGLISH COURTS

9 Exch. 341, 156 Eng.Rep. 145 (1854)

> *Eng.Rep.* is an abbreviation for *English Reports, Full Reprint,* a
> series of reports containing selected decisions made in English
> courts between 1378 and 1865.

> *Exch.* is an abbreviation for *English Exchequer Reports*, which includes the
> original reports of cases decided in England's Court of Exchequer.

STATUTORY AND OTHER CITATIONS

18 U.S.C. Section 1961(1)(A)

> *U.S.C.* denotes *United States Code*, the codification of *United States
> Statutes at Large*. The number 18 refers to the statute's U.S.C. title number
> and 1961 to its section number within that title. The number 1 in parentheses
> refers to a subsection within the section, and the letter A in parentheses
> to a subsection within the subsection.

UCC 2–206(1)(b)

> *UCC* is an abbreviation for *Uniform Commercial Code*. The first number 2 is
> a reference to an article of the UCC, and 206 to a section within that article.
> The number 1 in parentheses refers to a subsection within the section, and
> the letter b in parentheses to a subsection within the subsection.

Restatement (Third) of Torts, Section 6

> *Restatement (Third) of Torts* refers to the third edition of the American
> Law Institute's *Restatement of the Law of Torts*. The number 6 refers to a
> specific section.

17 C.F.R. Section 230.505

> *C.F.R.* is an abbreviation for *Code of Federal Regulations*, a compilation of
> federal administrative regulations. The number 17 designates the regulation's
> title number, and 230.505 designates a specific section within that title.

research projects or to gain additional legal information, the following sections will provide useful insights into how to read and understand case law.

Case Titles and Terminology

The title of a case, such as *Adams v. Jones,* indicates the names of the parties to the lawsuit. The *v.* in the case title stands for *versus,* which means "against." In the trial

• *Exhibit* 1A–2 **How to Read Citations, Continued**

WESTLAW® CITATIONS[b]

2011 WL 213420

WL is an abbreviation for Westlaw. The number 2011 is the year of the document that can be found with this citation in the Westlaw database. The number 213420 is a number assigned to a specific document. A higher number indicates that a document was added to the Westlaw database later in the year.

UNIFORM RESOURCE LOCATORS (URLs)

http://www.westlaw.com[c]

The suffix *com* is the top level domain (TLD) for this Web site. The TLD *com* is an abbreviation for "commercial," which usually means that a for-profit entity hosts (maintains or supports) this Web site.

westlaw is the host name—the part of the domain name selected by the organization that registered the name. In this case, West registered the name. This Internet site is the Westlaw database on the Web.

www is an abbreviation for "World Wide Web." The Web is a system of Internet servers that support documents formatted in *HTML* (hypertext markup language) and other formats as well.

http://www.uscourts.gov

This is "The Federal Judiciary Home Page." The host is the Administrative Office of the U.S. Courts. The TLD *gov* is an abbreviation for "government." This Web site includes information and links from, and about, the federal courts.

http://www.law.cornell.edu/index.html

This part of a URL points to a Web page or file at a specific location within the host's domain. This page is a menu with links to documents within the domain and to other Internet resources.

This is the host name for a Web site that contains the Internet publications of the Legal Information Institute (LII), which is a part of Cornell Law School. The LII site includes a variety of legal materials and links to other legal resources on the Internet. The TLD *edu* is an abbreviation for "educational institution" (a school or a university).

http://www.ipl2.org/div/news

This part of the URL points to a static *news* page at this Web site, which provides links to online newspapers from around the world.

div is an abbreviation for "division," which is the way that ipl2 tags the content on its Web site as relating to a specific topic.

The site *ipl2* was formed from the merger of the Internet Public Library and the Librarians' Internet Index. It is an online service that provides reference resources and links to other information services on the Web. The site is supported chiefly by the *iSchool* at Drexel College of Information Science and Technology. The TLD *org* is an abbreviation for "organization" (normally nonprofit).

b. Many court decisions that are not yet published or that are not intended for publication can be accessed through Westlaw, an online legal database.

c. The basic form for a URL is "service://hostname/path." The Internet service for all of the URLs in this text is *http* (hypertext transfer protocol). Because most Web browsers add this prefix automatically when a user enters a host name or a hostname/path, we have generally omitted the *http://* from the URLs listed in this text.

court, Adams was the plaintiff—the person who filed the suit. Jones was the defendant. If the case is appealed, however, the appellate court will sometimes place the name of the party appealing the decision first, so the case may be called *Jones v. Adams*. Because some reviewing courts retain the trial court order of names, it is often impossible to distinguish the plaintiff from the defendant in the title of a reported appellate court decision. You must carefully read the facts of each case to identify the parties.

The following terms and phrases are frequently encountered in court opinions and legal publications. Because it is important to understand what these terms and phrases mean, we define and discuss them here.

PARTIES TO LAWSUITS   As mentioned previously, the party initiating a lawsuit is referred to as the *plaintiff* or *petitioner,* depending on the nature of the action, and the party against whom a lawsuit is brought is the *defendant* or *respondent.* Lawsuits frequently involve more than one plaintiff and/or defendant. When a case is appealed from the original court or jurisdiction to another court or jurisdiction, the party appealing the case is called the *appellant.* The *appellee* is the party against whom the appeal is taken. (In some appellate courts, the party appealing a case is referred to as the *petitioner,* and the party against whom the suit is brought or appealed is called the *respondent.*)

JUDGES AND JUSTICES   The terms *judge* and *justice* are usually synonymous and represent two designations given to judges in various courts. All members of the United States Supreme Court, for example, are referred to as justices, and justice is the formal title often given to judges of appellate courts, although this is not always the case. In New York, a *justice* is a judge of the trial court (which is called the Supreme Court), and a member of the Court of Appeals (the state's highest court) is called a *judge.* The term *justice* is commonly abbreviated to J., and *justices,* to JJ. A Supreme Court case might refer to Justice Sotomayor as Sotomayor, J., or to Chief Justice Roberts as Roberts, C.J.

DECISIONS AND OPINIONS   Most decisions reached by reviewing, or appellate, courts are explained in written *opinions.* The opinion contains the court's reasons for its decision, the rules of law that apply, and the judgment. When all judges or justices unanimously agree on an opinion, the opinion is written for the entire court and can be deemed a *unanimous opinion.* When there is not a unanimous agreement, a *majority opinion* is written. The majority opinion outlines the view supported by the majority of the judges or justices deciding the case.

Often, a judge or justice who wishes to make or emphasize a point that was not made or emphasized in the unanimous or majority opinion will write a *concurring opinion.* This means that the judge or justice agrees, or concurs, with the majority's decision, but for different reasons. When there is not a unanimous opinion, a *dissenting opinion* presents the views of one or more judges who disagree with the majority's decision. The dissenting opinion is important because it may form the basis of the arguments used years later in overruling the precedential majority opinion. Occasionally, a court issues a *per curiam* (Latin for "by the court") opinion, which does not indicate the judge or justice who authored the opinion.

A Sample Court Case

Knowing how to read and analyze a court opinion is an essential step in undertaking accurate legal research. A further step involves "briefing" the case. Legal researchers routinely brief cases by summarizing and reducing the texts of the opinions to their essential elements. (For instructions on how to brief a case, go to Appendix A at the end of this text.) The cases contained within the chapters of this text have already been analyzed and partially briefed by the authors, and the essential aspects of each case are presented in a convenient format consisting of three basic sections: *Background and Facts, In the Words of the Court* (excerpts from the court's opinion), and *Decision and Remedy,* as shown in Exhibit 1A–3 on pages 28–30, which has also been annotated to illustrate the kind of information that is contained in each section. In the remaining chapters of this book, this basic case format is often expanded to include special introductory sections or special comments or considerations that follow the cases.

The sample court case we present and annotate in Exhibit 1A–3 is one that the Superior Court of New Jersey, Appellate Division—a state intermediate appellate court—decided in 2011. On behalf of Edward Fehr's boat, the *Gina Ariella,* Jack Aydelotte entered the Sterling Harbor Duke of Fluke Tournament in New Jersey. One of the issues before the court was the propriety of the *Gina Ariella's* disqualification from the tournament based on the judges' decision that Aydelotte had submitted "bad fish" in the competition for one of the prizes.

You will note that triple asterisks (* * *) and quadruple asterisks (* * * *) frequently appear in the opinion. The triple asterisks indicate that we have deleted a few words or sentences from the opinion for the sake of readability or brevity. Quadruple asterisks mean that an entire paragraph (or more) has been omitted. Additionally, when the opinion cites another case or legal source, the citation to the case or other source has been omitted to save space and to improve the flow of the text. These editorial practices are continued in the other court opinions presented in this book. In addition, whenever we present a court opinion that includes a term or phrase that may not be readily understandable, a bracketed definition or paraphrase has been added.

THE SAMPLE COURT CASE STARTS ON THE NEXT PAGE.

● *Exhibit* 1A-3 **A Sample Court Case**

This section contains the citation—the name of the case, the name of the court that heard the case, reporters in which the court's opinion can be found, and the year of the decision.

FEHR v. ALGARD

Superior Court of New Jersey, Appellate Division

__ A.3d __ (2011).

This line provides the name of the justice (or judge) who authored the court's opinion. *Per curiam* means "by the court" and distinguishes an opinion of the whole court from one that a single judge wrote.

PER CURIAM. [By the Whole Court]

* * * *

The court's opinion can be divided into three sections. The first section, which begins with this paragraph, summarizes the factual background of the case. The court identifies the parties and describes the events leading up to the trial and appeal. The decision of the lower court is included, as well as the issue to be decided by the appellate court.

Defendant Cathy Algard is the owner of defendant Sterling Harbor Motel & Marina Inc. (SHM), trading as Sterling Harbor Bait & Tackle, which is the sponsor of the Sterling Harbor Duke of Fluke Tournament (Tournament).

* * * *

* * * Each year, SHM sponsors the Tournament, which attracts more than one hundred contestants. A number of cash prizes in various categories are awarded. * * * This controversy entails two of those prize awards. The first, the "single heaviest **fluke** prize," given to the contestant

A *fluke* in this context is a flatfish, such as a flounder. *Fluke* has other meanings in the fishing industry—it can refer to part of an anchor, a harpoon, or a whale's tail. (*Fluke* can also refer to accidental success.)

who catches the heaviest live flounder, and the second, the "five heaviest fluke prize," given to the boat catching the five flounder with the greatest combined weight.

The contest rules listed in the Tournament brochure are few. * * * Rule 12 states:

> * * * Any fish entered in the contest is subject to disqualification if a judge decides it bears suspicious marks or characteristics.

The rules brochure also includes the registration [form]. Appearing directly below a registrant's information and above the space provided for the captain's signature, is the following statement:

> * * * Anyone who is found to have provided false information is subject to immediate disqualification including the rest of the anglers aboard said vessel.

The 2007 Tournament was held in Wildwood on July 14, 2007, and monitored by three judges: George and Cathy Algard, and Kenneth Greenling. Plaintiff's boat, the *Gina Ariella*, was registered for the Tournament by Jack Aydelotte.

● *Exhibit* 1A–3 **A Sample Court Case—Continued**

To *sue* is to file a lawsuit and begin the process of resolving a dispute through the court system.

A *contract* is an agreement between two or more parties that can be enforced in court. In a contract, each party agrees to perform, or to refrain from performing, some act now or in the future. The offer of a prize in a contest by its sponsors can become a binding contract in favor of a contestant who complies with the rules.

A *breach* is the breaking of a legal obligation that one person owes to another or to society. A *breach of contract* is a failure to perform the obligations of a contract without a legal excuse.

A *summary judgment* is a judgment that a court enters without beginning or continuing a trial. This judgment can be entered only if no facts are in dispute and the only question is how the law applies to the facts.

The section of the court's opinion that begins with this paragraph contains the court's decision and reasoning on the issue before it. An appellate court's decision is often phrased with reference to the decision of the lower court from which the case was appealed. For example, an appellate court may "affirm" or "reverse" a lower court's ruling. A court's rationale indicates the relevant laws and legal principles, and the court's reasoning that led to its conclusion. The reasoning in this case covered the contract that existed between the contest's sponsors and contestants, and the terms of that contract, which consisted of the contest rules.

Construction in this context means interpretation.

During weigh-in, Aydelotte, on behalf of the *Gina Ariella*, presented the fish to be considered for prizes. First, he offered a six-pound, four-ounce flounder for the single heaviest fluke award. The fish was tagged and placed in a cooler. Next, Aydelotte * * * submitted * * * fish * * * for consideration for the heaviest five fluke award.

As Aydelotte placed the fish in the weigh-in tray, [George] Algard was the first judge to see them. He stated:

> * * * Those fish were not caught that day because I don't know of anything that you can do to make a fish look that bad in eight hours.

Greenling next looked at the fish presented by Aydelotte. He refused to complete the weigh-in, disallowed all five fish and dumped them onto the asphalt parking lot. * * * Algard told Aydelotte "you are disqualified. Don't ever come back here again."

* * * *

Plaintiff **sued** [in a New Jersey state court] alleging, among other things, **breach of contract.**

* * * *

* * * The trial court determined Rule 12 disqualified the "bad fish" but did not support the disqualification of plaintiff and his boat. The court determined plaintiff caught the heaviest fluke, and [in a **summary judgment**] awarded [Fehr] the prize money and the right to assume the title: "2007 Duke of Fluke."

* * * *

In granting summary judgment, the trial judge found the terms of the contract were unambiguous.

* * * *

If we find the terms * * * are clear and unambiguous, there is no room for **construction** and the court must enforce those terms as written, giving them their plain, ordinary meaning. However, if the terms of the contract are susceptible to at least two reasonable alternative interpretations, an ambiguity

(Continued)

● *Exhibit* **1A–3 A Sample Court Case–Continued**

Evidence is proof offered at trial–in the form of testimony, documents, records, exhibits, objects, and the like–to convince the court or jury of the truth of a contention. In this case, *extrinsic* evidence is proof that is outside the express terms of the contract between these parties.

An *offer* is a promise or commitment to perform (or refrain from performing) some specified act.

A *fact finder* is a person or persons who hear testimony from witnesses or otherwise determine and report the facts concerning an event, situation, or dispute. This may be a judge, a jury, or a person appointed by a court.

Every party to a contract is bound by a duty of good faith and fair dealing in its performance. Good faith conduct is conduct that is honest, fair, and reasonable in accord with the parties' agreed purpose and their justified expectations. To act in *bad faith* is to do something that undercuts the right of one of the parties to receive the benefits of the contract.

In the third major section of the opinion, which consists of a single paragraph that begins here, the court states its decision and gives its order.

To *reverse* a judgment is to reject or overrule the judgment that was rendered in the lower court.

To *remand* is to send back. Here the appellate court sent this case back to the trial court to give the parties the opportunity to prove their claims.

exists. In that case, a court may look to **extrinsic evidence** as an aid to interpretation.

* * * *

Plaintiff rejects the need for testimony, arguing there is no ambiguity in the contract. * * * Plaintiff reminds us he first offered his heaviest fluke, which was not rejected, but in fact was weighed and retained by the judges. Viewing this event in isolation, plaintiff appears to have met all requirements of the Tournament rules and defendants' failure to pay was a breach of contract.

Conversely, defendants contend the contest rules along with the [statement] appearing above the captain's signature together form its **offer.** Defendants argue that [the rules] could * * * reasonably be understood to provide that cheating is a basis for disqualification and release from the Tournament.

* * * *

Following our review, we conclude there is enough of an ambiguity in the document forming the parties' agreement to overcome summary judgment and to allow the **fact finder** to decide whether the terms of the contract were breached.

* * * *

* * * Here, the facts, when viewed most indulgently to defendants, demonstrate plaintiff's conduct attempted to dupe the judges. The order of plaintiff's submissions for prizes should not allow the first fish to be considered for an award, if, in fact, he then tried to weigh-in day old fish. We additionally note that * * * if the judges are found to have acted in **bad faith** and exceeded the rules in making a decision, plaintiff may prevail.

We **reverse** the grant of summary judgment to plaintiff and **remand** for further proceedings.

Chapter 2

> "New occasions teach new duties."
>
> —James Russell Lowell, 1819–1891
> (American editor, poet, and diplomat)

Ethics and Business Decision Making

Chapter Objectives

After reading this chapter, you should be able to answer the following questions:

1. **What is business ethics, and why is it important?**

2. **How can business leaders encourage their companies to act ethically?**

3. **How do duty-based ethical standards differ from outcome-based ethical standards?**

4. **What are six guidelines that an employee can use to evaluate whether his or her actions are ethical?**

5. **What types of ethical issues might arise in the context of international business transactions?**

(John Elk III/Lonely Planet Images/Getty Images)

In the early part of the first decade of the 2000s, ethics scandals erupted throughout corporate America. Heads of major corporations (some of which no longer exist) were tried for fraud, conspiracy, grand larceny, and obstruction of justice. Former multimillionaires (and even billionaires) who once ran multinational corporations are now serving sentences in federal penitentiaries. The giant energy company Enron in particular dominated headlines. Its investors lost around $60 billion when the company ceased to exist.

Fast-forward to 2009. One man, Bernard Madoff, was convicted of bilking investors out of more than $65 billion through a Ponzi scheme[1] that he had perpetrated for decades. Madoff's victims included not just naïve retirees but also some of the world's largest and best-known financial institutions, such as the Royal Bank of Scotland, France's BNP Paribas, Spain's Banco Santander, and Japan's Nomura. And ethical lapses were not limited to Madoff. In 2010, the Securities and Exchange Commission imposed its largest-ever penalty against a Wall Street firm when it fined Goldman Sachs Group, Inc., $550 million for misleading investors in its marketing materials. Ethical problems in many financial institutions contributed to the onset of the deepest recession since the Great Depression of the 1930s. Not only did some $9 trillion in investment capital evaporate, but millions of workers lost their jobs.

---

1. A Ponzi scheme is a type of illegal pyramid scheme named after Charles Ponzi, who duped thousands of New England residents into investing in a postage-stamp speculation scheme in the 1920s.

The point is clear: the scope and scale of corporate unethical behavior, especially in the financial sector, skyrocketed in the first decade of the twenty-first century—with enormous repercussions for everyone, not just in the United States, but around the world. As the chapter-opening quotation on the previous page states, "New occasions teach new duties." Indeed, the ethics scandals of the last fifteen years have taught businesspersons all over the world that business ethics cannot be taken lightly. Acting ethically in a business context can mean billions of dollars—made or lost—for corporations, shareholders, and employees, and can have far-reaching effects on society and the global economy.

Business Ethics

Ethics   Moral principles and values applied to social behavior.

As you might imagine, business ethics is derived from the concept of ethics. **Ethics** can be defined as the study of what constitutes right or wrong behavior. It is the branch of philosophy that focuses on morality and the way in which moral principles are derived and applied to one's conduct in daily life. Ethics has to do with questions relating to the fairness, justness, rightness, or wrongness of an action.

Business Ethics   Ethics in a business context; a consensus as to what constitutes right or wrong behavior in the world of business and the application of moral principles to situations that arise in a business setting.

Business ethics focuses on what constitutes right or wrong behavior in the business world and on how businesspersons apply moral and ethical principles to situations that arise in the workplace. Because business decision makers often address more complex ethical dilemmas than they face in their personal lives, business ethics is more complicated than personal ethics.

Why Is Business Ethics Important?

To see why business ethics is so important, reread the first paragraph of this chapter. All of the corporate executives who are sitting behind bars could have avoided this outcome had they engaged in ethical decision making during their careers. As a result of their crimes, all of their companies suffered losses, and some were forced to enter bankruptcy, causing thousands of workers to lose their jobs.

If the executives had acted ethically, the corporations, shareholders, and employees of those companies would not have paid such a high price. Thus, an in-depth understanding of business ethics is important to the long-run viability of a corporation, the well-being of officers and directors, and the firm's employees. Finally, unethical corporate decision making can negatively affect suppliers, consumers, the community, and society as a whole.

Moral Minimum   The minimum degree of ethical behavior expected of a business firm, which is usually defined as compliance with the law.

The Moral Minimum

The minimum acceptable standard for ethical business behavior—known as the **moral minimum**—normally is considered to be compliance with the law. In many corporate scandals, had most of the businesspersons involved simply followed the law, they would not have gotten into trouble. Note, though, that in the interest of preserving personal freedom, as well as for practical reasons, the law does not—and cannot—codify all ethical requirements.

As they make business decisions, businesspersons must remember that just because an action is legal does not necessarily make it ethical. For instance, no law specifies the salaries that publicly held corporations can pay their officers. Nevertheless, if a corporation pays its officers an excessive amount relative to other employees, or to what officers at other corporations are paid, the executives' compensation might be challenged as unethical. (Executive bonuses can also present ethical problems—see the discussion later in this chapter.)

"But in the business world, failure is rewarded with big bailouts."

Short-Run Profit Maximization

Some people argue that a corporation's only goal should be profit maximization, which will be reflected in a higher market value. When all firms strictly adhere to the goal of profit maximization, resources tend to flow to where they are most highly valued by society. Thus, in theory, profit maximization ultimately leads to the most efficient allocation of scarce resources.

Corporate executives and employees have to distinguish, however, between *short-run* and *long-run* profit maximization. In the short run, a company may increase its profits by continuing to sell a product even though it knows that the product is defective. In the long run, though, because of lawsuits, large settlements, and bad publicity, such unethical conduct will cause profits to suffer. Thus, business ethics is consistent only with long-run profit maximization. An overemphasis on short-term profit maximization is the most common reason that ethical problems occur in business.

CASE EXAMPLE 2.1   When the powerful narcotic painkiller OxyContin was first marketed, its manufacturer, Purdue Pharma, claimed that it was unlikely to lead to drug addiction or abuse. Internal company documents later showed that the company's executives knew that OxyContin could be addictive, but they kept this risk a secret to boost sales and maximize short-term profits. In 2007, Purdue Pharma and three former executives pleaded guilty to criminal charges that they misled regulators, patients, and physicians about OxyContin's risks of addiction. Purdue Pharma agreed to pay $600 million in fines and other payments. The three former executives agreed to pay $34.5 million in fines and were barred from federal health programs for a period of fifteen years—a ruling that was upheld by an administrative law judge in 2009. Thus, the company's focus on maximizing profits in the short run led to unethical conduct that hurt profits in the long run.[2] ●

The following case provides an example of unethical—and illegal—conduct designed to enhance a company's short-term outlook that in the end destroyed the firm.

─────────────

2. *United States v. Purdue Frederick Co.*, 495 F. Supp.2d 569 (W.D.Va. 2007).

Case 2.1   **Skilling v. United States**

Supreme Court of the United States, ___ U.S. ___, 130 S.Ct. 2896, 177 L.Ed.2d 619 (2010).

COMPANY PROFILE   *In the 1990s, Enron Corporation was an international, multibillion-dollar enterprise consisting of four businesses that bought and sold energy, owned energy networks, and bought and sold bandwidth capacity. "Wholesale," the division that bought and sold energy wholesale, was the most profitable and accounted for 90 percent of Enron's revenues. Jeffrey Skilling–Enron's president and its chief operating officer, and a member of its board of directors–boasted at a conference with financial analysts in January 2001 that Enron's retail energy and bandwidth sales divisions had "sustainable high earnings power." Skilling became Enron's chief executive officer (CEO) in February 2001.*

BACKGROUND AND FACTS   In August 2001, Jeffrey Skilling resigned his position as Enron's CEO. Four months later, Enron filed for bankruptcy. An investigation uncovered a conspiracy to deceive investors about Enron's finances to ensure that its stock price remained high. Among other things, Skilling had shifted more than $2 billion in losses from Enron's struggling divisions to Wholesale. He had overstated Enron's profits in calls to investors and in press releases. To hide more losses, he had arranged deals between Enron's executives and third parties, which he falsely portrayed to Enron's accountants and to the Securities and Exchange Commission as producing income. Skilling was convicted in a federal district court of various crimes, including conspiring to commit fraud to deprive Enron and its shareholders of the "honest services" of its employees. He was sentenced to 292 months' imprisonment and three years' supervised release, and ordered to pay $45 million in restitution. Skilling appealed, and the U.S. Court of Appeals for the Fifth Circuit affirmed the trial court's ruling. Skilling

Case 2.1–Continues next page ➡

"It's easy to make a buck. It's a lot tougher to make a difference."

Tom Brokaw, 1940–present
(American television journalist)

Case 2.1–Continued

Jeffrey Skilling (left) and Enron's former chief executive officer, Kenneth Lay (right). Of what were they guilty?

appealed to the United States Supreme Court, arguing, among other things, that the honest-services statute is unconstitutionally vague or, in the alternative, that his conduct did not fall within the statute's compass.

IN THE WORDS OF THE COURT . . . Justice *GINSBURG* delivered the opinion of the Court.

* * * *

[In 1988,] Congress enacted a new statute "specifically to cover * * * the intangible right of honest services" [as a "scheme or artifice to defraud" in laws prohibiting mail and wire fraud].

* * * *

[Before 1988,] the "vast majority" of the honest-services cases involved offenders who, in violation of a fiduciary duty participated in bribery or kickback schemes.

* * * The honest-services doctrine had its genesis [origin] in prosecutions involving bribery allegations.

In view of this history, there is no doubt that Congress intended [the law] to reach *at least* bribes and kickbacks. Reading the statute to proscribe [rule out] a wider range of offensive conduct, we acknowledge, would raise the due process concerns underlying the vagueness doctrine. To preserve the statute without transgressing [breaching] constitutional limitations, we now hold that [the statute] criminalizes *only* the bribe-and-kickback core of the [case law prior to 1988]. [Emphases added by the Court.]

* * * *

The government did not, at any time, allege that Skilling solicited or accepted side payments from a third party in exchange for making * * * misrepresentations [concerning Enron's fiscal health]. It is therefore clear that, as we read [the statute], Skilling did not commit honest-services fraud.

Because the indictment alleged three objects of the conspiracy—honest-services wire fraud, money-or-property wire fraud, and securities fraud—Skilling's conviction is flawed. This determination, however, does not necessarily require reversal of the conspiracy conviction * * *. We leave this dispute for resolution on remand.

DECISION AND REMEDY   The United States Supreme Court vacated the federal appellate court's ruling that Skilling's actions had violated the honest-services statute. The Court remanded the case for further proceedings to determine how its decision would affect the other charges against Skilling.

THE ETHICAL DIMENSION   *During Skilling's tenure at Enron, the mood among the employees was upbeat because the company's future prospects appeared "rosy." Among other things, many employees invested all their pension funds in Enron stock. Is there anything unethical about this situation? Discuss.*

MANAGERIAL IMPLICATIONS   *Just because the Court has reduced the scope of the honest-services fraud doctrine does not mean that federal prosecutors will be unable to indict businesspersons who flagrantly violate ethical business standards. There are more than four thousand federal crimes on the books today. Consequently, the federal government will continue to pursue actions that it deems illegal business practices. The government will simply charge those who are its targets with other federal crimes.*

"Gray Areas" in the Law

In many situations, business firms can predict with a fair amount of certainty whether a given action would be legal. For instance, firing an employee solely because of that person's race or gender would clearly violate federal laws prohibiting employment discrimination. In some situations, though, the legality of a particular action may be less clear. In part, this is because there are so many laws regulating business that it is increasingly possible to violate one of them without realizing it. The law also contains numerous "gray areas," making it difficult to predict with certainty how a court will apply a given law to a particular action.

In addition, many rules of law require a court to determine what is "foreseeable" or "reasonable" in a particular situation. Because a business has no way of predicting how a specific court will decide these issues, decision makers need to proceed with caution and evaluate an action and its consequences from an ethical perspective. The same problem often occurs in cases involving the Internet because it is often unclear how a court will apply existing laws in the context of cyberspace. Generally, if a company can demonstrate that it acted in good faith and responsibly in the circumstances, it has a better chance of successfully defending its action in court or before an administrative law judge.

If a company discovers that a manager has behaved unethically or engaged in misconduct, the company should take prompt remedial action. The following case illustrates what can happen when a manager fails to follow the standards that apply to other employees.

Case 2.2   Mathews v. B and K Foods, Inc.

Missouri Court of Appeals, 332 S.W.3d 273 (2011).

BACKGROUND AND FACTS   Dianne Mathews was employed as a floral manager by B and K Foods, Inc. On July 15, 2010, her employment was terminated for submitting falsified time cards. On July 17, Mathews filed an application with the state for unemployment compensation (see Chapter 17). B and K objected, arguing that Mathews was not entitled to unemployment benefits because she had been discharged for misconduct in connection with work. At an administrative hearing held by the unemployment commission, the chief executive officer of B and K testified that it was company policy to deduct thirty minutes each day from the time sheets of employees, including managers, for a lunch break. When an individual was "not able to clock out for lunch" and worked straight through, that person could fill out a "no lunch" sheet for the day. Payroll would then add thirty minutes back to the person's work time. Mathews allegedly sometimes turned in "no lunch" sheets to cover time when she was running personal errands instead of working. Mathews admitted that she knew about the "no lunch" sheet policy and had used it on occasion but contended that her conduct was warranted. She claimed that a former employee who was a higher-level manager at B and K had told her that it was unnecessary to adjust her time card when she spent a few minutes on a personal errand. The unemployment commission concluded that Mathews was disqualified from seeking unemployment benefits due to misconduct. Mathews appealed.

IN THE WORDS OF THE COURT . . .
William W. FRANCIS, Jr., Judge.

* * * *

"Misconduct" which would disqualify an employee from unemployment benefits is defined as:

> An act of wanton or willful disregard of the employer's interest, a deliberate violation of the employer's rules, a disregard of standards of behavior which the employer has the right to expect of his or her employee * * * .

Section 288.030.1(23).

"'*Work-related misconduct*' *must involve a willful violation of the rules or standards of the employer.*" * * * To willfully disregard Employer's interests, Claimant [Mathews] first had to be aware of the requirement, and then knowingly or consciously violate it. [Emphasis added.]

* * * *

Substantial evidence supported a finding that Claimant's conduct of falsifying her timecard record by turning in a "no lunch sheet"

for time she had left the store to run a personal errand was a willful or deliberate violation of Employer's policy. First, Claimant herself testified she was familiar with the "no lunch sheet" and verified it was her practice during 2009 not to take a lunch break every day and to complete and turn in a "no lunch sheet" for each day. The "no lunch sheet" allowed managers to be compensated for *working* through their lunch breaks. Additionally, as a manager, Claimant was responsible for enforcing Employer's lunch policy with her subordinate employees. Mr. Gerard [the top corporate executive at B and K] testified they had no choice but to terminate Claimant because she was in a higher position and had a responsibility to enforce the lunch policy. Thus, Claimant was well aware of Employer's lunch policy when she made the affirmative choice to turn in a "no lunch sheet" for the time she spent running a personal errand.

* * * *

* * * Here, Claimant's knowledge of Employer's "no lunch sheet" policy is especially apparent because Claimant herself testified to her familiarity with it and she was responsible for enforcing the policy regularly with employees under her direct supervision.

Claimant's actions of turning in "no lunch sheets" and thereby claiming pay status for time she was out of the store conducting personal errands were a direct violation of Employer's policy. Claimant's conduct goes beyond a mere lack of judgment as evidence established she knew her behavior was inappropriate and against Employer's interest. * * * Accordingly, we affirm the decision of the Commission.

DECISION AND REMEDY   A state intermediate appellate court affirmed the decision of the state unemployment commission. The court found that the employer had met its burden of proving that Matthews had engaged in work-related misconduct, which disqualified her from receiving unemployment benefits.

WHAT IF THE FACTS WERE DIFFERENT?   *Suppose that Mathews had not admitted to knowing about the "no lunch sheet" policy. Would the result in this case have been different? Why or why not?*

Case 2.2–Continues next page ➡

Case 2.2–Continued

MANAGERIAL IMPLICATIONS   *Any employer that discovers a manager is not following stated company policies should take immediate action to correct the situation. Although a company does not always need to terminate the manager for misconduct, as was done in this case, it must act decisively because its action will have a significant impact on workplace ethics. A company that allows managers to engage in unethical conduct without consequences sends a message to subordinate employees that such behavior is tolerated. Managers must live by the same rules as employees and face the same consequences when they fail to do so.*

The Importance of Ethical Leadership

Talking about ethical business decision making is meaningless if management does not set standards. Furthermore, managers must apply the same standards to themselves as they do to the employees of the company.

ATTITUDE OF TOP MANAGEMENT   One of the most important ways to create and maintain an ethical workplace is for top management to demonstrate its commitment to ethical decision making. A manager who is not totally committed to an ethical workplace rarely succeeds in creating one. Management's behavior, more than anything else, sets the ethical tone of a firm. Employees take their cues from management. **CASE EXAMPLE 2.2**   Devon, a SureTek employee, observes his manager cheating on her expense account. Devon quickly understands that such behavior is acceptable. Later, when Devon is promoted to a managerial position, he "pads" his expense account as well, knowing that he is unlikely to face sanctions for doing so. ●

> *"What you do speaks so loudly that I cannot hear what you say."*
>
> Ralph Waldo Emerson, 1803–1882
> (American essayist and poet)

Managers who set unrealistic production or sales goals increase the probability that employees will act unethically. If a sales quota can be met only through high-pressure, unethical sales tactics, employees will try to act "in the best interest of the company" and will continue to behave unethically.

A manager who looks the other way when she or he knows about an employee's unethical behavior also sets an example—one indicating that ethical transgressions will be accepted. Managers have found that discharging even one employee for ethical reasons has a tremendous impact as a deterrent to unethical behavior in the workplace.

BEHAVIOR OF OWNERS AND MANAGERS   Business owners and managers sometimes take more active roles in fostering unethical and illegal conduct. This may indicate to their co-owners, co-managers, employees, and others that unethical business behavior will be tolerated.

Business owners' misbehavior can have negative consequences for themselves and their business. Not only can a court sanction the business owners and managers, but it can also issue an injunction that prevents them from engaging in similar patterns of conduct in the future.

CASE EXAMPLE 2.3   Douglas and Brian Baum, along with their father, ran an asset recovery business. The Baums researched various unclaimed funds, tried to locate the rightful owners, and received either a finder's fee or the right to some or all of the funds recovered. The Baums convinced investors—through misrepresentation—to file a meritless lawsuit in a federal district court in Texas. The court later determined that the Baums had maliciously attempted to extort funds and sanctioned them for pretending to be lawyers, lying to the investors and the court, and generally abusing the judicial system. The judge also issued a permanent injunction against all three Baums to prohibit them from filing claims related to the same case without express permission from the judge. When the Baums continued their business in the same manner, the judge expanded the injunction to apply to all claims filed in Texas. The

Baums appealed, claiming that the court lacked the power to expand the injunction. The appellate court ruled that federal courts have the power to enjoin (prevent) plaintiffs from future filings when those plaintiffs consistently abuse the court system and harass their opponents.[3] ●

The following case shows how a manager's sexist attitudes and actions affected the workplace environment. The case also underscores the limitations of the law with respect to this type of unethical business behavior.

3. *Baum v. Blue Moon Ventures, LLC*, 513 F.3d 181 (5th Cir. 2008).

Case 2.3 Krasner v. HSH Nordbank AG[a]

United States District Court, Southern District of New York, 680 F.Supp.2d 502 (2010).

(AP Photo/Axel Heimken)

BACKGROUND AND FACTS

David Krasner worked in the New York branch of HSH Nordbank AG (HSH), an international commercial bank headquartered in Germany. Krasner claimed that his supervisor, Roland Kiser, fostered an atmosphere "infected with overt sexism." According to Krasner, career advancement was based on "sexual favoritism," and women's advancement was governed by a "casting couch." Krasner alleged that Kiser and other male supervisors promoted a sexist and demeaning image of women in the workplace. Krasner also stated that Kiser pressured male subordinates, such as Krasner, to go to strip clubs with him when on business trips abroad. Krasner repeatedly objected to Kiser's and other supervisors' sexist attitudes, and particularly to Kiser's relationship with a female employee, Melissa Campfield. According to Krasner, Campfield was promoted at the expense of the "career advancement and reputations of other far more senior and qualified employees," including Krasner. Krasner complained both to Kiser and to the company's human resources department that Kiser's actions were violating the company's ethics policy. HSH investigated Krasner's complaints but found no violation of the law or of its own ethics policy. Shortly thereafter, Krasner was summarily terminated. Krasner sued HSH and Kiser in a federal district court, alleging that the defendants had discriminated against him on the basis of gender in violation of Title VII of the Civil Rights Act of 1964.[b] The defendants moved to dismiss the case.

IN THE WORDS OF THE COURT . . .

Gerard E. LYNCH, Circuit Judge.

* * * *

The substantive anti-discrimination provision of Title VII prohibits employers from "discriminat[ing] against any individual with respect

a. *AG* stands for *Actiengesellschaft*, a German term denoting a corporation.
b. Title VII of the federal Civil Rights Act of 1964 prohibits employment discrimination on the basis of race, color, national origin, religion, or gender—see Chapter 18.

to his compensation, terms, conditions, or privileges of employment, because of such individual's * * * sex." *"One form of gender discrimination prohibited by Title VII is sexual harassment that results in a 'hostile or abusive work environment.' "* Under this doctrine, even if an *"employee does not experience a specific negative action,"* he may have a viable claim under Title VII for sexual discrimination where *"the harassment is so pervasive that it changes the conditions of employment."* [Emphasis added.]

* * * *

Krasner's discrimination claim is founded on allegations that he was subject to a sexually hostile work environment through a combination of "(1) widespread sexual favoritism resulting from Kiser's affair with Campfield; (2) widespread sexual favoritism resulting from other affairs at [HSH]; and (3) sexually harassing and offensive conduct perpetrated by Kiser * * * unrelated to sexual affairs." In addressing these contentions, the parties argue as though a hostile environment is something that exists in some absolute way, like poisonous chemicals in the air, affecting everyone who comes in contact with it. In doing so, the parties all but ignore the prohibited causal factor requirement, which is critical to liability.

Title VII does not prohibit employers from maintaining nasty, unpleasant workplaces, or even ones that are unpleasant for reasons that are sexual in nature. Rather, it prohibits employers from discriminating against an employee (including by subjecting him or her to hostile working conditions) "because of such individual's * * * sex."

* * * *

An examination of Krasner's allegations reveals that he does not contend that he was disparaged or badly treated or subjected to an unpleasant work atmosphere in any way because he is a man. Rather, his complaint is primarily that Kiser and other supervisors advanced a demeaning view of women in the workplace, which Krasner was exposed to and found "objectionable," and which denied "him the opportunity to work in an employment setting free of unlawful harassment."

* * * *

Case 2.3–Continues next page ⇒

Case 2.3–Continued

* * * Krasner's claim fails because "none of the alleged acts of harassment committed directly against [Krasner]"—either when viewed in isolation or in conjunction with any potential discrimination against women—"support a claim that [he] is being harassed because he is a *male* employee." The primary animator of the complaint is what Krasner terms the "egregious effects of Kiser's favoritism" towards Campfield upon plaintiff himself.

Assuming that these actions * * * systematically and pervasively altered the conditions of Krasner's working environment sufficiently to satisfy the objective component of a hostile environment claim, the claim must nevertheless fail because the complaint does not allege that these incidents are in any way related to his gender. Krasner does not allege, and proffers [presents, or offers] no facts that remotely suggest, that a female supervisor in his position would not have experienced exactly the same consequences from Kiser's preferential treatment of Campfield.

DECISION AND REMEDY　　The federal district court granted the defendants' motions to dismiss the complaint. Krasner had no cause of action for gender discrimination under Title VII because he had not demonstrated that the defendants' treatment of him was based on his gender.

WHAT IF THE FACTS WERE DIFFERENT?　　*Assume that a female employee experienced the same type of treatment that Krasner faced. Would the female employee succeed in a Title VII claim of gender-based discrimination? Why or why not?*

MANAGERIAL IMPLICATIONS　　*Just because Krasner's case was dismissed does not mean that the working environment at HSH was appropriate. The treatment of employees might have been legal, but it was not ethical. Managers should always be on the lookout for situations like the ones described in this case and should attempt to rectify them—at the very least, to avoid similar lawsuits. In addition, human resources policies should explicitly forbid such behavior.*

Creating Ethical Codes of Conduct

One of the most effective ways of setting a tone of ethical behavior within an organization is to create an ethical code of conduct. A well-written code of ethics explicitly states a company's ethical priorities and demonstrates the company's commitment to ethical behavior.

This chapter features a foldout exhibit showing the code of ethics of Costco Wholesale Corporation as an example. This code of conduct indicates Costco's commitment to legal compliance, as well as to the welfare of its members (those who purchase its goods), its employees, and its suppliers. The code also details some specific ways in which the interests and welfare of these different groups will be protected. You can also see that Costco acknowledges that by protecting these groups' interests, it realize its "ultimate goal"—rewarding its shareholders with maximum shareholder value.

ETHICS TRAINING FOR EMPLOYEES　　For an ethical code to be effective, its provisions must be clearly communicated to employees. Most large companies have implemented ethics training programs, in which managers discuss with employees on a face-to-face basis the firm's policies and the importance of ethical conduct. Some firms hold periodic ethics seminars during which employees can openly discuss any ethical problems that they may be experiencing and learn how the firm's ethical policies apply to those specific problems. Smaller firms should also offer some form of ethics training to employees because if a firm is accused of an ethics violation, the court will consider the presence or absence of such training in evaluating the firm's conduct.

Preventing Legal Disputes

To avoid disputes over ethical violations, you should first create an ethical code that is written in clear and understandable language. The code should establish specific procedures that employees can follow if they have questions or complaints. It should assure employees that their jobs will be secure and that they will not face reprisals if they do file a complaint. A well-written code might also include examples to clarify what the company considers to be acceptable and unacceptable conduct. You should also hold periodic training meetings so that you can explain to employees face to face why ethics is important to the company.

THE SARBANES-OXLEY ACT AND WEB-BASED REPORTING SYSTEMS   The Sarbanes-Oxley Act of 2002[4] requires companies to set up confidential systems so that employees and others can "raise red flags" about suspected illegal or unethical auditing and accounting practices. (Excerpts from the Sarbanes-Oxley Act with explanatory comments appear in Appendix D of this text.)

Some companies have implemented online reporting systems to accomplish this goal. In one such system, employees can click on an icon on their computers that anonymously links them with EthicsPoint, an organization based in Portland, Oregon. Through EthicsPoint, employees can report suspicious accounting practices, sexual harassment, and other possibly unethical behavior. EthicsPoint, in turn, alerts management personnel or the audit committee at the designated company to the possible problem. Those who have used the system say that it is less inhibiting than calling a company's toll-free number.

▶ Ethical Transgressions by Financial Institutions

One of the best ways to learn the ethical responsibilities inherent in operating a business is to look at the mistakes made by other companies. In the following subsections, we describe some of the worst ethical failures of financial institutions during the latter part of the first decade of the 2000s. Many of these ethical wrongdoings received wide publicity and raised public awareness of the need for ethical leadership throughout all businesses.

Corporate Stock Buybacks

Stock Buyback   A company's purchase of shares of its own stock on the open market.

Stock Option   An agreement that grants the owner the option to buy a given number of shares of stock, usually within a set time period.

Lehman Brothers was an investment banking firm that had been in business for more than 150 years. When the U.S. Treasury refused to bail out the firm in 2008, it went bankrupt. Were its stock buybacks earlier that same year unethical? Why or why not?

By now, you are probably aware that in 2008 and 2009 many well-known financial companies in the United States either went bankrupt, were taken over by the federal government, or were bailed out by U.S. taxpayers. What most people do not know is that those same corporations were using their own cash funds to prop up the value of their stock in the years just before the economic crisis started in 2008.

The theory behind a **stock buyback** is simple—the management of a corporation believes that the market price of its shares is "below their fair value." Therefore, instead of issuing dividends to shareholders or reinvesting profits, management uses the company's funds to buy its shares in the open market, thereby boosting the price of the stock. From 2005 to 2007, stock buybacks for the top five hundred U.S. corporations added up to $1.4 *trillion*.

Who benefits from stock buybacks? The main individual beneficiaries are corporate executives who have been given **stock options,** which enable them to buy shares of the corporation's stock at a set price. When the market price rises above that level, the executives can profit by selling their shares. Although stock buybacks are legal and can serve legitimate purposes, they can easily be abused if managers use them just to increase the stock price in the short term so that they can profit from their options without considering the long-term needs of the company.

In the investment banking business, which almost disappeared entirely in the latter half of 2008, stock buybacks were particularly egregious. In the first half of 2008, Lehman Brothers Holdings was buying back its own stock—yet in September of that year, it

---
4. 15 U.S.C. Sections 7201 *et seq.*

filed for bankruptcy. According to financial writer Liam Denning, Lehman's buybacks were "akin to giving away the fire extinguisher even as your house begins to fill with smoke." Goldman Sachs, another investment bank, bought back $15 billion of its stock in 2007. By the end of 2008, U.S. taxpayers had provided $10 billion in bailout funds to that same company.

Startling Executive Decisions at American International Group

For years, New York–based American International Group (AIG) was a respected, conservative worldwide insurance company. Then, during the early 2000s, it decided to enter an area in which it had little expertise—the issuance of insurance contracts guaranteeing certain types of complicated financial contracts. When many of those insured contracts failed, AIG experienced multibillion-dollar losses. Finally, the company sought a federal bailout that eventually amounted to almost $200 billion of U.S. taxpayers' funds.

While some company executives were testifying before Congress after receiving the funds, other AIG executives spent almost $400,000 on a retreat at a resort in California. In essence, U.S. taxpayers were footing the bill. To most observers, such arrogance was as incomprehensible as it was unethical.

Executive Bonuses

Until the economic crisis began in 2008, the bonuses paid in the financial industry did not make headlines. After all, times were good, and why shouldn't those responsible for record company earnings be rewarded? When investment banks and commercial banks began to fail, however, or had to be bailed out or taken over by the federal government, executive bonuses became an issue of paramount importance.

Certainly, the system of rewards in banking became perverse during the early 2000s. Executives and others in the industry were paid a percentage of their firm's profits, no matter how risky their investment actions had been. In other words, commissions and bonuses were based on sales of risky assets to investors. These included securities based on subprime mortgages, collateralized debt obligations, and other mortgages.

When the subprime mortgage crisis started, the worldwide house of cards came tumbling down, but those who had created and sold those risky assets suffered no liability—and even received bonuses. Of course, some of those firms that had enjoyed high short-run returns from their risky investments—and paid bonuses based on those profits—found themselves facing bankruptcy.

Consider Lehman Brothers before its bankruptcy. Its chief executive officer, Richard Fuld, Jr., earned almost $500 million between 2000 and the firm's demise in 2008. Even after Lehman Brothers entered bankruptcy, its new owners, Barclays and Nomura, legally owed $3.5 billion in bonuses to employees still on the payroll. In 2006, Goldman Sachs awarded its employees a total of $16.5 billion in bonuses, or an average of almost $750,000 for each employee.

By 2007, profits on Wall Street had already begun to drop—sometimes dramatically. Citigroup's profits, for example, were down 83 per-

Speaker of the House Nancy Pelosi presents the American Recovery and Reinvestment Act (the economic stimulus bill) before it was passed by Congress and signed into law by President Barack Obama in 2009. One provision in that act restricted bonuses that can be paid by companies receiving bailout funds from the U.S. government. Why did the government seek to restrict bonus payments in the financial industry?

(EPA/Michael Reynolds/Corbis)

cent from the previous year. Bonuses, in contrast, declined by less than 5 percent. The bonus payout in 2007 for all Wall Street firms combined was $33.2 billion.

▶ Approaches to Ethical Reasoning

Ethical Reasoning A reasoning process in which an individual links his or her moral convictions or ethical standards to the particular situation at hand.

Each individual, when faced with a particular ethical dilemma, engages in **ethical reasoning**—that is, a reasoning process in which the individual examines the situation at hand in light of his or her moral convictions or ethical standards. Businesspersons do likewise when making decisions with ethical implications.

How do business decision makers decide whether a given action is the "right" one for their firms? What ethical standards should be applied? Broadly speaking, ethical reasoning relating to business traditionally has been characterized by two fundamental approaches. One approach defines ethical behavior in terms of duty, which also implies certain rights. The other approach determines what is ethical in terms of the consequences, or outcome, of any given action. We examine each of these approaches here.

In addition to the two basic ethical approaches, several theories have been developed that specifically address the social responsibility of corporations. Because these theories also influence today's business decision makers, we conclude this section with a short discussion of the different views of corporate social responsibility.

Duty-Based Ethics

Duty-based ethical standards often are derived from revealed truths, such as religious precepts. They can also be derived through philosophical reasoning.

"When I do good, I feel good. When I do bad, I feel bad. And that's my religion."

Abraham Lincoln, 1809–1865
(Sixteenth president of the United States, 1861–1865)

RELIGIOUS ETHICAL STANDARDS In the Judeo-Christian tradition, which is the dominant religious tradition in the United States, the Ten Commandments of the Old Testament establish fundamental rules for moral action. Other religions have their own sources of revealed truth. Religious rules generally are absolute with respect to the behavior of their adherents. **EXAMPLE 2.4** The commandment "Thou shalt not steal" is an absolute mandate for a person who believes that the Ten Commandments reflect revealed truth. Even a benevolent motive for stealing (such as Robin Hood's) cannot justify the act because the act itself is inherently immoral and thus wrong. ●

Categorical Imperative A concept developed by the philosopher Immanuel Kant as an ethical guideline for behavior. In deciding whether an action is right or wrong, or desirable or undesirable, a person should evaluate the action in terms of what would happen if everybody else in the same situation, or category, acted the same way.

KANTIAN ETHICS Duty-based ethical standards may also be derived solely from philosophical reasoning. The German philosopher Immanuel Kant (1724–1804), for example, identified some general guiding principles for moral behavior based on what he believed to be the fundamental nature of human beings. Kant believed that human beings are qualitatively different from other physical objects and are endowed with moral integrity and the capacity to reason and conduct their affairs rationally. Therefore, a person's thoughts and actions should be respected. When human beings are treated merely as a means to an end, they are being treated as the equivalent of objects and are being denied their basic humanity.

A central theme in Kantian ethics is that individuals should evaluate their actions in light of the consequences that would follow if *everyone* in society acted in the same way. This **categorical imperative** can be applied to any action. **EXAMPLE 2.5** Suppose that you are deciding whether to cheat on an examination. If you have adopted Kant's categorical imperative, you will decide *not* to cheat because if everyone cheated, the examination (and the entire education system) would be meaningless. ●

THE PRINCIPLE OF RIGHTS   Because a duty cannot exist without a corresponding right, duty-based ethical standards imply that human beings have basic rights. The principle that human beings have certain fundamental rights (to life, liberty, and the pursuit of happiness, for example) is deeply embedded in Western culture. As discussed in Chapter 1, the natural law tradition embraces the concept that certain actions (such as killing another person) are morally wrong because they are contrary to nature (the natural desire to continue living). Those who adhere to this **principle of rights,** or "rights theory," believe that a key factor in determining whether a business decision is ethical is how that decision affects the rights of others. These others include the firm's owners, its employees, the consumers of its products or services, its suppliers, the community in which it does business, and society as a whole.

A potential dilemma for those who support rights theory, however, is that there are often conflicting rights and people may disagree on which rights are most important. When considering all those affected by a business decision, for example, how much weight should be given to employees relative to shareholders, customers relative to the community, or employees relative to society as a whole?

In general, rights theorists believe that whichever right is stronger in a particular circumstance takes precedence. **EXAMPLE 2.6**   A firm can either keep a manufacturing plant open, saving the jobs of twelve workers, or shut the plant down and avoid contaminating a river with pollutants that would endanger the health of tens of thousands of people. In this situation, a rights theorist can easily choose which group to favor. Not all choices are so clear-cut, however. •

Outcome-Based Ethics: Utilitarianism

"The greatest good for the greatest number" is a paraphrase of the major premise of the utilitarian approach to ethics. **Utilitarianism** is a philosophical theory developed by Jeremy Bentham (1748–1832) and modified by John Stuart Mill (1806–1873)—both British philosophers. In contrast to duty-based ethics, utilitarianism is outcome oriented. It focuses on the consequences of an action, not on the nature of the action itself or on any set of preestablished moral values or religious beliefs.

Under a utilitarian model of ethics, an action is morally correct, or "right," when, among the people it affects, it produces the greatest amount of good for the greatest number. When an action affects the majority adversely, it is morally wrong. Applying the utilitarian theory thus requires (1) a determination of which individuals will be affected by the action in question; (2) a **cost-benefit analysis,** which involves an assessment of the negative and positive effects of alternative actions on these individuals; and (3) a choice among alternative actions that will produce maximum societal utility (the greatest positive net benefits for the greatest number of individuals).

Corporate Social Responsibility

For many years, groups concerned with civil rights, employee safety and welfare, consumer protection, environmental preservation, and other causes have pressured corporate America to behave in a responsible manner with respect to these causes. Thus was born the concept of **corporate social responsibility**—the idea that those who run corporations can and should act ethically and be accountable to society for their actions. Just what constitutes corporate social responsibility has been debated for some time, and there are a number of different theories today.

STAKEHOLDER APPROACH   One view of corporate social responsibility stresses that corporations have a duty not just to shareholders, but also to other groups

Principle of Rights The principle that human beings have certain fundamental rights (to life, liberty, and the pursuit of happiness, for example). Those who adhere to this "rights theory" believe that a key factor in determining whether a business decision is ethical is how that decision affects the rights of various groups, including employees, customers, and suppliers.

Utilitarianism An approach to ethical reasoning that evaluates behavior in light of the consequences of that behavior for those who will be affected by it, rather than on the basis of any absolute ethical or moral values. In utilitarian reasoning, a "good" decision is one that results in the greatest good for the greatest number of people affected by the decision.

Cost-Benefit Analysis A decision-making technique that involves weighing the costs of a given action against the benefits of that action.

Corporate Social Responsibility The idea that corporations can and should act ethically and be accountable to society for their actions.

affected by corporate decisions ("stakeholders"). Under this approach, a corporation would consider the impact of its decision on the firm's employees, customers, creditors, suppliers, and the community in which the corporation operates. The reasoning behind this "stakeholder view" is that in some circumstances, one or more of these other groups may have a greater stake in company decisions than the shareholders do. Although this may be true, as mentioned earlier in this chapter, it is often difficult to decide which group's interests should receive greater weight if the interests conflict.

EXAMPLE 2.7 During 2008–2010, layoffs numbered in the millions. Nonetheless, some corporations succeeded in reducing labor costs without layoffs. To avoid slashing their workforces, these employers turned to alternatives such as four-day workweeks, unpaid vacations and voluntary furloughs, wage freezes, pension cuts, and flexible work schedules. Some companies asked for and received from their workers 1 percent wage cuts to prevent layoffs. Companies finding alternatives to layoffs included computer maker Dell (extended unpaid holidays), network router manufacturer Cisco Systems (four-day workweeks and end-of-year shutdowns), electronics giant Motorola (salary cuts), and automaker Honda (voluntary unpaid vacation time). Professor Jennifer Chatman remarked, "Organizations are trying to cut costs in the name of avoiding layoffs. It's not just that organizations are saying 'we're cutting costs,' they're saying: 'we're doing this to keep from losing people.'"[5] ●

CORPORATE CITIZENSHIP Another theory of social responsibility argues that corporations should behave as good citizens by promoting goals that society deems worthwhile and by taking positive steps toward solving social problems. The idea is that because business controls so much of the wealth and power of this country, business, in turn, has a responsibility to society to use that wealth and power in socially beneficial ways.. Under a corporate citizenship view, companies are judged on how much they donate to social causes, as well as how they conduct their operations with respect to employment discrimination, human rights, environmental concerns, and similar issues.

Bill Gates, founder and former chairman of Microsoft, Inc., with his wife, Melinda, at a press conference concerning their charity foundation. Gates indicated that he would launch a campaign to encourage the wealthiest Chinese to sign up for philanthropic endeavors. They also announced a $34 million grant to the Global Network for Neglected Tropical Diseases. How do their charitable actions reflect on the business community at large?

(Fabrice Coffrini/AFP/Getty Images)

A Way of Doing Business. A survey of U.S. executives undertaken by the Boston College Center for Corporate Citizenship found that more than 70 percent of those polled agreed that corporate citizenship must be treated as a priority. More than 60 percent said that good corporate citizenship added to their companies' profits. Strategist Michelle Bernhart has argued that corporate social responsibility cannot attain its maximum effectiveness unless it is treated as a way of doing business rather than as a special program.

Not all socially responsible activities can benefit a corporation, however. Corporate responsibility is most successful when a company undertakes activities that are relevant and significant to its stakeholders and related to its business operations. **EXAMPLE 2.8** The Brazilian firm Companhia Vale do Rio Doce is one of the world's largest diversified metals and mining companies. In 2008, it invested more than $150 million in social projects, including health care, infrastructure, and education. At the same time, it invested

---

5. Jennifer Chatman is a professor at the Hass School of Business at the University of California–Berkeley. This quotation is from Matt Richtel, "Some Firms Use Scalpel, Not Ax, to Cut Costs," *The New York Times*, December 28, 2008.

more than $300 million in environmental protection. One of its projects involves the rehabilitation of native species in the Amazon valley. To that end, it is planting almost 200 million trees in an attempt to restore 1,150 square miles of land where cattle breeding and farming have caused deforestation. ● (For a discussion on how "managerial accounting" can be an effective social responsibility tool for large companies, see this chapter's *Linking the Law to Managerial Accounting* feature on page 48.)

The Employee Recruiting and Retention Advantage.   A key corporate stakeholder is a company's workforce, which may include potential employees—job seekers. Surveys of college students about to enter the job market confirm that young people are looking for socially responsible employers. Younger workers generally are altruistic. They want to work for a company that allows them to participate in community projects. Corporations that engage in meaningful social activities find that they retain workers longer, particularly younger ones. **EXAMPLE 2.9**   At the accounting firm PKF Texas, employees support a variety of business, educational, and philanthropic organizations. As a result, this company is able to recruit and retain a younger workforce. Its average turnover rate is half the industry average. ●

▶ Making Ethical Business Decisions

As Dean Krehmeyer, executive director of the Business Roundtable's Institute for Corporate Ethics, once said, "Evidence strongly suggests being ethical—doing the right thing—pays." Instilling ethical business decision making into the fabric of a business organization is no small task, though, even if ethics "pays." The job is to encourage people to understand that they have to think more broadly about how their decisions will affect employees, shareholders, customers, and even the community. Great companies, such as Enron and the worldwide accounting firm Arthur Andersen, were brought down by the unethical behavior of a few. A two-hundred-year-old British investment bank, Barings Bank, was destroyed by the actions of one employee and a few of his friends. Clearly, ensuring that all employees get on the ethical business decision-making "bandwagon" is crucial in today's fast-paced world.

The George S. May International Company has provided six basic guidelines to help corporate employees judge their actions. Each employee—no matter what her or his level in the organization—should evaluate her or his actions using the following six guidelines:

1. *The law.* Is the action you are considering legal? If you do not know the laws governing the action, then find out. Ignorance of the law is no excuse.
2. *Rules and procedures.* Are you following the internal rules and procedures that have already been laid out by your company? They have been developed to avoid problems. Is what you are planning to do consistent with your company's policies and procedures? If not, stop.
3. *Values.* Laws and internal company policies reinforce society's values. You might wish to ask yourself whether you are attempting to find a loophole in the law or in your company's policies. Next, you have to ask yourself whether you are following the "spirit" of the law as well as the letter of the law or the internal policy.
4. *Conscience.* If you feel any guilt, let your conscience be your guide. Alternatively, ask yourself whether you would be happy to be interviewed by the national news media about the actions you are going to take.
5. *Promises.* Every business organization is based on trust. Your customers believe that your company will do what it is supposed to do. The same is true for your

> *"Never let your sense of morals prevent you from doing what is right."*
>
> Isaac Asimov, 1920–1992
> (Russian-born writer and scientist)

suppliers and employees. Will your actions live up to the commitments you have made to others, both inside the business and outside?

6. *Heroes.* We all have heroes who are role models for us. Is what you are planning on doing an action that your "hero" would take? If not, how would your hero act? That is how you should be acting.

▶ Practical Solutions to Corporate Ethics Questions

Corporate ethics officers and ethics committees require a practical method to investigate and solve specific ethics problems. Ethics consultant Leonard H. Bucklin of Corporate-Ethics.US has devised a procedure that he calls Business Process Pragmatism.[6] It involves the following five steps:

1. *Inquiry.* Of course, an understanding of the facts must be the initial action. The parties involved might include the mass media, the public, employees, or customers. At this stage of the process, the ethical problem or problems are specified. A list of relevant ethical principles is created.

2. *Discussion.* Here, a list of action options is developed. Each option carries with it certain ethical principles. Finally, resolution goals should also be listed.

3. *Decision.* Working together, those participating in the process create a consensus decision, or a consensus plan of action for the corporation.

4. *Justification.* Does the consensus solution withstand moral scrutiny? At this point in the process, reasons should be attached to each proposed action or series of actions. Will the stakeholders involved accept these reasons?

5. *Evaluation.* Do the solutions to the corporate ethics issue satisfy corporate values, community values, and individual values? Ultimately, can the consensus resolution withstand moral scrutiny of the decisions made and the process used to reach those decisions?

> *"Next to doing the right thing, the most important thing is to let people know you are doing the right thing."*
>
> John D. Rockefeller, 1839–1897
> (American industrialist and philanthropist)

▶ Business Ethics on a Global Level

Given the various cultures and religions throughout the world, it is not surprising that conflicts in ethics frequently arise between foreign and U.S. businesspersons. **EXAMPLE 2.10** In certain countries, the consumption of alcohol and specific foods is forbidden for religious reasons. Under such circumstances, it would be thoughtless and imprudent for a U.S. businessperson to invite a local business contact out for a drink. ●

The role played by women in other countries may also present some difficult ethical problems for firms doing business internationally. Equal employment opportunity is a fundamental public policy in the United States, and Title VII of the Civil Rights Act of 1964 prohibits discrimination against women in the employment context (see Chapter 18). Some other countries, however, offer little protection for women against gender discrimination in the workplace, including sexual harassment.

We look here at how laws governing workers in other countries, particularly developing countries, have created some especially difficult ethical problems for U.S. sellers of goods manufactured in foreign countries. We also examine some of the ethical ramifications of laws prohibiting U.S. businesspersons from bribing foreign officials to obtain favorable business contracts.

---

6. Corporate-Ethics.US and Business Process Pragmatism are registered trademarks.

Monitoring the Employment Practices of Foreign Suppliers

Many U.S. businesses contract with companies in developing nations to produce goods, such as shoes and clothing, because the wage rates in those nations are significantly lower than wages in the United States. Yet what if a foreign company exploits its workers—by hiring women and children at below-minimum-wage rates, for example, or by requiring its employees to work long hours in a workplace full of health hazards? What if the company's supervisors routinely engage in workplace conduct that is offensive to women?

Given today's global communications network, few companies can assume that their actions in other nations will go unnoticed by "corporate watch" groups that discover and publicize unethical corporate behavior. (For a discussion of how the Internet has increased the ability of critics to publicize a corporation's misdeeds, see this chapter's *Online Developments* feature below.) As a result, U.S. businesses today usually take steps to avoid such adverse publicity—either by refusing to deal with certain suppliers or by arranging to monitor their suppliers' workplaces to make sure that the employees are not being mistreated.

The Foreign Corrupt Practices Act

Another ethical problem in international business dealings has to do with the legitimacy of certain "side" payments to government officials. In the United States, the majority of contracts are formed within the private sector. In many foreign countries,

Online Developments

Corporate Reputations under Attack

In the pre-Internet days, disgruntled employees and customers wrote letters of complaint to corporate management or to the editors of local newspapers. Occasionally, an investigative reporter would write an exposé of alleged corporate misdeeds. Today, those unhappy employees and customers have gone online. To locate them, just type in the name of any major corporation. You will find electronic links to blogs, wikis, message boards, and online communities—many of which post unadorned criticisms of corporate giants. Some dissatisfied employees and consumers have even created rogue Web sites that mimic the look of the target corporation's official Web site, except that the rogue sites feature chat rooms and postings of "horror stories" about the corporation.

Damage to Corporate Reputations

Clearly, by providing a forum for complaints, the Internet has increased the potential for damage to the reputation of any major (or minor) corporation. Now a relatively small number of unhappy employees, for example, may make the entire world aware of a single incident that is not at all representative of how the corporation ordinarily operates.

Special Interest Groups Go on the Attack

Special interest groups are also using the Internet to attack corporations they do not like. Rather than writing letters or giving speeches to a limited audience, a special interest group can now go online and mercilessly "expose" what it considers to be a corporation's "bad practices." Wal-Mart and Nike in particular have been frequent targets for advocacy groups that believe those corporations exploit their workers.

Online Attacks: Often Inaccurate, but Probably Legal

Corporations often point out that many of the complaints and charges leveled against them are unfounded or exaggerated. Sometimes, management has tried to argue that the online attacks are libelous. The courts, however, disagree. To date, most courts have regarded online attacks simply as expressions of opinion and therefore a form of speech protected by the First Amendment.

In contrast, if employees breach company rules against the disclosure of internal financial information or trade secrets, the courts have been willing to side with the employers. Note, also, that having a clear set of written guidelines about what employees can do when they blog or generate other online content can provide a strong basis for successful lawsuits against inappropriate employee online disclosures.

FOR CRITICAL ANALYSIS

How might online attacks actually help corporations in the long run? (Hint: Some online criticisms might be accurate.)

however, government officials make the decisions on most major construction and manufacturing contracts because of extensive government regulation and control over trade and industry. Side payments to government officials in exchange for favorable business contracts are not unusual in such countries, where they are not considered to be unethical. In the past, U.S. corporations doing business in these countries largely followed the dictum "When in Rome, do as the Romans do."

In the 1970s, however, the U.S. press, and government officials as well, uncovered a number of business scandals involving large side payments by U.S. corporations to foreign representatives for the purpose of securing advantageous international trade contracts. In response to this unethical behavior, in 1977 Congress passed the Foreign Corrupt Practices Act[7] (FCPA), which prohibits U.S. businesspersons from bribing foreign officials to secure advantageous contracts.

PROHIBITION AGAINST THE BRIBERY OF FOREIGN OFFICIALS The first part of the FCPA applies to all U.S. companies and their directors, officers, shareholders, employees, and agents. This part prohibits the bribery of officials of foreign governments if the purpose of the payment is to get the officials to act in their official capacity to provide business opportunities.

The FCPA does not prohibit payment of substantial sums to minor officials whose duties are ministerial. These payments are often referred to as "grease," or facilitating payments. They are meant to accelerate the performance of administrative services that might otherwise be carried out at a slow pace. Thus, for example, if a firm makes a payment to a minor official to speed up an import licensing process, the firm has not violated the FCPA.

Generally, the act, as amended, permits payments to foreign officials if such payments are lawful within the foreign country. The act also does not prohibit payments to private foreign companies or other third parties unless the U.S. firm knows that the payments will be passed on to a foreign government in violation of the FCPA. Business firms that violate the FCPA may be fined up to $2 million. Individual officers or directors who violate the act may be fined up to $100,000 (the fine cannot be paid by the company) and may be imprisoned for up to five years.

ACCOUNTING REQUIREMENTS In the past, bribes were often concealed in corporate financial records. Thus, the second part of the FCPA is directed toward accountants. All companies must keep detailed records that "accurately and fairly" reflect the company's financial activities. In addition, all companies must have an accounting system that provides "reasonable assurance" that all transactions entered into by the company are accounted for and legal. These requirements assist in detecting illegal bribes. The FCPA further prohibits any person from making false statements to accountants or false entries in any record or account.

---

7. 15 U.S.C. Sections 78dd-1 *et seq.*

"Never doubt that a small group of committed citizens can change the world; indeed, it is the only thing that ever has."

Margaret Mead, 1901–1978
(American anthropologist)

Reviewing . . . Ethics and Business Decision Making

Isabel Arnett was promoted to CEO of Tamik, Inc., a pharmaceutical company that manufactures a vaccine called Kafluk, which supposedly provides some defense against bird flu. The company began marketing Kafluk throughout Asia. After numerous media reports that bird flu might soon become a worldwide epidemic, the demand for Kafluk increased, sales soared, and Tamik earned record profits. Tamik's CEO, Arnett, then

(Continued)

began receiving disturbing reports from Southeast Asia that in some patients, Kafluk had caused psychiatric disturbances, including severe hallucinations, and heart and lung problems. Arnett was informed that six children in Japan had committed suicide by jumping out of windows after receiving the vaccine. To cover up the story and prevent negative publicity, Arnett instructed Tamik's partners in Asia to offer cash to the Japanese families whose children had died in exchange for their silence. Arnett also refused to authorize additional research within the company to study the potential side effects of Kafluk. Using the information presented in the chapter, answer the following questions.

1. This scenario illustrates one of the main reasons why ethical problems occur in business. What is that reason?
2. Would a person who adheres to the principle of rights consider it ethical for Arnett not to disclose potential safety concerns and to refuse to perform additional research on Kafluk? Why or why not?
3. If Kafluk prevented fifty Asian people who were exposed to bird flu from dying, would Arnett's conduct in this situation be ethical under a utilitarian cost-benefit analysis? Why or why not?
4. Did Tamik or Arnett violate the Foreign Corrupt Practices Act in this scenario? Why or why not?

Linking the Law *to Managerial Accounting*
Managing a Company's Reputation

While in business school, all of you must take basic accounting courses. Accounting generally is associated with developing balance sheets and profit-and-loss statements, but it can also be used as a support system to provide information that can help managers do their jobs correctly. Enter managerial accounting, which involves the provision of accounting information for a company's internal use. Managerial accounting is used within a company for planning, controlling, and decision making.

Increasingly, managerial accounting is also being used to *manage corporate reputations.* To this end, more than 2,500 multinationals now release to the public large quantities of managerial accounting information.

Internal Reports Designed for External Scrutiny

Some large companies refer to the managerial accounting information that they release to the public as their corporate sustainability reports. Dow Chemical Company, for example, issues its Global Reporting Initiative Sustainability Report annually. So does Waste Management, Inc., which calls its report "The Color of Our World."

Other corporations call their published documents social responsibility reports. The antivirus software company Symantec Corporation issued its first corporate responsibility report in 2008. The report demonstrated the company's focus on critical environmental, social, and governance issues. Among other things, Symantec pointed out that it had adopted the Calvert Women's Principles, the first global code of corporate conduct designed to empower, advance, and invest in women worldwide.

A smaller number of multinationals provide what they call citizenship reports. For example, in 2010 General Electric (GE)

released its Sixth Annual Citizenship Report, which it calls "Renewing Responsibilities." GE's emphasis is on energy and climate change, demographics, growth markets, and financial markets. It even has a Web site that provides detailed performance metrics (www.ge.com/citizenship).

The Hitachi Group releases an Annual Corporate Social Responsibility Report, which outlines its environmental strategy, including its attempts to reduce carbon dioxide emissions (so-called greenhouse gases). It typically discusses human rights policy and its commitment to human rights awareness.

Why Use Managerial Accounting to Manage Reputations?

We live in an age of information. The advent of 24/7 cable news networks, Internet bloggers, and online newspapers guarantees that any news, whether positive or negative, about a corporation will be known throughout the world almost immediately. Consequently, corporations want to manage their reputations by preparing and releasing the news that the public, their shareholders, and government officials will receive. In a world in which corporations are often blamed for anything bad that happens, corporations are finding that managerial accounting information can provide a useful counterweight. To this end, some corporations have combined their social responsibility reports with their traditional financial accounting information. When a corporation's reputation is on the line, the future is at stake.

FOR CRITICAL ANALYSIS

Valuable company resources are used to create and publish corporate social responsibility reports. Under what circumstances can a corporation justify such expenditures?

Key Terms

business ethics 32	ethical reasoning 41	stock buyback 39
categorical imperative 41	ethics 32	stock option 39
corporate social responsibility 42	moral minimum 32	utilitarianism 42
cost-benefit analysis 42	principle of rights 42	

 Chapter Summary: Ethics and Business Decision Making

Business Ethics (See pages 32–39.)	1. *Ethics*—Business ethics focuses on how moral and ethical principles are applied in the business context. 2. *The moral minimum*—Lawful behavior is the moral minimum. The law has its limits, though, and some actions may be legal but not ethical. 3. *Short-term profit maximization*—One of the more pervasive reasons why ethical breaches occur is the focus on short-term profit maximization. Executives should distinguish between short-run and long-run profit goals and focus on maximizing profits over the long run because only long-run profit maximization is consistent with business ethics. 4. *Legal uncertainties*—It may be difficult to predict with certainty whether particular actions are legal, given the numerous and frequent changes in the laws regulating business and the "gray areas" in the law. 5. *The importance of ethical leadership*—Management's commitment and behavior are essential in creating an ethical workplace. Management's behavior, more than anything else, sets the ethical tone of a firm and influences the behavior of employees. 6. *Ethical codes*—Most large firms have ethical codes or policies and training programs to help employees determine whether certain actions are ethical. In addition, the Sarbanes-Oxley Act requires firms to set up confidential systems so that employees and others can report suspected illegal or unethical auditing or accounting practices.
Ethical Transgressions by Financial Institutions (See pages 39–41.)	During the first decade of the 2000s, corporate wrongdoing among U.S. financial firms escalated. They sold increasingly risky assets to investors and invested in such assets themselves to increase short-term profits. Abusive use of stock buybacks and stock options also proliferated. When the economic crisis began, some investment banking firms such as Lehman Brothers Holdings were forced into bankruptcy, and others including Goldman Sachs had to accept bailout funds from the U.S. government. The insurance giant AIG also had to be saved from bankruptcy with federal bailout funds. Nevertheless, the firms continued to pay exorbitant bonuses, which fueled public outrage, as the U.S. taxpayers had to pay the price through the federal bailouts and a deepening nationwide recession.
Approaches to Ethical Reasoning (See pages 41–44.)	1. *Duty-based ethics*—Ethics based on religious beliefs; philosophical reasoning, such as that of Immanuel Kant; and the basic rights of human beings (the principle of rights). A potential problem for those who support the latter approach is deciding which rights are more important in a given situation. Management constantly faces ethical conflicts and trade-offs when considering all those affected by a business decision. 2. *Outcome-based ethics (utilitarianism)*—Ethics based on philosophical reasoning, such as that of John Stuart Mill. Applying this theory requires a cost-benefit analysis, weighing the negative effects against the positive and deciding which course of action produces the best outcome. 3. *Corporate social responsibility*—A number of theories based on the idea that corporations can and should act ethically and be accountable to society for their actions. These include the stakeholder approach and corporate citizenship.
Making Ethical Business Decisions (See pages 44–45.)	Making ethical business decisions is crucial in today's legal environment. Doing the right thing pays off in the long run, both in terms of increasing profits and avoiding negative publicity and the potential for bankruptcy. We provide six guidelines for making ethical business decisions on pages 44 and 45.

(Continued)

Chapter Summary: Ethics and Business Decision Making, Continued

Practical Solutions to Corporate Ethics Questions (See page 45.)	Corporate ethics officers and ethics committees require a practical method to investigate and solve specific ethics problems. For a pragmatic five-step procedure to solve ethical problems recommended by one expert, see page 45.
Business Ethics on a Global Level (See pages 45–47.)	Businesses must take account of the many cultural, religious, and legal differences among nations. Notable differences relate to the role of women in society, employment laws governing workplace conditions, and the practice of giving side payments to foreign officials to secure favorable contracts.

ExamPrep

ISSUE SPOTTERS

1. Delta Tools, Inc., markets a product that under some circumstances is capable of seriously injuring consumers. Does Delta have an ethical duty to remove this product from the market, even if the injuries occur only when the product is misused? Why or why not?
2. Acme Corporation decides to respond to what it sees as a moral obligation to correct for past discrimination by adjusting pay differences among its employees. Does this raise an ethical conflict among Acme's employees? Between Acme and its employees? Between Acme and its shareholders? Explain your answers.

—**Check your answers to these questions against the answers provided in Appendix G.**

BEFORE THE TEST

Go to **www.cengagebrain.com**, enter the ISBN number "9781111530617," and click on "Find" to locate this textbook's Web site. Then, click on "Access Now" under "Study Tools," and select "Chapter 2" at the top. There you will find an "Interactive Quiz" that you can take to assess your mastery of the concepts in this chapter, as well as "Flashcards" and a "Glossary" of important terms.

For Review

1. What is business ethics, and why is it important?
2. How can business leaders encourage their companies to act ethically?
3. How do duty-based ethical standards differ from outcome-based ethical standards?
4. What are six guidelines that an employee can use to evaluate whether his or her actions are ethical?
5. What types of ethical issues might arise in the context of international business transactions?

Questions and Case Problems

2–1. Business Ethics. Jason Trevor owns a commercial bakery in Blakely, Georgia, that produces a variety of goods sold in grocery stores. Trevor is required by law to perform internal tests on food produced at his plant to check for contamination. Three times in 2011, the tests of food products that contained peanut butter were positive for salmonella contamination. Trevor was not required to report the results to U.S. Food and Drug Administration officials, however, so he did not. Instead, Trevor instructed his employees to simply repeat the tests until the outcome was negative. Therefore, the products that had originally tested positive for salmonella were eventually shipped out to retailers. Five people who ate Trevor's baked goods in 2011 became seriously ill, and one person died from salmonella poisoning. Even though Trevor's conduct was legal, was it unethical for him to sell goods that had once tested positive for salmonella? If Trevor had followed the six basic guidelines for making ethical business decisions, would he still have sold the contaminated goods? Why or why not?

2–2. **Question with Sample Answer. Ethical Duties.** Shokun Steel Co. owns many steel plants. One of its plants is much older than the others. Equipment at that plant is outdated and inefficient, and the costs of production are now two times higher than at any of Shokun's other plants. The company cannot raise the price of steel because of competition, both domestic and international. The plant employs more than a thousand workers and is located in Twin Firs, Pennsylvania, which has a population of about 45,000. Shokun is contemplating whether to close the plant. What factors should the firm consider in making its decision? Will the firm violate any ethical duties if it closes the plant? Analyze these questions from the two basic perspectives on ethical reasoning discussed in this chapter.

—**For a sample answer to Question 2–2, go to Appendix E at the end of this text.**

2–3. **Ethical Conduct.** Unable to pay more than $1.2 billion in debt, Big Mountain Metals, Inc., filed a petition to declare bankruptcy in a federal bankruptcy court in July 2009. Big Mountain's creditors included Bank of New London and Suzuki Bank, among others. The court appointed Morgan Crawford to work as a "disinterested" (neutral) party with Big Mountain and the creditors to resolve their disputes. The court set an hourly fee as Crawford's compensation. Crawford told the banks that he wanted them to pay him an additional percentage fee based on the "success" he attained in finding "new value" to pay Big Mountain's debts. He said that without such a deal, he would not perform his mediation duties. Suzuki Bank agreed, but the other banks disputed the deal, although no one told the court. In October 2010, Crawford asked the court for nearly $2.5 million in compensation, including the hourly fees, which totaled about $531,000, and the percentage fees. Big Mountain and others asked the court to deny Crawford any fees on the basis that he had improperly negotiated "secret side agreements." How did Crawford violate his duties as a "disinterested" party? Should he be denied compensation? Why or why not?

2–4. **Corporate Social Responsibility.** Methamphetamine (meth) is an addictive, synthetic drug made chiefly in small toxic labs (STLs) in homes, tents, barns, or hotel rooms. The manufacturing process is dangerous, often resulting in explosions, burns, and toxic fumes. The government has spent considerable resources to find and eradicate STLs, imprison meth dealers and users, treat addicts, and provide services for families affected by these activities. Meth cannot be made without ephedrine or pseudoephedrine, which are ingredients in cold and allergy medications. Arkansas has one of the highest numbers of STLs in the United States. In an effort to recoup the costs of dealing with the meth epidemic, twenty counties in Arkansas filed a suit in a federal district court against Pfizer, Inc., and other companies that make or distribute cold and allergy medications. What is the defendants' ethical responsibility in this case, and to whom do they owe it? Why?

[*Ashley County, Arkansas v. Pfizer, Inc.,* 552 F.3d 659 (8th Cir. 2009)]

2–5. **Business Ethics on a Global Scale.** In the 1990s, Pfizer, Inc., developed a new antibiotic called Trovan (trovafloxacin mesylate). Tests showed that in animals Trovan had life-threatening side effects, including joint disease, abnormal cartilage growth, liver damage, and a degenerative bone condition. In 1996, an epidemic of bacterial meningitis swept across Nigeria. Pfizer sent three U.S. physicians to test Trovan on children who were patients in Nigeria's Infectious Disease Hospital. Pfizer did not obtain the patients' consent, alert them to the risks, or tell them that Médecins Sans Frontières (Doctors without Borders) was providing an effective conventional treatment at the same site. Eleven children died in the experiment, and others were left blind, deaf, paralyzed, or brain damaged. Rabi Abdullahi and other Nigerian children filed a suit in a U.S. federal district court against Pfizer, alleging a violation of a customary international law norm prohibiting involuntary medical experimentation on humans. Did Pfizer violate any ethical standards? What might Pfizer have done to avert the consequences? Explain. [*Abdullahi v. Pfizer, Inc.,* 562 F.3d 163 (2d Cir. 2009)]

2–6. **Case Problem with Sample Answer. Violation of Internal Ethical Codes.** Havensure, LLC, an insurance broker, approached York International to determine whether it could provide insurance to York at a better rate than it currently was paying. York allowed Havensure to study its policies. Havensure realized that Prudential, an insurance provider for York, had a hidden broker fee in its premium that it used to pay the broker universal life resources (ULR) that provided the Prudential policy for York. Havensure told York that it could provide insurance at a lower price, so York had Havensure send requests for proposals to various insurance companies. To keep York's business, Prudential offered to match the lowest rate quoted, but Prudential told York that it would have to continue to buy the policy through the broker ULR, and not through Havensure. York agreed. Havensure then sued Prudential for wrongful interference with a business relationship (see Chapter 5). The trial court held for Prudential. Havensure appealed. The appeals court held that what Prudential did, by having a hidden fee for a broker, violated its ethical code and may have violated New York insurance law, but Havensure still had no case. Does it make sense that a firm violating its own rules, as well as possibly violating the law, has no obligation for the loss it may have imposed on another firm that is trying to compete for business? Explain your answer. [*Havensure, LLC v. Prudential Insurance,* 595 F.3d 312 (6th Cir. 2010)]

—**To view a sample answer for Case Problem 2–6, go to Appendix F at the end of this text.**

2–7. **Ethical Misconduct.** Frank A. Pasquale used the Social Security number of his father, Frank F. Pasquale, to obtain a credit card, which he used to charge a $7,500 item. Although he was employed by his father's firm, the son also collected unemployment benefits. Later, the son, claiming to act on behalf of Frank Pasquale Limited Partnership, misrepresented his status to obtain a $350,000 loan. His father—the only person authorized to borrow funds on behalf of the partnership—was unaware of his son's misdeeds. The loan went into default. When the father learned of the fraud, he confronted his son, who produced forged documents to show that the loan had been paid. Adams Associates, LLC, which had acquired the unpaid loan from the original lender, filed a suit in a New Jersey state court against the father and the son for damages. During the trial, another family member testified to the son's general "lack of ethics." Did the son deserve this characterization? Should the court issue a judgment against the father and the son? Explain. [*Adams Associates, LLC v. Frank Pasquale Limited Partnership,* __ A.3d __ (2011)]

2–8.   **A Question of Ethics. Copyright.** *Steven Soderbergh is the Academy Award–winning director of* Erin Brockovich, Traffic, *and many other films. CleanFlicks, LLC, filed a suit in a federal district court against Soderbergh, fifteen other directors, and the Directors Guild of America. The plaintiff asked the court to rule that it had the right to sell DVDs of the defendants' films altered without the defendants' consent to delete scenes of "sex, nudity, profanity and gory violence." CleanFlicks sold or rented the edited DVDs under the slogan "It's About Choice" to consumers, sometimes indirectly through retailers. It would not sell to retailers that made unauthorized copies of the edited films. The defendants, with DreamWorks, LLC, and seven other movie studios that own the copyrights to the films, filed a counterclaim against CleanFlicks and others engaged in the same business, alleging copyright infringement (see Chapter 8). Those filing the counterclaim asked the court to prevent CleanFlicks and the others from making and marketing altered versions of the films. [CleanFlicks of Colorado, LLC v. Soderbergh, 433 F.Supp.2d 1236 (D.Colo. 2006)]*

1. Movie studios often edit their films to conform to content and other standards and sell the edited versions to network television and other commercial buyers. In this case, however, the studios objected when CleanFlicks edited the films and sold the altered versions directly to consumers. Similarly, CleanFlicks made unauthorized copies of the studios' DVDs to edit the films, but objected to others' making unauthorized copies of the altered versions. Is there anything unethical about these apparently contradictory positions? Why or why not?

2. CleanFlicks and its competitors asserted, among other things, that they were making "fair use" of the studios'

copyrighted works. They argued that by their actions "they are criticizing the objectionable content commonly found in current movies and that they are providing more socially acceptable alternatives to enable families to view the films together, without exposing children to the presumed harmful effects emanating from the objectionable content." If you were the judge, how would you view this argument? Is a court the appropriate forum for making determinations of public or social policy? Explain.

2–9.   **Critical-Thinking Managerial Question.** Assume that you are a high-level manager for a shoe manufacturer. You know that your firm could increase its profit margin by producing shoes in Indonesia, where you could hire women for $100 a month to assemble them. You also know that human rights advocates recently accused a competing shoe manufacturer of engaging in exploitative labor practices because the manufacturer sold shoes made by Indonesian women for similarly low wages. You personally do not believe that paying $100 a month to Indonesian women is unethical because you know that in their country, $100 a month is a better-than-average wage rate. Assuming that the decision is yours to make, should you have the shoes manufactured in Indonesia and make higher profits for your company? Should you instead avoid the risk of negative publicity and the consequences of that publicity for the firm's reputation and subsequent profits? Are there other alternatives? Discuss fully.

2–10.   **Video Question. *Pharzime, Scene 1 and Scene 2.*** Access the videos using the instructions provided below to answer the following questions.

1. In *Scene 1*, employees discuss whether to market their company's drug as a treatment for other conditions—even though it has only been approved for treating epilepsy. One employee argues that marketing the drug for more than the one treatment will increase the company's short-term profits and that obtaining approval for the other treatments will take too long. What theory describes this perspective?

2. In *Scene 2*, a new sales rep discusses the company's off-label marketing strategy with a veteran sales rep. Is it unethical or illegal for a sales rep to represent that he is a doctor when he has a doctorate in chemistry but is not actually a physician? Explain.

—To watch the videos, go to **www.cengagebrain.com** and register the access code that came with your new book or log in to your existing account. Select the link for either the "Business Law Digital Video Library Online Access" or "Business Law CourseMate," and then click on "Complete Video List" to find the videos for this chapter (Videos 79 and 80).

Chapter 3

Courts and Alternative Dispute Resolution

> "An eye for an eye will make the whole world blind."
>
> —Mahatma Gandhi, 1869–1948
> (Indian political and spiritual leader)

Contents

Chapter Objectives

After reading this chapter, you should be able to answer the following questions:

1. What is judicial review? How and when was the power of judicial review established?

2. Before a court can hear a case, it must have jurisdiction. Over what must it have jurisdiction? How are the courts applying traditional jurisdictional concepts to cases involving Internet transactions?

3. What is the difference between a trial court and an appellate court?

4. What is discovery, and how does electronic discovery differ from traditional discovery?

5. What are three alternative methods of resolving disputes?

(John Elk III/Lonely Planet Images/Getty Images)

Every society needs to have an established method for resolving disputes. Without one, as Mahatma Gandhi implied in the chapter-opening quotation, the biblical "eye for an eye" would lead to anarchy. This is particularly true in the business world—nearly every businessperson will face a lawsuit at some time in his or her career. For this reason, anyone involved in business needs to have an understanding of court systems in the United States, as well as the various methods of dispute resolution that can be pursued outside the courts.

In this chapter, after examining the judiciary's overall role in the American governmental scheme, we discuss some basic requirements that must be met before a party may bring a lawsuit before a particular court. We then look at the court systems of the United States in some detail and, to clarify judicial procedures, follow a hypothetical case through a state court system. Throughout this chapter, we indicate how court doctrines and procedures are being adapted to the needs of a cyber age. The chapter concludes with an overview of some alternative methods of settling disputes, including online dispute resolution.

▶ The Judiciary's Role in American Government

As you learned in Chapter 1, the body of American law includes the federal and state constitutions, statutes passed by legislative bodies, administrative law, and the case decisions and legal principles that form the common law. These laws would be

(AP Photo/Nati Harnik)

The head of Nebraska's highest court delivers his State of the Judiciary address to that state's lawmakers. What is the main duty of the judiciary in the American governmental system?

Judicial Review   The process by which a court decides on the constitutionality of legislative enactments and actions of the executive branch.

Jurisdiction   The authority of a court to hear and decide a specific case.

meaningless, however, without the courts to interpret and apply them. This is the essential role of the judiciary—the courts—in the American governmental system: to interpret and to apply the law.

Judicial Review

As the branch of government entrusted with interpreting the laws, the judiciary can decide, among other things, whether the laws or actions of the other two branches are constitutional. The process for making such a determination is known as **judicial review.** The power of judicial review enables the judicial branch to act as a check on the other two branches of government, in line with the checks-and-balances system established by the U.S. Constitution. (Today, nearly all nations with constitutional democracies, including Canada, France, and Germany, have some form of judicial review.)

The Origins of Judicial Review in the United States

The power of judicial review was not mentioned in the Constitution, but the concept was not new at the time the nation was founded. Indeed, before 1789 state courts had already overturned state legislative acts that conflicted with state constitutions. Many of the founders expected the United States Supreme Court to assume a similar role with respect to the federal Constitution. Alexander Hamilton and James Madison both emphasized the importance of judicial review in their essays urging the adoption of the new Constitution. When was the doctrine of judicial review established? See this chapter's *Landmark in the Legal Environment* feature on the facing page for the answer.

 Basic Judicial Requirements

Before a court can hear a lawsuit, certain requirements must first be met. These requirements relate to *jurisdiction, venue,* and *standing to sue.* We examine each of these important concepts here.

Jurisdiction

In Latin, *juris* means "law," and *diction* means "to speak." Thus, the term **jurisdiction** literally means "the power to speak the law." Before any court can hear a case, it must have jurisdiction over the person (or company) against whom the suit is brought (the defendant) or over the property involved in the suit. The court must also have jurisdiction over the subject matter of the dispute.

JURISDICTION OVER PERSONS OR PROPERTY   Generally, a court can exercise personal jurisdiction (*in personam* jurisdiction) over any person or business that resides in a certain geographic area. A state trial court, for example, normally has jurisdictional authority over residents (including businesses) in a particular area of the state, such as a county or district. A state's highest court (often called the state supreme court)[1] has jurisdiction over all residents of that state.

---

1. As will be discussed shortly, a state's highest court is frequently referred to as the state supreme court, but there are exceptions. For example, in New York, the supreme court is a trial court.

Landmark in the Legal Environment *Marbury v. Madison* (1803)

The *Marbury v. Madison*[a] decision is widely viewed as a cornerstone of constitutional law. When Thomas Jefferson defeated the incumbent president, John Adams, in the presidential elections of 1800, Adams feared the Jeffersonians' antipathy toward business and toward a strong national government. Adams therefore rushed to "pack" the judiciary with loyal Federalists (those who believed in a strong national government) by appointing what came to be called "midnight judges" just before he left office. All of the fifty-nine judicial appointment letters had to be certified and delivered, but Adams's secretary of state (John Marshall) was able to deliver only forty-two of them before Jefferson took over as president. Jefferson refused to order his secretary of state, James Madison, to deliver the remaining commissions.

Marshall's Dilemma   William Marbury and three others to whom the commissions had not been delivered sought a writ of *mandamus* (an order directing a government official to fulfill a duty) from the United States Supreme Court, as authorized by the Judiciary Act of 1789. As fate would have it, John Marshall had just been appointed chief justice of the Supreme Court. Marshall faced a dilemma: If he ordered the commissions delivered, the new secretary of state (Madison) could simply refuse to deliver them—and the Court had no way to compel him to act. At the same time, if Marshall simply allowed the new administration to do as it wished, the Court's power would be severely eroded.

Marshall's Decision   Marshall masterfully fashioned his decision to enlarge the power of the Supreme Court by affirming the Court's power of judicial review. He stated, "It is emphatically the province and duty of the Judicial Department to say what the law is. . . . If two laws conflict with each other, the courts must decide on the operation of each. . . . If a law is in opposition to the Constitution . . . [t]he Court must determine which of these conflicting rules governs the case."

Marshall's decision did not require anyone to do anything. He concluded that the highest court did not have the power to issue a writ of *mandamus* in this particular case. Although the Judiciary Act of 1789 specified that the Supreme Court could issue writs of *mandamus* as part of its original jurisdiction, Article III of the Constitution, which spelled out the Court's original jurisdiction, did not mention writs of *mandamus*. Because Congress did not have the right to expand the Supreme Court's jurisdiction, this section of the Judiciary Act of 1789 was unconstitutional—and thus void. To this day, the *Marbury* decision continues to stand as a judicial and political masterpiece.

• Application to Today's Legal Environment   *Since the* Marbury v. Madison *decision, the power of judicial review has remained unchallenged and today is exercised by both federal and state courts. If the courts did not have the power of judicial review, the constitutionality of Congress's acts could not be challenged in court—a congressional statute would remain law unless changed by Congress. The courts of other countries that have adopted a constitutional democracy often cite this decision as a justification for judicial review.*

---
a. 5 U.S. (1 Cranch) 137, 2 L.Ed. 60 (1803).

A court can also exercise jurisdiction over property that is located within its boundaries. This kind of jurisdiction is known as *in rem* jurisdiction, or "jurisdiction over the thing." **EXAMPLE 3.1**   A dispute arises over the ownership of a boat in dry dock in Fort Lauderdale, Florida. The boat is owned by an Ohio resident, over whom a Florida court normally cannot exercise personal jurisdiction. The other party to the dispute is a resident of Nebraska. In this situation, a lawsuit concerning the boat could be brought in a Florida state court on the basis of the court's *in rem* jurisdiction. •

Long Arm Statute   A state statute that permits a state to obtain personal jurisdiction over nonresident defendants. A defendant must have certain "minimum contacts" with that state for the statute to apply.

Long Arm Statutes. Under the authority of a state **long arm statute,** a court can exercise personal jurisdiction over certain out-of-state defendants based on activities that took place within the state. Before exercising long arm jurisdiction over a nonresident, however, the court must be convinced that the defendant had sufficient contacts, or *minimum contacts,* with the state to justify the jurisdiction.[2] Generally, this means that the defendant must have enough of a connection to the state for the judge to conclude that it is fair for the state to exercise power over the defendant.

---
2. The minimum-contacts standard was established in *International Shoe Co. v. State of Washington,* 326 U.S. 310, 66 S.Ct. 154, 90 L.Ed. 95 (1945).

This Xbox is made from numerous components, many of which are manufactured in different countries. If a defect in one of those foreign-manufactured components causes injury, can the user sue the foreign manufacturer in her or his state of residence? Why or why not?

If an out-of-state defendant caused an automobile accident or sold defective goods within the state, for instance, a court usually will find that minimum contacts exist to exercise jurisdiction over that defendant.

CASE EXAMPLE 3.2   After an Xbox game system caught fire in Bonnie Broquet's home in Texas and caused substantial personal injuries, Broquet filed a lawsuit in a Texas court against Ji-Haw Industrial Company, a nonresident company that made the Xbox components. Broquet alleged that Ji-Haw's components were defective and had caused the fire. Ji-Haw argued that the Texas court lacked jurisdiction over it, but in 2008, a state appellate court held that the Texas long arm statute authorized the exercise of jurisdiction over the out-of-state defendant.[3] • Similarly, a state may exercise personal jurisdiction over a nonresident defendant who is sued for breaching a contract that was formed within the state, even when that contract was negotiated over the phone or through online and offline correspondence.

Corporate Contacts. Because corporations are considered legal persons, courts use the same principles to determine whether it is fair to exercise jurisdiction over a corporation.[4] A corporation normally is subject to personal jurisdiction in the state in which it is incorporated, has its principal office, and is doing business. Courts apply the minimum-contacts test to determine if they can exercise jurisdiction over out-of-state corporations.

The minimum-contacts requirement usually is met if the corporation advertises or sells its products within the state, or places its goods into the "stream of commerce" with the intent that the goods be sold in the state. **EXAMPLE 3.3**   A business is incorporated under the laws of Maine but has a branch office and manufacturing plant in Georgia. The corporation also advertises and sells its products in Georgia. These activities would likely constitute sufficient contacts with the state of Georgia to allow a Georgia court to exercise jurisdiction over the corporation. •

Some corporations, however, do not sell or advertise products or place any goods in the stream of commerce. Determining what constitutes minimum contacts in these situations can be more difficult. In the following case, the defendant was a New Jersey corporation that performed machining services on component parts that it received from a North Carolina firm. The North Carolina firm claimed that the services were defective and sued for breach of contract in a North Carolina court. The question before the court was whether the New Jersey firm had minimum contacts with North Carolina.

---

3. *Ji-Haw Industrial Co. v. Broquet,* 2008 WL 441822 (Tex.App.—San Antonio 2008).

4. In the eyes of the law, corporations are "legal persons"—entities that can sue and be sued. See Chapter 15.

Case 3.1   **Southern Prestige Industries, Inc. v. Independence Plating Corp.**

Court of Appeals of North Carolina, 690 S.E.2d 768 (2010).
www.nccourts.org[a]

BACKGROUND AND FACTS   Independence Plating Corporation (the defendant) is a New Jersey corporation that provides

---

a. In the right-hand column of the page, click on "Court Opinions." When that page opens, select the year 2010 under the heading "Court of Appeals Opinions." Scroll down to February 2, 2010, and click on the case title under "Unpublished Opinions" to access the opinion. The North Carolina court system maintains this Web site.

metal-coating services. Its only office and all of its personnel are located in New Jersey. It does not advertise out of state, but had a long-standing business relationship with Kidde Aerospace in North Carolina (filing under the name Southern Prestige Industries). For almost a year, Independence and Kidde engaged in frequent transactions. On November 18, 2008, Kidde initiated an action for breach of contract in a North Carolina state court, alleging defects in the metal-plating process carried out by Independence. Independence filed a motion to dismiss for

Case 3.1–Continued

lack of personal jurisdiction, which the trial court denied. Independence appealed, arguing that it had insufficient contacts with North Carolina for the state to exercise jurisdiction.

IN THE WORDS OF THE COURT . . .
CALABRIA, Judge.
* * * *

In order to satisfy due process requirements, there must be "certain minimum contacts [between the nonresident defendant and the forum state—that is, the state in which the court is located] such that the maintenance of the suit does not offend 'traditional notions of fair play and substantial justice.' " In order to establish minimum contacts with North Carolina, the defendant must have purposefully availed itself of the privilege of conducting activities within the forum state and invoked the benefits and protections of the laws of North Carolina. The relationship between the defendant and the forum state must be such that the defendant should reasonably anticipate being haled into a North Carolina court.
* * * *

* * * *Our courts look at the following factors in determining whether minimum contacts exist: (1) the quantity of the contacts, (2) the nature and quality of the contacts, (3) the source and connection of the cause of action to the contacts, (4) the interest of the forum state, and (5) the convenience to the parties.* [Emphasis added.]

In the instant case, the trial court found that the parties "had an ongoing business relationship characterized by frequent transactions between July 27, 2007, and April 25, 2008, as reflected by thirty-two purchase orders." Plaintiff would ship machined parts to defendant, who would then anodize the parts and return them to plaintiff in

North Carolina. Defendant sent invoices totaling $21,018.70 to plaintiff in North Carolina, and these invoices were paid from plaintiff's corporate account at a North Carolina bank. Plaintiff filed a breach of contract action against defendant because the machined parts that were shipped to defendant from North Carolina and then anodized by defendant and shipped back to North Carolina were defective.
* * * *

* * * After examining the ongoing relationship between the parties, the nature of their contacts, the interest of the forum state, the convenience of the parties, and the cause of action, we conclude defendant has "purposely availed" itself of the benefits of doing business in North Carolina and "should reasonably anticipate being haled" into a North Carolina court. We hold that defendant has sufficient minimum contacts with North Carolina to justify the exercise of personal jurisdiction over defendant without violating the due process clause.

DECISION AND REMEDY   The North Carolina appellate court affirmed the trial court's decision. Independence had sufficient minimum contacts with North Carolina to justify the state's exercise of personal jurisdiction.

WHAT IF THE FACTS WERE DIFFERENT?   *Suppose that the two parties had engaged in a single business transaction. Would the outcome of this case have been the same? Why or why not?*

THE ETHICAL DIMENSION   *Was it fair for the North Carolina courts to require a New Jersey company to litigate in North Carolina? Explain.*

Probate Court   A state court of limited jurisdiction that conducts proceedings relating to the settlement of a deceased person's estate.

Bankruptcy Court   A federal court of limited jurisdiction that handles only bankruptcy proceedings, which are governed by federal bankruptcy law.

JURISDICTION OVER SUBJECT MATTER   Jurisdiction over subject matter is a limitation on the types of cases a court can hear. In both the federal and state court systems, there are courts of *general* (unlimited) *jurisdiction* and courts of *limited jurisdiction.* An example of a court of general jurisdiction is a state trial court or a federal district court. An example of a state court of limited jurisdiction is a probate court. **Probate courts** are state courts that handle only matters relating to the transfer of a person's assets and obligations after his or her death, including matters relating to the custody and guardianship of children. An example of a federal court of limited subject-matter jurisdiction is a bankruptcy court. **Bankruptcy courts** handle only bankruptcy proceedings, which are governed by federal bankruptcy law (see Chapter 12).

A court's jurisdiction over subject matter is usually defined in the statute or constitution creating the court. In both the federal and state court systems, a court's subject-matter jurisdiction can be limited not only by the subject of the lawsuit but also by the amount in controversy, by whether a case is a felony (a more serious type of crime) or a misdemeanor (a less serious type of crime), or by whether the proceeding is a trial or an appeal.

ORIGINAL AND APPELLATE JURISDICTION   The distinction between courts of original jurisdiction and courts of appellate jurisdiction normally lies in whether the case is being heard for the first time. Courts having original jurisdiction are courts of the first instance, or trial courts—that is, courts in which lawsuits begin, trials take place, and evidence is presented. In the federal court system, the *district courts* are trial courts. In the various state court systems, the trial courts are known by various names, as will be discussed shortly.

The key point here is that any court having original jurisdiction is normally known as a trial court. Courts having appellate jurisdiction act as reviewing courts, or appellate courts. In general, cases can be brought before appellate courts only on appeal from an order or a judgment of a trial court or other lower court.

JURISDICTION OF THE FEDERAL COURTS   Because the federal government is a government of limited powers, the jurisdiction of the federal courts is limited. Federal courts have subject-matter jurisdiction in two situations.

Federal Questions.   Article III of the U.S. Constitution establishes the boundaries of federal judicial power. Section 2 of Article III states that "[t]he judicial Power shall extend to all Cases, in Law and Equity, arising under this Constitution, the Laws of the United States, and Treaties made, or which shall be made, under their Authority." This clause means that whenever a plaintiff's cause of action is based, at least in part, on the U.S. Constitution, a treaty, or a federal law, then a **federal question** arises, and the case comes under the judicial power of the federal courts. Any lawsuit involving a federal question, such as a person's rights under the U.S. Constitution, can originate in a federal court. Note that in a case based on a federal question, a federal court will apply federal law.

> **Federal Question**   A question that pertains to the U.S. Constitution, acts of Congress, or treaties. A federal question provides a basis for federal jurisdiction.

Diversity of Citizenship.   Federal district courts can also exercise original jurisdiction over cases involving **diversity of citizenship.** The most common type of diversity jurisdiction has two requirements:[5] (1) the plaintiff and defendant must be residents of different states, and (2) the dollar amount in controversy must exceed $75,000. For purposes of diversity jurisdiction, a corporation is a citizen of both the state in which it is incorporated and the state in which its principal place of business is located. A case involving diversity of citizenship can be filed in the appropriate federal district court. If the case starts in a state court, it can sometimes be transferred, or "removed," to a federal court. A large percentage of the cases filed in federal courts each year are based on diversity of citizenship.

As noted, a federal court will apply federal law in cases involving federal questions. In a case based on diversity of citizenship, in contrast, a federal court will apply the relevant state law (which is often the law of the state in which the court sits).

> **Diversity of Citizenship**   Under Article III, Section 2, of the U.S. Constitution, a basis for federal district court jurisdiction over a lawsuit between (1) citizens of different states, (2) a foreign country and citizens of a state or of different states, or (3) citizens of a state and citizens or subjects of a foreign country. The amount in controversy must be more than $75,000 before a federal district court can take jurisdiction in such cases.

EXCLUSIVE VERSUS CONCURRENT JURISDICTION   When both federal and state courts have the power to hear a case, as is true in lawsuits involving diversity of citizenship, **concurrent jurisdiction** exists. When cases can be tried only in federal courts or only in state courts, **exclusive jurisdiction** exists. Federal courts have exclusive jurisdiction in cases involving federal crimes, bankruptcy, patents, and copyrights; in suits against the United States; and in some areas of admiralty law (law governing transportation on ocean waters). State courts also have exclusive jurisdiction over certain subject matter—for example, divorce and adoption.

> **Concurrent Jurisdiction**   Jurisdiction that exists when two different courts have the power to hear a case. For example, some cases can be heard in a federal or a state court.

> **Exclusive Jurisdiction**   Jurisdiction that exists when a case can be heard only in a particular court or type of court.

---

5. Diversity jurisdiction also exists in cases between (1) a foreign country and citizens of a state or of different states and (2) citizens of a state and citizens or subjects of a foreign country. These bases for diversity jurisdiction are less commonly used.

When either a federal court or a state court can exercise jurisdiction, a party has a choice of courts in which to bring a suit. A number of factors can affect a party's decision to litigate in a federal or a state court, such as the availability of different remedies, the distance to the respective courthouses, or the experience or reputation of a particular judge. For example, if the dispute involves a trade secret, a party might conclude that a federal court—which has exclusive jurisdiction over copyrights, patents, and trademarks—would have more expertise in the matter.

A party might also choose a federal court over a state court if he or she is concerned about bias in a state court. In contrast, a plaintiff might choose to litigate in a state court if it has a reputation for awarding substantial amounts of damages or if the judge is perceived as being pro-plaintiff. The concepts of exclusive jurisdiction and concurrent jurisdiction are illustrated in Exhibit 3–1 below.

Jurisdiction in Cyberspace

The Internet's capacity to bypass political and geographic boundaries undercuts the traditional basis on which courts assert personal jurisdiction. As already discussed, for a court to compel a defendant to come before it, there must be at least minimum contacts—the presence of a salesperson within the state, for example. Are there sufficient minimum contacts if the defendant's only connection to a jurisdiction is an ad on a Web site originating from a remote location?

THE "SLIDING-SCALE" STANDARD The courts have developed a standard—called a "sliding-scale" standard—for determining when the exercise of jurisdiction over an out-of-state defendant is proper. In developing this standard, the courts have identified three types of Internet business contacts: (1) substantial business conducted over the Internet (with contracts and sales, for example); (2) some interactivity through a Web site; and (3) passive advertising. Jurisdiction is proper for the first category, improper for the third, and may or may not be appropriate for the second.[6] An

---

6. For a leading case on this issue, see *Zippo Manufacturing Co. v. Zippo Dot Com, Inc.,* 952 F.Supp. 1119 (W.D.Pa. 1997).

• *Exhibit* **3–1 Exclusive and Concurrent Jurisdiction**

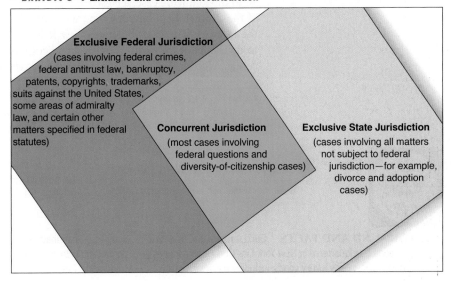

Exclusive Federal Jurisdiction
(cases involving federal crimes, federal antitrust law, bankruptcy, patents, copyrights, trademarks, suits against the United States, some areas of admiralty law, and certain other matters specified in federal statutes)

Concurrent Jurisdiction
(most cases involving federal questions and diversity-of-citizenship cases)

Exclusive State Jurisdiction
(cases involving all matters not subject to federal jurisdiction—for example, divorce and adoption cases)

Internet communication is typically considered passive if people have to voluntarily access it to read the message, and active if it is sent to specific individuals.

In certain situations, even a single contact can satisfy the minimum-contacts requirement. **CASE EXAMPLE 3.4** A Louisiana resident, Daniel Crummey, purchased a used recreational vehicle (RV) from sellers in Texas after viewing numerous photos of it on eBay. The sellers' statements on eBay claimed that "everything works great on this RV and will provide comfort and dependability for years to come. This RV will go to Alaska and back without problems!" Crummey picked up the RV in Texas, but on the drive home, the RV stopped running. He filed a suit in Louisiana against the sellers alleging that the vehicle was defective, but the sellers claimed that the Louisiana court lacked jurisdiction. Because the sellers had used eBay to market and sell the RV to a Louisiana buyer—and had regularly used eBay to sell vehicles to remote parties in the past—the court found that jurisdiction was proper.[7] ●

Preventing Legal Disputes

Those of you with an entrepreneurial spirit may be eager to establish Web sites to promote products and solicit orders. Be aware, however, that you can be sued in states in which you have never been physically present if you have had sufficient contacts with residents of those states over the Internet. Before you create a Web site that is the least bit interactive, you need to consult an attorney to find out whether you will be subjecting yourself to jurisdiction in every state. Becoming informed about the extent of your potential exposure to lawsuits in various locations is an important part of preventing litigation.

INTERNATIONAL JURISDICTIONAL ISSUES   Because the Internet is global in scope, it obviously raises international jurisdictional issues. The world's courts seem to be developing a standard that echoes the minimum-contacts requirement applied by U.S. courts. Most courts are indicating that minimum contacts—doing business within the jurisdiction, for example—are enough to compel a defendant to appear and that a physical presence is not necessary. The effect of this standard is that a business firm has to comply with the laws in any jurisdiction in which it targets customers for its products. This situation is complicated by the fact that many countries' laws on particular issues—free speech, for example—are very different from U.S. laws.

In the following case, a New York–based maker of designer goods sued a resident of the People's Republic of China who was allegedly selling counterfeit goods over the Internet. The case illustrates how federal courts apply a sliding-scale standard to determine if they can exercise jurisdiction over a foreign defendant whose only contact with the United States is through a Web site.

---

7. *Crummey v. Morgan*, 965 So.2d 497 (La.App.1 Cir. 2007). But note that a single sale on eBay does not necessarily confer jurisdiction. Jurisdiction depends on whether the seller regularly uses eBay as a means for doing business with remote buyers. See *Boschetto v. Hansing*, 539 F.3d 1011 (9th Cir. 2008).

Case 3.2   **Gucci America, Inc. v. Wang Huoqing**

United States District Court, Northern District of California, ___ F.Supp.3d ___ (2011).

BACKGROUND AND FACTS   Gucci America, Inc., is a New York corporation headquartered in New York City. Gucci manufactures and distributes high-quality luxury goods, including footwear, belts, sunglasses, handbags, and wallets, which are sold worldwide. In connection with its products, Gucci uses twenty-one federally registered trademarks (trademark law will be discussed in Chapter 8). Gucci

Case 3.2–Continued

also operates a number of boutiques, some of which are located in California. Wang Huoqing, a resident of the People's Republic of China, operates numerous Web sites. When Gucci discovered that Huoqing's Web sites offered for sale counterfeit goods–products that bear Gucci's trademarks but are not genuine Gucci articles–it hired a private investigator in San Jose, California, to buy goods from the Web sites. The investigator purchased a wallet that was labeled Gucci but was counterfeit. Gucci filed a trademark infringement lawsuit against Huoqing in a federal district court in California seeking damages and an injunction to prevent further infringement. Huoqing was notified of the lawsuit via e-mail (see the discussion of *service of process* later in the chapter) but did not appear in court. Gucci asked the court to enter a default judgment–that is, a judgment entered when the defendant fails to appear–but the court first had to determine whether it had personal jurisdiction over Huoqing based on the Internet sales.

IN THE WORDS OF THE COURT . . .
Joseph C. *SPERO*, United States Magistrate Judge.
    * * * *

* * * Under California's long-arm statute, federal courts in California may exercise jurisdiction to the extent permitted by the Due Process Clause of the Constitution. The Due Process Clause allows federal courts to exercise jurisdiction where * * * the defendant has had sufficient minimum contacts with the forum to subject him or her to the specific jurisdiction of the court. The courts apply a three-part test to determine whether specific jurisdiction exists:

> (1) The nonresident defendant must do some act or consummate some transaction with the forum or perform some act by which he purposefully avails himself of the privilege of conducting activities in the forum, thereby invoking the benefits and protections of its laws; (2) the claim must be one which arises out of or results from the defendant's forum-related activities; and (3) exercise of jurisdiction must be reasonable.

    * * * *

In order to satisfy the first prong of the test for specific jurisdiction, a defendant must have either purposefully availed itself of [taken advantage of] the privilege of conducting business activities within the forum or purposefully directed activities toward the forum. *Purposeful availment typically consists of action taking place in the forum that invokes the benefits and protections of the laws of the forum, such as executing or performing a contract within the forum.* To show purposeful availment, a plaintiff must show that the defendant "engage[d] in some form of affirmative conduct allowing or promoting the transaction of business within the forum state." * * * [Emphasis added.]

"In the Internet context, the Ninth Circuit utilizes a sliding scale analysis under which 'passive' websites do not create sufficient contacts to establish purposeful availment, whereas interactive websites may create sufficient contacts, depending on how interactive the website is." * * * *Personal jurisdiction is appropriate where an entity is conducting business over the Internet and has offered for sale and sold its products to forum residents.* [Emphasis added.]

Here, the allegations and evidence presented by Plaintiffs in support of the Motion are sufficient to show purposeful availment on the part of Defendant Wang Huoqing. Plaintiffs have alleged that Defendant operates "fully interactive Internet websites operating under the Subject Domain Names" and have presented evidence in the form of copies of web pages showing that the websites are, in fact, interactive. * * * Additionally, Plaintiffs allege Defendant is conducting counterfeiting and infringing activities within this Judicial District and has advertised and sold his counterfeit goods in the State of California. * * * Plaintiffs have also presented evidence of one actual sale within this district, made by investigator Robert Holmes from the website bag2do.cn. * * * Finally, Plaintiffs have presented evidence that Defendant Wang Huoqing owns or controls the twenty-eight websites listed in the Motion for Default Judgment. * * * Such commercial activity in the forum amounts to purposeful availment of the privilege of conducting activities within the forum, thus invoking the benefits and protections of its laws. Accordingly, the Court concludes that Defendant's contacts with California are sufficient to show purposeful availment.

DECISION AND REMEDY   The U.S. District Court for the Northern District of California held that it had personal jurisdiction over the foreign defendant, Wang Huoqing. The court entered a default judgment against Huoqing and granted Gucci an injunction.

WHAT IF THE FACTS WERE DIFFERENT?   *Suppose that Gucci had not presented evidence that Wang Huoqing had made one actual sale through his Web site to a resident (the private investigator) of the court's district. Would the court still have found that it had personal jurisdiction over Huoqing? Why or why not?*

THE LEGAL ENVIRONMENT DIMENSION   *Is it relevant to the analysis of jurisdiction that Gucci America's principal place of business is in New York rather than California? Explain.*

Venue

Venue   The geographic district in which a legal action is tried and from which the jury is selected.

Jurisdiction has to do with whether a court has authority to hear a case involving specific persons, property, or subject matter. **Venue**[8] is concerned with the most appropriate physical location for a trial. Two state courts (or two federal courts) may

---

8. Pronounced *ven-yoo*.

have the authority to exercise jurisdiction over a case, but it may be more appropriate or convenient to hear the case in one court than in the other.

Basically, the concept of venue reflects the policy that a court trying a suit should be in the geographic neighborhood (usually the county) where the incident leading to the lawsuit occurred or where the parties involved in the lawsuit reside. Venue in a civil case typically is where the defendant resides, whereas venue in a criminal case normally is where the crime occurred.

Pretrial publicity or other factors, though, may require a change of venue to another community, especially in criminal cases when the defendant's right to a fair and impartial jury has been impaired. **EXAMPLE 3.5** Police raided a compound of Mormon polygamists in Texas and removed many children from the ranch. Authorities suspected that some of the girls were being sexually and physically abused. The raid received a great deal of media attention, and people living in the nearby towns would likely have been influenced by this publicity. In this situation, if the government filed criminal charges against a member of the religious sect, that individual might request—and would probably receive—a change of venue to another location. ●

Standing to Sue

Standing to Sue The requirement that an individual must have a sufficient stake in a controversy before he or she can bring a lawsuit. The plaintiff must demonstrate that he or she has been either injured or threatened with injury.

Justiciable Controversy A controversy that is not hypothetical or academic but real and substantial; a requirement that must be satisfied before a court will hear a case.

Before a person can bring a lawsuit before a court, the party must have **standing to sue,** or a sufficient stake in the matter to justify seeking relief through the court system. In other words, to have standing, a party must have a legally protected and tangible interest at stake in the litigation. The party bringing the lawsuit must have suffered a harm, or have been threatened by a harm, as a result of the action about which she or he has complained. Standing to sue also requires that the controversy at issue be a **justiciable[9] controversy**—a controversy that is real and substantial, as opposed to hypothetical or academic. As Chief Justice John Roberts of the United States Supreme Court recently noted, a lack of standing is like Bob Dylan's line in the song "Like a Rolling Stone": "When you got nothing, you got nothing to lose."[10]

CASE EXAMPLE 3.6 James Bush visited the Federal Bureau of Investigation's (FBI's) office in San Jose, California, on two occasions in December 2007. He filled out complaint forms indicating that he was seeking records under the Freedom of Information Act regarding a police brutality claim and the FBI's failure to investigate it. In August 2008, Bush filed a suit against the U.S. Department of Justice in an attempt to compel the FBI to provide the requested records. The court dismissed the lawsuit on the ground that no justiciable controversy existed. Bush had failed to comply with the requirements of the FOIA when he filled out the forms, so the FBI was not obligated to provide any records. Thus, there was no actual controversy for the court to decide.[11] ●

Note that in some situations a person may have standing to sue on behalf of another person, such as a minor or a mentally incompetent person. **EXAMPLE 3.7** Three-year-old Emma suffers serious injuries as a result of a defectively manufactured toy. Because Emma is a minor, her parent or legal guardian can bring a lawsuit on her behalf. ●

---

9. Pronounced jus-*tish*-uh-bul.

10. The chief justice stated, "The absence of any substantive recovery means that respondents cannot benefit from the judgment they seek and thus lack Article III standing." He then quoted Bob Dylan's lyrics from "Like a Rolling Stone," on *Highway 61 Revisited* (Columbia Records, 1965). This was the first time that a member of the Supreme Court cited rock lyrics in an opinion. See *Sprint Communications Co. v. APCC Services, Inc.,* 554 U.S. 269, 128 S.Ct. 2531, 171 L.Ed.2d 424 (2008).

11. *Bush v. Department of Justice,* 2008 WL 5245046 (N.D.Cal. 2008).

▶ The State and Federal Court Systems

As mentioned earlier in this chapter, each state has its own court system. Additionally, there is a system of federal courts. Even though there are fifty-two court systems—one for each of the fifty states, one for the District of Columbia, plus a federal system—similarities abound. Exhibit 3–2 below illustrates the basic organizational structure characteristic of the court systems in many states. The exhibit also shows how the federal court system is structured. Keep in mind that the federal courts are not superior to the state courts—they are simply an independent system of courts, which derives its authority from Article III, Sections 1 and 2, of the U.S. Constitution. We turn now to an examination of these court systems, beginning with the state courts.

The State Court Systems

Typically, a state court system will include several levels, or tiers, of courts. As indicated in Exhibit 3–2 below, state courts may include (1) trial courts of limited jurisdiction, (2) trial courts of general jurisdiction, (3) appellate courts, and (4) the state's highest court (often called the state supreme court). Generally, any person who is a party to a lawsuit has the opportunity to plead the case before a trial court and then, if he or she loses, before at least one level of appellate court. Only if the case involves a federal statute or a federal constitutional issue may the decision of a state supreme court on that issue be further appealed to the United States Supreme Court.

The states use various methods to select judges for their courts: in most states, judges are elected, but in some states, they are appointed. Usually, states specify the number of years that a judge will serve. In contrast, as you will read shortly, judges in the federal court system are appointed by the president of the United States and, if they are confirmed by the Senate, hold office for life—unless they engage in blatantly illegal conduct.

"Although it's nothing serious, let's keep an eye on it to make sure it doesn't turn into a major lawsuit."

● *Exhibit* **3–2** **The State and Federal Court Systems**

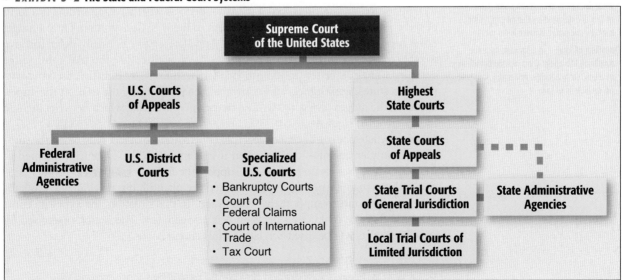

TRIAL COURTS   Trial courts are exactly what their name implies—courts in which trials are held and testimony taken. State trial courts have either general or limited jurisdiction. Trial courts that have general jurisdiction as to subject matter may be called county, district, superior, or circuit courts.[12] The jurisdiction of these courts is often determined by the size of the county in which the court sits. State trial courts of general jurisdiction have jurisdiction over a wide variety of subjects, including both civil disputes and criminal prosecutions. (In some states, trial courts of general jurisdiction may hear appeals from courts of limited jurisdiction.)

Some courts of limited jurisdiction are called special inferior trial courts or minor judiciary courts. **Small claims courts** are inferior trial courts that hear only civil cases involving claims of less than a certain amount, such as $5,000 (the amount varies from state to state). Suits brought in small claims courts are generally conducted informally, and lawyers are not required (in a few states, lawyers are not even allowed). Another example of an inferior trial court is a local municipal court that hears mainly traffic cases. Decisions of small claims courts and municipal courts may sometimes be appealed to a state trial court of general jurisdiction. Other courts of limited jurisdiction as to subject matter include domestic relations or family courts, which handle primarily divorce actions and child-custody disputes, and probate courts, as mentioned earlier. A few states have even established Islamic law courts, which are courts of limited jurisdiction that serve the American Muslim community. (See this chapter's *Beyond Our Borders* feature on the facing page for a discussion of the rise of Islamic law courts.)

APPELLATE, OR REVIEWING, COURTS   Every state has at least one court of appeals (appellate court, or reviewing court), which may be an intermediate appellate court or the state's highest court. About three-fourths of the states have intermediate appellate courts. Generally, courts of appeals do not conduct new trials in which evidence is submitted and witnesses are examined. Rather, an appellate court panel of three or more judges reviews the record of the case on appeal, which includes a transcript of the trial proceedings, and determines whether the trial court committed an error.

Usually, appellate courts focus on questions of law, not questions of fact. A **question of fact** deals with what really happened in regard to the dispute being tried—such as whether a party actually burned a flag. A **question of law** concerns the application or interpretation of the law—such as whether flag-burning is a form of speech protected by the First Amendment to the U.S. Constitution. Only a judge, not a jury, can rule on questions of law. Appellate courts normally defer (or give weight) to a trial court's findings on questions of fact because the trial court judge and jury were in a better position to evaluate testimony by directly observing witnesses' gestures, appearance, and nonverbal behavior during the trial. At the appellate level, the judges review the written transcript of the trial, which does not include these nonverbal elements.

An appellate court will challenge a trial court's finding of fact only when the finding is clearly erroneous—that is, when it is contrary to the evidence presented at trial—or when there is no evidence to support the finding. **EXAMPLE 3.8**   A jury concludes that a manufacturer's product harmed the plaintiff, but no evidence was submitted to the court to support that conclusion. In this situation, the appellate court will hold that the trial court's decision was erroneous. • The options exercised by appellate courts will be discussed later in this chapter.

Small Claims Court   A special court in which parties may litigate small claims (such as $5,000 or less). Attorneys are not required in small claims courts and, in some states, are not allowed to represent the parties.

Question of Fact   In a lawsuit, an issue that involves only disputed facts, and not what the law is on a given point. Questions of fact are decided by the jury in a jury trial (by the judge if there is no jury).

Question of Law   In a lawsuit, an issue involving the application or interpretation of a law. Only a judge, not a jury, can rule on questions of law.

---

12. The name in Ohio is court of common pleas, and the name in New York is supreme court.

Beyond Our Borders | Islamic Law Courts Abroad and at Home

As discussed in Chapter 1, Islamic law is one of the world's three most common legal systems, along with civil law and common law. In most Islamic countries, the law is based on *sharia,* a system of law derived from the Qur'an as well as the sayings and doings of Muhammad and his companions. *Sharia* means "way" and provides the legal framework for many aspects of Muslim life, including politics, banking, business, family, economics, and social issues.

Islamic Law in Britain and Canada

In 2008, the archbishop of Canterbury–the leader of the Church of England–argued that it was time for Britain to consider "crafting a just and constructive relationship between Islamic law and the statutory law of the United Kingdom." Even before the archbishop made his proposal, *sharia* was already being applied in Britain via councils that rule on Islamic civil justice through a number of mosques in that country. These councils arbitrate disputes between British Muslims involving child custody, property, employment, and housing. Of course, the councils do not deal with criminal law or with any civil issues that would put *sharia* in direct conflict with British statutory law. Most Islamic law cases involve marriage or divorce.

In late 2008, Britain officially sanctioned the authority of *sharia* judges to rule on

divorce and financial disputes between couples. Britain now has five officially recognized *sharia* courts that have the full power of their equivalent courts within the traditional British judicial system.

As early as 2003 in Ontario, Canada, a group of Canadian Muslims established a judicial tribunal using *sharia.* To date, this tribunal has resolved only marital disagreements and some other civil disputes. Initially, there was some heated debate about whether Canada should or even legally could allow *sharia* law to be applied to any aspect of Canadian life or business. Under Ontario law, however, the regular judicial system must uphold such agreements as long as they are voluntary and negotiated through an arbitrator. Any agreements that violate Canada's Charter of Rights and Freedoms are not upheld in the traditional judicial system.

Canadian Muslims have also created the Islamic Institute of Civil Justice to oversee *sharia* tribunals that arbitrate family disputes among Muslims.

Islamic Law Courts in the United States

About the time that Britain was formally recognizing Islamic law courts, a controversy about the same issue erupted in Detroit, Michigan, where there is a large American Muslim community. Courts in Texas and Minnesota had already ruled

on the legality of arbitration clauses that require recourse to Islamic law courts. In the Texas case, an American Muslim couple were married and received a "Society of Arlington Islamic Marriage Certificate." A number of years later, a dispute arose over marital property and the nonpayment of a "dowry for the bride." The parties involved had signed an arbitration agreement in which all claims and disputes were to be submitted to arbitration in front of the Texas Islamic Court in Richardson, Texas. A Texas appeals court ruled that the arbitration agreement was valid and enforceable.[a]

The case in Minnesota involved an Islamic arbitration committee decision that was contested by one of the parties who had agreed to arbitrate any differences before the committee. Again, the appeals court affirmed the arbitration award.[b]

For Critical Analysis
One of the arguments against allowing sharia *courts in the United States is that we would no longer have a common legal framework within our society. Do you agree or disagree? Why?*

---

a. *Jabri v. Qaddura,* 108 S.W.3d 404 (Tex.App.–Fort Worth 2003).

b. *Abd Alla v. Mourssi,* 680 N.W.2d 569 (Minn.App. 2004).

BE CAREFUL The decisions of a state's highest court are final on questions of state law.

HIGHEST STATE COURTS   The highest appellate court in a state is usually called the supreme court but may be called by some other name. For example, in both New York and Maryland, the highest state court is called the court of appeals. The decisions of each state's highest court are final on all questions of state law. Only when issues of federal law are involved can a decision made by a state's highest court be overruled by the United States Supreme Court.

The Federal Court System

The federal court system is basically a three-tiered model consisting of (1) U.S. district courts (trial courts of general jurisdiction) and various courts of limited jurisdiction, (2) U.S. courts of appeals (intermediate courts of appeals), and (3) the United States Supreme Court. Unlike state court judges, who are usually elected, federal court judges—including the justices of the Supreme Court—are appointed by the president of the United States and confirmed by the U.S. Senate. All federal judges receive lifetime appointments because under Article III they "hold their offices during Good Behavior."

U.S. DISTRICT COURTS   At the federal level, the district court is the equivalent of a state trial court of general jurisdiction. There is at least one federal district court in every state. The number of judicial districts can vary over time, primarily owing to population changes and corresponding caseloads. There are ninety-four federal judicial districts. U.S. district courts have original jurisdiction in federal matters. Federal cases typically originate in district courts. There are other courts with original, but special (or limited), jurisdiction, such as the federal bankruptcy courts and others shown in Exhibit 3–2 on page 63.

U.S. COURTS OF APPEALS   In the federal court system, there are thirteen U.S. courts of appeals—also referred to as U.S. circuit courts of appeals. The federal courts of appeals for twelve of the circuits, including the U.S. Court of Appeals for the District of Columbia Circuit, hear appeals from the federal district courts located within their respective judicial circuits. The Court of Appeals for the Thirteenth Circuit, called the Federal Circuit, has national appellate jurisdiction over certain types of cases, such as cases involving patent law and cases in which the U.S. government is a defendant.

The decisions of the circuit courts of appeals are final in most cases, but appeal to the United States Supreme Court is possible. Exhibit 3–3 on the facing page shows the geographic boundaries of the U.S. circuit courts of appeals and the boundaries of the U.S. district courts within each circuit.

THE UNITED STATES SUPREME COURT   The highest level of the three-tiered model of the federal court system is the United States Supreme Court. According to the language of Article III of the U.S. Constitution, there is only one national Supreme Court. All other courts in the federal system are considered "inferior." Congress is empowered to create other inferior courts as it deems necessary. The inferior courts that Congress has created include the second tier in our model—the U.S. courts of appeals—as well as the district courts and any other courts of limited, or specialized, jurisdiction.

The United States Supreme Court consists of nine justices. Although the Supreme Court has original, or trial, jurisdiction in rare instances (set forth in Article III, Section 2), most of its work is as an appeals court. The Supreme Court can review any case decided by any of the federal courts of appeals, and it also has appellate authority over some cases decided in the state courts.

Appeals to the Supreme Court. To bring a case before the Supreme Court, a party requests that the Court issue a writ of *certiorari*. A **writ of *certiorari***[13] is an order issued by the Supreme Court to a lower court requiring the latter to send it the record of the case for review. The Court will not issue a writ unless at least four of the nine justices approve of it. This is called the **rule of four.** Whether the Court will issue a writ of *certiorari* is entirely within its discretion. The Court is not required to issue one, and most petitions for writs are denied. (Although thousands of cases are filed with the Supreme Court each year, it hears, on average, fewer than one hundred of

Writ of *Certiorari*   A writ from a higher court asking a lower court for the record of a case.

Rule of Four   A rule of the United States Supreme Court under which the Court will not issue a writ of *certiorari* unless at least four justices approve of the decision to issue the writ.

---

13. Pronounced sur-shee-uh-*rah*-ree.

● *Exhibit* **3-3** Boundaries of the U.S. Courts of Appeals and U.S. District Courts

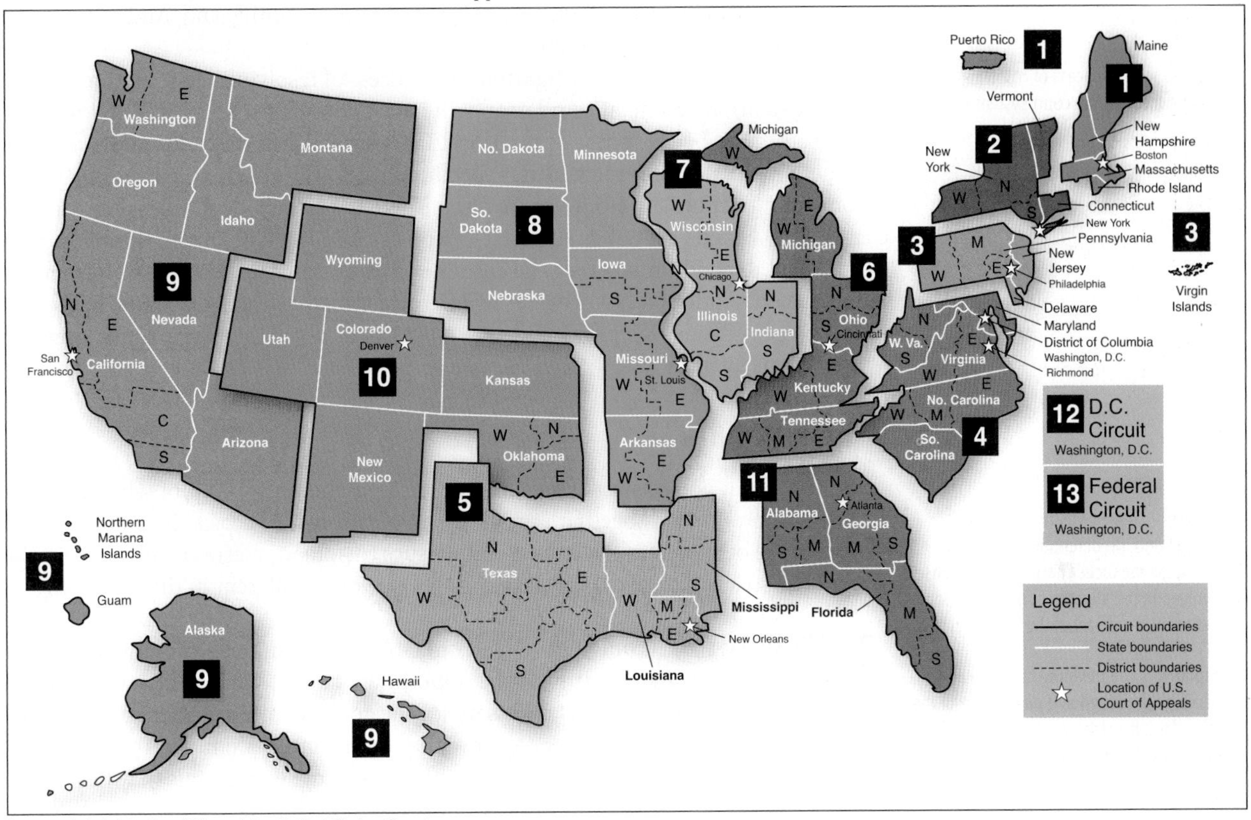

Source: Administrative Office of the United States Courts.

these cases.)[14] A denial is not a decision on the merits of a case, nor does it indicate agreement with the lower court's opinion. Furthermore, a denial of the writ has no value as a precedent.

Petitions Granted by the Court. Typically, the Court grants petitions when cases raise important constitutional questions or when the lower courts are issuing conflicting decisions on a significant issue. The justices, however, never explain their reasons for hearing certain cases and not others, so it is difficult to predict which cases the Court will select.

● Following a State Court Case

"Lawsuit: A machine which you go into as a pig and come out of as a sausage."
Ambrose Bierce, 1842–1914
(American journalist)

To illustrate the procedures that would be followed in a civil lawsuit brought in a state court, we present a hypothetical case and follow it through the state court system. The case involves an automobile accident in which Kevin Anderson, driving a Lexus, struck Lisa Marconi, driving a Ford Taurus. The accident occurred at the intersection of Wilshire Boulevard and Rodeo Drive in Beverly Hills, California. Marconi suffered personal injuries, incurring medical and hospital expenses as well

---

14. From the mid-1950s through the early 1990s, the United States Supreme Court reviewed more cases per year than it has in the last few years. In the Court's 1982–1983 term, for example, the Court issued opinions in 151 cases. In contrast, in its 2010–2011 term, the Court issued opinions in only 84 cases.

as lost wages for four months. Anderson and Marconi are unable to agree on a settlement, and Marconi sues Anderson. Marconi is the plaintiff, and Anderson is the defendant. Both are represented by lawyers.

During each phase of the **litigation** (the process of resolving a lawsuit through the court system), Marconi and Anderson will have to observe strict procedural requirements. A large body of law—procedural law—establishes the rules and standards for determining disputes in courts. Procedural rules are very complex, and they vary from court to court and from state to state. There is a set of federal rules of procedure as well as various sets of rules for state courts. Additionally, the applicable procedures will depend on whether the case is a civil or criminal proceeding. Generally, the Marconi-Anderson civil lawsuit will involve the procedures discussed in the following subsections. Keep in mind that attempts to settle the case may be ongoing throughout the trial.

Litigation The process of resolving a dispute through the court system.

The Pleadings

The complaint and answer (and the counterclaim and reply)—all of which are discussed below—taken together are called the **pleadings.** The pleadings inform each party of the other's claims and specify the issues (disputed questions) involved in the case. The style and form of the pleadings may be quite different in different states.

Pleadings Statements made by the plaintiff and the defendant in a lawsuit that detail the facts, charges, and defenses involved in the litigation. The complaint and answer are part of the pleadings.

THE PLAINTIFF'S COMPLAINT Marconi's suit against Anderson commences when her lawyer files a **complaint** with the appropriate court. The complaint contains a statement alleging (1) the facts necessary for the court to take jurisdiction, (2) a brief summary of the facts necessary to show that the plaintiff is entitled to a remedy,[15] and (3) a statement of the remedy the plaintiff is seeking. Complaints may be lengthy or brief, depending on the complexity of the case and the rules of the jurisdiction.

Complaint The pleading made by a plaintiff alleging wrongdoing on the part of the defendant; the document that, when filed with a court, initiates a lawsuit.

After the complaint has been filed, the sheriff, a deputy of the county, or another *process server* (one who delivers a complaint and summons) serves a **summons** and a copy of the complaint on defendant Anderson. The summons notifies Anderson that he must file an answer to the complaint with both the court and the plaintiff's attorney within a specified time period (usually twenty to thirty days). The summons also informs Anderson that failure to answer may result in a **default judgment** for the plaintiff, meaning the plaintiff could be awarded the damages alleged in her complaint. Service of process is essential in our legal system. No case can proceed to a trial unless the plaintiff can prove that he or she has properly served the defendant.

Summons A document informing a defendant that a legal action has been commenced against her or him and that the defendant must appear in court on a certain date to answer the plaintiff's complaint.

Default Judgment A judgment entered by a court against a defendant who has failed to appear in court to answer or defend against the plaintiff's claim.

Answer Procedurally, a defendant's response to the plaintiff's complaint.

THE DEFENDANT'S ANSWER The defendant's **answer** either admits the statements or allegations set forth in the complaint or denies them and outlines any defenses that the defendant may have. If Anderson admits to all of Marconi's allegations in his answer, the court will enter a judgment for Marconi. If Anderson denies any of Marconi's allegations, the litigation will go forward.

Anderson can deny Marconi's allegations and set forth his own claim that Marconi was in fact negligent and therefore owes him compensation for the damage to his Lexus. This is appropriately called a **counterclaim.** If Anderson files a counterclaim, Marconi will have to answer it with a pleading, normally called a **reply,** which has the same characteristics as an answer.

Counterclaim A claim made by a defendant in a civil lawsuit against the plaintiff. In effect, the defendant is suing the plaintiff.

Reply Procedurally, a plaintiff's response to a defendant's answer.

---

15. The factual allegations in a complaint must be enough to raise a right to relief above the speculative level; they must plausibly suggest that the plaintiff is entitled to a remedy. *Bell Atlantic Corp. v. Twombly,* 550 U.S. 544, 127 S.Ct. 1955, 167 L.Ed.2d 929 (2007).

Anderson can also admit the truth of Marconi's complaint but raise new facts that may result in dismissal of the action. This is called raising an *affirmative defense*. For example, Anderson could assert the expiration of the time period under the relevant *statute of limitations* (a state or federal statute that sets the maximum time period during which a certain action can be brought or rights enforced) as an affirmative defense.

Motion to Dismiss   A **motion to dismiss** requests the court to dismiss the case for stated reasons. Grounds for dismissal of a case include improper delivery of the complaint and summons, improper venue, and the plaintiff's failure to state a claim for which a court could grant relief (a remedy). For instance, if Marconi had suffered no injuries or losses as a result of Anderson's negligence, Anderson could move to have the case dismissed because Marconi would not have stated a claim for which relief could be granted.

> **Motion to Dismiss**   A pleading in which a defendant asserts that the plaintiff's claim fails to state a cause of action (that is, has no basis in law) or that there are other grounds on which the suit should be dismissed. Although the defendant normally is the party requesting a dismissal, either the plaintiff or the court can also make a motion to dismiss the case.

If the judge grants the motion to dismiss, the plaintiff generally is given time to file an amended complaint. If the judge denies the motion, the suit will go forward, and the defendant must then file an answer. Note that if Marconi wishes to discontinue the suit because, for example, an out-of-court settlement has been reached, she can likewise move for dismissal. The court can also dismiss the case on its own motion.

Pretrial Motions

Either party may attempt to get the case dismissed before trial through the use of various pretrial motions. We have already mentioned the motion to dismiss. Two other important pretrial motions are the motion for judgment on the pleadings and the motion for summary judgment.

At the close of the pleadings, either party may make a **motion for judgment on the pleadings,** or on the merits of the case. The judge will grant the motion only when there is no dispute over the facts of the case and the sole issue to be resolved is a question of law. In deciding on the motion, the judge may consider only the evidence contained in the pleadings.

> **Motion for Judgment on the Pleadings**   A motion by either party to a lawsuit at the close of the pleadings requesting the court to decide the issue solely on the pleadings without proceeding to trial. The motion will be granted only if no facts are in dispute.

> **Motion for Summary Judgment**   A motion requesting the court to enter a judgment without proceeding to trial. The motion can be based on evidence outside the pleadings and will be granted only if no facts are in dispute.

In contrast, in a **motion for summary judgment,** the court may consider evidence outside the pleadings, such as sworn statements (affidavits) by parties or witnesses, or other documents relating to the case. Either party can make a motion for summary judgment. As with the motion for judgment on the pleadings, a motion for summary judgment will be granted only if there are no genuine questions of fact and the sole question is a question of law.

Discovery

Before a trial begins, each party can use a number of procedural devices to obtain information and gather evidence about the case from the other party or from third parties. The process of obtaining such information is known as **discovery.** Discovery includes gaining access to witnesses, documents, records, and other types of evidence.

> **Discovery**   A phase in the litigation process during which the opposing parties may obtain information from each other and from third parties prior to trial.

The Federal Rules of Civil Procedure and similar rules in the states set forth the guidelines for discovery activity. Generally, discovery is allowed regarding any matter that is not privileged and is relevant to the claim or defense of any party. Discovery rules also attempt to protect witnesses and parties from undue harassment and to safeguard privileged or confidential material from being disclosed. If a discovery request involves privileged or confidential business information, a court can deny the request and can limit the scope of discovery in a number of ways. For instance, a court can require the party to submit the materials to the judge in a sealed envelope so that the judge can decide if they should be disclosed to the opposing party. A court may sanction parties who do not comply with discovery rules.

Discovery prevents surprises at trial by giving parties access to evidence that might otherwise be hidden. This allows both parties to learn as much as they can about what to expect at a trial before they reach the courtroom. It also serves to narrow the issues so that trial time is spent on the main questions in the case.

DEPOSITIONS AND INTERROGATORIES   Discovery can involve the use of depositions or interrogatories, or both. A **deposition** is sworn testimony by a party to the lawsuit or any witness. The person being deposed (the deponent) answers questions asked by the attorneys, and the questions and answers are recorded by an authorized court official and sworn to and signed by the deponent. (Occasionally, written depositions are taken when witnesses are unable to appear in person.) The answers given to depositions will, of course, help the attorneys prepare their cases. They can also be used in court to impeach (challenge the credibility of) a party or a witness who changes her or his testimony at the trial. In addition, the answers given in a deposition can be used as testimony if the witness is not available at trial.

> **Deposition**   The testimony of a party to a lawsuit or a witness taken under oath before a trial.

Interrogatories are written questions for which written answers are prepared and then signed under oath. The main difference between interrogatories and written depositions is that interrogatories are directed to a party to the lawsuit (the plaintiff or the defendant), not to a witness, and the party can prepare answers with the aid of an attorney. The scope of interrogatories is broader because parties are obligated to answer the questions, even if that means disclosing information from their records and files.

> **Interrogatories**   A series of written questions for which written answers are prepared by a party to a lawsuit, usually with the assistance of the party's attorney, and then signed under oath.

REQUESTS FOR OTHER INFORMATION   A party can serve a written request on the other party for an admission of the truth on matters relating to the trial. Any matter admitted under such a request is conclusively established for the trial. For example, Marconi can ask Anderson to admit that he was driving at a speed of forty-five miles an hour. A request for admission saves time at trial because the parties will not have to spend time proving facts on which they already agree.

A party can also gain access to documents and other items not in her or his possession in order to inspect and examine them. Likewise, a party can gain "entry upon land" to inspect the premises. Anderson's attorney, for example, normally can gain permission to inspect and photocopy Marconi's car repair bills.

When the physical or mental condition of one party is in question, the opposing party can ask the court to order a physical or mental examination. If the court issues the order, which it will do only if the need for the information outweighs the right to privacy of the person to be examined, the opposing party can obtain the results of the examination.

ELECTRONIC DISCOVERY   Any relevant material, including information stored electronically, can be the object of a discovery request. The federal rules and most state rules now specifically allow all parties to obtain electronic "data compilations." Electronic evidence, or **e-evidence,** includes all types of computer-generated or electronically recorded information, such as e-mail, voice mail, spreadsheets, document preparation systems, and other data. E-evidence can reveal significant facts that are not discoverable by other means. For example, computers automatically record certain information about files—such as who created the file and when, and who accessed, modified, or transmitted it—on their

> **E-Evidence**   Evidence that consists of computer-generated or electronically recorded information, including e-mail, voice mail, spreadsheets, document preparation systems, and other data.

hard drives. This information can be obtained only from the file in its electronic format—not from printed-out versions.

The Federal Rules of Civil Procedure deal with the preservation, retrieval, and production of electronic data. Although traditional means, such as interrogatories and depositions, are still used to find out about the e-evidence, a party must usually hire an expert to retrieve evidence in its electronic format. The expert uses software to reconstruct e-mail exchanges and establish who knew what and when they knew it. The expert can even recover files that the user thought had been deleted from a computer.

Electronic discovery, or e-discovery, has significant advantages over paper discovery. Back-up copies of documents and e-mail can provide useful—and often quite damaging—information about how a particular matter progressed over several weeks or months. E-discovery can uncover the proverbial smoking gun that leads to litigation success, but it is also time consuming and expensive, especially when lawsuits involve large firms with multiple offices. Also, many firms are finding it difficult to fulfill their duty to preserve e-evidence from a vast number of sources. For a discussion of some of the problems associated with preserving e-evidence for discovery, see this chapter's *Online Developments* feature on the following page.

Pretrial Conference

Either party or the court can request a pretrial conference, or hearing. Usually, the hearing consists of an informal discussion between the judge and the opposing attorneys after discovery has taken place. The purpose of the hearing is to explore the possibility of a settlement without trial and, if this is not possible, to identify the matters that are in dispute and to plan the course of the trial.

Jury Selection

A trial can be held with or without a jury. The Seventh Amendment to the U.S. Constitution guarantees the right to a jury trial for cases in *federal* courts when the amount in controversy exceeds $20, but this guarantee does not apply to state courts. Most states have similar guarantees in their own constitutions (although the threshold dollar amount is higher than $20). The right to a trial by jury does not have to be exercised, and many cases are tried without a jury. In most states and in federal courts, one of the parties must request a jury in a civil case, or the judge presumes the parties waive the right.

Before a jury trial commences, a jury must be selected. The jury selection process is known as **voir dire**.[16] During *voir dire* in most jurisdictions, attorneys for the plaintiff and the defendant ask prospective jurors oral questions to determine whether a potential jury member is biased or has any connection with a party to the action or with a prospective witness. In some jurisdictions, the judge may do all or part of the questioning based on written questions submitted by counsel for the parties.

During *voir dire*, a party may challenge a prospective juror *peremptorily*—that is, ask that an individual not be sworn in as a juror without providing any reason. Alternatively, a party may challenge a prospective juror *for cause*—that is, provide a reason why an individual should not be sworn in as a juror. If the judge grants the challenge, the individual is asked to step down. A prospective juror may not be excluded from the jury by the use of discriminatory challenges, however, such as those based on racial criteria or gender.

---

16. Pronounced vwahr *deehr.*

> *"The judicial system is the most expensive machine ever invented for finding out what happened and what to do about it."*
>
> Irving R. Kaufman, 1910–1992
> (American jurist)

Voir Dire An Old French phrase meaning "to speak the truth." In legal language, the process in which the attorneys question prospective jurors to learn about their backgrounds, attitudes, biases, and other characteristics that may affect their ability to serve as impartial jurors.

TAKE NOTE A prospective juror cannot be excluded solely on the basis of his or her race or gender.

Online Developments

The Duty to Preserve E-Evidence for Discovery

Today, less than 0.5 percent of new information is created on paper. Instead of sending letters and memos, people send e-mails and text messages, creating a massive amount of electronically stored information (ESI). The law requires parties to preserve ESI whenever there is a "reasonable anticipation of litigation."

Why Companies Fail to Preserve E-Evidence

Preserving e-evidence can be a challenge, though, particularly for large corporations that have electronic data scattered across multiple networks, servers, desktops, laptops, handheld devices, and even home computers. Although many companies have policies regarding back-up of office e-mail and computer systems, these may cover only a fraction of the e-evidence requested in a lawsuit.

Technological advances further complicate the situation. Users of BlackBerrys, for example, can configure them so that messages are transmitted with limited or no archiving rather than going through a company's servers and being recorded. How can a company preserve e-evidence that is never on its servers? In one case, the court held that a company had a duty to preserve transitory "server log data," which exist only temporarily on a computer's memory.[a]

Potential Sanctions and Malpractice Claims

A court may impose sanctions (such as fines) on a party that fails to preserve electronic evidence or to comply with e-discovery requests. A firm may be sanctioned if it provides e-mails without the attachments, does not produce all of the e-evidence requested, or fails to suspend its automatic e-mail deletion procedures.[b] Nearly 25 percent of the reported opinions on e-discovery in 2008 involved sanctions for failure to preserve e-evidence.[c] Attorneys who fail to properly advise their clients concerning the duty to preserve e-evidence also often face sanctions and malpractice claims.[d]

Lessons from Intel

A party that fails to preserve e-evidence may even find itself at such a disadvantage that it will settle a dispute rather than continue litigation. For example, Advanced Micro Devices, Inc. (AMD), sued Intel Corporation, one of the world's largest microprocessor suppliers, for violating antitrust laws. Immediately after the lawsuit was filed, Intel began collecting and preserving the ESI on its servers. Although the company instructed its employees to retain documents and e-mails related to competition with AMD, many employees saved only copies of the e-mails that they had received and not e-mails that they had sent. In addition, Intel did not stop its automatic e-mail deletion system, causing other information to be lost. In the end, although Intel produced data that were equivalent to "somewhere in the neighborhood of a pile [of paper] 137 miles high," its failure to preserve e-evidence led it to settle the dispute in 2008.[e]

FOR CRITICAL ANALYSIS

How might a large company protect itself from allegations that it intentionally failed to preserve electronic data?

a. See *Columbia Pictures v. Brunnell,* 2007 WL 2080419 (C.D.Cal. 2007).

b. See, for example, *John B. v. Goetz,* 531 F.3d 448 (6th Cir. 2008); and *Wingnut Films, Ltd. v. Katija Motion Pictures,* 2007 WL 2758571 (C.D.Cal. 2007).

c. Sheri Qualters, "25% of Reported E-Discovery Opinions in 2008 Involved Sanction Issues," *National Law Journal,* December 12, 2008.

d. See, for example, *Qualcomm, Inc. v. Broadcom Corp.,* 539 F.Supp.2d 1214 (S.D.Cal. 2007).

e. See *In re Intel Corp. Microprocessor Antitrust Litigation,* 2008 WL 2310288 (D.Del. 2008). See also *Adams v. Gateway, Inc.,* 2006 WL 2563418 (D. Utah 2006).

The Trial

At the beginning of the trial, the attorneys present their opening arguments, setting forth the facts that they expect to prove during the trial. Then the plaintiff's case is presented. In our hypothetical case, Marconi's lawyer would introduce evidence (relevant documents, exhibits, and the testimony of witnesses) to support Marconi's position. The defendant has the opportunity to challenge any evidence introduced and to cross-examine any of the plaintiff's witnesses.

At the end of the plaintiff's case, the defendant's attorney has the opportunity to ask the judge to direct a verdict for the defendant on the ground that the plaintiff has presented no evidence that would justify the granting of the plaintiff's remedy. This is called a **motion for a directed verdict** (known in federal courts as a *motion*

Motion for a Directed Verdict In a jury trial, a motion for the judge to take the decision out of the hands of the jury and to direct a verdict for the party who filed the motion on the ground that the other party has not produced sufficient evidence to support her or his claim.

for judgment as a matter of law). If the motion is not granted (it seldom is granted), the defendant's attorney then presents the evidence and witnesses for the defendant's case. At the conclusion of the defendant's case, the defendant's attorney has another opportunity to make a motion for a directed verdict. The plaintiff's attorney can challenge any evidence introduced and cross-examine the defendant's witnesses.

EXPERT WITNESSES   Both the plaintiff and the defendant may present testimony from one or more expert witnesses—such as forensic scientists, physicians, and psychologists—as part of their cases. An expert witness is a person who, by virtue of education, training, skill, or experience, has scientific, technical, or other specialized knowledge in a particular area beyond that of an average person. In Marconi's case, her attorney might hire an accident reconstruction specialist to establish Anderson's negligence or a physician to confirm the extent of Marconi's injuries.

Normally, witnesses can testify only about the facts of a case—that is, what they personally observed. When witnesses are qualified as experts in a particular field, however, they can offer their opinions and conclusions about the evidence in that field. Expert testimony is an important component of litigation today. Because numerous experts are available for hire and expert testimony is powerful and effective with juries, there is tremendous potential for abuse. Therefore, in federal courts and most state courts, judges act as gatekeepers to ensure that the experts are qualified and that their opinions are based on scientific knowledge. If a party believes that the opponent's witness is not qualified as an expert in the relevant field, that party can make a motion asking the judge to exclude this evidence and prevent the expert witness from testifying in front of the jury.

In the following case, a federal district court had refused to allow an expert to testify as to his opinion at trial because the plaintiff had failed to file a discovery report outlining the expert's testimony and credentials. The appellate court had to decide whether to reverse the trial court's decision regarding the expert's testimony.

Case 3.3   Downey v. Bob's Discount Furniture Holdings, Inc.

United States Court of Appeals, First Circuit, 633 F.3d 1 (2011).

BACKGROUND AND FACTS   Yvette Downey bought a children's bedroom set from Bob's Discount Furniture Holdings, Inc., in 2004. Soon, Downey and her daughter, Ashley Celester, began to experience skin irritation. In July 2005, they discovered insects in their home, and some of the bugs were on Ashley's body. Downey immediately called Allegiance Pest Control and spoke to Edward Gordinier, a licensed and experienced exterminator. Gordinier inspected Downey's home that day. He found bedbugs throughout the house and identified Ashley's bedroom set as the main source of the infestation. Downey informed Bob's about the problem. Although Bob's retrieved the bedroom set and refunded the purchase price, it refused to pay for the costs of extermination or any other damages. Downey and her daughter filed a lawsuit in a federal district court seeking compensation for health problems, emotional distress, and economic loss. Before the trial, the plaintiffs named Gordinier as a witness but did not submit a written report describing his anticipated testimony or specifying his

qualifications. Rule 26 of the Federal Rules of Civil Procedure requires that a written report be filed for an expert witness who is retained or specially employed to provide expert testimony. The plaintiffs asserted that Gordinier had not been specially employed as an expert and, therefore, no such disclosures were required. The defendants argued that Gordinier could not testify as to his expert opinion because the plaintiffs had not filed a written report. The district court agreed with the defendants and allowed Gordinier to testify only about the facts, such as his inspection of the premises, not about his opinion of the source of the bedbug infestation. The court granted a judgment for the defendants based, in part, on their claim that the plaintiffs had not proved that the furniture was infested with bedbugs when it was delivered. The plaintiffs appealed.

Case 3.3–Continues next page ➡

Case 3.3–Continued

IN THE WORDS OF THE COURT . . .
SELYA, Circuit Judge.
* * * *

* * * Rule 26 "is an integral part of the machinery devised to facilitate the management of pretrial discovery." Among other things, the rule provides for wide-ranging pretrial disclosures in connection with anticipated expert testimony. *At its most basic level, the rule obligates a party who wishes to offer expert testimony to disclose "the identity of any witness it may use at trial to present evidence under Federal Rule of Evidence 702, 703, or 705."* In the case at hand, the plaintiffs seasonably [within a reasonable time period] complied with this identification requirement, naming Gordinier as a potential expert witness regarding causation. [Emphasis added.]

Other, more stringent disclosure requirements pertain to a witness who is "retained or specially employed to provide expert testimony in the case or . . . whose duties as the party's employee regularly involve giving expert testimony." The proponent of a witness falling into this subset must submit to the opposing party "a written report containing, [among other things,] detailed information as to the qualifications and intended testimony of the witness."
* * * *

As the text of Rule 26(a)(2)(B) makes plain, the rule covers two types of experts: (i) "retained or specially employed" experts who meet certain criteria and (ii) employees of a party who meet certain criteria. Because there is no suggestion that Gordinier was regularly employed by the plaintiffs, the lens of our inquiry narrows to whether he was "retained or specially employed."

The circumstances suggest that he was not. For one thing, there is no evidence that Gordinier was a person who held himself out for hire as a purveyor of expert testimony. For another thing, there is no evidence that he was charging a fee for his testimony.

Interpreting the words "retained or specially employed" in a common-sense manner, consistent with their plain meaning, we conclude that as long as an expert was not retained or specially employed in connection with the litigation, and his opinion about causation is premised on personal knowledge and observations made in the course of treatment, no report is required under the terms of Rule 26(a)(2)(B).
* * * *

DECISION AND REMEDY   The U.S. Court of Appeals for the First Circuit held that Gordinier was not the type of expert witness for whom a report was required. Therefore, the court reversed the district court's judgment and remanded the case for a new trial.

THE LEGAL ENVIRONMENT DIMENSION   *Why can only an expert testify about the source of a bedbug infestation?*

THE ETHICAL DIMENSION   *Is it fair to require plaintiffs who hire expert witnesses to pay for and submit written reports that specify what the experts will say at trial? Why or why not?*

CLOSING ARGUMENTS   After the defense concludes its presentation, the attorneys present their closing arguments, each urging a verdict in favor of her or his client. The judge instructs the jury in the law that applies to the case (these instructions are often called *charges*), and the jury retires to the jury room to deliberate on a verdict. In the Marconi-Anderson case, the jury will not only decide for the plaintiff or for the defendant but, if it finds for the plaintiff, will also decide on the amount of the **award** (the compensation to be paid to her).

Posttrial Motions

After the jury has rendered its verdict, either party may make a posttrial motion. If Marconi wins and Anderson's attorney has previously moved for a directed verdict, Anderson's attorney may make a **motion for judgment *n.o.v.*** (from the Latin *non obstante veredicto,* which means "notwithstanding the verdict"—called a *motion for judgment as a matter of law* in the federal courts). Such a motion will be granted only if the jury's verdict was unreasonable and erroneous. If the judge grants the motion, the jury's verdict will be set aside, and a judgment will be entered in favor of the opposite party (Anderson).

Alternatively, Anderson could make a **motion for a new trial,** asking the judge to set aside the adverse verdict and to hold a new trial. The motion will be granted if, after looking at all the evidence, the judge is convinced that the jury was in error but does not feel that it is appropriate to grant judgment for the other side. A judge can also grant a new trial on the basis of newly discovered evidence, misconduct by the participants or

Award   In litigation, the amount of monetary compensation awarded to a plaintiff in a civil lawsuit as damages. In the context of alternative dispute resolution, the decision rendered by an arbitrator.

Motion for Judgment *n.o.v.*   A motion requesting the court to grant judgment in favor of the party making the motion on the ground that the jury's verdict against him or her was unreasonable and erroneous.

Motion for a New Trial   A motion asserting that the trial was so fundamentally flawed (because of error, newly discovered evidence, prejudice, or another reason) that a new trial is necessary to prevent a miscarriage of justice.

the jury during the trial (such as when an attorney or jury member has made prejudicial and inflammatory remarks), or error by the judge.

The Appeal

Assume here that any posttrial motion is denied and that Anderson appeals the case. (If Marconi wins but receives a smaller monetary award than she sought, she can appeal also.) Keep in mind, though, that a party cannot appeal a trial court's decision simply because he or she is dissatisfied with the outcome of the trial. A party must have legitimate grounds to file an appeal, meaning that he or she must be able to claim that the lower court committed an error. If Anderson has grounds to appeal the case, a notice of appeal must be filed with the clerk of the trial court within a prescribed time. Anderson now becomes the appellant, or petitioner, and Marconi becomes the appellee, or respondent.

FILING THE APPEAL   Anderson's attorney files the record on appeal with the appellate court. The record includes the pleadings, the trial transcript, the judge's rulings on motions made by the parties, and other trial-related documents. Anderson's attorney will also provide the reviewing court with a condensation of the record, known as an *abstract,* and a brief. The **brief** is a formal legal document outlining the facts and issues of the case, the judge's rulings or jury's findings that should be reversed or modified, the applicable law, and arguments on Anderson's behalf (citing applicable statutes and relevant cases as precedents). Briefs can be filed electronically in many jurisdictions (see the discussion of electronic filing on the next page).

Marconi's attorney will file an answering brief. Anderson's attorney can file a reply to Marconi's brief, although it is not required. The reviewing court then considers the case.

APPELLATE REVIEW   As mentioned earlier, a court of appeals does not hear evidence. Rather, it reviews the record for errors of law. Its decision concerning a case is based on the record on appeal, the abstracts, and the attorneys' briefs. The attorneys can present oral arguments, after which the case is taken under advisement. In general, appellate courts do not reverse findings of fact unless the findings are unsupported or contradicted by the evidence.

An appellate court has the following options after reviewing a case:

1. The court can *affirm* the trial court's decision.
2. The court can *reverse* the trial court's judgment if it concludes that the trial court erred or that the jury did not receive proper instructions.
3. The appellate court can *remand* (send back) the case to the trial court for further proceedings consistent with its opinion on the matter.
4. The court might also affirm or reverse a decision *in part.* For example, the court might affirm the jury's finding that Anderson was negligent but remand the case for further proceedings on another issue (such as the extent of Marconi's damages).
5. An appellate court can also *modify* a lower court's decision. If the appellate court decides that the jury awarded an excessive amount in damages, for example, the court might reduce the award to a more appropriate, or fairer, amount.

APPEAL TO A HIGHER APPELLATE COURT   If the reviewing court is an intermediate appellate court, the losing party may decide to appeal to

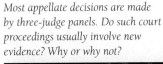

Brief   A formal legal document prepared by a party's attorney for the appellant or the appellee (in answer to the appellant's brief) and submitted to an appellate court when a case is appealed. The appellant's brief outlines the facts and issues of the case, the judge's rulings or jury's findings that should be reversed or modified, the applicable law, and the arguments on the client's behalf.

Most appellate decisions are made by three-judge panels. Do such court proceedings usually involve new evidence? Why or why not?

the state supreme court (the highest state court). Such a petition corresponds to a petition for a writ of *certiorari* from the United States Supreme Court. Although the losing party has a right to ask (petition) a higher court to review the case, the party does not have a right to have the case heard by the higher appellate court.

Appellate courts normally have discretionary power and can accept or reject an appeal. Like the United States Supreme Court, in general state supreme courts deny most appeals. If the appeal is granted, new briefs must be filed before the state supreme court, and the attorneys may be allowed or requested to present oral arguments. Like the intermediate appellate court, the supreme court may reverse or affirm the appellate court's decision or remand the case. At this point, the case typically has reached its end (unless a federal question is at issue and one of the parties has legitimate grounds to seek review by a federal appellate court).

Enforcing the Judgment

The uncertainties of the litigation process are compounded by the lack of guarantees that any judgment will be enforceable. Even if a plaintiff wins an award of damages in court, the defendant may not have sufficient assets or insurance to cover that amount. Usually, one of the factors considered before a lawsuit is initiated is whether the defendant has sufficient assets to cover the amount of damages sought, should the plaintiff win the case.

The Courts Adapt to the Online World

We have already mentioned that the courts have attempted to adapt traditional jurisdictional concepts to the online world. Not surprisingly, the Internet has also brought about changes in court procedures and practices, including new methods for filing pleadings and other documents and issuing decisions and opinions. Some jurisdictions are exploring the possibility of cyber courts, in which legal proceedings could be conducted totally online.

Electronic Filing

The federal court system has now implemented its electronic filing system, Case Management/Electronic Case Files (CM/ECF), in nearly all of the federal courts. The system is available in federal district, appellate, and bankruptcy courts, as well as the Court of International Trade and the Court of Federal Claims. More than 33 million cases are on the CM/ECF system. Users can create a document using conventional software, save it as a PDF file, then log on to a court's Web site and submit the PDF to the court via the Internet. Access to the electronic documents filed on CM/ECF is available through a system called PACER (Public Access to Court Electronic Records), which is a service of the U.S. Judiciary.

More than 60 percent of the states have some form of electronic filing. Some states, including Arizona, California, Colorado, Delaware, Mississippi, New Jersey, New York, and Nevada, offer statewide e-filing systems. Generally, when electronic filing is available, it is optional. Nonetheless, some state courts have now made e-filing mandatory in certain types of disputes, such as complex civil litigation.

Courts Online

Most courts today have sites on the Web. Of course, each court decides what to make available at its site. Some courts display only the names of court personnel and office phone numbers. Others add court rules and forms. Many appellate court sites include judicial decisions, although the decisions may remain online for only a limited time. In addition, in some states, such as California and Florida, court clerks offer information about the court's **docket** (the court's schedule of cases to be heard) and other searchable databases online.

Appellate court decisions are often posted online immediately after they are rendered. Recent decisions of the U.S. courts of appeals, for example, are available online at their Web sites. The United States Supreme Court also has an official Web site and publishes its opinions there immediately after they are announced to the public. In fact, even decisions that are designated as unpublished opinions by the appellate courts are often published online (as discussed in the *Online Developments* feature in Chapter 1 on page 9).

Cyber Courts and Proceedings

Someday, litigants may be able to use cyber courts, in which judicial proceedings take place only on the Internet. The parties to a case could meet online to make their arguments and present their evidence. This might be done with e-mail submissions, through video cameras, in designated chat rooms, at closed sites, or through the use of other Internet facilities. These courtrooms could be efficient and economical. We might also see the use of virtual lawyers, judges, and juries—and possibly the replacement of court personnel with computer software.

Already the state of Michigan has passed legislation creating cyber courts that will hear cases involving technology issues and high-tech businesses. The state of Wisconsin recently enacted a rule authorizing the use of videoconferencing in both civil and criminal trials, at the discretion of the trial court.[17] In some situations, a Wisconsin judge can allow videoconferencing even over the objection of the parties, provided certain operational criteria are met.

The courts may also use the Internet in other ways. In a groundbreaking decision, for instance, a Florida county court granted "virtual" visitation rights in a couple's divorce proceeding. Each parent was ordered to set up a computerized videoconferencing system so that the child could visit with the parent who did not have custody via the Internet at any time.

 Alternative Dispute Resolution

Litigation is an expensive and time-consuming process. Because of the backlog of cases pending in many courts, several years may pass before a case is actually tried. For these and other reasons, more and more businesspersons are turning to **alternative dispute resolution (ADR)** as a means of settling their disputes.

The great advantage of ADR is its flexibility. It ranges from the parties sitting down together to attemp to work out their differences to multinational corporations agreeing to resolve a dispute through a formal hearing before a panel of experts. Normally, the parties themselves can control how they will attempt to settle their dispute, what procedures will be used, whether a neutral third party will be present or make a decision, and whether that decision will be legally binding or nonbinding.

Today, more than 90 percent of cases are settled before trial through some form of ADR. Indeed, most states either require or encourage parties to undertake ADR prior to trial. Many federal courts have instituted ADR programs as well. In the following

Docket The list of cases entered on a court's calendar and thus scheduled to be heard by the court.

Alternative Dispute Resolution (ADR) The resolution of disputes in ways other than those involved in the traditional judicial process. Negotiation, mediation, and arbitration are forms of ADR.

---

17. Wisconsin Statute Section 751.12.

pages, we examine the basic forms of ADR. Keep in mind, though, that new methods of ADR—and new combinations of existing methods—are constantly being devised and employed.

Negotiation

Negotiation A process in which parties attempt to settle their dispute informally, with or without attorneys to represent them.

The simplest form of ADR is **negotiation,** in which the parties attempt to settle their dispute informally, with or without attorneys to represent them. Attorneys frequently advise their clients to negotiate a settlement voluntarily before they proceed to trial. Parties may even try to negotiate a settlement during a trial, or after the trial but before an appeal. Negotiation traditionally involves just the parties themselves and (typically) their attorneys. The attorneys, though, are advocates—they are obligated to put their clients' interests first.

Mediation

Mediation A method of settling disputes outside the courts by using the services of a neutral third party, who acts as a communicating agent between the parties and assists them in negotiating a settlement.

In **mediation,** a neutral third party acts as a mediator and works with both sides in the dispute to facilitate a resolution. The mediator talks with the parties separately as well as jointly and emphasizes their points of agreement in an attempt to help the parties evaluate their options. Although the mediator may propose a solution (called a *mediator's proposal*), he or she does not make a decision resolving the matter. States that require parties to undergo ADR before trial often offer mediation as one of the ADR options or (as in Florida) the only option.

One of the main advantages of mediation is that it is not as adversarial as litigation. In trials, the parties "do battle" with each other in the courtroom, trying to prove one another wrong, while the judge is usually a passive observer. In mediation, the mediator takes an active role and attempts to bring the parties together so that they can come to a mutually satisfactory resolution. The mediation process tends to reduce the hostility between the disputants, allowing them to resume their former relationship without bad feelings. For this reason, mediation is often the preferred form of ADR for disputes involving business partners, employers and employees, or other parties involved in long-term relationships.

EXAMPLE 3.9 Two business partners, Mark Shalen and Charles Rowe, have a dispute over how the profits of their firm should be distributed. If the dispute is litigated, the parties will be adversaries, and their respective attorneys will emphasize how the parties' positions differ, not what they have in common. In contrast, when the dispute is mediated, the mediator emphasizes the common ground shared by Shalen and Rowe and helps them work toward agreement. The two men can work out the distribution of profits without damaging their continuing relationship as partners. ●

Arbitration

Arbitration The settling of a dispute by submitting it to a disinterested third party (other than a court), who renders a decision that is (most often) legally binding.

A more formal method of ADR is **arbitration,** in which an arbitrator (a neutral third party or a panel of experts) hears a dispute and imposes a resolution on the parties. Arbitration is unlike other forms of ADR because the third party hearing the dispute makes a decision for the parties. Exhibit 3–4 on the facing page outlines the basic differences among the three traditional forms of ADR. Usually, the parties in arbitration agree that the third party's decision will be *legally binding,* although the parties can also agree to *nonbinding* arbitration. (Arbitration that is mandated by the courts often is nonbinding.) In nonbinding arbitration, the parties can go forward with a lawsuit if they do not agree with the arbitrator's decision.

● *Exhibit* 3–4 **Basic Differences in the Traditional Forms of Alternative Dispute Resolution**

TYPE OF ADR	DESCRIPTION	NEUTRAL THIRD PARTY PRESENT	WHO DECIDES THE RESOLUTION
Negotiation	The parties meet informally with or without their attorneys and attempt to agree on a resolution.	No	The parties themselves reach a resolution.
Mediation	A neutral third party meets with the parties and emphasizes points of agreement to help them resolve their dispute.	Yes	The parties decide the resolution, but the mediator may suggest or propose a resolution.
Arbitration	The parties present their arguments and evidence before an arbitrator at a hearing, and the arbitrator renders a decision resolving the parties' dispute.	Yes	The arbitrator imposes a resolution on the parties that may be either binding or nonbinding.

Arbitration Clause   A clause in a contract that provides that, in the event of a dispute, the parties will submit the dispute to arbitration rather than litigate the dispute in court.

Supporters of a union that represents firefighters stage a protest during a contract dispute with the city of Philadelphia. An arbitration panel ruled in favor of the union and ordered a wage increase, and the city appealed.

(Courtesy of the Philadelphia Fire Fighters' Union)

In some respects, formal arbitration resembles a trial, although usually the procedural rules are much less restrictive than those governing litigation. In the typical arbitration, the parties present opening arguments and ask for specific remedies. Evidence is then presented, and witnesses may be called and examined by both sides. The arbitrator then renders a decision, which is called an *award.*

An arbitrator's award is usually the final word on the matter. Although the parties may appeal an arbitrator's decision, a court's review of the decision will be much more restricted in scope than an appellate court's review of a trial court's decision. The general view is that because the parties were free to frame the issues and set the powers of the arbitrator at the outset, they cannot complain about the results. The award will be set aside only if the arbitrator's conduct or "bad faith" substantially prejudiced the rights of one of the parties, if the award violates an established public policy, or if the arbitrator exceeded her or his powers (arbitrated issues that the parties did not agree to submit to arbitration).

ARBITRATION CLAUSES AND STATUTES   Just about any commercial matter can be submitted to arbitration. Frequently, parties include an **arbitration clause** in a contract (a written agreement—see Chapter 9), providing that any dispute that arises under the contract will be resolved through arbitration rather than through the court system. Parties can also agree to arbitrate a dispute after the dispute arises.

Most states have statutes (often based in part on the Uniform Arbitration Act of 1955) under which arbitration clauses will be enforced, and some state statutes compel arbitration of certain types of disputes, such as those involving public employees. At the federal level, the Federal Arbitration Act (FAA), enacted in 1925, enforces arbitration clauses in contracts involving maritime activity and interstate commerce (though its applicability to employment contracts has been controversial, as discussed in a later subsection). Because of the breadth of the commerce clause (see Chapter 4), arbitration agreements involving transactions only slightly connected to the flow of interstate commerce may fall under the FAA.[18]

CASE EXAMPLE 3.10   Vincent Concepcion and others sued their cell phone provider, AT&T Mobility, LLC, in a federal court in California. The customers claimed that AT&T had committed fraud when it offered a free phone to anyone who signed up for its cell phone service, but then charged each customer approximately $30 in sales tax on the retail value of the free phone. Each contract included an arbitration clause and

---

18. See, for example, *Buckeye Check Cashing, Inc. v. Cardegna,* 546 U.S. 440, 126 S.Ct. 1204, 163 L.Ed.2d 1038 (2006).

required plaintiffs to bring claims as individuals, not as part of a class action (a form of lawsuit in which an individual files a claim against the defendant on behalf of a large number of plaintiffs). Nevertheless, the plaintiffs joined together in a class-action lawsuit, and AT&T filed a motion to compel arbitration. The district court denied the motion, finding that the arbitration clause was unfair under California case law, which held that class-action waivers in arbitration clauses were unfair in consumer contracts. On appeal, a federal appellate court also refused to compel arbitration, and AT&T appealed to the United States Supreme Court. In 2011, the Supreme Court reversed and remanded the case for trial. The Supreme Court held that the Federal Arbitration Act preempted California's judicial rule against class arbitration waivers in consumer contracts. The decision is a major victory for companies because the high court essentially held that arbitration clauses must be enforced even if they are considered unfair under state law.[19] ●

THE ISSUE OF ARBITRABILITY   Notice that in Case Example 3.10 above, the issue before the United States Supreme Court was *not* the basic controversy (whether it was fraud to charge sales tax on a cell phone that was advertised as free) but rather the issue of arbitrability—that is, whether the matter was one that had to be resolved by separate arbitration proceedings under the arbitration clause. Such actions, in which one party files a motion to compel arbitration, often occur when a dispute arises over an agreement that contains an arbitration clause. If the court finds that the subject matter in controversy is covered by the agreement to arbitrate—even when the claim involves the violation of a statute, such as an employment statute—then a party may be compelled to arbitrate the dispute. Usually, a court will allow the claim to be arbitrated if the court, in interpreting the statute, can find no legislative intent to the contrary.

No party, however, will be ordered to submit a particular dispute to arbitration unless the court is convinced that the party consented to do so.[20] Additionally, the courts will not compel arbitration if it is clear that the prescribed arbitration rules and procedures are inherently unfair to one of the parties.

The terms of an arbitration agreement can limit the types of disputes that the parties agree to arbitrate. When the parties do not specify limits, however, disputes can arise as to whether a particular matter is covered by the arbitration agreement, and then the court will have to resolve the issue of arbitrability.

MANDATORY ARBITRATION IN THE EMPLOYMENT CONTEXT   A significant question in the last several years has concerned mandatory arbitration clauses in employment contracts. Many claim that employees' rights are not sufficiently protected when workers are forced, as a condition of being hired, to agree to arbitrate all disputes and thus waive their rights under statutes specifically designed to protect employees. The United States Supreme Court, however, has generally held that mandatory arbitration clauses in employment contracts are enforceable.

CASE EXAMPLE 3.11   In a landmark decision, *Gilmer v. Interstate/Johnson Lane Corp.*,[21] the Supreme Court held that a claim brought under a federal statute prohibiting age discrimination (see Chapter 18) could be subject to arbitration. The Court concluded that the employee had waived his right to sue when he agreed, as part of a required registration application to be a securities representative with the New

KEEP IN MIND   Litigation—even of a dispute over whether a particular matter should be submitted to arbitration—can be time consuming and expensive.

---

19. *AT&T Mobility, LLC v. Concepcion,* ___ U.S.___, 131 S.Ct. 1740, 179 L.Ed.2d 742 (2011).

20. See, for example, *Wright v. Universal Maritime Service Corp.,* 525 U.S. 70, 119 S.Ct. 391, 142 L.Ed.2d 361 (1998).

21. 500 U.S. 20, 111 S.Ct. 1647, 114 L.Ed.2d 26 (1991).

York Stock Exchange, to arbitrate "any dispute, claim, or controversy" relating to his employment. ●

Providers of ADR Services

ADR services are provided by both government agencies and private organizations. A major provider of ADR services is the American Arbitration Association (AAA). Most of the largest U.S. law firms are members of this nonprofit association. Cases brought before the AAA are heard by an expert or a panel of experts in the area relating to the dispute and usually are settled quickly. The AAA has a special team devoted to resolving large, complex disputes across a wide range of industries.

Hundreds of for-profit firms around the country also provide various forms of dispute-resolution services. Typically, these firms hire retired judges to conduct arbitration hearings or otherwise assist parties in settling their disputes. The judges follow procedures similar to those of the federal courts and use similar rules. Generally, each party to the dispute pays a filing fee and a designated fee for a hearing session or conference.

Online Dispute Resolution

Online Dispute Resolution (ODR) The resolution of disputes with the assistance of organizations that offer dispute-resolution services via the Internet.

An increasing number of companies and organizations offer dispute-resolution services using the Internet. The settlement of disputes in these online forums is known as **online dispute resolution (ODR).** The disputes have most commonly involved disagreements over the rights to domain names (Web site addresses—see Chapter 8) or over the quality of goods sold via the Internet, including goods sold through Internet auction sites.

ODR may be best suited for resolving small- to medium-sized business liability claims, which may not be worth the expense of litigation or traditional ADR. Rules being developed in online forums, however, may ultimately become a code of conduct for everyone who does business in cyberspace. Most online forums do not automatically apply the law of any specific jurisdiction. Instead, results are often based on general, universal legal principles. As with most offline methods of dispute resolution, any party may appeal to a court at any time if the ADR is nonbinding arbitration.

Interestingly, some cities are using ODR as a means of resolving claims against them. **EXAMPLE 3.12** New York City has used Cybersettle.com to resolve auto accident, sidewalk, and other personal-injury claims made against the city. Cybersettle. com provides services for negotiating settlements over the Internet. Using this system, parties with complaints submit their claims, and the city submits its offers confidentially via the Internet. Whenever an offer exceeds the claim, a settlement is reached, and the plaintiff gets to keep half of the difference between his or her claim and the city's offer as a bonus. ●

 Reviewing . . . Courts and Alternative Dispute Resolution

Stan Garner resides in Illinois and promotes boxing matches for SuperSports, Inc., an Illinois corporation. Garner created the promotional concept of the "Ages" fights—a series of three boxing matches pitting an older fighter (George Foreman) against a younger fighter. The concept included titles for each of the three fights ("Challenge of the Ages," "Battle of the Ages," and "Fight of the Ages"), as well as promotional epithets to characterize the two fighters ("the Foreman Factor"). Garner contacted Foreman and his manager, who both reside in Texas, to sell

(Continued)

the idea, and they arranged a meeting at Caesar's Palace in Las Vegas, Nevada. At some point in the negotiations, Foreman's manager signed a nondisclosure agreement prohibiting him from disclosing Garner's promotional concepts unless they signed a contract. Nevertheless, after negotiations fell through, Foreman used Garner's "Battle of the Ages" concept to promote a subsequent fight. Garner filed a lawsuit against Foreman and his manager in a federal district court in Illinois, alleging breach of contract. Using the information presented in the chapter, answer the following questions.

1. On what basis might the federal district court in Illinois exercise jurisdiction in this case?
2. Does the federal district court have original or appellate jurisdiction?
3. Suppose that Garner had filed his action in an Illinois state court. Could an Illinois state court exercise personal jurisdiction over Foreman or his manager? Why or why not?
4. Assume that Garner had filed his action in a Nevada state court. Would that court have personal jurisdiction over Foreman or his manager? Explain.

 ## Key Terms

alternative dispute resolution (ADR) 77	e-evidence 70	motion to dismiss 69
answer 68	exclusive jurisdiction 58	negotiation 78
arbitration 78	federal question 58	online dispute resolution (ODR) 81
arbitration clause 79	interrogatories 70	pleadings 68
award 74	judicial review 54	probate court 57
bankruptcy court 57	jurisdiction 54	question of fact 64
brief 75	justiciable controversy 62	question of law 64
complaint 68	litigation 68	reply 68
concurrent jurisdiction 58	long arm statute 55	rule of four 66
counterclaim 68	mediation 78	small claims court 64
default judgment 68	motion for a directed verdict 72	standing to sue 62
deposition 70	motion for a new trial 74	summons 68
discovery 69	motion for judgment *n.o.v.* 74	venue 61
diversity of citizenship 58	motion for judgment on the pleadings 69	*voir dire* 71
docket 77	motion for summary judgment 69	writ of *certiorari* 66

 ## Chapter Summary: Courts and Alternative Dispute Resolution

The Judiciary's Role in American Government (See pages 53–54.)	The role of the judiciary—the courts—in the American governmental system is to interpret and apply the law. Through the process of judicial review—determining the constitutionality of laws—the judicial branch acts as a check on the executive and legislative branches of government.

Basic Judicial Requirements (See pages 54–62.)	1. *Jurisdiction*—Before a court can hear a case, it must have jurisdiction over the person against whom the suit is brought or the property involved in the suit, as well as jurisdiction over the subject matter.
	  a. Limited versus general jurisdiction—Limited jurisdiction exists when a court is limited to a specific subject matter, such as probate or divorce. General jurisdiction exists when a court can hear any kind of case.
	  b. Original versus appellate jurisdiction—Courts that have authority to hear a case for the first time (trial courts) have original jurisdiction. Courts of appeals, or reviewing courts, have appellate jurisdiction. Generally, appellate courts do not have original jurisdiction.
	  c. Federal jurisdiction—Arises (1) when a federal question is involved (when the plaintiff's cause of action is based, at least in part, on the U.S. Constitution, a treaty, or a federal law) or (2) when a case involves diversity of citizenship and the amount in controversy exceeds $75,000.

Chapter Summary: Courts and Alternative Dispute Resolution, Continued

Basic Judicial Requirements— Continued	d. Concurrent versus exclusive jurisdiction—Concurrent jurisdiction exists when two different courts have authority to hear the same case. Exclusive jurisdiction exists when only state courts or only federal courts have authority to hear a case. 2. *Jurisdiction in cyberspace*—Because the Internet does not have physical boundaries, traditional jurisdictional concepts have been difficult to apply in cases involving online activities. Courts are developing standards for determining when jurisdiction over a Web site owner or operator located in another state is proper. 3. *Venue*—Venue has to do with the most appropriate location for a trial. 4. *Standing to sue*—A requirement that a party must have a legally protected and tangible interest at stake sufficient to justify seeking relief through the court system. The controversy at issue must also be a justiciable controversy—one that is real and substantial, as opposed to hypothetical or academic.

The State and Federal Court Systems (See pages 63–67.)	1. *Trial courts*—Courts of original jurisdiction, in which legal actions are initiated.
	  a. State—Courts of general jurisdiction can hear any case. Courts of limited jurisdiction include domestic relations courts, probate courts, traffic courts, and small claims courts.
	  b. Federal—The federal district court is the equivalent of the state trial court. Federal courts of limited jurisdiction include the U.S. Tax Court, the U.S. Bankruptcy Court, and the U.S. Court of Federal Claims.
	
	2. *Intermediate appellate courts*—Courts of appeals, or reviewing courts; generally without original jurisdiction. Many states have an intermediate appellate court. In the federal court system, the U.S. circuit courts of appeals are the intermediate appellate courts.
	
	3. *Supreme (highest) courts*—Each state has a supreme court, although it may be called by some other name. Appeal from the state supreme court to the United States Supreme Court is possible only if the case involves a federal question. The United States Supreme Court is the highest court in the federal court system.

Following a State Court Case (See pages 67–76.)	Rules of procedure prescribe the way in which disputes are handled in the courts. Rules differ from court to court, and separate sets of rules exist for federal and state courts, as well as for criminal and civil cases. A civil court case in a state court would involve the following procedures:
	
	1. *The pleadings*—
	  a. Complaint—Filed by the plaintiff with the court to initiate the lawsuit; served with a summons on the defendant.
	  b. Answer—A response to the complaint in which the defendant admits or denies the allegations made by the plaintiff; may assert a counterclaim or an affirmative defense.
	  c. Motion to dismiss—A request to the court to dismiss the case for stated reasons, such as the plaintiff's failure to state a claim for which relief can be granted.
	
	2. *Pretrial motions (in addition to the motion to dismiss)*—
	  a. Motion for judgment on the pleadings—May be made by either party; will be granted if the parties agree on the facts and the only question is how the law applies to the facts. The judge bases the decision solely on the pleadings.
	  b. Motion for summary judgment—May be made by either party; will be granted if the parties agree on the facts. The judge applies the law in rendering a judgment. The judge can consider evidence outside the pleadings when evaluating the motion.
	
	3. *Discovery*—The process of gathering evidence concerning the case. Discovery involves depositions, interrogatories, and various requests for information. Discovery may also involve electronically recorded information, such as e-mail, voice mail, word-processing documents, and other data compilations.
	
	4. *Pretrial conference*—Either party or the court can request a pretrial conference to identify the matters in dispute after discovery has taken place and to plan the course of the trial.
	
	5. *Trial*—Following jury selection (*voir dire*), the trial begins with opening statements from both parties' attorneys. The following events then occur:

(Continued)

Chapter Summary: Courts and Alternative Dispute Resolution, Continued

Following a State Court Case—Continued	a. The plaintiff's introduction of evidence (including the testimony of witnesses) supporting the plaintiff's position. The defendant's attorney can challenge evidence and cross-examine witnesses.
	b. The defendant's introduction of evidence (including the testimony of witnesses) supporting the defendant's position. The plaintiff's attorney can challenge evidence and cross-examine witnesses.
	c. Closing arguments by the attorneys in favor of their respective clients, the judge's instructions to the jury, and the jury's verdict.
	6. *Posttrial motions—*
	  a. Motion for judgment *n.o.v.* ("notwithstanding the verdict")—Will be granted if the judge is convinced that the jury was in error.
	  b. Motion for a new trial—Will be granted if the judge is convinced that the jury was in error; can also be granted on the grounds of newly discovered evidence, misconduct by the participants during the trial, or error by the judge.
	7. *Appeal*—Either party can appeal the trial court's judgment to an appropriate court of appeals. After reviewing the record on appeal, the appellate court holds a hearing and renders its opinion.

The Courts Adapt to the Online World (See pages 76–77.)	Nearly all of the federal appellate courts and bankruptcy courts and a majority of the federal district courts have implemented electronic filing systems.
Alternative Dispute Resolution (See pages 77–81.)	1. *Negotiation*—The parties come together, with or without attorneys to represent them, and try to reach a settlement without the involvement of a third party. 2. *Mediation*—The parties themselves reach an agreement with the help of a neutral third party, called a mediator. The mediator may propose a solution but does not make a decision resolving the matter. 3. *Arbitration*—A more formal method of ADR in which the parties submit their dispute to a neutral third party, the arbitrator, who renders a decision. The decision may or may not be legally binding. 4. *Providers of ADR services*—Both nonprofit and for-profit firms provide ADR services. 5. *Online dispute resolution*—A number of organizations now offer this service through online forums.

 ExamPrep

ISSUE SPOTTERS

1. Sue contracts with Tom to deliver a quantity of computers to Sue's Computer Store. They disagree over the amount, the delivery date, the price, and the quality. Sue files a suit against Tom in a state court. Their state requires that their dispute be submitted to mediation or nonbinding arbitration. If the dispute is not resolved, or if either party disagrees with the decision of the mediator or arbitrator, will a court hear the case? Explain.

2. At the trial, after Sue calls her witnesses, offers her evidence, and otherwise presents her side of the case, Tom has at least two choices between courses of action. Tom can call his first witness. What else might he do?

—**Check your answers to these questions against the answers provided in Appendix G.**

BEFORE THE TEST

Go to **www.cengagebrain.com**, enter the ISBN number "9781111530617," and click on "Find" to locate this textbook's Web site. Then, click on "Access Now" under "Study Tools," and select "Chapter 3" at the top. There you will find an "Interactive Quiz" that you can take to assess your mastery of the concepts in this chapter, as well as "Flashcards" and a "Glossary" of important terms.

 For Review

1. What is judicial review? How and when was the power of judicial review established?

2. Before a court can hear a case, it must have jurisdiction. Over what must it have jurisdiction? How are the courts applying traditional jurisdictional concepts to cases involving Internet transactions?

3. What is the difference between a trial court and an appellate court?
4. What is discovery, and how does electronic discovery differ from traditional discovery?
5. What are three alternative methods of resolving disputes?

Questions and Case Problems

3–1. Standing. Jack and Maggie Turton bought a house in Jefferson County, Idaho, located directly across the street from a gravel pit. A few years later, the county converted the pit to a landfill. The landfill accepted many kinds of trash that cause harm to the environment, including major appliances, animal carcasses, containers with hazardous content warnings, leaking car batteries, and waste oil. The Turtons complained to the county, but the county did nothing. The Turtons then filed a lawsuit against the county alleging violations of federal environmental laws pertaining to groundwater contamination and other pollution. Do the Turtons have standing to sue? Why or why not?

3–2. **Question with Sample Answer. Jurisdiction.** Marya Callais, a citizen of Florida, sustained numerous injuries when she was walking along a busy street in Tallahassee and a large crate flew off a passing truck and hit her. She experienced a great deal of pain and suffering, incurred significant medical expenses, and could not work for six months. She wishes to sue the trucking firm for $300,000 in damages. The firm's headquarters are in Georgia, although the company does business in Florida. In what court may Callais bring suit—a Florida state court, a Georgia state court, or a federal court? What factors might influence her decision?

—**For a sample answer to Question 3–2, go to Appendix E at the end of this text.**

3–3. Discovery. Advance Technology Consultants, Inc. (ATC), contracted with RoadTrac, LLC, to provide software and client software systems for the products of global positioning satellite (GPS) technology being developed by RoadTrac. RoadTrac agreed to provide ATC with hardware with which ATC's software would interface. Problems soon arose, however, and RoadTrac filed a lawsuit against ATC alleging breach of contract. During discovery, RoadTrac requested ATC's customer lists and marketing procedures. ATC objected to providing this information because RoadTrac and ATC had become competitors in the GPS industry. Should a party to a lawsuit have to hand over its confidential business secrets as part of a discovery request? Why or why not? What limitations might a court consider imposing before requiring ATC to produce this material?

3–4. Arbitration. Thomas Baker and others who bought new homes from Osborne Development Corp. sued for multiple defects in the houses they purchased. When Osborne sold the homes, it paid for them to be in a new home warranty program administered by Home Buyers Warranty (HBW). When the company enrolled a home with HBW, it paid a fee and filled out a form that stated the following: "By signing below, you acknowledge that you . . . CONSENT TO THE TERMS OF THESE DOCUMENTS INCLUDING THE BINDING ARBITRATION PROVISION contained therein." HBW then issued warranty booklets to the new homeowners that stated: "Any and all claims, disputes and controversies by or between the Homeowner, the Builder, the Warranty Insurer and/or HBW . . . shall be submitted to arbitration." Were the new homeowners bound by the arbitration agreement, or could they sue the builder, Osborne, in court? Explain. [*Baker v. Osborne Development Corp.,* 159 Cal.App.4th 884, 71 Cal.Rptr.3d 854 (Cal.App. 2008)]

3–5. **Case Problem with Sample Answer. Arbitration Clause.** Kathleen Lowden sued cellular phone company T-Mobile USA, Inc., contending that its service agreements were not enforceable under Washington state law. Lowden moved to create a class-action lawsuit, in which her claims would extend to similarly affected customers. She contended that T-Mobile had improperly charged her fees beyond the advertised price of service and charged her for roaming calls that should not have been classified as roaming. T-Mobile moved to force arbitration in accordance with provisions that were clearly set forth in the service agreement. The agreement also specified that no class-action lawsuit could be brought, so T-Mobile asked the court to dismiss the class-action request. Was T-Mobile correct that Lowden's only course of action would be to file arbitration personally? Explain. [*Lowden v. T-Mobile USA, Inc.,* 512 F.3d 1213 (9th Cir. 2008)]

—**To view a sample answer for Case Problem 3–5, go to Appendix F at the end of this text.**

3–6. Discovery. Rita Peatie filed a suit in a Connecticut state court in October 2004 against Wal-Mart Stores, Inc., to recover for injuries to her head, neck, and shoulder. Peatie claimed that she had been struck two years earlier by a metal cylinder falling from a store ceiling. The parties agreed to nonbinding arbitration. Ten days before the hearing in January 2006, the plaintiff asked for, and was granted, four more months to conduct discovery. On the morning of the rescheduled hearing, she asked for more time, but the court denied this request. The hearing was held, and the arbitrator ruled in Wal-Mart's favor. Peatie filed a motion for a new trial, which was granted. Five months later, she sought through discovery to acquire any photos, records, and reports held by Wal-Mart regarding her alleged injury. The court issued a "protective order" against the request, stating that the time for discovery had long been over. On the day of the trial—four years after the alleged injury—the plaintiff asked the court to lift the order. Should the court do it? Why or why not?

[*Peatie v. Wal-Mart Stores, Inc.,* 112 Conn.App. 8, 961 A.2d 1016 (2009)]

3–7. Arbitration. PRM Energy Systems, Inc. (PRM), owned technology patents and licensed Primenergy to use and to sublicense the technology in the United States. The agreement stated that all disputes would be settled by arbitration. Kobe Steel of Japan was interested in using the technology at its U.S. subsidiary; PRM directed Kobe to talk to Primenergy about that. Kobe talked to PRM directly about using the technology in Japan, but no agreement was reached. Primenergy then agreed to let Kobe use the technology in Japan without telling PRM. The dispute between PRM and Primenergy about Kobe went to arbitration as required by the license agreement. PRM sued Primenergy for fraud and theft of trade secrets. PRM also sued Kobe for using the technology in Japan without its permission. The district court ruled that PRM had to take all complaints about Primenergy to arbitration. PRM also had to take its complaint about Kobe to arbitration because the complaint involved a sublicense Kobe was granted by Primenergy. PRM appealed, contending that the fraud and theft of trade secrets went beyond the license agreement with Primenergy and that Kobe had no right to demand arbitration because it never had a right to use the technology under a license from PRM. Is PRM correct, or must all matters go to arbitration? Explain. [*PRM Energy Systems v. Primenergy,* 592 F.3d 830 (8th Cir. 2010)]

3–8. Arbitration. From 1983 to 2002, Bruce Matthews played football in the National Football League (NFL) for the Houston Oilers and the Tennessee Titans. As part of his player contract, Matthews had agreed to submit any disputes with the NFL to final and binding arbitration. He had also signed a contract with the Titans stating that Tennessee law would determine all employment issues and matters related to workers' compensation benefits. Five years after he left the NFL, Matthews filed a workers' compensation claim (see Chapter 17) in California. The Titans and the NFL Management Council filed a grievance against Matthews, and the dispute was arbitrated. The arbitrator ruled that Matthews could pursue a workers' compensation claim in California but that the claim must proceed under Tennessee law. If California did not apply Tennessee law, then Matthews would be required to withdraw his claim. Unsatisfied with this ruling, the National Football League Players Association—on behalf of Matthews and all NFL players—filed a lawsuit asking the court to vacate the arbi-

tration award. For what reasons will a court set aside an arbitrator's award? Should the court set aside the award in this case? Explain. [*National Football League Players Association v. National Football League Management Council,* ___ F.Supp.2d ___ (S.D.Cal. 2011)]

3–9. **A Question of Ethics. Agreement to Arbitrate.** *Nellie Lumpkin, who suffered from various illnesses, including dementia, was admitted to the Picayune Convalescent Center, a nursing home. Because of her mental condition, her daughter, Beverly McDaniel, filled out the admissions paperwork and signed the admissions agreement. It included a clause requiring parties to submit to arbitration any disputes that arose. After Lumpkin left the center two years later, she sued, through her husband, for negligent treatment and malpractice during her stay. The center moved to force the matter to arbitration. The trial court held that the arbitration agreement was not enforceable. The center appealed.* [Covenant Health & Rehabilitation of Picayune, LP v. Lumpkin, *23 So.3d 1092 (Miss.App. 2009)]*

1. Should a dispute involving medical malpractice be forced into arbitration? This is a claim of negligent care, not a breach of a commercial contract. Is it ethical for medical facilities to impose such a requirement? Is there really any bargaining over such terms?

2. Should a person with limited mental capacity be held to the arbitration clause agreed to by the next-of-kin who signed on behalf of that person?

3–10. **Video Question.** *Jurisdiction in Cyberspace.* Access the video using the instructions provided below to answer the following questions.

1. What standard would a court apply to determine whether it has jurisdiction over the out-of-state computer firm in the video?

2. What factors is a court likely to consider in assessing whether sufficient contacts existed when the only connection to the jurisdiction is through a Web site?

3. How do you think the court would resolve the issue in this case?

—To watch this video, go to **www.cengagebrain.com** and register the access code that came with your new book or log in to your existing account. Select the link for either the "Business Law Digital Video Library Online Access" or "Business Law CourseMate," and then click on "Complete Video List" to find the video for this chapter (Video 1).

Chapter 4

Constitutional Authority to Regulate Business

> "The United States Constitution has proved itself the most marvelously elastic compilation of rules of government ever written."
>
> —Franklin D. Roosevelt, 1882–1945
> (Thirty-second president of the United States, 1933–1945)

Contents

Chapter Objectives

After reading this chapter, you should be able to answer the following questions:

1. What is the basic structure of the U.S. government?
2. What constitutional clause gives the federal government the power to regulate commercial activities among the various states?
3. What constitutional clause allows laws enacted by the federal government to take priority over conflicting state laws?
4. What is the Bill of Rights? What freedoms does the First Amendment guarantee?
5. Where in the Constitution can the due process clause be found?

(John Elk III/Lonely Planet Images/Getty Images)

The U.S. Constitution is brief.[1] It contains only about seven thousand words—less than one-third of the number of words in the average state constitution. Perhaps its brevity explains why it has proved to be so "marvelously elastic," as Franklin Roosevelt pointed out in the chapter-opening quotation, and why it has survived for more than two hundred years—longer than any other written constitution in the world.

Laws that govern business have their origin in the lawmaking authority granted by this document, which is the supreme law in this country. As mentioned in Chapter 1, neither Congress nor any state can enact a law that is in conflict with the Constitution. In this chapter, we first look at some basic constitutional concepts and clauses and their significance for business. Then we examine how certain fundamental freedoms guaranteed by the Constitution affect businesspersons and the workplace.

We also examine privacy rights, which are protected by the Constitution and have come to the forefront in recent years. The Internet has significantly expanded the amount of information that the public can access about individuals. This is an area of growing concern, particularly as information concerning lawsuits and criminal records is widely available online.

---

1. See Appendix B for the full text of the U.S. Constitution.

The Constitutional Powers of Government

Following the Revolutionary War, the states created a *confederal* form of government in which the states had the authority to govern themselves and the national government could exercise only limited powers. When problems arose because the nation was facing an economic crisis and state laws interfered with the free flow of commerce, a national convention was called, and the delegates drafted the U.S. Constitution. This document, after its ratification by the states in 1789, became the basis for an entirely new form of government.

A Federal Form of Government

The new government created by the U.S. Constitution reflected a series of compromises made by the convention delegates on various issues. Some delegates wanted sovereign power to remain with the states, whereas others wanted the national government alone to exercise sovereign power. The end result was a compromise—a **federal form of government** in which the national government and the states *share* sovereign power.

The Constitution sets forth specific powers that can be exercised by the national government and provides that the national government has the implied power to undertake actions necessary to carry out its expressly designated powers (or *enumerated powers*). All other powers are expressly "reserved" to the states or to the people under the Tenth Amendment to the Constitution.

In part because of this provision of the Tenth Amendment, state governments have the authority to regulate affairs within their borders as part of their inherent sovereignty. State regulatory powers are often referred to as **police powers.** The term does not relate solely to criminal law enforcement but rather refers to the broad right of state governments to regulate private activities to protect or promote the public order, health, safety, morals, and general welfare. Fire and building codes, antidiscrimination laws, parking regulations, zoning restrictions, licensing requirements, and thousands of other state statutes covering almost every aspect of life have been enacted pursuant to states' police powers. Local governments, including cities, also exercise police powers. Generally, state laws enacted pursuant to a state's police powers carry a strong presumption of validity.

The Separation of Powers

To make it difficult for the national government to use its power arbitrarily, the Constitution divided the national government's powers among the three branches of government. The legislative branch makes the laws, the executive branch enforces the laws, and the judicial branch interprets the laws. Each branch performs a separate function, and no branch may exercise the authority of another branch.

Additionally, a system of **checks and balances** allows each branch to limit the actions of the other two branches, thus preventing any one branch from exercising too much power. The following are examples of these checks and balances:

1. The legislative branch (Congress) can enact a law, but the executive branch (the president) has the constitutional authority to veto that law.
2. The executive branch is responsible for foreign affairs, but treaties with foreign governments require the advice and consent of the Senate.

Federal Form of Government A system of government in which the states form a union and the sovereign power is divided between the central government and the member states.

Police Powers Powers possessed by the states as part of their inherent sovereignty. These powers may be exercised to protect or promote the public order, health, safety, morals, and general welfare.

Checks and Balances The principle under which the powers of the national government are divided among three separate branches—the executive, legislative, and judicial branches—each of which exercises a check on the actions of the others.

After the president signs legislation into law, what responsibilities remain with the executive branch?

(AP Photo/Ron Edmonds)

3. Congress determines the jurisdiction of the federal courts, and the president appoints federal judges, with the advice and consent of the Senate, but the judicial branch has the power to hold actions of the other two branches unconstitutional.[2]

The Commerce Clause

To prevent states from establishing laws and regulations that would interfere with trade and commerce among the states, the Constitution expressly delegated to the national government the power to regulate interstate commerce. Article I, Section 8, of the U.S. Constitution expressly permits Congress "[t]o regulate Commerce with foreign Nations, and among the several States, and with the Indian Tribes." This clause, referred to as the **commerce clause,** has had a greater impact on business than any other provision in the Constitution.

Commerce Clause The provision in Article I, Section 8, of the U.S. Constitution that gives Congress the power to regulate interstate commerce.

Initially, the commerce power was interpreted as being limited to *interstate* commerce (commerce among the states) and not applicable to *intrastate* commerce (commerce within a state). In 1824, however, in *Gibbons v. Ogden* (see this chapter's *Landmark in the Legal Environment* feature on the next page), the United States Supreme Court held that commerce within a state could also be regulated by the national government as long as the commerce *substantially affected* commerce involving more than one state.

THE EXPANSION OF NATIONAL POWERS UNDER THE COMMERCE CLAUSE In *Gibbons v. Ogden,* the Supreme Court expanded the commerce clause to regulate activities that "substantially affect interstate commerce." As the nation grew and faced new kinds of problems, the commerce clause became a vehicle for the additional expansion of the national government's regulatory powers. Even activities that seemed purely local came under the regulatory reach of the national government if those activities were deemed to substantially affect interstate commerce. **CASE EXAMPLE 4.1** In 1942, in *Wickard v. Filburn,*[3] the Supreme Court held that wheat production by an individual farmer intended wholly for consumption on his own farm was subject to federal regulation. The Court reasoned that the home consumption of wheat reduced the market demand for wheat and thus could have a substantial effect on interstate commerce. •

THE COMMERCE CLAUSE TODAY Today, the national government continues to rely on the commerce clause for its constitutional authority to regulate business activities in the United States. The breadth of the commerce clause permits the national government to legislate in areas in which Congress has not explicitly been granted power. In the last twenty years, however, the Supreme Court has begun to curb somewhat the national government's regulatory authority under the commerce clause. In 1995, the Court held—for the first time in sixty years—that Congress had exceeded its regulatory authority under the commerce clause. The Court struck down an act that banned the possession of guns within one thousand feet of any school because the act attempted to regulate an area that had "nothing to do with

---

2. See the *Landmark in the Legal Environment* feature on page 55 in Chapter 3 on *Marbury v. Madison,* 5 U.S. (1 Cranch) 137, 2 L.Ed. 60 (1803), a case in which the doctrine of judicial review was clearly enunciated by Chief Justice John Marshall.
3. 317 U.S. 111, 63 S.Ct. 82, 87 L.Ed. 122 (1942).

Landmark in the Legal Environment — *Gibbons v. Ogden* (1824)

The commerce clause of the U.S. Constitution gives Congress the power "[t]o regulate Commerce with foreign Nations, and among the several States, and with the Indian Tribes." Prior to the commerce clause, states tended to restrict commerce within and beyond their borders, which hampered trade by making market exchanges inefficient and costly. The goal of the clause was to unify the states' commerce policies and to improve the efficiency of exchanges. The problem was that although the commerce clause gave Congress some authority to regulate trade among the states, the extent of that power was unclear. What exactly does "to regulate commerce" mean? What does "commerce" entail? These questions came before the United States Supreme Court in 1824 in the case of *Gibbons v. Ogden.*[a]

Background In 1803, Robert Fulton, the inventor of the steamboat, and Robert Livingston, who was the ambassador to France, secured a monopoly on steam navigation on the waters in the state of New York from the New York legislature. Their monopoly extended to interstate waterways—those areas of water that stretch between states. Fulton and Livingston licensed Aaron Ogden, a former governor of New Jersey and a U.S. senator, to operate steam-powered ferryboats between New York and New Jersey.

Thomas Gibbons operated a ferry service between New Jersey and New York, which had been licensed by Congress under a 1793 act regulating the coastal trade. Although the federal government had licensed Gibbons to operate boats in interstate waters, he did not have the state of New York's permission to compete with Ogden in that area. Ogden sued Gibbons. The New York state courts granted Ogden's request for an injunction—an order prohibiting Gibbons from operating in New York waters. Gibbons appealed the decision to the United States Supreme Court.

Marshall's Decision The issue before the Court was whether the law regulated commerce that was "among the several states." The Court ruled against Ogden's monopoly, reversing the injunction against Gibbons. The opinion was written by John Marshall, the chief justice of the Supreme Court and an advocate of a strong national government. In the decision, Marshall defined the word *commerce* as used in the commerce clause to mean all commercial intercourse—that is, all business dealings that affect more than one state.

This broader definition includes navigation. Marshall not only expanded the definition of commerce but also validated and increased the power of the national legislature to regulate commerce. Said Marshall, "What is this power? It is the power . . . to prescribe the rule by which commerce is to be governed." Marshall held that the power to regulate interstate commerce is an exclusive power of the national government and that this power includes the power to regulate any intrastate commerce that substantially affects interstate commerce.

• Application to Today's Legal Environment *Marshall's broad definition of the commerce power established the foundation for the expansion of national powers in the years to come. Today, the national government continues to rely on the commerce clause for its constitutional authority to regulate business activities. Marshall's conclusion that the power to regulate interstate commerce was an exclusive power of the national government has also had significant consequences. By implication, this means that a state cannot regulate activities that extend beyond its borders, such as out-of-state online gambling operations that affect the welfare of in-state citizens. It also means that state regulations over in-state activities normally will be invalidated if the regulations substantially burden interstate commerce.*

a. 22 U.S. (9 Wheat.) 1, 6 L.Ed. 23 (1824).

commerce."[4] Subsequently, the Court invalidated key portions of two other federal acts on the ground that they exceeded Congress's commerce clause authority.[5]

In one notable case, however, the Supreme Court did allow the federal government to regulate noncommercial activities taking place wholly within a state's borders. **CASE EXAMPLE 4.2** About a dozen states have adopted laws that legalize marijuana for medical purposes. Marijuana possession, however, is illegal under the federal Controlled Substances Act (CSA).[6] After the federal government seized the marijuana that two seriously ill California women were using on the advice of their physicians, the women filed a lawsuit. They argued that it was unconstitutional for

4. The United States Supreme Court held the Gun-Free School Zones Act of 1990 to be unconstitutional in *United States v. Lopez,* 514 U.S. 549, 115 S.Ct. 1624, 131 L.Ed.2d 626 (1995).
5. See *Printz v. United States,* 521 U.S. 898, 117 S.Ct. 2365, 138 L.Ed.2d 914 (1997), involving the Brady Handgun Violence Prevention Act of 1993; and *United States v. Morrison,* 529 U.S. 598, 120 S.Ct. 1740, 146 L.Ed.2d 658 (2000), concerning the federal Violence Against Women Act of 1994.
6. 21 U.S.C. Sections 801 *et seq.*

(Creative Commons)

This store in Los Angeles advertises the sale of medical marijuana, which is legal under California state law. Does federal law also apply? Why or why not?

the federal statute to prohibit them from using marijuana for medical purposes that were legal within the state. The Supreme Court, however, held that Congress has the authority to prohibit the *intra*state possession and noncommercial cultivation of marijuana as part of a larger regulatory scheme (the CSA).[7] In other words, state medical marijuana laws do not insulate the users from federal prosecution. ●

THE "DORMANT" COMMERCE CLAUSE   The United States Supreme Court has interpreted the commerce clause to mean that the national government has the *exclusive* authority to regulate commerce that substantially affects trade and commerce among the states. This express grant of authority to the national government, which is often referred to as the "positive" aspect of the commerce clause, implies a negative aspect—that the states do not have the authority to regulate interstate commerce. This negative aspect of the commerce clause is often referred to as the "dormant" (implied) commerce clause.

The dormant commerce clause comes into play when state regulations affect interstate commerce. In this situation, the courts normally weigh the state's interest in regulating a certain matter against the burden that the state's regulation places on interstate commerce. Because courts balance the interests involved, it can be extremely difficult to predict the outcome in a particular case.

In the following case, the court had to decide whether a state law discriminated against out-of-state wineries in violation of the dormant commerce clause.

---

7. *Gonzales v. Raich*, 545 U.S. 1, 125 S.Ct. 2195, 162 L.Ed.2d 1 (2005).

Case 4.1   **Family Winemakers of California v. Jenkins[a]**

United States Court of Appeals, First Circuit, 592 F.3d 1 (2010).

BACKGROUND AND FACTS   Since the 1930s, most states, including Massachusetts, have used a three-tier system to control the sale of alcoholic beverages within their borders. Producers can sell beverages only to licensed in-state wholesalers. Licensed wholesalers can sell only to licensed retailers, such as stores, taverns, restaurants, and bars. Nonetheless, many states also allow alcoholic beverages to be shipped directly to consumers in their states. Direct shipping offers economic advantages to small wineries throughout the country. It also benefits consumers because it eliminates wholesaler and retailer price markups. In 2006, Massachusetts passed a law that bases wineries' eligibility for direct shipping licenses on whether they are *small* or *large*. Presumably, this system does not distinguish between in-state and out-of-state wineries. Large wineries are defined as those that produce more than 30,000 gallons per year. These wineries must choose between using the existing three-tier system or selling directly to consumers. Small wineries can use both systems simultaneously and therefore have a competitive advantage. Family Winemakers

of California argued that this law has a discriminatory effect. Family pointed out that 98 percent of all wine in the United States is produced by "large" wineries and that all of these wineries are located outside Massachusetts. Under the law, "small" wineries within Massachusetts can use multiple distribution methods not available to "large" out-of-state wineries. Family argued that the law's true purpose was "to ensure that Massachusetts wineries obtained advantages over their out-of-state counterparts." A federal district court agreed and prevented enforcement of the statute. Massachusetts appealed.

IN THE WORDS OF THE COURT . . .
LYNCH, Chief Judge.
   * * * *

   * * * Plaintiffs argue that Massachusetts's choice of 30,000 gallons as the demarcation [separation] point between "small" and "large" wineries, along with [a] production exception for fruit wine, has both a discriminatory effect and purpose. The discriminatory effect is because [the law's] definition of "large" wineries encompasses the wineries which produce 98 percent of all wine in the United States, all of which

---

a. The case was brought against Eddie J. Jenkins, the chair of the Massachusetts Alcoholic Beverages Control Commission, in his official capacity.

Case 4.1–Continues next page ➡

Case 4.1–Continued

are located out-of-state and all of which are deprived of the benefits of combining distribution methods. All wines produced in Massachusetts, on the other hand, are from "small" wineries that can use multiple distribution methods.

* * * *

* * * *State laws that alter conditions of competition to favor in-state interests over out-of-state competitors in a market have long been subject to invalidation.* [Emphasis added.]

* * * Here, the totality of the evidence introduced by plaintiffs demonstrates that [the law's] preferential treatment of "small" wineries that produce 30,000 gallons or less of grape wine is discriminatory. Its effect is to significantly alter the terms of competition between in-state and out-of-state wineries to the detriment of the out-of-state wineries that produce 98 percent of the country's wine.

[The 2006 law] confers a clear competitive advantage to "small" wineries, which include all Massachusetts's wineries, and creates a comparative disadvantage for "large" wineries, none of which are in Massachusetts. "Small" wineries that obtain a * * * license can use direct shipping to consumers, retailer distribution, and wholesaler distribution simultaneously. Combining these distribution methods allows "small" wineries to sell their full range of wines at maximum efficiency because they serve complementary markets. "Small" wineries that produce higher-volume wines can continue distributing

those wines through wholesaler relationships. They can obtain new markets for all their wines by distributing their wines directly to retailers, including individual bars, restaurants, and stores. They can also use direct shipping to offer their full range of wines directly to Massachusetts consumers, resulting in greater overall sales.

DECISION AND REMEDY   The U.S. Court of Appeals for the First Circuit affirmed the trial court's decision. The court concluded that the 2006 Massachusetts statute regulating wineries purposefully discriminated against out-of-state commerce in violation of the commerce clause.

WHAT IF THE FACTS WERE DIFFERENT?   *Suppose that most "small" wineries, as defined by the Massachusetts law, were located out of state. How could the law be discriminatory in that situation?*

THE ETHICAL DIMENSION   *People who favor laws that prohibit direct-to-consumer shipping of alcoholic beverages, particularly wine, claim that such laws prevent minors from having easy access to alcoholic beverages. Is this argument sufficiently strong to justify states' prohibiting such shipments within their borders? Why or why not?*

The Supremacy Clause

Supremacy Clause   The requirement in Article VI of the U.S. Constitution that provides that the Constitution, laws, and treaties of the United States are "the supreme Law of the Land." Under this clause, state and local laws that directly conflict with federal law will be rendered invalid.

Preemption   A doctrine under which certain federal laws preempt, or take precedence over, conflicting state or local laws.

Article VI of the Constitution provides that the Constitution, laws, and treaties of the United States are "the supreme Law of the Land." This article, commonly referred to as the **supremacy clause,** is important in the ordering of state and federal relationships. When there is a direct conflict between a federal law and a state law, the state law is rendered invalid. Because some powers are *concurrent* (shared by the federal government and the states), however, it is necessary to determine which law governs in a particular circumstance.

Preemption occurs when Congress chooses to act exclusively in a concurrent area. In this circumstance, a valid federal statute or regulation will take precedence over a conflicting state or local law or regulation on the same general subject. Often, it is not clear whether Congress, in passing a law, intended to preempt an entire subject area against state regulation. In these situations, the courts must determine whether Congress intended to exercise exclusive power over a given area. No single factor is decisive as to whether a court will find preemption. Generally, congressional intent to preempt will be found if a federal law regulating an activity is so pervasive, comprehensive, or detailed that the states have little or no room to regulate in that area. Also, when a federal statute creates an agency—such as the National Labor Relations Board—to enforce the law, the agency's rulings on matters that come within its jurisdiction will likely preempt state laws.

CASE EXAMPLE 4.3   The United States Supreme Court heard a case involving a man who alleged that he had been injured by a faulty medical device (a balloon catheter that had been inserted into his artery following a heart attack). The Court found that the Medical Device Amendments of 1976 had included a preemption provision and that the device had passed the U.S. Food and Drug Administration's rigorous premarket approval process. Therefore, the Court ruled that the federal regulation of medical devices preempted the injured party's state common law claims for negligence, strict liability, and implied warranty (see Chapters 5 and 11).[8] ●

▶ Business and the Bill of Rights

The importance of having a written declaration of the rights of individuals eventually caused the first Congress of the United States to enact twelve amendments to the Constitution and submit them to the states for approval. The first ten of these amendments, commonly known as the **Bill of Rights,** were adopted in 1791 and embody a series of protections for the individual against various types of interference by the federal government.[9] Some constitutional protections apply to business entities as well. For example, corporations exist as separate legal entities, or legal persons, and enjoy many of the same rights and privileges as natural persons do. Summarized here are the protections guaranteed by these ten amendments (see Appendix B for the complete text of each amendment):

Bill of Rights The first ten amendments to the U.S. Constitution.

1. The First Amendment guarantees the freedoms of religion, speech, and the press and the rights to assemble peaceably and to petition the government.
2. The Second Amendment guarantees the right to keep and bear arms.
3. The Third Amendment prohibits, in peacetime, the lodging of soldiers in any house without the owner's consent.
4. The Fourth Amendment prohibits unreasonable searches and seizures of persons or property.
5. The Fifth Amendment guarantees the rights to indictment (formal accusation) by grand jury, to due process of law, and to fair payment when private property is taken for public use. The Fifth Amendment also prohibits compulsory self-incrimination and double jeopardy (trial for the same crime twice).
6. The Sixth Amendment guarantees the accused in a criminal case the right to a speedy and public trial by an impartial jury and with counsel. The accused has the right to cross-examine witnesses against him or her and to solicit testimony from witnesses in his or her favor.
7. The Seventh Amendment guarantees the right to a trial by jury in a civil (noncriminal) case involving at least twenty dollars.[10]
8. The Eighth Amendment prohibits excessive bail and fines, as well as cruel and unusual punishment.
9. The Ninth Amendment establishes that the people have rights in addition to those specified in the Constitution.
10. The Tenth Amendment establishes that those powers neither delegated to the federal government nor denied to the states are reserved for the states.

"The way I see it, the Constitution cuts both ways. The First Amendment gives you the right to say what you want, but the Second Amendment gives me the right to shoot you for it."

BE CAREFUL Although most of these rights apply to actions of the states, some of them apply only to actions of the federal government.

We will look closely at several of these amendments in Chapter 6, in the context of criminal law and procedures. In this chapter, we examine two important guarantees of the First Amendment—freedom of speech and freedom of religion.

---

8. *Riegel v. Medtronic, Inc.,* 552 U.S. 312, 128 S.Ct. 999, 169 L.Ed.2d 892 (2008).

9. One of the proposed amendments was ratified more than two hundred years later (in 1992) and became the Twenty-seventh Amendment to the Constitution. See Appendix B.

10. Twenty dollars was forty days' pay for the average person when the Bill of Rights was written.

Limits on Federal and State Governmental Actions

As originally intended, the Bill of Rights limited only the powers of the national government. Over time, however, the United States Supreme Court "incorporated" most of these rights into the protections against state actions afforded by the Fourteenth Amendment to the Constitution. That amendment, passed in 1868 after the Civil War, provides, in part, that "[n]o State shall . . . deprive any person of life, liberty, or property, without due process of law." Starting in 1925, the Supreme Court began to define various rights and liberties guaranteed in the national Constitution as constituting "due process of law," which was required of state governments under the Fourteenth Amendment. Today, most of the rights and liberties set forth in the Bill of Rights apply to state governments as well as to the national government.

The rights secured by the Bill of Rights are not absolute. Many of the rights guaranteed by the first ten amendments are described in very general terms. For example, the Second Amendment states that people have a right to keep and bear arms, but it does not explain the extent of this right. As the Supreme Court noted in 2008, this does not mean that people can "keep and carry any weapon whatsoever in any manner whatsoever and for whatever purpose."[11] Legislatures can prohibit the carrying of concealed weapons or certain types of weapons, such as machine guns. Ultimately, it is the Supreme Court, as the final interpreter of the Constitution, that gives meaning to these rights and determines their boundaries. (For a discussion of how the Supreme Court may consider other nations' laws when determining the appropriate balance of individual rights, see this chapter's *Beyond Our Borders* feature on the facing page.)

The First Amendment—Freedom of Speech

A democratic form of government cannot survive unless people can freely voice their political opinions and criticize governmental actions or policies. Freedom of speech, particularly political speech, is thus a prized right, and traditionally the courts have protected this right to the fullest extent possible.

Symbolic Speech   Nonverbal expressions of beliefs. Symbolic speech, which includes gestures, movements, and articles of clothing, is given substantial protection by the courts.

Symbolic speech—gestures, movements, articles of clothing, and other forms of expressive conduct—is also given substantial protection by the courts. The Supreme Court held that the burning of the American flag to protest government policies is a constitutionally protected form of expression.[12] Similarly, wearing a T-shirt with a photo of a presidential candidate is a constitutionally protected form of expression. The test is whether a reasonable person would interpret the conduct as conveying some sort of message. **EXAMPLE 4.4**   As a form of expression, Bryan has gang signs tattooed on his torso, arms, neck, and legs. If a reasonable person would interpret this conduct as conveying a message, then it might be a protected form of symbolic speech. ●

"If the freedom of speech is taken away, then dumb and silent we may be led like sheep to the slaughter."

George Washington, 1732–1799
(First president of the United States, 1789–1797)

REASONABLE RESTRICTIONS   Expression—oral, written, or symbolized by conduct—is subject to reasonable restrictions. A balance must be struck between a government's obligation to protect its citizens and those citizens' exercise of their rights. Reasonableness is analyzed on a case-by-case basis. If a restriction imposed by the government is content neutral, then a court may allow it. To be content neutral, the restriction must be aimed at combating some secondary societal problem,

---

11. *District of Columbia v. Heller,* 554 U.S. 570, 128 S.Ct. 2783, 171 L.Ed.2d 637 (2008).
12. See *Texas v. Johnson,* 491 U.S. 397, 109 S.Ct. 2533, 105 L.Ed.2d 342 (1989).

Beyond Our Borders | The Impact of Foreign Law on the United States Supreme Court

As noted in the text, the United States Supreme Court interprets and gives meaning to the rights provided in the U.S. Constitution. Determining the appropriate balance of rights and protections stemming from the Constitution is not an easy task, especially because society's perceptions and needs change over time. The justices on the Supreme Court are noticeably influenced by the opinions and beliefs of U.S. citizens. This is particularly true when the Court is faced with issues of freedom of speech or religion, obscenity, or privacy.

Changing views on controversial topics, such as privacy in an era of terrorist threats or the rights of gay men and lesbians, may affect the way the Supreme Court decides a

These demonstrators show their appreciation for the United States Supreme Court's decision in Lawrence v. Texas—the first Supreme Court case that referenced foreign law in its published majority decision. Do all Supreme Court justices agree that it is appropriate to use foreign law in U.S. judicial decisions? Why or why not?

case. But should the Court also consider other nations' laws and world opinion when balancing individual rights in the United States?

Over the past ten years, justices on the Supreme Court have increasingly considered foreign law when deciding issues of national importance. For example, in 2003—for the first time ever—foreign law was cited in a majority opinion of the Supreme Court (references to foreign law had appeared in footnotes and dissents on a few occasions in the past). The case was a controversial one in which the Court struck down laws that prohibited oral and anal sex between consenting adults of the same sex. In the majority opinion (an opinion that the majority of justices have signed), Justice Anthony Kennedy mentioned that the European Court of Human Rights and other foreign courts have consistently acknowledged that homosexuals have a right "to engage in intimate, consensual conduct."[a]

In 2005, the Court again looked at foreign law when deciding whether the death penalty was an appropriate

---

a. *Lawrence v. Texas,* 539 U.S. 558, 123 S.Ct. 2472, 156 L.Ed.2d 508 (2003). Other cases in which the Court has referenced foreign law include *Grutter v. Bollinger,* 539 U.S. 306, 123 S.Ct. 2325, 156 L.Ed.2d 304 (2003), in the dissent; and *Atkins v. Virginia,* 536 U.S. 304, 122 S.Ct. 2242, 153 L.Ed.2d 335 (2002), in footnote 21 to the majority opinion.

punishment for juveniles.[b] Then, in 2008, a majority of the Supreme Court justices concluded that the U.S. Constitution applied to foreign nationals who were apprehended by U.S. authorities as enemy combatants and detained at Guantánamo Bay, Cuba.[c] Although the Bush administration contended that noncitizens held abroad had no constitutional rights, the Court found that these detainees had the same constitutional rights to contest their detention as citizens did.

The practice of looking at foreign law has many critics, including Justice Antonin Scalia, who believes that foreign views are irrelevant to rulings on U.S. law. Other Supreme Court justices, however, including Justice Stephen Breyer, believe that in our increasingly global community we should not ignore the laws and court decisions of the rest of the world.

For Critical Analysis

Should U.S. courts, and particularly the United States Supreme Court, look to other nations' laws for guidance when deciding important issues—including those involving rights granted by the Constitution? If so, what impact might this have on their decisions? Explain.

---

b. *Roper v. Simmons,* 543 U.S. 551, 125 S.Ct. 1183, 161 L.Ed.2d 1 (2005).

c. *Boumediene v. Bush,* 553 U.S. 723, 128 S.Ct. 2229, 171 L.Ed.2d 41 (2008).

---

such as crime, and not at suppressing the expressive conduct or its message. **CASE EXAMPLE 4.5**   Courts have often protected nude dancing as a form of symbolic expression. Nevertheless, the courts typically allow content-neutral laws that ban all public nudity. A man was charged with dancing nude at an annual anti-Christmas protest in Harvard Square in Cambridge, Massachusetts, under a statute banning public displays of open and gross lewdness. The man argued that the statute was overbroad and unconstitutional, and a trial court agreed. On appeal, however, a state appellate court upheld the statute as constitutional in situations in which there was an unsuspecting or unwilling audience.[13] ●

---

13. *Commonwealth v. Ora,* 451 Mass. 125, 883 N.E.2d 1217 (2008).

(Clay Good/ZUMA Press)

Students at Juneau-Douglas High School in Alaska unfurled this banner during an off-campus, school-sanctioned event. Why did the United States Supreme Court rule that the school could suspend the students responsible for this action?

The United States Supreme Court has also held that schools may restrict students' free speech at school events. **CASE EXAMPLE 4.6** Some high school students held up a banner saying "Bong Hits 4 Jesus" at an off-campus but school-sanctioned event. The majority of the Court ruled that school officials did not violate the students' free speech rights when they confiscated the banner and suspended the students for ten days. Because the banner could reasonably be interpreted as promoting drugs, the Court concluded that the school officials' actions were justified. Several justices disagreed, however, noting that the majority's holding creates a special exception that will allow schools to censor any student speech that mentions drugs.[14] ●

CORPORATE POLITICAL SPEECH Political speech by corporations also falls within the protection of the First Amendment. **CASE EXAMPLE 4.7** Many years ago, the United States Supreme Court reviewed a Massachusetts statute that prohibited corporations from making political contributions or expenditures that individuals were permitted to make. The Court ruled that the Massachusetts law was unconstitutional because it violated the right of corporations to freedom of speech.[15] ● The Court has also held that a law prohibiting a corporation from using bill inserts to express its views on controversial issues violated the First Amendment.[16]

Corporate political speech continues to be given significant protection under the First Amendment. In 2010, the Court overturned a twenty-year-old precedent when it ruled that corporations can spend freely to support or oppose candidates for president and Congress.[17] (See the *Landmark in the Legal Environment* feature on page 436 of Chapter 15 for a discussion of this important case.)

REMEMBER The First Amendment guarantee of freedom of speech applies only to *government* restrictions on speech.

COMMERCIAL SPEECH The courts also give substantial protection to *commercial speech,* which consists of communications—primarily advertising and marketing—made by business firms that involve only their commercial interests. The protection given to commercial speech under the First Amendment is not as extensive as that afforded to noncommercial speech, however. A state may restrict certain kinds of advertising, for instance, in the interest of protecting consumers from being misled by the advertising practices. States also have a legitimate interest in the beautification of roadsides, and this interest allows states to place restraints on billboard advertising.

Generally, a restriction on commercial speech will be considered valid as long as it (1) seeks to implement a substantial government interest, (2) directly advances that interest, and (3) goes no further than necessary to accomplish its objective.

At issue in the following case was whether a government agency had unconstitutionally restricted commercial speech when it prohibited the inclusion of a certain illustration on beer labels.

---

14. *Morse v. Frederick,* 551 U.S. 393, 127 S.Ct. 2618, 168 L.Ed.2d 290 (2007).
15. *First National Bank of Boston v. Bellotti,* 435 U.S. 765, 98 S.Ct. 1407, 55 L.Ed.2d 707 (1978).
16. *Consolidated Edison Co. v. Public Service Commission,* 447 U.S. 530, 100 S.Ct. 2326, 65 L.Ed.2d 319 (1980).
17. *Citizens United v. Federal Election Commission,* 558 U.S. 50, 130 S.Ct. 876, 175 L.Ed.2d 753 (2010).

Case 4.2 **Bad Frog Brewery, Inc. v. New York State Liquor Authority**

United States Court of Appeals, Second Circuit, 134 F.3d 87 (1998).
www.findlaw.com/casecode/index.html[a]

(Courtesy of Bad Frog Beer)

BACKGROUND AND FACTS Bad Frog Brewery, Inc., makes and sells alcoholic beverages. Some of the beverages feature labels with a drawing of a frog making the gesture generally known as "giving the finger." Bad Frog's authorized New York distributor, Renaissance Beer Company, applied to the New York State Liquor Authority (NYSLA) for brand label approval, as required by state law before the beer could be sold in New York. The NYSLA denied the application, in part, because "the label could appear in grocery and convenience stores, with obvious exposure on the shelf to children of tender age." Bad Frog filed a suit in a federal district court against the NYSLA, asking for, among other things, an injunction against the denial of the application. The court granted summary judgment in favor of the NYSLA. Bad Frog appealed to the U.S. Court of Appeals for the Second Circuit.

IN THE WORDS OF THE COURT . . .
Jon O. NEWMAN, Circuit Judge.
* * * *

* * * To support its asserted power to ban Bad Frog's labels [NYSLA advances] * * * the State's interest in "protecting children from vulgar and profane advertising" * * * .

[This interest is] substantial * * * . *States have a compelling interest in protecting the physical and psychological well-being of minors* * * * . [Emphasis added.]
* * * *

* * * NYSLA endeavors to advance the state interest in preventing exposure of children to vulgar displays by taking only the limited step of barring such displays from the labels of alcoholic beverages. *In view of the wide currency of vulgar displays throughout contemporary society, including comic books targeted directly at children, barring*

such displays from labels for alcoholic beverages cannot realistically be expected to reduce children's exposure to such displays to any significant degree. [Emphasis added.]

* * * If New York decides to make a substantial effort to insulate children from vulgar displays in some significant sphere of activity, at least with respect to materials likely to be seen by children, NYSLA's label prohibition might well be found to make a justifiable contribution to the material advancement of such an effort, but its currently isolated response to the perceived problem, applicable only to labels on a product that children cannot purchase, does not suffice. * * * A state must demonstrate that its commercial speech limitation is part of a substantial effort to advance a valid state interest, not merely the removal of a few grains of offensive sand from a beach of vulgarity.
* * * *

* * * Even if we were to assume that the state materially advances its asserted interest by shielding children from viewing the Bad Frog labels, it is plainly excessive to prohibit the labels from all use, including placement on bottles displayed in bars and taverns where parental supervision of children is to be expected. Moreover, to whatever extent NYSLA is concerned that children will be harmfully exposed to the Bad Frog labels when wandering without parental supervision around grocery and convenience stores where beer is sold, that concern could be less intrusively dealt with by placing restrictions on the permissible locations where the appellant's products may be displayed within such stores.

DECISION AND REMEDY The U.S. Court of Appeals for the Second Circuit reversed the judgment of the district court and remanded the case for the entry of a judgment in favor of Bad Frog. The NYSLA's ban on the use of the labels lacked a "reasonable fit" with the state's interest in shielding minors from vulgarity, and the NYSLA did not adequately consider alternatives to the ban.

WHAT IF THE FACTS WERE DIFFERENT? *If Bad Frog had sought to use the offensive label to market toys instead of beer, would the court's ruling likely have been the same? Explain your answer.*

THE LEGAL ENVIRONMENT DIMENSION *Whose interests are advanced by the banning of certain types of advertising?*

---

a. Under the heading "US Courts of Appeals-Opinions and Resources," click on "2nd Circuit Court of Appeals." Enter "Bad Frog Brewery" in the "Party Name Search" box, and click on "search." On the resulting page, click on the case name to access the opinion.

Unprotected Speech. The United States Supreme Court has made it clear that certain types of speech will not be given any protection under the First Amendment. Speech that harms the good reputation of another, or defamatory speech (see Chapter 5), will not be protected. Speech that violates criminal laws (such as threatening speech) is not constitutionally protected. Other unprotected speech includes fighting words, or words that are likely to incite others to respond violently.

Obscene Speech. The First Amendment, as interpreted by the Supreme Court, also does not protect obscene speech. Establishing an objective definition of obscene speech has proved difficult, however, and the Court has grappled with this problem from time to time. In *Miller v. California*,[18] the Supreme Court created a test for legal obscenity, which involved a set of requirements that must be met for material to be legally obscene. Under this test, material is obscene if (1) the average person finds that it violates contemporary community standards; (2) the work taken as a whole appeals to a prurient (arousing or obsessive) interest in sex; (3) the work shows patently offensive sexual conduct; and (4) the work lacks serious redeeming literary, artistic, political, or scientific merit.

Because community standards vary widely, the *Miller* test has had inconsistent application, and obscenity remains a constitutionally unsettled issue. Numerous state and federal statutes make it a crime to disseminate and possess obscene materials, including child pornography.

Online Obscenity. Congress's first two attempts at protecting minors from pornographic materials on the Internet—the Communications Decency Act (CDA) of 1996[19] and the Child Online Protection Act (COPA) of 1998[20]—failed. Ultimately, the United States Supreme Court struck down both the CDA and COPA as unconstitutional restraints on speech, largely because the wording of these acts was overbroad and would restrict nonpornographic materials.[21]

In 2000, Congress enacted the Children's Internet Protection Act (CIPA),[22] which requires public schools and libraries to block adult content from access by children by installing **filtering software** on computers. Such software is designed to prevent persons from viewing certain Web sites by responding to a site's Internet address or its **meta tags,** or key words. CIPA was also challenged on constitutional grounds, but in 2003 the Supreme Court held that the act did not violate the First Amendment. The Court concluded that because libraries can disable the filters for any patrons who ask, the system is reasonably flexible and does not burden free speech to an unconstitutional extent.[23]

Because of the difficulties of policing the Internet, as well as the constitutional complexities of prohibiting online obscenity through legislation, it remains a continuing problem worldwide. The Federal Bureau of Investigation established an Anti-Porn Squad to target and prosecute companies that distribute child pornography in cyberspace. The Federal Communications Commission has also passed new obscenity regulations for television networks. For a discussion of how the law is evolving, see this chapter's *Online Developments* feature on the facing page.

The First Amendment—Freedom of Religion

The First Amendment states that the government may neither establish any religion nor prohibit the free exercise of religious practices. The first part of this constitutional provision is referred to as the **establishment clause,** and the second part is

Filtering Software   A computer program that is designed to block access to certain Web sites, based on their content. The software blocks the retrieval of a site whose URL or key words are on a list within the program.

Meta Tag   A key word in a document that can serve as an index reference to the document. On the Web, search engines return results based, in part, on these tags in Web documents.

Establishment Clause   The provision in the First Amendment to the U.S. Constitution that prohibits the government from establishing any state-sponsored religion or enacting any law that promotes religion or favors one religion over another.

---

18. 413 U.S. 15, 93 S.Ct. 2607, 37 L.Ed.2d 419 (1973).

19. 47 U.S.C. Section 223(a)(1)(B)(ii).

20. 47 U.S.C. Section 231.

21. See *Reno v. American Civil Liberties Union,* 521 U.S. 844, 117 S.Ct. 2329, 138 L.Ed.2d 874 (1997); *Ashcroft v. American Civil Liberties Union,* 535 U.S. 564, 122 S.Ct. 1700, 152 L.Ed.2d 771 (2002); and *American Civil Liberties Union v. Ashcroft,* 322 F.3d 240 (3d Cir. 2003).

22. 17 U.S.C. Sections 1701–1741.

23. *United States v. American Library Association,* 539 U.S. 194, 123 S.Ct. 2297, 156 L.Ed.2d 221 (2003).

Online Developments

The Supreme Court Upholds a Law That Prohibits Pandering Virtual Child Pornography

Millions of pornographic images of children are available on the Internet. Some are images of actual children engaged in sexual activity. Others are virtual (computer-generated) pornography—that is, images made to look like children engaged in sexual acts. Whereas child pornography is illegal, the United States Supreme Court has ruled that virtual pornography is legally protected under the First Amendment because it does not involve the exploitation of real children.[a] In its ruling, the Supreme Court struck down as overly broad, and therefore unconstitutional, provisions of the Child Pornography Prevention Act of 1996 (CPPA). Among other things, the act prohibited any visual depiction including a "computer-generated image" that "is, or appears to be, of a minor engaging in sexually explicit conduct."

This ruling and the difficulty in distinguishing between real and virtual pornography have created problems for prosecutors. Before they can convict someone of disseminating child pornography on the Internet, they must prove that the images depict real children. To help remedy this problem, Congress enacted the Protect Act of 2003 (here, *Protect* stands for "Prosecutorial Remedies and Other Tools to end the Exploitation of Children Today").[b]

The Protect Act's Pandering Provisions

One of the Protect Act's many provisions prohibits misrepresenting virtual child pornography as actual child pornography. The act makes it a crime to knowingly advertise, present, distribute, or solicit "any material or purported material in a manner that reflects the belief, or that is intended to cause another to believe, that the material or purported material" is illegal child pornography.[c] Thus, it may be a crime to intentionally distribute virtual child pornography.

The Protect Act's "pandering" provision was challenged in a subsequent case, *United States v. Williams.*[d] The defendant, Michael Williams, sent a message to an Internet chat room that

read "Dad of Toddler has 'good' pics of her an [*sic*] me for swap of your toddler pics." A law enforcement agent responded by sending a private message to Williams that contained photos of a college-aged female, which were computer altered to look like photos of a ten-year-old girl. Williams requested explicit photos of the girl, but the agent did not respond. After that, Williams sent another public message that accused the agent of being a cop and included a hyperlink containing seven pictures of minors engaging in sexually explicit conduct.

Williams was arrested and charged with possession of child pornography and pandering material that appeared to be child pornography. He claimed that the Protect Act's pandering provision was—like its predecessor (the CPPA)—unconstitutionally overbroad and vague. (He later pleaded guilty to the charges but preserved the issue of constitutionality for appeal.)

Is the Protect Act Constitutional?

On appeal, the federal appellate court held that the pandering provision of the Protect Act was unconstitutional because it criminalized speech regarding child pornography. The court reasoned that, under the act, a person who distributes innocent pictures via the Internet (such as sending an e-mail labeled "good pictures of the kids in bed") could be penalized for offering child pornography.

The United States Supreme Court reversed that decision, ruling that the Protect Act was neither unconstitutionally overbroad nor impermissibly vague. The Court held that the statute was valid because it does not prohibit a substantial amount of protected speech. Rather, the act generally prohibits offers to provide, and requests to obtain, child pornography—both of which are unprotected speech. Thus, the act's pandering provisions remedied the constitutional defects of the CPPA, which had made it illegal to possess virtual child pornography.

a. *Ashcroft v. Free Speech Coalition,* 553 U.S. 234, 122 S.Ct. 1389, 152 L.Ed.2d 403 (2002).
b. 18 U.S.C. Section 2252A(a)(5)(B).
c. 18 U.S.C. Section 2252A(a)(3)(B).
d. 553 U.S. 285, 128 S.Ct. 1830, 170 L.Ed.2d 650 (2008).

FOR CRITICAL ANALYSIS

Why should it be illegal to "pander" virtual child pornography when it is not illegal to possess it?

Free Exercise Clause The provision in the First Amendment to the U.S. Constitution that prohibits the government from interfering with people's religious practices or forms of worship.

known as the **free exercise clause.** Government action, both federal and state, must be consistent with this constitutional mandate.

THE ESTABLISHMENT CLAUSE The establishment clause prohibits the government from establishing a state-sponsored religion, as well as from passing laws that promote (aid or endorse) religion or show a preference for one religion over another. Although the establishment clause involves the separation of church and state, it does not require a complete separation. Rather, it requires the government to accommodate religions. Federal or state laws that do not promote or place a significant burden on religion are constitutional even if they have some impact on religion. For a government law or policy to be constitutional, it must not have the primary effect of promoting or inhibiting religion.

Establishment clause cases often involve such issues as the legality of allowing or requiring school prayers, using state-issued vouchers to pay tuition at religious schools, and teaching creation theories versus evolution. In 2007, for instance, several taxpayers challenged the Bush administration's faith-based initiative expenditures as violating the establishment clause. President George W. Bush had issued executive orders creating a White House office to ensure that faith-based community groups were eligible to compete for federal financial support. Ultimately, however, the United States Supreme Court dismissed the action because the taxpayers did not have a sufficient stake in the controversy (called *standing*—see Chapter 3) to bring a lawsuit challenging executive orders.[24] (Taxpayers do have standing to challenge legislation in court.) The high court never ruled on the establishment clause issue.

Religious displays on public property have often been challenged as violating the establishment clause, and the United States Supreme Court has ruled on several such cases. Generally, the Court has focused on the proximity of the religious display to nonreligious symbols, such as reindeer and candy canes, or to symbols from different religions, such as a menorah (a nine-branched candelabrum used in celebrating Hanukkah). **CASE EXAMPLE 4.8**　The Supreme Court took a slightly different approach in a dispute that involved a six-foot-tall monument of the Ten Commandments on the Texas State Capitol grounds. The Court held that the monument did not violate the establishment clause because the Ten Commandments had historical, as well as religious, significance.[25] ●

The following case illustrates some of the factors that courts consider when deciding establishment clause cases.

(Creative Commons)

This monument displaying the Ten Commandments is located outside the Texas State Capitol. Why did the United States Supreme Court determine that it did not violate the establishment clause of the First Amendment to the U.S. Constitution?

---

24. *Hein v. Freedom from Religion Foundation, Inc.,* 551 U.S. 587, 127 S.Ct. 2553, 168 L.Ed.2d 424 (2007). *Standing* is a basic requirement for any plaintiff to file or maintain a cause of action.
25. *Van Orden v. Perry,* 545 U.S. 677, 125 S.Ct. 2854, 162 L.Ed.2d 607 (2005).

Case 4.3　Trunk v. City of San Diego

United States Court of Appeal, Ninth Circuit, 629 F.3d 1099 (2011).

BACKGROUND AND FACTS　Mount Soledad is a prominent hill in the La Jolla community of San Diego, California. There has been a cross on top of Mount Soledad since 1913. The cross is more than forty feet tall and is visible from miles away. Although the cross stood alone for most of its history, since the late 1990s it has been the centerpiece of a war memorial. This memorial features six walls around the base of the cross and more than two thousand stone plaques honoring individual veterans and groups of soldiers. The site was privately owned until 2006, when Congress authorized the property's transfer to the federal government "to

preserve a historically significant war memorial." Shortly after the federal government took possession, Steve Trunk and the Jewish War Veterans filed lawsuits claiming that the cross display violated the establishment clause because it endorsed the Christian religion. The lawsuits were later consolidated (joined together). A federal district court determined that Congress had acted with a secular (nonreligious) purpose in acquiring the memorial and that the memorial did not have the effect of advancing religion. The court granted a summary judgment in favor of the government. The plaintiffs appealed.

Case 4.3–Continued

IN THE WORDS OF THE COURT . . .
McKEOWN, Circuit Judge:
* * * *

The heart of this controversy is the primary effect of the Memorial. The question is * * * whether "it would be objectively reasonable for the government action to be construed as sending primarily a message of either endorsement or disapproval of religion." By "endorsement," we are not concerned with all forms of government approval of religion * * * but rather those acts that send the stigmatic [pertaining to a stigma] message to nonadherents "that they are outsiders, not full members of the political community, and an accompanying message to adherents that they are insiders, favored members. . . ." [Emphasis added.]
* * * *

We begin by considering the potential meanings of the Latin cross that serves as the centerpiece and most imposing element of the Mount Soledad Memorial. We have repeatedly recognized that "the Latin cross is the preeminent symbol of Christianity."

The cross is also "exclusively a Christian symbol, and not a symbol of any other religion."
* * * *

Significantly, the cross never became a default headstone in military cemeteries in the United States. A visitor to Arlington or another national cemetery does not encounter a multitude of crosses * * *.
* * * *

Prior decisions inform us of just a handful of other standalone crosses that have been dedicated as war memorials on public land. These prior decisions do little to establish that the cross is a prevalent symbol to commemorate veterans.

In sum, the uncontested facts are that the cross has never been used as a default grave marker for veterans buried in the United States, that very few war memorials include crosses or other religious imagery, and that even those memorials containing crosses tend to subordinate the cross to patriotic or other secular symbols. The record contains not a single clear example of a memorial cross akin to the Mount Soledad Cross * * *. There is simply "no evidence . . . that the cross has been widely embraced by"–or even applied to–"non-Christians as a secular symbol of death" or of sacrifice in military service.
* * * *

The question, then, is whether the entirety of the Mount Soledad Memorial, when understood against the background of its particular history and setting, projects a government endorsement of Christianity. We conclude it does * * *. The Memorial has a long history of religious use and symbolism that is inextricably intertwined with its commemorative message. This history, combined with the history of La Jolla and the prominence of the Cross in the Memorial, leads us to conclude that a reasonable observer would perceive the Memorial as projecting a message of religious endorsement, not simply secular memorialization.
* * * *

La Jolla–where the Memorial is located and serves as a prominent landmark–has a history of anti-Semitism that reinforces the Memorial's sectarian effect. The record contains various documents reporting "long-standing, culturally entrenched anti-Semitism" in La Jolla from the 1920s through about 1970.
* * * *

Overall, a reasonable observer viewing the Memorial would be confronted with an initial dedication for religious purposes, its long history of religious use, widespread public recognition of the Cross as a Christian symbol, and the history of religious discrimination in La Jolla. These factors cast a long shadow of sectarianism over the Memorial that has not been overcome by the fact that it is also dedicated to fallen soldiers, or by its comparatively short history of secular events.

The Memorial's physical setting amplifies the message of endorsement and exclusion projected by its history and usage. Despite the recent addition of secular elements, the Cross remains the Memorial's central feature [and] physically dominates the site.

DECISION AND REMEDY   The U.S. Court of Appeals for the Ninth Circuit ruled that the memorial as a whole violates the establishment clause. The court reversed the lower court's decision and remanded the case with instructions to enter a judgment in favor of Trunk and the Jewish War Veterans.

WHAT IF THE FACTS WERE DIFFERENT?   *Suppose that the cross had been only six feet tall and that the memorial had not had a long history of religious use. Would the outcome have been different? Why or why not?*

THE LEGAL ENVIRONMENT DIMENSION   *Can a religious display that is located on private property violate the establishment clause? Explain.*

Beware   The free exercise clause applies only to the actions of the state and federal governments. Nevertheless, under federal employment laws (see Chapter 17), employers may be required to accommodate their employees' religious beliefs, at least to a reasonable extent.

THE FREE EXERCISE CLAUSE   The free exercise clause guarantees that a person can hold any religious belief that she or he wants, or a person can have no religious belief. The constitutional guarantee of personal religious freedom restricts only the actions of the government and not those of individuals or private businesses.

When religious *practices* work against public policy and the public welfare, however, the government can act. For instance, the government can require that a child receive certain types of vaccinations or medical treatment when the child's life is in danger—regardless of the child's or parent's religious beliefs. When public safety is an issue, an individual's religious beliefs often have to give way to the government's interests in protecting the public. **EXAMPLE 4.9** According to the Muslim faith, it is a religious violation for a woman to appear in public without a scarf, known as a *hijab,* over her head. Due to public safety concerns, many courts today do not allow the wearing of any headgear (hats or scarves) in courtrooms. In 2008, a Muslim woman was prevented from entering a courthouse with her husband in Douglasville, Georgia, because she refused to remove her scarf. As she left, she uttered an expletive at the court official and was arrested and brought before the judge, who ordered her to serve ten days in jail. Similar incidents have occurred in other states. ●

According to the United States Supreme Court, the free exercise clause protects the use of a controlled substance in the practice of a sincerely held religious belief. **CASE EXAMPLE 4.10** A religious sect in New Mexico follows the practices of a Brazil-based church. Its members ingest hoasca tea as part of a ritual to connect with and better understand God. Hoasca tea, which is brewed from plants native to the Amazon rain forest, contains an illegal hallucinogenic drug, dimethyltryptamine (DMT), that is regulated by the federal Controlled Substances Act. When federal drug agents confiscated the church's shipment of hoasca tea as it entered the country, the church members filed a lawsuit claiming that the confiscation violated their right to freely exercise their religion. Ultimately, the Supreme Court agreed, ruling that the government had failed to demonstrate a sufficiently compelling interest in barring the sect's sacramental use of hoasca.[26] ●

Due Process and Equal Protection

Two other constitutional guarantees of great significance to Americans are mandated by the due process clauses of the Fifth and Fourteenth Amendments and the equal protection clause of the Fourteenth Amendment.

Due Process

Due Process Clause The provisions in the Fifth and Fourteenth Amendments to the U.S. Constitution that guarantee that no person shall be deprived of life, liberty, or property without due process of law. Similar clauses are found in most state constitutions.

Both the Fifth and the Fourteenth Amendments provide that no person shall be deprived "of life, liberty, or property, without due process of law." The **due process clause** of each of these constitutional amendments has two aspects—procedural and substantive. Note that the due process clause applies to "legal persons," such as corporations, as well as to individuals.

PROCEDURAL DUE PROCESS Procedural due process requires that any government decision to take life, liberty, or property must be made fairly—that is, the government must give a person proper notice and an opportunity to be heard. Fair procedures must be used in determining whether a person will be subjected to punishment or have some burden imposed on him or her. Fair procedure has been interpreted as requiring that the person have at least an opportunity to object to a proposed action before a fair, neutral decision maker (who need not be a judge). **EXAMPLE 4.11** In most states, a driver's license is construed as a property interest. Therefore, the state must provide some sort of opportunity for a person to object before her or his license is suspended or terminated. ●

---

26. *Gonzales v. O Centro Espirita Beneficente Uniao Do Vegetal,* 546 U.S. 418, 126 S.Ct. 1211, 163 L.Ed.2d 1017 (2006).

Preventing Legal Disputes

Many of the constitutional protections discussed in this chapter have become part of our culture in the United States. Due process, especially procedural due process, has become synonymous with what Americans consider "fair." For this reason, if you wish to avoid legal disputes, you should consider giving due process to anyone who might object to some of your business decisions or actions, whether that person is an employee, a partner, an affiliate, or a customer. For instance, it is prudent to give ample notice of new policies to all affected persons and to allow them at least an opportunity to express their opinions on the matter. Providing an opportunity to be heard is often the ideal way to make people feel that they are being treated fairly. People are less likely to sue a businessperson or firm that they believe is fair and listens to both sides of an issue.

SUBSTANTIVE DUE PROCESS Substantive due process protects an individual's life, liberty, or property against certain government actions regardless of the fairness of the procedures used to implement them. Substantive due process limits what the government may do in its legislative and executive capacities. Legislation must be fair and reasonable in content and must further a legitimate governmental objective. Only when state conduct is arbitrary or shocks the conscience, however, will it rise to the level of violating substantive due process.

If a law or other governmental action limits a fundamental right, it will be held to violate substantive due process unless it promotes a compelling or overriding state interest. Fundamental rights include interstate travel, privacy, voting, marriage and family, and all First Amendment rights. Thus, a state must have a substantial reason for taking any action that infringes on a person's free speech rights. In situations not involving fundamental rights, a law or action does not violate substantive due process if it rationally relates to any legitimate governmental end. It is almost impossible for a law or action to fail the "rationality" test. Under this test, almost any government regulation of business will be upheld as reasonable.

Equal Protection Clause The provision in the Fourteenth Amendment to the U.S. Constitution that guarantees that a state may not "deny to any person within its jurisdiction the equal protection of the laws." This clause mandates that the state governments must treat similarly situated individuals in a similar manner.

Equal Protection

Under the Fourteenth Amendment, a state may not "deny to any person within its jurisdiction the equal protection of the laws." The United States Supreme Court has used the due process clause of the Fifth Amendment to make the **equal protection clause** applicable to the federal government as well. Equal protection means that the government must treat similarly situated individuals in a similar manner.

Both substantive due process and equal protection require review of the substance of the law or other governmental action rather than review of the procedures used. When a law or action limits the liberty of all persons to do something, it may violate substantive due process. When a law or action limits the liberty of some persons but not others, it may violate the equal protection clause.

The city of Portland, Oregon, passed an anticamping ordinance to rid itself of homeless camps like the one under this city bridge. Could the homeless argue that the city ordinance violated their substantive due process rights, including the right to shelter?

(L.E. Baskow/Portland Tribune)

EXAMPLE 4.12 If a law prohibits all advertising on the sides of trucks, it raises a substantive due process question. If it makes an exception to allow truck owners to advertise their own businesses, it raises an equal protection issue. •

In an equal protection inquiry, when a law or action distinguishes between or among individuals, the basis for the distinction—that is, the classification—is examined. Depending on the classification, the courts apply different levels of scrutiny, or "tests," to determine whether the law or action violates the equal protection clause. The courts use one of three standards: *strict scrutiny, intermediate scrutiny,* or the *"rational basis" test.*

STRICT SCRUTINY If a law or action prohibits or inhibits some persons from exercising a fundamental right, the law or action will be subject to "strict scrutiny" by the courts. Under this standard, the classification must be necessary to promote a *compelling state interest.* Also, if the classification is based on a *suspect trait*—such as race, national origin, or citizenship status—it must be necessary to promote a compelling government interest. Compelling state interests include remedying past unconstitutional or illegal discrimination, but do not include correcting the general effects of "society's discrimination." **EXAMPLE 4.13** For a city to give preference to minority applicants in awarding construction contracts, it normally must identify past unconstitutional or illegal discrimination against minority construction firms. Because the policy is based on suspect traits (race and national origin), it will violate the equal protection clause *unless* it is necessary to promote a compelling state interest. • Generally, few laws or actions survive strict-scrutiny analysis by the courts.

INTERMEDIATE SCRUTINY The standard of intermediate scrutiny is applied in cases involving gender discrimination or discrimination against illegitimate children (children born out of wedlock). Laws using gender or legitimacy classifications must be *substantially related to important government objectives.* **EXAMPLE 4.14** An important government objective is preventing illegitimate teenage pregnancies. Because males and females are not similarly situated in this regard—only females can become pregnant—a law that punishes men but not women for statutory rape will be upheld even though it treats men and women unequally. •

The state also has an important objective in establishing time limits (called *statutes of limitation*) for how long after an event a particular type of action can be brought. Nevertheless, the limitation period must be substantially related to the important objective of preventing fraudulent or outdated claims. **EXAMPLE 4.15** A state law requires illegitimate children to bring paternity suits within six years of their births in order to seek support from their fathers. A court will strike down this law if legitimate children are allowed to seek support from their parents at any time because distinguishing between support claims on the basis of legitimacy is not related to the important government objective of preventing fraudulent or outdated claims. •

THE "RATIONAL BASIS" TEST In matters of economic and social welfare, a classification will be considered valid if there is any conceivable "rational basis" on which the classification might relate to a *legitimate government interest.* It is almost impossible for a law or action to fail the rational basis test. **EXAMPLE 4.16** A city ordinance that in effect prohibits all pushcart vendors, except a specific few, from operating in a particular area of the city will be upheld if the city offers a rational basis—such as reducing traffic in that area—for the ordinance. In contrast, a law that provides unemployment benefits only to people over six feet tall would clearly fail the rational basis test because it could not further any legitimate government interest. •

> *"Our Constitution protects aliens, drunks, and U.S. senators."*
>
> Will Rogers, 1879–1935
> (American humorist)

▶ Privacy Rights

The U.S. Constitution does not explicitly mention a general right to privacy. In a 1928 Supreme Court case, *Olmstead v. United States,*[27] Justice Louis Brandeis stated in his dissent that the right to privacy is "the most comprehensive of rights and the right

---

27. 277 U.S. 438, 48 S.Ct. 564, 72 L.Ed. 944 (1928).

most valued by civilized men." The majority of the justices at that time, however, did not agree with Brandeis. It was not until the 1960s that the Supreme Court endorsed the view that the Constitution protects individual privacy rights. In a landmark 1965 case, *Griswold v. Connecticut,*[28] the Supreme Court held that a constitutional right to privacy was implied by the First, Third, Fourth, Fifth, and Ninth Amendments.

> *"There was, of course, no way of knowing whether you were being watched at any given moment."*
>
> George Orwell, 1903–1950
> (Author, from his famous novel *1984*)

Federal Statutes Affecting Privacy Rights

In the 1960s, Americans were sufficiently alarmed by the accumulation of personal information in government files that they pressured Congress to pass laws permitting individuals to access their files. Congress responded in 1966 with the Freedom of Information Act, which allows any person to request copies of any information on her or him contained in federal government files. In 1974, Congress passed the Privacy Act, which also gives persons the right to access such information. Since then, Congress has passed numerous other laws protecting individuals' privacy rights with respect to financial transactions, electronic communications, and other activities in which personal information may be gathered and stored by organizations. Some of the major federal laws protecting privacy rights are listed and described in Exhibit 4–1 below. (Note that state constitutions and statutes also protect individual's privacy rights.)

28. 381 U.S. 479, 85 S.Ct. 1678, 14 L.Ed.2d 510 (1965).

● *Exhibit* **4–1 Federal Legislation Relating to Privacy**

TITLE	PROVISIONS CONCERNING PRIVACY
Freedom of Information Act (1966)	Provides that individuals have a right to obtain access to information about them collected in government files.
Family and Educational Rights and Privacy Act (1974)	Limits access to computer-stored records of education-related evaluations and grades in private and public colleges and universities.
Privacy Act (1974)	Protects the privacy of individuals about whom the federal government has information. Under this act, agencies that use or disclose personal information must make sure that the information is reliable and guard against its misuse. Individuals must be able to find out what data concerning them the agency is compiling and how the data will be used. In addition, the agency must give individuals a means to correct inaccurate data and must obtain their consent before using the data for any other purpose.
Tax Reform Act (1976)	Preserves the privacy of personal financial information.
Right to Financial Privacy Act (1978)	Prohibits financial institutions from providing the federal government with access to a customer's records unless the customer authorizes the disclosure.
Electronic Communications Privacy Act (1986)	Prohibits the interception of information communicated by electronic means.
Driver's Privacy Protection Act (1994)	Prevents states from disclosing or selling a driver's personal information without the driver's consent.
Health Insurance Portability and Accountability Act (1996)	Prohibits the use of a consumer's medical information for any purpose other than that for which such information was provided, unless the consumer expressly consents to the use.
Financial Services Modernization Act (Gramm-Leach-Bliley Act) (1999)	Prohibits the disclosure of nonpublic personal information about a consumer to an unaffiliated third party unless strict disclosure and opt-out requirements are met.

Since the 1990s, one of individuals' major concerns has been how to protect privacy rights in cyberspace and to safeguard private information that may be revealed online (including credit-card numbers and financial information). The increasing value of personal information for online marketers—who are willing to pay a high price for such information to those who collect it—has exacerbated the situation.

MEDICAL INFORMATION   Responding to the growing need to protect the privacy of individuals' health records—particularly computerized records—Congress passed the Health Insurance Portability and Accountability Act (HIPAA) of 1996.[29] This act defines and limits the circumstances in which an individual's "protected health information" may be used or disclosed.

HIPAA also requires health-care providers and health-care plans, including certain employers who sponsor health plans, to inform patients of their privacy rights and of how their personal medical information may be used. The act also states that a person's medical records generally may not be used for purposes unrelated to health care—such as marketing, for example—or disclosed to others without the individual's permission. Covered entities must formulate written privacy policies, designate privacy officials, limit access to computerized health data, physically secure medical records with lock and key, train employees and volunteers on their privacy policies, and sanction those who violate the policies. In 2009, Congress expanded HIPAA provisions to apply to *vendors* (who maintain personal health records for health-care providers) and to electronic records shared by multiple medical providers. Congress also authorized the Federal Trade Commission to enforce HIPAA and pursue violators.[30]

COURT RECORDS   As mentioned in the chapter introduction, the online dissemination of information concerning civil and criminal cases raises new privacy issues. Although court proceedings have always been a matter of public record, previously persons had to go to a courthouse to examine the physical records. Now, technological improvements in information sharing allow civil and criminal justice records to be shared, synthesized, sold, and analyzed electronically. From anywhere in the world, private individuals, businesses, and other organizations can instantly access court records either directly in a state database or from a private data firm.

Moreover, states earn substantial revenue by selling certain records—such as residents' criminal history and tax records—to private data firms. This revenue makes it unlikely that the states will refrain from selling such information in the future. Although most states have some privacy protections in place, once the information leaves the state's control, it can be given to anyone and used for any purpose. Additionally, if a state sells inaccurate or incomplete information to a company, there may be no way of correcting inaccuracies after the information has been sold.

The advent of electronically available court documents raises difficult questions about how to protect a person's privacy. Court records (and police reports) frequently disclose the names and addresses of witnesses and victims, and may also include their date of birth, ethnicity, Social Security number, credit information, and details about their children and family. Criminals might use this information to perpetrate identity theft (see Chapter 6) or to intimidate or harass a witness or victim. Employers and landlords may use the information to screen potential applicants. An employer might decide not to hire a person who was involved in a civil or criminal case, and a

> "The things most people want to know about are usually none of their business."
>
> George Bernard Shaw, 1856–1950
> (Irish dramatist and socialist)

---

29. HIPAA was enacted as Pub. L. No. 104-191 (1996) and is codified in 29 U.S.C.A. Sections 1181 *et seq.*

30. These provisions were part of the American Recovery and Reinvestment Act (ARRA) of 2009, popularly known as the stimulus law. See 45 C.F.R. Sections 164.510 and 164.512(f)(2).

landlord might not rent property to that person. (Even the victims in domestic violence cases, for example, may find that employers are reluctant to offer them jobs.) When mistakes occur, they can be devastating, as when a person's Social Security number is associated with a criminal or a person is misidentified as a sex offender.

Courts may order certain criminal records, such as a conviction for underage drinking or drug possession, to be sealed (not available to the public) or expunged (removed). But if the record has already been sold to a private data firm or been posted on the Internet, how can it be removed, and who is responsible for any harm it has caused and may cause in the future?

THE USA PATRIOT ACT   The USA Patriot Act was passed by Congress in the wake of the terrorist attacks of September 11, 2001, and then reauthorized in 2006.[31] The Patriot Act has given government officials increased authority to monitor Internet activities (such as e-mail and Web site visits) and to gain access to personal financial information and student information. Law enforcement officials may now track the telephone and e-mail communications of one party to find out the identity of the other party or parties. To gain access to these communications, the government must certify that the information likely to be obtained by such monitoring is relevant to an ongoing criminal investigation but does not need to provide proof of any wrongdoing.[32] Privacy advocates argue that this law adversely affects the constitutional rights of all Americans, and it has been widely criticized in the media.

PRETEXTING   A *pretext* is a false motive put forth to hide the real motive, and *pretexting* is the process of obtaining information by false means. Pretexters may try to obtain personal data by claiming that they are conducting a survey for a research firm, a political party, or even a charity. In 1999, Congress passed the Gramm-Leach-Bliley Act,[33] which made pretexting to obtain financial information illegal. Initially, it was not clear whether that law prohibited lying to obtain *nonfinancial* information for purposes other than identity theft.

EXAMPLE 4.17   Patricia C. Dunn was once the chair of Hewlett-Packard. To find out who had leaked confidential company information to the press, Dunn hired private investigators who used false pretenses to access individuals' personal cell phone records. Dunn claimed that she had not been aware of the investigators' methods. Although criminal charges that were brought against her were later dropped, several civil lawsuits followed. In 2007, the company paid $14.5 million in fines to settle a lawsuit filed by the California attorney general. In 2008, Hewlett-Packard reached a settlement with the New York Times Company and three *BusinessWeek* magazine journalists in connection with the scandal. •

To clarify the law on pretexting to gain access to phone records, Congress enacted the Telephone Records and Privacy Protection Act.[34] This act makes it a federal crime to pretend to be someone else or to make false representations for the purpose of obtaining another person's confidential phone records. The Federal Trade Commission investigates and prosecutes violators, who can be fined and sentenced to up to ten years in prison.

---

31. The Uniting and Strengthening America by Providing Appropriate Tools Required to Intercept and Obstruct Terrorism Act of 2001, also known as the USA Patriot Act, was enacted as Pub. L. No. 107-56 (2001) and reauthorized by Pub. L. No. 109-173 (2006).

32. See, for example, *American Civil Liberties Union v. National Security Agency,* 493 F.3d 644 (6th Cir. 2007).

33. Also known as the Financial Services Modernization Act, Pub. L. No. 106-102 (1999), 113 Stat. 1338, codified in numerous sections of 12 U.S.C.A. and 15 U.S.C.A.

34. Pub. L. No. 109-476, (2007), 120 Stat. 3568, codified at 18 U.S.C.A. Section 1039.

Other Laws Affecting Privacy

State constitutions and statutes also protect individuals' privacy rights, often to a significant degree. Privacy rights are also protected under tort law (see Chapter 5). Additionally, the Federal Trade Commission has played an active role in protecting the privacy rights of online consumers (see Chapter 20). The protection of employees' privacy rights, particularly with respect to electronic monitoring practices, is an area of growing concern (see Chapter 17).

 Reviewing . . . Constitutional Authority to Regulate Business

A state legislature enacted a statute that required any motorcycle operator or passenger on the state's highways to wear a protective helmet. Jim Alderman, a licensed motorcycle operator, sued the state to block enforcement of the law. Alderman asserted that the statute violated the equal protection clause because it placed requirements on motorcyclists that were not imposed on other motorists. Using the information presented in the chapter, answer the following questions.

1. Why does this statute raise equal protection issues instead of substantive due process concerns?
2. What are the three levels of scrutiny that the courts use in determining whether a law violates the equal protection clause?
3. Which standard, or test, of scrutiny would apply to this situation? Why?
4. Applying this standard, or test, is the helmet statute constitutional? Why or why not?

 Key Terms

Bill of Rights 93	establishment clause 98	police powers 88
checks and balances 88	federal form of government 88	preemption 92
commerce clause 89	filtering software 98	supremacy clause 92
due process clause 102	free exercise clause 99	symbolic speech 94
equal protection clause 103	meta tag 98	

 Chapter Summary: Constitutional Authority to Regulate Business

The Constitutional Powers of Government (See pages 88–89.)	1. *A federal form of government*–The U.S. Constitution established a federal form of government, in which government powers are shared by the national government and the state governments. At the national level, government powers are divided among the legislative, executive, and judicial branches. 2. *The regulatory powers of the states*–The Tenth Amendment reserves to the states all powers not expressly delegated to the national government. Under their police powers, state governments may regulate private activities in order to protect or promote the public order, health, safety, morals, and general welfare.
The Commerce Clause (See pages 89–92.)	1. *The expansion of national powers*–The commerce clause expressly permits Congress to regulate commerce. Over time, courts expansively interpreted this clause, thereby enabling the national government to wield extensive powers over the economic life of the nation. 2. *The commerce power today*–Today, the commerce power authorizes the national government, at least theoretically, to regulate every commercial enterprise in the United States. In recent years, the Supreme Court has reined in somewhat the national government's regulatory powers under the commerce clause. 3. *The "dormant" commerce clause*–If state regulations substantially interfere with interstate commerce, they will be held to violate the "dormant" commerce clause of the U.S. Constitution. The positive aspect of the commerce clause, which gives the national government the exclusive authority to regulate interstate commerce, implies a "dormant" aspect–that the states do *not* have this power.

Chapter Summary: Constitutional Authority to Regulate Business, Continued

The Supremacy Clause (See pages 92–93.)	The U.S. Constitution provides that the Constitution, laws, and treaties of the United States are "the supreme Law of the Land." Whenever a state law directly conflicts with a federal law, the state law is rendered invalid.
Business and the Bill of Rights (See pages 93–102.)	The Bill of Rights, which consists of the first ten amendments to the U.S. Constitution, was adopted in 1791 and embodies a series of protections for individuals—and, in some instances, business entities—against various types of interference by the federal government. Today, most of the protections apply against state governments as well. Freedoms guaranteed by the First Amendment that affect businesses include the following: 1. *Freedom of speech*—Speech, including symbolic speech, is given the fullest possible protection by the courts. Corporate political speech and commercial speech also receive substantial protection under the First Amendment. Certain types of speech, such as defamatory speech and lewd or obscene speech, are not protected under the First Amendment. Government attempts to regulate unprotected forms of speech in the online environment have, to date, met with numerous challenges. 2. *Freedom of religion*—Under the First Amendment, the government may neither establish any religion (the establishment clause) nor prohibit the free exercise of religion (the free exercise clause).
Due Process and Equal Protection (See pages 102–104.)	1. *Due process*—Both the Fifth and the Fourteenth Amendments provide that no person shall be deprived of "life, liberty, or property, without due process of law." Procedural due process requires that any government decision to take life, liberty, or property must be made fairly, using fair procedures. Substantive due process focuses on the content of legislation. Generally, a law that limits a fundamental right violates substantive due process unless the law promotes a compelling state interest, such as public safety. 2. *Equal protection*—Under the Fourteenth Amendment, a law or action that limits the liberty of some persons but not others may violate the equal protection clause. Such a law may be deemed valid, however, if there is a rational basis for the discriminatory treatment of a given group or if the law substantially relates to an important government objective.
Privacy Rights (See pages 104–108.)	Americans are increasingly concerned about privacy issues raised by Internet-related technology. The Constitution does not contain a specific guarantee of a right to privacy, but such a right has been derived from guarantees found in several constitutional amendments. A number of federal statutes protect privacy rights. Privacy rights are also protected by many state constitutions and statutes.

 ExamPrep

ISSUE SPOTTERS

1. Can a state, in the interest of energy conservation, ban all advertising by power utilities if conservation could be accomplished by less restrictive means? Why or why not?
2. Would it be a violation of equal protection for a state to impose a higher tax on out-of-state companies doing business in the state than on in-state companies if the only reason for the tax is to protect the local firms from out-of-state competition? Explain.

—**Check your answers to these questions against the answers provided in Appendix G.**

BEFORE THE TEST

Go to **www.cengagebrain.com**, enter the ISBN number "9781111530617," and click on "Find" to locate this textbook's Web site. Then, click on "Access Now" under "Study Tools," and select "Chapter 4" at the top. There you will find an "Interactive Quiz" that you can take to assess your mastery of the concepts in this chapter, as well as "Flashcards" and a "Glossary" of important terms.

For Review

1. What is the basic structure of the U.S. government?
2. What constitutional clause gives the federal government the power to regulate commercial activities among the various states?
3. What constitutional clause allows laws enacted by the federal government to take priority over conflicting state laws?
4. What is the Bill of Rights? What freedoms does the First Amendment guarantee?
5. Where in the Constitution can the due process clause be found?

Questions and Case Problems

4–1. Freedom of Speech. A mayoral election is about to be held in a large U.S. city. One of the candidates is Luis Delgado, and his campaign supporters wish to post campaign signs on lampposts and utility poles throughout the city. A city ordinance, however, prohibits the posting of any signs on public property. Delgado's supporters contend that the city ordinance is unconstitutional because it violates their rights to free speech. What factors might a court consider in determining the constitutionality of this ordinance?

4–2. Question with Sample Answer. Free Exercise Clause. Thomas worked in the nonmilitary operations of a large firm that produced both military and nonmilitary goods. When the company discontinued the production of nonmilitary goods, Thomas was transferred to the plant producing military equipment. Thomas left his job, claiming that it violated his religious principles to participate in the manufacture of goods to be used in destroying life. In effect, he argued, the transfer to the military equipment plant forced him to quit his job. He was denied unemployment compensation by the state because he had not been effectively "discharged" by the employer but had voluntarily terminated his employment. Did the state's denial of unemployment benefits to Thomas violate the free exercise clause of the First Amendment? Explain.

—**For a sample answer to Question 4–2, go to Appendix E at the end of this text.**

4–3. Commerce Clause. Suppose that Georgia enacts a law requiring the use of contoured rear-fender mudguards on trucks and trailers operating within its state lines. The statute further makes it illegal for trucks and trailers to use straight mudguards. In thirty-five other states, straight mudguards are legal. Moreover, in the neighboring state of Florida, straight mudguards are explicitly required by law. There is some evidence suggesting that contoured mudguards might be a little safer than straight mudguards. Discuss whether this Georgia statute would violate the commerce clause of the U.S. Constitution.

4–4. Equal Protection. With the objectives of preventing crime, maintaining property values, and preserving the quality of urban life, New York City enacted an ordinance to regulate the locations of commercial establishments that featured adult entertainment. The ordinance expressly applied to female, but not male, topless entertainment. Adele Buzzetti owned the Cozy Cabin, a New York City cabaret that featured female topless dancers. Buzzetti and an anonymous dancer filed a suit in a federal district court against the city, asking the court to block the enforcement of the ordinance. The plaintiffs argued, in part, that the ordinance violated the equal protection clause. Under the equal protection clause, what standard applies to the court's consideration of this ordinance? Under this test, how should the court rule? Why?

4–5. Case Problem with Sample Answer. Freedom of Speech. For decades, New York City has had to deal with the vandalism and defacement of public property caused by unauthorized graffiti. Among other attempts to stop the damage, in December 2005 the city banned the sale of aerosol spray-paint cans and broad-tipped indelible markers to persons under twenty-one years of age and prohibited them from possessing such items on property other than their own. By May 1, 2006, five people—all under age twenty-one—had been cited for violations of these regulations, while 871 individuals had been arrested for actually making graffiti. Artists who wished to create graffiti on legal surfaces, such as canvas, wood, and clothing, included college student Lindsey Vincenty, who was studying visual arts. Unable to buy her supplies in the city or to carry them in the city if she bought them elsewhere, Vincenty and others filed a suit in a federal district court on behalf of themselves and other young artists against Michael Bloomberg, the city's mayor, and others. The plaintiffs claimed that, among other things, the new rules violated their right to freedom of speech. They asked the court to enjoin the rules' enforcement. Should the court grant this request? Why or why not? [*Vincenty v. Bloomberg,* 476 F.3d 74 (2d Cir. 2007)]

—**To view a sample answer for Case Problem 4–5, go to Appendix F at the end of this text.**

4–6. Due Process. In 2006, the Russ College of Engineering and Technology of Ohio University announced that an investigation had found "rampant and flagrant plagiarism" in the theses of mechanical engineering graduate students. Faculty singled out for "ignoring their ethical responsibilities and contributing to an atmosphere of negligence toward issues of academic misconduct" included Jay Gunasekera, professor of mechanical engineering and chair of the department. These findings were publicized in a press conference. The university then prohibited Gunasekera from advising graduate students. He filed a suit in a federal district court against Dennis Irwin, the dean of Russ College, and others, for violating his "due-process rights when they publicized accusations about his role in plagiarism by his graduate student advisees without providing him with a meaningful opportunity to clear his name" in public. Irwin asked the court to dismiss the suit. What does due process require in these circumstances? Why? [*Gunasekera v. Irwin,* 551 F.3d 461 (6th Cir. 2009)]

4–7. Commerce Clause. Under the federal Sex Offender Registration and Notification Act (SORNA), sex offenders must register as sex offenders and update their registration when they travel from one state to another. David Hall, a convicted sex offender in New York, moved from New York to Virginia, where he lived for part of a year. When he returned to New York, he was charged with the federal offense of failing to register as a sex offender while in Virginia, as required by SORNA. In his defense, he claimed that SORNA was unconstitutional because Congress had no authority to criminalize interstate travel since no commerce was involved. The district court dismissed the indictment. The government appealed, contending that the statute is valid under the commerce clause. Does that contention seem reasonable? Why or why not? [*United States v. Hall,* 591 F.3d 83 (2d Cir. 2010)]

4–8. Establishment Clause. James DeWeese, an Ohio judge, hung two posters in his courtroom, one showing the Bill of Rights and the other showing the Ten Commandments. The American Civil Liberties Union (ACLU) brought an action against DeWeese in a federal district court. The ACLU alleged that the Ten Commandments poster violated the establishment clause and requested an injunction to prevent DeWeese from continuing to display the poster in his courtroom. The

district court ruled in the ACLU's favor. DeWeese appealed to the U.S. Court of Appeals for the Sixth Circuit, claiming that his purpose in displaying the Ten Commandments poster was not to promote religion. Rather, he claimed to be expressing his views about two warring legal philosophies that motivate behavior and consequences—moral relativism and moral absolutism (which was represented by the Ten Commandments). DeWeese also stated that he used the poster "occasionally in educational efforts" when speaking to community groups to "express his belief that God is the ultimate authority." Does displaying a poster of the Ten Commandments in a courtroom violate the establishment clause? Why or why not? How should the federal appellate court rule? [*American Civil Liberties Union of Ohio Foundation, Inc. v. DeWeese,* 633 F.3d 424 (6th Cir. 2011)]

4–9. **A Question of Ethics. Free Speech.** *Aric Toll owns and manages the Balboa Island Village Inn, a restaurant and bar in Newport Beach, California. Anne Lemen owns the "Island Cottage," a residence across an alley from the inn. Lemen often complained to the authorities about excessive noise and the behavior of the inn's customers, whom she called "drunks" and "whores." Lemen referred to Theresa Toll, Aric's wife, as "Madam Whore." Lemen told the inn's bartender Ewa Cook that Cook "worked for Satan," was "Satan's wife," and was "going to have Satan's children." She told the inn's neighbors that it was "a whorehouse" with "prostitution going on inside" and that it sold illegal drugs, sold alcohol to minors, made "sex videos," was involved in child pornography, had "Mafia connections," encouraged "lesbian activity," and stayed open until 6:00 a.m. Lemen also voiced her complaints to potential customers, and the inn's sales dropped more than 20 percent. The inn filed a suit in a California state court against Lemen, asserting defamation and other claims. [Balboa Island Village Inn, Inc. v. Lemen, 40 Cal.4th 1141, 57 Cal.Rptr.3d 320 (2007)]*

1. Are Lemen's statements about the inn's owners, customers, and activities protected by the U.S. Constitution? Should such statements be protected? In whose favor should the court rule? Why?

2. Did Lemen behave unethically in the circumstances of this case? Explain.

Chapter 5

Torts and Cyber Torts

"Two wrongs do
not make a right."
—English Proverb

Contents

Chapter Objectives

After reading this chapter, you should be able to answer the following questions:

1. What is a tort?

2. What is the purpose of tort law? What are two basic categories of torts?

3. What are the four elements of negligence?

4. What is meant by strict liability? In what circumstances is strict liability applied?

5. What is a cyber tort, and how are tort theories being applied in cyberspace?

(John Elk III/Lonely Planet Images/Getty Images)

Tort A civil wrong not arising from a breach of contract; a breach of a legal duty that proximately causes harm or injury to another.

Torts are wrongful actions (the word *tort* is French for "wrong"). Most of us agree with the chapter-opening quotation above—two wrongs do not make a right. Tort law is our nation's attempt to right a wrong. Through tort law, society tries to ensure that those who have suffered injuries as a result of the wrongful conduct of others receive compensation from the wrongdoers. Although some torts, such as assault and trespass, originated in the English common law, the field of tort law continues to expand. As new ways to commit wrongs are discovered, such as the use of the Internet to commit wrongful acts, the courts are extending tort law to cover these wrongs.

As you will see in later chapters, many of the lawsuits brought by or against business firms are based on the tort theories discussed in this chapter. Some of the torts examined here can occur in any context, including the business environment. Others, traditionally referred to as **business torts,** involve wrongful interference with the business rights of others. Business torts include such vague concepts as *unfair competition* and *wrongfully interfering with the business relations of another.*

Business Tort Wrongful interference with another's business rights.

Cyber Tort A tort committed in cyberspace.

Torts committed via the Internet are sometimes referred to as **cyber torts.** We look at how the courts have applied traditional tort law to wrongful actions in the online environment in the concluding pages of this chapter.

The Basis of Tort Law

Damages Money sought as a remedy for a breach of contract or a tortious action.

Two notions serve as the basis of all torts: wrongs and compensation. Tort law is designed to compensate those who have suffered a loss or injury due to another person's wrongful act. In a tort action, one person or group brings a personal suit against another person or group to obtain compensation (monetary **damages**) or other relief for the harm suffered.

The Purpose of Tort Law

Generally, the purpose of tort law is to provide remedies for the invasion of various *protected interests.* Society recognizes an interest in personal physical safety, and tort law provides remedies for acts that cause physical injury or interfere with physical security and freedom of movement. Society recognizes an interest in protecting real and personal property, and tort law provides remedies for acts that cause destruction or damage to property. Society also recognizes an interest in protecting certain intangible interests, such as personal privacy, family relations, reputation, and dignity, and tort law provides remedies for invasion of these protected interests.

Damages Available in Tort Actions

Because the purpose of tort law is to compensate the injured party for the damage suffered, it is important to have a basic understanding of the types of damages that plaintiffs seek in tort actions.

Compensatory Damages A monetary award equivalent to the actual value of injuries or damage sustained by the aggrieved party.

COMPENSATORY DAMAGES **Compensatory damages** are intended to compensate or reimburse a plaintiff for actual losses—to make the plaintiff whole and put her or him in the same position that she or he would have been in had the tort not occurred. Compensatory damages awards are often broken down into *special damages* and *general damages.*

Special damages compensate the plaintiff for quantifiable monetary losses, such as medical expenses, lost wages and benefits (now and in the future), extra costs, the loss of irreplaceable items, and the costs of repairing or replacing damaged property. **CASE EXAMPLE 5.1** Seaway Marine Transport operates the *Enterprise,* a large cargo ship, which has twenty-two hatches for storing coal. When the *Enterprise* positioned itself to receive a load of coal on the shores of Lake Erie in Ohio, it struck a land-based coal-loading machine operated by Bessemer & Lake Erie Railroad Company. A federal court found Seaway liable for negligence and awarded $522,000 in special damages to compensate Bessemer for the cost of repairing the harm to the loading boom.[1] ●

General damages compensate individuals (not companies) for the nonmonetary aspects of the harm suffered, such as pain and suffering. A court might award general damages for physical or emotional pain and suffering, loss of companionship, loss of consortium (losing the emotional and physical benefits of a spousal relationship), disfigurement, loss of reputation, or loss or impairment of mental or physical capacity.

Punitive Damages Monetary damages that may be awarded to a plaintiff to punish the defendant and deter similar conduct in the future.

PUNITIVE DAMAGES Occasionally, **punitive damages** may also be awarded in tort cases to punish the wrongdoer and deter others from similar wrongdoing. Punitive damages are appropriate only when the defendant's conduct was particularly

---

1. *Bessemer & Lake Erie Railroad Co. v. Seaway Marine Transport,* 596 F.3d 357 (6th Cir. 2010).

egregious (bad) or reprehensible (unacceptable). Usually, this means that punitive damages are available mainly in intentional tort actions and only rarely in negligence lawsuits (*intentional torts* and *negligence* will be explained later in the chapter). They may be awarded, however, in suits involving *gross negligence,* which can be defined as an intentional failure to perform a manifest duty in reckless disregard of the consequences of such a failure for the life or property of another.

Courts exercise great restraint in granting punitive damages to plaintiffs in tort actions, because punitive damages are subject to the limitations imposed by the due process clause of the U.S. Constitution (discussed in Chapter 4). The United States Supreme Court has held that a punitive damages award that is grossly excessive furthers no legitimate purpose and violates due process requirements.[2] Consequently, an appellate court will sometimes reduce the amount of punitive damages awarded to a plaintiff on the ground that it is excessive and thereby violates the due process clause.[3]

Typically, appellate courts look at the ratio of the compensatory and punitive damages awarded to a plaintiff to determine whether the punitive damages award is grossly excessive. Nevertheless, as the following case illustrates, there is no strict formula for determining whether a punitive damages award is so excessive that it violates due process.

---

2. *State Farm Mutual Automobile Insurance Co. v. Campbell,* 538 U.S. 408, 123 S.Ct. 1513, 155 L.Ed.2d 585 (2003).

3. See, for example, *Buell-Wilson v. Ford Motor Co.,* 160 Cal.App.4th 1107, 73 Cal.Rptr.3d 277 (2008).

Case 5.1 **Hamlin v. Hampton Lumber Mills, Inc.**

Supreme Court of Oregon, 349 Or. 526, 246 P.3d 1121 (2011).

BACKGROUND AND FACTS Hampton Lumber Mills, Inc., operates a lumber mill in Oregon. Ken Hamlin, a temporary employee, was injured while working at the mill. The company never instructed Hamlin on how to "lock out" the machinery to clear jams safely and avoid injury. Nor did it issue him the locks necessary to do so. Instead, Hamlin was told to watch the other employees and to do what they did. On the night he was injured, Hamlin was told to stand in a specified location, which later was determined to be unsafe. When a board became wedged between a conveyor belt and a bin, Hamlin was told to grab the board, and the machinery caught his glove and mangled his thumb. Hamlin was hospitalized and unable to work for four months. During that time, the mill twice told Hamlin that his job was secure. The agency through which he had been hired also informed Hamlin that under Oregon law he had the right to be reinstated when he recovered. During his recovery, Hamlin received workers' compensation benefits, and he filed a complaint with the Oregon Occupational Safety and Health Administration (OR-OSHA, see Chapter 17). When he was ready to work, the mill refused to reinstate him on the ground that he was a "safety risk." Hamlin filed an action against the mill for failing to reinstate him and claimed that the mill was retaliating against him for filing a complaint with OR-OSHA. A jury awarded him lost wages of $6,000 and punitive damages of $175,000.

The mill appealed, claiming that the punitive damages award was so "grossly excessive" that it violated due process. The appellate court agreed, finding that the ratio between the punitive and compensatory damages (plus interest) awarded in the case was 22:1—well outside the 4:1 ratio that the defendant asserted was appropriate in such cases. Hamlin appealed to the state supreme court.

IN THE WORDS OF THE COURT . . .
WALTERS, J. [Justice]
    * * * *

On review, plaintiff argues that the Court of Appeals erred in applying the ratio guidepost too strictly. Plaintiff contends that when, as in this case, a compensatory damages award is small, a punitive damages award that is more than a single-digit multiplier of the compensatory damages award is constitutionally permissible. Plaintiff also asserts that, because defendant's conduct violated a statute, and particularly a statute prohibiting discrimination against a worker, its conduct is more than moderately reprehensible.
    * * * *

In deciding whether the compensatory damages award is small, we are mindful, just as the Supreme Court has been, that the process of identifying due process limits demands flexibility and a consideration

Case 5.1–Continued

of the facts and circumstances that each case presents. Just as the Supreme Court has been unwilling to draw a rigid dividing line between constitutional and unconstitutional ratios, we are unwilling to draw a rigid line between "small" and "substantial" compensatory damages awards.

* * * *

In this case, $6,000 in lost wages is a relatively small recovery that we would not expect to serve an admonitory [deterrent], as well as a compensatory, function. * * * Evidence in the record indicates that, in the year in which it violated [the Oregon statute], defendant employed approximately 380 workers, that its net worth was approximately $10 million, and that its gross profit was approximately $2.8 million. We conclude, therefore, that the fact that the ratio between punitive and compensatory damages is greater than a single digit does not, in itself, indicate that the punitive damages that the jury awarded were "grossly excessive."

* * * *

Having decided that the punitive damages award in this case may exceed a single-digit multiplier of the compensatory damages award without violating due process, we still must decide whether the amount of punitive damages actually awarded–$175,000–is, nevertheless, "grossly excessive." In that regard, we note first that the jury's award is different in order of magnitude from the multimillion dollar, three-digit multiplier, punitive damages awards that the Supreme Court invalidated as "grossly excessive" * * * . The punitive damages award in this case is less than $200,000 and is a low double-digit (22:1) multiplier of the compensatory damages award.

* * * *

In this case, the compensatory damages are small and the ratio between the punitive and compensatory damages–22:1–is in the low double digits. That ratio is higher than would be constitutionally permissible if the compensatory damages were more substantial, but is not so high that it makes the award "grossly excessive." The amount of the punitive damages award–$175,000–also is not so high that we can say that it exceeds, rather than serves, this state's interests in deterring and punishing the violation of [the Oregon statute]. We hold that the Court of Appeals erred in reversing the jury's punitive damages verdict, and we reinstate it. [Emphasis added.]

DECISION AND REMEDY   The Supreme Court of Oregon reversed the decision of the state appellate court and allowed Hamlin to recover the full amount of punitive damages awarded by the jury.

THE ETHICAL DIMENSION   *Two justices filed a dissenting opinion that stated "the identified exception to the ratio guidepost is not for all 'small' damages awards, but only for those that also involve particularly egregious misconduct–which is not true in this case." Do you agree that the employer's conduct was not particularly egregious? Why or why not?*

THE LEGAL ENVIRONMENT DIMENSION   *Why has the United States Supreme Court declined to articulate a hard-and-fast rule for when the ratio between compensatory and punitive damages is too great?*

Tort Reform

Critics of the current tort law system contend that it encourages trivial and unfounded lawsuits, which clog the courts, and is unnecessarily costly. In particular, they say, damages awards are often excessive and bear little relationship to the actual damage suffered. Such large awards encourage plaintiffs and their lawyers to bring frivolous suits. The result, in the critics' view, is a system that disproportionately rewards a few plaintiffs while imposing a "tort tax" on business and society as a whole. Furthermore, the tax manifests itself in other ways. Because physicians, hospitals, and pharmaceutical companies are worried about medical malpractice suits, they have changed their behavior. Physicians, for example, order more tests than necessary, adding to the nation's health-care costs.

TORT REFORM GOALS   Critics wish to reduce both the number of tort cases brought each year and the amount of damages awarded. They advocate (1) limiting the amount of both punitive damages and general damages that can be awarded; (2) capping the amount that attorneys can collect in contingency fees (attorneys' fees that are based on a percentage of the damages awarded to the client); and (3) requiring the losing party to pay both the plaintiff's and the defendant's expenses to discourage the filing of meritless suits.

TORT REFORM LEGISLATION   The federal government and a number of states have begun to take some steps toward tort reform. At the federal level, the Class Action Fairness Act of 2005[4] shifted jurisdiction over large interstate tort and product liability class-action lawsuits (lawsuits filed by a large number of plaintiffs) from the state courts to the federal courts. The intent was to prevent plaintiffs' attorneys from *forum shopping*—looking for a state court known to be sympathetic to their clients' cause and predisposed to award large damages in class-action suits.

At the state level, more than twenty states have placed caps ranging from $250,000 to $750,000 on general damages, especially in medical malpractice suits. See this chapter's *Insight into Ethics* feature below for a discussion of some unintended

---

4. 28 U.S.C. Sections 1453, 1711–1715.

Insight into Ethics   Some Consequences of Caps on Medical Malpractice Awards

As part of the effort to curb excessive tort litigation, many states have enacted limits on the amount of general noneconomic damages that can be awarded. (Noneconomic damages include damages for pain and suffering, emotional distress, inconvenience, physical impairment, disfigurement, and the like.) Some states also specifically limit damages awards in medical malpractice (professional negligence) cases.

Limitations on Damages

Although placing such caps on damages awards may seem a logical way to reduce the number of negligence cases filed, it raises issues of fairness. Why should a plaintiff who loses a limb, for example, not be able to obtain adequate monetary damages for the mental anguish associated with such an injury? The limits also encourage plaintiffs' attorneys to find ways to avoid these caps, such as by suing defendants (including nurses and other health-care professionals) to whom the caps do not apply.

More than half of the states now limit damages awards in medical malpractice cases. For example, California caps noneconomic damages in medical malpractice cases at $250,000—even if the plaintiff dies.[a] States hope that these limitations will reduce the frequency and size of malpractice claims and thereby reduce health-care expenditures, although there is no definitive scientific evidence showing that damages caps lower health-care costs.[b]

Michigan Nurse Sued for Negligence

As an example of how ethical issues can result from caps on medical malpractice claims, consider what happened in one

Michigan case. A fifty-two-year-old Michigan farmer developed a blood clot in his leg and underwent emergency surgery at a hospital to remove it. After the surgery, a health-care professional removed an epidural catheter (a tube that enables painkillers to pass into the space surrounding the spinal cord). Eleven minutes later, a nurse came in and gave the patient a blood thinner called heparin. According to the standard of care for this procedure, heparin should not be given until at least one hour after an epidural catheter has been removed to ensure that the catheter site has sufficient time to stop bleeding.

In this situation, the heparin was given too soon and was given continuously for the next twenty-four hours. As a result, the patient experienced bleeding into the epidural space under his skin, and pressure built up in his spinal column. The hospital physicians and nurses failed to recognize the problem, and he was left with a permanent spinal cord injury and paralysis. Because of Michigan's cap on malpractice awards,[c] though, the negligent physician and the hospital responsible for his lifelong injuries were able to settle the claims against them for the legislatively mandated maximum of $717,000 for pain and suffering (and $1.1 million in economic damages). Because the cap did not apply to the nurse's negligence, however, the plaintiff could potentially collect unlimited damages from the nurse.

FOR CRITICAL ANALYSIS
Insight into the Social Environment

If plaintiffs can still collect significant amounts of economic damages, will the limits on noneconomic damages be effective at reducing the number of negligence lawsuits filed? Why or why not?

---

a. See California Civil Code Section 3333.2.
b. Fred J. Hellinger and William E. Encinosa, "The Impact of State Laws Limiting Malpractice Damage Awards on Health Care Expenditures," *American Journal of Public Health,* August 2006, pp. 1375–1381.

c. Michigan Compiled Laws Section 600.1483.

consequences of these laws. More than thirty states have limited punitive damages, and some have imposed outright bans.

Classifications of Torts

There are two broad classifications of torts: *intentional torts* and *unintentional torts* (torts involving negligence). The classification of a particular tort depends largely on how the tort occurs (intentionally or negligently) and the surrounding circumstances. In the following pages, you will read about these two classifications of torts.

 Intentional Torts against Persons

Intentional Tort   A wrongful act knowingly committed.

Tortfeasor   One who commits a tort.

An **intentional tort,** as the term implies, requires *intent*. The **tortfeasor** (the one committing the tort) must intend to commit an act, the consequences of which interfere with the personal or business interests of another in a way not permitted by law. An evil or harmful motive is not required—in fact, the actor may even have a beneficial motive for committing what turns out to be a tortious act. In tort law, intent means only that the actor intended the consequences of his or her act or knew with substantial certainty that certain consequences would result from the act. The law generally assumes that individuals intend the *normal* consequences of their actions. Thus, forcefully pushing another—even if done in jest and without any evil motive—is an intentional tort if injury results, because the object of a strong push can ordinarily be expected to fall down.

This section discusses intentional torts against persons, which include assault and battery, false imprisonment, infliction of emotional distress, defamation, invasion of the right to privacy, appropriation, fraudulent misrepresentation, abusive or frivolous litigation, and wrongful interference.

Assault and Battery

Assault   Any word or action intended to make another person fearful of immediate physical harm; a reasonably believable threat.

An **assault** is any intentional and unexcused threat of immediate harmful or offensive contact, including words or acts that create in another person a reasonable apprehension of harmful contact. An assault can be completed even if there is no actual contact with the plaintiff, provided that the defendant's conduct creates a reasonable apprehension of imminent harm in the plaintiff. Tort law aims to protect individuals from having to expect harmful or offensive contact.

Battery   The unexcused, harmful or offensive, intentional touching of another.

The *completion* of the act that caused the apprehension, if it results in harm to the plaintiff, is a **battery,** which is defined as an unexcused and harmful or offensive physical contact *intentionally* performed. **EXAMPLE 5.2**   Ivan threatens Jean with a gun and then shoots her. The pointing of the gun at Jean is an assault. The firing of the gun (if the bullet hits Jean) is a battery. ● The contact can be harmful, or it can be merely offensive (such as an unwelcome kiss). Physical injury need not occur. The contact can involve any part of the body or anything attached to it—for example, a hat, a purse, or a chair in which one is sitting. Whether the contact is offensive or not is determined by the *reasonable person standard*.[5] The contact can be made by the defendant directly, or it can occur as a result of a force set in motion by the defendant, such as throwing a rock or distributing poisoned food.

---

5. The reasonable person standard is an objective test of how a reasonable person would have acted under the same circumstances. See "The Duty of Care and Its Breach" later in this chapter on pages 129–130.

If the plaintiff shows that there was contact, and the jury (or judge, if there is no jury) agrees that the contact was offensive, then the plaintiff has a right to compensation. A plaintiff may be compensated for the emotional harm or loss of reputation resulting from a battery, as well as for physical harm. A defendant may raise a number of legally recognized defenses (reasons why the plaintiff should not obtain damages) that justify his or her conduct, including self-defense and defense of others.

False Imprisonment

False imprisonment is the intentional confinement or restraint of another person's activities without justification. False imprisonment interferes with the freedom to move without restraint. The confinement can be accomplished through the use of physical barriers, physical restraint, or threats of physical force. Moral pressure or threats of future harm do not constitute false imprisonment. It is essential that the person under restraint does not wish to be restrained.

Businesspersons are often confronted with suits for false imprisonment after they have attempted to confine a suspected shoplifter for questioning. Under the "privilege to detain" granted to merchants in most states, a merchant can use *reasonable force* to detain or delay a person suspected of shoplifting the merchant's property. Although laws pertaining to this privilege vary from state to state, generally any detention must be conducted in a *reasonable* manner and for only a *reasonable* length of time. Undue force or unreasonable detention can lead to liability for the business.

Intentional Infliction of Emotional Distress

The tort of *intentional infliction of emotional distress* can be defined as an intentional act involving extreme and outrageous conduct that results in severe emotional distress to another. To be **actionable** (capable of serving as the ground for a lawsuit), the act must be so extreme and outrageous that it exceeds the bounds of decency accepted by society. **EXAMPLE 5.3** A father attacks a man who has had consensual sexual relations with the father's nineteen-year-old daughter. The father handcuffs the man to a steel pole and threatens to castrate and kill him unless he leaves town immediately. The father's conduct may be sufficiently extreme and outrageous to be actionable as an intentional infliction of emotional distress. ●

Courts in most jurisdictions are wary of emotional distress claims and confine them to truly outrageous behavior. Generally, repeated annoyances (such as those experienced by a person who is being stalked), coupled with threats, are sufficient to support a claim. Acts that cause indignity or annoyance alone usually are not enough.

Note that when the outrageous conduct consists of speech about a public figure, the First Amendment's guarantee of freedom of speech also limits emotional distress claims. **CASE EXAMPLE 5.4** *Hustler* magazine once printed a fake advertisement that showed a picture of the Reverend Jerry Falwell and described him as having lost his virginity to his mother in an outhouse while he was drunk. Falwell sued the magazine for intentional infliction of emotional distress and won, but the United States Supreme Court overturned the decision. The Court held that creators of parodies of public figures are protected under the First Amendment from intentional infliction of emotional distress claims. (The Court applied the same standards that apply to public figures in defamation lawsuits, discussed next).[6] ●

Actionable Capable of serving as the basis of a lawsuit. An actionable claim can be pursued in a lawsuit or other court action.

---

6. *Hustler Magazine, Inc. v. Falwell,* 485 U.S. 46, 108 S.Ct. 876, 99 L.Ed.2d 41 (1988). For another example of how the courts protect parody, see *Busch v. Viacom International, Inc.,* 477 F.Supp.2d 764 (N.D.Tex. 2007), involving a fake endorsement of televangelist Pat Robertson's diet shake.

Defamation

As discussed in Chapter 4, the freedom of speech guaranteed by the First Amendment to the U.S. Constitution is not absolute. In interpreting the First Amendment, the courts must balance free speech rights against other strong social interests, including society's interest in preventing and redressing attacks on reputation. (Nations with fewer free speech protections have seen an increase in defamation lawsuits targeting U.S. journalists as defendants. See this chapter's *Beyond Our Borders* feature below for a discussion of this trend.)

Defamation Anything published or publicly spoken that causes injury to another's good name, reputation, or character.

Libel Defamation in writing or other form having the quality of permanence (such as a digital recording).

Slander Defamation in oral form.

Defamation of character involves wrongfully hurting a person's good reputation. The law has imposed a general duty on all persons to refrain from making *false, defamatory statements of fact* about others. Breaching this duty in writing or other permanent form (such as a digital recording) involves the tort of **libel.** Breaching this duty orally involves the tort of **slander.** The tort of defamation can also arise when a false statement of fact is made about a person's product, business, or legal ownership rights to property.

Beyond Our Borders Libel Tourism

As mentioned earlier, U.S. plaintiffs sometimes engage in forum shopping by trying to have their complaints heard by a particular court that is likely to be sympathetic to their claims. *Libel tourism* is essentially forum shopping on an international scale. Rather than filing a defamation lawsuit in the United States, where the freedoms of speech and press are strongly protected, a plaintiff files it in a foreign jurisdiction where there is a greater chance of winning.

Libel tourism has increased in recent years, particularly in England and Wales, where it is easier for plaintiffs to win libel cases—even those involving sham claims. In England, the law of defamation assumes that the offending speech is false (libelous), and the writer or author (the defendant) must prove that it is true in order to prevail. In contrast, U.S. law presumes that the speech is true (not libelous), and the plaintiff has the burden of proving that the statements are false.

The Threat of Libel Tourism

Libel tourism can have a chilling effect on the speech of U.S. journalists and authors because the fear of liability in other nations may prevent them from freely discussing topics of profound public importance. Libel tourism could even increase the threat to our nation's security if it discourages authors from writing about persons supporting or financing terrorism or other dangerous activities.

The threat of libel tourism captured media attention when Khalid bin Mahfouz, a Saudi Arabian businessman, sued U.S. resident Dr. Rachel Ehrenfeld. In her book *Funding Evil: How Terrorism Is Financed—and How to Stop It,* Ehrenfeld claimed that Mahfouz finances Islamic terrorist groups.

Mahfouz filed the lawsuit in a court in London, England, which took jurisdiction because twenty-three copies of the book had been sold online to residents of the United Kingdom. Ehrenfeld did not go to the English court to defend herself, and a judgment of $225,000 was entered against her. She then countersued Mahfouz in a U.S. court in an attempt to show that she was protected under the First Amendment and had not committed libel, but that case was dismissed for lack of jurisdiction.[a]

The U.S. Response

In response to the *Ehrenfeld* case, the New York state legislature enacted the Libel Terrorism Reform Act in 2008.[b] This act enables New York courts to assert jurisdiction over anyone who obtains a foreign libel judgment against a writer or publisher living in New York State. It also prevents courts from enforcing foreign libel judgments unless the foreign country provides equal or greater free speech protection than is available in the United States and New York.

In 2008, the federal government proposed similar legislation, the Libel Terrorism Protection Act, but it has not yet become law.

For Critical Analysis

Why do we need special legislation designed to control foreign libel claims against U.S. citizens? Explain.

---

a. *Ehrenfeld v. Mahfouz,* 518 F.3d 102 (2d Cir. 2008).

b. McKinney's Consolidated Laws of New York Sections 302 and 5304.

Often at issue in defamation lawsuits (including online defamation, which will be discussed later in this chapter) is whether the defendant made a statement of fact or a *statement of opinion.*[7] Statements of opinion normally are not actionable because they are protected under the First Amendment. In other words, making a negative statement about another person is not defamation unless the statement is false and represents something as a fact (for example, "Lane cheats on his taxes") rather than a personal opinion (for example, "Lane is a jerk").

Whether an attorney's statement to a reporter about another attorney constituted fact or opinion was at issue in the following case.

---

7. See, for example, *Lott v. Levitt,* 469 F.Supp.2d 575 (N.D.Ill. 2007).

| Case 5.2 | **Orlando v. Cole** |

Appeals Court of Massachusetts, 76 Mass.App.Ct. 1112, 921 N.E. 2d 566 (2010).

BACKGROUND AND FACTS   In February 2005, Joseph Orlando, an attorney, was representing a high school student who had sued her basketball coach for sexual assault. The coach, Thomas Atwater, was apparently an acquaintance of Orlando's. After the alleged incident and before he had retained an attorney, Atwater approached Orlando and admitted that he had committed the assault. Atwater signed an affidavit to that effect and then made a full confession to the police. A few days later, Orlando spoke to two newspaper reporters, who were preparing an article about the incident. He gave them a copy of Atwater's affidavit and explained the circumstances under which Atwater gave the affidavit. Before publishing the article, the reporters asked Garrick Cole, who was now representing Atwater, for Cole's comments. Cole responded that the affidavit was "inaccurate" and called Orlando's actions "deceitful" and "fraudulent." Both Orlando's and Cole's comments were reported together in various publications. Orlando sued Cole for slander in a Massachusetts state court. He alleged that Cole's comments were false, that they described conduct undertaken by Orlando in his profession and business, and that they imputed "an unfitness for or a misconduct in his office or employment." Orlando claimed that he had suffered harm to his reputation as an attorney as a result of Cole's comments. The trial court granted Cole's motion to dismiss the complaint, and Orlando appealed.

IN THE WORDS OF THE COURT . . .
By the Court (McHUGH, VUONO & MEADE, JJ. [Justices]).
    * * * *
We begin with a threshold inquiry into whether the comments are "'reasonably susceptible of a defamatory connotation [implication],'" so as to warrant their submission to a jury to determine if in fact the defamatory connotation was conveyed. *A statement is defamatory*

in the circumstances if it discredits a person in the minds of any considerable and respectable class of the community." [Emphasis added.]

We now turn to whether Cole's statements were ones of fact, or opinion, or a combination of both. "The determination whether a statement is one of fact or opinion is generally considered a question of law." The distinction is critical because "under the First Amendment there is no such thing as a false idea. However pernicious [destructive] an opinion may seem, we depend for its correction not on the conscience of judges and juries but on the competition of other ideas. But there is no constitutional value in false statements of fact."

To determine whether a statement is opinion, a court must "examine the statement in its totality in the context in which it was uttered or published." In doing so, "the court must consider all the words used, not merely a particular phrase or sentence. In addition, the court must give weight to cautionary terms used by the person publishing the statement. Finally, the court must consider all of the circumstances surrounding the statement, including the medium by which the statement is disseminated and the audience to which it is published." If the "average reader" could understand the allegedly libelous statements as either fact or opinion, the determination is for the jury.

Cole's allegations that the affidavit signed by Atwater was "inaccurate" and that Orlando's conduct was "fraudulent" and "deceitful" are factual because they are capable of being proved false. These comments were not presented as opinions nor accompanied by any cautionary language. Even if we were to conclude that these statements were an expression of opinion, they appear to be based on undisclosed defamatory facts, namely the unreported private communications between Cole and his new client, Atwater. "Defamation can occur by innuendo as well as by explicit assertion." As previously noted, the terms imply misconduct. Because, within the context of the article, a reader could view Cole's comments as based

Case 5.2–Continued

on undisclosed defamatory facts, they are not protected under the First Amendment.

DECISION AND REMEDY   The Appeals Court of Massachusetts reversed the judgment of the trial court and remanded the case for further proceedings. The comments at issue were susceptible of a defamatory connotation, and therefore the case should go forward.

THE LEGAL ENVIRONMENT DIMENSION   *Why would Cole have made such explicit comments to reporters, knowing that his words would be reproduced in the media?*

THE ETHICAL DIMENSION   *Are there any circumstances under which one professional should publicly describe another professional's actions as "deceitful" and "fraudulent"? Explain your answer.*

THE PUBLICATION REQUIREMENT   The basis of the tort of defamation is the publication of a statement or statements that hold an individual up to contempt, ridicule, or hatred. *Publication* here means that the defamatory statements are communicated to persons other than the defamed party. **EXAMPLE 5.5**   If Thompson writes Andrews a private letter accusing him of embezzling funds, the action does not constitute libel. If Peters falsely states that Gordon is dishonest and incompetent when no one else is around, the action does not constitute slander. In neither situation was the message communicated to a third party. •

The courts generally have held that even dictating a letter to a secretary constitutes publication, although the publication may be *privileged* (privileged communications will be discussed on the next page). Moreover, if a third party merely overhears defamatory statements by chance, the courts usually hold that this also constitutes publication. Defamatory statements made via the Internet are also actionable, as you will read later in this chapter. Note further that any individual who republishes or repeats defamatory statements is liable even if that person reveals the source of such statements.

DAMAGES FOR LIBEL   Once a defendant's liability for libel is established, general damages are presumed as a matter of law. As mentioned earlier, general damages are designed to compensate the plaintiff for nonspecific harms such as disgrace or dishonor in the eyes of the community, humiliation, injured reputation, and emotional distress—harms that are difficult to measure. In other words, to recover damages in a libel case, the plaintiff need not prove that she or he was actually injured in any way as a result of the libelous statement.

> *"My initial response was to sue her for defamation of character, but then I realized that I had no character."*
>
> Charles Barkley, 1963–present
> (National Basketball Association player, 1984–2000)

DAMAGES FOR SLANDER   In contrast to cases alleging libel, in a case alleging slander, the plaintiff must prove *special damages* to establish the defendant's liability. In other words, the plaintiff must show that the slanderous statement caused the plaintiff to suffer actual economic or monetary losses. Unless this initial hurdle of proving special damages is overcome, a plaintiff alleging slander normally cannot go forward with the suit and recover any damages. This requirement is imposed in cases involving slander because slanderous statements have a temporary quality. In contrast, a libelous (written) statement has the quality of permanence, can be circulated widely, and usually results from some degree of deliberation on the part of the author.

Exceptions to the burden of proving special damages in cases alleging slander are made for certain types of slanderous statements. If a false statement constitutes "slander *per se,*" no proof of special damages is required for it to be actionable. Four types of utterances are considered to be slander *per se:*

1. A statement that another has a particular type of disease (historically, leprosy and sexually transmitted diseases, but now also including allegations of mental illness).

2. A statement that another has committed improprieties while engaging in a business, profession, or trade.

3. A statement that another has committed or has been imprisoned for a serious crime.

4. A statement that a person (usually only unmarried persons and sometimes only women) is unchaste or has engaged in serious sexual misconduct.

DEFENSES AGAINST DEFAMATION   Truth is normally an absolute defense against a defamation charge. In other words, if the defendant in a defamation suit can prove that his or her allegedly defamatory statements were true, normally no tort has been committed. Other defenses to defamation may exist if the statement is privileged or concerns a public figure. Note that the majority of defamation actions in the United States are filed in state courts, and the states may differ both in how they define defamation and in the particular defenses they allow, such as privilege.

Privileged Communications. In some circumstances, a person will not be liable for defamatory statements because she or he enjoys a **privilege**, or immunity. Privileged communications are of two types: absolute and qualified.[8] Only in judicial proceedings and certain government proceedings is an *absolute* privilege granted. Thus, statements made in a courtroom by attorneys and judges during a trial are absolutely privileged, as are statements made by government officials during legislative debate.

In other situations, a person will not be liable for defamatory statements because he or she has a *qualified*, or conditional, privilege. An employer's statements in written evaluations of employees are an example of a qualified privilege. Generally, if the statements are made in good faith and the publication is limited to those who have a legitimate interest in the communication, the statements fall within the area of qualified privilege. The concept of conditional privilege rests on the assumption that in some situations, the right to know or speak is superior to the right not to be defamed. Only if the privilege is abused or the statement is knowingly false or malicious will the person be liable for damages.

Public Figures. Public officials who exercise substantial governmental power and any persons in the public limelight are considered *public figures*. In general, public figures are considered fair game, and false and defamatory statements about them that appear in the media will not constitute defamation unless the statements are made with **actual malice**.[9] To be made with actual malice, a statement must be made *with either knowledge of falsity or a reckless disregard of the truth*. Statements made about public figures, especially when the statements are made via a public medium, are usually related to matters of general interest. They are made about people who substantially affect all of us. Furthermore, public figures generally have some access to a public medium for answering disparaging (belittling, discrediting) falsehoods about themselves, whereas private individuals do not. For these reasons, public figures have a greater burden of proof in defamation cases (they must prove actual malice) than do private individuals.

CASE EXAMPLE 5.6   Lynne Spears, the mother of pop star Britney Spears, wrote a book in which she claimed that Sam Lutfi, Britney's former business manager,

Privilege   A legal right, exemption, or immunity granted to a person or a class of persons. In the context of defamation, an absolute privilege immunizes the person making the statements from a lawsuit, regardless of whether the statements were malicious.

Actual Malice   The deliberate intent to cause harm, which exists when a person makes a statement either knowing that it is false or showing a reckless disregard for whether it is true. In a defamation suit, a statement made about a public figure normally must be made with actual malice for the plaintiff to recover damages.

---

8. Note that the term *privileged communication* in this context is not the same as privileged communication between a professional, such as an attorney, and his or her client.

9. *New York Times Co. v. Sullivan*, 376 U.S. 254, 84 S.Ct. 710, 11 L.Ed.2d 686 (1964). See also *Tomblin v. WCHS-TV8*, 2011 WL 1789770 (4th Cir. 2011).

contributed to a mental breakdown that Britney experienced in 2008. Among other things, the book stated that Lutfi hid psychiatric drugs in Britney's food, disabled her cars and phones, and stole funds from her bank accounts. Lutfi filed a lawsuit for defamation and asserted that Lynne's statements were untrue, disparaging, and made with actual malice. A Los Angeles trial court found that Lutfi was a public figure and had presented enough evidence in his complaint for the case to go forward to trial. Lynne appealed, but the appellate court affirmed the ruling and refused to dismiss Lufti's complaint.[10] ●

Invasion of the Right to Privacy

A person has a right to solitude and freedom from prying public eyes—in other words, to privacy. As discussed in Chapter 4, the Supreme Court has held that a fundamental right to privacy is implied by various amendments to the U.S. Constitution. Some state constitutions also explicitly provide for privacy rights. In addition, a number of federal and state statutes have been enacted to protect individual rights in specific areas. Tort law also safeguards these rights through the tort of *invasion of privacy*. Generally, to successfully sue for invasion, a person must have a reasonable expectation of privacy, and the invasion must be highly offensive. Four acts can qualify as an invasion of privacy:

1. *Appropriation of identity.* Under the common law, using a person's name, picture, or other likeness for commercial purposes without permission is a tortious invasion of privacy. Most states today have also enacted statutes prohibiting appropriation (discussed further in the next subsection).
2. *Intrusion into an individual's affairs or seclusion.* For example, invading someone's home or illegally searching someone's briefcase is an invasion of privacy. The tort has been held to extend to eavesdropping by wiretap, the unauthorized scanning of a bank account, compulsory blood testing, and window peeping.
3. *False light.* Publication of information that places a person in a false light is another category of invasion of privacy. This could be a story attributing to the person ideas not held or actions not taken by the person. (Publishing such a story could involve the tort of defamation as well.)
4. *Public disclosure of private facts.* This type of invasion of privacy occurs when a person publicly discloses private facts about an individual that an ordinary person would find objectionable or embarrassing. A newspaper account of a private citizen's sex life or financial affairs could be an actionable invasion of privacy, even if the information revealed is true, because it is *not* a matter of legitimate public concern. Note, however, that news reports about public figures' personal lives are often not actionable because they *are* considered of legitimate public concern. For instance, when U.S. Congressman Anthony Weiner posted partially nude photos of himself on Twitter in 2011, it was of legitimate public concern. In contrast, the same inappropriate online communications by a neighbor might not be of legitimate public concern.

Appropriation

Appropriation In tort law, the use by one person of another person's name, likeness, or other identifying characteristic without permission and for the benefit of the user.

The use by one person of another person's name, likeness, or other identifying characteristic, without permission and for the benefit of the user, constitutes the tort of **appropriation.** Under the law, an individual's right to privacy normally includes the right to the exclusive use of her or his identity.

---

10. *Lutfi v. Spears,* 2010 WL 4723437 (2010).

(AP Photo/Diane Bondareff)

Robert Burck bills himself as The Naked Cowboy and performs regularly in New York City's Times Square. He has licensed his name and likeness to Chevrolet and to other companies. Given his fame, was he able to prevent Mars, Inc., maker of M&M candy, from appropriating his likeness for an animated billboard commercial?

CASE EXAMPLE 5.7   Vanna White, the hostess of the popular television game show *Wheel of Fortune,* brought a case against Samsung Electronics America, Inc. Without White's permission, Samsung had included in an advertisement a robotic image dressed in a wig, gown, and jewelry, posed in a scene that resembled the *Wheel of Fortune* set, in a stance for which White is famous. The court held in White's favor, holding that the tort of appropriation does not require the use of a celebrity's name or likeness. The court stated that Samsung's robot ad left "little doubt" as to the identity of the celebrity whom the ad was meant to depict.[11] ●

Courts may differ as to the degree of likeness that is required to impose liability for the tort of appropriation, however. Some courts have held that even when an animated character in a video or a video game is made to look like an actual person, there are not enough similarities to constitute appropriation. **CASE EXAMPLE 5.8**   The Naked Cowboy, Robert Burck, has been a street entertainer in New York City's Times Square for more than ten years. He performs for tourists wearing only a white cowboy hat, white cowboy boots, and white underwear and carrying a guitar strategically placed to give the illusion of nudity. Burck has become a well-known persona, appearing in television shows, movies, and video games, and has licensed his name and likeness to several companies, including Chevrolet. When Mars, Inc., the maker of M&M candy, began using a video on billboards in Times Square that depicted a blue M&M dressed up exactly like The Naked Cowboy, Burck sued for appropriation. In 2008, a federal district court held that Mars's creation of a cartoon character dressed in The Naked Cowboy's signature costume did not amount to appropriation by use of Burck's "portrait or picture." (Burck was allowed to continue his lawsuit against Mars for allegedly violating trademark law—to be discussed in Chapter 8.)[12] ●

Fraudulent Misrepresentation

A misrepresentation leads another to believe in a condition that is different from the condition that actually exists. This is often accomplished through a false or incorrect statement. Although persons sometimes make misrepresentations accidentally because they are unaware of the existing facts, the tort of **fraudulent misrepresentation,** or fraud, involves *intentional* deceit for personal gain. The tort includes several elements:

Fraudulent Misrepresentation   Any misrepresentation, either by misstatement or by omission of a material fact, knowingly made with the intention of deceiving another and on which a reasonable person would and does rely to his or her detriment.

1. The misrepresentation of facts or conditions with knowledge that they are false or with reckless disregard for the truth.
2. An intent to induce another to rely on the misrepresentation.
3. Justifiable reliance by the deceived party.
4. Injuries suffered as a result of the reliance.
5. A causal connection between the misrepresentation and the injury suffered.

Puffery   A salesperson's often exaggerated claims concerning the quality of property offered for sale. Such claims involve opinions rather than facts and are not considered to be legally binding promises or warranties.

For fraud to occur, more than mere **puffery,** or *seller's talk,* must be involved. Fraud exists only when a person represents as a fact something she or he knows is untrue. For example, it is fraud to claim that a roof does not leak when one knows it does. Facts are objectively ascertainable, whereas seller's talk is not. "I am the best accountant in town" is seller's talk. The speaker is not trying to represent something as fact because the term *best* is a subjective, not an objective, term.

Normally, the tort of misrepresentation or fraud occurs only when there is reliance on a *statement of fact.* Sometimes, however, reliance on a *statement of opinion* may involve the tort of misrepresentation if the individual making the statement of opinion has a superior knowledge of the subject matter. For instance, when a lawyer

11. *White v. Samsung Electronics America, Inc.,* 971 F.2d 1395 (9th Cir. 1992).
12. *Burck v. Mars, Inc.,* 571 F.Supp.2d 446 (S.D.N.Y. 2008). See also *Kirby v. Sega of America, Inc.,* 144 Cal. App.4th 47, 50 Cal.Rptr.3d 607 (2006).

makes a statement of opinion about the law in a state in which the lawyer is licensed to practice, a court would construe reliance on such a statement to be equivalent to reliance on a statement of fact.

Abusive or Frivolous Litigation

Persons or businesses generally have a right to sue when they have been injured. In recent years, however, more and more plaintiffs have filed meritless lawsuits simply to harass the defendant. Defending oneself in legal proceedings can be costly, time consuming, and emotionally draining. Tort law recognizes that people have a right not to be sued without a legally just and proper reason, and therefore it protects individuals from the misuse of litigation. Torts related to abusive litigation include malicious prosecution and abuse of process.

If a party initiates a lawsuit out of malice and without probable cause (a legitimate legal reason), and ends up losing the suit, that party can be sued for *malicious prosecution*. In some states, the plaintiff (who was the defendant in the first proceeding) must also prove injury other than the normal costs of litigation, such as lost profits. *Abuse of process* can apply to any person using a legal process against another in an improper manner or to accomplish a purpose for which it was not designed. The key difference between the torts of abuse of process and malicious prosecution is the level of proof required to succeed.

Abuse of process does not require the plaintiff to prove malice or show that the defendant (who was previously the plaintiff) lost in a prior legal proceeding.[13] In addition, an abuse of process claim is not limited to prior litigation. It can be based on the wrongful use of subpoenas, court orders to attach or seize real property, or other types of formal legal process.

Wrongful Interference

Business torts involving wrongful interference are generally divided into two categories: wrongful interference with a contractual relationship and wrongful interference with a business relationship.

WRONGFUL INTERFERENCE WITH A CONTRACTUAL RELATIONSHIP   Three elements are necessary for *wrongful interference with a contractual relationship* to occur:

1. A valid, enforceable contract must exist between two parties.
2. A third party must know that this contract exists.
3. The third party must *intentionally* induce a party to breach the contract.

CASE EXAMPLE 5.9   A landmark case involved an opera singer, Joanna Wagner, who was under contract to sing for a man named Lumley for a specified period of years. A man named Gye, who knew of this contract, nonetheless "enticed" Wagner to refuse to carry out the agreement, and Wagner began to sing for Gye. Gye's action constituted a tort because it wrongfully interfered with the contractual relationship between Wagner and Lumley.[14] (Of course, Wagner's refusal to carry out the agreement also entitled Lumley to sue Wagner for breach of contract.) •

The body of tort law relating to intentional interference with a contractual relationship has expanded greatly in recent years. In principle, any lawful contract can be the basis for an action of this type. The contract could be between a firm and its

---

13. See *Bernhard-Thomas Building Systems, LLC v. Dunican*, 918 A.2d 889 (Conn.App. 2007); and *Hewitt v. Rice*, 154 P.3d 408 (Colo. 2007).
14. *Lumley v. Gye*, 118 Eng.Rep. 749 (1853).

employees or a firm and its customers. Sometimes, a competitor draws away one of a firm's key employees. To recover damages from the competitor, the original employer must show that the competitor knew of the contract's existence and intentionally induced the breach.

EXAMPLE 5.10   Sutter is under contract to do gardening work on Carlin's estate every week for fifty-two weeks at a specified price per week. Mellon, who needs gardening services and knows nothing about the Sutter-Carlin contract, contacts Sutter and offers to pay a wage substantially higher than that offered by Carlin. Sutter breaches his contract with Carlin so that he can work for Mellon. Carlin cannot sue Mellon because Mellon knew nothing of the Sutter-Carlin contract and was totally unaware that the higher wage he offered induced Sutter to breach that contract. ●

WRONGFUL INTERFERENCE WITH A BUSINESS RELATIONSHIP   Businesspersons devise countless schemes to attract customers. They are prohibited, however, from unreasonably interfering with another's business in their attempts to gain a share of the market.

There is a difference between competitive methods and predatory behavior—actions undertaken with the intention of unlawfully driving competitors completely out of the market. Attempting to attract customers in general is a legitimate business practice, whereas specifically targeting the customers of a competitor is more likely to be predatory. **EXAMPLE 5.11**   A shopping mall contains two athletic shoe stores: Joe's and SneakerSprint. Joe's cannot station an employee at the entrance of SneakerSprint to divert customers by telling them that Joe's will beat SneakerSprint's prices. This type of activity constitutes the tort of wrongful interference with a business relationship, which is commonly considered to be an unfair trade practice. If this type of activity were permitted, Joe's would reap the benefits of SneakerSprint's advertising. ●

REMEMBER   What society and the law consider permissible often depends on the circumstances.

DEFENSES TO WRONGFUL INTERFERENCE   A person can avoid liability for the tort of wrongful interference with a contractual or business relationship by showing that the interference was justified or permissible. Bona fide competitive behavior is a permissible interference even if it results in the breaking of a contract. **EXAMPLE 5.12**   If Antonio's Meats advertises so effectively that it induces Sam's Restaurant to break its contract with Burke's Meat Company, Burke's Meat Company will be unable to recover against Antonio's Meats on a wrongful interference theory. After all, the public policy that favors free competition through advertising outweighs any possible instability that such competitive activity might cause in contractual relations. ● Although luring customers away from a competitor through aggressive marketing and advertising strategies obviously interferes with the competitor's relationship with its customers, courts typically allow such activities in the spirit of competition.

Intentional Torts against Property

REMEMBER   It is the intent to do an act that is important in tort law, not the motive behind the intent.

Intentional torts against property include trespass to land, trespass to personal property, conversion, and disparagement of property. These torts are wrongful actions that interfere with individuals' legally recognized rights with regard to their land or personal property. The law distinguishes real property from personal property (see Chapter 22). *Real property* is land and things "permanently" attached to the land. *Personal property* consists of all other items, which are basically movable. Thus, a house and lot are real property, whereas the furniture inside a house is personal property. Cash and stocks and bonds are also personal property.

Trespass to Land

Trespass to Land The entry onto, above, or below the surface of land owned by another without the owner's permission or legal authorization.

A **trespass to land** occurs anytime a person, without permission, enters onto, above, or below the surface of land that is owned by another; causes anything to enter onto the land; or remains on the land or permits anything to remain on it. Actual harm to the land is not an essential element of this tort because the tort is designed to protect the right of an owner to exclusive possession of her or his property. Common types of trespass to land include walking or driving on someone else's land, shooting a gun over the land, throwing rocks at a building that belongs to someone else, building a dam across a river and thereby causing water to back up on someone else's land, and constructing a building so that part of it is on an adjoining landowner's property.

TRESPASS CRITERIA, RIGHTS, AND DUTIES Before a person can be a trespasser, the real property owner (or other person in actual and exclusive possession of the property) must establish that person as a trespasser. For example, "posted" trespass signs expressly establish as a trespasser a person who ignores these signs and enters onto the property. A guest in your home is not a trespasser—unless she or he has been asked to leave but refuses. Any person who enters onto your property to commit an illegal act (such as a thief entering a lumberyard at night to steal lumber) is established impliedly as a trespasser, without posted signs.

At common law, a trespasser is liable for damages caused to the property and generally cannot hold the owner liable for injuries sustained on the premises. This common law rule is being abandoned in many jurisdictions in favor of a *reasonable duty of care* rule that varies depending on the status of the parties. For instance, a landowner may have a duty to post a notice that guard dogs patrol the property. Also, under the *attractive nuisance* doctrine, children do not assume the risks of the premises if they are attracted to the property by some object, such as a swimming pool, an abandoned building, or a sand pile. Trespassers normally can be removed from the premises through the use of reasonable force without the owner's being liable for assault, battery, or false imprisonment.

DEFENSES AGAINST TRESPASS TO LAND One defense to a claim of trespass to land is to show that the trespass was warranted—for example, that the trespasser entered the property to assist someone in danger. Another defense is for the trespasser to show that he or she had a license to come onto the land. A *licensee* is one who is invited (or allowed to enter) onto the property of another for the licensee's benefit. A person who enters another's property to read an electric meter, for example, is a licensee. When you purchase a ticket to attend a movie or sporting event, you are licensed to go onto the property of another to view that movie or event. Note that licenses to enter are *revocable* by the property owner. If a property owner asks a meter reader to leave and the meter reader refuses to do so, the meter reader at that point becomes a trespasser.

Trespass to Personal Property

Trespass to Personal Property The unlawful taking or harming of another's personal property; interference with another's right to the exclusive possession of his or her personal property.

Whenever an individual wrongfully takes or harms the personal property of another or otherwise interferes with the lawful owner's possession of personal property, **trespass to personal property** occurs (also called *trespass to chattels* or *trespass to personalty*[15]). In this context, harm means not only destruction of the property, but also anything that diminishes its value, condition, or quality. Trespass to personal property involves

---

15. Pronounced *per-sun-ul-tee.*

intentional meddling with a possessory interest, including barring an owner's access to personal property. **EXAMPLE 5.13**   Kelly takes Ryan's business law book as a practical joke and hides it so that Ryan is unable to find it for several days before the final examination. Here, Kelly has engaged in a trespass to personal property. (Kelly has also committed the tort of *conversion*—to be discussed next.) ●

A complete defense to a claim of trespass to personal property is to show that the trespass was warranted. Most states, for example, allow automobile repair shops to hold a customer's car (under an *artisan's lien,* as will be discussed in Chapter 12) when the customer refuses to pay for repairs already completed.

Conversion

Conversion   Wrongfully taking or retaining possession of an individual's personal property and placing it in the service of another.

Whenever a person wrongfully possesses or uses the personal property of another without permission, the tort of **conversion** occurs. Any act that deprives an owner of personal property (including electronic data) or the use of that property without that owner's permission and without just cause can be conversion. **CASE EXAMPLE 5.14**   Jafar Vossoughi, an expert in applied mechanics and experimental biomechanics, taught at the University of the District of Columbia (UDC). Vossoughi set up a laboratory on campus to conduct research and continued working at the lab even after his employment contract expired. In 2000, without Vossoughi's knowledge, UDC cleaned out the laboratory and threw away most of its contents. Vossoughi sued UDC for conversion, seeking damages for the loss of his course materials, unpublished research data, unique scientific instruments, and other items. Vossoughi won and was awarded $1.65 million. On appeal, the court upheld this award as a reasonable estimate of the value of the property based on the time it would take Vossoughi to duplicate the work.[16] ●

Often, when conversion occurs, a trespass to personal property also occurs because the original taking of the personal property from the owner was a trespass and wrongfully retaining it is conversion. Conversion is the civil side of crimes related to theft, but it is not limited to theft. Even if the rightful owner consented to the initial taking of the property, so there was no theft or trespass, failure to return the personal property may still be conversion. **EXAMPLE 5.15**   Chen borrows Mark's iPad to use while traveling home from school for the holidays. When Chen returns to school, Mark asks for his iPad back. Chen tells Mark that she gave it to her little brother for Christmas. In this situation, Mark can sue Chen for conversion, and Chen will have to either return the iPad or pay damages equal to its value. ●

KEEP IN MIND   In tort law, the underlying motive for an act does not matter. What matters is the intent to do the act that results in the tort.

Note that conversion can occur even if a person mistakenly believed that she or he was entitled to the goods. In other words, good intentions are not a defense against conversion. Someone who buys stolen goods, for example, can be liable for conversion even if he or she did not know that the goods were stolen. If the true owner brings a tort action against the buyer, the buyer must either return the property to the owner or pay the owner the full value of the property, despite having already paid the purchase price to the thief. A successful defense against the charge of conversion is that the purported owner does not, in fact, own the property or does not have a right to possess it that is superior to the right of the holder.

Disparagement of Property

Disparagement of Property   An economically injurious falsehood made about another's product or property; a general term for torts that are more specifically referred to as *slander of quality* or *slander of title.*

Disparagement of property occurs when economically injurious falsehoods are made about another's product or property, not about another's reputation. Disparagement of property is a general term for torts specifically referred to as *slander*

---

16. *Trustees of University of District of Columbia v. Vossoughi,* 963 A.2d 1162 (D.C.App. 2009).

Slander of Quality (Trade Libel) The publication of false information about another's product, alleging that it is not what its seller claims.

of quality or *slander of title*. Publication of false information about another's product, alleging that it is not what its seller claims, constitutes the tort of **slander of quality**, or **trade libel.** To establish trade libel, the plaintiff must prove that the improper publication caused a third party to refrain from dealing with the plaintiff and that the plaintiff sustained economic damages (such as lost profits) as a result.

An improper publication may be both a slander of quality and defamation of character. For example, a statement that disparages the quality of a product may also, by implication, disparage the character of the person who would sell such a product.

Slander of Title The publication of a statement that denies or casts doubt on another's legal ownership of any property, causing financial loss to that property's owner.

When a publication denies or casts doubt on another's legal ownership of any property, and the property's owner suffers a financial loss as a result, the tort of **slander of title** may exist. Usually, this is an intentional tort in which someone knowingly publishes an untrue statement about property with the intent of discouraging a third party from dealing with the person slandered. For instance, a car dealer would have difficulty attracting customers after competitors published a notice that the dealer's stock consisted of stolen automobiles.

▶ Unintentional Torts (Negligence)

The tort of **negligence** occurs when someone suffers injury because of another's failure to live up to a required *duty of care*. In contrast to intentional torts, in torts involving negligence, the tortfeasor neither wishes to bring about the consequences of the act nor believes that they will occur. The actor's conduct merely creates a *risk* of such consequences. If no risk is created, there is no negligence. Moreover, the risk must be foreseeable—that is, it must be such that a reasonable person engaging in the same activity would anticipate the risk and guard against it. In determining what is reasonable conduct, courts consider the nature of the possible harm.

Negligence The failure to exercise the standard of care that a reasonable person would exercise in similar circumstances.

Many of the actions discussed earlier in the chapter in the section on intentional torts constitute negligence if the element of intent is missing. **EXAMPLE 5.16** Juan walks up to Maya and intentionally shoves her. Maya falls and breaks an arm as a result. In this situation, Juan has committed an intentional tort (assault and battery). If Juan carelessly bumps into Maya, however, and she falls and breaks an arm as a result, Juan's action will constitute negligence. In either situation, Juan has committed a tort. ●

To succeed in a negligence action, the plaintiff must prove each of the following:

1. *Duty.* That the defendant owed a duty of care to the plaintiff.
2. *Breach.* That the defendant breached that duty.
3. *Causation.* That the defendant's breach caused the plaintiff to suffer an injury.
4. *Damages.* That the injury suffered by the plaintiff is legally recognizable.

We discuss each of these four elements of negligence next.

The Duty of Care and Its Breach

Duty of Care The duty of all persons, as established by tort law, to exercise a reasonable amount of care in their dealings with others. Failure to exercise due care, which is normally determined by the reasonable person standard, constitutes the tort of negligence.

Central to the tort of negligence is the concept of a **duty of care.** The basic principle underlying the duty of care is that people in society are free to act as they please so long as their actions do not infringe on the interests of others.

When someone fails to comply with the duty to exercise reasonable care, a potentially tortious act may have been committed. Failure to live up to a standard of care may be an act (accidentally setting fire to a building) or an omission (neglecting to put out a campfire). It may be a careless act or a carefully performed but nevertheless dangerous act that results in injury. Courts consider the nature of the act (whether it is outrageous or commonplace), the manner in which the act was performed (cautiously versus heedlessly), and the nature of the injury (whether it is serious or slight).

THE REASONABLE PERSON STANDARD　　Tort law measures duty by the **reasonable person standard.** In determining whether a duty of care has been breached, the courts ask how a reasonable person would have acted in the same circumstances. The reasonable person standard is said to be (though in an absolute sense it cannot be) objective. It is not necessarily how a particular person would act. It is society's judgment on how people *should* act. If the so-called reasonable person existed, he or she would be careful, conscientious, even tempered, and honest. The courts frequently use this hypothetical reasonable person in decisions relating to other areas of law as well. That individuals are required to exercise a reasonable standard of care in their activities is a pervasive concept in business law, and many of the issues discussed in subsequent chapters of this text have to do with this duty.

In negligence cases, the degree of care to be exercised varies, depending on the defendant's occupation or profession, her or his relationship with the plaintiff, and other factors. Generally, whether an action constitutes a breach of the duty of care is determined on a case-by-case basis. The outcome depends on how the judge (or jury, if it is a jury trial) decides a reasonable person in the position of the defendant would act in the particular circumstances of the case.

THE DUTY OF LANDOWNERS　　Landowners are expected to exercise reasonable care to protect persons coming onto their property from harm. As mentioned earlier, in some jurisdictions, landowners are held to owe a duty to protect even trespassers against certain risks. Landowners who rent or lease premises to tenants (see Chapter 22) are expected to exercise reasonable care to ensure that the tenants and their guests are not harmed in common areas, such as stairways, entryways, and laundry rooms.

Duty to Warn Business Invitees of Risks. Retailers and other firms that explicitly or implicitly invite persons to come onto their premises are usually charged with a duty to exercise reasonable care to protect those persons, who are considered **business invitees.** **EXAMPLE 5.17**　Liz enters a supermarket, slips on a wet floor, and sustains injuries as a result. The owner of the supermarket would be liable for damages if, when Liz slipped, there was no sign warning that the floor was wet. A court would hold that the business owner was negligent because the owner failed to exercise a reasonable degree of care in protecting the store's customers against foreseeable risks about which the owner knew or *should have known*. That a patron might slip on the wet floor and be injured was a foreseeable risk. The owner should have taken care to avoid this risk and warned the customer of it (by posting a sign or setting out orange cones, for example). ●

The landowner also has a duty to discover and, within a reasonable amount of time, remove any hidden dangers that might injure a customer or other invitee. Store owners have a duty to protect customers from potentially slipping and injuring themselves on merchandise that has fallen off the shelves.

Obvious Risks Provide an Exception. Some risks, of course, are so obvious that the owner need not warn of them. For instance, a business owner does not need

---

Reasonable Person Standard　The standard of behavior expected of a hypothetical "reasonable person"; the standard against which negligence is measured and that must be observed to avoid liability for negligence.

Business Invitee　A person, such as a customer or a client, who is invited onto business premises by the owner of those premises for business purposes.

"A little neglect may breed great mischief."
Benjamin Franklin, 1706–1790
(American politician and inventor)

to warn customers to open a door before attempting to walk through it. Other risks, however, may seem obvious to a business owner but may not be so in the eyes of another, such as a child. In addition, even if a risk is obvious, that does not necessarily excuse a business owner from the duty to protect its customers from foreseeable harm.

CASE EXAMPLE 5.18 Giorgio's Grill, a restaurant in Hollywood, Florida, becomes a nightclub after hours. At those times, traditionally, as the manager of Giorgio's knew, the staff and customers threw paper napkins into the air as the music played. The napkins landed on the floor, but no one picked them up. One night, Jane Izquierdo went to Giorgio's. Although she had been to the club on other occasions and knew about the napkin-throwing tradition, she slipped and fell, breaking her leg. She sued Giorgio's for negligence but lost at trial because a jury found that the risk of slipping on the napkins was obvious. A state appellate court reversed, however, holding that the obviousness of a risk does not discharge a business owner's duty to its invitees to maintain the premises in a safe condition.[17] ●

Preventing Legal Disputes

It can be difficult to determine whether a risk is obvious. Because you can be held liable if you fail to discover hidden dangers on business premises that could cause injuries to customers, you should post warnings of any conceivable risks on the property. Be vigilant and frequently reassess potential hazards. Train your employees to be on the lookout for possibly dangerous conditions at all times and to notify a superior immediately if they notice an unsafe situation. Remember that a finding of liability in a single lawsuit can leave a small enterprise close to bankruptcy. To prevent potential negligence liability, make sure that your business premises are as safe as possible for all persons who might be there, including children, senior citizens, and individuals with disabilities.

THE DUTY OF PROFESSIONALS If an individual has knowledge or skill superior to that of an ordinary person, the individual's conduct must be consistent with that status. Because professionals—including physicians, dentists, architects, engineers, accountants, lawyers, and others—are required to have a certain level of knowledge and training, a higher standard of care applies. In determining whether professionals have exercised reasonable care, the law takes their training and expertise into account. Thus, an accountant's conduct is judged not by the reasonable person standard, but by the reasonable accountant standard.

If a professional violates her or his duty of care toward a client, the professional may be sued for **malpractice**, which is essentially professional negligence. For example, a patient might sue a physician for *medical malpractice*. A client might sue an attorney for *legal malpractice*.

Malpractice Professional misconduct or the lack of the requisite degree of skill as a professional. Negligence—the failure to exercise due care—on the part of a professional, such as a physician, is commonly referred to as malpractice.

Causation

Another element necessary to a negligence action is *causation*. If a person fails in a duty of care and someone suffers an injury, the wrongful activity must have caused the harm for the activity to be considered a tort. In deciding whether there is causation, the court must address two questions:

1. *Is there causation in fact?* Did the injury occur because of the defendant's act, or would it have occurred anyway? If an injury would not have occurred without the defendant's act, then there is causation in fact. **Causation in fact** can usually be determined by the *but for* test: "but for" the wrongful act, the injury would not

Causation in Fact An act or omission without which an event would not have occurred.

---

17. *Izquierdo v. Gyroscope, Inc.*, 946 So.2d 115 (Fla.App. 2007).

have occurred. Theoretically, causation in fact is limitless. One could claim, for example, that "but for" the creation of the world, a particular injury would not have occurred. Thus, as a practical matter, the law has to establish limits, and it does so through the concept of proximate cause.

Proximate Cause Legal cause, which exists when the connection between an act and an injury is strong enough to justify imposing liability.

NOTE Proximate cause can be thought of as a question of social policy. Should the defendant be made to bear the loss instead of the plaintiff?

2. *Was the act the proximate cause of the injury?* **Proximate cause,** or legal cause, exists when the connection between an act and an injury is strong enough to justify imposing liability. Courts use proximate cause to limit the scope of the defendant's liability to a subset of the total number of potential plaintiffs that might have been harmed by the defendant's actions. **EXAMPLE 5.19** Ackerman carelessly leaves a campfire burning. The fire not only burns down the forest but also sets off an explosion in a nearby chemical plant that spills chemicals into a river, killing all the fish for a hundred miles downstream and ruining the economy of a tourist resort. Should Ackerman be liable to the resort owners? To the tourists whose vacations were ruined? These are questions of proximate cause that a court must decide. ●

Both of these questions must be answered in the affirmative for liability in tort to arise. If a defendant's action constitutes causation in fact but a court decides that the action was not the proximate cause of the plaintiff's injury, the causation requirement has not been met—and the defendant normally will not be liable to the plaintiff.

Questions of proximate cause are linked to the concept of foreseeability because it would be unfair to impose liability on a defendant unless the defendant's actions created a foreseeable risk of injury. Probably the most cited case on proximate cause is the *Palsgraf* case, which is discussed in this chapter's *Landmark in the Legal Environment* feature on the facing page. In determining the issue of proximate cause, the court addressed the following question: Does a defendant's duty of care extend only to those who may be injured as a result of a foreseeable risk, or does it extend also to a person whose injury could not reasonably be foreseen?

The Injury Requirement and Damages

For a tort to have been committed, the injury the plaintiff suffered must be a *legally recognizable* injury. To recover damages (receive compensation), the plaintiff must have suffered some loss, harm, wrong, or invasion of a protected interest. Essentially, the purpose of tort law is to compensate for legally recognized injuries resulting from wrongful acts. If no legally recognizable harm or injury results from a given negligent action, there is nothing to compensate—and no tort exists. **EXAMPLE 5.20** If you carelessly bump into a passerby, who stumbles and falls as a result, you may be liable in tort if the passerby is injured in the fall. If the person is unharmed, however, there normally cannot be a suit for damages because no injury was suffered. ●

Compensatory damages are the norm in negligence cases. As noted earlier, a court will award punitive damages only if the defendant's conduct was grossly negligent, reflecting an intentional failure to perform a duty with reckless disregard of the consequences to others.

Defenses to Negligence

Defendants often defend against negligence claims by asserting that the plaintiffs failed to prove the existence of one or more of the required elements for negligence. Additionally, there are three basic *affirmative* defenses in negligence cases (defenses that a defendant can use to avoid liability even if the facts are as the plaintiff state): *assumption of risk*, *superseding cause*, and *contributory and comparative negligence*.

Stella Liebeck was awarded several million dollars by a jury after she accidentally spilled a cup of hot McDonald's coffee on her lap. McDonald's appealed, and the award was reduced. Does such an award constitute compensatory damages?

(AP Photo/Joe Marquette)

Landmark in the Legal Environment **Palsgraf v. Long Island Railroad Co. (1928)**

In 1928, the New York Court of Appeals (that state's highest court) issued its decision in *Palsgraf v. Long Island Railroad Co.*,[a] a case that has become a landmark in negligence law and proximate cause.

The Facts of the Case The plaintiff, Palsgraf, was waiting for a train on a station platform. A man carrying a small package wrapped in newspaper was rushing to catch a train that had begun to move away from the platform. As the man attempted to jump aboard the moving train, he seemed unsteady and about to fall. A railroad guard on the train car reached forward to grab him, and another guard on the platform pushed him from behind to help him board the train. In the process, the man's package fell on the railroad tracks and exploded, because it contained fireworks. The repercussions of the explosion caused scales at the other end of the train platform to fall on Palsgraf, who was injured as a result. She sued the railroad company for damages in a New York state court.

The Question of Proximate Cause At the trial, the jury found that the railroad guards were negligent in their conduct. On appeal, the question before the New York Court of Appeals was whether the conduct of the railroad guards was the proximate cause of Palsgraf's injuries. In other words, did the guards' duty of care extend to Palsgraf, who was outside the zone of danger and whose injury could not reasonably have been foreseen?

The court stated that the question of whether the guards were negligent *with respect to Palsgraf* depended on whether her injury was *reasonably foreseeable* to the railroad guards. Although the guards may have acted negligently with respect to the man boarding the train, this had no bearing on the question of their negligence with respect to Palsgraf. This was not a situation in which a person commited an act so potentially harmful (for example, firing a gun at a building) that he or she would be held responsible for any harm that resulted. The court stated that here "there was nothing in the situation to suggest to the most cautious mind that the parcel wrapped in newspaper would spread wreckage through the station." The court thus concluded that the railroad guards were not negligent with respect to Palsgraf because her injury was not reasonably foreseeable.

• **Application to Today's Legal Environment** *The Palsgraf case established foreseeability as the test for proximate cause. Today, the courts continue to apply this test in determining proximate cause—and thus tort liability for injuries. Generally, if the victim of a harm or the consequences of a harm done are unforeseeable, there is no proximate cause. Note, though, that in the online environment, distinctions based on physical proximity, such as the "zone of danger" cited by the court in this case, are largely inapplicable.*

a. 248 N.Y. 339, 162 N.E. 99 (1928).

Assumption of Risk A doctrine under which a plaintiff may not recover for injuries or damage suffered from risks he or she knows of and has voluntarily assumed.

ASSUMPTION OF RISK A plaintiff who voluntarily enters into a risky situation, knowing the risk involved, will not be allowed to recover. This is the defense of **assumption of risk.** The requirements of this defense are (1) knowledge of the risk and (2) voluntary assumption of the risk. The risk can be assumed by express agreement, or the assumption of risk can be implied by the plaintiff's knowledge of the risk and subsequent conduct. Courts do not apply the assumption of risk doctrine in emergency situations, however. Nor does it apply when a statute protects a class of people (such as employees) from harm and a member of the class is injured by the harm.

The assumption of risk defense frequently is asserted when the plaintiff is injured during recreational activities that involve known risk, such as skiing and skydiving. Note that assumption of risk can apply not only to participants in sporting events, but also to spectators and bystanders who are injured while attending those events.

CASE EXAMPLE 5.21 Delinda Taylor, who was a Seattle Mariners fan, took her sons to see a baseball game. They arrived early so that they could watch the players warm up and get their autographs. Taylor was standing by her seat near the foul line watching Mariners pitcher Freddie Garcia throwing the ball with another player. When she looked away from the field, an errant ball got past Garcia and struck Taylor in the face, causing serious injuries. She filed a negligence lawsuit against the Mariners to recover for her injuries. The Mariners asserted the defense of assumption of risk. The court ruled that Taylor was familiar with baseball and that she knew about and had voluntarily assumed the risk of getting hit by a thrown baseball.[18] ●

In the following case, a homeowner who had hired a contractor to remodel his home fell through a hole in the floor during the construction. The issue was whether the homeowner had primarily assumed the risk of injury and was therefore barred from recovering for negligence on the part of the contractor and a subcontractor.

---

18. *Taylor v. Baseball Club of Seattle, LP,* 132 Wash.App. 32, 130 P.3d 835 (2006); see also *Allred v. Capital Area Soccer League, Inc.,* 669 S.E.2d 777 (N.C.App. 2008).

Case 5.3   Wolf v. Don Dingmann Construction, Inc.

Court of Appeals of Minnesota, __ N.W.2d __ (2011).

BACKGROUND AND FACTS   Michael John Wolf contracted with Lumber One, Cold Spring, Inc., to remodel his home. Lumber One in turn awarded a subcontract to Don Dingmann Construction, Inc. Wolf lived in the house during the construction, and he was present at the job site on most days. Part of the project, which Wolf designed, included the construction of a loft. A ventilation pipe was to go from a fireplace in the den up through the loft. During construction, at Wolf's direction, the subcontractor left a large opening in the loft's floor to accommodate the pipe. One Friday, the subcontractor's owner, Don Dingmann, suggested removing the temporary stairs that led to the loft to prevent risk of injury over the weekend because guardrails had not yet been installed at the loft's edges. Wolf declined. The following Monday, while Dingmann was working in the loft, he saw Wolf climb the stairs from the den into the loft. A few minutes later, he found Wolf lying unconscious on the ground below the hole in the loft floor. Wolf filed a lawsuit in district court, alleging that Lumber One and Don Dingmann had negligently caused his fall. The defendants moved for summary judgment, arguing that they owed no duty to Wolf because the danger was open and obvious and because Wolf had assumed the risks associated with his presence on the job site. The district court agreed and granted summary judgment for the contractors. Wolf appealed.

IN THE WORDS OF THE COURT . . .
WRIGHT, Judge.
        * * * *

The undisputed facts establish that Wolf had personal knowledge and appreciation of the risk of falling. Wolf was familiar with the jobsite because he designed the loft, he lived in the home during construction, and he inspected the jobsite regularly. In his deposition testimony, Wolf stated that he knew better than to fall down a hole, he had been on construction sites before, and a person entering a construction site should be cautious. It is also undisputed that Dingmann and Wolf discussed taking safety precautions regarding the loft because it lacked guardrails. But Wolf declined them as

unnecessary. This evidence not only indicates that Wolf had the authority to veto safety decisions, but also that he appreciated the risk presented by the construction site's condition.

Wolf voluntarily chose to engage in the risk rather than avoid it. It was common for Wolf to inspect the work, and a photograph taken the same day as the accident established that he had stood on the unfinished loft when it was in the same condition as it was when he fell. Wolf went up to the loft on the morning of his fall to check the work on the walls, describing his reason for doing so as being "nosey." The record reflects that Wolf climbed up to the loft for no reason other than his curiosity. In doing so, he undertook the risk voluntarily and relieved the contractors of their legal duty of care. [Emphasis added.]

Wolf argues that secondary assumption of risk rather than primary assumption of risk applies here, thereby creating a genuine issue of material fact to be resolved by a jury. For secondary assumption of risk to apply, there must be an absence of consent to absolve Lumber One and the subcontractor of their duty. "A plaintiff consents to relieve the defendant of his duty when the plaintiff voluntarily enters into a relationship in which the plaintiff assumes well-known, incidental risks." Although primary assumption of risk is most often applied to spectators at or participants in athletic activities, the undisputed facts establish that *Wolf had experience at construction sites, knowledge of the incidental risks associated with construction sites generally, and knowledge of the risks associated with this particular construction site.* These circumstances warrant application of primary assumption of risk here. Because Wolf manifested his consent to relieve the contractors of their duty and thereby assumed the well-known, incidental risks associated with entering an elevated construction site that included a 42-by-42-inch hole, he primarily assumed the inherent risk of falling that gave rise to his injuries. [Emphasis added.]

DECISION AND REMEDY   The state intermediate appellate court affirmed the lower court's judgment. Wolf undertook the risk voluntarily, which relieved the contractors of their legal duty of care.

Case 5.3–Continued

He was aware of the risk of falling, he was familiar with the jobsite, and he discussed safety precautions with the contractors, but declined them.

WHAT IF THE FACTS WERE DIFFERENT? *Suppose that Dingmann and Wolf had not discussed taking safety precautions*

because of the loft's lack of guardrails. Would the result have been different? Why or why not?

THE ETHICAL DIMENSION *Should courts apply the doctrine of assumption of the risk to children? Discuss.*

Superseding Cause An unforeseeable intervening event may break the connection between a wrongful act and an injury to another. If so, the event acts as a *superseding cause*—that is, it relieves a defendant of liability for injuries caused by the intervening event. **EXAMPLE 5.22** Derrick, while riding his bicycle, negligently hits Julie, who is walking on the sidewalk. As a result of the impact, Julie falls and fractures her hip. While she is waiting for help to arrive, a small aircraft crashes nearby and explodes, and some of the fiery debris hits her, causing her to sustain severe burns. Derrick will be liable for Julie's fractured hip because the risk of hitting her with his bicycle was foreseeable. Normally, Derrick will not be liable for the burns caused by the plane crash—because the risk of a plane's crashing nearby and injuring Julie was not foreseeable. ●

Contributory and Comparative Negligence All individuals are expected to exercise a reasonable degree of care in looking out for themselves. In the past, under the common law doctrine of **contributory negligence,** a plaintiff who was also negligent (failed to exercise a reasonable degree of care) could not recover anything from the defendant. Under this rule, no matter how insignificant the plaintiff's negligence was relative to the defendant's negligence, the plaintiff was precluded from recovering any damages. Today, only a few jurisdictions still hold to this doctrine.

In most states, the doctrine of contributory negligence has been replaced by a **comparative negligence** standard. Under this standard, both the plaintiff's and the defendant's negligence are computed, and the liability for damages is distributed accordingly. Some jurisdictions have adopted a "pure" form of comparative negligence that allows the plaintiff to recover, even if the extent of his or her fault is greater than that of the defendant. For example, if the plaintiff was 80 percent at fault and the defendant 20 percent at fault, the plaintiff may recover 20 percent of his or her damages. Many states' comparative negligence statutes, however, contain a "50 percent" rule under which the plaintiff recovers nothing if she or he was more than 50 percent at fault. Following this rule, a plaintiff who is 35 percent at fault could recover 65 percent of his or her damages, but a plaintiff who is 65 percent at fault could recover nothing.

Contributory Negligence A rule in tort law that completely bars the plaintiff from recovering any damages if the damage suffered is partly the plaintiff's own fault; used in a minority of states.

Comparative Negligence A rule in tort law that reduces the plaintiff's recovery in proportion to the plaintiff's degree of fault, rather than barring recovery completely; used in the majority of states.

Special Negligence Doctrines and Statutes

There are a number of special doctrines and statutes relating to negligence. We examine a few of them here.

Res Ipsa Loquitur Generally, in lawsuits involving negligence, the plaintiff has the burden of proving that the defendant was negligent. In certain situations,

Res Ipsa Loquitur   A doctrine under which negligence may be inferred simply because an event occurred, if it is the type of event that would not occur in the absence of negligence. Literally, the term means "the facts speak for themselves."

however, under the doctrine of ***res ipsa loquitur***[19] (meaning "the facts speak for themselves"), the courts may infer that negligence has occurred. Then the burden of proof rests on the defendant—to prove she or he was *not* negligent. This doctrine is applied only when the event creating the damage or injury is one that ordinarily would occur only as a result of negligence.

CASE EXAMPLE 5.23   Mary Gubbins undergoes abdominal surgery and following the surgery has nerve damage in her spine near the area of the operation. She is unable to walk or stand for months, and even after regaining some use of her legs through physical therapy, her mobility is impaired and she experiences pain. In her subsequent negligence lawsuit, Gubbins can assert *res ipsa loquitur,* because the injury would never have occurred in the absence of the surgeon's negligence.[20] ●

NEGLIGENCE *PER SE*

Negligence Per Se   An action or failure to act in violation of a statutory requirement.

Certain conduct, whether it consists of an action or a failure to act, may be treated as **negligence *per se*** (*per se* means "in or of itself"). Negligence *per se* may occur if an individual violates a statute or ordinance and thereby causes the kind of harm that the statute was intended to prevent. The statute must clearly set out what standard of conduct is expected, when and where it is expected, and of whom it is expected. The standard of conduct required by the statute is the duty that the defendant owes to the plaintiff, and a violation of the statute is the breach of that duty.

CASE EXAMPLE 5.24   A Delaware statute states that anyone "who operates a motor vehicle and who fails to give full time and attention to the operation of the vehicle" is guilty of inattentive driving. Michael Moore was cited for inattentive driving after he collided with Debra Wright's car when he backed a truck out of a parking space. Moore paid the ticket, which meant that he pleaded guilty to violating the statute. The day after the accident, Wright began having back pain, which eventually required surgery. She sued Moore for damages, alleging negligence *per se*. The Delaware Supreme Court ruled that the inattentive driving statute sets forth a sufficiently specific standard of conduct to warrant application of negligence *per se*.[21] ●

"DANGER INVITES RESCUE" DOCTRINE

Sometimes, a person who is trying to avoid harm—such as an individual who swerves to avoid a head-on collision with a drunk driver—ends up causing harm to another (such as a cyclist riding in the bike lane) as a result. In those situations, the original wrongdoer (the drunk driver in this scenario) is liable to anyone who is injured, even if the injury actually resulted from another person's attempt to escape harm. The "danger invites rescue" doctrine extends the same protection to a person who is trying to rescue another from harm—the original wrongdoer is liable for injuries to an individual attempting a rescue. The idea is that the rescuer should not be held liable for any damages because he or she did not cause the danger and because danger invites rescue.

EXAMPLE 5.25   Ludley, while driving down a street, fails to see a stop sign because he is trying to break up a squabble between his two young children in the car's back seat. Salter, on the curb near the stop sign, realizes that Ludley is about to hit a pedestrian and runs into the street to push the pedestrian out of the way. If Ludley's vehicle hits Salter instead, Ludley will be liable for Salter's injury, as well as for *any* injuries the other pedestrian sustained. ● Whether rescuers injure themselves, the person rescued, or even a stranger, the original wrongdoer will still be liable.

---

19. Pronounced *rehz ihp*-suh *low*-kwuh-tuhr.
20. *Gubbins v. Hurson,* 885 A.2d 269 (D.C. 2005).
21. *Wright v. Moore,* 931 A.2d 405 (Del.Supr. 2007).

SPECIAL NEGLIGENCE STATUTES   A number of states have enacted statutes prescribing duties and responsibilities in certain circumstances. For example, most states now have what are called **Good Samaritan statutes.**[22] Under these statutes, someone who is aided voluntarily by another cannot turn around and sue the "Good Samaritan" for negligence. These laws were passed largely to protect physicians and medical personnel who voluntarily render medical services in emergency situations to those in need, such as individuals hurt in car accidents. Indeed, the California Supreme Court has interpreted the state's Good Samaritan statute to mean that a person who renders nonmedical aid is not immune from liability.[23] Thus, only medical personnel and persons rendering medical aid in emergencies are protected in California.

Good Samaritan Statute   A state statute stipulating that persons who provide emergency services to, or rescue, someone in peril cannot be sued for negligence, unless they act recklessly, thereby causing further harm.

Many states have also passed **dram shop acts,**[24] under which a tavern owner or bartender may be held liable for injuries caused by a person who became intoxicated while drinking at the bar or who was already intoxicated when served by the bartender. Some states' statutes also impose liability on *social hosts* (persons hosting parties) for injuries caused by guests who became intoxicated at the hosts' homes. Under these statutes, it is unnecessary to prove that the tavern owner, bartender, or social host was negligent. Thus, if Jane hosts a Super Bowl party at which Brett, a minor, sneaks alcoholic drinks, Jane is potentially liable for damages resulting from Brett's drunk driving after the party.

Dram Shop Act   A state statute that imposes liability on the owners of bars and taverns, as well as those who serve alcoholic drinks to the public, for injuries resulting from accidents caused by intoxicated persons when the sellers or servers of alcoholic drinks contributed to the intoxication.

▶ Strict Liability

Another category of torts is called **strict liability,** or *liability without fault.* Intentional torts and torts of negligence involve acts that depart from a reasonable standard of care and cause injuries. Under the doctrine of strict liability, a person who engages in certain activities can be held responsible for any harm that results to others even if the person used the utmost care. Thus, liability for injury is imposed for reasons other than fault.

Strict Liability   Liability regardless of fault. In tort law, strict liability is imposed on those engaged in abnormally dangerous activities, on persons who keep dangerous animals, and on manufacturers or sellers that introduce into commerce goods that are unreasonably dangerous when in a defective condition.

Abnormally Dangerous Activities

Strict liability for damages proximately caused by an abnormally dangerous, or ultrahazardous, activity is one application of strict liability. Courts apply the doctrine of strict liability in these situations because of the extreme risk of the activity. Abnormally dangerous activities are those that involve a high risk of serious harm to persons or property that cannot be completely guarded against by the exercise of reasonable care. Examples of such activities include blasting and storing explosives. Even if blasting with dynamite is performed with all reasonable care, there is still a risk of injury. Balancing that risk against the potential for harm, it seems reasonable to ask the person engaged in the activity to pay for injuries caused by that activity. Although there is no fault, there is still responsibility because of the dangerous nature of the undertaking.

---

22. These laws derive their name from the Good Samaritan story in the Bible. In the story, a traveler who had been robbed and beaten lay along the roadside, ignored by those passing by. Eventually, a man from the country of Samaria (the "Good Samaritan") stopped to render assistance to the injured person.

23. *Van Horn v. Watson,* 45 Cal.4th 322, 197 P.3d 164, 86 Cal.Rptr.3d 350 (2008).

24. Historically, a *dram* was a small unit of liquid, and distilled spirits (strong alcoholic liquor) were sold in drams. Thus, a dram shop was a place where liquor was sold in drams.

Other Applications of Strict Liability

Persons who keep wild animals are strictly liable for any harm inflicted by the animals. The basis for applying strict liability is that if wild animals escape from confinement, they pose a serious risk of harm to people in the vicinity. An owner of domestic animals (such as dogs, cats, cows, or sheep) may be strictly liable for harm caused by those animals if the owner knew, or should have known, that the animals were dangerous or had a propensity to harm others.

A significant application of strict liability is in the area of product liability—liability of manufacturers and sellers for harmful or defective products. Liability here is a matter of social policy and is based on two factors: (1) the manufacturing company can better bear the cost of injury because it can spread the cost throughout society by increasing prices of goods, and (2) the manufacturing company is making a profit from its activities and therefore should bear the cost of injury as an operating expense. We will discuss product liability in greater detail in Chapter 11.

Cyber Torts—Online Defamation

Torts can also be committed in the online environment. To date, most *cyber torts* have involved defamation, so this discussion will focus on how the traditional tort law concerning defamation is being adapted to apply to online defamation.

Identifying the Author of Online Defamation

An initial issue raised by online defamation was simply discovering who was committing it. In the real world, identifying the author of a defamatory remark generally is an easy matter, but suppose that a business firm has discovered that defamatory statements about its policies and products are being posted in an online forum. Such forums allow anyone—customers, employees, or crackpots—to complain about a firm that they dislike while remaining anonymous.

Therefore, a threshold barrier to anyone who seeks to bring an action for online defamation is discovering the identity of the person who posted the defamatory message. An Internet service provider (ISP)—a company that provides connections to the Internet—can disclose personal information about its customers only when ordered to do so by a court. Consequently, businesses and individuals are increasingly bringing lawsuits against "John Does" (John Doe, Jane Doe, and the like are fictitious names used in lawsuits when the identity of a party is not known or when a party wishes to conceal his or her name for privacy reasons). Then, using the authority of the courts, the plaintiffs can obtain from the ISPs the identity of the persons responsible for the defamatory messages.

Liability of Internet Service Providers

Recall from the discussion of defamation earlier in this chapter that those who repeat or otherwise disseminate defamatory statements made by others can be held liable for defamation. Thus, newspapers, magazines, and radio and television stations can be subject to liability for defamatory content that they publish or broadcast, even though the content was prepared or created by others. Applying this rule to cyberspace, however, raises an important issue: Should ISPs be regarded as publishers and therefore be held liable for defamatory messages that are posted by their users in online forums or other arenas?

U.S. film director Woody Allen sued a clothing company, known for its racy ads featuring scantily clad models, for using his image on the Internet. Can the Internet service provider through which the offending ads were directed be held liable?

(AP Photo/Manu Fernandez)

Before 1996, the courts grappled with this question. Then Congress passed the Communications Decency Act (CDA), which states that "no provider or user of an interactive computer service shall be treated as the publisher or speaker of any information provided by another information content provider."[25] Thus, under the CDA, ISPs generally are treated differently from publishers in other media and are not liable for publishing defamatory statements that come from a third party.[26] Although the courts generally have construed the CDA as providing a broad shield to protect ISPs from liability for third-party content, recently some courts have started establishing some limits to CDA immunity.[27]

---

25. 47 U.S.C. Section 230.

26. For a leading case on this issue, see *Zeran v. America Online, Inc.,* 129 F.3d 327 (4th Cir. 1997); *cert.* denied, 524 U.S. 937, 118 S.Ct. 2341, 141 L.Ed.2d 712 (1998). See also *Noah v. AOL Time Warner, Inc.,* 261 F.Supp.2d 532 (E.D.Va. 2003); and *Doe v. Bates,* 2006 WL 3813758 (E.D.Tex. 2006).

27. See, for example, *Fair Housing Council of San Fernando Valley v. Roommate.com, LLC,* 521 F.3d 1157 (9th Cir. 2008).

 ## Reviewing . . . Torts and Cyber Torts

Two sisters, Darla and Irene, are partners in an import business located in a small town in Rhode Island. Irene is also campaigning to be the mayor of their town. Both sisters travel to other countries to purchase the goods they sell at their retail store. Irene buys Indonesian goods, and Darla buys goods from Africa. After a tsunami destroys many of the Indonesian towns where Irene usually purchases goods, she phones one of her contacts there and asks him to procure some items and ship them to her. He informs her that it will be impossible to buy these items now because the townspeople are being evacuated due to a water shortage. Irene is angry and tells her contact that if he cannot purchase the goods, he should just take them without paying for them after the town has been evacuated. Darla overhears her sister's instructions and is outraged. They have a falling-out, and Darla decides that she no longer wishes to be in business with her sister. Using the information presented in the chapter, answer the following questions.

1. Suppose that Darla tells several of her friends about Irene's instructing her contact to take goods without paying for them after the tsunami. If Irene files a tort action against Darla alleging slander, will her suit be successful? Why or why not?

2. Now suppose that Irene wins the election and becomes the city's mayor. Darla then writes a letter to the editor of the local newspaper disclosing Irene's misconduct. If Irene accuses Darla of committing libel, what defenses could Darla assert?

3. If Irene accepts goods shipped from Indonesia that were wrongfully obtained, has she committed an intentional tort against property? Explain.

4. Suppose now that Darla was in the store one day with an elderly customer, Betty Green, who was looking for a graduation gift for her granddaughter. When Darla went to the counter to answer the phone, Green continued to wander around the store and eventually went through an open door into the stockroom area, where she fell over some boxes on the floor and fractured her hip. Green files a negligence action against the store. Did Darla breach her duty of care? Why or why not?

 ## Key Terms

actionable 118	assumption of risk 133	causation in fact 131
actual malice 122	battery 117	comparative negligence 135
appropriation 123	business invitee 130	compensatory damages 113
assault 117	business tort 112	contributory negligence 135

Chapter Summary: Torts and Cyber Torts

Intentional Torts against Persons (See pages 117–126.)	1. *Assault and battery*—An assault is an unexcused and intentional act that causes another person to be apprehensive of immediate harm. A battery is an assault that results in physical contact. 2. *False imprisonment*—The intentional confinement or restraint of another person's movement without justification. 3. *Intentional infliction of emotional distress*—An intentional act involving extreme and outrageous conduct that results in severe emotional distress to another. 4. *Defamation (libel or slander)*—A false statement of fact, not made under privilege, that is communicated to a third person and that causes damage to a person's reputation. For public figures, the plaintiff must also prove actual malice. 5. *Invasion of the right to privacy*—The use of a person's name or likeness for commercial purposes without permission, wrongful intrusion into a person's private activities, publication of information that places a person in a false light, or disclosure of private facts that an ordinary person would find objectionable. 6. *Appropriation*—The use of another person's name, likeness, or other identifying characteristic, without permission and for the benefit of the user. Courts disagree on the degree of likeness required. 7. *Fraudulent misrepresentation*—A false representation made by one party, through misstatement of facts or through conduct, with the intention of deceiving another and on which the other reasonably relies to his or her detriment. 8. *Abusive or frivolous litigation*—If a party initiates a lawsuit out of malice and without probable cause (a legitimate legal reason), and ends up losing the suit, that party can be sued for the tort of *malicious prosecution.* When a person uses a legal process against another in an improper manner or to accomplish a purpose for which it was not designed, that person can be sued for *abuse of process.* 9. *Wrongful interference*—The knowing, intentional interference by a third party with an enforceable contractual relationship or an established business relationship between other parties for the purpose of advancing the economic interests of the third party.
Intentional Torts against Property (See pages 126–129.)	1. *Trespass to land*—The invasion of another's real property without consent or privilege. 2. *Trespass to personal property*—Unlawfully damaging or interfering with the owner's right to use, possess, or enjoy her or his personal property. 3. *Conversion*—Wrongfully taking personal property from its rightful owner or possessor and placing it in the service of another. 4. *Disparagement of property*—Any economically injurious falsehood that is made about another's product or property; an inclusive term for the torts of slander of quality and slander of title.
Unintentional Torts (Negligence) (See pages 129–137.)	1. *Negligence*—The careless performance of a legally required duty or the failure to perform a legally required act. Elements that must be proved are that a legal duty of care exists, that the defendant breached that duty, and that the breach caused a legally recognizable injury to another.

Chapter Summary: Torts and Cyber Torts, Continued

Unintentional Torts (Negligence)—Continued	2. *Defenses to negligence*—The basic affirmative defenses in negligence cases are assumption of risk, superseding cause, and contributory or comparative negligence.
	3. *Special negligence doctrines and statutes*—
	  a. *Res ipsa loquitur*—A doctrine under which a plaintiff need not prove negligence on the part of the defendant because "the facts speak for themselves."
	  b. Negligence *per se*—A type of negligence that may occur if a person violates a statute or an ordinance and the violation causes another to suffer the kind of injury that the statute or ordinance was intended to prevent.
	  c. Special negligence statutes—State statutes that prescribe duties and responsibilities in certain circumstances, the violation of which will impose civil liability. Dram shop acts and Good Samaritan statutes are examples of special negligence statutes.

Strict Liability (See pages 137–138.)	Under the doctrine of strict liability, a person may be held liable, regardless of the degree of care exercised, for damages or injuries caused by her or his product or activity. Strict liability includes liability for harms caused by abnormally dangerous activities, by dangerous animals, and by defective products (product liability).
Cyber Torts— Online Defamation (See pages 138–139.)	General tort principles are being extended to cover cyber torts, or torts that occur in cyberspace, such as online defamation. Federal and state statutes may also apply to certain forms of cyber torts. For example, under the federal Communications Decency Act of 1996, Internet service providers are not liable for defamatory messages posted by their subscribers.

 ExamPrep

ISSUE SPOTTERS

1. Jana leaves her truck's motor running while she enters a Kwik-Pik Store. The truck's transmission engages, and the vehicle crashes into a gas pump, starting a fire that spreads to a warehouse on the next block. The warehouse collapses, causing its billboard to fall and injure Lou, a bystander. Can Lou recover from Jana? Why or why not?
2. A water pipe bursts, flooding Metal Fabrication Company's utility room and tripping the circuit breakers on a panel in the room. Metal Fabrication contacts Nouri, a licensed electrician with five years' experience, to check the damage and turn the breakers back on. Without testing for short circuits, which Nouri knows that he should do, he tries to switch on a breaker. He is electrocuted, and his wife sues Metal Fabrication for damages, alleging negligence. What might the firm successfully claim in defense?

—**Check your answers to these questions against the answers provided in Appendix G.**

BEFORE THE TEST

Go to **www.cengagebrain.com**, enter the ISBN number "9781111530617," and click on "Find" to locate this textbook's Web site. Then, click on "Access Now" under "Study Tools," and select "Chapter 5" at the top. There you will find an "Interactive Quiz" that you can take to assess your mastery of the concepts in this chapter, as well as "Flashcards" and a "Glossary" of important terms.

 For Review

1. What is a tort?
2. What is the purpose of tort law? What are two basic categories of torts?
3. What are the four elements of negligence?
4. What is meant by strict liability? In what circumstances is strict liability applied?
5. What is a cyber tort, and how are tort theories being applied in cyberspace?

Questions and Case Problems

5–1. Liability to Business Invitees. Kim went to Ling's Market to pick up a few items for dinner. It was a stormy day, and the wind had blown water through the market's door each time it opened. As Kim entered through the door, she slipped and fell in the rainwater that had accumulated on the floor. The manager knew of the weather conditions but had not posted any sign to warn customers of the water hazard. Kim injured her back as a result of the fall and sued Ling's for damages. Can Ling's be held liable for negligence? Discuss.

5–2. Question with Sample Answer. Wrongful Interference. Lothar owns a bakery. He has been trying to obtain a long-term contract with the owner of Martha's Tea Salons for some time. Lothar starts an intensive advertising campaign on radio and television and in the local newspaper. The advertising is so persuasive that Martha decides to break her contract with Harley's Bakery so that she can patronize Lothar's bakery. Is Lothar liable to Harley's Bakery for the tort of wrongful interference with a contractual relationship? Is Martha liable for this tort? Why or why not?

—For a sample answer to Question 5–2, go to Appendix E at the end of this text.

5–3. Negligence. Shannon's physician gives her some pain medication and tells her not to drive after taking it because the medication induces drowsiness. In spite of the doctor's warning, Shannon decides to drive to the store while on the medication. Owing to her lack of alertness, she fails to stop at a traffic light and crashes into another vehicle, causing a passenger in that vehicle to be injured. Is Shannon liable for the tort of negligence? Why or why not?

5–4. Defenses to Negligence. Mitsubishi Motors North America, Inc., operates an auto plant in Normal, Illinois. In 2003, TNT Logistics Corp. coordinated deliveries of auto parts to the plant and DeKeyser Express, Inc., transported the parts. On January 21, TNT told DeKeyser to transport three pallets of parts from Trelleborg YSH, Inc., to the plant. DeKeyser dispatched its driver Lola Camp. At Trelleborg's loading dock, Camp noticed that the pallets would fit inside the trailer only if they were stacked. Camp was concerned that the load might shift during transport. A DeKeyser dispatcher, Ken Kasprzak, and a TNT supervisor, Alan Marten, told her that she would not be liable for any damage. Trelleborg loaded the pallets. Camp drove to TNT's dock in Normal. When she opened the trailer door, the top pallet slipped. Trying to close the door to prevent its fall, Camp injured her shoulder and arm. She filed a suit against TNT and Trelleborg, claiming negligence. What is their defense? Discuss. [*Camp v. TNT Logistics Corp.,* 553 F.3d 502 (7th Cir. 2009)]

5–5. Negligence and Multiparty Liability. Alice Banks was injured when a chair she was sitting on at an Elks Club collapsed.

As a result of Banks's injury, Dr. Robert Boyce performed surgery on her back, fusing certain vertebrae. Boyce fused the wrong vertebrae, however, and had to perform a second surgery to correct the error. Then, during rehabilitation at a nursing home, Banks developed a serious infection that required additional surgeries and extensive care and treatment. She sued the Elks Club and Boyce for negligence. The Elks Club and Boyce filed motions against each other and also sued the nursing home. After complicated holdings by lower courts, the Tennessee high court reviewed the matter. Did the Elks Club have primary liability for all injuries suffered by Banks after the initial accident, or did each defendant separately contribute to Banks's injuries? Explain your answer. [*Banks v. Elks Club Pride of Tennessee,* 301 S.W.3d 214 (Tenn. 2010)]

5–6. Case Problem with Sample Answer. Libel and Invasion of Privacy. The *Northwest Herald,* a newspaper in Illinois, received e-mail reports regularly from area police departments about criminal arrests. The paper published that information, which is proper because it is public record. One day, the newspaper received an e-mail that stated that Carolene Eubanks had been charged with theft and obstruction of justice. The paper included this information in an issue that was to be published four days later. Several hours later, the police issued another e-mail, which explained that Eubanks had not been charged with anything. Instead, the person charged was Barbara Bradshaw. Due to a long weekend, the second e-mail was not noticed until after the paper had been published. The following day, five days after the e-mails had been received, a correction was published. Eubanks sued the paper for libel and for invasion of privacy. Do you think Eubanks has a good case for either tort? Why or why not? [*Eubanks v. Northwest Herald Newspapers,* 397 Ill.App.3d 746, 922 N.E.2d 1196 (2010)]

—To view a sample answer for Case Problem 5–6, go to Appendix F at the end of this text.

5–7. Proximate Cause. Sixteen-year-old Galen Stoller was killed at a railroad crossing when an AMTRAK passenger train hit the vehicle he was driving on a county road in Rowe, New Mexico. His parents, Maida Henderson and Ken Stoller, filed a lawsuit against Burlington Northern & Santa Fe Railroad Corporation (BNSF), among others. The parents accused the railroad of negligence in the design and maintenance of the crossing. Specifically, they claimed that the railroad had failed to (1) clear excessive vegetation from the crossing area and (2) install active warning devices (such as flashing lights, bells, or gates to warn of approaching trains). The crossing was marked with a stop sign and a railroad-crossing symbol. Submitted photos revealed that the sign was unobstructed. Although it was clear that Galen's car was on the tracks when the train collided with the vehicle, the parties disputed whether Galen had stopped at the stop sign. New Mexico law requires "a traveler approaching an open, unguarded railroad crossing . . . to stop, look and listen for trains using the tracks." Under state law, a driver's failure to "stop, look and listen" will be deemed the sole proximate cause of the collision, unless sufficient evidence exists from which a jury could conclude that the railroad was also negligent. The district court granted a summary judgment in favor of the railroad, and the plaintiffs appealed. Was there sufficient evidence that the railroad was negligent? How should the appellate court rule concerning the proximate cause of the accident? Explain. [*Henderson v. National Railroad Passenger Corp.*, __ F.3d __ (10th Cir. 2011)]

5–8. Wrongful Interference. Medtronic, Inc., is a diversified medical technology company that develops therapies to treat a variety of medical conditions. The market is highly competitive, and Medtronic competes nationally and internationally with St. Jude Medical S.C., Inc. James Hughes worked for Medtronic as a district sales manager in Birmingham, Alabama. Hughes's employment contract prohibited him from working on competitors' products for one year after leaving Medtronic. After thirteen years with Medtronic, Hughes sought and accepted employment as a sales director for St. Jude in Orlando, Florida. In their negotiations, representatives of St. Jude told Hughes that they believed his employment contract with Medtronic was unenforceable. Medtronic filed a lawsuit in a Minnesota state court against St. Jude, alleging wrongful interference. Which type of wrongful interference tort was most likely the basis for this lawsuit? What are its elements and defenses? Should the defendant be held liable? Why or why not? [*Medtronic, Inc. v. Hughes*, __ N.W.2d __ (Minn.App. 2011)]

5–9. A Question of Ethics. Dram Shop Acts. Donald and Gloria Bowden hosted a late afternoon cookout at their home in South Carolina, inviting mostly business acquaintances. Justin Parks, who was nineteen years old, attended the party. Alcoholic beverages were available to all of the guests, even those who, like Parks, were not minors but were underage. Parks consumed alcohol at the party and left with other guests. One of these guests detained Parks at the guest's home to give Parks time to "sober up." Parks then drove himself from this guest's home and was killed in a one-car accident. At the time of death, he had a blood alcohol content of 0.291 percent, which exceeded the state's limit for driving a motor vehicle. Linda Marcum, Parks's mother, filed a suit in a South Carolina state court against the Bowdens and others, alleging that they were negligent. [*Marcum v. Bowden*, 372 S.C. 452, 643 S.E.2d 85 (2007)]

1. Considering the principles discussed in this chapter, what are arguments in favor of, and against, holding social hosts liable in this situation? Explain.

2. The states vary widely in assessing liability and imposing sanctions in the circumstances described in this problem. In other words, justice is not equal for parents and other social hosts who serve alcoholic beverages to underage individuals. Why is that?

5–10. Video Question. *Jaws: The Bite That's Right.* Access the video using the instructions provided below to answer the following questions.

1. In the video, the mayor (Murray Hamilton) and a few other men try to persuade Chief Brody (Roy Scheider) not to close the town's beaches. If Brody keeps the beaches open and a swimmer is injured or killed because he failed to warn swimmers about the potential shark danger, has Brody committed the tort of negligence? Explain.

2. Can Chief Brody be held liable for any injuries or deaths to swimmers under the doctrine of strict liability? Why or why not?

3. Suppose that Chief Brody goes against the mayor's instructions and warns townspeople to stay off the beach. Nevertheless, several swimmers do not heed his warning and are injured as a result. What defense or defenses could Brody raise under these circumstances if he is sued for negligence?

—To watch this video, go to **www.cengagebrain.com** and register the access code that came with your new book or log in to your existing account. Select the link for either the "Business Law Digital Video Library Online Access" or "Business Law CourseMate," and then click on "Complete Video List" to find the video for this chapter (Video 56).

Chapter 6

Criminal Law and Cyber Crime

> "The crime problem is getting really serious. The other day, the Statue of Liberty had both hands up."
>
> —Jay Leno, 1950–present
> (American comedian and television host)

Contents

Chapter Objectives

After reading this chapter, you should be able to answer the following questions:

1. **What two elements must exist before a person can be held liable for a crime? Can a corporation commit crimes?**

2. **What are five broad categories of crimes? What is white-collar crime?**

3. **What defenses might be raised by criminal defendants to avoid liability for criminal acts?**

4. **What constitutional safeguards exist to protect persons accused of crimes?**

5. **How has the Internet expanded opportunities for identity theft?**

(John Elk III/Lonely Planet Images/Getty Images)

Criminal law is an important part of the legal environment of business. Various sanctions are used to bring about a society in which individuals engaging in business can compete and flourish. These sanctions include damages for various types of tortious conduct (see Chapter 5), damages for breach of contract (see Chapter 10), and equitable remedies (see Chapters 1 and 10). Additional sanctions are imposed under criminal law. Many statutes regulating business provide for criminal as well as civil sanctions.

As noted in the chapter-opening quotation above, crime is a serious problem in the United States, and some fear that the nation's economic difficulties will lead to even higher crime rates. Moreover, the government's ability to pay for prisons has declined due to the economic slowdown. Many prisons are at twice their capacity, and inmates are not receiving adequate medical care. Overcrowding became so severe in California prisons that in 2011 the United States Supreme Court ruled that conditions there violated the Eighth Amendment's prohibition against cruel and unusual punishment.[1] As a result, 46,000 inmates had to be released from California prisons.

In this chapter, following a brief summary of the major differences between criminal and civil law, we look at how crimes are classified and what elements must be

---

1. See *Brown v. Plata*, ___ U.S. ___, 131 S.Ct. 1910, 179 L.Ed.2d 969 (2011).

present for criminal liability to exist. We then examine various categories of crimes, the defenses that can be raised to avoid liability for criminal actions, and the rules of criminal procedure. We conclude the chapter with a discussion of crimes that occur in cyberspace, often referred to as *cyber crime.*

 Civil Law and Criminal Law

Remember from Chapter 1 that *civil law* spells out the duties that exist between persons or between persons and their governments, excluding the duty not to commit crimes. Contract law, for example, is part of civil law. The whole body of tort law, which deals with the infringement by one person on the legally recognized rights of another, is also an area of civil law.

Crime A wrong against society set forth in a statute and, if committed, punishable by society through fines and/or imprisonment–and, in some cases, death.

Criminal law, in contrast, has to do with crime. A **crime** can be defined as a wrong against society set forth in a statute and, if committed, punishable by society through fines and/or imprisonment—and, in some cases, death. (Although crimes in our nation are defined by statute, this is not necessarily true in other societies. For a discussion of how some residents of Afghanistan and Pakistan base their criminal law on a tribal code, see this chapter's *Beyond Our Borders* feature below.) As mentioned in Chapter 1, because crimes are *offenses against society as a whole,* criminals are prosecuted by a public official, such as a district attorney (D.A.), rather than by the crime victims. Victims often report the crime to the police, but ultimately it is the D.A.'s office that decides whether to file criminal charges and to what extent to pursue the prosecution or carry out additional investigation.

 Beyond Our Borders **An Absence of Codified Criminal Law: The Pushtun Way**

The mountainous area spanning the border between southwestern Afghanistan and northwestern Pakistan is one of the most remote regions in the world. It is the home of about 28 million Pushtuns. With a well-below-average literacy rate and a population spread thinly over vast mountain ranges and steppes, the Pushtuns have shown little interest in written, codified criminal law. Instead, for millennia they have relied on a tribal code of ethics known as *Pushtunwali* to regulate behavior in their society.

The fundamental value of *Pushtunwali* is *nang,* or honor. A person who loses *nang* is effectively rejected by the community. A Pushtun's *nang* is closely related to his property–that is, his money, his land, and his women. If any of these are dishonored, the Pushtun is required by the code to take revenge. In one

recent example, a Pushtun businessman's daughter eloped against his wishes, fleeing to the Afghan capital of Kabul with her boyfriend. The businessman sold his land, tracked the couple to Kabul, and killed his daughter's lover. He promised to do the

Pakistani human rights activists held a protest over "honor" killings. Every year, mainly in rural areas in Pakistan, more than 4,000 people are killed in the name of family honor.

same to his daughter, who sought refuge with a Western human rights organization.

Under the rules of *Pushtunwali,* tribal councils called *jirga* are convened on a semiregular basis to moderate disputes. *Jirga* are composed of *spingeeri* ("white beards"), who make their decisions based on history, custom, and their own experience. At a recent *jirga,* after a Pushtun named Khan admitted to killing every male member of a rival family, the *spingeeri* decided that his punishment would be the destruction of two of his homes and a fine of 500,000 rupees (about $8,500).

For Critical Analysis
Should foreign governments pressure the Pushtuns to modify their criminal laws so that they are more in keeping with "modern" values? Why or why not?

Key Differences between Civil Law and Criminal Law

Because the state has extensive resources at its disposal when prosecuting criminal cases, there are procedural safeguards to protect the rights of defendants. We look here at one of these safeguards—the higher burden of proof that applies in a criminal case—as well as the harsher sanctions for criminal acts than for civil wrongs. Exhibit 6–1 below summarizes these and other key differences between civil law and criminal law.

BURDEN OF PROOF   In a civil case, the plaintiff usually must prove his or her case by a *preponderance of the evidence.* Under this standard, the plaintiff must convince the court that, based on the evidence presented by both parties, it is more likely than not that the plaintiff's allegation is true.

In a criminal case, in contrast, the state must prove its case **beyond a reasonable doubt.** If the jury views the evidence in the case as reasonably permitting either a guilty or a not guilty verdict, then the jury's verdict must be *not* guilty. In other words, the government (prosecutor) must prove beyond a reasonable doubt that the defendant committed every essential element of the offense with which she or he is charged. If the jurors are not convinced of the defendant's guilt beyond a reasonable doubt, they must find the defendant not guilty. Note also that in a criminal case, the jury's verdict normally must be unanimous—agreed to by all members of the jury—to convict the defendant.[2] (In a civil trial by jury, in contrast, typically only three-fourths of the jurors need to agree.)

CRIMINAL SANCTIONS   The sanctions imposed on criminal wrongdoers are also harsher than those that are applied in civil cases. Remember from Chapter 5 that the purpose of tort law is to allow persons harmed by the wrongful acts of others to obtain compensation from the wrongdoer rather than to punish the wrongdoer. In contrast, criminal sanctions are designed to punish those who commit crimes and to deter others from committing similar acts in the future. Criminal sanctions include

Beyond a Reasonable Doubt   The standard of proof used in criminal cases. If there is any reasonable doubt that a criminal defendant committed the crime with which she or he has been charged, then the verdict must be "not guilty."

---

2. Note that there are exceptions—a few states allow jury verdicts that are not unanimous. Arizona, for example, allows six of eight jurors to reach a verdict in criminal cases. Louisiana and Oregon have also relaxed the requirement of unanimous jury verdicts.

● *Exhibit* **6–1 Key Differences between Civil Law and Criminal Law**

ISSUE	CIVIL LAW	CRIMINAL LAW
Party who brings suit	The person who suffered harm.	The state.
Wrongful act	Causing harm to a person or to a person's property.	Violating a statute that prohibits some type of activity.
Burden of proof	Preponderance of the evidence.	Beyond a reasonable doubt.
Verdict	Three-fourths majority (typically).	Unanimous (almost always).
Remedy	Damages to compensate for the harm or a decree to achieve an equitable result.	Punishment (fine, imprisonment, or death).

fines as well as the much harsher penalty of the loss of one's liberty by incarceration in a jail or prison. The harshest criminal sanction is, of course, the death penalty.

Civil Liability for Criminal Acts

Some torts, such as assault and battery, provide a basis for a criminal prosecution as well as a tort action. **EXAMPLE 6.1**   Joe is walking down the street, minding his own business, when suddenly a passerby attacks him. In the ensuing struggle, the attacker stabs Joe several times, seriously injuring him. A police officer restrains and arrests the wrongdoer. In this situation, the attacker may be subject to both criminal prosecution by the state and a tort lawsuit brought by Joe. ● Exhibit 6–2 on the following page illustrates how the same act can result in both a tort action and a criminal action against the wrongdoer.

▶ Criminal Liability

Two elements must exist simultaneously for a person to be convicted of a crime: (1) the performance of a prohibited act and (2) a specified state of mind or intent on the part of the actor. Additionally, to establish criminal liability, there must be a *concurrence* between the act and the intent. In other words, these two elements must occur together.

The Criminal Act

Actus Reus   A guilty (prohibited) act. The commission of a prohibited act is one of the two essential elements required for criminal liability, the other element being the intent to commit a crime.

Every criminal statute prohibits certain behavior. Most crimes require an act of *commission,* meaning that a person must *do* something in order to be accused of a crime. In criminal law, a prohibited act is referred to as the ***actus reus***,[3] or guilty act. In some situations, an act of *omission* can be a crime, but only when a person has a legal duty to perform the omitted act, such as failing to file a tax return.

The *guilty act* requirement is based on one of the premises of criminal law—that a person is punished for harm done to society. For a crime to exist, the guilty act must cause some harm to a person or to property. Thinking about killing someone or about stealing a car may be wrong, but the thoughts do no harm until they are translated into action. Of course, a person can be punished for attempting murder or robbery, but normally only if he or she took substantial steps toward the criminal objective.

State of Mind

Mens Rea   Mental state, or intent. Normally, a wrongful mental state is as necessary as a wrongful act to establish criminal liability. What constitutes such a mental state varies according to the wrongful action. Thus, for murder, the *mens rea* is the intent to take a life.

A wrongful mental state (***mens rea***)[4] generally is required to establish criminal liability. What constitutes such a mental state varies according to the wrongful action. For murder, the act is the taking of a life, and the mental state is the intent to take life. For theft, the guilty act is the taking of another person's property, and the mental state involves both the knowledge that the property belongs to another and the intent to deprive the owner of it.

CRIMINAL NEGLIGENCE OR RECKLESSNESS   A court can also find that the required mental state is present when a defendant's acts are reckless or criminally negligent. A defendant is *criminally reckless* if he or she consciously disregards a

---

3. Pronounced *ak*-tuhs *ray*-uhs.
4. Pronounced *mehns ray*-uh.

• *Exhibit* 6-2 **Tort Lawsuit and Criminal Prosecution for the Same Act**

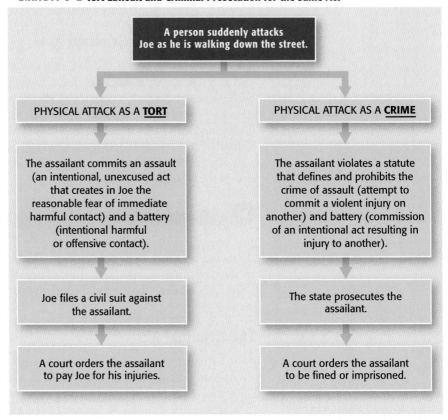

substantial and unjustifiable risk. *Criminal negligence* involves the mental state in which the defendant deviates from the standard of care that a reasonable person would use under the same circumstances. The defendant is accused of taking an unjustified, substantial, and foreseeable risk that resulted in harm. Under the Model Penal Code, criminal negligence has occurred if the defendant *should have foreseen* the risk, even if she or he was not actually aware of it.[5]

A homicide is classified as *involuntary manslaughter* when it results from an act of criminal negligence and there is no intent to kill. For example, in 2010, Dr. Conrad Murray, the personal physician of pop star Michael Jackson, was charged with involuntary manslaughter after a coroner determined that Jackson's sudden death in 2009 was the result of drug intoxication. Murray had given Jackson propofol, a powerful anesthetic normally used in surgery, as a sleep aid on the night of his death, even though he knew that Jackson had already taken other sedatives.

STRICT LIABILITY AND OVERCRIMINALIZATION   In recent years, an increasing number of laws and regulations have imposed criminal sanctions for strict liability crimes—that is, offenses that do not require a wrongful mental state to establish criminal liability. The federal criminal code now lists more than four thousand

---

5. Model Penal Code Section 2.02(2)(d).

criminal offenses, many of which do not require a specific mental state. There are also at least ten thousand federal rules that can be enforced through criminal sanctions, and many of these rules do not require intent. Strict liability crimes are particularly common in environmental laws, laws aimed at combating illegal drugs, and other laws affecting public health, safety, and welfare. Under federal law, for example, tenants can be evicted from public housing if one of their relatives or guests used illegal drugs—regardless of whether the tenant knew or should have known about the drug activity.[6]

Many states have also enacted laws that punish behavior as criminal without the need to show criminal intent. Under Arizona law, for instance, a hunter who shoots an elk outside the area specified by the permit has committed a crime, regardless of the hunter's intent or knowledge of the law.[7]

Although proponents of such laws argue that they are necessary to protect the public and the environment, critics say the laws have led to *overcriminalization,* or the use of criminal law to solve social problems, such as illegal drug use. These critics argue that the removal of the requirement of intent, or malice, from criminal offenses increases the likelihood that people will commit crimes unknowingly—and perhaps even innocently. When an honest mistake can lead to a criminal conviction, the idea that a crime is a wrong against society is undermined.

Corporate Criminal Liability

As will be discussed in Chapter 15, a *corporation* is a legal entity created under the laws of a state. At one time, it was thought that a corporation could not incur criminal liability because, although a corporation is a legal person, it can act only through its agents (corporate directors, officers, and employees). Therefore, the corporate entity itself could not "intend" to commit a crime. Over time, this view has changed. Obviously, corporations cannot be imprisoned, but they can be fined or denied certain legal privileges (such as a license).

LIABILITY OF THE CORPORATE ENTITY Today, corporations normally are liable for the crimes committed by their agents and employees within the course and scope of their employment. For such criminal liability to be imposed, the prosecutor typically must show that the corporation could have prevented the act or that a supervisor within the corporation authorized or had knowledge of the act. In addition, corporations can be criminally liable for failing to perform specific duties imposed by law.

CASE EXAMPLE 6.2 A prostitution ring, the Gold Club, was operating out of Economy Inn and Scottish Inn motels in West Virginia. A motel manager gave discounted rates to the prostitutes, and they paid him in cash. The corporation that owned the motels received a portion of the funds generated by the Gold Club's illegal operations. At trial, a jury found that the corporation was criminally liable because a supervisor within the corporation—the motel manager—knew of the prostitution and the corporation allowed it to continue.[8] ●

---

6. See, for example, *Department of Housing and Urban Development v. Rucker,* 535 U.S. 125, 122 S.Ct. 1230, 152 L.Ed.2d 258 (2002).

7. See, for example, *State v. Slayton and Remmert,* 1 CA-SA 06-0208 (Ariz.Ct.App. 2007).

8. The motel manager was sentenced to fifteen months in prison, and the corporation was ordered to forfeit the Scottish Inn property. *United States v. Singh,* 518 F.3d 236 (4th Cir. 2008).

LIABILITY OF CORPORATE OFFICERS AND DIRECTORS   Corporate directors and officers are personally liable for the crimes they commit, regardless of whether the crimes were committed for their personal benefit or on the corporation's behalf. Additionally, corporate directors and officers may be held liable for the actions of employees under their supervision. Under what has become known as the *responsible corporate officer doctrine,* a court may impose criminal liability on a corporate officer regardless of whether she or he participated in, directed, or even knew about a given criminal violation.

CASE EXAMPLE 6.3   The Roscoe family owned The Customer Company, a corporation that operated an underground storage tank that leaked gasoline. After the leak occurred, an employee, John Johnson, notified the state environmental agency, and the Roscoes hired an environmental services firm to clean up the spill. The clean-up did not occur immediately, however, and the state sent many notices to John Roscoe, a corporate officer, warning him that the company was violating federal and state laws. Roscoe gave the letters to Johnson, who passed them on to the environmental services firm, but nothing was cleaned up. The state eventually filed criminal charges against the corporation and the Roscoes individually, and they were convicted. On appeal, the court affirmed the Roscoes' convictions under the responsible corporate officer doctrine. The Roscoes were in positions of responsibility, they had influence over the corporation's actions, and their failure to act caused a violation of environmental laws.[9] ●

Preventing Legal Disputes

If you become a corporate officer or director at some point in your career, you need to be aware that you can be held liable for the crimes of your subordinates. You should always be familiar with any criminal statutes relevant to the corporation's particular industry or trade. Also, make sure that corporate employees are trained in how to comply with the multitude of applicable laws, particularly environmental laws and health and safety regulations, which frequently involve criminal sanctions.

▶ Types of Crimes

Federal, state, and local laws provide for the classification and punishment of hundreds of thousands of different criminal acts. Traditionally, though, crimes have been grouped into five broad categories, or types: violent crime (crimes against persons), property crime, public order crime, white-collar crime, and organized crime. Within each of these categories, crimes may also be separated into more than one classification. Note also that many crimes may be committed in cyberspace, as well as the physical world. When they occur in the virtual world, we refer to them as cyber crimes, as discussed later in the chapter.

Violent Crime

Robbery   The act of forcefully and unlawfully taking personal property of any value from another. Force or intimidation is usually necessary for an act of theft to be considered a robbery.

Crimes against persons, because they cause others to suffer harm or death, are referred to as *violent crimes.* Murder is a violent crime. So, too, is sexual assault, or rape. **Robbery**—defined as the taking of cash, personal property, or any other article of value from a person by means of force or fear—is another violent crime. Typically,

---

9. The Roscoes and the corporation were sentenced to pay penalties of $2,493,250. *People v. Roscoe,* 169 Cal.App.4th 829, 87 Cal.Rptr.3d 187 (3 Dist. 2008).

(Jewel Samad/AFP/Getty Images)

Police have cordoned off a crime scene after a shooting in Covina, California. What are the other categories of crimes besides violent crime?

states impose more severe penalties for *aggravated robbery*—robbery with the use of a deadly weapon.

Assault and battery, which were discussed in Chapter 5 in the context of tort law, are also classified as violent crimes. Remember that assault can involve an object or force put into motion by a person. **EXAMPLE 6.4** In 2009, on the anniversary of an abortion rights ruling, a man drove his vehicle into an abortion clinic building in Saint Paul, Minnesota. The police arrested him for aggravated assault, even though no one was injured. ●

Each of these violent crimes is further classified by degree, depending on the circumstances surrounding the criminal act. These circumstances include the intent of the person who committed the crime, whether a weapon was used, and (in cases other than murder) the level of pain and suffering experienced by the victim.

Property Crime

The most common type of criminal activity is property crime—crimes in which the goal of the offender is to obtain some form of economic gain or to damage property. Robbery is a form of property crime, as well as a violent crime, because the offender seeks to gain the property of another. We look here at a number of other crimes that fall within the general category of property crime. (Note also that many types of cyber crime, discussed later in this chapter, are forms of property crime as well.)

Burglary The unlawful entry or breaking into a building with the intent to commit a felony. (Some state statutes expand this to include the intent to commit any crime.)

BURGLARY Traditionally, **burglary** was defined under the common law as breaking and entering the dwelling of another at night with the intent to commit a felony. Originally, the definition was aimed at protecting an individual's home and its occupants. Most state statutes have eliminated some of the requirements found in the common law definition. The time of day at which the breaking and entering occurs, for example, is usually immaterial. State statutes frequently omit the element of breaking, and some states do not require that the building be a dwelling. When a deadly weapon is used in a burglary, the person can be charged with *aggravated burglary* and punished more severely.

Larceny The wrongful taking and carrying away of another person's personal property with the intent to permanently deprive the owner of the property. Some states classify larceny as either grand or petit, depending on the property's value.

LARCENY Under the common law, the crime of **larceny** involved the unlawful taking and carrying away of someone else's personal property with the intent to permanently deprive the owner of possession. Put simply, larceny is stealing or theft. Whereas robbery involves force or fear, larceny does not. Therefore, picking pockets is larceny, not robbery. Similarly, taking company products and supplies home for personal use without authorization is larceny. (Note that a person who commits larceny generally can also be sued under tort law because the act of taking possession of another's property involves a trespass to personal property.)

Most states have expanded the definition of property that is subject to larceny statutes. Stealing computer programs or computer time may constitute larceny even though the "property" consists of magnetic impulses. So, too, can the theft of natural gas or Internet and television cable service. The common law distinguished between grand and petit larceny depending on the value of the property taken. Many states have abolished this distinction, but in those that have not, grand larceny (or theft) is a felony, and petit larceny (or theft) is a misdemeanor.

OBTAINING GOODS BY FALSE PRETENSES It is a criminal act to obtain goods by means of false pretenses, such as buying groceries with a check knowing that you have insufficient funds to cover it or offering to sell someone the latest iPad knowing

(Creative Commons)

This California home was damaged by arson. If the owner of the home hired someone to burn it down, what crimes has the owner committed?

Arson The intentional burning of another's building. Some statutes have expanded this to include any real property regardless of ownership and the destruction of property by other means—for example, by explosion.

Forgery The fraudulent making or altering of any writing in a way that changes the legal rights and liabilities of another.

that you do not actually own the iPad. Statutes dealing with such illegal activities vary widely from state to state.

RECEIVING STOLEN GOODS   It is a crime to receive stolen goods. The recipient of such goods need not know the true identity of the owner or the thief. All that is necessary is that the recipient knows or should have known that the goods are stolen, which implies an intent to deprive the owner of those goods.

ARSON   The willful and malicious burning of a building (and, in some states, personal property) owned by another is the crime of **arson.** At common law, arson traditionally applied only to burning down another person's house. The law was designed to protect human life. Today, arson statutes have been extended to cover the destruction of any building, regardless of ownership, by fire or explosion.

Every state has a special statute that covers the act of burning a building for the purpose of collecting insurance. **EXAMPLE 6.5**   Benton owns an insured apartment building that is falling apart. If he sets fire to it himself or pays someone else to do so, he is guilty not only of arson but also of defrauding the insurer, which is attempted larceny. ● Of course, the insurer need not pay the claim when insurance fraud is proved.

FORGERY   The fraudulent making or altering of any writing (including electronic records) in a way that changes the legal rights and liabilities of another is **forgery.** **EXAMPLE 6.6**   Without authorization, Severson signs Bennett's name to the back of a check made out to Bennett and attempts to cash it. Severson has committed the crime of forgery. ● Forgery also includes changing trademarks, falsifying public records, counterfeiting, and altering a legal document.

Public Order Crime

Historically, societies have always outlawed activities that are considered to be contrary to public values and morals. Today, the most common public order crimes include public drunkenness, prostitution, gambling, and illegal drug use.

These crimes are sometimes referred to as victimless crimes because they normally harm only the offender. From a broader perspective, however, they are deemed detrimental to society as a whole because they may create an environment that gives rise to property and violent crimes. **EXAMPLE 6.7**   A man flying from Texas to California on a commercial airliner becomes angry and yells obscenities at a flight attendant when a beverage cart strikes his knee. After the pilot diverts the plane and makes an unscheduled landing at a nearby airport, police remove the passenger and arrest him. If the man is subsequently found guilty of the public order crime of interfering with a flight crew, he may be sentenced to more than two years in prison. ●

White-Collar Crime

White-Collar Crime Nonviolent crime committed by individuals or corporations to obtain a personal or business advantage.

Crimes that typically occur only in the business context are popularly referred to as **white-collar crimes.** Although there is no official definition of white-collar crime, the term is commonly used to mean an illegal act or series of acts committed by an individual or business entity using some nonviolent means. Usually, this kind of crime is committed in the course of a legitimate occupation. Corporate crimes fall into this category. In addition, certain property crimes, such as larceny and forgery, may also be white-collar crimes if they occur within the business context.

EMBEZZLEMENT   When a person who is entrusted with another person's funds or property fraudulently appropriates it, **embezzlement** occurs. Typically, embezzlement is carried out by an employee who steals funds. Banks are particularly prone to this problem, but embezzlement can occur in any firm. In a number of businesses, corporate officers or accountants have fraudulently converted funds for their own benefit and then "fixed" the books to cover up their crime. Embezzlement is not larceny, because the wrongdoer does not physically take the property from the possession of another, and it is not robbery, because force or fear is not used.

Embezzlement occurs whether the embezzler takes the funds directly from the victim or from a third person. If the financial officer of a large corporation pockets checks from third parties that were given to her to deposit into the corporate account, she is embezzling. Frequently, an embezzler takes a relatively small amount at one time but does so repeatedly over a long period. This might be done by underreporting income or deposits and embezzling the remaining amount, for example, or by creating fictitious persons or accounts and writing checks to them from the corporate account. Even an employer's failure to remit state withholding taxes that were collected from employee wages can constitute embezzlement.

Practically speaking, an embezzler who returns what has been taken may not be prosecuted because the owner is unwilling to take the time to make a complaint, cooperate with the state's investigative efforts, and appear in court. Also, the owner may not want the crime to become public knowledge. Nevertheless, the intent to return the embezzled property—or its actual return—is not a defense to the crime of embezzlement, as the following case illustrates.

Embezzlement The fraudulent appropriation of funds or other property by a person to whom the funds or property has been entrusted.

"It was beautiful and simple as all truly great swindles are."
O. Henry, 1862–1910
(American writer)

Case 6.1   People v. Sisuphan

Court of Appeal of California, First District, 181 Cal.App.4th 800, 104 Cal.Rptr.3d 654 (2010).

If a Toyota dealership's employee returns embezzled funds, should he still be prosecuted?

BACKGROUND AND FACTS
Lou Sisuphan was the director of finance at a Toyota dealership. His responsibilities included managing the financing contracts for vehicle sales and working with lenders to obtain payments. Sisuphan complained repeatedly to management about the performance and attitude of one of the finance managers, Ian McClelland. The general manager, Michael Christian, would not terminate McClelland "because he brought a lot of money into the dealership." One day, McClelland accepted $22,600 in cash and two checks totaling $7,275.51 from a customer in payment for a car. McClelland placed the cash, the checks, and a copy of the receipt in a large envelope. As he tried to drop the envelope into the safe through a mechanism at its top, the envelope became stuck. While McClelland went for assistance, Sisuphan wiggled

the envelope free and kept it. On McClelland's return, Sisuphan told him that the envelope had dropped into the safe. When the payment turned up missing, Christian told all the managers he would not bring criminal charges if the payment was returned within twenty-four hours. After the twenty-four-hour period had lapsed, Sisuphan told Christian that he had taken the envelope, and he returned the cash and checks to Christian. Sisuphan claimed that he had no intention of stealing the payment but had taken it to get McClelland fired. Christian fired Sisuphan the next day, and the district attorney later charged Sisuphan with embezzlement. After a jury trial, Sisuphan was found guilty. Sisuphan appealed, arguing that the trial court had erred by excluding evidence that he had returned the payment. The trial court had concluded that the evidence was not relevant because return of the property is not a defense to embezzlement.

Case 6.1–Continues next page ➡

Case 6.1–Continued

IN THE WORDS OF THE COURT . . .
JENKINS, J. [Judge]
* * * *

Fraudulent intent is an essential element of embezzlement. Although restoration of the property is not a defense, evidence of repayment may be relevant to the extent it shows that a defendant's intent at the time of the taking was not fraudulent. Such evidence is admissible "only when [a] defendant shows a relevant and probative [tending to prove] link in his subsequent actions from which it might be inferred his original intent was innocent." The question before us, therefore, is whether evidence that Sisuphan returned the money reasonably tends to prove he lacked the requisite intent at the time of the taking. [Emphasis added.]

Section 508 [of the California Penal Code], which sets out the offense of which Sisuphan was convicted, provides: "Every clerk, agent, or servant of any person who fraudulently appropriates to his own use, or secretes with a fraudulent intent to appropriate to his own use, any property of another which has come into his control or care by virtue of his employment * * * is guilty of embezzlement." Sisuphan denies he ever intended "to use the [money] to financially better himself, even temporarily" and contends the evidence he sought to introduce showed "he returned the [money] without having appropriated it to his own use in any way." He argues that this evidence negates fraudulent intent because it supports his claim that he took the money to get McClelland fired and acted "to help his company by drawing attention to the inadequacy and incompetency of an employee." We reject these contentions.

In determining whether Sisuphan's intent was fraudulent at the time of the taking, the issue is not whether he intended to spend the money, but whether he intended to use it for a purpose other than that for which the dealership entrusted it to him. *The offense of embezzlement contemplates a principal's entrustment of property to an agent for certain purposes and the agent's breach of that trust by acting outside his authority in his use of the property.* * * * Sisuphan's undisputed purpose–to get McClelland fired–was beyond the scope of his responsibility and therefore outside the trust afforded him by the dealership. Accordingly, even if the proffered [submitted] evidence shows he took the money for this purpose, it does not tend to prove he lacked fraudulent intent, and the trial court properly excluded this evidence. [Emphasis added.]

DECISION AND REMEDY   The California appellate court affirmed the trial court's decision. The fact that Sisuphan had returned the payment was irrelevant. He was guilty of embezzlement.

THE LEGAL ENVIRONMENT DIMENSION   *Why was Sisuphan convicted of embezzlement instead of larceny? What is the difference between these two crimes?*

THE ETHICAL DIMENSION   *Given that Sisuphan returned the cash, was it fair for the dealership's general manager to terminate Sisuphan's employment? Why or why not?*

MAIL AND WIRE FRAUD   One of the most potent weapons against white-collar criminals is the Mail Fraud Act of 1990.[10] Under this act, it is a federal crime (mail fraud) to use the mails to defraud the public. Illegal use of the mails must involve (1) mailing or causing someone else to mail a writing—something written, printed, or photocopied—for the purpose of executing a scheme to defraud and (2) a contemplated or an organized scheme to defraud by false pretenses.

Federal law also makes it a crime to use wire (for example, the telephone), radio, or television transmissions to defraud.[11] Violators may be fined up to $1,000, imprisoned for up to five years, or both. If the violation affects a financial institution, the violator may be fined up to $1 million, imprisoned for up to thirty years, or both.

CASE EXAMPLE 6.8   Gabriel Sanchez and Timothy Lyons set up six charities and formed a fund-raising company, North American Acquisitions (NAA), to solicit donations on the charities' behalf through telemarketing. NAA raised more than $6 million, of which less than $5,000 was actually spent on charitable causes. The telemarketers kept 80 percent of the donated funds as commissions, the NAA took 10 percent, and most of the rest went to Sanchez, who spent the funds on himself. Lyons and Sanchez were both prosecuted for mail fraud and sentenced to fifteen years in prison. They appealed. A federal appellate court affirmed their convictions,

---

10. 18 U.S.C. Sections 1341–1342.
11. 18 U.S.C. Section 1343.

(AP Photo/Kathy Willens)

Bernard Madoff (center) leaves a U.S. district court in New York. Over a thirty-year period, he engaged in the largest Ponzi scheme ever, bilking his clients and others out of $65 billion. Why were his criminal actions not a type of larceny?

ruling that the government can use these antifraud laws to prohibit professional fund-raisers from obtaining funds through false pretenses or by making false statements.[12] ●

Although most fraudulent schemes involve cheating the victim out of tangible property (funds), it can also be a crime to deprive a person of an intangible right to another's honest services. For a discussion of "honest-services fraud," see this chapter's *Insight into Ethics* feature on the next page.

BRIBERY   The crime of bribery involves offering to give something of value to someone in an attempt to influence that person, who usually, but not always, is a public official, to act in a way that serves a private interest. Three types of bribery are considered crimes: bribery of public officials, commercial bribery, and bribery of foreign officials. As an element of the crime of bribery, intent must be present and proved. The bribe itself can be anything the recipient considers to be valuable. Realize that the *crime of bribery occurs when the bribe is offered*—it is not required that the bribe be accepted. *Accepting a bribe* is a separate crime.

Commercial bribery involves corrupt dealings between private persons or businesses. Typically, people make commercial bribes to obtain proprietary information, cover up an inferior product, or secure new business. Industrial espionage sometimes involves commercial bribes. **EXAMPLE 6.9** Kent works at the firm of Jacoby & Meyers. He offers to pay Laurel, an employee in a competing firm, in exchange for that firm's trade secrets and price schedules. Kent has committed commercial bribery. ● So-called kickbacks, or payoffs for special favors or services, are a form of commercial bribery in some situations. Bribing foreign officials to obtain favorable business contracts is a crime. The Foreign Corrupt Practices Act of 1977 was passed to curb the use of bribery by U.S. businesspersons in securing foreign contracts.

BANKRUPTCY FRAUD   Federal bankruptcy law (see Chapter 12) allows individuals and businesses to be relieved of oppressive debt through bankruptcy proceedings. Numerous white-collar crimes may be committed during the many phases of a bankruptcy proceeding. A creditor, for example, may file a false claim against the debtor. Also, a debtor may attempt to protect assets from creditors by fraudulently transferring property to favored parties. For instance, a company-owned automobile may be "sold" at a bargain price to a trusted friend or relative. Closely related to the crime of fraudulent transfer of property is the crime of fraudulent concealment of property, such as hiding gold coins.

THE THEFT OF TRADE SECRETS AND OTHER INTELLECTUAL PROPERTY   As will be discussed in Chapter 8, trade secrets constitute a form of intellectual property that can be extremely valuable for many businesses. The Economic Espionage Act of 1996[13] made the theft of trade secrets a federal crime. The act also made it a federal crime to buy or possess trade secrets of another person, knowing that the trade secrets were stolen or otherwise acquired without the owner's authorization.

Violations of the act can result in steep penalties. An individual who violates the act can be imprisoned for up to ten years and fined up to $500,000. If a

---

12. *United States v. Lyons,* 569 F.3d 995 (9th Cir. 2009).
13. 18 U.S.C. Sections 1831–1839.

Insight into Ethics — Prosecuting White-Collar Crime with the Honest-Services Fraud Law

What do former Enron chief executive officer (CEO) Jeffrey Skilling, former Hollinger International CEO Conrad Black, and former Illinois governor Rod Blagojevich have in common? They, along with thousands of other individuals, had been charged under the "honest-services fraud" law. Indeed, 95 percent of the high-profile, white-collar crime cases in recent years have involved individuals who have been charged under this law.

What Is the Honest-Services Fraud Law?

The honest-services fraud law dates back to 1988 and consists of only twenty-eight words. The law, set forth in Section 1346 of Title XVIII of the *United States Code,* is broad enough to encompass just about every conceivable white-collar criminal act. Consequently, it has allowed federal prosecutors to attempt to impose criminal penalties on a broad swath of misconduct by public officials and employees, as well as private employees and corporate directors and officers. The key to the law is that it requires individuals to provide the "intangible right of honest services" to their employers.

Critics point out that the law is used when the purported crime committed is "fuzzy." When a businessperson is charged with honest-services fraud, there is often a nagging question as to whether the actions involved were truly a crime or just aggressive business behavior.

How Congress Got Involved

Under the U.S. Constitution, the federal government does not have the power to punish fraud directly, but it does have the power to regulate the U.S. mails and interstate commerce. In the 1970s, federal prosecutors started using the federal laws against mail and wire fraud whenever such actions deprived someone of funds or property. Then, a federal prosecutor used the legal theory that a fraudulent action to deprive the public of "honest services" is equivalent to a theft of intangible rights. In 1987, however, the United States Supreme Court rejected this concept of honest services.[a]

Not happy with the Court's ruling, federal prosecutors pleaded with Congress to pass a new law. Congress subsequently created a law stating that any scheme to deprive another of honest services will be considered a scheme to defraud. Courts have at times described honest-services fraud as simply the situation in which the public does not get what it wants and deserves—that is, honest, faithful, disinterested services from employees, whether they be public or private.

Interestingly, criminal fraud requires that a victim be cheated out of tangible property, such as funds. Honest-services fraud changes that concept. It involves depriving the victim of an intangible right to another's honest services.

The Law Has Been Applied Widely

Federal prosecutors have used the honest-services fraud law since 1988 in a variety of situations. In Texas, federal prosecutors successfully brought a charge against three coaches at Baylor University (a private school) for scheming to obtain scholarships for players. In California, federal prosecutors have used the honest-services legal theory to investigate the hierarchy of the Catholic Archdiocese of Los Angeles. Top church officials are being accused of covering up sexual abuse of minors by priests.

The United States Supreme Court Decides

In 2010, the United States Supreme Court issued a ruling that could have a major impact on white-collar crime and political fraud cases in the future. The Court ruled that the honest-services fraud law could not be used against Jeffrey Skilling, who had been convicted for his role in the collapse of Enron.[b] According to the Court, honest-services fraud can be applied only in cases that involve bribes and kickbacks. Because there was no evidence that Skilling had solicited or accepted side payments from a third party in exchange for making misrepresentations about the company, he did not commit honest-services fraud.

The Court did not overturn Skilling's conviction, however. Instead, the Court left it up to the lower court to determine whether Skilling's conviction could be upheld on other grounds. In addition, the Court remanded the honest-services fraud conviction of Conrad Black—who defrauded his media company—for the same reason.[c] In fact, the Court remanded numerous honest-services fraud cases for reconsideration in light of its decision. On remand, nevertheless, many of these convictions have been allowed to stand.[d]

FOR CRITICAL ANALYSIS
Insight into the Social Environment

Does the prosecution of high-profile white-collar defendants for honest-services fraud really deter future criminal conduct? Why or why not?

---

a. *McNally v. United States,* 483 U.S. 350, 107 S.Ct. 2875, 97 L.Ed.2d 292 (1987).

b. *Skilling v. United States,* ___ U.S. ___, 130 S.Ct. 2896, 177 L.Ed.d 619 (2010). See Case 2.1 on pages 33 and 34 of Chapter 2.

c. See *Black v. United States,* ___ U.S. ___, 130 S.Ct. 2963, 177 L.Ed.2d 695 (2010).

d. See, for example, *United States v. Alcorn,* 638 F.3d 819 (8th Cir. 2011); and *United States v. Pelisamen,* 641 F.3d 399 (9th Cir. 2011).

corporation or other organization violates the act, it can be fined up to $5 million. Additionally, the law provides that any property acquired as a result of the violation, such as airplanes and automobiles, along with any property used in the commission of the violation, such as computers and other electronic devices, are subject to criminal *forfeiture*—meaning that the government can take the property. A theft of trade secrets conducted via the Internet, for example, could result in the forfeiture of every computer or other device used to commit or facilitate the crime.

The unauthorized copying and use of intellectual property, such as books, films, music, and software—commonly known as pirating—is also a crime under federal law. It has been estimated that 35 percent of all business software is pirated, as is nearly 95 percent of downloaded music. In the United States, digital pirates can be criminally prosecuted under the Digital Millennium Copyright Act.[14] An individual who violates the act for purposes of financial gain can be imprisoned for up to five years and fined up to $500,000 on a first offense. The punishment doubles for any subsequent offense.

INSIDER TRADING   An individual who obtains *inside information*—that is, information that has not been made available to the public—about the plans of a publicly listed corporation can often make stock-trading profits by purchasing or selling corporate securities based on the information. Insider trading is a violation of securities law and will be considered more fully in Chapter 24.

Organized Crime

As mentioned, white-collar crime takes place within the confines of the legitimate business world. *Organized crime,* in contrast, operates *illegitimately* by, among other things, providing illegal goods and services. For organized crime, the traditional preferred markets are gambling, prostitution, illegal narcotics, and loan sharking (lending at higher than legal interest rates), along with counterfeiting and credit-card scams.

MONEY LAUNDERING   The profits from organized crime and illegal activities amount to billions of dollars a year, particularly the profits from illegal drug transactions and, to a lesser extent, from racketeering, prostitution, and gambling. Under federal law, banks, savings and loan associations, and other financial institutions are required to report currency transactions involving more than $10,000. Consequently, those who engage in illegal activities face difficulties in depositing their cash profits from illegal transactions.

As an alternative to simply storing cash from illegal transactions in a safe-deposit box, wrongdoers and racketeers have invented ways to launder "dirty" money through legitimate businesses to make it "clean." **Money laundering** is engaging in financial transactions to conceal the identity, source, or destination of illegally gained funds.

Money Laundering   Engaging in financial transactions to conceal the identity, source, or destination of illegally gained funds.

EXAMPLE 6.10   Harris, a successful drug dealer, becomes a partner with a restaurateur. Little by little, the restaurant shows increasing profits. As a partner in the restaurant, Harris is able to report the "profits" of the restaurant as legitimate income on which he pays federal and state taxes. He can then spend those funds without worrying that his lifestyle may exceed the level possible with his reported income. •

---

14. 17 U.S.C. Sections 2301 *et seq.*

Joseph "Joey the Clown" Lombardo is a reputed mob boss in Chicago. The federal government successfully prosecuted him as a leader of that city's major organized crime family and for the murder of a government witness in a union pension fraud case. How do members of organized crime entities typically obtain revenues for their organization?

Felony A crime—such as arson, murder, rape, or robbery—that carries the most severe sanctions, ranging from one year in a state or federal prison to the death penalty.

Misdemeanor A lesser crime than a felony, punishable by a fine or incarceration in jail for up to one year.

Petty Offense In criminal law, the least serious kind of criminal offense, such as a traffic or building-code violation.

THE RACKETEER INFLUENCED AND CORRUPT ORGANIZATIONS ACT   In 1970, in an effort to curb the apparently increasing entry of organized crime into the legitimate business world, Congress passed the Racketeer Influenced and Corrupt Organizations Act (RICO).[15] The statute, which was enacted as part of the Organized Crime Control Act, makes it a federal crime to (1) use income obtained from racketeering activity to purchase any interest in an enterprise, (2) acquire or maintain an interest in an enterprise through racketeering activity, (3) conduct or participate in the affairs of an enterprise through racketeering activity, or (4) conspire to do any of the preceding activities.

RICO incorporates by reference twenty-six separate types of federal crimes and nine types of state felonies and declares that if a person commits two of these offenses, he or she is guilty of "racketeering activity." Under the criminal provisions of RICO, any individual found guilty is subject to a fine of up to $25,000 per violation, imprisonment for up to twenty years, or both. Additionally, the statute provides that those who violate RICO may be required to forfeit (give up) any assets, in the form of property or cash, that were acquired as a result of the illegal activity or that were "involved in" or an "instrumentality of" the activity.

In the event of a RICO violation, the government can seek civil penalties, including the divestiture of a defendant's interest in a business (called forfeiture) or the dissolution of the business. Moreover, in some cases, the statute allows private individuals to sue violators and potentially recover three times their actual losses (treble damages), plus attorneys' fees, for business injuries caused by a violation of the statute. This is perhaps the most controversial aspect of RICO and one that continues to cause debate in the nation's federal courts.

Classification of Crimes

Depending on their degree of seriousness, crimes typically are classified as felonies or misdemeanors. **Felonies** are serious crimes punishable by death or by imprisonment for more than a year. Many states also define different degrees of felony offenses and vary the punishment according to the degree. **Misdemeanors** are less serious crimes, punishable by a fine or by confinement for up to a year. In most jurisdictions, **petty offenses** are considered to be a subset of misdemeanors. Petty offenses are minor violations, such as jaywalking and violations of building codes. Even for petty offenses, however, a guilty party can be put in jail for a few days, fined, or both, depending on state or local law.

▶ Defenses to Criminal Liability

Persons charged with crimes may be relieved of criminal liability if they can show that their criminal actions were justified under the circumstances. In certain circumstances, the law may also allow a person to be excused from criminal liability because she or he lacks the required mental state. We look at several of the defenses to criminal liability here.

Note that procedural violations, such as obtaining evidence without a valid search warrant, may also operate as defenses. As you will read later in this chapter, evidence obtained in violation of a defendant's constitutional rights normally may not be admitted in court. If the evidence is suppressed, then there may be no basis for prosecuting the defendant.

---

15. 18 U.S.C. Sections 1961–1968.

Justifiable Use of Force

Self-Defense The legally recognized privilege to protect oneself or one's property against injury by another. The privilege of self-defense usually applies only to acts that are reasonably necessary to protect oneself, one's property, or another person.

Probably the best-known defense to criminal liability is **self-defense.** Other situations, however, also justify the use of force: the defense of one's dwelling, the defense of other property, and the prevention of a crime. In all of these situations, it is important to distinguish between deadly and nondeadly force. *Deadly force* is likely to result in death or serious bodily harm. *Nondeadly force* is force that reasonably appears necessary to prevent the imminent use of criminal force.

Generally speaking, people can use the amount of nondeadly force that seems necessary to protect themselves, their dwellings, or other property or to prevent the commission of a crime. Deadly force can be used in self-defense if the defender *reasonably believes* that imminent death or grievous bodily harm will otherwise result, if the attacker is using unlawful force (an example of lawful force is that exerted by a police officer), and if the defender has not initiated or provoked the attack. Deadly force normally can be used to defend a dwelling only if the unlawful entry is violent and the person believes deadly force is necessary to prevent imminent death or great bodily harm. In some jurisdictions, however, deadly force can also be used if the person believes it is necessary to prevent the commission of a felony in the dwelling. Many states are expanding the situations in which the use of deadly force can be justified (see this chapter's *Management Perspective* feature on the next page for further discussion).

Necessity

Sometimes, criminal defendants can be relieved of liability by showing that a criminal act was necessary to prevent an even greater harm. **EXAMPLE 6.11** Trevor is a convicted felon and, as such, is legally prohibited from possessing a firearm. While he and his wife are in a convenience store, a man draws a gun, points it at the cashier, and asks for all the cash. Afraid that the man will start shooting, Trevor grabs the gun and holds onto it until police arrive. In this situation, if Trevor is charged with possession of a firearm, he can assert the defense of necessity. •

Insanity

Donna Boston is the mother of Michael Delodge, shown with her in the photo she is holding. Delodge was the boyfriend of Sheila LaBarre, who murdered him, claiming that she was "an angel sent from God" to punish pedophiles. The jury rejected her insanity defense. What are some of the tests for sanity?

A person who suffers from a mental illness may be incapable of the state of mind required to commit a crime. Thus, insanity can be a defense to a criminal charge. Note that an insanity defense does not allow a person to avoid prison. It simply means that if the defendant successfully proves insanity, she or he will be placed in a mental institution.

The courts have had difficulty deciding what the test for legal insanity should be, and psychiatrists as well as lawyers are critical of the tests used. Almost all federal courts and some states use the relatively liberal substantial capacity test set forth in the Model Penal Code:

> A person is not responsible for criminal conduct if at the time of such conduct as a result of mental disease or defect he or she lacks substantial capacity either to appreciate the wrongfulness of his [or her] conduct or to conform his [or her] conduct to the requirements of the law.

Some states use the *M'Naghten* test,[16] under which a criminal defendant is not responsible if, at the time of the offense, he or she did not know the nature and quality of the act or did not know that the act was wrong. Other states use the

---

16. A rule derived from *M'Naghten's Case*, 8 Eng.Rep. 718 (1843).

Management Perspective   Can a Businessperson Use Deadly Force to Prevent a Crime on the Premises?

Management Faces a Legal Issue

Traditionally, the justifiable use of force, or self-defense, doctrine required prosecutors to distinguish between deadly and nondeadly force. In general, state laws have allowed individuals to use the amount of *nondeadly force* that is reasonably necessary to protect themselves or their dwellings, businesses, or other property. Most states have allowed a person to use *deadly force* only when the person reasonably believed that imminent death or bodily harm would otherwise result. Additionally, the attacker had to be using unlawful force, and the defender had to have no other possible response or alternative way out of the life-threatening situation.

What the Courts Say

Today, many states still have "duty-to-retreat" laws. Under these laws, when a person's home is invaded or an assailant approaches, the person is required to retreat and cannot use deadly force unless her or his life is in danger.[a] Other states, however, are taking a very different approach and expanding the occasions when deadly force can be used in self-defense. Because such laws allow or even encourage the defender to stay and use force, they are known as "stand-your-ground" laws.

Florida, for example, enacted a statute in 2005 that allows the use of deadly force to prevent the commission of a "forcible felony," including not only murder but also such crimes as robbery, carjacking, and sexual battery.[b] Under this law, a Florida resident has a right to shoot an intruder in his or her home or a would-be carjacker even if there is no physical threat to the owner's safety. Similar laws that eliminate the duty to retreat have been passed in at least thirteen other states, including Arizona, Georgia, Idaho, Indiana, Kansas, Kentucky, Louisiana, Michigan, Oklahoma, South Carolina, South Dakota, Tennessee, and Texas.

In a number of states, a person may use deadly force to prevent someone from breaking into his or her home, car, or place of business. For example, courts in Louisiana now allow a person who is lawfully in a home, car, or place of business to use deadly force to repel an attack without imposing any duty to retreat.[c] Courts in Connecticut allow the use of deadly force not only to prevent a person from unlawful entry, but also when reasonably necessary to prevent arson or some other violent crime from being committed on the premises.[d]

Implications for Managers

The stand-your-ground laws that many states have enacted often include places of business as well as homes and vehicles. Consequently, businesspersons in those states can be less concerned about the duty-to-retreat doctrine. In addition, business liability insurance often costs less in states without a duty to retreat, because many statutes provide that the business owner is not liable in a civil action for injuries to the attacker. Even in states that impose a duty to retreat, there is no duty to retreat if doing so would increase rather than diminish the danger. Nevertheless, business owners should use deadly force only as a last resort to prevent the commission of crime at their business premises.

---

a. See, for example, *State v. Sandoval,* 342 Or. 506, 156 P.3d 60 (2007).
b. Florida Statutes Section 776.012.

c. See, for example, *State v. Johnson,* 948 So.2d 1229 (La.App. 3d Cir. 2007); and Lousiana Statutes Annotated Section 14:20.
d. See, for example, *State v. Terwilliger,* 105 Conn.App. 219, 937 A.2d 735 (2008); and Connecticut General Statutes Section 53a-20.

---

irresistible-impulse test. A person operating under an irresistible impulse may know an act is wrong but cannot refrain from doing it. Under any of these tests, proving insanity is extremely difficult. For this reason, the insanity defense is rarely used and usually is not successful.

Mistake

Everyone has heard the saying "Ignorance of the law is no excuse." Ordinarily, ignorance of the law or a mistaken idea about what the law requires is not a valid defense. A *mistake of fact,* as opposed to a *mistake of law,* can excuse criminal responsibility if it negates the mental state necessary to commit a crime. **EXAMPLE 6.12** If Oliver Wheaton mistakenly walks off with Julie Tyson's briefcase because he thinks it is his, there is no crime. Theft requires knowledge that the property belongs to another. (If

Wheaton's act causes Tyson to incur damages, however, she may sue him in a civil action for trespass to personal property or conversion—torts that were discussed in Chapter 5.) ●

Duress

Duress   Unlawful pressure brought to bear on a person, causing the person to perform an act that she or he would not otherwise have performed.

Duress exists when the *wrongful threat* of one person induces another person to perform an act that she or he would not otherwise have performed. In such a situation, duress is said to negate the mental state necessary to commit a crime because the defendant was forced or compelled to commit the act. Duress can be used as a defense to most crimes except murder. The states vary in how duress is defined and what types of crimes it can excuse, however. Generally, to successfully assert duress as a defense, the defendant must reasonably believe in the immediate danger, and the jury (or judge) must conclude that the defendant's belief was reasonable.

Entrapment

Entrapment   In criminal law, a defense in which the defendant claims that he or she was induced by a public official–usually an undercover agent or police officer–to commit a crime that he or she would not otherwise have committed.

Entrapment is a defense designed to prevent police officers or other government agents from enticing persons to commit crimes in order to later prosecute them for those crimes. In the typical entrapment case, an undercover agent *suggests* that a crime be committed and somehow pressures or induces an individual to commit it. The agent then arrests the individual for the crime.

For entrapment to succeed as a defense, both the suggestion and the inducement must take place. The defense is intended not to prevent law enforcement agents from setting a trap for an unwary criminal but rather to prevent them from pushing the individual into it. The crucial issue is whether the person who committed a crime was predisposed to commit the illegal act or did so because the agent induced it.

Statute of Limitations

With some exceptions, such as for the crime of murder, statutes of limitations apply to crimes just as they do to civil wrongs. In other words, the state must initiate criminal prosecution within a certain number of years. If a criminal action is brought after the statutory time period has expired, the accused person can raise the statute of limitations as a defense.

Immunity

Self-Incrimination   The giving of testimony that may subject the testifier to criminal prosecution. The Fifth Amendment to the U.S. Constitution protects against self-incrimination by providing that no person "shall be compelled in any criminal case to be a witness against himself."

Plea Bargaining   The process by which a criminal defendant and the prosecutor in a criminal case work out a mutually satisfactory disposition of the case, subject to court approval; usually involves the defendant's pleading guilty to a lesser offense in return for a lighter sentence.

At times, the government may wish to obtain information from a person accused of a crime. Accused persons are understandably reluctant to give information if it will be used to prosecute them, and they cannot be forced to do so. The privilege against **self-incrimination** is guaranteed by the Fifth Amendment to the U.S. Constitution, which reads, in part, "nor shall [any person] be compelled in any criminal case to be a witness against himself." When the state wishes to obtain information from a person accused of a crime, the state can grant *immunity* from prosecution or agree to prosecute for a less serious offense in exchange for the information. Once immunity is given, the person can no longer refuse to testify on Fifth Amendment grounds because he or she now has an absolute privilege against self-incrimination.

Often, a grant of immunity from prosecution for a serious crime is part of the **plea bargaining** between the defendant and the prosecuting attorney. The defendant may be convicted of a lesser offense, while the state uses the defendant's testimony to prosecute accomplices for serious crimes carrying heavy penalties.

Constitutional Safeguards and Criminal Procedures

Criminal law brings the power of the state, with all its resources, to bear against the individual. Criminal procedures are designed to protect the constitutional rights of individuals and to prevent the arbitrary use of power on the part of the government.

The U.S. Constitution provides specific safeguards for those accused of crimes, as mentioned in Chapter 4. Most of these safeguards protect individuals against state government actions, as well as federal government actions, by virtue of the due process clause of the Fourteenth Amendment. These protections include the following:

1. The Fourth Amendment protection from unreasonable searches and seizures.
2. The Fourth Amendment requirement that no warrant for a search or an arrest be issued without probable cause.
3. The Fifth Amendment requirement that no one be deprived of "life, liberty, or property without due process of law."
4. The Fifth Amendment prohibition against **double jeopardy**—that is, trying someone twice for the same criminal offense.[17] (The prohibition against double jeopardy means that once a criminal defendant is found not guilty of a particular crime, the government may not indict that person again and retry him or her for the same crime.)
5. The Fifth Amendment requirement that no person be required to be a witness against (incriminate) himself or herself.
6. The Sixth Amendment guarantees of a speedy trial, a trial by jury, a public trial, the right to confront witnesses, and the right to a lawyer at various stages in some proceedings.
7. The Eighth Amendment prohibitions against excessive bail and fines and against cruel and unusual punishment. Under this amendment, prison officials are required to provide humane conditions of confinement, including adequate food, clothing, shelter, and medical care.

Fourth Amendment Protections

The Fourth Amendment protects the "right of the people to be secure in their persons, houses, papers, and effects." Before searching or seizing private property, law enforcement officers must obtain a **search warrant**—an order from a judge or other public official authorizing the search or seizure.

To obtain a search warrant, law enforcement officers must convince a judge that they have reasonable grounds, or **probable cause,** to believe a search will reveal a specific illegality. Probable cause requires the officers to have trustworthy evidence that would convince a reasonable person that the proposed search or seizure is more likely justified than not. Furthermore, the Fourth Amendment prohibits general warrants. It requires a particular description of what is to be searched or seized. General searches through a person's belongings are impermissible. The search cannot extend

Double Jeopardy   A situation occurring when a person is tried twice for the same criminal offense; prohibited by the Fifth Amendment to the U.S. Constitution.

Search Warrant   An order granted by a public authority, such as a judge, that authorizes law enforcement personnel to search particular premises or property.

Probable Cause   Reasonable grounds for believing that a person should be arrested or searched.

A police officer pats down a homeless man in Madison, Wisconsin. What document provides the most safeguards for this man?

(Charles Osgood/Chicago Tribune/MCT/Landov)

---

17. The prohibition does not preclude the crime victim from bringing a *civil* suit against that same person to recover damages, however. Additionally, a state's prosecution of a crime will not prevent a separate federal prosecution of the same crime, and vice versa.

beyond what is described in the warrant. Although search warrants require specificity, if a search warrant is issued for a person's residence, items that are in that residence may be searched even if they do not belong to that individual.

Because of the strong governmental interest in protecting the public, a warrant normally is not required for the seizure of spoiled or contaminated food. Nor are warrants required for searches of businesses in such highly regulated industries as liquor, guns, and strip mining. The standard used for highly regulated industries is sometimes applied in other contexts as well.

The Exclusionary Rule

Exclusionary Rule In criminal procedure, a rule under which any evidence that is obtained in violation of the accused's rights guaranteed by the Fourth, Fifth, and Sixth Amendments to the U.S. Constitution, as well as any evidence derived from illegally obtained evidence, will not be admissible in court.

Under what is known as the **exclusionary rule,** all evidence obtained in violation of the constitutional rights spelled out in the Fourth, Fifth, and Sixth Amendments, as well as all evidence derived from illegally obtained evidence, normally must be excluded from the trial. Evidence derived from illegally obtained evidence is known as the "fruit of the poisonous tree." For example, if a confession is obtained after an illegal arrest, the arrest is "the poisonous tree," and the confession, if "tainted" by the arrest, is the "fruit."

The purpose of the exclusionary rule is to deter police from conducting warrantless searches and engaging in other misconduct. The rule is sometimes criticized because it can lead to injustice. Many a defendant has "gotten off on a technicality" because law enforcement personnel failed to observe procedural requirements. Even though a defendant may be obviously guilty, if the evidence of that guilt was obtained improperly (without a valid search warrant, for example), it normally cannot be used against the defendant in court.

If a suspect is arrested on the basis of a police officer's mistaken belief that there is an outstanding arrest warrant for that individual, should evidence found during a search incident to the arrest be excluded from the trial? This question arose in the following case.

Case 6.2 | **Herring v. United States**

Supreme Court of the United States, 555 U.S. 135, 129 S.Ct. 695, 172 L.Ed.2d 496 (2009).
www.findlaw.com/casecode/supreme.html[a]

Bennie Herring.

(Coffee County Sheriff's Office)

BACKGROUND AND FACTS
The Dale County, Alabama, sheriff's office maintains copies of arrest warrants in a computer database. When a warrant is recalled, Sharon Morgan, the warrant clerk, enters this information in the database and also throws out the physical copy. In July 2004, Sandy Pope, the warrant clerk in the sheriff's department in neighboring Coffee County, asked Morgan if there were any outstanding warrants for the arrest of Bennie Herring. Morgan checked her database and told Pope that there was a warrant. Coffee County officers arrested

Herring. A search revealed methamphetamine in his pocket and an illegal gun in his truck. Meanwhile, Morgan learned that a mistake had been made: the warrant had been recalled. Herring was charged in a federal district court with illegal possession of a gun and drugs. He filed a motion to exclude the evidence on the ground that his arrest had been illegal. The court denied the motion, the U.S. Court of Appeals for the Eleventh Circuit affirmed the denial, and Herring appealed.

IN THE WORDS OF THE COURT . . .
Chief Justice *ROBERTS* delivered the opinion of the Court.

* * * *

* * * We have repeatedly rejected the argument that exclusion [of evidence] is a necessary consequence of a Fourth Amendment

a. In the "Browse Supreme Court Opinions" section, click on "2009." On that page, scroll to the name of the case and click on it to access the opinion. FindLaw maintains this Web site.

Case 6.2–Continues next page ⇒

Case 6.2–Continued

violation. Instead we have focused on the efficacy [efficiency] of the rule in deterring Fourth Amendment violations in the future.

In addition, the benefits of deterrence must outweigh the costs. * * * The principal cost of applying the rule is, of course, letting guilty and possibly dangerous defendants go free.

* * * *

* * * *Evidence should be suppressed only if it can be said that the law enforcement officer had knowledge, or may properly be charged with knowledge, that the search was unconstitutional under the Fourth Amendment.* [Emphasis added.]

* * * *

Indeed, the abuses that gave rise to the exclusionary rule featured *intentional* conduct that was patently unconstitutional. [Emphasis added.]

* * * An error that arises from nonrecurring and attenuated [diluted] negligence is * * * far removed from the core concerns that led us to adopt the rule in the first place.

To trigger the exclusionary rule, police conduct must be sufficiently deliberate that exclusion can meaningfully deter it, and sufficiently culpable [blameworthy] that such deterrence is worth the price paid by the justice system. As laid out in our cases, the exclusionary rule serves to deter deliberate, reckless, or grossly negligent conduct, or in some circumstances recurring or systemic negligence. The error in this case does not rise to that level.

* * * *

* * * [In a previous case, we held that] negligent police miscommunications in the course of acquiring a warrant do not provide a basis to rescind a warrant and render a search or arrest invalid. Here, the miscommunications occurred in a different context–after the warrant had been issued and recalled–but that fact should not require excluding the evidence obtained.

* * * *

We do not suggest that all recordkeeping errors by the police are immune from the exclusionary rule. In this case, however, the conduct at issue was not so objectively culpable as to require exclusion.

DECISION AND REMEDY   The United States Supreme Court affirmed the lower court's judgment. The exclusionary rule does not apply when a police mistake leading to an unlawful search is the result of an isolated instance of negligence.

WHAT IF THE FACTS WERE DIFFERENT?   *Suppose that the warrant for Herring's arrest had still been outstanding but had been based on false information. Should the standards applied in this case apply in those circumstances? Explain.*

THE LEGAL ENVIRONMENT DIMENSION   *What does the decision in this case mean for businesses that are subjected to searches by law enforcement personnel?*

The *Miranda* Rule

REMEMBER   Once a suspect has been informed of his or her rights, anything that person says can be used as evidence in a trial.

In *Miranda v. Arizona*, a case decided in 1966, the United States Supreme Court established the rule that individuals who are arrested must be informed of certain constitutional rights, including their Fifth Amendment right to remain silent and their Sixth Amendment right to counsel. If the arresting officers fail to inform a criminal suspect of these constitutional rights, any statements the suspect makes normally will not be admissible in court. Because of its importance in criminal procedure, the *Miranda* case is presented as this chapter's *Landmark in the Legal Environment* feature on the facing page.

Over time, as part of a continuing attempt to balance the rights of accused persons against the rights of society, the United States Supreme Court has carved out numerous exceptions to the *Miranda* rule. For example, the Court has recognized a "public safety" exception, holding that certain statements—such as statements concerning the location of a weapon—are admissible even if the defendant was not given *Miranda* warnings. Additionally, a suspect must unequivocally and assertively request to exercise his or her right to counsel in order to stop police questioning. Saying "Maybe I should talk to a lawyer" during an interrogation after being taken into custody is not enough. Police officers are not required to decipher the suspect's intentions in such situations.

Criminal Process

As mentioned, a criminal prosecution differs significantly from a civil case in several respects. These differences reflect the desire to safeguard the rights of the individ-

Landmark in the Legal Environment   *Miranda v. Arizona* (1966)

The United States Supreme Court's decision in *Miranda v. Arizona*[a] has been cited in more court decisions than any other case in the history of American law. Through television shows and other media, the case has also become familiar to most of the adult population in the United States.

The case arose after Ernesto Miranda was arrested in his home, on March 13, 1963, for the kidnapping and rape of an eighteen-year-old woman. Miranda was taken to a police station in Phoenix, Arizona, and questioned by two police officers. Two hours later, the officers emerged from the interrogation room with a written confession signed by Miranda.

Rulings by the Lower Courts   The confession was admitted into evidence at the trial, and Miranda was convicted and sentenced to prison for twenty to thirty years. Miranda appealed his conviction, claiming that he had not been informed of his constitutional rights. He did not assert that he was innocent of the crime or that his confession was false or made under duress. He claimed only that he would not have confessed if he had been advised of his right to remain silent and to have an attorney.

The Supreme Court of Arizona held that Miranda's constitutional rights had not been violated and affirmed his conviction. In its decision, the court emphasized that Miranda had not specifically requested an attorney.

---

a. 384 U.S. 436, 86 S.Ct. 1602, 16 L.Ed.2d 694 (1966).

The Supreme Court's Decision   The *Miranda* case was subsequently consolidated with three other cases involving similar issues and reviewed by the United States Supreme Court. In its decision, the Court stated that whenever an individual is taken into custody, "the following measures are required: He must be warned prior to any questioning that he has the right to remain silent, that anything he says can be used against him in a court of law, that he has the right to the presence of an attorney, and that if he cannot afford an attorney one will be appointed for him prior to any questioning if he so desires."

If the accused waives his or her rights to remain silent and to have counsel present, the government must be able to demonstrate that the waiver was made knowingly, intelligently, and voluntarily.

• Application to Today's Legal Environment   *Today, both on television and in the real world, police officers routinely advise suspects of their "Miranda rights" on arrest. When Ernesto Miranda himself was later murdered, the suspected murderer was "read his Miranda rights." Interestingly, this decision has also had ramifications for criminal procedure in Great Britain. British police officers are required, when making arrests, to inform suspects, "You do not have to say anything. But if you do not mention now something which you later use in your defense, the court may decide that your failure to mention it now strengthens the case against you. A record will be made of everything you say, and it may be given in evidence if you are brought to trial."*

---

ual against the state. Here, we discuss three phases of the criminal process—arrest, indictment or information, and trial—in more detail.

ARREST   Before a warrant for arrest can be issued, there must be probable cause to believe that the individual in question has committed a crime. As discussed earlier, *probable cause* can be defined as a substantial likelihood that the person has committed or is about to commit a crime. Note that probable cause involves a likelihood, not just a possibility. Arrests can be made without a warrant if there is no time to get one, but the action of the arresting officer is still judged by the standard of probable cause.

Indictment   A charge by a grand jury that a named person has committed a crime.

Grand Jury   A group of citizens called to decide, after hearing the state's evidence, whether a reasonable basis (probable cause) exists for believing that a crime has been committed and that a trial ought to be held.

INDICTMENT OR INFORMATION   Individuals must be formally charged with having committed specific crimes before they can be brought to trial. If issued by a grand jury, this charge is called an **indictment**.[18] A **grand jury** usually consists of more jurors than the ordinary trial jury. A grand jury does not determine the guilt or innocence of an accused party. Rather, its function is to hear the state's evidence and to determine whether a reasonable basis (probable cause) exists for believing that a crime has been committed and that a trial ought to be held.

---

18. Pronounced in-*dyte*-ment.

Usually, grand juries are used in cases involving serious crimes, such as murder. For lesser crimes, an individual may be formally charged with a crime by what is called an **information,** or criminal complaint. An information will be issued by a government prosecutor if the prosecutor determines that there is sufficient evidence to justify bringing the individual to trial.

TRIAL   At a criminal trial, the accused person does not have to prove anything. The entire burden of proof is on the prosecutor (the state). As mentioned earlier, the prosecution must show that, based on all the evidence presented, the defendant's guilt is established *beyond a reasonable doubt.* If there is a reasonable doubt as to whether a criminal defendant committed the crime with which she or he has been charged, then the verdict must be "not guilty." Note that giving a verdict of "not guilty" is not the same as stating that the defendant is innocent. It merely means that not enough evidence was properly presented to the court to prove guilt beyond a reasonable doubt. Courts have complex rules about what types of evidence may be presented and how the evidence may be brought out in criminal cases. These rules are designed to ensure that evidence in trials is relevant, reliable, and not prejudicial toward the defendant.

SENTENCING GUIDELINES   In 1984, Congress passed the Sentencing Reform Act. This act created the U.S. Sentencing Commission, which was charged with the task of standardizing sentences for federal crimes. The commission's guidelines, which became effective in 1987, established a range of possible penalties for each federal crime and required the judge to select a sentence from within that range. In other words, the guidelines originally established a mandatory system because judges were not allowed to deviate from the specified sentencing range. Some federal judges felt uneasy about imposing long prison sentences on certain criminal defendants, particularly first-time offenders and those convicted of offenses involving small quantities of illegal drugs.[19]

> "In school, every period ends with a bell. Every sentence ends with a period. Every crime ends with a sentence."
> Steven Wright, 1955–present
> (American comedian)

In 2005, the United States Supreme Court held that certain provisions of the federal sentencing guidelines were unconstitutional. **CASE EXAMPLE 6.13**   Freddie Booker was arrested with 92.5 grams of crack cocaine in his possession. Booker admitted to police that he had sold an additional 566 grams of crack cocaine, but he was never charged with, or tried for, possessing this additional quantity. Nevertheless, under the federal sentencing guidelines the judge was required to sentence Booker to twenty-two years in prison. The Court ruled that this sentence was unconstitutional because a jury did not find beyond a reasonable doubt that Booker had possessed the additional 566 grams of crack.[20] ●

Essentially, the Court's ruling changed the federal sentencing guidelines from mandatory to advisory. Depending on the circumstances of the case, a federal trial judge may now depart from the guidelines if he or she believes that it is reasonable to do so. Sentencing guidelines still exist and provide for enhanced punishment for certain types of crimes, including white-collar crimes, violations of the Sarbanes-Oxley Act (see Chapter 2), and violations of securities laws.[21] In 2009, the Court considered the sentencing guidelines again and held that a sentencing judge cannot presume that a sentence within the applicable guidelines is reasonable.[22] The judge must take into

---

19. See, for example, *United States v. Angelos,* 345 F.Supp.2d 1227 (D. Utah 2004).
20. *United States v. Booker,* 543 U.S. 220, 125 S.Ct. 738, 160 L.Ed.2d 621 (2005).
21. The sentencing guidelines were amended in 2003, as required under the Sarbanes-Oxley Act of 2002, to impose stiffer penalties for corporate securities fraud—see Chapter 24.
22. *Nelson v. United States,* 555 U.S. 350, 129 S.Ct. 890, 172 L.Ed.2d 719 (2009).

account the various sentencing factors that apply to an individual defendant. When the defendant is a business firm, these factors include the company's history of past violations, management's cooperation with federal investigators, and the extent to which the firm has undertaken specific programs and procedures to prevent criminal activities by its employees.

 ## Cyber Crime

Computer Crime   Any wrongful act that is directed against computers and computer parts or that involves the wrongful use or abuse of computers or software.

The U.S. Department of Justice broadly defines **computer crime** as any violation of criminal law that involves knowledge of computer technology for its perpetration, investigation, or prosecution. A number of the white-collar crimes discussed earlier in this chapter, such as fraud, embezzlement, and the theft of intellectual property, are now committed with the aid of computers and are thus considered computer crimes.

Cyber Crime   A crime that occurs online, in the virtual community of the Internet, as opposed to the physical world.

Many computer crimes fall under the broad label of **cyber crime,** which describes any criminal activity occurring via a computer in the virtual community of the Internet. Most cyber crimes are not "new" crimes. Rather, they are existing crimes in which the Internet is the instrument of wrongdoing. Here we look at several types of activity that constitute cyber crimes against persons or property. Other cyber crimes will be discussed in later chapters as they relate to particular topics, such as consumer law or investor protection.

Cyber Fraud

As pointed out in Chapter 5, fraud is any misrepresentation knowingly made with the intention of deceiving another and on which a reasonable person would and does rely to her or his detriment. **Cyber fraud,** then, is fraud committed over the Internet. Frauds that were once conducted solely by mail or phone can now be found online, and new technology has led to increasingly creative ways to commit fraud.

Cyber Fraud   Any misrepresentation knowingly made over the Internet with the intention of deceiving another and on which a reasonable person would and does rely to his or her detriment.

Sometimes, Internet fraud is just an electronic version of frauds formerly perpetrated by mail. **EXAMPLE 6.14**   The "Nigerian letter fraud scam" is perhaps the longest-running Internet fraud. In this swindle, con artists send e-mails promising the recipients a percentage if they will send funds to help fictitious officials from Nigeria transfer millions of nonexistent dollars to Western banks. Some versions of the scam reflect current events. In these scams, the e-mails may ask for financial help in retrieving the fortune of a loved one or an associate who perished in the conflict in Iraq or Afghanistan or during the earthquake in Japan. •

ONLINE AUCTION FRAUD   Online auction fraud, in its most basic form, is a simple process. A person puts up an expensive item for auction, on either a legitimate or a fake auction site, and then refuses to send the product after receiving payment. Or, as a variation, the wrongdoer may provide the purchaser with an item that is worth less than the one offered in the auction. The larger online auction sites, such as eBay, try to protect consumers against such schemes by providing warnings about deceptive sellers or offering various forms of insurance. The nature of the Internet, however, makes it nearly impossible to completely block fraudulent auction activity. Because users can assume multiple identities, it is very difficult to pinpoint fraudulent sellers—they will simply change their screen names with each auction.

ONLINE RETAIL FRAUD   Somewhat similar to online auction fraud is online retail fraud, in which consumers pay directly (without bidding) for items that are never delivered. Because most consumers will purchase items only from reputable, well-known sites such as Amazon.com, criminals have had to take advantage of some of the complexities of cyberspace to lure unknowing customers. As with other forms of online fraud, it is difficult to determine the actual extent of online sales fraud, but anecdotal evidence suggests that it is a substantial problem.

CASE EXAMPLE 6.15   Jeremy Jaynes grossed more than $750,000 per week selling nonexistent or worthless products such as "penny stock pickers" and "Internet history erasers." By the time he was arrested, he had amassed an estimated $24 million from his various fraudulent schemes.[23] ●

Cyber Theft

In cyberspace, thieves are not subject to the physical limitations of the "real" world. A thief can steal data stored in a networked computer with Internet access from anywhere on the globe. Only the speed of the connection and the thief's computer equipment limit the quantity of data that can be stolen.

Identity Theft   The theft of identity information, such as a person's name, driver's license number, or Social Security number. The information is then usually used to access the victim's financial resources.

IDENTITY THEFT   Not surprisingly, there has been a marked increase in identity theft in recent years. **Identity theft** occurs when the wrongdoer steals a form of identification—such as a name, date of birth, or Social Security number—and uses the information to access the victim's financial resources. This crime existed to a certain extent before the widespread use of the Internet. Thieves would rifle through garbage to find credit-card or bank account numbers and then use those numbers to purchase goods or to withdraw funds from the victims' accounts.

The Internet has provided even easier access to private data. Frequent Web surfers surrender a wealth of information about themselves without knowing it. Many Web sites use "cookies" to collect data on those who visit their sites. The data may include the areas of the site the user visits and the links on which the user clicks. Furthermore, Web browsers often store information such as the consumer's name and e-mail address. Finally, every time a purchase is made online, the item is linked to the purchaser's name, allowing Web retailers to amass a database of who is buying what.

In the following case, the defendant was charged with identity theft and mail fraud (discussed earlier) stemming from his role in a scheme to file fraudulent claims for unemployment benefits. The court had to decide whether to suppress evidence of the crime that officers found at the defendant's girlfriend's house.

PLEASE REMAIN ON HOLD WHILE WE COMPLETE THE FINAL DETAILS OF THE THEFT OF YOUR IDENTITY.

A COURTESY CALL

©Jack Ziegler/Condé Nast Publications/www.cartoonbank.com).

23. *Jaynes v. Commonwealth of Virginia*, 276 Va.App. 443, 666 S.E.2d 303 (2008).

Case 6.3   **United States v. Oliver**

United States Court of Appeals, Fifth Circuit, 630 F.3d 397 (2011).
www.ca5.uscourts.gov/Opinions.aspx[a]

BACKGROUND AND FACTS   Lonnie Oliver, Jr., was arrested by officers investigating a scheme to file fraudulent claims for unemployment benefits. Oliver and others were suspected of gaining

access to people's names, Social Security numbers, and other identifiers, and using this information to file for and receive unemployment benefits. After he was read his *Miranda* rights, Oliver confessed to his role in the scheme. Oliver also consented to a search of his car, but he refused to consent to a search of his home. Oliver's co-defendant then told the police that Oliver had stored a laptop computer and a cardboard box containing items related to the scheme at the apartment of Oliver's girlfriend, Erica Armstrong. Acting on this information,

---

a. Under the heading "Search for opinions where," type "01-10133" in the "and/or Docket number is:" box and click on "Search." In the result, click on the docket number to access the opinion. The U.S. Court of Appeals for the Fifth Circuit maintains this Web site.

Case 6.3–Continued

several agents went to Armstrong's apartment, and she gave them the box and the laptop computer. Inside the box, officers found hundreds of personal identifiers, including names, dates of birth, and Social Security numbers of victims, along with credit and debit cards. They also found a notebook labeled "business ideas" with Oliver's notes for the scheme. After the laptop was seized, officers obtained a warrant to search its contents and found evidence that Oliver had used it to submit fraudulent unemployment claims. Oliver filed a motion to suppress the evidence in the cardboard box on the ground that it had been obtained unconstitutionally because he had not consented to the search. Further, he claimed that the evidence found on the laptop should also be excluded as "fruit of the poisonous tree" because the warrant to search the laptop was issued on the basis of an affidavit that relied, in part, on the evidence in the box. The district court denied the motion. Oliver appealed.

IN THE WORDS OF THE COURT . . .
CRONE, District Judge:
* * * *

At the suppression hearing, Armstrong stated she observed Oliver—who told her he worked from home—using a laptop and a notebook. According to Armstrong, she first became aware of Oliver's cardboard box when, before traveling out of town, he informed her that he had left it in her apartment under her bed. * * * After Oliver had not been in contact with Armstrong for several days, she looked through the box for information to contact him. In the box, Armstrong found a notebook, a ziplock bag containing credit cards, a white envelope containing identification cards, and other loose paperwork resembling tax documents. Later that day, Agent McReynolds arrived at her apartment inquiring about Oliver. Armstrong did not reveal, and federal authorities were unaware, that Armstrong had already searched the box when she handed it over to McReynolds and agents subsequently examined its contents.
* * * *

Where a private individual examines the contents of a closed container, a subsequent search of the container by government officials does not constitute an unlawful search for purposes of the Fourth Amendment as long as the government search does not exceed the scope of the private search. [Emphasis added.]

When confronted with situations where, as here, the police search items found within a residence after a private search has already been conducted, a defendant may retain a reasonable expectation of privacy following the private search under certain circumstances. To determine whether a defendant's reasonable expectation of privacy survives a private search, "consideration must be given to whether the activities of the home's occupants or the circumstances within the home at the time of the private search created *a risk of intrusion by the private party that was reasonably foreseeable."* "If indeed the private party's intrusion was reasonably foreseeable (based on such activities or circumstances), the occupant will no longer possess a reasonable expectation of privacy in the area or thing searched, and the subsequent police search will not trigger the Fourth Amendment."
* * * *

In the present case, * * * Armstrong readily and willingly gave Agent McReynolds the box, which she had already searched, as it was not locked or otherwise safeguarded and was left in her dining room. *Oliver's decision to leave his unsecured cardboard box in an easily accessible and common area of the apartment for several days without notifying or otherwise communicating his whereabouts to Armstrong made it reasonably foreseeable that she would examine his belongings, including the box, to look for a way to contact him.* Given these circumstances, the court finds that the initial private search, which was reasonably foreseeable, and the searcher's act, later that day, of voluntarily giving authorities the box, in which no reasonable expectation of privacy remained, rendered the subsequent police search permissible under the Fourth Amendment. [Emphasis added.]
* * * *

Oliver also objects to the district court's ruling that the contents of the laptop computer were admissible under the independent source doctrine. Evidence not obtained as a result of police illegality, but rather through a legal, independent source, need not be suppressed.

Oliver contends that Agent McReynolds's affidavit in support of the warrant relied on evidence that was illegally obtained. * * * As correctly noted by the district court, unlawfully obtained evidence need not be suppressed if officials later reseize the evidence from a "distinct, untainted source." Even without mentioning the original seizure of the laptop, the affidavit contains sufficient information to make the resulting warrant a distinct, untainted source, permitting agents to reseize and search the laptop. In her affidavit, McReynolds relies on information provided by Oliver and Henson (the co-defendant), who both admitted to using a laptop computer to submit fraudulent unemployment claims. McReynolds also states in the affidavit that Henson revealed the location of the laptop—Armstrong's apartment. She also recounts Armstrong's statements that Oliver used the laptop while looking at documents later found by federal agents to contain identifying information for various individuals. *In this circumstance, the affidavit contained sufficient independent information to make the resulting warrant a distinct, untainted source that permitted the agents to reseize and search the laptop lawfully.* [Emphasis added.]

DECISION AND REMEDY The federal appellate court affirmed the lower court's decision that the searches of the box and the laptop computer were legal and that the evidence found therefore was admissible. Because there was sufficient (admissible) evidence to support aggravated identity theft, Oliver pleaded guilty.

WHAT IF THE FACTS WERE DIFFERENT? *Suppose that Armstrong had not looked through the cardboard box before the police searched it. Would the box's contents have been admissible? Why or why not?*

THE LEGAL ENVIRONMENT DIMENSION *Why was the evidence in the box crucial to the government's prosecution of Oliver?*

Phishing The attempt to acquire financial data, passwords, or other personal information from consumers by sending e-mail messages that purport to be from a legitimate business, such as a bank or a credit-card company.

Trojan Horse A computer program that appears to perform a legitimate function but in fact performs a malicious function that allows the sender to gain unauthorized access to the user's computer; named after the wooden horse that enabled the Greek forces to gain access to the city of Troy in the ancient story.

Vishing A variation of phishing that involves some form of voice communication. The consumer receives either an e-mail or a phone call from someone claiming to be from a legitimate business and asking for personal information. Instead of being asked to respond by e-mail as in phishing, the consumer is asked to call a phone number.

PHISHING   A distinct form of identity theft known as **phishing** has added a different wrinkle to the practice. In a phishing attack, the perpetrators "fish" for financial data and passwords from consumers by posing as a legitimate business such as a bank or credit-card company. The "phisher" sends an e-mail asking the recipient to "update" or "confirm" vital information, often with the threat that an account or some other service will be discontinued if the information is not provided. Once the unsuspecting individual enters the information, the phisher can use it to masquerade as that person or to drain his or her bank or credit account.

EXAMPLE 6.16 Customers of Wachovia Bank (now owned by Wells Fargo) received official-looking e-mails telling them to type in personal information on a Web form to complete a mandatory installation of a new Internet security certificate. But the Web site was bogus. When people filled out the forms, their computers were infected with a **Trojan horse** that funneled their data to a computer server. The cyber criminals then sold the data. Another scheme targeted small-business owners, among others. E-mails purportedly from the Internal Revenue Service requested bank account information for direct deposit of federal tax refunds, but, of course, the refunds never came. ●

VISHING   When phishing involves some form of voice communication, the scam is known as **vishing.** In one variation, the consumer receives an e-mail saying there is a problem with an account and that she or he should call a certain telephone number to resolve the problem. Sometimes, the e-mail even says that a telephone call is being requested so that the recipient will know that this is not a phishing attempt. Of course, the goal is to get the consumer to divulge passwords and account information during the call. In one scheme, e-mails seemingly from the Federal Bureau of Investigation (FBI) asked recipients to call a special telephone number and provide account information. Vishing scams use Voice over Internet Protocol (VoIP) service, which enables telephone calls to be made over the Internet. Such calls are inexpensive and enable scammers to hide their identity easily.

EMPLOYMENT FRAUD   Cyber criminals also look for victims at online job-posting sites. Claiming to be an employment officer in a well-known company, the criminal sends bogus e-mail messages to job seekers. The message asks the unsuspecting job seeker to reveal enough information to allow for identity theft. **CASE EXAMPLE 6.17** The job site Monster.com had to ask all of its users to change their passwords because cyber thieves had broken into its databases to steal user identities, passwords, and other data. The theft of 4.5 million users' personal information from Monster.com was one of Britain's largest cyber theft cases.[24] ●

CREDIT-CARD CRIME ON THE WEB   Credit-card theft was mentioned previously in connection with identity theft. An important point to note, however, is that stolen credit cards are much more likely to hurt merchants and credit-card issuers (such as banks) than consumers. In most situations, the legitimate holders of credit cards are not held responsible for the costs of purchases made with a stolen number (see Chapter 20). That means the financial burden must be borne either by the merchant or by the credit-card company. Most credit-card issuers require merchants to cover the costs—especially if the address to which the goods are sent does not match the billing address of the credit card.

---

24. John Bingham, "Monster.com Hacking Follows Tradition of Cyber Theft," *Telegraph.co.uk.,* January 28, 2009.

(AP Photo/Steve Helber)

This member of the State Police Computer Evidence Recovery Unit in Richmond, Virginia, works on extracting criminal evidence from a hard drive. Increasingly, cities are establishing cyber crime investigation centers.

Hacker   A person who uses one computer to break into another.

Botnet   A network of computers that have been appropriated without the knowledge of their owners and used to spread harmful programs via the Internet; short for *robot network.*

Malware   Any program that is harmful to a computer or a computer user; for example, worms and viruses.

Worm   A computer program that can automatically replicate itself over a network such as the Internet and interfere with the normal use of a computer. A worm does not need to be attached to an existing file to move from one network to another.

Virus   A computer program that can replicate itself over a network, such as the Internet, and interfere with the normal use of a computer. A virus cannot exist as a separate entity and must attach itself to another program to move through a network.

Additionally, companies take risks by storing their online customers' credit-card numbers. By doing so, companies can provide quicker service because a consumer can make a purchase by providing a code or clicking on a particular icon without entering a lengthy card number. These electronic warehouses are quite tempting to cyber thieves, however. **EXAMPLE 6.18**   Several years ago, an unknown person was able to gain access to computerized records at CardSystems Solutions, a company in Tucson, Arizona, that processes credit-card transactions for small Internet businesses. The breach exposed 40 million credit-card numbers.[25] ●

Hacking

A **hacker** is someone who uses one computer to break into another. The danger posed by hackers has increased significantly because of **botnets,** or networks of computers that have been appropriated by hackers without the knowledge of their owners. A hacker will secretly install a program on thousands, if not millions, of personal computer "robots," or "bots," that allows him or her to forward transmissions to an even larger number of systems.

EXAMPLE 6.19   In 2011, someone hacked into Sony Corporation's PlayStation 3 video gaming and entertainment networks. The incident forced the company to temporarily shut down its online gaming services and affected more than 100 million online accounts that provide gaming, chat, and music streaming services. ●

MALWARE   Botnets are one of the latest forms of **malware,** a term that refers to any program that is harmful to a computer or, by extension, a computer user. A **worm,** for example, is a software program that is capable of reproducing itself as it spreads from one computer to the next. **EXAMPLE 6.20**   In 2009, within three weeks, the computer worm called "Conflicker" spread to more than 1 million personal computers around the world. It was transmitted to some computers through the use of Facebook and Twitter. This worm also infected servers and devices plugged into infected computers via USB ports, such as iPods and USB flash drives. ●

A **virus,** another form of malware, is also able to reproduce itself, but must be attached to an "infested" host file to travel from one computer network to another. For example, hackers are now capable of corrupting banner ads that use Adobe's Flash Player. When an Internet user clicks on the banner ad, a virus is installed. Worms and viruses can be programmed to perform a number of functions, such as prompting host computers to continually "crash" and reboot, or otherwise infect the system.

NEW SERVICE-BASED HACKING AVAILABLE AT LOW COST   A recent trend in business computer applications is the use of "software as a service." Instead of buying software to install on a computer, the user connects to Web-based software. The user can write e-mails, edit spreadsheets, and the like using his or her Web browser. Cyber criminals have adapted this method and now offer "crimeware as a service."

A would-be thief no longer has to be a computer hacker to create a botnet or steal banking information and credit-card numbers. He or she can rent the online services of cyber criminals to do the work on such sites as NeoSploit. The thief can even target individual groups, such as U.S. physicians or British attorneys. The cost of renting a Web site to do the work is only a few cents per target computer.

---

25. The Federal Trade Commission (FTC) brought charges against the company, which ultimately reached a settlement with the FTC.

CYBERTERRORISM Hackers who break into computers without authorization often commit cyber theft, but sometimes their principal aim is to prove how smart they are by gaining access to others' password-protected computers. **Cyberterrorists** are hackers who, rather than trying to gain attention, strive to remain undetected so that they can exploit computers for a serious impact. Just as "real" terrorists destroyed the World Trade Center towers and a portion of the Pentagon on September 11, 2001, cyberterrorists might explode "logic bombs" to shut down central computers. Such activities obviously can pose a danger to national security.

Cyberterrorists, as well as hackers, may target businesses. The goals of a hacking operation might include a wholesale theft of data, such as a merchant's customer files, or the monitoring of a computer to discover a business firm's plans and transactions. A cyberterrorist might also want to insert false codes or data. For example, the processing control system of a food manufacturer could be changed to alter the levels of ingredients so that consumers of the food would become ill.

A cyberterrorist attack on a major financial institution, such as the New York Stock Exchange or a large bank, could leave securities or money markets in flux and seriously affect the daily lives of millions of citizens. Similarly, any prolonged disruption of computer, cable, satellite, or telecommunications systems due to the actions of expert hackers would have serious repercussions on business operations—and national security—on a global level.

> **Cyberterrorist** A person who uses the Internet to attack or sabotage businesses and government agencies with the purpose of disrupting infrastructure systems.

Spam

Businesses and individuals alike are targets of **spam,** or unsolicited "junk e-mails" that flood virtual mailboxes with advertisements, solicitations, and other messages. Considered relatively harmless in the early days of the Internet's popularity, by 2012 spam accounted for roughly 75 percent of all e-mails. Far from being harmless, the unwanted files can wreak havoc on business operations.

> **Spam** Bulk e-mails, particularly of commercial advertising, sent in large quantities without the consent of the recipients.

STATE REGULATION OF SPAM In an attempt to combat spam, thirty-six states have enacted laws that prohibit or regulate its use. Many state laws that regulate spam require the senders of e-mail ads to instruct the recipients on how they can "opt out" of further e-mail ads from the same sources. For instance, in some states an unsolicited e-mail ad must include a toll-free phone number or return e-mail address through which the recipient can contact the sender to request that no more ads be e-mailed.

> *"Speech is not free when it comes postage due."*
> Jim Nitchals, 1962–1998
> (Spam fighter and computer programmer)

THE FEDERAL CAN-SPAM ACT In 2003, Congress enacted the Controlling the Assault of Non-Solicited Pornography and Marketing (CAN-SPAM) Act, which took effect on January 1, 2004. The legislation applies to any "commercial electronic mail messages" that are sent to promote a commercial product or service. Significantly, the statute preempts state antispam laws except for those provisions in state laws that prohibit false and deceptive e-mailing practices.

Generally, the act permits the use of unsolicited commercial e-mail but prohibits certain types of spamming activities, including the use of a false return address and the use of false, misleading, or deceptive information when sending e-mail. The statute also prohibits the use of "dictionary attacks"—sending messages to randomly generated e-mail addresses—and the "harvesting" of e-mail addresses from Web sites with specialized software.

CASE EXAMPLE 6.21 In 2007, federal officials arrested Robert Alan Soloway, considered one of the world's most prolific spammers. Because Soloway had been using botnets to send out hundreds of millions of unwanted e-mails, he was charged under anti–identity theft laws for the appropriation of other people's domain names, among other crimes. In 2008, Soloway, known as the "Spam King," pleaded guilty to mail fraud and failure to pay taxes.[26] ● Arresting prolific spammers, however, has done little to curb spam, which continues to flow at a rate of 70 billion messages per day.

THE U.S. SAFE WEB ACT After the CAN-SPAM Act of 2003 prohibited false and deceptive e-mails originating in the United States, spamming from servers located in other nations increased. These cross-border spammers generally were able to escape detection and legal sanctions because the Federal Trade Commission (FTC) lacked the authority to investigate foreign spamming.

Congress sought to rectify the situation by enacting the U.S. Safe Web Act of 2006 (also known as the Undertaking Spam, Spyware, and Fraud Enforcement with Enforcers Beyond Borders Act). The act allows the FTC to cooperate and share information with foreign agencies in investigating and prosecuting those involved in Internet fraud and deception, including spamming, spyware, and various Internet frauds. It also provides Internet service providers (ISPs) with a "safe harbor" (immunity from liability) for supplying information to the FTC concerning possible unfair or deceptive conduct in foreign jurisdictions.

Prosecution of Cyber Crime

The "location" of cyber crime (cyberspace) has raised new issues in the investigation of crimes and the prosecution of offenders. A threshold issue is, of course, jurisdiction. A person who commits an act against a business in California, where the act is a cyber crime, might never have set foot in California but might instead reside in New York, or even in Canada, where the act may not be a crime. If the crime was committed via e-mail, the question arises as to whether the e-mail would constitute sufficient minimum contacts (see Chapter 3) for the victim's state to exercise jurisdiction over the perpetrator.

Identifying the wrongdoer can also be difficult. Cyber criminals do not leave physical traces, such as fingerprints or DNA samples, as evidence of their crimes. Even electronic "footprints" can be hard to find and follow. For example, e-mail may be sent through a remailer, an online service that guarantees that a message cannot be traced to its source.

For these reasons, laws written to protect physical property are often difficult to apply in cyberspace. Nonetheless, governments at both the state and the federal level have taken significant steps toward controlling cyber crime, both by applying existing criminal statutes and by enacting new laws that specifically address wrongs committed in cyberspace.

The Computer Fraud and Abuse Act

Perhaps the most significant federal statute specifically addressing cyber crime is the Counterfeit Access Device and Computer Fraud and Abuse Act of 1984 [27] (commonly known as the Computer Fraud and Abuse Act, or CFAA). Among other things, this act provides that a person who accesses a computer online, without authority, to obtain classified, restricted, or protected data (or attempts to do so) is subject to criminal prosecution. Such data could include financial and credit records, medical records, legal files, military and national security files, and other confidential

26. "'Spam King of Seattle' Soloway Pleads Guilty," *SC Magazine,* March 17, 2008: n.p. Web.
27. 18 U.S.C. Section 1030.

information in government or private computers. The crime has two elements: accessing a computer without authority and taking the data.

This theft is a felony if it is committed for a commercial purpose or for private financial gain, or if the value of the stolen data (or computer time) exceeds $5,000. Penalties include fines and imprisonment for up to twenty years. A victim of computer theft can also bring a civil suit against the violator to obtain damages, an injunction, and other relief.

For a discussion of a case involving students who were accused of violating the CFAA, see this chapter's *Online Developments* feature below.

Online Developments

Can Students Who Gain Unauthorized Access to an Online Antiplagiarism Service Be Subject to the Computer Fraud and Abuse Act?

The Computer Fraud and Abuse Act is primarily a criminal statute in that its main purpose is to deter computer hackers. Nevertheless, in certain circumstances, private parties may bring a civil suit alleging a violation of the act. One case arose when four high school students were required to submit written assignments to an online antiplagiarism service, which then archived the students' work.

Fighting Student Plagiarism

Instructors in high schools, colleges, and universities worldwide face a plagiarism problem of epic proportions. Any student can access various online sources from which work can be plagiarized. As a result, several companies, including iParadigms, LLC, have created software and other services to help instructors detect plagiarism. One of iParadigms' products is Turnitin Plagiarism Detection Service. Instructors can require their students to submit written assignments to Turnitin, which then compares the students' work with more than 10 billion Web pages; 70 million student papers; 10,000 newspapers, magazines, and scholarly journals; plus thousands of books. Students who submit their work to Turnitin must agree to allow iParadigms to archive their papers in the Turnitin master file.

Does Gaining Unauthorized Access to an Online Service Violate the Computer Fraud and Abuse Act?

Four high school students who were required to submit their assignments to Turnitin filed a suit in a federal district court, claiming that the archiving of their papers infringed their copyright interests. The court found that the archiving of the papers qualified as a "fair use" and thus did not infringe the students' copyright interests (see Chapter 8 for a full discussion of copyright law). Hence, the court granted summary judgment for iParadigms, LLC, a decision that was upheld on appeal by the U.S. Court of Appeals for the Fourth Circuit.[a]

Meanwhile, iParadigms had counterclaimed, alleging that one of the high school students had gained unauthorized access to the company's online services in violation of the Computer Fraud and Abuse Act. Using a password and login ID obtained via the Internet, the student had registered and submitted papers to Turnitin, misrepresenting himself as a student of a university that he had never attended.

Was this a violation of the Computer Fraud and Abuse Act? The federal district court did not believe so. On appeal, though, the decision was reversed and remanded. The appellate court observed that iParadigms had to spend costly resources to determine whether there was a glitch in its online registration program. These expenses fell under the economic damages part of the act, which defines loss as:

> any reasonable cost to any victim, including the cost of responding to an offense, conducting a damage assessment, and restoring . . . the system . . . to its condition prior to the offense, and any revenue lost, cost incurred, or other consequential damages incurred because of interruption to service.[b]

The federal appeals court also ruled in iParadigms' favor on a separate counterclaim, finding that the defendant had violated the Virginia Computer Crimes Act.[c] The consequential damages presented by iParadigms fit within the "any damages" language of the Virginia law.

FOR CRITICAL ANALYSIS

What might have motivated the four high school students to bring their lawsuit?

---

a. *A.V. ex rel. Vanderhye v. iParadigms, LLC,* 562 F.3d 630 (4th Cir. 2009).

b. 18 U.S.C. Section 1030(a)(11).

c. Virginia Code Annotated Sections 18.2-152.3 and 18.2-152.6.

Reviewing . . . Criminal Law and Cyber Crime

One day, Kendra Donahue received an e-mail advertisement offering a free sample bottle of a "superfood" nutritional supplement made from acai berries, which are supposed to boost energy and aid weight loss. She clicked on the link to place an order and filled out an online form with her name, address, and credit-card number to pay for the shipping charges. Although Donahue read the terms displayed, nothing on the page indicated that she was signing up for a monthly shipment. Shortly before the bottle of pills arrived, Donahue received a phone call from her credit-card company asking if she had authorized a charge on her credit card at a grocery store in Israel. She told the company representative that she had not. When Donahue received her credit-card statement, she found a number of other unauthorized charges. A month later, she received a second bottle of the supplement in the mail and then discovered that her credit card had been charged $85 for this shipment. She called the 800 number on the invoice, but no one answered, so she contacted the seller via the Internet. An online agent at the seller's Web site indicated that she would cancel future monthly shipments to Donahue (but claimed that the terms were posted at the Web site). In order to obtain a refund, however, Donahue would have to pay to ship the bottle back to a post office box in Florida. If the bottle arrived within fifteen days, the company would refund the charges. When asked about the unauthorized charges on Donahue's card, the seller's agent claimed that the company did not sell her credit-card information to any third party or have any contacts with Israel. Using the information presented in the chapter, answer the following questions.

1. What is the term for the type of e-mail that Donahue received offering a sample of the nutritional supplement?
2. Assuming that the information contained in the e-mail was not false or misleading, did it violate any federal law? Why or why not?
3. Is it clear that the company that sold the acai berry supplement to Donahue was engaged in a crime relating to her credit card? Why or why not?
4. Suppose that when Donahue clicked on the link in the e-mail, malicious software was downloaded onto her computer. Whenever Donahue subsequently typed in her personal information online, that program then recorded the keystrokes and sent the data to cyber crooks. What crime has been committed, and why might it be difficult to prosecute?

 ## Key Terms

actus reus 147
arson 152
beyond a reasonable doubt 146
botnet 171
burglary 151
computer crime 167
crime 145
cyber crime 167
cyber fraud 167
cyberterrorist 172
double jeopardy 162
duress 161
embezzlement 153
entrapment 161

exclusionary rule 163
felony 158
forgery 152
grand jury 165
hacker 171
identity theft 168
indictment 165
information 166
larceny 151
malware 171
mens rea 147
misdemeanor 158
money laundering 157
petty offense 158

phishing 170
plea bargaining 161
probable cause 162
robbery 150
search warrant 162
self-defense 159
self-incrimination 161
spam 172
Trojan horse 170
virus 171
vishing 170
white-collar crime 152
worm 171

 ## Chapter Summary: Criminal Law and Cyber Crime

Civil Law and Criminal Law (See pages 145–147.)	1. *Civil law*—Spells out the duties that exist between persons or between citizens and their governments, excluding the duty not to commit crimes.

(Continued)

Chapter Summary: Criminal Law and Cyber Crime, *Continued*

Civil Law and Criminal Law—Continued	2. *Criminal law*—Has to do with crimes, which are wrongs against society defined in statutes and, if committed, punishable by society through fines and/or imprisonment—and, in some cases, death. Because crimes are *offenses against society as a whole,* they are prosecuted by a public official, not by victims.
	3. *Key differences*—An important difference between civil and criminal law is that the standard of proof is higher in criminal cases (see Exhibit 6–1 on page 146 for other differences between civil and criminal law).
	4. *Civil liability for criminal acts*—A criminal act may give rise to both criminal liability and tort liability (see Exhibit 6–2 on page 148 for an example of criminal and tort liability for the same act).
Criminal Liability (See pages 147–150.)	1. *Guilty act*—In general, some form of harmful act must be committed for a crime to exist.
	2. *Intent*—An intent to commit a crime, or a wrongful mental state, is generally required for a crime to exist.
	3. *Liability of corporations*—Corporations normally are liable for the crimes committed by their agents and employees within the course and scope of their employment. Corporations cannot be imprisoned, but they can be fined or denied certain legal privileges.
	4. *Liability of corporate officers and directors*—Corporate directors and officers are personally liable for the crimes they commit and may be held liable for the actions of employees under their supervision.
Types of Crimes (See pages 150–158.)	1. Crimes fall into five general categories: violent crime, property crime, public order crime, white-collar crime, and organized crime.
	a. Violent crimes are those that cause others to suffer harm or death, including murder, assault and battery, sexual assault (rape), and robbery.
	b. Property crimes are the most common form of crime. The offender's goal is to obtain some economic gain or to damage property. This category includes burglary, larceny, obtaining goods by false pretenses, receiving stolen property, arson, and forgery.
	c. Public order crimes are acts, such as public drunkenness, prostitution, gambling, and illegal drug use, that a statute has established are contrary to public values and morals.
	d. White-collar crimes are illegal acts committed by a person or business using nonviolent means to obtain a personal or business advantage. Usually, such crimes are committed in the course of a legitimate occupation. Embezzlement, mail and wire fraud, bribery, bankruptcy fraud, the theft of trade secrets, and insider trading are examples of this category of crime.
	e. Organized crime is a form of crime conducted by groups operating illegitimately to satisfy the public's demand for illegal goods and services (such as gambling or illegal narcotics). This category of crime also includes money laundering and racketeering (RICO) violations.
	2. Each type of crime may also be classified according to its degree of seriousness. Felonies are serious crimes punishable by death or by imprisonment for more than one year. Misdemeanors are less serious crimes punishable by fines or by confinement for up to one year.
Defenses to Criminal Liability (See pages 158–161.)	Defenses to criminal liability include justifiable use of force, necessity, insanity, mistake, duress, entrapment, and the statute of limitations. Also, in some cases defendants may be relieved of criminal liability, at least in part, if they are given immunity.
Constitutional Safeguards and Criminal Procedures (See pages 162–167.)	1. *Fourth Amendment*—Provides protection against unreasonable searches and seizures and requires that probable cause exist before a warrant for a search or an arrest can be issued.
	2. *Fifth Amendment*—Requires due process of law, prohibits double jeopardy, and protects against self-incrimination.
	3. *Sixth Amendment*—Provides guarantees of a speedy trial, a trial by jury, a public trial, the right to confront witnesses, and the right to counsel.
	4. *Eighth Amendment*—Prohibits excessive bail and fines, and cruel and unusual punishment.
	5. *Exclusionary rule*—A criminal procedural rule that prohibits the introduction at trial of any evidence obtained in violation of constitutional rights, as well as any evidence derived from the illegally obtained evidence.

Chapter Summary: Criminal Law and Cyber Crime, Continued

Constitutional Safeguards and Criminal Procedures— Continued	6. *Miranda rule*—A rule set forth by the Supreme Court in *Miranda v. Arizona* holding that individuals who are arrested must be informed of certain constitutional rights, including their right to counsel. 7. *Criminal process*—Procedures governing arrest, indictment, and trial for a crime are designed to safeguard the rights of the individual against the state. The federal government has established sentencing laws or guidelines, which are no longer mandatory but provide a range of penalties for each federal crime.
Cyber Crime **(See pages 167–174.)**	1. *Cyber fraud*—The crime of cyber fraud occurs when misrepresentations are knowingly made over the Internet to deceive another. Two widely reported forms of cyber crime are online auction fraud and online retail fraud. 2. *Cyber theft*—In cyberspace, thieves can steal data from anywhere in the world. Their task is made easier by the fact that many e-businesses store information such as the consumer's name, e-mail address, and credit-card numbers. Phishing, vishing, and employment fraud are variations of identity theft. 3. *Credit-card crime*—The financial burden of stolen credit-card numbers falls on merchants and credit-card issuers more than on consumers. 4. *Hacking*—A hacker is a person who uses one computer to break into another. Malware is any program that is harmful to a computer or, by extension, a computer user. Worms, viruses, and botnets are examples. Some hackers simply want to prove how smart they are, but others have more malicious purposes. Cyberterrorists aim to cause serious problems for computer systems. They may target businesses to find out a firm's plans or transactions, or insert false codes or data to damage a firm's product. A cyberterrorist attack on a major U.S. financial institution or telecommunications system could have serious repercussions, including jeopardizing national security. 5. *Spam*—Unsolicited junk e-mail accounts for about three-quarters of all e-mails. Laws to combat spam have been enacted by thirty-six states and the federal government, but the flow of spam continues. In 2006, Congress enacted the U.S. Safe Web Act to address spam that originates from other nations. 6. *Prosecution of cyber crime*—Prosecuting cyber crime is more difficult than prosecuting traditional crime. Identifying the wrongdoer through electronic footprints left on the Internet is complicated, and jurisdictional issues may arise when the suspect lives in another jurisdiction or nation. A significant federal statute addressing cyber crime is the Computer Fraud and Abuse Act of 1984.

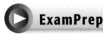 **ExamPrep**

ISSUE SPOTTERS

1. Daisy takes her roommate's credit card, intending to charge expenses that she incurs on a vacation. Her first stop is a gas station, where she uses the card to pay for gas. With respect to the gas station, has she committed a crime? If so, what is it?
2. Without permission, Ben downloads consumer credit files from a computer belonging to Consumer Credit Agency. He then sells the data to Dawn. Has Ben committed a crime? If so, what is it?

—**Check your answers to these questions against the answers provided in Appendix G.**

BEFORE THE TEST

Go to **www.cengagebrain.com**, enter the ISBN number "9781111530617," and click on "Find" to locate this textbook's Web site. Then, click on "Access Now" under "Study Tools," and select "Chapter 6" at the top. There you will find an "Interactive Quiz" that you can take to assess your mastery of the concepts in this chapter, as well as "Flashcards" and a "Glossary" of important terms.

For Review

1. What two elements must exist before a person can be held liable for a crime? Can a corporation commit crimes?
2. What are five broad categories of crimes? What is white-collar crime?
3. What defenses might be raised by criminal defendants to avoid liability for criminal acts?
4. What constitutional safeguards exist to protect persons accused of crimes?
5. How has the Internet expanded opportunities for identity theft?

Questions and Case Problems

6–1. Types of Cyber Crimes. The following situations are similar, but each represents a variation of a particular crime. Identify the crime and point out the differences in the variations.

1. Chen, posing fraudulently as Diamond Credit Card Co., sends an e-mail to Emily, stating that the company has observed suspicious activity in her account and has frozen the account. The e-mail asks her to reregister her credit-card number and password to reopen the account.

2. Claiming falsely to be Big Buy Retail Finance Co., Conner sends an e-mail to Dino, asking him to confirm or update his personal security information to prevent his Big Buy account from being discontinued.

3. Felicia posts her résumé on GotWork.com, an online job-posting site, seeking a position in business and managerial finance and accounting. Hayden, who misrepresents himself as an employment officer with International Bank & Commerce Corp., sends her an e-mail asking for more personal information.

6–2. **Question with Sample Answer. Cyber Scam.** Kayla, a student at Learnwell University, owes $20,000 in unpaid tuition. If Kayla does not pay the tuition, Learnwell will not allow her to graduate. To obtain the funds to pay the debt, she sends e-mail letters to people that she does not personally know asking for financial help to send Milo, her disabled child, to a special school. In reality, Kayla has no children. Is this a crime? If so, which one?
—For a sample answer to Question 6–2, go to Appendix E at the end of this text.

6–3. White-Collar Crime. Helm Instruction Co. in Maumee, Ohio, makes custom electrical control systems. In September 1998, Helm hired Patrick Walsh to work as comptroller. Walsh soon developed a close relationship with Richard Wilhelm, Helm's president, who granted Walsh's request to hire Shari Price as an assistant. Wilhelm was not aware that Walsh and Price were engaged in an extramarital affair. Over the next five years, Walsh and Price spent more than $200,000 of Helm's money on themselves. Among other things, Walsh drew unauthorized checks on Helm's accounts to pay his personal credit cards and issued to Price and himself unauthorized salary increases, overtime payments, and tuition reimbursement payments, altering Helm's records to hide the payments. After an investigation, Helm officials confronted Walsh. He denied the affair with Price, claimed that his unauthorized use of Helm's funds was an "interest-free loan," and argued that it was less of a burden on the company to pay his credit cards than to give him the salary increases to which he felt he was entitled. Did Walsh commit a crime? If so, what crime did he commit? Discuss. [*State v. Walsh,* 113 Ohio App.3d 1515, 866 N.E.2d 513 (6 Dist. 2007)]

6–4. Credit Cards. Oleksiy Sharapka ordered merchandise online using stolen credit cards. He had the items sent to outlets of Mail Boxes, Etc., and then arranged for someone to deliver the items to his house. He subsequently shipped the goods overseas, primarily to Russia. Sharapka was indicted in a federal district court. At the time of his arrest, government agents found in his possession, among other things, more than three hundred stolen credit-card numbers, including numbers issued by American Express. There was evidence that he had used more than ten of the American Express numbers to buy goods worth between $400,000 and $1 million from at least fourteen vendors. Did Sharapka commit any crimes? If so, who were his victims? Explain. [*United States v. Sharapka,* 526 F.3d 58 (1st Cir. 2008)]

6–5. Intellectual Property. Jiri Klimecek was a member of a group that overrode copyright protection in movies, video games, and software, and made them available for download online. Klimecek bought and installed hardware and software to set up a computer server and paid half of the monthly service charges to connect the server to the Internet. He knew that users around the world could access the server to upload and download copyrighted works (discussed in Chapter 8). He obtained access to Czech movies and music to make them available. Klimecek was indicted in a federal district court for copyright infringement. He claimed that he had not understood the full scope of the operation. Did Klimecek commit a crime? If so, was he a "minor participant" entitled to a reduced sentence? Explain. [*United States v. Klimecek,* __ F.3d __ (7th Cir. 2009)]

6–6. **Case Problem with Sample Answer. Fourth Amendment.** Three police officers, including Maria Trevizo, were on patrol in Tucson, Arizona, near a neighborhood associated with the Crips gang, when they pulled over a car with suspended registration. Each officer talked to one of the three occupants. Trevizo spoke with Lemon Johnson, who was wearing clothing consistent with Crips membership. Visible in his jacket pocket was a police scanner, and he said that he had served time in prison for burglary. Trevizo asked him to get out of the car and patted him down "for officer safety." She found a gun. Johnson was charged in an Arizona state court with illegal possession of a weapon. What standard should apply to an officer's pat-down of a passenger during a traffic stop? Should a search warrant be required? Could a search proceed solely on the basis of probable cause? Would a reasonable suspicion short of probable cause be sufficient? Discuss. [*Arizona v. Johnson*, 555 U.S. 323, 129 S.Ct. 781, 172 L.Ed.2d 694 (2009)]

—**To view a sample answer for Case Problem 6–6, go to Appendix F at the end of this text.**

6–7. Sentencing Guidelines. Paul Wilkinson worked for a company that sold fuel to various military bases. He paid an employee of a competitor to provide him with information about bids for contracts for which both companies were bidding. The information enabled Wilkinson to rig the bids and win contracts. When the scam was uncovered, he was indicted for conspiracy to defraud the government, to commit wire fraud, and to steal trade secrets. He pleaded guilty to the charges under a plea arrangement. Given the nature of the offenses, the federal sentencing guidelines provide for a prison term of fifty-one to sixty-three months with no possibility of probation. Due to Wilkinson's cooperation, the prosecution recommended fifty-one months. His attorney argued for a term of ten to sixteen months. The judge sentenced Wilkinson to three years' probation and eight hundred hours of community service, but no prison term. The government appealed, arguing that the sentence was too light and thus violated the sentencing guidelines. Can a trial judge give such a light sentence under the sentencing guidelines? Explain your answer. [*United States v. Wilkinson*, 590 F.3d 259 (4th Cir. 2010)]

6–8. Fourth Amendment. While awaiting trial, Charles E. Byrd was held in a minimum-security jail. Several fights had broken out at the jail, and the guards suspected that some of the inmates possessed contraband. One day, a team of officers wearing T-shirts and jeans showed up at the jail. They ordered the inmates to form a line and then took several inmates at a time into a room for a strip search. Byrd was ordered to remove all his clothing except his boxer shorts. A female officer searched Byrd while several male officers stood by watching. During the search, the officer felt around Byrd's inner and outer thighs, felt across his genitals on the outside of his boxer shorts, and squeezed his buttocks to check his anus for drugs. Byrd later filed a grievance with the jail and then a lawsuit against the sheriff's department, claiming that the search was unreasonable and violated his Fourth Amendment rights. Is a cross-gender strip search constitutionally unreasonable if no immediate emergency exists? Why or why not? When would such a search be permissible? [*Byrd v. Maricopa County Sheriff's Department*, 629 F.3d. 1135 (9th Cir. 2011)]

6–9. A Question of Ethics. Identity Theft. *Davis Omole had good grades in high school, played on the football and chess teams, and went on to college. Twenty-year-old Omole was also one of the chief architects of a scheme through which more than one hundred individuals were defrauded. Omole worked at a cell phone store, where he stole customers' personal information. He and others used the stolen identities to create one hundred different accounts on eBay, through which they held more than three hundred auctions listing for sale items that they did not own and did not intend to sell—cell phones, plasma televisions, stereos, and more. They collected $90,000 through these auctions. To avoid getting caught, they continuously closed and opened the eBay accounts, activated and deactivated cell phone and e-mail accounts, and changed mailing addresses and post office boxes. Omole, who had previously been convicted in a state court for Internet fraud, was convicted in a federal district court of identity theft and wire fraud. [United States v. Omole, 523 F.3d 691 (7th Cir. 2008)]*

1. Before Omole's trial, he sent e-mails to his victims, ridiculing them and calling them stupid for having been cheated. During his trial, he displayed contempt for the court. What do these factors show about Omole's ethics?

2. Under the federal sentencing guidelines, Omole could have been imprisoned for more than eight years, but he received a sentence of only three years, two of which were the mandatory sentence for identity theft. Was this sentence too lenient? Explain.

6–10. Video Question. *Twelve Angry Men.* Access the video using the instructions provided below to answer the following questions.

1. The jurors are deliberating on whether to convict the defendant. One juror says that at the beginning of the trial he felt that the defendant was guilty and that "nobody proved otherwise." Does a criminal defendant have to offer evidence of his or her innocence? What must the prosecution show to establish that a defendant is guilty? How does the burden of proof differ in criminal and civil cases?

2. It is clear that all of the jurors except one (Henry Fonda) believe that the defendant is guilty. How many jurors does it usually take to render a verdict in a criminal case?

3. When the holdout juror says that under the U.S. Constitution "the defendant does not even have to open his mouth," to which provision is he referring?

—To watch this video, go to **www.cengagebrain.com** and register the access code that came with your new book or log in to your existing account. Select the link for either the "Business Law Digital Video Library Online Access" or "Business Law CourseMate," and then click on "Complete Video List" to find the video for this chapter (Video 70).

Chapter 7

International Law in a Global Economy

> "The merchant has no country."
>
> —Thomas Jefferson, 1743–1826
> (Third president of the United States, 1801–1809)

Chapter Objectives

After reading this chapter, you should be able to answer the following questions:

1. **What is the principle of comity, and why do courts deciding disputes involving a foreign law or judicial decree apply this principle?**

2. **What is the act of state doctrine? In what circumstances is this doctrine applied?**

3. **Under the Foreign Sovereign Immunities Act of 1976, on what bases might a foreign state be considered subject to the jurisdiction of U.S. courts?**

4. **In what circumstances will U.S. antitrust laws be applied extraterritorially?**

5. **Do U.S. laws prohibiting employment discrimination apply in all circumstances to U.S. employees working for U.S. employers abroad?**

(John Elk III/Lonely Planet Images/Getty Images)

International business transactions are not unique to the modern world. Indeed, commerce has always crossed national borders, as President Thomas Jefferson noted in the chapter-opening quotation above. What is new in our day is the dramatic growth in world trade and the emergence of a global business community. Because exchanges of goods, services, and ideas on a global level are now routine, students of business law and the legal environment should be familiar with the laws pertaining to international business transactions. Future businesspersons should also be aware that in response to the latest economic recession, the U.S. government has undertaken an initiative to encourage exports of goods and services to foreign markets by U.S. companies. Accordingly, we examine this recent initiative in this chapter.

Laws affecting the international legal environment of business include both international law and national law. **International law** can be defined as a body of law—formed as a result of international customs, treaties, and organizations—that governs relations among or between nations. International law may be public, creating standards for the nations themselves, or it may be private, establishing international standards for private transactions that cross national borders. *National law* is the law of a particular nation, such as Brazil, Germany, Japan, or the United States.

In this chapter, we examine how both international law and national law frame business operations in the global context. We also look at some selected areas relating

International Law The law that governs relations among nations. International customs, treaties, and organizations are important sources of international law.

to business activities in a global context, including international sales contracts, civil dispute resolution, letters of credit, and investment protection. We conclude the chapter with a discussion of the application of certain U.S. laws in a transnational setting.

▶ International Law—Sources and Principles

The major difference between international law and national law is that government authorities can enforce national law. What government, however, can enforce international law? By definition, a *nation* is a sovereign entity—meaning that there is no higher authority to which that nation must submit. If a nation violates an international law and persuasive tactics fail, other countries or international organizations have no recourse except to take coercive actions—from severance of diplomatic relations and boycotts to, as a last resort, war—against the violating nation.

In essence, international law attempts to reconcile the need of each country to be the final authority over its own affairs with the desire of nations to benefit economically from trade and harmonious relations with one another. Sovereign nations can, and do, voluntarily agree to be governed in certain respects by international law for the purpose of facilitating international trade and commerce, as well as civilized discourse. As a result, a body of international law has evolved.

Sources of International Law

Basically, there are three sources of international law: international customs, treaties and international agreements, and international organizations and conferences. We look at each of these sources here.

INTERNATIONAL CUSTOMS   One important source of international law consists of the international customs that have evolved among nations in their relations with one another. Article 38(1) of the Statute of the International Court of Justice refers to an international custom as "evidence of a general practice accepted as law." The legal principles and doctrines that you will read about shortly are rooted in international customs and traditions that have evolved over time in the international arena.

TREATIES AND INTERNATIONAL AGREEMENTS   Treaties and other explicit agreements between or among foreign nations provide another important source of international law. A **treaty** is an agreement or contract between two or more nations that must be authorized and ratified by the supreme power of each nation. Under Article II, Section 2, of the U.S. Constitution, the president has the power "by and with the Advice and Consent of the Senate, to make Treaties, provided two-thirds of the Senators present concur."

Treaty   In international law, a formal written agreement negotiated between two nations or among several nations. In the United States, all treaties must be approved by the Senate.

A *bilateral* agreement, as the term implies, is an agreement formed by two nations to govern their commercial exchanges or other relations with one another. A *multilateral* agreement is formed by several nations. For example, regional trade associations such as the Andean Community, the Association of Southeast Asian Nations, and the European Union are the result of multilateral trade agreements.

INTERNATIONAL ORGANIZATIONS   In international law, the term **international organization** generally refers to an organization that is composed mainly of officials of member nations and usually established by treaty. The United States is a member

International Organization   Any membership group that operates across national borders. These organizations can be governmental organizations, such as the United Nations, or nongovernmental organizations, such as the Red Cross.

Archbishop Desmond Tutu speaks at the United Nations. How is the United Nations a source of international law?

of more than one hundred multilateral and bilateral organizations, including at least twenty through the United Nations. These organizations adopt resolutions, declarations, and other types of standards that often require nations to behave in a particular manner. The General Assembly of the United Nations, for example, has adopted numerous nonbinding resolutions and declarations that embody principles of international law. Disputes involving these resolutions and declarations may be brought before the International Court of Justice. That court, however, normally has authority to settle legal disputes only when nations voluntarily submit to its jurisdiction.

The United Nations Commission on International Trade Law has made considerable progress in establishing uniformity in international law as it relates to trade and commerce. One of the commission's most significant creations to date is the 1980 Convention on Contracts for the International Sale of Goods (CISG). The CISG is similar to Article 2 of the Uniform Commercial Code. It is designed to settle disputes between parties to sales contracts if the parties have not agreed otherwise in their contracts. The CISG governs only sales contracts between trading partners in nations that have ratified the CISG.

International Principles and Doctrines

Over time, a number of legal principles and doctrines have evolved and have been employed by the courts of various nations to resolve or reduce conflicts that involve a foreign element. The three important legal principles discussed next are based primarily on courtesy and respect, and are applied in the interests of maintaining harmonious relations among nations.

Comity The principle by which one nation defers to and gives effect to the laws and judicial decrees of another nation. This recognition is based primarily on respect.

THE PRINCIPLE OF COMITY Under the principle of **comity,** one nation will defer to and give effect to the laws and judicial decrees of another country, as long as they are consistent with the law and public policy of the accommodating nation.

CASE EXAMPLE 7.1 Karen Goldberg's husband was killed in a terrorist bombing in Israel. She filed a lawsuit in a federal court in New York against UBS AG, a Switzerland-based global financial services company with many offices in the United States. Goldberg claimed that UBS was liable under the U.S. Anti-Terrorism Act for aiding and abetting the murder of her husband because it provided financial services to the international terrorist organizations responsible for his murder. UBS argued that the case should be transferred to a court in Israel, which would offer a remedy "substantially the same" as the one available in the United States. The court refused to transfer the case, however, because that would require an Israeli court to take evidence and judge the emotional damage suffered by Goldberg, "raising distinct concerns of comity and enforceability." U.S. courts hesitate to impose U.S. law on foreign courts when such law is "an unwarranted intrusion" on the policies governing a foreign nation's judicial system.[1] ●

One way to understand the principle of comity (and the *act of state doctrine,* which will be discussed shortly) is to consider the relationships among the states in our federal form of government. Each state honors (gives "full faith and credit" to) the contracts, property deeds, wills, and other legal obligations formed in other states, as well as judicial decisions with respect to such obligations. On a global basis, nations similarly attempt to honor judgments rendered in other countries when it is feasible to do so. Of course, in the United States the states are constitutionally required to honor other states' actions whereas internationally, nations are not *required* to honor the actions of other nations.

---

1. *Goldberg v. UBS AG,* 690 F.Supp.2d 92 (E.D.N.Y. 2010).

Act of State Doctrine A doctrine providing that the judicial branch of one country will not examine the validity of public acts committed by a recognized foreign government within its own territory.

THE ACT OF STATE DOCTRINE The **act of state doctrine** provides that the judicial branch of one country will not examine the validity of public acts committed by a recognized foreign government within its own territory.

A government controls the natural resources, such as oil reserves, within its territory. It can decide to exploit the resources or preserve them, or to establish a balance between exploitation and preservation. Does the act of state doctrine apply to such decisions even though they may affect market prices in other countries? That was the question in the following case.

Case 7.1 **Spectrum Stores, Inc. v. Citgo Petroleum Corp.**

United States Court of Appeals, Fifth District, 632 F.3d 938 (2011).
www.ca5.uscourts.gov[a]

BACKGROUND AND FACTS Spectrum Stores, Inc., and other U.S. gasoline retailers (the plaintiffs) filed a suit against Citgo Petroleum Corporation and other oil production companies in a federal district court. The plaintiffs alleged that the defendants had conspired to fix the prices of crude oil and refined petroleum products in the United States, primarily by limiting the production of crude oil. Citgo is owned by the national oil company of Venezuela, and most of the other defendants are owned entirely or in part by Venezuela or Saudi Arabia. Both nations are members of the Organization of Petroleum Exporting Countries (OPEC), which was formed by several oil-rich nations "to ensure the stabilization of oil markets in order to secure an efficient, economic and regular supply of petroleum." Spectrum sought damages, an injunction, and other relief. The court dismissed the suit, and Spectrum appealed.

IN THE WORDS OF THE COURT . . .
E. Grady *JOLLY*, Circuit Judge:
* * * *

Under the act of state doctrine, the courts of one country will not sit in judgment on the acts of the government of another, done within its own territory. The doctrine is grounded in the principle that juridical review of acts of state of a foreign power could embarrass the conduct of foreign relations by the political branches of the government.
* * * *

* * * Adjudication of this suit would necessarily call into question the acts of foreign governments with respect to exploitation of their natural resources. * * * Exploitation of natural resources is an inherently sovereign function.

* * * The availability of oil has become a significant factor in international relations * * * . The United States has a grave interest in the petro-politics of the Middle East and * * * the foreign policy arms

of the executive and legislative branches are intimately involved in this sensitive area.

* * * The granting of any relief to Appellants would effectively order foreign governments to dismantle their chosen means of exploiting the valuable natural resources within their sovereign territories. *Recognizing that the judiciary is neither competent nor authorized to frustrate the longstanding foreign policy of the political branches by wading so brazenly into the sphere of foreign relations, we decline to sit in judgment of the acts of the foreign states that comprise OPEC.* [Emphasis added.]
* * * *

We sum up: Appellants, retailers of gasoline products in the United States, have asked [this court] to adjudicate the merits of their * * * claims against oil production companies that have allegedly participated in a conspiracy to fix prices. Reducing their claims to basics, Appellants allege a conspiracy that is orchestrated by the sovereign member nations of OPEC. * * * Any ruling on the merits of this case would, by its core essence, impermissibly interfere with the Executive Branch's longstanding policy of engaging with OPEC nations regarding the global supply of oil through diplomacy instead of private litigation. * * * Adjudication of Appellants' claims is precluded by the act of state doctrine.

DECISION AND REMEDY The U.S. Court of Appeals for the Fifth Circuit affirmed the lower court's judgment. Granting relief to the plaintiffs would effectively order foreign governments to dismantle their chosen means of exploiting the resources within their own territories. Under the act of state doctrine, a U.S. court will not rule on the validity of a foreign government's acts within its own territory.

THE POLITICAL DIMENSION *If the judicial branch does not have the authority to rule on matters of foreign policy, which branch of government does? Explain.*

THE GLOBAL DIMENSION *Suppose that a U.S. court declared that a foreign nation's act was illegal. Would such a declaration encroach on foreign policy matters falling under the authority of other branches of government? Why or why not?*

---

a. In the left column, in the "Opinions" section, click on "Opinions Page." On the next page, in the "Search for opinions where:" section, in the "and/or Docket number is:" box, type "09-20084" and click on "Search." In the result, click on the docket number to access the opinion. The U.S. Court of Appeals for the Fifth Circuit maintains this Web site.

(AP Photo/Carlos Hernandez)

In 2009, President Hugo Chávez of Venezuela ordered the expropriation of a rice-processing plant owned by the U.S. food company Cargill, Inc. What would determine if this action was an expropriation or a confiscation?

Expropriation   The seizure by a government of a privately owned business or personal property for a proper public purpose and with just compensation.

Confiscation   A government's taking of a privately owned business or personal property without a proper public purpose or an award of just compensation.

Sovereign Immunity   A doctrine that immunizes foreign nations from the jurisdiction of U.S. courts when certain conditions are satisfied.

When a Foreign Government Takes Private Property. The act of state doctrine can have important consequences for individuals and firms doing business with, and investing in, other countries. This doctrine is frequently employed in cases involving **expropriation,** which occurs when a government seizes a privately owned business or privately owned goods for a proper public purpose and awards just compensation. When a government seizes private property for an illegal purpose and without just compensation, the taking is referred to as a **confiscation.** The line between these two forms of taking is sometimes blurred because of differing interpretations of what is illegal and what constitutes just compensation.

EXAMPLE 7.2   Flaherty, Inc., a U.S. company, owns a mine in Brazil. The government of Brazil seizes the mine for public use and claims that the profits Flaherty has already realized from the mine constitute just compensation. Flaherty disagrees, but the act of state doctrine may prevent that company's recovery in a U.S. court. •

Note that in a case alleging that a foreign government has wrongfully taken the plaintiff's property, the defendant government has the burden of proving that the taking was an expropriation, not a confiscation.

Doctrine May Immunize a Foreign Government's Actions. When applicable, both the act of state doctrine and the doctrine of *sovereign immunity,* which we discuss next, tend to shield foreign nations from the jurisdiction of U.S. courts. As a result, firms or individuals who own property overseas generally have little legal protection against government actions in the countries where they operate.

THE DOCTRINE OF SOVEREIGN IMMUNITY   When certain conditions are satisfied, the doctrine of **sovereign immunity** immunizes foreign nations from the jurisdiction of U.S. courts. In 1976, Congress codified this rule in the Foreign Sovereign Immunities Act (FSIA).[2] The FSIA exclusively governs the circumstances in which an action may be brought in the United States against a foreign nation, including attempts to attach (take legal action against, see Chapter 12) a foreign nation's property. Because the law is jurisdictional in nature, a plaintiff has the burden of showing that a defendant is not entitled to sovereign immunity.

Section 1605 of the FSIA sets forth the major exceptions to the jurisdictional immunity of a foreign state. A foreign state is not immune from the jurisdiction of U.S. courts in the following situations:

1. When the foreign state has waived its immunity either explicitly or by implication.
2. When the foreign state has engaged in commercial activity within the United States or in commercial activity outside the United States that has "a direct effect in the United States."[3]
3. When the foreign state has committed a tort in the United States or has violated certain international laws.

In applying the FSIA, questions frequently arise as to whether an entity is a "foreign state" and what constitutes a "commercial activity." Under Section 1603 of the

---

2. 28 U.S.C. Sections 1602–1611.
3. See, for example, *O'Bryan v. Holy See,* 556 F.3d 361 (6th Cir. 2009).

FSIA, a *foreign state* includes both a political subdivision of a foreign state and an instrumentality of a foreign state. Section 1603 broadly defines a *commercial activity* as a regular course of commercial conduct, transaction, or act that is carried out by a foreign state within the United States. Section 1603, however, does not describe the particulars of what constitutes a commercial activity. Thus, the courts are left to decide whether a particular activity is governmental or commercial in nature.

▶ Doing Business Internationally

Export The sale of goods and services by domestic firms to buyers located in other countries.

A U.S. domestic firm can engage in international business transactions in a number of ways. The simplest way is for U.S. firms to **export** their goods and services to markets abroad. Alternatively, a U.S. firm can establish foreign production facilities so as to be closer to the foreign market or markets in which its products are sold. The advantages may include lower labor costs, fewer government regulations, and lower taxes and trade barriers. A domestic firm can also obtain revenues by licensing its technology to an existing foreign company or by selling franchises to overseas entities.

Exporting

"Commerce is the great civilizer. We exchange ideas when we exchange fabrics."

Robert G. Ingersoll, 1833–1899
(American politician and orator)

Exporting can take two forms: direct exporting and indirect exporting. In *direct exporting,* a U.S. company signs a sales contract with a foreign purchaser that provides for the conditions of shipment and payment for the goods. (How payments are made in international transactions will be discussed later in this chapter.) If sufficient business develops in a foreign country, a U.S. corporation may set up a specialized marketing organization in that foreign market by appointing a foreign agent or a foreign distributor. This is called *indirect exporting.*

When a U.S. firm desires to limit its involvement in an international market, it will typically establish an *agency relationship* with a foreign firm. (*Agency* will be discussed in Chapter 16.) The foreign firm then acts as the U.S. firm's agent and can enter into contracts in the foreign location on behalf of the principal (the U.S. company).

Distribution Agreement A contract between a seller and a distributor of the seller's products setting out the terms and conditions of the distributorship.

DISTRIBUTORSHIPS When a foreign country represents a substantial market, a U.S. firm may wish to appoint a distributor located in that country. The U.S. firm and the distributor enter into a **distribution agreement,** which is a contract between the seller and the distributor setting out the terms and conditions of the distributorship. These terms and conditions—for example, price, currency of payment, availability of supplies, and method of payment—primarily involve contract law. Disputes concerning distribution agreements may involve jurisdictional or other issues, as well as contract law, which will be discussed later in this chapter.

THE NATIONAL EXPORT INITIATIVE Although the United States is one of the world's major exporters, exports make up a much smaller share of annual output in the United States than they do in our most important trading partners. This is because the United States has not promoted exports as actively as many other nations have.

In an effort to increase U.S. exports, in 2010 the Obama administration created the National Export Initiative (NEI) with a goal of doubling U.S. exports by 2015. Some commentators believe that another goal of the NEI is to reduce outsourcing—the practice of having manufacturing or other activities performed in lower-wage countries such as China and India. Especially in view of the stubbornly high U.S. unemployment rate, there is increasing concern that U.S. jobs are being shipped overseas.

Export Promotion. An important component of the NEI is the Export Promotion Cabinet, which consists of officials from sixteen government agencies and departments. All cabinet members must submit detailed plans to the president, outlining the steps that they will take to increase U.S. exports.

The U.S. Commerce Department plays a leading role in the NEI, and hundreds of its trade experts serve as advocates to help some twenty thousand U.S. companies increase their export sales. In addition, the Commerce Department and other cabinet members will work to promote U.S. exports in the high-growth developing markets of Brazil, China, and India. The members will also identify market opportunities in fast-growing sectors, such as environmental goods and services, biotechnology, and renewable energy.

Increased Export Financing. Under the NEI, the Export-Import Bank of the United States is increasing the financing that it makes available to small and medium-sized businesses by 50 percent. In the initial phase, the bank added hundreds of new small-business clients that sell a wide variety of products, from sophisticated polymers to date palm trees and nanotechnology-based cosmetics. In addition, the administration has proposed that $30 billion be used to boost lending to small businesses, especially for export purposes.

Preventing Legal Disputes

In light of the National Export Initiative, managers in companies that are now outsourcing or thinking of doing so may wish to reconsider. Increasingly, the federal government is taking a stance against outsourcing. As long as unemployment remains high in the United States, the emphasis will be on the creation of jobs at home. These efforts will often be backed by subsidies and access to federally supported borrowing initiatives.

Manufacturing Abroad

An alternative to direct or indirect exporting is the establishment of foreign manufacturing facilities. Typically, U.S. firms establish manufacturing plants abroad if they believe that doing so will reduce their costs—particularly for labor, shipping, and raw materials—and enable them to compete more effectively in foreign markets. Foreign firms have done the same in the United States. Sony, Nissan, and other Japanese manufacturers have established U.S. plants to avoid import duties that the U.S. Congress may impose on Japanese products entering this country.

A U.S. firm may license a foreign manufacturing company to use its copyrighted, patented, or trademarked intellectual property or trade secrets. Like any other licensing agreement (see Chapter 8), a licensing agreement with a foreign-based firm calls for a payment of royalties on some basis—such as so many cents per unit produced or a certain percentage of profits from units sold in a particular geographic territory. As will be discussed in Chapter 14, franchising is a well-known form of licensing. **EXAMPLE 7.3**   The Coca-Cola Bottling Company licenses firms worldwide to employ (and keep confidential) its secret formula for the syrup used in its soft drink. In return, the foreign firms licensed to make the syrup pay Coca-Cola a percentage of the income earned from the sale of the soft drink. ● Once a

The Coca-Cola Bottling Company licenses firms throughout the world to produce its soft drinks. All such firms must keep Coca-Cola's syrup formula a secret. Why would foreign companies choose to pay for a license with Coca-Cola rather than create their own competitive soft drinks?

firm's trademark is known worldwide, the firm may experience increased demand for other products it manufactures or sells—obviously an important consideration.

Another way to expand into a foreign market is to establish a wholly owned subsidiary firm in a foreign country. When a wholly owned subsidiary is established, the parent company, which remains in the United States, retains complete ownership of all the facilities in the foreign country, as well as complete authority and control over all phases of the operation. A U.S. firm can also expand into international markets through a joint venture. In a joint venture, the U.S. company owns only part of the operation. The rest is owned either by local owners in the foreign country or by another foreign entity. All of the firms involved in a joint venture share responsibilities, as well as profits and liabilities.

Regulation of Specific Business Activities

Doing business abroad can affect the economies, foreign policies, domestic policies, and other national interests of the countries involved. For this reason, nations impose laws to restrict or facilitate international business. Controls may also be imposed by international agreements. Here, we discuss how different types of international activities are regulated.

Investment Protections

Firms that invest in foreign nations face the risk that the foreign government may take possession of the investment property. Expropriation, as already mentioned, occurs when property is taken and the owner is paid just compensation for what is taken. Expropriation generally does not violate observed principles of international law. Such principles are usually violated, however, when a government confiscates property without compensation (or without adequate compensation). Few remedies are available for confiscation of property by a foreign government. Claims are often resolved by lump-sum settlements after negotiations between the United States and the taking nation.

To counter the deterrent effect that the possibility of confiscation may have on potential investors, many countries guarantee that foreign investors will be compensated if their property is taken. A guaranty can take the form of statutory laws or provisions in international treaties. As further protection for foreign investments, some countries provide insurance for their citizens' investments abroad.

Export Controls

NOTE Most countries restrict exports for the same reasons: to protect national security, to further foreign policy objectives, and to prevent the spread of nuclear weapons.

The U.S. Constitution provides in Article I, Section 9, that "No Tax or Duty shall be laid on Articles exported from any State." Thus, Congress cannot impose any export taxes. Congress can, however, use a variety of other devices to control exports. Congress may set export quotas on various items, such as grain being sold abroad. Under the Export Administration Act of 1979,[4] the flow of technologically advanced products and technical data can be restricted.

---

4. 50 U.S.C. Sections 2401–2420.

While restricting certain exports, the United States (and other nations) also uses devices such as export incentives and subsidies to stimulate other exports and thereby aid domestic businesses. Under the Export Trading Company Act of 1982,[5] U.S. banks are encouraged to invest in export trading companies, which are formed when exporting firms join together to export a line of goods. The U.S. Export-Import Bank provides financial assistance, consisting primarily of credit guaranties given to commercial banks that in turn lend funds to U.S. exporting companies.

Import Controls

All nations have restrictions on imports, and the United States is no exception. Restrictions include strict prohibitions, quotas, and tariffs. Under the Trading with the Enemy Act of 1917,[6] for instance, no goods may be imported from nations that have been designated enemies of the United States. Other laws prohibit the importation of illegal drugs, books that urge insurrection against the United States, and agricultural products that pose dangers to domestic crops or animals. The import of goods that infringe U.S. patents is also prohibited. The International Trade Commission investigates allegations that imported goods infringe U.S. patents and imposes penalties if necessary.

QUOTAS AND TARIFFS   Limits on the amounts of goods that can be imported are known as **quotas.** At one time, the United States had legal quotas on the number of automobiles that could be imported from Japan. Today, Japan "voluntarily" restricts the number of automobiles exported to the United States. **Tariffs** are taxes on imports. A tariff usually is a percentage of the value of the import, but it can be a flat rate per unit (for example, per barrel of oil). Tariffs raise the prices of goods, causing some consumers to purchase more domestically manufactured goods and fewer imported goods. (For a discussion of tariffs and other considerations for businesses going global, see this chapter's *Linking the Law to Marketing* feature on page 199.)

Sometimes, countries impose tariffs on goods from a particular nation in retaliation for political acts. **EXAMPLE 7.4**   In 2009, Mexico imposed tariffs of 10 to 20 percent on ninety products exported from the United States in retaliation for the Obama administration's cancellation of a cross-border trucking program. The program had been instituted to comply with a provision in the North American Free Trade Agreement (discussed shortly) that was intended to eventually grant Mexican trucks full access to U.S. highways. U.S truck drivers opposed the program, however, and consumer protection groups claimed that the Mexican trucks posed safety issues. Because the Mexican tariffs were imposed annually on $2.4 billion of U.S. goods, in 2011 President Barack Obama negotiated a deal that allowed Mexican truckers to enter the United States. In exchange, Mexico agreed to suspend half of the tariffs immediately and the remainder when the first Mexican hauler complied with the new U.S. requirements.The agreement officially ended the ban on Mexican trucks crossing the U.S. border. ●

In the following case, an importer provided invoices that understated the value of its imports and resulted in lower tariffs than would have been paid on the full value of the goods. Was this fraud or negligence?

"The notion dies hard that in some sort of way exports are patriotic but imports are immoral."

Lord Harlech, 1918–1985
(English writer)

Quota   A set limit on the amount of goods that can be imported.

Tariff   A tax on imported goods.

"Tariff: a scale of taxes on imports, designed to protect the domestic producer against the greed of his consumer."

Ambrose Bierce, 1842–1914
(American journalist)

---

5. 15 U.S.C. Sections 4001, 4003.
6. 12 U.S.C. Section 95a.

Case 7.2 United States v. Inn Foods, Inc.

United States Court of Appeals, Federal Circuit, 560 F.3d 1338 (2009).
www.cafc.uscourts.gov[a]

COMPANY PROFILE *Inn Foods, Inc. (www.innfoods.com), was established in 1976 as a subsidiary of the VPS Companies, Inc. Inn Foods imports frozen fruits and vegetables into the United States from sources worldwide. At its plants in California and Texas, the company blends, custom packages, co-packs, flavors, and seasons vegetables, pasta, potatoes, rice, fruits, and other food products. Each year, Inn Foods sells more than 157 million pounds of food. Its customers include buyers in the food service industry, industrial food markets, and retail food markets at locations around the globe.*

A company importing frozen produce uses a double-invoicing system to undervalue its purchases and reduce its tariff payments. Is this fraud?

BACKGROUND AND FACTS

Between 1987 and 1990, Inn Foods imported frozen produce from six Mexican growers who agreed to issue invoices that understated the value of the produce. For each understated invoice, Inn Foods sent an order confirmation that estimated the produce's actual market value. Inn Foods later remitted the difference to the growers. Through this double-invoicing system, Inn Foods undervalued its purchases by approximately $3.5 million and paid lower tariff taxes as a result. During an investigation by U.S. Customs and Border Protection, Inn Foods's accounting supervisor denied the existence of the double invoices. The federal government filed an action in the U.S. Court of International Trade against Inn Foods. The court held the defendant liable for fraud and assessed the amount of the unpaid taxes—$624,602.55—plus an additional penalty of $7.5 million. Inn Foods appealed, claiming that it had acted negligently, not fraudulently.

IN THE WORDS OF THE COURT . . .
DYK, Circuit Judge.
* * * *

Initially we note that the record fully supports the trade court's determination that Inn Foods knew that the invoice for each shipment of produce was grossly undervalued, and hence false. The Mexican grower sent Inn Foods a copy of the undervalued "factura" invoice; that "factura" invoice was used to value the entries for

Customs purposes. There was evidence that the growers specifically informed Inn Foods of the undervaluation. As the trade court noted, for example, a letter * * * from one of the Mexican growers stated that "we ship * * * Broccoli Spears at 0.50/lb " but that "my invoice * * * will read * * * 0.28/lb." Moreover, upon receipt of the undervalued factura, a * * * manager * * * adjusted the prices to reflect the true and higher estimate. This higher amount was entered into Inn Foods's accounting system. Inn Foods then sent an order confirmation to the Mexican grower with the higher price, retaining a copy of both the undervalued and true invoices for its files. *Thus, one invoice served to bring the produce into the United States at a reduced cost and * * * the second to keep accurate accounting records.* [Emphasis added.]

The existence of the double invoices was also concealed. * * * [For example] during the initial Customs investigation, Inn Foods's accounting supervisor—with what must have been full knowledge of the falsity of the statement—denied outright the existence of a second invoice reflecting a price higher than the amount reported to Customs. This concealment, too, points strongly to fraudulent intent.

The record also makes clear, and Inn Foods does not contest, that Inn Foods knew the false invoices would be used to enter goods into the United States.
* * * *

In sum, we agree that the evidence supports the trade court's finding of fraudulent intent with regard to the basic double-invoicing scheme.

DECISION AND REMEDY
The U.S. Court of Appeals for the Federal Circuit affirmed the lower court's judgment. The evidence showed that Inn Foods "knowingly entered goods by means of a material false statement."

WHAT IF THE FACTS WERE DIFFERENT?
Suppose that after Inn Foods learned of the investigation, the company told U.S. Customs and Border Protection that it was working to correct the "errors" and would "advise" as soon as that happened. Would this have undercut the government's case? Why or why not?

THE LEGAL ENVIRONMENT DIMENSION
Inn Foods passed on the cost savings from the lower duties to the growers when it paid them the difference between the understated value of the products and their actual value. Should this in any way absolve Inn Foods of liability for fraud? Explain your answer.

---

a. In the link at the bottom of the page, click on "Opinions & Orders." On that page, type in "Inn Foods, Inc." in the "Search By:" box. In the result, click on the case name to access the opinion. The U.S. Court of Appeals for the Federal Circuit maintains this Web site.

ANTIDUMPING DUTIES The United States has laws specifically directed at what it sees as unfair international trade practices. **Dumping,** for example, is the sale of imported goods at "less than fair value." *Fair value* is usually determined by the price of those goods in the exporting country. Foreign firms that engage in dumping in the United States hope to undersell U.S. businesses to obtain a larger share of the U.S. market. To prevent this, an extra tariff—known as an *antidumping duty*—may be assessed on the imports.

Two U.S. government agencies are instrumental in imposing antidumping duties: the International Trade Commission (ITC) and the International Trade Administration (ITA). The ITC assesses the effects of dumping on domestic businesses and then makes recommendations to the president concerning temporary import restrictions. The ITA, which is part of the Department of Commerce, decides whether imports were sold at less than fair value. The ITA's determination establishes the amount of antidumping duties, which are set to equal the difference between the price charged in the United States and the price charged in the exporting country. A duty may be retroactive to cover past dumping.

Minimizing Trade Barriers

Restrictions on imports are also known as *trade barriers.* The elimination of trade barriers is sometimes seen as essential to the world's economic well-being. Most of the world's leading trading nations are members of the World Trade Organization (WTO), which was established in 1995. To minimize trade barriers among nations, each member country of the WTO is required to grant **normal trade relations (NTR) status** (formerly known as most-favored-nation status) to other member countries. This means each member is obligated to treat other members at least as well as it treats the country that receives its most favorable treatment with regard to imports or exports. Various regional trade agreements and associations also help to minimize trade barriers between nations.

THE EUROPEAN UNION (EU) The European Union (EU) arose out the 1957 Treaty of Rome, which created the Common Market, a free trade zone comprising the nations of Belgium, France, Italy, Luxembourg, the Netherlands, and West Germany. Today, the EU is a single integrated trading unit made up of twenty-seven European nations.

The EU has gone a long way toward creating a new body of law to govern all of the member nations—although some of its efforts to create uniform laws have been confounded by nationalism. The council and the commission issue regulations, or directives, that define EU law in various areas, such as environmental law, product liability, anticompetitive practices, and corporations. The directives normally are binding on all member countries.

THE NORTH AMERICAN FREE TRADE AGREEMENT (NAFTA) The North American Free Trade Agreement (NAFTA) created a regional trading unit consisting of Canada, Mexico, and the United States. The goal of NAFTA is to eliminate tariffs among these three countries on substantially all goods by reducing the tariffs incrementally over a period of time. NAFTA gives the three countries a competitive advantage by retaining tariffs on goods imported from countries outside the NAFTA trading unit. Additionally, NAFTA provides for the elimination of barriers that traditionally have prevented the cross-border movement of services, such as financial and transportation services. NAFTA also attempts to eliminate citizenship

In 1992, the heads of Canada, Mexico, and the United States, along with their chief negotiators, signed a draft of the North American Free Trade Agreement, which took effect two years later. Who benefits from such an agreement?

requirements for the licensing of accountants, attorneys, physicians, and other professionals.

THE CENTRAL AMERICA–DOMINICAN REPUBLIC–UNITED STATES FREE TRADE AGREEMENT (CAFTA-DR)   The Central America–Dominican Republic–United States Free Trade Agreement (CAFTA-DR) was formed by Costa Rica, the Dominican Republic, El Salvador, Guatemala, Honduras, Nicaragua, and the United States. Its purpose is to reduce tariffs and improve market access among all of the signatory nations. Legislatures from all seven countries have approved the CAFTA-DR, despite significant opposition in certain nations.

Bribing Foreign Officials

Giving cash or in-kind benefits to foreign government officials to obtain business contracts and other favors is often considered normal practice. To reduce such bribery by representatives of U.S. corporations, Congress enacted the Foreign Corrupt Practices Act in 1977.[7] This act was discussed in Chapter 6.

▶ Commercial Contracts in an International Setting

An international contract should be in writing. For an example of an actual international sales contract from Starbucks Coffee Company, refer to the foldout exhibit at the end of Chapter 11.

Contract Clauses

Language and legal differences among nations can create special problems for parties to international contracts when disputes arise. To avoid these problems, parties should include special provisions in the contract that designate the language of the contract, where any disputes will be resolved, and the substantive law that will be applied in settling any disputes. Parties to international contracts should also indicate in their contracts what acts or events will excuse the parties from performance under the contract and whether disputes under the contract will be arbitrated or litigated.

Choice-of-Language Clause   A clause in a contract designating the official language by which the contract will be interpreted in the event of a future disagreement over the contract's terms.

CHOICE OF LANGUAGE   A deal struck between a U.S. company and a company in another country normally involves two languages. Typically, many phrases in one language are not readily translatable into another. Consequently, the complex contractual terms involved may not be understood by one party in the other party's language. To make sure that no disputes arise out of this language problem, an international sales contract should have a **choice-of-language clause** designating the official language by which the contract will be interpreted in the event of disagreement. Note also that some nations have mandatory language requirements. In France, for instance, certain legal documents, such as the prospectuses used in securities offerings (see Chapter 24), must be written in French. In addition,

---

7. 15 U.S.C. Sections 78m–78ff.

contracts with any state or local authority in France, instruction manuals, and warranties for goods and services offered for sale in France must be written in French. To avoid disputes, know the law of the jurisdiction before you enter into any agreements in that nation.

CHOICE OF FORUM   When a dispute arises, litigation may be pursued in courts of different nations. There are no universally accepted rules as to which court has jurisdiction over a particular subject matter or parties to a dispute. Consequently, parties to an international transaction should always include in the contract a **forum-selection clause** indicating what court, jurisdiction, or tribunal will decide any disputes arising under the contract. It is especially important to indicate the specific court that will have jurisdiction. The forum does not necessarily have to be within the geographic boundaries of the home nation of either party.

Forum-Selection Clause   A provision in a contract designating the court, jurisdiction, or tribunal that will decide any disputes arising under the contract.

   CASE EXAMPLE 7.5   Garware Polyester, Ltd., based in Mumbai, India, developed and made plastics and high-tech polyester film. Intermax Trading Corporation, based in New York, acted as Garware's North American sales agent and sold its products on a commission basis. Garware and Intermax had executed a series of agency agreements under which the courts of Mumbai, India, would have exclusive jurisdiction over any disputes relating to their agreement. When Intermax fell behind in its payments to Garware, Garware filed a lawsuit in a U.S. court to collect the balance due, claiming that the forum-selection clause did not apply to sales of warehoused goods. The court, however, sided with Intermax. Because the forum-selection clause was valid and enforceable, Garware had to bring its complaints against Intermax in a court in India.[8] ●

CHOICE OF LAW   A contractual provision designating the applicable law—such as the law of Germany or the United Kingdom or California—is called a **choice-of-law clause**. Every international contract typically includes a choice-of-law clause. At common law (and in European civil law systems), parties are allowed to choose the law that will govern their contractual relationship, provided that the law chosen is the law of a jurisdiction that has a substantial relationship to the parties and to the international business transaction.

Choice-of-Law Clause   A clause in a contract designating the law (such as the law of a particular state or nation) that will govern the contract.

   Under Section 1–105 of the Uniform Commercial Code (see Chapter 11), parties may choose the law that will govern the contract as long as the choice is "reasonable." Article 6 of the United Nations Convention on Contracts for the International Sale of Goods, however, imposes no limitation on the parties' choice of what law will govern the contract. The 1986 Hague Convention on the Law Applicable to Contracts for the International Sale of Goods—often referred to as the Choice-of-Law Convention—allows unlimited autonomy in the choice of law. The Hague Convention indicates that whenever a contract does not specify a choice of law, the governing law is that of the country in which the *seller's* place of business is located.

FORCE MAJEURE CLAUSE   Every contract, particularly those involving international transactions, should have a ***force majeure* clause**. *Force majeure* is a French term meaning "impossible or irresistible force"—sometimes loosely identified as "an act of God." In international business contracts, *force majeure* clauses commonly stipulate that in addition to acts of God, a number of other eventualities

***Force Majeure* Clause**   A provision in a contract stipulating that certain unforeseen events–such as war, political upheavals, or acts of God–will excuse a party from liability for nonperformance of contractual obligations.

---

8. *Garware Polyester, Ltd. v. Intermax Trading Corp.,* ___ F.Supp.2d ___ (S.D.N.Y. 2001); see also *Laasko v. Xerox Corp.,* 566 F.Supp.2d 1018 (C.D.Cal. 2008).

(such as government orders or embargoes) may excuse a party from liability for nonperformance.

Civil Dispute Resolution

International contracts frequently include arbitration clauses. By means of such clauses, the parties agree in advance to be bound by the decision of a specified third party in the event of a dispute, as discussed in Chapter 3. (For an example of an arbitration clause in an international contract, refer to the foldout exhibit at the end of Chapter 11.) The United Nations Convention on the Recognition and Enforcement of Foreign Arbitral Awards (often referred to as the New York Convention) assists in the enforcement of arbitration clauses, as do provisions in specific treaties among nations. The New York Convention has been implemented in nearly one hundred countries, including the United States.

If a sales contract does not include an arbitration clause, litigation may occur. If the contract contains forum-selection and choice-of-law clauses, the lawsuit will be heard by a court in the specified forum and decided according to that forum's law. If no forum and choice of law have been specified, however, legal proceedings will be more complex and attended by much more uncertainty. For instance, litigation may take place in two or more countries, with each country applying its own choice-of-law rules to determine the substantive law that will be applied to the particular transactions. Even if a plaintiff wins a favorable judgment in a lawsuit litigated in the plaintiff's country, there is no way to predict whether courts in the defendant's country will enforce the judgment. (For further discussion of this issue, see this chapter's *Beyond Our Borders* feature on the following page.)

Payment Methods for International Transactions

Currency differences between nations and the geographic distance between parties to international sales contracts add a degree of complexity to international sales that does not exist in the domestic market. Because international contracts involve greater financial risks, special care should be taken in drafting these contracts to specify both the currency in which payment is to be made and the method of payment.

Foreign Exchange Market A worldwide system in which foreign currencies are bought and sold.

Monetary Systems

Although our national currency, the U.S. dollar, is one of the primary forms of international currency, any U.S. firm undertaking business transactions abroad must be prepared to deal with one or more other currencies. After all, a Japanese firm may want to be paid in Japanese yen for goods and services sold outside Japan. Both firms therefore must rely on the convertibility of currencies.

Currencies are convertible when they can be freely exchanged one for the other at some specified market rate in a **foreign exchange market.** Foreign exchange markets make up a worldwide system for the buying and selling of foreign currencies. The foreign exchange rate is simply the price of a unit of one country's currency in terms of another country's currency. For example, if today's exchange rate is one hundred Japanese yen for one dollar, that means that anybody with one hundred yen

To do business internationally, buyers and sellers rely on foreign exchange markets. Why don't companies just accept other countries' currencies as payment?

(Anthony Edwards/Getty Images)

Beyond Our Borders   Arbitration versus Litigation

One of the reasons many businesspersons find it advantageous to include arbitration clauses in their international contracts is that arbitration awards are usually easier to enforce than court judgments. As mentioned, the New York Convention provides for the enforcement of arbitration awards in those countries that have signed the convention. In contrast, the enforcement of court judgments normally depends on the principle of comity and bilateral agreements providing for such enforcement.

How the principle of comity is applied varies from one nation to another, though, and many countries have not signed bilateral agreements agreeing to enforce judgments rendered in U.S. courts. Furthermore, a U.S. court may not enforce a foreign court's judgment if it conflicts with U.S. laws or policies, especially if the case involves important constitutional rights such as freedom of the press or freedom of religion. For example, a U.S.

federal appellate court refused to enforce the judgment of a British court in a libel (defamation) case. The court pointed out that the judgment was contrary to the public policy of the United States, which generally favors a much broader and more protective freedom of the press than has ever been provided by English law.[a]

Similarly, a U.S. court refused to enforce a French default judgment against Viewfinder, Inc., a U.S. firm that operated a Web site. The firm's Web site posted photographs from fashion shows and information about the fashion industry. Several French clothing designers filed an action in a French court alleging that the Web site showed photos of their clothing designs. Because Viewfinder defaulted

and did not appear in the French court to contest the allegations, the French court awarded the designers the equivalent of more than $175,000. When the designers came to the United States to enforce the judgment, Viewfinder asserted a number of arguments as to why the U.S. court should not enforce the French judgment. Ultimately, Viewfinder convinced the U.S. court that its conduct on the Web site was protected expression under the First Amendment.[b]

For Critical Analysis
What might be some other advantages of arbitrating disputes involving international transactions? Are there any disadvantages?

---

a. *Matusevitch v. Telnikoff,* 159 F.3d 636 (D.C.Cir. 1998). Note that a U.S. court may be less likely to have public-policy concerns when enforcing a foreign judgment based on a contract. See, for example, *Society of Lloyd's v. Siemon-Netto,* 457 F.3d 94 (C.A.D.C. 2006).

b. *Sarl Louis Feraud International v. Viewfinder, Inc.,* 489 F.3d 474 (2d Cir. 2007).

---

can obtain one dollar, and vice versa. Like other prices, the exchange rate is set by the forces of supply and demand.

Frequently, a U.S. company can rely on its domestic bank to take care of all international transfers of funds. Commercial banks often transfer funds internationally through their **correspondent banks** in other countries. **EXAMPLE 7.6**   A customer of Citibank wishes to pay a bill in euros to a company in Paris. Citibank can draw a bank check payable in euros on its account in Crédit Agricole, a Paris correspondent bank, and then send the check to the French company to which its customer owes the funds. Alternatively, Citibank's customer can request a wire transfer of the funds to the French company. Citibank instructs Crédit Agricole by wire to pay the necessary amount in euros. ●

Correspondent Bank A bank in which another bank has an account (and vice versa) for the purpose of facilitating fund transfers.

Letters of Credit

Letter of Credit A written instrument, usually issued by a bank on behalf of a customer or other person, in which the issuer promises to honor drafts or other demands for payment by third parties in accordance with the terms of the instrument.

Because buyers and sellers engaged in international business transactions are frequently separated by thousands of miles, special precautions are often taken to ensure performance under the contract. Sellers want to avoid delivering goods for which they might not be paid. Buyers desire the assurance that sellers will not be paid until there is evidence that the goods have been shipped. Thus, **letters of credit** are frequently used to facilitate international business transactions.

PARTIES TO A LETTER OF CREDIT   In a simple letter-of-credit transaction, the *issuer* (a bank) agrees to issue a letter of credit and to ascertain whether the *beneficiary* (seller) performs certain acts. In return, the *account party* (buyer) promises to reimburse the issuer for the amount paid to the beneficiary. The transaction may also involve an *advising bank* that transmits information and a *paying bank* that expedites payment under the letter of credit. See Exhibit 7–1 below for an illustration of a letter-of-credit transaction.

Under a letter of credit, the issuer is bound to pay the beneficiary (seller) when the beneficiary has complied with the terms and conditions of the letter of credit. The beneficiary looks to the issuer, not to the account party (buyer), when it presents the documents required by the letter of credit. Typically, the letter of credit will require that the beneficiary deliver a *bill of lading* to the issuing bank to prove that shipment has been made. A letter of credit assures the beneficiary (seller) of payment and at the same time assures the account party (buyer) that payment will not be made until the beneficiary has complied with the terms and conditions of the letter of credit.

DON'T FORGET   A letter of credit is independent of the underlying contract between the buyer and the seller.

THE VALUE OF A LETTER OF CREDIT   The basic principle behind letters of credit is that payment is made against the documents presented by the beneficiary and not against the facts that the documents purport to reflect. Thus, in a letter-of-credit

● *Exhibit* **7–1 A Letter-of-Credit Transaction**

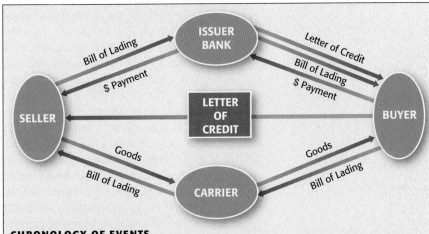

CHRONOLOGY OF EVENTS

1. Buyer contracts with issuer bank to issue a letter of credit, which sets forth the bank's obligation to pay on the letter of credit and buyer's obligation to pay the bank.

2. Letter of credit is sent to seller informing seller that on compliance with the terms of the letter of credit (such as presentment of necessary documents—in this example, a bill of lading), the bank will issue payment for the goods.

3. Seller delivers goods to carrier and receives a bill of lading.

4. Seller delivers the bill of lading to issuer bank and, if the document is proper, receives payment.

5. Issuer bank delivers the bill of lading to buyer.

6. Buyer delivers the bill of lading to carrier.

7. Carrier delivers the goods to buyer.

8. Buyer settles with issuer bank.

transaction, the issuer does not police the underlying contract. A letter of credit is independent of the underlying contract between the buyer and the seller. Eliminating the need for banks (issuers) to inquire into whether actual contractual conditions have been satisfied greatly reduces the costs of letters of credit. Moreover, the use of a letter of credit protects both buyers and sellers.

 ## U.S. Laws in a Global Context

The internationalization of business raises questions about the extraterritorial application of a nation's laws—that is, the effect of the country's laws outside its boundaries. To what extent do U.S. domestic laws apply to other nations' businesses? To what extent do U.S. domestic laws apply to U.S. firms doing business abroad? Here, we discuss the extraterritorial application of certain U.S. laws, including antitrust laws, tort laws, and laws prohibiting employment discrimination.

U.S. Antitrust Laws

U.S. antitrust laws (to be discussed in Chapter 23) have a wide application. They may *subject* firms in foreign nations to their provisions, as well as *protect* foreign consumers and competitors from violations committed by U.S. citizens. Section 1 of the Sherman Act—the most important U.S. antitrust law—provides for the extraterritorial effect of the U.S. antitrust laws. The United States is a major proponent of free competition in the global economy. Thus, any conspiracy that has a *substantial effect* on U.S. commerce is within the reach of the Sherman Act. The law applies even if the violation occurs outside the United States, and foreign governments as well as businesses can be sued for violations.

Before U.S. courts will exercise jurisdiction and apply antitrust laws, however, it must be shown that the alleged violation had a substantial effect on U.S. commerce. **CASE EXAMPLE 7.7**   An investigation by the U.S. government revealed that a number of companies that manufactured and sold thermal fax paper on the global market had met in Japan and reached a price-fixing agreement (an agreement to set prices—see Chapter 23). A Florida company that uses thermal fax paper filed a lawsuit against New Oji Paper Company, a Japan-based manufacturer that had participated in the conspiracy. Although New Oji is based in a foreign nation, it sold fax paper in the United States. Thus, its agreement to sell paper at above-normal prices throughout North America had a substantial restraining effect on U.S. commerce. Therefore, the Supreme Court of Florida ruled that it had jurisdiction over New Oji, even though all of the price-fixing activities took place outside the United States.[9] ●

International Tort Claims

The international application of tort liability is growing in significance and controversy. An increasing number of U.S. plaintiffs are suing foreign (or U.S.) entities for torts that these entities have allegedly committed overseas. Often, these cases involve human rights violations by foreign governments. The Alien Tort Claims Act (ATCA),[10] adopted in 1789, allows even foreign citizens to bring civil suits in U.S. courts for injuries caused by violations of international law or a treaty of the United States.

---

9. *Execu-Tech Business Systems, Inc. v. New Oji Paper Co.,* 752 So.2d 582 (Fla. 2000).

10. 28 U.S.C. Section 1350.

Since 1980, plaintiffs have increasingly used the ATCA to bring actions against companies operating in other countries. ATCA actions have been brought against companies doing business in nations such as Colombia, Ecuador, Egypt, Guatemala, India, Indonesia, Nigeria, and Saudi Arabia. Some of these cases have involved alleged environmental destruction. In addition, mineral companies in Southeast Asia have been sued for collaborating with oppressive government regimes.

The following case involved claims against hundreds of corporations that allegedly "aided and abetted" the government of South Africa in maintaining its apartheid (racially discriminatory) regime.

Case 7.3 Khulumani v. Barclay National Bank, Ltd.

United States Court of Appeals, Second Circuit, 504 F.3d 254 (2007).[a]

BACKGROUND AND FACTS The Khulumani plaintiffs, along with other plaintiff groups, filed class-action claims on behalf of victims of apartheid-related atrocities, human rights violations, crimes against humanity, and unfair and discriminatory forced-labor practices. The plaintiffs brought this action in federal district court under the Alien Tort Claims Act (ATCA) against a number of corporations, including Bank of America, Barclay National Bank, Citigroup, Credit Suisse Group, General Electric, and IBM. The district court dismissed the plaintiffs' complaints in their entirety. The court held that the plaintiffs had failed to establish subject-matter jurisdiction under the ATCA. The plaintiffs appealed to the U.S. Court of Appeals for the Second Circuit.

IN THE WORDS OF THE COURT . . .
PER CURIAM. [By the Whole Court]
    * * * *

    * * * [This court] vacate[s] the district court's dismissal of the plaintiffs' ATCA claims because the district court erred in holding that aiding and abetting violations of customary international law cannot provide a basis for ATCA jurisdiction. *We hold that * * * a plaintiff may plead a theory of aiding and abetting liability under the ATCA.* * * * [The majority of the judges on the panel that heard this case agreed on the result but differed on the reasons, which were presented in two concurring opinions. One judge believed that liability on these facts is "well established in international law," citing such examples as the Rome Statute of the International Criminal Court. Another judge stated that according to Section 876(b) of the *Restatement (Second) of Torts,* liability could be assessed in part for "facilitating the commission of human rights violations by providing the principal tortfeasor with

the tools, instrumentalities, or services to commit those violations."]
[Emphasis added.]
    * * * *

    * * * We decline to affirm the dismissal of plaintiffs' ATCA claims on the basis of the prudential concerns[b] raised by the defendants. * * * The Supreme Court [has] identified two different respects in which courts should consider prudential concerns [exercise great caution and carefully evaluate international norms and potential adverse foreign policy consequences] in deciding whether to hear claims brought under the ATCA.[c] First, * * * courts should consider prudential concerns in the context of determining whether to recognize a cause of action under the ATCA. Specifically, * * * the determination whether a norm is sufficiently definite to support a cause of action should (and, indeed, inevitably must) involve an element of judgment about the practical consequences of making that cause available to litigants in the federal courts. Second, * * * in certain cases, other prudential principles might operate to limit the availability of relief in the federal courts for violations of customary international law.
    * * * *

    One such principle * * * [is] a policy of case-specific deference to the political branches [of the U.S. government]. *This policy of judicial*

---

b. The term *prudential concerns* refers to the defendants' arguments that the plaintiffs do not have standing to pursue their case in a U.S. court. Here, *prudential* means that the arguments are based on judicially (or legislatively) created principles rather than on the constitutionally based requirements set forth in Article III of the U.S. Constitution (the case or controversy clause).

c. The court is referring to the decision of the United States Supreme Court in *Sosa v. Alvarez-Machain,* 542 U.S. 692, 124 S.Ct. 2739, 159 L.Ed.2d 718 (2004). In the *Sosa* case, the Supreme Court outlined the need for caution in deciding actions under the ATCA and said that the "potential implications for the foreign relations of the United States of recognizing such causes should make courts particularly wary of impinging [encroaching] on the discretion of the Legislative and Executive Branches in managing foreign affairs."

---

a. See also 509 F.3d 148 (2d Cir. 2007), in which the court denied the defendants' motion for a stay; and *American Isuzu Motors, Inc. v. Ntsebeza,* 553 U.S. 1028, 128 S.Ct. 2424, 171 L.Ed.2d 225 (2008), in which the United States Supreme Court had to affirm the Second Circuit's decision in this case because it was unable to hear the appeal in the following term.

Case 7.3—Continues next page ➡

Case 7.3–Continued

deference to the Executive Branch on questions of foreign policy has long been established under the prudential justiciability [appropriate for a court to resolve] doctrine known as the political question doctrine. Another prudential doctrine that the defendants raise in this case is international comity. This doctrine * * * asks whether adjudication of the case by a United States court would offend amicable working relationships with a foreign country. [Emphasis added.]

DECISION AND REMEDY   The U.S. Court of Appeals for the Second Circuit vacated the district court's dismissal of the plaintiffs'

claims and remanded the case for further proceedings. According to the reviewing court, a plaintiff may plead a theory of aiding and abetting liability under the Alien Tort Claims Act.

THE LEGAL ENVIRONMENT DIMENSION   *What are the ramifications of the ruling for the defendants?*

THE ETHICAL DIMENSION   *Should the companies cited as defendants have refused all business dealings with South Africa while that country's white government imposed unjust restrictions on the majority black African population during apartheid? Explain.*

Antidiscrimination Laws

Laws in the United States prohibit discrimination on the basis of race, color, national origin, religion, gender, age, and disability, as will be discussed in Chapter 18. These laws, as they affect employment relationships, generally apply extraterritorially. U.S. employees working abroad for U.S. employers are protected under the Age Discrimination in Employment Act of 1967. The Americans with Disabilities Act of 1990, which requires employers to accommodate the needs of workers with disabilities, also applies to U.S. nationals working abroad for U.S. firms.

In addition, the major law regulating employment discrimination—Title VII of the Civil Rights Act of 1964—applies extraterritorially to all U.S. employees working for U.S. employers abroad. U.S. employers must abide by U.S. discrimination laws unless to do so would violate the laws of the country where their workplaces are located. This "foreign laws exception" prevents employers from being subjected to conflicting laws.

 ### Reviewing . . . International Law in a Global Economy

Robco, Inc., was a Florida arms dealer. The armed forces of Honduras contracted to purchase weapons from Robco over a six-year period. After the government was replaced and a democracy installed, the Honduran government sought to reduce the size of its military, and its relationship with Robco deteriorated. Honduras refused to honor the contract by purchasing the inventory of arms, which Robco could sell only at a much lower price. Robco filed a suit in a federal district court in the United States to recover damages for this breach of contract by the government of Honduras. Using the information provided in the chapter, answer the following questions.

1. Should the Foreign Sovereign Immunities Act preclude this lawsuit? Why or why not?
2. Does the act of state doctrine bar Robco from seeking to enforce the contract? Explain.
3. Suppose that before this lawsuit, the new government of Honduras had enacted a law making it illegal to purchase weapons from foreign arms dealers. What doctrine might lead a U.S. court to dismiss Robco's case in that situation?
4. Now suppose that the U.S. court hears the case and awards damages to Robco, but the government of Honduras has no assets in the United States that can be used to satisfy the judgment. Under which doctrine might Robco be able to collect the damages by asking another nation's court to enforce the U.S. judgment?

Linking the Law *to Marketing*
Going Global

Since the end of World War II, international trade in goods and services has grown dramatically. Today, U.S. exports amount to more than 14 percent of the U.S. gross domestic product. In your marketing classes in business school, you will learn about domestic marketing. If you work for many U.S. firms, though, you will also need to know about marketing on a global basis.

Legal and Economic Constraints on Global Marketing Campaigns

If you are the global marketing manager for your company, you will need to be aware of the following legal considerations that we outlined in this chapter:

- **Tariffs**—Before you embark on a marketing campaign in any country, you should determine what tariffs may be imposed on your company's products. If your company must pay relatively high tariffs and compete against domestic producers who obviously face no tariffs, you may be wasting your time. No matter how good your marketing campaign is, those tariffs could cause your company's products to be priced out of the market.

- **Quotas**—The United States has strict quotas on imports of textiles, sugar, and many dairy products. Other countries have quotas, too. If those quotas are highly restrictive, there is no point in trying to sell your company's products in those countries.

- **Exchange controls**—When your company exports to another country, that country has to pay for those U.S.-made goods in dollars. Sometimes, governments impose restrictions on the amount of dollars that may be purchased in the foreign exchange market to pay for goods from the United States. You may find that some exchange controls are so restrictive that it is not worthwhile to attempt to sell your company's products in a particular country.

- **Trade agreements**—You must also determine whether any trade agreements apply to trade between the United States and the target countries. Some countries may have signed bilateral or international trade agreements that make it particularly attractive for you to attempt to market your company's products in those countries. You should consult a specialist in international trade agreements to find out precisely how those agreements can help your company.

Global Marketing Standardization

In the past, multinational organizations generally employed different marketing strategies for the various countries in which they sold their products. They attempted to adapt the product features, advertising, and packaging to fit the culture of each country.

The trend today, according to former Harvard professor Ted Levitt, is toward "global marketing." Levitt, who devised the notion of global marketing standardization, or a global vision, contends that advances in communication and technology have created a "small" world. By this he means that consumers everywhere want the same items that they have seen in popular movies exported from the United States, for example, or featured on the Internet.

Coca-Cola, McDonald's, and Colgate-Palmolive are some of the companies that use global marketing standardization. They produce globally standardized products that are marketed more or less the same way throughout the world.

Global Marketing the Standard Way—Considering Each Culture Separately

No matter how "small" the world has become, countries still have different sets of shared values that affect their citizens' preferences. Therefore, as a global marketing manager, you will have to become intimately acquainted with the cultures of the countries where you conduct marketing campaigns.

Samsonite, for example, found this out the hard way. It used an advertising campaign with an image of its luggage being carried on a magic flying carpet. Only after it conducted focus groups did it learn that most Middle Eastern consumers thought that Samsonite was selling carpets. Green Giant learned to its dismay that it could not use its logo with a man in a green hat in parts of Asia—because in those areas a green hat signifies a man who has an unfaithful wife.

Similarly, the translation of names and slogans into other languages is fraught with pitfalls. Toyota had to drop the "2" from its model MR2 in France because the combination of sounds sounded like a French swear word. Mitsubishi Motors had to rename one of its models in Spanish-speaking countries because the original name described a sexual activity.

FOR CRITICAL ANALYSIS

Why should a global marketing manager consult local attorneys in other countries before creating a marketing campaign?

Key Terms

act of state doctrine 183	dumping 190	international organization 181
choice-of-language clause 191	export 185	letter of credit 194
choice-of-law clause 192	expropriation 184	normal trade relations (NTR) status 190
comity 182	*force majeure* clause 192	quota 188
confiscation 184	foreign exchange market 193	sovereign immunity 184
correspondent bank 194	forum-selection clause 192	tariff 188
distribution agreement 185	international law 180	treaty 181

Chapter Summary: International Law in a Global Economy

International Law— Sources and Principles (See pages 181–185.)	1. *The principle of comity*—Under this principle, nations give effect to the laws and judicial decrees of other nations for reasons of courtesy and international harmony. 2. *The act of state doctrine*—A doctrine under which U.S. courts avoid passing judgment on the validity of public acts committed by a recognized foreign government within its own territory. 3. *The doctrine of sovereign immunity*—When certain conditions are satisfied, foreign nations are immune from U.S. jurisdiction under the Foreign Sovereign Immunities Act of 1976. Exceptions are made when a foreign state (a) has waived its immunity either explicitly or by implication, (b) has engaged in commercial activity within the United States, or (c) has committed a tort within the United States.
Doing Business Internationally (See pages 185–187.)	U.S. domestic firms may engage in international business transactions in several ways. These include (1) exporting, which may involve foreign agents or distributors, and (2) manufacturing abroad through licensing arrangements, franchising operations, wholly owned subsidiaries, or joint ventures.
Regulation of Specific Business Activities (See pages 187–191.)	In the interests of their economies, foreign policies, domestic policies, or other national priorities, nations impose laws that restrict or facilitate international business. Such laws regulate foreign investments, exporting, and importing. The World Trade Organization attempts to minimize trade barriers among nations, as do regional trade agreements and associations, including the European Union and the North American Free Trade Agreement.
Commercial Contracts in an International Setting (See pages 191–193.)	International business contracts often include choice-of-language, forum-selection, and choice-of-law clauses to reduce the uncertainties associated with interpreting the language of the agreement and dealing with legal differences. Most domestic and international contracts include *force majeure* clauses. They commonly stipulate that acts of God and certain other events may excuse a party from liability for nonperformance of the contract. Arbitration clauses are also frequently found in international contracts.
Payment Methods for International Transactions (See pages 193–196.)	1. *Currency conversion*—Because nations have different monetary systems, payment on international contracts requires currency conversion at a rate specified in a foreign exchange market. 2. *Correspondent banking*—Correspondent banks facilitate the transfer of funds from a buyer in one country to a seller in another. 3. *Letters of credit*—Letters of credit facilitate international transactions by ensuring payment to sellers and assuring buyers that payment will not be made until the sellers have complied with the terms of the letters of credit. Typically, compliance occurs when a bill of lading is delivered to the issuing bank.
U.S. Laws in a Global Context (See pages 196–198.)	1. *Antitrust laws*—U.S. antitrust laws may be applied beyond the borders of the United States. Any conspiracy that has a substantial effect on commerce within the United States may be subject to the Sherman Act, even if the violation occurs outside the United States. 2. *Antidiscrimination laws*—The major U.S. laws prohibiting employment discrimination, including Title VII of the Civil Rights Act of 1964, the Age Discrimination in Employment Act of 1967, and the Americans with Disabilities Act of 1990, cover U.S. employees working abroad for U.S. firms—*unless* to apply the U.S. laws would violate the laws of the host country.

ExamPrep

ISSUE SPOTTERS

1. Café Rojo, Ltd., an Ecuadoran firm, agrees to sell coffee beans to Dark Roast Coffee Company, a U.S. firm. Dark Roast accepts the beans but refuses to pay. Café Rojo sues Dark Roast in an Ecuadoran court and is awarded damages, but Dark Roast's assets are in the United States. Under what circumstances would a U.S. court enforce the judgment of the Ecuadoran court?

2. Gems International, Ltd., is a foreign firm that has a 12 percent share of the U.S. market for diamonds. To capture a larger share, Gems offers its products at a below-cost discount to U.S. buyers (and inflates the prices in its own country to make up the difference). How can this attempt to undersell U.S. businesses be defeated?

—**Check your answers to these questions against the answers provided in Appendix G.**

BEFORE THE TEST

Go to **www.cengagebrain.com**, enter the ISBN number "9781111530617," and click on "Find" to locate this textbook's Web site. Then, click on "Access Now" under "Study Tools," and select "Chapter 7" at the top. There you will find an "Interactive Quiz" that you can take to assess your mastery of the concepts in this chapter, as well as "Flashcards" and a "Glossary" of important terms.

 For Review

1. What is the principle of comity, and why do courts deciding disputes involving a foreign law or judicial decree apply this principle?

2. What is the act of state doctrine? In what circumstances is this doctrine applied?

3. Under the Foreign Sovereign Immunities Act of 1976, on what bases might a foreign state be considered subject to the jurisdiction of U.S. courts?

4. In what circumstances will U.S. antitrust laws be applied extraterritorially?

5. Do U.S. laws prohibiting employment discrimination apply in all circumstances to U.S. employees working for U.S. employers abroad?

 Questions and Case Problems

7–1. Letters of Credit. The Swiss Credit Bank issued a letter of credit in favor of Antex Industries to cover the sale of 92,000 electronic integrated circuits manufactured by Electronic Arrays. The letter of credit specified that the chips would be transported to Tokyo by ship. Antex shipped the circuits by air. Payment on the letter of credit was dishonored because the shipment by air did not fulfill the precise terms of the letter of credit. Should a court compel payment? Explain.

7–2. **Question with Sample Answer. Dumping.** The U.S. pineapple industry alleged that producers of canned pineapple from the Philippines were selling their canned pineapple in the United States for less than its fair market value (dumping). The Philippine producers also exported other products, such as pineapple juice and juice concentrate, that used separate parts of the same fresh pineapple, so they shared raw material costs, according to the producers' own financial records. To determine fair value and antidumping duties, the plaintiffs argued that a court should calculate the Philippine producers' cost of production and allocate a portion of the shared fruit costs to the canned fruit. The result of this allocation showed that more than 90 percent of the canned fruit sales were below the cost of production. Is this a reasonable approach to determining the production costs and fair market value of canned pineapple in the United States? Why or why not?

—**For a sample answer to Question 7–2, go to Appendix E at the end of this text.**

7–3. Dumping. A newspaper printing press system is more than one hundred feet long, stands four or five stories tall, and weighs 2 million pounds. Only about ten of the systems are sold each year in the United States. Because of the size and cost, a newspaper may update its system, rather than replace it, by buying "additions." By the 1990s, Goss International Corp. was the only domestic maker of the equipment in the United States and represented the entire U.S. market. Tokyo Kikai Seisakusho (TKSC), a Japanese corporation, makes the systems in Japan. In the 1990s, TKSC began to compete in the U.S. market, forcing Goss to cut its prices below cost. TKSC's tactics included offering its customers "secret" rebates on prices that were ultimately substantially less than the products' actual market value in Japan. According to TKSC office memos, the goal was to "win completely this survival game" against Goss, the "enemy." Goss filed a suit in a federal district court against TKSC and others, alleging illegal dumping. At what point does a foreign firm's attempt to compete with a domestic manufacturer in the United States become illegal dumping? Was that point reached in this case? Discuss. [*Goss International Corp. v. Man Roland Druckmaschinen Aktiengesellschaft,* 434 F.3d 1081 (8th Cir. 2006)]

7–4. Comity. Jan Voda, M.D., a resident of Oklahoma City, Oklahoma, owns three U.S. patents related to guiding catheters for use in interventional cardiology, as well as corresponding foreign patents issued by the European Patent Office, Canada, France, Germany, and Great Britain. Voda filed a suit in a federal district court against Cordis Corp., a U.S. firm, alleging infringement of the U.S. patents under U.S. patent law and of the corresponding foreign patents under the patent laws of the various foreign countries. Cordis admitted, "The XB catheters have been sold domestically and internationally since 1994. The XB catheters were manufactured in Miami Lakes, Florida, from 1993 to 2001 and have been manufactured in Juarez, Mexico, since 2001." Cordis argued, however, that Voda could not assert infringement claims under foreign patent law because the court did not have jurisdiction over such claims. Which of the important international legal principles discussed in this chapter would be most likely to apply in this case? How should the court apply it? Explain. [*Voda v. Cordis Corp.,* 476 F.3d 887 (Fed.Cir. 2007)]

7–5. **Case Problem with Sample Answer. Sovereign Immunity.** When Ferdinand Marcos was president of the Republic of the Philippines, he put assets into a company called Arelma. Its holdings are in New York. A group of plaintiffs, referred to as the Pimentel class, brought a class-action suit in a U.S. district court for human rights violations by Marcos. They won a judgment of $2 billion and sought to attach (take legal action against) Arelma's assets to help pay the judgment. At the same time, the Republic of the Philippines established a commission to recover property wrongfully taken by Marcos. A court in the Philippines was determining whether Marcos's property, including Arelma, should be forfeited to the Republic or to other parties. The Philippine government, in opposition to the Pimentel judgment, moved to dismiss the U.S. court proceedings. The district court refused, and the U.S. Court of Appeals for the Ninth Circuit agreed that the Pimentel class should take the assets. The Republic of the Philippines appealed. What are the key international legal issues? [*Republic of the Philippines v. Pimentel,* 553 U.S. 851, 128 S. Ct. 2180, 171 L.Ed.2d 131 (2008)]

—To view a sample answer for Case Problem 7–5, go to Appendix F at the end of this text.

7–6. Dumping. The fuel for nuclear power plants is low-enriched uranium (LEU). LEU consists of feed uranium enriched by energy to a certain assay—the percentage of the isotope necessary for a nuclear reaction. The amount of energy is described by an industry standard as a "separative work unit" (SWU). A nuclear utility may buy LEU from an enricher, or the utility may provide an enricher with feed uranium and pay for the SWUs necessary to produce LEU. Under an SWU contract, the LEU returned to the utility may not be exactly the uranium the utility provided. This is because feed uranium is fungible and trades like a commodity (such as wheat or corn), and profitable enrichment requires the constant processing of undifferentiated stock. LEU imported from foreign enrichers, including Eurodif, S.A., was purportedly being sold in the United States for "less than fair value." Does this constitute dumping? Explain. If so, what could be done to prevent it? [*United States v. Eurodif, S.A.,* 555 U.S. 305, 129 S.Ct. 878, 172 L.Ed.2d 679 (2009)]

7–7. International Agreements and Jurisdiction. The plaintiffs in this case were descendants of Holocaust victims who had lived in various countries in Europe. Before the Holocaust, the plaintiffs' ancestors had purchased insurance policies from Assicurazioni Generali, S.P.A., an Italian insurance company. When Generali refused to pay benefits under the policies, the plaintiffs, who were U.S. citizens and the beneficiaries of these policies, sued for breach of the insurance contracts. Due to certain agreements among nations after World War II, such lawsuits could not be filed for many years. In 2000, however, the United States agreed that Germany could establish a foundation—the International Commission on Holocaust-Era Insurance Claims, or ICHEIC—that would compensate victims who had suffered losses at the hands of the Germans during the war. Whenever a German company was sued in a U.S. court based on a Holocaust-era claim, the U.S. government would inform the court that the matter should be referred to the ICHEIC as the exclusive forum and remedy for the resolution. There was no such agreement with Italy, however. The plaintiffs sued the Italy-based Generali in a U.S. district court. The court dismissed the suit, and the plaintiffs appealed. Did the plaintiffs have to take their claim to the ICHEIC rather than sue in a U.S. court? Why or why not? [*In re Assicurazioni Generali, S.P.A.,* 592 F.3d 113 (2d Cir. 2010)]

7–8. Sovereign Immunity. Bell Helicopter Textron, Inc., designs, makes, and sells helicopters with distinctive and famous trade dress that identifies them as Bell aircraft. Bell also owns the helicopters' design patents. Bell's Model 206 Series includes the Jet Ranger. Thirty-six years after Bell developed the Jet Ranger, the Islamic Republic of Iran began to make and sell counterfeit Model 206 Series helicopters and parts. Iran's counterfeit versions—the Shahed 278 and the

Shahed 285—use Bell's *trade dress* (see Chapter 8). The Shahed aircraft was promoted at an international air show in Iran to aircraft customers. Bell filed a suit in a federal district court against Iran, alleging violations of trademark and patent laws. Is Iran—a foreign nation—exempt in these circumstances from the jurisdiction of U.S. courts? Explain. [*Bell Helicopter Textron, Inc. v. Islamic Republic of Iran,* 764 F.Supp.2d 122 (D.D.C. 2011)]

7–9. 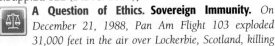 **A Question of Ethics. Sovereign Immunity.** *On December 21, 1988, Pan Am Flight 103 exploded 31,000 feet in the air over Lockerbie, Scotland, killing all 259 passengers and crew on board and 11 people on the ground. Among those killed was Roger Hurst, a U.S. citizen. An investigation determined that a portable radio-cassette player packed in a brown Samsonite suitcase smuggled onto the plane was the source of the explosion. The explosive device was constructed with a digital timer specially made for, and bought by, Libya. Abdel Basset Ali Al-Megrahi, a Libyan government official and an employee of the Libyan Arab Airline (LAA), was convicted by the Scottish High Court of Justiciary on criminal charges that he had planned and executed the bombing in association with members of the Jamahiriya Security Organization (JSO)—an agency of the Libyan government that performs security and intelligence functions—or the Libyan military. Members of the victims' families filed a suit in a U.S. federal district court against the JSO, the LAA, Al-Megrahi, and others. The plaintiffs claimed violations of U.S. federal law, including the Anti-Terrorism Act, and state law, including the intentional infliction of emotional distress.* [*Hurst v. Socialist People's Libyan Arab Jamahiriya,* 474 F.Supp.2d 19 (D.D.C. 2007)]

1. Under what doctrine, codified in which federal statute, might the defendants claim to be immune from the jurisdiction of a U.S. court? Should this law include an exception for "state-sponsored terrorism"? Why or why not?

2. The defendants agreed to pay $2.7 billion, or $10 million per victim, to settle all claims for "compensatory death damages." The families of eleven victims, including Hurst, were excluded from the settlement because they were "not wrongful death beneficiaries under applicable state law." These plaintiffs continued the suit. The defendants filed a motion to dismiss. Should the motion be granted on the ground that the settlement bars the plaintiffs' claims? Explain.

7–10. **Video Question. *International: Letter of Credit.*** Access the video using the instructions provided below to answer the following questions.

1. Do banks always require the same documents to be presented in letter-of-credit transactions? If not, who dictates what documents will be required in the letter of credit?

2. At what point does the seller receive payment in a letter-of-credit transaction?

3. What assurances does a letter of credit provide to the buyer and the seller involved in the transaction?

—To watch this video, go to **www.cengagebrain.com** and register the access code that came with your new book or log in to your existing account. Select the link for either the "Business Law Digital Video Library Online Access" or "Business Law CourseMate," and then click on "Complete Video List" to find the video for this chapter (Video 55).

UNIT ONE Cumulative Business Hypothetical

CompTac, Inc., which is headquartered in San Francisco, California, is one of the leading software manufacturers in the United States. The company invests millions of dollars in research and development of new software applications and computer games, which are sold worldwide. It also has a large service department and has taken great pains to offer its customers excellent support services.

1. CompTac routinely purchases some of the materials necessary to produce its computer games from a New York firm, Electrotex, Inc. A dispute arises between the two firms, and CompTac wants to sue Electrotex for breach of contract. Can CompTac bring the suit in a California state court? Can CompTac bring the suit in a federal court? Explain.

2. A customer at one of CompTac's retail stores stumbles over a crate in the parking lot and breaks her leg. The crate had just moments before fallen off a CompTac truck that was delivering goods from a CompTac warehouse to the store. The customer sues CompTac, alleging negligence. Will she succeed in her suit? Why or why not?

3. Roban Electronics, a software manufacturer and one of CompTac's major competitors, has been trying to convince one of CompTac's key employees, Jim Baxter, to come to work for Roban. Roban knows that Baxter has a written employment contract with CompTac, which Baxter would breach if he left CompTac before the contract expired. Baxter goes to work for Roban, and the departure of its key employee causes CompTac to suffer substantial losses due to delays in completing new software. Can CompTac sue Roban to recoup some of these losses? If so, on what ground?

4. One of CompTac's employees in its accounting division, Alan Green, has a gambling problem. To repay a gambling debt of $10,000, Green decides to "borrow" some money from CompTac to cover the debt. Using his "hacking" skills and his knowledge of CompTac account numbers, Green electronically transfers CompTac funds into his personal checking account. A week later, he is luckier at gambling and uses the same electronic procedures to transfer funds from his personal checking account to the relevant CompTac account. Has Green committed any crimes? If so, what are they?

5. One of CompTac's best-selling products is a computer game that includes some extremely violent actions. Groups of parents, educators, and consumer activists have bombarded CompTac with letters and e-mail messages calling on the company to stop selling the product. CompTac executives are concerned about the public outcry, but at the same time they realize that the game is a major source of profits. If it ceased marketing the game, the company could go bankrupt. If you were a CompTac decision maker, what would your decision be in this situation? How would you justify your decision from an ethical perspective?

6. CompTac wants to sell one of its best-selling software programs to An Phat Company, a firm located in Ho Chi Minh City, Vietnam. CompTac is concerned, however, that after an initial purchase, An Phat will duplicate the software without permission (and in violation of U.S. copyright laws) and sell the illegal bootleg software to other firms in Vietnam. How can CompTac protect its software from being pirated by An Phat Company?

The Commercial Environment

(Quaziefoto/Creative Commons)

Chapter 8

Intellectual Property and Internet Law

> "The Internet is just a world passing around notes in a classroom."
>
> —Jon Stewart, 1962–present
> (American comedian and host of *The Daily Show*)

Contents

Chapter Objectives

After reading this chapter, you should be able to answer the following questions:

1. What is intellectual property?
2. Why does the law protect trademarks and patents?
3. What laws protect authors' rights in the works they generate?
4. What are trade secrets, and what laws offer protection for this form of intellectual property?
5. What steps have been taken to protect intellectual property rights in today's digital age?

(Quaziefoto/Creative Commons)

Intellectual Property Property resulting from intellectual, creative processes.

Intellectual property is any property resulting from intellectual, creative processes—the products of an individual's mind. Although it is an abstract term for an abstract concept, intellectual property is nonetheless familiar to almost everyone. The information contained in books and computer files is intellectual property. The software you use, the movies you see, and the music you listen to are all forms of intellectual property.

A significant concern for many businesspersons is the need to protect their rights in intellectual property, which may be more valuable than their physical property, such as machines and buildings. Consider, for instance, the importance of intellectual property rights to technology companies, such as Apple, Inc., the maker of the iPhone and the iPad. Such companies derive most of their profits from their intellectual property rights, which is why Apple sued its rival Samsung Electronics Company in 2011. Apple claims that Samsung's Galaxy line of mobile phones and tablets (which run Google's Android software) copy the look, design, and user interface of Apple's iPhone and iPad. Although Apple is one of Samsung's biggest customers and buys many of its components from Samsung, in this instance Apple is concerned about protecting its revenue from iPhone and iPad sales from competing Android products.

The need to protect creative works was first recognized in Article I, Section 8, of the U.S. Constitution (see Appendix B), and statutory protection of these rights began in the 1940s. Laws protecting patents, trademarks, and copyrights are explicitly designed to protect and reward inventive and artistic creativity. These laws continue to evolve to meet the challenges of modern society.

In today's global economy, however, protecting intellectual property in one country is no longer sufficient. Therefore, the United States is participating in international agreements to secure ownership rights in intellectual property in other countries. Because the Internet allows the world to "pass around notes" so quickly, as Jon Stewart joked in the chapter-opening quotation on the previous page, protecting these rights in today's online environment has proved particularly challenging.

Trademarks and Related Property

Trademark A distinctive mark, motto, device, or emblem that a manufacturer stamps, prints, or otherwise affixes to the goods it produces so that they may be identified on the market and their origins made known. Once a trademark is established (under the common law or through registration), the owner is entitled to its exclusive use.

A **trademark** is a distinctive mark, motto, device, or emblem that a manufacturer stamps, prints, or otherwise affixes to the goods it produces so that they may be identified on the market and their origins made known. At common law, the person who used a symbol or mark to identify a business or product was protected in the use of that trademark. Clearly, by using another's trademark, a business could lead consumers to believe that its goods were made by the other business. The law seeks to avoid this kind of confusion. (For information on how companies use trademarks and service marks, see this chapter's *Linking the Law to Marketing* feature on page 230.)

In the following classic case concerning Coca-Cola, the defendants argued that the Coca-Cola trademark was entitled to no protection under the law because the term did not accurately represent the product.

Classic Case 8.1   **Coca-Cola Co. v. Koke Co. of America**

Supreme Court of the United States, 254 U.S. 143, 41 S.Ct. 113, 65 L.Ed. 189 (1920).
www.findlaw.com/casecode/supreme.html[a]

This advertisement from the 1890s shows model Hilda Clark in formal attire. The ad is entitled "Drink Coca-Cola 5¢."

(Wikimedia Commons and The Library of Congress)

COMPANY PROFILE
John Pemberton, an Atlanta pharmacist, invented a caramel-colored, carbonated soft drink in 1886. His bookkeeper, Frank Robinson, named the beverage Coca-Cola after two of the ingredients, coca leaves and kola nuts. Asa Candler bought the Coca-Cola Company in 1891 and, within seven years, had made the soft drink available throughout the United States, as well as in parts of Canada and Mexico. Candler continued to sell Coke aggressively and to open up new markets, reaching Europe before 1910. In doing

so, however, he attracted numerous competitors, some of whom tried to capitalize directly on the Coke name.

BACKGROUND AND FACTS The Coca-Cola Company brought an action in a federal district court to enjoin other beverage companies from using the words *Koke* and *Dope* for their products. The defendants contended that the Coca-Cola trademark was a fraudulent representation and that Coca-Cola was therefore not entitled to any help from the courts. By use of the Coca-Cola name, the defendants alleged, the Coca-Cola Company represented that the beverage contained cocaine (from coca leaves). The district court granted the injunction, but the federal appellate court reversed. The Coca-Cola Company appealed to the United States Supreme Court.

IN THE WORDS OF THE COURT . . .
Mr. Justice *HOLMES* delivered the opinion of the Court.
    * * * *

    * * * Before 1900 the beginning of [Coca-Cola's] good will was more or less helped by the presence of cocaine, a drug that, like alcohol or caffein or opium, may be described as a deadly poison or as a valuable item of the pharmacopœa [collection of pharmaceuticals] according to the [purposes of the speaker]. * * * After the Food and

---

a. This is the "US Supreme Court Opinions" page within the Web site of the "FindLaw Internet Legal Resources" database. This page provides several options for accessing an opinion. Because you know the citation for this case, you can go to the "Citation Search" box, type in the appropriate volume and page numbers for the *United States Reports* ("254" and "143," respectively, for the *Coca-Cola* case), and click on "Search."

Case 8.1–Continues next page ➡

Classic Case 8.1–Continued

Drug Act of June 30, 1906, if not earlier, long before this suit was brought, it was eliminated from the plaintiff's compound.

* * * Since 1900 the sales have increased at a very great rate corresponding to a like increase in advertising. The name now characterizes a beverage to be had at almost any soda fountain. It means a single thing coming from a single source, and well known to the community. It hardly would be too much to say that the drink characterizes the name as much as the name the drink. In other words Coca-Cola probably means to most persons the plaintiff's familiar product to be had everywhere rather than a compound of particular substances. * * * Before this suit was brought the plaintiff had advertised to the public that it must not expect and would not find cocaine, and had eliminated everything tending to suggest cocaine effects except the name and the picture of the leaves and nuts, which probably conveyed little or nothing to most who saw it. It appears to us that it would be going too far to deny the plaintiff relief against a palpable fraud because possibly here and there an ignorant person might call for the drink with the hope for incipient cocaine intoxication. The plaintiff's position must be judged by the facts as they were when the suit was begun, not by the facts of a different condition and an earlier time.

DECISION AND REMEDY   The United States Supreme Court upheld the district court's injunction. The competing beverage companies were enjoined from calling their products "Koke." The Court did not prevent them from calling their products "Dope," however.

WHAT IF THE FACTS WERE DIFFERENT?   *Suppose that Coca-Cola had been trying to make the public believe that its product contained cocaine. Would the result in the case likely have been different? Explain your answer.*

IMPACT OF THIS CASE ON TODAY'S LAW   *In this early case, the United States Supreme Court made it clear that trademarks and trade names (and nicknames for those marks and names, such as the nickname "Coke" for "Coca-Cola") that are in common use receive protection under the common law. This holding is significant historically because it is the predecessor to the federal statute later passed to protect trademark rights (the Lanham Act of 1946, to be discussed shortly).*

Statutory Protection of Trademarks

Statutory protection of trademarks and related property is provided at the federal level by the Lanham Act of 1946.[1] The Lanham Act was enacted, in part, to protect manufacturers from losing business to rival companies that used confusingly similar trademarks. The act incorporates the common law of trademarks and provides remedies for owners of trademarks who wish to enforce their claims in federal court. Many states also have trademark statutes.

TRADEMARK DILUTION   Before 1995, federal trademark law prohibited only the unauthorized use of the same mark on competing—or on noncompeting but "related"—goods or services. Protection was given only when the unauthorized use would likely confuse consumers as to the origin of those goods and services. In 1995, Congress amended the Lanham Act by passing the Federal Trademark Dilution Act,[2] which allowed trademark owners to bring a suit in federal court for trademark *dilution*. Trademark dilution laws protect "distinctive" or "famous" trademarks (such as Jergens, McDonald's, Dell, and Apple) from certain unauthorized uses even when the use is on noncompeting goods or is unlikely to confuse. More than half of the states have also enacted trademark dilution laws.

USE OF A SIMILAR MARK MAY CONSTITUTE TRADEMARK DILUTION   A famous mark may be diluted not only by the use of an *identical* mark but also by the use of a *similar* mark, provided that it reduces the value of the famous mark.[3] **CASE EXAMPLE 8.1** Samantha Lundberg opened a coffee shop under the name "Sambuck's Coffeehouse"

---

1. 15 U.S.C. Sections 1051–1128.
2. 15 U.S.C. Section 1125.
3. See *Moseley v. V Secret Catalogue, Inc.*, 537 U.S. 418, 123 S.Ct. 1115, 155 L.Ed.2d 1 (2003).

This coffee shop in Astoria, Oregon, used to be named "Sambuck's Coffeehouse" until Starbucks successfully sued for trademark dilution. Why would Starbucks spend the resources necessary to sue a single coffee shop in a small town?

in Astoria, Oregon, even though she knew that "Starbucks" was one of the larger coffee chains in the nation. When Starbucks Corporation filed a dilution lawsuit, the federal court ruled that use of the "Sambuck's" mark constituted trademark dilution because it created confusion for consumers. Not only was there a "high degree" of similarity between the marks, but also both companies provided coffee-related services through "stand-alone" retail stores. Therefore, the use of the similar mark (Sambuck's) reduced the value of the famous mark (Starbucks).[4] ●

Trademark Registration

Trademarks may be registered with the state or with the federal government. To register for protection under federal trademark law, a person must file an application with the U.S. Patent and Trademark Office in Washington, D.C. A mark can be registered (1) if it is currently in commerce or (2) if the applicant intends to put the mark into commerce within six months.

In special circumstances, the six-month period can be extended by thirty months, giving the applicant a total of three years from the date of notice of trademark approval to make use of the mark and file the required use statement. Registration is postponed until the mark is actually used. Nonetheless, during this waiting period, the applicant's trademark is protected against a third party who has neither used the mark previously nor filed an application for it. Registration is renewable between the fifth and sixth years after the initial registration and every ten years thereafter (every twenty years for trademarks registered before 1990).

Trademark Infringement

Registration of a trademark with the U.S. Patent and Trademark Office gives notice on a nationwide basis that the trademark belongs exclusively to the registrant. The registrant is also allowed to use the symbol ® to indicate that the mark has been registered. Whenever someone else uses that trademark in its entirety or copies it to a substantial degree, intentionally or unintentionally, the trademark has been *infringed* (used without authorization).

When a trademark has been infringed, the owner has a cause of action against the infringer. To succeed in a trademark infringement action, the owner must show that the defendant's use of the mark created a likelihood of confusion about the origin of the defendant's goods or services. The owner need not prove that the infringer acted intentionally or that the trademark was registered (although registration does provide proof of the date of inception of the trademark's use).

The most commonly granted remedy for trademark infringement is an *injunction* to prevent further infringement. Under the Lanham Act, a trademark owner that successfully proves infringement can recover actual damages, plus the profits that the infringer wrongfully received from the unauthorized use of the mark. A court can also order the destruction of any goods bearing the unauthorized trademark. In some situations, the trademark owner may also be able to recover attorneys' fees.

---

4. *Starbucks Corp. v. Lundberg*, 2005 WL 3183858 (D.Or. 2005).

Distinctiveness of the Mark

A central objective of the Lanham Act is to reduce the likelihood that consumers will be confused by similar marks. For that reason, only those trademarks that are deemed sufficiently distinctive from all competing trademarks will be protected.

STRONG MARKS   Fanciful, arbitrary, or suggestive trademarks are generally considered to be the most distinctive (strongest) trademarks because they are normally taken from outside the context of the particular product and thus provide the best means of distinguishing one product from another. Fanciful trademarks include invented words, such as "Xerox" for one manufacturer's copiers and "Kodak" for another company's photographic products. Arbitrary trademarks use common words that would not ordinarily be associated with the product, such as "Dutch Boy" as a name for paint.

A single letter used in a particular style can be an arbitrary trademark. **CASE EXAMPLE 8.2**   Sports entertainment company ESPN sued Quiksilver, Inc., a maker of surfer clothing, alleging trademark infringement. ESPN claimed that Quiksilver had used on its clothing the stylized "X" mark that ESPN uses in connection with the "X Games," a competition focusing on extreme action sports such as skateboarding and snowboarding. Quiksilver filed counterclaims for trademark infringement and dilution, arguing that it had a long history of using the stylized X on its products. ESPN created the X Games in the mid-1990s, and Quiksilver had been using the X mark since 1994. ESPN, which had trademark applications pending for the stylized X, asked the court to dismiss Quiksilver's counterclaims. In 2008, a federal district court held that the X on Quiksilver's clothing was clearly an arbitrary mark. Noting that "the two Xs are similar enough that a consumer might well confuse them," the court refused to dismiss Quiksilver's claims and allowed the dispute to go to trial.[5] ●

Suggestive trademarks bring to mind something about a product without describing the product directly. For instance, "Dairy Queen" suggests an association between its products and milk, but it does not directly describe ice cream. "Blu-ray" is a suggestive mark that is associated with the high-quality, high-definition video contained on a particular optical data storage disc. Although blue-violet lasers are used to read blu-ray discs, the term *blu-ray* does not directly describe the disc.

SECONDARY MEANING   Descriptive terms, geographic terms, and personal names are not inherently distinctive and do not receive protection under the law *until* they acquire a secondary meaning. **CASE EXAMPLE 8.3**   Frosty Treats, Inc., sells frozen desserts out of ice cream trucks. The video game series Twisted Metal depicts an ice cream truck with a clown character on it that is similar to the clowns on Frosty Treats' trucks. In the last game of the series, the truck bears the label "Frosty Treats." Frosty Treats sued for trademark infringement, but the court held that "Frosty Treats" is a descriptive term that is not protected by trademark law unless it has acquired a secondary meaning. To establish secondary meaning, Frosty Treats would have had to show that the public recognized its trademark and associated it with a single source. Because Frosty Treats failed to do so, the court entered a judgment in favor of the video game producer.[6] ●

A secondary meaning arises when customers begin to associate a specific term or phrase, such as *London Fog*, with specific trademarked items (coats with "London Fog" labels) made by a particular company. Whether a secondary meaning becomes attached to a term or name usually depends on how extensively the product is advertised, the market for the product, the number of sales, and other factors. Once a

---

5. *ESPN, Inc. v. Quiksilver, Inc.,* 586 F.Supp.2d 219 (S.D.N.Y. 2008).
6. *Frosty Treats, Inc. v. Sony Computer Entertainment America, Inc.,* 426 F.3d 1001 (8th Cir. 2005).

secondary meaning is attached to a term or name, a trademark is considered distinctive and is protected. Even a color can qualify for trademark protection, as did the color schemes used by four state university sports teams, including Ohio State University and Louisiana State University.[7]

GENERIC TERMS   Generic terms are terms that refer to an entire class of products, such as *bicycle* and *computer*. Generic terms receive no protection, even if they acquire secondary meanings. A particularly thorny problem for a business arises when its trademark acquires generic use. For instance, *aspirin* and *thermos* were originally trademarked products, but today the words are used generically. Other trademarks that have acquired generic use include *escalator, trampoline, raisin bran, dry ice, lanolin, linoleum, nylon,* and *cornflakes*.[8]

Service, Certification, and Collective Marks

> **Service Mark**   A mark used in the sale or advertising of services to distinguish the services of one person from those of others. Titles, character names, and other distinctive features of radio and television programs may be registered as service marks.

A **service mark** is essentially a trademark that is used to distinguish the *services* (rather than the products) of one person or company from those of another. For instance, each airline has a particular mark or symbol associated with its name. Titles and character names used in radio and television are frequently registered as service marks.

> **Certification Mark**   A mark used by one or more persons, other than the owner, to certify the region, materials, mode of manufacture, quality, or other characteristic of specific goods or services.

Other marks protected by law include certification marks and collective marks. A **certification mark** is used by one or more persons, other than the owner, to certify the region, materials, mode of manufacture, quality, or other characteristic of specific goods or services. Certification marks include such marks as "Good Housekeeping Seal of Approval" and "UL Tested." When used by members of a cooperative, association, union, or other organization, a certification mark is referred to as a **collective mark.**

> **Collective Mark**   A mark used by members of a cooperative, association, union, or other organization to certify the region, materials, mode of manufacture, quality, or other characteristic of specific goods or services.

EXAMPLE 8.4   Collective marks appear at the ends of movie credits to indicate the various associations and organizations that participated in making the movie. The union marks found on the tags of certain products are also collective marks. ●

Trade Dress

> **Trade Dress**   The image and overall appearance of a product—for example, the distinctive decor, menu, layout, and style of service of a particular restaurant. Basically, trade dress is subject to the same protection as trademarks.

The term **trade dress** refers to the image and overall appearance of a product. Trade dress is a broad concept and can include all or part of the total image or overall impression created by a product or its packaging. **EXAMPLE 8.5**   The distinctive decor, menu, and style of service of a particular restaurant may be regarded as the restaurant's trade dress. Similarly, trade dress can include the layout and appearance of a mail-order catalogue, the use of a lighthouse as part of a golf hole's design, the fish shape of a cracker, or the G-shaped design of a Gucci watch. ●

Basically, trade dress is subject to the same protection as trademarks. In cases involving trade dress infringement, as in trademark infringement cases, a major consideration is whether consumers are likely to be confused by the allegedly infringing use.

Counterfeit Goods

Counterfeit goods copy or otherwise imitate trademarked goods, but they are not the genuine trademarked goods. The importation of goods bearing counterfeit (fake) trademarks poses a growing problem for U.S. businesses, consumers, and law enforcement.

---

7. *Board of Supervisors of LA State University v. Smack Apparel Co.,* 438 F.Supp.2d 653 (2006). See also *Qualitex Co. v. Jacobson Products Co.,* 514 U.S. 159, 115 S.Ct. 1300, 131 L.Ed.2d 248 (1995).

8. See, for example, *Boston Duck Tours, LP v. Super Duck Tours, LLC,* 531 F.3d 1 (1st Cir. 2008).

New York City mayor Michael Bloomberg stands amidst seized counterfeit goods in Chinatown's New Land Shopping Center. These included counterfeit Coach, Fendi, Prada, and Rolex goods. What sanctions can be imposed on those found guilty under current law?

In addition to having negative financial effects on legitimate businesses, sales of certain counterfeit goods, such as pharmaceuticals and nutritional supplements, can present serious public health risks. It is estimated that nearly 7 percent of the goods imported into the United States are counterfeit.

THE STOP COUNTERFEITING IN MANUFACTURED GOODS ACT

Congress enacted the Stop Counterfeiting in Manufactured Goods Act[9] (SCMGA) to combat counterfeit goods. The act made it a crime to intentionally traffic in, or attempt to traffic in, counterfeit goods or services, or to knowingly use a counterfeit mark on or in connection with goods or services. Before this act, the law did not prohibit the creation or shipment of counterfeit labels that were not attached to a product.[10] Therefore, counterfeiters would make labels and packaging bearing a fake trademark, ship the labels to another location, and then affix them to inferior products to deceive buyers. The SCMGA closed this loophole by making it a crime to traffic in counterfeit labels, stickers, packaging, and the like, whether or not they are attached to goods.

PENALTIES FOR COUNTERFEITING   Persons found guilty of violating the SCMGA may be fined up to $2 million or imprisoned for up to ten years (or more if they are repeat offenders). If a court finds that the statute was violated, it must order the defendant to forfeit the counterfeit products (which are then destroyed), as well as any property used in the commission of the crime. The defendant must also pay restitution to the trademark holder or victim in an amount equal to the victim's actual loss.

CASE EXAMPLE 8.6   Wajdi Beydoun pleaded guilty to conspiring to import cigarette-rolling papers from Mexico that were falsely marked as "Zig-Zags" and sell them in the United States. Beydoun was sentenced to prison and ordered to pay $566,267 in restitution. On appeal, the court affirmed the prison sentence but ordered the trial court to reduce the amount of restitution because it exceeded the actual loss suffered by the legitimate sellers of Zig-Zag rolling papers.[11] ●

Trade Names

Trade Name   A term that is used to indicate part or all of a business's name and that is directly related to the business's reputation and goodwill. Trade names are protected under the common law (and under trademark law, if the name is the same as the firm's trademarked product).

Trademarks apply to *products*. The term **trade name** is used to indicate part or all of a business's name, whether the business is a sole proprietorship, a partnership, or a corporation. Generally, a trade name is directly related to a business and its goodwill. A trade name may be protected as a trademark if it is the same as the company's trademarked product—for example, Coca-Cola. Unless it is also used as a trademark or service mark, a trade name cannot be registered with the federal government. Trade names are protected under the common law, however. As with trademarks, words must be unusual or fancifully used if they are to be protected as trade names. For instance, the courts held that the word *Safeway* was sufficiently fanciful to obtain protection as a trade name for a grocery chain.

---

9. Pub. L. No. 109-181 (2006), which amended 18 U.S.C. Sections 2318–2320.
10. See, for example, *Commonwealth v. Crespo,* 884 A.2d 960 (Pa. 2005).
11. *United States v. Beydoun,* 469 F.3d 102 (5th Cir. 2006).

▶ Cyber Marks

Cyber Mark A trademark in cyberspace.

In cyberspace, trademarks are sometimes referred to as **cyber marks.** We turn now to a discussion of how new laws and the courts are addressing trademark-related issues in cyberspace.

Domain Names

Domain Name The last part of an Internet address, such as "westlaw.com." The top level (the part of the name to the right of the period) indicates the type of entity that operates the site (*com* is an abbreviation for "commercial"). The second level (the part of the name to the left of the period) is chosen by the entity.

As e-commerce expanded worldwide, one issue that emerged involved the rights of a trademark owner to use the mark as part of a domain name. A **domain name** is part of an Internet address, such as "westlaw.com." Every domain name ends with a top level domain (TLD), which is the part to the right of the period that indicates the type of entity that operates the site (for example, *com* is an abbreviation for "commercial").

The second level domain (SLD)—the part of the name to the left of the period—is chosen by the business entity or individual registering the domain name. Competition for SLDs among firms with similar names and products has led to numerous disputes. By using the same, or a similar, domain name, parties have attempted to profit from a competitor's goodwill, sell pornography, offer for sale another party's domain name, or otherwise infringe on others' trademarks.

The Internet Corporation for Assigned Names and Numbers (ICANN), a nonprofit corporation, oversees the distribution of domain names and operates an online arbitration system. Due to numerous complaints, ICANN completely overhauled the domain name distribution system and began using a new system in 2009. One of the goals of the new system is to alleviate the problem of *cybersquatting.* **Cybersquatting** occurs when a person registers a domain name that is the same as, or confusingly similar to, the trademark of another and then offers to sell the domain name back to the trademark owner.

Cybersquatting The act of registering a domain name that is the same as, or confusingly similar to, the trademark of another and then offering to sell that domain name back to the trademark owner.

Anticybersquatting Legislation

During the 1990s, cybersquatting led to so much litigation that Congress passed the Anticybersquatting Consumer Protection Act (ACPA) of 1999, which amended the Lanham Act—the federal law protecting trademarks discussed earlier. The ACPA makes it illegal to "register, traffic in, or use" a domain name (1) if the name is identical or confusingly similar to the trademark of another and (2) if the person registering, trafficking in, or using the domain name has a "bad faith intent" to profit from that trademark.

THE ONGOING PROBLEM OF CYBERSQUATTING Despite the ACPA, cybersquatting continues to present a problem for businesses, largely because more TLDs are now available and many more companies are registering domain names. Indeed, domain name registrars have proliferated. These companies charge a fee to businesses and individuals to register new names and to renew annual registrations (often through automated software). Many of these companies also buy and sell expired domain names. Although all registrars are supposed to relay information about these transactions to ICANN and the other companies that keep a master list of domain names, this does not always occur. The speed at which domain names change hands and the difficulty in tracking mass automated registrations have created an environment in which cybersquatting can flourish.

Cybersquatters have also developed new tactics, such as *typosquatting* (registering a name that is a misspelling of a popular brand, for example, hotmial.com or myspac.com). Because many Internet users are not perfect typists, Web pages using these misspelled names can generate significant traffic. More traffic generally means increased profits (advertisers often pay Web sites based on the number of unique visits, or hits), which in turn provides incentive for more cybersquatters. Also, if the misspelling is significant, the trademark owner may have difficulty proving that the name is identical or confusingly similar to the owner's mark, as required by the ACPA.

Cybersquatting is costly for businesses, which must attempt to register all variations of a name to protect their domain name rights from would-be cybersquatters. Large corporations may have to register thousands of domain names across the globe just to protect their basic brands and trademarks.

APPLICABILITY OF THE ACPA AND SANCTIONS UNDER THE ACT   The ACPA applies to all domain name registrations of trademarks. Successful plaintiffs in suits brought under the act can collect actual damages and profits or elect to receive statutory damages that range from $1,000 to $100,000.

Although some companies have successfully sued under the ACPA, there are roadblocks to pursuing such lawsuits. Some domain name registrars offer privacy services that hide the true owners of Web sites, making it difficult for trademark owners to identify cybersquatters. Thus, before a trademark owner can bring a suit, he or she has to ask the court for a subpoena to discover the identity of the owner of the infringing Web site. Because of the high costs of court proceedings, discovery, and even arbitration, many disputes over cybersquatting are settled out of court.

Meta Tags

Search engines compile their results by looking through a Web site's key-word field. *Meta tags,* or key words, may be inserted into this field to increase the likelihood that a site will be included in search engine results, even though the site may have nothing to do with the inserted words. Using this same technique, one site may appropriate the key words of other sites with more frequent hits so that the appropriating site appears in the same search engine results as the more popular sites. Using another's trademark in a meta tag without the owner's permission, however, normally constitutes trademark infringement.

Some uses of another's trademark as a meta tag may be permissible if the use is reasonably necessary and does not suggest that the owner authorized or sponsored the use. **CASE EXAMPLE 8.7**   Terri Welles, a former model who had been "Playmate of the Year" in *Playboy* magazine, established a Web site that used the terms *Playboy* and *Playmate* as meta tags. Playboy Enterprises, Inc., which publishes *Playboy,* filed a suit seeking to prevent Welles from using these meta tags. The court determined that Welles's use of Playboy's meta tags to direct users to her Web site was permissible because it did not suggest sponsorship and there were no descriptive substitutes for the terms *Playboy* and *Playmate.*[12] ●

Dilution in the Online World

As discussed earlier, trademark *dilution* occurs when a trademark is used, without authorization, in a way that diminishes the distinctive quality of the mark. Unlike trademark infringement, a claim of dilution does not require proof that consumers are likely to be confused by a connection between the unauthorized use and the mark. For this reason,

---

12. *Playboy Enterprises, Inc. v. Welles,* 279 F.3d 796 (9th Cir. 2002). See also *Canfield v. Health Communications, Inc.,* 2008 WL 961318 (C.D.Cal. 2008).

the products involved do not have to be similar. **CASE EXAMPLE 8.8**   In the first case alleging dilution on the Web, a court prohibited the use of "candyland.com" as the URL for an adult site. The suit was brought by the maker of the Candyland children's game and owner of the Candyland mark. Although consumers were not likely to connect candyland.com with the children's game, the court reasoned that the sexually explicit adult site would dilute the value of the Candyland mark.[13] ●

Licensing

License In the context of intellectual property law, an agreement permitting the use of a trademark, copyright, patent, or trade secret for certain limited purposes.

One way to make use of another's trademark or other form of intellectual property, while avoiding litigation, is to obtain a license to do so. A **license** in this context is an agreement permitting the use of a trademark, copyright, patent, or trade secret for certain limited purposes. The party that owns the intellectual property rights and issues the license is the *licensor,* and the party obtaining the license is the *licensee.*

A license grants only the rights expressly described in the license agreement. A licensor might, for example, allow the licensee to use the trademark as part of its company name, or as part of its domain name, but not otherwise use the mark on any products or services. Disputes frequently arise over licensing agreements, particularly when the license involves uses on the Internet or in different nations.

CASE EXAMPLE 8.9   George V Restauration S.A. and others owned and operated the Buddha Bar Paris, a restaurant with an Asian theme in Paris, France. In 2005, one of the owners allowed Little Rest Twelve, Inc., to use the Buddha Bar trademark and its associated concept in New York City under the name *Buddha Bar NYC.* Little Rest paid royalties for its use of the Buddha Bar mark and advertised Buddha Bar NYC's affiliation with Buddha Bar Paris, a connection also noted on its Web site and in the media. When a dispute arose, the owners of Buddha Bar Paris withdrew their permission for Buddha Bar NYC's use of their mark, but Little Rest continued to use it. The owners of the mark filed a suit in a New York state court against Little Rest, and ultimately a state appellate court granted an injunction preventing Little Rest from using the mark.[14] ●

Preventing Legal Disputes

To avoid litigation, consult with an attorney before signing any licensing contract to make sure that the wording of the contract is very clear as to what rights are or are not being conveyed. Moreover, to prevent misunderstandings over the scope of the rights being acquired, determine whether any other parties hold licenses to use that particular intellectual property and the extent of those rights.

 ## Patents

Patent A government grant that gives an inventor the exclusive right or privilege to make, use, or sell his or her invention for a limited time period.

A **patent** is a grant from the government that gives an inventor the exclusive right to make, use, and sell an invention for a period of twenty years. Patents for designs, as opposed to inventions, are given for a fourteen-year period. For either a regular patent or a design patent, the applicant must demonstrate to the satisfaction of the U.S. Patent and Trademark Office that the invention, discovery, process, or design is *novel, useful,* and *not obvious* in light of current technology.

Until 2011, patent law in the United States differed from many other countries because the first person to invent a product or process obtained the patent rights

---

13. *Hasbro, Inc. v. Internet Entertainment Group, Ltd.,* 1996 WL 84858 (W.D.Wash. 1996).
14. *George V Restauration S.A. v. Little Rest Twelve, Inc.,* 58 A.D.3d 428, 871 N.Y.S.2d 65 (2009).

rather than the first person to file for a patent. It was often difficult to prove who invented an item first, however, which prompted Congress to change the system in 2011 by passing the America Invents Act. Now the first person to file an application for a patent on the product or process receives patent protection. In addition, under the new law there is a nine-month limit for challenging a patent on any ground.

The period of patent protection begins on the date when the patent application is filed, rather than when the patent is issued, which can sometimes be years later. After the patent period ends (either fourteen or twenty years later), the product or process enters the public domain, and anyone can make, sell, or use the invention without paying the patent holder.

Searchable Patent Databases

A significant development relating to patents is the availability online of the world's patent databases. The Web site of the U.S. Patent and Trademark Office (www.uspto. gov) provides searchable databases covering U.S. patents granted since 1976. The Web site of the European Patent Office (www.epo.org) provides online access to 50 million patent documents in more than seventy nations through a searchable network of databases. Businesses use these searchable databases in many ways. Patents are valuable assets, and businesses may need to perform patent searches to list or inventory their assets.

"To invent, you need a good imagination and a pile of junk."

Thomas Edison, 1847–1931
(American inventor)

What Is Patentable?

Under federal law, "[w]hoever invents or discovers any new and useful process, machine, manufacture, or composition of matter, or any new and useful improvement thereof, may obtain a patent therefor, subject to the conditions and requirements of this title."[15] As mentioned, to be patentable, the item must be novel, useful, and not obvious.

Almost anything is patentable, except the laws of nature,[16] natural phenomena, and abstract ideas (including algorithms[17]). (See this chapter's *Online Developments* feature on the facing page for a discussion of an important case in the ongoing debate over whether business processes should be patentable.) Even artistic methods, certain works of art, and the structures of storylines are patentable, provided that they are novel and not obvious.

Plants that are reproduced asexually (by means other than from seed), such as hybrid or genetically engineered plants, are patentable in the United States, as are genetically engineered (or cloned) microorganisms and animals. **CASE EXAMPLE 8.10** Monsanto, Inc., has been selling its patented genetically modified (GM) seeds to farmers as a way to achieve higher yields using fewer pesticides. Monsanto requires farmers who buy GM seeds to sign licensing agreements promising to plant the seeds for only one crop cycle and to pay a technology fee for each acre planted. To ensure compliance,

---

15. 35 U.S.C. Section 101.

16. Several justices of the United States Supreme Court indicated that they believed a process to diagnose vitamin deficiencies should not be patentable because allowing a patent would improperly give a monopoly over a scientific relationship, or law of nature. Nevertheless, the majority of the Court allowed the patent to stand. *Laboratory Corporation of America Holdings v. Metabolite Laboratories, Inc.,* 548 U.S. 124, 126 S.Ct. 2921, 165 L.Ed.2d 399 (2006).

17. An *algorithm* is a step-by-step procedure, formula, or set of instructions for accomplishing a specific task—such as the set of rules used by a search engine to rank the listings contained within its index in response to a particular query.

Online Developments

Should the Law Continue to Allow Business Process Patents?

At one time, it was difficult for developers and manufacturers of software to obtain patent protection because many software products simply automate procedures that can be performed manually. In other words, it was thought that computer programs did not meet the "novel" and "not obvious" requirements for patents. This changed in 1981 when the United States Supreme Court held that a patent could be obtained for a *process* that incorporates a computer program.[a] Then, in a landmark 1998 case, *State Street Bank & Trust Co. v. Signature Financial Group, Inc.,*[b] a federal appellate court ruled that business processes are patentable.

Skyrocketing Demand

After the *State Street* case, numerous firms applied for and received patents on business processes or methods. Walker Digital obtained a business process patent for its "Dutch auction" system, which allows Priceline.com users to name their own price for airline tickets and hotels. Amazon.com patented its "one-click" online payment system.

The U.S. Patent and Trademark Office (USPTO) has issued thousands of business process patents, and many more applications are clogging its system. These applications frequently involve ideas about a business process, blurring the distinction between ideas (which are not patentable) and processes (which are). In addition, because business process patents often involve fields that provide services, such as accounting and finance, determining when a process originated or who first developed it can be difficult. Consequently, business process patents are more likely to lead to litigation than patents on tangible inventions, such as machines.

The *In re Bilski* Decision
Significantly Limits Business Process Patents

In 2008, the same court that decided the *State Street* case made it more difficult to obtain patents for business processes when it

reversed its earlier decision and invalidated "pure" business process patents.[c] In the *In re Bilski* case, two men had applied for a patent for a process that uses transactions to hedge the risk in commodity trading. The USPTO denied their application because it was not limited to a particular machine and did not describe any method for working out which transactions to perform. The men appealed.

After soliciting input from numerous interest groups, the appellate court established a new test for business process patents. A business process patent is valid only if the process (1) is carried out by a particular machine or apparatus or (2) transforms a particular article into a different state or object. Because the men's process did not meet the machine-or-transformation test, the court affirmed the USPTO's decision.

One of the dissenting judges in the *Bilski* case, Judge Haldane Robert Mayer, would have done away with business process patents altogether. He lamented that "the patent system is intended to protect and promote advances in science and technology, not ideas about how to structure commercial transactions." In Mayer's view, these patents "do not promote 'useful arts' because they are not directed to any technological or scientific innovation." Although they may use technology, such as computers, the creative part of business methods is in the thought process rather than the technology.

FOR CRITICAL ANALYSIS

Some patent experts think that the Bilski *decision, and sentiments such as those expressed by Judge Mayer, may signal an end to all business process patents in the near future. Should business process patents be severely limited or eliminated? Why or why not?*

---

a. *Diamond v. Diehr,* 450 U.S. 175, 101 S.Ct. 1048, 67 L.Ed.2d 155 (1981).
b. 149 F.3d 1368 (Fed.Cir. 1998).

c. *In re Bilski,* 545 F.3d 943 (Fed.Cir. 2008).

Monsanto has assigned seventy-five employees to investigate and prosecute farmers who use the GM seeds illegally. Monsanto has filed more than ninety lawsuits against nearly 150 farmers in the United States and has been awarded more than $15 million in damages (not including out-of-court settlement amounts).[18] ●

---

18. See, for example, *Monsanto Co. v. Scruggs,* 459 F.3d 1328 (2006); *Monsanto Co. v. McFarling,* __ F.Supp.2d __ (E.D.Mo. 2005); and *Sample v. Monsanto Co.,* 283 F.Supp.2d 1088 (2003).

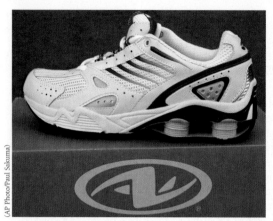

Wal-Mart creates private brands and markets them in its stores. This is a photo of a running shoe that it has created and sold. Nike has marketed a similarly constructed shoe for several years. Nike sued Wal-Mart for patent infringement because of the springlike device in the heel of the Wal-Mart version. What type of out-of-court settlement might the companies agree to?

Patent Infringement

If a firm makes, uses, or sells another's patented design, product, or process without the patent owner's permission, it commits the tort of patent infringement. Patent infringement may occur even though the patent owner has not put the patented product in commerce. Patent infringement may also occur even though not all features or parts of an invention are copied. (With respect to a patented process, however, all steps or their equivalent must be copied for infringement to exist.)

PATENT INFRINGEMENT SUITS AND HIGH-TECH COMPANIES

Obviously, companies that specialize in developing new technology stand to lose significant profits if someone "makes, uses, or sells" devices that incorporate their patented inventions. Because these firms hold numerous patents, they are frequently involved in patent infringement lawsuits (as well other types of intellectual property disputes). Many companies that make and sell electronics and computer software and hardware are based in foreign nations (for example, Samsung Electronics Company is a Korean firm). Foreign firms can apply for and obtain U.S. patent protection on items that they sell in the United States, just as U.S. firms can obtain protection in foreign nations where they sell goods.

Nevertheless, as a general rule, no patent infringement occurs under U.S. law when a product patented in the United States is made and sold in another country by another firm. The United States Supreme Court has narrowly construed patent infringement as it applies to exported software.

CASE EXAMPLE 8.11 AT&T Corporation holds a patent on a device used to digitally encode, compress, and process recorded speech. AT&T brought an infringement case against Microsoft Corporation, which admitted that its Windows operating system incorporated software code that infringed on AT&T's patent. The case reached the United States Supreme Court on the question of whether Microsoft's liability extended to computers made in another country. The Court held that it did not. Microsoft was liable only for infringement in the United States and not for the Windows-based computers produced in foreign locations. The Court reasoned that Microsoft had not "supplied" the software for the computers but had only electronically transmitted a master copy, which the foreign manufacturers then copied and loaded onto the computers.[19] ●

APPLE, INC. V. SAMSUNG ELECTRONICS CO.

As mentioned in the chapter introduction, Apple filed a lawsuit against Samsung in a federal court in 2011, alleging that Samsung's Galaxy mobile phones and tablets infringe on Apple's patents. The 373-page complaint actually contains numerous claims, including infringement of trade dress (that Samsung copied the "look and feel" of iPhones and iPads) and trademarks (that the icons used for many of the apps on Samsung's products are nearly identical to Apple's apps). The majority of the claims involve patent infringement, however. Apple claims that its design patents cover the graphical user interface (the display of icons on the home screen), the device's shell, and the screen and button design. It also claims that it has patents covering the way information is displayed on iPhones and other devices, the way windows pop open, and the way information is scaled and rotated, as well as other aspects such as the overlay windows and scrolling. Apple argues that Samsung's phones and tablets that use the Android system violate all of these patents. Although a court has ordered expedited discovery, this

---

19. *Microsoft Corp. v. AT&T Corp.,* 550 U.S. 437, 127 S.Ct. 1746, 167 L.Ed.2d 737 (2007).

litigation will likely take years to resolve because of the number of claims and the complexity of the issues.[20] ●

Remedies for Patent Infringement

If a patent is infringed, the patent holder may sue for relief in federal court. The patent holder can seek an injunction against the infringer and can also request damages for royalties and lost profits. In some cases, the court may grant the winning party reimbursement for attorneys' fees and costs. If the court determines that the infringement was willful, the court can triple the amount of damages awarded (treble damages).

In the past, permanent injunctions were routinely granted to prevent future infringement. In 2006, however, the United States Supreme Court ruled that patent holders are not automatically entitled to a permanent injunction against future infringing activities. According to the Supreme Court, a patent holder must prove that it has suffered irreparable injury and that the public interest would not be disserved by a permanent injunction.[21] This decision gives courts discretion to decide what is equitable in the circumstances and allows them to consider what is in the public interest rather than just the interests of the parties.

CASE EXAMPLE 8.12   In the first case applying this rule, a court found that although Microsoft had infringed on the patent of a small software company, the latter was not entitled to an injunction. According to the court, the small company was not irreparably harmed and could be adequately compensated by damages. Also, the public might suffer negative effects from an injunction because the infringement involved part of Microsoft's widely used Office suite software.[22] ●

 ## Copyrights

Copyright   The exclusive right of an author or originator of a literary or artistic production to publish, print, or sell that production for a statutory period of time. A copyright has the same monopolistic nature as a patent or trademark, but it differs in that it applies exclusively to works of art, literature, and other works of authorship (including computer programs).

A **copyright** is an intangible property right granted by federal statute to the author or originator of certain literary or artistic productions. The Copyright Act of 1976,[23] as amended, governs copyrights. Works created after January 1, 1978, are automatically given statutory copyright protection for the life of the author plus 70 years. For copyrights owned by publishing houses, the copyright expires 95 years from the date of publication or 120 years from the date of creation, whichever is first. For works by more than one author, the copyright expires 70 years after the death of the last surviving author.

Copyrights can be registered with the U.S. Copyright Office (www.copyright.gov) in Washington, D.C. A copyright owner no longer needs to place a © or *Copr.* or *Copyright* on the work, however, to have the work protected against infringement. Chances are that if somebody created it, somebody owns it.

What Is Protected Expression?

Works that are copyrightable include books, records, films, artworks, architectural plans, menus, music videos, product packaging, and computer software. To be protected, a work must be "fixed in a durable medium" from which it can be perceived, reproduced, or communicated. Protection is automatic. Registration is not required.

---

20. *Apple, Inc. v. Samsung Electronics Co.,* 2011 WL 1938154 (2011).
21. *eBay, Inc. v. MercExchange, LLC,* 547 U.S. 388, 126 S.Ct. 1837, 164 L.Ed.2d 641 (2006).
22. See *Z4 Technologies, Inc. v. Microsoft Corp.,* 434 F.Supp.2d 437 (2006).
23. 17 U.S.C. Sections 101 *et seq.*

To obtain protection under the Copyright Act, a work must be original and fall into one of the following categories:

1. Literary works (including newspaper and magazine articles, computer and training manuals, catalogues, brochures, and print advertisements).
2. Musical works and accompanying words (including advertising jingles).
3. Dramatic works and accompanying music.
4. Pantomimes and choreographic works (including ballets and other forms of dance).
5. Pictorial, graphic, and sculptural works (including cartoons, maps, posters, statues, and even stuffed animals).
6. Motion pictures and other audiovisual works (including multimedia works).
7. Sound recordings.
8. Architectural works.

SECTION 102 EXCLUSIONS   It is not possible to copyright an *idea*. Section 102 of the Copyright Act specifically excludes copyright protection for any "idea, procedure, process, system, method of operation, concept, principle, or discovery, regardless of the form in which it is described, explained, illustrated, or embodied." Thus, others can freely use the underlying ideas or principles embodied in a work. What is copyrightable is the particular way in which an idea is *expressed*. Whenever an idea and an expression are inseparable, the expression cannot be copyrighted. Generally, anything that is not an original expression will not qualify for copyright protection. Facts widely known to the public are not copyrightable. Page numbers are not copyrightable because they follow a sequence known to everyone. Mathematical calculations are not copyrightable.

> **BE CAREFUL**   If a creative work does not fall into a certain category, it might not be copyrighted, but it may be protected by other intellectual property law.

COMPILATIONS OF FACTS   Unlike ideas, *compilations* of facts are copyrightable. Under Section 103 of the Copyright Act, a compilation is a work formed by the collection and assembling of preexisting materials or of data that are selected, coordinated, or arranged in such a way that the resulting work as a whole constitutes an original work of authorship. The key requirement for the copyrightability of a compilation is originality. The White Pages of a telephone directory do not qualify for copyright protection because they simply list alphabetically names and telephone numbers. The Yellow Pages of a directory can be copyrightable, provided that the information is selected, coordinated, or arranged in an original way. Similarly, a compilation of information about yachts listed for sale may qualify for copyright protection.[24]

> *"Don't worry about people stealing an idea. If it's original and it's any good, you'll have to ram it down their throats."*
>
> Howard Aiken, 1900–1973
> (Engineer and pioneer in computing)

Copyright Infringement

Whenever the form or expression of an idea is copied, an infringement of copyright occurs. The reproduction does not have to be exactly the same as the original, nor does it have to reproduce the original in its entirety. If a substantial part of the original is reproduced, copyright infringement has occurred.

REMEDIES FOR COPYRIGHT INFRINGEMENT   Those who infringe copyrights may be liable for damages or criminal penalties. These range from actual damages or statutory damages, imposed at the court's discretion, to criminal proceedings for willful violations. Actual damages are based on the harm caused to the copyright

---

24. See, for example, *BUC International Corp. v. International Yacht Council, Ltd.,* 489 F.3d 1129 (11th Cir. 2007).

(AP Photo/Manny Garcia/Shepard Fairey)

Artist Shepard Fairey created a poster (right) of Barack Obama during the 2008 presidential campaign. Clearly, this poster was based on an Associated Press file photo of Obama taken by Manny Garcia (left). Did Fairey violate copyright law? Why or why not?

holder by the infringement, while statutory damages, not to exceed $150,000, are provided for under the Copyright Act. Criminal proceedings may result in fines and/or imprisonment. A court can also issue a permanent injunction against a defendant when the court deems it necessary to prevent future copyright infringement.

CASE EXAMPLE 8.13   Rusty Carroll operated an online term paper business, R2C2, Inc., that offered up to 300,000 research papers for sale at nine different Web sites. Individuals whose work was posted on these Web sites without their permission filed a lawsuit against Carroll for copyright infringement. A federal district court in Illinois ruled that an injunction was proper because the plaintiffs had shown that they had suffered irreparable harm and that monetary damages were inadequate to compensate them. Because Carroll had repeatedly failed to comply with court orders regarding discovery, the court found that the copyright infringement was likely to continue unless an injunction was issued. The court therefore issued a permanent injunction prohibiting Carroll and R2C2 from selling any term paper without sworn documentary evidence that the paper's author had given permission.[25] ●

THE "FAIR USE" EXCEPTION   An exception to liability for copyright infringement is made under the "fair use" doctrine. In certain circumstances, a person or organization can reproduce copyrighted material without paying royalties (fees paid to the copyright holder for the privilege of reproducing the copyrighted material). Section 107 of the Copyright Act provides as follows:

> [T]he fair use of a copyrighted work, including such use by reproduction in copies or phonorecords or by any other means specified by [Section 106 of the Copyright Act], for purposes such as criticism, comment, news reporting, teaching (including multiple copies for classroom use), scholarship, or research, is not an infringement of copyright. In determining whether the use made of a work in any particular case is a fair use the factors to be considered shall include–
>
> (1) the purpose and character of the use, including whether such use is of a commercial nature or is for nonprofit educational purposes;
> (2) the nature of the copyrighted work;
> (3) the amount and substantiality of the portion used in relation to the copyrighted work as a whole; and
> (4) the effect of the use upon the potential market for or value of the copyrighted work.

WHAT IS FAIR USE?   Because these guidelines are very broad, the courts determine whether a particular use is fair on a case-by-case basis. Thus, even if a person who reproduces copyrighted material believes the fair use exception applies, that person may still be committing a violation. In determining whether a use is fair, courts have often considered the fourth factor to be the most important.

CASE EXAMPLE 8.14   The owner of copyrighted music, BMG Music Publishing, granted a license to Leadsinger, Inc., a manufacturer of karaoke devices. The license gave Leadsinger permission to reproduce the sound recordings, but not to reprint the song lyrics, which appeared at the bottom of a TV screen when the karaoke device was used. BMG demanded that Leadsinger pay a "lyric reprint" fee and a "synchronization"

---

25. *Weidner v. Carroll*, No. 06-782-DRH, U.S. District Court for the Southern District of Illinois, January 21, 2010.

fee. Leadsinger refused to pay, claiming that its use of the lyrics was educational and thus did not constitute copyright infringement under the fair use exception. A federal appellate court disagreed. The court held that Leadsinger's display of the lyrics was not a fair use because it would have a negative effect on the value of the copyrighted work.[26] ●

THE FIRST SALE DOCTRINE   Section 109(a) of the Copyright Act—also known as the first sale doctrine—provides that "the owner of a particular copy or phonorecord lawfully made under [the Copyright Act], or any person authorized by such owner, is entitled, without the authority of the copyright owner, to sell or otherwise dispose of the possession of that copy or phonorecord." In other words, once a copyright owner sells or gives away a particular copy of a work, the copyright owner no longer has the right to control the distribution of that copy. Thus, for example, a person who buys a copyrighted book can sell it to another person.

In the following case, a music company had sent promotional CDs to a group of people in the music industry, including critics and radio programmers (disc jockeys). When those promotional CDs turned up for sale on the Internet, the company filed a lawsuit for copyright infringement. The issue was whether the music company had given up its right to control further distribution of the promotional CDs under the first sale doctrine.

---

26. *Leadsinger, Inc. v. BMG Music Publishing,* 512 F.3d 522 (9th Cir. 2008).

Case 8.2   UMG Recordings, Inc. v. Augusto

United States Court of Appeals, Ninth Circuit, 628 F.3d 1175 (2011).

COMPANY PROFILE   *Universal Music Group (UMG) is the world's largest music company. It is made up of two core businesses–music recording and music publishing. The company develops, markets, and distributes recorded music through a network of subsidiaries, joint ventures, and licensees in more than seventy countries. Founded in 1934, UMG was at first attached to the film studio Universal Pictures. It was separated from the studio in 2004, when the French media conglomerate Vivendi acquired the company. UMG is now a wholly owned subsidiary of Vivendi.*

BACKGROUND AND FACTS   UMG regularly ships specially produced promotional CDs to individuals such as music critics and radio programmers. The recipients have neither requested nor agreed to receive the CDs, and UMG does not receive payment for them. The CD labels state that the CDs are "the property of the record company," "licensed to the intended recipient," and for "Promotional Use Only–Not for Sale." Troy Augusto managed to obtain some of these promotional CDs from various sources and later sold them through online auction sites, such as eBay. After making several unsuccessful attempts to halt the auctions through eBay's dispute-resolution program, UMG filed a complaint in a federal district court alleging that Augusto had infringed UMG's copyrights. Augusto asserted that UMG's initial distribution of the CDs effectively transferred ownership of the CDs to the recipients. Thus, his resales

were permitted under the first sale doctrine. UMG argued that the statements on the CD's labels and the circumstances of their distribution granted only a license to each recipient, not a transfer of ownership. The district court granted summary judgment in favor of Augusto, and UMG appealed.

IN THE WORDS OF THE COURT . . .
CANBY, Circuit Judge:
* * * *

To establish a *prima facie* case of copyright infringement, a plaintiff must show (1) ownership of a valid copyright and (2) violation by the alleged infringer of at least one of the exclusive rights granted to copyright owners by the Copyright Act (the "Act"). Section 106 of the Act grants copyright owners, such as UMG, the exclusive right, among others, "to distribute copies or phonorecords of the copyrighted work to the public by sale or other transfer of ownership."

Although UMG, as the owner of the copyright, has exclusive rights in the promotional CDs, "[e]xemptions, compulsory licenses, and defenses found in the Copyright Act narrow [those] rights."
* * * *

* * * A copyright owner who transfers title in a particular copy to a purchaser or donee cannot prevent resale of that particular copy. We have recognized, however, that not every transfer of possession of a copy transfers title. *Particularly with regard to computer software,*

Case 8.2–Continued

we have recognized that copyright owners may create licensing arrangements so that users acquire only a license to use the particular copy of software and do not acquire title that permits further transfer or sale of that copy without the permission of the copyright owner. [Emphasis added.]

* * * We conclude that, under all the circumstances of the CDs' distribution, the recipients were entitled to use or dispose of them in any manner they saw fit, and UMG did not enter a license agreement for the CDs with the recipients. Accordingly, UMG transferred title to the particular copies of its promotional CDs and cannot maintain an infringement action against Augusto for his subsequent sale of those copies.

Our conclusion that the recipients acquired ownership of the CDs is based largely on the nature of UMG's distribution. First, the promotional CDs are dispatched to the recipients without any prior arrangement as to those particular copies. The CDs are not numbered, and no attempt is made to keep track of where particular copies are or what use is made of them. * * * *Although UMG places written restrictions in the labels of the CDs, it has not established that the restrictions on the CDs create a license agreement.* [Emphasis added.]

* * * *

UMG's distribution of the promotional CDs under the circumstances effected a sale (transfer of title) of the CDs to the recipients. Further sale of those copies was therefore permissible without UMG's authorization. The judgment of the district court dismissing UMG's copyright infringement action against Augusto is therefore

AFFIRMED.

DECISION AND REMEDY The federal appellate court held that UMG had conveyed title of the copyrighted promotional CDs to the recipients, rather than creating licenses. The court therefore affirmed the district court's order dismissing the copyright infringement action against Augusto.

THE LEGAL ENVIRONMENT DIMENSION *What could UMG have done to better protect its copyrights of the music on the promotional CDs?*

THE SOCIAL DIMENSION *What would be the implications for society if the first sale doctrine did not exist?*

Copyright Protection for Software

In 1980, Congress passed the Computer Software Copyright Act, which amended the Copyright Act of 1976 to include computer programs in the list of creative works protected by federal copyright law. Generally, the courts have extended copyright protection not only to those parts of a computer program that can be read by humans, such as the high-level language of a source code, but also to the binary-language object code of a computer program, which is readable only by the computer. Additionally, such elements as the overall structure, sequence, and organization of a program have been deemed copyrightable. Not all aspects of software are protected, however. For the most part, courts have not extended copyright protection to the "look and feel"—the general appearance, command structure, video images, menus, windows, and other screen displays—of computer programs.

Copyrights in Digital Information

Copyright law is probably the most important form of intellectual property protection on the Internet, largely because much of the material on the Web (software, for example) is copyrighted and in order to be transferred online, it must be "copied." Generally, anytime a party downloads software or music into a computer's random access memory, or RAM, without authorization, a copyright is infringed. Technology has vastly increased the potential for copyright infringement. **CASE EXAMPLE 8.15** In one case, a rap song that was included in the sound track of a movie had used only a few seconds from the guitar solo of another's copyrighted sound recording without permission. Nevertheless, a federal appellate court held that digitally sampling a copyrighted sound recording of any length constitutes copyright infringement.[27] ●

---

27. *Bridgeport Music, Inc. v. Dimension Films,* 410 F.3d 792 (6th Cir. 2005).

In 1998, Congress implemented the provisions of the World Intellectual Property Organization (WIPO) treaty by updating U.S. copyright law. The law—the Digital Millennium Copyright Act of 1998—is a landmark step in the protection of copyright owners and, because of the leading position of the United States in the creative industries, serves as a model for other nations. Among other things, the act established civil and criminal penalties for anyone who circumvents (bypasses—or gets around—through clever maneuvering, for example) encryption software or other technological antipiracy protection. Also prohibited are the manufacture, import, sale, and distribution of devices or services for circumvention.

MP3 and File-Sharing Technology

Soon after the Internet became popular, a few enterprising programmers created software to compress large data files, particularly those associated with music, so that they could more easily be transmitted online. The best-known compression and decompression system is MP3, which enables music fans to download songs or entire CDs onto their computers or onto portable listening devices, such as iPods. The MP3 system also made it possible for music fans to access other fans' files by engaging in file-sharing via the Internet.

Peer-to-Peer (P2P) Networking   The sharing of resources (such as files, hard drives, and processing styles) among multiple computers without the need for a central network server.

Distributed Network   A network that can be used by persons located (distributed) around the country or the globe to share computer files.

Cloud Computing   A subscription-based or pay-per-use service that, in real time over the Internet, extends a computer's software or storage capabilities. By using the services of large companies with excess storage and computing capacity, a company can increase its information technology capabilities without investing in new infrastructure, training new personnel, or licensing new software.

File-sharing is accomplished through **peer-to-peer (P2P) networking**. The concept is simple. Rather than going through a central Web server, P2P involves numerous personal computers (PCs) that are connected to the Internet. Individuals on the same network can access files stored on a single PC through a **distributed network**, which has parts dispersed in many locations. Persons scattered throughout the country or the world can work together on the same project by using file-sharing programs.

A newer method of sharing files via the Internet is **cloud computing**, which is essentially a subscription-based or pay-per-use service that extends a computer's software or storage capabilities. Cloud computing can deliver a single application through a browser to multiple users, or it may be a utility program to pool resources and provide data storage and virtual servers that can be accessed on demand. Apple, Amazon, Facebook, Google, IBM, and Sun Microsystems are using and developing cloud-computing services.

SHARING STORED MUSIC FILES   When file-sharing is used to download others' stored music files, copyright issues arise. Recording artists and their labels stand to lose large amounts of royalties and revenues if relatively few CDs are purchased and then made available on distributed networks, from which everyone can get them for free. **CASE EXAMPLE 8.16**   The issue of file-sharing infringement has been the subject of an ongoing debate since the highly publicized case of *A&M Records, Inc. v. Napster, Inc.*[28] Napster, Inc., operated a Web site with free software that enabled users to copy and transfer MP3 files via the Internet. When firms in the recording industry sued Napster, the court held that Napster was liable for contributory and vicarious[29] (indirect) copyright infringement because it had assisted others in obtaining unauthorized copies of copyrighted music. •

---

28. 239 F.3d 1004 (9th Cir. 2001).

29. *Vicarious (indirect) liability* exists when one person is subject to liability for another's actions. A common example occurs in the employment context, when an employer is held vicariously liable by third parties for torts committed by employees in the course of their employment.

In the following case, a group of recording companies sued an Internet user who had downloaded a number of their copyrighted songs. The user then shared the audio files with others via a P2P network. One of the issues before the court was whether the user was an "innocent infringer"—that is, whether she was innocent of copyright infringement because she was unaware that the works were copyrighted.

Case 8.3 Maverick Recording Co. v. Harper

United States Court of Appeals, Fifth Circuit, 598 F.3d 193 (2010).
www.ca5.uscourts.gov/Opinions/aspx[a]

Under what circumstances can an "innocent infringer" of copyrighted music files be prosecuted?

COMPANY PROFILE   *Recording star Madonna, others in the music business, and Time Warner created Maverick Records in 1992. Initially, the company saw great success with Alanis Morissette, The Prodigy, and Candlebox. It also created the soundtrack for the movie* The Matrix. *In a dispute over company management, Madonna and another co-owner were bought out. Today, Maverick is a wholly owned subsidiary of Warner Music Group.*

BACKGROUND AND FACTS
Maverick Recording Company and several other music-recording firms (the plaintiffs) hired MediaSentry to investigate the infringement of their copyrights over the Internet. During its investigation, MediaSentry discovered that Whitney Harper was using a computer program to share digital audio files with other users of a peer-to-peer network. The shared files included a number of the plaintiffs' copyrighted works. The plaintiffs sued Harper for copyright infringement and sought $750 per infringed work (the minimum amount of damages set forth in the Copyright Act). Harper had downloaded thirty-seven copyrighted audio files. Harper asserted that she was an "innocent" infringer, citing Section 504(c)(2) of the Copyright Act, which provides that when an infringer was not aware that his or her acts constituted copyright infringement, "the court in its discretion may reduce the award of statutory damages to a sum of not less than $200." The trial court granted summary judgment for the plaintiffs on the issue of copyright infringement and prevented Harper from further downloading and sharing of the copyrighted works. The court, however, awarded the plaintiffs only $200 per infringed work. Both parties appealed. Harper claimed that there was insufficient evidence of copyright infringement. The plaintiffs argued that the district court had erred by failing to rule out the innocent infringer defense as a matter of law.

IN THE WORDS OF THE COURT . . .
Edith Brown *CLEMENT*, Circuit Judge:
   * * * *

   The uncontroverted [noncontroversial] evidence is more than sufficient to compel a finding that Harper had downloaded the

files: there was no evidence from which a fact-finder could draw a reasonable inference that Harper had *not* downloaded them or that they were something other than audio files. * * * The district court properly rejected Harper's argument that the evidence of infringement was insufficient.
   * * * *

   * * * The district court held that there was a genuine issue of material fact as to whether Harper was an innocent infringer. * * * Harper averred [asserted] in an affidavit that she did not understand the nature of file-sharing programs and that she believed that listening to music from file-sharing networks was akin to listening to a noninfringing Internet radio station. The district court ruled that this assertion created a triable [capable of being tried before a jury or a judge] issue as to whether Harper's infringement was "innocent" under [Section 504(c)(2) of the Copyright Act].

   * * * We hold that the defense was unavailable to her as a matter of law. *The innocent infringer defense is limited by [Section 402(d) of the Copyright Act]: with one exception not relevant here, when a proper copyright notice "appears on the published * * * phonorecords to which a defendant * * * had access, then no weight shall be given to such a defendant's interposition of a defense based on innocent infringement in mitigation of actual or statutory damages."* [Emphasis added.]

   The district court acknowledged that Plaintiffs provided proper notice on each of the published phonorecords from which the audio files were taken. * * * Harper contended only that she was too young and naive to understand that the copyrights on published music applied to downloaded music.

   These arguments are insufficient to defeat the interposition [interference] of the [Section 402(d)] limitation on the innocent infringer defense. Harper's reliance on her own understanding of copyright law—or lack thereof—is irrelevant in the context of [Section 402(d)]. *The plain language of the statute shows that the infringer's knowledge or intent does not affect its application. Lack of legal sophistication cannot overcome a properly asserted [Section 402 (d)] limitation to the innocent infringer defense.* [Emphasis added.]
   * * * *

   In short, the district court found a genuine issue of fact as to whether Harper intended to infringe Plaintiffs' copyrights, but that issue was not material: [Section 402(d)] forecloses, as a matter of law, Harper's innocent infringer defense. Because the defense does not apply, Plaintiffs

---

a. In the box titled "and/or Title contains text," type in "Maverick." On the page that opens, click on the docket number beside the case title to access the opinion. The U.S. Court of Appeals for the Fifth Circuit maintains this Web site.

Case 8.3–Continues next page ➡

Case 8.3—Continued

are entitled to statutory damages. And because Plaintiffs requested the minimum statutory damages under [Section 504(c)(1)], Harper's culpability is not an issue and there are no issues left for trial. Plaintiffs must be awarded statutory damages of $750 per infringed work.

DECISION AND REMEDY   The U.S. Court of Appeals for the Fifth Circuit affirmed the trial court's finding of copyright liability, reversed its finding that the innocent infringer defense presented an issue for trial, and remanded the case for further proceedings consistent with the court's opinion. The appellate court concluded that the district court had erred by awarding damages of $200 per infringement because Harper was not an innocent infringer.

THE ETHICAL DIMENSION   *In this and other cases involving similar issues, the courts have held that when the published*

phonorecordings from which audio files were taken contained copyright notices, the innocent infringer defense does not apply. It is irrelevant that the notice is not provided in the online file. Is this fair? Explain.

MANAGERIAL IMPLICATIONS   *Owners and managers of firms in the business of recording and distributing music face a constant challenge in protecting their copyrights. This is particularly true for audio files in the online environment, where Internet users can easily download a copyrighted song and make it available to P2P file-sharing networks. Among other things, this means that recording companies must be ever vigilant in searching the Web to find infringing uses of works distributed online. Today, companies often hire antipiracy firms to investigate the illegal downloading of their copyrighted materials.*

THE EVOLUTION OF FILE-SHARING TECHNOLOGIES   After the *Napster* decision, the recording industry filed and won numerous lawsuits against companies that distribute online file-sharing software. Other companies then developed technologies that allow P2P network users to share stored music files, without paying a fee, more quickly and efficiently than ever. Software such as Morpheus, KaZaA, and LimeWire, for example, provides users with an interface that is similar to a Web browser.[30] When a user performs a search, the software locates a list of peers that have the file available for downloading. Because of the automated procedures, the companies do not maintain a central index and are unable to supervise whether users are exchanging copyrighted files.

In 2005, the United States Supreme Court clarified that companies that distribute file-sharing software intending that it be used to violate copyright laws can be liable for users' copyright infringement. **CASE EXAMPLE 8.17**   In *Metro-Goldwyn-Mayer Studios, Inc. v. Grokster, Ltd.,*[31] music and film industry organizations sued Grokster, Ltd., and StreamCast Networks, Inc., for contributory and vicarious copyright infringement. The Supreme Court held that anyone who distributes file-sharing software "with the object of promoting its use to infringe copyright, as shown by clear expression or other affirmative steps taken to foster infringement, . . . is liable for the resulting acts of infringement by third parties." • Although the music and film industries won the *Grokster* case, they have not been able to prevent new technology from enabling copyright infringement.

 Trade Secrets

> **Trade Secret** Information or a process that gives a business an advantage over competitors that do not know the information or process.

The law of trade secrets protects some business processes and information that are not or cannot be patented, copyrighted, or trademarked against appropriation by a competitor. A **trade secret** is basically information of commercial value. This may include customer lists, plans, research and development, pricing information,

---

30. Note that in 2005, KaZaA entered into a settlement agreement with four major music companies that had alleged copyright infringement. KaZaA agreed to offer only legitimate, fee-based music downloads in the future.

31. 545 U.S. 913, 125 S.Ct. 2764, 162 L.Ed.2d 781 (2005). Grokster, Ltd., later settled this dispute out of court and stopped distributing its software.

marketing techniques, and production methods—anything that makes an individual company unique and that would have value to a competitor.

Unlike copyright and trademark protection, protection of trade secrets extends both to ideas and to their expression. (For this reason, and because there are no registration or filing requirements for trade secrets, trade secret protection may be well suited for software.) Of course, the secret formula, method, or other information must be disclosed to some persons, particularly to key employees. Businesses generally attempt to protect their trade secrets by having all employees who use the process or information agree in their contracts, or in confidentiality agreements, never to divulge it.[32]

State and Federal Law on Trade Secrets

Under Section 757 of the *Restatement of Torts,* those who disclose or use another's trade secret, without authorization, are liable to that other party if (1) they discovered the secret by improper means or (2) their disclosure or use constitutes a breach of a duty owed to the other party. The theft of confidential business data by industrial espionage, as when a business taps into a competitor's computer, is a theft of trade secrets without any contractual violation and is actionable in itself.

Although trade secrets have long been protected under the common law, today most states' laws are based on the Uniform Trade Secrets Act, which has been adopted in forty-seven states. Additionally, in 1996 Congress passed the Economic Espionage Act, which made the theft of trade secrets a federal crime. (See Chapter 6, where we examined the provisions and significance of this act in the context of crimes related to business.)

Trade Secrets in Cyberspace

Today's computer technology undercuts a business firm's ability to protect its confidential information, including trade secrets. For instance, a dishonest employee could e-mail trade secrets in a company's computer to a competitor or a future employer. If e-mail is not an option, the employee might walk out with the information on a flash pen drive.

For a summary of trade secrets and other forms of intellectual property, see Exhibit 8–1 on the following page.

 International Protection for Intellectual Property

For many years, the United States has been a party to various international agreements relating to intellectual property rights. For example, the Paris Convention of 1883, to which 173 countries are signatory, allows parties in one country to file for patent and trademark protection in any of the other member countries. Other international agreements include the Berne Convention, the Agreement on Trade-Related Aspects of Intellectual Property Rights (or more simply, the TRIPS agreement), and the Madrid Protocol. To learn about a new international treaty being negotiated that will affect international property rights, see this chapter's *Beyond Our Borders* feature on page 229.

The Berne Convention

Under the Berne Convention of 1886, an international copyright agreement, if a U.S. citizen writes a book, every country that has signed the convention must recognize the U.S. author's copyright in the book. Also, if a citizen of a country that has

---

32. See, for example, *Verigy US, Inc. v. Mayder,* 2008 WL 564634 (N.D.Cal. 2008); and *Gleeson v. Preferred Sourcing, LLC,* 883 N.E.2d 164 (Ind.App. 2008).

• *Exhibit* 8–1 **Forms of Intellectual Property**

	DEFINITION	HOW ACQUIRED	DURATION	REMEDY FOR INFRINGEMENT
Patent	A grant from the government that gives an inventor exclusive rights to an invention.	By filing a patent application with the U.S. Patent and Trademark Office and receiving its approval.	Twenty years from the date of the application; for design patents, fourteen years.	Monetary damages, including royalties and lost profits, *plus* attorneys' fees. Damages may be tripled for intentional infringements.
Copyright	The right of an author or originator of a literary or artistic work, or other production that falls within a specified category, to have the exclusive use of that work for a given period of time.	Automatic (once the work or creation is put in tangible form). Only the *expression* of an idea (and not the idea itself) can be protected by copyright.	For authors: the life of the author, plus 70 years. For publishers: 95 years after the date of publication or 120 years after creation.	Actual damages plus profits received by the party who infringed *or* statutory damages under the Copyright Act, *plus* costs and attorneys' fees in either situation.
Trademark (service mark and trade dress)	Any distinctive word, name, symbol, or device (image or appearance), or combination thereof, that an entity uses to distinguish its goods or services from those of others. The owner has the exclusive right to use that mark or trade dress.	1. At common law, ownership created by use of the mark. 2. Registration with the appropriate federal or state office gives notice and is permitted if the mark is currently in use or will be within the next six months.	Unlimited, as long as it is in use. To continue notice by registration, the owner must renew by filing between the fifth and sixth years, and thereafter, every ten years.	1. Injunction prohibiting the future use of the mark. 2. Actual damages plus profits received by the party who infringed (can be increased under the Lanham Act). 3. Destruction of articles that infringed. 4. *Plus* costs and attorneys' fees.
Trade Secret	Any information that a business possesses and that gives the business an advantage over competitors (including formulas, lists, patterns, plans, processes, and programs).	Through the originality and development of the information and processes that constitute the business secret and are unknown to others.	Unlimited, so long as not revealed to others. Once revealed to others, it is no longer a trade secret.	Monetary damages for misappropriation (the Uniform Trade Secrets Act also permits punitive damages if willful), *plus* costs and attorneys' fees.

not signed the convention first publishes a book in one of the 164 countries that have signed, all other countries that have signed the convention must recognize that author's copyright. Copyright notice is not needed to gain protection under the Berne Convention for works published after March 1, 1989.

This convention and other international agreements have given some protection to intellectual property on a global level. None of them, however, has been as significant and far reaching in scope as the agreement discussed next.

The TRIPS Agreement

Representatives from more than one hundred nations signed the TRIPS agreement in 1994. The agreement established, for the first time, standards for the international protection of intellectual property rights, including patents, trademarks, and copyrights for movies, computer programs, books, and music. The

Beyond Our Borders   The Anti-Counterfeiting Trade Agreement

In 2008, the United States began negotiating a new international treaty with the European Union, Japan, and Switzerland. Over the next few years, these parties were joined by additional nations, including Australia, Canada, Jordan, Mexico, Morocco, New Zealand, Singapore, South Korea, and the United Arab Emirates. The final wording of the treaty was completed in 2010, and the parties are now developing domestic procedures that comply with its provisions. Once a nation has adopted appropriate procedures, it can ratify the treaty.

The treaty, called the Anti-Counterfeiting Trade Agreement (ACTA), establishes its own governing body that is separate and distinct from existing organizations, such as the World Trade Organization and the World Intellectual Property Organization. ACTA's goals are to increase international cooperation, facilitate the best law enforcement practices, and provide a legal framework to combat counterfeiting. The treaty applies not only to counterfeit

physical goods, such as medications, but also to pirated copyrighted works being distributed via the Internet and other information technology. In fact, an entire section of the treaty is devoted to protecting and enforcing intellectual property rights in the digital environment. The idea is to create a new standard of enforcement for intellectual property rights that goes beyond the TRIPS agreement and encourages international cooperation and information sharing among signatory countries.

Under ACTA's provisions, member nations are required to establish border measures that allow officials, on their own initiative, to examine commercial import and export shipments for counterfeit goods. Member nations can exclude personal luggage and small, noncommercial shipments from these procedures if they choose. The treaty neither requires nor prohibits random border searches of electronic devices, such as laptops and iPads, for infringing content. (Before the

specific terms of the treaty were released to the public in 2010, some had speculated that it might authorize random searches of such devices.) But, if border authorities reasonably believe that *any* goods in transit are counterfeit, the treaty allows them to keep the suspect goods unless the rights holder proves that the items are authentic and noninfringing.

In sum, the treaty establishes procedures for seizure, forfeiture, and destruction of infringing articles, and provides civil and criminal remedies against the infringers. It also allows member nations, in accordance with their own laws, to order online service providers to provide information about (including the identity of) suspected trademark and copyright infringers.

For Critical Analysis
Why did the parties negotiating ACTA take several years to disclose the details of the provisions under consideration?

TRIPS agreement provides that each member country must include in its domestic laws broad intellectual property rights and effective remedies (including civil and criminal penalties) for violations of those rights.

Generally, the TRIPS agreement forbids member nations from discriminating against foreign owners of intellectual property rights in the administration, regulation, or adjudication of those rights. In other words, a member nation cannot give its own nationals (citizens) favorable treatment without offering the same treatment to nationals of all member countries. **EXAMPLE 8.18** A U.S. software manufacturer brings a suit for the infringement of intellectual property rights under Germany's national laws. Because Germany is a member nation, the U.S. manufacturer is entitled to receive the same treatment as a German manufacturer. • Each member nation must also ensure that legal procedures are available for parties who wish to bring actions for infringement of intellectual property rights. Additionally, a related document established a mechanism for settling disputes among member nations.

The Madrid Protocol

In the past, one of the difficulties in protecting U.S. trademarks internationally was that registering a trademark in foreign countries was a time-consuming and expensive process. The filing fees and procedures for trademark registration vary significantly among individual countries. The Madrid Protocol, which was signed into law in 2003, may help to resolve these problems. The Madrid Protocol is an international treaty that has been signed by eighty-four countries. Under its provisions, a U.S. company wishing to register its trademark abroad can submit a single application and designate other member countries in which it would like to register the mark. The treaty was designed to reduce the costs of obtaining international trademark protection by more than 60 percent.

Although the Madrid Protocol may simplify and reduce the cost of trademark registration in foreign nations, whether it will provide significant benefits remains unclear. Even with an easier registration process, trademark owners must still be concerned that some member countries may not enforce the law and protect the mark.

Reviewing . . . Intellectual Property and Internet Law

Two computer science majors, Trent and Xavier, have an idea for a new video game, which they propose to call "Hallowed." They form a business and begin developing their idea. Several months later, Trent and Xavier run into a problem with their design and consult with a friend, Brad, who is an expert in creating computer source codes. After the software is completed but before Hallowed is marketed, a video game called Halo 2 is released for both the Xbox and PlayStation 3 systems. Halo 2 uses source codes similar to those of Hallowed and imitates Hallowed's overall look and feel, although not all the features are alike. Using the information presented in the chapter, answer the following questions.

1. Would the name *Hallowed* receive protection as a trademark or as trade dress?
2. If Trent and Xavier had obtained a business process patent on Hallowed, would the release of Halo 2 infringe on their patent? Why or why not?
3. Based only on the facts described above, could Trent and Xavier sue the makers of Halo 2 for copyright infringement? Why or why not?
4. Suppose that Trent and Xavier discover that Brad took the idea of Hallowed and sold it to the company that produced Halo 2. Which type of intellectual property issue does this raise?

Linking the Law *to Marketing*

Trademarks and Service Marks

In your marketing courses, you will learn about the importance of trademarks. As a marketing manager, you will be involved with creating trademarks or service marks for your firm, protecting existing marks, and ensuring that you do not infringe on anyone else's marks.

The Broad Range of Trademarks and Service Marks

The courts have held that trademarks and service marks consist of much more than well-known brand names, such as Sony and Apple. As a marketing manager, you will need to be aware that parts of a brand or other product identification often qualify for trademark protection.

Catchy phrases—Marketers have developed certain phrases that have become associated with their brands, such as Nike's "Just Do It!" Take care not to use another brand's catchy phrase in your own marketing program. Note, too, that not all phrases can become

part of a trademark or service mark. When a phrase is extremely common, the courts normally will not grant trademark or service mark protection to it. America Online, Inc., for example, was unable to protect its phrases "You have mail" and "You've got mail."

Abbreviations—The public sometimes abbreviates a well-known trademark. For instance, Budweiser beer became known as Bud and Coca-Cola as Coke. Do not use any name for a product or service that closely resembles a well-known abbreviation, such as Koke for a cola drink.

Shapes—The shape of a brand name, a service mark, or a container can take on exclusivity if the shape clearly aids in product or service identification. For example, just about everyone recognizes the shape of a Coca-Cola bottle.

Ornamental colors—Sometimes, color combinations can become part of a service mark or trademark. For example, the combination of bright orange and purple is associated with FedEx's unique identity.

(Continued)

The courts have protected this color combination. The same holds for the black-and-copper color combination of Duracell batteries.

Ornamental designs—Symbols and designs associated with a particular mark normally are protected, so do not attempt to copy them. For instance, Levi's places a small red tag on the left side of the rear pocket of its jeans.

Sounds—Sounds can also be protected. For example, the familiar roar of the Metro-Goldwyn-Mayer lion is protected.

When to Protect Your Trademarks and Service Marks

Once your company has established a trademark or a service mark, as a manager, you will have to decide how aggressively you wish to protect those marks. If you fail to protect them, your company faces the possibility that they will become generic. Remember that *aspirin, thermos, shredded wheat,* and many other familiar terms were once legally protected trademarks.

Protecting exclusive rights to a mark can be expensive, so you will have to determine how much it is worth to your company to protect your rights. Coca-Cola and Rolls-Royce run newspaper and magazine ads stating that their names are protected trademarks and cannot be used as generic terms. Occasionally, such ads threaten lawsuits against any competitors that infringe the trademarks. If you work in a small company, making such major expenditures to protect your trademarks and service marks will not be cost-effective.

FOR CRITICAL ANALYSIS

The U.S. Patent and Trademark Office requires that a registered trademark or service mark be put into commercial use within three years after the application has been approved. Why do you think the federal government put this requirement into place?

 Key Terms

certification mark 211	**distributed network** 224	**service mark** 211
cloud computing 224	**domain name** 213	**trade dress** 211
collective mark 211	**intellectual property** 206	**trade name** 212
copyright 219	**license** 215	**trade secret** 226
cyber mark 213	**patent** 215	**trademark** 207
cybersquatting 213	**peer-to-peer (P2P) networking** 224	

 Chapter Summary: Intellectual Property and Internet Law

Trademarks and Related Property (See pages 207–212.)	1. A *trademark* is a distinctive mark, motto, device, or emblem that a manufacturer stamps, prints, or otherwise affixes to the goods it produces so that they may be identified on the market and their origin vouched for. 2. The major federal statutes protecting trademarks and related property are the Lanham Act of 1946 and the Federal Trademark Dilution Act of 1995. Generally, to be protected, a trademark must be sufficiently distinctive from all competing trademarks. 3. *Trademark infringement* occurs when a person uses a mark that is the same as, or confusingly similar to, the protected trademark, service mark, trade name, or trade dress of another without permission when marketing goods or services.
Cyber Marks (See pages 212–215.)	A *cyber mark* is a trademark in cyberspace. Trademark infringement in cyberspace occurs when one person uses, in a domain name or in meta tags, a name that is the same as, or confusingly similar to, the protected mark of another.
Patents (See pages 215–219.)	1. A *patent* is a grant from the government that gives an inventor the exclusive right to make, use, and sell an invention for a period of twenty years (fourteen years for a design patent) from the date when the application for a patent is filed. To be patentable, an invention (or a discovery, process, or design) must be genuine, novel, useful, and not obvious in light of current technology. Computer software may be patented.

(Continued)

Chapter Summary: Intellectual Property and Internet Law, Continued

Patents—Continued	2. Almost anything is patentable, except the laws of nature, natural phenomena, and abstract ideas (including algorithms). Even business processes or methods are patentable if they relate to a machine or transformation. 3. *Patent infringement* occurs when a person uses or sells another's patented design, product, or process without the patent owner's permission. The patent holder can sue the infringer in federal court and request an injunction, but must prove irreparable injury to obtain a permanent injunction against the infringer. The patent holder can also request damages and attorneys' fees.
Copyrights (See pages 219–226.)	1. A *copyright* is an intangible property right granted by federal statute to the author or originator of certain literary or artistic productions. The Copyright Act of 1976, as amended, governs copyrights. 2. *Copyright infringement* occurs whenever the form or expression of an idea is copied without the permission of the copyright holder. An exception applies if the copying is deemed a "fair use." 3. To protect copyrights in digital information, Congress passed the Digital Millennium Copyright Act of 1998. 4. Technology that allows users to share files online often raises copyright infringement issues. 5. The United States Supreme Court has ruled that companies that provide file-sharing software to users can be held liable for contributory and vicarious copyright liability if they take affirmative steps to promote copyright infringement.
Trade Secrets (See pages 226–227.)	*Trade secrets* include customer lists, plans, research and development, and pricing information, for example. Trade secrets are protected under the common law and, in some states, under statutory law against misappropriation by competitors.
International Protection for Intellectual Property (See pages 227–230.)	Various international agreements provide international protection for intellectual property. A landmark agreement is the 1994 Agreement on Trade-Related Aspects of Intellectual Property Rights (TRIPS), which provides for enforcement procedures in all countries signatory to the agreement.

 ExamPrep

ISSUE SPOTTERS

1. Global Products develops, patents, and markets software. World Copies, Inc., sells Global's software without the maker's permission. Is this patent infringement? If so, how might Global save the cost of suing World for infringement and at the same time profit from World's sales?

2. In 2000, Eagle Corporation began marketing software under the mark "Eagle." In 2009, Eagle.com, Inc., a different company selling different products, begins to use "eagle" as part of its URL and registers it as a domain name. Can Eagle Corporation stop this use of "eagle"? If so, what must the company show?

—**Check your answers to these questions against the answers provided in Appendix G.**

BEFORE THE TEST

Go to **www.cengagebrain.com**, enter the ISBN number "9781111530617," and click on "Find" to locate this textbook's Web site. Then, click on "Access Now" under "Study Tools," and select "Chapter 8" at the top. There you will find an "Interactive Quiz" that you can take to assess your mastery of the concepts in this chapter, as well as "Flashcards" and a "Glossary" of important terms.

 For Review

1. What is intellectual property?
2. Why does the law protect trademarks and patents?
3. What laws protect authors' rights in the works they generate?

4. What are trade secrets, and what laws offer protection for this form of intellectual property?

5. What steps have been taken to protect intellectual property rights in today's digital age?

▶ Questions and Case Problems

8–1. Patent Infringement. John and Andrew Doney invented a hard-bearing device for balancing rotors. Although they registered their invention with the U.S. Patent and Trademark Office, it was never used as an automobile wheel balancer. Some time later, Exetron Corp. produced an automobile wheel balancer that used a hard-bearing device with a support plate similar to that of the Doneys' device. Given that the Doneys had not used their device for automobile wheel balancing, does Exetron's use of a similar device infringe on the Doneys' patent? Why or why not?

8–2. **Question with Sample Answer. Copyright Infringement.** In which of the following situations would a court likely hold Maruta liable for copyright infringement? Explain.

1. At the library, Maruta photocopies ten pages from a scholarly journal relating to a topic on which she is writing a term paper.

2. Maruta makes leather handbags and sells them in her small shop. She advertises her handbags as "Vutton handbags," hoping that customers will mistakenly assume that they were made by Vuitton, the well-known maker of high-quality luggage and handbags.

3. Maruta teaches Latin American history at a small university. She has a digital video recorder and frequently records television programs relating to Latin America and puts them on DVDs. She then takes the DVDs to her classroom so that her students can watch them.

—**For a sample answer to Question 8–2, go to Appendix E at the end of this text.**

8–3. Fair Use. Professor Littrell is teaching a summer seminar in business torts at State University. Several times during the course, he makes copies of relevant sections from business law texts and distributes them to his students. Littrell does not realize that the daughter of one of the textbook authors is a member of his seminar. She tells her father about Littrell's copying activities, which have taken place without her father's or his publisher's permission. Her father sues Littrell for copyright infringement. Littrell claims protection under the fair use doctrine. Who will prevail? Explain.

8–4. Trademarks. In 1969, Jack Masquelier, a professor of pharmacology, discovered a chemical antioxidant made from the bark of a French pine tree. The substance supposedly assists in nutritional distribution and blood circulation. Horphag Research, Ltd., began to sell the product under the name Pycnogenol, which Horphag registered as a trademark in 1993. Pycnogenol became one of the fifteen best-selling herbal supplements in the United States. In 1999, through the Web site www.healthierlife.com, Larry Garcia began to sell Masquelier's Original OPCs, a supplement derived from grape pits. Claiming that this product was the "true Pycnogenol," Garcia used the mark as a meta tag and a generic term, attributing the results of research on Horphag's product to Masquelier's and altering quotations from scientific literature to substitute the name of Masquelier's product for Horphag's. Customers who purchased Garcia's product contacted Horphag about it, only to learn that they had not bought Horphag's product. Others called Horphag to ask whether Garcia "was selling . . . real Pycnogenol." Horphag filed a suit in a federal district court against Garcia, alleging, among other things, that he was diluting Horphag's mark. What is trademark dilution? Did it occur here? Explain. [*Horphag Research, Ltd. v. Garcia*, 475 F.3d 1029 (9th Cir. 2007)]

8–5. **Case Problem with Sample Answer. Copyright.** Redwin Wilchcombe is a musician and music producer. In 2002, Wilchcombe met Jonathan Smith, known as Lil Jon, a member of Lil Jon & The East Side Boyz (LJESB). Lil Jon and LJESB are under contract to give TeeVee Toons, Inc. (TVT), all rights to LJESB's recordings and Lil Jon's songs. At Lil Jon's request, based on his idea, and with his suggestions, Wilchcombe composed, performed, and recorded a song titled "Tha Weedman" for LJESB's album *Kings of Crunk*. They did not discuss payment and Wilchcombe was not paid, but he was given credit on the album as a producer. By 2005, the album had sold 2 million copies. Wilchcombe filed a suit against TVT and the others, alleging copyright infringement. The defendants asserted that they had a license to use the song. Wilchcombe argued that he had never granted a license to anyone. Do these facts indicate that the defendants had a license to use Wilchcombe's song? If so, what does that mean for Wilchcombe's cause? Explain. [*Wilchcombe v. TeeVee Toons, Inc.*, 555 F.3d 949 (11th Cir. 2009)]

—**To view a sample answer for Case Problem 8–5, go to Appendix F at the end of this text.**

8–6. Trade Secrets. Peggy Hamilton was a major shareholder in Carbon Processing and Reclamation, LLC (CPR). After a dispute, she sold her interest in the company and signed a confidentiality agreement not to divulge company business to anyone. A year later, when William Jones, the owner of CPR, left on a trip, he let an employee, Jesse Edwards, drive his company car. There were boxes containing some detailed company records in the car. Edwards and his wife, Channon, were in the middle of a divorce, and she suspected him of hiding financial information from her. When Channon saw the boxes in the car her husband was driving, she got a car key from Hamilton, who still had one from when she was an owner. Channon used the key to get into the boxes of company information. Jones then sued Hamilton for breach of the confidentiality agreement, contending that allowing Channon to have access to the files was assisting in the theft of trade secrets. The trial court dismissed the claim, but Jones appealed. Could Hamilton's actions be the basis for a claim of trade secret violation? What factors should be taken into consideration? [*Jones v. Hamilton*, 53 So.3d 134 (Ala.Civ.App. 2010)]

8–7. Copyright Infringement. United Fabrics International, Inc., purchased a fabric design from an Italian design house, Contromoda, and registered a copyright to the design with the U.S. Copyright Office. When Macy's, Inc., began selling garments with a similar design, United filed a copyright infringement lawsuit against Macy's and others. In its defense, Macy's claimed that United did not own a valid copyright to the design. Ownership of a copyright is a requirement to establish an infringement claim. The district court held that the evidence was insufficient to establish United's ownership of the design and, for that reason, dismissed the action. United appealed, arguing that its copyright in the design should be presumptively valid because the copyright had been registered with the U.S. Copyright Office. How should the federal appellate court rule? Should the owner of a registered copyright have to prove that the copyright is valid to establish infringement? Or should the party contesting the validity of a copyright have to show that it is invalid? Explain your answer. [*United Fabrics International, Inc. v. C&J Wear, Inc.*, 630 F.3d 1255 (9th Cir. 2011)]

8–8. **A Question of Ethics. Copyright Infringement.** *Custom Copies, Inc., in Gainesville, Florida, is a copy shop that reproduces and distributes, for profit, on request, material published and owned by others. One of the copy shop's primary activities is the preparation and sale of coursepacks, which contain compilations of readings for college courses. For a particular coursepack, a teacher selects the readings and delivers a syllabus to the copy shop, which obtains the materials from a library, copies them, and then binds and sells the copies. Blackwell Publishing, Inc., in Malden, Massachusetts, publishes books and journals in medicine and other fields and owns the copyrights to these publications. Blackwell and others filed a suit in a federal district court against Custom Copies, alleging copyright infringement for its "routine and systematic reproduction of materials from plaintiffs' publications, without seeking permission," to compile coursepacks for classes at the University of Florida. The plaintiffs asked the court to issue an injunction and award them damages, as well as the profit from the infringement. The defendant filed a motion to dismiss*

the complaint. [*Blackwell Publishing, Inc. v. Custom Copies, Inc.*, __ F.Supp.2d __ (N.D.Fla. 2007)]

1. Custom Copies argued, in part, that it did not "distribute" the coursepacks. Does a copy shop violate copyright law if it only copies materials for coursepacks? Does the copying fall under the "fair use" exception? Should the court grant the defendants' motion? Why or why not?

2. What is the potential impact if copies of a book or journal are created and sold without the permission of, and the payment of royalties or a fee to, the copyright owner? Explain.

8–9. **Critical-Thinking Managerial Question.** Sync Computers, Inc., makes computer-related products under the brand name "Sync," which the company registers as a trademark. Without Sync's permission, E-Product Corp. embeds the Sync mark in E-Product's Web site, in black type on a blue background. This tag causes the E-Product site to be returned at the top of the list of results on a search engine query for "Sync." Does E-Product's use of the Sync mark as a meta tag without Sync's permission constitute trademark infringement? Explain.

8–10. **Video Question. *The Jerk.***
Access the video using the instructions provided below to answer the following questions.

1. In the video, Navin (Steve Martin) creates a special handle for Fox's (Bill Macy's) glasses. Can Navin obtain a patent or a copyright protecting his invention? Explain.

2. Suppose that after Navin legally protects his idea, Fox steals it and decides to develop it for himself, without Navin's permission. Has Fox committed infringement? If so, what kind: trademark, patent, or copyright?

3. Suppose that after Navin legally protects his idea, he realizes he doesn't have the funds to mass-produce the special handle. Navin therefore agrees to allow Fox to manufacture the product. Has Navin granted Fox a license? Explain.

4. Assume that Navin is able to manufacture his invention. What might Navin do to ensure that his product is identifiable and can be distinguished from other products?

—To watch this video, go to **www.cengagebrain.com** and register the access code that came with your new book or log in to your existing account. Select the link for either the "Business Law Digital Video Library Online Access" or "Business Law CourseMate," and then click on "Complete Video List" to find the video for this chapter (Video 66).

Chapter 9

Formation of Traditional and E-Contracts

> "All sensible people are selfish, and nature is tugging at every contract to make the terms of it fair."
>
> —Ralph Waldo Emerson, 1803–1882
> (American essayist and poet)

Contents

Chapter Objectives

After reading this chapter, you should be able to answer the following questions:

1. **What are the four basic requirements for the formation of a valid contract?**
2. **What elements are necessary for an effective acceptance?**
3. **What is the Uniform Electronic Transactions Act? What are some of the major provisions of this act?**
4. **What is consideration?**
5. **What is a convenant not to compete? When will such a covenant be enforceable?**

(Quaziefoto/Creative Commons)

Promise An assertion that something either will or will not happen in the future.

As Ralph Waldo Emerson observed in the chapter-opening quotation, people act in their own self-interest by nature, and this influences the terms they seek in their contracts. Contract law must therefore provide rules to determine which contract terms will be enforced and which promises must be kept. A **promise** is an assertion that something either will or will not happen in the future.

Like other types of law, contract law reflects our social values, interests, and expectations at a given point in time. It shows, for example, what kinds of promises our society thinks should be legally binding. It distinguishes between promises that create only *moral* obligations (such as a promise to take a friend to lunch) and promises that are legally binding (such as a promise to pay for merchandise purchased).

Contract law also demonstrates what excuses our society accepts for breaking certain types of promises. In addition, it shows what promises are considered to be contrary to public policy—against the interests of society as a whole—and therefore legally invalid. When the person making a promise is a child or is mentally incompetent, for example, a question will arise as to whether the promise should be enforced. Resolving such questions is the essence of contract law.

▶ An Overview of Contract Law

Before we look at the numerous rules that courts use to determine whether a particular promise will be enforced, it is necessary to understand some fundamental concepts of contract law. In this section, we describe the sources and general function of contract law and introduce the objective theory of contracts.

Sources of Contract Law

The common law governs all contracts except when it has been modified or replaced by statutory law, such as the Uniform Commercial Code (UCC),[1] or by administrative agency regulations. Contracts relating to services, real estate, employment, and insurance, for example, generally are governed by the common law of contracts.

Contracts for the sale and lease of goods, however, are governed by the UCC—to the extent that the UCC has modified general contract law. The relationship between general contract law and the law governing sales and leases of goods will be explored in Chapter 11. In this chapter and Chapter 10, covering the common law of contracts, we indicate briefly in footnotes the areas in which the UCC has significantly altered common law contract principles.

The Function of a Contract

No aspect of modern life is entirely free of contractual relationships. You acquire rights and obligations, for example, when you borrow funds, buy or lease a house, obtain insurance, form a business, and purchase goods or services. Contract law is designed to provide stability and predictability for both buyers and sellers in the marketplace.

Contract law assures the parties to private agreements that the promises they make will be enforceable. Clearly, many promises are kept because the parties involved feel a moral obligation to keep them or because keeping a promise is in their mutual self-interest. The **promisor** (the person making the promise) and the **promisee** (the person to whom the promise is made) may also decide to honor their agreement for other reasons. Nevertheless, the rules of contract law are often followed in business agreements to avoid potential problems.

By supplying procedures for enforcing private agreements, contract law provides an essential condition for the existence of a market economy. Without a legal framework of reasonably ensured expectations within which to plan and venture, businesspersons would be able to rely only on others' good faith. Duty and good faith are usually sufficient, but when dramatic price changes or adverse economic conditions make it costly to comply with a promise, these elements may not be enough. Contract law is necessary to ensure compliance with a promise or to entitle the innocent party to some form of relief.

The Definition of a Contract

A **contract** is "a promise or a set of promises for the breach of which the law gives a remedy, or the performance of which the law in some way recognizes as a duty."[2]

Promisor   A person who makes a promise.

Promisee   A person to whom a promise is made.

Contract   An agreement that can be enforced in court; formed by two or more competent parties who agree, for consideration, to perform or to refrain from performing some legal act now or in the future.

---

1. See Chapter 1 and Chapter 11 for further discussions of the significance and coverage of the UCC. Excerpts from the UCC are presented in Appendix C at the end of this book.
2. *Restatement (Second) of Contracts,* Section 1. As mentioned in Chapter 1, *Restatements of the Law* are scholarly books that restate the existing common law principles distilled from court opinions as a set of rules on a particular topic. Courts often refer to the *Restatements* for guidance.

Put simply, a contract is a legally binding agreement between two or more parties who agree to perform or to refrain from performing some act now or in the future. Generally, contract disputes arise when there is a promise of future performance. A party who fails to fulfill a contractual promise is subject to the sanctions of a court (see Chapter 10) and may be required to pay monetary damages or, in limited instances, to perform the promised act.

The Objective Theory of Contracts

Objective Theory of Contracts A theory under which the intent to form a contract will be judged by outward, objective facts (what the party said when entering into the contract, how the party acted or appeared, and the circumstances surrounding the transaction) as interpreted by a reasonable person, rather than by the party's own secret, subjective intentions.

In determining whether a contract has been formed, the element of intent is of prime importance. In contract law, intent is determined by the **objective theory of contracts.** This theory is that a party's intention to enter into a contract is judged by outward, objective facts as interpreted by a *reasonable person,* rather than by the party's own secret, subjective intentions. Objective facts include (1) what the party said when entering into the contract, (2) how the party acted or appeared, and (3) the circumstances surrounding the transaction. As will be discussed on page 241, intent to form a contract may be manifested by conduct, as well as by words, oral or written.

Freedom of Contract and Freedom from Contract

As a general rule, everyone has the ability to enter freely into contractual arrangements. This ability is called *freedom of contract,* a freedom protected by the U.S. Constitution in Article I, Section 10. Because freedom of contract is a fundamental public policy of the United States, courts rarely interfere with contracts that have been voluntarily made.

Of course, as in other areas of the law, there are many exceptions to the general rule. For example, illegal bargains, agreements that unreasonably restrain trade, and certain unfair contracts made between one party with a great amount of bargaining power and another with little power generally are not enforced. In addition, as you will read later in this chapter, certain contracts and clauses may not be enforceable if they are contrary to public policy, fairness, and justice. These exceptions provide *freedom from contract* for persons who may have been forced into making contracts unfavorable to themselves.

(AP Photo/Damian Dovarganes)

The manager of a Toyota dealership in Glendora, California, displays the same contract written in four different Asian languages (Chinese, Korean, Vietnamese, and Tagalog). Under a California consumer protection law, certain businesses, such as car dealers and apartment owners, whose employees orally negotiate contracts in these languages must provide written contracts in that same language. Why might it be important to the enforceability of a written contract that the consumer can actually read its provisions?

Requirements of a Valid Contract

The following four requirements must be met for a valid contract to exist. If any of these elements is lacking, no contract will have been formed. (Each requirement will be explained more fully later in this chapter.)

1. *Agreement.* An agreement to form a contract includes an *offer* and an *acceptance.* One party must offer to enter into a legal agreement, and another party must accept the terms of the offer.
2. *Consideration.* Any promises made by the parties must be supported by legally sufficient and bargained-for consideration (something of value received or promised to convince a person to make a deal).
3. *Contractual capacity.* Both parties entering into the contract must have the contractual capacity to do so. The law must recognize them as possessing characteristics that qualify them as competent parties.

4. *Legality.* The contract's purpose must be to accomplish some goal that is legal and not against public policy.

Defenses to the Enforceability of a Contract

Even if all of the elements of a valid contract are present, a contract may be unenforceable if the following requirements are not met:

1. *Voluntary consent.* The apparent consent of both parties must be voluntary. For example, if a contract was formed as a result of fraud, a mistake, or duress, the contract may not be enforceable.
2. *Form.* The contract must be in whatever form the law requires—for example, some contracts must be in writing to be enforceable.

The failure to fulfill either requirement may be raised as a *defense* to the enforceability of an otherwise valid contract, as will be discussed in Chapter 10.

Types of Contracts

There are numerous types of contracts. They are categorized based on legal distinctions as to their formation, performance, and enforceability. Exhibit 9–1 below illustrates three classifications, or categories, of contracts based on their mode of formation.

Contract Formation

These three classifications of contracts are based on how and when a contract is formed. The best way to explain each type of contract is to compare the various types, as we do in the following pages.

BILATERAL VERSUS UNILATERAL CONTRACTS   Every contract involves at least two parties. The **offeror** is the party making the offer. The **offeree** is the party to whom the offer is made. The offeror always promises to do or not to do something and thus is also a promisor. Whether the contract is classified as *bilateral* or *unilateral* depends on what the offeree must do to accept the offer and bind the offeror to a contract.

Bilateral Contracts. If the offeree can accept simply by promising to perform, the contract is a **bilateral contract.** Hence, a bilateral contract is a "promise for a promise." For example, a contract in which one person agrees to buy another person's automobile

Offeror   A person who makes an offer.

Offeree   A person to whom an offer is made.

Bilateral Contract   A type of contract that arises when a promise is given in exchange for a return promise.

• *Exhibit* **9–1 Classifications Based on Contract Formation**

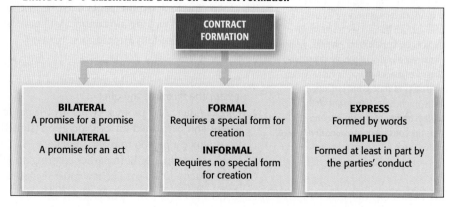

for a specified price is a bilateral contract. No performance, such as the payment of funds or delivery of goods, need take place for a bilateral contract to be formed. The contract comes into existence at the moment the promises are exchanged.

EXAMPLE 9.1 Javier offers to buy Ann's digital camera for $200. Javier tells Ann that he will give her the cash for the camera on the following Friday, when he gets paid. Ann accepts Javier's offer and promises to give him the camera when he pays her on Friday. Javier and Ann have formed a bilateral contract. •

Unilateral Contracts. If the offer is phrased so that the offeree can accept only by completing the contract performance, the contract is a **unilateral contract.** Hence, a unilateral contract is a "promise for an act." In other words, the contract is formed not at the moment when promises are exchanged but rather when the contract is *performed.*

CASE EXAMPLE 9.2 Applicants for vacancies in the police department in Providence, Rhode Island, first completed a series of tests. The city then sent the most qualified applicants a letter that said it was "a conditional offer of employment" and informed the applicants that they could attend the police training academy if they passed a medical exam. Meanwhile, a new chief of police revised the selection process and rejected some of those who had received this letter. The rejected applicants sued, claiming that the city had breached its contract. The court held that the letter was a unilateral offer that the plaintiffs had accepted by passing the required medical exam. The court ordered the city to allow the plaintiffs to attend the police academy.[3] •

Contests, lotteries, and other competitions involving prizes are examples of offers to form unilateral contracts. If a person complies with the rules of the contest—such as by submitting the right lottery number at the right place and time—a unilateral contract is formed, binding the organization offering the prize to a contract to perform as promised in the offer. If the person fails to comply with the contest rules, however, no binding contract is formed. See this chapter's *Insight into Ethics* feature below

> **Unilateral Contract** A contract that results when an offer can be accepted only by the offeree's performance.

---

3. *Ardito v. City of Providence,* 263 F.Supp.2d 358 (D.R.I. 2003).

 Insight into Ethics   **Is It Right for a Company to Change the Prize Offered in a Contest?**

Courts have historically treated contests as unilateral contracts. Unilateral contracts typically cannot be modified by the offeror after the offeree has begun to perform. But this principle may not apply to contest terms if the company sponsoring the contest reserves the right to cancel the contest or change its terms at any time, as Donna Englert learned to her dismay.

Englert entered the "Quarter Million Dollar Challenge" contest sponsored by Nutritional Sciences, LLC. Contestants were to use Nutritional Sciences' products and training plans for thirteen weeks to lose weight and get fit. A panel of judges would then pick winners in certain categories based on their success in transforming their bodies. When Englert was chosen as female runner-up in her age group, she thought that she would receive the advertised prize of $1,500 cash and $500 worth of Nutritional Sciences' products. Instead, the company sent her a "challenge winner agreement" for $250 cash and $250 worth of products. Englert refused to sign the agreement and filed a lawsuit alleging breach of contract. The state trial court dismissed her claim, and she appealed.

The state appellate court observed that the contestant's compliance with the rules of a contest is necessary to form a binding unilateral contract. Here, the contest rules stipulated that "all winners must agree to the regulations outlined specifically for winners before claiming championship or money." Next to this statement was an asterisk corresponding to a note reserving the right of Nutritional Sciences to cancel the contest or alter its terms at any time. Because of this provision, the court ruled that Nutritional Sciences did not breach the contract when it changed the cash prize from $1,500 to $250.[a]

FOR CRITICAL ANALYSIS
Insight into the Social Environment

Why would a company that changes its advertised prizes have to worry about its reputation?

---

a. *Englert v. Nutritional Sciences, LLC,* 2008 WL 4416597 (Ohio App. 2008).

for a discussion of whether a company can change the advertised prize after the contestants have completed the contest.

In the following case, the court was asked to determine if an employer owed a bonus to a former employee. One issue for the court was whether the parties' employment contract was bilateral or unilateral.

Case 9.1   Schwarzrock v. Remote Technologies, Inc.

Court of Appeals of Minnesota, __ N.W.2d __ (2011).
www.lawlibrary.state.mn.us/archive[a]

BACKGROUND AND FACTS   Remote Technologies, Inc., is a Minnesota-based manufacturer of home-theater and home-automation controls. Remote employs product trainers to conduct training sessions for its dealers. Nick Schwarzrock contacted Remote to apply for employment. Remote offered Schwarzrock a position as a trainer and sent him a letter, stating that the compensation was "$60,000 per year salary, plus bonus." The day after starting work, Schwarzrock signed an employment agreement (EA) that expressly "superseded all previous correspondence." The EA stated, in part, that the salary "constitutes the full and exclusive . . . compensation for . . . the performance of all Employee's promises." Less than three months later, Baker fired Schwarzrock for "lots of reasons." Schwarzrock filed a suit in a Minnesota state court against Remote, claiming that he was owed a bonus and alleging breach of contract, among other things. On this claim, the court held that there was no breach of contract and that the bonus was discretionary. Schwarzrock appealed.

IN THE WORDS OF THE COURT . . .
CONNOLLY, Judge.
  * * * *

  * * * The [lower] court held that there can be no breach of contract where respondent [Remote] abided by the terms of the parties' agreement and that appellant [Schwarzrock] "cannot ignore the blatant terms of the EA to which he clearly assented."
  * * * *

An offer of employment on particular terms for an unspecified duration generally creates a binding unilateral contract once it is accepted by the employee. Here, respondent offered appellant a position as a national product trainer on particular terms, which included compensation, for an unspecified amount of time. Although appellant alleges that his "compensation package was an essential term of a bilateral negotiated contract," he provides no support for the alleged bilateral nature of the contract. [Emphasis added.]

The EA presented appellant with another unilateral offer of employment, which explained that the * * * "bonus" was discretionary: "Employee understands and agrees that any additional compensation to Employee (whether a bonus or other form of additional compensation) shall rest in the sole discretion of [the employer] * * * ." Appellant signed the EA and continued working for respondent.

In the case of unilateral contracts for employment, where an * * * employee retains employment with knowledge of new or changed conditions, the new or changed conditions may become a contractual obligation. In this manner, an original employment contract may be modified or replaced by a subsequent unilateral contract. *The employee's retention of employment constitutes acceptance of the offer of a unilateral contract; by continuing to stay on the job, although free to leave, the employee supplies the necessary consideration for the offer.* [Emphasis added.]
  * * * *

It is well established that where contracts relating to the same transaction are put into several instruments they will be read together and each will be construed with reference to the other. * * * Respondent intended to offer appellant both a specified salary and a bonus program; the offer letter and the EA do not contradict each other on these terms. Reading them together, we conclude that the plain terms of the parties' agreement stated that payment of the bonus was within respondent's discretion.

DECISION AND REMEDY   The state intermediate appellate court affirmed the lower court's judgment. Remote's letter may have implied that a bonus was not discretionary, but the EA clarified or modified the offer by clearly stating that it was. Schwarzrock accepted this unilateral offer when he signed the EA and continued working.

WHAT IF THE FACTS WERE DIFFERENT?   *Suppose that the court had ruled that Schwarzrock was employed under a bilateral contract, as he alleged. Would the result have been different? Explain.*

THE ECONOMIC DIMENSION   *Why does an employer make bonuses and other forms of additional compensation discretionary? Discuss.*

---

a. In the "Court of Appeals Opinions" box, click on "Index by Docket Number." On that page, in the "Unpublished & Order Opinions" box, select "Docket No. 10-* * * *." On the next page, scroll to "A10-473" to view the opinion. The Minnesota State Law Library maintains this Web site.

Revocation of Offers for Unilateral Contracts. A problem arises in unilateral contracts when the promisor attempts to *revoke* (cancel) the offer after the promisee has begun performance but before the act has been completed.

EXAMPLE 9.3 Roberta offers to buy Ed's sailboat, moored in San Francisco, on delivery of the boat to Roberta's dock in Newport Beach, three hundred miles south of San Francisco. Ed rigs the boat and sets sail. Shortly before his arrival at Newport Beach, Ed receives a radio message from Roberta withdrawing her offer. Roberta's offer is to form a unilateral contract, and only Ed's delivery of the sailboat at her dock is an acceptance. ●

In contract law, offers normally are *revocable* (capable of being taken back, or canceled) until accepted. Under the traditional view of unilateral contracts, Roberta's revocation would terminate the offer. But because the revocation of an offer to form a unilateral contract can have a harsh effect on the offeree, the modern-day view is that once performance has been *substantially* undertaken, the offeror cannot revoke the offer. Thus, in our example, even though Ed has not yet accepted the offer by complete performance, Roberta is prohibited from revoking it. Ed can deliver the boat and bind Roberta to the contract.

FORMAL VERSUS INFORMAL CONTRACTS   Another classification system divides contracts into formal contracts and informal contracts. **Formal contracts** require a special form or method of formation to be enforceable. For example, letters of credit, which frequently are used in international sales contracts (see Chapter 7), are a type of formal contract because a special form and language are required to create them.

> **Formal Contract**   A contract that by law requires a specific form for its validity.

Informal contracts (also called *simple contracts*) include all other contracts. No special form is required (except for certain types of contracts that must be in writing), as the contracts usually are based on their substance rather than their form. Typically, businesspersons put their contracts in writing to ensure that there is some proof of a contract's existence should problems arise.

> **Informal Contract**   A contract that does not require a specified form or formality to be valid.

EXPRESS VERSUS IMPLIED CONTRACTS   Contracts may also be categorized as express or implied by the conduct of the parties. In an **express contract,** the terms of the agreement are fully and explicitly stated in words, oral or written. A signed lease for an apartment or a house is an express written contract. If a classmate accepts your offer to sell your textbooks from last semester for $300, an express oral contract has been made.

> **Express Contract**   A contract in which the terms of the agreement are stated in words, oral or written.

A contract that is implied from the conduct of the parties is called an **implied contract.** This type of contract differs from an express contract in that the *conduct* of the parties, rather than their words, creates and defines at least some of the terms of the contract. Normally, if the following requirements are met, a court will hold that an implied contract was formed:

> **Implied Contract**   A contract formed in whole or in part from the conduct of the parties (as opposed to an express contract).

1. The plaintiff furnished some service or property.
2. The plaintiff expected to be paid for that service or property, and the defendant knew or should have known that payment was expected (by using the objective-theory-of-contracts test discussed on page 237).
3. The defendant had a chance to reject the services or property and did not.

> **KEEP IN MIND**   Not every contract is a document with "Contract" printed in block letters at the top. A contract can be expressed in a letter, a memo, or another document.

EXAMPLE 9.4 You need an accountant to fill out your tax return this year, so you search the Web and find an accounting firm located in your neighborhood. You drop by the firm's office, talk to an accountant, and learn what fees will be charged.

Thirteen-year-old classical singing star Faryl Smith (center) was a finalist on the television show Britain's Got Talent. *Her debut CD was a hit in the United Kingdom and in the United States. Here, she is signing a recording contract with Universal Classics and Jazz label. What requirements must be met to make this contract valid?*

The next day, you return and give the receptionist all of the necessary information and documents, such as canceled checks and W-2 forms. Then you walk out the door without saying anything expressly to the accountant. In this situation, you have entered into an implied contract to pay the accountant the usual and reasonable fees for her accounting services. The contract is implied by your conduct and by hers. She expects to be paid for completing your tax return. By bringing in the records she will need to do the work, you have implied an intent to pay for her services. ●

Contract Performance

Contracts are also classified according to their state of performance. A contract that has been fully performed on both sides is called an **executed contract.** A contract that has not been fully performed on either side is called an **executory contract.** If one party has fully performed but the other has not, the contract is said to be executed on the one side and executory on the other, but the contract is still classified as executory.

EXAMPLE 9.5   You agreed to buy ten tons of coal from Western Coal Company. Western has delivered the coal to your steel mill, where it is now being burned. At this point, the contract is an executory contract—it is executed on the part of Western and executory on your part. After you pay Western for the coal, the contract will be executed on both sides. ●

Contract Enforceability

A **valid contract** has the four elements necessary for contract formation: (1) an agreement (offer and acceptance) (2) supported by legally sufficient consideration (3) for a legal purpose and (4) made by parties who have the legal capacity to enter into the contract. Valid contracts may be enforceable, voidable, or unenforceable. Additionally, a contract may be referred to as a *void contract.*

Executed Contract   A contract that has been completely performed by both parties.

Executory Contract   A contract that has not yet been fully performed.

Valid Contract   A contract that results when the elements necessary for contract formation are present.

Voidable Contract   A contract that may be legally avoided (canceled) at the option of one or both of the parties.

VOIDABLE CONTRACTS   A **voidable contract** is a *valid* contract but one that can be avoided at the option of one or both of the parties. The party having the option can elect either to avoid any duty to perform or to *ratify* (make valid) the contract. If the contract is avoided, both parties are released from it. If it is ratified, both parties must fully perform their respective legal obligations.

As a general rule, for example, contracts made by minors are voidable at the option of the minor (as will be discussed later in this chapter). Additionally, contracts entered into under fraudulent conditions are voidable at the option of the defrauded party. Contracts entered into under legally defined duress or undue influence are also voidable (see Chapter 10).

Unenforceable Contract   A valid contract rendered unenforceable by some statute or law.

UNENFORCEABLE CONTRACTS   An **unenforceable contract** is one that cannot be enforced because of certain legal defenses against it. Such a contract is valid in that it satisfies the legal requirements of a contract, but it has been rendered unenforceable by some statute or law. For example, some contracts must be in writing. If they are not, they will not be enforceable except in certain exceptional circumstances.

Void Contract   A contract having no legal force or binding effect.

VOID CONTRACTS   A **void contract** is no contract at all. The terms *void* and *contract* are contradictory. None of the parties has any legal obligations if a contract is void. A contract can be void because, for example, one of the parties was previously determined by a court to be legally insane (and thus lacked the legal capacity to enter into a contract) or because the purpose of the contract was illegal.

Agreement

Regardless of whether a contract is formed in the traditional way by exchanging paper documents or online by exchanging electronic messages or documents, an essential element for contract formation is **agreement**—the parties must agree on the terms of the contract. Ordinarily, agreement is evidenced by two events: an *offer* and an *acceptance*. One party offers a certain bargain to another party, who then accepts that bargain.

Requirements of the Offer

An **offer** is a promise or commitment to perform or refrain from performing some specified act in the future. Recall that the party making an offer is called the *offeror*, and the party to whom the offer is made is called the *offeree*. Three elements are necessary for an offer to be effective:

1. There must be a serious, objective intention by the offeror.
2. The terms of the offer must be reasonably certain, or definite, so that the parties and the court can ascertain the terms of the contract.
3. The offer must be communicated to the offeree.

Once an effective offer has been made, the offeree's acceptance of that offer creates a legally binding contract (providing the other essential elements for a valid and enforceable contract are present).

INTENTION The first requirement for an effective offer is a serious, objective intention on the part of the offeror. Intent is not determined by the *subjective* intentions, beliefs, or assumptions of the offeror. Rather, it is determined by what a reasonable person in the offeree's position would conclude the offeror's words and actions meant. Offers made in obvious anger, jest, or undue excitement do not meet the serious-and-objective-intent test. Because these offers are not effective, an offeree's acceptance does not create an agreement.

The concept of intention can be further clarified through an examination of the types of statements that are *not* offers. We look at these expressions and statements in the subsections that follow. In the classic case presented next, the court considered whether an offer made "after a few drinks" met the serious-intent requirement.

Agreement A meeting of two or more minds in regard to the terms of a contract; usually broken down into two events—an offer by one party to form a contract and an acceptance of the offer by the person to whom the offer is made.

Offer A promise or commitment to perform or refrain from performing some specified act in the future.

***Classic* Case 9.2** | **Lucy v. Zehmer**

Supreme Court of Appeals of Virginia, 196 Va. 493, 84 S.E.2d 516 (1954).

BACKGROUND AND FACTS W. O. Lucy and A. H. Zehmer had known each other for fifteen to twenty years. For some time, Lucy had been wanting to buy Zehmer's farm. Zehmer had always told Lucy that he was not interested in selling. One night, Lucy stopped in to visit with the Zehmers at a restaurant they operated. Lucy said to Zehmer, "I bet you wouldn't take $50,000 for that place." Zehmer replied, "Yes, I would, too; you wouldn't give fifty." Throughout the evening, the conversation returned to the sale of the farm. At the same time, the parties were drinking whiskey. Eventually, Zehmer wrote up an agreement, on the back of a restaurant check, for the sale of the

(Supreme Court of Appeals of Virginia)

The receipt from Ye Olde Virginnie Restaurant on which is written: "We hereby agree to sell to W. O. Lucy the Ferguson Farm complete for $50,000.00, title satisfactory to buyer," and signed by the defendants, A. H. and Ida Zehmer.

Case 9.2–Continues next page ➡

Classic Case 9.2–Continued

farm, and he asked his wife, Ida, to sign it–which she did. When Lucy brought an action in a Virginia state court to enforce the agreement, Zehmer argued that he had been "high as a Georgia pine" at the time and that the offer had been made in jest: "two doggoned drunks bluffing to see who could talk the biggest and say the most." Lucy claimed that he had not been intoxicated and did not think Zehmer had been, either, given the way Zehmer handled the transaction. The trial court ruled in favor of the Zehmers, and Lucy appealed.

IN THE WORDS OF THE COURT . . .
BUCHANAN, J. [Justice] delivered the opinion of the court.

* * * *

In his testimony, Zehmer claimed that he "was high as a Georgia pine," and that the transaction "was just a bunch of two doggoned drunks bluffing to see who could talk the biggest and say the most." That claim is inconsistent with his attempt to testify in great detail as to what was said and what was done.

* * * *

The appearance of the contract, the fact that it was under discussion for forty minutes or more before it was signed; Lucy's objection to the first draft because it was written in the singular, and he wanted Mrs. Zehmer to sign it also; the rewriting to meet that objection and the signing by Mrs. Zehmer; the discussion of what was to be included in the sale, the provision for the examination of the title, the completeness of the instrument that was executed, the taking possession of it by Lucy with no request or suggestion by either of the defendants that he give it back, are facts which furnish persuasive evidence that the execution of the contract was a serious business transaction rather than a casual, jesting matter as defendants now contend.

* * * *

In the field of contracts, as generally elsewhere, *we must look to the outward expression of a person as manifesting his intention rather than to his secret and unexpressed intention.* The law imputes to a person an intention corresponding to the reasonable meaning of his words and acts. [Emphasis added.]

* * * *

Whether the writing signed by the defendants and now sought to be enforced by the complainants was the result of a serious offer by Lucy and a serious acceptance by the defendants, or was a serious offer by Lucy and an acceptance in secret jest by the defendants, in either event it constituted a binding contract of sale between the parties.

DECISION AND REMEDY   The Supreme Court of Virginia determined that the writing was an enforceable contract and reversed the ruling of the lower court. The Zehmers were required by court order to follow through with the sale of the Ferguson Farm to the Lucys.

WHAT IF THE FACTS WERE DIFFERENT?   *Suppose that the day after Lucy signed the agreement, he decided that he did not want the farm after all, and Zehmer sued Lucy to perform the contract. Would this change in the facts alter the court's decision that Lucy and Zehmer had created an enforceable contract? Why or why not?*

IMPACT OF THIS CASE ON TODAY'S LAW   *This is a classic case in contract law because it so clearly illustrates the objective theory of contracts with respect to determining whether an offer was intended. Today, the objective theory of contracts continues to be applied by the courts, and the* Lucy v. Zehmer *decision is routinely cited as a significant precedent in this area.*

Expressions of Opinion. An expression of opinion is not an offer. It does not demonstrate an intention to enter into a binding agreement. **CASE EXAMPLE 9.6**   Hawkins took his son to McGee, a physician, and asked McGee to operate on the son's hand. McGee said that the boy would be in the hospital three or four days and that the hand would *probably* heal a few days later. The son's hand did not heal for a month, but nonetheless the father did not win a suit for breach of contract. The court held that McGee did not make an offer to heal the son's hand in three or four days. He merely expressed an opinion as to when the hand would heal.[4] ●

BE CAREFUL   An opinion is not an offer and not a contract term. Goods or services can be "perfect" in one party's opinion and "poor" in another's.

Statements of Future Intent. A statement of an *intention* to do something in the future is not an offer. **EXAMPLE 9.7**   If Samir says, "*I plan* to sell my stock in Novation, Inc., for $150 per share," no contract is created if John "accepts" and tenders $150 per share for the stock. Samir has merely expressed his intention to enter into a future contract for the sale of the stock. If John accepts and tenders the $150 per share, no contract is formed, because a reasonable person would conclude that Samir was only *thinking about* selling his stock, not *promising* to sell it. ●

Preliminary Negotiations. A request or invitation to negotiate is not an offer but only an expression of a willingness to discuss the possibility of entering into a

---

4. *Hawkins v. McGee*, 84 N.H. 114, 146 A. 641 (1929).

(Paul Friel/Creative Commons)

A $27 million Harrier fighter jet that was offered as a prize in PepsiCo's "Drink Pepsi—Get Stuff" ad campaign. Although the offer was a fanciful jest by PepsiCo, one consumer took the offer seriously and attempted to fulfill the terms for the prize. Is PepsiCo's "offer" of the jet enforceable?

KEEP IN MIND Advertisements are not binding, but they cannot be deceptive.

"I fear explanations explanatory of things explained."

Abraham Lincoln, 1809–1865
(Sixteenth president of the United States, 1861–1865)

contract. Examples are statements such as "Will you sell Forest Acres?" and "I wouldn't sell my car for less than $8,000." A reasonable person would not conclude that such statements indicated an intention to enter into binding obligations. Likewise, when the government and private firms need to have construction work done, they invite contractors to submit bids. The *invitation* to submit bids is not an offer, and a contractor does not bind the government or private firm by submitting a bid. (The bids that the contractors submit are offers, however, and the government or private firm can bind the contractor by accepting the bid.)

Advertisements, Catalogues, and Circulars. In general, advertisements, mail-order catalogues, price lists, and circular letters (meant for the general public) are treated as invitations to negotiate, not as offers to form a contract. **CASE EXAMPLE 9.8** An advertisement on the *Science*NOW Web site asked readers to submit "news tips," which the organization would then investigate for possible inclusion in its magazine or on the Web site. Erik Trell, a professor and physician, submitted a manuscript in which he claimed to have solved a famous mathematical problem. When *Science*NOW did not publish the information, Trell filed a lawsuit for breach of contract. He claimed that the *Science*NOW ad was an offer, which he had accepted by submitting his manuscript. The court dismissed Trell's suit, holding that the ad was not an offer, but merely an invitation.[5] ●

Price lists are another form of invitation to negotiate or trade. A seller's price list is not an offer to sell at that price but merely an invitation to the buyer to offer to buy at that price. In fact, the seller usually puts "prices subject to change" on the price list. Only in rare circumstances will a price quotation be construed as an offer.

Although most advertisements and the like are treated as invitations to negotiate, this does not mean that an advertisement can never be an offer. On some occasions, courts have construed advertisements to be offers because the ads contained definite terms that invited acceptance (such as an ad offering a reward for the return of a lost dog).

Agreements to Agree. Traditionally, agreements to agree—that is, agreements to agree to the material terms of a contract at some future date—were not considered to be binding contracts. The modern view, however, is that agreements to agree may be enforceable agreements (contracts) if it is clear that the parties intend to be bound by the agreements. In other words, under the modern view the emphasis is on the parties' intent rather than on form.

CASE EXAMPLE 9.9 After a customer was injured and nearly drowned on a water ride at one of its amusement parks, Six Flags, Inc., filed a lawsuit against the manufacturer that had designed the ride. The defendant manufacturer claimed that there was no binding contract between the parties, only preliminary negotiations that were never formalized into a contract to construct the ride. The court, however, held that a faxed document specifying the details of the water ride, along with the parties' subsequent actions (beginning construction and handwriting notes on the fax), was sufficient to show an intent to be bound. Because of the court's finding, the manufacturer was required to provide insurance for the water ride at Six Flags, and its insurer was required to defend Six Flags in the personal-injury lawsuit that arose out of the incident.[6] ●

---

5. *Trell v. American Association for the Advancement of Science,* __ F.Supp.2d __ (W.D.N.Y. 2007).
6. *Six Flags, Inc. v. Steadfast Insurance Co.,* 474 F.Supp.2d 201 (D.Mass. 2007).

Increasingly, the courts are holding that a preliminary agreement constitutes a binding contract if the parties have agreed on all essential terms and no disputed issues remain to be resolved.[7] In contrast, if the parties agree on certain major terms but leave other terms open for further negotiation, a preliminary agreement is binding only in the sense that the parties have committed themselves to negotiate the undecided terms in good faith in an effort to reach a final agreement.[8]

Preventing Legal Disputes

To avoid potential legal disputes, be cautious when drafting a memorandum that outlines a preliminary agreement or understanding with another party. If all the major terms are included, a court might hold that the agreement is binding even though you intended it to be only a tentative agreement. One way to avoid being bound is to include in the writing the points of disagreement, as well as those points on which you and the other party agree. Alternatively, you could add a disclaimer to the memorandum stating that, although you anticipate entering a contract in the future, neither party intends to be legally bound to the terms that were discussed. That way, the other party cannot claim that you have already reached an agreement on all essential terms.

DEFINITENESS   The second requirement for an effective offer involves the definiteness of its terms. An offer must have reasonably definite terms so that a court can determine if a breach has occurred and give an appropriate remedy. The specific terms required depend, of course, on the type of contract. Generally, a contract must include the following terms, either expressed in the contract or capable of being reasonably inferred from it:

1. The identification of the parties.
2. The identification of the object or subject matter of the contract (also the quantity, when appropriate), including the work to be performed, with specific identification of such items as goods, services, and land.
3. The consideration to be paid.
4. The time of payment, delivery, or performance.

An offer may invite an acceptance to be worded in such specific terms that the contract is made definite. **EXAMPLE 9.10**   Marcus Business Machines contacts your corporation and offers to sell "from one to ten MacCool copying machines for $1,600 each; state number desired in acceptance." Your corporation agrees to buy two copiers. Because the quantity is specified in the acceptance, the terms are definite, and the contract is enforceable. ●

COMMUNICATION   The third requirement for an effective offer is communication—the offer must be communicated to the offeree. **EXAMPLE 9.11**   Tolson advertises a reward for the return of her lost cat. Dirk, not knowing of the reward, finds the cat and returns it to Tolson. Ordinarily, Dirk cannot recover the reward because an essential element of a reward contract is that the one who claims the reward must have known it was offered. A few states would allow recovery of the reward, but not on contract principles—Dirk would be allowed to recover on the basis that it would be unfair to deny him the reward just because he did not know about it. ●

Termination of the Offer

The communication of an effective offer to an offeree gives the offeree the power to transform the offer into a binding, legal obligation (a contract) by an acceptance.

---

7. See, for example, *Basis Technology Corp. v. Amazon.com, Inc.*, 71 Mass.App.Ct. 291, 878 N.E.2d 952 (2008).
8. See, for example, *MBH, Inc. v. John Otte Oil & Propane, Inc.*, 727 N.W.2d 238 (Neb.App. 2007); and *Barrand v. Whataburger, Inc.*, 214 S.W.3d 122 (Tex.App.—Corpus Christi 2006).

This power of acceptance does not continue forever, though. It can be terminated by either the *action of the parties* or by *operation of law.* Termination by the action of the parties can involve a revocation by the offeror or a rejection or counteroffer by the offeree.

Revocation In contract law, the withdrawal of an offer by the offeror. Unless the offer is irrevocable, it can be revoked at any time prior to acceptance without liability.

TERMINATION BY ACTION OF THE OFFEROR   The offeror's act of withdrawing an offer is referred to as **revocation.** Unless an offer is irrevocable, the offeror usually can revoke the offer (even if he or she has promised to keep the offer open), as long as the revocation is communicated to the offeree before the offeree accepts. Revocation may be accomplished by an express repudiation of the offer (for example, with a statement such as "I withdraw my previous offer of October 17") or by the performance of acts that are inconsistent with the existence of the offer and that are made known to the offeree.

EXAMPLE 9.12   Michelle offers to sell some land to Gary. A month passes, and Gary, who has not accepted the offer, learns that Michelle has sold the property to Liam. Because Michelle's sale of the land to Liam is inconsistent with the continued existence of the offer to Gary, the offer to Gary is effectively revoked. •

The general rule followed by most states is that a revocation becomes effective when the offeree or the offeree's *agent* (see page 472) actually receives it. Therefore, a letter of revocation mailed on April 1 and delivered at the offeree's residence or place of business on April 3 becomes effective on April 3.

BE CAREFUL The way in which a response to an offer is phrased can determine whether the offer is accepted or rejected.

TERMINATION BY ACTION OF THE OFFEREE   If the offeree rejects the offer—by words or by conduct—the offer is terminated. Any subsequent attempt by the offeree to accept will be construed as a new offer, giving the original offeror (now the offeree) the power of acceptance. Like a revocation, a rejection of an offer is effective only when it is actually received by the offeror or the offeror's agent. **EXAMPLE 9.13** Goldfinch Farms offers to sell specialty Maitake mushrooms to a Japanese buyer, Kinoko Foods. If Kinoko rejects the offer by sending a letter via U.S. mail, the rejection will not be effective (and the offer will not be terminated) until Goldfinch receives the letter. • Merely inquiring about an offer does not constitute rejection.

Counteroffer An offeree's response to an offer in which the offeree rejects the original offer and at the same time makes a new offer.

A **counteroffer** is a rejection of the original offer and the simultaneous making of a new offer. **EXAMPLE 9.14**   Burke offers to sell his home to Lang for $270,000. Lang responds, "Your price is too high. I'll offer to purchase your house for $250,000." Lang's response is called a counteroffer because it rejects Burke's offer to sell at $270,000 and creates a new offer by Lang to purchase the home at a price of $250,000. •

Mirror Image Rule A common law rule that requires that the terms of the offeree's acceptance adhere exactly to the terms of the offeror's offer for a valid contract to be formed.

At common law, the **mirror image rule** requires that the offeree's acceptance match the offeror's offer exactly. In other words, the terms of the acceptance must "mirror" those of the offer. If the acceptance materially changes or adds to the terms of the original offer, it will be considered not an acceptance but a counteroffer—which, of course, need not be accepted. The original offeror can, however, accept the terms of the counteroffer and create a valid contract.[9]

TERMINATION BY OPERATION OF LAW   The power of the offeree to transform the offer into a binding, legal obligation can be terminated by operation of law through the occurrence of any of the following events:

1. Lapse of time.
2. Destruction of the specific subject matter of the offer.

---

9. The mirror image rule has been greatly modified in regard to sales contracts. Section 2–207 of the UCC provides that a contract is formed if the offeree makes a definite expression of acceptance (such as signing the form in the appropriate location), even though the terms of the acceptance modify or add to the terms of the original offer (see Chapter 11).

3. Death or incompetence of the offeror or the offeree.

4. Supervening illegality of the proposed contract. (A statute or court decision that makes an offer illegal automatically terminates the offer.)

An offer terminates automatically by law when the period of time *specified in the offer* has passed. If the offer states that it will be left open until a particular date, then the offer will terminate at midnight on that day. If the offer states that it will be left open for a number of days, such as ten days, this time period normally begins to run when the offer is actually received by the offeree, not when it is formed or sent.

If the offer does not specify a time for acceptance, the offer terminates at the end of a *reasonable* period of time, which is determined by the subject matter of the contract, business and market conditions, and other relevant circumstances. An offer to sell farm produce, for example, will terminate sooner than an offer to sell farm equipment because farm produce is perishable and subject to greater fluctuations in market value.

IRREVOCABLE OFFERS   Although most offers are revocable, some can be made irrevocable. Increasingly, courts refuse to allow an offeror to revoke an offer when the offeree has changed position because of justifiable reliance on the offer (under the doctrine of *promissory estoppel*—see page 261). In some circumstances, "firm offers" made by merchants may also be considered irrevocable (see Chapter 11).

Another form of irrevocable offer is an option contract. An **option contract** is created when an offeror promises to hold an offer open for a specified period of time in return for a payment (consideration) given by the offeree. An option contract takes away the offeror's power to revoke an offer for the period of time specified in the option. If no time is specified, then a reasonable period of time is implied.

Option contracts frequently are used in conjunction with the sale of real estate. **EXAMPLE 9.15**   Tyrell agrees to lease a house from Jackson, the property owner. The lease contract includes a clause stating that Tyrell is paying an additional $15,000 for an option to purchase the property within a specified period of time. If Tyrell decides not to purchase the house after the specified period has lapsed, he loses the $15,000, and Jackson is free to sell the property to another buyer. ●

Option Contract   A contract under which the offeror cannot revoke the offer for a stipulated time period.

Acceptance

An **acceptance** is a voluntary act by the offeree that shows assent, or agreement, to the terms of an offer. The offeree's act may consist of words or conduct. The acceptance must be unequivocal and must be communicated to the offeror. Generally, only the person to whom the offer is made or that person's agent can accept the offer and create a binding contract.

Acceptance   A voluntary act by the offeree that shows assent, or agreement, to the terms of an offer; may consist of words or conduct.

UNEQUIVOCAL ACCEPTANCE   To exercise the power of acceptance effectively, the offeree must accept unequivocally. This is the mirror image rule. If the acceptance is subject to new conditions or if its terms materially change the original offer, the acceptance may be deemed a counteroffer that implicitly rejects the original offer.

Certain terms, when included in an acceptance, will not change the offer sufficiently to constitute rejection. **EXAMPLE 9.16**   In response to an art dealer's offer to sell a painting, the offeree, Ashton Gibbs, replies, "I accept. Please send a written contract." Gibbs is requesting a written contract but is not making it a condition for acceptance. Therefore, the acceptance is effective without the written contract. In contrast, if Gibbs replies, "I accept *if* you send a written contract," the acceptance is expressly conditioned on the request for a writing, and the statement is not an acceptance but a counteroffer. (Notice how important each word is!)[10] ●

SILENCE AS ACCEPTANCE   Ordinarily, silence cannot constitute acceptance, even if the offeror states, "By your silence and inaction, you will be deemed to have accepted this offer." This general rule applies because an offeree should not be put under a burden of liability to act affirmatively in order to reject an offer. No consideration—that is, nothing of value—has passed to the offeree to impose such a liability.

In some instances, however, the offeree does have a duty to speak. If so, his or her silence or inaction will operate as an acceptance. Silence may be an acceptance when an offeree takes the benefit of offered services even though he or she had an opportunity to reject them and knew that they were offered with the expectation of compensation.

EXAMPLE 9.17   John is a student who earns extra income by washing store windows. John taps on the window of a store, catches the attention of the store's manager, and points to the window and raises his cleaner, signaling that he will be washing the window. The manager does nothing to stop him. Here, the store manager's silence constitutes an acceptance, and an implied contract is created. The store is bound to pay a reasonable value for John's work. ●

Silence can also operate as an acceptance when the offeree has had prior dealings with the offeror. If a merchant, for example, routinely receives shipments from a supplier and in the past has always notified the supplier when defective goods are rejected, then silence constitutes acceptance.

Also, if a buyer solicits an offer specifying that certain terms and conditions are acceptable, and the seller makes the offer in response to the solicitation, the buyer has a duty to reject—that is, a duty to tell the seller that the offer is not acceptable. Failure to reject (silence) will operate as an acceptance.

COMMUNICATION OF ACCEPTANCE   In a bilateral contract, communication of acceptance is necessary because acceptance is in the form of a promise (not performance), and the contract is formed when the promise is made (rather than when the act is performed). Communication of acceptance is not necessary if the offer dispenses with the requirement, however, or if the offer can be accepted by silence.[11]

Because a unilateral contract calls for the full performance of some act, acceptance is usually evident, and notification is unnecessary. Nevertheless, exceptions do exist, such as when the offeror requests notice of acceptance or has no way of determining whether the requested act has been performed.

In the following case, the court had to decide whether a party's failure to respond to a settlement offer constituted acceptance.

---

10. For sales contracts, the UCC provides that an acceptance may still be effective even if some terms are added. The new terms are simply treated as proposals for additions to the contract, unless both parties are merchants. If the parties are merchants, the additional terms (with some exceptions) become part of the contract [UCC 2–207(2)].

11. Under UCC 2–206(1)(b), an order or other offer to buy goods that are to be promptly shipped may be treated as either a bilateral or a unilateral offer and can be accepted by a promise to ship or by actual shipment.

Case 9.3   Powerhouse Custom Homes, Inc. v. 84 Lumber Co.

Court of Appeals of Georgia, 307 Ga.App. 605, 705 S.E.2d 704 (2011).

BACKGROUND AND FACTS   Powerhouse Custom Homes, Inc., entered into a credit agreement to obtain building materials from 84 Lumber Company. Eventually, Powerhouse owed 84 Lumber a balance of $95,260.42 under the agreement. When Powerhouse failed to pay, 84 Lumber filed a suit in a Georgia state court to collect. Before the trial, 84 Lumber filed a discovery request for admission with respect to the debt. (As discussed in Chapter 3, a request for admission is a written request that a party admit certain facts—in this case, facts concerning the existence and amount of the debt.) Powerhouse did not respond to the request, which meant that the facts included in the request were deemed admitted. Later, while taking part in court-ordered mediation, the parties agreed to a deadline for objections to any agreements they might reach during mediation. Powerhouse then proposed to pay a sum less than the amount owed, but 84 Lumber did not respond to this proposal before the deadline. Afterward, 84 Lumber filed a motion for summary judgment with the trial court. The court granted summary judgment in 84 Lumber's favor for the entire debt. Powerhouse appealed, arguing that 84 Lumber had accepted its proposal to pay a lesser amount by not objecting to it before the agreed-on deadline had elapsed.

IN THE WORDS OF THE COURT . . .
MILLER, Presiding Judge.

* * * *

Under Georgia law, an agreement alleged to be in settlement and compromise of a pending lawsuit must meet the same requisites of formation and enforceability as any other contract. In this regard, it is well settled that an agreement between two parties will occur only when the minds of the parties meet at the same time, upon the same subject matter, and in the same sense. * * * *An answer to an offer will not amount to an acceptance, so as to result in a contract, unless it is unconditional and identical with the terms of the offer. To constitute a contract, the offer must be accepted unequivocally and without variance of any sort. Absent such mutual agreement, there is no enforceable contract as between the parties.* [Emphasis added.]

* * * Powerhouse * * * merely set forth a "proposal," amounting to a settlement offer that was subject to acceptance or rejection by

84 Lumber. It is undisputed that 84 Lumber did not communicate acceptance of the proposal. It thus follows that no settlement agreement was reached.

Nevertheless, in support [of the] contention that a settlement had occurred, Powerhouse * * * relies upon the provision of the mediation agreement that established a 10-day deadline for objections. Reliance upon this provision, however, is misplaced. The 10-day deadline provision for objections could only apply if an agreement had in fact been reached by acceptance of the proposal. Since 84 Lumber did not accept the proposal, no settlement agreement was reached and the 10-day deadline provision was inapplicable.

Moreover, because Powerhouse * * * failed to respond or object to the request for admissions, the pertinent facts and legal conclusions set forth in the request were deemed admitted * * * . The admissions conclusively established that Powerhouse * * * owed 84 Lumber the principal amount of $95,260.42 under the open account; that Powerhouse * * * had defaulted by failing to pay the debt owed; and that Powerhouse * * * owed accrued interest on the debt * * * , plus * * * post-judgment interest, attorney fees, and costs. These admissions left no genuine issue of material fact on 84 Lumber's complaint and thus, 84 Lumber was entitled to judgment.

DECISION AND REMEDY   A state intermediate appellate court affirmed the lower court's judgment. 84 Lumber had not agreed to Powerhouse's proposal, so the ten-day deadline did not apply. Powerhouse had not responded to 84 Lumber's request for admissions, so its facts were deemed admitted. Powerhouse was liable for the entire debt, plus interest, fees, and costs.

THE LEGAL ENVIRONMENT DIMENSION   *Would it have been possible for the court to interpret the deadline provision as meaning that one party's failure to object by the deadline constituted an acceptance? Explain.*

THE ECONOMIC DIMENSION   *Why do judgments often include awards of interest, attorneys' fees, and costs?*

Mailbox Rule   A rule providing that an acceptance of an offer becomes effective on dispatch (on being placed in an official mailbox), if mail is, expressly or impliedly, an authorized means of communication of acceptance to the offeror.

MODE AND TIMELINESS OF ACCEPTANCE   Acceptance in bilateral contracts must be timely. The general rule is that acceptance in a bilateral contract is timely if it is made before the offer is terminated. Problems may arise, though, when the parties involved are not dealing face to face. In such situations, the offeree should use an authorized mode of communication.

The Mailbox Rule.   Acceptance takes effect, thus completing formation of the contract, at the time the offeree sends or delivers the communication via the mode expressly or impliedly authorized by the offeror. This is the so-called **mailbox rule,**

also called the *deposited acceptance rule,* which the majority of courts follow. Under this rule, if the authorized mode of communication is the mail, then an acceptance becomes valid when it is dispatched (placed in the control of the U.S. Postal Service)—*not* when it is received by the offeror.

The mailbox rule does not apply to instantaneous forms of communication, such as face-to-face, telephone, or fax. There is still some uncertainty in the courts as to whether e-mail should be considered an instantaneous form of communication to which the mailbox rule does not apply. If the parties have agreed to conduct transactions electronically and if the Uniform Electronic Transactions Act (UETA—see page 256) applies, then e-mail is considered sent when it either leaves the sender's control or is received by the recipient. This rule, which takes the place of the mailbox rule when the UETA applies, essentially allows an e-mail acceptance to become effective when sent (as it would if sent by U.S. mail).

Authorized Means of Communication. A means of communicating acceptance can be expressly authorized by the offeror or impliedly authorized by the facts and circumstances surrounding the situation. An acceptance sent by means not expressly or impliedly authorized normally is not effective until it is received by the offeror.

When an offeror specifies how acceptance should be made (for example, by overnight delivery), express authorization is said to exist, and the contract is not formed unless the offeree uses that specified mode of acceptance. Moreover, both offeror and offeree are bound in contract the moment this means of acceptance is employed. **EXAMPLE 9.18**   Shaylee & Perkins, a Massachusetts firm, offers to sell a container of antique furniture to Leaham's Antiques in Colorado. The offer states that Leaham's must accept the offer via FedEx overnight delivery. The acceptance is effective (and a binding contract is formed) the moment that Leaham's gives the overnight envelope containing the acceptance to the FedEx driver. ●

If the offeror does not expressly authorize a certain mode of acceptance, then acceptance can be made by any reasonable means. Courts look at the prevailing business usages and the surrounding circumstances to determine whether the mode of acceptance used was reasonable. Usually, the offeror's choice of a particular means in making the offer implies that the offeree can use *the same or a faster* means for acceptance. Thus, if the offer is made via priority mail, it would be reasonable to accept the offer via priority mail or by a faster method, such as by fax or overnight delivery.

Substitute Method of Acceptance. If the offeror authorizes a particular method of acceptance, but the offeree accepts by a different means, the acceptance may still be effective if the substituted method serves the same purpose as the authorized means. The use of a substitute method of acceptance is not effective on dispatch, though, and no contract will be formed until the acceptance is received by the offeror. Thus, if an offer specifies FedEx overnight delivery but the offeree accepts by overnight delivery from another carrier, such as UPS, the acceptance will still be effective, but not until the offeror receives it.

▶ E-Contracts

E-Contract A contract that is formed electronically.

Numerous contracts are formed online. Electronic contracts, or **e-contracts,** must meet the same basic requirements (agreement, consideration, capacity, and legality) as paper contracts. Disputes concerning e-contracts, however, tend to center on contract terms and whether the parties voluntarily agreed to those terms.

Online contracts may be formed not only for the sale of goods and services but also for *licensing*. The "sale" of software generally involves a license, or a right to use the software, rather than the passage of title (ownership rights) from the seller to the buyer. **EXAMPLE 9.19**   Galynn wants to obtain software that will allow her to work on spreadsheets on her BlackBerry. She goes online and purchases GridMagic. During the transaction, she has to click on several on-screen "I agree" boxes to indicate that she understands that she is purchasing only the right to use the software and will not obtain any ownership rights. After she agrees to these terms (the licensing agreement), she can download the software. •

As you read through the following subsections, keep in mind that although we typically refer to the offeror and the offeree as a *seller* and a *buyer,* in many online transactions these parties would be more accurately described as a *licensor* and a *licensee.*

Online Offers

Sellers doing business via the Internet can protect themselves against contract disputes and legal liability by creating offers that clearly spell out the terms that will govern their transactions if the offers are accepted. All important terms should be conspicuous and easy to view.

DISPLAYING THE OFFER   The seller's Web site should include a hypertext link to a page containing the full contract so that potential buyers are made aware of the terms to which they are assenting. The contract generally must be displayed online in a readable format, such as a twelve-point typeface. All provisions should be reasonably clear. **EXAMPLE 9.20**   Netquip sells heavy equipment, such as trucks and trailers, on its Web site. Because Netquip's pricing schedule is very complex, the full schedule must be provided and explained on the Web site. In addition, the terms of the sale (such as any warranties and the refund policy) must be fully disclosed. •

PROVISIONS TO INCLUDE   An important rule to keep in mind is that the offeror controls the offer and thus the resulting contract. The seller should therefore determine the terms she or he wants to include in a contract and provide for them in the offer. In some instances, a standardized contract form may suffice. At a minimum, an online offer should include the following provisions:

1. A clause that clearly indicates what constitutes the buyer's agreement to the terms of the offer, such as a box containing the words "I accept" that the buyer can click on to indicate acceptance. (Mechanisms for accepting online offers will be discussed in detail later in this chapter.)

2. A provision specifying how payment for the goods (including any applicable taxes) must be made.

3. A statement of the seller's refund and return policies.

4. Disclaimers of liability for certain uses of the goods. For example, an online seller of business forms may add a disclaimer that the seller does not accept responsibility for the buyer's reliance on the forms rather than on an attorney's advice.

5. A provision specifying the remedies available to the buyer if the goods are found to be defective or if the contract is otherwise breached. Any limitation of remedies should be clearly spelled out.

6. A statement indicating how the seller will use the information gathered about the buyer.

7. Provisions relating to dispute settlement, such as an arbitration clause or a *forum-selection clause* (discussed on the facing page).

DISPUTE-SETTLEMENT PROVISIONS   Online offers frequently include provisions relating to dispute settlement. For example, the offer might include an arbitration clause specifying that any dispute arising under the contract will be arbitrated in a designated forum.

Forum-Selection Clause A provision in a contract designating the court, jurisdiction, or tribunal that will decide any disputes arising under the contract.

Many online contracts also contain a **forum-selection clause** indicating the forum, or location (such as a court or jurisdiction), for the resolution of any dispute arising under the contract. As discussed in Chapter 3, significant jurisdictional issues may occur when parties are at a great distance, as they often are when they form contracts via the Internet. A forum-selection clause will help to avert future jurisdictional problems and also help to ensure that the seller will not be required to appear in court in a distant state.

Some online contracts may also include a *choice-of-law clause* specifying that any dispute arising out of the contract will be settled in accordance with the law of a particular jurisdiction, such as a state or country. Choice-of-law clauses are particularly common in international contracts, but they may also appear in e-contracts to specify which state's laws will govern in the United States.

Online Acceptances

The *Restatement (Second) of Contracts* states that parties may agree to a contract "by written or spoken words or by other action or by failure to act."[12] The UCC, which governs sales contracts, has a similar provision. Section 2–204 of the UCC states that any contract for the sale of goods "may be made in any manner sufficient to show agreement, including conduct by both parties which recognizes the existence of such a contract."

Click-on Agreement An agreement that arises when a buyer, engaging in a transaction on a computer, indicates assent to be bound by the terms of an offer by clicking on a button that says, for example, "I agree."

Shrink-Wrap Agreement An agreement whose terms are expressed in a document located inside a box in which goods (usually software) are packaged.

CLICK-ON AGREEMENTS   The courts have used these provisions to conclude that a binding contract can be created by conduct, including the act of clicking on a box indicating "I accept" or "I agree" to accept an online offer. The agreement resulting from such an acceptance is often called a **click-on agreement** (also referred to as a *click-on license* or *click-wrap agreement*). Exhibit 9–2 shows a portion of a typical click-on agreement that accompanies a software package.

Generally, the law does not require that the parties have read all of the terms in a contract for it to be effective. Therefore, clicking on a box that states "I agree" to certain terms can be enough. The terms may be contained on a Web site through which the buyer is obtaining goods or services, or they may appear on a computer screen when software is loaded from a CD-ROM or DVD or downloaded from the Internet.

SHRINK-WRAP AGREEMENTS   A **shrink-wrap agreement** (or *shrink-wrap license*) is an agreement whose terms are expressed inside a box in which the goods are packaged. (The term *shrink-wrap* refers to the plastic that covers the box.) Usually, the party who opens the box is told that she or he agrees to the terms by keeping whatever is in the box. Similarly,

• *Exhibit* **9–2 A Click-on Agreement Sample**
This exhibit illustrates an online offer to form a contract. To accept the offer, the user simply scrolls down the page and clicks on the "I Accept" button.

---

12. *Restatement (Second) of Contracts,* Section 19.

when the purchaser opens a software package, he or she agrees to abide by the terms of the limited license agreement.

EXAMPLE 9.21 John orders a new computer from a national company, which ships the computer to him. Along with the computer, the box contains an agreement setting forth the terms of the sale, including what remedies are available. The document also states that John's retention of the computer for longer than thirty days will be construed as an acceptance of the terms. •

In most instances, a shrink-wrap agreement is not between a retailer and a buyer, but between the manufacturer of the hardware or software and the ultimate buyer-user of the product. The terms generally concern warranties, remedies, and other issues associated with the use of the product.

Shrink-Wrap Agreements and Enforceable Contract Terms. In some cases, courts have enforced the terms of shrink-wrap agreements in the same way as the terms of other contracts. These courts have reasoned that by including the terms with the product, the seller proposed a contract that the buyer could accept by using the product after having an opportunity to read the terms.

Shrink-Wrap Terms That May Not Be Enforced. Sometimes, however, courts have refused to enforce certain terms in shrink-wrap agreements because the buyer did not expressly consent to them. An important factor is when the parties form their contract.

Suppose that a buyer orders a product over the telephone. If the contract is formed at that time and the seller does not mention terms such as an arbitration clause or a forum-selection clause, clearly the buyer has not expressly consented to these terms. If the clauses are included in the shrink-wrap agreement, a court may conclude that they are proposals for additional terms, and not part of the original contract, because the buyer did not discover them until *after* the contract was formed.

Browse-Wrap Term A term or condition of use that is presented to an Internet user at the time certain products, such as software, are being downloaded but that need not be agreed to (by clicking "I agree," for example) before the user is able to install or use the product.

BROWSE-WRAP TERMS Like the terms of a click-on agreement, **browse-wrap terms** can occur in a transaction conducted over the Internet. Unlike a click-on agreement, however, browse-wrap terms do not require an Internet user to assent to the terms before, say, downloading or using certain software. In other words, a person can install the software without clicking "I agree" to the terms of a license. Browse-wrap terms are often unenforceable because they do not satisfy the agreement requirement of contract formation.[13]

E-Signature Technologies

E-Signature As defined by the Uniform Electronic Transactions Act, "an electronic sound, symbol, or process attached to or logically associated with a record and executed or adopted by a person with the intent to sign the record."

Today, numerous technologies allow electronic documents to be signed. An **e-signature** has been defined as "an electronic sound, symbol, or process attached to or logically associated with a record and executed or adopted by a person with the intent to sign the record."[14] Thus, e-signatures include encrypted digital signatures, names (intended as signatures) at the ends of e-mail messages, and "clicks" on a Web page if the click includes the identification of the person.

The technologies for creating e-signatures generally fall into one of two categories, *digitized handwritten signatures* and *digital signatures based on a public-key infrastructure*. A digitized signature is a graphical image of a handwritten signature that

---

13. See, for example, *Jesmer v. Retail Magic, Inc.,* 863 N.Y.S.2d 737 (2008).
14. This definition is from the Uniform Electronic Transactions Act (see pages 256–258).

An e-signature.

is often created using a digital pen and pad, such as an ePad, and special software. The strokes of a person's signature can be measured by software to authenticate the signature (this is referred to as signature dynamics).

In a public-key infrastructure (such as an asymmetric cryptosystem), two mathematically linked but different keys are generated—a private signing key and a public validation key. A digital signature is created when the signer uses the private key to create a unique mark on an electronic document. The appropriate software enables the recipient of the document to use the public key to verify the identity of the signer. A **cybernotary,** or legally recognized certification authority, issues the key pair, identifies the owner of the keys, and certifies the validity of the public key. The cybernotary also serves as a repository for public keys.

Federal Law on E-Signatures and E-Documents

Cybernotary A legally recognized authority that can certify the validity of digital signatures.

In 2000, Congress enacted the Electronic Signatures in Global and National Commerce Act (E-SIGN Act),[15] which provides that no contract, record, or signature may be "denied legal effect" solely because it is in electronic form. In other words, under this law, an electronic signature is as valid as a signature on paper, and an e-document can be as enforceable as a paper one.

For an e-signature to be enforceable, the contracting parties must have agreed to use electronic signatures. For an electronic document to be valid, it must be in a form that can be retained and accurately reproduced.

The E-SIGN Act does not apply to all types of documents, however. Court papers, divorce decrees, evictions, foreclosures, health-insurance terminations, prenuptial agreements, and wills are exempt. Also, the only agreements governed by the UCC that fall under this law are those covered by Articles 2 and 2A and UCC 1–107 and 1–206. Despite these limitations, the E-SIGN Act significantly expanded the possibilities for contracting online.

As will be discussed in Chapter 20, the Fair and Accurate Credit Transactions (FACT) Act of 2003[16] was passed to combat identity theft. One provision of the FACT Act involves how credit-card receipts should be handled to avoid fraud. See this chapter's *Management Perspective* feature on the following page for more details on how this provision may affect online transactions.

Partnering Agreements

Partnering Agreement An agreement between a seller and a buyer who frequently do business with each other concerning the terms and conditions that will apply to all subsequently formed electronic contracts.

One way that online sellers and buyers can prevent disputes over signatures in their e-contracts, as well as disputes over the terms and conditions of those contracts, is to form partnering agreements. In a **partnering agreement,** a seller and a buyer who frequently do business with each other agree in advance on the terms and conditions that will apply to all transactions subsequently conducted electronically. The partnering agreement can also establish special access and identification codes to be used by the parties when transacting business electronically.

A partnering agreement reduces the likelihood that disputes will arise under the contract because the buyer and the seller have agreed in advance to the terms and

---

15. 15 U.S.C. Sections 7001 *et seq.*
16. 15 U.S.C. Sections 1681 *et seq.*

Management Perspective   E-Mailed Credit-Card Receipts

Management Faces a Legal Issue

As consumers engage in more transactions on the Internet, retailers are printing out fewer credit-card receipts than they did previously. Merchants who do print out paper receipts must follow strict guidelines. The Fair and Accurate Credit Transactions (FACT) Act of 2003 prohibits merchants from printing more than the last five digits of the card number or the expiration date on any receipt provided to the cardholder at the point of sale of the transaction. This prohibition applies only to receipts that are "electronically printed." Congress did not specifically indicate what is meant by the words *electronically printed.* Thus, online retailers have faced the legal issue of whether e-mailed receipts are subject to the FACT Act's so-called truncation (shortening) requirement.

What the Courts Say

The question is whether a Web page screen shot counts as a receipt under the FACT Act. At least two court cases have examined this issue. The first one involved reservations for rental motorcycles. The motorcycle rental store sent out an online reservation confirmation that included credit cards' expiration dates on the renters' computer screens. The plaintiffs contended that the confirmations they received were "electronically printed" receipts subject to the FACT

Act's truncation requirement. The defendant moved for summary judgment on the ground that the receipts did not violate the act. The court granted the motion, observing that "[w]hen one refers to a printed receipt, what springs to mind is a tangible document."[a]

A similar case concerned the online sale of contact lenses by a popular telemarketing and online retailer. Again, the plaintiff received an e-mail confirmation that included his credit card's expiration date, and again, the court sided with the defendant. The court pointed out that the legislative history of the FACT Act clearly shows that Congress intended this law to apply to physically printed paper receipts. The FACT Act "makes no use of terms like 'Internet' or 'e-mail' that would signal an intent to reach paperless receipts transmitted to the consumer via e-mail."[b]

Implications for Managers

At this time, credit-card receipts sent via e-mail by online retailers appear not to be subject to the FACT Act's truncation requirement. Nonetheless, the prudent online retailer might wish to conform to the FACT Act provisions simply as a good business practice. After all, hackers can sometimes illegally access e-mail correspondence. Moreover, Congress may amend the FACT Act to include e-mail receipts because online retailing is growing dramatically in the United States and elsewhere.

---

a. *Kelleher v. Eaglerider, Inc.,* 2010 WL 4386837 (N.D.Ill. 2010).
b. *Shlahtichman v. 1-800 Contacts, Inc.,* 615 F.3d 794 (7th Cir. 2010).

---

conditions that will accompany each sale. Furthermore, if a dispute does arise, a court or arbitration forum will be able to refer to the partnering agreement when determining the parties' intent.

 ## The Uniform Electronic Transactions Act

Although most states have laws governing e-signatures and other aspects of electronic transactions, these laws are far from uniform. In an attempt to create more uniformity among the states, in 1999 the National Conference of Commissioners on Uniform State Laws and the American Law Institute promulgated the Uniform Electronic Transactions Act (UETA). To date, the UETA has been adopted, at least in part, by forty-eight states.

The primary purpose of the UETA is to remove barriers to e-commerce by giving the same legal effect to electronic records and signatures as is given to paper documents and signatures. As mentioned earlier, the UETA broadly defines an *e-signature* as "an electronic sound, symbol, or process attached to or logically associated with a record and executed or adopted by a person with the intent to sign the record."[17]

---

17. UETA 102(8).

Record According to the Uniform Electronic Transactions Act, information that is either inscribed on a tangible medium or stored in an electronic or other medium and is retrievable.

A **record** is "information that is inscribed on a tangible medium or that is stored in an electronic or other medium and is retrievable in perceivable [visual] form."[18]

The UETA does not create new rules for electronic contracts but rather establishes that records, signatures, and contracts may not be denied enforceability solely due to their electronic form. The UETA does not apply to all writings and signatures. It covers only electronic records and electronic signatures *relating to a transaction*. A *transaction* is defined as an interaction between two or more people relating to business, commercial, or governmental activities.[19]

The act specifically does not apply to wills or testamentary trusts or to transactions governed by the UCC (other than those covered by Articles 2 and 2A).[20] In addition, the provisions of the UETA allow the states to exclude its application to other areas of law.

The Federal E-SIGN Act and the UETA

When Congress passed the E-SIGN Act in 2000, a year after the UETA was presented to the states for adoption, a significant issue was to what extent the federal E-SIGN Act preempted the UETA as adopted by the states. The E-SIGN Act[21] refers explicitly to the UETA and provides that if a state has enacted the uniform version of the UETA, it is not preempted by the E-SIGN Act. In other words, if the state has enacted the UETA without modification, state law will govern. The problem is that many states have enacted nonuniform (modified) versions of the UETA, largely for the purpose of excluding other areas of state law from the UETA's terms. The E-SIGN Act specifies that those exclusions will be preempted to the extent that they are inconsistent with the E-SIGN Act's provisions.

The E-SIGN Act, however, explicitly allows the states to enact alternative requirements for the use of electronic records or electronic signatures. Generally, however, the requirements must be consistent with the provisions of the E-SIGN Act, and the state must not give greater legal status or effect to one specific type of technology. Additionally, if a state enacts alternative requirements *after* the E-SIGN Act was adopted, the state law must specifically refer to the E-SIGN Act. The relationship between the UETA and the E-SIGN Act is illustrated in Exhibit 9–3 on the next page.

Highlights of the UETA

The UETA will not apply to a transaction unless each of the parties has previously agreed to conduct transactions by electronic means. The agreement need not be explicit, however, and it may be implied by the conduct of the parties and the surrounding circumstances.[22] It may be reasonable to infer that a person who gives out a business card with an e-mail address on it has consented to transact business electronically. The party's agreement may also be inferred from a letter or other writing, as well as from some verbal communication. A person who has previously agreed to an electronic transaction can also withdraw his or her consent and refuse to conduct further business electronically.

---

18. UETA 102(15).
19. UETA 2(12) and 3.
20. UETA 3(b).
21. 15 U.S.C. Section 7002(2)(A)(i).
22. UETA 5(b).

• *Exhibit* 9–3 **The E-SIGN Act and the UETA**

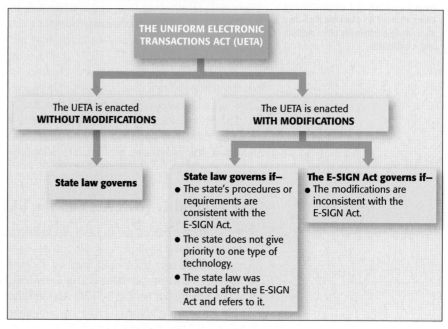

Under the UETA, if an electronic record or signature is the act of a particular person, the record or signature may be attributed to that person. If a person types her or his name at the bottom of an e-mail purchase order, that name will qualify as a "signature" and be attributed to the person whose name appears.

Note that the UETA states that the effect of a record is to be determined from the context and surrounding circumstances. In other words, a record may have legal effect even if no one has signed it. **EXAMPLE 9.22**   Jack Darby sends a fax to Corina Scott. The fax contains a letterhead identifying Darby as the sender, but Darby's signature does not appear on the faxed document. Depending on the circumstances, the fax may be attributed to Darby. •

The UETA does not contain any express provisions about what constitutes fraud or whether an agent is authorized to enter a contract. Under the UETA, other state laws control if any issues relating to agency, authority, forgery, or contract formation arise. If existing state law requires a document to be notarized, the UETA provides that this requirement is satisfied by the electronic signature of a notary public or other person authorized to verify signatures.

 Consideration

The fact that a promise has been made does not mean the promise can or will be enforced. Under common law, a primary basis for the enforcement of promises is consideration, which, as mentioned on page 237, is the second requirement for the formation of a valid contract. **Consideration** usually is defined as the value (such as cash) given in return for a promise (in a bilateral contract) or in return for a performance (in a unilateral contract).

Consideration   Generally, the value given in return for a promise or a performance. The consideration, which must be present to make the contract legally binding, must be something of legally sufficient value and bargained for.

Elements of Consideration

Often, consideration is broken down into two parts: (1) something of *legally sufficient value* must be given in exchange for the promise, and (2) usually, there must be a *bargained-for exchange.*

LEGALLY SUFFICIENT VALUE   The "something of legally sufficient value" may consist of (1) a promise to do something that one has no prior legal duty to do, (2) the performance of an action that one is otherwise not obligated to undertake, or (3) the refraining from an action that one has a legal right to undertake (called a *forbearance*).

Consideration in bilateral contracts normally consists of a promise in return for a promise, as explained earlier. In contrast, unilateral contracts involve a promise in return for a performance. **EXAMPLE 9.23** Anita says to her neighbor, "When you finish painting the garage, I will pay you $100." Anita's neighbor paints the garage. The act of painting the garage is the consideration that creates Anita's contractual obligation to pay her neighbor $100. •

What if, in return for a promise to pay, a person refrains from pursuing harmful habits (a forbearance), such as the use of tobacco and alcohol? In most situations, such forbearance constitutes legally sufficient consideration for a promise.[23]

BARGAINED-FOR EXCHANGE   The second element of consideration is that it must provide the basis for the bargain struck between the contracting parties. The item of value must be given or promised by the promisor (offeror) in return for the promisee's promise, performance, or promise of performance.

This element of bargained-for exchange distinguishes contracts from gifts. **EXAMPLE 9.24** Roberto says to his son, "In consideration of the fact that you are not as wealthy as your brothers, I will pay you $5,000." The fact that the word *consideration* is used does not, by itself, mean that consideration has been given. Indeed, this is not an enforceable promise because the son does not have to do anything in order to receive the promised $5,000. Because the son does not need to give Roberto something of legal value in return for his promise, there is no bargained-for exchange. Rather, Roberto has simply stated his motive for giving his son a gift. •

Adequacy of Consideration

Adequacy of consideration involves how much consideration is given. Essentially, it concerns the fairness of the bargain. On the surface, when the items exchanged are of unequal value, fairness would appear to be an issue. A court generally will not question the adequacy of consideration, however, based solely on a comparison of values of the things exchanged. Something need not be of direct economic or financial value to be regarded as legally sufficient consideration.

Under the doctrine of freedom of contract, courts leave it up to the parties to decide what something is worth, and parties usually are free to bargain as they wish. If people could sue merely because they had entered into an unwise contract, the courts would be overloaded with frivolous suits.

---

23. For a classic case holding that a person's promise to refrain from using alcohol and tobacco was sufficient consideration, see *Hamer v. Sidway,* 124 N.Y. 538, 27 N.E. 256 (1891).

Nevertheless, a large disparity in the amount or value of the consideration exchanged may raise a red flag, causing a court to look more closely at the bargain. This is because shockingly inadequate consideration can indicate that fraud, duress, or undue influence was involved or that the element of bargained-for exchange was lacking. Judges are uneasy about enforcing unequal bargains and generally try to make sure that no defect in a contract's formation negates mutual assent.

Agreements That Lack Consideration

Sometimes, one of the parties (or both parties) to an agreement may think that consideration has been exchanged when in fact it has not. Here, we look at some situations in which the parties' promises or actions do not qualify as contractual consideration.

PREEXISTING DUTY   Under most circumstances, a promise to do what one already has a legal duty to do does not constitute legally sufficient consideration. The pre-existing legal duty may be imposed by law or may arise out of a previous contract. A sheriff, for example, cannot collect a reward for providing information leading to the capture of a criminal if the sheriff already has a legal duty to capture the criminal.

Likewise, if a party is already bound by contract to perform a certain duty, that duty cannot serve as consideration for a second contract. **EXAMPLE 9.25** Bauman-Bache, Inc., begins construction on a seven-story office building and after three months demands an extra $75,000 on its contract. If the extra $75,000 is not paid, the contractor will stop working. The owner of the land, finding no one else to complete the construction, agrees to pay the extra $75,000. The agreement is unenforceable because it is not supported by legally sufficient consideration. Bauman-Bache had a preexisting contractual duty to complete the building. •

Unforeseen Difficulties. The preexisting duty rule is intended to prevent extortion and the "holdup game." If, during performance of a contract, extraordinary difficulties arise that were totally unforeseen at the time the contract was formed, a court may allow an exception to the rule.

Suppose that in Example 9.25 above Bauman-Bache had asked for the extra $75,000 because it encountered a rock formation that no one knew existed, and the landowner had agreed to pay the extra amount to excavate the rock. In this situation, the court may refrain from applying the preexisting duty rule and enforce the agreement to pay the extra $75,000. Note, however, that for the rule to be waived, the difficulties must be truly unforeseen and not be the types of risks ordinarily assumed in business. In the example above, if the construction was taking place in an area where rock formations were common, a court would likely enforce the preexisting duty rule on the basis that Bauman-Bache had assumed the risk that it would encounter rock.

Rescission and New Contract. The law recognizes that two parties can mutually agree to rescind, or cancel, their contract, at least to the extent that it is executory (still to be carried out). **Rescission**[24] is the unmaking of a contract so as to return the parties to the positions they occupied before the contract was made. Sometimes, parties rescind a contract and make a new contract at the same time. When this occurs, it is often difficult to determine whether there was consideration for the new contract, or whether the parties had a preexisting duty under the previous contract.

Rescission   A remedy whereby a contract is canceled and the parties are returned to the positions they occupied before the contract was made; may be effected through the mutual consent of the parties, by their conduct, or by court decree.

---

24. Pronounced reh-*sih*-zhen.

If a court finds there was a preexisting duty, then the new contract will be invalid because there was no consideration.

PAST CONSIDERATION   Promises made in return for actions or events that have already taken place are unenforceable. These promises lack consideration in that the element of bargained-for exchange is missing. In short, a person can bargain for something to take place now or in the future but not for something that has already taken place. Therefore, *past consideration* is no consideration.

Suppose that Elsie, a real estate agent, does her friend Judy a favor by selling Judy's house and not charging a commission. Later, Judy says to Elsie, "In return for your generous act, I will pay you $3,000." This promise involves past consideration. Consequently, a court would not enforce it. Judy is simply creating a situation in which she presents a gift to Elsie.

CASE EXAMPLE 9.26   Jamil Blackmon became friends with Allen Iverson when Iverson was a high school student who showed tremendous promise as an athlete. One evening, Blackmon suggested that Iverson use "The Answer" as a nickname in the summer league basketball tournaments. Blackmon said that Iverson would be "The Answer" to all of the National Basketball Association's woes. Later that night, Iverson said that he would give Blackmon 25 percent of any proceeds from the merchandising of products that used "The Answer" as a logo or a slogan. Because Iverson's promise was made in return for past consideration, it was unenforceable. In effect, Iverson stated his intention to give Blackmon a gift.[25] ●

Promissory Estoppel

Promissory Estoppel   A doctrine that applies when a promisor makes a clear and definite promise on which the promisee justifiably relies; such a promise is binding if justice will be better served by the enforcement of the promise.

Under the doctrine of **promissory estoppel** (also called *detrimental reliance*), a person who has reasonably and substantially relied on the promise of another may be able to obtain some measure of recovery. This doctrine is applied in a wide variety of contexts in which a promise is otherwise unenforceable, such as when a promise is not supported by consideration. Under this doctrine, a court may enforce an otherwise unenforceable promise to avoid the injustice that would otherwise result. For the doctrine to be applied, the following elements are required:

1. There must be a clear and definite promise.
2. The promisor should have expected that the promisee would rely on the promise.
3. The promisee reasonably relied on the promise by acting or refraining from some act.
4. The promisee's reliance was definite and resulted in substantial detriment.
5. Enforcement of the promise is necessary to avoid injustice.

If these requirements are met, a promise may be enforced even though it is not supported by consideration. In essence, the promisor will be *estopped* (prevented) from asserting the lack of consideration as a defense.

▶ Contractual Capacity

Contractual Capacity   The threshold mental capacity required by the law for a party who enters into a contract to be bound by that contract.

In addition to agreement and consideration, for a contract to be deemed valid, the parties to the contract must have **contractual capacity**—the legal ability to enter into a contractual relationship. Courts generally presume the existence of contractual

---

25. *Blackmon v. Iverson,* 324 F.Supp.2d 602 (E.D.Pa. 2003).

capacity. In some situations, however, when a person is young, intoxicated, or mentally incompetent, capacity is lacking or may be questionable.

Minors

Today, in almost all states, the *age of majority* (when a person is no longer a minor) for contractual purposes is eighteen years.[26] In addition, some states provide for the termination of minority on marriage. Minority status may also be terminated by a minor's *emancipation,* which occurs when a child's parent or legal guardian relinquishes the legal right to exercise control over the child. Normally, minors who leave home to support themselves are considered emancipated. Several jurisdictions permit minors themselves to petition a court for emancipation. For business purposes, a minor may petition a court to be treated as an adult.

The general rule is that a minor can enter into any contract that an adult can, provided that the contract is not one prohibited by law for minors (for example, the sale of tobacco or alcoholic beverages). A contract entered into by a minor, however, is voidable at the option of that minor, subject to certain exceptions.

The legal avoidance, or setting aside, of a contractual obligation is referred to as *disaffirmance.* To disaffirm, a minor must express his or her intent, through words or conduct, not to be bound to the contract. The minor must disaffirm the entire contract, not merely a portion of it. For example, the minor cannot decide to keep part of the goods purchased under a contract and return the remaining goods.

Intoxication

Intoxication is a condition in which a person's normal capacity to act or think is inhibited by alcohol or some other drug. A contract entered into by an intoxicated person can be either voidable or valid (and thus enforceable). If the person was sufficiently intoxicated to lack mental capacity, then the agreement may be voidable even if the intoxication was purely voluntary. If, despite intoxication, the person understood the legal consequences of the agreement, the contract will be enforceable. For the contract to be voidable, the person must prove that the intoxication impaired her or his reason and judgment so severely that she or he did not comprehend the legal consequences of entering into the contract.

Mental Incompetence

If a court has previously determined that a person is mentally incompetent and has appointed a guardian to represent the individual, any contract made by the mentally incompetent person is *void*—no contract exists. Only the guardian can enter into binding legal obligations on behalf of the mentally incompetent person.

If a court has not previously judged a person to be mentally incompetent, the contract may be *voidable* if the person did not know he or she was entering into the contract or lacked the mental capacity to comprehend its nature, purpose, and consequences. A contract entered into by a mentally incompetent person (whom a court has not previously declared incompetent) may also be *valid* if the person had capacity *at the time the contract was formed.*

---

26. The age of majority may still be twenty-one for other purposes, such as the purchase and consumption of alcohol.

▶ Legality

Legality is the fourth requirement for a valid contract to exist. For a contract to be valid and enforceable, it must be formed for a legal purpose. A contract to do something that is prohibited by federal or state statutory law is illegal and, as such, void from the outset and thus unenforceable. A contract or a clause in a contract can also be illegal even in the absence of a specific statute prohibiting the action promised by the contract. Additionally, a contract to commit a tortious act—such as an agreement to engage in fraudulent misrepresentation (see Chapter 10)—is contrary to public policy and therefore illegal and unenforceable.

Contracts Contrary to Statute

Any contract to commit a crime (see Chapter 6) is a contract in violation of a statute. Thus, a contract to sell illegal drugs in violation of criminal laws is unenforceable, as is a contract to cover up a corporation's violation of the Sarbanes-Oxley Act (see Chapter 2). Similarly, a contract to smuggle undocumented workers from another country into the United States for an employer is illegal (see Chapter 17), as is a contract to dump hazardous waste in violation of environmental laws (see Chapter 21). If the object or performance of the contract is rendered illegal by statute *after* the contract has been entered into, the contract is considered to be discharged by law. (See the discussion of impossibility or impracticability of performance in Chapter 10 on page 289.)

USURY Almost every state has a statute that sets the maximum rate of interest that can be charged for different types of transactions, including ordinary loans. A lender who makes a loan at an interest rate above the lawful maximum commits *usury*. Although usurious contracts are illegal, most states simply limit the interest that the lender may collect on the contract to the lawful maximum interest rate in that state. In a few states, the lender can recover the principal amount of the loan but no interest.

GAMBLING Gambling is the creation of risk for the purpose of assuming it. Traditionally, the states have deemed gambling contracts illegal and thus void. All states have statutes that regulate gambling, and many states allow certain forms of gambling, such as horse racing, poker machines, and charity-sponsored bingo. In addition, nearly all states allow state-operated lotteries and gambling on Native American reservations. Even in states that permit certain types of gambling, though, courts often find that gambling contracts are illegal.

CASE EXAMPLE 9.27 Casino gambling is legal in Louisiana, as are video poker machines. Nevertheless, Louisiana courts refused to enforce certain contracts relating to the installation of video poker machines. Gaming Venture, Inc. (GVI), had entered into two contracts with Tastee Restaurant Corporation: a licensing agreement and an agreement that authorized GVI to install poker machines in various Tastee locations. When several Tastee restaurants refused to install the machines, GVI sued for breach of contract. The state appellate court held that the two agreements were illegal gambling contracts and therefore void because GVI had failed to get the prior approval of the state video gaming commission.[27] ●

---

27. *Gaming Venture, Inc. v. Tastee Restaurant Corp.*, 996 So.2d 515 (La.App. 5 Cir. 2008).

LICENSING STATUTES All states require members of certain professions—including physicians, lawyers, real estate brokers, accountants, architects, electricians, and stockbrokers—to have licenses. Some licenses are obtained only after extensive schooling and examinations, which indicate to the public that a special skill has been acquired. Others require only that the applicant be of good moral character and pay a fee.

Whether a contract with an unlicensed person is legal and enforceable depends on the purpose of the licensing statute. If the statute's purpose is to protect the public from unauthorized practitioners (such as unlicensed attorneys and electricians), then a contract involving an unlicensed practitioner is generally illegal and unenforceable. If the statute's purpose is merely to raise government revenues, however, a contract with an unlicensed person (such as a landscape architect or a massage therapist) may be enforced and the unlicensed practitioner fined.

Contracts Contrary to Public Policy

Although contracts involve private parties, some are not enforceable because of the negative impact they would have on society. Examples include a contract to commit a civil wrong, such as invading another person's privacy (see Chapter 4), and a contract to commit an immoral act, such as selling a child. We look here at other types of business contracts that are often said to be *contrary to public policy.*

CONTRACTS IN RESTRAINT OF TRADE Contracts in restraint of trade (anticompetitive agreements) usually adversely affect the public policy that favors competition in the economy. Typically, such contracts also violate one or more federal or state antitrust statutes (see Chapter 23). An exception is recognized when the restraint is reasonable and is contained in an ancillary (secondary, or subordinate) clause in a contract. Such restraints often are included in contracts for the sale of an ongoing business and employment contracts.

Covenants Not to Compete and the Sale of an Ongoing Business. Many contracts involve a type of restraint called a **covenant not to compete,** or a restrictive covenant (promise). A covenant not to compete may be created when a seller agrees not to open a new store in a certain geographic area surrounding the old store. Such an agreement enables the seller to sell, and the purchaser to buy, the goodwill and reputation of an ongoing business without having to worry that the seller will open a competing business a block away. Provided the restrictive covenant is reasonable and is an ancillary part of the sale of an ongoing business, it is enforceable.

Covenant Not to Compete
A contractual promise of one party to refrain from competing with another party for a certain period of time and within a certain geographic area.

Covenants Not to Compete in Employment Contracts. Sometimes, agreements not to compete (also referred to as *noncompete agreements*) are included in employment contracts. People in middle- or upper-level management positions commonly agree not to work for competitors or start competing businesses for a specified period of time after termination of employment. Such agreements are legal in most states so long as the specified period of time is not excessive and the geographic restriction is reasonable. What constitutes a reasonable time period may be shorter in the online environment than in conventional employment contracts because the restrictions apply worldwide. To be reasonable, a restriction on competition must protect a legitimate business interest and must not be any greater than necessary to protect that interest.

CASE EXAMPLE 9.28 Improv West Associates is the founder of the Improv Comedy Club and owner of the "Improv" trademark. Comedy Club, Inc. (CCI), owns and operates restaurants and comedy clubs. Improv West granted CCI an exclusive license to open four Improv clubs per year in 2001, 2002, and 2003. CCI further promised to open eight additional clubs. Their agreement prohibited CCI from opening any non-Improv comedy clubs "in the contiguous United States" until 2019. A dispute arose when CCI failed to open the additional Improv clubs, and CCI lost its right to open more Improv Clubs. A federal appellate court ruled that the covenant not to compete was unenforceable, however. The court held that the covenant was unreasonable because of its "dramatic geographic and temporal [relating to time] scope."[28] ●

Occasionally, depending on the jurisdiction, courts will *reform* covenants not to compete to make the terms more reasonable and then enforce the reformed covenant. Courts usually resort to contract *reformation* only when necessary to prevent undue burdens or hardships.

UNCONSCIONABLE CONTRACTS   A court does not ordinarily look at the fairness or equity of a contract. For example, the courts generally do not inquire into the adequacy of consideration. Persons are assumed to be reasonably intelligent, and the courts will not come to their aid just because they have made an unwise bargain. In certain circumstances, however, bargains are so oppressive that the courts relieve innocent parties of part or all of their duties. Such bargains are deemed **unconscionable**[29] because they are so unscrupulous or grossly unfair as to be "void of conscience."[30] A contract can be unconscionable on either procedural or substantive grounds.

Procedural Unconscionability. *Procedural unconscionability* often involves inconspicuous print, unintelligible language (legalese), or the lack of an opportunity to read the contract or ask questions about its meaning. It can also occur when there is such disparity in bargaining power between the two parties that the weaker party's consent is not voluntary. This type of situation often involves an adhesion contract. An *adhesion contract* is written exclusively by one party (usually, the seller or creditor) and presented to the other (usually, the buyer or borrower) on a take-it-or-leave-it basis. Only those adhesion contracts that unreasonably favor the drafter are unconscionable.

Substantive Unconscionability. *Substantive unconscionability* characterizes contracts that are oppressive or overly harsh. Courts generally focus on provisions that deprive one party of the benefits of the agreement or leave that party without a remedy for nonperformance by the other. For example, a contract clause that gives the business entity free access to the courts but requires the other party to arbitrate any dispute with the firm may be unconscionable. Contracts drafted by insurance companies and cell phone providers have been struck down as substantively unconscionable when they included provisions that were overly harsh or one sided.[31]

EXCULPATORY CLAUSES   Often closely related to the concept of unconscionability are **exculpatory clauses,** which release a party from liability in the event of monetary or physical injury *no matter who is at fault*. Indeed, courts sometimes refuse to enforce such clauses on the ground that they are unconscionable. Exculpatory clauses found in rental agreements for commercial property frequently are held to be contrary to public policy, and such clauses are almost always unenforceable in

Unconscionable   A contract or clause that is void on the basis of public policy because one party, as a result of his or her disproportionate bargaining power, is forced to accept terms that are unfairly burdensome and that unfairly benefit the dominating party.

Exculpatory Clause   A clause that releases a contractual party from liability in the event of monetary or physical injury, no matter who is at fault.

---

28. *Comedy Club, Inc. v. Improv West Associates,* 535 F.3d 1277 (9th Cir. 2009).
29. Pronounced un-*kon*-shun-uh-bul.
30. The UCC incorporated the concept of unconscionability in Sections 2–302 and 2A–108. These provisions, which apply to contracts for the sale or lease of goods, will be discussed in Chapter 11.
31. See, for example, *Gatton v. T-Mobile USA, Inc.,* 152 Cal.App.4th 571, 61 Cal.Rptr.3d 344 (2007); and *Aul v. Golden Rule Insurance Co.,* 737 N.W.2d 24 (Wis.App. 2007).

residential property leases. Courts also usually hold that exculpatory clauses are against public policy in the employment context. Thus, employers frequently cannot enforce exculpatory clauses in contracts with employees or independent contractors (see Chapter 17) to avoid liability for work-related injuries.[32]

Although courts view exculpatory clauses with disfavor, they do enforce such clauses when they do not contravene public policy, are not ambiguous, and do not claim to protect parties from liability for intentional misconduct. Businesses such as health clubs, racetracks, amusement parks, skiing facilities, horse-rental operations, golf-cart concessions, and skydiving organizations frequently use exculpatory clauses to limit their liability for patrons' injuries.

---

32. See, for example, *Speedway SuperAmerica, LLC v. Erwin*, 250 S.W.3d 339 (2008).

Reviewing . . . Formation of Traditional and E-Contracts

Ted and Betty Hyatt live in California, a state that provides extensive statutory protection for consumers. The Hyatts decided to buy a computer so that they could use e-mail to stay in touch with their grandchildren, who live in another state. Over the phone, they ordered a computer from CompuEdge, Inc. When the box arrived, it was sealed with a brightly colored sticker warning that the terms enclosed within the box would govern the sale unless the customer returned the computer within thirty days. Among those terms was a clause that required any disputes to be resolved in Tennessee state courts. The Hyatts then signed up for Internet service through CyberTool, an Internet service provider. They downloaded CyberTool's software and clicked on the "quick install" box that allowed them to bypass CyberTool's "Terms of Service" page. It was possible to read this page by scrolling to the next screen, but the Hyatts did not realize this. The terms included a clause that stated all disputes were to be submitted to a Virginia state court. As soon as the Hyatts attempted to e-mail their grandchildren, they experienced problems using CyberTool's e-mail service, which continually stated that the network was busy. They also were unable to receive the photos sent by their grandchildren. Using the information presented in the chapter, answer the following questions.

1. Did the Hyatts accept the list of contract terms included in the computer box? Why or why not? What is the name used for this type of e-contract?
2. What type of agreement did the Hyatts form with CyberTool?
3. Suppose that the Hyatts experienced trouble with the computer's components after they had used the computer for two months. What factors will a court consider in deciding whether to enforce the forum-selection clause? Would a court be likely to enforce the clause in this contract? Why or why not?
4. Are the Hyatts bound by the contract terms specified on CyberTool's "Terms of Service" page that they did not read? Which of the required elements for contract formation might the Hyatts claim were lacking? How might a court rule on this issue?

Linking the Law *to Marketing*
Customer Relationship Management

Increasingly, the contracting process is moving online. Online offers for millions of goods and services populate large and small Web sites. The vast amount of data collected from online shoppers has pushed *customer relationship management* (CRM) to the forefront. CRM is a marketing strategy that allows companies to acquire information about customers' wants, needs, and behaviors. They can then use that information to build customer relationships and loyalty. The focus of CRM is understanding customers as individuals rather than simply as a group of consumers. As Exhibit 9–4 shows, CRM is a closed system that uses feedback from customers to build relationships.

(Continued)

• *Exhibit* 9–4 **A Customer Relationship Management Cycle**

- Understand interactions with current customers.
- Create a customer database with customer-buying habits.
- Use information technology to store all customer data.
- Identify customer wants and needs.
- Determine how to leverage customer information.

Two Examples—Netflix and Amazon

If you use Netflix.com, you choose DVDs based on your individual preferences. Netflix asks you to rate movies you have rented on a scale of one to five. Using a computer algorithm, Netflix then creates an individualized rating system that predicts how you will rate thousands of different movies. By applying your individual rating system to movies you have not seen, Netflix is able to suggest movies that you might like. Amazon.com uses similar technology to recommend books and music that you might wish to buy. Amazon sends out numerous "personalized" e-mails with suggestions based on its customers' individualized-buying habits. For both Netflix and Amazon, CRM allows for a focused marketing effort, rather than the typical shotgun approach used by spam advertising on the Internet.

CRM in Online versus Traditional Companies

For online companies, all customer information has some value because the cost of obtaining it, analyzing it, and utilizing it is so small. In contrast, for traditional companies obtaining data to be used for CRM requires a different process that is much more costly. An automobile company, for example, obtains customer information from a variety of sources, including customer surveys and online inquiries. Integrating, storing, and managing such information makes CRM much more expensive for traditional companies than for online companies.

FOR CRITICAL ANALYSIS

Online companies not only target individual customers, but they also utilize each customer's buying habits to create generalized marketing campaigns. Might any privacy issues arise as an online company creates a database to be used for generalized marketing campaigns? Explain.

 Key Terms

Chapter Summary: Formation of Traditional and E-Contracts

An Overview of Contract Law (See pages 236–238.)	1. *Sources of contract law*–The common law governs all contracts except when it has been modified or replaced by statutory law, such as the Uniform Commercial Code (UCC), or by administrative agency regulations. The UCC governs contracts for the sale or lease of goods (see Chapter 11). 2. *The definition of a contract*–A contract is an agreement that can be enforced in court. It is formed by two or more competent parties who agree to perform or to refrain from performing some act now or in the future. 3. *Objective theory of contracts*–In contract law, intent is determined by objective facts, not by the personal or subjective intent, or belief, of a party. 4. *Requirements of a valid contract*–The four requirements of a valid contract are agreement, consideration, capacity, and legality. 5. *Defenses to the enforceability of a contract*–Even if the four requirements of a valid contract are met, a contract may be unenforceable if it lacks voluntary consent or is not in the required form.
Types of Contracts (See pages 238–243.)	1. *Bilateral*–A promise for a promise. 2. *Unilateral*–A promise for an act (acceptance is the completed–or substantial–performance of the contract by the offeree). 3. *Formal*–Requires a special form for contract formation. 4. *Informal*–Requires no special form for contract formation. 5. *Express*–Formed by words (oral, written, or a combination). 6. *Implied*–Formed at least in part by the conduct of the parties. 7. *Executed*–A fully performed contract. 8. *Executory*–A contract not yet fully performed. 9. *Valid*–A contract that results when the elements necessary for contract formation exist, including an agreement (an offer and an acceptance), consideration, parties with capacity, and a legal purpose. 10. *Voidable*–A contract that may be legally avoided (canceled) at the option of one or both of the parties. 11. *Unenforceable*–A valid contract rendered unenforceable by some statute or legal defense. 12. *Void*–A contract that has no legal force or binding effect.
Agreement– Requirements of the Offer (See pages 243–246.)	1. *Intent*–There must be a serious, objective intention by the offeror to become bound by the offer. Nonoffer situations include (a) expressions of opinion; (b) statements of intention; (c) preliminary negotiations; (d) generally, advertisements, catalogues, price lists, and circulars; and (e) traditionally, agreements to agree in the future. 2. *Definiteness*–The terms of the offer must be sufficiently definite to be ascertainable by the parties or by a court. 3. *Communication*–The offer must be communicated to the offeree.
Agreement– Termination of the Offer (See pages 246–248.)	1. *By action of the parties*–An offer can be revoked or withdrawn at any time before acceptance without liability. A counteroffer is a rejection of the original offer and the making of a new offer. 2. *By operation of law*–An offer can terminate by (a) lapse of time, (b) destruction of the subject matter, (c) death or incompetence of the parties, or (d) supervening illegality.
Acceptance (See pages 248–251.)	1. Can be made only by the offeree or the offeree's agent. 2. Must be unequivocal. Under the common law (mirror image rule), if new terms or conditions are added to the acceptance, it will be considered a counteroffer. 3. Acceptance of a unilateral offer is effective on full performance of the requested act. Generally, no communication is necessary. 4. Acceptance of a bilateral offer can be communicated by the offeree by any authorized mode of communication and is effective on dispatch. If the offeror does not specify the mode of communication, acceptance can be made by any reasonable means. Usually, the same means used by the offeror or a faster means can be used.

Chapter Summary: Formation of Traditional and E-Contracts, Continued

E-Contracts– **Online Offers** (See pages 252–253.)	The terms of contract offers presented via the Internet should be as inclusive as the terms in an offer made in a written (paper) document. The offer should be displayed in an easily readable format and should include some mechanism, such as an "I agree" or "I accept" box, by which the customer can accept the offer. Because jurisdictional issues frequently arise with online transactions, the offer should include dispute-settlement provisions and a forum-selection clause.
E-Contracts– **Online Acceptances** (See pages 253–254.)	1. *Click-on agreement*—An agreement created when a buyer, completing a transaction on a computer, is required to indicate her or his assent to be bound by the terms of an offer by clicking on a box that says, for example, "I agree." The courts have enforced click-on agreements, holding that by clicking on "I agree," the offeree has indicated acceptance by conduct. 2. *Shrink-wrap agreement*—An agreement whose terms are expressed inside a box in which the goods are packaged. The party who opens the box is informed that, by keeping the goods that are in the box, he or she agrees to the terms of the shrink-wrap agreement. The courts have often enforced shrink-wrap agreements, even if the purchaser-user of the goods did not read the terms of the agreement. A court may deem a shrink-wrap agreement unenforceable, however, if the buyer learns of the shrink-wrap terms after the parties entered into the agreement.
E-Contracts– **E-Signatures** (See pages 254–256.)	An e-signature is "an electronic sound, symbol, or process attached to or logically associated with a record and executed or adopted by a person with the intent to sign the record." 1. *E-signature technologies*—The two main categories are digitized handwritten signatures and digital signatures based on a public-key infrastructure. 2. *Federal law on e-signatures and e-documents*—The Electronic Signatures in Global and National Commerce Act (E-SIGN Act) of 2000 gave validity to e-signatures by providing that no contract, record, or signature may be "denied legal effect" solely because it is in an electronic form. 3. *Partnering agreements*—To reduce the likelihood that disputes will arise under their e-contracts, parties who frequently do business with each other online may form a partnering agreement, setting out the terms and conditions that will apply to all their subsequent electronic transactions.
The Uniform Electronic Transactions Act (UETA) (See pages 256–258.)	This uniform act has been adopted, at least in part, by most states, to create rules to support the enforcement of e-contracts. The UETA provides for the validity of e-signatures and may ultimately create more uniformity among the states in this respect. Under the UETA, contracts entered into online, as well as other documents, are presumed to be valid. The UETA does not apply to certain transactions governed by the UCC or to wills or testamentary trusts.

Consideration
(See pages 258–261.)
	Sufficient consideration is the second requirement for the formation of a valid contract. Consideration is the value given in exchange for a promise.
	1. *Elements of consideration*—Consideration is often broken down into two parts:
	  a. Something of *legally sufficient value* must be given in exchange for the promise. This may consist of a promise, an act, or a forbearance.
	  b. There must be a *bargained-for exchange*.
	2. *Adequacy of consideration*—Adequacy of consideration relates to how much consideration is given and whether a fair bargain was reached. Courts will inquire into the adequacy of consideration (whether the consideration is legally sufficient) only when fraud, undue influence, or duress may be involved or a bargained-for exchange may be lacking.
	3. *Agreements that lack consideration*—Consideration is lacking in the following situations:
	  a. *Preexisting duty*—Consideration is not legally sufficient if a party by law or by contract already has a preexisting duty to perform the action being offered as consideration for a new contract.
	  b. *Past consideration*—Actions or events that have already taken place do not constitute legally sufficient consideration.
	4. *Promissory estoppel*—In some situations, when injustice can be avoided only by enforcing a promise that would otherwise be unenforceable, the doctrine of promissory estoppel may allow a contract to be enforced.

(Continued)

Chapter Summary: Formation of Traditional and E-Contracts, Continued

Contractual Capacity (See pages 261–262.)	Capacity is the third requirement necessary to form a valid contract. 1. *Minors*—A minor is a person who has not yet reached the age of majority. In virtually all states, the age of majority is eighteen for contract purposes. Contracts with minors are voidable at the option of the minor. 2. *Intoxication*—A contract with an intoxicated person is enforceable if, despite being intoxicated, the person understood the legal consequences of entering into the contract. A contract entered into by an intoxicated person is voidable at the option of the intoxicated person if the person was sufficiently intoxicated to lack mental capacity, even if the intoxication was voluntary. 3. *Mental incompetence*—A contract made by a person whom a court has previously determined to be mentally incompetent is void. Only a guardian can enter into a contract on behalf of an incompetent person.

Legality (See pages 263–266.)	Legality is the fourth requirement for a valid contract to exist.
	 1. *Contracts contrary to statute*—For a contract to be valid and enforceable, it must be formed for a legal purpose. A contract to do something that is prohibited by federal or state statutory law is illegal and, as such, void from the outset and thus unenforceable. Contracts contrary to statute include contracts to commit crimes as well as contracts that violate other laws, such as state laws setting the maximum interest rate that can be charged by a lender. They also include gambling contracts and some contracts with unlicensed professionals.
	 2. *Contracts contrary to public policy*—Contracts that are contrary to public policy are also not enforceable on the grounds of illegality.
	    a. Contracts to reduce or restrain free competition are illegal and prohibited by statutes. An exception is a *covenant not to compete,* which is enforceable if the terms are secondary to a contract (such as a contract for the sale of a business or an employment contract) and are reasonable as to time and area of restraint.
	    b. When a contract or contract clause is so unfair that it is oppressive to one party, it may be deemed unconscionable. As such, it is illegal and cannot be enforced.
	    c. An exculpatory clause is a clause that releases a party from liability in the event of monetary or physical injury, no matter who is at fault. In certain situations, exculpatory clauses may be contrary to public policy and thus unenforceable.

 ExamPrep

ISSUE SPOTTERS

1. Joe advertises in the *New York Times* that he will pay $5,000 to anyone giving him information as to the whereabouts of Elaine. Max sees a copy of the ad in a Tokyo newspaper, in Japanese, and sends Joe the requested information. Does Max get the reward? Why or why not?
2. Applied Products, Inc., does business with Beltway Distributors, Inc., online. Under the Uniform Electronic Transactions Act, what determines the effect of the electronic documents evidencing the parties' deal? Is a party's "signature" necessary? Explain.

—**Check your answers to these questions against the answers provided in Appendix G.**

BEFORE THE TEST

Go to **www.cengagebrain.com**, enter the ISBN number "9781111530617," and click on "Find" to locate this textbook's Web site. Then, click on "Access Now" under "Study Tools," and select "Chapter 9" at the top. There you will find an "Interactive Quiz" that you can take to assess your mastery of the concepts in this chapter, as well as "Flashcards" and a "Glossary" of important terms.

For Review

1. What are the four basic requirements for the formation of a valid contract?
2. What elements are necessary for an effective acceptance?
3. What is the Uniform Electronic Transactions Act? What are some of the major provisions of this act?
4. What is consideration?
5. What is a covenant not to compete? When will such a covenant be enforceable?

Questions and Case Problems

9–1. Agreement. Ball writes to Sullivan and inquires how much Sullivan is asking for a specific forty-acre tract of land Sullivan owns. Sullivan replies to Ball with a letter stating, "I will not take less than $60,000 for the forty-acre tract as specified." Ball immediately sends Sullivan a fax stating, "I accept your offer for $60,000 for the forty-acre tract as specified." Discuss whether Ball can hold Sullivan to a contract for sale of the land.

9–2. Online Acceptance. Anne is a reporter for the *Daily Business Journal,* a print publication consulted by investors and other businesspersons. She often uses the Internet to perform research for the articles that she writes for the publication. While visiting the Web site of Cyberspace Investments Corp., Anne reads a pop-up window that states, "Our business newsletter, *E-Commerce Weekly,* is available at a one-year subscription rate of $5 per issue. To subscribe, enter your e-mail address below and click 'SUBSCRIBE.' By subscribing, you agree to the terms of the subscriber's agreement. To read this agreement, click 'AGREEMENT.'" Anne enters her e-mail address, but does not click on "AGREEMENT" to read the terms. Has Anne entered into an enforceable contract to pay for *E-Commerce Weekly?* Explain.

9–3. Offer and Acceptance. Carrie offered to sell a set of legal encyclopedias to Antonio for $300. Antonio said that he would think about her offer and let her know his decision the next day. Norvel, who had overheard the conversation between Carrie and Antonio, said to Carrie, "I accept your offer" and gave her $300. Carrie gave Norvel the books. The next day, Antonio, who had no idea that Carrie had already sold the books to Norvel, told Carrie that he accepted her offer. Has Carrie breached a valid contract with Antonio? Explain.

9–4. Offer and Acceptance. In 1996, Troy Blackford was gambling at Prairie Meadows Casino when he destroyed a slot machine. After pleading guilty to criminal mischief, Blackford was banned from the casino. In 1998, Blackford was found in the casino, escorted out, and charged with trespass. In 2006, he gambled at the casino again and won $9,387. When Blackford went to collect his winnings, casino employees learned who he was and refused to pay. He sued for breach of contract, contending that he and the casino had an enforceable contract because he had accepted its offer to gamble. The casino argued that it had not made an offer and in fact had banned Blackford from the premises. The trial court held in favor of the casino. The appellate court reversed and ordered a new trial. The casino appealed to the Iowa high court for review. Did the casino make a valid offer to Blackford to gamble and thus create an enforceable contract between them? Explain your answer. [*Blackford v. Prairie Meadows Racetrack and Casino,* 778 N.W.2d 184 (Sup.Ct. Iowa 2010)]

9–5. Types of Contracts. Kim Panenka asked to borrow $4,750 from her sister, Kris, so that Kim could make her mortgage payment. Kris deposited a check for that amount into Kim's bank account. Hours later, Kim asked to borrow another $1,100. Kris took a cash advance on her credit card and deposited this amount into Kim's account. About a week later, Kim asked Kris for $845.40 to pay a dental bill. Kris paid the bill by credit card. After Kris asked for repayment several times and did not receive payment, she filed a suit against her sister in a Wisconsin state court. At the trial, Kim admitted that she had asked for the various amounts and that the funds had not been a gift, but she testified that the sisters had a long history of paying for things for each other without expecting repayment. Kris countered that she had "loaned" Kim these amounts. Can the court impose a contract between the sisters? Explain. [*Panenka v. Panenka,* 331 Wis.2d 731, 795 N.W.2d 493 (2011)]

9–6. Acceptance. In August, Kathy Wright entered into a written agreement with a real estate agent, Jennifer Crilow, to sell certain real estate in Ohio. The agreement ran until February 28. A "protection period" provision in the agreement stated that if the property sold within six months after the agreement expired to a party who had been shown the property during the term of the agreement, Crilow would be paid a commission. In January, Crilow switched agencies and asked Wright to sign a new contract. They orally agreed on the terms, which included an expiration date of April 30. Crilow sent Wright a written copy of the agreement. Wright crossed out the protection period provision and signed and returned the copy. Crilow filed it without reviewing it. Before April 30, Crilow showed Wright's property to Michael Ballway. Less than six months later—after the agreement had expired but within the protection period—Ballway bought the property. Crilow filed a suit against Wright in an Ohio state court seeking a commission on the sale. Did the parties' contract include the protection period provision? Does Wright owe Crilow a commission? Explain. [*Crilow v. Wright,* __ Ohio App.3d __, __ N.E.2d __ (5 Dist. 2011)]

9–7. Case Problem with Sample Answer. Licensing Statutes. PEMS Co. International, Inc., agreed to find a buyer for Rupp Industries, Inc. A commission of 2 percent of the purchase price was to be paid by the buyer. PEMS analyzed Rupp's operational and financial conditions, paid legal fees, carefully managed Rupp's confidential data, and screened more than a dozen potential buyers. Using PEMS's services, an investment group that became Rupp Industries Acquisition, Inc. (RIA), acquired key information about Rupp and bought the company for $20 million. RIA changed Rupp's name to Temp-Air, Inc. No one paid PEMS's commission. PEMS filed a suit in a Minnesota state court against Temp-Air, alleging breach of contract. Temp-Air responded that PEMS had been acting as a broker in the transaction without having obtained a broker's license. Thus, because state law required a broker to have a license, PEMS was barred from maintaining this suit. PEMS argued that it had acted not as a broker but as a "finder." The applicable statute defines a broker as any person who deals with the sale of a business. What determines whether a contract with an unlicensed person is enforceable? Assuming that the statute in this case was intended to protect the public, can PEMS collect its commission? Explain. [*PEMS Co. International, Inc. v. Temp-Air, Inc.,* __ N.W.2d __ (Minn.App. 2011)]

—To view a sample answer for Case Problem 9–7, go to Appendix F at the end of this text.

9–8. Consideration. In March 1997, Leonard Kranzler loaned Lewis Saltzman $100,000. Saltzman signed a written memo that stated, "Loaned to Lewis Saltzman $100,000 to be paid back with interest." Saltzman made fifteen payments on the loan, but these payments did not cover the entire amount. The last payment was made in July 2005. In June 2007—more than ten years after the date of the loan but less than two years after the date of the last payment—Kranzler filed a suit in an Illinois state court against Saltzman, seeking to recover the outstanding principal and interest. Saltzman admitted that he had borrowed the funds and had made payments on the loan, but he claimed that Kranzler's complaint was barred by a ten-year statute of limitations. Does Kranzler need to prove a new promise with new consideration to collect the unpaid debt? Explain. [*Kranzler v. Saltzman,* 347 Ill.Dec. 519, 942 N.E.2d 722 (1 Dist. 2011)]

9–9. A Question of Ethics. Promissory Estoppel. Claudia Aceves obtained a loan of $845,000 to buy a home in Los Angeles, California. Less than two years into the loan, Aceves could no longer afford the monthly payments. U.S. Bank, which held her mortgage, declared her in default and notified her that it planned to foreclose on her home. (Foreclosure is a process that allows a lender to repossess and sell the property that secures a loan.) Aceves filed for bankruptcy. Filing a petition in bankruptcy automatically stays, or suspends, any action by a mortgagee (lender) against the debtor. Aceves hoped to set up a new, affordable schedule of payments. On learning of the filing, U.S. Bank offered to modify Aceves's mortgage if she would forgo bankruptcy. In reliance on that promise, she allowed the bankruptcy court to lift the automatic stay. Once the stay was lifted, the bank did not work with Aceves to modify her loan. Instead, it foreclosed on her home and initiated eviction proceedings. She filed a lawsuit in a California state court against the bank, alleging a cause of action for promissory estoppel. [*Aceves v. U.S. Bank, N.A.,* 192 Cal.App.4th 218, 120 Cal.Rptr.3d 507 (2 Dist. 2011)]

1. Is Aceves likely to succeed in her claim of promissory estoppel? Why or why not? How does this theory relate to the ethical principles discussed in Chapter 2?

2. Did either the borrower or the lender—or both—behave unethically in the circumstances of this case? Explain.

9–10. Video Question. *Jack's Restaurant, Scene 2.* Access the video using the instructions provided below to answer the following questions.

1. In regard to the sale of Jack's Restaurant, Jack (the seller) said that he was going to retain the rights to the restaurant's frozen food line. The buyers, however, thought that their sales agreement included the rights to all of the restaurant's signature dishes—whether fresh or frozen. Did the parties have an "agreement to agree" on the terms of the sale of the restaurant? Why or why not?

2. Suppose that Jack had previously offered to sell the restaurant to these particular buyers and they had all agreed on the price and date for delivery. Would such an offer meet the definiteness requirement, even if no terms pertained to the frozen food line? Explain.

—To watch this video, go to www.cengagebrain.com and register the access code that came with your new book or log in to your existing account. Select the link for either the "Business Law Digital Video Library Online Access" or "Business Law CourseMate," and then click on "Complete Video List" to find the video for this chapter (Video 77).

Chapter 10

Contract Performance, Breach, and Remedies

> "Men keep their engagements when it is to the advantage of both not to break them."
>
> —Solon, Sixth century B.C.E.
> (Athenian legal reformer)

Chapter Objectives

After reading this chapter, you should be able to answer the following questions:

1. In what types of situations might voluntary consent to a contract's terms be lacking?
2. What are the elements of fraudulent misrepresentation?
3. What is substantial performance?
4. What is the standard measure of compensatory damages when a contract is breached?
5. What equitable remedies can a court grant, and in what circumstances will a court consider granting them?

(Quaziefoto/Creative Commons)

As pointed out in the chapter-opening quotation above, a contract will not be broken so long as "it is to the advantage of both" parties not to break it. In a perfect world, every party who signed a contract would perform his or her duties completely and in a timely fashion, thereby discharging (terminating) the contract. In the real world, however, things frequently become complicated. Certainly, events often occur that may affect our performance or our ability to perform contractual duties. Just as rules are necessary to determine when a legally enforceable contract exists, so also are they required to determine when one of the parties can justifiably say, "I have fully performed, so I am now discharged from my obligations under this contract."

Additionally, the parties to a contract need to know what remedies are available to them if one party decides that he or she does not want to, or cannot, perform as promised. A *remedy* is the relief provided for an innocent party when the other party has breached the contract. It is the means employed to enforce a right or to redress an injury. The most common remedies available to a nonbreaching party include damages, rescission and restitution, specific performance, and reformation, all of which will be examined later in this chapter.

Voluntary Consent

Two parties, each with full legal capacity and for a legal purpose, have entered into a contract that is supported by consideration. The contract thus meets the four requirements for a valid contract that were specified in Chapter 9. Nonetheless, the contract may be unenforceable if the parties have not voluntarily consented to its terms.

Lack of **voluntary consent** (assent) can be used as a defense to the contract's enforceability. Voluntary consent may be lacking because of a mistake, fraudulent misrepresentation, undue influence, or duress—in other words, because there is no true "meeting of the minds." In this section, we examine problems relating to voluntary consent.

Voluntary Consent The knowing and voluntary agreement to the terms of a contract. If a contract is formed as a result of a mistake, misrepresentation, undue influence, or duress, voluntary consent is lacking, and the contract will be voidable.

Mistakes

We all make mistakes, so it is not surprising that mistakes are made when contracts are formed. It is important to distinguish between *mistakes of fact* and *mistakes of value or quality*. Only a mistake of fact may allow a contract to be avoided.

If a mistake concerns the future market value or quality of the object of the contract, the mistake is one of value, and either party can normally enforce the contract. **EXAMPLE 10.1** Chi buys a violin from Bev for $250. Although the violin is very old, neither party believes that it is extremely valuable. Later, however, an antiques dealer informs the parties that the violin is rare and worth thousands of dollars. Although both parties were mistaken, the mistake is not a mistake of fact that warrants contract rescission. ●

Mistakes of fact occur in two forms—bilateral and unilateral. A **bilateral mistake** is made by both of the contracting parties. A **unilateral mistake** is made by only one of the parties. We look next at these two types of mistakes and illustrate them graphically in Exhibit 10–1 below.

Bilateral Mistake A mistake that occurs when both parties to a contract are mistaken about the same material fact.

Unilateral Mistake A mistake that occurs when one party to a contract is mistaken as to a material fact.

BILATERAL (MUTUAL) MISTAKES   A bilateral, or mutual, mistake occurs when both parties are mistaken as to some *material fact*—that is, a fact important to the subject matter of the contract. When a bilateral mistake occurs, the contract can be rescinded, or canceled, by either party. **CASE EXAMPLE 10.2** Steven Simkin married Laura Blank in 1973. When the couple divorced in 2006, they agreed to split their assets equally. At the time of the agreement, both parties believed that they owned

● *Exhibit* **10–1 Mistakes of Fact**

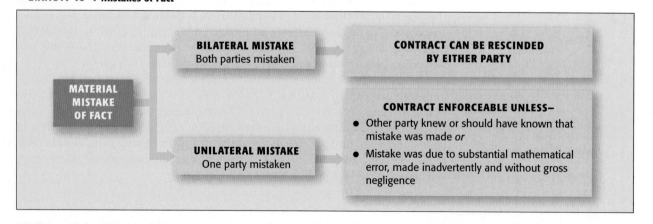

an account with Bernard L. Madoff Investment Securities worth $5.4 million. Simkin kept the account in the divorce agreement, paying more than $6.5 million to Blank (including $2.7 million to offset the funds in the Madoff account). It was later discovered that there were no funds in the Madoff account because of a Ponzi scheme (see page 31). Simkin filed a lawsuit seeking rescission of the divorce agreement due to mutual mistake. Blank filed a motion to dismiss, which the lower court granted. Simkin appealed. A New York appellate court reversed, concluding that Simkin had stated a claim for a bilateral mistake. Because both parties had been mistaken concerning a material fact—that the Madoff account was their largest asset—the divorce settlement could possibly be rescinded (depending on the outcome after a full trial).[1] •

A word or term in a contract may be subject to more than one reasonable interpretation. In that situation, if the parties to the contract attach materially different meanings to the term, their mutual mistake of fact may allow the contract to be rescinded.

CASE EXAMPLE 10.3 In 1864, Wichelhaus agreed to buy a shipment of Surat cotton from Raffles, "to arrive 'Peerless' from Bombay." There were two ships named *Peerless* sailing from Bombay, India, however. Wichelhaus was referring to the *Peerless* that sailed in October, but Raffles meant a different *Peerless* that sailed in December. When Raffles tried to deliver the goods in December, Wichelhaus refused to accept them, and a lawsuit followed. The court held in favor of Wichelhaus, concluding that a mutual mistake had been made because the parties had attached materially different meanings to an essential term of the contract—that is, which ship *Peerless* was to transport the goods.[2] •

In the following case, the court had to grapple with the question of whether a mutual mistake of fact had occurred.

---

1. *Simkin v. Blank,* 80 A.D.3d 401, 915 N.Y.S.2d 47 (N.Y.A.D. 1 Dept. 2011).
2. *Raffles v. Wichelhaus,* 159 Eng.Rep. 375 (1864).

Case 10.1 **L&H Construction Co. v. Circle Redmont, Inc.**

District Court of Appeal of Florida, Fifth District, 55 So.3d 630 (2011).
www.5dca.org/opinions.shtml[a]

BACKGROUND AND FACTS L&H Construction Company was a general contractor involved in the renovation of the Thomas Edison historic site in West Orange, New Jersey, for the National Park Service. L&H contracted with Circle Redmont, Inc., which is based in Melbourne, Florida, to make a cast-iron staircase and a glass flooring system. Redmont originally proposed to "engineer, fabricate, and install" the staircase and flooring system. During negotiations, however, installation and its costs were cut from the deal. The final agreement stated that payment was due on "Supervision of Installation" instead of "Completion of Installation." Nevertheless, the final agreement also stated that Redmont would "engineer, fabricate, and install." Later, Redmont claimed that this was a mistake. L&H

insisted that installation was included. L&H filed a suit in a Florida state court against Redmont. The court found that the word *install* in the phrase "engineer, fabricate, and install" was the result of a mutual mistake. L&H appealed.

IN THE WORDS OF THE COURT . . .
PER CURIAM. [By the Whole Court]
* * * *

A mistake is mutual when the parties agree to one thing and then, due to either a scrivener's error [an error made by the person copying the document] or inadvertence [carelessness], express something different in the written instrument. * * * [Emphasis added.]

Clearly, the final contract between L&H and Redmont was ambiguous. While the final * * * proposal stated that Redmont was

---

a. In the "Search Opinions" section, in the "Search for this:" box, type "Redmont" and click on "Submit." In the result, click on the appropriate link to view the opinion. The Florida Fifth District Court of Appeal maintains this Web site.

Case 10.1—Continues next page ⇨

Case 10.1–Continued

to "engineer, fabricate and install" the staircase and flooring system, [the agreement also] states that the final $40,000 progress payment was "Due upon Supervision of Installation." The trial court allowed the parties to present some parol evidence to establish the parties' true intent and subsequently found the contract contained a mutual mistake as to whether Redmont was to install, or merely supervise, the installation of the product. This was an issue that could have been decided for or against either party and we cannot say the trial court's findings of fact were unsupported by competent, substantial evidence. Although the face of the contract clearly reflected a duty to install, Redmont's witnesses' testimony supported the trial court's finding that it was the express understanding between Redmont and L&H that Redmont would only supervise, and not provide complete installation of the staircase and flooring system.

Redmont's witnesses testified that L&H knew that installation was being deleted as a means of saving money for L&H. Redmont's installation supervisor testified that the final * * * proposal was specifically worked up to schedule the progress payments toward the end of the job pursuant to L&H's president's request, and that L&H had decided that it wanted only installation supervision, and the contract price reflected installation supervision, not complete installation. Redmont's [chief financial officer] further testified that L&H was aware that Redmont was not going to install the product "because L&H's president had asked us to take the installation out to save money."

Moreover, Redmont's president testified that he spoke directly with L&H's president regarding Redmont's supervision of installation and it was decided that Redmont would only provide installation supervision. * * * Redmont's president also reiterated [repeated] that he had direct conversations with L&H's president where he said, "Fred, how can we save me some money here and what can we do?" The weight to be given to the testimony turned on the witnesses' credibility, a matter exclusively within the trial court's province.

DECISION AND REMEDY   A state intermediate appellate court upheld the lower court's ruling that the use of the word *install* in the parties' agreement was a mutual mistake. The appellate court reversed the lower court's final judgment in Redmont's favor on other grounds, however.

WHAT IF THE FACTS WERE DIFFERENT?   *Suppose that Redmont had intentionally misled L&H to believe that installation was included in the price. Would the court's decision on the mutual mistake issue have been different? Discuss.*

THE ECONOMIC DIMENSION   *The parties performed as agreed, with Redmont working on schedule and L&H making timely payments, until the issue of installation arose. Assuming that no further disputes arose, what might be the appropriate remedy?*

UNILATERAL MISTAKES   A unilateral mistake occurs when only one of the contracting parties makes a mistake as to some material fact. The general rule is that a unilateral mistake does not afford the party making the mistake any right to relief from the contract. **EXAMPLE 10.4** DeVinck intends to sell her motor home for $32,500. When she learns that Benson is interested in buying a used motor home, she prepares an e-mail offering to sell the vehicle to him. When writing the e-mail, however, DeVinck mistakenly keys in the price of $23,500. After receiving the offer, Benson immediately sends DeVinck an e-mail accepting the offer. Even though DeVinck intended to sell her motor home for $32,500, her unilateral mistake falls on her. She is bound in contract to sell the motor home to Benson for $23,500. ●

There are at least two exceptions to this general rule. First, if the *other* party to the contract knows or should have known that a mistake of fact was made, the contract may not be enforceable. **EXAMPLE 10.5** In Example 10.4 above, if Benson knew that DeVinck intended to sell her motor home for $32,500, then DeVinck's unilateral mistake (stating $23,500 in her offer) may render the resulting contract unenforceable. ● The second exception arises when a unilateral mistake of fact was due to a mathematical mistake in addition, subtraction, division, or multiplication and was made inadvertently and without gross (extreme) negligence. If a contractor's bid was significantly low because he or she made a mistake in addition when totaling the estimated costs, any contract resulting from the bid may be rescinded, or canceled. Of course, in both situations, the mistake must still involve some material fact.

Fraudulent Misrepresentation

In the context of contract law, fraud affects the genuineness of the innocent party's consent to the contract. Thus, the transaction is not voluntary in that it does not involve mutual assent. When an innocent party is fraudulently induced to enter into a contract, the contract usually can be avoided because that party has not voluntarily consented to its terms. Normally, the innocent party can either rescind the contract and be restored to his or her original position or enforce the contract and seek damages for any injuries resulting from the fraud.

Generally, fraudulent misrepresentation refers only to misrepresentation that is consciously false and is intended to mislead another. The perpetrator of the fraudulent misrepresentation knows or believes that the assertion is false or knows that she or he does not have a basis (stated or implied) for the assertion. Typically, fraudulent misrepresentation consists of the following elements:

Scienter Knowledge on the part of the misrepresenting party that material facts have been falsely represented or omitted with an intent to deceive.

1. A misrepresentation of a material fact.
2. An intent to deceive, called *scienter*.[3]
3. The justifiable reliance of the innocent party on the misrepresentation.

To collect damages, a party must have been harmed as a result of the misrepresentation. Fraudulent misrepresentation can also occur in the online environment. For a case involving allegations that Yahoo fraudulently posted online personal ads, see this chapter's *Online Developments* feature on the next page. Because curbing Internet fraud is a major challenge in today's world, we will explore the topic further in Chapter 20, in the context of consumer law.

HOW MISREPRESENTATION CAN OCCUR Misrepresentation can occur by words or actions, but it must concern a material fact. **EXAMPLE 10.6** The statement "This sculpture was created by Michelangelo" is a misrepresentation of fact if another artist sculpted the statue. • Misrepresentation also arises when a party takes specific action to conceal a fact that is material to the contract. Therefore, if a seller, by her or his actions, prevents a buyer from learning of some fact that is material to the contract, such behavior constitutes misrepresentation by conduct.

CASE EXAMPLE 10.7 Actor Tom Selleck contracted to purchase a horse named Zorro for his daughter from Dolores Cuenca. Cuenca acted as though Zorro was fit to ride in competitions, when in reality the horse suffered from a medical condition. Selleck filed a lawsuit against Cuenca for wrongfully concealing the horse's condition, and a jury awarded Selleck more than $187,000 for Cuenca's misrepresentation by conduct.[4] •

A woman browses through some online personal ads. Individuals who post their profiles on an Internet dating site may exaggerate their attractive traits and may even make statements about themselves that they know to be false. But what happens when Yahoo or Google makes fraudulent misrepresentations about its dating-services users?

(Bill Stryker)

RELIANCE ON THE MISREPRESENTATION To constitute fraud, the deceived party must have a justifiable reason for relying on the misrepresentation, and the misrepresentation must be an important factor in inducing the party to enter into the contract. Reliance is not justified if the innocent party knows the true facts or relies on obviously extravagant statements. **EXAMPLE 10.8** If a used-car dealer tells you, "This old Cadillac will get over sixty miles to the gallon," you normally would not be justified in relying on this statement. Suppose, however, that Merkel, a bank director, induces O'Connell, a codirector, to sign a statement that

---

3. Pronounced sy-*en*-ter.
4. *Selleck v. Cuenca*, Case No. GIN056909, North County of San Diego, California, decided September 9, 2009.

Online Developments

Online Personals—Fraud and Misrepresentation Issues

Keying the words *online personals* into the Google search engine will return more than 35 million hits, including Match.com, Chanceforlove.com, Widowsorwidowers.com, Makefriendsonline.com, and Yahoo! Personals. Yahoo! Personals, which calls itself the "top online dating site," offers two options. One, aimed at people looking for casual dates, allows users to create their own profiles, browse member profiles, and exchange e-mail or instant messages. The second option, called Yahoo! Personals Primer, is for people who want serious relationships. Users must take a relationship test. Then they can use Yahoo's computerized matching system to "zero in on marriage material." With this service, users can chat on the phone as well as exchange e-mail.

The Thorny Problem of Misrepresentation

When singles (and others) create their profiles for online dating services, they tend to exaggerate their more appealing features and downplay or omit their less attractive attributes. All users of such services are aware that the profiles may not correspond exactly with reality, but they do assume that the profiles are not complete misrepresentations. In 2006, nonetheless, Robert Anthony, individually and on behalf of others, brought a suit against Yahoo in federal district court, alleging fraud and negligent misrepresentation, among other things.

In his complaint, Anthony claimed that Yahoo was not just posting fictitious or exaggerated profiles submitted by users but was deliberately and intentionally originating, creating, and perpetuating false and/or nonexistent profiles. According to Anthony, many profiles used the exact same phrases "with such unique diction and vernacular [language] that such a random occurrence would not be possible." Anthony also argued that some photo images had multiple identities—that is, the same photo appeared in several different profiles. He also alleged that Yahoo continued to circulate profiles of "actual, legitimate former subscribers whose subscriptions had expired." Finally, Anthony claimed that when a subscription neared its end date, Yahoo would send the subscriber a fake profile, heralding it as a "potential 'new match.' "

Did Yahoo Have Immunity?

Yahoo asked the court to dismiss the complaint on the grounds that the lawsuit was barred by the Communications Decency Act (CDA) of 1996.[a] As discussed in Chapter 4, the CDA shields Internet service providers from liability for any information submitted by another information content provider. In other words, an interactive computer service cannot be held liable under state law as a publisher of information that originates from a third party information content provider. The CDA defines an information content provider as "any person or entity that is responsible, in whole or in part, for the creation or development of information provided through the Internet or any other interactive computer service."[b]

The court rejected Yahoo's claim that it had immunity under the CDA and held that Yahoo had become an information content provider itself when it created bogus user profiles. The court observed that there is no case precedent for immunizing a defendant from liability if *it* creates tortious content. Thus, the court denied Yahoo's motion to dismiss and allowed Anthony's claims of fraud and negligent misrepresentation to proceed to trial.[c]

FOR CRITICAL ANALYSIS

Assume that Anthony had contacted various users of Yahoo's online dating service only to discover that each user's profile exaggerated the user's physical appearance, intelligence, and occupation. Would Anthony prevail if he brought a lawsuit for fraudulent misrepresentation against Yahoo in that situation? Why or why not?

---

a. 47 U.S.C. Section 230.
b. 47 U.S.C. Section 230(f)(3).
c. *Anthony v. Yahoo!, Inc.,* 421 F.Supp.2d 1257 (N.D.Cal. 2006). See also *Doe v. SexSearch.com,* 502 F.Supp.2d 719 (N.D. Ohio 2007); and *Fair Housing Council of San Fernando Valley v. Roommate.com, LLC,* 521 F.3d 1157 (9th Cir. 2008).

---

the bank's assets will satisfy its liabilities by telling O'Connell, "We have plenty of assets to satisfy our creditors." This statement is false. If O'Connell knows the true facts or, as a bank director, should know the true facts, he is not justified in relying on Merkel's statement. If O'Connell does not know the true facts, however, *and has no way of finding them out,* he may be justified in relying on the statement. ●

> **REMEMBER** An opinion is not a contract offer, nor a contract term, nor fraud.

The same rule applies to defects in property sold. If the defects are of the kind that would be obvious on inspection, the buyer cannot justifiably rely on the seller's representations. If the defects are hidden or latent, the buyer is justified in relying on the seller's statements.

Should employers also be held liable for misrepresentations they make to prospective employees? See this chapter's *Insight into Ethics* feature below for a discussion of this issue.

Undue Influence

Undue influence arises from special kinds of relationships in which one party can greatly influence another party, thus overcoming that party's free will. A contract entered into under excessive or undue influence lacks voluntary assent and is therefore voidable.

In various types of relationships, one party may have an opportunity to dominate and unfairly influence another party. Minors and elderly people, for example, are often under the influence of guardians (persons who are legally responsible for others). If a guardian induces a young or elderly ward (the person whom the guardian looks after) to enter into a contract that benefits the guardian, undue influence may have been exerted. Undue influence can arise from a number of confidential or fiduciary relationships: attorney-client, physician-patient, parent-child, husband-wife, or trustee-beneficiary.

The essential feature of undue influence is that the party being taken advantage of does not exercise free will in entering into a contract. It is not enough that a person is elderly or suffers from some mental or physical impairment. There must be clear and convincing evidence that the person did not act of her or his free will.

Duress

Agreement to the terms of a contract is not voluntary if one of the parties is forced into the agreement. The use of threats to force a party to enter into a contract is referred to as *duress*. In addition, blackmail or extortion to induce consent to a

---

Insight into Ethics **How Much Information Must Employers Disclose to Prospective Employees?**

One of the problems employers face is that it is not always clear what information they should disclose to prospective employees. To lure qualified workers, employers are often tempted to "promise the moon" and paint their companies' prospects as bright. Employers must be careful, though, to avoid any conduct that could be interpreted by a court as intentionally deceptive. In particular, they must avoid making any statements about their companies' future prospects or financial health that they know to be false. If they do make a false statement on which a prospective employee relies to her or his detriment, they may be sued for fraudulent misrepresentation.

In one case, for example, an employee accepted a job with a brokerage firm because he relied on assurances that the firm was not about to be sold. In fact, negotiations to sell the firm were under way at the time he was hired. The employee filed a fraud claim against the firm and won, and the trial court awarded him more than $6 million in damages.[a]

In another case, Kevin Helmer filed a fraud lawsuit against Bingham Toyota Isuzu and Bob Clark, his supervisor at the firm. Helmer claimed that Clark fraudulently induced him to leave his job with another Toyota dealership by making false promises about the amount of compensation that he would receive at Bingham Toyota. A jury found in Helmer's favor, awarding him $450,913 in compensatory damages and $1.5 million in punitive damages. (Later, the court reduced the punitive damages award to $675,000.)[b]

FOR CRITICAL ANALYSIS
Insight into the Legal Environment

Why would an employer risk the possibility of a lawsuit by providing a prospective employee with false information?

---

a. *McConkey v. AON Corp.,* 354 N.J.Super. 25, 804 A.2d 572 (A.D. 2002).

b. *Helmer v. Bingham Toyota Isuzu,* 129 Cal.App.4th 1121, 29 Cal.Rptr.3d 136 (2005).

contract constitutes duress. Duress is both a defense to the enforcement of a contract and a ground for the rescission of a contract.

To establish duress, there must be proof of a threat to do something that the threatening party has no right to do. Generally, for duress to occur, the threatened act must be wrongful or illegal and must render the person incapable of exercising free will. A threat to exercise a legal right, such as the right to sue someone, ordinarily does not constitute duress.

▶ The Statute of Frauds—Writing Requirement

Another defense to the enforceability of a contract is *form*—that is, some contracts need to be in writing. Every state has a statute, modeled after an old English act, that stipulates what types of contracts must be in writing. Although the statutes vary slightly from state to state, all states require certain types of contracts to be in writing or evidenced by a written (or electronic) memorandum signed by the party against whom enforcement is sought, unless certain exceptions apply. In this text, we refer to these statutes collectively as the **Statute of Frauds.**

Statute of Frauds A state statute under which certain types of contracts must be in writing to be enforceable.

The actual name of the Statute of Frauds is misleading because it neither applies to fraud nor invalidates any type of contract. Rather, it denies *enforceability* to certain contracts that do not comply with its requirements. (Note that in some states, an oral contract that would otherwise be unenforceable under the Statute of Frauds may be enforced under the doctrine of promissory estoppel.)

The following types of contracts are said to fall "within" or "under" the Statute of Frauds and therefore require a writing:

1. Contracts involving interests in land.
2. Contracts that cannot by their terms be performed within one year from the day after the date of formation.
3. Collateral, or secondary, contracts, such as promises to answer for the debt or duty of another and promises by the administrator or executor of an estate to pay a debt of the estate personally—that is, out of his or her own pocket.
4. Promises made in consideration of marriage.
5. Under the Uniform Commercial Code (UCC—see Chapter 11), contracts for the sale of goods priced at $500 or more.

"The pen is mightier than the sword, and considerably easier to write with."
Marty Feldman, 1934–1982
(English actor and comedian)

A writing can consist of any confirmation, invoice, sales slip, check, fax, or e-mail—or such items in combination. The written contract need not consist of a single document to constitute an enforceable contract. One document may incorporate another document by expressly referring to it. Several documents may form a single contract if they are physically attached—such as by staple, paper clip, or glue—or even if they are only placed in the same envelope. To be legally sufficient, the writing need only contain the essential terms of the contract, not every term. (See the *Linking the Law to Business Communication* feature on page 301.)

▶ Third Party Rights

Once it has been determined that a valid and legally enforceable contract exists, attention can turn to the rights and duties of the parties to the contract. A contract is a private agreement between the parties who have entered into it, and traditionally these parties alone have rights and liabilities under the contract. This principle is referred to as *privity of contract*. A *third party*—one who is not a direct party to a particular contract—normally does not have rights under that contract.

There are exceptions to the rule of privity of contract. One exception allows a party to a contract to transfer the rights or duties arising from the contract to another person through an *assignment* (of rights) or a *delegation* (of duties). Another exception involves a *third party beneficiary contract*—a contract in which the parties to the contract intend that the contract benefit a third party.

Assignments

In a bilateral contract, the two parties have corresponding rights and duties. One party has a *right* to require the other to perform some task, and the other has a *duty* to perform it. The transfer of contractual *rights* to a third party is known as an **assignment.** When rights under a contract are assigned unconditionally, the rights of the *assignor*[5] (the party making the assignment) are extinguished. The third party (the *assignee,*[6] or party receiving the assignment) has a right to demand performance from the other original party to the contract (the *obligor*). The assignee takes only those rights that the assignor originally had.

> **Assignment** The act of transferring to another all or part of one's rights arising under a contract.

As a general rule, all rights can be assigned. Exceptions are made, however, in some circumstances. If a statute expressly prohibits assignment of a particular right, that right cannot be assigned. When a contract is *personal* in nature, the rights under the contract cannot be assigned unless all that remains is a money payment. A right cannot be assigned if assignment will materially increase or alter the risk or duties of the obligor. If a contract stipulates that a right cannot be assigned, then ordinarily the right cannot be assigned.

Although generally a contract can, by its terms, prohibit any assignment of the contract, this rule has several exceptions:

1. A contract cannot prevent an assignment of the right to receive money. This exception exists to encourage the free flow of money and credit in modern business settings.
2. The assignment of rights in real estate often cannot be prohibited because such a prohibition is contrary to public policy. Prohibitions of this kind are called restraints against *alienation* (transfer of land ownership).
3. The assignment of *negotiable instruments* (which include checks and promissory notes) cannot be prohibited.
4. In a contract for the sale of goods, the right to receive damages for breach of contract or for payment of an account owed may be assigned even though the sales contract prohibits such assignment.

Delegations

> **Delegation** The transfer of a contractual duty to a third party. The party delegating the duty (the delegator) to the third party (the delegatee) is still obliged to perform on the contract should the delegatee fail to perform.

Just as a party can transfer rights through an assignment, a party can also transfer duties. The transfer of contractual *duties* to a third party is known as a **delegation.** Normally, a delegation of duties does not relieve the party making the delegation (the *delegator*) of the obligation to perform in the event that the party to whom the duty has been delegated (the *delegatee*) fails to perform. No special form is required to create a

---

5. Pronounced uh-*sye*-nore.
6. Pronounced uh-*sye*-nee.

valid delegation of duties. As long as the delegator expresses an intention to make the delegation, it is effective—the delegator need not even use the word *delegate*.

As a general rule, any duty can be delegated. Delegation is prohibited, however, in the following circumstances:

1. When special trust has been placed in the obligor (the person contractually obligated to perform).
2. When performance depends on the personal skill or talents of the obligor.
3. When performance by a third party will vary materially from that expected by the obligee (the one to whom performance is owed) under the contract.
4. When the contract expressly prohibits delegation.

If a delegation of duties is enforceable, the obligee must accept performance from the delegatee. The obligee can legally refuse performance from the delegatee only if the duty is one that cannot be delegated.

As mentioned, a valid delegation of duties does not relieve the delegator of obligations under the contract. Thus, if the delegatee fails to perform, the delegator is still liable to the obligee.

Third Party Beneficiaries

Third Party Beneficiary One for whose benefit a promise is made in a contract but who is not a party to the contract.

Intended Beneficiary A third party for whose benefit a contract is formed. An intended beneficiary can sue the promisor if such a contract is breached.

Incidental Beneficiary A third party who incidentally benefits from a contract but whose benefit was not the reason the contract was formed. An incidental beneficiary has no rights in a contract and cannot sue to have the contract enforced.

Another exception to the doctrine of privity of contract occurs when the original parties to the contract intend at the time of contracting that the contract performance directly benefit a third person. In this situation, the third person becomes a **third party beneficiary** of the contract. As an **intended beneficiary** of the contract, the third party has legal rights and can sue the promisor directly for breach of contract.

The benefit that an **incidental beneficiary** receives from a contract between two parties is unintentional. Because the benefit is unintentional, an incidental beneficiary cannot sue to enforce the contract. **CASE EXAMPLE 10.9** Spectators at the infamous boxing match in which Mike Tyson was disqualified for biting his opponent's ear sued Tyson and the fight's promoters for a refund on the basis of breach of contract. The spectators claimed that they were third party beneficiaries of the contract between Tyson and the fight's promoters. The court, however, held that the spectators could not sue because they were not in contractual privity with the defendants. Any benefits they received from the contract were incidental to the contract, and according to the court, the spectators got what they paid for: "the right to view whatever event transpired."[7] ●

 Performance and Discharge

Discharge The termination of an obligation. In contract law, discharge occurs when the parties have fully performed their contractual obligations or when events, conduct of the parties, or operation of law releases the parties from performance.

Performance In contract law, the fulfillment of one's duties arising under a contract with another; the normal way of discharging one's contractual obligations.

The most common way to **discharge**, or terminate, one's contractual duties is by the **performance** of those duties. For example, a buyer and seller have a contract for the sale of a 2012 Lexus for $42,000. This contract will be discharged on the performance by the parties of their obligations under the contract—the buyer's payment of $42,000 to the seller and the seller's transfer of possession of the Lexus to the buyer.

The duty to perform under a contract may be *conditioned* on the occurrence or nonoccurrence of a certain event, or the duty may be *absolute*. In this section, we look at conditions of performance and the degree of performance required. We then

---

7. *Castillo v. Tyson*, 268 A.D.2d 336, 701 N.Y.S.2d 423 (Sup.Ct.App.Div. 2000).

examine some other ways in which a contract can be discharged, including discharge by agreement of the parties and discharge by operation of law.

Conditions of Performance

In most contracts, promises of performance are not expressly conditioned or qualified. Instead, they are *absolute promises.* They must be performed, or the parties promising the acts will be in breach of contract. **EXAMPLE 10.10** JoAnne contracts to sell Alfonso a painting for $10,000. The parties' promises are unconditional: JoAnne's transfer of the painting to Alfonso and Alfonso's payment of $10,000 to JoAnne. The payment does not have to be made if the painting is not transferred. •

> **Condition**   A qualification, provision, or clause in a contractual agreement, the occurrence or nonoccurrence of which creates, suspends, or terminates the obligations of the contracting parties.

In some situations, however, contractual promises are conditioned. A **condition** is a possible future event, the occurrence or nonoccurrence of which will trigger the performance of a legal obligation or terminate an existing obligation under a contract. If the condition is not satisfied, the obligations of the parties are discharged. **EXAMPLE 10.11** Alfonso, from the previous example, offers to purchase JoAnne's painting only if an independent appraisal indicates that it is worth at least $10,000. JoAnne accepts Alfonso's offer. Their obligations (promises) are conditioned on the outcome of the appraisal. Should this condition not be satisfied (for example, if the appraiser deems the value of the painting to be only $5,000), their obligations to each other are discharged and cannot be enforced. •

> **Condition Precedent**   In a contractual agreement, a condition that must be met before a party's promise becomes absolute.

A condition that must be fulfilled before a party's promise becomes absolute is called a **condition precedent.** The condition precedes the absolute duty to perform. For instance, insurance contracts frequently specify that certain conditions, such as passing a physical examination, must be met before the insurance company will be obligated to perform under the contract.

Sometimes, a lease of real property (see Chapter 22) includes an option to buy that property. The lease in the following case required timely rent payments as a condition of exercising such an option, but the lessee often failed to make the payments on time. The court had to decide whether the lessee could still exercise the option even though it had not strictly complied with the condition precedent.

Case 10.2	**Pack 2000, Inc. v. Cushman**

Appellate Court of Connecticut, 126 Conn.App. 339, 11 A.3d 181 (2011).
www.jud.state.ct.us[a]

COMPANY PROFILE   *The first Midas muffler repair shop opened in Macon, Georgia, in 1956. Within ten years, Midas had added shock absorber services and expanded beyond the United States into the European market. By 1986, Midas had added brake services and opened shops around the world. Today, with more than 1,700 locations, Midas is a leader in muffler and exhaust services. It also offers comprehensive programs for tires, auto maintenance, and commercial fleet services. Recently, the company has renewed its focus on its franchise and real estate businesses.*

BACKGROUND AND FACTS   Eugene Cushman agreed to transfer two Midas muffler shops to Pack 2000, Inc. The deal included leases for the real estate on which the shops were located. Each lease provided Pack with an option to buy the leased real estate subject to certain conditions. Pack was to pay rent by the first day of each month, make payments on the notes by the eighth day of each month, and pay utilities and other accounts on time. Pack, however, was often late in making these payments. The utility and phone companies threatened to cut off services, an insurance company canceled Pack's liability coverage, and other

a. In the left column, in the "Opinions" pull-out menu, click on "Appellate Court." On that page, in the "Search the Archives:" section, click on "Appellate Court Archive." In the result, click on "2011." Scroll to the "Published in Connecticut Law Journal–2/1/11" section, and click on the docket number next to the title of the case to view the opinion. The Connecticut judicial branch maintains this Web site.

Case 10.2–Continues next page ⇒

Case 10.2–Continued

delinquencies prompted collection calls and letters. When Pack sought to exercise the options to buy the real estate, Cushman responded that Pack had not complied with the conditions. Pack filed a suit in a Connecticut state court against Cushman, seeking specific performance of the options. The court rendered a judgment in Pack's favor. Cushman appealed.

IN THE WORDS OF THE COURT . . .
LAVERY, J. [Judge]
* * * *

When a lease provides the lessee with the option to purchase realty subject to certain terms and conditions, the right of the lessee to exercise the option is contingent on the lessee's strict compliance with those terms and conditions.
* * * *

The defendant [Cushman] claims that the plaintiff [Pack 2000] has lost its right to exercise the options at issue because it has not strictly complied with the conditions precedent to the defendant's duty to perform. A condition precedent is a fact or event which the parties intend must exist or take place before there is a right to performance. * * * *Whether the performance of a certain act by a party to a contract is a condition precedent to the duty of the other party to act depends on the intent of the parties as expressed in the contract and read in the light of the circumstances surrounding the execution of the instrument.* [Emphasis added.]

In the present case, the two lease agreements provide that the defendant's duty to perform under the terms of the options is conditioned on the plaintiff's "compliance with the terms and conditions of the Lease, the Letter of Intent, and Management Agreement * * * ." Additionally, the management agreement provides

that the plaintiff must be in "full compliance with the management agreement" in order to exercise the options to purchase the defendant's realty. Under the terms of these agreements, the plaintiff is required to make periodic payments to the defendant and to certain third parties by specified deadlines. We conclude, therefore, that the plaintiff's right to exercise the options is subject to a condition precedent—namely, the timely submission of the aforementioned payments.

Upon our review of the record, we find ample support for the * * * finding that the plaintiff was often late in making the required payments. Accordingly, * * * the plaintiff did not strictly comply with the terms and conditions of its agreements with the defendant. We conclude, therefore, that the plaintiff did not have the right to exercise the options to purchase the defendant's realty because the plaintiff was not in strict compliance with the contracts that set forth the terms of the options.

DECISION AND REMEDY A state intermediate appellate court reversed the lower court's judgment and remanded the case for the entry of a judgment for Cushman, the defendant. A party retains its right to exercise an option to buy real estate only by strict compliance with the conditions precedent to its exercise of the option. In this case, Pack did not strictly comply with those conditions.

WHAT IF THE FACTS WERE DIFFERENT? *Suppose that Pack had not made any late payments. Would the result in this case have been different? Explain.*

THE ECONOMIC DIMENSION *Why are rent and other payments due under a lease subject to strict time deadlines?*

Discharge by Performance

Tender An unconditional offer to perform an obligation by a person who is ready, willing, and able to do so.

The great majority of contracts are discharged by performance. The contract comes to an end when both parties fulfill their respective duties by performing the acts they have promised. Performance can also be accomplished by tender. **Tender** is an unconditional offer to perform by a person who is ready, willing, and able to do so. Therefore, a seller who places goods at the disposal of a buyer has tendered delivery and can demand payment. A buyer who offers to pay for goods has tendered payment and can demand delivery of the goods. Once performance has been tendered, the party making the tender has done everything possible to carry out the terms of the contract. If the other party then refuses to perform, the party making the tender can sue for breach of contract.

There are two basic types of performance—*complete performance* and *substantial performance*. In addition, a contract may stipulate that performance must meet the personal satisfaction of either the contracting party or a third party. Such a provision must be considered in determining whether the performance rendered satisfies the contract.

> *"There are occasions
> and causes and why and
> wherefore in all things."*
> —William Shakespeare, 1564–1616
> (English dramatist and poet)

COMPLETE PERFORMANCE   When a party performs exactly as agreed, there is no question as to whether the contract has been performed. When a party's performance is perfect, it is said to be complete.

Normally, conditions expressly stated in a contract must be fully satisfied for complete performance to take place. For example, most construction contracts require the builder to meet certain specifications. If the specifications are conditions, complete performance is required to avoid *material breach* (see page 286). If the conditions are met, the other party to the contract must then fulfill her or his obligation to pay the builder. If the specifications are not conditions and if the builder, without the other party's permission, fails to comply with the specifications, performance is not complete. What effect does such a failure have on the other party's obligation to pay? The answer is part of the doctrine of substantial performance.

SUBSTANTIAL PERFORMANCE   A party who in good faith performs substantially all of the terms of a contract can enforce the contract against the other party under the doctrine of substantial performance. Note that good faith is required. Intentionally failing to comply with the terms is a breach of the contract.

To qualify as substantial performance, the performance must not vary greatly from the performance promised in the contract, and it must create substantially the same benefits as those promised in the contract. If the omission, variance, or defect in performance is unimportant and can easily be compensated for by awarding damages, a court is likely to hold that the contract has been substantially performed.

EXAMPLE 10.12   A couple contracts with a construction company to build a house. The contract specifies that Brand X plasterboard be used for the walls. The builder cannot obtain Brand X plasterboard, and the buyers are on holiday in the mountains of Peru and unreachable. The builder decides to install Brand Y instead, which he knows is identical in quality and durability to Brand X plasterboard. All other aspects of construction conform to the contract. In this situation, a court will likely hold that the builder has substantially performed his end of the bargain, and therefore the couple will be obligated to pay the builder. The court might award the couple damages for the use of a different brand of plasterboard, but the couple would still have to pay the contractor the contract price, less the amount of damages. ●

Courts decide whether the performance was substantial on a case-by-case basis, examining all of the facts of the particular situation. If performance is substantial, the other party's duty to perform remains absolute (except that the party can sue for damages due to the minor deviation).

CASE EXAMPLE 10.13   Wisconsin Electric Power Company (WEPCO) contracted with Union Pacific Railroad to transport coal to WEPCO from mines in Colorado. The contract required WEPCO to notify Union Pacific monthly of how many tons of coal (below a certain maximum) it wanted to have shipped the next month. Union Pacific was to make "good faith reasonable efforts" to meet the schedule. The contract also required WEPCO to supply the railcars. When WEPCO did not supply the railcars, Union Pacific used its own railcars and delivered 84 percent of the requested coal. A federal appellate court held that in this situation, the delivery of 84 percent of the contracted amount constituted substantial performance.[8] ●

A woman shakes hands with a salesperson after agreeing to purchase a car. Suppose that the agreement is conditioned on the dealer's installing certain optional equipment. When the woman returns to the dealership the following day, she discovers that the optional features have not been installed. Is she still obligated to buy the car? Why or why not?

(Brian Teutsch/Creative Commons)

---

8. *Wisconsin Electric Power Co. v. Union Pacific Railroad Co.*, 557 F.3d 504 (7th Cir. 2009).

PERFORMANCE TO THE SATISFACTION OF ANOTHER   Contracts often state that completed work must personally satisfy one of the parties or a third person. The question is whether this satisfaction becomes a condition precedent, requiring actual personal satisfaction or approval for discharge, or whether the test of satisfaction is performance that would satisfy a *reasonable person* (substantial performance).

When the subject matter of the contract is personal, a contract to be performed to the satisfaction of one of the parties is conditioned, and performance must actually satisfy that party. For example, contracts for portraits, works of art, and tailoring are considered personal. Therefore, only the personal satisfaction of the party fulfills the condition—unless a court finds the party is expressing dissatisfaction just to avoid payment or otherwise is not acting in good faith.

Most other contracts need to be performed only to the satisfaction of a reasonable person unless they *expressly state otherwise.* When such contracts require performance to the satisfaction of a third party (for example, "to the satisfaction of Robert Ames, the supervising engineer"), the courts are divided. A majority of courts require the work to be satisfactory to a reasonable person, but some courts hold that the personal satisfaction of the third party designated in the contract (Robert Ames, in this example) must be met. Again, the personal judgment must be made honestly, or the condition will be excused.

Breach of Contract   The failure, without legal excuse, of a promisor to perform the obligations of a contract.

Different brands of construction supplies displayed at a site. If a contract for the construction of a house specifies a particular brand, can a different brand of comparable quality be substituted? Why or why not?

MATERIAL BREACH OF CONTRACT   A **breach of contract** is the nonperformance of a contractual duty. The breach is *material* when performance is not at least substantial. If there is a material breach, then the nonbreaching party is excused from the performance of contractual duties and has a cause of action to sue for damages resulting from the breach. If the breach is *minor* (not material), the nonbreaching party's duty to perform can sometimes be suspended until the breach has been remedied, but the duty to perform is not entirely excused. Once the minor breach has been corrected, the nonbreaching party must resume performance of the contractual obligations undertaken.

Any breach entitles the nonbreaching party to sue for damages, but only a material breach discharges the nonbreaching party from the contract. The policy underlying these rules allows contracts to go forward when only minor problems occur but allows them to be terminated if major difficulties arise.

CASE EXAMPLE 10.14   Su Yong Kim sold an apartment building in Portland, Oregon, to a group of buyers. At the time of the sale, the building's plumbing violated the city's housing code. The contract therefore provided that Kim would correct the plumbing code violations within eight months after signing the contract. A year after the contract was signed, Kim still had not made the necessary repairs, and the new owners were being fined by the city for continuing plumbing code violations. The buyers stopped making payments under the contract, and the dispute ended up in court. The court found that Kim's failure to make the required repairs was a material breach of the contract because it defeated the purpose of the contract. The buyers had purchased the building to lease it out to tenants, but instead were losing tenants and paying fines to the city due to the substandard plumbing. Because Kim's breach was material, the buyers were not obligated to continue to make payments under the contract.[9] ●

9. *Kim v. Park,* 192 Or.App. 365, 86 P.3d 63 (2004).

ANTICIPATORY REPUDIATION OF A CONTRACT Before either party to a contract has a duty to perform, one of the parties may refuse to perform her or his contractual obligations. This is called **anticipatory repudiation**.[10] When anticipatory repudiation occurs, it is treated as a material breach of contract, and the nonbreaching party is permitted to bring an action for damages immediately, even though the scheduled time for performance under the contract may still be in the future. Until the nonbreaching party treats this early repudiation as a breach, however, the breaching party can retract the anticipatory repudiation by proper notice and restore the parties to their original obligations.

An anticipatory repudiation is treated as a present, material breach for two reasons. First, the nonbreaching party should not be required to remain ready and willing to perform when the other party has already repudiated the contract. Second, the nonbreaching party should have the opportunity to seek a similar contract elsewhere and may have the duty to do so to minimize his or her loss.

Quite often, an anticipatory repudiation occurs when market prices change significantly, making performance of the contract extremely unfavorable to one of the parties. **EXAMPLE 10.15** Shasta Manufacturing Company contracts to manufacture and sell 100,000 personal computers to New Age, Inc., a computer retailer with one hundred outlet stores. Delivery is to be made two months from the date of the contract. One month later, three suppliers of computer parts raise their prices to Shasta. Because of these higher prices, Shasta stands to lose $500,000 if it sells the computers to New Age at the contract price. Shasta writes to New Age, stating that it cannot deliver the 100,000 computers at the agreed-on contract price. Even though you might sympathize with Shasta, its letter is an anticipatory repudiation of the contract, allowing New Age the option of treating the repudiation as a material breach and proceeding immediately to pursue remedies, even though the contract delivery date is still a month away. ●

Discharge by Agreement

Any contract can be discharged by agreement of the parties. The agreement can be contained in the original contract, or the parties can form a new contract for the express purpose of discharging the original contract.

DISCHARGE BY RESCISSION *Rescission* is the process by which a contract is canceled or terminated and the parties are returned to the positions they occupied prior to forming it. For **mutual rescission** to take place, the parties must make another agreement that also satisfies the legal requirements for a contract. There must be an offer, an acceptance, and consideration. Ordinarily, if the parties agree to rescind the original contract, their promises not to perform the acts stipulated in the original contract will be legal consideration for the second contract (the rescission).

Oral agreements to rescind executory contracts (in which neither party has performed) generally are enforceable, even if the original agreement was in writing. Under the Uniform Commercial Code, however, an agreement rescinding a contract for the sale of goods, regardless of price, must be in writing if the contract requires a written rescission. Also, agreements to rescind contracts involving transfers of realty must be in writing.

When one party has fully performed, an agreement to cancel the original contract normally will not be enforceable. Because the performing party has received no

Anticipatory Repudiation An assertion or action by a party indicating that he or she will not perform an obligation that the party is contractually obligated to perform at a future time.

REMEMBER The risks that prices will fluctuate and values will change are ordinary business risks for which the law normally does not provide relief.

Mutual Rescission An agreement between the parties to cancel their contract, releasing the parties from further obligations under the contract. The object of the agreement is to restore the parties to the positions they would have occupied had no contract ever been formed.

---

10. *Restatement (Second) of Contracts,* Section 253; and UCC 2–610 and 2–611.

consideration for the promise to call off the original bargain, additional consideration is necessary.

DISCHARGE BY NOVATION   A contractual obligation may also be discharged through novation. A **novation** occurs when both of the parties to a contract agree to substitute a third party for one of the original parties. The requirements of a novation are as follows:

1. A previous valid obligation.
2. An agreement by all the parties to a new contract.
3. The extinguishing of the old obligation (discharge of the prior party).
4. A new contract that is valid.

> **Novation**   The substitution, by agreement, of a new contract for an old one, with the rights under the old one being terminated. Typically, novation involves the substitution of a new party for one of the original parties to the contract.

EXAMPLE 10.16   Union Corporation contracts to sell its pharmaceutical division to British Pharmaceuticals, Ltd. Before the transfer is completed, Union, British Pharmaceuticals, and a third company, Otis Chemicals, execute a new agreement to transfer all of British Pharmaceuticals' rights and duties in the transaction to Otis Chemicals. As long as the new contract is supported by consideration, the novation will discharge the original contract (between Union and British Pharmaceuticals) and replace it with the new contract (between Union and Otis Chemicals). ●

A novation expressly or impliedly revokes and discharges a prior contract. The parties involved may expressly state in the new contract that the old contract is now discharged. If the parties do not expressly discharge the old contract, it will be impliedly discharged if the new contract's terms are inconsistent with the old contract's terms.

DISCHARGE BY SETTLEMENT AGREEMENT   A *compromise,* or settlement agreement, that arises out of a genuine dispute over the obligations under an existing contract will be recognized at law. Such an agreement will be substituted as a new contract, and it will either expressly or impliedly revoke and discharge the obligations under any prior contract. In contrast to a novation, a settlement agreement does not involve a third party. Rather, the two original parties to the contract form a different agreement to substitute for the original one.

DISCHARGE BY ACCORD AND SATISFACTION   For a contract to be discharged by accord and satisfaction, the parties must agree to accept performance that is different from the performance originally promised. An *accord* is a contract to perform some act to satisfy an existing contractual duty. The duty has not yet been discharged. A *satisfaction* is the performance of the accord agreement. An accord and its satisfaction discharge the original contractual obligation.

Once the accord has been made, the original obligation is merely suspended. The obligor (the one owing the obligation) can discharge the obligation by performing either the obligation agreed to in the accord or the original obligation. If the obligor refuses to perform the accord, the obligee (the one to whom performance is owed) can bring action on the original obligation or seek a decree compelling specific performance on the accord.

EXAMPLE 10.17   Frazer obtains a judgment against Ling for $8,000. Later, both parties agree that the judgment can be satisfied by Ling's transfer of his automobile to Frazer. This agreement to accept the auto in lieu of $8,000 is the accord. If Ling transfers the car to Frazer, the accord is fully performed, and the debt is discharged. If Ling refuses to transfer the car, the accord is breached. Because the original obligation is merely suspended, Frazer can sue Ling to enforce the original judgment for $8,000 or bring an action for breach of the accord. ●

Discharge by Operation of Law

"Law is a practical matter."
—Roscoe Pound, 1870–1964
(American jurist)

Under certain circumstances, contractual duties may be discharged by operation of law. These circumstances include material alteration of the contract, the running of the statute of limitations, bankruptcy, and the impossibility or impracticability of performance.

ALTERATION OF THE CONTRACT   To discourage parties from altering written contracts, the law operates to allow an innocent party to be discharged when the other party has materially altered a written contract without consent. For example, contract terms such as quantity or price might be changed without the knowledge or consent of all parties. If so, the party who was not involved in the alteration can treat the contract as discharged or terminated.

STATUTES OF LIMITATIONS   As mentioned earlier in this text, statutes of limitations restrict the period during which a party can sue on a particular cause of action. After the applicable limitations period has passed, a suit can no longer be brought. For example, the limitations period for bringing suits for breach of oral contracts is usually two to three years; for written contracts, four to five years; and for recovery of amounts awarded in judgments, ten to twenty years, depending on state law. Suits for breach of a contract for the sale of goods generally must be brought within four years after the cause of action has accrued. By their original agreement, the parties can reduce this four-year period to not less than one year, but they cannot agree to extend it.

BANKRUPTCY   A proceeding in bankruptcy attempts to allocate the assets a debtor owns to creditors in a fair and equitable fashion. Once the assets have been allocated, the debtor receives a *discharge in bankruptcy*. A discharge in bankruptcy will ordinarily bar creditors from enforcing most of their contracts with the debtor. Partial payment of a debt *after* discharge in bankruptcy will not revive the debt. (Bankruptcy will be discussed in detail in Chapter 12.)

IMPOSSIBILITY OR IMPRACTICABILITY OF PERFORMANCE   After a contract has been made, performance may become impossible in an objective sense. This is known as **impossibility of performance** and may discharge a contract.

Impossibility of Performance   A doctrine under which a party to a contract is relieved of his or her duty to perform when performance becomes objectively impossible or totally impracticable (through no fault of either party).

Objective Impossibility of Performance. *Objective impossibility* ("It can't be done") must be distinguished from *subjective impossibility* ("I'm sorry, I simply can't do it"). Two examples of subjective impossibility are the inability to deliver goods on time because of a freight car shortage and the inability to make payment on time because the bank is closed. In effect, the party in each of these situations is saying, "It is impossible for me to perform," not "It is impossible for anyone to perform." Accordingly, such excuses do not discharge a contract, and the nonperforming party is normally held in breach of contract. Three basic types of situations, however, generally qualify as grounds for the discharge of contractual obligations based on impossibility of performance:[11]

1. *When one of the parties to a personal contract dies or becomes incapacitated prior to performance.* **EXAMPLE 10.18**   Fred, a famous dancer, contracts with Ethereal Dancing Guild to play a leading role in its new ballet. Before the ballet can be

---

11. *Restatement (Second) of Contracts,* Sections 262–266; and UCC 2–615.

performed, Fred becomes ill and dies. His personal performance was essential to the completion of the contract. Thus, his death discharges the contract and his estate's liability for his nonperformance. ●

2. *When the specific subject matter of the contract is destroyed.* **EXAMPLE 10.19** A-1 Farm Equipment agrees to sell Gudgel the green tractor on its lot and promises to have it ready for Gudgel to pick up on Saturday. On Friday night, however, a truck veers off the nearby highway and smashes into the tractor, destroying it beyond repair. Because the contract was for this specific tractor, A-1's performance is rendered impossible owing to the accident. ●

3. *When a change in law renders performance illegal.* **CASE EXAMPLE 10.20** A contract to build an apartment building becomes impossible to perform when the zoning laws are changed to prohibit the construction of residential rental property at the planned location. A contract to paint a bridge using lead paint becomes impossible when the government passes new regulations forbidding the use of lead paint on bridges.[12] ●

Temporary Impossibility. An occurrence or event that makes performance temporarily impossible operates to suspend performance until the impossibility ceases. Then, ordinarily, the parties must perform the contract as originally planned. If, however, the lapse of time and the change in circumstances surrounding the contract make it substantially more burdensome for the parties to perform the promised acts, the contract is discharged. For instance, actor Gene Autry was drafted into the U.S. Army in 1942. Being drafted rendered his contract with a movie production company temporarily impossible to perform, and it was suspended until the end of World War II. When Autry got out of the army, the purchasing power of the dollar had declined so much that performance of the contract would have been substantially burdensome to him. Therefore, the contract was discharged.[13]

CASE EXAMPLE 10.21 On August 22, 2005, Keefe Hurwitz contracted to sell his home in Madisonville, Louisiana, to Wesley and Gwendolyn Payne for a price of $241,500. On August 26—just four days after the parties signed the contract—Hurricane Katrina made landfall and caused extensive property damage to the house. The cost of repairs was estimated at $60,000 and Hurwitz would have to make the repairs before the *closing date* (see Chapter 22). Hurwitz did not have the funds and refused to pay $60,000 for the repairs only to sell the property to the Paynes for the previously agreed-on price of $241,500. The Paynes filed a lawsuit to enforce the contract. Hurwitz claimed that Hurricane Katrina had made it impossible for him to perform and had discharged his duties under the contract. The court, however, ruled that Hurricane Katrina had caused only a temporary impossibility. Hurwitz was required to pay for the necessary repairs and to perform the contract as written. In other words, he could not obtain a higher purchase price to offset the cost of the repairs.[14] ●

Commercial Impracticability. When a supervening event does not render performance objectively impossible, but does make it much more difficult or expensive to perform, the courts may excuse the parties' obligations under the contract. For someone to invoke the doctrine of **commercial impracticability** successfully, however,

Commercial Impracticability A doctrine under which a court may excuse the parties from performing a contract when the performance becomes much more difficult or costly due to an event that the parties did not foresee or anticipate at the time the contract was made.

---

12. *M. J. Paquet, Inc. v. New Jersey Department of Transportation,* 171 N.J. 378, 794 A.2d 141 (2002).

13. See *Autry v. Republic Productions,* 30 Cal.2d 144, 180 P.2d 888 (1947).

14. *Payne v. Hurwitz,* 978 So.2d 1000 (La.App. 1st Cir., 2008).

the anticipated performance must become significantly more difficult or costly than originally contemplated at the time the contract was formed.[15]

In addition, the reason for the added burden of performing must not have been foreseeable. **CASE EXAMPLE 10.22** In one case, the court allowed a party to rescind a contract for the sale of land because of a potential problem with contaminated groundwater under the land. The court found that "the potential for substantial and unbargained-for" liability made contract performance economically impracticable.[16] ● (See this chapter's *Beyond Our Borders* feature below for a discussion of Germany's approach to impracticability and impossibility of performance.)

Frustration of Purpose A court-created doctrine under which a party to a contract will be relieved of his or her duty to perform when the objective purpose for performance no longer exists due to reasons beyond that party's control.

Frustration of Purpose. A theory closely allied with the doctrine of commercial impracticability is the doctrine of **frustration of purpose.** In principle, a contract will be discharged if supervening circumstances make it impossible to attain the purpose both parties had in mind when making the contract.

As with commercial impracticability and impossibility, the supervening event must not have been reasonably foreseeable at the time the contract was formed. In contrast to impracticability, which usually involves an event that increases the cost or difficulty of performance, frustration of purpose typically involves an event that decreases the value of what a party receives under the contract.[17]

See Exhibit 10–2 on the following page for a summary of the ways in which a contract can be discharged.

 ## Damages for Breach of Contract

A breach of contract entitles the nonbreaching party to sue for monetary damages. Damages are designed to compensate a party for harm suffered as a result of another's wrongful act. In the context of contract law, damages compensate the nonbreaching party for the loss of the bargain, including lost profits. Often, courts say that innocent parties are to be placed in the position they would have occupied had the contract been fully performed.

---

15. *Restatement (Second) of Contracts,* Section 264.
16. *Cape-France Enterprises v. Estate of Peed,* 305 Mont. 513, 29 P.3d 1011 (2001).
17. See, for example, *East Capitol View Community Development Corp. v. Robinson,* 941 A.2d 1036 (D.C.App. 2008).

 Beyond Our Borders **Impossibility or Impracticability of Performance in Germany**

In the United States, when a party alleges that contract performance is impossible or impracticable because of circumstances unforeseen at the time the contract was formed, a court will either discharge the party's contractual obligations or hold the party to the contract. In other words, if a court agrees that the contract is impossible or impracticable to perform, the remedy is to rescind (cancel) the contract. Under German law, however, a court may adjust the terms of (reform) a contract in light of economic developments. If an unforeseen event affects the foundation of the agreement, the court can alter the contract's terms in view of the disruption in expectations, thus making the contract fair for both parties.

For Critical Analysis
When a contract becomes impossible or impracticable to perform, which remedy would a businessperson prefer—rescission or reformation? Explain your answer.

• *Exhibit* **10-2 Contract Discharge**

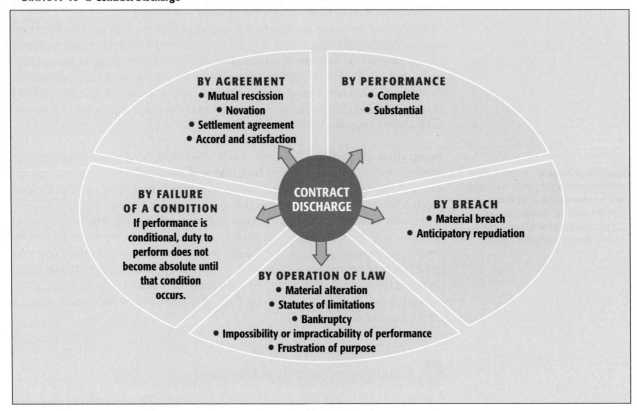

Types of Damages

There are basically four broad categories of damages:

1. Compensatory (to cover direct losses and costs).
2. Consequential (to cover indirect and foreseeable losses).
3. Punitive (to punish and deter wrongdoing).
4. Nominal (to recognize wrongdoing when no monetary loss is shown).

Compensatory and punitive damages were discussed in Chapter 5 in the context of tort law. Here, we look at compensatory and consequential damages in the context of contract law.

COMPENSATORY DAMAGES   Damages that compensate the nonbreaching party for the *loss of the bargain* are known as *compensatory damages*. These damages compensate the injured party only for damages actually sustained and proved to have arisen directly from the loss of the bargain caused by the breach of contract. They simply replace what was lost because of the wrong or damage. The standard measure of compensatory damages is the difference between the value of the breaching party's promised performance under the contract and the value of her or his actual performance. This amount is reduced by any loss that the injured party has avoided, however.

EXAMPLE 10.23　Wilcox contracts to perform certain services exclusively for Hernandez during the month of March for $4,000. Hernandez cancels the contract and is in breach. Wilcox is able to find another job during the month of March but can earn only $3,000. He can sue Hernandez for breach and recover $1,000 as compensatory damages. Wilcox can also recover from Hernandez the amount that he spent to find the other job. ● Expenses that are caused directly by a breach of contract—such as those incurred to obtain performance from another source—are known as *incidental damages*.

The measurement of compensatory damages varies by type of contract. Certain types of contracts deserve special mention. They are contracts for the sale of goods, the sale of land, and construction.

Sale of Goods. In a contract for the sale of goods, the usual measure of compensatory damages is an amount equal to the difference between the contract price and the market price at the time and place at which the goods were to be delivered or tendered.[18] **EXAMPLE 10.24**　Chrylon Corporation contracts to buy ten model UTS network servers from an XEXO Corporation dealer for $8,000 each. The dealer, however, fails to deliver the ten servers to Chrylon. The market price of the servers at the time the buyer learns of the breach is $8,150. Chrylon's measure of damages is therefore $1,500 (10 × $150) plus any incidental damages (expenses) caused by the breach. ● In a situation in which the buyer breaches and the seller has not yet produced the goods, compensatory damages normally equal lost profits on the sale, not the difference between the contract price and the market price.

Sale of Land. Ordinarily, because each parcel of land is unique, the remedy for a seller's breach of a contract for a sale of real estate is specific performance—that is, the buyer is awarded the parcel of property for which she or he bargained. When this remedy is unavailable (for example, when the seller has sold the property to someone else), or when the buyer is the breaching party, the measure of damages is ordinarily the same as in contracts for the sale of goods—that is, the difference between the contract price and the market price of the land. The majority of states follow this rule.

Construction Contracts. The measure of damages in a building or construction contract varies depending on which party breaches and when the breach occurs. If the owner breaches *before performance has begun,* the contractor can recover only the profits that would have been made on the contract (that is, the total contract price less the cost of materials and labor). If the owner breaches *during performance,* the contractor can recover the profits plus the costs incurred in partially constructing the building. If the owner breaches *after the construction has been completed,* the contractor can recover the entire contract price, plus interest.

When the construction contractor breaches the contract—either by failing to undertake construction or by stopping work partway through the project—the measure of damages is the cost of completion, which includes reasonable compensation for any delay in performance. If the contractor finishes late, the measure of damages is the loss of use.

"The duty to keep a contract at common law means a prediction that you must pay damages if you do not keep it—and nothing else."

—Oliver Wendell Holmes, Jr., 1841–1935
(Associate justice of the United States Supreme Court, 1902–1932)

---

18. See UCC 2–708 and 2–713.

How should a court rule when the performance of both parties—the construction contractor and the owner—falls short of what their contract required? That was the issue in the following case.

Case 10.3   Jamison Well Drilling, Inc. v. Pfeifer

Court of Appeals of Ohio, Third District, 2011 Ohio 521 (2011).

BACKGROUND AND FACTS   Jamison Well Drilling, Inc., contracted to drill a water well for Ed Pfeifer in Crawford County, Ohio. Pfeifer agreed to pay Jamison $4,130 for the labor and supplies. Jamison drilled the well and installed a storage tank. The Ohio Department of Health requires that a well be lined with a minimum of twenty-five vertical feet of casing, but Jamison installed only eleven feet of casing in the drilled well. The county health department later tested the water in the well for bacteria and repeatedly found that the levels were too high. The state health department investigated and discovered that the well's casing did not comply with its requirements. The department ordered that the well be abandoned and sealed. Pfeifer used the storage tank but paid Jamison nothing. Jamison filed a suit in an Ohio state court against Pfeifer to recover the contract price and other costs. The court entered a judgment for Jamison for $970 for the storage tank. Jamison appealed.

IN THE WORDS OF THE COURT . . .
WILLAMOWSKI, J. [Judge]
    * * * *

The parties in this case entered into a contract * * * in which the Plaintiff was to drill a well for the Defendant for Four Thousand One Hundred Thirty and 00/100 Dollars ($4,130.00). There were additional charges and discounts applied to this figure which resulted in the Plaintiff seeking Four Thousand Nine Hundred Thirty-three and 00/100 Dollars ($4,933.00).

Evidence presented at the hearing indicated that the Ohio Department of Health determined that the well was not in compliance with the State law and must be sealed. Due to this fact, there is sufficient evidence to indicate that the Plaintiff is not entitled to the full contract price.

Despite not being entitled to a full contract price, the Plaintiff installed certain material on the Defendant's property. A review of "Exhibit B" (an invoice provided to the Defendant by the Plaintiff) reveals that a 400-gallon tank was installed by the Plaintiff. The cost of this tank was Nine Hundred Seventy and 00/100 Dollars ($970.00). * * * *While the Plaintiff was not entitled to his full contract price, it would be unfair to allow the Defendant to keep the tank without paying for it * * *.* [Emphasis added.]

Since Jamison's actions caused the well to be in noncompliance * * *, Jamison is responsible for the well having to be abandoned and sealed. Although Pfeifer assumed the risk that the well would be unusable due to low production of water, he contracted for a well that would comply with all statutory and administrative requirements. This well had to be abandoned because it did not comply with Ohio law. There was no evidence presented that Pfeifer assumed the risk that the well would have to be abandoned due to noncompliance. Thus, *Jamison is not entitled to recover for the labor and materials as set forth in the contract as the contract was not completed as intended.* [Emphasis added.]

However, * * * Jamison should be permitted to recover the cost of the storage tank which Pfeifer was able to use. The value of the tank was set forth in Exhibit B which was admitted into evidence. Pfeifer testified that he was using the tank. * * * Therefore, the trial court did not abuse its discretion in reaching its decision.

DECISION AND REMEDY   A state intermediate appellate court affirmed the lower court's decision. The judgment struck a balance that recognized the completed project had value and the storage tank was functional, but the well was not usable.

WHAT IF THE FACTS WERE DIFFERENT?   *Suppose that Pfeifer had paid Jamison for the work before the well was ordered sealed and had later filed a suit to recover for breach of contract. What would have been the measure of damages?*

THE LEGAL ENVIRONMENT DIMENSION   *What did Jamison most likely offer as proof of damages? Was this proof sufficient, or should an expert have testified? Explain.*

Consequential Damages   Special damages that compensate for a loss that does not directly or immediately result from the breach (for example, lost profits). For the plaintiff to collect consequential damages, they must have been reasonably foreseeable at the time the breach or injury occurred.

CONSEQUENTIAL DAMAGES   Foreseeable damages that result from a party's breach of contract are referred to as **consequential damages,** or *special damages.* Consequential damages differ from compensatory damages in that they are caused by special circumstances beyond the contract itself. They flow from the consequences, or results, of a breach. When a seller fails to deliver goods, knowing that the buyer is planning to use or resell those goods immediately, consequential damages are awarded for the loss of profits from the planned resale.

EXAMPLE 10.25 Gilmore contracts to have a specific item shipped to her—one that she desperately needs to repair her printing press. In her contract with the shipper, Gilmore states that she must receive the item by Monday or she will not be able to print her paper and will lose $950. If the shipper is late, Gilmore normally can recover the consequential damages caused by the delay (that is, the $950 in losses). ●

NOTE A seller who does not wish to take on the risk of consequential damages can limit the buyer's remedies via contract.

To recover consequential damages, the breaching party must know (or have reason to know) that special circumstances will cause the nonbreaching party to suffer an additional loss. When was this rule first enunciated? See this chapter's *Landmark in the Legal Environment* feature on the next page for a discussion of *Hadley v. Baxendale*, a case decided in England in 1854.

Preventing Legal Disputes

It is sometimes impossible to prevent contract disputes. You should realize at the outset, though, that collecting damages through a court judgment requires litigation, which can be expensive and time consuming. Also, keep in mind that court judgments are often difficult to enforce, particularly if the breaching party does not have sufficient assets to pay the damages awarded. For these reasons, most parties choose to settle their contract disputes before trial rather than litigate in hopes of being awarded—and being able to collect—damages (or other remedies). Another alternative you should consider is mediation, which can help reduce the cost of resolving a dispute and may allow for the possibility of future business transactions between the parties.

Mitigation of Damages

In most situations, when a breach of contract occurs, the innocent injured party is held to a duty to mitigate, or reduce, the damages that he or she suffers. Under this doctrine of **mitigation of damages**, the duty owed depends on the nature of the contract.

Mitigation of Damages A rule requiring a plaintiff to do whatever is reasonable to minimize the damages caused by the defendant.

In the majority of states, a person whose employment has been wrongfully terminated has a duty to mitigate damages incurred because of the employer's breach of the employment contract. In other words, a wrongfully terminated employee has a duty to take a similar job if it is available. If the employee fails to do this, the damages received will be equivalent to the employee's salary less the income she or he would have received in a similar job obtained by reasonable means. Normally, the employee is under no duty to take a job that is not of the same type and rank.

CASE EXAMPLE 10.26 Harry De La Concha was employed by Fordham University. De La Concha claimed that he had been injured in an altercation with Fordham's director of human resources and filed for workers' compensation benefits. (These benefits are available for on-the-job injuries regardless of fault, as you will read in Chapter 17.) Fordham then fired De La Concha, who sought to be reinstated by arguing that he had been terminated in retaliation for filing a workers' compensation claim. The New York state workers' compensation board held that De La Concha had failed to mitigate his damages because he had not even looked for another job, and a state court affirmed the decision. Because De La Concha had failed to mitigate his damages, any compensation he received would be reduced by the amount he could have obtained from other employment.[19] ●

"A long dispute means that both parties are wrong."
—Voltaire, 1694–1778
(French author)

Some states require a landlord to use reasonable means to find a new tenant if a tenant abandons the premises and fails to pay rent. If an acceptable tenant becomes available, the landlord is required to lease the premises to him or her to mitigate

---

19. *De La Concha v. Fordham University*, 814 N.Y.S.2d 320, 28 A.3d 963 (2006).

Landmark in the Legal Environment   *Hadley v. Baxendale* (1854)

The rule that notice of special ("consequential") circumstances must be given if consequential damages are to be recovered was first enunciated in *Hadley v. Baxendale*,[a] a landmark case decided in 1854.

Case Background   This case involved a broken crankshaft used in a flour mill run by the Hadley family in Gloucester, England. The crankshaft attached to the steam engine in the mill broke, and the shaft had to be sent to a foundry located in Greenwich so that a new shaft could be made to fit the other parts of the engine.

The Hadleys hired Baxendale, a common carrier, to transport the shaft from Gloucester to Greenwich. Baxendale received payment in advance and promised to deliver the shaft the following day. It was not delivered for several days, however. As a consequence, the mill was closed during those days because the Hadleys had no extra crankshaft on hand to use. The Hadleys sued Baxendale to recover the profits they lost during that time. Baxendale contended that the loss of profits was "too remote."

In the mid-1800s, it was common knowledge that large mills, such as that run by the Hadleys, normally had more than one crankshaft in case the main one broke and had to be repaired, as happened in this situation. It is against this background that the parties argued their respective positions on whether the damages resulting from loss of profits while the crankshaft was out for repair were "too remote" to be recoverable.

---

a.   9 Exch. 341, 156 Eng.Rep. 145 (1854).

The Issue before the Court and the Court's Ruling   The crucial issue before the court was whether the Hadleys had informed the carrier, Baxendale, of the special circumstances surrounding the crankshaft's repair. Specifically, did Baxendale know at the time of the contract that the mill would have to shut down while the crankshaft was being repaired?

In the court's opinion, the only circumstances communicated by the Hadleys to Baxendale at the time the contract was made were that the item to be transported was a broken crankshaft of a mill and that the Hadleys were the owners and operators of that mill. The court concluded that these circumstances did not reasonably indicate that the mill would have to stop operations if the delivery of the crankshaft was delayed.

• Application to Today's Legal Environment   *Today, the rule enunciated by the court in this case still applies. When damages are awarded, compensation is given only for those injuries that the defendant could reasonably have foreseen as a probable result of the usual course of events following a breach. If the injury complained of is outside the usual and foreseeable course of events, the plaintiff must show specifically that the defendant had reason to know the facts and foresee the injury. This rule applies to contracts in the online environment as well. For example, suppose that a Web merchant loses business (and profits) due to a computer system's failure. If the failure was caused by malfunctioning software, the merchant normally may recover the lost profits from the software maker if these consequential damages were foreseeable.*

---

the damages recoverable from the former tenant. The former tenant is still liable for the difference between the amount of the rent under the original lease and the rent received from the new tenant. If the landlord has not taken reasonable steps to find a new tenant, a court will likely reduce any award by the amount of rent the landlord could have received had he or she done so.

Liquidated Damages versus Penalties

A **liquidated damages** provision in a contract specifies that a certain dollar amount is to be paid in the event of a future default or breach of contract. (*Liquidated* means determined, settled, or fixed.) Liquidated damages differ from penalties. A **penalty** specifies a certain amount to be paid in the event of a default or breach of contract and is designed to penalize the breaching party. Liquidated damages provisions normally are enforceable. In contrast, if a court finds that a provision calls for a penalty, the agreement as to the amount will not be enforced, and recovery will be limited to actual damages.[20]

Liquidated Damages   An amount, stipulated in a contract, that the parties to the contract believe to be a reasonable estimate of the damages that will occur in the event of a breach.

Penalty   A contractual clause that states that a certain amount of monetary damages will be paid in the event of a future default or breach of contract. The damages are a punishment for a default and not an accurate measure of compensation for the contract's breach. The agreement as to the penalty amount will not be enforced, and recovery will be limited to actual damages.

---

20.   This is also the rule under the UCC. See UCC 2–718(1).

To determine whether a particular provision is for liquidated damages or for a penalty, the court must answer two questions:

1. At the time the contract was formed, was it apparent that damages would be difficult to estimate in the event of a breach?
2. Was the amount set as damages a reasonable estimate and not excessive?[21]

If the answers to both questions are yes, the provision normally will be enforced. If either answer is no, the provision usually will not be enforced. Liquidated damages provisions are frequently used in construction contracts because it is difficult to estimate the amount of damages that would be caused by a delay in completing the work. **EXAMPLE 10.27** Ray Curl is a construction contractor. He enters into a contract with a developer to build a home in a new subdivision. The contract includes a clause that requires Curl to pay $300 for every day he is late in completing the project. This is a liquidated damages provision because it specifies a reasonable amount that Curl must pay to the developer if his performance is late. •

Equitable Remedies

In some situations, damages are an inadequate remedy for a breach of contract. In these cases, the nonbreaching party may ask the court for an equitable remedy. Equitable remedies include rescission and restitution, specific performance, and reformation. Additionally, a court acting in the interests of equity may sometimes step in and impose contractual obligations in an effort to prevent the unjust enrichment of one party at the expense of another.

Rescission and Restitution

As discussed earlier in this chapter, *rescission* is essentially an action to undo, or cancel, a contract—to return nonbreaching parties to the positions that they occupied prior to the transaction.[22] When fraud, mistake, duress, or failure of consideration is present, rescission is available. Rescission may also be available by statute. The failure of one party to perform under a contract entitles the other party to rescind the contract. The rescinding party must give prompt notice to the breaching party.

To rescind a contract, both parties generally must make **restitution** to each other by returning goods, property, or funds previously conveyed. If the physical property or goods can be returned, they must be. If the property or goods have been consumed, restitution must be made in an equivalent dollar amount.

Essentially, restitution involves the recapture of a benefit conferred on the defendant that has unjustly enriched her or him. **EXAMPLE 10.28** Andrea pays $32,000 to Myles in return for his promise to design a house for her. The next day, Myles calls Andrea and tells her that he has taken a position with a large architectural firm in another state and cannot design the house. Andrea decides to hire another architect that afternoon. Andrea can obtain restitution of $32,000 because Myles has received an unjust benefit of $32,000. •

Restitution may be appropriate when a contract is rescinded, but the right to restitution is not limited to rescission cases. For example, restitution might be available

Restitution An equitable remedy under which a person is restored to his or her original position prior to loss or injury, or placed in the position he or she would have been in had the breach not occurred.

CONTRAST Restitution offers several advantages over traditional damages. First, restitution may be available in situations when damages cannot be proved or are difficult to prove. Second, restitution can be used to recover specific property. Third, restitution sometimes results in a greater overall award.

---

21. *Restatement (Second) of Contracts,* Section 356(1).
22. The rescission discussed here refers to *unilateral* rescission, in which only one party wants to undo the contract. In *mutual* rescission, both parties agree to undo the contract. Mutual rescission discharges the contract, whereas unilateral rescission generally is available as a remedy for breach of contract.

when there has been misconduct by a party in a confidential or other special relationship and sometimes even in criminal cases.

Specific Performance

Specific Performance   An equitable remedy requiring exactly the performance that was specified in a contract; usually granted only when money damages would be an inadequate remedy and the subject matter of the contract is unique (for example, real property).

The equitable remedy of **specific performance** calls for the performance of the act promised in the contract. This remedy is attractive to a nonbreaching party because it provides the exact bargain promised in the contract. It also avoids some of the problems inherent in a suit for damages, such as collecting a judgment and arranging another contract. In addition, the actual performance may be more valuable than the monetary damages.

Normally, however, specific performance will not be granted unless the party's legal remedy (monetary damages) is inadequate. For this reason, contracts for the sale of goods rarely qualify for specific performance. The legal remedy—monetary damages—is ordinarily adequate in such situations because substantially identical goods can be bought or sold in the market. Only if the goods are unique will a court grant specific performance. For example, paintings, sculptures, or rare books or coins are so unique that monetary damages will not enable a buyer to obtain substantially identical substitutes in the market.

SALE OF LAND   A court may grant specific performance to a buyer in an action for a breach of contract involving the sale of land. In this situation, the legal remedy of monetary damages may not compensate the buyer adequately because every parcel of land is unique: the same land in the same location obviously cannot be obtained elsewhere. Only when specific performance is unavailable (such as when the seller has sold the property to someone else) will monetary damages be awarded instead.

CASE EXAMPLE 10.29 Howard Stainbrook entered into a contract to sell Trent Low forty acres of mostly timbered land for $45,000. Low agreed to pay for a survey of the property and other costs in addition to the price. He gave Stainbrook a check for $1,000 to show his intent to fulfill the contract. One month later, Stainbrook died. His son David became the executor of the estate. After he discovered that the timber on the property was worth more than $100,000, David asked Low to withdraw his offer to buy the forty acres. Low refused and filed a suit against David seeking specific performance of the contract. The court found that because Low had substantially performed his obligations under the contract and offered to perform the rest, he was entitled to specific performance.[23] •

Suppose that a seller contracts to sell some valuable coins to a buyer. If the seller breaches the contract, would specific performance be an appropriate remedy for the buyer to seek? Why or why not?

(Axel Buhrmann, Creative Commons)

CONTRACTS FOR PERSONAL SERVICES   Personal-service contracts require one party to work personally for another party. Courts normally refuse to grant specific performance of contracts for personal services. This is because to order a party to perform personal services against his or her will amounts to a type of involuntary servitude (slavery), which is contrary to the public policy expressed in the Thirteenth Amendment to the Constitution. Moreover, the courts do not want to monitor contracts for personal services.

EXAMPLE 10.30 If you contract with a brain surgeon to perform brain surgery on you and the surgeon refuses to perform, the court will not compel (and you certainly would not want) the surgeon to perform under these circumstances. There is no way the court can ensure meaningful performance in such a situation. •

---

23. *Stainbrook v. Low*, 842 N.E.2d 386 (Ind.App. 2006).

Reformation

Reformation   A court-ordered correction of a written contract so that it reflects the true intentions of the parties.

Reformation is an equitable remedy used when the parties have *imperfectly* expressed their agreement in writing. Reformation enables a court to modify, or rewrite, the contract to reflect the parties' true intentions. Courts order reformation most often when fraud or mutual mistake is present. **EXAMPLE 10.31** Carson contracts to buy a forklift from Shelley, but the written contract refers to a crane. Thus, a mutual mistake has occurred, and a court could reform the contract so that the writing conforms to the parties' original intention as to the piece of equipment being sold. ● Exhibit 10–3 below graphically presents the remedies, including reformation, that are available to the nonbreaching party.

Courts frequently reform contracts in two other situations. The first occurs when two parties who have made a binding oral contract agree to put the oral contract in writing but, in doing so, make an error in stating the terms. Usually, the courts allow into evidence the correct terms of the oral contract, thereby reforming the written contract. The second situation occurs when the parties have executed a written covenant not to compete (see Chapter 9). If the covenant not to compete is for a valid and legitimate purpose (such as the sale of a business) but the area or time restraints are unreasonable, some courts will reform the restraints by making them reasonable and will enforce the entire contract as reformed. Other courts, however, will throw out the entire restrictive covenant as illegal.

Recovery Based on Quasi Contract

Quasi Contract   A fictional contract imposed on parties by a court in the interests of fairness and justice; usually imposed to avoid the unjust enrichment of one party at the expense of another.

In some situations, when no actual contract exists, a court may step in to prevent one party from being unjustly enriched at the expense of another party. **Quasi contract** is a legal theory under which an obligation is imposed in the absence of an agreement. It allows the courts to act as if a contract exists when there is no actual contract or agreement between the parties. The courts can also use this theory when the parties entered a contract that is unenforceable for some reason.

Quasi-contractual recovery is often granted when one party has partially performed under a contract that is unenforceable. It provides an alternative to suing for damages and allows the party to recover the reasonable value of the partial performance. **EXAMPLE 10.32** Ericson contracts to build two oil derricks for Petro Industries. The derricks are to be built over a period of three years, but the parties do not create a written contract. Therefore, the Statute of Frauds will bar the enforcement of the contract. After Ericson completes one derrick, Petro Industries informs him that it will not pay for the derrick. Ericson can sue Petro Industries under the theory of quasi contract. ●

● *Exhibit* **10–3 Remedies for Breach of Contract**

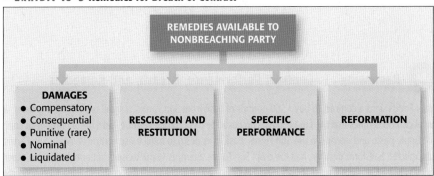

To recover on quasi contract, the party seeking recovery must show the following:

1. The party conferred a benefit on the other party.
2. The party conferred the benefit with the reasonable expectation of being paid.
3. The party did not act as a volunteer in conferring the benefit.
4. The party receiving the benefit would be unjustly enriched by retaining the benefit without paying for it.

 ## Election of Remedies

In many cases, a nonbreaching party has several remedies available. Because the remedies may be inconsistent with one another, the common law of contracts requires the party to choose which remedy to pursue. This is called *election of remedies.* The purpose of the doctrine of election of remedies is to prevent double recovery.

EXAMPLE 10.33 Jefferson agrees to sell his land to Adams. Then Jefferson changes his mind and repudiates the contract. Adams can sue for compensatory damages or for specific performance. If Adams receives damages as a result of the breach, she should not also be granted specific performance of the sales contract because that would mean she would unfairly end up with both the land and the damages. The doctrine of election of remedies requires Adams to choose the remedy she wants, and it eliminates any possibility of double recovery. •

In contrast, remedies under the Uniform Commercial Code (UCC) are cumulative. They include all of the remedies available under the UCC for breach of a sales or lease contract.[24] We will discuss these UCC provisions in Chapter 11.

 ## Contract Provisions Limiting Remedies

A contract may include provisions stating that no damages can be recovered for certain types of breaches or that damages must be limited to a maximum amount. The contract may also provide that the only remedy for breach is replacement, repair, or refund of the purchase price. Provisions stating that no damages can be recovered are called *exculpatory clauses.* Provisions that affect the availability of certain remedies are called *limitation-of-liability clauses.*

Whether these contract provisions and clauses will be enforced depends on the type of breach that is excused by the provision. Normally, a provision excluding liability for fraudulent or intentional injury will not be enforced. Likewise, a clause excluding liability for illegal acts or violations of law will not be enforced. A clause excluding liability for negligence may be enforced in certain cases, however. When an exculpatory clause for negligence is contained in a contract made between parties who have roughly equal bargaining positions, the clause usually will be enforced.

---

24. See UCC 2–703 and 2–711.

 ## Reviewing . . . Contract Performance, Breach, and Remedies

Val's Foods signs a contract to buy 1,500 pounds of basil from Sun Farms, a small organic herb grower, as long as an independent organization inspects and certifies that the crop contains no pesticide or herbicide residue. Val's has a number of contracts with different restaurant chains to supply pesto and intends to use Sun Farms' basil in its pesto to fulfill these contracts. While Sun Farms is preparing to harvest the basil, an unexpected hailstorm destroys half the crop. Sun Farms attempts to purchase additional basil from other farms, but it is late in the season and the price is twice the normal market price. Sun Farms is too small to absorb this cost and immediately notifies Val's that it will not fulfill the contract. Using the information presented in the chapter, answer the following questions.

1. Suppose that the basil does not pass the chemical-residue inspection. Which concept discussed in the chapter might allow Val's to refuse to perform the contract in this situation?
2. Under which legal theory or theories might Sun Farms claim that its obligation under the contract has been discharged by operation of law? Discuss fully.
3. Suppose that Sun Farms contacts every basil grower in the country and buys the last remaining chemical-free basil anywhere. Nevertheless, Sun Farms is able to ship only 1,475 pounds to Val's. Would this fulfill Sun Farms' obligations to Val's? Why or why not?
4. Now suppose that Sun Farms sells its operations to Happy Valley Farms. As a part of the sale, all three parties agree that Happy Valley will provide the basil as stated under the original contract. What is this type of agreement called? Does it discharge the obligations of any of the parties? Explain.

Linking the Law *to Business Communication*
When E-Mails Become Enforceable Contracts

Most business students must take a course in business communication. These courses cover the planning and preparation of oral and written communications, including electronic messages. Indeed, e-mails have become so pervasive that an increasing number of contracts are created via e-mail.

Voluntary Consent and Mistakes

One defense to contract enforceability is a lack of voluntary consent, sometimes due to mistakes. Often, when a mistake is unilateral, the courts will still enforce the contract. Consequently, your e-mail communications can result in an enforceable contract even if you make a typographic error in, say, a dollar amount. If you are making an offer or an acceptance via e-mail, you should treat that communication as carefully as if you were writing or typing it on a sheet of paper. Today, unfortunately, many individuals in the business world treat e-mails somewhat casually. Remember that you are creating an enforceable contract if you make an offer or an acceptance via e-mail, and reread your e-mails several times before you hit the send button.

The Sufficiency of the Writing

In this chapter, you also learned about the Statute of Frauds. The legal definitions of written memoranda and signatures have changed in our electronic age. Today, an e-mail definitely constitutes a writing. A writing can also be a series of e-mail exchanges between two parties. In other words, five e-mail exchanges taken together may form a single contract. (In the past, before e-mails and faxes, this applied to written communications on pieces of paper that were stapled or clipped together.) If one or more e-mails name the parties, identify the subject matter, and lay out the consideration, a court normally will accept those e-mails as constituting a writing sufficient to satisfy the Statute of Frauds.

The Importance of Clear, Precise E-Mail Language

In addition to typographic errors, casually written e-mails may contain ambiguities and miscommunications. Nevertheless, those e-mails may create an enforceable contract, whether you intended it or not. Therefore, all of your business e-mails should be carefully written.

At a minimum, when you are e-mailing business contacts, you should:

1. **Create a precise and informative subject line.** Rather than saying "we should discuss" or "important information," be specific in the subject line of the e-mail, such as "change delivery date for portable generators."
2. **Repeat the subject within the body of the e-mail message.** In the actual e-mail message, avoid phrases with indefinite antecedents such as "This is . . . ." Good business e-mail communication involves a repetition of most of the subject line. That way, if your recipient skips the subject line, the message will still be clear.
3. **Focus on a limited number of subjects, usually one.** Do not ramble and discuss a variety of topics in your e-mail. If necessary, send e-mails on different topics.
4. **Create e-mails that are just as attractive as if they were written on letterhead.** Obviously, e-mails that have no particular format, no paragraphs, bad grammar, misspellings, and incorrect punctuation create a negative impression. More important, if your language is not precise, you may find that you have created an enforceable contract when you did not intend to do so. At a minimum, use the spelling and grammar checker in your word-processing program.
5. **Proofread your work.** This aspect of e-mail communications is so important that it is worth repeating. Proofreading your e-mails before you hit the send button is the most important step that you can take to avoid contract misinterpretations.

FOR CRITICAL ANALYSIS

Sometimes, in contract disputes, one party produces a printout of an e-mail that supposedly was sent, but the other party contends that it was never received. How can the sender avoid this problem?

Key Terms

Chapter Summary: Contract Performance, Breach, and Remedies

Voluntary Consent
(See pages 274–280.)
	1. *Mistakes*—
	   a. *Bilateral (mutual) mistakes*—When both parties are mistaken about the same material fact, such as identity, either party can avoid the contract. If the mistake concerns value or quality, either party can enforce the contract.
	   b. *Unilateral mistakes*—Generally, the party making the mistake is bound by the contract *unless* (a) the other party knows or should have known of the mistake or (b) the mistake is an inadvertent mathematical error—such as an error in addition or subtraction—committed without gross negligence.
	2. *Fraudulent misrepresentation*—When fraud occurs, usually the innocent party can enforce or avoid the contract. To obtain damages, the innocent party must have suffered an injury.
	3. *Undue influence*—Undue influence arises from special relationships in which one party can greatly influence another party, thus overcoming that party's free will. Usually, the contract is voidable.
	4. *Duress*—Duress is the use of a threat, such as the threat of violence or serious economic loss, to force a party to enter a contract. The party forced to enter the contract can rescind the contract.

The Statute of Frauds—Writing Requirement (See page 280.)	The following types of contracts fall under the Statute of Frauds and must be in writing to be enforceable: 1. Contracts involving interests in land. 2. Contracts that cannot by their terms be performed within one year from the day after the date of formation. 3. Collateral, or secondary, contracts, such as promises to answer for the debt or duty of another. 4. Promises made in consideration of marriage. 5. Under the UCC, contracts for the sale of goods priced at $500 or more.
Third Party Rights (See pages 280–282.)	1. *Assignments*—An assignment is the transfer of rights under a contract to a third party. The third party to whom the rights are assigned has a right to demand performance from the other original party to the contract. Generally, all rights can be assigned, but there are a few exceptions, such as when a statute prohibits assignment or when the contract calls for personal services. 2. *Delegations*—A delegation is the transfer of duties under a contract to a third party, who then assumes the obligation of performing the contractual duties previously held by the one making the delegation. As a general rule, any duty can be delegated, except in a few situations, such as when the contract expressly prohibits delegation or when performance depends on the personal skills of the original party. 3. *Third party beneficiaries*—A third party beneficiary is one who benefits from a contract between two other parties. If the party was an intended beneficiary, then the third party has legal rights and can sue the promisor directly to enforce the contract. If the contract benefits the third party unintentionally, then the third party cannot sue to enforce the contract.

Chapter Summary: Contract Performance, Breach, and Remedies, Continued

Performance and Discharge (See pages 282–291.)	1. *Conditions of performance*—Contract obligations are sometimes subject to conditions. A condition is a possible future event, the occurrence or nonoccurrence of which will trigger the performance of a contract obligation or terminate an existing obligation. A condition that must be fulfilled before a party's promise becomes absolute is called a *condition precedent.*
	2. *Discharge by performance*—A contract may be discharged by complete (strict) performance or by substantial performance. In some instances, performance must be to the satisfaction of another. Totally inadequate performance constitutes a material breach of contract. An anticipatory repudiation of a contract allows the other party to sue immediately for breach of contract.
	3. *Discharge by agreement*—Parties may agree to discharge their contractual obligations in several ways:
	   a. *By rescission*—The parties mutually agree to rescind (cancel) the contract.
	   b. *By novation*—A new party is substituted for one of the primary parties to a contract.
	   c. *By settlement agreement*—The parties agree to a new contract that replaces the old contract as a means of settling a dispute.
	   d. *By accord and satisfaction*—The parties agree to render and accept performance different from that on which they originally agreed.
	4. *Discharge by operation of law*—Parties' obligations under contracts may be discharged by operation of law owing to one of the following:
	   a. Contract alteration.
	   b. Statutes of limitations.
	   c. Bankruptcy.
	   d. Impossibility or impracticability of performance, including frustration of purpose.

Damages for Breach of Contract (See pages 291–297.)	Damages are the legal remedy designed to compensate the nonbreaching party for the loss of the bargain. By awarding monetary damages, the court tries to place the parties in the positions that they would have occupied had the contract been fully performed.
	1. *Compensatory damages*—Damages that compensate the nonbreaching party for injuries actually sustained and proved to have arisen directly from the loss of the bargain resulting from the breach of contract.
	   a. In breached contracts for the sale of goods, the usual measure of compensatory damages is the difference between the contract price and the market price.
	   b. In breached contracts for the sale of land, the measure of damages is ordinarily the same as in contracts for the sale of goods.
	2. *Consequential damages*—Damages resulting from special circumstances beyond the contract itself—the damages flow only from the consequences of a breach. For a party to recover consequential damages, the damages must be the foreseeable result of a breach of contract, and the breaching party must have known at the time the contract was formed that special circumstances existed that would cause the nonbreaching party to incur additional loss on breach of the contract. Also called *special damages.*
	3. *Mitigation of damages*—The nonbreaching party frequently has a duty to *mitigate* (lessen or reduce) the damages incurred as a result of the contract's breach.
	4. *Liquidated damages*—Damages that may be specified in a contract as the amount to be paid to the nonbreaching party in the event the contract is breached in the future. Clauses providing for liquidated damages are enforced if the damages were difficult to estimate at the time the contract was formed and if the amount stipulated is reasonable. If the amount is construed to be a penalty, the clause will not be enforced.

Equitable Remedies (See pages 297–300.)	1. *Rescission*—A remedy whereby a contract is canceled and the parties are restored to the positions that they occupied prior to the transaction. Available when fraud, a mistake, duress, or failure of consideration is present. The rescinding party must give prompt notice of the rescission to the breaching party.

(Continued)

Chapter Summary: Contract Performance, Breach, and Remedies, Continued

Equitable Remedies– Continued	2. *Restitution*–When a contract is rescinded, both parties must make restitution to each other by returning the goods, property, or funds previously conveyed. Restitution prevents the unjust enrichment of the parties.
	3. *Specific performance*–An equitable remedy calling for the performance of the act promised in the contract. This remedy is available only in special situations–such as those involving contracts for the sale of unique goods or land–in which monetary damages would be an inadequate remedy. Specific performance is not available as a remedy in breached contracts for personal services.
	4. *Reformation*–An equitable remedy allowing a contract to be "reformed," or rewritten, to reflect the parties' true intentions. Available when an agreement is imperfectly expressed in writing.
	5. *Recovery based on quasi contract*–An equitable theory imposed by the courts to prevent unjust enrichment in a situation in which no enforceable contract exists. The party seeking recovery must show the following:
	a. A benefit was conferred on the other party.
	b. The party conferring the benefit did so with the expectation of being paid.
	c. The benefit was not volunteered.
	d. Retaining the benefit without paying for it would result in the unjust enrichment of the party receiving the benefit.
Election of Remedies (See page 300.)	A common law doctrine under which a nonbreaching party must choose one remedy from those available. This doctrine prevents double recovery. Under the UCC, remedies are cumulative for the breach of a contract for the sale of goods.
Contract Provisions Limiting Remedies (See page 300.)	A contract may provide that no damages (or only a limited amount of damages) can be recovered in the event the contract is breached. Clauses excluding liability for fraudulent or intentional injury or for illegal acts cannot be enforced. Clauses excluding liability for negligence may be enforced if both parties hold roughly equal bargaining power.

ExamPrep

ISSUE SPOTTERS

1. Ira, a famous and wealthy musician, dies. Jen, his widow, sells their farm to Kris, who asks what should be done with all the "junk" on the property. Jen says that Kris can do whatever he wants with it. Unknown to Jen or Kris, in a cabinet in the house are the master tapes for an unreleased album. Can Kris keep the tapes? Why or why not?

2. Ready Foods contracts to buy two hundred carloads of frozen pizzas from Speedy Distributors. Before Ready or Speedy starts performing, can either party call off the deal? What if Speedy has already shipped the pizzas? Explain your answers.

—**Check your answers to these questions against the answers provided in Appendix G.**

BEFORE THE TEST

Go to **www.cengagebrain.com**, enter the ISBN number "9781111530617," and click on "Find" to locate this textbook's Web site. Then, click on "Access Now" under "Study Tools," and select "Chapter 10" at the top. There you will find an "Interactive Quiz" that you can take to assess your mastery of the concepts in this chapter, as well as "Flashcards" and a "Glossary" of important terms.

For Review

1. In what types of situations might voluntary consent to a contract's terms be lacking?
2. What are the elements of fraudulent misrepresentation?

3. What is substantial performance?

4. What is the standard measure of compensatory damages when a contract is breached?

5. What equitable remedies can a court grant, and in what circumstances will a court consider granting them?

 ## Questions and Case Problems

10–1. Substantial Performance. The Caplans own a real estate lot, and they contract with Faithful Construction, Inc., to build a house on it for $360,000. The specifications list "all plumbing bowls and fixtures . . . to be Crane brand." The Caplans leave on vacation, and during their absence Faithful is unable to buy and install Crane plumbing fixtures. Instead, Faithful installs Kohler brand fixtures, an equivalent in the industry. On completion of the building contract, the Caplans inspect the work, discover the substitution, and refuse to accept the house, claiming Faithful has breached the conditions set forth in the specifications. Discuss fully the Caplans' claim.

10–2. Discharge by Agreement. Junior owes creditor Iba $1,000, which is due and payable on June 1. Junior has been in a car accident, has missed a great deal of work, and consequently will not have the funds on June 1. Junior's father, Fred, offers to pay Iba $1,100 in four equal installments if Iba will discharge Junior from any further liability on the debt. Iba accepts. Is this transaction a novation or an accord and satisfaction? Explain.

10–3. Impossibility of Performance. In the following situations, certain events take place after the formation of contracts. Discuss which of these contracts are discharged because the events render the contracts impossible to perform.

  1. Jimenez, a famous singer, contracts to perform in your nightclub. He dies prior to performance.

  2. Raglione contracts to sell you her land. Just before title is to be transferred, she dies.

  3. Oppenheim contracts to sell you one thousand bushels of apples from her orchard in the state of Washington. Because of a severe frost, she is unable to deliver the apples.

  4. Maxwell contracts to lease a service station for ten years. His principal income is from the sale of gasoline. Because of an oil embargo by foreign oil-producing nations, gasoline is rationed, cutting sharply into Maxwell's gasoline sales. He cannot make his lease payments.

10–4. Quasi Contract. Middleton Motors, Inc., a struggling Ford dealership in Madison, Wisconsin, sought managerial and financial assistance from Lindquist Ford, Inc., a successful Ford dealership in Bettendorf, Iowa. While the two dealerships negotiated the terms for the services and a cash infusion, Lindquist sent Craig Miller, its general manager, to assume control of Middleton. After about a year, the parties had not agreed on the terms, Lindquist had not invested any money, Middleton had not made a profit, and Miller was fired without being paid. Lindquist and Miller filed a suit in a federal district court against Middleton based on quasi contract, seeking to recover Miller's pay for his time. What are the requirements to recover on a theory of quasi contract? Which of these requirements is most likely to be disputed in this case? Why? [*Lindquist Ford, Inc. v. Middleton Motors, Inc.,* 557 F.3d 469 (7th Cir. 2009)]

10–5. Condition Precedent. Just Homes, LLC (JH), hired Mike Building & Contracting, Inc., to do $1.35 million worth of renovation work on three homes. Community Preservation Corp. (CPC) supervised Mike's work on behalf of JH. The contract stated that in the event of a dispute, JH would have to obtain the project architect's certification to justify terminating Mike. As construction progressed, relations between Mike and CPC worsened. At a certain point in the project, Mike requested partial payment, and CPC recommended that JH not make it. Mike refused to continue work without further payment. JH evicted Mike from the project. Mike sued for breach of contract. JH contended that it had the right to terminate the contract due to CPC's negative reports and Mike's failure to agree with the project's engineer. Mike moved for summary judgment for the amounts owed for work performed, claiming that JH had not fulfilled the condition precedent—that is, JH never obtained the project architect's certification for Mike's termination. Which of the two parties involved breached the contract? Explain your answer. [*Mike Building & Contracting, Inc. v. Just Homes, LLC,* 27 Misc.3d 833, 901 N.Y.S.2d 458 (2010)]

10–6. **Case Problem with Sample Answer. Liquidated Damages and Penalties.** Planned Pethood Plus, Inc., is a veterinarian-owned clinic. It borrowed $389,000 from KeyBank at an interest rate of 9.3 percent per year for ten years. The loan had a "prepayment penalty" clause that clearly stated that if the loan was repaid early, a specific formula would be used to assess a lump-sum payment to extinguish the obligation. The sooner the loan was paid off, the higher the prepayment penalty. After a year, the veterinarians decided to pay off the loan. KeyBank invoked a prepayment penalty of $40,525.92, which was equal to 10.7 percent of the balance due. The veterinarians sued, contending that the prepayment requirement was unenforceable because it was a penalty. The bank countered that the amount was not a penalty but liquidated damages and that the sum was reasonable. The trial court agreed with the bank, and the veterinarians appealed. Was the loan's prepayment charge reasonable, and should it have been enforced? Why or why not? [*Planned Pethood Plus, Inc. v. KeyCorp, Inc.,* 228 P.3d 262 (Colo.App. 2010)]

—To view a sample answer for Case Problem 10–6, go to Appendix F at the end of this text.

10–7. Conditions of Performance. James Maciel leased an apartment in Regent Village, a university-owned housing facility for Regent University (RU) students in Virginia Beach, Virginia. The lease ran until the end of the fall semester. Maciel had an option to renew the lease semester by semester as long as he maintained his status as an RU student. When Maciel completed his coursework for the spring semester, he told RU that he intended to withdraw. The university told him that he could stay in the apartment until May 31, the final day of the spring semester. Maciel asked for two additional weeks, but the university denied the request. On June 1, RU changed the locks on the apartment. Maciel entered through a window and e-mailed the university that he planned to stay "for another one or two weeks." Charged in a Virginia state court with trespassing, Maciel argued that he had "legal authority" to occupy the apartment. Was Maciel correct? Explain. [*Maciel v. Commonwealth,* __ S.E.2d __ (Va.App. 2011)]

10–8. Damages. Before buying a house in Rockaway, New Jersey, Dean and Donna Testa hired Ground Systems, Inc. (GSI), to inspect the sewage and water disposal system. Steve Austin, the GSI inspector, told Dean that the system included a tank, a distribution box, pipes, and a leach field (where contaminants are removed from the sewage). Austin's written report described a split system with a watertight septic tank and a separate kitchen and laundry wastewater tank. The Testas bought the house. Ten years later, when they tried to sell the house, a prospective buyer withdrew from the sale after receiving an inspection report that evaluated the septic system as "unsatisfactory." The Testas arranged for the installation of a new system. During the work, Dean saw that the old system was not as Austin had described—there was no distribution box or leach field, and there was only one tank, which was not watertight. The Testas filed a suit in a New Jersey state court against GSI, alleging breach of contract. If GSI was liable, what would be the measure of the damages? [*Testa v. Ground Systems, Inc.,* 206 N.J. 330, 20 A.3d 435 (2011)]

10–9. **A Question of Ethics. Conditions.** *King County, Washington, hired Frank Coluccio Construction Co. (FCCC) to act as general contractor for a public works project involving the construction of a small utility tunnel under the Duwamish Waterway. FCCC hired Donald B. Murphy Contractors, Inc. (DBM), as a subcontractor. DBM was responsible for constructing an access shaft at the eastern end of the tunnel. Problems arose during construction, including a "blow-in" of the access shaft that caused it to fill with water, soil, and debris. FCCC and DBM incurred substantial expenses from the repairs and delays. Under the project contract, King County was supposed to buy an insurance policy to "insure against physical loss or damage by perils included under an 'All-Risk' Builder's Risk policy." Any claim under this policy was to be filed through the insured. King County, which had general property damage insurance, did not obtain an all-risk builder's risk policy. For the losses attributable to the blow-in, FCCC and DBM submitted builder's risk claims, which the county denied. FCCC filed a suit in a Washington state court against King County, alleging, among other claims, breach of contract. [Frank Coluccio Construction Co. v. King County, 136 Wash.App. 751, 150 P.3d 1147 (Div. 1 2007)]*

1. King County's property damage policy specifically excluded, at the county's request, coverage of tunnels. The county drafted its contract with FCCC to require the all-risk builder's risk policy and authorize itself to "sponsor" claims. When FCCC and DBM filed their claims, the county secretly colluded with its property damage insurer to deny payment. What do these facts indicate about the county's ethics and legal liability in this situation?

2. Could DBM, as a third party to the contract between King County and FCCC, maintain an action on the contract against King County? Discuss.

3. All-risk insurance is a promise to pay on the "fortuitous" happening of a loss or damage from any cause except those that are specifically excluded. Payment usually is not made on a loss that, at the time the insurance was obtained, the claimant subjectively knew would occur. If a loss results from faulty workmanship on the part of a contractor, should the obligation to pay under an all-risk policy be discharged? Explain.

10–10. **Video Question. *Midnight Run.*** Access the video using the instructions provided below to answer the following questions.

1. Eddie (Joe Pantoliano) and Jack (Robert De Niro) negotiate a contract for Jack to find the Duke, a mob accountant who embezzled funds, and bring him back for trial. Assume that the contract is valid. If Jack breaches the contract by failing to bring in the Duke, what kinds of remedies, if any, can Eddie seek? Explain your answer.

2. Would the equitable remedy of specific performance be available to either Jack or Eddie in the event of a breach? Why or why not?

3. Now assume that the contract between Eddie and Jack is unenforceable. Nevertheless, Jack performs his side of the bargain (brings in the Duke). Does Jack have any legal recourse in this situation? Why or why not?

—To watch this video, go to **www.cengagebrain.com** and register the access code that came with your new book or log in to your existing account. Select the link for either the "Business Law Digital Video Library Online Access" or "Business Law CourseMate," and then click on "Complete Video List" to find the video for this chapter (Video 57).

Chapter 11

Sales, Leases, and Product Liability

> "I am for free commerce with all nations."
>
> —George Washington, 1732–1799
> (First president of the United States, 1789–1797)

Contents

Chapter Objectives

After reading this chapter, you should be able to answer the following questions:

1. How do Article 2 and Article 2A of the UCC differ? What types of transactions does each article cover?

2. Under the UCC, if an offeree includes additional or different terms in an acceptance, will a contract result? If so, what happens to these terms?

3. What remedies are available to a seller or lessor when the buyer or lessee breaches the contract? What remedies are available to a buyer or lessee if the seller or lessor breaches the contract?

4. What implied warranties arise under the UCC?

5. What are the elements of a cause of action in strict product liability?

(Quaziefoto/Creative Commons)

When we turn to contracts for the sale and lease of goods, we move away from common law principles and into the area of statutory law. State statutory law governing sales and lease transactions is based on the Uniform Commercial Code (UCC), which, as mentioned in Chapter 1, has been adopted as law by all of the states.[1] The goal of the UCC is to simplify and streamline commercial transactions, allowing parties to form sales and lease contracts without observing the same degree of formality used in forming other types of contracts. By facilitating commercial transactions, the UCC reflects the sentiment expressed in the chapter-opening quotation above—free commerce will benefit our nation.

This chapter opens with a look at the broad scope of Articles 2 and 2A. Article 2 of the UCC establishes the requirements to form sales contracts, and we describe how these laws differ from the common law of contracts. Article 2 also stipulates the duties and obligations of parties to sales contracts, although parties normally can agree to terms different from those stated in the UCC. Article 2A covers similar issues for lease contracts. Because of its importance in commercial transactions, we have included Article 2 in Appendix C of this text.

---

1. Louisiana has not adopted Articles 2 and 2A, however.

After examining the formation of sales and lease contracts, we look at the performance required in such contracts and the remedies available if a contract is breached. We also examine the warranties, both express and implied, that can arise in contracts to sell or lease goods. Actions for breach of warranty are a subset of product liability claims, which we discuss in the final pages of this chapter.

▶ The Scope of Article 2—The Sale of Goods

Sales Contract   A contract for the sale of goods under which the ownership of goods is transferred from a seller to a buyer for a price.

Article 2 of the UCC (as adopted by state statutes) governs **sales contracts,** or contracts for the sale of goods. To facilitate commercial transactions, Article 2 modifies some of the common law contract requirements that were discussed in the previous chapters. To the extent that it has not been modified by the UCC, however, the common law of contracts (including the requirements for agreement, consideration, capacity, and legality) also applies to sales contracts.

In general, the rule is that whenever a conflict arises between a common law contract rule and the state statutory law based on the UCC, the UCC controls. In other words, when a UCC provision addresses a certain issue, the UCC rule governs, but when the UCC is silent, the common law governs. The relationship between general contract law and the law governing sales of goods is illustrated in Exhibit 11–1 below. (For a discussion of some problems surrounding state taxation of sales that take place over the Internet, see this chapter's *Online Developments* feature on the facing page.)

In regard to Article 2, keep two points in mind. First, Article 2 deals with the sale of *goods* and does not cover items such as real property (real estate) and services. Thus, if the subject matter of a dispute is goods, the UCC governs. If it is real estate or services, the common law applies. Second, in some situations, the rules may vary, depending on whether the buyer or the seller is a *merchant*. We look now at how the UCC defines a *sale*, *goods*, and *merchant status*.

● *Exhibit* **11–1 The Law Governing Contracts**
This exhibit graphically illustrates the relationship between general contract law and statutory law (UCC Articles 2 and 2A) governing contracts for the sale and lease of goods. Sales contracts are not governed exclusively by Article 2 of the UCC but are also governed by general contract law whenever it is relevant and has not been modified by the UCC.

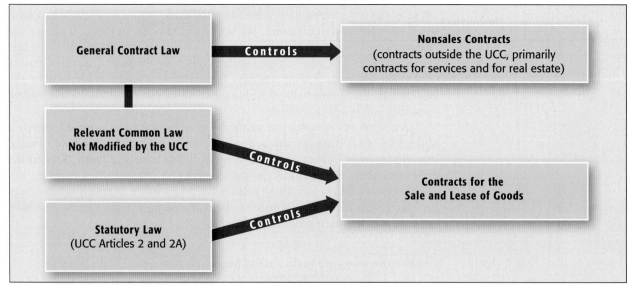

Online Developments

The Thorny Issue of Taxing Internet Sales

From the very beginning of e-commerce, cities and states have complained that they are losing millions, if not billions, of dollars of potential tax revenues because e-commerce companies generally do not collect state and local sales taxes. Although most states have laws requiring their residents to report purchases from other states and to pay taxes on those purchases (so-called use taxes), few (if any) U.S. consumers ever comply with these laws.

Certainly, the possibility of avoiding sales taxes has likely contributed to the growth of e-commerce. Not surprisingly, retailers with investment in physical sales outlets have complained to local, state, and federal governments about this "sales tax inequity."

Local Governments Are Suing Online Travel Companies

One recent trend in the effort to collect taxes from e-commerce has focused on online travel companies, including Travelocity, Priceline. com, Hotels.com, and Orbitz.com. By 2011, at least a dozen cities, including Atlanta, Charleston, Philadelphia, and San Antonio, had filed suits claiming that the online travel companies owed taxes on hotel reservations that they had booked. All of the cities involved in the suits impose hotel occupancy taxes. In Atlanta, for example, the local statute authorizes the city to devise "a rate of taxation, the manner of imposition, payment, and collection of the tax, and all other procedures related to the tax."[a]

At issue in the lawsuits is not whether the online travel companies owe hotel occupancy tax, but rather the amount of tax that they owe and the procedure that should be used to collect it. Online travel companies, such as Hotels.com, typically purchase blocks of hotel rooms at a wholesale rate and subsequently resell the rooms to customers at a marked-up retail rate, keeping the difference as profit. The company forwards to the hotel an amount

intended to cover the hotel occupancy tax on the wholesale price of the rooms sold. The hotel then remits to the city taxing authority the tax on the rooms sold by the online travel agency. Thus, the online travel companies do not remit taxes directly to any city authorities.

In calculating the amount of tax owed, the online travel companies assess the occupancy tax rates on the wholesale prices of the rooms, rather than the retail prices that they charge. The cities claim that the online travel companies should be assessing the hotel occupancy tax on the retail prices of the rooms. The cities also want the online companies to register with the local jurisdictions and to collect and remit the required taxes directly.

What the Courts Have Been Deciding

More than a dozen cases have been brought against online travel agencies, but so far the courts have been divided. Many of these cases have been brought in federal district courts, and those courts have often ruled in favor of the cities.[b]

Some state courts have also upheld the cities' claims. In one case, for example, the Supreme Court of Georgia reversed the lower court's dismissal and remanded the case for trial on Atlanta's claim concerning the city's hotel tax ordinance.[c] Given that most cities and counties have found themselves in dire financial straits during the latest recession, we can expect to see more such suits around the country.

FOR CRITICAL ANALYSIS

Why do you think that cities and states have not brought similar lawsuits against e-commerce retailers such as Amazon.com?

---

a. OCGA Section 48-13-53, which is the Enabling Statutes for the city of Atlanta.

b. See, for example, *City of Goodlettsville v. Priceline.com, Inc.,* 605 F.Supp.2d 982 (M.D.Tenn. 2009); and *City of Findlay v. Hotels.com,* 561 F.Supp.2d 917 (N.D. Ohio 2008).

c. *City of Atlanta v. Hotels.com, L.P.,* 285 Ga. 231, 674 S.E.2d 898 (2009).

What Is a Sale?

Sale The passing of title to property from the seller to the buyer for a price.

Tangible Property Property that has physical existence and can be distinguished by the senses of touch and sight.

Intangible Property Property that cannot be seen or touched but exists only conceptually, such as corporate stocks and bonds. Article 2 of the UCC does not govern intangible property.

The UCC defines a **sale** as "the passing of title [evidence of ownership rights] from the seller to the buyer for a price" [UCC 2–106(1)]. The price may be payable in cash (or its equivalent, such as a check or credit card) or in other goods or services.

What Are Goods?

To be characterized as a *good*, an item of property must be *tangible*, and it must be *movable*. **Tangible property** has physical existence—it can be touched or seen. **Intangible property**—such as corporate stocks and bonds, patents and copyrights, and ordinary contract rights—has only conceptual existence and thus does not come under Article 2. A *movable* item can be carried from place to place. Hence, real estate is excluded from Article 2.

Goods associated with real estate can fall within the scope of Article 2, however [UCC 2–107]. For example, a contract for the sale of minerals, oil, or gas is a contract for the sale of goods if *severance, or separation, is to be made by the seller.* Similarly, a contract for the sale of growing crops or timber to be cut is a contract for the sale of goods *regardless of who severs them.*

In cases involving contracts in which goods and services are combined, the courts generally use the **predominant-factor test** to determine whether a contract is primarily for the sale of goods or for the sale of services. If a court decides that a mixed contract is primarily a goods contract, *any* dispute, even a dispute over the services portion, will be decided under the UCC.

EXAMPLE 11.1 An accounting firm contracts to purchase customized software from Micro Systems. The contract states that half of the purchase price is for Micro's professional services and the other half is for the goods (the software). If a court determines that the contract is predominantly for the software, rather than the customizing services, the court will hold that the transaction falls under Article 2. Conversely, if the court finds that the services are predominant, it will hold that the transaction is not governed by the UCC. •

> **Predominant-Factor Test** A test courts use to determine whether a contract is primarily for the sale of goods or for the sale of services.

Who Is a Merchant?

Article 2 governs the sale of goods in general. It applies to sales transactions between all buyers and sellers. In addition, the UCC imposes certain special business standards on merchants because of their commercial expertise.[2] Such standards do not apply to the casual or inexperienced seller or buyer (consumer). Section 2–104 sets forth three ways in which merchant status can arise:

1. A merchant is a person who *deals in goods of the kind* involved in the sales contract. Thus, a retailer, a wholesaler, or a manufacturer is a merchant of the goods sold in his or her business. A merchant for one type of goods is not necessarily a merchant for another type. For example, a sporting goods retailer is a merchant when selling tennis rackets but not when selling a used computer.

2. A merchant is a person who, by occupation, holds himself or herself out as having knowledge and skill unique to the practices or goods involved in the transaction. This broad definition may include banks or universities as merchants.

3. A person who *employs a merchant as a broker, agent, or other intermediary* has the status of merchant in that transaction. Hence, if an art collector hires a broker to purchase or sell art for her, the collector is considered a merchant in the transaction.

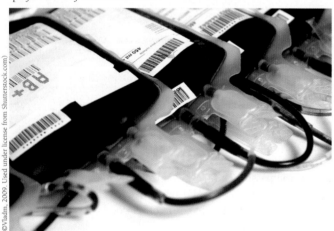

Is providing blood to a patient during an operation a "sale of goods" or the "performance of a medical service"?

---

2. The provisions that apply only to merchants deal principally with the Statute of Frauds, firm offers, confirmatory memoranda, warranties, and contract modification. These special rules reflect expedient business practices commonly known to merchants in the commercial setting. They will be discussed later in this chapter.

Merchant A person who is engaged in the purchase and sale of goods. Under the UCC, a person who deals in goods of the kind involved in the sales contract or who holds herself or himself out as having skill or knowledge peculiar to the practices or goods being purchased or sold.

Lease Under Article 2A of the UCC, a transfer of the right to possess and use goods for a period of time in exchange for payment.

Lease Agreement In regard to the lease of goods, an agreement in which one person (the lessor) agrees to transfer the right to the possession and use of property to another person (the lessee) in exchange for rental payments.

Lessor A person who transfers the right to the possession and use of goods to another in exchange for rental payments.

Lessee A person who acquires the right to the possession and use of another's goods in exchange for rental payments.

In summary, a person is a **merchant** when she or he, acting in a mercantile capacity, possesses or uses an expertise specifically related to the goods being sold. This basic distinction is not always clear-cut. For example, state courts appear to be split on whether farmers should be considered merchants.

The Scope of Article 2A—Leases

In the past few decades, leases of personal property (goods) have become increasingly common. Consumers and business firms lease automobiles, industrial equipment, items for use in the home (such as floor polishers), and many other types of goods. Article 2A of the UCC was created to fill the need for uniform guidelines in this area.

Article 2A covers any transaction that creates a **lease** of goods or a sublease of goods [UCC 2A–102, 2A–103(1)(k)]. Article 2A is essentially a repetition of Article 2, except that it applies to leases of goods rather than sales of goods and thus varies to reflect differences between sales and lease transactions. (Note that Article 2A is not concerned with leases of real property, such as land or buildings.)

Article 2A defines a **lease agreement** as a lessor and lessee's bargain with respect to the lease of goods, as found in their language and as implied by other circumstances [UCC 2A–103(1)(k)]. A **lessor** is one who transfers the right to the possession and use of goods under a lease [UCC 2A–103(1)(p)]. A **lessee** is one who acquires the right to the possession and use of goods under a lease [UCC 2A–103(1)(o)]. In other words, the lessee is the party who is leasing the goods from the lessor. Article 2A applies to all types of leases of goods. Special rules apply to certain types of leases, however, including consumer leases and finance leases.

A company offers to lease automobiles. All such leases are governed by Article 2 of the UCC. What leases are not governed by the UCC?

(S. Jones/Creative Commons)

The Formation of Sales and Lease Contracts

Article 2 and Article 2A of the UCC modify common law rules for the formation of sales and lease contracts in several ways. Remember, though, that parties to sales contracts are basically free to establish whatever terms they wish. The UCC comes into play only when the parties have failed to provide in their contract for a contingency that later gives rise to a dispute. The UCC makes this clear time and again by using such phrases as "unless the parties otherwise agree" or "absent a contrary agreement by the parties."

The foldout exhibit that follows this chapter shows an actual sales contract used by Starbucks Coffee Company. The contract illustrates many of the terms and clauses that typically are contained in contracts for the sale of goods.

Offer

In general contract law, the moment a definite offer is met by an unqualified acceptance, a binding contract is formed. In commercial sales transactions, the verbal exchanges, correspondence, and actions of the parties may not reveal exactly when a binding contractual obligation arises. The UCC states that an agreement sufficient to constitute a contract can exist even if the moment of its making is undetermined [UCC 2–204(2), 2A–204(2)].

OPEN TERMS   Remember from Chapter 9 that under the common law of contracts, an offer must be definite enough for the parties (and the courts) to ascertain its essential terms when it is accepted. In contrast, the UCC states that a sales or lease contract will not fail for indefiniteness even if one or more terms are left open as long as (1) the parties intended to make a contract and (2) there is a reasonably certain basis for the court to grant an appropriate remedy [UCC 2–204(3), 2A–204(3)]. Normally, under Article 2 the only term that must be specified is the quantity—because there is almost no way to determine objectively what is a reasonable quantity of goods for someone to buy.

In contrast, a court can objectively determine a reasonable price for particular goods by looking at the market. Thus, if the parties have not agreed on a price, the court will determine a "reasonable price at the time for delivery" [UCC 2–305(1)]. If the parties do not specify payment terms, payment is due at the time and place at which the buyer is to receive the goods [UCC 2–310(a)]. When no delivery terms are specified, the buyer normally takes delivery at the seller's place of business [UCC 2–308(a)].

CONTRAST   The common law requires that the parties make their terms definite before they have a contract. The UCC applies general commercial standards to make the terms of a contract definite.

Preventing Legal Disputes

If a business owner leaves certain terms of a sales or lease contract open, the UCC allows a court to supply the missing terms. Although this can sometimes be advantageous (to establish that a contract existed, for instance), it can also be a major disadvantage. If a party fails to state a price in the contract offer, for example, a court will impose a reasonable price by looking at the market price of similar goods *at the time of delivery.* Thus, instead of receiving the usual price for the goods, a business will receive what a court considers a reasonable price when the goods are delivered. Therefore, when goods are being sold or leased, the contract should clearly state any terms that are essential to the bargain, particularly the price. It is generally better to establish the terms of a contract than to leave it up to a court to determine what terms are reasonable after a dispute has arisen.

MERCHANT'S FIRM OFFER   Under common law contract principles, an offer can be revoked at any time before acceptance. The UCC has an exception that applies only to **firm offers** for the sale or lease of goods made by a merchant (regardless of whether or not the offeree is a merchant). A firm offer arises when a merchant gives assurances *in a signed writing* that the offer will remain open. A firm offer is irrevocable without the necessity of consideration for the stated period or, if no definite period is stated, a reasonable period (neither to exceed three months) [UCC 2–205, 2A–205].

EXAMPLE 11.2   Osaka, a used-car dealer, writes a letter to Bennett on January 1, stating, "I have a used 2010 Suzuki on the lot that I'll sell you for $20,500 any time between now and January 31." By January 18, Osaka has heard nothing from Bennett, so he sells the Suzuki to another person. On January 23, Bennett tenders $20,500 to Osaka and asks for the car. When Osaka tells him the car has already been sold, Bennett claims that Osaka has breached a valid contract. Bennett is right. Osaka is a merchant of used cars and assured Bennett in a signed writing that he would keep his offer open until the end of January. Thus, Bennett's acceptance on January 23 created a contract, which Osaka breached. ●

Firm Offer   An offer (by a merchant) that is irrevocable without the necessity of consideration for a stated period of time or, if no definite period is stated, for a reasonable time (neither period to exceed three months). A firm offer by a merchant must be in writing and must be signed by the offeror.

Acceptance

BE AWARE   The UCC provides that acceptance can be made by any means of communication that is reasonable under the circumstances.

Acceptance of an offer to buy, sell, or lease goods generally may be made in any reasonable manner and by any reasonable means. The UCC permits acceptance of an offer to buy goods "either by a prompt *promise* to ship or by the prompt or current shipment of conforming or nonconforming goods" [UCC 2–206(1)(b)]. *Conforming goods* accord with the contract's terms, whereas *nonconforming goods* do not.

The prompt shipment of nonconforming goods constitutes both an acceptance, which creates a contract, and a breach of that contract. This rule does not apply if the seller **seasonably** (within a reasonable amount of time) notifies the buyer that the nonconforming shipment is offered only as an *accommodation,* or as a favor. The notice of accommodation must clearly indicate to the buyer that the shipment does not constitute an acceptance and, thus, that no contract has been formed.

EXAMPLE 11.3 McFarrell Pharmacy orders five cases of Johnson & Johnson 3-by-5-inch gauze pads from H.T. Medical Supply, Inc. If H.T. ships five cases of Xeroform 3-by-5-inch gauze pads instead, the shipment acts as both an acceptance of McFarrell's offer and a *breach* of the resulting contract. McFarrell may sue H.T. for any appropriate damages. If, however, H.T. notifies McFarrell that the Xeroform gauze pads are being shipped *as an accommodation*—because H.T. has only Xeroform pads in stock—the shipment will constitute a counteroffer, not an acceptance. A contract will be formed only if McFarrell accepts the Xeroform gauze pads. •

COMMUNICATION OF ACCEPTANCE   Under the common law, because a unilateral offer invites acceptance by a performance, the offeree need not notify the offeror of performance unless the offeror would not otherwise know about it. In other words, a unilateral offer can be accepted by beginning performance. The UCC is more stringent than the common law in this regard because it requires notification. Under the UCC, if the offeror is not notified within a reasonable time that the offeree has accepted the contract by beginning performance, then the offeror can treat the offer as having lapsed before acceptance [UCC 2–206(2), 2A–206(2)].

ADDITIONAL TERMS   Recall that under the common law, the mirror image rule requires that the terms of the acceptance exactly match those of the offer. The UCC dispenses with the mirror image rule. Generally, the UCC takes the position that if the offeree's response indicates a *definite* acceptance of the offer, a contract is formed even if the acceptance includes additional or different terms from those contained in the offer [UCC 2–207(1)]. Whether the additional terms become part of the contract depends, in part, on whether the parties are nonmerchants or merchants.

Rules When One Party or Both Parties Are Nonmerchants. If one (or both) of the parties is a *nonmerchant,* the contract is formed according to the terms of the original offer submitted by the original offeror and not according to the additional terms of the acceptance [UCC 2–207(2)].

EXAMPLE 11.4 Tolsen offers in writing to sell his iPad and thirteen additional apps to Valdez for $1,500. Valdez faxes a reply to Tolsen stating, "I accept your offer to purchase your iPad and thirteen additional apps for $1,500. I *would like* a box of laser printer paper and two extra toner cartridges to be included in the purchase price." Valdez has given Tolsen a definite expression of acceptance (creating a contract), even though the acceptance also *suggests* an added term for the offer. Because Tolsen is not a merchant, the additional term is merely a proposal (suggestion), and Tolsen is not legally obligated to comply with that term. •

In the following case, the court had to decide whether an additional term that appeared in the invoice sent with the goods was part of the parties' contract. This additional term was a forum-selection clause (see page 253).

Seasonably   Within a specified time period or, if no period is specified, within a reasonable time.

"Business, more than any other occupation, is a continual dealing with the future; it is a continual calculation, an instinctive exercise in foresight."

Henry R. Luce, 1898–1967
(U.S. editor and publisher)

Case 11.1   **Office Supply Store.com v. Kansas City School Board**

Missouri Court of Appeals, 334 S.W.3d 574 (2011).
www.courts.mo.gov [a]

BACKGROUND AND FACTS   Office Supply Store.com is a domain name registered to Office Supply Store, Inc., a corporation based in Bellevue, Washington. Employees of the Kansas City School District in Missouri allegedly ordered $17,642.54 worth of office supplies—without the authority or approval of their employer—from Office Supply Store.com. The Office Supply invoice that was sent with the goods after the order had been placed identified Los Angeles, California, as the "legal venue" for deciding disputes. When the goods were not paid for, Office Supply filed a suit against the Kansas City School Board and others, including some of the district's employees, in a California state court. The defendants did not respond. The court entered a default judgment in Office Supply's favor for more than $30,000 in damages, interest, attorneys' fees, and court costs. Office Supply asked a Missouri state court to formally register the judgment so that it could be enforced. The defendants appealed this registration.

IN THE WORDS OF THE COURT . . .
Alok *AHUJA*, Judge.
    * * * *

    Office Supply * * * argues that the School District consented to the jurisdiction of California's courts. In making this argument, Office Supply relies on the sample invoice it submitted to the trial court, which states (in what appears to be 5- or 6-point type) that Legal Venue is Los Angeles, California.

    This fine-print statement on Office Supply's invoices cannot establish personal jurisdiction. As a general proposition, a defendant can consent to personal jurisdiction by entering into a contract containing a valid forum selection clause. But here, Office Supply has provided no evidence that the School District ever agreed to Office Supply's choice of forum. Instead, the forum selection language appears only on invoices sent by Office Supply to the School District after the shipment of the School District's purchases had already been made.

---

a. In the "Quick Links" column, click on "Opinions & Minutes." On the next page, in the "Missouri Court of Appeals, Western District" row, click on "opinions." On that page, type "Office Supply" in the "Step 2. Search Opinions:" box, and click on "Search." In the result, click on the case title to access the opinion. The Missouri courts maintain this Web site.

    Both Missouri and California have adopted Section 2–207 of the * * * Uniform Commercial Code (the "UCC"), which provides:

> (1) A definite and seasonable expression of acceptance or a written confirmation which is sent within a reasonable time operates as an acceptance even though it states terms additional to or different from those offered or agreed upon, unless acceptance is expressly made conditional on assent to the additional or different terms.
> (2) The additional terms are to be construed as proposals for addition to the contract.

    Under Section 2–207 as adopted in both Missouri and California, Office Supply's invoices were effective to confirm the parties' agreement to a purchase transaction, despite the inclusion in the invoices of an additional forum selection term. But the additional term did not thereby become part of the parties' contract. It does not appear that the School District would be deemed a "merchant" of office supplies under the UCC definition. If the School District is not a "merchant," under Section 2–207(2) the additional forum-selection term stated in Office Supply's invoice must be construed simply as a proposal for an addition to the contract. There is no evidence that the School District agreed to the forum selection clause, and Office Supply's attempted reliance on it must accordingly fail. [Emphasis added.]

DECISION AND REMEDY   A state intermediate appellate court reversed the lower court's decision. Additional terms included in an invoice sent by a seller to a nonmerchant buyer with the purchased goods do not become part of the parties' contract unless the buyer expressly agrees to them.

THE ETHICAL DIMENSION   *Should the court have allowed the default judgment to be registered so that it could have been enforced? Why or why not?*

THE ECONOMIC DIMENSION   *Why would a business such as Office Supply Store.com want to include a forum-selection clause in its contracts with buyers?*

Rules When Both Parties Are Merchants. The drafters of the UCC created a special rule for merchants to avoid the "battle of the forms," which occurs when two merchants exchange separate standard forms containing different contract terms. Under UCC 2–207(2), in contracts *between merchants*, the additional terms *automatically* become part of the contract unless one of the following conditions exists:

1. The original offer expressly limited acceptance to its terms.
2. The new or changed terms materially alter the contract.
3. The offeror objects to the new or changed terms within a reasonable period of time.

Generally, if the modification does not involve an unreasonable element of surprise or hardship for the offeror, the court will hold that the modification did not materially alter the contract. Courts also consider the parties' prior dealings and course of performance when determining whether the alteration is material.

Consideration

The common law rule that a contract requires consideration also applies to sales and lease contracts. Unlike the common law, however, the UCC does not require a contract modification to be supported by new consideration. An agreement modifying a contract for the sale or lease of goods "needs no consideration to be binding" [UCC 2–209(1), 2A–208(1)]. Of course, a contract modification must be sought in good faith [UCC 1–304].

The Statute of Frauds

The UCC contains Statute of Frauds provisions covering sales and lease contracts. Under these provisions, sales contracts for goods priced at $500 or more and lease contracts requiring payments of $1,000 or more must be in writing to be enforceable [UCC 2–201(1), 2A–201(1)]. (These low threshold amounts may eventually be raised.)

BE AWARE It has been proposed that the UCC be revised to eliminate the Statute of Frauds.

To satisfy the UCC's Statute of Frauds provisions, a writing or a memorandum need only indicate that the parties intended to form a contract and be signed by the party against whom enforcement is sought. The contract normally will not be enforceable beyond the quantity of goods shown in the writing, however. All other terms can be proved in court by oral testimony. For leases, the writing must reasonably identify and describe the goods leased and the lease term.

An artisan creates a specially designed "bowl within a bowl" out of one piece of clay. If a restaurant orally contracts with the artisan to create twenty of the specially designed bowls for use in its business at a price of $800, will the contract have to be in writing to be enforceable? Why or why not?

(AP Photo/*The Saginaw News*/Jeff Schrier)

SPECIAL RULES FOR CONTRACTS BETWEEN MERCHANTS   Once again, the UCC provides a special rule for merchants in sales transactions (there is no corresponding rule for leases under Article 2A). Merchants can satisfy the Statute of Frauds if, after the parties have agreed orally, one of the merchants sends a signed written confirmation of the terms to the other merchant within a reasonable time. Unless the merchant who receives the confirmation objects in writing to its contents within ten days after receipt, the contract is enforceable, even though the receiving merchant has not signed anything [UCC 2–201(2)]. Generally, courts hold that an e-mail confirmation is sufficient.

EXAMPLE 11.5   Alfonso, a merchant-buyer in Cleveland, contracts over the telephone to purchase $4,000 worth of spare aircraft parts from Goldstein, a merchant-seller in New York City. Two days later, Goldstein sends a written, signed confirmation detailing the terms of the oral contract, and Alfonso subsequently receives it. If Alfonso does not notify Goldstein in writing of his objection to the contents of the confirmation within ten days of receipt, Alfonso cannot raise the Statute of Frauds as a defense against the enforcement of the oral contract. ●

EXCEPTIONS   The UCC defines three exceptions to the writing requirements of the Statute of Frauds:

1. *Specially manufactured goods.* An oral contract will still be enforceable if it is for goods that are specially manufactured for a particular buyer and the seller has substantially started manufacturing the goods.

2. *Partial performance.* An oral contract that has been partially performed (such as when some of the contracted goods have been paid for and accepted) will be enforceable to the extent that it has been performed.

3. *Admissions.* When the party against whom enforcement is sought admits to making an oral contract, the contract is enforceable, but only as to the quantity of goods that the party admitted. **CASE EXAMPLE 11.6** Gerald Lindgren, a farmer, agreed by phone to sell his crops to Glacial Plains Cooperative. The parties reached four oral agreements: two for the delivery of soybeans and two for the delivery of corn. Lindgren made the soybean deliveries and part of the first corn delivery, but he sold the rest of his corn to another dealer. Glacial Plains bought corn elsewhere, paying a higher price, and then sued Lindgren for breach of contract. In papers filed with the court, Lindgren acknowledged his oral agreements with Glacial Plains and admitted that he did not fully perform. The court applied the admissions exception and held that the four agreements were enforceable.[3] ●

▶ Performance of Sales and Lease Contracts

The performance required under a sales or lease contract consists of the duties and obligations each party has under the terms of the contract. The basic obligation of the seller or lessor is to transfer and deliver the goods as stated in the contract, and the basic duty of the buyer or lessee is to accept and pay for the goods.

Keep in mind that "duties and obligations" under the terms of the contract include those specified by the agreement, by custom, and by the UCC. Thus, parties to a sales or lease contract may be bound not only by terms they expressly agreed on, but also by terms implied by custom, such as a customary method of weighing or measuring particular goods. In addition, the UCC sometimes imposes terms on parties to a sales contract, such as the requirement that a seller find a substitute carrier to deliver goods to the buyer if the agreed-on carrier becomes unavailable. In this section, we examine the basic performance obligations of the parties under a sales or lease contract.

The obligations of good faith and commercial reasonableness underlie every sales and lease contract. The UCC's good faith provision, which can never be disclaimed, reads as follows: "Every contract or duty within this Act imposes an obligation of good faith in its performance or enforcement" [UCC 1–304]. *Good faith* means honesty in fact. For a merchant, it means honesty in fact and the observance of reasonable commercial standards of fair dealing in the trade [UCC 2–103(1)(b)]. In other words, merchants are held to a higher standard of performance or duty than are nonmerchants.

Obligations of the Seller or Lessor

Conforming Goods Goods that conform to contract specifications.

Tender of Delivery Under the Uniform Commercial Code, a seller's or lessor's act of placing conforming goods at the disposal of the buyer or lessee and giving the buyer or lessee whatever notification is reasonably necessary to enable the buyer or lessee to take delivery.

As stated, the basic duty of the seller or lessor is to deliver the goods called for under the contract to the buyer or lessee. Goods that conform to the contract description in every way are called **conforming goods.** To fulfill the contract, the seller or lessor must either deliver or tender delivery of conforming goods to the buyer or lessee. **Tender of delivery** occurs when the seller or lessor makes conforming goods available to the buyer or lessee and gives the buyer or lessee whatever notification is reasonably necessary to enable the buyer or lessee to take delivery [UCC 2–503(1), 2A–508(1)].

---

3. *Glacial Plains Cooperative v. Lindgren,* 759 N.W.2d 661 (Minn.App. 2009).

A vendor unloads boxes of produce at a store on San Francisco's Clement Street. Tender of delivery occurs when the seller or lessor delivers all goods called for in the contract at a reasonable hour and keeps them available for a reasonable period of time to enable the buyer to take possession of them. Under what circumstances can the goods be delivered in more than one lot?

Tender must occur at a *reasonable hour* and in a *reasonable manner.* For example, a seller cannot call the buyer at 2:00 A.M. and say, "The goods are ready. I'll give you twenty minutes to get them." Unless the parties have agreed otherwise, the goods must be tendered for delivery at a reasonable hour and kept available for a reasonable period of time to enable the buyer to take possession of them [UCC 2–503(1)(a)]. Normally, all goods called for by a contract must be tendered in a single delivery—unless the parties have agreed that the goods may be delivered in several lots or *installments* [UCC 2–307, 2–612, 2A–510].

PLACE OF DELIVERY The buyer and seller (or lessor and lessee) may agree that the goods will be delivered to a particular destination where the buyer or lessee will take possession. If the contract does not designate the place of delivery, then the goods must be made available to the buyer at the *seller's place of business* or, if the seller has none, the *seller's residence* [UCC 2–308(a)]. If, at the time of contracting, the parties know that the goods identified to the contract are located somewhere other than the seller's business, then the *location of the goods* is the place for their delivery [UCC 2–308(b)].

THE PERFECT TENDER RULE The seller or lessor has an obligation to ship or tender *conforming goods,* which the buyer or lessee is then obligated to accept and pay for according to the terms of the contract [UCC 2–507]. Under the common law, the seller was obligated to deliver goods that conformed to the terms of the contract in every detail. This was called the **perfect tender rule.** The UCC preserves the perfect tender doctrine by stating that if goods or tender of delivery fails *in any respect* to conform to the contract, the buyer or lessee has the right to accept the goods, reject the entire shipment, or accept part and reject part [UCC 2–601, 2A–509].

For example, a lessor contracts to lease fifty Comclear monitors to be delivered at the lessee's place of business on or before October 1. On September 28, the lessor discovers that it has only thirty Comclear monitors in inventory but will have another twenty Comclear monitors within the next two weeks. The lessor tenders delivery of the thirty Comclear monitors on October 1, with the promise that the other monitors will be delivered within two weeks. Because the lessor has failed to make a perfect tender of fifty Comclear monitors, the lessee has the right to reject the entire shipment and hold the lessor in breach.

Because of the rigidity of the perfect tender rule, several exceptions to the rule have been created. Some of these exceptions are discussed next.

Perfect Tender Rule A rule under which a seller or lessor is required to deliver goods that conform perfectly to the requirements of the contract. A tender of nonconforming goods automatically constitutes a breach of contract.

Cure The right of a party who tenders nonconforming performance to correct that performance within the contract period.

Cure. The UCC does not specifically define the term **cure,** but it refers to the right of the seller or lessor to repair, adjust, or replace defective or nonconforming goods [UCC 2–508, 2A–513]. When any delivery is rejected because of nonconforming goods and the time for performance has not yet expired, the seller or lessor can attempt to "cure" the defect *within the contract time for performance* [UCC 2–508(1), 2A–513(1)]. To do so, the seller or lessor must seasonably notify the buyer or lessee

A seller or lessor may sometimes tender nonconforming goods, say, blue pens for black pens. What options does the buyer or lessee have when confronted with a tender of nonconforming goods?

of the intention to cure. Once the time for performance under the contract has expired, the seller or lessor can still exercise the right to cure if he or she has *reasonable grounds to believe that the nonconforming tender will be acceptable to the buyer or lessee* [UCC 2–508(2), 2A–513(2)].

The right to cure substantially restricts the right of the buyer or lessee to reject goods. For example, if a lessee refuses a tender of goods as nonconforming but does not disclose the nature of the defect to the lessor, the lessee cannot later assert the defect as a defense if the defect is one that the lessor could have cured. Generally, buyers and lessees must act in good faith and state specific reasons for refusing to accept goods [UCC 2–605, 2A–514].

Substitution of Carriers. When an agreed-on manner of delivery (such as the use of a particular carrier to transport the goods) becomes impracticable or unavailable through no fault of either party, but a commercially reasonable substitute is available, this substitute performance is sufficient tender to the buyer and must be used [UCC 2–614(1)].

Commercial Impracticability. As discussed in Chapter 10 on page 290, events unforeseen by either party when a contract was made may make performance commercially impracticable. When this occurs, the perfect tender rule no longer applies. According to UCC 2–615(a) and 2A–405(a), a delay in delivery or nondelivery in whole or in part is not a breach if performance has been made impracticable "by the occurrence of a contingency the nonoccurrence of which was a basic assumption on which the contract was made." The seller or lessor must, however, notify the buyer or lessee as soon as practicable that there will be a delay or nondelivery.

The doctrine of commercial impracticability does not extend to problems that could have been foreseen. An increase in cost resulting from inflation, for instance, does not in and of itself excuse performance, as this kind of foreseeable risk is ordinarily assumed by a seller or lessor conducting business.[4] The nonoccurrence of the contingency must have been a basic assumption on which the contract was made [UCC 2–615, 2A–405].

Destruction of Identified Goods. Sometimes, an unexpected event, such as a fire, totally destroys goods through no fault of either party and before risk passes to the buyer or lessee. In such a situation, *if the goods were identified at the time the contract was formed,* the parties are excused from performance [UCC 2–613, 2A–221]. If the goods are only partially destroyed, however, the buyer or lessee can inspect them and either treat the contract as void or accept the damaged goods with a reduction in the contract price.

Assurance and Cooperation. The UCC provides that if one of the parties to a contract has "reasonable grounds" to believe that the other party will not perform as contracted, she or he may *in writing* "demand adequate assurance of due performance" from the other party. Until such assurance is received, she or he may "suspend" further performance without liability. What constitutes "reasonable grounds" is

"Resolve to perform what you ought; perform without fail what you resolve."

Benjamin Franklin, 1706–1790
(American politician and inventor)

---

4. For a classic case on this issue, see *Maple Farms, Inc. v. City School District of Elmira,* 76 Misc.2d 1080, 352 N.Y.S.2d 784 (1974).

determined by commercial standards. If such assurances are not forthcoming within a reasonable time (not to exceed thirty days), the failure to respond may be treated as a *repudiation* of the contract [UCC 2–609, 2A–401].

CASE EXAMPLE 11.7 Two companies that made road-surfacing materials, Koch Materials and Shore Slurry Seal, Inc., entered into a contract. Koch obtained a license to use Novachip, a special material made by Shore, and Shore agreed to buy all of its asphalt from Koch for the next seven years. A few years into the contract term, Shore notified Koch that it was planning to sell its assets to Asphalt Paving Systems, Inc. Koch demanded assurances that Asphalt Paving would continue the deal, but Shore refused to provide assurances. The court held that Koch could treat Shore's failure to give assurances as a repudiation and sue Shore for breach of contract.[5] ●

Sometimes, the performance of one party depends on the cooperation of the other. The UCC provides that when such cooperation is not forthcoming, the other party can suspend his or her own performance without liability and hold the uncooperative party in breach or proceed to perform the contract in any reasonable manner [UCC 2–311(3)].

Obligations of the Buyer or Lessee

Once the seller or lessor has adequately tendered delivery, the buyer or lessee is obligated to accept the goods and pay for them according to the terms of the contract.

PAYMENT In the absence of any specific agreements, the buyer or lessee must make payment at the time and place the goods are *received* [UCC 2–310(a), 2A–516(1)]. When a sale is made on credit, the buyer is obliged to pay according to the specified credit terms (for example, 60, 90, or 120 days), not when the goods are received. The credit period usually begins on the *date of shipment* [UCC 2–310(d)]. Under a lease contract, a lessee must make the lease payment that was specified in the contract [UCC 2A–516(1)].

Payment can be made by any means agreed on between the parties—cash or any other method generally acceptable in the commercial world. If the seller demands cash when the buyer offers a check, credit card, or the like, the seller must allow the buyer reasonable time to obtain legal tender [UCC 2–511].

RIGHT OF INSPECTION Unless the parties otherwise agree, or for C.O.D. (collect on delivery) transactions, the buyer or lessee has an absolute right to inspect the goods before making payment. This right allows the buyer or lessee to verify that the goods tendered or delivered conform to the contract. Inspection can take place at any reasonable place and time and in any reasonable manner. If the goods are not as ordered, the buyer or lessee has no duty to pay. *An opportunity for inspection is therefore a condition precedent to the right of the seller or lessor to enforce payment* [UCC 2–513(1), 2A–515(1)].

CASE EXAMPLE 11.8 Jessie Romero wanted to buy a new Silverado pickup from Scoggin-Dickey Chevrolet-Buick, Inc. In their contracts, Romero agreed, among other things, that he would supply two trade-in vehicles. Romero did not have the vehicles with him when he signed the contract but said that their combined value

---

5. *Koch Materials Co. v. Shore Slurry Seal, Inc.,* 205 F.Supp.2d 324 (D.N.J. 2002).

was $15,000. Romero took possession of the truck, but when he brought in the trade-in vehicles, the dealership inspected them and determined that they had very little commercial value. The dealership then refused to go through with the deal, took back the pickup, and offered to partially refund Romero's down payment. Romero rejected the offer and filed a lawsuit to enforce the contract. The court found that the dealership had a right to inspect the goods (trade-in vehicles) identified in the contract at any reasonable place and time prior to payment or acceptance. In this case, the dealership had inspected the vehicles on their delivery and had determined that they did not conform to the description in the contract. The contract was conditioned on the acceptance of the trade-in vehicles, and the dealership was entitled to reject nonconforming goods and thereby cancel the contract.[6] ●

ACCEPTANCE   A buyer or lessee demonstrates acceptance of the delivered goods by doing any of the following:

1. If, after having had a reasonable opportunity to inspect the goods, the buyer or lessee signifies to the seller or lessor that the goods either are conforming or are acceptable in spite of their nonconformity [UCC 2–606(1)(a), 2A–515(1)(a)].
2. If the buyer or lessee has had a reasonable opportunity to inspect the goods and has *failed to reject* them within a reasonable period of time, then acceptance is presumed [UCC 2–602(1), 2–606(1)(b), 2A–515(1)(b)].
3. In sales contracts, if the buyer *performs any act inconsistent with the seller's ownership,* then the buyer will be deemed to have accepted the goods. For example, any use or resale of the goods—except for the limited purpose of testing or inspecting the goods—generally constitutes an acceptance [UCC 2–606(1)(c)].

If some of the goods delivered do not conform to the contract and the seller or lessor has failed to cure, the buyer or lessee can make a *partial* acceptance [UCC 2–601(c), 2A–509(1)]. The same is true if the nonconformity was not reasonably discoverable before acceptance. (In the latter situation, the buyer or lessee may be able to revoke the acceptance, as will be discussed later in this chapter.)

A buyer or lessee cannot accept less than a single commercial unit, however. The UCC defines a *commercial unit* as a unit of goods that, by commercial usage, is viewed as a "single whole" for purposes of sale, and its division would materially impair the character of the unit, its market value, or its use [UCC 2–105(6), 2A–103(1)(c)]. A commercial unit can be a single article (such as a machine), a set of articles (such as a suite of furniture or an assortment of sizes), a quantity (such as a bale, a gross, or a carload), or any other unit treated in the trade as a single whole.

Anticipatory Repudiation

What if, before the time for contract performance, one party clearly communicates to the other the intention not to perform? Such an action is a breach of the contract by anticipatory repudiation. When anticipatory repudiation occurs, the nonbreaching party has a choice of two responses: (1) treat the repudiation as a final breach by pursuing a remedy or (2) wait to see if the repudiating party will decide to honor the contract despite the avowed intention to renege [UCC 2–610, 2A–402]. In either situation, the nonbreaching party may suspend performance.

The UCC permits the breaching party to "retract" his or her repudiation (subject to some limitations). This can be done by any method that clearly indicates the

---

6. *Romero v. Scoggin-Dickey Chevrolet-Buick, Inc.,* __ S.W.3d __ (Tex.App. 2010).

party's intent to perform. Once retraction is made, the rights of the repudiating party under the contract are reinstated. There can be no retraction, however, if since the time of the repudiation the other party has canceled or materially changed position or otherwise indicated that the repudiation is final [UCC 2–611, 2A–403].

EXAMPLE 11.9   On April 1, Cora, who owns a small inn, purchases a suite of furniture from Horton's Furniture Warehouse. The contract states, "Delivery must be made on or before May 1." On April 10, Horton's informs Cora that it cannot make delivery until May 10 and asks her to consent to the modified delivery date. In this situation, Cora has the option of either treating the notice of late delivery as a final breach of contract and pursuing a remedy or agreeing to the changed delivery date. Suppose that Cora does neither for two weeks. On April 24, Horton's informs Cora that it will be able to deliver the furniture by May 1 after all. In effect, Horton's has retracted its repudiation, reinstating the rights and obligations of the parties under the original contract. Note that if after the repudiation Cora had indicated that she was canceling the contract, Horton's would not have been able to retract its repudiation. •

▶ Remedies for Breach of Sales and Lease Contracts

When one party fails to carry out the performance promised in a contract, a breach occurs, and the aggrieved party looks for remedies. These remedies range from retaining the goods to requiring the breaching party's performance under the contract. The general purpose of these remedies is to put the aggrieved party "in as good a position as if the other party had fully performed." Remedies under the UCC are *cumulative* in nature. In other words, an innocent party to a breached sales or lease contract is not limited to one exclusive remedy. (Of course, a party still may not recover twice for the same harm.)

Remedies of the Seller or Lessor

NOTE   A buyer or lessee breaches a contract by wrongfully rejecting the goods, wrongfully revoking acceptance, refusing to pay, or repudiating the contract.

When the buyer or lessee is in breach, the remedies available to the seller or lessor depend on the circumstances at the time of the breach, such as which party has possession of the goods. If the goods are in the buyer's or lessee's possession, the seller or lessor can sue to recover the purchase price of the goods or the lease payments due [UCC 2–709(1), 2A–529(1)]. If the breach occurs before the goods have been delivered to the buyer or lessee, the seller or lessor has the right to pursue the remedies discussed next.

THE RIGHT TO CANCEL THE CONTRACT   If the buyer or lessee breaches the contract, the seller or lessor can choose to cancel (rescind) the contract [UCC 2–703(f), 2A–523(1)(a)]. The seller must notify the buyer or lessee of the cancellation, and at that point all remaining obligations of the seller or lessor are discharged. The buyer or lessee is not discharged from all remaining obligations, however. He or she is in breach, and the seller or lessor can pursue remedies available under the UCC for breach.

THE RIGHT TO WITHHOLD DELIVERY   In general, sellers and lessors can withhold or discontinue performance of their obligations under sales or lease contracts when the buyers or lessees are in breach. This is true whether a buyer or lessee has wrongfully rejected or revoked acceptance of contract goods (rejection and revocation of acceptance will be discussed later), failed to make a payment, or repudiated the contract [UCC 2–703(a), 2A–523(1)(c)]. The seller or lessor can also refuse to deliver the goods to a buyer or lessee who is insolvent (unable to pay debts as they become due), unless the buyer or lessee pays in cash [UCC 2–702(1), 2A–525(1)].

THE RIGHT TO RESELL OR DISPOSE OF THE GOODS   A seller or lessor who is still in possession of the goods when a breach occurs can resell or dispose of the goods. The seller can retain any profits made as a result of the sale and can hold the buyer or lessee liable for any loss [UCC 2–703(d), 2–706(1), 2A–523(1)(e), 2A–527(1)]. The seller must give the original buyer reasonable notice of the resale, unless the goods are perishable or will rapidly decline in value [UCC 2–706(2), (3)].

When the goods contracted for are unfinished at the time of breach, the seller or lessor can either (1) cease manufacturing the goods and resell them for scrap or salvage value or (2) complete the manufacture and resell or dispose of them, holding the buyer or lessee liable for any deficiency. In choosing between these alternatives, the seller or lessor must exercise reasonable commercial judgment to mitigate the loss and obtain maximum value from the unfinished goods [UCC 2–704(2), 2A–524(2)]. Any resale of the goods must be made in good faith and in a commercially reasonable manner.

THE RIGHT TO RECOVER THE PURCHASE PRICE OR THE LEASE PAYMENTS DUE   Under the UCC, an unpaid seller or lessor can bring an action to recover the purchase price or payments due under the lease contract, plus incidental damages [UCC 2–709(1), 2A–529(1)]. If a seller or lessor is unable to resell or dispose of goods and sues for the contract price or lease payments due, the goods must be held for the buyer or lessee. The seller or lessor can resell or dispose of the goods at any time prior to collection (of the judgment) from the buyer or lessee, but must credit the net proceeds from the sale to the buyer or lessee.

EXAMPLE 11.10   Southern Realty contracts to purchase one thousand pens with its name inscribed on them from Gem Point. When Gem Point tenders delivery of the pens, Southern Realty wrongfully refuses to accept them. In this situation, Gem Point can bring an action for the purchase price because it delivered conforming goods, and Southern Realty refused to accept or pay for the goods. Gem Point obviously cannot resell the pens inscribed with the buyer's business name, so this situation falls under UCC 2–709. Gem Point is required to make the pens available for Southern Realty, but can resell them (in the event that it can find a buyer) at any time before collecting the judgment from Southern Realty. ●

THE RIGHT TO RECOVER DAMAGES   If a buyer or lessee repudiates a contract or wrongfully refuses to accept the goods, a seller or lessor can maintain an action to recover the damages that were sustained. Ordinarily, the amount of damages equals the difference between the contract price or lease payments and the market price or lease payments at the time and place of tender of the goods, plus incidental damages [UCC 2–708(1), 2A–528(1)].

Remedies of the Buyer or Lessee

Like the remedies available to sellers and lessors, the remedies of buyers and lessees depend on the circumstances existing at the time of the breach. If the seller or lessor refuses to deliver the goods or the buyer or lessee has rejected the goods, the remedies available to the buyer or lessee include those discussed next.

THE RIGHT TO CANCEL THE CONTRACT   When a seller or lessor fails to make proper delivery or repudiates the contract, the buyer or lessee can cancel, or rescind, the contract. On notice of cancellation, the buyer or lessee is relieved of any further obligations under the contract but retains all rights to other remedies against the seller [UCC 2–711(1), 2A–508(1)(a)]. (The right to cancel the contract is also available to a buyer or lessee who has rightfully rejected goods or revoked acceptance, as will be discussed shortly.)

THE RIGHT TO OBTAIN THE GOODS ON INSOLVENCY   If a buyer or lessee has made a partial or full payment for goods that are in the possession of a seller or lessor who is or becomes insolvent, the buyer or lessee has a right to obtain the goods. To exercise this right, the goods must be identified to the contract, and the buyer or lessee must pay any remaining balance of the price to the seller or lessor [UCC 2–502, 2A–522].

THE RIGHT TO OBTAIN SPECIFIC PERFORMANCE   A buyer or lessee can obtain specific performance when the goods are unique and the remedy at law is inadequate [UCC 2–716(1), 2A–521(1)]. Ordinarily, a successful suit for monetary damages is sufficient to place a buyer or lessee in the position he or she would have occupied if the seller or lessor had fully performed.

When the contract is for the purchase of a particular work of art or a similarly unique item, however, monetary damages may not be sufficient. Under these circumstances, equity will require that the seller or lessor perform exactly by delivering the particular goods identified to the contract (a remedy of specific performance).

CASE EXAMPLE 11.11   Doreen Houseman and Eric Dare bought a house together and a pedigreed dog. When the couple separated, they agreed that Dare would keep the house (and pay Houseman for her interest in it) and Houseman would keep the dog. Houseman allowed Dare to take the dog for visits, but after one visit, Dare kept the dog. Houseman filed a lawsuit seeking specific performance of their agreement. The court found that because pets have special subjective value to their owners, a dog can be unique goods. Thus, an award of specific performance was appropriate.[7] ●

Cover Under the UCC, a remedy that allows the buyer or lessee, on the seller's or lessor's breach, to obtain the goods, in good faith and within a reasonable time, from another seller or lessor and substitute them for the goods due under the contract.

THE RIGHT OF COVER   In certain situations, buyers and lessees can protect themselves by obtaining **cover**—that is, by purchasing or leasing other goods to substitute for those due under the contract. This option is available when the seller or lessor repudiates the contract or fails to deliver the goods, or when a buyer or lessee has rightfully rejected goods or revoked acceptance.

In obtaining cover, the buyer or lessee must act in good faith and without unreasonable delay [UCC 2–712, 2A–518]. After purchasing or leasing substitute goods, the buyer or lessee can recover damages from the seller or lessor. The measure of damages is the difference between the cost of cover and the contract price (or lease payments), plus incidental and consequential damages, less the expenses (such as delivery costs) that were saved as a result of the breach [UCC 2–712, 2–715, 2A–518]. Consequential damages are any losses suffered by the buyer or lessee that the seller or lessor could have foreseen at the time of contract formation and any injury to the buyer's or lessee's person or property proximately resulting from the contract's breach [UCC 2–715(2), 2A–520(2)].

Buyers and lessees are not required to cover, and failure to do so will not bar them from using any other remedies available under the UCC. A buyer or lessee who fails to cover, however, may *not* be able to collect consequential damages that could have been avoided by purchasing or leasing substitute goods.

---

7. *Houseman v. Dare*, 405 N.J.Super. 538, 966 A.2d 24 (2009).

Replevin An action to recover identified goods in the hands of a party who is wrongfully withholding them from the other party.

THE RIGHT TO REPLEVY GOODS

Buyers and lessees also have the right to replevy goods. **Replevin**[8] is an action to recover specific goods in the hands of a party who is wrongfully withholding them from the other party. Under the UCC, the buyer or lessee can replevy goods subject to the contract if the seller or lessor has repudiated or breached the contract. To maintain an action to replevy goods, usually buyers and lessees must show that they are unable to cover for the goods after a reasonable effort [UCC 2–716(3), 2A–521(3)].

THE RIGHT TO RECOVER DAMAGES

If a seller or lessor repudiates the sales contract or fails to deliver the goods, the buyer or lessee can sue for damages. The measure of recovery is the difference between the contract price (or lease payments) and the market price of (or lease payments that could be obtained for) the goods at the time the buyer (or lessee) *learned* of the breach. The market price or market lease payments are determined at the place where the seller or lessor was supposed to deliver the goods. The buyer or lessee can also recover incidental and consequential damages, less the expenses that were saved as a result of the breach [UCC 2–713, 2A–519].

RECALL Consequential damages compensate for a loss (such as lost profits) that is not direct but was reasonably foreseeable at the time of the breach.

In the following case, a sales contract was breached less than a month after the parties entered into it. The market price of the goods was equal to the contract price, but the buyer had also paid a commercial trucking company to pick up the goods. The question before the court was whether the shipping amount could be included in the damages.

---

8. Pronounced ruh-*pleh*-vun.

Case 11.2   Les Entreprises Jacques Defour & Fils, Inc. v. Dinsick Equipment Corp.

United States District Court, Northern District of Illinois, ___ F.Supp.2d ___ (2011).

BACKGROUND AND FACTS Les Entreprises Jacques Defour & Fils, Inc., is a Canadian corporation in the business of highway construction. Its principal place of business is in Baie-Saint-Paul, Quebec, Canada. Dinsick Equipment Corporation is a U.S. firm that sells new and used industrial equipment from its base of operations in Plainfield, Illinois. Les Entreprises contracted to buy a 30,000-gallon industrial tank from Dinsick and wired the price of $70,000 directly to the seller's bank account. Less than a week later, Dinsick told Les Entreprises that the tank could be picked up in Joplin, Missouri. The buyer paid Xaak Transport, Inc., to pick up the tank, but when Xaak went to Joplin, the tank was not there. Les Entreprises paid Xaak $7,459 for its services and then contacted Dinsick, which agreed to reimburse the $70,000. When Dinsick did not refund the price, however, Les Entreprises filed a suit in a federal district court against the seller.

IN THE WORDS OF THE COURT . . .
Morton **DENLOW**, * * * Judge.
  * * * *

To establish a breach of contract claim, a plaintiff must establish (1) the existence of a valid and enforceable contract; (2) substantial performance by the plaintiff; (3) a breach by the defendant; and (4) resultant damages.

In this case, it is undisputed that Plaintiff [Les Entreprises] and Defendant [Dinsick] entered into an agreement for the purchase of an industrial tank and that Defendant failed to deliver the tank. Plaintiff provided the completed invoice statement Defendant billed to him listing the sale of one 30,000-gallon industrial tank at the price of $70,000, and the wiring information for payment purposes. *This act of depositing the full payment into Defendant's bank account prior to receiving the tank demonstrated substantial performance by Plaintiff. Defendant's failure to make the tank available for acceptance breached the terms of the contract. This breach coupled with the failure to reimburse Plaintiff for the non-delivery resulted in damages to Plaintiff for the purchase price of the tank.* [Emphasis added.]

The only question remaining is whether Plaintiff may recover incidental damages for the $7,459 Plaintiff paid Xaak to transport the industrial tank. Under the Illinois Uniform Commercial Code, "incidental damages resulting from a seller's breach include expenses reasonably incurred in the inspection, receipt, transportation, and care and custody of the goods rightfully rejected, any commercially reasonable charges, expenses or commissions in connection with effecting cover and any other reasonable expenses incident to the delay or other breach." For instance, courts have previously awarded incidental damages for the increased shipment costs of goods purchased as cover for a breach.

Case 11.2–Continued

Here, the expenses Plaintiff paid to Xaak for its services were reasonable under the circumstances. The original invoice for the sale of the tank included the clause "no freight included," which would imply to a reasonable person that the buyer would have to provide the transportation costs of the item. Thus, upon Defendant's notification that the tank was ready for pick-up in Joplin, it was reasonable for Plaintiff to send some means of transportation to retrieve the tank. Because the shipping costs were integral to performance of the contract, they were "reasonable expenses incident to the * * * breach."

DECISION AND REMEDY   The court issued a judgment in Les Entreprises' favor. Dinsick had breached the contract, and Les

Entreprises was entitled to compensatory damages of $70,000 and incidental damages of $7,459 for the transport.

THE TECHNOLOGICAL DIMENSION   *What did the act of wiring the full payment directly into the seller's bank account demonstrate? Could the buyer have used other methods to accomplish the same purpose? Explain.*

THE GLOBAL DIMENSION   *On what basis could the court exercise jurisdiction in this case? Explain.*

When the Seller or Lessor Delivers Nonconforming Goods

When the seller or lessor delivers nonconforming goods, the buyer or lessee has several remedies available under the UCC.

THE RIGHT TO REJECT THE GOODS   If either the goods or the tender of the goods by the seller or lessor fails to conform to the contract *in any respect*, the buyer or lessee can reject the goods in whole or in part [UCC 2–601, 2A–509]. If the buyer or lessee rejects the goods, she or he may then obtain cover, cancel the contract, or sue for damages for breach of contract, just as if the seller or lessor had refused to deliver the goods.

CASE EXAMPLE 11.12 Jorge Jauregui contracted to buy a Kawai RX5 piano from Bobb's Piano Sales. Bobb's represented that the piano was in new condition and qualified for the manufacturer's warranty. Jauregui paid the contract price, but the piano was delivered with "unacceptable damage," according to Jauregui, who videotaped its condition. Jauregui rejected the piano and filed a lawsuit for breach of contract. The court ruled that Bobb's had breached the contract by delivering nonconforming goods. Jauregui was entitled to damages equal to the contract price with interest, plus the sales tax, delivery charge, and attorneys' fees.[9] ●

The buyer or lessee must reject the goods within a reasonable amount of time after delivery and must seasonably notify the seller or lessor [UCC 2–602(1), 2A–509(2)]. When rejecting goods, the buyer or lessee must also designate defects that would have been apparent to the seller or lessor on reasonable inspection. Failure to do so precludes the buyer or lessee from using such defects to justify rejection or to establish breach when the seller could have cured the defects if they had been disclosed in a timely fashion [UCC 2–605, 2A–514]. A *merchant buyer or lessee* who rightfully rejects goods has a good faith obligation to follow any reasonable instructions received from the seller or lessor with respect to the goods [UCC 2–603, 2A–511].

REVOCATION OF ACCEPTANCE   Acceptance of the goods precludes the buyer or lessee from exercising the right of rejection, but it does not necessarily prevent the buyer or lessee from pursuing other remedies. In certain circumstances, a buyer or lessee is permitted to *revoke* her or his acceptance of the goods. Acceptance of a lot or a commercial unit can be revoked if the nonconformity *substantially* impairs the

---

9. *Jauregui v. Bobb's Piano Sales & Service, Inc.*, 922 So.2d 303 (Fla.App. 2006).

An employee at a retail establishment sorts through boxes of nonconforming goods that will be returned to the manufacturers. If the merchant-buyer is following the seller's instructions for rejecting the goods, who should bear the cost of having employees perform this task?

(Photo Courtesy of KBToys.com and eToys.com)

value of the lot or unit and if one of the following factors is present:

1. Acceptance was predicated on the reasonable assumption that the nonconformity would be cured, and it has not been cured within a reasonable time [UCC 2–608(1)(a), 2A–517(1)(a)].
2. The buyer or lessee did not discover the nonconformity before acceptance, either because it was difficult to discover before acceptance or because assurances made by the seller or lessor that the goods were conforming kept the buyer or lessee from inspecting the goods [UCC 2–608(1)(b), 2A–517(1)(b)].

Revocation of acceptance is not effective until notice is given to the seller or lessor. Notice must occur within a reasonable time after the buyer or lessee either discovers or *should have discovered* the grounds for revocation.

THE RIGHT TO RECOVER DAMAGES FOR ACCEPTED GOODS   A buyer or lessee who has accepted nonconforming goods may also keep the goods and recover damages caused by the breach. To do so, the buyer or lessee must notify the seller or lessor of the breach within a reasonable time after the defect was or should have been discovered [UCC 2–607, 2–714, 2–717, 2A–519].

CASE EXAMPLE 11.13   James Fitl attended a sports-card show in California, where he met Mark Strek, an exhibitor at the show. Fitl bought a 1952 Mickey Mantle Topps baseball card for $17,750 from Strek, who had represented that the card was in near-mint condition. Strek delivered the card to Fitl in Nebraska, and Fitl placed it in a safe-deposit box. Two years later, Fitl sent the card to a sports-card grading service, which told Fitl that the card was ungradable because it had been discolored and doctored. Fitl complained to Strek, who refused to refund the purchase price because of the amount of time that had gone by. Fitl then filed a lawsuit, and the court awarded him $17,750, plus his court costs. Strek appealed. The Nebraska Supreme Court affirmed Fitl's right to recover damages. The court held that Fitl had reasonably relied on Strek's representation that the card was "authentic," which it was not, and that Fitl had given Strek timely notice of the card's defects when they were discovered.[10] ●

Additional Provisions Affecting Remedies

The parties to a sales or lease contract can vary their respective rights and obligations by contractual agreement. For example, a seller and buyer can expressly provide for remedies in addition to those provided in the UCC. The parties can also specify remedies in lieu of those provided in the UCC, or they can change the measure of damages. As under the common law of contracts, they may also include clauses providing for liquidated damages in the event of a breach or a delay in performance (see page 282 in Chapter 10).

Additionally, a seller can stipulate that the buyer's only remedy on the seller's breach will be repair or replacement of the item, or the seller can limit the buyer's remedy to

---

10. *Fitl v. Strek*, 269 Neb. 51, 690 N.W.2d 605 (2005).

return of the goods and refund of the purchase price. In sales and lease contracts, an agreed-on remedy is in addition to those provided in the UCC unless the parties expressly agree that the remedy is exclusive of all others [UCC 2–719(1), 2A–503(1), (2)].

▶ Sales and Lease Warranties

Warranty is an age-old concept. In sales and lease law, a warranty is an assurance or guarantee by the seller or lessor of certain facts concerning the goods being sold or leased. The UCC has numerous rules governing product warranties as they occur in sales and lease contracts.

Because a warranty imposes a duty on the seller or lessor, a breach of warranty is a breach of the seller's or lessor's promise. Assuming that the parties have not agreed to limit or modify the remedies available, if the seller or lessor breaches a warranty, the buyer or lessee can sue to recover damages from the seller or lessor. Under some circumstances, a breach of warranty can allow the buyer or lessee to cancel the agreement.

Title Warranties

Under the UCC, three types of title warranties—*good title, no liens,* and *no infringements*—can automatically arise in sales and lease contracts [UCC 2–312, 2A–211]. Normally, a seller or lessor can disclaim or modify these title warranties only by including *specific language* in the contract. For example, sellers may assert that they are transferring only such rights, title, and interest as they have in the goods.

In most sales, sellers warrant that they have good and valid title to the goods sold and that the transfer of the title is rightful [UCC 2–312(1)(a)]. A second warranty of title protects buyers and lessees who are *unaware* of any encumbrances (claims, charges, or liabilities—usually called *liens*[11]) against goods at the time the contract is made [UCC 2–312(1)(b), 2A–211(1)]. This warranty protects buyers who, for example, unknowingly purchase goods that are subject to a creditor's security interest (a *security interest* is an interest in the goods that secures payment or performance of an obligation—see Chapter 12). If a creditor legally repossesses the goods from a buyer *who had no actual knowledge of the security interest,* the buyer can recover from the seller for breach of warranty. (A buyer who has *actual knowledge of a security interest* has no recourse against a seller.) Article 2A affords similar protection for lessees [UCC 2A–211(1)].

Finally, when the seller or lessor is a merchant, he or she automatically warrants that the buyer or lessee takes the good *free of infringements.* In other words, a merchant promises that the goods delivered are free from any copyright, trademark, or patent claims of a third person [UCC 2–312(3), 2A–211(2)].

Express Warranties

Express Warranty A seller's or lessor's oral or written promise, ancillary to an underlying sales or lease agreement, as to the quality, description, or performance of the goods being sold or leased.

A seller or lessor can create an **express warranty** by making representations concerning the quality, condition, description, or performance potential of the goods. Under UCC 2–313 and 2A–210, express warranties arise when a seller or lessor indicates any of the following:

1. That the goods conform to any *affirmation* (a declaration that something is true) *of fact* or *promise* that the seller or lessor makes to the buyer or lessee about the

---

11. Pronounced *leens.* Liens will be discussed in Chapter 12.

goods. Such affirmations or promises are usually made during the bargaining process. Statements such as "these drill bits will *easily* penetrate stainless steel—and without dulling" are express warranties.

2. That the goods conform to any *description* of them. For example, a label that reads "Crate contains one 150-horsepower diesel engine" or a contract that calls for the delivery of a "wool coat" creates an express warranty that the content of the goods sold conforms to the description.

3. That the goods conform to any *sample or model* of the goods shown to the buyer or lessee.

Express warranties can be found in a seller's or lessor's advertisement, brochure, or promotional materials, in addition to being made orally or in an express warranty provision in a sales or lease contract.

BASIS OF THE BARGAIN   To create an express warranty, a seller or lessor does not have to use formal words such as *warrant* or *guarantee*. It is only necessary that a reasonable buyer or lessee would regard the representation as being part of the basis of the bargain [UCC 2–313(2), 2A–210(2)]. The UCC does not define "basis of the bargain," however, and it is a question of fact in each case whether a representation was made at such a time and in such a way that it induced the buyer or lessee to enter into the contract. Therefore, if an express warranty is not intended, the marketing agent or salesperson should not promise too much.

STATEMENTS OF OPINION AND VALUE   Only statements of fact create express warranties. A seller or lessor who makes a statement that merely relates to the value or worth of the goods, or states an opinion about or recommends the goods, does not create an express warranty [UCC 2–313(2), 2A–210(2)].

Suppose that a seller claims, "This is the best used car to come along in years. It has four new tires and a 250-horsepower engine rebuilt this year." The seller has made several *affirmations of fact* that can create a warranty: the automobile has an engine, it has a 250-horsepower engine, the engine was rebuilt this year, there are four tires on the automobile, and the tires are new.

The seller's *opinion* that the vehicle is "the best used car to come along in years," however, is known as *puffery* and creates no warranty. (**Puffery** is an expression of opinion by a seller or lessor that is not made as a representation of fact.) It is not always easy to determine whether a statement constitutes an express warranty or puffery. The reasonableness of the buyer's or lessee's reliance appears to be the controlling criterion in many cases.

CASE EXAMPLE 11.14   A tobacco farmer read an advertisement for Chlor-O-Pic, a chemical fumigant, which stated that, if applied as directed, Chlor-O-Pic would give "season-long control with application in fall, winter, or spring" against black shank disease, a fungal disease that destroys tobacco crops. The farmer bought Chlor-O-Pic and applied it as directed to his tobacco crop. Nonetheless, the crop developed black shank disease. The farmer sued the manufacturer of Chlor-O-Pic, arguing that he had purchased the product in reliance on a "strong promise" of "season-long control." The court found that the manufacturer's strong promise had created an express warranty and that the farmer was entitled to the value of the damaged crop.[12] ●

Puffery A seller's or lessor's exaggerated claims concerning the quality of goods. Such claims involve opinions rather than facts and are not considered to be legally binding promises or warranties.

---

12. *Triple E, Inc. v. Hendrix & Dail, Inc.,* 344 S.C. 186, 543 S.E.2d 245 (2001). See also *Nomo Agroindustrial Sa De CV v. Enza Zaden North America, Inc.,* 492 F.Supp.2d 1175 (D.Ariz. 2007).

Implied Warranties

Implied Warranty A warranty that the law derives by implication or inference from the nature of the transaction or the relative situation or circumstances of the parties.

An **implied warranty** is one that *the law derives* by inference from the nature of the transaction or the relative situations or circumstances of the parties. Under the UCC, merchants impliedly warrant that the goods they sell or lease are merchantable and, in certain circumstances, fit for a particular purpose. In addition, an implied warranty may arise from a course of dealing or usage of trade. We examine these three types of implied warranties in the following subsections.

IMPLIED WARRANTY OF MERCHANTABILITY Every sale or lease of goods made *by a merchant* who deals in goods of the kind sold or leased automatically gives rise to an **implied warranty of merchantability** [UCC 2–314, 2A–212].

Implied Warranty of Merchantability A warranty that goods being sold or leased are reasonably fit for the ordinary purpose for which they are sold or leased, are properly packaged and labeled, and are of fair quality. The warranty automatically arises in every sale or lease of goods made by a merchant who deals in goods of the kind sold or leased.

EXAMPLE 11.15 A merchant who is in the business of selling ski equipment makes an implied warranty of merchantability every time he sells a pair of skis. A neighbor selling her skis at a garage sale does not (because she is not in the business of selling goods of this type). •

To be *merchantable,* goods must be "reasonably fit for the ordinary purposes for which such goods are used." They must be of at least average, fair, or medium-grade quality. "Merchantable" food, for instance, is food that is fit to eat on the basis of consumer expectations [UCC 2–314(1)]. The goods must also be adequately packaged and labeled, and they must conform to the promises or affirmations of fact made on the container or label, if any.

CASE EXAMPLE 11.16 Darrell Shoop bought a Dodge Dakota truck that had been manufactured by DaimlerChrysler Corporation. Almost immediately, he had problems with the truck. During the first eighteen months, the engine, suspension, steering, transmission, and other components required repairs twelve times, including at least five times for the same defect, which remained uncorrected. Shoop eventually traded in the truck and filed a lawsuit against DaimlerChrysler for breach of the implied warranty of merchantability. The court held that Shoop could maintain an action against DaimlerChrysler and use the fact that the truck had required a significant number of repairs as evidence that it was unmerchantable.[13] •

Implied Warranty of Fitness for a Particular Purpose A warranty that goods sold or leased are fit for a particular purpose. The warranty arises when any seller or lessor knows the particular purpose for which a buyer or lessee will use the goods and knows that the buyer or lessee is relying on the skill and judgment of the seller or lessor to select suitable goods.

IMPLIED WARRANTY OF FITNESS FOR A PARTICULAR PURPOSE The **implied warranty of fitness for a particular purpose** arises when any seller or lessor (merchant or nonmerchant) knows the particular purpose for which a buyer or lessee will use the goods *and* knows that the buyer or lessee is relying on the skill and judgment of the seller or lessor to select suitable goods [UCC 2–315, 2A–213].

A "particular purpose" of the buyer or lessee differs from the "ordinary purpose for which goods are used" (merchantability). Goods can be merchantable but unfit for a particular purpose. **EXAMPLE 11.17** You need a gallon of paint to match the color of your living room walls—a light shade somewhere between coral and peach. You take a sample to your local hardware store and request a gallon of paint of that color. Instead, you are given a gallon of bright blue paint. Here, the salesperson has not breached any warranty of implied merchantability—the bright blue paint is of high quality and suitable for interior walls—but he or she has breached an implied warranty of fitness for a particular purpose. •

A seller or lessor is not required to have actual knowledge of the buyer's or lessee's particular purpose, so long as the seller or lessor "has reason to know" the purpose.

---

13. *Shoop v. DaimlerChrysler Corp.,* 371 Ill.App.3d 1058, 864 N.E.2d 785, 309 Ill.Dec. 544 (2007).

For an implied warranty to be created, however, the buyer or lessee must have *relied* on the skill or judgment of the seller or lessor in selecting or furnishing suitable goods.

WARRANTIES IMPLIED FROM PRIOR DEALINGS OR TRADE CUSTOM   Implied warranties can also arise (or be excluded or modified) as a result of **course of dealing** or **usage of trade** [UCC 2–314(3), 2A–212(3)]. In the absence of evidence to the contrary, when both parties to a sales or lease contract have knowledge of a well-recognized trade custom, the courts will infer that both parties intended for that trade custom to apply to their contract.

EXAMPLE 11.18   Suppose that it is an industrywide custom to lubricate new cars before they are delivered to buyers. Latoya buys a new car from Bender Chevrolet. After the purchase, Latoya discovers that Bender failed to lubricate the car before delivering it to her. In this situation, Latoya can hold the dealer liable for damages resulting from the breach of an implied warranty. (This, of course, would also be negligence on the part of the dealer.) ●

Warranty Disclaimers

The UCC generally permits warranties to be disclaimed or limited by specific and unambiguous language, provided that the buyer or lessee is protected from surprise. The manner in which a seller or lessor can disclaim warranties varies depending on the type of warranty. All oral express warranties can be disclaimed by including in the contract a written (or an electronically recorded) disclaimer in language that is clear and conspicuous, and called to a buyer's or lessee's attention [UCC 2–316(1), 2A–214(1)]. Note, however, that a buyer or lessee must be made aware of any warranty disclaimers or modifications *at the time the contract is formed.*

Generally, unless circumstances indicate otherwise, the implied warranties of merchantability and fitness are disclaimed by expressions such as "as is" or "with all faults."[14] The phrase must be one that in common understanding for *both* parties calls the buyer's or lessee's attention to the fact that there are no implied warranties [UCC 2–316(3)(a), 2A–214(3)(a)].

To specifically disclaim an implied warranty of merchantability, a seller or lessor must mention the word *merchantability* [UCC 2–316(2), 2A–214(2)]. The disclaimer need not be written, but if it is, the writing (or record) must be conspicuous [UCC 2–316(2), 2A–214(4)]. To specifically disclaim an implied warranty of fitness for a particular purpose, the disclaimer *must* be in a writing (or record) and must be conspicuous. The word *fitness* does not have to be mentioned. Conspicuous terms include words set in capital letters, in a larger font size, or in a different color so as to be set off from the surrounding text.

▶ Product Liability

Those who make, sell, or lease goods can be held liable for physical harm or property damage that those goods cause to a consumer, user, or bystander. This is called **product liability.** Product liability claims may be based on the warranty theories just discussed, as well as on the theories of negligence, misrepresentation, and strict liability.

---

14. Note that some states have laws that forbid "as is" sales. Other states do not allow disclaimers of warranties of merchantability for consumer goods.

Course of Dealing   Prior conduct between parties to a contract that establishes a common basis for their understanding.

Usage of Trade   Any practice or method of dealing having such regularity of observance in a place, vocation, or trade as to justify an expectation that it will be observed with respect to the transaction in question.

REMEMBER   If a seller or lessor carefully refrains from making any promise or affirmation of fact relating to the goods, describing the goods, or using a model or sample, no express warranty is created.

Product Liability   The legal liability of manufacturers, sellers, and lessors of goods to consumers, users, and bystanders for injuries or damage that are caused by the goods.

Negligence

Chapter 5 defined *negligence* as the failure to exercise the degree of care that a reasonable, prudent person would have exercised under the circumstances. If a manufacturer fails to exercise "due care" to make a product safe, a person who is injured by the product may sue the manufacturer for negligence. The manufacturer must exercise due care in designing the product, selecting the materials, using the appropriate production process, assembling the product, and placing adequate warnings on the label informing the user of dangers of which an ordinary person might not be aware. The duty of care also extends to the inspection and testing of any purchased products that are used in the final product sold by the manufacturer.

RECALL The elements of negligence include a duty of care, a breach of the duty, and an injury to the plaintiff proximately caused by the breach.

A product liability action based on negligence does not require privity of contract between the injured plaintiff and the defendant manufacturer. As discussed in Chapter 9, *privity of contract* refers to the relationship that exists between the promisor and the promisee of a contract. (Privity is the reason that only the parties to a contract normally can enforce that contract.) In the context of product liability law, privity is not required. This means that a person who was injured by a defective product need not be the one who actually purchased the product to maintain a negligence suit against the manufacturer or seller of the product.

Misrepresentation

When a user or consumer is injured as a result of a manufacturer's or seller's fraudulent misrepresentation, the basis of liability may be the tort of fraud. The intentional mislabeling of packaged cosmetics, for instance, or the intentional concealment of a product's defects would constitute fraudulent misrepresentation. The misrepresentation must concern a material fact, and the seller must have intended to induce the buyer's reliance on the misrepresentation. Misrepresentation on a label or advertisement is enough to show an intent to induce the reliance of anyone who may use the product. In addition, the buyer must have relied on the misrepresentation.

Strict Product Liability

Suppose that Ford Motor Company installs Firestone tires on all new Ford Explorers. The tires are defective and cause numerous accidents involving people driving new Explorers. Who should bear the costs of the resulting injuries (Ford, Firestone, or the drivers' insurance companies), and why?

(AP Photo/Eric Gay)

Under the doctrine of strict liability, people may be liable for the results of their acts regardless of their intentions or their exercise of reasonable care. In addition, liability does not depend on privity of contract. The law imposes strict product liability as a matter of public policy. This public policy rests on the threefold assumption that (1) consumers should be protected against unsafe products; (2) manufacturers and distributors should not escape liability for faulty products simply because they are not in privity of contract with the ultimate user of those products; and (3) manufacturers, sellers, and lessors of products generally are in a better position than consumers to bear the costs associated with injuries caused by their products—costs that they can ultimately pass on to all consumers in the form of higher prices.

California was the first state to impose strict product liability in tort on manufacturers. In a landmark decision, *Greenman v. Yuba Power Products, Inc.,*[15] the California Supreme Court set out the

---

15. 59 Cal.2d 57, 377 P.2d 897, 27 Cal.Rptr. 697 (1963).

reason for applying tort law rather than contract law in cases involving consumers injured by defective products. According to the court, the "purpose of such liability is to ensure that the costs of injuries resulting from defective products are borne by the manufacturers . . . rather than by the injured persons who are powerless to protect themselves." Today, the majority of states recognize strict product liability, although some state courts limit its application to situations involving personal injuries (rather than property damage).

Public policy may be expressed in a statute or in the common law. Sometimes, public policy may be revealed in a court's interpretation of a statute, as in the following case.

Case 11.3   Bruesewitz v. Wyeth, LLC

Supreme Court of the United States, __ U.S. __, 131 S.Ct. 1068, 179 L.Ed.2d 1 (2011).
www.supremecourt.gov [a]

COMPANY PROFILE   *Wyeth, LLC—a subsidiary of Pfizer, Inc.— is an international pharmaceutical and health-care company with its corporate headquarters in Madison, New Jersey. Wyeth develops, makes, and markets medical therapies, clinical programs, nutritional supplements, prescription drugs, and other health-care products, including over-the-counter medications. Wyeth was incorporated in 1926. In 1994, the company bought Lederle Laboratories, which had been making the diphtheria, tetanus, and pertussis (DTP) vaccine for children since 1948.*

BACKGROUND AND FACTS   When Hannah Bruesewitz was six months old, her pediatrician administered a dose of the DTP vaccine according to the Centers for Disease Control's recommended childhood immunization schedule. Within twenty-four hours, Hannah began to experience seizures. She suffered more than one hundred seizures during the next month. Her doctors diagnosed her with "residual seizure disorder" and "developmental delay." Hannah's parents, Russell and Robalee Bruesewitz, filed a claim for relief in the U.S. Court of Federal Claims under the National Childhood Vaccine Injury Act (NCVIA) of 1986, which set up a no-fault compensation program for persons injured by vaccines. The claim was denied. The Bruesewitzes then filed a suit in a Pennsylvania state court against Wyeth, LLC, the maker of the vaccine, alleging strict product liability. The suit was moved to a federal district court. The court held that the claim was preempted by the NCVIA, which includes provisions protecting manufacturers from liability for "a vaccine's unavoidable, adverse side effects." The U.S. Court of Appeals for the Third Circuit affirmed the district court's judgment. The Bruesewitzes appealed to the United States Supreme Court.

IN THE WORDS OF THE COURT . . .
Justice *SCALIA* delivered the opinion of the Court.
* * * *

In the 1970's and 1980's vaccines became, one might say, victims of their own success. They had been so effective in preventing infectious diseases that the public became much less alarmed at the threat of those diseases, and much more concerned with the risk of injury from the vaccines themselves.

Much of the concern centered around vaccines against * * * DTP, which were blamed for children's disabilities * * * . This led to a massive increase in vaccine-related tort litigation. * * * This destabilized the DTP vaccine market, causing two of the three domestic manufacturers to withdraw.
* * * *

To stabilize the vaccine market and facilitate compensation, Congress enacted the NCVIA in 1986. The Act establishes a no-fault compensation program designed to work faster and with greater ease than the civil tort system. A person injured by a vaccine, or his legal guardian, may file a petition for compensation in the United States Court of Federal Claims.
* * * *

Successful claimants receive compensation for medical, rehabilitation, counseling, special education, and vocational training expenses; diminished earning capacity; pain and suffering; and $250,000 for vaccine-related deaths. Attorney's fees are provided * * * . These awards are paid out of a fund created by a * * * tax on each vaccine dose.

The *quid pro quo* [something done in exchange] for this, designed to stabilize the vaccine market, was the provision of significant tort-liability protections for vaccine manufacturers. * * * *Manufacturers are generally immunized from liability * * * * if they have complied with all regulatory requirements * * * . And most relevant to the present case, the Act expressly eliminates liability for a vaccine's unavoidable, adverse side effects.* [Emphasis added.]
* * * *

---

a. In the "Supreme Court Documents" column, in the "Opinions" pull-down menu, select "Bound Volumes." On the next page, in the "For Search Term:" box, type "Bruesewitz" and click on "Search." In the result, click on the name of the case to access the opinion. The United States Supreme Court maintains this Web site.

Case 11.3–Continued

The Act's structural *quid pro quo* leads to the * * * conclusion: The vaccine manufacturers fund from their sales an informal, efficient compensation program for vaccine injuries; in exchange they avoid costly tort litigation.

DECISION AND REMEDY The United States Supreme Court affirmed the lower court's judgment. The NCVIA preempted the Bruesewitzes' claim against Wyeth for compensation for the injury to their daughter caused by the DTP vaccine's side effects. The Court stated that the NCVIA's compensation program strikes a balance between paying victims harmed by vaccines and protecting the vaccine industry from collapsing under the costs of tort liability.

THE ECONOMIC DIMENSION *What public policy do the provisions of the NCVIA reflect?*

THE POLITICAL DIMENSION *If the public wants to change the policy outlined in this case, which branch of the government—and at what level—should the public lobby to make the change? Why?*

REQUIREMENTS FOR STRICT LIABILITY After the *Restatement (Second) of Torts* was issued in 1964, Section 402A became a widely accepted statement of how the doctrine of strict liability should be applied to sellers of goods (including manufacturers, processors, assemblers, packagers, bottlers, wholesalers, distributors, retailers, and lessors). The bases for an action in strict liability that are set forth in Section 402A of the *Restatement* can be summarized by the following six requirements. Depending on the jurisdiction, if these requirements are met, a manufacturer's liability to an injured party can be almost unlimited.

1. The product must be in a *defective condition* when the defendant sells it.
2. The defendant must normally be engaged in the *business of selling* (or otherwise distributing) that product.
3. The product must be *unreasonably dangerous* to the user or consumer because of its defective condition (in most states).
4. The plaintiff must incur *physical harm* to self or property by use or consumption of the product.
5. The defective condition must be the *proximate cause* of the injury or damage.
6. The *goods must not have been substantially changed* from the time the product was sold to the time the injury was sustained.

Proving a Defective Condition. Under these requirements, in any action against a manufacturer, seller, or lessor, the plaintiff does not have to show why or in what manner the product became defective. The plaintiff does, however, have to prove that the product was defective at the time it left the hands of the seller or lessor and that this defective condition made it "unreasonably dangerous" to the user or consumer. If the product was delivered in a safe condition and subsequent mishandling made it harmful to the user, the seller or lessor usually is not strictly liable.

Unreasonably Dangerous Product
In product liability law, a product that is defective to the point of threatening a consumer's health and safety. A product will be considered unreasonably dangerous if it is dangerous beyond the expectation of the ordinary consumer or if a less dangerous alternative was economically feasible for the manufacturer, but the manufacturer failed to produce it.

Unreasonably Dangerous Products. The *Restatement* recognizes that many products cannot possibly be made entirely safe for all consumption, and thus holds sellers or lessors liable only for products that are *unreasonably* dangerous. A court may consider a product so defective as to be an **unreasonably dangerous product** in either of the following situations.

1. The product is dangerous beyond the expectation of the ordinary consumer.
2. A less dangerous alternative was economically feasible for the manufacturer, but the manufacturer failed to produce it.

Sony manufactured defective lithium-ion cell batteries, some of which caught on fire. Dell and other computer companies bought these Sony batteries for use in their laptop computers. To what extent is Sony liable? To what extent are Dell and other laptop makers that purchased these batteries liable?

As will be discussed next, a product may be unreasonably dangerous for several reasons.

PRODUCT DEFECTS—RESTATEMENT (THIRD) OF TORTS   In 1997, the American Law Institute issued the *Restatement (Third) of Torts: Products Liability.* This *Restatement* defines the three types of product defects that have traditionally been recognized in product liability law—manufacturing defects, design defects, and inadequate warnings.

Manufacturing Defects. According to Section 2(a) of the *Restatement (Third) of Torts: Products Liability,* a product "contains a manufacturing defect when the product departs from its intended design even though all possible care was exercised in the preparation and marketing of the product." Basically, a manufacturing defect is a departure from a product's design specifications that results in products that are physically flawed, damaged, or incorrectly assembled. A glass bottle that is made too thin and explodes in a consumer's face has a manufacturing defect.

Usually, such defects occur when a manufacturer fails to assemble, test, or adequately check the quality of a product. Liability is imposed on the manufacturer (and on the wholesaler and retailer) regardless of whether the manufacturer's quality control efforts were "reasonable." The idea behind holding defendants strictly liable for manufacturing defects is to encourage greater investment in product safety and stringent quality control standards. (For more information on how effective quality control procedures can help businesses reduce their potential legal liability for breached warranties and defective products, see the *Linking the Law to Management* feature on pages 339 and 340.)

CASE EXAMPLE 11.19   Kevin Schmude purchased an eight-foot ladder and used it to install radio-frequency shielding in a hospital room. While Schmude was standing on the ladder, it collapsed, and he was seriously injured. He filed a lawsuit against the ladder's maker, Tricam Industries, Inc., based on a manufacturing defect. Experts testified that when the ladder was assembled, the preexisting holes in the top cap did not properly line up with the holes in the rear right rail and backing plate. As a result of the misalignment, the rivet at the rear legs of the ladder was more likely to fail. A jury concluded that this manufacturing defect made the ladder unreasonably dangerous and awarded Schmude more than $677,000 in damages.[16] •

Design Defects. Unlike a product with a manufacturing defect, a product with a design defect is made in conformity with the manufacturer's design specifications, but nevertheless results in injury to the user because the design itself is flawed. The product's design creates an unreasonable risk to the user. A product "is defective in design when the foreseeable risks of harm posed by the product could have been reduced or avoided by the adoption of a reasonable alternative design by the seller or other distributor, or a predecessor in the commercial chain of distribution, and the omission of the alternative design renders the product not reasonably safe."[17]

To successfully assert a design defect, a plaintiff has to show that a reasonable alternative design was available and that the defendant's failure to adopt the alternative design rendered the product unreasonably dangerous. In other words, a manufacturer or other defendant is liable only when the harm was reasonably preventable.

---

16. *Schmude v. Tricam Industries, Inc.,* 550 F.Supp.2d 846 (E.D.Wis. 2008).
17. *Restatement (Third) of Torts: Products Liability,* Section 2(b).

(Nelson Pavlosky/Creative Commons)

Segway, Inc., manufacturer of the Segway® Personal Transporter, voluntarily recalled all of its transporters to fix a software problem that could cause users to fall and injure themselves. What would a person injured as a result of such malfunctioning software have to prove to establish that the device had a design defect?

According to the *Restatement,* a court can consider a broad range of factors, including the magnitude and probability of the foreseeable risks as well as the relative advantages and disadvantages of the product as it was designed and as it could have been designed. Basically, most courts engage in a risk-utility analysis, determining whether the risk of harm from the product as designed outweighs its utility to the user and to the public.

CASE EXAMPLE 11.20 Jodie Bullock smoked cigarettes manufactured by Philip Morris for forty-five years. When she was diagnosed with lung cancer, Bullock brought a product liability suit against Philip Morris. She presented evidence that by the late 1950s, scientists had proved that smoking caused lung cancer. Nonetheless, Philip Morris had issued full-page announcements stating that there was no proof that smoking caused cancer and that "numerous scientists" questioned "the validity of the statistics." At trial, the judge instructed the jury to consider the gravity of the danger posed by the design, as well as the likelihood that the danger would cause injury. The jury found that there was a defect in the design of the cigarettes and that they had been negligently designed. It awarded Bullock $850,000 in compensatory damages and $28 million in punitive damages. Philip Morris appealed, claiming that no evidence had been offered to show that there was a safer design for cigarettes, but the reviewing court found that the jury had been properly instructed. The court affirmed the award but remanded the case for a reconsideration of the proper amount of punitive damages.[18] ●

Inadequate Warnings. A product may also be deemed defective because of inadequate instructions or warnings. A product will be considered defective "when the foreseeable risks of harm posed by the product could have been reduced or avoided by the provision of reasonable instructions or warnings by the seller or other distributor, or a predecessor in the commercial chain of distribution, and the omission of the instructions or warnings renders the product not reasonably safe."[19] Generally, a seller must also warn consumers of the harm that can result from the *foreseeable misuse* of its product.

Important factors for a court to consider include the risks of a product, the "content and comprehensibility" and "intensity of expression" of warnings and instructions, and the "characteristics of expected user groups." Courts apply a "reasonableness" test to determine if the warnings adequately alert consumers to the product's risks. For example, children will likely respond more readily to bright, bold, simple warning labels, while educated adults might need more detailed information.

There is no duty to warn about risks that are obvious or commonly known. Warnings about such risks do not add to the safety of a product and could even detract from it by making other warnings seem less significant. The obviousness of a risk and a user's decision to proceed in the face of that risk may be a defense in a product liability suit based on a warning defect (defenses will be discussed on page 337).

An action alleging that a product is defective due to an inadequate label can be based on state law. (For a discussion of a case involving a state law that required warning labels on violent video games, see this chapter's *Insight into Ethics* feature on the following page.)

MARKET-SHARE LIABILITY Ordinarily, in all product liability claims, a plaintiff must prove that the defective product that caused his or her injury was the product of a specific defendant. In a few situations, however, courts have dropped this

---

18. *Bullock v. Philip Morris USA, Inc.,* 159 Cal.App.4th 655, 71 Cal.Rptr.3d 775 (2008).
19. *Restatement (Third) of Torts: Products Liability,* Section 2(c).

Insight into Ethics   Warning Labels for Video Games

The video game industry uses a voluntary rating system that includes six age-specific labels. Should video game makers also be required to attach labels to their games that warn parents of excessive violence?

California's Video Game Law

When California legislated its warning labels requirement, video software dealers sued. The California act defined a violent video game as one in which "the range of options available to a player includes killing, maiming, dismembering, or sexually assaulting an image of a human being." While agreeing that some video games are unquestionably violent by everyday standards, the trial court pointed out that many video games are based on popular novels or motion pictures and have complex plot lines.

Accordingly, the court found that the definition of a violent video game was unconstitutionally vague and thus violated the First Amendment's guarantee of freedom of speech. The court also noted the existence of the voluntary rating system. The state appealed, but the U.S. Court of Appeals for the Ninth Circuit also found that the statute's definition of a violent video game was unconstitutionally broad.[a] The state appealed again.

The United States Supreme Court's Decision

In 2011, the United States Supreme Court affirmed the decision in favor of video game and software industries. The Court noted that video games are entitled to First Amendment protection. Because California had failed to show that the statute was justified by a compelling government interest and that the law was narrowly tailored to serve that interest, the Court ruled that the statute was unconstitutional.[b]

FOR CRITICAL ANALYSIS
Insight into the Social Environment

Why would some legislators believe that the voluntary six age-specific labeling system for video games is not sufficient to protect minors?

---

a. *Video Software Dealers Association v. Schwarzenegger,* 556 F.3d 950 (9th Cir. 2009).

b. *Brown v. Entertainment Merchants Association,* ___ U.S. ___, 131 S.Ct. 2729, 180 L.Ed.2d 708 (2011).

---

requirement when plaintiffs could not prove which of many distributors of a harmful product supplied the particular product that caused the injuries.

CASE EXAMPLE 11.21 John Smith suffered from hemophilia. Because of his condition, Smith received injections of a blood protein known as antihemophiliac factor (AHF) concentrate. Smith later tested positive for the acquired immune deficiency syndrome (AIDS) virus. Because it was not known which manufacturer was responsible for the particular AHF received by Smith, the court held that all of the manufacturers of AHF could be held liable under the theory of **market-share liability.**[20] ● Under a theory of market-share liability, all firms that manufactured and distributed the product during the period in question are held liable for the plaintiff's injuries in proportion to the firms' respective shares of the market for that product during that period.

Courts in many jurisdictions do not recognize this theory of liability, believing that it deviates too significantly from traditional legal principles. In jurisdictions that do recognize market-share liability, it is usually applied in cases involving drugs or chemicals, when it is difficult or impossible to determine which company made a particular product.

Market-Share Liability A theory under which liability is shared among all firms that manufactured and distributed a particular product during a certain period of time. This form of liability sharing is used only when the true source of the harmful product is unidentifiable.

OTHER APPLICATIONS OF STRICT LIABILITY Almost all courts extend the strict liability of manufacturers and other sellers to injured bystanders. **EXAMPLE 11.22** A forklift that Trent is operating will not go into reverse, and as a result, it runs into a bystander. In this situation, the bystander can sue the manufacturer of the defective forklift under strict liability (and possibly bring a negligence action against the forklift operator as well). ●

Strict liability also applies to suppliers of component parts. **EXAMPLE 11.23** Toyota buys brake pads from a subcontractor and puts them in Corollas without changing

---

20. *Smith v. Cutter Biological, Inc.,* 72 Haw. 416, 823 P.2d 717 (1991). See also *In re Methyl Tertiary Butyl Ether (MTBE) Products Liability Litigation,* 447 F.Supp.2d 289 (S.D.N.Y. 2006).

their composition. If those pads are defective, both the supplier of the brake pads and Toyota will be held strictly liable for the injuries caused by the defects. •

Defenses to Product Liability

Defendants in product liability suits can raise a number of defenses. One defense, of course, is to show that there is no basis for the plaintiff's claim. For example, in a product liability case based on negligence, if a defendant can show that the plaintiff has *not* met the requirements (such as causation) for an action in negligence, generally the defendant will not be liable.

Similarly, in a case involving strict product liability, a defendant can claim that the plaintiff failed to meet one of the requirements. If the defendant, for instance, establishes that the goods were altered after they were sold, the defendant normally will not be held liable. A defendant may also assert that the *statute of limitations* (see Chapter 1) for a product liability claim has lapsed.[21] In addition, defendants may assert the defenses discussed next.

ASSUMPTION OF RISK Assumption of risk can sometimes be used as a defense in a product liability action. To establish such a defense, the defendant must show that (1) the plaintiff knew and appreciated the risk created by the product defect and (2) the plaintiff voluntarily assumed the risk, even though it was unreasonable to do so. (See Chapter 5 for a more detailed discussion of assumption of risk.)

PRODUCT MISUSE Similar to the defense of voluntary assumption of risk is that of product misuse, which occurs when a product is used for a purpose for which it was not intended. The courts have severely limited this defense, however, and it is now recognized as a defense only when the particular use was not reasonably foreseeable. If the misuse is foreseeable, the seller must take measures to guard against it.

COMPARATIVE NEGLIGENCE (FAULT) Developments in the area of comparative negligence, or fault (discussed in Chapter 5), have also affected the doctrine of strict liability. In the past, the plaintiff's conduct was not a defense to liability for a defective product. Today, courts in many jurisdictions consider the negligent or intentional actions of both the plaintiff and the defendant when apportioning liability and awarding damages.[22]

Thus, a defendant may be able to limit at least some of its liability for injuries caused by its defective product if it can show that the plaintiff's misuse of the product contributed to the injuries. When proved, comparative negligence differs from other defenses in that it does not completely absolve the defendant of liability, but it can reduce the amount of damages that will be awarded to the plaintiff.

CASE EXAMPLE 11.24 Dan Smith, a mechanic in Alaska, was not wearing a hard hat at work when he was asked to start the diesel engine of an air compressor. Because the compressor was an older model, he had to prop open a door to start it. When Smith got the engine started, the door fell from its position and hit his head. The injury caused him to suffer from seizures and epilepsy. Smith sued the manufacturer, claiming that the engine was defectively designed. The manufacturer argued that Smith had been negligent by failing to wear his hard hat and by propping the door open in an unsafe manner. Smith's attorney claimed that the plaintiff's ordinary negligence could not be used as a defense in product liability cases, but the Alaska Supreme

---

21. Similar state statutes, called *statutes of repose,* place outer time limits on product liability actions.
22. See, for example, *Industrial Risk Insurers v. American Engineering Testing, Inc.,* 318 Wis.2d 148, 769 N.W.2d 82 (Wis.App. 2009).

Court disagreed. Alaska, like many other states, allows comparative negligence to be raised as a defense in product liability lawsuits.[23] ●

COMMONLY KNOWN DANGERS   The dangers associated with certain products (such as sharp knives and guns) are so commonly known that manufacturers need not warn users of those dangers. If a defendant succeeds in convincing the court that a plaintiff's injury resulted from a commonly known danger, the defendant normally will not be liable.

CASE EXAMPLE 11.25   A classic case on this issue involved a plaintiff who was injured when an elastic exercise rope that she had purchased slipped off her foot and struck her in the eye, causing a detachment of the retina. The plaintiff claimed that the manufacturer should be liable because it had failed to warn users that the exercise rope might slip off a foot in such a manner. The court stated that to hold the manufacturer liable in these circumstances "would go beyond the reasonable dictates of justice in fixing the liabilities of manufacturers." After all, stated the court, "[a]lmost every physical object can be inherently dangerous or potentially dangerous in a sense. . . . A manufacturer cannot manufacture a knife that will not cut or a hammer that will not mash a thumb or a stove that will not burn a finger. The law does not require [manufacturers] to warn of such common dangers."[24] ●

KNOWLEDGEABLE USER   A related defense is the *knowledgeable user* defense. If a particular danger (such as electrical shock) is or should be commonly known by particular users of the product (such as electricians), the manufacturer of electrical equipment need not warn these users of the danger.

CASE EXAMPLE 11.26   The parents of a group of teenagers who had become overweight and developed health problems filed a product liability lawsuit against McDonald's, claiming that the fast-food chain should be held liable for failing to warn customers of the adverse health effects of eating its food products. The court rejected this claim, however, based on the knowledgeable user defense. The court found that it is well known that the food at McDonald's contains high levels of cholesterol, fat, salt, and sugar and is therefore unhealthful. The court's opinion, which thwarted numerous future lawsuits against fast-food restaurants, stated: "If consumers know (or reasonably should know) the potential ill health effects of eating at McDonald's, they cannot blame McDonald's if they, nonetheless, choose to satiate [satisfy] their appetite with a surfeit [excess] of supersized McDonald's products."[25] ●

---

23. *Smith v. Ingersoll-Rand Co.*, 14 P.3d 990 (Alaska 2000). See also *Winschel v. Brown*, 171 P.3d 142 (Alaska 2007).

24. *Jamieson v. Woodward & Lothrop*, 247 F.2d 23, 101 D.C.App. 32 (1957).

25. *Pelman v. McDonald's Corp.*, 237 F.Supp.2d 512 (S.D.N.Y. 2003).

 ## Reviewing . . . Sales, Leases, and Product Liability

Guy Holcomb owns and operates Oasis Goodtime Emporium, an adult entertainment establishment. Holcomb wanted to create an adult Internet system for Oasis that would offer customers adult theme videos and "live" chat room programs using performers at the club. On May 10, Holcomb signed a work order authorizing Crossroads Consulting Group (CCG) "to deliver a working prototype of a customer chat system, demonstrating the integration of live video and chatting in a Web browser." In exchange for creating the prototype, Holcomb agreed to pay CCG $64,697. On May 20, Holcomb signed an additional work order in the amount of $12,943 for CCG to install a customized firewall system. The work orders stated that Holcomb would make monthly installment payments to CCG, and both parties expected the work would be finished by September. Due to unforeseen problems largely attributable to system configuration and software incompatibility, the project required more time than anticipated. By the end of the summer, the Web site was still not ready, and Holcomb had fallen behind in the payments to CCG. CCG was threatening to cease work and file suit for breach of contract unless the bill was paid. Rather than make further payments, Holcomb wanted to abandon the Web site project. Using the information presented in the chapter, answer the following questions.

1. Would a court be likely to decide that the transaction between Holcomb and CCG was covered by the Uniform Commercial Code (UCC)? Why or why not?
2. Would a court be likely to consider Holcomb a merchant under the UCC? Why or why not?
3. Did the parties have a valid contract under the UCC? Explain.
4. Suppose that Holcomb and CCG meet in October in an attempt to resolve their problems. At that time, the parties reach an oral agreement that CCG will continue to work without demanding full payment of the past-due amounts and Holcomb will pay CCG $5,000 per week. Assuming that the contract falls under the UCC, is the oral agreement enforceable? Why or why not?

Linking the Law *to Management*
Quality Control

In this chapter, you learned that breaches of warranties and manufacturing and design defects can give rise to liability. Although it is possible to minimize liability through warranty disclaimers and various defenses to product liability claims, all businesspersons know that such disclaimers and defenses do not necessarily fend off expensive lawsuits.

The legal issues surrounding product liability and warranties relate directly to quality control. As all of your management courses will emphasize, quality control is an important concern for every manager in all organizations. Companies that have cost-effective quality control systems produce products with fewer manufacturing and design defects. As a result, these companies incur fewer potential and actual warranty and product liability lawsuits.

Three Types of Quality Control

Most management systems involve three types of quality control— preventive, concurrent, and feedback. They apply at different stages of the process: preventive quality control occurs before the process begins, concurrent control takes place during the process, and feedback control occurs after it is finished.

In a typical manufacturing process, for example, preventive quality control might involve inspecting raw materials before they are put into the production process. Once the process begins, measuring and monitoring devices constantly assess quality standards as part of a concurrent quality control system. When the standards are not being met, employees correct the problem.

Once the manufacturing is completed, the products undergo a final quality inspection as part of the feedback quality control system. Of course, there are economic limits to how complete the final inspection will be. A refrigerator can be tested for an hour, a day, or a year. Management faces a trade-off. The less the refrigerator is tested, the sooner it gets to market and the faster the company receives its payment. The shorter the testing period, however, the higher the probability of a defect that will cost the manufacturer because of its expressed or implied warranties.

Total Quality Management (TQM)

Some managers attempt to reduce warranty and product liability costs by relying on a concurrent quality control system known as total quality management (TQM). This is an organization-wide effort to infuse quality into every activity in a company through continuous improvement.

Quality circles are a popular TQM technique. These are groups of six to twelve employees who volunteer to meet regularly to discuss problems and how to solve them. In a continuous-stream manufacturing process, for example, a quality circle might consist of workers from different phases in the production process. Quality circles lead to changes in the production process that affect workers who are actually on the production line.

Benchmarking is another technique used in TQM. In benchmarking, a company continuously measures its products against those of its toughest competitors or the industry leaders in order to identify areas for improvement. In the automobile industry, benchmarking enabled several Japanese firms to overtake U.S. automakers in terms of quality. Some argue that Toyota gained worldwide market share by effectively using this type of quality control management system.

Another TQM system is called *Six Sigma*. Motorola introduced the quality principles in this system in the late 1980s, but Six Sigma has

(Continued)

now become a generic term for a quality control approach that takes nothing for granted. It is based on a five-step methodology: define, measure, analyze, improve, and control. Six Sigma controls emphasize discipline and a relentless attempt to achieve higher quality (and lower costs). A possible impediment to a company's instituting a Six Sigma program is that it requires a major commitment from top management because it may involve widespread changes throughout the entire organization.

FOR CRITICAL ANALYSIS

Quality control leads to fewer defective products and fewer lawsuits. Consequently, managers know that quality control is important to their company's long-term financial health. At the same time, the more quality control that managers impose on their organization, the higher the average cost per unit of whatever is produced and sold. How does a manager decide how much quality control to undertake?

 Key Terms

conforming goods 316	intangible property 309	puffery 328
course of dealing 330	lease 311	replevin 324
cover 323	lease agreement 311	sale 309
cure 317	lessee 311	sales contract 308
express warranty 327	lessor 311	seasonably 313
firm offer 312	market-share liability 336	tangible property 309
implied warranty 329	merchant 311	tender of delivery 316
implied warranty of fitness	perfect tender rule 317	unreasonably dangerous
for a particular purpose 329	predominant-factor test 310	product 333
implied warranty	product liability 330	usage of trade 330
of merchantability 329		

 Chapter Summary: Sales, Leases, and Product Liability

The Scope of Articles 2 (Sales) and 2A (Leases) (See pages 308–311.)	1. *Article 2 (sales)*—Article 2 of the UCC governs contracts for the sale of goods (tangible, movable personal property). The common law of contracts also applies to sales contracts to the extent that the common law has not been modified by the UCC. If there is a conflict between a common law rule and the UCC, the UCC controls. Special rules apply to merchants. 2. *Article 2A (leases)*—Article 2A governs contracts for the lease of goods. Except that it applies to leases, instead of sales, of goods, Article 2A is essentially a repetition of Article 2 and varies only to reflect differences between sales and lease transactions.

The Formation of Sales and Lease Contracts (See pages 311–316.)	1. *Offer*—
	  a. Not all terms have to be included for a contract to be formed (only the quantity term must be specified).
	  b. The price does not have to be included for a contract to be formed.
	  c. Particulars of performance can be left open.
	  d. A written and signed offer by a *merchant,* covering a period of three months or less, is irrevocable without payment of consideration.
	2. *Acceptance*—
	  a. Acceptance may be made by any reasonable means of communication. It is effective when dispatched.
	  b. An offer can be accepted by a promise to ship or by prompt shipment of conforming goods, or by prompt shipment of nonconforming goods if not accompanied by a notice of accommodation.
	  c. Acceptance by performance requires notice within a reasonable time. Otherwise, the offer can be treated as lapsed.

Chapter Summary: Sales, Leases, and Product Liability, Continued

The Formation of Sales and Lease Contracts– Continued	d. A definite expression of acceptance creates a contract even if the terms of the acceptance differ from those of the offer, unless the different terms in the acceptance are expressly conditioned on the offeror's assent to those terms.
	3. *Consideration*–A modification of a contract for the sale of goods does not require consideration.
	4. *The Statute of Frauds*–
	a. All contracts for the sale of goods priced at $500 or more must be in writing. A writing is sufficient as long as it indicates a contract between the parties and is signed by the party against whom enforcement is sought. A contract is not enforceable beyond the quantity shown in the writing.
	b. When written confirmation of an oral contract *between merchants* is not objected to in writing by the receiver within ten days, the contract is enforceable.
	c. Exceptions to the Statute of Frauds are made when the goods are specially manufactured, when the contract has been partially performed, and when there have been admissions.
Performance of Sales and Lease Contracts (See pages 316–321.)	1. The seller or lessor must tender *conforming goods* to the buyer or lessee. Tender must take place at a *reasonable hour* and in a *reasonable manner.* Under the perfect tender doctrine, the seller or lessor must tender goods that conform exactly to the terms of the contract [UCC 2–503(1), 2A–508(1)].
	2. If the seller or lessor tenders nonconforming goods prior to the performance date and the buyer or lessee rejects them, the seller or lessor may cure (repair or replace the goods) within the contract time for performance [UCC 2–508(1), 2A–513(1)]. If the seller or lessor has reasonable grounds to believe the buyer or lessee would accept the tendered goods, on the buyer's or lessee's rejection the seller or lessor has a reasonable time to substitute conforming goods without liability [UCC 2–508(2), 2A–513(2)].
	3. If the agreed-on means of delivery becomes impracticable or unavailable, the seller must substitute an alternative means (such as a different carrier) if one is available [UCC 2–614(1)].
	4. When performance becomes commercially impracticable owing to circumstances that were not foreseeable when the contract was formed, the perfect tender rule no longer holds [UCC 2–615, 2A–405].
	5. On tender of delivery by the seller or lessor, the buyer or lessee must pay for the goods at the time and place the goods are received, unless the sale is made on credit.
	6. The buyer or lessee can manifest acceptance of delivered goods expressly in words or by conduct or by failing to reject the goods after a reasonable period of time following inspection or after having had a reasonable opportunity to inspect them [UCC 2–606(1), 2A–515(1)]. A buyer will be deemed to have accepted goods if he or she performs any act inconsistent with the seller's ownership [UCC 2–606(1)(c)].
	7. If, before the time for performance, either party clearly indicates to the other an intention not to perform, this is called anticipatory repudiation. Under UCC 2–610 and 2A–402, the nonbreaching party may either treat the breach as final by pursuing a remedy or wait and hope that the other party will perform. In either situation, the nonbreaching party may suspend performance.
Remedies for Breach of Sales and Lease Contracts (See pages 321–327.)	1. *Remedies of the seller or lessor*–When a buyer or lessee breaches the contract, a seller or lessor can withhold or discontinue performance. If the seller or lessor is still in possession of the goods, the seller or lessor can resell or dispose of the goods and hold the buyer or lessee liable for any loss [UCC 2–703(d), 2–706(1), 2A–523(1)(e), 2A–527(1)]. If the goods cannot be resold or disposed of, an unpaid seller or lessor can bring an action to recover the purchase price or payments due under the contract, plus incidental damages [UCC 2–709(1), 2A–529(1)]. If the buyer or lessee repudiates the contract or wrongfully refuses to accept goods, the seller or lessor can recover the damages that were sustained.
	2. *Remedies of the buyer or lessee*–When the seller or lessor breaches, the buyer or lessee can choose from a number of remedies, including the following:
	a. Obtain specific performance (when the goods are unique and when the remedy at law is inadequate) [UCC 2–716(1), 2A–521(1)].

(Continued)

Chapter Summary: Sales, Leases, and Product Liability, Continued

Remedies for Breach of Sales and Lease Contracts–Continued	b. Obtain cover (in certain situations) [UCC 2–712, 2A–518]. c. Sue to recover damages [UCC 2–713, 2A–519]. d. Reject the goods [UCC 2–601, 2A–509]. e. Revoke acceptance (in certain circumstances) [UCC 2–608, 2A–517]. f. Accept the goods and recover damages [UCC 2–607, 2–714, 2–717, 2A–519]. 3. The parties can agree to vary their respective rights and remedies in their agreement. If the contract states that a remedy is exclusive, then that is the sole remedy.

Sales and Lease Warranties (See pages 327–330.)	1. *Title warranties*–The seller or lessor automatically warrants that he or she has good title, and that there are no liens or infringements on the property being sold or leased.
	 2. *Express warranties*–An express warranty arises under the UCC when a seller or lessor indicates, as part of the basis of the bargain, that the goods conform to any of the following:
	   a. An affirmation or promise of fact.
	   b. A description of the goods.
	   c. A sample shown to the buyer or lessee [UCC 2–313, 2A–210].
	 3. *Implied warranties*–
	   a. The implied warranty of merchantability automatically arises when the seller or lessor is a merchant who deals in the kind of goods sold or leased. The seller or lessor warrants that the goods sold or leased are of proper quality, are properly labeled, and are reasonably fit for the ordinary purposes for which such goods are used [UCC 2–314, 2A–212].
	   b. The implied warranty of fitness for a particular purpose arises when the buyer's or lessee's purpose or use is expressly or impliedly known by the seller or lessor and the buyer or lessee purchases or leases the goods in reliance on the seller's or lessor's selection [UCC 2–315, 2A–213].
	 4. Warranties, both express and implied, can be disclaimed or qualified by a seller or lessor, but disclaimers generally must be specific and unambiguous, and often must be in writing.

Product Liability (See pages 330–338.)	1. *Liability based on negligence*–The manufacturer must use due care in designing the product, selecting materials, using the appropriate production process, assembling and testing the product, and placing adequate warnings on the label or product. Privity of contract is not required. A manufacturer is liable for failure to exercise due care to any person who sustains an injury proximately caused by a negligently made (defective) product.
	 2. *Strict liability requirements*–
	   a. The defendant must sell the product in a defective condition.
	   b. The defendant must normally be engaged in the business of selling that product.
	   c. The product must be unreasonably dangerous to the user or consumer because of its defective condition (in most states).
	   d. The plaintiff must incur physical harm to self or property by use or consumption of the product.
	   e. The defective condition must be the proximate cause of the injury or damage.
	   f. The goods must not have been substantially changed from the time the product was sold to the time the injury was sustained.
	 3. *Product defects*–A product may be defective in three basic ways:
	   a. In its manufacture.
	   b. In its design.
	   c. In the instructions or warnings that come with it.
	 4. *Market-share liability*–When plaintiffs cannot prove which of many distributors of a defective product supplied the particular product that caused the plaintiffs' injuries, some courts apply market-share liability. All firms that manufactured and distributed the harmful product during the period in question are then held liable for the plaintiffs' injuries in proportion to the firms' respective shares of the market, as directed by the court.

Chapter Summary: Sales, Leases, and Product Liability, Continued

Product Liability–Continued	5. *Other applications of strict liability*—Manufacturers and other sellers are liable for harms suffered by bystanders as a result of defective products. Suppliers of component parts are strictly liable for defective parts that, when incorporated into a product, cause injuries to users.
	6. *Defenses to product liability*—
	  a. Assumption of risk—The user or consumer knew of the risk of harm and voluntarily assumed it.
	  b. Product misuse—The user or consumer misused the product in a way unforeseeable by the manufacturer.
	  c. Comparative negligence—Liability may be distributed between the plaintiff and the defendant under the doctrine of comparative negligence if the plaintiff's misuse of the product contributed to the risk of injury.
	  d. Commonly known dangers—If a defendant succeeds in convincing the court that a plaintiff's injury resulted from a commonly known danger, such as the danger associated with using a sharp knife, the defendant will not be liable.
	  e. Knowledgeable user—If a particular danger is or should be commonly known by particular users of the product, the manufacturer of the product need not warn these users of the danger.

ExamPrep

ISSUE SPOTTERS

1. E-Design, Inc., orders 150 computer desks. Fav-O-Rite Supplies, Inc., ships 150 printer stands. Is this an acceptance of the offer or a counteroffer? If it is an acceptance, is it a breach of the contract? What if Fav-O-Rite told E-Design it was sending the printer stands as "an accommodation"?
2. Rim Corporation makes tire rims and sells them to Superior Vehicles, Inc., which installs them on cars. One set of rims is defective, which an inspection would reveal. Superior does not inspect the rims. The car with the defective rims is sold to Town Auto Sales, which sells the car to Uri. Soon, the car is in an accident caused by the defective rims, and Uri is injured. Is Superior Vehicles liable? Explain your answer.

—**Check your answers to these questions against the answers provided in Appendix G.**

BEFORE THE TEST

Go to **www.cengagebrain.com**, enter the ISBN number "9781111530617," and click on "Find" to locate this textbook's Web site. Then, click on "Access Now" under "Study Tools," and select "Chapter 11" at the top. There you will find an "Interactive Quiz" that you can take to assess your mastery of the concepts in this chapter, as well as "Flashcards" and a "Glossary" of important terms.

For Review

1. How do Article 2 and Article 2A of the UCC differ? What types of transactions does each article cover?
2. Under the UCC, if an offeree includes additional or different terms in an acceptance, will a contract result? If so, what happens to these terms?
3. What remedies are available to a seller or lessor when the buyer or lessee breaches the contract? What remedies are available to a buyer or lessee if the seller or lessor breaches the contract?
4. What implied warranties arise under the UCC?
5. What are the elements of a cause of action in strict product liability?

Questions and Case Problems

11–1. Additional Terms. Strike offers to sell Bailey one thousand shirts for a stated price. The offer declares that shipment will be made by the Dependable Truck Line. Bailey replies, "I accept your offer for one thousand shirts at the price quoted. Delivery to be by Yellow Express Truck Line." Both Strike and Bailey are merchants. Three weeks later, Strike ships the shirts by the Dependable Truck Line, and Bailey refuses shipment. Strike sues for breach of contract. Bailey claims (a) that there never was a contract because the reply, which included a modification of carriers, did not constitute an acceptance and (b) that even if there had been a contract, Strike would have been in breach because it shipped the shirts by Dependable, contrary to the contract terms. Discuss fully Bailey's claims.

11–2. Product Liability. Carmen buys a television set manufactured by AKI Electronics. She is going on vacation, so she takes the set to her mother's house for her mother to use. Because the set is defective, it explodes, causing considerable damage to her mother's house. Carmen's mother sues AKI for the damage to her house. Discuss the theories under which Carmen's mother can recover from AKI.

11–3. Anticipatory Repudiation. Topken has contracted to sell Lorwin five hundred washing machines of a certain model at list price. Topken is to ship the goods on or before December 1. Topken produces one thousand washing machines of this model but has not yet prepared Lorwin's shipment. On November 1, Lorwin repudiates the contract. Discuss the remedies available to Topken.

11–4. Defenses to Product Liability. Terry Kunkle and VanBuren High hosted a Christmas party in Berkeley County, South Carolina. Guests had drinks and hors d'oeuvres at a residence and adjourned to dinner in a barn across a public road. Brandon Stroud ferried the guests to the barn in a golf car made by Textron, Inc. The golf car was not equipped with lights, and Textron did not warn against its use on public roads at night. South Carolina does not require golf cars to be equipped with lights, but does ban their operation on public roads at night. As Stroud attempted to cross the road at 8:30 P.M., his golf car was struck by a vehicle driven by Joseph Thornley. Stroud was killed. His estate filed a suit in a South Carolina state court against Textron, alleging strict product liability and product liability based on negligence. The estate claimed that the golf car was defective and unreasonably dangerous. What might Textron assert in its defense? Explain. [*Moore v. Barony House Restaurant, LLC,* 382 S.C. 35, 674 S.E.2d 500 (S.C.App. 2009)]

11–5. Product Liability. Yun Tung Chow tried to unclog a floor drain in the kitchen of the restaurant where he worked. He used a drain cleaner called Lewis Red Devil Lye that contained crystalline sodium hydroxide. The product label said to wear eye protection, to put one tablespoon of lye directly into the drain, and to keep your face away from the drain because there could be dangerous backsplash. Not wearing eye protection, Chow mixed three spoonfuls of lye in a can and poured that mixture down the drain while bending over it. Liquid splashed back into his face, causing injury. He sued for product liability based on inadequate warnings and a design defect. The trial court granted summary judgment to the manufacturer. Chow appealed. An expert for Chow stated that the product was defective because it had a tendency to backsplash. Is that a convincing argument? Why or why not? [*Yun Tung Chow v. Reckitt & Coleman, Inc.,* 69 A.D.3d 413, 891 N.Y.S.2d 402 (N.Y.A.D. 1 Dept. 2010)]

11–6. Breach and Damages. Before Chad DeRosier could build a house on his undeveloped property, he needed to have some fill dirt deposited on the land. Utility Systems of America, Inc., was doing roadwork nearby, and DeRosier asked Utility if it would like to deposit extra fill dirt on his property. Utility said it would, and DeRosier obtained the necessary permit. The permit was for 1,500 cubic yards of fill dirt, the amount that DeRosier needed. DeRosier gave Utility a copy of the permit. Later, DeRosier found 6,500 cubic yards of fill dirt on his land and had to have 5,000 cubic yards of it removed. Utility denied responsibility but said that it would remove the fill dirt for $9,500. DeRosier filed a suit against Utility and hired another company to remove the fill dirt and to do certain foundation work. He paid $46,629 to that contractor. The district court held that Utility had breached its contract and ordered it to pay DeRosier $22,829 in general damages and $8,000 in consequential damages. Utility appealed. In view of the fact that Utility charged nothing for the fill dirt, did a breach of contract occur? If a breach occurred, should the damages be greater than $9,500? Can consequential damages be justified? Discuss. [*DeRosier v. Utility Systems of America, Inc.,* 780 N.W.2d 1 (Minn.App. 2010)]

11–7. Case Problem with Sample Answer. Remedies of the Buyer. Woodridge USA Properties, LP, bought eighty-seven commercial truck trailers under a contract with southeast Trailer Mart (STM), Inc. Southeastern Freight Lines, Inc., owned the lot in Atlanta, Georgia, where the trailers were stored. Gerald McCarty, an independent sales agent who arranged the deal, showed Woodridge the documents of title. They did not indicate that Woodridge was the buyer. Woodridge asked McCarty to hold the documents and sell the trailers for Woodridge. Within three months, all of the trailers had been sold, but McCarty had not given the proceeds to Woodridge. Woodridge—without mentioning the title documents—asked STM to refund the contract price. STM refused. Later, Woodridge filed a suit in a federal district court against STM, claiming that the title documents had been defective and seeking damages. Does Woodridge have a right to recover damages for accepted goods? What would be the measure of the damages? Explain. [*Woodridge USA Properties, L.P. v. Southeast Trailer Mart, Inc.,* ___ F.3d ___ (11th Cir. 2011)]

—**To view a sample answer for Case Problem 11–7, go to Appendix F at the end of this text.**

11–8.   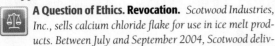 **A Question of Ethics. Revocation.** *Scotwood Industries, Inc., sells calcium chloride flake for use in ice melt products. Between July and September 2004, Scotwood delivered thirty-seven shipments of flake to Frank Miller & Sons, Inc. After each delivery, Scotwood billed Miller, which paid thirty-five of the invoices and processed 30 to 50 percent of the flake. In August, Miller began complaining about the product's quality. Scotwood assured Miller that it would remedy the situation. Finally, in October, Miller told Scotwood, "This is totally unacceptable. We are willing to discuss Scotwood picking up the material." Miller claimed that the flake was substantially defective because it was chunked. Calcium chloride maintains its purity for up to five years, but if it is exposed to and absorbs moisture, it chunks and becomes unusable. In response to Scotwood's suit to collect payment on the unpaid invoices, Miller filed a counterclaim in a federal district court for breach of contract, seeking to recover based on revocation of acceptance, among other things. [Scotwood Industries, Inc. v. Frank Miller & Sons, Inc., 435 F.Supp.2d 1160 (D.Kan. 2006)]*

1. What is revocation of acceptance? How does a buyer effectively exercise this option? Do the facts in this case support this theory as a ground for Miller to recover damages? Why or why not?

2. Is there an ethical basis for allowing a buyer to revoke acceptance of goods and recover damages? If so, is there an ethical limit to this right? Discuss.

11–9.   **Video Question. *Matilda.***

Access the video using the instructions provided below to answer the following questions.

1. What warranties of title arise in sales of used cars by dealers?

2. A father (Danny DeVito) uses a tool to turn back the numbers on a vehicle's odometer. When he sells this car, if he tells the buyer the mileage is only 60,000, knowing that it is really 120,000, has he breached an express warranty? If the seller did not make any oral statements about the car's mileage, could the buyer claim an express warranty existed? Explain.

3. What would a person who buys the car in the video have to show to prove that the seller breached the implied warranty of merchantability?

—To watch this video, go to **www.cengagebrain.com** and register the access code that came with your new book or log in to your existing account. Select the link for either the "Business Law Digital Video Library Online Access" or "Business Law CourseMate," and then click on "Complete Video List" to find the video for this chapter (Video 71).

Chapter 12

Creditor-Debtor Relations and Bankruptcy

> "Capitalism without bankruptcy is like Christianity without hell."
>
> —Frank Borman, 1928–present
> (U.S. astronaut and businessman)

Contents

Chapter Objectives

After reading this chapter, you should be able to answer the following questions:

1. What is a prejudgment attachment? What is a writ of execution? How does a creditor use these remedies?

2. What is garnishment? When might a creditor undertake a garnishment proceeding?

3. In a bankruptcy proceeding, what constitutes the debtor's estate in property? What property is exempt from the estate under federal bankruptcy law?

4. What is the difference between an exception to discharge and an objection to discharge?

5. In a Chapter 11 reorganization, what is the role of the debtor in possession?

(Quazieforo/Creative Commons)

Normally, creditors have no problem collecting the debts owed to them. When disputes arise over the amount owed, however, or when the debtor simply cannot or will not pay, what happens? What remedies are available to creditors when debtors default (fail to pay as promised)?

In this chapter, we first focus on some basic laws that assist the creditor and debtor in resolving their dispute without resorting to bankruptcy or mortgage foreclosure (see Chapter 13). We then examine the process of bankruptcy, which is the last resort in resolving creditor-debtor problems in a capitalist society, as the chapter-opening quotation implies. We look at the different types of relief available to debtors under federal bankruptcy law and discuss the basic bankruptcy procedures required for each type of relief. Our discussion specifically includes changes that resulted from the Bankruptcy Reform Act of 2005.

Laws Assisting Creditors

Both the common law and statutory laws create various rights and remedies for creditors. Here, we discuss some of these rights and remedies.

Liens

Lien A claim against specific property to satisfy a debt.

A **lien** is an encumbrance on (claim against) property to satisfy a debt or protect a claim for the payment of a debt. Creditors' liens may arise under statutory law or under the common law. Statutory liens include *mechanic's liens,* whereas *artisan's liens* were recognized at common law. *Judicial liens* arise when a creditor attempts to collect on a debt before or after a judgment is entered by a court.

Liens can be an important tool for creditors because they generally take priority over other claims, except those of creditors who have a *perfected security interest* in the same property. (A *security interest* is an interest in a debtor's personal property—called *collateral*—that a seller, lender, or other creditor takes to secure payment of an obligation. *Perfection,* which is generally accomplished by filing a financing statement with a state official, is the legal process by which a creditor protects its security interest from the claims of others.) In fact, unless a statute provides otherwise, the holders of mechanic's and artisan's liens normally take priority even over creditors who have a perfected security interest in the property.

For liens other than mechanic's and artisan's liens, priority depends on whether the lien was obtained before the other creditor perfected its security interest. If the lien was obtained first, the lienholder has priority, but if the security interest was perfected first, the party with the perfected security interest has priority.

MECHANIC'S LIEN   When a person contracts for labor, services, or materials to be furnished for the purpose of making improvements on real property (land and things attached to the land, such as buildings and trees—see Chapter 22) but does not immediately pay for the improvements, the creditor can file a **mechanic's lien** on the property. This creates a special type of debtor-creditor relationship in which the real estate itself becomes security for the debt.

Mechanic's Lien A statutory lien on the real property of another to ensure payment for work performed and materials furnished for the repair or improvement of real property, such as a building.

EXAMPLE 12.1   A painter agrees to paint a homeowner's house for an agreed-on price to cover labor and materials. If the homeowner refuses to pay for the work or pays only a portion of the charges, a mechanic's lien against the property can be created. The painter is the lienholder, and the real property is encumbered (burdened) with a mechanic's lien for the amount owed. If the homeowner does not pay the lien, the property can be sold to satisfy the debt. Notice of the foreclosure (the process by which the creditor deprives the debtor of his or her property) and sale must be given to the debtor in advance, however. •

State law governs the procedures that must be followed to create a mechanic's lien. Generally, the lienholder must file a written notice of lien against the particular property involved. The notice must be filed within a specific time period, normally measured from the last date on which materials or labor were provided (usually within 60 to 120 days). If the property owner fails to pay the debt, the lienholder is entitled to foreclose on the real estate for which the work or materials were provided and to sell it to satisfy the amount of the debt.

In the following case, a contractor attempted to foreclose on a piece of property under a mechanic's lien. The property owner claimed to be unaware of any work done by the contractor. Could this prevent the foreclosure?

Sometimes, homeowners contract for significant improvements to their structures. When a homeowner fails to pay those individuals or companies that provided labor and materials for the renovations, a mechanic's lien *is automatically created. Why do mechanic's liens have priority over perfected security interests?*

(AP Photo/*Columbus Ledger-Enquirer*/Joe Paul)

Case 12.1   BHP Land Services, Inc. v. Seymour

Superior Court of Connecticut, __ A.3d __ (2011).

BACKGROUND AND FACTS   Jean Seymour lived in Barkhamsted, Connecticut, but she also owned a house, a horse barn, and several acres of land in Enfield. Jean's daughter, Jennifer, lived on the Enfield property, which she called the RoundTuit Ranch. Jennifer boarded, trained, and sold horses on the ranch. Jean paid the property taxes and the mortgage but did not participate in the RoundTuit business. Jennifer did not pay rent, but she paid the costs of the business, including snow plowing and house repairs. Jennifer hired BHP Land Services, Inc., to remove tree stumps and grade two acres for $2,450 per acre. When the work was done, Jennifer paid the bill. The next year, she hired BHP to do similar work on another nine acres at the same price per acre. When Jennifer did not pay the bill, BHP filed a suit in a Connecticut state court against Jean, who responded that she had never authorized the work.

IN THE WORDS OF THE COURT . . .
KLACZAK, Lawrence C., J.T.R. [Judge Trial Referee[a]]
    * * * *

In this case the plaintiff in its [complaint] seeks to foreclose a mechanic's lien on a parcel of property known as 100 Fletcher Road, Enfield, Connecticut.
    * * * *

A mechanic's lien is available to one who has a claim for services rendered for the improvement of a plot of land. The owner of the land upon which improvement is made, or someone having authority, must have consented to the services having been rendered. [Emphasis added.]
    * * * *

Jean Seymour had given her daughter apparent carte blanche authority to operate the ranch as she saw fit * * * when this clearing

---

a. A judge trial referee is a judge who has been designated by the chief justice of the Connecticut Supreme Court to hear a certain case.

work was done. Any improvements to the property inured [came in effect] to Jean's benefit as the record owner. Jennifer also acted as her mother's agent when they appeared at [the Enfield] Inland Wetland Agency regarding the grading, clearing and seeding project on the property.

Clearly, on that occasion, Jean represented that Jennifer could act as her agent and, further, she (Jean), was obviously aware that work was expected to be done which would enhance the property. The Court concludes that Jean permitted Jennifer to act as the agent of the property owner. Jennifer had the authority to do work on the property without any authorization from Jean and she had unfettered authority to act as the agent of the owner.

The complaint sufficiently alleges * * * facts to substantiate an order to foreclose the mechanic's lien, and the evidence as discussed herein supports the Court's finding.
    * * * *

Judgment shall enter against the defendant in the amount of $26,250, which was the * * * price for the work done.

DECISION AND REMEDY   The court found that Jennifer Seymour had the authority to act as her mother's agent (see Chapter 16) and have work done on the property. Therefore, the court issued a judgment in BHP's favor and ordered a hearing to determine the terms of the foreclosure, as well as its fees and costs.

THE ECONOMIC DIMENSION   *What should Jean do next—appeal the court's decision, settle with BHP for the amount of the judgment, or go through the foreclosure process? Explain.*

THE LEGAL ENVIRONMENT DIMENSION   *When no actual contract exists, under what theory may a court step in to prevent a property owner from being unjustly enriched by the work, labor, or services of a contractor?*

Artisan's Lien   A possessory lien given to a person who has made improvements and added value to another person's personal property as security for payment for services performed.

ARTISAN'S LIEN   An **artisan's lien** is a security device created at common law through which a creditor can recover payment from a debtor for labor and materials furnished for the repair or improvement of personal property. In contrast to a mechanic's lien, an artisan's lien is *possessory*. This means that the lienholder ordinarily must have retained possession of the property and have expressly or impliedly agreed to provide the services on a cash, not a credit, basis. The lien remains in existence as long as the lienholder maintains possession, and the lien is terminated once possession is voluntarily surrendered—unless the surrender is only temporary.

EXAMPLE 12.2   Selena leaves her diamond ring at the jeweler's to be repaired and to have her initials engraved on the band. In the absence of an agreement, the jeweler can keep the ring until she pays for the services. Should Selena fail to pay, the jeweler has a lien on her ring for the amount of the bill and normally can sell the ring in satisfaction of the lien. ●

Modern statutes permit the holder of an artisan's lien to foreclose and sell the property subject to the lien to satisfy payment of the debt. As with a mechanic's lien, the holder of an artisan's lien is required to give notice to the owner of the property prior to foreclosure and sale. The sale proceeds are used to pay the debt and the costs of the legal proceedings, and the surplus, if any, is paid to the former owner.

JUDICIAL LIENS   When a debt is past due, a creditor can bring a legal action against the debtor to collect the debt. If the creditor is successful in the action, the court awards the creditor a judgment against the debtor (usually for the amount of the debt plus any interest and legal costs incurred in obtaining the judgment). Frequently, however, the creditor is unable to collect the awarded amount.

To help ensure that a judgment in the creditor's favor will be collectible, the creditor is permitted to request that certain nonexempt property of the debtor be seized to satisfy the debt. (Under state or federal statutes, certain property is exempt from attachment by creditors. Additionally, many judgments are uncollectible because of bankruptcy exemptions.) A court's order to seize the debtor's property is known as a *writ of attachment* if it is issued before a judgment in the creditor's favor. If the order is issued after a judgment, it is referred to as a *writ of execution*.

Writ of Attachment. In the context of judicial liens, **attachment** is a court-ordered seizure and taking into custody of property prior to the securing of a judgment for a past-due debt. Attachment rights are created by state statutes. Normally, attachment is a *prejudgment* remedy occurring either at the time a lawsuit is filed or immediately afterward. To attach before judgment, a creditor must comply with the specific state's statutory restrictions and requirements. The due process clause of the Fourteenth Amendment to the U.S. Constitution also applies and requires that the debtor be given notice and an opportunity to be heard (see Chapter 4).

The creditor must have an enforceable right to payment of the debt under law and must follow certain procedures. Otherwise, the creditor can be liable for damages for wrongful attachment. She or he must file with the court an *affidavit* (a written or printed statement, made under oath or sworn to) stating that the debtor is in default and indicating the statutory grounds under which attachment is sought. The creditor must also post a bond to cover at least the court costs, the value of the loss of use of the good suffered by the debtor, and the value of the property attached. When the court is satisfied that all the requirements have been met, it issues a **writ of attachment,** which directs the sheriff or another public officer to seize nonexempt property. If the creditor prevails at trial, the seized property can be sold to satisfy the judgment.

Writ of Execution. If the creditor wins at trial and the debtor will not or cannot pay the judgment, the creditor is entitled to go back to the court and request a **writ of execution.** This writ is a court order directing the sheriff to seize (levy) and sell any of the debtor's nonexempt real or personal property that is within the court's geographic jurisdiction (usually the county in which the courthouse

Attachment   In the context of judicial liens, a court-ordered seizure and taking into custody of property prior to the securing of a judgment for a past-due debt.

Writ of Attachment   A court's order, issued prior to a trial to collect a debt, directing the sheriff or another public officer to seize nonexempt property of the debtor. If the creditor prevails at trial, the seized property can be sold to satisfy the judgment.

Writ of Execution   A court's order, issued after a judgment has been entered against a debtor, directing the sheriff to seize and sell any of the debtor's nonexempt real or personal property.

The bank that loaned funds for the purchase of this boat can bring a legal action to collect the debt. Once a judgment against the debtor is rendered, what happens next?

(AP Photo/Jeffrey M. Boan)

is located). The proceeds of the sale are used to pay the judgment, accrued interest, and the costs of the sale. Any excess is paid to the debtor. The debtor can pay the judgment and redeem the nonexempt property any time before the sale takes place.

Garnishment

Garnishment   A legal process used by a creditor to collect a debt by seizing property of the debtor (such as wages) that is being held by a third party (such as the debtor's employer).

An order for **garnishment** permits a creditor to collect a debt by seizing property of the debtor that is being held by a third party. In a garnishment proceeding, the third party— the person or entity that the court is ordering to garnish an individual's property—is called the *garnishee*. Typically, a garnishee is the debtor's employer, and the creditor is seeking a judgment so that part of the debtor's usual paycheck will be paid to the creditor.

In some situations, however, the garnishee is a third party that holds funds belonging to the debtor (such as a bank) or has possession of, or exercises control over, other types of property belonging to the debtor. A creditor can garnish almost all types of property—including tax refunds, pensions, and trust funds—so long as the property is not exempt from garnishment and is in the possession of a third party.

CASE EXAMPLE 12.3   Helen Griffin failed to pay a debt she owed to Indiana Surgical Specialists. Indiana Surgical filed a lawsuit to collect, and Griffin did not answer the complaint or appear in court. The court issued a default judgment in favor of Indiana Surgical and a garnishment order to withhold the appropriate amount from Griffin's earnings until her debt was paid. At the time, Griffin was working as a subcontractor driving for a courier service. She claimed that her wages could not be garnished because she was an independent contractor, and not an employee (see Chapter 17 for a discussion of independent-contractor status). Ultimately, an Indiana intermediate appellate court held that payments for the services of an independent contractor fall within the definition of earnings and can be garnished.[1] ●

GARNISHMENT PROCEEDINGS   Because state law governs garnishment actions, the procedures differ from state to state. Garnishment can be a prejudgment remedy, requiring a hearing before a court, but it is most often a postjudgment remedy. In some states, the creditor needs to obtain only one order of garnishment, which then applies continuously to the debtor's wages until the entire debt is paid. In other states, the creditor must go back to court for a separate order of garnishment for each pay period.

LAWS LIMITING THE AMOUNT OF WAGES SUBJECT TO GARNISHMENT   Both federal and state laws limit the amount that can be taken from a debtor's weekly take-home pay through garnishment proceedings.[2] Federal law provides a minimal framework to protect debtors from suffering unduly when paying judgment debts.[3] State laws also provide dollar exemptions, and these amounts are often larger than those provided by federal law. Under federal law, an employer cannot dismiss an employee because his or her wages are being garnished.

---

1. *Indiana Surgical Specialists v. Griffin,* 867 N.E.2d 260 (Ind.App. 2007).
2. Some states (for example, Texas) do not permit garnishment of wages by private parties except under a child-support order.
3. For example, the federal Consumer Credit Protection Act of 1968, 15 U.S.C. Sections 1601–1693r, provides that a debtor can retain either 75 percent of disposable earnings per week or a sum equivalent to thirty hours of work paid at federal minimum-wage rates, whichever is greater.

Creditors' Composition Agreements

Creditors may contract with the debtor for discharge of the debtor's liquidated debts (debts that are definite, or fixed, in amount) on payment of a sum less than that owed. These agreements are called **creditors' composition agreements,** or simply *composition agreements,* and usually are held to be enforceable.

Suretyship and Guaranty

Creditors' Composition Agreement An agreement formed between a debtor and his or her creditors in which the creditors agree to accept a lesser sum than that owed by the debtor in full satisfaction of the debt.

When a third person promises to pay a debt owed by another in the event the debtor does not pay, either a *suretyship* or a *guaranty* relationship is created. Suretyship and guaranty provide creditors with the right to seek payment from the third party if the primary debtor defaults on her or his obligations. Exhibit 12–1 below illustrates the relationship between a suretyship or guaranty party and the creditor. At common law, there were significant differences in the liability of a surety and a guarantor, as discussed in the following subsections. Today, however, the distinctions outlined here have been abolished in some states.

Suretyship An express contract in which a third party to a debtor-creditor relationship (the surety) promises to be primarily responsible for the debtor's obligation.

Surety A person, such as a cosigner on a note, who agrees to be primarily responsible for the debt of another.

SURETY A contract of strict **suretyship** is a promise made by a third person to be responsible for the debtor's obligation. It is an express contract between the **surety** (the third party) and the creditor. The surety in the strictest sense is primarily liable for the debt of the principal. The creditor need not exhaust all legal remedies against the principal debtor before holding the surety responsible for payment. The creditor can demand payment from the surety from the moment the debt is due.

EXAMPLE 12.4 Roberto Delmar wants to borrow from the bank to buy a used car. Because Roberto is still in college, the bank will not lend him the funds unless his father, José Delmar, who has dealt with the bank before, will cosign the note (add his signature to the note, thereby becoming a surety and thus jointly liable for payment of the debt). When José Delmar cosigns the note, he becomes primarily liable to the bank. On the note's due date, the bank can seek payment from either Roberto or José Delmar, or both jointly. ●

● *Exhibit* **12–1 Suretyship and Guaranty Parties**
In a suretyship or guaranty arrangement, a third party promises to be responsible for a debtor's obligations. A third party who agrees to be responsible for the debt even if the primary debtor does not default is known as a surety; a third party who agrees to be *secondarily* responsible for the debt—that is, responsible only if the primary debtor defaults—is known as a guarantor. A promise of guaranty (a collateral, or secondary, promise) normally must be in writing to be enforceable.

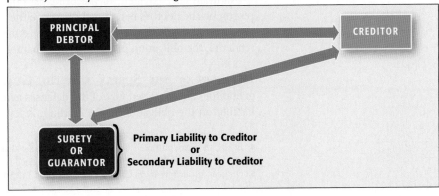

Guarantor   A person who agrees to satisfy the debt of another (the debtor) only after the principal debtor defaults. Thus, a guarantor's liability is secondary.

GUARANTY   With a suretyship arrangement, the surety is *primarily* liable for the debtor's obligation. With a guaranty arrangement, the **guarantor**—the third person making the guaranty—is *secondarily* liable. The guarantor can be required to pay the obligation *only after the principal debtor defaults,* and default usually takes place only after the creditor has made an attempt to collect from the debtor.

EXAMPLE 12.5   BX Enterprises, a small corporation, needs to borrow funds to meet its payroll. The bank is skeptical about the creditworthiness of BX and requires Dawson, its president, who is a wealthy businessperson and the owner of 70 percent of BX Enterprises, to sign an agreement making himself personally liable for payment if BX does not pay off the loan. As a guarantor of the loan, Dawson cannot be held liable until BX Enterprises is in default. •

Under the Statute of Frauds, a guaranty contract between the guarantor and the creditor must be in writing to be enforceable unless the *main purpose rule* applies.[4] At common law, a suretyship agreement did not need to be in writing to be enforceable, and oral surety agreements were sufficient. Today, however, some states require a writing (or electronic record) to enforce a suretyship.

Normally, a guaranty contract that is in a signed writing is presumed to be valid and enforceable. **CASE EXAMPLE 12.6**   Nam Koo Kim created Majestic Group Korea, Ltd., to open a restaurant. Majestic borrowed $1.5 million from Overseas Private Investment Corporation to finance the restaurant. Kim and his wife, Hee Sun, issued personal guaranties for the loan. When Majestic defaulted on the debt, Overseas sued Kim and his wife, seeking payment from them personally. Hee Sun claimed that she did not understand her full liability under the guaranty at the time that she signed it. A New York appellate court found that the guaranty had clearly specified that Hee Sun was personally guaranteeing full payment on the loan. Because there was no fraud, duress, or other wrongdoing by a party to the contract, the court held that Hee Sun's signature on the guaranty was binding and enforceable.[5] •

ACTIONS THAT RELEASE THE SURETY AND THE GUARANTOR   Basically, the same actions will release a surety or a guarantor from an obligation. If a material modification is made in the terms of the original contract between the principal debtor and the creditor—without the consent of the surety or guarantor—the surety or guarantor's obligation will be discharged. (The extent to which the surety or guarantor is discharged depends on whether he or she was compensated and to what extent he or she suffered a loss from the modification.)

Similarly, if a debt is secured by collateral and the creditor surrenders the collateral to the debtor or impairs the collateral without the consent of the surety or guarantor, these acts can reduce the obligation of the surety or guarantor.

Naturally, any payment of the principal obligation by the debtor or by another person on the debtor's behalf will discharge the surety or guarantor from the obligation. Even if the creditor refused to accept payment of the principal debt when it was tendered, the obligation of the surety or guarantor can be discharged.

DEFENSES OF THE SURETY AND THE GUARANTOR   Generally, the surety or guarantor can also assert any of the defenses available to a principal debtor to avoid liability on the obligation to the creditor. A few exceptions do exist, however. The

---

4. Briefly, the main purpose rule, or exception, provides that if the main purpose of the guaranty agreement is to benefit the guarantor, then the contract need not be in writing to be enforceable.

5. *Overseas Private Investment Corp. v. Kim,* 69 A.D.3d 1185, 895 N.Y.S.2d 217 (N.Y.A.D. 2010).

surety or guarantor cannot assert the principal debtor's incapacity or bankruptcy as a defense, nor can the surety assert the statute of limitations as a defense.

Obviously, a surety or guarantor may also have her or his own defenses—for example, her or his own incapacity or bankruptcy. If the creditor fraudulently induced the surety to guarantee the debt of the debtor, the surety can assert fraud as a defense. In most states, the creditor has a legal duty to inform the surety, before the formation of the suretyship contract, of material facts known by the creditor that would substantially increase the surety's risk. Failure to so inform may constitute fraud and renders the suretyship obligation voidable.

RIGHTS OF THE SURETY AND THE GUARANTOR   Usually, when the surety or guarantor pays the debt owed to the creditor, the surety or guarantor is entitled to certain rights. Because the rights of the surety and guarantor are basically the same, the following discussion applies to both.

Right of Subrogation The right of a person to stand in the place of (be substituted for) another, giving the substituted party the same legal rights that the original party had.

The Right of Subrogation. The surety has the legal **right of subrogation.** Simply stated, this means that any right the creditor had against the debtor now becomes the right of the surety. Included are creditor rights in bankruptcy, rights to collateral possessed by the creditor, and rights to judgments secured by the creditor. In short, the surety now stands in the shoes of the creditor and may pursue any remedies that were available to the creditor against the debtor.

Right of Reimbursement The legal right of a person to be restored, repaid, or indemnified for costs, expenses, or losses incurred or expended on behalf of another.

The Right of Reimbursement. The surety has a **right of reimbursement** from the debtor. Basically, the surety is entitled to receive from the debtor all outlays made on behalf of the suretyship arrangement. Such outlays can include expenses incurred, as well as the actual amount of the debt paid to the creditor.

Co-Surety A joint surety; a person who assumes liability jointly with another surety for the payment of an obligation.

Right of Contribution The right of a co-surety who pays more than her or his proportionate share on a debtor's default to recover the excess paid from other co-sureties.

The Right of Contribution. Two or more sureties are called **co-sureties.** When one surety pays more than her or his proportionate share on a debtor's default, that surety is entitled to recover the amount paid above her or his obligation from the other co-sureties. This is the **right of contribution.** Generally, a co-surety's liability either is determined by agreement between the co-sureties or, in the absence of an agreement, is specified in the suretyship contract itself.

EXAMPLE 12.7 Two co-sureties are obligated under a suretyship contract to guarantee the debt of a debtor. Together, the sureties' maximum liability is $25,000. As specified in the suretyship contract, Surety A's maximum liability is $15,000, and surety B's is $10,000. The debtor owes $10,000 and is in default. Surety A pays the creditor the entire $10,000. In the absence of any agreement between the two co-sureties, Surety A can recover $4,000 from Surety B ($10,000/$25,000 × $10,000 = $4,000). ●

Preventing Legal Disputes

Business owners and managers should be careful when signing guaranty contracts and explicitly indicate that they are signing on behalf of a company rather than personally. If corporate officers or directors sign a guaranty without indicating that they are signing as representatives of the corporation, they might be held personally liable. Although a guaranty contract may be preferable to a suretyship contract in some states because it creates secondary rather than primary liability, a guaranty still involves substantial risk. Depending on the wording of a guaranty contract, the extent of the guarantor's liability may be unlimited or may continue over a series of transactions. Any business owner should be absolutely clear about the potential liability before agreeing to serve as a guarantor and should contact an attorney for guidance.

▶ Protection for Debtors

The law protects debtors as well as creditors. Certain property of the debtor, for example, is exempt under state law from creditors' actions. Consumer protection statutes (see Chapter 20) also protect debtors' rights. Of course, bankruptcy laws, which will be discussed shortly, are designed specifically to assist debtors in need of help.

In most states, certain types of real and personal property are exempt from execution or attachment. State exemption statutes usually include both real and personal property.

Exempted Real Property

Homestead Exemption A law permitting a debtor to retain the family home, either in its entirety or up to a specified dollar amount, free from the claims of unsecured creditors or trustees in bankruptcy.

Probably the most familiar exemption for real property is the **homestead exemption.** Each state permits the debtor to retain the family home, either in its entirety or up to a specified dollar amount, free from the claims of unsecured creditors or trustees in bankruptcy. (Note that federal bankruptcy law now places a cap on the amount that debtors filing bankruptcy can claim is exempt under their state's homestead exemption—see page 363.)

EXAMPLE 12.8 Beere owes Veltman $40,000. The debt is the subject of a lawsuit, and the court awards Veltman a judgment of $40,000 against Beere. Beere's home is valued at $50,000, and the homestead exemption is $25,000. There are no outstanding mortgages or other liens on his home. To satisfy the judgment debt, Beere's family home is sold at public auction for $45,000. The proceeds of the sale are distributed as follows:

1. Beere is given $25,000 as his homestead exemption.
2. Veltman is paid $20,000 toward the judgment debt, leaving a $20,000 deficiency judgment (that is, "leftover debt") that can be satisfied from any other nonexempt property (personal or real) that Beere may own, if permitted by state law. ●

In a few states, statutes allow the homestead exemption only if the judgment debtor has a family. If a judgment debtor does not have a family, a creditor may be entitled to collect the full amount realized from the sale of the debtor's home. In addition, the homestead exemption interacts with other areas of law and can sometimes operate to cancel out a portion of a lien on a debtor's real property.

CASE EXAMPLE 12.9 Antonio Stanley purchased a modular home from Yates Mobile Services Corporation. When Stanley failed to pay the purchase price of the home, Yates obtained a judicial lien against Stanley's property in the amount of $165,138.05. Stanley then filed for bankruptcy and asserted the homestead exemption. The court found that Stanley was entitled to avoid the lien to the extent that it impaired his exemption. Using a bankruptcy law formula, the court determined that the total impairment was $143,639.05 and that Stanley could avoid paying this amount to Yates. Thus, Yates was left with a judicial lien on Stanley's home in the amount of $21,499.[6] ●

Exempted Personal Property

Personal property that is most often exempt from satisfaction of judgment debts includes the following:

1. Household furniture up to a specified dollar amount.
2. Clothing and certain personal possessions, such as family pictures or a Bible.

Under most state laws, certain personal property is exempt from satisfaction of judgment debts. Commonly, clothing is exempt. Under what circumstances might clothing not be exempt?

(©Shannon West, 2009. Used under license from Shutterstock.com)

---

6. *In re Stanley,* 2010 WL 2103441 (M.D.N.C. 2010).

3. A vehicle (or vehicles) for transportation (at least up to a specified dollar amount).
4. Certain classified animals, usually livestock but including pets.
5. Equipment that the debtor uses in a business or trade, such as tools or professional instruments, up to a specified dollar amount.

▶ Bankruptcy Law

Bankruptcy law in the United States has two goals—to protect a debtor by giving him or her a fresh start, free from creditors' claims, and to provide a fair means of distributing a debtor's assets to creditors. Bankruptcy law is federal law, but state laws on secured transactions, liens, judgments, and exemptions also play a role in federal bankruptcy proceedings. (For a discussion of how bankruptcy law affects consumers and businesses, see the *Linking the Law to Economics* feature on page 375.)

Bankruptcy law (called the Bankruptcy Code, or simply, the Code) prior to 2005 was based on the Bankruptcy Reform Act of 1978, as amended. In 2005, Congress enacted bankruptcy reform legislation that significantly overhauled certain provisions of the Bankruptcy Code for the first time in twenty-five years.[7] One of the major goals of this legislation was to require more consumers to pay as many of their debts as they possibly could, instead of having those debts fully extinguished in bankruptcy.

Bankruptcy Courts

Bankruptcy proceedings are held in federal bankruptcy courts, which are under the authority of U.S. district courts, and rulings by bankruptcy courts can be appealed to the district courts. A bankruptcy court holds proceedings that are required to administer the estate of the debtor in bankruptcy. (The *estate* consists of the debtor's assets, as will be discussed shortly.) A bankruptcy court can conduct a jury trial if the appropriate district court has authorized it and if the parties to the bankruptcy consent to a jury trial.

Types of Bankruptcy Relief

The Bankruptcy Code is contained in Title 11 of the *United States Code* (U.S.C.) and has eight "chapters." Chapters 1, 3, and 5 of the Code include general definitional provisions, as well as provisions governing case administration, creditors, the debtor, and the estate. These three chapters of the Code normally apply to all types of bankruptcies.

Four chapters of the Code set forth the most important types of relief that debtors can seek.

1. Chapter 7 provides for *liquidation* proceedings—that is, the selling of all nonexempt assets and the distribution of the proceeds to the debtor's creditors.
2. Chapter 11 governs reorganizations.
3. Chapter 12 (for family farmers and family fishermen) and Chapter 13 (for individuals) provide for adjustment of the debts of parties with regular incomes.[8]

---

7. The full title of the act is the Bankruptcy Abuse Prevention and Consumer Protection Act of 2005, Pub. L. No. 109-8, 119 Stat. 23 (April 20, 2005).
8. There are no Chapters 2, 4, 6, 8, or 10 in Title 11. Such "gaps" are not uncommon in the *United States Code*. They occur because, when a statute is enacted, chapter numbers (or other subdivisional unit numbers) are sometimes reserved for future use. A gap may also appear if a law has been repealed.

Note that a debtor (except for a municipality) need not be insolvent[9] to file for bankruptcy relief under the Code. Anyone obligated to a creditor can declare bankruptcy.

Special Requirements for Consumer-Debtors

Consumer-Debtor An individual whose debts are primarily consumer debts (debts for purchases made primarily for personal or household use).

A **consumer-debtor** is a debtor whose debts result primarily from the purchase of goods for personal, family, or household use. To ensure that a consumer-debtor is aware of the types of relief available, the Code requires that the clerk of the court give all consumer-debtors written notice of the general purpose, benefits, and costs of each chapter under which they might proceed. In addition, the clerk must provide consumer-debtors with information on the types of services available from credit counseling agencies. In practice, most of these steps are handled by an attorney, not by court clerks.

▶ Chapter 7—Liquidation

Liquidation The sale of all of the nonexempt assets of a debtor and the distribution of the proceeds to the debtor's creditors.

Liquidation under Chapter 7 of the Bankruptcy Code is probably the most familiar type of bankruptcy proceeding and is often referred to as an *ordinary,* or *straight, bankruptcy.* Put simply, a debtor in a liquidation bankruptcy turns all assets over to a *bankruptcy trustee,* a person appointed by the court to manage the debtor's funds. The trustee sells the nonexempt assets and distributes the proceeds to creditors. With certain exceptions, the remaining debts are then **discharged** (extinguished), and the debtor is released from the obligation to pay the debts.

Discharge In bankruptcy proceedings, the release of a debtor from all debts that are provable, except those specifically excepted by statute.

Any "person"—defined as including individuals, partnerships, and corporations[10]—may be a debtor in a liquidation proceeding. A husband and wife may file jointly for bankruptcy under a single petition. Insurance companies, banks, railroads, savings and loan associations, investment companies licensed by the Small Business Administration, and credit unions *cannot* be debtors in a liquidation bankruptcy, however. Other chapters of the Code or other federal or state statutes apply to them.

Petition in Bankruptcy The document that is filed with a bankruptcy court to initiate bankruptcy proceedings. The official forms required for a petition in bankruptcy must be completed accurately, sworn to under oath, and signed by the debtor.

A straight bankruptcy can be commenced by the filing of either a voluntary or an involuntary **petition in bankruptcy**—the document that is filed with a bankruptcy court to initiate bankruptcy proceedings. If a debtor files the petition, the bankruptcy is voluntary. If one or more creditors file a petition to force the debtor into bankruptcy, the bankruptcy is involuntary. We discuss both voluntary and involuntary bankruptcy proceedings under Chapter 7 in the following subsections.

Voluntary Bankruptcy

To bring a voluntary petition in bankruptcy, the debtor files official forms designated for that purpose in the bankruptcy court. Current bankruptcy law specifies that before debtors can file a petition, they must receive credit counseling from an approved nonprofit agency within the 180-day period preceding the date of filing. Debtors filing a Chapter 7 petition must include a certificate proving that they have

---

9. The inability to pay debts as they come due is known as *equitable* insolvency. A *balance-sheet* insolvency, which exists when a debtor's liabilities exceed assets, is not used as the test for filing for relief. Thus, it is possible for debtors to petition voluntarily for bankruptcy even though their assets far exceed their liabilities. This situation may occur when a debtor's cash-flow problems become severe.

10. The definition of *corporation* includes unincorporated companies and associations. It also covers labor unions.

received individual or group counseling from an approved agency within the last 180 days (roughly six months).

A consumer-debtor who is filing for liquidation bankruptcy must confirm the accuracy of the petition's contents. The debtor must also state in the petition, at the time of filing, that he or she understands the relief available under other chapters of the Code and has chosen to proceed under Chapter 7. Attorneys representing consumer-debtors must file an affidavit stating that they have informed the debtors of the relief available under each chapter of the Code. In addition, the attorneys must reasonably attempt to verify the accuracy of the consumer-debtors' petitions and schedules (described below). Failure to do so is considered perjury.

CHAPTER 7 SCHEDULES   The voluntary petition must contain the following schedules:

1. A list of both secured and unsecured creditors, their addresses, and the amount of debt owed to each. (A *secured* creditor is one who received an interest in collateral—personal property of the debtor—as security for payment of the debt.)
2. A statement of the financial affairs of the debtor.
3. A list of all property owned by the debtor, including property that the debtor claims is exempt.
4. A list of current income and expenses.
5. A certificate of credit counseling (as discussed previously).
6. Proof of payments received from employers within sixty days prior to the filing of the petition.
7. A statement of the amount of monthly income, itemized to show how the amount is calculated.
8. A copy of the debtor's federal income tax return for the most recent year ending immediately before the filing of the petition.

The official forms must be completed accurately, sworn to under oath, and signed by the debtor. To conceal assets or knowingly supply false information on these schedules is a crime under the bankruptcy laws.

With the exception of tax returns, failure to file the required schedules within forty-five days after the filing of the petition (unless an extension of up to forty-five days is granted) will result in an automatic dismissal of the petition. The debtor has up to seven days before the date of the first creditors' meeting to provide a copy of the most recent tax returns to the trustee.

TAX RETURNS DURING BANKRUPTCY   In addition, a debtor may be required to file a tax return at the end of each tax year while the case is pending and to provide a copy to the court. This may be done at the request of the court or of the **U.S. trustee**—a government official who performs administrative tasks that a bankruptcy judge would otherwise have to perform, including supervising the work of the bankruptcy trustee. Any *party in interest* (a party, such as a creditor, who has a valid interest in the outcome of the proceedings) may make this request as well. Debtors may also be required to file tax returns during Chapter 11 and 13 bankruptcies.

U.S. Trustee   A government official who performs certain administrative tasks that a bankruptcy judge would otherwise have to perform.

SUBSTANTIAL ABUSE AND THE MEANS TEST   In the past, a bankruptcy court could dismiss a Chapter 7 petition for relief (discharge of debts) if the use of Chapter 7 would constitute a "substantial abuse" of bankruptcy law. Today, the law provides a *means test* to determine a debtor's eligibility for Chapter 7. The purpose of the test is to keep upper-income people from abusing the bankruptcy process by filing for Chapter 7, as was thought to have happened in the past. The test forces more people to file for Chapter 13 bankruptcy rather than have their debts discharged under Chapter 7.

The Basic Formula. A debtor wishing to file for bankruptcy must complete the means test to determine whether she or he qualifies for Chapter 7. The debtor's average monthly income in recent months is compared with the median income in the geographic area in which the person lives. (The U.S. Trustee Program provides these data at its Web site.) If the debtor's income is below the median income, the debtor usually is allowed to file for Chapter 7 bankruptcy, as there is no presumption of bankruptcy abuse.

Applying the Means Test to Future Disposable Income.   If the debtor's income is above the median income, then further calculations must be made to determine whether the person will have sufficient disposable income in the future to repay at least some of his or her unsecured debts. *Disposable income* is calculated by subtracting living expenses and secured debt payments, such as mortgage payments, from monthly income.

In making this calculation, the debtor's recent monthly income is presumed to continue for the next sixty months. Living expenses are the amounts allowed under formulas used by the Internal Revenue Service (IRS). The IRS allowances include modest allocations for food, clothing, housing, utilities, transportation (including a car payment), health care, and other necessities. (The U.S. Trustee Program's Web site also provides these amounts.) The allowances do not include expenditures for items such as cell phones and cable television service.

Once future disposable income has been estimated, that amount is used to determine whether the debtor will have income that could be applied to unsecured debts. To a large extent, this process follows the prior law on substantial abuse. The court may also consider the debtor's bad faith or other circumstances indicating abuse.

ADDITIONAL GROUNDS FOR DISMISSAL   As noted, a debtor's voluntary petition for Chapter 7 relief may be dismissed for substantial abuse or for failing to provide the necessary documents (such as schedules and tax returns) within the specified time. In addition, a motion to dismiss a Chapter 7 filing might be granted in two other situations. First, if the debtor has been convicted of a violent crime or a drug-trafficking offense, the victim can file a motion to dismiss the voluntary petition. Second, if the debtor fails to pay postpetition domestic-support obligations (which include child and spousal support), the court may dismiss the debtor's petition.

ORDER FOR RELIEF   If the voluntary petition for bankruptcy is found to be proper, the filing of the petition will itself constitute an **order for relief.** (An order for relief is a court's grant of assistance to a petitioner.) Once a consumer-debtor's voluntary petition has been filed, the trustee and creditors must be given notice of the order for relief by mail not more than twenty days after entry of the order.

Order for Relief   A court's grant of assistance to a complainant. In bankruptcy proceedings, the order relieves the debtor of the immediate obligation to pay the debts listed in the bankruptcy petition.

Involuntary Bankruptcy

An involuntary bankruptcy occurs when the debtor's creditors force the debtor into bankruptcy proceedings.[11] For an involuntary action to be filed, the following

---

11. An involuntary case cannot be filed against a charitable institution or a farmer (an individual or business that receives more than 50 percent of gross income from farming operations).

requirements must be met: If the debtor has twelve or more creditors, three or more of these creditors having unsecured claims totaling at least $14,425 must join in the petition. If a debtor has fewer than twelve creditors, one or more creditors having a claim totaling $14,425 or more may file.[12]

If the debtor challenges the involuntary petition, a hearing will be held, and the bankruptcy court will enter an order for relief if it finds either of the following:

1. The debtor is not paying debts as they come due.
2. A general receiver, assignee, or custodian took possession of, or was appointed to take charge of, substantially all of the debtor's property within 120 days before the filing of the petition.

If the court grants an order for relief, the debtor will be required to supply the same information in the bankruptcy schedules as in a voluntary bankruptcy.

An involuntary petition should not be used as an everyday debt-collection device, and the Code provides penalties for the filing of frivolous petitions against debtors. Petitioning creditors may be required to pay the costs and attorneys' fees incurred by the debtor in defending against the petition. If the petition was filed in bad faith, damages can be awarded for injury to the debtor's reputation.

Automatic Stay

Automatic Stay   In bankruptcy proceedings, the suspension of virtually all litigation and other action by creditors against the debtor or the debtor's property; the stay is effective the moment the debtor files a petition in bankruptcy.

The moment a petition, either voluntary or involuntary, is filed, an **automatic stay,** or suspension, of almost all actions by creditors against the debtor or the debtor's property normally goes into effect. In other words, once a petition has been filed, creditors cannot contact the debtor by phone or mail or start any legal proceedings to recover debts or to repossess property. (In some circumstances, a secured creditor or other party in interest may petition the bankruptcy court for relief from the automatic stay, as will be discussed shortly.)

The Code provides that if a creditor *knowingly* violates the automatic stay (a willful violation), any injured party, including the debtor, is entitled to recover actual damages, costs, and attorneys' fees, and may be awarded punitive damages as well. Until the bankruptcy proceeding is closed or dismissed, the automatic stay prohibits a creditor from taking any act to collect, assess, or recover a claim against the debtor that arose before the filing of the petition.

THE ADEQUATE PROTECTION DOCTRINE   Underlying the Code's automatic-stay provision for a secured creditor is a concept known as *adequate protection.* The *adequate protection doctrine,* among other things, protects secured creditors from losing their security as a result of the automatic stay. The bankruptcy court can provide adequate protection by requiring the debtor or trustee to make periodic cash payments or a one-time cash payment (or to provide additional collateral or replacement liens) to the extent that the stay may actually cause the value of the property to decrease.

EXCEPTIONS TO THE AUTOMATIC STAY   The Code provides several exceptions to the automatic stay. Collection efforts can continue for domestic-support obligations, which include any debt owed to or recoverable by a spouse, a former spouse, a child of the debtor, that child's parent or guardian, or a governmental unit. In addition, proceedings against the debtor related to divorce, child custody or visitation,

---

12. 11 U.S.C. Section 303. The amounts stated are in accordance with those computed on April 1, 2010.

domestic violence, and support enforcement are not stayed. Also excepted are investigations by a securities regulatory agency (see Chapter 24) and certain statutory liens for property taxes.

LIMITATIONS ON THE AUTOMATIC STAY   A secured creditor or other party in interest can petition the bankruptcy court for relief from the automatic stay. If a creditor or other party requests relief from the stay, the stay will automatically terminate sixty days after the request, unless the court grants an extension or the parties agree otherwise. Also, the automatic stay on secured debts, such as a financed automobile, will terminate thirty days after the petition is filed if the debtor filed a bankruptcy petition that was dismissed within the prior year. Any party in interest can request that the court extend the stay by showing that the filing is in good faith.

If the debtor had two or more bankruptcy petitions dismissed during the prior year, the Code presumes bad faith, and the automatic stay does *not* go into effect until the court determines that the petition was filed in good faith. In addition, the automatic stay on secured property terminates forty-five days after the creditors' meeting (to be discussed shortly) unless the debtor redeems or reaffirms certain debts (*reaffirmation* will be discussed later in this chapter). In other words, the debtor cannot keep the secured property, even if she or he continues to make payments on it, without reinstating the rights of the secured party to collect on the debt.

Bankruptcy Estate

On the commencement of a liquidation proceeding under Chapter 7, a *bankruptcy estate* (sometimes called an *estate in property*) is created. This task is performed by the bankruptcy trustee, as described next. The estate consists of all the debtor's interests in property currently held, wherever located. It also includes *community property*—that is, property jointly owned by a husband and wife in certain states—property transferred in a transaction voidable by the trustee, proceeds and profits from the property of the estate, and certain after-acquired property. Interests in certain property—such as gifts, inheritances, property settlements (from a divorce), and life insurance death proceeds—to which the debtor becomes entitled *within 180 days after filing* may also become part of the estate. Withholdings for employee benefit plan contributions are excluded from the estate.

Generally, though, the filing of a bankruptcy petition fixes a dividing line: property acquired prior to the filing of the petition becomes property of the estate, and property acquired after the filing of the petition (except as just noted) remains the debtor's.

The Bankruptcy Trustee

Promptly after the order for relief in the liquidation proceeding has been entered, a *bankruptcy trustee* is appointed. The basic duty of the bankruptcy trustee is to collect and reduce to cash the property in the bankruptcy estate that is not exempt. (Exemptions will be discussed later in the chapter.) The trustee is held accountable for administering the debtor's estate to preserve the interests of both the debtor and unsecured creditors. To enable the trustee to accomplish this duty, the Code gives the trustee certain powers, stated in both general and specific terms. These powers must be exercised within two years of the order for relief.

DUTIES FOR MEANS TESTING   The trustee is required to promptly review all materials filed by the debtor to determine if there is substantial abuse. Within ten days after the first meeting of the creditors (held soon after the order for relief is granted, as discussed later), the trustee must file a statement indicating whether the case is presumed to be an abuse under the means test. When there is a presumption of abuse, the trustee must either file a motion to dismiss the petition (or convert it to a Chapter 13 case) or file a statement setting forth the reasons why a motion would not be appropriate.

THE TRUSTEE'S POWERS   The trustee has the power to require persons holding the debtor's property at the time the petition is filed to deliver the property to the trustee.[13] To enable the trustee to implement this power, the Code provides that the trustee has rights *equivalent* to those of certain other parties, such as a creditor who has a judicial lien. This power of a trustee, which is equivalent to that of a lien creditor, is known as *strong-arm power.*

In addition, the trustee has specific *powers of avoidance*—that is, the trustee can set aside (avoid) a sale or other transfer of the debtor's property, taking it back as a part of the debtor's estate. These powers include voidable rights available to the debtor, preferences, and fraudulent transfers by the debtor. Each is discussed in more detail below. In addition, a trustee can avoid certain statutory liens (creditors' claims against the debtor's property).

The debtor shares most of the trustee's avoidance powers. Thus, if the trustee does not take action to enforce one of the rights just mentioned, the debtor in a liquidation bankruptcy can enforce that right.

VOIDABLE RIGHTS   A trustee steps into the shoes of the debtor. Thus, any reason that a debtor can use to obtain the return of her or his property can be used by the trustee as well. These grounds include fraud, duress, incapacity, and mutual mistake.

EXAMPLE 12.10   Ben sells his boat to Tara. Tara gives Ben a check, knowing that she has insufficient funds in her bank account to cover the check. Tara has committed fraud. Ben has the right to avoid that transfer and recover the boat from Tara. If Ben files for bankruptcy relief under Chapter 7, the trustee can exercise the same right to recover the boat from Tara, and the boat becomes a part of the debtor's estate. ●

Preference In bankruptcy proceedings, property transfers or payments made by the debtor that favor (give preference to) one creditor over others. The bankruptcy trustee is allowed to recover payments made both voluntarily and involuntarily to one creditor in preference over another.

PREFERENCES   A debtor is not permitted to transfer property or to make a payment that favors—or gives a **preference** to—one creditor over others. The trustee is allowed to recover payments made both voluntarily and involuntarily to one creditor in preference over another.

To have made a preferential payment that can be recovered, an *insolvent* debtor must have transferred property, for a *preexisting* debt, within *ninety days* prior to the filing of the bankruptcy petition. The transfer must have given the creditor more than the creditor would have received as a result of the bankruptcy proceedings. The Code presumes that a debtor is insolvent during the ninety-day period before filing a petition.

Preferred Creditor One who has received a preferential transfer from a debtor.

If a **preferred creditor** (one who has received a preferential transfer from the debtor) has sold the property to an innocent third party, the trustee cannot recover the property from the innocent party. The trustee generally can force the preferred creditor to pay the value of the property, however.

---

13. Usually, though, the trustee takes constructive, rather than actual, possession of the debtor's property. For example, to obtain control of a debtor's business inventory, a trustee might change the locks on the doors to the business and hire a security guard.

Preferences to Insiders. Sometimes, the creditor receiving the preference is an *insider*—an individual, a partner, a partnership, a corporation, or an officer or a director of a corporation (or a relative of one of these) who has a close relationship with the debtor. In this situation, the avoidance power of the trustee is extended to transfers made within *one year* before filing. (If the transfer was fraudulent, as will be discussed shortly, the trustee can avoid transfers made within *two years* before filing.) Note, however, that if the transfer occurred before the ninety-day period, the trustee is required to prove that the debtor was insolvent at the time it occurred or that the transfer was made to or for the benefit of an insider.

What Constitutes a Preference? Not all transfers are preferences. To be a preference, the transfer must be made for something other than current consideration. Most courts generally assume that payment for services rendered *within fifteen days* before the payment is not a preference. If a creditor receives payment in the ordinary course of business from an individual or business debtor, such as payment of last month's cell phone bill, the bankruptcy trustee cannot recover the payment. To be recoverable, a preference must be a transfer for an antecedent (preexisting) debt, such as a year-old landscaping bill. In addition, the Code permits a consumer-debtor to transfer any property to a creditor up to a total value of $5,850 without the transfer's constituting a preference. Payment of domestic-support debts does not constitute a preference.

FRAUDULENT TRANSFERS The trustee may avoid fraudulent transfers or obligations if they (1) were made within two years of the filing of the petition or (2) were made with actual intent to hinder, delay, or defraud a creditor. For example, a debtor who is thinking about petitioning for bankruptcy sells her gold jewelry, worth $10,000, to a friend for $500. The friend agrees that in the future he will "sell" the collection back to the debtor for the same amount. This is a fraudulent transfer that the trustee can undo.

Transfers made for less than reasonably equivalent consideration are also vulnerable if the debtor thereby became insolvent or was left engaged in business with an unreasonably small amount of capital. When a fraudulent transfer is made outside the Code's two-year limit, creditors may seek alternative relief under state laws. Some state laws may allow creditors to recover for transfers made up to three years before the filing of a petition. Courts have even held that severance payments—that is, compensation paid to an employee who is fired—can constitute a fraudulent transfer under the Code.[14]

Exemptions

As just described, the trustee takes control over the debtor's property in a Chapter 7 bankruptcy, but an individual debtor is entitled to exempt (exclude) certain property from the bankruptcy. The Bankruptcy Code exempts the following property:[15]

1. Up to $21,625 in equity in the debtor's residence and burial plot (the homestead exemption).
2. Interest in a motor vehicle up to $3,450.

---

14. See, for example, *In the Matter of TransTexas Gas Corp.*, 597 F.3d 298 (5th Cir. 2010).
15. The dollar amounts stated in the Bankruptcy Code are adjusted automatically every three years on April 1 based on changes in the Consumer Price Index. The adjusted amounts are rounded to the nearest $25. The amounts stated are in accordance with those computed on April 1, 2010.

3. Interest, up to $550 for a particular item, in household goods and furnishings, wearing apparel, appliances, books, animals, crops, and musical instruments (the aggregate total of all items is limited to $11,525).
4. Interest in jewelry up to $1,450.
5. Interest in any other property up to $1,150, plus any unused part of the $21,625 homestead exemption up to $10,825.
6. Interest in any tools of the debtor's trade up to $2,175.
7. A life insurance contract owned by the debtor (other than a credit life insurance contract).
8. Certain interests in accrued dividends and interest under, or loan value of, life insurance contracts owned by the debtor, not to exceed $11,525.
9. Professionally prescribed health aids.
10. The right to receive Social Security and certain welfare benefits, alimony and support, certain retirement funds and pensions, and education savings accounts held for specific periods of time.
11. The right to receive certain personal-injury and other awards up to $21,625.

Individual states have the power to pass legislation precluding debtors from using the federal exemptions within the state. A majority of the states have done this. In those states, debtors may use only state, not federal, exemptions. In the rest of the states, an individual debtor (or a husband and wife filing jointly) may choose either the exemptions provided under state law or the federal exemptions.

The Homestead Exemption

The 2005 reforms significantly changed the law for those debtors seeking to use state homestead exemption statutes (see page 354). In six states, including Florida and Texas, homestead exemptions allowed debtors petitioning for bankruptcy to shield *unlimited* amounts of equity in their homes from creditors. The Bankruptcy Code now places limits on the amount that can be claimed as exempt in bankruptcy. In addition, a debtor must have lived in a state for two years before filing the bankruptcy petition to use the state homestead exemption (prior law required only six months).

In general, if the debtor acquired the homestead within three and a half years preceding the date of filing, the maximum equity exempted is $146,450, even if state law would permit a higher amount. Note, however, that a debtor who has violated securities laws, been convicted of a felony, or engaged in certain other intentional misconduct may not be able to claim the exemption.

Creditors' Meeting and Claims

Within a reasonable time after the order for relief has been granted (not less than twenty days or more than forty days), the trustee must call a meeting of the creditors listed in the schedules filed by the debtor. The bankruptcy judge does not attend this meeting. The debtor is required to attend (unless excused by the court) and to submit to examination under oath by the creditors and the trustee. At the meeting, the debtor is questioned under oath to ensure that he or she is aware of the potential consequences of bankruptcy and of relief available under the different chapters of the Bankruptcy Code.

To be entitled to receive a portion of the debtor's estate, each creditor normally files a *proof of claim* with the bankruptcy court clerk within ninety days of the creditors' meeting.[16] The proof of claim lists the creditor's name and address, as well as the amount that the creditor asserts is owed to the creditor by the debtor. A creditor need not file a proof of claim if the debtor's schedules list the creditor's claim as liquidated (exactly determined) and the creditor does not dispute the amount of the claim. A proof of claim is necessary if there is any dispute concerning the claim.

Distribution of Property

In the next step in a Chapter 7 bankruptcy, the trustee distributes the bankruptcy estate to the creditors, following specific rules provided in the Code for the distribution of the debtor's property. These rules are discussed next and illustrated in Exhibit 12–2 below.

In the distribution of the debtor's estate, secured creditors take priority over unsecured creditors. Within thirty days of filing a liquidation petition or before the date of the first meeting of the creditors (whichever is first), a consumer-debtor must file with the clerk a statement of intention with respect to the secured collateral. The statement must indicate whether the debtor will retain the collateral or surrender it to the secured party. Also, if applicable, the debtor must specify whether the collateral will be claimed as exempt property and whether the debtor intends to redeem the property or reaffirm the debt secured by the collateral. The trustee is obligated to enforce the debtor's statement within forty-five days after it is filed.

In a bankruptcy case in which the debtor has no assets (called a "no-asset case"), creditors are notified of the debtor's petition for bankruptcy but are instructed not to file a claim. In no-asset cases, the unsecured creditors will receive no payment, and most, if not all, of these debts will be discharged.

DISTRIBUTION TO SECURED CREDITORS   As discussed earlier, secured creditors are creditors who received an interest in collateral to secure a debtor's payment or

---

16. This ninety-day rule applies in Chapter 12 and Chapter 13 bankruptcies as well.

● *Exhibit* **12–2 Collection and Distribution of Property in Most Voluntary Bankruptcies**
This exhibit illustrates the property that might be collected in a debtor's voluntary bankruptcy and how it might be distributed to creditors. Involuntary bankruptcies and some voluntary bankruptcies could include additional types of property and other creditors.

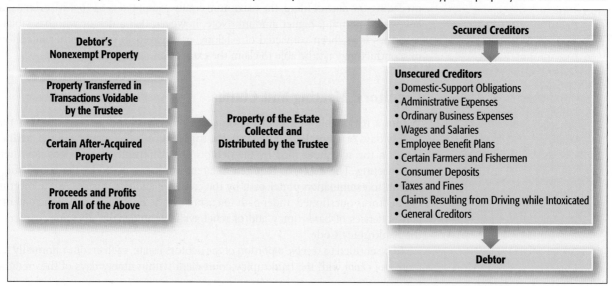

performance. If the collateral is surrendered to the secured party, the secured creditor can enforce the security interest either by accepting the property in full satisfaction of the debt or by selling the collateral and using the proceeds to pay off the debt. Thus, the secured party has priority over unsecured parties as to the proceeds from the disposition of the collateral. Should the collateral be insufficient to cover the secured debt owed, the secured creditor becomes an unsecured creditor for the difference.

DISTRIBUTION TO UNSECURED CREDITORS   Bankruptcy law establishes an order of priority for classes of debts owed to *unsecured* creditors, and they are paid in the order of their priority. Each class must be fully paid before the next class is entitled to any of the remaining proceeds. If there are insufficient proceeds to pay fully all the creditors in a class, the proceeds are distributed *proportionately* to the creditors in that class, and classes lower in priority receive nothing.

In almost all Chapter 7 bankruptcies, the funds will be insufficient to pay all creditors. Note that claims for domestic-support obligations, such as child support and alimony, have the highest priority among unsecured claims, so these debts must be paid first. If any amount remains after the priority classes of creditors have been satisfied, it is turned over to the debtor.

Discharge

From the debtor's point of view, the primary purpose of liquidation is to obtain a fresh start through a discharge of debts. Certain debts, however, are not dischargeable in bankruptcy. Also, certain debtors may not qualify to have all debts discharged in bankruptcy. These situations are discussed next.

EXCEPTIONS TO DISCHARGE   Discharge of a debt may be denied because of the nature of the claim or the conduct of the debtor. A court will not discharge claims that are based on a debtor's willful or malicious conduct or fraud, or claims related to property or funds that the debtor obtained by false pretenses, embezzlement, or larceny. Any monetary judgment against the debtor for driving while intoxicated cannot be discharged in bankruptcy. When a debtor fails to list a creditor on the bankruptcy schedules, that creditor's claims are not dischargeable because the creditor was not notified of the bankruptcy.

BE AWARE Often, a discharge in bankruptcy—even under Chapter 7—does not free a debtor of *all* of her or his debts.

Claims that are not dischargeable in a liquidation bankruptcy include amounts due to the government for taxes, fines, or penalties, and any amounts borrowed to pay these debts.[17] Domestic-support obligations and property settlements arising from a divorce or separation cannot be discharged. Certain student loans or educational debts are not dischargeable (unless payment of the loans imposes an "undue hardship" on the debtor and the debtor's dependents), nor are amounts due on a retirement account loan. Consumer debts for purchasing luxury items worth more than $600 and cash advances totaling more than $875 generally are not dischargeable.

OBJECTIONS TO DISCHARGE   In addition, a bankruptcy court may deny the discharge based on the debtor's conduct. In such a situation, the assets of the debtor are

---

17. Taxes accruing within three years prior to bankruptcy are nondischargeable, including federal and state income taxes, employment taxes, taxes on gross receipts, property taxes, excise taxes, customs duties, and any other taxes for which the government claims the debtor is liable in some capacity. See 11 U.S.C. Sections 507(a)(8), 523(a)(1).

still distributed to the creditors, but the debtor remains liable for the unpaid portion of all claims. Grounds for a denial of discharge of the debtor include the following:

1. The debtor's concealment or destruction of property with the intent to hinder, delay, or defraud a creditor.
2. The debtor's fraudulent concealment or destruction of financial records.
3. The grant of a discharge to the debtor within eight years before the petition was filed.
4. The debtor's failure to complete the required consumer education course.
5. Proceedings in which the debtor could be found guilty of a felony (basically, a court may not discharge any debt until the completion of felony proceedings against the debtor).

EFFECT OF A DISCHARGE The primary effect of a discharge is to void, or set aside, any judgment on a discharged debt and prohibit any action to collect a discharged debt. A discharge does not affect the liability of a co-debtor. (For a discussion of how some debts that were discharged in bankruptcy have still appeared on debtors' credit reports, see this chapter's *Insight into Ethics* feature below.)

On petition by the trustee or a creditor, the bankruptcy court can, within one year, revoke the discharge decree if it is discovered that the debtor acted fraudulently or dishonestly during the bankruptcy proceedings. The revocation renders the discharge void, allowing creditors not satisfied by the distribution of the debtor's estate to proceed with their claims against the debtor.

Insight into Ethics   The Debt That Never Goes Away

When a bankruptcy judge discharges certain debts, they are no longer supposed to appear on debtors' credit reports. Nonetheless, many credit-card companies and other creditors have been keeping debts active even after they have been discharged in bankruptcy. Not surprisingly, some aggressive entrepreneurs have found a way to profit from this practice. Companies with names such as eCast Settlement and Max Recovery purchase discharged debt obligations at pennies on the dollar. Then they pursue the debtors and pressure them to pay the debts even though they have been discharged. Some of these companies have been successful enough to become publicly traded on the New York Stock Exchange.

The fact that discharged debt does not have a zero dollar value indicates that some consumers have been repaying these debts. As the number of bankruptcies rose during the latest recession, the market price of fully discharged Chapter 7 debt actually increased—to about seven cents on the dollar.

One federal district court judge, though, has had enough. In a class-action lawsuit, plaintiffs claimed that credit reporting agencies had violated the federal Fair Credit Reporting Act (see Chapter 20)

by failing to follow reasonable procedures that ensured accurate reporting of debts discharged in Chapter 7 bankruptcies. The court agreed and ordered the agencies to revise their procedures.[a] Today, credit agencies must automatically report all prebankruptcy debt as "discharged," unless the debt is nondischargable. Although the purchasers of discharged debt may still attempt to pressure consumers into paying debts that they do not owe, the change in the credit bureaus' procedures may give consumers additional help in their efforts to rebuild their lives after bankruptcy.

FOR CRITICAL ANALYSIS
Insight into the Economic Environment

About six years ago, one could buy debt that had been discharged in bankruptcy for less than five cents on the dollar. Why has the price increased to seven cents on the dollar?

---

a. *White v. Experian Information Solutions,* No. 05-CV-1-70 DOC (C.D.Cal. 2008).

Reaffirmation of Debt

Reaffirmation Agreement An agreement between a debtor and a creditor in which the debtor reaffirms, or promises to pay, a debt dischargeable in bankruptcy. To be enforceable, the agreement must be made prior to the discharge of the debt by the bankruptcy court.

An agreement to pay a debt dischargeable in bankruptcy is called a **reaffirmation agreement.** A debtor may wish to pay a debt—for example, a debt owed to a family member, physician, bank, or some other creditor—even though the debt could be discharged in bankruptcy.

To be enforceable, a reaffirmation agreement must be made before the debtor is granted a discharge. The agreement must be signed and filed with the court. Court approval is required unless the debtor is represented by an attorney during the negotiation of the reaffirmation and submits the proper documents and certifications. Even when the debtor is represented by an attorney, court approval may be required if it appears that the reaffirmation will result in undue hardship on the debtor. When court approval is required, a separate hearing will take place. The court will approve the reaffirmation only if it finds that the agreement will not result in undue hardship to the debtor and that the reaffirmation is consistent with the debtor's best interests.

To discourage creditors from engaging in abusive reaffirmation practices, the law provides specific language for disclosures that must be given to debtors entering into reaffirmation agreements. Among other things, these disclosures explain that the debtor is not required to reaffirm any debt, but that liens on secured property, such as mortgages and cars, will remain in effect even if the debt is not reaffirmed.

The reaffirmation agreement must disclose the amount of the debt reaffirmed, the rate of interest, the date payments begin, and the right to rescind. The disclosures also caution the debtor: "Only agree to reaffirm a debt if it is in your best interest. Be sure you can afford the payments you agree to make." The original disclosure documents must be signed by the debtor, certified by the debtor's attorney, and filed with the court at the same time as the reaffirmation agreement. A reaffirmation agreement that is not accompanied by the original signed disclosures will not be effective.

▶ Chapter 11—Reorganization

The type of bankruptcy proceeding most commonly used by corporate debtors is the Chapter 11 *reorganization.* In a reorganization, the creditors and the debtor formulate a plan under which the debtor pays a portion of the debts and is discharged of the remainder. The debtor is allowed to continue in business. Although this type of bankruptcy is generally a corporate reorganization, any debtor (except a stockbroker or a commodities broker) who is eligible for Chapter 7 relief is eligible for relief under Chapter 11. Railroads are also eligible.

In 1994, Congress established a "fast-track" Chapter 11 procedure for small-business debtors whose liabilities do not exceed $2.19 million and who do not own or manage real estate. The fast track enables a debtor to avoid the appointment of a creditors' committee and also shortens the filing periods and relaxes certain other requirements. Because the process is shorter and simpler, it is less costly.

The same principles that govern the filing of a liquidation (Chapter 7) petition apply to reorganization (Chapter 11) proceedings. The case may be brought either voluntarily or involuntarily. The automatic-stay provisions and adequate protection doctrine apply in reorganizations as well. An exception from the automatic stay is triggered if the debtor files for bankruptcy again within two years and new grounds for dismissal (such as substantial abuse) or conversion of the case are established.

Workouts

Workout An out-of-court agreement between a debtor and creditors in which the parties work out a payment plan or schedule under which the debtor's debts can be discharged.

In some instances, to avoid bankruptcy proceedings, creditors may prefer private, negotiated adjustments of creditor-debtor relations, also known as **workouts.** Often, these out-of-court workouts are much more flexible and thus more conducive to a speedy settlement. Speed is critical because delay is one of the most costly elements in any bankruptcy proceeding. Another advantage of workouts is that they avoid the various administrative costs of bankruptcy proceedings.

Creditors' Best Interests

After a petition for Chapter 11 bankruptcy has been filed, a bankruptcy court, after notice and a hearing, can dismiss or suspend all proceedings at any time if dismissal or suspension would better serve the interests of the creditors. The Bankruptcy Code also allows a court, after notice and a hearing, to dismiss a case under reorganization "for cause." Cause includes the absence of a reasonable likelihood of rehabilitation, the inability to effect a plan, and an unreasonable delay by the debtor that is prejudicial to (may harm the interests of) creditors.[18]

Debtor in Possession

Debtor in Possession (DIP) In Chapter 11 bankruptcy proceedings, a debtor who is allowed to continue in possession of the estate in property (the business) and to continue business operations.

On entry of the order for relief, the debtor generally continues to operate the business as a **debtor in possession (DIP).** The court, however, may appoint a trustee (often referred to as a *receiver*) to operate the debtor's business if gross mismanagement of the business is shown or if appointing a trustee is in the best interests of the estate.

The DIP's role is similar to that of a trustee in a liquidation. The DIP is entitled to avoid preferential payments made to creditors and fraudulent transfers of assets. The DIP has the power to decide whether to cancel or assume obligations under prepetition executory contracts (those that are not yet performed) or unexpired leases. Cancellation of executory contracts or unexpired leases can be a substantial benefit to a Chapter 11 debtor. The DIP can also exercise a trustee's strong-arm powers (see page 361). **EXAMPLE 12.11** Five years ago, before a national recession, APT Corporation leased an office building for a twenty-year term. Now, APT can no longer afford to pay the rent due under the lease and has filed for Chapter 11 reorganization. In this situation, the DIP can cancel the lease so that APT will not be required to continue paying the substantial rent for the building for fifteen more years. ●

Creditors' Committees

As soon as practicable after the entry of the order for relief, a creditors' committee of unsecured creditors is appointed.[19] This committee often is composed of the biggest suppliers to the business. The committee may consult with the trustee or the DIP concerning the administration of the case or the formulation of the plan. Additional creditors' committees may be appointed to represent special interest creditors.

Generally, no orders affecting the estate will be entered without the consent of the committee or a hearing in which the judge is informed of the committee's position. As mentioned earlier, businesses with debts of less than $2.19 million that do not

---

18. See 11 U.S.C. Section 1112(b). Debtors are not prohibited from filing successive petitions, however. A debtor whose petition is dismissed, for example, can file a new Chapter 11 petition (which may be granted unless it is filed in bad faith).

19. If the debtor has filed a reorganization plan accepted by the creditors, the trustee may decide not to call a meeting of the creditors.

own or manage real estate can avoid creditors' committees. In these cases, orders can be entered without a committee's consent.

The Reorganization Plan

A reorganization plan to rehabilitate the debtor is a plan to conserve and administer the debtor's assets in the hope of an eventual return to successful operation and solvency. The plan must be fair and equitable and must do the following:

1. Designate classes of claims and interests.
2. Specify the treatment to be afforded the classes. (The plan must provide the same treatment for all claims in a particular class.)
3. Provide an adequate means for execution. (Individual debtors are required to utilize postpetition assets as necessary to execute the plan.)
4. Provide for payment of tax claims over a five-year period.

FILING THE PLAN Only the debtor may file a plan within the first 120 days after the date of the order for relief. This period may be extended, but not beyond eighteen months from the date of the order for relief. If the debtor does not meet the 120-day deadline or obtain an extension, and if the debtor fails to procure the required creditor consent (discussed below) within 180 days, any party may propose a plan. The plan need not provide for full repayment to unsecured creditors. Instead, creditors receive a percentage of each dollar owed to them by the debtor. If a small-business debtor chooses to avoid a creditors' committee, the time for the debtor's filing is 180 days.

ACCEPTANCE AND CONFIRMATION OF THE PLAN Once the plan has been developed, it is submitted to each class of creditors for acceptance. For the plan to be adopted, each class that is adversely affected by the plan must accept it. A class has accepted the plan when a majority of the creditors, representing two-thirds of the amount of the total claim, vote to approve it. Confirmation is conditioned on the debtor's certification that all postpetition domestic-support obligations have been paid in full.

Even when all classes of creditors accept the plan, the court may refuse to confirm it if it is not "in the best interests of the creditors." The plan can also be modified on the request of the debtor, the trustee, the U.S. trustee, or a holder of an unsecured claim. If an unsecured creditor objects to the plan, specific rules apply to the value of property to be distributed under the plan. Tax claims must be paid over a five-year period.

Even if only one class of creditors has accepted the plan, the court may still confirm the plan under the Code's so-called **cram-down provision.** In other words, the court may confirm the plan over the objections of a class of creditors. Before the court can exercise this right of cram-down confirmation, it must be demonstrated that the plan does not discriminate unfairly against any creditors and is fair and equitable.

DISCHARGE The plan is binding on confirmation. The law provides, however, that confirmation of a plan does not discharge an individual debtor. *For individual debtors, the plan must be completed before discharge will be granted,* unless the court orders otherwise. For all other debtors, the court may order discharge at any time after the plan is confirmed. At this time, the debtor is given a reorganization discharge from all claims not protected under the plan. This discharge does not apply to any claims that would be denied discharge under liquidation.

Cram-Down Provision A provision of the Bankruptcy Code that allows a court to confirm a debtor's Chapter 11 reorganization plan even though only one class of creditors has accepted it. To use this provision, the court must demonstrate that the plan does not discriminate unfairly against any creditors and is fair and equitable.

Bankruptcy Relief under Chapter 12 and Chapter 13

In addition to bankruptcy relief through liquidation (Chapter 7) and reorganization (Chapter 11), the Code also provides for family-farmer and family-fisherman debt adjustments (Chapter 12) and individuals' repayment plans (Chapter 13).

Chapter 12—Family Farmers and Fishermen

In 1986, to help relieve economic pressure on small farmers, Congress created Chapter 12 of the Bankruptcy Code. In 2005, Congress extended this protection to family fishermen, modified its provisions somewhat, and made it a permanent chapter in the Bankruptcy Code. For purposes of Chapter 12, a *family farmer* is one whose gross income is at least 50 percent farm dependent and whose debts are at least 50 percent farm related.[20] The total debt must not exceed $3,792,650. A partnership or a close corporation (see Chapters 14 and 15) that is at least 50 percent owned by the farm family can also qualify as a family farmer.[21]

A *family fisherman* is one whose gross income is at least 50 percent dependent on commercial fishing operations and whose debts are at least 80 percent related to commercial fishing. The total debt for a family fisherman must not exceed $1,757,475. As with family farmers, a partnership or close corporation can also qualify.

FILING THE PETITION   The procedure for filing a family-farmer or family-fisherman bankruptcy plan is very similar to the procedure for filing a repayment plan under Chapter 13. The debtor must file a plan not later than ninety days after the order for relief. The filing of the petition acts as an automatic stay against creditors' and co-obligors' actions against the estate. A farmer or fisherman who has already filed a reorganization or repayment plan may convert the plan to a Chapter 12 plan. The debtor may also convert a Chapter 12 plan to a liquidation plan.

CONTENT AND CONFIRMATION OF THE PLAN   The content of a plan under Chapter 12 can be modified by the debtor but, except for cause, must be confirmed or denied within forty-five days of the filing of the plan.

Court confirmation of the plan is the same as for a repayment plan. In summary, the plan must provide for payment of secured debts at the value of the collateral. If the secured debt exceeds the value of the collateral, the remaining debt is unsecured. For unsecured debtors, the plan must be confirmed if either the value of the property to be distributed under the plan equals the amount of the claim or the plan provides that all of the debtor's disposable income to be received in a three-year period (or longer, by court approval) will be applied to making payments. Completion of payments under the plan discharges all debts provided for by the plan.

Chapter 13—Individuals' Repayment Plan

Chapter 13 of the Bankruptcy Code provides for the "Adjustment of Debts of an Individual with Regular Income." Individuals (not partnerships or corporations) with regular income who owe fixed (liquidated) unsecured debts of less than $360,475 or fixed secured debts of less than $1,081,400 may take advantage of bankruptcy repay-

---

20. Note that the Bankruptcy Code defines a *family farmer* and a *farmer* differently. To be a farmer, a person or business must receive 50 percent of gross income from a farming operation that the person or business owns or operates.

21. For a corporation or partnership to qualify under Chapter 12, at least 80 percent of the value of the firm's assets must consist of assets related to the farming operation.

ment plans. Among those eligible are salaried employees; sole proprietors; and individuals who live on welfare, Social Security benefits, fixed pensions, or investment income. Many small-business debtors have a choice of filing under either Chapter 11 or Chapter 13. Repayment plans offer some advantages because they are typically less expensive and less complicated than reorganization or liquidation proceedings.

FILING THE PETITION A Chapter 13 repayment plan case can be initiated only by the filing of a voluntary petition by the debtor or by the conversion of a Chapter 7 petition (because of a finding of substantial abuse under the means test, for example). Certain liquidation and reorganization cases may be converted to Chapter 13 with the consent of the debtor.[22] A trustee, who will make payments under the plan, must be appointed. On the filing of a repayment plan petition, the automatic stay previously discussed takes effect. Although the stay applies to all or part of the debtor's consumer debt, it does not apply to any business debt incurred by the debtor or to any domestic-support obligations.

GOOD FAITH REQUIREMENT The Bankruptcy Code imposes the requirement of good faith on a debtor at both the time of the filing of the petition and the time of the filing of the plan. The Code does not define good faith, but if the circumstances as a whole indicate bad faith, a court can dismiss a debtor's Chapter 13 petition.

CASE EXAMPLE 12.12 Roger and Pauline Buis operated an air show business under the name Otto Airshows with a helicopter decorated as "Otto the Clown." After the Buises accused a competitor of safety lapses, the competitor won a defamation lawsuit against the Buises and Otto Airshows. The Buises then stopped doing business as Otto Airshows and formed a new firm, Prop and Rotor Aviation, Inc., to which they leased the Otto equipment. Within a month, they filed a bankruptcy petition under Chapter 13. The plan and the schedules did not mention the lawsuit, the equipment lease, and several other items. The court therefore dismissed the Buises' petition due to bad faith. The debtors had not included all of their assets and liabilities on their initial petition, and they had timed its filing to avoid payment on the defamation judgment.[23] •

THE REPAYMENT PLAN A plan of rehabilitation by repayment must provide for the following:

1. The turning over to the trustee of such future earnings or income of the debtor as is necessary for execution of the plan.
2. Full payment through deferred cash payments of all claims entitled to priority, such as taxes.[24]
3. Identical treatment of all claims within a particular class. (The Code permits the debtor to list co-debtors, such as guarantors or sureties, as a separate class.)

The repayment plan may provide for payment of all obligations in full or for payment of a lesser amount. The debtor must begin making payments under the proposed plan within thirty days after the plan has been filed and must continue to make "timely" payments from her or his disposable income. If the debtor fails to make timely payments or to commence payments within the thirty-day period, the court can convert the case to a liquidation bankruptcy or dismiss the petition.

---

22. A Chapter 13 repayment plan may be converted to a Chapter 7 liquidation either at the request of the debtor or, under certain circumstances, "for cause" by a creditor. A Chapter 13 case may be converted to a Chapter 11 case after a hearing.
23. *In re Buis,* 337 Bankr. 243 (N.D.Fla. 2006).
24. As with a Chapter 11 reorganization plan, full repayment of all claims is not always required.

The length of the payment plan can be three or five years, depending on the debtor's family income. If the debtor's family income is greater than the median family income in the relevant geographic area under the means test, the term of the proposed plan must be five years.[25] The term may not exceed five years.

In putting together a repayment plan, a debtor must apply the means test to identify the amount of disposable income that will be available to repay creditors. The debtor is allowed to deduct certain expenses from monthly income to arrive at this amount. Can a debtor who owns a car outright claim the costs of car ownership as an expense? That was the issue in the following case.

---

25. See 11 U.S.C. Section 1322(d) for details.

Case 12.2   **Ransom v. FIA Card Services, N.A.**

Supreme Court of the United States, __ U.S. __, 131 S.Ct. 716, 178 L.Ed.2d 603 (2011).
www.supremecourt.gov [a]

BACKGROUND AND FACTS   Jason Ransom filed a petition in a federal bankruptcy court to declare bankruptcy under Chapter 13. Among his assets, Ransom reported a Toyota Camry that he owned free of any debt. In listing monthly expenses for the means test, he claimed a deduction of $471 for car ownership and a separate deduction of $388 for car-operating costs. Based on his means-test calculations, Ransom proposed a five-year plan that would repay about 25 percent of his unsecured debt. He listed FIA Card Services, N.A., as an unsecured creditor. FIA objected to Ransom's plan, arguing that he should not have claimed the car-ownership allowance because he did not make payments on his car. The court agreed with FIA and issued a decision in its favor. A Bankruptcy Appellate Panel and the U.S. Court of Appeals for the Ninth Circuit affirmed the decision. Ransom appealed to the United States Supreme Court.

IN THE WORDS OF THE COURT . . .
Justice *KAGAN* delivered the opinion of the Court.
* * * *

[Under the Bankruptcy Code] a debtor may claim not all, but only "applicable" expense amounts * * * .
* * * *

What makes an expense amount "applicable" * * * (appropriate, relevant, suitable, or fit) is most naturally understood to be its correspondence to an individual debtor's financial circumstances. * * * A debtor may claim a deduction * * * only if that deduction is appropriate for him. And a deduction is so appropriate * * * only if the debtor will incur that kind of expense during the life of the plan.

If Congress had * * * omitted the term "applicable" * * * all debtors would be eligible to claim a deduction for each category [listed in the tables of standardized expense amounts that a debtor can claim as reasonable living expenses and shield from creditors]. Interpreting the

statute to require a threshold determination of eligibility ensures that the term "applicable" carries meaning, as each word in a statute should.

This reading draws support from the statute's context and purpose. The Code initially defines a debtor's disposable income as his "current monthly income * * * less amounts reasonably necessary to be expended." The statute then instructs that "amounts reasonably necessary to be expended * * * shall be determined in accordance with" the means test. Because Congress intended the means test to approximate the debtor's reasonable expenditures on essential items, a debtor should be required to qualify for a deduction by actually incurring an expense in the relevant category.

Finally, consideration of the [Bankruptcy Code's] purpose strengthens our reading of the term "applicable." *Congress designed the means test to measure debtors' disposable income and, in that way, to ensure that they repay creditors the maximum they can afford. This purpose is best achieved by interpreting the means test, consistent with the statutory text, to reflect a debtor's ability to afford repayment.* [Emphasis added.]
* * * *

Because Ransom owns his vehicle free and clear of any encumbrance, he incurs no expense in the "Ownership Costs" category * * * . Accordingly, the car-ownership expense amount is not "applicable" to him.

DECISION AND REMEDY   The United States Supreme Court affirmed the lower court's decision. A debtor who does not make loan or lease payments may not take a car-ownership deduction. In Ransom's case, the ultimate result was that confirmation of his repayment plan was denied. (Confirmation of repayment plans is discussed on page 373.)

THE ECONOMIC DIMENSION   *Should debtors with older vehicles be allowed to take an additional deduction for operating expenses? Explain.*

THE CULTURAL DIMENSION   *What argument might be made in favor of allowing a debtor who lives outside an area with mass transit to claim a deduction in the "Ownership Costs" category for a car that he or she owns free and clear?*

---

a. In the "Supreme Court Documents" column, in the "Opinions" pull-down menu, select "Bound Volumes." On the next page, in the "For Search Term:" box, type "Ransom" and click on "Search." In the result, click on the name of the case to access the opinion. The United States Supreme Court maintains this Web site.

CONFIRMATION OF THE PLAN   After the plan is filed, the court holds a confirmation hearing, at which interested parties (such as creditors) may object to the plan. The hearing must be held at least twenty days, but no more than forty-five days, after the meeting of the creditors. The debtor must have filed all prepetition tax returns and paid all postpetition domestic-support obligations before a court will confirm any plan. The court will confirm a plan with respect to each claim of a secured creditor under any of the following circumstances:

1. If the secured creditors have accepted the plan.
2. If the plan provides that secured creditors retain their liens until there is payment in full or until the debtor receives a discharge.
3. If the debtor surrenders the property securing the claims to the creditors.

BE CAREFUL   Courts, trustees, and creditors carefully monitor Chapter 13 debtors. If payments are not made, a court can require that the debtor explain why and may allow a creditor to take back her or his property.

DISCHARGE   After the completion of all payments, the court grants a discharge of all debts provided for by the repayment plan. Except for allowed claims not provided for by the plan, certain long-term debts provided for by the plan, certain tax claims, payments on retirement accounts, and claims for domestic-support obligations, all other debts are dischargeable. Under current law, debts related to injury or property damage caused while driving under the influence of alcohol or drugs are nondischargeable.

In the following case, a debtor had proposed to discharge some of his student loan debt in a Chapter 13 repayment plan. Certain student loan debts can be discharged under Chapter 13, but only if the court finds that payment of the debt would constitute an "undue hardship" for the debtor. Due to an oversight by the creditor and an error by the bankruptcy court, the plan was approved and subsequently confirmed without the required finding of "undue hardship." The United States Supreme Court had to decide whether these problems rendered the discharge of the debt void.

Case 12.3 | **United Student Aid Funds, Inc. v. Espinosa**

Supreme Court of the United States, ____ U.S. ____, 130 S.Ct. 1367, 176 L.Ed.2d 158 (2010).
www.supremecourt.gov [a]

When can Chapter 13 bankruptcy extinguish a student loan debt?

BACKGROUND AND FACTS   Francisco Espinosa filed a petition for an individual repayment plan under Chapter 13 of the Bankruptcy Code. The plan proposed that Espinosa would repay only the principal of his student loan debt and that the interest on the loan would be discharged once the principal was repaid. Under Chapter 13, a student loan cannot be discharged unless the bankruptcy court finds that payment of the debt would constitute an undue hardship for the debtor. Notwithstanding this requirement, no undue hardship hearing was requested by the debtor, by the court, or by the creditor, United Student Aid Funds (United). The creditor received notice of the plan but did not object to it—nor did the creditor file an appeal after the bankruptcy court subsequently

confirmed the plan. Years later, however, United filed a motion under Federal Rule of Civil Procedure 60(b)(4) asking the bankruptcy court to rule that its order confirming the plan was void because the order was issued in violation of the laws and rules governing bankruptcy. The court denied United's petition and ordered the creditor to cease its collection efforts. The creditor appealed to the U.S. District Court for the District of Arizona, and the district court reversed the bankruptcy court's ruling. On further appeal, the U.S. Court of Appeals for the Ninth Circuit reversed the district court's judgment. United appealed to the United States Supreme Court.

IN THE WORDS OF THE COURT . . .
Justice *THOMAS* delivered the opinion of the Court.
* * * *

A discharge under Chapter 13 "is broader than the discharge received in any other chapter." Chapter 13 nevertheless restricts or prohibits entirely the discharge of certain types of debts. As relevant here, [Section] 1328(a) [of the Bankruptcy Code] provides that when a debtor has completed the repayments required by a confirmed plan, a bankruptcy court "shall grant the debtor a discharge of all

---

a. In the "Supreme Court Documents" column, in the "Opinions" pull-down menu, select "Bound Volumes." On the next page, in the "For Search Term:" box, type "Espinosa" and click on "Search." In the result, click on the name of the case to access the opinion. The United States Supreme Court maintains this Web site.

Case 12.3–Continues next page ➡

Case 12.3–Continued

debts provided for by the plan or disallowed under Section 502 of this title, except," *inter alia* [among others], "any debt * * * of the kind specified in [Section] 523(a)(8). [That section], in turn, specifies certain student loan debts "unless excepting such debt from discharge * * * would impose an undue hardship on the debtor and the debtor's dependents." * * * *[The] Bankruptcy Rules require a party seeking to determine the dischargeability of a student loan debt to commence an adversary proceeding by serving a summons and complaint on affected creditors.* We must decide whether the Bankruptcy Court's order confirming Espinosa's plan is "void" under Federal Rule of Civil Procedure 60(b)(4) because the Bankruptcy Court confirmed the plan without complying with these requirements. [Emphasis added.]

The Bankruptcy Court's order confirming Espinosa's proposed plan was a final judgment, from which United [Student Aid Funds] did not appeal. * * * Rule 60(b)(4)–the provision under which United brought this motion–authorizes the court to relieve a party from a final judgment if "the judgment is void."

* * * *

"A judgment is not void" * * * "simply because it is or may have been erroneous." Similarly, a motion under Rule 60(b)(4) is not a substitute for a timely appeal. Instead, Rule 60(b)(4) applies only in the rare instance where a judgment is premised either on a certain type of jurisdictional error or on a violation of due process that deprives a party of notice or the opportunity to be heard.

* * * *

Unable to demonstrate a jurisdictional error or a due process violation, United and the Government, as *amicus* [friend of the court], urge us to expand the universe of judgment defects that support Rule 60(b)(4) relief. Specifically, they contend that the Bankruptcy Court's confirmation order is void because the court lacked statutory authority to confirm Espinosa's plan absent a finding of undue hardship.

* * * *

*Given the Code's clear * * * requirement for an undue hardship determination, the Bankruptcy Court's failure to find undue hardship before confirming Espinosa's plan was a legal error. But the order remains enforceable and binding on United because United had* notice of the error and failed to object or timely appeal. [Emphasis added.]

United's response–that it had no obligation to object to Espinosa's plan until Espinosa served it with the summons and complaint the Bankruptcy Rules require–is unavailing [ineffective]. Rule 60(b)(4) does not provide a license for litigants to sleep on their rights. United had actual notice of the filing of Espinosa's plan, its contents, and the Bankruptcy Court's subsequent confirmation of the plan. In addition, United filed a proof of claim regarding Espinosa's student loan debt, thereby submitting itself to the Bankruptcy Court's jurisdiction with respect to that claim. United therefore forfeited its arguments regarding the validity of service or the adequacy of the Bankruptcy Court's procedures by failing to raise a timely objection in that court.

DECISION AND REMEDY   The United States Supreme Court affirmed the judgment of the U.S. Court of Appeals for the Ninth Circuit. The bankruptcy court's confirmation order concerning Espinosa's Chapter 13 repayment plan was not void, and the student loan debt was thus discharged.

THE ETHICAL DIMENSION   *At one point, United argued that if the Court failed to declare the bankruptcy court's order void, it would encourage dishonest debtors to abuse the Chapter 13 process. How might such abuse occur, and should the possibility of such abuse affect the Court's decision?*

MANAGERIAL IMPLICATIONS   *Business owners and managers should be aware that courts generally have little sympathy for those who "sleep on their rights." In this case, the creditor could have objected to the plan, but it did not. The creditor also could have appealed the confirmation order, but it did not. Only years later did the creditor seek to have the confirmation order declared void. If a client or other debtor petitions for bankruptcy relief, businesspersons should protect their rights by responding promptly to any notices from the debtor or the bankruptcy court.*

 ## Reviewing . . . Creditor-Debtor Relations and Bankruptcy

Three months ago, Janet Hart's husband of twenty years died of cancer. Although he had medical insurance, he left Janet with outstanding medical bills of more than $50,000. Janet has worked at the local library for the past ten years, earning $1,500 per month. Since her husband's death, Janet also has received $1,500 in Social Security benefits and $1,100 in life insurance proceeds every month, giving her a monthly income of $4,300. After she pays the mortgage payment of $1,500 and the amounts due on other debts each month, Janet barely has enough left to buy groceries for her family (she has two teenaged daughters at home). She decides to file for Chapter 7 bankruptcy, hoping for a fresh start. Using the information provided in the chapter, answer the following questions.

1. What must Janet do before filing a petition for relief under Chapter 7?
2. How much time does Janet have after filing the bankruptcy petition to submit the required schedules? What happens if Janet does not meet the deadline?
3. Assume that Janet files a petition under Chapter 7. Further assume that the median family income in the state in which Janet lives is $49,300. What steps would a court take to determine whether Janet's petition is presumed to be "substantial abuse" under the means test?

4. Suppose that the court determines that no presumption of substantial abuse applies in Janet's case. Nevertheless, the court finds that Janet does have the ability to pay at least a portion of the medical bills out of her disposable income. What would the court likely order in that situation?

Linking the Law *to Economics*

The Effects of Bankruptcy Law on Consumers and Businesses

The economic crisis that started in late 2007 led to a significant increase in bankruptcy filings by U.S. consumers and businesses. In 2008, bankruptcy filings by consumers were up by more than 30 percent. In the same year, 136 publicly traded U.S. companies filed for bankruptcy, an increase of 74 percent from a year earlier. In a typical month in 2009, about 100,000 consumers filed for bankruptcy protection.

Bankruptcy in the United States is permitted under Article I, Section 8, of the U.S. Constitution, which authorizes Congress to enact "uniform Laws on the subject of Bankruptcies throughout the United States." In your business law or legal environment course, you learn about the types of bankruptcy and their procedures. In your economics courses, you learn about how bankruptcy law affects the behavior of individuals and businesses.

Bankruptcy Law Can Change the Incentives Facing Consumers

Before the framing of the U.S. Constitution, there were debtors' prisons in the United States, and debtors who could not pay their debts were sometimes sent to prison. The threat of going to prison certainly caused consumers to borrow less and to make a great effort to repay what they owed. Today, of course, we no longer have debtors' prisons, so consumers who are unable to pay their debts know that although they may be ruined financially if they have to file for bankruptcy, they will not go to prison.

It goes without saying that the easier and less costly it is for consumers to declare bankruptcy and effectively "start over with a clean slate," the more debt they will demand and the less they will worry about repaying their creditors. Indeed, one of the reasons that the bankruptcy reform law was enacted in 2005 was to prevent abuse of the bankruptcy process. According to some, it had become too easy for consumers to avoid paying their debts in full.

Bankruptcy Law Also Affects the Incentives of Businesses That Lend

Consumers typically obtain credit from banks, credit-card companies, auto loan companies, finance companies, and major retailers. These lending entities end up charging a competitive interest rate because the market for consumer credit is highly competitive. That competitive interest rate includes a risk premium to cover the consumer debt that is never repaid. Consequently, the easier it is for consumers to file for bankruptcy and wipe out their debts, the higher the risk to the lenders. In other words, the more forgiving the bankruptcy laws are, the more the lending entities will charge consumers for credit. As you learn in your economics courses, all government actions that change incentives lead to other changes in the economy. In this situation, laws that are more favorable to borrowers are by definition less favorable to lenders. The result is higher market interest rates for loans.

FOR CRITICAL ANALYSIS
In what ways do bankruptcy laws benefit the economy as a whole?

 Key Terms

Chapter Summary: Creditor-Debtor Relations and Bankruptcy

LAWS ASSISTING CREDITORS	
Liens (See pages 347–350.)	1. *Mechanic's lien*—A nonpossessory, filed lien on an owner's real estate for labor, services, or materials furnished to or used to make improvements on the realty. 2. *Artisan's lien*—A possessory lien on an owner's personal property for labor performed or value added. 3. *Judicial liens*— a. Writ of attachment—A court-ordered seizure of property prior to a court's final determination of the creditor's rights to the property. Attachment is available only on the creditor's posting of a bond and strict compliance with the applicable state statutes. b. Writ of execution—A court order directing the sheriff to seize (levy) and sell a debtor's nonexempt real or personal property to satisfy a court's judgment in the creditor's favor.
Garnishment (See page 350.)	A collection remedy that allows the creditor to attach a debtor's funds (such as wages owed or bank accounts) and property that are held by a third person.
Creditors' Composition Agreements (See page 351.)	A contract between a debtor and his or her creditors by which the debtor's debts are discharged by payment of a sum less than the amount that is actually owed.
Suretyship and Guaranty (See pages 351–353.)	Under contract, a third person agrees to be primarily or secondarily liable for the debt owed by the principal debtor. A creditor can turn to this third person for satisfaction of the debt.
LAWS ASSISTING DEBTORS	
Exemptions (See pages 354–355.)	Certain property of a debtor is exempt from creditors' actions under state laws. Each state permits a debtor to retain the family home, either in its entirety or up to a specified dollar amount, free from the claims of unsecured creditors or trustees in bankruptcy (homestead exemption).

BANKRUPTCY—A COMPARISON OF CHAPTERS 7, 11, 12, AND 13			
Issue	**Chapter 7**	**Chapter 11**	**Chapters 12 and 13**
Purpose	Liquidation.	Reorganization.	Adjustment.
Who Can Petition	Debtor (voluntary) or creditors (involuntary).	Debtor (voluntary) or creditors (involuntary).	Debtor (voluntary) only.
Who Can Be a Debtor	Any "person" (including partnerships and corporations) except railroads, insurance companies, banks, savings and loan institutions, investment companies licensed by the U.S. Small Business Administration, and credit unions. Farmers and charitable institutions cannot be involuntarily petitioned.	Any debtor eligible for Chapter 7 relief; railroads are also eligible.	*Chapter 12*—Any family farmer (one whose gross income is at least 50 percent farm dependent and whose debts are at least 50 percent farm related) or family fisherman (one whose gross income is at least 50 percent dependent on and whose debts are at least 80 percent related to commercial fishing) or any partnership or close corporation at least 50 percent owned by a family farmer or fisherman, when total debt does not exceed $3,792,650 for a family farmer and $1,757,475 for a family fisherman.

Chapter Summary: Creditor-Debtor Relations and Bankruptcy, Continued

Issue	Chapter 7	Chapter 11	Chapters 12 and 13
Who Can Be a Debtor—Continued			*Chapter 13*—Any individual (not partnerships or corporations) with regular income who owes fixed (liquidated) unsecured debts of less than $360,475 or fixed secured debts of less than $1,081,400.
Procedure Leading to Discharge	Nonexempt property is sold with proceeds to be distributed (in order) to priority groups. Dischargeable debts are terminated.	Plan is submitted. If it is approved and followed, debts are discharged.	Plan is submitted and must be approved if the value of the property to be distributed equals the amount of the claims or if the debtor turns over disposable income for a three- or five-year period. If the plan is followed, debts are discharged.
Advantages	On liquidation and distribution, most debts are discharged, and the debtor has an opportunity for a fresh start.	Debtor continues in business. Creditors can either accept the plan, or it can be "crammed down" on them. The plan allows for the reorganization and liquidation of debts over the plan period.	Debtor continues in business or possession of assets. If the plan is approved, most debts are discharged after a three-year period.

ExamPrep

ISSUE SPOTTERS

1. Joe contracts with Larry of Midwest Roofing to fix Joe's roof. Joe pays half of the contract price in advance. Larry and Midwest complete the job, but Joe refuses to pay the rest of the price. What can Larry and Midwest do?
2. Ogden is a vice president of Plumbing Service, Inc. (PSI). On May 1, Ogden loans PSI $10,000. On June 1, the firm repays the loan. On July 1, PSI files for bankruptcy. Quentin is appointed trustee. Can Quentin recover the $10,000 paid to Ogden on June 1? Explain.

—**Check your answers to these questions against the answers provided in Appendix G.**

BEFORE THE TEST

Go to **www.cengagebrain.com**, enter the ISBN number "9781111530617," and click on "Find" to locate this textbook's Web site. Then, click on "Access Now" under "Study Tools," and select "Chapter 12" at the top. There you will find an "Interactive Quiz" that you can take to assess your mastery of the concepts in this chapter, as well as "Flashcards" and a "Glossary" of important terms.

For Review

1. What is a prejudgment attachment? What is a writ of execution? How does a creditor use these remedies?
2. What is garnishment? When might a creditor undertake a garnishment proceeding?
3. In a bankruptcy proceeding, what constitutes the debtor's estate in property? What property is exempt from the estate under federal bankruptcy law?
4. What is the difference between an exception to discharge and an objection to discharge?
5. In a Chapter 11 reorganization, what is the role of the debtor in possession?

Questions and Case Problems

12–1. Mechanic's Lien. Grant is the owner of a relatively old home valued at $45,000. He notices that the bathtubs and fixtures in both bathrooms are leaking and need to be replaced. He contracts with Jane's Plumbing to replace the bathtubs and fixtures. Jane replaces them, and on June 1 she submits her bill of $4,000 to Grant. Because of financial difficulties, Grant does not pay the bill. Grant's only asset is his home, but his state's homestead exemption is $40,000. Discuss fully Jane's remedies in this situation.

12–2. Voluntary versus Involuntary Bankruptcy. Burke has been a rancher all her life, raising cattle and crops. Her ranch is valued at $500,000, almost all of which is exempt under state law. Burke has eight creditors and a total indebtedness of $70,000. Two of her largest creditors are Oman ($30,000 owed) and Sneed ($25,000 owed). The other six creditors have claims of less than $5,000 each. A drought has ruined all of Burke's crops and forced her to sell many of her cattle at a loss. She cannot pay off her creditors.

1. Under the Bankruptcy Code, can Burke, with a $500,000 ranch, voluntarily petition herself into bankruptcy? Explain.

2. Could either Oman or Sneed force Burke into involuntary bankruptcy? Explain.

12–3. Preferences. Peaslee is not known for his business sense. He started a greenhouse and nursery business two years ago, and because of his lack of experience, he soon was in debt to a number of creditors. On February 1, Peaslee borrowed $5,000 from his father to pay some of these creditors. On May 1, Peaslee paid back the $5,000, depleting his entire working capital. One creditor, the Cool Springs Nursery Supply Corp., extended credit to Peaslee on numerous purchases. Cool Springs pressured Peaslee for payment, and on July 1, Peaslee paid Cool Springs half the amount owed. On September 1, Peaslee voluntarily petitioned himself into bankruptcy. The trustee in bankruptcy claimed that both Peaslee's father and Cool Springs must turn over to the debtor's estate the amounts Peaslee paid to them. Discuss fully the trustee's claims.

12–4. Bankruptcy. Cathy Coleman took out loans to complete her college education. After graduation, Coleman was irregularly employed as a teacher before filing a petition in a federal bankruptcy court under Chapter 13. The court confirmed a five-year plan under which Coleman was required to commit all of her disposable income to paying the student loans. Less than a year later, she was laid off. Still owing more than $100,000 to Educational Credit Management Corp., Coleman asked the court to discharge the debt on the ground that it would be undue hardship for her to pay it. Under Chapter 13, when is a debtor normally entitled to a discharge? Are student loans dischargeable? If not, is "undue hardship" a legitimate ground for an exception? With respect to a debtor, what is the goal of

bankruptcy? With these facts and principles in mind, what argument could be made in support of Coleman's request? [*In re Coleman,* 560 F.3d 1000 (9th Cir. 2009)]

12–5. Discharge in Bankruptcy. Caroline McAfee loaned $400,000 to Carter Oaks Crossing. Joseph Harman, president of Carter Oaks Crossing, signed a promissory note providing that the company would repay the amount with interest in installments beginning in 1999 and ending by 2006. Harman signed a personal guaranty for the note. Carter Oaks Crossing defaulted on the note, so McAfee sued Harman for payment under the guaranty. Harman moved for summary judgment on the ground that McAfee's claim against him had been discharged in his Chapter 7 bankruptcy case, filed after 1999 but before the default on the note. The guaranty was not listed among Harman's debts in the bankruptcy filing. Would the obligation under the guaranty have been discharged in bankruptcy, as Harman claimed? Why or why not? [*Harman v. McAfee,* 302 Ga.App. 698, 691 S.E.2d 586 (2010)]

12–6. Liens. Autolign Manufacturing Group, Inc., was a plastic injection molder that made parts for the auto industry. Because of a fire at its plant, Autolign subcontracted its work to several other companies to produce parts for its customers. Autolign provided the subcontractors with molds it owned so that they could produce the exact parts needed. After the subcontractors produced the parts, Autolign sold them to automakers. Shortly afterward, Autolign ceased operations. The subcontractors sued Autolign for breach of contract, claiming that they were never paid for the parts that they had produced for Autolign. The subcontractors asserted a statutory "molder's lien" on the molds in their possession. A molder's lien is similar to an artisan's lien in that it is possessory, but it was established by a Michigan statute rather than common law. One of Autolign's creditors, Wamco 34, Ltd., argued that the molds were its property because the molds were used to secure repayment of a debt that Autolign owed to Wamco. The trial court held that Wamco was a secured creditor and that its interest had priority over the plaintiffs' lien in the molds. The subcontractors appealed. Which party had the superior claim? Explain your answer. [*Delta Engineered Plastics, LLC v. Autolign Manufacturing Group, Inc.,* 286 Mich.App. 115, 777 N.W.2d 502 (2010)]

12–7. Case Problem with Sample Answer. Protection for Debtors. Bill and Betty Ma owned one-half of a two-unit residential building in San Francisco, California. Betty and her mother lived in one of the units, and Bill lived in China. Mei-Fang Zhang (and others) obtained a judgment in a federal district court against Bill Ma (and others, including Wei-Man Raymond Tse) based on a claim that they had been the victims of a foreign currency trading scam operated by Bill Ma and others. The judgment was more than $1 million. Zhang asked the court for a writ of execution, directing the sheriff to seize and sell the Mas' building. California state law allows a $100,000 homestead exemption free from the claims of creditors, if the debtor or the debtor's spouse lives in the home. A greater exemption of $175,000 is allowed if either of these persons lives in the home *and* is disabled and "unable to engage in gainful employment." Bill Ma argued that he was "unable to engage in gainful employment as a waiter or a driver" because of "gout and dizziness" and claimed a homestead exemption of $175,000. To how much of an exemption is Bill entitled? Why? How will the proceeds from the sale be distributed? [*Zhang v. Tse*, __ F.Supp.2d __ (N.D.Cal. 2011)]

—**To view a sample answer for Case Problem 12–7, go to Appendix F at the end of this text.**

12–8. Discharge in Bankruptcy. Monica Sexton filed a petition in a federal bankruptcy court under Chapter 13. One of her creditors was Friedman's Jewelers of Savannah, Georgia. Her schedules misclassified Friedman's claim as $800 of unsecured debt. Within days, Friedman's filed proof of a secured claim for $300 and an unsecured claim for $462.26. Eventually, Friedman's was sent payments of about $300 by check. None of these checks was cashed, however, because Friedman's had filed its own bankruptcy petition under Chapter 11. As a result, Bankruptcy Receivables Management (BRM) had bought Friedman's unpaid accounts, and the checks had not been forwarded to BRM. In the meantime, Sexton had received a discharge on the completion of her plan, but BRM was not notified. BRM wrote to Sexton's attorney to ask about the status of her case, but received no response. BRM then wrote to Sexton, demanding that she surrender the collateral on its claim. Sexton asked the court to impose sanctions on BRM for violating the discharge order. Was Sexton's debt to Friedman's dischargeable? What is the effect of a discharge? Should BRM be sanctioned? Discuss. [*In re Sexton*, __ Bankr. __ (E.D.N.C. 2011)]

12–9. **A Question of Ethics. Guaranty.** *73-75 Main Avenue, LLC, agreed to lease a portion of the commercial property at 73 Main Avenue, Norwalk, Connecticut, to PP Door Enterprise, Inc. Nan Zhang, as manager of PP Door, signed the lease agreement. The lessor required the principal officers of PP Door to execute personal guaranties. In addition, the principal officers agreed to provide the lessor with credit*

information. Apparently, both the lessor and the principals of PP Door signed the lease and guaranty agreements that were sent to PP Door's office. When PP Door failed to make monthly payments, 73-75 Main Avenue filed a suit against PP Door and its owner, Ping Ying Li. At trial, Li testified that she was the sole owner of PP Door but denied that Zhang was its manager. She also denied signing the guaranty agreement. She claimed that she had signed the credit authorization form because Zhang had told her he was too young to have good credit. Li claimed to have no knowledge of the lease agreement. She did admit, however, that she had paid the rent. She claimed that Zhang had been in a car accident and had asked her to help pay his bills, including the rent at 73 Main Avenue. Li further testified that she did not see the name PP Door on the storefront of the leased location. [73-75 Main Avenue, LLC v. PP Door Enterprise, Inc., *120 Conn.App. 150, 991 A.2d 650 (2010)*]

1. Li argued that she was not liable on the lease agreement because Zhang was not authorized to bind her to the lease. Do the facts support Li? Why or why not?

2. Li claimed that the guaranty for rent was not enforceable against her. Why might the court agree?

12–10. **Video Question. *Field of Dreams.*** Access the video using the instructions provided below to answer the following questions.

1. Before this scene, the movie makes clear that Ray (Kevin Costner) is unable to pay his bills, but he has not filed a voluntary petition for bankruptcy. What would be required for Ray's creditors to force him into an involuntary bankruptcy?

2. If Ray did file a voluntary petition for a Chapter 7 bankruptcy, what exemptions might protect him from "losing everything" and being evicted, as the man indicated in this scene? How much equity in the farm home could Ray claim as exempt if he filed the petition?

3. What are the requirements for Ray to qualify as a family farmer under Chapter 12 of the Bankruptcy Code?

4. How would the results of a Chapter 12 bankruptcy differ from those of a Chapter 7 bankruptcy for Ray?

—To watch this video, go to **www.cengagebrain.com** and register the access code that came with your new book or log in to your existing account. Select the link for either the "Business Law Digital Video Library Online Access" or "Business Law CourseMate," and then click on "Complete Video List" to find the video for this chapter (Video 73).

Chapter 13

Mortgages and Foreclosures after the Recession

> "These days America is looking like the Bernie Madoff of economies: For many years it was held in respect, even awe, but it turns out to have been a fraud all along."
>
> —Paul Krugman, 1953–present
> (American columnist and winner of the Nobel Prize in economics)

(Quaziefoto/Creative Commons)

Chapter Objectives

After reading this chapter, you should be able to answer the following questions:

1. What is a subprime mortgage? How does it differ from a standard fixed-rate mortgage? What is a home equity loan?

2. When is private mortgage insurance required? Which party does it protect?

3. Does the Truth-in-Lending Act (TILA) apply to all mortgages? How do the TILA provisions protect borrowers and curb abusive practices by mortgage lenders?

4. What is a short sale? How might a short sale be more advantageous than a mortgage foreclosure for a borrower, and what impact does it have on the balance owed to the lender on the mortgage loan?

5. In a mortgage foreclosure, what legal rights do mortgage holders have if the sale proceeds are insufficient to pay the underlying debt?

During the early years of the twenty-first century, the United States experienced one of the biggest real estate bubbles in its history as housing prices in many areas increased at unprecedented rates. The bubble started to shrink in 2006 and was still deflating in 2011. As a result of the collapse of the housing market and the financial crisis that accompanied it, the United States and much of the rest of the world suffered through what is now called the Great Recession.

Although several years have passed since the housing crisis and recession began, the real estate market is still in turmoil. Many people have lost their homes to foreclosure because they could not make the payments on their *mortgages*—the loans that borrowers obtain to purchase homes. Others can afford the payments but choose not to pay because they owe more on the properties than those properties are worth.

As the problems drag on, it has become apparent that the entire mortgage process during the bubble years was fraught with fraud, as the chapter-opening quotation above suggests. In June 2011, for example, Bank of America announced that it would pay as much as $20 billion to settle claims involving mortgage-backed securities the bank had sold as safe investments. In fact, the securities were actually based on mortgages granted to borrowers who had little, if any, ability to repay their loans (see Chapter 24 for more on securities fraud). Other major mortgage companies, including Citigroup, JPMorgan Chase, and Wells Fargo, faced similar fraud claims. In the meantime, complaints about fraud in the mortgage foreclosure process by both borrowers and lenders have risen—in fact, they were up 31 percent in the first quarter of 2011.[1]

This chapter examines the rights and obligations that apply to homeowners and their lenders. It begins with a discussion of mortgages, which lenders provide to enable borrowers to purchase real property (*real property* will be discussed in Chapter 22). Next, we examine the laws that protect borrowers when they obtain mortgages. The chapter concludes with a discussion of the options that lenders and homeowners have when homeowners cannot continue to make their mortgage payments.

▶ Mortgages

Mortgage　A written document that gives a creditor (the mortgagee) an interest in, or lien on, the debtor's (mortgagor's) real property as security for a debt.

When individuals purchase real property, they typically borrow funds from a financial institution for part or all of the purchase price. A **mortgage** is a written instrument that gives the creditor (the *mortgagee*) an interest in, or lien on, the property being acquired by the debtor (the *mortgagor*) as security for the debt's payment. Here, we look first at the different types of mortgages, including some new varieties that helped to inflate the housing bubble. Then we consider some of the ways that creditors protect their interest in the property and examine some of the more important provisions in a typical mortgage document.

Types of Mortgages

Mortgage loans are contracts, and as such, they come in a variety of forms. Lenders offer various types of mortgages to meet the needs of different borrowers. In recent decades, the expansion of home ownership became a political goal, and lenders were encouraged to become more creative in devising new types of mortgages. In many instances, these new mortgages were aimed at borrowers who could not qualify for traditional mortgages and lacked the funds to make a **down payment** (the part of the purchase price that is paid up front).

Down Payment　The part of the purchase price of real property that is paid up front, reducing the amount of the loan or mortgage.

In general, these mortgages, which include some adjustable-rate mortgages, interest-only mortgages, and balloon mortgages, feature a low initial interest rate. Often, the borrower hopes to refinance—pay off the original mortgage and obtain a new one at more favorable terms—within a few years. When the housing bubble burst and house prices began to decline, however, refinancing became more difficult than many borrowers had anticipated.

Fixed-Rate Mortgage　A standard mortgage with a fixed, or unchanging, rate of interest. The loan payments on these mortgages remain the same for the duration of the loan.

FIXED-RATE MORTGAGES　*Fixed-rate mortgages* are the simplest mortgage loans. A **fixed-rate mortgage** is a standard mortgage with a fixed, or unchanging, rate of interest. Payments on the loan remain the same for the duration of the mortgage, which ranges from fifteen to forty years. Lenders determine the interest rate based on a variety of factors, including the borrower's credit history, credit score, income, and debts. Today, for a borrower to qualify for a standard fixed-rate mortgage loan, lenders typically require that the monthly mortgage payment (including principal, interest, taxes, and insurance) not exceed 28 percent of the person's gross income.

Adjustable-Rate Mortgage (ARM)　A mortgage in which the rate of interest paid by the borrower changes periodically, often with reference to a predetermined government interest rate (the index).

ADJUSTABLE-RATE MORTGAGES　The rate of interest paid by the borrower changes periodically with an **adjustable-rate mortgage (ARM)**. Typically, the initial

---

1. This figure is according to the Financial Crimes Enforcement Network, a U.S. Treasury bureau that tracks illegal financial activity.

interest rate for an ARM is set at a relatively low fixed rate for a specified period, such as a year or three years. After that time, the interest rate adjusts annually or by some other period, such as biannually or monthly. ARMs generally are described in terms of the initial fixed period and the adjustment period. For example, if the interest rate is fixed for three years and then adjusts annually, the mortgage is called a 3/1 ARM, whereas if the rate adjusts annually after five years, the mortgage is a 5/1 ARM.

The interest rate adjustment is calculated by adding a certain number of percentage points (called the margin) to an index rate (one of various government interest rates). The margin and index rate are specified in the mortgage loan documents. **EXAMPLE 13.1** Greta and Marcus obtain a 3/1 ARM to purchase a home. After three years, when the first adjustment is to be made, the index rate is 6 percent. If the margin specified in the loan documents is 3 percentage points, the fully indexed interest rate for the ARM would be 9 percent. ● Most ARMs, however, have lifetime interest rate caps that limit the amount that the rate can rise over the duration of the loan.

Some ARMs also have caps that stipulate the maximum increase that can occur at any particular adjustment period. **EXAMPLE 13.2** In the Greta and Marcus example above, if the initial interest rate was 5 percent and the loan stipulated that the rate could rise no more than 3 percentage points in one adjustment period, the interest rate after three years would increase to 8 percent, not 9 percent, because of the cap. ● Note that the interest rate could be adjusted downward as well as upward. If the index rate was 1 percent, the adjusted rate would potentially fall to 4 percent, although some ARMs also limit the amount that the rate can fall.

INTEREST-ONLY (IO) MORTGAGES With an **interest-only (IO) mortgage,** the borrower can choose to pay only the interest portion of the monthly payments and forgo paying any of the principal for a specified period of time. (IO loans can be for fixed-rate or adjustable-rate mortgages.) This IO payment usually is available for three to ten years. After the IO payment option is exhausted, the borrower's payment increases to include payments on the principal.

SUBPRIME MORTGAGES During the late 1990s and the first decade of the 2000s, *subprime lending* increased significantly. A **subprime mortgage** is a loan made to a borrower who does not qualify for a standard mortgage. Often, such borrowers have poor credit scores or high current *debt-to-income ratios*—that is, the total amount owed as a percentage of current after-tax income. Subprime mortgages are riskier than traditional mortgages and have a higher default rate. Consequently, lenders charge a higher interest rate for subprime loans. Subprime mortgages can be fixed-rate, adjustable-rate, or IO loans. Subprime lending allows many people who could not otherwise purchase real property to do so, but at a higher risk to the lender.

CONSTRUCTION LOANS A **construction loan** is similar to a mortgage in many ways—for example, this type of loan comes in all varieties, including fixed-rate and adjustable-rate loans. Rather than purchasing an existing home, the borrower uses the funds from a construction loan to build a new home. Construction loans are often set up with a schedule of "draws." **EXAMPLE 13.3** Joel and Jennie borrow funds to purchase real estate and build a home. The first draw of funds pays for the land. Subsequent draws occur when the foundation is laid, when the framing for the structure is finished, when the exterior is completed, and finally when the interior is completed and the contractor turns the house over to the couple for occupancy. ●

"My problem lies in reconciling my gross habits with my net income."

Errol Flynn, 1909–1959
(Australian-born actor)

Interest-Only (IO) Mortgage A mortgage that gives the borrower the option of paying only the interest portion of the monthly payment and forgoing the payment of principal for a specified period of time. After the IO payment option is exhausted, the borrower's payment increases to include payments on the principal.

Subprime Mortgage A high-risk loan made to a borrower who does not qualify for a standard mortgage because of his or her poor credit rating or high debt-to-income ratio. Lenders typically charge a higher interest rate on subprime mortgages.

Construction Loan A loan obtained by a borrower to finance the building of a new home. Construction loans are often set up to release funds at particular stages of the project.

Balloon Mortgage A loan that allows the debtor to make small monthly payments for an initial period, such as eight years, but then requires a large balloon payment for the entire remaining balance of the mortgage loan at the end of that period.

BALLOON MORTGAGES Similar to an ARM, a **balloon mortgage** starts with low payments for a specified period, usually seven to ten years. At the end of that period, a large balloon payment for the entire balance of the mortgage loan is due. Because the balloon payment is often very large, many borrowers refinance when this payment is due. A potential disadvantage is that the lender will set the interest rate of the refinanced loan at whatever the market dictates at that time. As a result, the payments may be higher than they would have been if the buyer had initially obtained a fixed-rate mortgage instead of a balloon mortgage.

HYBRID AND REVERSE MORTGAGES A variety of other less common mortgages are also available. One example is a **hybrid mortgage** (also called a *two-step mortgage*), which starts as a fixed-rate mortgage and then converts into an ARM.

Hybrid Mortgage A mortgage that starts as a fixed-rate mortgage and then converts to an adjustable-rate mortgage.

Reverse Mortgage A loan product typically provided to older homeowners that allows them to extract funds (in either a lump sum or multiple payments) for the equity in their home. The mortgage does not need to be repaid until the home is sold or the owner leaves or dies.

With a **reverse mortgage,** instead of borrowing from a bank to buy a home, existing homeowners receive funds for the equity, or value, in their home. The mortgage does not need to be repaid until the home is sold or the owner dies. Reverse mortgages are geared toward older borrowers (over the age of sixty-two) who have substantial equity in their homes. By converting a portion of that equity into cash, the homeowners can supplement their retirement income.

Home Equity Loans

Home equity refers to the portion of a home's value that is "paid off." **EXAMPLE 13.4** If Susanna has a home valued at $200,000 and owes the bank $120,000 on her mortgage, she has 40 percent equity in her house ($80,000/$200,000 = 40 percent). With a **home equity loan,** a bank accepts the borrower's equity as *collateral,* which can be seized if the loan is not repaid on time. If Susanna takes out a $30,000 home equity loan, the amount is added to the amount of her mortgage ($30,000 + $120,000 = $150,000), so she now has only $50,000 (25 percent) equity in her $200,000 home. ●

Home Equity Loan A loan in which the lender accepts a person's home equity (the portion of the home's value that is paid off) as collateral, which can be seized if the loan is not repaid on time.

Borrowers often take out home equity loans to obtain funds to renovate the property itself. Others obtain home equity loans to pay off debt, such as credit-card debt, that carries a higher interest rate than they will pay on the home equity loan. This strategy can lead to problems, however, if the borrower cannot keep up the payments. Many Americans who lost their homes during the Great Recession were able to pay their original mortgage loans, but not their home equity loans. From the lender's perspective, a home equity loan is riskier than a mortgage loan because home equity loans are *subordinated,* which means that they take a lower priority in any proceeding that occurs if the homeowner fails to make the payments on the primary mortgage.

Creditor Protection

"People are living longer than ever before, a phenomenon undoubtedly made necessary by the 30-year mortgage."

Doug Larson, 1926–present
(American columnist)

When creditors grant mortgages, they are advancing a significant amount of funds for a number of years. Consequently, creditors take a number of steps to protect their interest. One precaution is to require debtors to obtain private mortgage insurance if they do not make a down payment of at least 20 percent of the purchase price. For example, if a borrower makes a down payment of only 5 percent of the purchase price, the creditor might require insurance covering 15 percent of the cost. Then, if the debtor defaults, the creditor repossesses the house and receives reimbursement from the insurer for the covered portion of the loan.

In addition, the creditor will record the mortgage with the appropriate office in the county where the property is located. Recording ensures that the creditor is officially on record as holding an interest in the property. A lender that fails to record a mortgage could find itself in the position of an unsecured creditor.

Mortgages normally are lengthy documents that include a number of provisions. Many of these provisions are aimed at protecting the creditor's investment.

Statute of Frauds   Because a mortgage involves a transfer of real property, it must be in writing to comply with the Statute of Frauds (see page 280 in Chapter 10). Most mortgages today are highly formal documents with similar formats, but a mortgage is not required to follow any particular form. Indeed, as long as the mortgage satisfies the Statute of Frauds, it generally will be effective.

Important Mortgage Provisions   Mortgage documents ordinarily contain all or most of the following terms:

1. *The terms of the underlying loan.* These include the loan amount, the interest rate, the period of repayment, and other important financial terms, such as the margin and index rate for an ARM. Many lenders include a **prepayment penalty clause,** which requires the borrower to pay a penalty if the mortgage is repaid in full within a certain period. A prepayment penalty helps to protect the lender should the borrower refinance within a short time after obtaining a mortgage.

2. *Provisions relating to the maintenance of the property.* Because the mortgage conveys an interest in the property to the lender, the lender will require the borrower to maintain the property in such a way that the lender's investment is protected.

3. *A statement obligating the borrower to maintain* **homeowners' insurance** *(also known as* hazard insurance*) on the property.* This type of insurance protects the lender's interest in the event of a loss due to certain hazards, such as fire or storm damages.

4. *A list of the nonloan financial obligations to be borne by the borrower.* For example, the borrower typically is required to pay all property taxes, assessments, and other claims against the property.

5. *A provision requiring that the borrower pay certain obligations.* For example, a borrower may be required to pay some or all of the taxes, insurance, assessments, or other expenses associated with the property in advance or through the lender. In this way, the lender is assured that the funds for these expenses will be available when the bills come due.

Although a record number of homeowners have failed to keep up with their mortgage payments in recent years, courts have continued to enforce the terms of plainly written financing documents. In today's more protective environment, borrowers cannot avoid the clear meaning of terms in financing documents, even when the effect may be harsh.

Prepayment Penalty Clause   A clause in a mortgage loan contract that requires the borrower to pay a penalty if the mortgage is repaid in full within a certain period. A prepayment penalty helps to protect the lender if the borrower refinances within a short time after obtaining a mortgage.

Homeowners' Insurance   Insurance that protects a homeowner's property against damage from storms, fire, and other hazards. Lenders may require that a borrower carry homeowners' insurance on mortgaged property.

▶ Real Estate Financing Law

During the real estate boom in the first years of the 2000s, some lenders were less than honest with borrowers about the loan terms the latter were signing. As a result, many individuals failed to understand how much the monthly payments on ARMs, interest-only mortgages, and other exotic types of loans might increase. In addition, fees and penalties often were not properly disclosed. In an effort to provide more protection for borrowers, Congress and the Federal Reserve Board have instituted a number of new requirements, mostly in the form of required disclosures. Here, we examine some of the more important statutes that provide protection for borrowers. First, though, we look at some of the practices that led to the enactment of these statutes.

Predatory Lending and Other Improper Practices

"Mortgage: a house with a guilty conscience."

Anonymous

The general term *predatory lending* is often used to describe situations in which borrowers are the victims of loan terms or lending procedures that are excessive, deceptive, or not properly disclosed. Predatory lending typically occurs during the loan origination process. It includes a number of practices ranging from failure to disclose terms to providing misleading information to outright dishonesty.

Two specific types of improper practices are often at the core of a violation. *Steering and targeting* occurs when the lender manipulates a borrower into accepting a loan product that benefits the lender but is not the best loan for the borrower. For instance, a lender may steer a borrower toward an ARM, even though the buyer qualifies for a fixed-rate mortgage. *Loan flipping* occurs when a lender convinces a homeowner to refinance soon after obtaining a mortgage. Such early refinancing rarely benefits the homeowner and may, in fact, result in prepayment penalties.

The Truth-in-Lending Act (TILA)

The Truth-in-Lending Act (TILA) of 1968[2] requires lenders to disclose the terms of a loan in clear, readily understandable language so that borrowers can make rational choices. (We will discuss the TILA in more detail in Chapter 20 in the context of consumer law.) With respect to real estate transactions, the TILA applies only to residential loans.

Annual Percentage Rate (APR) The cost of credit on a yearly basis, typically expressed as an annual percentage.

REQUIRED DISCLOSURES The major terms that must be disclosed under the TILA include the loan principal; the interest rate at which the loan is made; the **annual percentage rate,** or **APR** (the actual cost of the loan on a yearly basis); and all fees and costs associated with the loan. The TILA requires that these disclosures be made on standardized forms and based on uniform formulas of calculation. Certain types of loans—including ARMs, reverse mortgages, open-ended home equity loans, and high-interest loans—have specially tailored disclosure requirements. The Mortgage Disclosure Improvement Act of 2008[3] amended the TILA to strengthen the disclosures required for ARMs, which, as mentioned earlier, played a leading role in the recent real estate meltdown.

PROHIBITIONS AND REQUIREMENTS The TILA prohibits certain lender abuses and creates certain borrower rights. Among the prohibited practices is the charging of prepayment penalties on most subprime mortgages and home equity loans.

Appraiser An individual who specializes in determining the value of certain real or personal property.

The TILA also addresses other unfair, abusive, or deceptive home mortgage–lending practices. For example, lenders may not coerce an **appraiser** (an individual who specializes in determining the value of specified real or personal property) into misstating the value of a property on which a loan is to be issued. Also, a loan cannot be advertised as a fixed-rate loan if, in fact, its rate or payment amounts will change.

---

2. 15 U.S.C. Sections 1601–1693r.

3. The Mortgage Disclosure Improvement Act is contained in Sections 2501 through 2503 of the Housing and Economic Recovery Act of 2008, Pub. L. No. 110-289, enacted on July 30, 2008. Congress then amended its provisions as part of the Emergency Economic Stabilization Act of 2008 (also known as the Bailout Bill), Pub. L. No. 110-343, enacted on October 3, 2008.

Right to Rescind. A mortgage cannot be finalized until at least seven days after a borrower has received the TILA paperwork. Even if all required disclosures are provided, the TILA gives the borrower the right to rescind (cancel) a mortgage within three business days. According to the 2008 amendments, Sunday is the only day of the week that is not a business day. If the lender fails to provide material TILA disclosures, including the three-day right to rescind, the rescission period lasts up to three years.

Written Representations. The TILA requirements apply to the written materials the lender provides, not to any oral representations. If a lender provides the required TILA disclosures, a borrower who fails to read the relevant documents cannot claim fraud, even if the lender orally misrepresented the terms of the loan.

CASE EXAMPLE 13.5 Patricia Ostolaza and José Diaz owned a home on which they had two mortgage loans and a home equity line of credit provided by Bank of America. Anthony Falcone called them and said that he could refinance their mortgages in a manner that would reduce their monthly payments. Falcone said that he represented Bank of America when in fact he represented Countrywide Home Loans, Inc. At the *closing* (see page 633) of the new loan, the homeowners were given all of the relevant documents, including the TILA disclosure statement. The documents accurately stated the monthly payment under the new loan, which was higher than the couple's original payments. The homeowners later filed a lawsuit against Falcone and Countrywide Bank, alleging fraud. The trial court dismissed the suit, and the appellate court upheld the dismissal because the homeowners had been given the opportunity to read all of the relevant documents, but had not done so.[4] ●

Protection for High-Cost Mortgage Loan Recipients

In the last twenty years, lenders have provided many high-cost and high-fee mortgage products to people who could not easily obtain credit under other loan programs. These loans are commonly known as HOEPA loans, named after the Home Ownership and Equity Protection Act (HOEPA) of 1994,[5] which amended the TILA to create this special category of loans. The rules pertaining to HOEPA loans are contained in Section 32 of *Regulation Z,* enacted by the Federal Reserve Board to implement the TILA (see Chapter 20).

A loan can qualify for protection under HOEPA either because it carries a high rate of interest or because it entails high fees for the borrower. HOEPA applies if the APR disclosed for the loan exceeds the interest rates of **Treasury securities** (or bonds) of comparable maturity by more than 8 percentage points for a first mortgage and 10 percentage points for a second mortgage. HOEPA can also apply when the total fees paid by the consumer exceed 8 percent of the loan amount or a set dollar amount (based on changes in the Consumer Price Index), whichever is larger.

Treasury Securities Government debt issued by the U.S. Department of the Treasury. The interest rate on Treasury securities is often used as a baseline for measuring the rate on loan products with higher interest rates.

SPECIAL CONSUMER PROTECTIONS If a loan qualifies for HOEPA protection, the consumer must receive several disclosures in addition to those required by the TILA. The lender must disclose the APR, the regular payment amount, and any required balloon payments. For loans with a variable rate of interest, the lender must disclose that the rate and monthly payments may increase and state the potential maximum monthly payment. These disclosures must be provided at least three business days before the loan is finalized.

---

4. *Ostolaza-Diaz v. Countrywide Bank, N.A.,* 2010 WL 95145 (4th Cir. 2010).
5. 15 U.S.C. Sections 1637 and 1647.

In addition, the lender must provide a written notice stating that the consumer need not complete the loan simply because he or she received the disclosures or signed the loan application. Borrowers must also be informed that they could lose their home (and all funds invested in it) if they default on the loan.

HOEPA also prohibits lenders from engaging in certain practices, such as requiring balloon payments for loans with terms of five years or less. Loans that result in negative amortization are also prohibited. **Negative amortization** occurs when the monthly payments are insufficient to cover the interest due on the loan. The difference is then added to the principal, so the balance owed on the loan increases over time.

> **Negative Amortization** This occurs when the payment made by the borrower is less than the interest due on the loan and the difference is added to the principal. As a result, the balance owed on the loan increases rather than decreases over time.

REMEDIES AND LIABILITIES For HOEPA violations, consumers can obtain damages in an amount equal to all finance charges and fees paid if the lender's failure to disclose is deemed material. Any failure to comply with HOEPA provisions also extends the borrower's right to rescind the loan for up to three years.

Whether a particular loan is covered by HOEPA and thus is entitled to the statute's significant protections can have important ramifications because it can determine whether a borrower can recover on a lender's failure to comply with HOEPA's provisions and the amount of the recovery. In the following case, a consumer attempted to recover from a lender for alleged violations of the TILA and HOEPA.

Case 13.1   In re Kitts

United States Bankruptcy Court, District of Utah, 447 Bankr. 330 (2011).

BACKGROUND AND FACTS Facing the loss of his family's home in Park City, Utah, to creditors, Brian Kitts sought to refinance the debt. He entered into two mortgage loan agreements for $1.35 million and $39,603.47, respectively, with Winterfox, LLC. As part of the deal, Kitts paid $87,500 in "loan origination fees." Kitts defaulted on the loans and filed a petition in a federal bankruptcy court to declare bankruptcy. He also filed a complaint against Winterfox to recover damages for alleged violations of the federal Truth-in-Lending Act (TILA). The court dismissed the action, but on appeal, a federal district court ruled that Winterfox had failed to make certain required disclosures. The district court remanded the case for "further fact finding concerning damages" for violation of the TILA, as well as for Kitts's request for attorneys' fees.

IN THE WORDS OF THE COURT . . .
Joel T. *MARKER*, Bankruptcy Judge.
* * * *

* * * Both loans qualify as high-cost mortgages [covered by HOEPA] from an interest-rate standpoint based on evidence regarding the APRs of those loans.
* * * *

* * * Based on the facts that Winterfox made two loans to the Debtor, provided no disclosures at all, and attempted in this litigation to cover up its failure to disclose with fabricated documents, the Court concludes that the maximum statutory damages of $2,000 for each violation are appropriate for total statutory damages of $4,000.
* * * *

On the issue of finance charges in connection with the Winterfox loans, the parties do not dispute the fact that Winterfox charged $87,500 in "loan origination fees" to the Debtor * * * . The parties also do not dispute that the $87,500 was paid from the Winterfox loan proceeds rather than being paid out of pocket by the Debtor. *The major dispute is over the purely legal question of whether finance charges that are paid from the loan proceeds, rather than finance charges paid out of pocket by the Debtor, qualify as "finance charges paid by the consumer" under [the TILA].* Winterfox also argues in the alternative that finance charges should not be awarded as damages because its "failure to comply [with HOEPA] is not material." [Emphasis added.]

Finance charges qualify as compensable damages under [HOEPA]. * * * This view comports with both the formal nature of the underlying financial transaction as well as the remedial nature of TILA and the equity protection purpose of HOEPA. [Emphasis added.]

Winterfox's failure to provide any of the required disclosures constitutes a material failure to comply with [HOEPA]. Accordingly, the Court awards the [plaintiff] damages of $87,500 for the Debtor's finance charges.

Case 13.1–Continues next page ⇨

Case 13.1–Continued

* * * *

The Court's task in determining a "reasonable" [attorneys'] fee is a difficult one. * * * Based on the underlying administration of the main bankruptcy case, the relative complexity of the issues in this adversary proceeding, the contributions of both parties to the length and expense of this adversary proceeding, the [plaintiff's] ultimate degree of success on the merits before the Court and the District Court, and the relative billing rates of the [plaintiff's] counsel, the Court finds that 750 hours is a reasonable number of hours spent in prosecution of this adversary proceeding at $200/hour for a total fee and cost award of $150,000.

DECISION AND REMEDY   The court concluded that HOEPA covered the Winterfox loans. The plaintiff was awarded statutory TILA

damages of $4,000, $87,500 for the finance charges paid in connection with the loans, and $150,000 for attorneys' fees.

THE ECONOMIC DIMENSION   *Why would a borrower who is relatively sophisticated (as the court found that Kitts was) and can afford to buy a million-dollar home, agree to pay such high loan origination fees?*

THE LEGAL ENVIRONMENT DIMENSION   *The TILA, HOEPA, and other consumer-protection laws exist to protect purchasers from "unscrupulous" lenders or sellers. As consumers become better informed about these issues, will these laws still be needed? Discuss.*

Protection for Higher-Priced Mortgage Loans

In 2008, the Federal Reserve Board enacted an amendment to Regulation Z that created a second category of expensive loans, called Higher-Priced Mortgage Loans (HPMLs). Only mortgages secured by a consumer's principal home qualify to receive the HPML designation.

REQUIREMENTS TO QUALIFY   To be an HPML, a mortgage must have an APR that exceeds the *average prime offer rate* for a comparable transaction by 1.5 percentage points or more if the loan is a first lien on a dwelling. (The **average prime offer rate** is the rate offered to the best-qualified borrowers as established by a survey of lenders.) If the loan is secured by a subordinate lien on a home, then the APR must exceed the average prime offer rate by 3.5 percentage points or more in order to be considered an HPML.

Average Prime Offer Rate   The mortgage rate offered to the best-qualified borrowers as established by a survey of lenders.

Mortgages excluded from coverage include those for the initial construction of a home, temporary or *bridge loans* that are one year or shorter in duration, home equity lines of credit, and reverse mortgages. (**Bridge loans** are short-term loans that allow a buyer to make a down payment on a new home before selling her or his current home.)

Bridge Loan   A short-term loan that allows a buyer to make a down payment on a new home before selling her or his current home. The current home is used as collateral.

SPECIAL PROTECTIONS FOR CONSUMERS   As with a HOEPA loan, consumers receiving an HPML receive additional protections. First, lenders cannot make an HPML based on the value of the consumer's home without verifying the consumer's ability to repay the loan. This verification is typically accomplished through review of the consumer's financial records such as tax returns, bank account statements, and payroll records. The creditor must also verify the consumer's other credit obligations.

Second, prepayment penalties are severely restricted for HPMLs. Prepayment penalties are allowed only if they are limited to two years, and they will not even apply if the source of the prepayment funds is a refinancing by the creditor or the creditor's affiliate. Additionally, lenders must establish *escrow accounts* for borrowers' payments for homeowners' insurance and property taxes for all first mortgages. (An escrow account holds funds to be paid to a third party—see Chapter 22.) Finally, lenders cannot structure a loan specifically to evade the HPML protections.

Default   The act of failing to pay a debt, perform an obligation, or appear in court when legally required to do so. A court can enter a default judgment against a defendant who fails to appear in court to answer or defend against a plaintiff's claim.

 ## Foreclosures

Foreclosure   A proceeding in which a mortgagee either takes title to or forces the sale of the mortgagor's property in satisfaction of a debt.

If a homeowner **defaults,** or fails to make mortgage payments, the lender has the right to foreclose on the mortgaged property. **Foreclosure** is a process that allows a lender to legally repossess and auction off the property that is securing

(AP Photo/Mel Evans)

Foreclosure occurs after the mortgagor fails to make timely payments. The methods of foreclosure are state-specific. What are the two methods by which a lender can foreclose on property for which the underlying loan is in default?

Forbearance An agreement between a lender and a borrower in which the lender agrees to temporarily cease requiring mortgage payments, delay foreclosure, or accept smaller payments than previously scheduled.

Workout Agreement A formal contract in which a debtor and his or her creditors agree to negotiate a payment plan for the amount due on the loan instead of proceeding to foreclosure.

Short Sale A sale of real property by a borrower for an amount that is less than the balance owed on the mortgage loan. The lender must consent to the sale, and the borrower usually must show some financial hardship.

a loan.[6] Foreclosure is expensive and time consuming, however, and generally benefits neither the borrower, who loses his or her home, nor the lender, which faces the prospect of a loss on its loans. Therefore, various methods to avoid foreclosure have been developed. We look first at some of these methods and then turn to the foreclosure process itself.

How to Avoid Foreclosure

In the past, especially during the Great Depression of the 1930s, a number of alternatives to foreclosure were developed. More recently, as foreclosures were more common than at any time since the Great Depression, Congress has intervened to aid in the modification of mortgage loans.

FORBEARANCE AND WORKOUT AGREEMENTS The first preforeclosure option a borrower has is called forbearance. **Forbearance** is the postponement, for a limited time, of part or all of the payments on a loan in jeopardy of foreclosure. Such payment waivers had their origins in the Great Depression. A lender grants forbearance when it expects that, during the forbearance period, the borrower can solve the problem by securing a new job, selling the property, or finding another acceptable solution.

When a borrower fails to make payments as required, the lender may attempt to negotiate a workout. As noted in Chapter 12, a *workout* is a voluntary process to cure the default in some fashion. The parties may even create a formal **workout agreement**—a written document that describes the rights and responsibilities of the parties as they try to resolve the default without proceeding to foreclosure. In such an agreement, the lender will likely agree to delay seeking foreclosure or other legal rights. In exchange, the borrower may agree to provide to the lender financial information on which a workout might be constructed.

Whether a workout is possible or preferable to foreclosure depends on many factors, including the value of the property, the amount of the unpaid principal, the market in which the property will be sold, the relationship of the lender and the borrower, and the financial condition of the borrower.

HOUSING AND URBAN DEVELOPMENT ASSISTANCE A lender may be able to work with the borrower to obtain an interest-free loan from the U.S. Department of Housing and Urban Development (HUD) to bring the mortgage current. HUD assistance may be available if the loan is at least four months (but not more than twelve months) delinquent, if the property is not in foreclosure, and if the borrower is able to make full mortgage payments. When the lender files a claim, HUD pays the lender the amount necessary to make the mortgage current. The borrower executes a note to HUD, and a lien for the second loan is placed on the property. The promissory note is interest free and comes due if the property is sold.

SHORT SALES When a borrower is unable to make mortgage payments, the lender may agree to a **short sale**—that is, a sale of the property for less than the balance due on the mortgage loan. The borrower must obtain the lender's permission for the short

---

6. Lenders other than those holding a first mortgage on a property may also foreclose. For example, a roofing company holding a mechanic's lien for the unpaid cost of a new roof can foreclose on the property.

sale, and typically she or he has to show some hardship, such as the loss of a job, a decline in the value of the home, a divorce, or a death in the household. The lender receives the proceeds of the sale, and the borrower still owes the balance of the debt to the lender, unless the lender specifically agrees to forgive the remaining debt. In 2007, Congress passed the Mortgage Forgiveness Debt Relief Act,[7] which eliminated income taxes on the forgiven debt. (Ordinarily, forgiven debt must be reported as income that is subject to federal income tax.)

A short sale can offer several advantages. Although the borrower's credit rating is affected, the negative impact is less than it would be with a foreclosure, which generally remains on the borrower's credit report for seven years.[8] The short sale process also avoids the expense of foreclosure for the lender and the trauma of being evicted from the home for the homeowner. But because the lender often has approval rights in a short sale, the sale process can take much longer than a standard real estate transaction. In addition, although the parties' losses are mitigated, the borrower still loses her or his home.

SALE AND LEASEBACK   In some situations, the homeowner may be able to sell the property to an investor who is looking for an income property. The owner sells the property to the investor and then leases it back at an amount that is less than the monthly mortgage payment. The owner-seller uses the proceeds of the sale to pay off the mortgage and still has the use and possession of the property. In some circumstances, this strategy can also be used to raise capital when there is no risk of loss of the property.

"The gap in our economy is between what we have and what we think we ought to have–and that is a moral problem, not an economic one."

Paul Heyne, 1931–2000
(American economist)

HOME AFFORDABLE MODIFICATION PROGRAM   In 2009, the U.S. Treasury Department launched the Home Affordable Modification Program (HAMP) to encourage private lenders to modify mortgages so as to lower the monthly payments of borrowers who are in default. The program may share in the costs of modifying the loan and provides incentives to lenders based on successful loan modification. A series of steps must be taken to determine debtor eligibility, the appropriate method for reducing the mortgage burden, and the possibility of forbearance of part of the mortgage loan.

Determination If a Homeowner Qualifies. HAMP modifications are not available for every mortgage. To qualify, the loan must have originated on or before January 1, 2009, the home must be occupied by the owner, and the unpaid balance may not exceed $729,750 for a single-unit property.[9] The homeowner must be facing financial hardship and be either more than sixty days late on mortgage payments or at risk of imminent default. Homeowners are required to verify their hardship through appropriate documentation.

In addition, the home must be the homeowner's primary residence. Investor-owned homes, vacant homes, and condemned properties are not eligible under the program. Borrowers in active litigation related to their mortgage may take advantage of the program without waiving their legal rights.

Steps Taken to Alleviate the Mortgage Burden. The purpose of HAMP is not to force lenders to forgive all high-risk mortgages, but rather to reduce monthly mortgage payments to a level that the homeowner can reasonably pay. The goal is to reduce the debtor's mortgage payment to 31 percent of his or her gross monthly income.

---

7. Pub. L. No. 110-142, December 7, 2007.

8. Credit reporting agencies also claim that a foreclosure looks much worse on a credit report than a bankruptcy.

9. Higher limits are allowed for properties with two to four units.

The loan is then restructured by adding any delinquencies (such as accrued interest, past-due taxes, or unpaid insurance premiums) to the principal amount. This increases the number of payments but eliminates the delinquencies by spreading them over the life of the loan. Once the loan is restructured, lenders try to incrementally lower the mortgage interest rate to a level at which the payments are less than 31 percent of the debtor's income. If the lender cannot reach the 31 percent target by lowering the interest rate to 2 percent, then the lender can **reamortize** the loan (change the way the payments are configured), extending the schedule of payments for up to forty years.

Borrowers who qualify under HAMP then begin a ninety-day trial period to determine their ability to make three modified monthly mortgage payments. If they succeed, the lender offers them permanent modifications.

VOLUNTARY CONVEYANCE   Under some circumstances, the parties might benefit from a **deed in lieu of foreclosure,** by which the property is conveyed (transferred) to the lender in satisfaction of the mortgage. A property that is worth close to the outstanding loan principal and on which no other loans have been taken might be the subject of such a conveyance.

Although the lender faces the risk that it may ultimately sell the property for less than the loan amount, the lender avoids the time, risk, and expense of foreclosure litigation. The borrower who gives the property to the lender without a fight also avoids the foreclosure process and may preserve a better credit rating than if he or she had been forced to give up the property involuntarily.

FRIENDLY FORECLOSURE   Another way for the parties to avoid a contested foreclosure is to engage in a friendly foreclosure. In such a transaction, the borrower in default agrees to submit to the court's jurisdiction, to waive any defenses as well as the right to appeal, and to cooperate with the lender. This process takes longer than a voluntary conveyance, but all of the parties have greater certainty as to the finality of the transaction with respect to others who might have a financial interest in the property.

PREPACKAGED BANKRUPTCY   Bankruptcy allows a borrower to escape payment of some debts (see Chapter 12). A prepackaged bankruptcy allows a debtor to negotiate terms with all of her or his creditors in advance. The package of agreements is then submitted to the bankruptcy court for approval. This approach to bankruptcy will likely save considerable time and expense for all parties involved, although the creditors are also likely to receive less than full payment on their particular debts.

The Foreclosure Procedure

If all efforts to find another solution fail, the lender will proceed to foreclosure—a process that dates back to English law. A formal foreclosure is necessary to extinguish the borrower's *equitable right of redemption* (discussed later). Generally, two types of foreclosure are used in the United States: **judicial foreclosure** and **power of sale foreclosure.** In a judicial foreclosure, which is available in all states, a court supervises the process. In a power of sale foreclosure, the lender is allowed to foreclose on and sell the property without judicial supervision.

Only a few states permit power of sale foreclosures because borrowers have less protection when a court does not supervise the process. In these states, lenders must strictly comply with the terms of the state statute governing power of sale foreclosures. The following case turned on whether two banks that had foreclosed on certain properties had the right to do so under the power of sale foreclosure law of Massachusetts.

Reamortize   Restart the amortization schedule (a table of the periodic payments the borrower makes to pay off a debt), changing the way the payments are configured.

Deed in Lieu of Foreclosure   An alternative to foreclosure in which the mortgagor voluntarily conveys the property to the lender in satisfaction of the mortgage.

Judicial Foreclosure   A court-supervised foreclosure proceeding in which the court determines the validity of the debt and, if the borrower is in default, issues a judgment for the lender.

Power of Sale Foreclosure   A foreclosure procedure that is not court supervised and is available only in some states.

Case 13.2   U.S. Bank National Association v. Ibanez

Supreme Judicial Court of Massachusetts, 458 Mass. 637, 941 N.E.2d 40 (2011).

America experiences more foreclosures.

BACKGROUND AND FACTS   Mortgage, Inc., issued Antonio Ibanez a $103,500 home loan, and Option One Mortgage issued Mark and Tammy LaRace a $129,000 home loan. Each of the loans subsequently changed hands several times through various banks, as is common in the mortgage-lending industry. Both Ibanez and the LaRaces defaulted on their mortgages. U.S. Bank National Association foreclosed on the Ibanez mortgage, and Wells Fargo foreclosed on the LaRace mortgage. Both banks published notices of the foreclosure sales in a newspaper, as required by statute, and then bought the homes at the foreclosure auctions. Both banks purchased the properties for significantly less than the purported market value. At the time of the foreclosures, each bank represented that it was the "owner (assignee) and holder" of the mortgage. The banks filed separate lawsuits in a Massachusetts state court seeking a declaration that the banks now owned the properties. Neither bank, however, produced any signed documents showing that the mortgage had been properly assigned to it before the foreclosure sale. U.S. Bank received a written assignment of the mortgage more than a year after the foreclosure sale, and Wells Fargo received an assignment ten months after the sale. The court held that the banks, which were not the original mortgagees, had failed to show that they were holders of the mortgages at the time of the foreclosures. The banks appealed, and the cases were consolidated for appeal.

IN THE WORDS OF THE COURT . . .

GANT, J. [Justice]
* * * *

Recognizing the substantial power that the statutory scheme affords to a mortgage holder to foreclose *without immediate judicial oversight, we adhere to the familiar rule that "one who sells under a power [of sale] must follow strictly its terms. If he fails to do so there is no valid execution of the power, and the sale is wholly void."* [Emphasis added.]

One of the terms of the power of sale that must be strictly adhered to is the restriction on who is entitled to foreclose. The "statutory power of sale" can be exercised by "the mortgagee or his executors, administrators, successors or assigns." * * * *Any effort to foreclose by a party lacking "jurisdiction and authority" to carry out a foreclosure under these statutes is void.* [Emphasis added.]
* * * *

For the plaintiffs [U.S. Bank and Wells Fargo] to obtain the judicial declaration of clear title that they seek, they had to prove their authority to foreclose under the power of sale and show their compliance with the requirements on which this authority rests. Here, the plaintiffs were not the original mortgagees to whom the power of sale was granted; rather, they claimed the authority to foreclose as the eventual assignees of the original mortgagees. Under the plain

language of [the relevant state statutes] the plaintiffs had the authority to exercise the power of sale contained in the Ibanez and LaRace mortgages only if they were the assignees of the mortgages at the time of the notice of sale and the subsequent foreclosure sale.
* * * *

Focusing first on the Ibanez mortgage, U.S. Bank argues that it was assigned the mortgage under the trust agreement[a] described in [a memorandum submitted as evidence], but it did not submit a copy of this trust agreement to the judge. * * * U.S. Bank did not produce the schedule of loans and mortgages that was an exhibit to that agreement, so it failed to show that the Ibanez mortgage was among the mortgages to be assigned by that agreement. Finally, even if there were an executed trust agreement with the required schedule, U.S. Bank failed to furnish any evidence that the entity assigning the mortgage—Structured Asset Securities Corporation—ever held the mortgage to be assigned. The last assignment of the mortgage on record was from Rose Mortgage to Option One; nothing was submitted to the judge indicating that Option One ever assigned the mortgage to anyone before the foreclosure sale. Thus, based on the documents submitted to the judge, Option One, not U.S. Bank, was the mortgage holder at the time of the foreclosure, and U.S. Bank did not have the authority to foreclose the mortgage.

Turning to the LaRace mortgage, Wells Fargo claims that, before it issued the foreclosure notice, it was assigned the LaRace mortgage under the PSA [a pooling and servicing agreement that it had submitted to the court]. * * * But the mortgage loan schedule Wells Fargo submitted failed to identify with adequate specificity the LaRace mortgage as one of the mortgages assigned in the PSA. Moreover, Wells Fargo provided the judge with no document that reflected that the ABFC [Asset Backed Funding Corporation, the assignor in the transaction] held the LaRace mortgage that it was purportedly [supposedly] assigning in the PSA. As with the Ibanez loan, the record holder of the LaRace loan was Option One, and nothing was submitted to the judge which demonstrated that the LaRace loan was ever assigned by Option One to another entity before the publication of the notice and the sale.

DECISION AND REMEDY   The Supreme Judicial Court of Massachusetts affirmed the lower court's ruling in favor of the defendants (Ibanez and the LaRaces). U.S. Bank had failed to show that the Ibanez mortgage was among the mortgages assigned by the trust agreement. Wells Fargo had failed to demonstrate that it was the holder of the LaRace mortgage. Thus, the banks did not have the authority to foreclose, and the foreclosure sales were invalid.

THE ECONOMIC DIMENSION   *After the court's ruling, the price of Wells Fargo's stock dropped by about 3.4 percent. Why would a court's decision regarding a few mortgages affect the company's stock price?*

---

a. In recent years, due to the large numbers of foreclosures, banks and mortgage companies have increasingly transferred some of their mortgages in default into mortgage-backed trusts, or pools.

Case 13.2—Continued

MANAGERIAL IMPLICATIONS   *There was no dispute that the mortgagors of the properties (Ibanez and the LaRaces) had defaulted on their obligations and that the mortgaged properties were subject to foreclosure. The question was whether the lenders had kept proper records to prove that they held the mortgages on the properties at the time of the notice and sale. The two banks failed to show that they had received assignments of the mortgages. The court noted that a foreclosing entity can provide either (1) a complete* chain of assignments linking it to the record holder of the mortgage or (2) a single assignment from the record holder of the mortgage. But because these banks had exhibited what the court characterized as "utter carelessness" in documenting the titles to their assets, they lost the case. This should be a lesson to all business owners and managers to keep their records and paperwork in order, particularly with regard to ownership of assets.

ACCELERATION CLAUSES   In a strict foreclosure, the lender may seek only the amount of the missed payments, not the entire loan amount. Therefore, lenders often include an *acceleration clause* in their loan documents. An **acceleration clause** allows the lender to call the entire loan due—even if only one payment is late or missed. Thus, with an acceleration clause, the lender can foreclose only once on the entire amount of the loan rather than having to foreclose on smaller amounts over a period of time as each payment is missed.

Acceleration Clause A clause in a mortgage loan contract that makes the entire loan balance become due if the borrower misses or is late in making only one monthly mortgage payment.

NOTICE OF DEFAULT AND OF SALE   To initiate a foreclosure, a lender must record a **notice of default** with the appropriate county office. The borrower is then on notice of a possible foreclosure and can take steps to pay the loan and cure the default. If the loan is not paid within a reasonable time (usually three months), the borrower will receive a **notice of sale**. In addition, the notice of sale usually is posted on the property, recorded with the county, and published in a newspaper.

Notice of Default A formal notice to a borrower that he or she is in default on mortgage payments and may face foreclosure if the payments are not brought up to date. The notice is filed by the lender in the county where the property is located.

Notice of Sale A formal notice to a borrower who is in default on a mortgage that the mortgaged property will be sold in a foreclosure proceeding. The notice is sent to the borrower and is typically recorded with the county, posted on the property, and published in a newspaper.

The property is then sold in an auction on the courthouse steps at the time and location indicated in the notice of sale. The buyer generally has to pay cash within twenty-four hours for the property. If the procedures are not followed precisely, the parties may have to resort to litigation to establish clear ownership of the property. The following case illustrates how the notice requirements work.

Case 13.3   **Mitchell v. Valteau**

Court of Appeal of Louisiana, Fourth Circuit, 30 So.3d 1108 (2010).
www.la4th.org/Opinions.aspx[a]

(© Flickr/Creative Commons/Jacob Ruff)

A sheriff delivers a writ of seizure.

BACKGROUND AND FACTS   In 2001, Dr. Pamela Mitchell borrowed $143,724 to purchase a house and lot. The loan was secured by a mortgage on the property. The mortgage provided for the sale of the property in the event of a default. In 2006, Mitchell defaulted on her mortgage payments. The lending bank commenced a foreclosure proceeding, and the trial court ordered the issuance of a writ of seizure and sale. On January 23, 2007, Mitchell was served personally with a notice of seizure and the date of the sheriff's sale. Subsequently, the lending bank and Mitchell entered into a repayment agreement that postponed the seizure and sale. Mitchell made two payments and then was unable to comply with the payment terms of the new agreement. The trial court ordered that the original petition be amended and that an amended writ of seizure be issued, which the sheriff completed. The sheriff was unable to serve Mitchell at her residence on seven occasions, however. Therefore, the court appointed a receiver who accepted the service of process on Mitchell's behalf. On January 3, 2008, the property was sold at a sheriff's sale. Several months later, Mitchell filed a petition to annul the judicial sale and to ask for damages for wrongful seizure against the sheriff, Paul Valteau, as well as the lending bank and others. The bank filed a motion for summary judgment, which the trial court granted. Mitchell appealed.

---

a. From the search mode choices, select "Search Cases by Published Date." When that page opens, select "Click for Calendar." Using the arrow at the top of the calendar, go to January 2010, select "27," and then click on "Search." Scroll through the list at the bottom of the page to the case title and click on "Download" to access the opinion. The Louisiana court system maintains this Web site.

Case 13.3—Continues next page ➡

Case 13.3–Continued

IN THE WORDS OF THE COURT . . .
Patricia Rivet MURRAY, Judge.
* * * *

A creditor seeking to enforce a mortgage or privilege on property by executory process must file a petition praying for the seizure and sale of the property affected by the mortgage or privilege. * * * In this case, [the bank] filed a petition for executor process and attached thereto authentic evidence satisfying all three requirements for obtaining an order of seizure and sale: a copy of the note, mortgage agreement, and a certified copy of the assignment of the mortgage note to it. * * * It is undisputed that Dr. Mitchell was served with the initial notice of seizure. Dr. Mitchell, however, contends that the sheriff also was required to serve her with the amended notice of seizure from which her property was seized and sold. [Emphasis added.]

Resolution of the issue of whether service of the amended notice of seizure was required turns on construction of several * * * statutory provisions. La. C.C.P. Art. [Louisiana Code of Civil Procedure Article] 2721 provides that the sheriff must serve upon the defendant "a written notice of the seizure of the property. ["] La. C.C.P. Art. 2293(B) also provides that the sheriff shall serve "a notice of seizure."
* * * *

Construing La. R.S. [Louisiana Revised Statutes] 13:3852 and La. C.C.P. Art. 2293(B) * * * [a prior court] rejected a debtor's argument that she was entitled to a second notice of seizure when the first sale was delayed.
* * * *

The situation in this case is analogous to the situation presented in the [referenced] case. Dr. Mitchell defaulted on her loan agreement and [the bank] established its right to proceed by executory process to seize and sell the Property. Dr. Mitchell was served with a notice of seizure. Thereafter, she entered into the repayment agreement, [which] expressly provided that the executor proceeding would be placed on hold for the time the repayment agreement was in place. The agreement also provided for the resumption of the foreclosure in the event of a default in its terms, which Dr. Mitchell acknowledged occurred. When the executory proceeding was resumed, there was no obligation to serve Dr. Mitchell with another notice of seizure.

DECISION AND REMEDY The Louisiana appellate court upheld the trial court's decision. There was no obligation to serve Mitchell with another notice of seizure.

THE ETHICAL DIMENSION *What is the underlying purpose for requiring lenders to serve a written notice of seizure of property? Was the court's holding fair to Mitchell? Why or why not?*

THE LEGAL ENVIRONMENT DIMENSION *How might the lender have avoided the dispute in this case?*

Deficiency Judgment A judgment against the borrower for the amount of debt remaining unpaid after the collateral is sold.

DEFICIENCY JUDGMENTS If any equity remains after the foreclosed property is sold, the borrower is often able to keep the difference between the sale price and the mortgage amount. If the sale amount is not enough to cover the loan amount, the lender (in the majority of states) can ask a court for a **deficiency judgment.** A deficiency judgment requires the borrower to make up the difference to the lender over time. Note that some states do not allow deficiency judgments for mortgaged residential real estate.

Redemption Rights

Borrowers in every state have the right to purchase the property after default by paying the full amount of the debt, plus any interest and costs that have accrued, before the foreclosure sale. This is referred to as the buyer's **equitable right of redemption.** Equitable redemption allows a defaulting borrower to gain title and regain possession of a property.[10] The idea behind equitable redemption is that it is only fair, or equitable, for the borrower to have a chance to regain possession after default. Although many critics question the utility of this right, all states still allow for an equitable right of redemption.

Some states have passed laws that entitle a borrower to repurchase property even *after* a judicial foreclosure.[11] This is called a **statutory right of redemption,** and it may

Equitable Right of Redemption The right of a borrower who is in default on a mortgage loan to redeem or purchase the property prior to foreclosure proceedings.

Statutory Right of Redemption A right provided by statute in some states that allows borrowers to redeem or repurchase their property after a judicial foreclosure for a limited period of time.

---

10. Note that a foreclosure proceeding is the legal means by which a lender terminates the borrower's equitable right of redemption.

11. This right of redemption is not available after a power of sale foreclosure.

be exercised even if the property was purchased at auction by a third party. Generally, the borrower may exercise this right for up to one year from the time the house is sold at a foreclosure sale.[12] The borrower[13] must pay the price at which the house was sold at the foreclosure sale (the redemption price), plus taxes, interest, and assessments, as opposed to the balance owed on the foreclosed loan.

Some states allow the borrower to retain possession of the property after the foreclosure sale until the statutory redemption period ends. If the borrower does not exercise the right of redemption, the new buyer receives title to and possession of the property. The statutes creating this right were enacted to drive up sale prices at foreclosure auctions on the theory that third parties would offer prices too high for defaulting borrowers to afford. Instead, in many states, the statutory right of redemption has created a strong disincentive for potential buyers to tie up their funds in an uncertain transaction.

---

12. Some states do not allow a borrower to waive the statutory right of redemption. This means that a buyer at auction must wait one year to obtain title to, and possession of, a foreclosed property.

13. Some states also allow the spouse of a defaulting borrower or creditors holding liens on the property to purchase the property under the statutory right of redemption.

 Reviewing . . . Mortgages and Foreclosures after the Recession

Al and Betty Smith's home is valued at $200,000. They have paid off their mortgage and own the house outright—that is, they have 100 percent home equity. They lost most of their savings when the stock market declined during the Great Recession. Now they want to start a new business and need funds, so they decide to obtain a home equity loan. They borrow $150,000 for ten years at an interest rate of 12 percent. On the date they take out the loan, a ten-year Treasury bond is yielding 3 percent. The Smiths pay a total of $10,000 in fees to Alpha Bank. The Smiths are not given any notice that they can lose their home if they do not meet their obligations under the loan. Two weeks after completing the loan, the Smiths change their minds and want to rescind the loan.

1. Is the Smiths' loan covered by the Truth-in-Lending Act as amended by the Home Ownership and Equity Protection Act? Why or why not?

2. Do the Smiths have a right to rescind the loan two weeks after the fact, or are they too late? Explain.

3. Assume now that Alpha Bank gave the Smiths all of the required notices before the loan was completed. If all other facts remain the same, do the Smiths have a right to rescind? Discuss your answer.

4. Suppose now that the Smiths never rescind the loan and that they default four years later while still owing Alpha Bank $120,000. The bank forecloses and raises only $110,000 when the house is sold at auction. If the state where the Smiths live follows the rule in most states, can Alpha Bank seek the remaining $10,000 from the Smiths?

 Key Terms

acceleration clause 393	deed in lieu of foreclosure 391	hybrid mortgage 383	reamortize 391
adjustable-rate	default 388	interest-only (IO) mortgage 382	reverse mortgage 383
mortgage (ARM) 381	down payment 381	judicial foreclosure 391	short sale 389
annual percentage	equitable right of	mortgage 381	statutory right of
rate (APR) 385	redemption 394	negative amortization 387	redemption 394
appraiser 385	fixed-rate mortgage 381	notice of default 393	subprime mortgage 382
average prime offer rate 388	forbearance 389	notice of sale 393	Treasury securities 386
balloon mortgage 383	foreclosure 388	power of sale foreclosure 391	workout agreement 389
bridge loan 388	home equity loan 383	prepayment penalty	
construction loan 382	homeowners' insurance 384	clause 384	

Chapter Summary: Mortgages and Foreclosures after the Recession

Mortgages (See pages 381–384.)	1. *Types of mortgages*—A mortgage loan is a contract between a creditor (mortgagee) and a borrower (mortgagor). A down payment is the part of the purchase price that is paid up front. There are many types of mortgages, including: 　a. Fixed-rate mortgages, which are standard mortgages with a fixed rate of interest and payments that stay the same for the duration of the loan. 　b. Adjustable-rate mortgages (ARMs), in which the interest rate changes periodically, usually starting low and increasing over time. 　c. Interest-only mortgages, which allow borrowers to pay only the interest portion of the monthly payments for a limited time, after which the size of the payment increases. 　d. Subprime mortgages, which carry higher rates of interest because they are made to borrowers who do not qualify for standard mortgages. 　e. Construction loans, which finance the building of a new house and are often set up to release funds at particular stages of the project. 2. *Creditor protection*—When creditors grant mortgages, they take a number of steps to protect their interests. They may require private mortgage insurance if borrowers do not make a down payment of at least 20 percent of the home's purchase price. A creditor also usually records the mortgage with the county in which the property is located to notify all others of its interest in the property. Several provisions typically included in the mortgage contract also protect the lenders' interests. These include prepayment penalty clauses and clauses requiring the borrower to maintain homeowners' insurance.
Real Estate Financing Law (See pages 384–388.)	1. *Predatory lending*—This term describes situations in which borrowers are the victims of loan terms or lending procedures that are excessive, deceptive, or not properly disclosed. 　a. Steering and targeting occurs when a lender manipulates a borrower into a loan that benefits the lender but is not the best loan for the borrower. 　b. Loan flipping occurs when a lender convinces a borrower to refinance soon after a mortgage term begins. 2. *Truth-in-Lending Act (TILA)*—This federal statute requires mortgage lenders to disclose the terms of a loan in clear, readily understandable language on standardized forms. 　a. Terms that must be disclosed include the loan principal, the interest rate at which the loan is made, the annual percentage rate, and all fees and costs. 　b. The TILA prohibits certain unfair lender practices, such as charging prepayment penalties on most subprime mortgages and home equity loans and coercing an appraiser into misstating the value of property. 　c. A borrower has the right to rescind a mortgage within three business days. If a lender does not provide the required disclosures, the rescission period runs for three years. 3. *High-cost mortgages*—The Home Ownership and Equity Protection Act (HOEPA) of 1994 created a special category of high-cost and high-fee mortgage products. Rules for the loans are in Regulation Z. 　a. HOEPA rules apply to loans that carry a high rate of interest or entail high fees. 　b. In addition to the TILA disclosures, HOEPA requires lenders to make several other disclosures. These include the APR; the regular payment amount; any balloon payments; that the home may be lost if the borrower defaults; that the rate and payment amounts of variable-rate loans may increase; and what the maximum increase could be. HOEPA also prohibits short-term loans requiring balloon payments and loans that result in negative amortization. 　c. On a lender's material failure to disclose, a consumer may receive damages equal to all finance charges and fees paid. If a lender fails to comply with HOEPA, the borrower's right to rescind is extended to three years. 4. *Higher-priced mortgages*—A 2008 amendment to Regulation Z gave protection to consumers of a second category of expensive loans called Higher-Priced Mortgage Loans (HPMLs). To qualify as an HPML, a mortgage must have an APR that exceeds the average prime offer rate by a certain amount for a comparable transaction.

Chapter Summary: Mortgages and Foreclosures after the Recession, Continued

Foreclosures
(See pages 388–395.)
	If a borrower defaults, or fails to pay a loan, the lender can foreclose on the mortgaged property. The foreclosure process allows a lender to repossess and auction the property. A foreclosure can be expensive and remains on a borrower's credit report for seven years.
	1. *Ways to avoid foreclosure proceedings*—
	  a. A forbearance and workout agreement.
	  b. An interest-free loan from the U.S. Department of Housing and Urban Development.
	  c. A short sale.
	  d. A sale to an investor and leaseback to the former owner.
	  e. A modification of monthly payments under the Home Affordable Modification Program.
	  f. A deed in lieu of foreclosure.
	  g. A friendly foreclosure.
	  h. A prepackaged bankruptcy.
	2. *Foreclosure procedures*—
	  a. In a judicial foreclosure, which is available in all states, a court supervises the process.
	  b. In a power of sale foreclosure, which is permitted in only a few states, the lender can foreclose on and sell the property without judicial supervision.
	  c. An acceleration clause allows a lender to call an entire loan due, even if only one payment is late or missed.
	  d. To initiate a foreclosure, a lender records a notice of default with the county. If the amount due on the loan is not paid, the borrower receives a notice of sale, which also usually appears in a newspaper and is posted on the property.
	  e. Borrowers in every state have the equitable right to purchase the property after default by paying the full amount of the debt, plus any accrued interest and costs, before the foreclosure sale. In some states, a borrower has a statutory right to repurchase the property even after a judicial sale.
	  f. If the sale proceeds do not cover the amount of the loan, the lender can ask a court for a deficiency judgment. Some states do not permit deficiency judgments for mortgaged residential property.
	3. *Redemption rights*—
	  a. Equitable right of redemption—In all of the states, borrowers have the right to purchase the property after default by paying the full amount of the debt, plus any interest and costs that have accrued, before the foreclosure sale.
	  b. Statutory right of redemption—Some states allow borrowers to repurchase property even *after* a judicial foreclosure.

 ExamPrep

ISSUE SPOTTERS

1. Ruth Ann borrows $175,000 from Sunny Valley Bank to buy a home. Federal law regulates primarily the terms of the mortgage that must be disclosed in writing in clear, readily understandable language. What are the major terms that must be disclosed under the Truth-in-Lending Act?

2. Tanner borrows $150,000 from Southeast Credit Union to buy a home, which secures the loan. Two years into the term, Tanner stops making payments on the loan. After six months without payments, Southeast informs Tanner that he is in default and that it will proceed to foreclosure. What is foreclosure, and what is the usual procedure?

—**Check your answers to these questions against the answers provided in Appendix G.**

BEFORE THE TEST

Go to **www.cengagebrain.com**, enter the ISBN number "9781111530617," and click on "Find" to locate this textbook's Web site. Then, click on "Access Now" under "Study Tools," and select "Chapter 13" at the top. There you will find an "Interactive Quiz" that you can take to assess your mastery of the concepts in this chapter, as well as "Flashcards" and a "Glossary" of important terms.

For Review

1. What is a subprime mortgage? How does it differ from a standard fixed-rate mortgage? What is a home equity loan?
2. When is private mortgage insurance required? Which party does it protect?
3. Does the Truth-in-Lending Act (TILA) apply to all mortgages? How do the TILA provisions protect borrowers and curb abusive practices by mortgage lenders?
4. What is a short sale? How might a short sale be more advantageous than a mortgage foreclosure for a borrower, and what impact does it have on the balance owed to the lender on the mortgage loan?
5. In a mortgage foreclosure, what legal rights do mortgage holders have if the sale proceeds are insufficient to pay the underlying debt?

 Questions and Case Problems

13–1. Disclosure Requirements. Rancho Mortgage, Inc., is planning a new advertising campaign designed to attract home-buyers in a difficult economic environment. Rancho wants to promote its new loan product, which offers a fixed interest rate for the first five years and then switches to a variable rate of interest. Rancho believes that Spanish-speaking homebuyers have been underserved in recent years, and it wants to direct its ads to that market. What must Rancho say (and not say) in its advertising campaigns about the structure of the loan product, and in what language? What language should Rancho use in its Truth-in-Lending disclosures? Why?

13–2. Real Estate Financing. Jane Lane refinanced her mortgage with Central Equity, Inc. Central Equity split the transaction into two separate loan documents with separate Truth-in-Lending disclosure statements and settlement statements. Two years later, Lane sought to exercise her right to rescission under the Home Ownership and Equity Protection Act (HOEPA), but Central Equity refused. Central Equity responded that the original transactions comprised two separate loan transactions and because neither loan imposed sufficient fees and costs to trigger HOEPA, its protections did not apply. Lane claims that if the costs and fees were combined into a single transaction (which Lane expected the loan to be), they would surpass the HOEPA threshold and trigger its protections. In turn, because Central Equity did not provide the necessary disclosures under HOEPA, Lane argues that she can properly rescind under its provisions. Is Lane correct? Does loan splitting allow the lender to count each loan transaction with a borrower separately for HOEPA purposes? Why or why not?

13–3. Lender's Options. In 2008, Frank relocated and purchased a home in a beautiful mountain town. The home was five years old, and Frank purchased it for $450,000. He paid $90,000 as a down payment and financed the remaining $360,000 of the purchase price with a loan from Bank of Town. Frank signed mortgage documents that gave Bank of Town a mortgage interest in the home. Frank made payments on the loan for three years. But the housing market declined significantly, and Frank's home is now valued at only $265,000. The balance due on his loan is $354,000. In addition to the decline in housing prices, the economy has slowed, and the booming business that Frank started when he bought the home has experienced a decrease in revenues. It seems inevitable that Frank will not be able to make his mortgage payments. Discuss Bank of Town's options in this situation.

13–4. Home Ownership and Equity Protection Act. Michael and Edith Jones owned a home that went into foreclosure. During this time, they were contacted by a representative of Rees-Max, whose notice read: "There are only a few months to go in your redemption period! Your options to save the equity in your home are fading. Call me immediately for a no-bull, no-obligation assessment of your situation. Even if you have been 'promised' by a mortgage broker or investor that they will help, CALL ME . . . ." The Joneses contacted Rees-Max, and they entered into a sale and lease-back transaction. Rees-Max would purchase the property from the Joneses, the Joneses would lease the property for a few months, and then the Joneses would purchase the property back from Rees-Max on a contract. The property was appraised at $278,000 and purchased by Rees-Max for $214,000, with more than $30,000 in fees. The Joneses disputed these fees, and Rees-Max moved to evict them. The agreement did not use the terms *debt, security,* or *mortgage,* and the documents stated that no security interest was granted. Does this transaction constitute a mortgage that would receive protection under the Truth-in-Lending Act and the Home Ownership and Equity Protection Act? Why or why not? [*Jones v. Rees-Max, LLC,* 514 F.Supp.2d 1139 (D.Minn. 2007)]

13–5. Right of Rescission. George and Mona Antanuos obtained a mortgage loan secured with rental property from the First National Bank of Arizona. At the closing, they received from the bank a "Notice of Right to Cancel," informing them of their three-day rescission period under the Truth-in-Lending Act (TILA). The following day, according to the Antanuoses, they informed the lender via fax that they wished to exercise their right to rescind. The lender refused to rescind the agreement. George and Mona sued the bank. In federal court, the Antanuoses did not dispute that a consumer's right to rescind under the TILA applies only to the consumer's original dwelling and that they had used their commercial property as a security interest. Instead, the Antanuoses argued that the bank was prohibited from denying them the rescission right because they relied to their detriment on the bank's disclosure, which would have been required under the TILA. Would the court be convinced? Explain. [*Antanuos v. First National Bank of Arizona,* 508 F.Supp.2d 466 (E.D.Va. 2007)]

13–6. Mortgage Foreclosure. In January 2003, Gary Ryder and Washington Mutual Bank, F.A., executed a note in which Ryder promised to pay $2,450,000, plus interest at a rate that could vary from month to month. The amount of the first payment was $10,933. The note was to be paid in full by February 1, 2033. A mortgage on Ryder's real property at 345 Round Hill Road in Greenwich, Connecticut, in favor of the bank secured his obligations under the note. The note and mortgage required that he pay the taxes on the property, which he did not do in 2004 and 2005. The bank notified him that he was in default and, when he failed to act, paid $50,095.92 in taxes, penalties, interest, and fees. Other disputes arose between the parties, and Ryder filed a suit in a federal district court against the bank, alleging, in part, breach of contract. He charged, among other things, that some of his timely payments were not processed and were subjected to incorrect late fees, forcing him to make excessive payments and ultimately resulting in "nonpayment by Ryder." The bank filed a counterclaim, seeking to foreclose on the mortgage. What should a creditor be required to prove to foreclose on mortgaged property? What would be a debtor's most effective defense? Which party in this case is likely to prevail on the bank's counterclaim? Why? [*Ryder v. Washington Mutual Bank, F.A.,* 501 F.Supp.2d 311 (D.Conn. 2007)]

13–7. **Case Problem with Sample Answer. Wrongful Foreclosure.** After the debtors experienced a series of bankruptcies and foreclosures, Wells Fargo Home Mortgage, the mortgagee, foreclosed on the debtors' home and purchased it for $33,500. The debtors then filed a complaint against Wells Fargo and certain related entities, claiming wrongful foreclosure and breach of contract. The debtors sought damages, specific performance, and other remedies. The dispute grew out of a loan note for $51,300 that the debtors had executed with Southern Atlantic Financial Services, Inc. In exchange for that loan, the debtors gave Southern Atlantic a security interest in their home. Southern Atlantic transferred its interest in the property and the note to GE Capital Mortgage Services, Inc. On September 30, 2000, Wells Fargo Home Mortgage started servicing this loan for GE. Wells Fargo acquired the loan from GE on December 1, 2004. When the debtors did not make all of the required payments, Wells Fargo sought relief from

a stay to file a foreclosure because the debtors were in arrears on the mortgage. The parties agreed that Wells Fargo could have relief from the stay if the debtors failed to make all future payments. Claiming default, Wells Fargo then filed a foreclosure and bought the property at the sale. The debtors filed a complaint alleging that the price paid was shockingly insufficient and constituted wrongful foreclosure and a breach of fiduciary duty. Under what circumstances is a foreclosure sale unfair? Does a foreclosure sale have to realize the market price for the property? The amount owed on the note? Discuss. [*In re Sharpe,* 425 Bankr. 620 (N.D.Ala. 2010)]

—To view a sample answer for Case Problem 13–7, go to Appendix F at the end of this text.

13–8. Foreclosure on Mortgage and Liens. LaSalle Bank loaned $8 million to Cypress Creek to build an apartment complex. The loan was secured by a mortgage. Cypress Creek hired contractors to provide concrete work, plumbing, carpentry, and other construction services. Cypress Creek went bankrupt, owing LaSalle $3 million. The contractors recorded mechanic's liens when they did not get paid for their work. The property was sold to LaSalle at a sheriff's sale for $1.3 million. The contractors claimed that they should be paid the amounts they were owed out of the $1.3 million and that the mechanic's liens should be satisfied before any funds were distributed to LaSalle for its mortgage. The trial court distributed the $1.3 million primarily to LaSalle, with only a small fraction going to the contractors. Do the liens come before the mortgage in priority of payment? Discuss. [*LaSalle Bank v. Cypress Creek,* ___ N.E.2d ___ (Ill.App.3d 2011)]

13–9. **A Question of Ethics. Predatory Lending.** *Peter Sutton owned a home that was subject to two mortgages, but his only source of income was a $1,080 monthly Social Security benefit. In an effort to reduce his mortgage payments, which exceeded $1,400 per month, he sought a refinancing loan through an Apex Mortgage Services mortgage broker. According to Sutton, the broker led him to believe that he could receive, from Countrywide Home Loans, Inc., a refinancing loan with payments of $428 per month. The broker, however, ultimately arranged for Sutton to receive an adjustable-rate loan from Countrywide. The loan required monthly payments that started at more than $1,000 per month and were subject to further increases. Sutton also alleged that the broker reported his monthly income as four times the actual amount and failed to inform Sutton about the existence of a prepayment penalty. Sutton signed forms stating that he agreed to the terms of the loan arranged by the broker. He claimed, however, that he did not understand the terms of the loan until after the closing. As compensation for brokering Sutton's loan, Countrywide paid Apex $7,270, which included a yield-spread premium of $4,710. (A yield-spread premium is a form of compensation paid to a broker by a lender for providing a borrower with a loan that carries an interest rate above the lender's par rate.) Sutton sued the broker and lender claiming violations of federal law. [*Sutton v. Countrywide Home Loans, Inc.,* ___ F.3d ___ (11th Cir. 2009)]*

1. Who is ethically responsible for Sutton's predicament? To what extent does Sutton have a duty to read and understand what he signs? Discuss.
2. Sutton argued that because the broker provided services that were of no value to Sutton, the broker should not receive the yield-spread premium. Do you agree? Why or why not?

3. Did Countrywide, the lender, have any ethical obligation to monitor the activities of the broker? Would the result have been different if Countrywide had intervened before the documents were signed? Explain.

UNIT TWO Cumulative Business Hypothetical

Samuel Polson has an idea for a new software application. Polson hires an assistant and invests a considerable amount of his own time and funds developing the application. To manufacture and market his application and develop other software, Polson needs financial capital.

1. Polson borrows $5,000 from his friend Michael Brant. Polson promises to repay Brant the $5,000 in three weeks. Brant, in urgent need of funds, borrows $5,000 from his friend Mary Viva and assigns his rights to the $5,000 Polson owes him to Viva in return for the loan. Viva notifies Polson of the assignment. Polson pays Brant the $5,000 on the date stipulated in their contract. Brant refuses to give the $5,000 to Viva, and Viva sues Polson. Is Polson obligated to pay Viva $5,000 also? Discuss.

2. Polson learns that a competitor, Trivan, Inc., has already filed for a patent on a nearly identical program and has manufactured and sold the software to some customers. Polson learns from a reliable source that Trivan paid Polson's assistant a substantial sum to obtain a copy of the program. What legal recourse does Polson have against Trivan? Discuss fully.

3. While Polson is developing his idea and founding his business, he has no income. To meet expenses, Polson and his wife begin a home-based baking business for which he orders and has installed a new model X23 McIntyre oven from a local company, Western Heating Appliances. One day, Polson is baking croissants. When he opens the oven, part of the door becomes detached. As he struggles with the door, his hands are badly burned, and he is unable to work for several months. Polson later learns that the hinge mechanism on the door was improperly installed. He wants to sue the oven's manufacturer to recover damages, including consequential damages for lost profits. In a product liability suit against the manufacturer, under what legal principles and doctrines might Polson recover damages? Discuss fully.

4. During the course of the events described in the preceding questions, the payments on Polson's mortgage, his various credit-card debts, and some loans that he took out to pay for his son's college tuition continue to come due. As his software business begins to generate revenue, Polson files for Chapter 7 liquidation. Polson hopes to be rid of his personal debts entirely, even though he believes he could probably pay his creditors off over a four-year period if he scrimped and used every cent available. Are all of Polson's personal debts dischargeable under Chapter 7, including the debts incurred for his son's education? Given that Polson could foreseeably pay off his debts over a four-year period, will the court allow Polson to obtain relief under Chapter 7? Why or why not?

5. Denied a discharge in bankruptcy under Chapter 7, Polson still needs funds to pay his debts and capital to sustain his software business. His home is valued at $200,000. He owes $100,000 on a mortgage on the property. To obtain funds, Polson refinances the loan through Omni Bank, borrowing $200,000 for twenty years at an interest rate of 5.25 percent. During the lending process, Omni's loan officer fails to provide Polson with all of the required disclosures. On the day of the loan, a twenty-year Treasury bond is yielding 2.25 percent. Polson pays $5,500 in fees to the bank. Three months later, with a sudden spike in the software business, Polson wants to cancel the mortgage. Can he rescind the loan? Why or why not?

Unit Three

Business and Employment

Chapter 14

Small Business Organizations

Contents

- **Sole Proprietorships**
- **Partnerships**
- **Limited Liability Partnerships**
- **Limited Partnerships**
- **Limited Liability Companies**
- **Franchises**

Chapter Objectives

After reading this chapter, you should be able to answer the following questions:

1. **What advantages and disadvantages are associated with the sole proprietorship?**

2. **What is meant by joint and several liability? Why is this often considered to be a disadvantage of doing business as a general partnership?**

3. **What advantages do limited liability partnerships offer to entrepreneurs that are not offered by general partnerships?**

4. **What are the key differences between the rights and liabilities of general partners and those of limited partners?**

5. **How are limited liability companies formed, and who decides how they will be managed and operated?**

Entrepreneur One who initiates and assumes the financial risk of a new business enterprise and undertakes to provide or control its management.

Many Americans would agree with Frank Scully's comment in the chapter-opening quotation above that to succeed in business one must "go out on a limb." Certainly, an entrepreneur's primary motive for undertaking a business enterprise is to make profits. An **entrepreneur** is by definition one who initiates and assumes the financial risks of a new enterprise and undertakes to provide or control its management.

One of the questions faced by anyone who wishes to start a business is what form of business organization should be chosen for the business endeavor. In making this determination, the entrepreneur needs to consider a number of factors. Among the most important are (1) ease of creation, (2) the liability of the owners, (3) tax considerations, and (4) the need for capital. In studying this unit on business and employment, keep these factors in mind as you read about the various business organizational forms available to entrepreneurs.

Traditionally, entrepreneurs have used three major forms to structure their business enterprises: the sole proprietorship, the partnership, and the corporation. In this chapter, we examine the forms of business most often used by small business enterprises, including two of these traditional forms—sole proprietorships and partnerships—as well as variations on partnerships, limited liability companies, and franchises. In Chapter 15, we will discuss the third major traditional form of business—the corporation—and summarize and compare aspects of all the business organizations that have been discussed.

Sole Proprietorships

Sole Proprietorship The simplest form of business organization, in which the owner is the business. The owner reports business income on his or her personal income tax return and is legally responsible for all debts and obligations incurred by the business.

The simplest form of business organization is a **sole proprietorship.** In this form, the owner is the business. Thus, anyone who does business without creating a separate business organization has a sole proprietorship. More than two-thirds of all U.S. businesses are sole proprietorships. They are usually small enterprises—about 99 percent of the sole proprietorships in the United States have revenues of less than $1 million per year. Sole proprietors can own and manage any type of business, ranging from an informal, home-office undertaking to a large restaurant or construction firm. Today, a number of online businesses that sell goods and services nationwide are organized as sole proprietorships.

Advantages of the Sole Proprietorship

A major advantage of the sole proprietorship is that the proprietor owns the entire business and has a right to receive all of the profits (because he or she assumes all of the risk). In addition, it is often easier and less costly to start a sole proprietorship than to start any other kind of business, as few legal formalities are involved.[1] One does not need to file any documents with the government to start a sole proprietorship (though a state business license may be required to operate certain businesses).

This form of business organization also allows more flexibility than does a partnership or a corporation. The sole proprietor is free to make any decision she or he wishes concerning the business—including whom to hire, when to take a vacation, and what kind of business to pursue. In addition, the proprietor can sell or transfer all or part of the business to another party at any time and does not need approval from anyone else (as would be required from partners in a partnership or, normally, from shareholders in a corporation).

A sole proprietor pays only personal income taxes (including self-employment tax, which consists of Social Security and Medicare taxes) on the business's profits, which are reported as personal income on the proprietor's personal income tax return. Sole proprietors are also allowed to establish certain retirement accounts that are tax-exempt until the funds are withdrawn.

Disadvantages of the Sole Proprietorship

"Always tell yourself: The difference between running a business and ruining a business is I."

Anonymous

The major disadvantage of the sole proprietorship is that the proprietor alone bears the burden of any losses or liabilities incurred by the business enterprise. In other words, the sole proprietor has unlimited liability, or legal responsibility, for all obligations incurred in doing business. Any lawsuit against the business or its employees can lead to unlimited personal liability for the owner of a sole proprietorship. Creditors can go after the owner's personal assets to satisfy any business debts. This unlimited liability is a major factor to be considered in choosing a business form.

EXAMPLE 14.1 Sheila Fowler operates a golf shop business as a sole proprietorship. The shop is located near one of the best golf courses in the country. A professional golfer, Dean Maheesh, is seriously injured when a display of golf clubs, which one of Fowler's employees has failed to secure, falls on him. If Maheesh sues Fowler's shop (a sole proprietorship) and wins, Fowler's personal liability could easily exceed the

---

1. Although starting a sole proprietorship involves relatively few legal formalities compared with other business organizational forms, even small sole proprietorships may need to comply with certain zoning requirements, obtain appropriate licenses, and the like.

(Salim Fadhley/Creative Commons)

This woman is creating floral arrangements. She owns the business by herself. What are the advantages of doing business as a sole proprietorship?

limits of her insurance policy. In this situation, not only might Fowler lose her business, but she could also lose her house, her car, and any other personal assets that can be attached to pay the judgment. ●

The sole proprietorship also has the disadvantage of lacking continuity on the death of the proprietor. When the owner dies, so does the business—it is automatically dissolved. Another disadvantage is that the proprietor's opportunity to raise capital is limited to personal funds and the funds of those who are willing to make loans.

▶ Partnerships

A *partnership* arises from an agreement, express or implied, between two or more persons to carry on a business for profit. Partners are co-owners of a business and have joint control over its operation and the right to share in its profits.

Partnerships are governed both by common law concepts—in particular, those relating to agency (discussed in Chapter 16)—and by statutory law. The National Conference of Commissioners on Uniform State Laws has drafted the Uniform Partnership Act (UPA), which governs the operation of partnerships *in the absence of express agreement* and has done much to reduce controversies in the law relating to partnerships. In other words, the partners are free to establish rules for their partnership that differ from those stated in the UPA.

The UPA has undergone several major revisions since it was first issued in 1914. Except for Louisiana, every state has adopted the UPA. The majority of states have adopted the most recent version of the UPA, which was issued in 1994 and amended in 1997 to provide limited liability for partners in a limited liability partnership. We therefore base our discussion of the UPA in this chapter on the 1997 version of the act.

Agency Concepts and Partnership Law

When two or more persons agree to do business as partners, they enter into a special relationship with one another. To an extent, their relationship is similar to an agency relationship because each partner is deemed to be the agent of the other partners and of the partnership. The common law agency concepts you will read about in Chapter 16 thus apply—specifically, the imputation of knowledge of, and responsibility for, acts done within the scope of the partnership relationship. In their relations with one another, partners, like agents, are bound by fiduciary ties.

In one important way, however, partnership law is distinct from agency law. A partnership is based on a voluntary contract between two or more competent persons who agree to contribute financial capital, labor, and skill to a business with the understanding that profits and losses will be shared. In a nonpartnership agency relationship, the agent usually does not have an ownership interest in the business, nor is he or she obliged to bear a portion of the ordinary business losses.

When Does a Partnership Exist?

Conflicts sometimes arise over whether a business enterprise is legally a partnership, especially in the absence of a formal, written partnership agreement. The UPA defines a **partnership** as "an association of two or more persons to carry on as co-owners

Partnership An agreement by two or more persons to carry on, as co-owners, a business for profit.

Partnerships offer advantages, but they also have disadvantages—the main one being the unlimited personal liability of all partners. Some large accounting firms have therefore gone to great lengths to reduce potential partner liability. Shown here is an annual meeting of Ernst & Young, a firm with more than 140,000 employees in 140 countries. This accounting services business has created separate legal entities to provide services to clients, thereby reducing exposure to liability for the acts of employees working in other countries for clients.

(Rob Lee/Creative Commons)

a business for profit" [UPA 101(6)]. Note that under the UPA a corporation is a "person" [UPA 101(10)]. The *intent* to associate is a key element of a partnership, and a person cannot join a partnership unless all of the other partners consent [UPA 401(i)].

In resolving disputes over whether partnership status exists, courts usually look for the following three essential elements, which are implicit in the UPA's definition of a partnership:

1. A sharing of profits and losses.
2. A joint ownership of the business.
3. An equal right to be involved in the management of the business.

Joint ownership of property, obviously, does not in and of itself create a partnership. In fact, the sharing of gross revenues and even profits from such ownership is usually not enough to create a partnership [UPA 202(c)(1), (2)]. **EXAMPLE 14.2** Chiang and Burke jointly own a piece of rural property. They lease the land to a farmer, with the understanding that—in lieu of set rental payments—they will receive a share of the profits from the farming operation conducted by the farmer. This arrangement normally would not make Chiang, Burke, and the farmer partners. ●

KEEP IN MIND Forming a partnership requires two or more persons. Other forms of business can be organized by a single individual.

Note, though, that although the sharing of profits from ownership of property does not prove the existence of a partnership, sharing *both profits and losses* usually does. **EXAMPLE 14.3** Two sisters, Zoe and Cienna, buy a restaurant together, open a joint bank account from which they pay for expenses and supplies, and share the net profits that the restaurant generates. Zoe manages the restaurant and Cienna handles the bookkeeping. After eight years, Cienna stops doing the bookkeeping and does no other work for the restaurant. Zoe, who is now operating the restaurant by herself, no longer wants to share the profits with Cienna. She offers to buy her sister out, but the two cannot agree on a fair price. When Cienna files a lawsuit, a question arises as to whether the two sisters were partners in the restaurant. In this situation, a court would find that a partnership existed because the sisters shared management responsibilities, had joint accounts, and shared the profits and the losses of the restaurant equally. ●

Entity versus Aggregate Theory of Partnerships

At common law, a partnership was treated only as an aggregate of individuals and never as a separate legal entity. Thus, at common law a suit could never be brought by or against the firm in its own name. Instead, each individual partner had to sue or be sued.

Today, in contrast, a majority of the states follow the UPA and treat a partnership as an entity for most purposes. For example, a partnership usually can sue or be sued, collect judgments, and have all accounting procedures in the name of the partnership entity [UPA 201, 307(a)]. As an entity, a partnership may hold the title to real or personal property in its name rather than in the names of the individual partners. Additionally, federal procedural laws permit the partnership to be treated as an entity in suits in federal courts and bankruptcy proceedings.

For federal income tax purposes, however, the partnership is treated as an aggregate of the individual partners rather than a separate legal entity. The partnership is a pass-through entity and not a taxpaying entity. A **pass-through entity** is a business entity that has no tax liability because the entity's income is passed through to the owners, who pay taxes on it. Thus, the income or losses the partnership incurs are "passed through" the entity framework and attributed to the partners on their individual tax returns. The partnership itself has no tax liability and is responsible only for filing an **information return** with the Internal Revenue Service. In other words, the firm itself pays no taxes. A partner's profit from the partnership (whether distributed or not) is taxed as individual income to the individual partner.

Pass-Through Entity   A business entity that has no tax liability. The entity's income is passed through to the owners, and the owners pay taxes on the income.

Information Return   A tax return submitted by a partnership that only reports the income and losses earned by the business. The partnership as an entity does not pay taxes on the income received by the partnership.

Partnership Formation

As a general rule, an agreement to form a partnership can be *oral, written,* or *implied by conduct.* Some partnership agreements, however, must be in writing to be legally enforceable under the Statute of Frauds (see Chapter 10 for details). A written partnership agreement, called **articles of partnership,** can include almost any terms that the parties wish, unless they are illegal or contrary to public policy or statute [UPA 103]. The agreement usually specifies the name and location of the business, the duration of the partnership, the purpose of the business, each partner's share of the profits, how the partnership will be managed, and how assets will be distributed on dissolution, among other things.

Articles of Partnership   A written agreement that sets forth each partner's rights and obligations with respect to the partnership.

DURATION OF THE PARTNERSHIP   The partnership agreement can specify the duration of the partnership by stating that it will continue until a certain date or the completion of a particular project. A partnership that is specifically limited in duration is called a *partnership for a term.* Generally, withdrawing from a partnership for a term prematurely (prior to the expiration date) constitutes a breach of the agreement, and the responsible partner can be held liable for any resulting losses [UPA 602(b) (2)]. If no fixed duration is specified, the partnership is a *partnership at will.*

PARTNERSHIP BY ESTOPPEL   Occasionally, persons who are not partners may nevertheless hold themselves out as partners and make representations that third parties rely on in dealing with them. In such a situation, a court may conclude that a *partnership by estoppel* exists. The law does not confer any partnership rights on these persons, but it may impose liability on them. This is also true when a partner represents, expressly or impliedly, that a nonpartner is a member of the firm [UPA 308].

CASE EXAMPLE 14.4 Gary Chavers operated Chavers Welding and Construction (CWC). His sons Reggie and Mark worked in the business as well. CWC contracted with Epsco, Inc., to provide payroll and employee services. Initially, Epsco collected payments for its services each week, but later Epsco extended credit to CWC, which the Chaverses had represented was a partnership. Eventually, when CWC's account was more than $80,000 delinquent, Epsco filed a lawsuit to recover payment. Gary filed for bankruptcy, and his obligation to Epsco was discharged. Reggie and Mark claimed that their father owned CWC as a sole proprietor and that they were not partners in the business. The court, however, held that the sons were liable for CWC's debts based on partnership by estoppel. Because the Chaverses had represented to Epsco that CWC was a partnership and Epsco had relied on this representation when extending credit, the sons could not claim that no partnership existed.[2] ●

Rights of Partners

The rights of partners in a partnership relate to the following areas: management, interest in the partnership, compensation, inspection of books, accounting, and property. In the absence of provisions to the contrary in the partnership agreement, the law imposes the rights discussed here.

MANAGEMENT RIGHTS In a general partnership, all partners have equal rights in managing the partnership [UPA 401(f)]. Unless the partners agree otherwise, each partner has one vote in management matters *regardless of the proportional size of his or her interest in the firm.* Often, in a large partnership, partners agree to delegate daily management responsibilities to a management committee made up of one or more of the partners.

Decisions on ordinary matters connected with partnership business are made by majority rule, unless the agreement specifies otherwise. Decisions that significantly affect the nature of the partnership or that are not apparently for carrying on the ordinary course of the partnership business, or business of the kind, however, require the *unanimous* consent of the partners [UPA 301(2), 401(i), (j)]. Unanimous consent is typically required for such decisions as whether to admit new partners, amend the articles of partnership, engage in a new business, or undertake any act that would make further conduct of the partnership impossible.

INTEREST IN THE PARTNERSHIP Each partner is entitled to the proportion of business profits and losses that is designated in the partnership agreement. If the agreement does not apportion profits (indicate how the profits will be shared), the UPA provides that profits will be shared equally. If the agreement does not apportion losses, losses will be shared in the same ratio as profits [UPA 401(b)].

EXAMPLE 14.5 The partnership agreement for Rico and Brent provides for capital contributions of $60,000 from Rico and $40,000 from Brent, but it is silent as to how Rico and Brent will share profits or losses. In this situation, Rico and Brent will share both profits and losses equally. If their partnership agreement provided for profits to be shared in the same ratio as capital contributions, however, 60 percent of the profits would go to Rico, and 40 percent of the profits would go to Brent. If their partnership agreement was silent as to losses, losses would be shared in the same ratio as profits (60 percent and 40 percent, respectively). ●

"Forty for you, sixty for me—and equal partners we will be."

Anonymous

---

2. *Chavers v. Epsco, Inc.,* 352 Ark. 65, 98 S.W.3d 421 (2003).

Partners examine accounting records. Are there any restrictions on the right of a partner to inspect his or her firm's books and records? Why or why not?

COMPENSATION Devoting time, skill, and energy to partnership business is a partner's duty and generally is not a compensable service. Rather, as mentioned, a partner's income from the partnership takes the form of a distribution of profits according to the partner's share in the business. Partners can, of course, agree otherwise. For instance, the managing partner of a law firm often receives a salary—in addition to her or his share of profits—for performing special administrative duties, such as managing the office or personnel.

INSPECTION OF BOOKS Partnership books and records must be kept at the firm's principal business office and be accessible to all partners. Each partner has the right to receive (and the corresponding duty to produce) full and complete information concerning the conduct of all aspects of partnership business [UPA 403]. Every partner is entitled to inspect all books and records on demand and to make copies of the materials.

ACCOUNTING OF PARTNERSHIP ASSETS OR PROFITS An accounting of partnership assets or profits is required to determine the value of each partner's share in the partnership. An accounting can be performed voluntarily, or it can be compelled by court order. Under UPA 405(b), a partner has the right to bring an action for an accounting during the term of the partnership, as well as on the partnership's dissolution and winding up (see page 413).

PROPERTY RIGHTS Property acquired by a partnership is the property of the partnership and not of the partners individually [UPA 203]. Partnership property includes all property that was originally contributed to the partnership and anything later purchased by the partnership or in the partnership's name (except in rare circumstances) [UPA 204]. A partner may use or possess partnership property only on behalf of the partnership [UPA 401(g)]. A partner is *not* a co-owner of partnership property and has no right to sell, mortgage, or transfer partnership property to another. (A partner can assign her or his right to a share of the partnership profits to another to satisfy a debt, however.)

Duties and Liabilities of Partners

The duties and liabilities of partners are basically derived from agency law (discussed in Chapter 16). Each partner is an agent of every other partner and acts as both a principal and an agent in any business transaction within the scope of the partnership agreement. Each partner is also a general agent of the partnership in carrying out the usual business of the firm "or business of the kind carried on by the partnership" [UPA 301(1)]. Thus, every act of a partner concerning partnership business and "business of the kind," and every contract signed by that partner in the partnership's name, bind the firm.

One significant disadvantage associated with a traditional partnership is that partners are *personally* liable for the debts of the partnership. Moreover, the liability is essentially unlimited because the acts of one partner in the ordinary course of business subject the other partners to personal liability [UPA 305]. We examine here the fiduciary duties of partners, the authority of partners, and the liability of partners.

FIDUCIARY DUTIES   The fiduciary duties a partner owes to the partnership and the other partners are the duty of loyalty and the duty of care [UPA 404(a)]. The duty of loyalty requires a partner to account to the partnership for "any property, profit, or benefit" derived by the partner from the partnership's business or the use of its property [UPA 404(b)]. A partner must also refrain from competing with the partnership in business or dealing with the firm as an adverse party. A partner's duty of care involves refraining from "grossly negligent or reckless conduct, intentional misconduct, or a knowing violation of law" [UPA 404(c)].

These duties may not be waived or eliminated in the partnership agreement, and in fulfilling them, each partner must act consistently with the obligation of good faith and fair dealing, which applies to all contracts, including partnership agreements [UPA 103(b), 404(d)]. The agreement can specify acts that the partners agree will violate a fiduciary duty.

Note that a partner may pursue his or her own interests without automatically violating these duties [UPA 404(e)]. The key is whether the partner has disclosed the interest to the other partners. **EXAMPLE 14.6**   Jayne Trell, a partner at Jacoby & Meyers, owns a shopping mall. Trell may vote against a partnership proposal to open a competing mall, provided that she has fully disclosed her interest in the existing shopping mall to the other partners at the firm. ●

A partner can breach his or her duty of loyalty by self-dealing, misusing partnership property, disclosing trade secrets, or usurping a partnership business opportunity. The following case is a classic example.

> *"Surround yourself with partners who are better than you are."*
>
> David Ogilvy, 1911–1999
> (Scottish advertising executive)

Classic Case 14.1   Meinhard v. Salmon

Court of Appeals of New York, 249 N.Y. 458, 164 N.E. 545 (1928).
www.nycourts.gov/reporter/Index.htm[a]

(©Ugurhan Betin/iStockphoto)

BACKGROUND AND FACTS   Walter Salmon negotiated a twenty-year lease for the Hotel Bristol in New York City. To pay for the conversion of the building into shops and offices, Salmon entered into an agreement with Morton Meinhard to assume half of the cost. They agreed to share the profits and losses from the joint venture (a *joint venture* is similar to a partnership but typically is created for a single project, whereas a partnership usually involves an ongoing business), but Salmon was to have the sole power to manage the building. Less than four months before the end of the lease term, the building's owner Elbridge Gerry approached Salmon about a

project to raze the converted structure, clear five adjacent lots, and construct a single building across the whole property. Salmon agreed and signed a new lease in the name of his own business, Midpoint Realty Company, without telling Meinhard. When Meinhard learned of the deal, he filed a suit in a New York state court against Salmon. From a judgment in Meinhard's favor, Salmon appealed.

IN THE WORDS OF THE COURT . . .
CARDOZO, C.J. [Chief Justice]
  * * * *

Joint adventurers, like copartners, owe to one another, while the enterprise continues, the duty of the finest loyalty. Many forms of conduct permissible in a work-a-day world for those acting at arm's length are forbidden to those bound by fiduciary ties. * * * Not honesty alone, but the punctilio [strict observance of details] of an honor the most sensitive, is then the standard of behavior. As to this there has developed a tradition that is unbending and inveterate [entrenched]. Uncompromising rigidity has been the attitude of courts * * * when petitioned to undermine the rule of undivided loyalty.

---

a. In the links at the bottom of the page, click on "Archives." In the result, scroll to the name of the case and click on it to access the opinion. The New York State Law Reporting Bureau maintains this Web site.

Case 14.1—Continues next page ➡

Classic Case 14.1—Continued

* * * The trouble about [Salmon's] conduct is that he excluded his coadventurer from any chance to compete, from any chance to enjoy the opportunity for benefit.

* * * The very fact that Salmon was in control with exclusive powers of direction charged him the more obviously with the duty of disclosure, [because] only through disclosure could opportunity be equalized.

* * * Authority is, of course, abundant that one partner may not appropriate to his own use a renewal of a lease, though its term is to begin at the expiration of the partnership. The lease at hand with its many changes is not strictly a renewal. Even so, the standard of loyalty for those in trust relations is without the fixed divisions of a graduated scale. * * * *A man obtaining [an]* * * * *opportunity* * * * *by the position he occupies as a partner is bound by his obligation to his copartners in such dealings not to separate his interest from theirs, but, if he acquires any benefit, to communicate it to them. Certain it is also that there may be no abuse of special opportunities growing out of a special trust as manager or agent.* [Emphasis added.]

* * * Very likely [Salmon] assumed in all good faith that with the approaching end of the venture he might ignore his coadventurer and take the extension for himself. He had given to the enterprise time and labor as well as money. He had made it a success. Meinhard, who had given money, but neither time nor labor, had already been richly paid. * * * [But] Salmon had put himself in a position in which thought of

self was to be renounced, however hard the abnegation [self-denial]. He was much more than a coadventurer. He was a managing coadventurer. For him and for those like him the rule of undivided loyalty is relentless and supreme.

DECISION AND REMEDY   The Court of Appeals of New York held that Salmon breached his fiduciary duty by failing to inform Meinhard of the business opportunity and secretly taking advantage of it himself. The court granted Meinhard an interest "measured by the value of half of the entire lease."

WHAT IF THE FACTS WERE DIFFERENT?   *Suppose that Salmon had disclosed Gerry's proposal to Meinhard, who had said that he was not interested. Would the result in this case have been different? Explain.*

IMPACT OF THIS CASE ON TODAY'S LAW   *This landmark case involved a joint venture, not a partnership. At the time, a member of a joint venture had only the duty to refrain from actively subverting the rights of the other members. The decision in this case imposed the highest standard of loyalty on joint-venture members. The duty is now the same in both joint ventures and partnerships. The eloquent language in this case that describes the standard of loyalty is frequently quoted approvingly by courts in cases involving partnerships.*

AUTHORITY OF PARTNERS   Under the UPA and agency law, a partner has the authority to bind a partnership in contract. A partner may also subject the partnership to tort liability under agency principles. When a partner is carrying on partnership business or business of the kind with third parties in the usual way, both the partner and the firm share liability.

If a partner acts within the scope of her or his authority, the partnership is legally bound to honor the partner's commitments to third parties. The partnership will not be liable, however, if the third parties know that the partner had no authority to commit the partnership. Agency concepts that we explore in Chapter 16 relating to actual (express and implied) authority, apparent authority, and ratification also apply to partnerships. The extent of implied authority is generally broader for partners than for ordinary agents, though.

Joint Liability In partnership law, partners share liability for partnership obligations and debts. Thus, if a third party sues a partner on a partnership debt, the partner has the right to insist that the other partners be sued with him or her.

JOINT LIABILITY OF PARTNERS   Each partner in a partnership is jointly liable for the partnership's obligations. **Joint liability** means that a third party must sue all of the partners as a group, but each partner can be held liable for the full amount. Under the prior version of the UPA, which is still in effect in a few states, partners were subject to joint liability on partnership debts and contracts, but not on partnership debts arising from torts. If, for instance, a third party sues a partner on a partnership contract, the partner has the right to demand that the other partners be sued with her or him. In fact, if the third party does not sue all of the partners, the assets of the partnership cannot be used to satisfy the judgment. With joint liability, the partnership's assets must be exhausted before creditors can reach the partners' individual assets.[3]

JOINT AND SEVERAL LIABILITY OF PARTNERS   In the majority of states, under UPA 306(a), partners are jointly and severally (separately or individually) liable for all partnership obligations, including contracts, torts, and breaches of trust. **Joint and several liability** means that a third party may sue all of the partners together (jointly) or one or more of the partners separately (severally) at his or her option. All partners in a partnership can be held liable regardless of whether the partner participated in, knew about, or ratified the conduct that gave rise to the lawsuit. Normally, though, the partnership's assets must be exhausted before a creditor can enforce a judgment against a partner's separate assets [UPA 307(d)].

A judgment against one partner severally (separately) does not extinguish the others' liability. Those not sued in the first action normally may be sued subsequently, unless the court in the first action held that the partnership was in no way liable. If a plaintiff is successful in a suit against a partner or partners, he or she may collect on the judgment only against the assets of those partners named as defendants. A partner who commits a tort may be required to indemnify (reimburse) the partnership for any damages it pays—unless the tort was committed in the ordinary course of the partnership's business.

CASE EXAMPLE 14.7   Nicole Moren was a partner in Jax Restaurant. After work one day, Moren was called back to the restaurant to help in the kitchen. She brought her two-year-old-son, Remington, and sat him on the kitchen counter. While she was making pizzas, Remington reached into the dough press. His hand was crushed, causing permanent injuries. Through his father, Remington filed a suit against the partnership for negligence. The partnership filed a complaint against Moren, arguing that it was entitled to indemnity (compensation or reimbursement) from Moren for her negligence. The court held in favor of Moren and ordered the partnership to pay damages to Remington. Moren was not required to indemnify the partnership because her negligence occurred in the ordinary course of the partnership's business.[4] •

Partner's Dissociation

Dissociation occurs when a partner ceases to be associated in the carrying on of the partnership business. Although a partner always has the *power* to dissociate from the firm, he or she may not have the *right* to dissociate. Dissociation normally entitles the partner to have his or her interest purchased by the partnership and terminates his or her actual authority to act for the partnership and to participate with the partners in running the business. Otherwise, the partnership continues to do business without the dissociating partner.[5]

EVENTS CAUSING DISSOCIATION   Under UPA 601, a partner can be dissociated from a partnership in any of the following ways:

1. By the partner's voluntarily giving notice of an "express will to withdraw."
2. By the occurrence of an event agreed to in the partnership agreement.

Joint and Several Liability   In partnership law, a doctrine under which a plaintiff can file a lawsuit against all of the partners together (jointly) or one or more of the partners separately (severally, or individually). All partners in a partnership can be held liable regardless of whether the partner participated in, knew about, or ratified the conduct that gave rise to the lawsuit.

Dissociation   The severance of the relationship between a partner and a partnership when the partner ceases to be associated with the carrying on of the partnership business.

---

3. For a case applying joint liability to partnerships, see *Shar's Cars, LLC v. Elder,* 97 P.3d 724 (Utah App. 2004).
4. *Moren v. Jax Restaurant,* 679 N.W.2d 165 (Minn.App. 2004).
5. Under the previous version of the UPA, when a partner dissociated from a partnership, the partnership was considered dissolved, its business had to be wound up, and the proceeds had to be distributed to creditors and among partners. The amendments to the UPA recognize that a partnership may not want to break up just because one partner has left the firm.

3. By a unanimous vote of the other partners under certain circumstances, such as when a partner transfers substantially all of her or his interest in the partnership, or when it becomes unlawful to carry on partnership business with that partner.

4. By order of a court or arbitrator if the partner has engaged in wrongful conduct that affects the partnership business, breached the partnership agreement or violated a duty owed to the partnership or the other partners, or engaged in conduct that makes it "not reasonably practicable to carry on the business in partnership with the partner" [UPA 601(5)].

5. By the partner's declaring bankruptcy, assigning his or her interest in the partnership for the benefit of creditors, or becoming physically or mentally incapacitated, or by the partner's death. Note that although the bankruptcy or death of a partner represents that partner's "dissociation" from the partnership, it is not an *automatic* ground for the partnership's dissolution (*dissolution* will be discussed shortly).

WRONGFUL DISSOCIATION   As mentioned, a partner has the power to dissociate from a partnership at any time, but if she or he lacks the right to dissociate, then the dissociation is considered wrongful under the law [UPA 602]. When a partner's dissociation is in breach of the partnership agreement, for instance, it is wrongful. **EXAMPLE 14.8**   Jenson & Burke's partnership agreement states that it is a breach of the agreement for any partner to assign partnership property to a creditor without the consent of the others. If a partner, Janis, makes such an assignment, she has not only breached the agreement but has also wrongfully dissociated from the partnership. ●   Similarly, if a partner refuses to perform duties required by the partnership agreement—such as accounting for profits earned from the use of partnership property—this breach can be treated as wrongful dissociation. A partner who wrongfully dissociates is liable to the partnership and to the other partners for damages caused by the dissociation.

EFFECTS OF DISSOCIATION   Dissociation (rightful or wrongful) terminates some of the rights of the dissociated partner, requires that the partnership purchase his or her interest, and alters the liability of both parties to third parties. On a partner's dissociation, his or her right to participate in the management and conduct of the partnership business terminates [UPA 603]. The partner's duty of loyalty also ends. A partner's duty of care continues only with respect to events that occurred before dissociation, unless the partner participates in winding up the partnership's business (to be discussed shortly). **EXAMPLE 14.9**   Amy Pearson, a partner who leaves an accounting firm, Bubb & Pearson, can immediately compete with the firm for new clients. She must exercise care in completing ongoing client transactions, however, and must account to the firm for any fees received from the old clients based on those transactions. ●

After a partner's dissociation, his or her interest in the partnership must be purchased according to the rules in UPA 701. The **buyout price** is based on the amount that would have been distributed to the partner if the partnership were wound up on the date of dissociation. Offset against the price are amounts owed by the partner to the partnership, including any damages for the partner's wrongful dissociation.

For two years after a partner dissociates from a continuing partnership, the partnership may be bound by the acts of the dissociated partner based on apparent authority [UPA 702]. In other words, the partnership may be liable to a third party with whom a dissociated partner enters into a transaction if the third party reasonably believed that the dissociated partner was still a partner. Similarly, a dissociated

Buyout Price   The amount payable to a partner on his or her dissociation from a partnership, based on the amount distributable to that partner if the firm were wound up on that date, and offset by any damages for wrongful dissociation.

partner may be liable for partnership obligations entered into during a two-year period following dissociation [UPA 703].

Partnership Termination

The same events that cause dissociation can result in the end of the partnership if the remaining partners no longer wish to (or are unable to) continue the partnership business. The termination of a partnership is referred to as **dissolution,** which essentially means the commencement of the winding up process. **Winding up** is the process of collecting, liquidating, and distributing the partnership assets.[6]

Dissolution The formal disbanding of a partnership or a corporation.

Winding Up The second of two stages in the termination of a partnership or corporation. Once the firm is dissolved, it continues to exist legally until the process of winding up all business affairs is complete.

DISSOLUTION Dissolution of a partnership generally can be brought about by acts of the partners, by operation of law, and by judicial decree [UPA 801]. Any partnership (including one for a fixed term) can be dissolved by the partners' agreement. Similarly, if the partnership agreement states that it will dissolve on a certain event, such as a partner's death or bankruptcy, then the occurrence of that event will dissolve the partnership. A partnership for a fixed term or a particular undertaking is dissolved by operation of law at the expiration of the term or on the completion of the undertaking. Under the UPA, a court may order dissolution when it becomes obviously impractical for the firm to continue—for example, if the business can only be operated at a loss [UPA 801(5)].

DON'T FORGET Secured creditors have priority over unsecured creditors to any assets that serve as collateral for a partnership's debts.

WINDING UP After dissolution, the partnership continues for the limited purpose of the winding up process. The partners cannot create new obligations on behalf of the partnership. They have authority only to complete transactions begun but not finished at the time of dissolution and to wind up the business of the partnership [UPA 803, 804(1)]. *Winding up* includes collecting and preserving partnership assets, discharging liabilities (paying debts), and accounting to each partner for the value of her or his interest in the partnership. Partners continue to have fiduciary duties to one another and to the firm during this process.

Both creditors of the partnership and creditors of the individual partners can make claims on the partnership's assets. In general, partnership creditors share proportionately with the partners' individual creditors in the assets of the partners' estates, which include their interests in the partnership. A partnership's assets are distributed according to the following priorities [UPA 807]:

If a partner becomes incapacitated or dies, how does this affect the existence of the partnership?

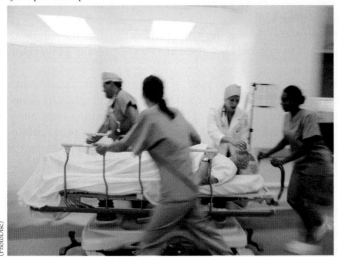

(PhotoDisc)

1. Payment of debts, including those owed to partner and nonpartner creditors.
2. Return of capital contributions and distribution of profits to partners.

If the partnership's liabilities are greater than its assets, the partners bear the losses—in the absence of a contrary agreement—in the same proportion in which

---

6. Although "winding down" would seem to describe more accurately the process of settling accounts and liquidating the assets of a partnership, "winding up" has been traditionally used in English and U.S. statutory and case law to denote this final stage of a partnership's existence.

they shared the profits (rather than, for example, in proportion to their contributions to the partnership's capital).

Preventing Legal Disputes

Before entering a partnership, agree on how the assets will be valued and divided in the event the partnership dissolves. Make express arrangements that will provide for a smooth dissolution. You and your partners can enter a buy-sell, or buyout, agreement, which provides that one or more partners will buy out the other or others, should the relationship deteriorate. Agreeing beforehand on who buys what, under what circumstances, and, if possible, at what price may eliminate costly negotiations or litigation later. Alternatively, your agreement can specify that one or more partners will determine the value of the interest being sold and that the other or others will decide whether to buy or sell.

 ## Limited Liability Partnerships

Limited Liability Partnership (LLP)
A hybrid form of business organization that is used mainly by professionals who normally do business in a partnership. Like a partnership, an LLP is a pass-through entity for tax purposes, but the personal liability of the partners is limited.

The **limited liability partnership (LLP)** is a hybrid form of business designed mostly for professionals, such as attorneys and accountants, who normally do business as partners in a partnership. In fact, nearly all the big accounting firms are LLPs. The major advantage of the LLP is that it allows a partnership to continue as a *pass-through entity* for tax purposes, but limits the personal liability of the partners. A special form of LLP is the *family limited liability partnership* (FLLP), in which the majority of the partners are persons related to each other, essentially as spouses, parents, grandparents, siblings, cousins, nephews, or nieces.

LLPs must be formed and operated in compliance with state statutes, which often include provisions of the UPA. The appropriate form must be filed with a state agency, and the business's name must include either "Limited Liability Partnership" or "LLP" [UPA 1001, 1002]. In addition, an LLP must file an annual report with the state to remain qualified as an LLP in that state [UPA 1003]. In most states, it is relatively easy to convert a traditional partnership into an LLP because the firm's basic organizational structure remains the same. Additionally, all of the statutory and common law rules governing partnerships still apply (apart from those modified by the state's LLP statute).

The LLP allows professionals to avoid personal liability for the malpractice of other partners. A partner in an LLP is still liable for her or his own wrongful acts, such as negligence, however. Also liable is the partner who supervised the party who committed a wrongful act. This generally is true for all types of partners and partnerships, not just LLPs.

Although LLP statutes vary from state to state, generally each state statute limits the liability of partners in some way. For example, Delaware law protects each innocent partner from the "debts and obligations of the partnership arising from negligence, wrongful acts, or misconduct." The UPA more broadly exempts partners from personal liability for any partnership obligation, "whether arising in contract, tort, or otherwise" [UPA 306(c)].

Limited Partnership (LP) A partnership consisting of one or more general partners (who manage the business and are liable to the full extent of their personal assets for debts of the partnership) and one or more limited partners (who contribute only assets and are liable only up to the extent of their contributions).

 ## Limited Partnerships

We now look at a business organizational form that limits the liability of *some* of its owners—the **limited partnership (LP).** LPs originated in medieval Europe and have been in existence in the United States since the early 1800s. In many ways,

LPs are like the general partnerships discussed earlier in this chapter, but they differ from general partnerships in several ways. Hence, they are sometimes referred to as *special partnerships.*

General Partner In a limited partnership, a partner who assumes responsibility for the management of the partnership and liability for all partnership debts.

Limited Partner In a limited partnership, a partner who contributes capital to the partnership but has no right to participate in the management and operation of the business. The limited partner assumes no liability for partnership debts beyond the capital contributed.

An LP consists of at least one **general partner** and one or more **limited partners.** A general partner assumes responsibility for managing the partnership and so has full responsibility for the partnership and for all of its debts. A limited partner contributes funds or other property and owns an interest in the firm but does not undertake any management responsibilities and is not personally liable for partnership debts beyond the amount of his or her investment. A limited partner can forfeit limited liability by taking part in the management of the business.

Until 1976, the law governing limited partnerships in all states except Louisiana was the Uniform Limited Partnership Act (ULPA). Since 1976, most states and the District of Columbia have adopted the revised version of the ULPA, known as the Revised Uniform Limited Partnership Act (RULPA). Because the RULPA is the dominant law governing limited partnerships in the United States, we will refer to it in the following discussion of limited partnerships.

Formation of the Limited Partnership

Certificate of Limited Partnership The basic document filed with a designated state official by which a limited partnership is formed.

In contrast to the informal, private, and voluntary agreement that usually suffices for a general partnership, the formation of a limited partnership is formal and public. The parties must follow specific statutory requirements and file a certificate with the state. A limited partnership must have at least one general partner and one limited partner, as mentioned previously. Additionally, the partners must sign a **certificate of limited partnership,** which requires information similar to that found in articles of incorporation (see Chapter 15), such as the name, mailing address, and capital contribution of each general and limited partner. The certificate usually is open to public inspection.

Liabilities of Partners in a Limited Partnership

General partners, unlike limited partners, are personally liable to the partnership's creditors. This policy can be circumvented in states that allow a corporation to be the general partner in a partnership. Because the corporation has limited liability by virtue of corporate laws, if a corporation is the general partner, no one in the limited partnership has personal liability.

NOTE A limited partner is liable to the extent of any contribution that she or he made to the partnership.

In contrast to the personal liability of general partners, the liability of a limited partner is limited to the capital that she or he contributes or agrees to contribute to the partnership [RULPA 502]. Limited partners enjoy limited liability so long as they do not participate in management [RULPA 303]. A limited partner who participates in management will be just as liable as a general partner to any creditor who transacts business with the limited partnership and believes, based on the limited partner's conduct, that he or she is a general partner [RULPA 303]. How much actual review and advisement a limited partner can engage in before being exposed to liability is an unsettled question.

Dissociation and Dissolution

A general partner has the power to voluntarily dissociate, or withdraw, from a limited partnership unless the partnership agreement specifies otherwise. A limited partner theoretically can withdraw from the partnership by giving six months' notice unless

> *"A friendship founded on business is a good deal better than a business founded on friendship."*
>
> John D. Rockefeller, 1839–1937
> (American industrialist)

the partnership agreement specifies a term, which most do. Also, some states have passed laws prohibiting the withdrawal of limited partners.

In a limited partnership, a general partner's voluntary dissociation from the firm normally will lead to dissolution *unless* all partners agree to continue the business. Similarly, the bankruptcy, retirement, death, or mental incompetence of a general partner will cause the dissociation of that partner and the dissolution of the limited partnership unless the other members agree to continue the firm [RULPA 801]. Bankruptcy of a limited partner, however, does not dissolve the partnership unless it causes the bankruptcy of the firm. Death or an assignment of the interest of a limited partner does not dissolve a limited partnership [RULPA 702, 704, 705]. A limited partnership can be dissolved by court decree [RULPA 802].

On dissolution, creditors' claims, including those of partners who are creditors, take first priority. After that, partners and former partners receive unpaid distributions of partnership assets and, except as otherwise agreed, amounts representing returns on their contributions and amounts proportionate to their shares of the distributions [RULPA 804].

▶ Limited Liability Companies

For many entrepreneurs and investors, the ideal business form would combine the tax advantages of the partnership form of business with the limited liability of the corporate enterprise. Although the limited partnership partially addresses these needs, the limited liability of limited partners is conditional: limited liability exists only so long as the limited partner does *not* participate in management.

Limited Liability Company (LLC)
A hybrid form of business enterprise that offers the limited liability of the corporation but the tax advantages of a partnership.

This is one reason that every state has adopted legislation authorizing a form of business organization called the **limited liability company (LLC).** The LLC is a hybrid form of business enterprise that offers the limited liability of the corporation but the tax advantages of a partnership. The origins and characteristics of this increasingly significant form of business organization are discussed in this chapter's *Landmark in the Legal Environment* feature on the facing page.

Like an LLP or LP, an LLC must be formed and operated in compliance with state law. About one-fourth of the states specifically require LLCs to have at least two owners, called **members.** In the rest of the states, although some LLC statutes are silent on this issue, one-member LLCs are usually permitted.

Member A person who has an ownership interest in a limited liability company.

Formation of an LLC

Articles of Organization The document filed with a designated state official by which a limited liability company is formed.

To form an LLC, **articles of organization** must be filed with a state agency—usually the secretary of state's office. Typically, the articles are required to set forth such information as the name of the business, its principal address, the name and address of a registered agent, the names of the owners, and information on how the LLC will be managed. The business's name must include the words "Limited Liability Company" or the initials "LLC." In addition to requiring that articles of organization be filed, a few states require that a notice of the intention to form an LLC be published in a local newspaper.

Sometimes, the future members of an LLC may enter into contracts on the entity's behalf before the LLC is formally formed. As you will read in Chapter 15, a similar process often occurs with corporations. Persons forming a corporation may enter into contracts during the process of incorporation but before the corporation becomes a legal entity. These contracts are referred to as preincorporation contracts.

Landmark in the Legal Environment — Limited Liability Company Statutes

In 1977, Wyoming became the first state to pass legislation authorizing the creation of a limited liability company (LLC). Although LLCs emerged in the United States in the late 1970s, they have been used for more than a century in various foreign jurisdictions, including several European and South American nations.

Taxation of LLCs   Despite Wyoming's adoption of an LLC statute, the tax status of LLCs in the United States was not clear until 1988, when the Internal Revenue Service (IRS) ruled that Wyoming LLCs would be taxed as partnerships instead of as corporations, providing that certain requirements were met. Before this ruling, only one additional state—Florida, in 1982—had authorized LLCs. The 1988 IRS ruling encouraged other states to enact LLC statutes, and in less than a decade, all states had done so.

IRS rules that went into effect in 1997 also encouraged more widespread use of LLCs in the business world. Under these rules, any unincorporated business is automatically taxed as a partnership unless it indicates otherwise on the tax form. The exceptions involve publicly traded companies, companies formed under a state incorporation statute, and certain foreign-owned companies. If a business chooses to be taxed as a corporation, it can indicate this preference by checking a box on the IRS form.

Foreign Entities May Be LLC Members   Part of the impetus behind the creation of LLCs in this country is that foreign investors are allowed to become LLC members. Generally, in an era increasingly characterized by global business efforts and investments, the LLC offers U.S. firms and potential investors from other countries greater flexibility and opportunities than are available through partnerships or corporations.

• **Application to Today's Legal Environment**   *Once it became clear that LLCs could be taxed as partnerships, the LLC form of business organization was widely adopted. Members could avoid the personal liability associated with the partnership form of business as well as the double taxation of the corporate form of business (see Chapter 15). Today, LLCs are a common form of business organization.*

Once the corporation is formed and adopts the preincorporation contract (by means of a *novation,* discussed in Chapter 10), it can then enforce the contract terms.

In dealing with the preorganization contracts of LLCs, courts may apply the well-established principles of corporate law relating to preincorporation contracts. **CASE EXAMPLE 14.10** 607 South Park, LLC, entered into a written agreement to sell a hotel to 607 Park View Associates, Ltd., whose general partner then assigned the rights to the hotel purchase to another company, 02 Development, LLC. At the time, 02 Development did not yet exist—it was legally created several months later. 607 South Park subsequently refused to sell the hotel to 02 Development, and 02 Development sued for breach of the purchase agreement. A California appellate court ruled that LLCs should be treated the same as corporations with respect to preorganization contracts. Although 02 Development did not exist when the agreement was executed, once it came into existence, it could enforce any preorganization contract made on its behalf.[7] •

Jurisdictional Requirements

One of the significant differences between LLCs and corporations has to do with federal jurisdictional requirements. Under the federal jurisdiction statute, a corporation is deemed to be a citizen of the state where it is incorporated and maintains its principal place of business. The statute does not mention the state citizenship of partnerships, LLCs, and other unincorporated associations, but the courts have tended to regard these entities as citizens of every state in which their members are citizens.

---

7. *02 Development, LLC v. 607 South Park, LLC,* 159 Cal.App.4th 609, 71 Cal.Rptr.3d 608 (2008). For a case in which a state court applied another corporate law principle (piercing the corporate veil) to LLCs, see *ORX Resources, Inc. v. MBW Exploration, LLC,* 32 So.3d 931 (La.App. 2010).

Stan Ovshinsky, founder of Ovonic Hydrogen Systems, LLC, a developer of alternative energy technologies. What are some of the advantages of doing business as an LLC instead of a corporation? Are there any disadvantages?

The state citizenship of an LLC may come into play when a party sues the LLC based on diversity of citizenship. Remember from Chapter 3 that when parties to a lawsuit are from different states and the amount in controversy exceeds $75,000, a federal court can exercise diversity jurisdiction. *Total* diversity of citizenship must exist, however. **EXAMPLE 14.11** Jen Fong, a citizen of New York, wishes to bring a suit against Skycel, an LLC formed under the laws of Connecticut. One of Skycel's members also lives in New York. Fong will not be able to bring a suit against Skycel in federal court on the basis of diversity jurisdiction because the defendant LLC is also a citizen of New York. The same would be true if Fong was bringing a suit against multiple defendants and one of the defendants lived in New York. •

Advantages of the LLC

The LLC offers many advantages to businesspersons, which is why this form of business organization has become increasingly popular.

LIMITED LIABILITY   A key advantage of the LLC is that the liability of members is limited to the amount of their investments. Although the LLC as an entity can be held liable for any loss or injury caused by the wrongful acts or omissions of its members, the members themselves generally are not personally liable.

TAXATION   Another advantage is the flexibility of the LLC in regard to taxation. An LLC that has *two or more members* can choose to be taxed either as a partnership or as a corporation. As you will read in Chapter 15, a corporate entity must pay income taxes on its profits, and the shareholders pay personal income taxes on profits distributed as dividends. An LLC that wants to distribute profits to its members may prefer to be taxed as a partnership to avoid the "double taxation" that is characteristic of the corporate entity.

Unless an LLC indicates that it wishes to be taxed as a corporation, the IRS automatically taxes it as a partnership. This means that the LLC as an entity pays no taxes. Rather, as in a partnership, profits are "passed through" the LLC to the members who then personally pay taxes on the profits. If an LLC's members want to reinvest the profits in the business, however, rather than distribute the profits to members, they may prefer that the LLC be taxed as a corporation. Corporate income tax rates may be lower than personal tax rates. Part of the attractiveness of the LLC is this flexibility with respect to taxation.

For federal income tax purposes, one-member LLCs are automatically taxed as sole proprietorships unless they indicate that they wish to be taxed as corporations. With respect to state taxes, most states follow the IRS rules.

MANAGEMENT AND FOREIGN INVESTORS   Still another advantage of the LLC for businesspersons is the flexibility it offers in terms of business operations and management—as will be discussed shortly. Finally, because foreign investors can participate in an LLC, the LLC form of business is attractive as a way to encourage investment. For a discussion of business organizations in other nations that are similar to the LLC, see this chapter's *Beyond Our Borders* feature on the facing page.

Disadvantages of the LLC

The main disadvantage of the LLC is that state LLC statutes are not uniform. Therefore, businesses that operate in more than one state may not receive consistent treatment in these states. Generally, though, most states apply to a foreign LLC

Beyond Our Borders | **Limited Liability Companies in Foreign Nations**

Limited liability companies are not unique to the United States. Many nations have business forms that provide limited liability, although these organizations may differ significantly from domestic LLCs.

In Germany, for example, the *GmbH*, or *Gesellschaft mit beschrankter Haftung* (which means "company with limited liability"), is a type of business entity that has been available since 1892. The GmbH is now the most widely used business form in Germany. A GmbH, however, is owned by shareholders and thus resembles a U.S. corporation in certain respects. German laws also impose numerous restrictions on the operations and business transactions of GmbHs, whereas LLCs in the United States are not even required to have an operating agreement.

Variants of the LLC form of business that limit the liability of owners are available today to businesspersons around the globe. Limited liability companies known as *limitadas* are common in many Latin American nations.

In France, *a société à responsabilité limitée* (meaning "society with limited liability") is an entity that provides business owners with limited liability. In 2002, the United Kingdom and Ireland passed laws that allow limited liability. Although these laws use the term *limited liability partnership,* the entities are similar to our domestic LLCs. In 2006, Japan enacted legislation that created a new type of business organization, called the *godo kaisha (GK),* which is also quite similar to a U.S. LLC. In most nations, some type of document that is similar to the LLC's articles of organization must be filed with the government to form the business.

Many countries limit the number of owners that such businesses may have, and some also require the member-owners to choose one or more persons who will manage the business affairs.

For Critical Analysis
Clearly, limited liability is an important aspect of doing business globally. Why might a nation limit the number of member-owners in a limited liability company?

(an LLC formed in another state) the law of the state where the LLC was formed. Difficulties can arise, nonetheless, when one state's court must interpret and apply another state's laws. In an attempt to create more uniformity among the states, in 1995 the National Conference of Commissioners on Uniform State Laws (NCCUSL) issued the Uniform Limited Liability Company Act (ULLCA), but less than one-fifth of the states adopted it. In 2006, the NCCUSL issued a revised version of this uniform law (the Re-ULLCA), which has been adopted in a few states.

The LLC Operating Agreement

Operating Agreement In a limited liability company, an agreement in which the members set forth the details of how the business will be managed and operated. State statutes typically give the members wide latitude in deciding for themselves the rules that will govern their organization.

The members of an LLC can decide how to operate the various aspects of the business by forming an **operating agreement** [ULLCA 103(a)]. Operating agreements typically contain provisions relating to management, how profits will be divided, the transfer of membership interests, whether the LLC will be dissolved on the death or departure of a member, and other important issues.

An operating agreement need not be in writing and indeed need not even be formed for an LLC to exist. Generally, though, LLC members should protect their interests by forming a written operating agreement. As with any business arrangement, disputes may arise over any number of issues. If there is no agreement covering the topic under dispute, such as how profits will be divided, the state LLC statute will govern the outcome. For example, most LLC statutes provide that if the members have not specified how profits will be divided, they will be divided equally among the members. Generally, when an issue is not covered by an operating agreement or by an LLC statute, the courts apply the principles of partnership law.

CASE EXAMPLE 14.12 Clifford Kuhn, Jr., and Joseph Tumminelli formed Touch of Class Limousine Service as an LLC. They did not create a written operating agreement but orally agreed that Kuhn would provide the financial backing and procure customers, and that Tumminelli would manage the company's day-to-day operations. Tumminelli embezzled $283,000 from the company after cashing customers' checks at Quick Cash, Inc., a local check-cashing service. Kuhn filed a lawsuit against Tumminelli, the banks, and others in a New Jersey state court to recover the embezzled funds. He argued that Quick Cash and the banks were liable because Tumminelli did not have the authority to cash the company's checks and convert the funds. The court, however, held that in the absence of a written operating agreement to the contrary, a member of an LLC, like a partner in a partnership, does have the authority to cash the firm's checks.[8] ●

Management of an LLC

Basically, there are two options for managing an LLC. The members may decide in their operating agreement to be either a "member-managed" LLC or a "manager-managed" LLC. Most LLC statutes and the ULLCA provide that unless the articles of organization specify otherwise, an LLC is assumed to be member managed [ULLCA 203(a)(6)].

In a *member-managed* LLC, all of the members participate in management, and decisions are made by majority vote [ULLCA 404(a)]. In a *manager-managed* LLC, the members designate a group of persons to manage the firm. The management group may consist of only members, both members and nonmembers, or only nonmembers.

FIDUCIARY DUTIES   Under the ULLCA, managers in a manager-managed LLC owe fiduciary duties to the LLC and its members, including the duty of loyalty and the duty of care [ULLCA 409(a), (h)], just as corporate directors and officers owe fiduciary duties to the corporation and its shareholders (see Chapter 15). Because not all states have adopted the ULLCA, though, some state statutes provide that managers owe fiduciary duties only to the LLC and not to the LLC's members individually. Although to whom the duty is owed may seem insignificant at first glance, it can have a dramatic effect on the outcome of litigation. (See this chapter's *Insight into Ethics* feature on the facing page for further discussion of this issue.)

In Alabama, where the following case arose, managers owe fiduciary duties to the LLC and its members.

---

8. *Kuhn v. Tumminelli*, 366 N.J.Super. 431, 841 A.2d 496 (2004).

> "*Business is the salt of life.*"
>
> Voltaire, 1694–1778
> (French author)

Case 14.2   Polk v. Polk

Court of Civil Appeals of Alabama, __ So.3d __ (2011).

BACKGROUND AND FACTS   Leslie Polk and his children, Yurii and Dusty Polk and Lezanne Proctor, formed Polk Plumbing, LLC, in Alabama. Leslie, Dusty, and Yurii performed commercial plumbing work, and Lezanne, an accountant, maintained the financial records and served as the office manager. After a couple of years, Yurii quit the firm. Eighteen months later, Leslie "fired" Dusty and Lezanne. He denied them access to the LLC's books and offices but continued to operate the business. Dusty and Lezanne filed a suit in an Alabama state court against Leslie, claiming breach of fiduciary duty. The court submitted the claim to a jury with the instruction that in Alabama employment relationships are "at will" (see Chapter 17). The court also told the jury that it could not consider the plaintiffs' "firing" as part of their claim. The jury awarded Dusty and Lezanne one dollar each in damages. They appealed, arguing that the judge's instructions to the jury were prejudicial—that is, that the instructions had substantially affected the outcome of the trial.

IN THE WORDS OF THE COURT . . .
MOORE, Judge.
* * * *

In this case, Dusty and Lezanne served as managers of the LLC. The LLC's Operating Agreement * * * provided that

> the Members may elect one or more of the Members to serve as Managers of the Company for the purpose of handling the day to day details of the Company. * * * The Managers shall serve for a period of one year or until their replacement or recall is voted by a majority of the Members.

Case 14.2–Continued

Based on the evidence presented at trial showing that the parties continued to act as managers of the LLC after the first year of operation, the foregoing contractual provision guaranteed that Dusty and Lezanne would remain managers until replaced or recalled by a vote of the majority of the members. Hence, their employment as managers of the LLC was not at will and the trial court erred in instructing the jury that it was. [Emphasis added.]

The trial court further erred in not allowing the jury to consider the circumstances of Dusty and Lezanne's "firing" as part of their breach-of-fiduciary-duty claim. * * * The record contains no evidence indicating that a vote was ever held to recall or replace Dusty and Lezanne. Rather, as Leslie testified, he simply acted in disregard of the terms of the Operating Agreement and instead rested on his right as the patriarch of the family to "fire" Dusty and Lezanne for, in his opinion, not working enough. Hence, * * * Leslie did not have the authority under the Operating Agreement to terminate the management positions of Dusty and Lezanne in the manner in which he did.

* * * *

By failing to instruct the jury that it also could consider Leslie's "firing" of Dusty and Lezanne as evidence in support of their breach-of-fiduciary-duty claim, we conclude that the trial court probably injuriously affected substantial rights of Dusty and Lezanne.

* * * *

Had the jury properly considered all the evidence supporting their breach-of-fiduciary-duty claim, it might have concluded that a higher amount of compensatory damages and possibly even punitive damages should have been awarded to Dusty and Lezanne.

DECISION AND REMEDY   A state intermediate appellate court reversed the lower court's judgment on the claim for breach of fiduciary duty and remanded the case for a new trial. The lower court committed reversible error by instructing the jury that Dusty and Lezanne's employment as managers was at will and by failing to instruct the jury that it could consider their "firing" as evidence in support of their claim.

WHAT IF THE FACTS WERE DIFFERENT?   *Suppose that Leslie owned a majority of the shares in Polk Plumbing. Could his "firing" of Dusty and Lezanne still be considered as evidence of a breach of fiduciary duty? Explain.*

THE LEGAL ENVIRONMENT DIMENSION   *Under what circumstances might the employment-at-will doctrine apply to the members of an LLC?*

DECISION-MAKING PROCEDURES   The members of an LLC can also set forth in their operating agreement provisions governing decision-making procedures. For instance, the agreement can include procedures for choosing or removing managers. Although most LLC statutes are silent on this issue, the ULLCA provides that members may choose and remove managers by majority vote [ULLCA 404(b)(3)].

 Insight into Ethics   **Fiduciary Duties of LLC Managers**

Fiduciary duties, such as the duty of loyalty and the duty of care, have an ethical component because they require a person to act honestly and faithfully toward another. In states that have adopted the ULLCA, the managers of a manager-managed LLC owe fiduciary duties to the members and thus basically are required to behave ethically toward them. In other states, however, the LLC statutes may not include such a requirement. Consequently, even when a manager has acted unfairly and unethically toward members, the members may not be able to sue the manager for a breach of fiduciary duties.

In North Carolina and Virginia, for example, the LLC statutes do not explicitly create fiduciary duties for managers to members. Instead, the statutes require that a manager exercise good business judgment in the best interests of the company. Because the statutes are silent on the manager's duty to members, in 2009 courts in those two states held that a manager-member owed fiduciary duties only to the LLC

and not to the other members.[a] In contrast, in two other cases decided in 2009, courts in Idaho and Kentucky held that a manager-member owed fiduciary duties to the LLC's other members and that the members could sue the manager for breaching fiduciary duties.[b]

FOR CRITICAL ANALYSIS
Insight into the Ethical Environment

Why wouldn't a manager always owe a fiduciary duty to the members of an LLC?

---

a. *Remora Investments, LLC v. Orr,* 277 Va. 316, 673 S.E.2d 845 (2009), applying Virginia Code Sections 13.1–1024.1; and *Kaplan v. O.K. Technologies, LLC,* 675 S.E.2d 133 (N.C.App. 2009), applying North Carolina General Statutes Section 57C-3-22(b).
b. *Bushi v. Sage Health Care, LLC,* 146 Idaho 764, 203 P.3d 694 (2009), applying Idaho Code Sections 30-6-101 *et seq.;* and *Patmon v. Hobbs,* 280 S.W.3d 589 (Ky.App. 2009), applying Kentucky Revised Statutes Section 275.170.

(PhotoDisc)

Members of a manager-managed LLC hold a formal members' meeting. What is the difference between a member-managed LLC and a manager-managed LLC? How are managers typically chosen?

Members may also specify in their agreement how voting rights will be apportioned. If they do not, LLC statutes in most states provide that voting rights are apportioned according to each member's capital contributions. Some states provide that, in the absence of an agreement to the contrary, each member has one vote.

Dissociation and Dissolution of an LLC

Recall that in the context of partnerships, *dissociation* occurs when a partner ceases to be associated in the carrying on of the business. The same concept applies to limited liability companies. A member of an LLC has the *power* to dissociate from the LLC at any time, but he or she may not have the *right* to dissociate. Under the ULLCA, the events that trigger a member's dissociation in an LLC are similar to the events causing a partner to be dissociated under the Uniform Partnership Act (UPA). These include voluntary withdrawal, expulsion by other members or by court order, bankruptcy, incompetence, and death. Generally, even if a member dies or otherwise dissociates from an LLC, the other members may continue to carry on LLC business, unless the operating agreement has contrary provisions.

DISSOCIATION   When a member dissociates from an LLC, he or she loses the right to participate in management and the right to act as an agent for the LLC. His or her duty of loyalty to the LLC also terminates, and the duty of care continues only with respect to events that occurred before dissociation. Generally, the dissociated member also has a right to have his or her interest in the LLC bought by the other members of the LLC. The LLC's operating agreement may contain provisions establishing a buyout price, but if it does not, the member's interest is usually purchased at a fair value. In states that have adopted the ULLCA, the LLC must purchase the interest at "fair" value within 120 days after the dissociation.

If the member's dissociation violates the LLC's operating agreement, it is considered legally wrongful, and the dissociated member can be held liable for damages caused by the dissociation. **EXAMPLE 14.13**   Chadwick and Barrel are members in an LLC. Chadwick manages the accounts, and Barrel, who has many connections in the community and is a skilled investor, brings in the business. If Barrel wrongfully dissociates from the LLC, the LLC's business will suffer, and Chadwick can hold Barrel liable for the loss of business resulting from her withdrawal. ●

DISSOLUTION   Regardless of whether a member's dissociation was wrongful or rightful, normally the dissociated member has no right to force the LLC to dissolve. The remaining members can opt to either continue or dissolve the business. Members can also stipulate in their operating agreement that certain events will cause dissolution, or they can agree that they have the power to dissolve the LLC by vote. As with partnerships, a court can order an LLC to be dissolved in certain circumstances, such as when the members have engaged in illegal or oppressive conduct, or when it is no longer feasible to carry on the business.

When an LLC is dissolved, any members who did not wrongfully dissociate may participate in the winding up process. To wind up the business, members must collect, liquidate, and distribute the LLC's assets. Members may preserve the assets for a reasonable time to optimize their return, and they continue to have the authority to perform reasonable acts in conjunction with winding up. In other words, the LLC will be bound by the reasonable acts of its members during the winding up process. Once all the LLC's assets have been sold, the proceeds are distributed to pay off debts to creditors first (including debts owed to members who are creditors of the LLC). The member's capital contributions are returned next, and any remaining amounts are then distributed to members in equal shares or according to their operating agreement.

▶ Franchises

Instead of setting up a business to market their own products or services, many entrepreneurs opt to purchase a franchise. A **franchise** is defined as any arrangement in which the owner of a trademark, a trade name, or a copyright licenses others to use the trademark, trade name, or copyright in the selling of goods or services. A **franchisee** (the purchaser of a franchise) is generally legally independent of the **franchisor** (the seller of the franchise). At the same time, the franchisee is economically dependent on the franchisor's integrated business system. In other words, a franchisee can operate as an independent businessperson but still obtain the advantages of a regional or national organization.

Today, franchising companies and their franchisees account for a significant portion of all retail sales in this country. Well-known franchises include 7-Eleven, Holiday Inn, and McDonald's.

Types of Franchises

Because the franchising industry is so extensive and so many different types of businesses sell franchises, it is difficult to summarize the many types of franchises that now exist. Generally, though, the majority of franchises fall into one of three classifications: distributorships, chain-style business operations, or manufacturing or processing-plant arrangements. We briefly describe these types of franchises here.

DISTRIBUTORSHIP A *distributorship* arises when a manufacturing concern (franchisor) licenses a dealer (franchisee) to sell its product. Often, a distributorship covers an exclusive territory. An example is an automobile dealership or beer distributorship.

EXAMPLE 14.14 Black Butte Beer Company distributes its brands of beer through a network of authorized wholesale distributors, each with an assigned territory. Marik signs a distributorship contract for the area from Gainesville to Ocala, Florida. If the contract states that Marik is the exclusive distributor in that area, then no other franchisee may distribute Black Butte beer in that region. ●

CHAIN-STYLE BUSINESS OPERATION In a *chain-style business operation,* a franchise operates under a franchisor's trade name and is identified as a member of a select group of dealers that engage in the franchisor's business. The franchisee is generally required to follow standardized or prescribed methods of operation. Often, the franchisor requires that the franchisee maintain certain standards of operation. In addition, sometimes the franchisee is obligated to obtain materials and supplies exclusively from the franchisor. Examples of this type of franchise are McDonald's and most other fast-food chains. Chain-style franchises are also common in

Franchise Any arrangement in which the owner of a trademark, trade name, or copyright licenses another to use that trademark, trade name, or copyright in the selling of goods or services.

Franchisee One receiving a license to use another's (the franchisor's) trademark, trade name, or copyright in the sale of goods and services.

Franchisor One licensing another (the franchisee) to use the owner's trademark, trade name, or copyright in the selling of goods or services.

Sometimes, individuals want to run their own businesses. They can do this as sole proprietors or as partners in a partnership. They can also get a head start on a business by buying a franchise for a well-known product, such as Domino's Pizza.

(*The Consumerist"/Creative Commons)

service-related businesses, including real estate brokerage firms, such as Century 21, and tax-preparing services, such as H&R Block, Inc.

MANUFACTURING OR PROCESSING-PLANT ARRANGEMENT   In a *manufacturing or processing-plant arrangement,* the franchisor transmits to the franchisee the essential ingredients or formula to make a particular product. The franchisee then markets the product either at wholesale or at retail in accordance with the franchisor's standards. Examples of this type of franchise are Coca-Cola and other soft-drink bottling companies.

Laws Governing Franchising

Because a franchise relationship is primarily a contractual relationship, it is governed by contract law. If the franchise exists primarily for the sale of products manufactured by the franchisor, the law governing sales contracts as expressed in Article 2 of the Uniform Commercial Code applies (see Chapter 11). Additionally, the federal government and most states have enacted laws governing certain aspects of franchising. Generally, these laws are designed to protect prospective franchisees from dishonest franchisors and to prohibit franchisors from terminating franchises without good cause.

FEDERAL REGULATION OF FRANCHISING   The federal government regulates franchising through laws that apply to specific industries and through the Franchise Rule, created by the Federal Trade Commission (FTC).

Industry-Specific Standards. Congress has enacted laws that protect franchisees in certain industries, such as automobile dealerships and service stations. These laws protect the franchisee from unreasonable demands and bad faith terminations of the franchise by the franchisor. If an automobile manufacturer-franchisor terminates a franchise because of a dealer-franchisee's failure to comply with unreasonable demands (for example, failure to attain an unrealistically high sales quota), the manufacturer may be liable for damages.[9] Similarly, federal law prescribes the conditions under which a franchisor of service stations can terminate the franchise.[10] Federal antitrust laws (see Chapter 23) also apply in certain circumstances to prohibit certain types of anticompetitive agreements.

The Franchise Rule. The FTC's Franchise Rule requires franchisors to disclose certain material facts that a prospective franchisee needs to make an informed decision concerning the purchase of a franchise.[11] The rule was designed to enable potential franchisees to weigh the risks and benefits of an investment. The rule requires the franchisor to make numerous written disclosures to prospective franchisees. For example, if a franchisor provides projected earnings figures, the franchisor must indicate whether the figures are based on actual data or hypothetical examples. If a franchisor makes sales or earnings projections based on actual data for a specific franchise location, the franchisor must disclose the number and percentage of its existing franchises that have achieved this result.

All representations made to a prospective franchisee must have a reasonable basis. Franchisors are also required to explain termination, cancellation, and renewal

(Baloo—Rex May/Cartoon Stock)

"Hi. Would you guys be interested in a Starbux franchise?"

---

9. Automobile Dealers' Franchise Act of 1965, also known as the Automobile Dealers' Day in Court Act, 15 U.S.C. Sections 1221 *et seq.*

10. Petroleum Marketing Practices Act (PMPA) of 1979, 15 U.S.C. Sections 2801 *et seq.*

11. 16 C.F.R. Part 436.

provisions of the franchise contract to potential franchisees before the agreement is signed. Those who violate the Franchise Rule are subject to substantial civil penalties, and the FTC can sue on behalf of injured parties to recover damages.

Can a franchisor satisfy the Franchise Rule by providing disclosures via the Internet? See this chapter's *Online Developments* feature below for a discussion of this topic.

STATE REGULATION OF FRANCHISING   State legislation varies but is often aimed at protecting franchisees from unfair practices and bad faith terminations by franchisors. Approximately fifteen states have laws similar to the federal rules requiring franchisors to provide presale disclosures to prospective franchisees.[12]

---

12. These states include California, Hawaii, Illinois, Indiana, Maryland, Michigan, Minnesota, New York, North Dakota, Oregon, Rhode Island, South Dakota, Virginia, Washington, and Wisconsin.

Online Developments

Satisfying the Federal Trade Commission's Franchise Rule in the Internet Age

The Federal Trade Commission (FTC) issued its Franchise Rule in 1978, when information normally was transmitted in a permanent form on paper. When Internet use became common in the 1990s, the FTC was faced with the possibility that franchisors might use Web sites to provide downloadable information to prospective franchisees. Was such online information the equivalent of an offer that requires compliance with the FTC's Franchise Rule? The FTC said yes.

In the 1990s, the FTC issued advisory opinions allowing electronic disclosures by CD-ROM and DVD, as long as the prospective franchisee was given the option of receiving the disclosure in electronic or paper format and chose electronic. The CD-ROM or DVD had to have a label indicating that it contained the disclosures required by the FTC and the date when it was issued. In 1999, the FTC began its formal rulemaking process to create regulations that would apply to online disclosures.[a]

Franchise.com and Others Get the Green Light

In 2001, Franchise.com, a marketer of existing franchises, became the first Web-based franchise operation to win the FTC's approval of its plan to provide electronic disclosure services for all of its franchisor advertisers. Franchise.com requires any franchisor that wishes to advertise on its Web site to provide a disclosure document containing the FTC's proposed cover-page statement regarding electronic disclosures. When a prospective franchisee comes to the Franchise.com Web site, he or she must agree to receive disclosures electronically by clicking on the appropriate

button. The prospect can then obtain information on a particular franchise through the Web site. Hyperlinks to written summary documents enable prospective franchisees to download or print the disclosure document for future reference.

In 2003, McGarry Internet, Ltd., of Dublin, Ireland, received similar approval. This company sends each prospective franchisee a Uniform Franchise Offering Circular via e-mail. In 2005, the FTC approved the request of VaultraNet, which had developed an Internet-based file delivery and signature system that it uses to provide disclosure documents to prospective franchisees.

Amendments to the Franchise Rule

In 2007, amendments to the Franchise Rule allowed franchisors to provide disclosure documents online as long as they met certain requirements. In 2008, the final amended version of the rule became mandatory. Prospective franchisees must be able to download or save all electronic disclosure documents. Additional disclosures are required about lawsuits that the franchisor has filed and any past settlement agreements.

A franchisor must also disclose whether the franchisor or an affiliate has the right to use other channels of distribution, such as the Internet, to make sales within the franchisee's territory. These amendments bring the federal rule into closer alignment with state franchise disclosure laws.

FOR CRITICAL ANALYSIS

Why do you think it took so long for the FTC to issue final rules about franchisors' use of the Internet?

---

a. 16 C.F.R. Part 436, 64 Fed.Reg. 57,294 (October 22, 1999).

State laws may also require that a disclosure document (known as the Franchise Disclosure Document, or FDD) be registered or filed with a state official, or they may require that the franchisor's advertising be submitted to the state for review or approval. To protect franchisees, a state law might require the disclosure of information such as the actual costs of operation, recurring expenses, and profits earned, along with data substantiating these figures. State deceptive trade practices acts (see Chapter 20) may also apply and prohibit certain types of actions on the part of franchisors.

To prevent arbitrary or bad faith terminations, state law may prohibit termination without "good cause" or require that certain procedures be followed in terminating a franchising relationship.

CASE EXAMPLE 14.15   FMS, Inc., entered into a franchise agreement with Samsung Construction Equipment North America to become an authorized dealership for the sale of Samsung brand construction equipment. Then Samsung sold its construction-equipment business to Volvo Construction Equipment North America, Inc., which was to continue selling Samsung brand equipment. Volvo did so for a while but then started modifying and rebranding construction equipment under its own name. When Volvo canceled FMS's franchise agreement, FMS filed a lawsuit alleging that Volvo, among other things, had violated Maine's franchise law, which prohibits termination of a franchise without "good cause." A federal appellate court, however, found that because Volvo was no longer manufacturing the Samsung brand equipment, it did have good cause to terminate FMS's franchise. If Volvo had continued making the Samsung brand equipment, the statute would have prevented it from terminating the FMS franchise, but the statute did not prohibit it from discontinuing the dealership as to the rebranded equipment.[13] ●

The Franchise Contract

The franchise relationship is defined by a contract between the franchisor and the franchisee. The franchise contract specifies the terms and conditions of the franchise and spells out the rights and duties of the franchisor and the franchisee. If either party fails to perform the contractual duties, that party may be subject to a lawsuit for breach of contract. Generally, statutes and case law governing franchising tend to emphasize the importance of good faith and fair dealing in franchise relationships.

PAYMENT FOR THE FRANCHISE   The franchisee ordinarily pays an initial fee or lump-sum price for the franchise license (the privilege of being granted a franchise). This fee is separate from the various products that the franchisee purchases from or through the franchisor.

In some industries, the franchisor relies heavily on the initial sale of the franchise for realizing a profit. In other industries, the continued dealing between the parties brings profit to both. In most situations, the franchisor will receive a stated percentage of the annual (or monthly) sales or annual volume of business done by the franchisee. The franchise agreement may also require the franchisee to pay a percentage of advertising costs and certain administrative expenses.

BUSINESS PREMISES   The franchise agreement may specify whether the premises for the business must be leased or purchased outright. In some instances, a building must be constructed or remodeled to meet the terms of the agreement. The

---

13. *FMS, Inc. v. Volvo Construction Equipment North America, Inc.,* 557 F.3d 758 (7th Cir. 2009).

The RJ Corporation of India signed a franchise agreement with Disney Consumer Products. What do you think some of the elements of that agreement were?

agreement usually will specify whether the franchisor supplies equipment and furnishings for the premises or whether this is the responsibility of the franchisee.

LOCATION OF THE FRANCHISE   Typically, the franchisor will determine the territory to be served. Some franchise contracts give the franchisee exclusive rights, or "territorial rights," to a certain geographic area. Other franchise contracts, though they define the territory allotted to a particular franchise, either specifically state that the franchise is nonexclusive or are silent on the issue of territorial rights.

Many franchise cases involve disputes over territorial rights, and the implied covenant of good faith and fair dealing often comes into play in this area of franchising. If the franchise contract does not grant exclusive territorial rights to a franchisee and the franchisor allows a competing franchise to be established nearby, the franchisee may suffer a significant loss in profits. In this situation, a court may hold that the franchisor's actions breached an implied covenant of good faith and fair dealing.

QUALITY CONTROL BY THE FRANCHISOR   Although the day-to-day operation of the franchise business is normally left to the franchisee, the franchise agreement may provide for the amount of supervision and control agreed on by the parties. When the franchisee prepares a product, such as food, or provides a service, such as a motel, the contract often provides that the franchisor will establish certain standards for the facility. Typically, the contract will state that the franchisor is permitted to make periodic inspections to ensure that the standards are being maintained so as to protect the franchise's name and reputation.

As a general rule, the validity of a provision permitting the franchisor to establish and enforce certain quality standards is unquestioned. Because the franchisor has a legitimate interest in maintaining the quality of the product or service to protect its name and reputation, it can exercise greater control in this area than would otherwise be tolerated.

Termination of the Franchise

The duration of the franchise is a matter to be determined between the parties. Sometimes, a franchise will start out for a short period, such as a year, so that the franchisor can determine whether it wants to stay in business with the franchisee. Other times, the duration of the franchise contract correlates with the term of the lease for the business premises, and both are renewable at the end of that period.

Usually, the franchise agreement will specify that termination must be "for cause," such as death or disability of the franchisee, insolvency of the franchisee, breach of the franchise agreement, or failure to meet specified sales quotas. Most franchise contracts provide that notice of termination must be given. If no set time for termination is specified, then a reasonable time, with notice, will be implied. A franchisee must be given reasonable time to wind up the business—that is, to do the accounting and return the copyright or trademark or any other property of the franchisor.

WRONGFUL TERMINATION   Because a franchisor's termination of a franchise often has adverse consequences for the franchisee, much franchise litigation involves claims of wrongful termination. Generally, the termination provisions of contracts are more favorable to the franchisor. This means that the franchisee, who normally invests a substantial amount of time and funds to make the franchise operation successful, may receive little or nothing for the business on termination. The franchisor owns the trademark and hence the business.

It is in this area that statutory and case law become important. The federal and state laws discussed earlier attempt, among other things, to protect franchisees from the arbitrary or unfair termination of their franchises by the franchisors.

THE IMPORTANCE OF GOOD FAITH AND FAIR DEALING   Generally, both statutory law and case law emphasize the importance of good faith and fair dealing in terminating a franchise relationship. In determining whether a franchisor has acted in good faith when terminating a franchise agreement, the courts usually try to balance the rights of both parties. If a court perceives that a franchisor has arbitrarily or unfairly terminated a franchise, the franchisee will be provided with a remedy for wrongful termination. If a franchisor's decision to terminate a franchise was made in the normal course of the franchisor's business operations, however, and reasonable notice of termination was given to the franchisee, in most instances a court will not consider the termination wrongful.

The importance of good faith and fair dealing in a franchise relationship is underscored by the consequences of the franchisor's acts in the following case.

Case 14.3   **Holiday Inn Franchising, Inc. v. Hotel Associates, Inc.**

Court of Appeals of Arkansas, 2011 Ark.App. 147 (2011).
opinions.aoc.arkansas.gov[a]

BACKGROUND AND FACTS   Buddy House was in the construction business in Arkansas and Texas. For decades, he collaborated on projects with Holiday Inns Franchising, Inc. Their relationship was characterized by good faith—many projects were undertaken without written contracts. At Holiday Inn's request, House inspected a hotel in Wichita Falls, Texas, to estimate the cost of getting it into shape. Holiday Inn wanted House to renovate the hotel and operate it as a Holiday Inn. House estimated that recovering the cost of renovation would take him more than ten years, so he asked for a franchise term longer than Holiday Inn's usual ten years. Holiday Inn refused, but said that if the hotel were run "appropriately," the term would be extended at the end of ten years. House bought the hotel, renovated it, and operated it as Hotel Associates, Inc. (HAI), generating substantial profits. He refused offers to sell it for as much as $15 million. Before the ten years had passed, Greg Aden, a Holiday Inn executive, developed a plan to license a different local hotel as a Holiday Inn instead of renewing House's franchise license. Aden stood to earn a commission from licensing the other hotel. No one informed House of Aden's plan. When the time came, HAI applied for an extension of its franchise, and Holiday Inn asked for major renovations. HAI spent $3 million to comply with this request. Holiday Inn did not renew HAI's

license, however, but instead granted a franchise to the other hotel. HAI sold its hotel for $5 million and filed a suit in an Arkansas state court against Holiday Inn, asserting fraud. The court awarded HAI compensatory and punitive damages. Holiday Inn appealed.

IN THE WORDS OF THE COURT . . .
Raymond R. *ABRAMSON*, Judge.
   * * * *

Generally, a mere failure to volunteer information does not constitute fraud. But *silence can amount to actionable fraud in some circumstances where the parties have a relation of trust or confidence, where there is inequality of condition and knowledge, or where there are other attendant circumstances.* * * * [Emphasis added.]

In this case, substantial evidence supports the existence of a duty on Holiday Inn's part to disclose the Aden [plan] to HAI. Buddy House had a long-term relationship with Holiday Inn characterized by honesty, trust, and the free flow of pertinent information. He testified that [Holiday Inn's] assurances at the onset of licensure [the granting of the license] led him to believe that he would be relicensed after ten years if the hotel was operated appropriately. Yet, despite Holiday Inn's having provided such an assurance to House, it failed to apprise House of an internal business plan * * * that advocated licensure of another facility instead of the renewal of his license. *A duty of disclosure may exist where information is peculiarly within the knowledge of one party and is of such a nature that the other party is justified in assuming its nonexistence.* Given House's history with Holiday Inn and the assurance

---

a. In the "Search Opinions" section, click on "Search Opinions by Docket Number." On that page, in the "Enter Docket Number:" box, type "CA10-21" and click on "Submit." In the result, click on the name of the case to access the opinion. The Arkansas Judiciary maintains this Web site.

Case 14.3–Continued

he received, we are convinced he was justified in assuming that no obstacles had arisen that jeopardized his relicensure. [Emphasis added.]

Holiday Inn asserts that it would have provided Buddy House with the Aden [plan] if he had asked for it. But, Holiday Inn cannot satisfactorily explain why House should have been charged with the responsibility of inquiring about a plan that he did not know existed. Moreover, several Holiday Inn personnel testified that Buddy House in fact should have been provided with the Aden plan. Aden himself stated that * * * House should have been given the plan. * * * In light of these circumstances, we see no ground for reversal on this aspect of HAI's cause of action for fraud.

DECISION AND REMEDY   The state intermediate appellate court affirmed the lower court's judgment and its award of compensatory damages. The appellate court increased the amount of punitive damages, however, citing Holiday Inn's "degree of reprehensibility."

THE ECONOMIC DIMENSION   *A jury awarded HAI $12 million in punitive damages. The trial court reduced this award to $1 million, but the appellate court reinstated the original award. What is the purpose of punitive damages? Did Holiday Inn's conduct warrant the $12 million punitive damages award? Explain.*

THE LEGAL ENVIRONMENT DIMENSION   *Why should House and HAI have been advised of Holiday Inn's plan to grant a franchise to a different hotel in their territory?*

 Reviewing . . . Small Business Organizations

A bridge on a prominent public roadway in the city of Papagos, Arizona, was deteriorating and in need of repair. The city posted notices seeking proposals for an artistic bridge design and reconstruction. Davidson Masonry, LLC, which was owned and managed by Carl Davidson and his wife, Marilyn Rowe, submitted a bid for a decorative concrete project that incorporated artistic metalwork. They contacted Shana Lafayette, a local sculptor who specialized in large-scale metal forms, to help them design the bridge. The city selected their bridge design and awarded them the contract for a commission of $184,000. Davidson Masonry and Lafayette then entered into an agreement to work together on the bridge project. Davidson Masonry agreed to install and pay for concrete and structural work, and Lafayette agreed to install the metalwork at her expense. They agreed that overall profits would be split, with 25 percent going to Lafayette and 75 percent going to Davidson Masonry. Lafayette designed numerous metal sculptures of salmon that were incorporated into colorful decorative concrete forms designed by Rowe, while Davidson performed the structural engineering. Using the information presented in the chapter, answer the following questions.

1. Would Davidson Masonry automatically be taxed as a partnership or a corporation? Explain.
2. Is Davidson Masonry a member-managed or manager-managed LLC? Explain.
3. Suppose that during construction, Lafayette had entered into an agreement to rent space in a warehouse that was close to the bridge so that she could work on her sculptures near the site where they would be installed. She entered into the contract without the knowledge or consent of Davidson Masonry. In this situation, would a court be likely to hold that Davidson Masonry was bound by the contract that Lafayette entered? Why or why not?
4. Now suppose that Rowe has an argument with her husband and wants to withdraw from being a member of Davidson Masonry. What is the term for such a withdrawal, and what effect does it have on the LLC?

 Key Terms

articles of organization 416	franchisee 423	limited partner 415
articles of partnership 406	franchisor 423	limited partnership (LP) 414
buyout price 412	general partner 415	member 416
certificate of limited partnership 415	information return 406	operating agreement 419
dissociation 411	joint and several liability 411	partnership 404
dissolution 413	joint liability 410	pass-through entity 406
entrepreneur 402	limited liability company (LLC) 416	sole proprietorship 403
franchise 423	limited liability partnership (LLP) 414	winding up 413

Chapter Summary: Small Business Organizations

Sole Proprietorships (See pages 403–404.)	The simplest form of business organization; used by anyone who does business without creating a separate organization. The owner is the business. The owner pays personal income taxes on all profits and is personally liable for all business debts.
Partnerships (See pages 404–414.)	1. A partnership is created by agreement of the parties. 2. A partnership is treated as an entity except for limited purposes. 3. Each partner pays a proportionate share of income taxes on the net profits of the partnership, whether or not they are distributed. The partnership files only an information return with the Internal Revenue Service. 4. Each partner has an equal voice in management unless the partnership agreement provides otherwise. 5. In the absence of an agreement, partners share profits equally and share losses in the same ratio as they share profits. 6. Partners have unlimited personal liability for partnership debts. 7. A partnership can be terminated by agreement or can be dissolved by action of the partners, operation of law (subsequent illegality), or court decree.
Limited Liability Partnerships (LLPs) (See page 414.)	1. *Formation*—LLPs must be formed in compliance with state statutes. Typically, an LLP is formed by professionals who normally work together as partners in a partnership. Under most state LLP statutes, it is relatively easy to convert a traditional partnership into an LLP. 2. *Liability of partners*—LLP statutes vary, but under the UPA, professionals generally can avoid personal liability for acts committed by other partners. Partners in an LLP continue to be liable for their own wrongful acts and for the wrongful acts of those whom they supervise.
Limited Partnerships (See pages 414–416.)	1. *Formation*—A certificate of limited partnership must be filed with the designated state official. The certificate must include information about the business, similar to the information included in articles of incorporation. The partnership consists of one or more general partners and one or more limited partners. 2. *Rights and liabilities of partners*—With some exceptions, the rights of partners are the same as the rights of partners in a general partnership. General partners have unlimited liability for partnership obligations. Limited partners are liable only to the extent of their contributions. 3. *Limited partners and management*—Only general partners can participate in management. Limited partners have no voice in management. If they do participate in management activities, they risk having liability as a general partner. 4. *Dissociation and dissolution*—Generally, a limited partnership can be dissolved in much the same way as an ordinary partnership. A general partner has the power to voluntarily dissociate unless the parties' agreement specifies otherwise. Some states limit the power of limited partners to voluntarily withdraw from the firm. The death or assignment of interest of a limited partner does not dissolve the partnership. Bankruptcy of a limited partner also will not dissolve the partnership unless it causes the bankruptcy of the firm.
Limited Liability Companies (LLCs) (See pages 416–422.)	1. *Formation*—Articles of organization must be filed with the appropriate state office—usually the office of the secretary of state—setting forth the name of the business, its principal address, the names of the owners (called members), and other relevant information. 2. *Advantages and disadvantages of the LLC*—Advantages of the LLC include limited liability, the option to be taxed as a partnership or as a corporation, and flexibility in deciding how the business will be managed and operated. The main disadvantage is the lack of uniformity in state LLC statutes. 3. *Operating agreement*—When an LLC is formed, the members decide, in an operating agreement, how the business will be managed and what rules will apply to the organization. 4. *Management*—An LLC may be managed by members only, by some members and some nonmembers, or by nonmembers only.

Chapter Summary: Small Business Organizations, Continued

Limited Liability Companies (LLCs)– Continued	5. *Dissociation and dissolution*–Members of an LLC have the power to dissociate from the LLC at any time, but they may not have the right to dissociate. Dissociation does not always result in the dissolution of an LLC. The remaining members can choose to continue the business. Dissociated members have a right to have their interest purchased by the other members. If the LLC is dissolved, the business must be wound up and the assets sold. Creditors are paid first, and then members' capital investments are returned. Any remaining proceeds are distributed to members.
Franchises (See pages 423–429.)	1. *Types of franchises–* a. Distributorship (for example, automobile dealerships). b. Chain-style operation (for example, fast-food chains). c. Manufacturing or processing-plant arrangement (for example, soft-drink bottling companies, such as Coca-Cola). 2. *Laws governing franchising–* a. Franchises are governed by contract law. b. Franchises are also governed by federal and state statutory and regulatory laws. 3. *The franchise contract*–The franchise relationship is defined by a contract between the franchisor and the franchisee. The contract normally spells out the following terms: a. Payment for the franchise–Ordinarily, the contract requires the franchisee (purchaser) to pay an initial fee or lump-sum price for the franchise license. b. Business premises and organization–Specifies whether the business premises will be leased or purchased by the franchisee. The franchisor may specify particular requirements for the form and capital structure of the business. c. Location of the franchise–Specifies the territory to be served by the franchisee. d. Quality control–The franchisor may require the franchisee to abide by certain standards of quality relating to the product or service offered. 4. *Termination of the franchise*–Usually, the contract provides for the date and/or conditions of termination of the franchise arrangement. Both federal and state statutes attempt to protect franchisees from franchisors who unfairly or arbitrarily terminate franchises.

 **ExamPrep**

ISSUE SPOTTERS

1. Gomer, Harry, and Ida are members of Jeweled Watches, LLC. What are their options with respect to the management of their firm?
2. Thirsty Bottling Company and U.S. Beverages, Inc. (USB), enter into a franchise agreement that states that the franchise may be terminated at any time "for cause." Thirsty fails to meet USB's specified sales quota. Does this constitute "cause" for termination? Why or why not?

—**Check your answers to these questions against the answers provided in Appendix G.**

BEFORE THE TEST

Go to **www.cengagebrain.com**, enter the ISBN number "9781111530617," and click on "Find" to locate this textbook's Web site. Then, click on "Access Now" under "Study Tools," and select "Chapter 14" at the top. There you will find an "Interactive Quiz" that you can take to assess your mastery of the concepts in this chapter, as well as "Flashcards" and a "Glossary" of important terms.

For Review

1. What advantages and disadvantages are associated with the sole proprietorship?
2. What is meant by joint and several liability? Why is this often considered to be a disadvantage of doing business as a general partnership?
3. What advantages do limited liability partnerships offer to entrepreneurs that are not offered by general partnerships?
4. What are the key differences between the rights and liabilities of general partners and those of limited partners?
5. How are limited liability companies formed, and who decides how they will be managed and operated?

Questions and Case Problems

14–1. Limited Liability Companies. John, Lesa, and Tabir form a limited liability company. John contributes 60 percent of the capital, and Lesa and Tabir each contribute 20 percent. Nothing is decided about how profits will be divided. John assumes that he will be entitled to 60 percent of the profits, in accordance with his contribution. Lesa and Tabir, however, assume that the profits will be divided equally. A dispute over the question arises, and ultimately a court has to decide the issue. What law will the court apply? In most states, what will result? How could this dispute have been avoided in the first place? Discuss fully.

14–2. **Question with Sample Answer. Dissolution of Limited Partnership.** Dorinda, Luis, and Elizabeth form a limited partnership. Dorinda is a general partner, and Luis and Elizabeth are limited partners. Consider each of the separate events below, and discuss fully which would constitute a dissolution of the limited partnership.

  1. Luis assigns his partnership interest to Ashley.
  2. Elizabeth is petitioned into involuntary bankruptcy.
  3. Dorinda dies.

  —For a sample answer to Question 14–2, go to Appendix E at the end of this text.

14–3. Partnership Formation. Daniel is the owner of a chain of shoe stores. He hires Rubya to be the manager of a new store, which is to open in Grand Rapids, Michigan. Daniel, by written contract, agrees to pay Rubya a monthly salary and 20 percent of the profits. Without Daniel's knowledge, Rubya represents himself to Classen as Daniel's partner, showing Classen the agreement to share profits. Classen extends credit to Rubya. Rubya defaults. Discuss whether Classen can hold Daniel liable as a partner.

14–4. Sole Proprietorship. Julie Anne Gaskill is an oral and maxillofacial surgeon in Bowling Green, Kentucky. Her medical practice is a sole proprietorship that consists of Gaskill as the sole surgeon and an office staff. She sees every patient, exercises all professional judgment and skill, and manages the business. When Gaskill and her spouse, John Robbins, initiated divorce proceedings in a Kentucky state court, her accountant estimated the value of the practice at $221,610, excluding goodwill. Robbins's accountant estimated the value at $669,075, including goodwill. (Goodwill is the ability or

reputation of a business to draw customers, get them to return, and contribute to future profitability.) How can a sole proprietor's reputation, skill, and relationships with customers be valued? Could these qualities be divided into "personal" and "enterprise" goodwill, with some goodwill associated with the business and some solely due to the personal qualities of the proprietor? If so, what might comprise each type? Is this an effective method for valuing Gaskill's practice? Discuss. [*Gaskill v. Robbins*, 282 S.W.3d 306 (Ky. 2009)]

14–5. Limited Partnership. James Carpenter contracted with Austin Estates, LP, to buy property in Texas. Carpenter asked Sandra McBeth to invest in the deal. He admitted that a dispute had arisen with the city of Austin over water for the property, but he assured her that it would not be a significant obstacle. McBeth agreed to invest $800,000 to hold open the option to buy the property. She became a limited partner in StoneLake Ranch, LP. Carpenter acted as the firm's general partner. Despite his assurances to McBeth, the purchase was delayed due to the water dispute. Unable to complete the purchase in a timely manner, Carpenter paid the $800,000 to Austin Estates without notifying McBeth. Later, Carpenter and others—*excluding* McBeth— bought the property and sold it at a profit. McBeth filed a suit in a Texas state court against Carpenter. What is the nature of the fiduciary duty that a general partner owes a limited partner? Did Carpenter breach that duty in this case? Explain. [*McBeth v. Carpenter*, 565 F.3d 171 (5th Cir. 2009)]

14–6. Fiduciary Duties of Partners. Karl Horvath, Hein Rüsen, and Carl Thomas formed a partnership, HRT Enterprises, to buy a vacant manufacturing plant and an annex building on eleven acres in Detroit, Michigan. HRT leased the plant to companies owned by the partners, including Horvath's Canadian-American Steel. When Horvath's firm missed three payments under its lease, HRT evicted it from the plant. Horvath objected but remained an HRT partner. Later, Rüsen and Thomas leased the entire plant to their company, Merkur Steel. Merkur then sublet the premises to City Steel and Merkur Technical Services—both of which were owned (or substantially owned) by Rüsen and Thomas. The rent these companies paid to Merkur was higher than the rent Merkur paid to HRT, which meant that Merkur profited from the arrangement. Rüsen and Thomas did not tell Horvath about the subleases. When Horvath learned of the deals, he filed a suit in a Michigan state court against HRT and the other partners for an accounting of their actions. Did Rüsen and Thomas breach their fiduciary duty to HRT and Horvath? Discuss. [*Horvath v. HRT Enterprises,* __ N.W.2d __ (2011)]

14–7. 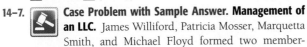 **Case Problem with Sample Answer. Management of an LLC.** James Williford, Patricia Mosser, Marquetta Smith, and Michael Floyd formed two member-managed limited liability companies—Bluewater Bay, LLC, and Bluewater Logistics, LLC (collectively Bluewater)—in Mississippi to bid on contracts related to the aftermath of Hurricane Katrina. Under Mississippi law, every member of a member-managed LLC is entitled to participate in managing the business. Under Bluewater's operating agreements, "a 75% Super Majority Vote of the members" could redeem any member's interest if the "member has either committed a felony or under any other circumstances that would jeopardise the company status" as a contractor. Bluewater had completed more than $5 million in contracts when Smith told Williford that he was "fired" and that she, Mosser, and Floyd were exercising their "super majority" right to buy him out. No reason was provided. Williford filed a suit in a Mississippi state court against Bluewater and the other members, who then told Williford that they had changed their minds about buying him out but that he was still fired. Did Smith, Mosser, and Floyd breach the state LLC statute, their fiduciary duties, or the Bluewater operating agreements? Discuss. [*Bluewater Logistics, LLC v. Williford,* 55 So.3d 148 (Miss. 2011)]

—**To view a sample answer for Case Problem 14–7, go to Appendix F at the end of this text.**

14–8. The Franchise Contract. Kubota Tractor Corp. makes farm, industrial, and outdoor equipment. Its franchise contracts allow Kubota to enter into dealership agreements with "others at any location." Kejzar Motors, Inc., is a Kubota dealer in Nacogdoches and Jasper, Texas. These two Kejzar stores operate as one dealership with two locations. Kubota granted a dealership to Michael Hammer in Lufkin, Texas, which lies between Kejzar's two store locations. Kejzar filed a suit in a Texas state court against Kubota. Kejzar asked for an injunction to prevent Kubota from locating a dealership in the same market area. Kejzar argued that the new location would cause it to suffer a significant loss of profits. Which party in a franchise relationship typically determines the territory served by a franchisee? Which legal principles come into play in this area? How do these concepts most likely apply in this case? Discuss. [*Kejzar Motors, Inc. v. Kubota Tractor Corp.,* 334 S.W.3d 351 (Tex.App.—Tyler 2011)]

14–9. **A Question of Ethics. Wrongful Dissociation.** *Elliot Willensky and Beverly Moran formed a partnership to renovate and "flip" (resell) some property. According to their agreement, Moran would finance the purchase and renovation of the property, and Willensky would provide labor and oversight of the renovation work. Moran would be reimbursed from the profits of the sale, and the remainder of the profits would be divided evenly. Any losses would also be divided evenly. Moran paid $240,000 for a house and planned to spend $60,000 for its renovation. The parties agreed that the renovation would be completed in six months. Willensky lived in the house during the renovation. More than a year later, the project still was not completed, and the cost was much more than the $60,000 originally planned. Willensky often failed to communicate with Moran, and when she learned that her funds were nearly exhausted and the house nowhere near completion, she became worried. She told Willensky that he would have to pay rent and utility bills if he wished to continue to live in the house. Shortly thereafter, Willensky left for Florida due to a family emergency, saying that he would return as soon as he could. He never returned, however, and Moran lost touch with him. Moran took over the project and discovered that Willensky had left numerous bills unpaid, spent money on excessive or unnecessary items, and misappropriated funds for his personal use. After completing the project, paying all expenses relating to the renovation (in all, the renovation costs came to $311,222), and selling the property, Moran brought an action in a Tennessee state court to dissolve the partnership and to recover damages from Willensky for breach of contract and wrongful dissociation from the partnership.* [*Moran v. Willensky,* ___ S.W.3d ___ (Tenn.Ct.App. 2010)]

1. Moran alleged that Willensky had wrongfully dissociated from the partnership. When did this dissociation occur? Why was his dissociation wrongful?
2. Which of Willensky's actions simply represent unethical behavior or bad management, and which constitute a breach of the agreement?

14–10. **Critical-Thinking Legal Environment Question.** Jordan Mendelson is interested in starting a kitchen franchise business. Customers will come to the business to assemble gourmet dinners and then take the prepared meals to their homes for cooking. The franchisor requires each store to use a specific layout and provides the recipes for various dinners, but the franchisee is not required to purchase the food products from the franchisor. What general factors should Mendelson consider before entering a contract to start such a franchise? Is location important? Are there any laws that Mendelson should consider due to the fact that this franchise involves food preparation and sales? If the franchisor does not insist on a specific type of business entity, should Mendelson operate this business as a sole proprietorship? Why or why not?

Chapter 15

Corporations

> "A corporation is an artificial being, invisible, intangible, and existing only in contemplation of law."
>
> —John Marshall, 1755–1835
> (Chief justice of the United States Supreme Court, 1801–1835)

Contents

Chapter Objectives

After reading this chapter, you should be able to answer the following questions:

1. What steps are involved in bringing a corporation into existence?
2. In what circumstances might a court disregard the corporate entity (pierce the corporate veil) and hold the shareholders personally liable?
3. What are the duties of corporate directors and officers?
4. Directors are expected to use their best judgment in managing the corporation. What must directors do to avoid liability for honest mistakes of judgment and poor business decisions?
5. What is a voting proxy? What is cumulative voting?

(©Svetlana Larina, 2009. Used under license from Shutterstock.com)

The corporation is a creature of statute. As John Marshall indicated in the chapter-opening quotation above, a corporation is an artificial being, existing only in law and neither tangible nor visible. Its existence generally depends on state law, although some corporations, especially public organizations, can be created under state or federal law. Each state has its own body of corporate law, and these laws are not entirely uniform.

The Model Business Corporation Act (MBCA) is a codification of modern corporation law that has been influential in the drafting and revision of state corporation statutes. Today, the majority of state statutes are guided by the revised version of the MBCA, which is often referred to as the Revised Model Business Corporation Act (RMBCA). Keep in mind, however, that corporation laws vary considerably, even among the states that have used the MBCA or the RMBCA as a basis for their statutes, and several states do not follow either act. Consequently, individual state corporation laws should be relied on rather than the MBCA or the RMBCA.

In this chapter, we examine the nature of the corporate form of business enterprise, the various classifications of corporations, and the formation and powers of today's corporations. We then consider the roles of corporate directors, officers, and shareholders.

▶ Corporate Nature and Classification

Corporation A legal entity formed in compliance with statutory requirements that is distinct from its shareholder-owners.

A **corporation** is a legal entity created and recognized by state law. It can consist of one or more *natural persons* (as opposed to the artificial *legal person* of the corporation) identified under a common name. A corporation can be owned by a single person, or it can have hundreds, thousands, or even millions of owners (shareholders). Although the corporation substitutes itself for its shareholders in conducting corporate business and in incurring liability, its authority to act and the liability for its actions are separate and apart from the individuals who own it.

A corporation is recognized as a "person," and it enjoys many of the same rights and privileges under state and federal law that natural persons enjoy. For example, corporations possess the same right of access to the courts as citizens and can sue or be sued. The constitutional guarantees of due process, free speech, and freedom from unreasonable searches and seizures also apply to corporations. Corporations also have a right under the First Amendment to fund political broadcasts—a topic discussed in this chapter's *Landmark in the Legal Environment* feature on the following page.

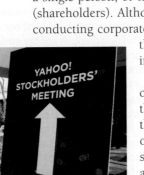

(AP Photo/Paul Sakuma)

Yahoo! has a shareholders' meeting once a year. To what extent do those attending have any say over what direction the company takes?

Corporate Personnel

In a corporation, the responsibility for the overall management of the firm is entrusted to a *board of directors,* whose members are elected by the shareholders. The board of directors hires *corporate officers* and other employees to run the daily business operations of the corporation.

CONTRAST The death of a sole proprietor results in the dissolution of a business. The death of a corporate shareholder, however, rarely causes the dissolution of a corporation.

When an individual purchases a share of stock in a corporation, that person becomes a shareholder and thus an owner of the corporation. Unlike the members of a partnership, the body of shareholders can change constantly without affecting the continued existence of the corporation. A shareholder can sue the corporation, and the corporation can sue a shareholder. Also, under certain circumstances, a shareholder can sue on behalf of a corporation, as discussed later in this chapter.

The Limited Liability of Shareholders

One of the key advantages of the corporate form is the limited liability of its owners (shareholders). Corporate shareholders normally are not personally liable for the obligations of the corporation beyond the extent of their investments. In certain limited situations, however, a court can *pierce the corporate veil* (see page 447) and impose liability on shareholders for the corporation's obligations. Additionally, to enable the firm to obtain credit, shareholders in small companies sometimes voluntarily assume personal liability, as guarantors, for corporate obligations.

Corporate Earnings and Taxation

Dividend A distribution to corporate shareholders of corporate profits or income, disbursed in proportion to the number of shares held.

Retained Earnings The portion of a corporation's profits that has not been paid out as dividends to shareholders.

When a corporation earns profits, it can either pass them on to shareholders in the form of **dividends** or retain them as profits. These **retained earnings,** if invested properly, will yield higher corporate profits in the future and thus cause the price of the company's stock to rise. Individual shareholders can then reap the benefits of these retained earnings in the capital gains that they receive when they sell their stock.

Landmark in the Legal Environment | ***Citizens United v. Federal Election Commission* (2010)**

In *Citizens United v. Federal Election Commission,*[a] the United States Supreme Court held that the First Amendment prohibits restrictions on corporate funding of independent political broadcasts in elections. The case involved the maker of a film called *Hillary: The Movie* that was critical of Hillary Clinton, who was a candidate for the Democratic presidential nomination at the time.

Background   Numerous efforts to reform campaign financing have been made over the years. In 2002, Congress enacted the McCain-Feingold Act, otherwise known as the Bipartisan Campaign Reform Act (BCRA). One provision of the BCRA prohibited corporations and unions from using their general treasury funds to make independent expenditures for speech that is an "electioneering communication" or for speech that expressly advocates the election or defeat of a candidate.[b] An electioneering communication is "any broadcast, cable, or satellite communication" that "refers to a clearly identified candidate for Federal office" and is made within thirty days of a primary election.

Citizens United, the maker of the anti-Hillary film, is a nonprofit political action corporation. Citizens planned to advertise the film on the Internet, sell it on DVD, and show it in a few theaters. Citizens anticipated that it would make *Hillary* available on television through video-on-demand within thirty days of primary elections, and was concerned about potential civil and criminal penalties for violating the BCRA. Citizens filed an action in federal court against the Federal Election Commission seeking a declaratory judgment that the BCRA was unconstitutional as applied to *Hillary*. The lower court granted judgment in favor of the Federal Election Commission, finding that the film had no purpose other than to discredit Clinton's candidacy. Citizens appealed.

A Surprising Decision   In a five-four decision, the United States Supreme Court struck down the provision of the BCRA that prohibited all corporations, both for profit and nonprofit, and unions from broadcasting "electioneering communications." In the majority opinion, Justice Anthony Kennedy stated: "All speakers, including individuals and the media, use money amassed from the economic marketplace to fund their speech. The First Amendment protects the resulting speech, even if it was enabled by economic transactions with persons or entities who disagree with the speaker's ideas." Four justices dissented, with Justice John Paul Stevens arguing that the Court's ruling "threatens to undermine the integrity of elected institutions across the Nation. The path it has taken to reach its outcome will, I fear, do damage to this institution."

The Court's ruling in the *Citizens United* case explicitly overruled two earlier Supreme Court decisions on election financing.[c] Only the portion of the BCRA that prohibited electioneering communications was affected, however. The Court upheld other provisions that require disclosures that identify the person or entity responsible for the content.

• Application to Today's Legal Environment   *The* Citizens United *decision effectively undid some of the hard-won legislation on campaign-finance reform. Many commentators—including President Barack Obama in his 2010 State of the Union address— claim that this decision will open the floodgates and allow huge corporations, including foreign-owed corporations, to influence our elections. Although federal law still prevents corporations and unions from contributing directly to campaigns, these entities can now fund advertising and other forms of communication that seek to persuade the voting public.*

---

a. 588 U.S. 50, 130 S.Ct. 876, 175 L.Ed.2d 753 (2010).
b. 2 U.S.C. Section 441b.

c. *Austin v. Michigan Chamber of Commerce,* 494 U.S. 652, 110 S.Ct. 1391, 108 L.Ed.2d 652 (1990); and *McConnell v. Federal Election Commission,* 540 U.S. 93, 124 S.Ct. 619, 157 L.Ed.2d 491 (2003).

Whether a corporation retains its profits or passes them on to the shareholders as dividends, those profits are subject to income tax by various levels of government. Failure to pay taxes can lead to severe consequences. The state can suspend the entity's corporate status until the taxes are paid or even dissolve the corporation for failing to pay taxes.

Another important aspect of corporate taxation is that corporate profits can be subject to double taxation. The company pays tax on its profits, and then if the profits are passed on to the shareholders as dividends, the shareholders must also pay income tax on them. The corporation normally does not receive a tax deduction for dividends it distributes to shareholders. This double-taxation feature is one of the major disadvantages of the corporate business form.

A taxation issue of increasing importance to corporations is whether they are required to collect state sales taxes on goods or services sold to consumers via the Internet. See this chapter's *Online Developments* feature on the following page for a discussion of this issue.

Torts and Criminal Acts

A corporation is liable for the torts committed by its agents or officers within the course and scope of their employment. This principle applies to a corporation exactly as it applies to the ordinary agency relationships that we will discuss in Chapter 16.

Recall from Chapter 6 that under modern criminal law, a corporation may be held liable for the criminal acts of its agents and employees, provided the punishment is one that can be applied to the corporation. Although corporations cannot be imprisoned, they can be fined. (Of course, corporate directors and officers can be imprisoned, and many have been in recent years.) In addition, under sentencing guidelines for crimes committed by corporate employees (white-collar crimes), corporate lawbreakers can face fines amounting to hundreds of millions of dollars.[1]

CASE EXAMPLE 15.1 Brian Gauthier was a truck driver who worked for Angelo Todesca Corporation. Gauthier drove the AT-56, a ten-wheel dump truck. Although Angelo's safety manual required its trucks to be equipped with back-up alarms that automatically sounded when the trucks were put into reverse, the AT-56's alarm was missing. Angelo ordered a new alarm but allowed Gauthier to continue driving the AT-56. At a worksite, when Gauthier backed up the AT-56 to dump its load, he struck and killed a police officer who was directing traffic through the site and facing away from the truck. The state charged Angelo and Gauthier with the crime of vehicular homicide. Angelo argued that a "corporation" could not be guilty of vehicular homicide because it cannot "operate" a vehicle. The court ruled that if an employee commits a crime "while engaged in corporate business that the employee has been authorized to conduct," a corporation can be held liable for the crime. Hence, the court held that Angelo was liable for Gauthier's negligent operation of the corporation's truck, which resulted in a person's death.[2] ●

Classification of Corporations

Corporations can be classified in several ways. The classification of a corporation normally depends on its location, purpose, and ownership characteristics, as described in the following subsections.

Domestic Corporation In a given state, a corporation that does business in, and is organized under the law of, that state.

Foreign Corporation In a given state, a corporation that does business in the state without being incorporated therein.

Alien Corporation A designation in the United States for a corporation formed in another country but doing business in the United States.

DOMESTIC, FOREIGN, AND ALIEN CORPORATIONS A corporation is referred to as a **domestic corporation** by its home state (the state in which it incorporates). A corporation formed in one state but doing business in another is referred to in the second state as a **foreign corporation.** A corporation formed in another country (say, Mexico) but doing business in the United States is referred to in the United States as an **alien corporation.**

A corporation does not have an automatic right to do business in a state other than its state of incorporation. In some instances, it must obtain a *certificate of authority* in any state in which it plans to do business. Once the certificate has been issued,

---

1. Note that the Sarbanes-Oxley Act of 2002, discussed in Chapter 2, stiffened the penalties for certain types of corporate crime and ordered the U.S. Sentencing Commission to revise the sentencing guidelines accordingly.
2. *Commonwealth v. Angelo Todesca Corp.*, 446 Mass. 128, 842 N.E.2d 930 (2006).

Online Developments

Economic Recession Fuels the "Amazon Tax" Debate

As discussed in the *Online Developments* feature in Chapter 11 on page 309, governments at the state and federal levels have long debated whether states should be able to collect sales taxes on online sales to in-state customers. State governments claim that their inability to tax online sales has caused them to lose billions of dollars in sales tax revenue. The issue has taken on new urgency as the states search desperately for revenue in the wake of the economic recession that began in December 2007.

Supreme Court Precedent Requires Physical Presence

In 1992, the United States Supreme Court ruled that no individual state can compel an out-of-state business that lacks a substantial physical presence (such as a warehouse, office, or retail store) within that state to collect and remit state taxes.[a] The Court recognized that Congress has the power to pass legislation requiring out-of-state corporations to collect and remit state sales taxes, but Congress so far has chosen not to tax Internet transactions. In fact, Congress temporarily prohibited the states from taxing Internet sales, and that ban was extended until 2014.[b] Thus, only online retailers that also have a physical presence within a state must collect state taxes on any Web sales made to residents of that state. (Otherwise, state residents are required to self-report their purchases and pay use taxes to the state, which rarely happens.)

New York Changed Its Definition of Physical Presence

In an effort to collect taxes on Internet sales made by out-of-state corporations, New York changed its tax laws in 2008 to redefine *physical presence.* Under the new law, if an online retailer pays any party within the state to solicit business for its products, that retailer has a physical presence in the state and must collect state taxes.[c] For example, Amazon.com, America's largest online retailer, pays thousands of associates in New York to post ads that link to Amazon's Web site. Consequently, the law requires Amazon to collect tax on any sales to New York residents.

Both Amazon and Overstock.com, a Utah corporation, filed lawsuits in 2009 claiming that the new law was unconstitutional. A New York court dismissed Amazon's case, finding that the law provided a sufficient basis for requiring collection of New York taxes. As long as the seller has a substantial connection with the state, the taxes need not derive from in-state activity. The court also observed that "out-of-state sellers can shield themselves from a tax-collection obligation by altogether prohibiting in-state solicitation activities . . . on their behalf."[d] As a result, Amazon now collects and pays state sales taxes on shipments to New York. Overstock canceled agreements with its New York affiliates.

The "Amazon Tax"

Since then, a number of states have changed their law on physical presence in an effort to collect sales tax from online retailers and close substantial gaps in their state budgets. These new laws, which many call the "Amazon tax" because they are largely aimed at Amazon, affect all online sellers (including Overstock.com and Drugstore.com)—especially those that pay affiliates to direct traffic to their Web sites. California enacted such a law in 2011, and Amazon quickly announced that it had canceled agreements with its California affiliates. By 2012, the Amazon tax had caused Amazon to end its arrangements with affiliates in Colorado, Illinois, North Carolina, and Rhode Island as well. When California officials insisted that its law still applied to Amazon because of other contacts with the state, such as the presence of a firm that handles some of Amazon's advertising, Amazon announced that it would support a proposed ballot initiative to repeal the law in 2012.

FOR CRITICAL ANALYSIS

Should the fact that an out-of-state corporation pays affiliates in a state to direct consumers to its Web site be sufficient to require the corporation to collect taxes on Web sales to state residents? Why or why not?

a. See *Quill Corp. v. North Dakota,* 504 U.S. 298, 112 S.Ct. 1904, 119 L.Ed.2d 91 (1992).
b. Internet Tax Freedom Act, Pub. L. No. 105-277; 47 U.S.C. Section 151 note (1998), extended to 2014 by Pub. L. No. 110-108.
c. New York Tax Law Section 1101(b)(8)(vi).
d. *Amazon.com, LLC v. New York State Department of Taxation and Finance,* 23 Misc.3d 418, 877 N.Y.S.2d 842 (2009); affirmed at 81 A.D.3d 183, 913 N.Y.S.2d 129 (2010).

NOTE   A private corporation is a voluntary association, but a public corporation is not.

the corporation generally can exercise in that state all of the powers conferred on it by its home state. If a foreign corporation does business in a state without obtaining a certificate of authority, the state can impose substantial fines and sanctions on the corporation, and sometimes even on its officers, directors, or agents. Note that most state statutes specify certain activities, such as soliciting orders via the Internet, that

AMTRAK is a public corporation. How does a public corporation differ from a private corporation?

are not considered doing business within the state. Thus, a foreign corporation normally does not need a certificate of authority to sell goods or services via the Internet or by mail.

PUBLIC AND PRIVATE CORPORATIONS　A public corporation is one formed by the government to meet some political or governmental purpose. Cities and towns that incorporate are common examples. In addition, many federal government organizations, such as the U.S. Postal Service, the Tennessee Valley Authority, and AMTRAK, are public corporations. Note that a public corporation is not the same as a *publicly held* corporation (often called a *public company*). A publicly held corporation is any corporation whose shares are publicly traded in securities markets, such as the New York Stock Exchange or the over-the-counter market.

In contrast to public corporations (*not* public companies), private corporations are created either wholly or in part for private benefit. Most corporations are private. Although they may serve a public purpose, as a public electric or gas utility does, they are owned by private persons rather than by the government.

NONPROFIT CORPORATIONS　Corporations formed for purposes other than making a profit are called *nonprofit* or *not-for-profit* corporations. Private hospitals, educational institutions, charities, and religious organizations, for example, are frequently organized as nonprofit corporations. The nonprofit corporation is a convenient form of organization that allows various groups to own property and to form contracts without exposing the individual members to personal liability.

CLOSE CORPORATIONS　Most corporate enterprises in the United States fall into the category of close corporations. A **close corporation** is one whose shares are held by members of a family or by relatively few persons. Close corporations are also referred to as *closely held, family,* or *privately held* corporations. Usually, the members of the small group constituting a close corporation are personally known to one another, and there is no trading market for the shares.

Close Corporation　A corporation whose shareholders are limited to a small group of persons, often only family members. In a close corporation, the shareholders' rights to transfer shares to others are usually restricted.

In practice, a close corporation is often operated like a partnership. Some states have enacted special statutory provisions that apply to close corporations. These provisions expressly permit close corporations to depart significantly from certain formalities required by traditional corporation law.[3]

Additionally, a provision added to the RMBCA in 1991 gives close corporations a substantial amount of flexibility in determining the rules by which they will operate [RMBCA 7.32]. If all of a corporation's shareholders agree in writing, the corporation can operate without directors, bylaws, annual or special shareholders' or directors' meetings, stock certificates, or formal records of shareholders' or directors' decisions.[4]

Management of Close Corporations. A close corporation has a single shareholder or a closely knit group of shareholders, who usually hold the positions of directors

---

3. For example, in some states (such as Maryland), a close corporation need not have a board of directors.

4. Shareholders cannot agree, however, to eliminate certain rights of shareholders, such as the right to inspect corporate books and records or the right to bring *derivative* actions (lawsuits on behalf of the corporation—discussed later in this chapter).

and officers. Management of a close corporation resembles that of a sole proprietorship or a partnership. As a corporation, however, the firm must meet all specific legal requirements set forth in state statutes.

To prevent a majority shareholder from dominating a close corporation, the corporation may require that more than a simple majority of the directors approve any action taken by the board. Typically, this would apply only to extraordinary actions, such as changing the amount of dividends or dismissing an employee-shareholder, and not to ordinary business decisions.

Transfer of Shares in Close Corporations. By definition, a close corporation has a small number of shareholders. Thus, the transfer of one shareholder's shares to someone else can cause serious management problems. The other shareholders may find themselves required to share control with someone they do not know or like.

EXAMPLE 15.2 Three brothers—Terry, Damon, and Henry Johnson—are the only shareholders of Johnson's Car Wash, Inc. Terry and Damon do not want Henry to sell his shares to an unknown third person. To avoid this situation, the corporation could restrict the transferability of shares to outside persons. Shareholders could be required to offer their shares to the corporation or the other shareholders before selling them to an outside purchaser. In fact, a few states have statutes that prohibit the transfer of close corporation shares unless certain persons—including shareholders, family members, and the corporation—are first given the opportunity to purchase the shares for the same price. ●

Control of a close corporation can also be stabilized through the use of a *shareholder agreement*. A shareholder agreement can provide that when one of the original shareholders dies, her or his shares of stock in the corporation will be divided in such a way that the proportionate holdings of the survivors, and thus their proportionate control, will be maintained. Courts are generally reluctant to interfere with private agreements, including shareholder agreements.

Misappropriation of Close Corporation Funds. Sometimes, a majority shareholder in a close corporation takes advantage of his or her position and misappropriates company funds. In such situations, the normal remedy for the injured minority shareholders is to have their shares appraised and to be paid the fair market value for them.

In the following case, a minority shareholder charged that the majority shareholders paid themselves excessive compensation in breach of their fiduciary duty.

Case 15.1   Rubin v. Murray

Appeals Court of Massachusetts, 79 Mass.App.Ct. 64, 943 N.E.2d 949 (2011).
www.massreports.com/OpinionArchive[a]

BACKGROUND AND FACTS   Olympic Adhesives, Inc., makes and sells industrial adhesives. John Murray, Stephen Hopkins, and Paul Ryan were the controlling shareholders of the company, as well as officers, directors, and employees. Merek Rubin was a minority

---

a. In the "Release date:" box, type "03/16/2011," and click on "submit." In the result, click on the appropriate link to view the opinion. The Reporter of Decisions for the Massachusetts Supreme Judicial Court and the Appeals Court maintains this Web site.

shareholder. Murray, Hopkins, and Ryan were paid salaries. Under Olympic's profit-sharing plan, one-third of its net operating income was paid into a fund that was distributed to employees, including Murray, Hopkins, and Ryan. Twice a year, Murray, Hopkins, and Ryan also paid themselves additional compensation—a percentage of the net profits after profit sharing, allocated according to their stock ownership. Over a fifteen-year period, the percentage grew from 75 percent to between 92 and 98 percent. During this time, the additional compensation totaled nearly $15 million. Rubin filed a suit in a Massachusetts state court against

Case 15.1—Continued

Murray, Hopkins, and Ryan, alleging that they had paid themselves excessive compensation and deprived him of his share of Olympic's profits in violation of their fiduciary duty to him as a minority shareholder. The court ordered the defendants to repay Olympic nearly $6 million to be distributed among its shareholders. The defendants appealed.

IN THE WORDS OF THE COURT . . .
KATZMANN, J. [Judge]
    * * * *

    [The trial] judge undertook to determine the reasonable compensation for top executives in a firm of Olympic's size and character, in order to determine the excess amounts that should be returned to the corporation. The defendants claim that the judge relied on speculative and insufficient evidence in determining what amounts constituted their reasonable compensation for the relevant years.

    * * * *A salary must bear a reasonable relation to the officer's ability and to the quantity and quality of the services he renders. In addition, compensation may be based to some extent on the profits resulting from their efforts.* [Emphasis added.]
    * * * *

    * * * The judge, relying on evidence that officer compensation fell between approximately four percent to seven percent of net sales for comparable companies * * * , and adding his own success premium based on the individual defendants' significant abilities and contributions, determined that fair and reasonable compensation for them was approximately ten percent of Olympic's average annual net sales. *Determining reasonable compensation based on a percentage of net profits, with his own adjustments for performance, was a*

permissible exercise of the judge's discretion. This amount the judge then confirmed with evidence of the average compensation for top officers in comparable firms. [Emphasis added.]
    * * * The judge could appropriately take into account that Murray, Olympic's president and treasurer, was vague in identifying a basis for determining distribution of additional compensation among the individual defendants and, when pressed by the judge, testified that Olympic used no numerical factors to set or apportion the additional compensation. The judge found it significant that amounts paid to the individual defendants in additional compensation corresponded to the percentage of their stock ownership, rather than to any enumerated performance factors bearing on the distribution, and he was entitled to reject Murray's explanation that the correlation was just a coincidence.

DECISION AND REMEDY   A state intermediate appellate court affirmed the lower court's judgment. The appellate court concluded that the findings as to the amounts that constituted reasonable compensation for the defendants were based on sufficient evidence and were not clearly erroneous.

WHAT IF THE FACTS WERE DIFFERENT?   *Suppose that Murray could have pinpointed a job-related basis for the distribution of the net profits among the defendants. Would the result have been different? Explain.*

THE ECONOMIC DIMENSION   *What are the tax consequences of passing corporate profits on to the shareholders as dividends?*

S Corporation A close business corporation that has met certain requirements set out in the Internal Revenue Code and thus qualifies for special income tax treatment. Essentially, an S corporation is taxed the same as a partnership, but its owners enjoy the privilege of limited liability.

S CORPORATIONS   A close corporation that meets the qualifying requirements specified in Subchapter S of the Internal Revenue Code can operate as an **S corporation.** If a corporation has S corporation status, it can avoid the imposition of income taxes at the corporate level while retaining many of the advantages of a corporation, particularly limited liability. Among the numerous requirements for S corporation status, the following are the most important:

1. The corporation must be a domestic corporation.
2. The corporation must not be a member of an affiliated group of corporations.
3. The shareholders of the corporation must be individuals, estates, or certain trusts. Partnerships and nonqualifying trusts cannot be shareholders. Corporations can be shareholders under certain circumstances.
4. The corporation must have no more than one hundred shareholders.
5. The corporation must have only one class of stock, although all shareholders do not have to have the same voting rights.
6. No shareholder of the corporation may be a nonresident alien.

    An S corporation is treated differently from a regular corporation for tax purposes. An S corporation is taxed like a partnership, so the corporate income passes through to the shareholders, who pay personal income tax on it. This treatment enables the S corporation to avoid the double taxation that is imposed on regular corporations. In addition, the shareholders' tax brackets may be lower than the tax bracket that the corporation would have been in if the tax had been imposed at the corporate level. This tax saving is particularly attractive when the corporation wants to accumulate earnings for some future business purpose. If the corporation has losses, the S election allows the shareholders to use the losses to offset other taxable income. Nevertheless, because the limited liability company and the limited liability partnership (see Chapter 14) offer similar tax advantages and greater flexibility, the S corporation has lost some of its significance.

CONTRAST Unlike the shareholders of most other corporations, the shareholders of professional corporations generally must be licensed professionals.

PROFESSIONAL CORPORATIONS   Professionals such as physicians, lawyers, dentists, and accountants can incorporate. Professional corporations typically are identified by the letters *S.C.* (service corporation), *P.C.* (professional corporation), or *P.A.* (professional association).

In general, the laws governing the formation and operation of professional corporations are similar to those governing ordinary business corporations. There are some differences in terms of liability, however, because the shareholder-owners are professionals who are held to a higher standard of conduct. For liability purposes, some courts treat a professional corporation somewhat like a partnership and hold each professional liable for any malpractice committed within the scope of the business by the others in the firm. With the exception of malpractice or a breach of duty to clients or patients, a shareholder in a professional corporation generally cannot be held liable for the torts committed by other professionals at the firm.

 Corporate Formation and Powers

Up to this point, we have discussed some of the general characteristics of corporations. We now examine the process by which corporations come into existence. Incorporating a business is much simpler today than it was twenty years ago, and many states allow businesses to incorporate via the Internet. If the owners of a partnership or sole proprietorship wish to expand the business, they may decide to incorporate because a corporation can obtain more capital by issuing shares of stock.

Promotional Activities

> *"A man to carry on a successful business must have imagination. He must see things as in a vision, a dream of the whole thing."*
> Charles M. Schwab, 1862–1939
> (American industrialist)

In the past, preliminary steps were taken to organize and promote the business prior to incorporating. Contracts were made with investors and others on behalf of the future corporation. Today, due to the relative ease of forming a corporation in most states, persons incorporating their business rarely, if ever, engage in preliminary promotional activities. Nevertheless, it is important for businesspersons to understand that they are personally liable for all preincorporation contracts made with investors, accountants, or others on behalf of the future corporation. This personal liability continues until the corporation assumes the preincorporation contracts by *novation* (discussed in Chapter 10).

EXAMPLE 15.3   Jade Sorrel contracts with an accountant, Ray Cooper, to provide tax advice for a proposed corporation, Blackstone, Inc. Cooper provides the services to Sorrel, knowing that the corporation has not yet been formed. Once Blackstone, Inc., is formed, Cooper sends an invoice to the corporation and to Sorrel personally, but the bill is not paid. Because Sorrel is personally liable for the preincorporation contract, Cooper can file a lawsuit against Sorrel for breaching the contract for accounting services. Cooper cannot seek to hold Blackstone, Inc., liable unless he has entered into a novation contract with the corporation. ●

Incorporation Procedures

Exact procedures for incorporation differ among states, but the basic steps are as follows: (1) select a state of incorporation, (2) secure the corporate name by confirming its availability, (3) prepare the articles of incorporation, and (4) file the articles of incorporation with the secretary of state accompanied by payment of the specified fees. These steps are discussed in more detail in the following subsections.

SELECT THE STATE OF INCORPORATION   The first step in the incorporation process is to select a state in which to incorporate. Because state corporation laws differ, individuals may look for the states that offer the most advantageous tax or other provisions. Another consideration is the fee that a particular state charges to incorporate, as well as the annual fees and the fees for specific transactions (such as stock transfers).

Delaware has historically had the least restrictive laws and provisions that favor corporate management. Consequently, many corporations, including a number of the largest, have incorporated there. Delaware's statutes permit firms to incorporate in that state and conduct business and locate their operating headquarters elsewhere. Most other states now permit this as well. Note, though, that close corporations, for reasons of convenience and cost, generally incorporate in the state where their principal shareholders live and work.

SECURE THE CORPORATE NAME   The choice of a corporate name is subject to state approval to ensure against duplication or deception. State statutes usually require that the secretary of state run a check on the proposed name in the state of incorporation. Some states require that the persons incorporating a firm, at their own expense, run a check on the proposed name, which can often be accomplished via Internet-based services. Once cleared, a name can be reserved for a short time, for a fee, pending the completion of the articles of incorporation. All corporate statutes require the corporation name to include the word *Corporation*, *Incorporated*, *Company*, or *Limited*, or abbreviations of these terms.

A new corporation's name cannot be the same as (or deceptively similar to) the name of an existing corporation doing business within the state. If those incorporating the firm contemplate doing business in other states—or over the Internet—they also need to check on existing corporate names in those states as well. In addition, because the firm will want to use its name as its Internet domain name, the persons incorporating the firm will need to make sure that the domain name is available by checking the database of domain names at the Internet Corporation for Assigned Names and Numbers (ICANN).

EXAMPLE 15.4   If an existing corporation is named Digital Synergy, Inc., the state is unlikely to allow a new corporation to choose the name Digital Synergy Company. That name is deceptively similar to the first and could impliedly transfer part of the goodwill established by the first corporate user to the second corporation, thereby infringing on the first company's trademark rights. In addition, the new corporation could not use Digital Synergy Company as a domain name if the existing corporation used Digital Synergy, Inc., as its domain name. ●

PREPARE THE ARTICLES OF INCORPORATION   The primary document needed to incorporate a business is the **articles of incorporation.** The articles include basic information about the corporation and serve as a primary source of authority for its future organization and business functions. The person or persons who execute

Articles of Incorporation   The document filed with the appropriate governmental agency, usually the secretary of state, when a business is incorporated. State statutes usually prescribe what kind of information must be contained in the articles of incorporation.

A new corporation must select a name that is not already in use and cannot be confused with an existing corporate name. What level of government usually approves corporate names?

(AP Photo/Al Behrman)

(sign) the articles are called *incorporators*. Generally, the articles of incorporation *must* include the following information [RMBCA 2.02]:

1. The name of the corporation.
2. The number of shares the corporation is authorized to issue.
3. The name and address of the corporation's initial registered agent.
4. The name and address of each incorporator.

In addition, the articles *may* set forth other information, such as the names and addresses of the initial board of directors, the duration and purpose of the corporation, a par value of shares of the corporation, and any other information pertinent to the rights and duties of the corporation's shareholders and directors. Articles of incorporation vary widely depending on the size and type of corporation and the jurisdiction. Frequently, the articles do not provide much detail about the firm's operations, which are spelled out in the company's **bylaws** (internal rules of management adopted by the corporation at its first organizational meeting).

Bylaws A set of governing rules adopted by a corporation or other association.

Shares of the Corporation. The articles must specify the number of shares of stock authorized for issuance. For instance, a company might state that the aggregate number of shares that the corporation has the authority to issue is five thousand. Large corporations often state a par value of each share, such as twenty cents per share, and specify the various types or classes of stock authorized for issuance. Sometimes, the articles set forth the capital structure of the corporation and other relevant information concerning equity, shares, and credit.

Registered Office and Agent. The corporation must indicate the location and address of its registered office within the state. Usually, the registered office is also the principal office of the corporation. The corporation must also give the name and address of a specific person who has been designated as an *agent* and can receive legal documents (such as orders to appear in court) on behalf of the corporation.

Incorporators. Each incorporator must be listed by name and address. The incorporators need not have any interest at all in the corporation, and sometimes signing the articles is their only duty. Many states do not have residency or age requirements for incorporators. States vary on the required number of incorporators—it can be as few as one or as many as three. Incorporators frequently participate in the first organizational meeting of the corporation.

Duration and Purpose. A corporation has perpetual existence unless the articles state otherwise. The RMBCA does not require a specific statement of purpose to be included in the articles. A corporation can be formed for any lawful purpose. Some incorporators choose to include a general statement of purpose "to engage in any lawful act or activity," while others opt to specify the intended business activities ("to engage in the production and sale of agricultural products," for example). It is increasingly common for the articles to state that the corporation is organized for "any legal business," with no mention of specifics, to avoid the need for future amendments to the corporate articles.

KEEP IN MIND Unlike the articles of incorporation, bylaws do not need to be filed with a state official.

Internal Organization. The articles can describe the internal management structure of the corporation, although this is usually included in the bylaws adopted after the corporation is formed. The articles of incorporation commence the corporation, whereas the bylaws are formed after commencement by the board of directors. Bylaws cannot conflict with the corporation statute or the articles of incorporation [RMBCA 2.06].

Under the RMBCA, shareholders may amend or repeal the bylaws. The board of directors may also amend or repeal the bylaws unless the articles of incorporation or provisions of the corporation statute reserve this power to the shareholders exclusively [RMBCA 10.20]. Typical bylaw provisions describe such matters as voting requirements for shareholders, the election of the board of directors, the methods of replacing directors, and the manner and time of holding shareholders' and board meetings. (These corporate activities will be discussed later in this chapter.)

FILE THE ARTICLES WITH THE STATE   Once the articles of incorporation have been prepared, signed, and authenticated by the incorporators, they are sent to the appropriate state official, usually the secretary of state, along with the required filing fee. In most states, the secretary of state then stamps the articles as "Filed" and returns a copy of the articles to the incorporators. Once this occurs, the corporation officially exists. (Note that some states issue a *certificate of incorporation,* which represents the state's authorization for the corporation to conduct business. This procedure was typical under the unrevised MBCA.)

First Organizational Meeting to Adopt Bylaws

After incorporation, the first organizational meeting must be held. Usually, the most important function of this meeting is the adoption of bylaws—the internal rules of management for the corporation. If the articles of incorporation named the initial board of directors, then the directors, by majority vote, call the meeting to adopt the bylaws and complete the company's organization. If the articles did not name the directors (as is typical), then the incorporators hold the meeting to elect the directors, adopt bylaws, and complete the routine business of incorporation (authorizing the issuance of shares and hiring employees, for example). The business transacted depends on the requirements of the state's corporation statute, the nature of the corporation, the provisions made in the articles, and the desires of the incorporators.

Improper Incorporation

The procedures for incorporation are very specific. If they are not followed precisely, others may be able to challenge the existence of the corporation. Errors in incorporation procedures can become important when, for example, a third party who is attempting to enforce a contract or bring a suit for a tort injury learns of them.

DE JURE AND DE FACTO CORPORATIONS   If a corporation has substantially complied with all conditions precedent to incorporation, the corporation is said to have *de jure* (rightful and lawful) existence. In most states and under RMBCA 2.03(b), the secretary of state's filing of the articles of incorporation is conclusive proof that all mandatory statutory provisions have been met [RMBCA 2.03(b)].

Sometimes, the incorporators fail to comply with all statutory mandates. If the defect is minor, such as an incorrect address listed on the articles of incorporation, most courts will overlook the defect and find that a corporation (*de jure*) exists. If the defect is substantial, however, such as a corporation's failure to hold an organizational meeting to adopt bylaws, the outcome will vary depending on the court. Some states, including Mississippi, New York, Ohio, and Oklahoma, still recognize the common law doctrine of *de facto* corporation, under which the corporation's status can be challenged by the state but not by third parties.[5]

Many state courts, however, have interpreted their states' version of the RMBCA as abolishing the common law doctrine of *de facto* corporations. These states include Alaska, Arizona, the District of Columbia, New Mexico, Minnesota, Oregon, South Dakota, Tennessee, Utah, and Washington. In those states, if there is a substantial defect in complying with the incorporation statute, the corporation does not legally exist, and the incorporators are personally liable.

CORPORATION BY ESTOPPEL   If a business holds itself out to others as being a corporation but has made no attempt to incorporate, the firm may be estopped (prevented) from denying corporate status in a lawsuit by a third party. This doctrine of corporation by estoppel is most commonly applied when a third party contracts with an entity that claims to be a corporation but has not filed articles of incorporation—or contracts with a person claiming to be an agent of a corporation that does not in fact exist. When justice requires, courts in some states will treat an alleged corporation as if it were an actual corporation for the purpose of determining rights and liabilities in particular circumstances. Recognition of corporate status does not extend beyond the resolution of the problem at hand.[6]

Corporate Powers

When a corporation is created, the express and implied powers necessary to achieve its purpose also come into existence. The express powers of a corporation are found in its articles of incorporation, in the law of the state of incorporation, and in the state and federal constitutions.

Corporate bylaws also establish the express powers of the corporation. Because state corporation statutes frequently provide default rules that apply if the company's bylaws are silent on an issue, it is important that the bylaws set forth the specific operating rules of the corporation. In addition, after the bylaws are adopted, the corporation's board of directors will pass resolutions that also grant or restrict corporate powers.

The following order of priority is used when conflicts arise among documents involving corporations:

1. The U.S. Constitution.
2. State constitutions.
3. State statutes.
4. The articles of incorporation.
5. Bylaws.
6. Resolutions of the board of directors.

IMPLIED POWERS   When a corporation is created, it acquires certain implied powers. Barring express constitutional, statutory, or other prohibitions, the corporation has the implied power to perform all acts reasonably appropriate and necessary to accomplish its corporate purposes. For this reason, a corporation has the implied power to borrow funds within certain limits, to lend funds, and to extend credit to those with whom it has a legal or contractual relationship.

To borrow funds, the corporation acts through its board of directors to authorize the loan. Most often, the president or chief executive officer of the corporation will

---

5. See, for example, *In re Hausman*, 13 N.Y.3d 408, 921 N.E.2d 191, 893 N.Y.S.2d 499 (2009).
6. See, for example, *Brown v. W. P. Media, Inc.*, 17 So.3d 1167 (Ala.Sup.Ct. 2009).

execute the necessary papers on behalf of the corporation. In so doing, corporate officers have the implied power to bind the corporation in matters directly connected with the *ordinary* business affairs of the enterprise. There is a limit to what a corporate officer can do, though. A corporate officer does not have the authority to bind the corporation to an action that will greatly affect the corporate purpose or undertaking, such as the sale of substantial corporate assets.

ULTRA VIRES DOCTRINE The term *ultra vires* means "beyond the power." In corporate law, acts of a corporation that are beyond its express or implied powers are *ultra vires* acts. Under Section 3.04 of the RMBCA, the shareholders can seek an injunction from a court to prevent the corporation from engaging in *ultra vires* acts. The attorney general in the state of incorporation can also bring an action to obtain an injunction against the *ultra vires* transactions or to institute dissolution proceedings against the corporation on the basis of *ultra vires* acts. The corporation or its shareholders (on behalf of the corporation) can seek damages from the officers and directors who were responsible for the *ultra vires* acts.

> **Ultra Vires** A Latin term meaning "beyond the powers"; in corporate law, acts of a corporation that are beyond its express and implied powers to undertake.

In the past, most cases dealing with *ultra vires* acts involved contracts made for unauthorized purposes. Now, however, most private corporations are organized for "any legal business" and do not state a specific purpose, so the *ultra vires* doctrine has declined in importance in recent years. Today, cases that allege *ultra vires* acts usually involve nonprofit corporations or municipal (public) corporations.

CASE EXAMPLE 15.5 Four men formed a nonprofit corporation to create the Armenian Genocide Museum & Memorial (AGM&M). The bylaws appointed them as trustees (similar to corporate directors) for life. One of the trustees, Gerard L. Cafesjian, became the chair and president of AGM&M. Eventually, the relationship among the trustees deteriorated, and Cafesjian resigned. The corporation then brought a suit claiming that Cafesjian had engaged in numerous *ultra vires* acts, self-dealing, and mismanagement. Among other things, although the bylaws required an 80 percent affirmative vote of the trustees to take action, Cafesjian had taken many actions without the board's approval. He had also entered into contracts for real estate transactions in which he had a personal interest. Because Cafesjian had taken actions that exceeded his authority and had failed to follow the rules set forth in the bylaws for board meetings, the court ruled that the corporation could go forward with its suit.[7] ●

▶ Piercing the Corporate Veil

Occasionally, the owners use a corporate entity to perpetrate a fraud, circumvent the law, or in some other way accomplish an illegitimate objective. In these situations, the court will ignore the corporate structure by **piercing the corporate veil** and exposing the shareholders to personal liability. Generally, when the corporate privilege is abused for personal benefit or when the corporate business is treated so carelessly that the corporation and the controlling shareholder are no longer separate entities, the court will require the owner to assume personal liability to creditors for the corporation's debts. In short, when the facts show that great injustice would result from the use of a corporation to avoid individual responsibility, a court will look behind the corporate structure to the individual shareholder.

> **Piercing the Corporate Veil** An action in which a court disregards the corporate entity and holds the shareholders personally liable for corporate debts and obligations.

---

7. *Armenian Assembly of America, Inc. v. Cafesjian*, 692 F.Supp.2d 20 (D.C. 2010).

Factors That Lead Courts to Pierce the Corporate Veil

The following are some of the factors that frequently cause the courts to pierce the corporate veil:

1. A party is tricked or misled into dealing with the corporation rather than the individual.
2. The corporation is set up never to make a profit or always to be insolvent, or it is too "thinly" capitalized—that is, it has insufficient capital at the time of formation to meet its prospective debts or other potential liabilities.
3. The corporation is formed to evade an existing legal obligation.
4. Statutory corporate formalities, such as holding required corporation meetings, are not followed.
5. Personal and corporate interests are **commingled** (mixed together) to such an extent that the corporation has no separate identity.

Commingle   To put funds or goods together into one mass so that they are mixed to such a degree that they no longer have separate identities. In corporate law, if personal and corporate interests are commingled to the extent that the corporation has no separate identity, a court may "pierce the corporate veil" and expose the shareholders to personal liability.

A Potential Problem for Close Corporations

The potential for corporate assets to be used for personal benefit is especially great in a close corporation, in which the shares are held by a single person or by only a few individuals, usually family members. In such a situation, the separate status of the corporate entity and the sole shareholder (or family-member shareholders) must be carefully preserved. Certain practices invite trouble for the one-person or family-owned corporation: the commingling of corporate and personal funds, the failure to hold board of directors' meetings and record the minutes, or the shareholders' continuous personal use of corporate property (for example, vehicles).

In the following case, a creditor asked the court to pierce the corporate veil and hold the sole shareholder-owner of the debtor corporation personally liable for a corporate debt.

Case 15.2   Schultz v. General Electric Healthcare Financial Services

Court of Appeals of Kentucky, ___ S.W.3d ___ (2010).

(Daniel Acker/Bloomberg/Getty Images)

A digital-imaging machine from General Electric.

BACKGROUND AND FACTS
Thomas Schultz was the president and sole shareholder-owner of Intra-Med Services, Inc., a Kentucky corporation that performed medical diagnostic-imaging services. Several General Electric Companies (collectively, GE) leased certain medical equipment to Intra-Med. When Intra-Med failed to make the required lease payments, GE sued Intra-Med to recover the payments. In 2004, the court entered a judgment in favor of GE for more than $4.7 million. GE was able to collect approximately $700,000 of the judgment. GE then learned of documents from another lawsuit that revealed Schultz had used Intra-Med assets for his own purposes. He had bought property using Intra-Med funds,

and when it was sold, he had kept the proceeds. GE intervened in the other lawsuit and filed a third party complaint against Schultz, seeking to pierce the corporate veil and hold him personally liable for the judgment against Intra-Med. GE requested a judgment in the amount of $1,150,000, allegedly the amount of Intra-Med funds that Schultz had used improperly. The trial court denied GE's request, stating that Schultz might have been entitled to some payments from Intra-Med because he had personally loaned the company $700,000. GE agreed to settle for $450,000, the difference between $1,150,000 and the claimed $700,000 loan. The court issued a judgment in GE's favor, and Schultz appealed.

IN THE WORDS OF THE COURT . . .
STUMBO, Judge.
* * * *

Mr. Schultz admitted several facts in his answer to GE's third-party complaint. The relevant admitted facts are: on November 15, 2004, GE

Case 15.2–Continued

was awarded a judgment in the amount of $4,746,921.80, plus interest, against Intra-Med; Mr. Schultz had knowledge of the GE judgment on or after November 15, 2005; on or about December of 1998, Mr. Schultz, individually, purchased real property located at 7405 New LaGrange Road, Louisville, KY 40242, using Intra-Med funds; Intra-Med did not receive any of the proceeds from the subsequent sale of the New LaGrange Road property in March of 2004; on or about October of 2000, Mr. Schultz, individually, purchased and improved real property located at 8700 Dixie Highway, Louisville, KY 40258, using Intra-Med funds; after entry of the GE judgment, Mr. Schultz sold the Dixie Highway property, which had been purchased and renovated by Mr. Schultz with Intra-Med funds, for $850,000; Intra-Med did not receive any of the proceeds from the sale of the Dixie Highway property; on or about May 24, 2001, Mr. Schultz, individually, purchased a marina slip for $23,000 with Intra-Med funds; and Intra-Med did not receive any of the proceeds from the subsequent sale of the marina slip. It is from these admitted facts that GE moved for a judgment on the pleadings.

"Three basic theories have been utilized to hold the shareholders of a corporation responsible for corporate liabilities. These have been labeled (1) the instrumentality theory; (2) the alter ego theory; and (3) the equity formulation." GE focused on the instrumentality theory in its motion.

> *Under the instrumentality theory three elements must be established in order to warrant a piercing of the corporate veil: (1) that the corporation was a mere instrumentality of the shareholder; (2) that the shareholder exercised control over the corporation in such a way as to defraud or to harm the plaintiff; and (3) that a refusal to disregard the corporate entity would subject the plaintiff to unjust loss. The courts adopting this test have been virtually unanimous in requiring that these three elements co-exist before the corporate veil will be pierced.* [Emphasis added.]

* * * *

The admitted facts * * * support the finding that the corporate veil should be pierced under the instrumentality theory. Mr. Schultz treated the corporation as a mere instrumentality by using corporate funds for his own individual purposes to purchase real estate and a boat slip. The admitted facts also demonstrate that Mr. Schultz harmed GE by using corporate funds as his own even after GE obtained a monetary judgment against Intra-Med. Money that could have been used to satisfy that judgment was used by Mr. Schultz for his own purposes. Finally, not piercing the corporate veil would subject GE to an unjust loss. As previously stated, money that could have been used to satisfy GE's judgment against Intra-Med was removed from the company and used elsewhere. GE has only been able to recover around $700,000 from a $4.7 million judgment. Piercing the corporate veil appears to be the only method for GE to recover its judgment.

DECISION AND REMEDY The Court of Appeals of Kentucky affirmed the trial court's judgment on the pleadings. The corporate veil of Intra-Med could be pierced to hold Schultz personally liable for the debt owed to GE.

WHAT IF THE FACTS WERE DIFFERENT? *Suppose that Schultz had turned over the proceeds from the sales of his properties to his corporation, Intra-Med, and used them to pay part or all of GE's judgment. In this situation, if the funds were insufficient to cover the debt, would the court have pierced the corporate veil to obtain the balance from Schultz personally? Explain.*

THE ETHICAL DIMENSION *Schultz argued that even if the corporate veil should be pierced, the $450,000 judgment against him was too much and should be reduced. How might the court have responded to this argument?*

 ## Directors and Officers

Corporate directors, officers, and shareholders all play different roles within the corporate entity. Sometimes, actions that may benefit the corporation as a whole do not coincide with the separate interests of the individuals making up the corporation. In such situations, it is important to know the rights and duties of all participants in the corporate enterprise and the ways in which conflicts among corporate participants are resolved.

Directors

The board of directors is the ultimate authority in every corporation. Directors have responsibility for all policymaking decisions necessary to the management of all corporate affairs. The board selects and removes the corporate officers, determines the capital structure of the corporation, and declares dividends. Each director has one vote, and customarily the majority rules. The general areas of responsibility of the board of directors are shown in Exhibit 15–1 on the following page.

Directors are sometimes inappropriately characterized as *agents,* (see Chapter 16) because they act on behalf of the corporation. No *individual* director, however, can act

• *Exhibit* **15–1 Directors' Management Responsibilities**

RESPONSIBILITIES	EXAMPLES
Authorize Major Corporate Policy Decisions	• Oversee major contract negotiations and management-labor negotiations. • Initiate negotiations on the sale or lease of corporate assets outside the regular course of business. • Decide whether to pursue new product lines or business opportunities.
Select and Remove Corporate Officers and Other Managerial Employees, and Determine Their Compensation	• Search for and hire corporate executives and determine the elements of their compensation packages, including stock options. • Supervise managerial employees and make decisions regarding their termination.
Make Financial Decisions	• Make decisions regarding the issuance of authorized shares and bonds. • Decide when to declare dividends to be paid to shareholders.

as an agent to bind the corporation, and as a group, directors collectively control the corporation in a way that no agent is able to control a principal. In addition, although directors occupy positions of trust and control over the corporation, they are not *trustees* because they do not hold title to property for the use and benefit of others.

There are few legal requirements concerning directors' qualifications. Only a handful of states impose minimum age and residency requirements. A director may be a shareholder, but this is not necessary (unless the articles of incorporation or bylaws require ownership).

ELECTION OF DIRECTORS   Subject to statutory limitations, the number of directors is set forth in the corporation's articles or bylaws. Historically, the minimum number of directors has been three, but today many states permit fewer. Normally, the incorporators appoint the first board of directors at the time the corporation is created. The initial board serves until the first annual shareholders' meeting. Subsequent directors are elected by a majority vote of the shareholders.

A director usually serves for a term of one year—from annual meeting to annual meeting. Most state statutes permit longer and staggered terms. A common practice is to elect one-third of the board members each year for a three-year term. In this way, there is greater management continuity. A director can be removed *for cause*— that is, for failing to perform a required duty—either as specified in the articles or bylaws or by shareholder action. If a director dies or resigns or if a new position is created through amendment of the articles or bylaws, either the shareholders or the board itself can fill the vacant position, depending on state law or the provisions of the bylaws.

BE AWARE   The articles of incorporation may provide that a director can be removed only for cause.

Note, however, that even when an election appears to be authorized by the bylaws, a court can invalidate it if the directors were attempting to manipulate the election in order to reduce the shareholders' influence. **CASE EXAMPLE 15.6** The bylaws of Liquid Audio, a Delaware corporation, authorized a board of five directors. Two directors on the board were elected each year. Another company offered to buy all of Liquid Audio's stock, but the board of directors rejected this offer. An election was coming up, and the directors feared that the shareholders would elect new directors who would allow the sale. The directors, therefore, amended the bylaws to increase the number of directors to seven, thereby diminishing the shareholders' influence in the vote. The shareholders filed an action challenging the election. The Delaware Supreme Court ruled that the directors' action was illegal because they had attempted to diminish the shareholders' right to vote effectively in an election of directors.[8] •

COMPENSATION OF DIRECTORS   In the past, corporate directors rarely were compensated, but today they are often paid at least nominal sums and may receive more

---

8. *MM Companies v. Liquid Audio, Inc.*, 813 A.2d 1118 (Del.Sup. 2003).

substantial compensation in large corporations because of the time, work, effort, and especially risk involved. Most states permit the corporate articles or bylaws to authorize compensation for directors. In fact, the RMBCA states that unless the articles or bylaws provide otherwise, the directors may set their own compensation [RMBCA 8.11]. Directors also gain through indirect benefits, such as business contacts and prestige, and other rewards, such as stock options.

In many corporations, directors are also chief corporate officers (president or chief executive officer, for example) and receive compensation in their managerial positions. A director who is also an officer of the corporation is referred to as an **inside director,** whereas a director who does not hold a management position is an **outside director.** Typically, a corporation's board of directors includes both inside and outside directors.

BOARD OF DIRECTORS' MEETINGS   The board of directors conducts business by holding formal meetings with recorded minutes. The dates of regular meetings are usually established in the articles or bylaws or by board resolution, and ordinarily no further notice is required. Special meetings can be called, with notice sent to all directors. Today, most states allow directors to participate in board of directors' meetings from remote locations via telephone or Web conferencing, provided that all the directors can simultaneously hear each other during the meeting [RMBCA 8.20].

Normally, a majority of the board of directors must be present to constitute a quorum [RMBCA 8.24]. (A **quorum** is the minimum number of members of a body of officials or other group that must be present in order for business to be validly transacted.) Some state statutes specifically allow corporations to set a quorum as less than a majority but not less than one-third of the directors.[9]

Once a quorum is present, the directors transact business and vote on issues affecting the corporation. Each director present at the meeting has one vote.[10] Ordinary matters generally require a simple majority vote, but certain extraordinary issues may require a greater-than-majority vote.

COMMITTEES OF THE BOARD OF DIRECTORS   When a board of directors has a large number of members and must deal with myriad complex business issues, meetings can become unwieldy. Therefore, the boards of large, publicly held corporations typically create committees, appoint directors to serve on individual committees, and delegate certain tasks to these committees. Committees focus on individual subjects and increase the efficiency of the board.

Two of the most common types of committees are the *executive committee* and the *audit committee.* An executive committee handles interim management decisions between board meetings. It is limited to making decisions about ordinary business matters, though, and does not have the power to declare dividends, amend the bylaws, or authorize the issuance of stock. The Sarbanes Oxley Act of 2002 requires all publicly held corporations to have an audit committee. The audit committee is responsible for the selection, compensation, and oversight of the independent public accountants that audit the firm's financial records.

RIGHTS OF DIRECTORS   A corporate director must have certain rights to function properly in that position and make informed policy decisions for the company.

Inside Director   A member of the board of directors who is also an officer of the corporation.

Outside Director   A member of the board of directors who does not hold a management position at the corporation.

Quorum   The number of members of a decision-making body that must be present before business may be transacted.

"I often feel like the director of a cemetery. I have a lot of people under me, but nobody listens!"

General James Gavin, 1907–1990
(U.S. Army lieutenant general)

---

9. See, for example, Delaware Code Annotated Title 8, Section 141(b), and New York Business Corporation Law Section 707, which both allow corporations to set a quorum at less than a majority.

10. Except in Louisiana, which allows a director to authorize another person to cast a vote in his or her place under certain circumstances.

The *right to participation* means that directors are entitled to participate in all board of directors' meetings and have a right to be notified of these meetings. Because the dates of regular board meetings are usually specified in the bylaws, as noted earlier, no notice of these meetings is required. If special meetings are called, however, notice is required unless waived by the director.

A director also has the *right of inspection,* which means that each director can access the corporation's books and records, facilities, and premises. Inspection rights are essential for directors to make informed decisions and to exercise the necessary supervision over corporate officers and employees. This right of inspection is almost absolute and cannot be restricted (by the articles, bylaws, or any act of the board).

When a director becomes involved in litigation by virtue of her or his position or actions, the director may also have a *right to indemnification* (reimbursement) for legal costs, fees, and damages incurred. Most states allow corporations to indemnify and purchase liability insurance for corporate directors [RMBCA 8.51].

Preventing Legal Disputes

Whenever businesspersons serve as corporate directors or officers, they may at some point become involved in litigation as a result of their positions. To protect against personal liability, directors or officers should take several steps. First, they should make sure that the corporate bylaws explicitly give them a right to indemnification (reimbursement) for any costs incurred as a result of litigation, as well as any judgments or settlements stemming from a lawsuit. Second, they should have the corporation purchase directors' and officers' liability insurance (D&O insurance). Having D&O insurance policies enables the corporation to avoid paying the substantial costs involved in defending a particular director or officer. The D&O policies offered by most private insurance companies have maximum coverage limits, so ensuring that the corporation is required to indemnify directors and officers in the event that the costs exceed the policy limits is very important.

Corporate Officers and Executives

Corporate officers and other executive employees are hired by the board of directors. At a minimum, most corporations have a president, one or more vice presidents, a secretary, and a treasurer. In most states, an individual can hold more than one office, such as president and secretary, and can be both an officer and a director of the corporation. In addition to carrying out the duties articulated in the bylaws, corporate and managerial officers act as agents of the corporation, and the ordinary rules of agency (discussed in Chapter 16) normally apply to their employment.

Corporate officers and other high-level managers are employees of the company, so their rights are defined by employment contracts. The board of directors normally can remove corporate officers at any time with or without cause and regardless of the terms of the employment contracts—although in so doing, the corporation may be liable for breach of contract.

The duties of corporate officers are similar to those of directors because both groups are involved in decision making and are in similar positions of control. We discuss those duties next.

Who hires corporate officers?

©GWImages, 2009. Used under license from Shutterstock.com

Duties and Liabilities of Directors and Officers

Directors and officers are deemed fiduciaries of the corporation because their relationship with the corporation and its shareholders is one of trust and confidence. As fiduciaries, directors and officers owe ethical—and legal—duties to the corporation and to the shareholders as a whole. These fiduciary duties include the duty of care and the duty of loyalty. (Directors and officers also have a duty not to destroy evidence in the event of a lawsuit involving the corporation.)

CONTRAST Shareholders own the corporation and directors make policy decisions, but the officers who run the corporation's daily business often have significant decision-making power.

DUTY OF CARE Directors and officers must exercise due care in performing their duties. The standard of *due care* has been variously described in judicial decisions and codified in many state corporation codes. Generally, a director or officer is expected to act in good faith, to exercise the care that an ordinarily prudent person would exercise in similar circumstances, and to act in what he or she considers to be the best interests of the corporation [RMBCA 8.30]. Directors and officers whose failure to exercise due care results in harm to the corporation or its shareholders can be held liable for negligence (unless the *business judgment rule* applies, as will be discussed shortly).

Duty to Make Informed and Reasonable Decisions. Directors and officers are expected to be informed on corporate matters and to conduct a reasonable investigation of the situation before making a decision. This means that they must do what is necessary to keep adequately informed: attend meetings and presentations, ask for information from those who have it, read reports, and review other written materials. In other words, directors and officers must investigate, study, and discuss matters and evaluate alternatives before making a decision. They cannot decide on the spur of the moment without adequate research.

Although directors and officers are expected to act in accordance with their own knowledge and training, they are also normally entitled to rely on information given to them by certain other persons. Most states and Section 8.30(b) of the RMBCA allow a director to make decisions in reliance on information furnished by competent officers or employees, professionals such as attorneys and accountants, and committees of the board of directors (on which the director does not serve). The reliance must be in good faith, of course, to insulate a director from liability if the information later proves to be inaccurate or unreliable.

"Executive ability is deciding quickly and getting somebody else to do the work."
J. C. Pollard, 1946–present
(British businessman)

Duty to Exercise Reasonable Supervision. Directors are also expected to exercise a reasonable amount of supervision when they delegate work to corporate officers and employees. **EXAMPLE 15.7** Dale, a corporate bank director, fails to attend any board of directors' meetings for five years. In addition, Dale never inspects any of the corporate books or records and generally fails to supervise the efforts of the bank president and the loan committee. Meanwhile, Brennan, the bank president, who is a corporate officer, makes various improper loans and permits large overdrafts. In this situation, Dale (the corporate director) can be held liable to the corporation for losses resulting from the unsupervised actions of the bank president and the loan committee. ●

Business Judgment Rule A rule that immunizes corporate management from liability for actions that result in corporate losses or damages if the actions are undertaken in good faith and are within both the power of the corporation and the authority of management to make.

THE BUSINESS JUDGMENT RULE Directors and officers are expected to exercise due care and to use their best judgment in guiding corporate management, but they are not insurers of business success. Under the **business judgment rule,** a corporate director or officer will not be liable to the corporation or to its shareholders for honest mistakes of judgment and bad business decisions. (Some say the business judgment rule provides too much protection for corporate decision makers—an issue that is discussed in this chapter's *Insight into Ethics* feature on the following page.)

Insight into Ethics   Is the Business Judgment Rule Overly Protective?

The business judgment rule generally insulates corporate decision makers from liability for bad decisions even though this may seem to contradict the goal of greater corporate accountability. Is the rule fair to shareholders?

Citigroup—An Example

In 2009, a Delaware court ruled against shareholders of Citigroup, Inc., who claimed that the bank's directors had breached their fiduciary duties. The shareholders alleged that the directors had caused Citigroup to continue to engage in subprime lending (see Chapter 13) despite the steady decline of the housing market, the dramatic increase in foreclosures, the collapse of other subprime lenders, and other red flags that should have warned Citigroup to change its practices.

    The shareholders claimed that the directors' failure to adequately protect the corporation's exposure to risk given these warning signs was a breach of their duties and resulted in significant losses to Citigroup. The court, however, found that "the warning signs alleged by plaintiffs are not evidence that the directors consciously disregarded their duties or otherwise acted in bad faith; at most they evidence that the directors made bad business decisions."[a] Thus, under the business judgment rule, the court dismissed the shareholders' claims of breach of fiduciary

duty. The court, however, did allow the shareholders to maintain a claim for waste based on the directors' approval of a compensation package for the company's chief executive officer.

Lyondell Chemical—Another Example

Another 2009 case also involved the business judgment rule. Early in 2007, a foreign firm had announced its intention to acquire Lyondell Chemical Company. Over the next several months, Lyondell's directors did nothing to prepare for a possible merger. They failed to research Lyondell's market value and made no attempt to seek out other potential buyers. The $13 billion cash merger was negotiated and finalized in less than one week in July 2007.

    At that time, the directors met for a total of only seven hours to discuss the transaction. Shortly afterward, shareholders filed a lawsuit alleging that the directors had breached their fiduciary duties by failing to maximize the sale price of the corporation. Nevertheless, the Delaware Supreme Court ruled that the directors were protected by the business judgment rule.[b]

FOR CRITICAL ANALYSIS
Insight into the Legal Environment

If courts were to ignore the business judgment rule, what might the consequences be?

---

a. *In re Citigroup, Inc., Shareholder Derivative Litigation,* 964 A.2d 106 (Del.Ch. 2009).

b. *Lyondell Chemical Co. v. Ryan,* 970 A.2d 235 (Del.Sup.Ct. 2009).

Courts give significant deference to the decisions of corporate directors and officers, and consider the reasonableness of a decision at the time it was made, without the benefit of hindsight. Thus, corporate decision makers are not subjected to second-guessing by shareholders or others in the corporation. The business judgment rule will apply as long as the director or officer:

1. Took reasonable steps to become informed about the matter.
2. Had a rational basis for his or her decision.
3. Did not have a conflict of interest between his or her personal interest and that of the corporation.

    In fact, unless there is evidence of bad faith, fraud, or a clear breach of fiduciary duties, most courts will apply the rule and protect directors and officers who make bad business decisions from liability for those choices. Consequently, if there is a reasonable basis for a business decision, a court is unlikely to interfere with that decision, even if the corporation suffers as a result.

    The business judgment rule does not apply when a director engages in fraud, dishonesty, or other intentional or reckless misconduct. **CASE EXAMPLE 15.8** The board of directors of the Chugach Alaska Corporation (CAC) split into two factions—one led by Sheri Buretta, who had chaired the board for several years, and the other by director Robert Henrichs. A coalition of directors voted to remove Buretta and install Henrichs. During his term, Henrichs acted without board approval, made decisions with only his supporters present, retaliated against directors who challenged his decisions, ignored board rules for conducting meetings, and refused to comply with bylaws that required a special shareholders' meeting in response to a shareholder petition. He also personally mistreated directors, shareholders, and employees. After six months, the board voted to reinstall Buretta. CAC filed a suit in an Alaska state court against Henrichs, alleging a breach of fiduciary duty. A jury found Henrichs liable, and the court barred him from serving on CAC's board for five years. The appellate court affirmed. Given the nature and seriousness of Henrichs's misconduct, the business judgment rule did not protect him.[11] ●

DUTY OF LOYALTY *Loyalty* can be defined as faithfulness to one's obligations and duties. In the corporate context, the duty of loyalty requires directors and officers to subordinate their personal interests to the welfare of the corporation. Directors cannot use corporate funds or confidential corporate information for personal advantage and must refrain from self-dealing. For instance, a director should not oppose a transaction that is in the corporation's best interest simply because its acceptance may cost the director her or his position. Cases dealing with the duty of loyalty typically involve one or more of the following:

1. Competing with the corporation.
2. Usurping (taking advantage of) a corporate opportunity.
3. Having an interest that conflicts with the interest of the corporation.
4. Using information that is not available to the public to make a profit trading securities (see *insider trading* on page 687 in Chapter 24).
5. Authorizing a corporate transaction that is detrimental to minority shareholders.
6. Selling control over the corporation.

The following classic case illustrates the conflict that can arise between a corporate official's personal interest and his or her duty of loyalty.

---

11. *Henrichs v. Chugach Alaska Corp.*, 250 P.3d 531 (Alaska Sup.Ct. 2011).

Classic Case 15.3 Guth v. Loft, Inc.

Supreme Court of Delaware, 23 Del.Ch. 255, 5 A.2d 503 (1939).

(Dalton Rowe/ Creative Commons)

Pepsi-Cola got its start when the head of Loft Candy Company usurped a corporate opportunity.

BACKGROUND AND FACTS Loft, Inc., made and sold candies, syrups, beverages, and food from its offices and plant in Long Island City, New York. Loft operated 115 retail outlets in several states and also sold its products wholesale. Charles Guth was Loft's president. Guth and his family owned Grace Company, which made syrups for soft drinks in a plant in Baltimore, Maryland. Coca-Cola Company supplied Loft with cola syrup. Unhappy with what he felt was Coca-Cola's high price, Guth entered into an agreement with Roy Megargel to acquire the trademark and formula for Pepsi-Cola and form Pepsi-

Cola Corporation. Neither Guth nor Megargel could finance the new venture, however, and Grace was insolvent. Without the knowledge of Loft's board, Guth used Loft's capital, credit, facilities, and employees to further the Pepsi enterprise. At Guth's direction, Loft made the concentrate for the syrup, which was sent to Grace to add sugar and water. Loft charged Grace for the concentrate but allowed forty months' credit. Grace charged Pepsi for the syrup but also granted substantial credit. Grace sold the syrup to Pepsi's customers, including Loft, which paid on delivery or within thirty days. Loft also paid for Pepsi's advertising. Finally, losing profits at its stores as a result of switching from Coca-Cola, Loft filed a suit in a Delaware state court

Classic Case 15.3—Continues next page ➡

Classic Case 15.3—Continued

against Guth, Grace, and Pepsi, seeking their Pepsi stock and an accounting. The court entered a judgment in the plaintiff's favor. The defendants appealed to the Delaware Supreme Court.

IN THE WORDS OF THE COURT . . .
LAYTON, **Chief Justice, delivering the opinion of the court:**
* * * *

Corporate officers and directors are not permitted to use their position of trust and confidence to further their private interests. * * * They stand in a fiduciary relation to the corporation and its stockholders. A public policy, existing through the years, and derived from a profound knowledge of human characteristics and motives, has established *a rule that demands of a corporate officer or director, peremptorily [not open for debate] and inexorably [unavoidably], the most scrupulous observance of his duty, not only affirmatively to protect the interests of the corporation committed to his charge, but also to refrain from doing anything that would work injury to the corporation* * * *. The rule that requires an undivided and unselfish loyalty to the corporation demands that there shall be no conflict between duty and self-interest. [Emphasis added.]
* * * *

* * * *If there is presented to a corporate officer or director a business opportunity which the corporation is financially able to undertake [that] is* * * * *in the line of the corporation's business and is of practical advantage to it* * * * *and, by embracing the opportunity, the self-interest of the officer or director will be brought into conflict with that of his corporation, the law will not permit him to seize the opportunity for himself.* * * * In such circumstances, * * * the corporation may elect to claim all of the benefits of the transaction for itself, and the law will impress a trust in favor of the corporation upon the property, interests and profits so acquired. [Emphasis added.]
* * * *

* * * The appellants contend that no conflict of interest between Guth and Loft resulted from his acquirement and exploitation of the Pepsi-Cola opportunity [and] that the acquisition did not place Guth in competition with Loft * * *. [In this case, however,] Guth was Loft, and Guth was Pepsi. He absolutely controlled Loft. His authority over

Pepsi was supreme. As Pepsi, he created and controlled the supply of Pepsi-Cola syrup, and he determined the price and the terms. What he offered, as Pepsi, he had the power, as Loft, to accept. Upon any consideration of human characteristics and motives, he created a conflict between self-interest and duty. He made himself the judge in his own cause. * * * Moreover, a reasonable probability of injury to Loft resulted from the situation forced upon it. Guth was in the same position to impose his terms upon Loft as had been the Coca-Cola Company.

* * * The facts and circumstances demonstrate that Guth's appropriation of the Pepsi-Cola opportunity to himself placed him in a competitive position with Loft with respect to a commodity essential to it, thereby rendering his personal interests incompatible with the superior interests of his corporation; and this situation was accomplished, not openly and with his own resources, but secretly and with the money and facilities of the corporation which was committed to his protection.

DECISION AND REMEDY　The Delaware Supreme Court upheld the judgment of the lower court. The state supreme court was "convinced that the opportunity to acquire the Pepsi-Cola trademark and formula, goodwill and business belonged to [Loft], and that Guth, as its President, had no right to appropriate the opportunity to himself."

WHAT IF THE FACTS WERE DIFFERENT?　*Suppose that Loft's board of directors had approved Pepsi-Cola's use of the company's personnel and equipment. Would the court's decision have been different? Discuss.*

IMPACT OF THIS CASE ON TODAY'S LAW　*This early Delaware decision was one of the first to set forth a test for determining when a corporate officer or director has breached the duty of loyalty. The test has two basic parts—whether the opportunity was reasonably related to the corporation's line of business, and whether the corporation was financially able to undertake the opportunity. The court also considered whether the corporation had an interest or expectancy in the opportunity and recognized that when the corporation had "no interest or expectancy, the officer or director is entitled to treat the opportunity as his own."*

> *"If it is not in the interest of the public, it is not in the interest of the business."*
>
> Joseph H. Defrees, 1812–1885
> (U.S. congressman)

DISCLOSURE OF POTENTIAL CONFLICTS OF INTEREST　Corporate directors often have many business affiliations, and a director may sit on the board of more than one corporation. Of course, directors are precluded from entering into or supporting businesses that operate in direct competition with corporations on whose boards they serve. Their fiduciary duty requires them to make a full disclosure of any potential conflicts of interest that might arise in any corporate transaction [RMBCA 8.60].

Sometimes, a corporation enters into a contract or engages in a transaction in which an officer or director has a personal interest. The director or officer must make a *full disclosure* of that interest and must abstain from voting on the proposed transaction.

EXAMPLE 15.9　Southwood Corporation needs office space. Lambert Alden, one of its five directors, owns the building adjoining the corporation's main office building. He negotiates a lease with Southwood for the space, making a full disclosure to

Southwood and the other four board directors. The lease arrangement is fair and reasonable, and it is unanimously approved by the other four directors. In this situation, Alden has not breached his duty of loyalty to the corporation, and thus the contract is valid. If it were otherwise, directors would be prevented from ever transacting business with the corporations they serve. •

Shareholders

The acquisition of a share of stock makes a person an owner and shareholder in a corporation. Thus, shareholders own the corporation. Although they have no legal title to corporate property, such as buildings and equipment, they do have an equitable (ownership) interest in the firm.

As a general rule, shareholders have no responsibility for the daily management of the corporation, even if they are ultimately responsible for choosing the board of directors, which does have such control. Ordinarily, corporate officers and directors owe no duty to individual shareholders unless some contract or special relationship exists between them in addition to the corporate relationship. Their duty is to act in the best interests of the corporation and its shareholder-owners as a whole. In turn, as you will read later in this chapter, controlling shareholders owe a fiduciary duty to minority shareholders. Normally, there is no legal relationship between shareholders and creditors of the corporation. Shareholders can be creditors of the corporation, though, and they have the same rights of recovery against the corporation as any other creditor.

Shareholders' Powers

BE AWARE Shareholders normally are not agents of the corporation.

Shareholders must approve fundamental changes affecting the corporation before the changes can be implemented. Hence, shareholders are empowered to amend the articles of incorporation (charter) and bylaws, approve a merger or the dissolution of the corporation, and approve the sale of all or substantially all of the corporation's assets. Some of these powers are subject to prior board approval.

Members of the board of directors are elected and removed by a vote of the shareholders. The first board of directors is either named in the articles of incorporation or chosen by the incorporators to serve until the first shareholders' meeting. From that time on, the selection and retention of directors are exclusively shareholder functions.

Directors usually serve their full terms. If the shareholders judge them unsatisfactory, they are simply not reelected. Shareholders have the inherent power, however, to remove a director from office for cause (such as for breach of duty or misconduct) by a majority vote.[12] As mentioned earlier, some state statutes (and some corporate articles) permit removal of directors without cause by the vote of a majority of the holders of outstanding shares entitled to vote.

Shareholders' Meetings

Shareholders' meetings must occur at least annually. In addition, special meetings can be called to deal with urgent matters. A corporation must notify its shareholders of the date, time, and place of an annual or special shareholders' meeting at least ten days, but not more than sixty days, before the meeting date [RMBCA 7.05].[13] Notice

Starbucks chair and chief executive officer Howard Schultz speaks to shareholders at the company's annual shareholders' meeting in Seattle, Washington. Do shareholders have any power over the actions of a corporation's board of directors?

(Robert Sorbo/Reuters /Landov)

---

12. A director can often demand court review of removal for cause.
13. A shareholder can waive the requirement of written notice by signing a waiver form or, in some states, by attending the meeting without protesting the lack of written notice.

of a special meeting must include a statement of the purpose of the meeting, and business transacted at the meeting is limited to that purpose.

PROXIES   It is usually not practical for owners of only a few shares of stock of publicly traded corporations to attend shareholders' meetings. Therefore, the law allows stockholders to either vote in person or appoint another person as their agent to vote their shares at the meeting. The signed appointment form or electronic transmission authorizing an agent to vote the shares is called a **proxy** (from the Latin *procurare,* meaning "to manage, take care of ").

Management often solicits proxies, but any person can solicit proxies to concentrate voting power. Proxies have been used by a group of shareholders as a device for taking over a corporation. Proxies normally are revocable (that is, they can be withdrawn), unless they are specifically designated as irrevocable. Under RMBCA 7.22(c), proxies last for eleven months, unless the proxy agreement provides for a longer period.

> **Proxy**   In corporate law, a written agreement between a stockholder and another party in which the stockholder authorizes the other party to vote the stockholder's shares in a certain manner.

SHAREHOLDER PROPOSALS   When shareholders want to change a company policy, they can put their idea up for a shareholder vote. They can do this by submitting a shareholder proposal to the board of directors and asking the board to include the proposal in the proxy materials that are sent to all shareholders before meetings.

The Securities and Exchange Commission (SEC), which regulates the purchase and sale of securities (see Chapter 24), has special provisions relating to proxies and shareholder proposals. SEC Rule 14a-8 provides that all shareholders who own stock worth at least $1,000 are eligible to submit proposals for inclusion in corporate proxy materials. The corporation is required to include information on whatever proposals will be considered at the shareholders' meeting along with proxy materials.

Under the SEC's e-proxy rules,[14] all public companies must post their proxy materials on the Internet and notify shareholders how to find that information. Although the law requires proxy materials to be posted online, public companies may still choose among several options—including paper documents or a DVD sent by mail—for actually delivering the materials to shareholders.

SHAREHOLDER VOTING   Shareholders exercise ownership control through the power of their votes. Corporate business matters are presented in the form of *resolutions,* which shareholders vote to approve or disapprove. Each shareholder is entitled to one vote per share of stock, although the articles of incorporation can exclude or limit voting rights, particularly for certain classes of shares. If a state statute requires specific voting procedures, the corporation's articles or bylaws must be consistent with the statute.

For shareholders to conduct business at a meeting, a quorum must be present. Generally, a quorum exists when shareholders holding more than 50 percent of the outstanding shares are present. In some states, obtaining the unanimous written consent of shareholders is a permissible alternative to holding a shareholders' meeting [RMBCA 7.25].

Once a quorum is present, voting can proceed. A majority vote of the shares represented at the meeting usually is required to pass resolutions. **EXAMPLE 15.10** Novo Pictures, Inc., has 10,000 outstanding shares of voting stock. Its articles of incorporation set the quorum at 50 percent of outstanding shares and provide that

---

14. 17 C.F.R. Parts 240, 249, and 274.

Shareholders in Wachovia Corporation leave a shareholders' meeting during which they voted on that company's takeover by Wells Fargo. Do shareholders who oppose takeovers have any rights?

BE CAREFUL   Once a quorum is present, a vote can be taken even if some shareholders leave without casting their votes.

a majority vote of the shares present is necessary to pass resolutions concerning ordinary matters. Therefore, for this firm, a quorum of shareholders representing 5,000 outstanding shares must be present at a shareholders' meeting to conduct business. If exactly 5,000 shares are represented at the meeting, a vote of at least 2,501 of those shares is needed to pass a resolution. If 6,000 shares are represented, a vote of 3,001 is required. •

At times, more than a simple majority vote is required either by a state statute or by the corporate articles. Extraordinary corporate matters, such as a merger, consolidation, or dissolution of the corporation, require a higher percentage of all corporate shares entitled to vote [RMBCA 7.27].

VOTING LISTS   The corporation prepares voting lists prior to each meeting of the shareholders. Ordinarily, only persons whose names appear on the corporation's shareholder records as owners are entitled to vote. The voting list contains the name and address of each shareholder as shown on the corporate records on a given cutoff, or record, date. (Under RMBCA 7.07, the record date may be as much as seventy days before the meeting.) The voting list also includes the number of voting shares held by each owner. The list is usually kept at the corporate headquarters and is available for shareholder inspection [RMBCA 7.20].

CUMULATIVE VOTING   Most states permit, and some require, shareholders to elect directors by *cumulative voting,* which is a voting method designed to allow minority shareholders to be represented on the board of directors. With cumulative voting, each shareholder is entitled to a total number of votes equal to the number of board members to be elected multiplied by the number of voting shares a shareholder owns. The shareholder can cast all of these votes for one candidate or split them among several nominees for director. All nominees stand for election at the same time. When cumulative voting is not required either by statute or under the articles, the entire board can be elected by a simple majority of shares at a shareholders' meeting.

Cumulative voting can best be understood through an example. **EXAMPLE 15.11**   A corporation has 10,000 shares issued and outstanding. The minority shareholders hold 3,000 shares, and the majority shareholders hold the other 7,000 shares. Three members of the board are to be elected. The majority shareholders' nominees are Acevedo, Barkley, and Craycik. The minority shareholders' nominee is Drake. Can Drake be elected by the minority shareholders?

If cumulative voting is allowed, the answer is yes. Together, the minority shareholders have 9,000 votes (the number of directors to be elected times the number of shares held by the minority shareholders equals 3 times 3,000, which equals 9,000 votes). All of these votes can be cast to elect Drake. The majority shareholders have 21,000 votes (3 times 7,000 equals 21,000 votes), but these votes have to be distributed among their three nominees. The principle of cumulative voting is that no matter how the majority shareholders cast their 21,000 votes, they will not be able to elect all three directors if the minority shareholders cast all of their 9,000 votes for Drake, as illustrated in Exhibit 15–2 on the following page. •

OTHER VOTING TECHNIQUES   Before a shareholders' meeting, a group of shareholders can agree in writing to vote their shares together in a specified manner. Such

● *Exhibit* **15–2 Results of Cumulative Voting**

BALLOT	MAJORITY SHAREHOLDERS' VOTES			MINORITY SHAREHOLDERS' VOTES	DIRECTORS ELECTED
	Acevedo	**Barkley**	**Craycik**	**Drake**	
1	10,000	10,000	1,000	9,000	Acevedo/Barkley/Drake
2	9,001	9,000	2,999	9,000	Acevedo/Barkley/Drake
3	6,000	7,000	8,000	9,000	Barkley/Craycik/Drake

agreements, called *shareholder voting agreements,* usually are held to be valid and enforceable. A shareholder can also appoint a voting agent and vote by proxy.

Rights of Shareholders

Shareholders possess numerous rights. A significant right—the right to vote their shares—has already been discussed. We now look at some additional rights of shareholders.

Stock Certificate   A certificate issued by a corporation evidencing the ownership of a specified number of shares in the corporation.

STOCK CERTIFICATES   A **stock certificate** is a certificate issued by a corporation that evidences ownership of a specified number of shares in the corporation. In jurisdictions that require the issuance of stock certificates, shareholders have the right to demand that the corporation issue certificates. In most states and under RMBCA 6.26, boards of directors may provide that shares of stock will be uncertificated—that is, no actual, physical stock certificates will be issued. When shares are uncertificated, the corporation may be required to send each shareholder a letter or some other form of notice that contains the same information that would normally appear on the face of stock certificates.

Stock is intangible personal property, and the ownership right exists independently of the certificate itself. If a stock certificate is lost or destroyed, ownership is not destroyed with it. A new certificate can be issued to replace one that has been lost or destroyed. Notice of shareholders' meetings, dividends, and operational and financial reports are all distributed according to the recorded ownership listed in the corporation's books, not on the basis of possession of the certificate.

Preemptive Rights   Rights held by shareholders that entitle them to purchase newly issued shares of a corporation's stock, equal in percentage to shares already held, before the stock is offered to any outside buyers. Preemptive rights enable shareholders to maintain their proportionate ownership and voice in the corporation.

PREEMPTIVE RIGHTS   Sometimes, the articles of incorporation grant preemptive rights to shareholders [RMBCA 6.30]. With **preemptive rights,** a shareholder receives a preference over all other purchasers to subscribe to or purchase a prorated share of a new issue of stock. In other words, a shareholder who is given preemptive rights can purchase the same percentage of the new shares being issued as she or he already holds in the company. This allows each shareholder to maintain her or his proportionate control, voting power, or financial interest in the corporation. Generally, preemptive rights apply only to additional, newly issued stock sold for cash, and the preemptive rights must be exercised within a specified time period, which is usually thirty days.

EXAMPLE 15.12   Tran Corporation authorizes and issues 1,000 shares of stock. Lebow purchases 100 shares, making her the owner of 10 percent of the company's stock. Subsequently, Tran, by vote of its shareholders, authorizes the issuance of another 1,000 shares (by amending the articles of incorporation). This increases its capital stock to a total of 2,000 shares. If preemptive rights have been provided, Lebow can purchase one additional share of the new stock being issued for each share she already owns—or 100 additional shares. Thus, she can own 200 of the 2,000 shares outstanding, and she

(PhotoDisc)

Stock certificates are displayed above. To be a shareholder, is it necessary to have physical possession of a stock certificate? Why or why not?

Stock Warrant   A certificate that grants the owner the option to buy a given number of shares of stock, usually within a set time period.

will maintain her relative position as a shareholder. If preemptive rights are not allowed, her proportionate control and voting power may be diluted from that of a 10 percent shareholder to that of a 5 percent shareholder because of the issuance of the additional 1,000 shares. •

Preemptive rights are most important in close corporations because each shareholder owns a relatively small number of shares but controls a substantial interest in the corporation. Without preemptive rights, it would be possible for a shareholder to lose his or her proportionate control over the firm.

STOCK WARRANTS   **Stock warrants** are rights to buy stock at a stated price by a specified date that are created by the company. Usually, when preemptive rights exist and a corporation is issuing additional shares, it issues its shareholders stock warrants. Warrants are often publicly traded on securities exchanges.

DIVIDENDS   As previously mentioned, a *dividend* is a distribution of corporate profits or income *ordered by the directors* and paid to the shareholders in proportion to their respective shares in the corporation. Dividends can be paid in cash, property, stock of the corporation that is paying the dividends, or stock of other corporations.[15]

State laws vary, but each state determines the general circumstances and legal requirements under which dividends are paid. State laws also control the sources of revenue to be used; only certain funds are legally available for paying dividends. Depending on state law, dividends may be paid from the following sources:

1. *Retained earnings.* All states allow dividends to be paid from retained earnings—the undistributed net profits earned by the corporation, including capital gains from the sale of fixed assets.
2. *Net profits.* A few states allow dividends to be issued from current net profits without regard to deficits in prior years.
3. *Surplus.* A number of states allow dividends to be paid out of any kind of surplus.

Illegal Dividends. Sometimes, dividends are improperly paid from an unauthorized account, or their payment causes the corporation to become insolvent. Generally, shareholders must return illegal dividends only if they knew that the dividends were illegal when the payment was received (or if the dividends were paid when the corporation was insolvent). Whenever dividends are illegal or improper, the board of directors can be held personally liable for the amount of the payment.

Directors' Failure to Declare a Dividend. When directors fail to declare a dividend, shareholders can ask a court to compel the directors to meet and to declare a dividend. To succeed, the shareholders must show that the directors have acted so unreasonably in withholding the dividend that their conduct is an abuse of their discretion.

Often, a corporation accumulates large cash reserves for a legitimate corporate purpose, such as expansion or research. The mere fact that the firm has sufficient

---

15. Technically, dividends paid in stock are not dividends. They maintain each shareholder's proportionate interest in the corporation.

earnings or surplus available to pay a dividend is not enough to compel directors to distribute funds that, in the board's opinion, should not be distributed. The courts are reluctant to interfere with corporate operations and will not compel directors to declare dividends unless abuse of discretion is clearly shown.

A General Motors shareholder asks a question at the company's annual stockholders' meeting. Shareholders also have a limited right to inspect and copy corporate books and records, provided the request is made in advance and is not impromptu in an open forum like a shareholders' meeting. What other limitations are placed on shareholders' inspection rights?

INSPECTION RIGHTS Shareholders in a corporation enjoy both common law and statutory inspection rights. The RMBCA provides that every shareholder is entitled to examine specified corporate records. The shareholder's right of inspection is limited, however, to the inspection and copying of corporate books and records for a *proper purpose,* provided the request is made in advance. The shareholder can inspect in person, or an attorney, accountant, or other authorized assistant can do so as the shareholder's agent.

The power of inspection is fraught with potential abuses, and the corporation is allowed to protect itself from them. For instance, a shareholder can properly be denied access to corporate records to prevent harassment or to protect trade secrets or other confidential corporate information. Some states require that a shareholder must have held his or her shares for a minimum period of time immediately preceding the demand to inspect or must hold a minimum number of outstanding shares. A shareholder who is denied the right of inspection can seek a court order to compel the inspection.

TRANSFER OF SHARES Corporate stock represents an ownership right in intangible personal property. The law generally recognizes the right to transfer stock to another person unless there are valid restrictions on its transferability. Although stock certificates are negotiable and freely transferable, transfer of stock in close corporations usually is restricted. These restrictions must be reasonable and may be set out in the bylaws or in a shareholder agreement. The existence of any restrictions on transferability must always be indicated on the face of the stock certificate.

When shares are transferred, a new entry is made in the corporate stock book to indicate the new owner. Until the corporation is notified and the entry is complete, all rights—including voting rights, the right to notice of shareholders' meetings, and the right to dividend distributions—remain with the current record owner.

RIGHTS ON DISSOLUTION When a corporation is dissolved and its outstanding debts and the claims of its creditors have been satisfied, the remaining assets are distributed to the shareholders in proportion to the percentage of shares owned by each shareholder. Certain classes of stock can be given priority. If no class of stock has been given preference in the distribution of assets on liquidation, then all of the stockholders share the remaining assets.

In some situations, shareholders can petition a court to have the corporation dissolved. The RMBCA permits any shareholder to initiate a dissolution proceeding in any of the following circumstances [RMBCA 14.30]:

1. The directors are deadlocked in the management of corporate affairs. The shareholders are unable to break that deadlock, and irreparable injury to the corporation is being suffered or threatened.

2. The acts of the directors or those in control of the corporation are illegal, oppressive, or fraudulent.
3. Corporate assets are being misapplied or wasted.
4. The shareholders are deadlocked in voting power and have failed, for a specified period (usually two annual meetings), to elect successors to directors whose terms have expired or would have expired with the election of successors.

THE SHAREHOLDER'S DERIVATIVE SUIT   When the corporation is harmed by the actions of a third party, the directors can bring a lawsuit in the name of the corporation against that party. If the corporate directors fail to bring a lawsuit, shareholders can do so "derivatively" in what is known as a **shareholder's derivative suit**. A shareholder cannot bring a derivative suit until ninety days after making a written demand on the corporation (the board of directors) to take suitable action [RMBCA 7.40]. Only if the directors refuse to take appropriate action can the derivative suit go forward.

> **Shareholder's Derivative Suit**   A suit brought by a shareholder to enforce a corporate cause of action against a third party.

The right of shareholders to bring a derivative action is especially important when the wrong suffered by the corporation results from the actions of corporate directors or officers. This is because the directors and officers would probably be unwilling to take any action against themselves. Nevertheless, a court will dismiss a derivative suit if the majority of directors or an independent panel determines in good faith that the lawsuit is not in the best interests of the corporation [RMBCA 7.44]. (Derivative actions are less common in other countries than in the United States, as this chapter's *Beyond Our Borders* feature below explains.)

When shareholders bring a derivative suit, they are not pursuing rights or benefits for themselves personally but are acting as guardians of the corporate entity. Therefore, if the suit is successful, any damages recovered normally go into the corporation's treasury, not to the shareholders personally. **EXAMPLE 15.13**   Zeon Corporation is owned by two shareholders, each holding 50 percent of the corporate shares. One of the shareholders wants to sue the other for misusing corporate assets or usurping corporate opportunities. In this situation, the plaintiff-shareholder will have to bring a shareholder's derivative suit (not a suit in his or her own name) because the alleged harm was suffered by Zeon, not by the plaintiff personally. Any damages awarded will go to the corporation, not to the plaintiff-shareholder. •

Beyond Our Borders   **Derivative Actions in Other Nations**

Today, most of the claims brought against directors and officers in the United States are those alleged in shareholders' derivative suits. Other nations, however, put more restrictions on the use of such suits. German law, for example, does not provide for derivative litigation, and a corporation's duty to its employees is just as significant as its duty to its shareholder-owners. The United Kingdom has no statute authorizing derivative actions, which are permitted only to challenge directors' actions that the shareholders could not legally ratify. Japan authorizes derivative actions but also permits a company to sue the plaintiff-shareholder for damages if the action is unsuccessful.

For Critical Analysis
Do corporations benefit from shareholders' derivative suits? If so, how?

Duties and Liabilities of Shareholders

One of the hallmarks of the corporate form of business organization is that shareholders are not personally liable for the debts of the corporation. If the corporation fails, shareholders can lose their investments, but generally that is the limit of their liability. As discussed earlier, in certain instances of fraud, undercapitalization, or careless observance of corporate formalities, a court will pierce the corporate veil and hold the shareholders individually liable. These situations are the exception, however, not the rule.

A shareholder can also be personally liable in certain other rare instances. One relates to illegal dividends, which were discussed previously. Another relates to *watered stock*. When a corporation issues shares for less than their fair market value, the shares are referred to as **watered stock.**[16] Usually, the shareholder who receives watered stock must pay the difference to the corporation (the shareholder is personally liable). In some states, the shareholder who receives watered stock may be liable to creditors of the corporation for unpaid corporate debts.

EXAMPLE 15.14 During the formation of a corporation, Gomez, one of the incorporators, transfers his property, Sunset Beach, to the corporation for 10,000 shares of stock. The stock has a specific face value (*par value*) of $100 per share, and thus the total price of the 10,000 shares is $1 million. After the property is transferred and the shares are issued, Sunset Beach is carried on the corporate books at a value of $1 million. On appraisal, it is discovered that the market value of the property at the time of transfer was only $500,000. The shares issued to Gomez are therefore watered stock, and he is liable to the corporation for the difference between the value of the shares and the value of the property. ●

Finally, in certain instances, a majority shareholder who engages in oppressive conduct or attempts to exclude minority shareholders from receiving certain benefits can be held personally liable. In these situations, majority shareholders owe a fiduciary duty to the minority shareholders. When a majority shareholder breaches her or his fiduciary duty to a minority shareholder, the minority shareholder can sue for damages.[17]

Watered Stock Shares of stock issued by a corporation for which the corporation receives, as payment, less than the stated value of the shares.

 ## Major Business Forms Compared

As mentioned in Chapter 14, when deciding which form of business organization to choose, businesspersons normally consider several factors. These factors include the ease of creation, the liability of the owners, tax considerations, and the ability to raise capital. Each major form of business organization offers distinct advantages and disadvantages with respect to these and other factors.

Exhibit 15–3 on pages 465 and 466 summarizes the essential advantages and disadvantages of each of the forms of business organization discussed in Chapter 14, as well as this chapter.

---

16. The phrase *watered stock* was originally used to describe cattle that were kept thirsty during a long drive and then were allowed to drink large quantities of water just before their sale. The increased weight of the "watered stock" allowed the seller to reap a higher profit.

17. See, for example, *Mazloom v. Mazloom*, 382 S.C. 307, 675 S.E.2d 746 (2009).

● *Exhibit* **15–3 Major Forms of Business Compared**

CHARACTERISTIC	SOLE PROPRIETORSHIP	PARTNERSHIP	CORPORATION
Method of Creation	Created at will by owner.	Created by agreement of the parties.	Authorized by the state under the state's corporation law.
Legal Position	Not a separate entity. Owner is the business.	A traditional partnership is a separate legal entity in most states.	Always a legal entity separate and distinct from its owners—a legal fiction for the purposes of owning property and being a party to litigation.
Liability	Unlimited liability.	Unlimited liability.	Limited liability of shareholders—shareholders are not liable for the debts of the corporation.
Duration	Determined by owner; automatically dissolved on owner's death.	Terminated by agreement of the partners, but can continue to do business even when a partner dissociates from the partnership.	Can have perpetual existence.
Transferability of Interest	Interest can be transferred, but individual's proprietorship then ends.	Although partnership interest can be assigned, assignee does not have full rights of a partner.	Shares of stock can be transferred.
Management	Completely at owner's discretion.	Each partner has a direct and equal voice in management unless expressly agreed otherwise in the partnership agreement.	Shareholders elect directors, who set policy and appoint officers.
Taxation	Owner pays personal taxes on business income.	Each partner pays pro rata share of income taxes on net profits, whether or not they are distributed.	Double taxation—corporation pays income tax on net profits, with no deduction for dividends, and shareholders pay income tax on disbursed dividends they receive.
Organizational Fees, Annual License Fees, and Annual Reports	None or minimal.	None or minimal.	All required.
Transaction of Business in Other States	Generally no limitation.	Generally no limitation.[a]	Normally must qualify to do business and obtain certificate of authority.
CHARACTERISTIC	LIMITED PARTNERSHIP	LIMITED LIABILITY COMPANY	LIMITED LIABILITY PARTNERSHIP
Method of Creation	Created by agreement to carry on a business for profit. At least one party must be a general partner and the other(s) limited partner(s). Certificate of limited partnership is filed. Charter must be issued by the state.	Created by an agreement of the member-owners of the company. Articles of organization are filed. Charter must be issued by the state.	Created by agreement of the partners. A statement of qualification for the limited liability partnership is filed.
Legal Position	Treated as a legal entity.	Treated as a legal entity.	Generally, treated same as a traditional partnership.

a. A few states have enacted statutes requiring that foreign partnerships qualify to do business within the state.

(Continued)

● *Exhibit* 15–3 Major Forms of Business Compared, Continued

CHARACTERISTIC	LIMITED PARTNERSHIP	LIMITED LIABILITY COMPANY	LIMITED LIABILITY PARTNERSHIP
Liability	Unlimited liability of all general partners. Limited partners are liable only to the extent of their capital contributions.	Member-owners' liability is limited to the amount of their capital contributions or investments.	Varies, but under the Uniform Partnership Act, liability of a partner for acts committed by other partners is limited.
Duration	By agreement in certificate, or by termination of the last general partner (retirement, death, and the like) or last limited partner.	Unless a single-member LLC, can have perpetual existence (same as a corporation).	Remains in existence until cancellation or revocation.
Transferability of Interest	Interest can be assigned (same as in a traditional partnership), but if assignee becomes a member with consent of other partners, certificate must be amended.	Member interests are freely transferable.	Interest can be assigned same as in a traditional partnership.
Management	General partners have equal voice or by agreement. Limited partners may not retain limited liability if they actively participate in management.	Member-owners can fully participate in management or can designate a group of persons to manage on behalf of the members.	Same as in a traditional partnership.
Taxation	Generally taxed as a partnership.	LLC is not taxed, and members are taxed personally on profits "passed through" the LLC.	Same as in a traditional partnership.
Organizational Fees, Annual License Fees, and Annual Reports	Organizational fee required, but others usually not required.	Organizational fee required. Others vary with states.	Fees are set by each state for filing statements of qualification, statements of foreign qualification, and annual reports.
Transaction of Business in Other States	Generally no limitation.	Generally no limitation, but may vary depending on state.	Must file a statement of foreign qualification before doing business in another state.

Reviewing . . . Corporations

David Brock is on the board of directors of Firm Body Fitness, Inc., which owns a string of fitness clubs in New Mexico. Brock owns 15 percent of the Firm Body stock, and he is also employed as a tanning technician at one of the fitness clubs. After the January financial report showed that Firm Body's tanning division was operating at a substantial net loss, the board of directors, led by Marty Levinson, discussed terminating the tanning operations. Brock successfully convinced a majority of the board that the tanning division was necessary to market the club's overall fitness package. By April, the tanning division's financial losses had risen. The board hired a business analyst who conducted surveys and determined that the tanning operations did not significantly increase membership. A shareholder, Diego Peñada, discovered that Brock owned stock in Sunglow, Inc., the company from which Firm Body purchased its tanning equipment. Peñada notified Levinson, who privately reprimanded Brock. Shortly afterward, Brock and Mandy Vail, who owned 37 percent of the Firm Body stock and also held shares of Sunglow, voted to replace Levinson on the board of directors. Using the information presented in the chapter, answer the following questions.

1. What duties did Brock, as a director, owe to Firm Body?
2. Does the fact that Brock owned shares in Sunglow establish a conflict of interest? Why or why not?
3. Suppose that Firm Body brought an action against Brock claiming that he had breached the duty of loyalty by not disclosing his interest in Sunglow to the other directors. What theory might Brock use in his defense?
4. Now suppose that Firm Body did not bring an action against Brock. What type of lawsuit might Peñada be able to bring based on these facts?

Key Terms

Chapter Summary: Corporations

Corporate Nature and Classification (See pages 435–442.)	A corporation is a legal entity distinct from its owners. Formal statutory requirements, which vary somewhat from state to state, must be followed in forming a corporation. 1. *Corporate parties*—The shareholders own the corporation. They elect a board of directors to govern the corporation. The board of directors hires corporate officers and other employees to run the daily business of the firm. 2. *Corporate taxation*—The corporation pays income tax on net profits, and shareholders pay income tax on the disbursed dividends that they receive from the corporation (double-taxation feature). 3. *Torts and criminal acts*—The corporation is liable for the torts committed by its agents or officers within the course and scope of their employment. In some circumstances, a corporation can be held liable (and be fined) for the criminal acts of its agents and employees. In certain situations, corporate officers may be held personally liable for corporate crimes. 4. *Domestic, foreign, and alien corporations*—A corporation is referred to as a *domestic corporation* within its home state (the state in which it incorporates). A corporation is referred to as a *foreign corporation* by any state that is not its home state. A corporation is referred to as an *alien corporation* if it originates in another country but does business in the United States. 5. *Public and private corporations*—A public corporation is one formed by a government (for example, cities, towns, and public projects). A private corporation is one formed wholly or in part for private benefit. Most corporations are private corporations. 6. *Nonprofit corporations*—Corporations formed without a profit-making purpose (for example, charitable, educational, and religious organizations and hospitals). 7. *Close corporations*—Corporations owned by a family or a relatively small number of individuals. Transfer of shares is usually restricted, and the corporation cannot make a public offering of its securities. 8. *S corporations*—Small domestic corporations (with no more than one hundred shareholders) that, under Subchapter S of the Internal Revenue Code, are given special tax treatment. These corporations allow shareholders to enjoy the limited legal liability of the corporate form but avoid its double-taxation feature. 9. *Professional corporations*—Corporations formed by professionals (for example, physicians and lawyers) to obtain the benefits of incorporation (such as limited liability).
Corporate Formation and Powers (See pages 442–447.)	1. *Promotional activities*—Preliminary promotional activities are rarely if ever taken today. A person who enters contracts with investors and others on behalf of the future corporation is personally liable on all preincorporation contracts. Liability remains until the corporation is formed and assumes the contract by novation. 2. *Incorporation procedures*—Exact procedures for incorporation differ among states, but the basic steps are as follows: (a) select a state of incorporation, (b) secure the corporate name by confirming its availability, (c) prepare the articles of incorporation, and (d) file the articles of incorporation with the secretary of state accompanied by payment of the specified fees.

(Continued)

Chapter Summary: Corporations, Continued

Corporate Formation and Powers—Continued	3. *Articles of incorporation*—The articles of incorporation must include the corporate name, the number of shares of stock the corporation is authorized to issue, the registered office and agent, and the names and addresses of the incorporators. The articles may (but are not required to) include additional information about the corporation's nature and purpose, duration, and internal organization. The state's filing of the articles of incorporation authorizes the corporation to conduct business.
	4. *The first organizational meeting*—A meeting is held after incorporation. The usual purpose of this meeting is to adopt the bylaws, or internal rules of the corporation, but other business, such as election of the board of directors may also take place.
	5. *Improper incorporation*—If a corporation has been improperly incorporated, the courts will sometimes impute corporate status to the firm by holding that it is a *de jure* corporation (cannot be challenged by the state or third parties) or a *de facto* corporation (can be challenged by the state but not by third parties). If a firm is neither a *de jure* nor a *de facto* corporation but represents itself to be a corporation and is sued as such by a third party, it may be held to be a corporation by estoppel.
	6. *Express powers*—The express powers of a corporation are found in the following laws and documents (listed according to their priority): federal constitution, state constitutions, state statutes, articles of incorporation, bylaws, and resolutions of the board of directors.
	7. *Implied powers*—Barring express constitutional, statutory, or other prohibitions, the corporation has the implied power to do all acts reasonably appropriate and necessary to accomplish its corporate purposes.
	8. *Ultra vires doctrine*—Any act of a corporation that is beyond its express or implied powers to undertake is an *ultra vires* act and may lead to a lawsuit by the shareholders, corporation, or state attorney general to enjoin or recover damages for the *ultra vires* acts.
Piercing the Corporate Veil (See pages 447–449)	To avoid injustice, courts may pierce the corporate veil and hold a shareholder or shareholders personally liable for a judgment against the corporation. This usually occurs only when the corporation was established to circumvent the law, when the corporate form is used for an illegitimate or fraudulent purpose, or when the controlling shareholders commingle their personal interests with those of the corporation to such an extent that the corporation no longer has a separate identity.
Directors and Officers (See pages 449–457.)	1. *Director*—Directors are responsible for all policymaking decisions necessary to the management of all corporate affairs (see Exhibit 15–1 on page 450). Directors usually serve a one-year term, although their terms can be longer or staggered. Compensation is usually specified in the corporate articles or bylaws. The board of directors conducts business by holding formal meetings with recorded minutes.
	2. *Rights of directors*—Directors' rights include the rights of participation, inspection, compensation, and indemnification.
	3. *Corporate officers and executives*—Corporate officers and other executive employees are normally hired by the board of directors and have the rights defined by their employment contracts. The duties of corporate officers are the same as those of directors.
	4. *Duty of care*—Directors and officers are obligated to act in good faith, to use prudent business judgment in the conduct of corporate affairs, and to act in the corporation's best interests. If a director fails to exercise this duty of care, she or he can be answerable to the corporation and to the shareholders for breaching the duty.
	5. *The business judgment rule*—This rule immunizes directors and officers from liability when they acted in good faith, acted in the best interests of the corporation, and exercised due care. For the rule to apply, the directors and officers must have made an informed, reasonable, and loyal decision.
	6. *Duty of loyalty*—Directors and officers have a fiduciary duty to subordinate their own interests to those of the corporation in matters relating to the corporation.
	7. *Conflicts of interest*—To fulfill their duty of loyalty, directors and officers must make a full disclosure of any potential conflicts between their personal interests and those of the corporation.

Chapter Summary: Corporations, Continued

Shareholders
(See pages 457–464.)
	1. *Shareholders' powers*—Shareholders' powers include the approval of all fundamental changes affecting the corporation and the election of the board of directors.
	2. *Shareholders' meetings*—Shareholders' meetings must occur at least annually. Special meetings can be called when necessary. Notice of the date, time, and place of the meeting (and its purpose, if it is specially called) must be sent to shareholders. Shareholders may vote by proxy (authorizing someone else to vote their shares) and may submit proposals to be included in the company's proxy materials sent to shareholders before meetings.
	3. *Shareholder voting*—Shareholder voting requirements and procedures are as follows:
	   a. A minimum number of shareholders (a quorum—generally, more than 50 percent of shares held) must be present at a meeting for business to be conducted. Resolutions are passed (usually) by simple majority vote.
	   b. The corporation must prepare voting lists of shareholders of record prior to each shareholders' meeting.
	   c. Cumulative voting may or may not be required or permitted. Cumulative voting gives minority shareholders a better chance to be represented on the board of directors.
	   d. A shareholder voting agreement (an agreement of shareholders to vote their shares together) is usually held to be valid and enforceable.
	4. *Rights of shareholders*—Shareholders have numerous rights, which may include the following:
	   a. The right to a stock certificate, preemptive rights, and the right to stock warrants (depending on the articles of incorporation).
	   b. The right to obtain a dividend (at the discretion of the directors).
	   c. The right to inspect the corporate records.
	   d. The right to transfer shares (this right may be restricted in close corporations).
	   e. The right to a share of corporate assets when the corporation is dissolved.
	   f. The right to sue on behalf of the corporation (bring a shareholder's derivative suit) when the directors fail to do so.
	5. *Duties and liabilities of shareholders*—Shareholders may be liable for the retention of illegal dividends and for the value of watered stock. In certain situations, majority shareholders may be regarded as having a fiduciary duty to minority shareholders and will be liable if that duty is breached.

 ExamPrep

ISSUE SPOTTERS

1. Name Brand, Inc., is a small business. Twelve members of a single family own all of its stock. Ordinarily, corporate income is taxed at the corporate and shareholder levels. How can Name Brand avoid this double taxation of income?
2. Wonder Corporation has an opportunity to buy stock in XL, Inc. The directors decide that instead of Wonder buying the stock, the directors will buy it. Yvon, a Wonder shareholder, learns of the purchase and wants to sue the directors on Wonder's behalf. Can she do it? Explain.

—**Check your answers to these questions against the answers provided in Appendix G.**

BEFORE THE TEST

Go to **www.cengagebrain.com**, enter the ISBN number "9781111530617," and click on "Find" to locate this textbook's Web site. Then, click on "Access Now" under "Study Tools," and select "Chapter 15" at the top. There you will find an "Interactive Quiz" that you can take to assess your mastery of the concepts in this chapter, as well as "Flashcards" and a "Glossary" of important terms.

For Review

1. What steps are involved in bringing a corporation into existence?
2. In what circumstances might a court disregard the corporate entity (pierce the corporate veil) and hold the shareholders personally liable?
3. What are the duties of corporate directors and officers?
4. Directors are expected to use their best judgment in managing the corporation. What must directors do to avoid liability for honest mistakes of judgment and poor business decisions?
5. What is a voting proxy? What is cumulative voting?

Questions and Case Problems

15–1. Preincorporation. Cummings, Okawa, and Taft are recent college graduates who want to form a corporation to manufacture and sell personal computers. Peterson tells them he will set in motion the formation of their corporation. First, Peterson makes a contract with Owens for the purchase of a piece of land for $20,000. Owens does not know of the prospective corporate formation at the time the contract is signed. Second, Peterson makes a contract with Babcock to build a small plant on the property being purchased. Babcock's contract is conditional on the corporation's formation. Peterson secures all necessary subscription agreements and capitalization, and he files the articles of incorporation. Discuss whether the newly formed corporation, Peterson, or both are liable on the contracts with Owens and Babcock. Is the corporation automatically liable to Babcock on formation? Explain.

15–2. Conflicts of Interest. Oxy Corp. is negotiating with the Wick Construction Co. for the renovation of the Oxy corporate headquarters. Wick, the owner of the Wick Construction Co., is also one of the five members of Oxy's board of directors. The contract terms are standard for this type of contract. Wick has previously informed two of the other directors of his interest in the construction company. Oxy's board approves the contract by a three-to-two vote, with Wick voting with the majority. Discuss whether this contract is binding on the corporation.

15–3. Fiduciary Duty of Officers. Designer Surfaces, Inc., supplied countertops to homeowners who shopped at stores such as Lowe's and Costco. The homeowners paid the store, which then contracted with Designer to fabricate and install the countertops. Designer bought materials from Arizona Tile, LLC, on an open account. Designer's only known corporate officers were Howard Berger and John McCarthy. Designer became insolvent and could not pay Arizona Tile for all the materials it had purchased, including materials for which Designer had already received payment from the retail stores. Arizona Tile sued Designer and won a default judgment, but the company had no funds. Arizona Tile then sued Berger and McCarthy personally for diverting company funds that Designer had received in trust for payment

to Arizona Tile. Arizona Tile argued that the use of the funds for other purposes was a breach of fiduciary duty. Berger and McCarthy argued that corporate law imposed neither a fiduciary duty on corporate officers nor personal liability for breach of a duty to suppliers of materials. Which argument is more credible and why? [*Arizona Tile, LLC v. Berger,* 223 Ariz. 491, 224 P.3d 988 (Ariz.App. 2010)]

15–4. Piercing the Corporate Veil. Smith Services, Inc., was a corporation solely owned by Tony Smith. Bear, Inc., owned and operated Laker Express, a fueling station in Kentucky. Smith charged fuel to an account at Laker Express and owed approximately $35,000. There was no written agreement indicating who was liable on the account in the event of default, but all invoices had been issued to Smith Services. Smith later dissolved Smith Services and continued to run his business as a sole proprietorship. When Laker Express sued Smith Services to collect on the debt, there were no assets in the corporation. Laker Express sued Tony Smith personally and asked the court to pierce the corporate veil, claiming that Smith was engaged in fraud and was using the corporate form only to protect himself. The trial court dismissed the case, and Laker Express appealed. Should the court pierce the corporate veil and hold Smith personally liable for the unpaid corporate debt? Why or why not? Or should Laker Express have been more careful when dealing with clients? Explain. [*Bear, Inc. v. Smith,* 303 S.W.3d 137 (Ky.App. 2010)]

15–5.   **Case Problem with Sample Answer. Rights of Shareholders.** Stanka Woods was the manager and sole member of Hair Ventures, LLC, which owned 3 million shares of stock in Biolustré, Inc. For several years, Woods and other Biolustré shareholders did not receive notices of shareholders' meetings or financial reports. Nevertheless, Woods learned that Biolustré planned to issue more stock, and her boyfriend, Daniel Davila, proposed that they meet with other shareholders to discuss the company's operations and oppose the issue. To obtain information regarding what was going on at Biolustré, Woods, through Hair Ventures, sent Biolustré a demand to examine its books and records. Biolustré did not respond.

Hair Ventures filed a suit in a Texas state court against the corporation, seeking an order to compel it to comply. Biolustré asserted that Hair Ventures' request was not for a proper purpose. Does a shareholder have a right to inspect corporate books and records? If so, what are the limits? Do any of those limits apply in this case? Explain. [*Biolustré Inc. v. Hair Ventures, LLC,* __ S.W.3d __ (Tex.App.—San Antonio 2011)]

—To view a sample answer for Case Problem 15–5, go to Appendix F at the end of this text.

15–6. Close Corporations. Mark Burnett and Kamran Pourgol were the only shareholders in a corporation that built and sold a house in North Hempstead, New York. The town revoked the certificate of occupancy on the ground that the house exceeded the amount of square footage allowed by the building permit. The corporation agreed with the buyers to pay a certain amount to renovate the house to conform with the permit and to obtain a new certificate of occupancy. Burnett, however, bought the house and then filed a suit in a New York state court against Pourgol. Burnett charged that Pourgol had submitted incorrect plans to the town without Burnett's knowledge, had assumed responsibility for the error in square footage in discussions with the buyers, had knowingly misrepresented the extent of the renovations, and had failed to undertake any work to fix the house. Do the charges indicate misconduct? How might this situation have been avoided? Discuss. [*Burnett v. Pourgol,* 83 A.D.3d 756, 921 N.Y.S.2d 280 (2011)]

15–7. **A Question of Ethics. Directors and Officers Duties.** *New Orleans Paddlewheels, Inc. (NOP), is a Louisiana corporation formed in 1982, when James Smith, Sr., and Warren Reuther were its only shareholders, with each holding 50 percent of the stock. NOP is part of a sprawling enterprise of tourism and hospitality companies in New Orleans. The positions on the board of each company were split equally between the Smith and Reuther families. At Smith's request, his son James Smith, Jr. (JES), became involved in the businesses. In 1999, NOP's board elected JES as president, to be in charge of day-to-day operations, and Reuther as chief executive officer (CEO), to be in charge of marketing and development. Over the next few years, animosity developed between Reuther and JES.*

In October 2001, JES terminated Reuther as CEO and denied him access to the offices and books of NOP and the other companies, literally changing the locks on the doors. At the next meetings of the boards of NOP and the overall enterprise, deadlock ensued, with the directors voting along family lines on every issue. Complaining that the meetings were a "waste of time," JES began to run the entire enterprise by taking advantage of an unequal balance of power on the companies' executive committees. In NOP's subsequent bankruptcy proceeding, Reuther filed a motion for the appointment of a trustee to formulate a plan for the firm's reorganization, alleging, among other things, misconduct by NOP's management. [In re New Orleans Paddlewheels, Inc., 350 Bankr. 667 (E.D.La. 2006)]

1. Was Reuther legally entitled to have access to the books and records of NOP and the other companies? JES maintained, among other things, that NOP's books were "a mess." Was JES's denial of that access unethical? Explain.

2. How would you describe JES's attempt to gain control of NOP and the other companies? Were his actions deceptive and self-serving in the pursuit of personal gain or legitimate and reasonable in the pursuit of a business goal? Discuss.

15–8. **Video Question. *Corporation or LLC: Which Is Better?*** Access the video using the instructions provided below to answer the following questions.

1. Compare the liability that Anna and Caleb would be exposed to as shareholders/owners of a corporation versus as members of a limited liability company (LLC).

2. How does the taxation of corporations and LLCs differ?

3. Given that Anna and Caleb conduct their business (Wizard Internet) over the Internet, can you think of any drawbacks to forming an LLC?

4. If you were in the position of Anna and Caleb, would you choose to create a corporation or an LLC? Why?

—To watch this video, go to **www.cengagebrain.com** and register the access code that came with your new book or log in to your existing account. Select the link for either the "Business Law Digital Video Library Online Access" or "Business Law CourseMate," and then click on "Complete Video List" to find the video for this chapter (Video 46).

Agency

> "[It] is a universal principle in the law of agency, that the powers of the agent are to be exercised for the benefits of the principal only, and not of the agent or of third parties."
>
> —Joseph Story, 1779–1845
> (Associate justice of the United States Supreme Court, 1811–1844)

Contents

Chapter Objectives

After reading this chapter, you should be able to answer the following questions:

1. What is the difference between an employee and an independent contractor?

2. How do agency relationships arise?

3. What duties do agents and principals owe to each other?

4. When is a principal liable for the agent's actions with respect to third parties? When is the agent liable?

5. What are some of the ways in which an agency relationship can be terminated?

Agency A relationship between two parties in which one party (the agent) agrees to represent or act for the other (the principal).

One of the most common, important, and pervasive legal relationships is that of **agency**. In an agency relationship between two parties, one of the parties, called the *agent,* agrees to represent or act for the other, called the *principal.* The principal has the right to control the agent's conduct in matters entrusted to the agent, and the agent must exercise his or her powers "for the benefits of the principal only," as Justice Joseph Story indicated in the chapter-opening quotation above. By using agents, a principal can conduct multiple business operations simultaneously in various locations. Thus, for example, contracts that bind the principal can be made at different places with different persons at the same time.

Agency relationships permeate the business world. Indeed, agency law is essential to the existence and operation of a corporate entity, because only through its agents can a corporation function and enter into contracts. A familiar example of an agent is a corporate officer who serves in a representative capacity for the owners of the corporation. In this capacity, the officer has the authority to bind the principal (the corporation) to a contract.

Agency Relationships

Section 1(1) of the *Restatement (Third) of Agency*[1] defines agency as "the fiduciary relation which results from the manifestation of consent by one person to another that the other shall act in his [or her] behalf and subject to his [or her] control, and consent by the other so to act." In other words, in a principal-agent relationship, the parties have agreed that the agent will act *on behalf and instead of* the principal in negotiating and transacting business with third parties.

The term **fiduciary** is at the heart of agency law. The term can be used both as a noun and as an adjective. When used as a noun, it refers to a person having a duty created by her or his undertaking to act primarily for another's benefit in matters connected with the undertaking. When used as an adjective, as in "fiduciary relationship," it means that the relationship involves trust and confidence.

Fiduciary As a noun, a person having a duty created by his or her undertaking to act primarily for another's benefit in matters connected with the undertaking. As an adjective, a relationship founded on trust and confidence.

Agency relationships commonly exist between employers and employees. Agency relationships may sometimes also exist between employers and independent contractors who are hired to perform special tasks or services.

Employer-Employee Relationships

Normally, all employees who deal with third parties are deemed to be agents. A salesperson in a department store, for instance, is an agent of the store's owner (the principal) and acts on the owner's behalf. Any sale of goods made by the salesperson to a customer is binding on the principal. Similarly, most representations of fact made by the salesperson with respect to the goods sold are binding on the principal.

Because employees who deal with third parties are generally deemed to be agents of their employers, agency law and employment law overlap considerably. Agency relationships, though, as will become apparent, can exist outside an employer-employee relationship and thus have a broader reach than employment laws do. Additionally, bear in mind that agency law is based on the common law. In the employment realm, many common law doctrines have been displaced by statutory law and government regulations relating to employment relationships.

Employment laws (state and federal) apply only to the employer-employee relationship. Statutes governing Social Security, withholding taxes, workers' compensation, unemployment compensation, workplace safety, employment discrimination, and the like (see Chapters 17 and 18) are applicable only if employer-employee status exists. *These laws do not apply to an independent contractor.*

An independent contractor communicates from a building site. What are some significant differences between employees and independent contractors?

Employer–Independent Contractor Relationships

Independent contractors are not employees because, by definition, those who hire them have no control over the details of their physical performance. Section 2 of the *Restatement (Third) of Agency* defines an **independent contractor** as follows:

Independent Contractor One who works for, and receives payment from, an employer but whose working conditions and methods are not controlled by the employer. An independent contractor is not an employee but may be an agent.

[An independent contractor is] a person who contracts with another to do something for him [or her] but who is not controlled by the other nor subject to the other's right to control with respect to his [or her] physical conduct in the performance of the undertaking. *He [or she] may or may not be an agent.* [Emphasis added.]

---

1. The *Restatement (Third) of Agency* is an authoritative summary of the law of agency and is often referred to by judges and other legal professionals.

"Keep up the good work, whatever it is, whoever you are."

Building contractors and subcontractors are independent contractors—a property owner does not control the acts of either of these professionals. Truck drivers who own their equipment and hire themselves out on a per-job basis are independent contractors, but truck drivers who drive company trucks on a regular basis are usually employees.

The relationship between a person or firm and an independent contractor may or may not involve an agency relationship. To illustrate: An owner of real estate who hires a real estate broker to negotiate a sale of his or her property not only has contracted with an independent contractor (the real estate broker) but also has established an agency relationship for the specific purpose of assisting in the sale of the property. Another example is an insurance agent, who is both an independent contractor and an agent of the insurance company for which she or he sells policies. (Note that an insurance *broker,* in contrast, normally is an agent of the person obtaining insurance and not of the insurance company.)

Determining Employee Status

The courts are frequently asked to determine whether a particular worker is an employee or an independent contractor. How a court decides this issue can have a significant effect on the rights and liabilities of the parties.

CRITERIA USED BY THE COURTS   In determining whether a worker has the status of an employee or an independent contractor, the courts often consider the following questions:

1. How much control can the employer exercise over the details of the work? (If an employer can exercise considerable control over the details of the work, this would indicate employee status. This is perhaps the most important factor weighed by the courts in determining employee status.)
2. Is the worker engaged in an occupation or business distinct from that of the employer? (If so, this points to independent-contractor status, not employee status.)
3. Is the work usually done under the employer's direction or by a specialist without supervision? (If the work is usually done under the employer's direction, this would indicate employee status.)
4. Does the employer supply the tools at the place of work? (If so, this would indicate employee status.)
5. For how long is the person employed? (If the person is employed for a long period of time, this would indicate employee status.)
6. What is the method of payment—by time period or at the completion of the job? (Payment by time period, such as once every two weeks or once a month, would indicate employee status.)
7. What degree of skill is required of the worker? (If little skill is required, this may indicate employee status.)

Sometimes, workers may benefit from having employee status—for tax purposes and to be protected under certain employment laws, for example. Employers are required to pay certain taxes, such as Social Security and unemployment taxes, for employees but not for independent contractors. Furthermore, as mentioned earlier, federal statutes governing employment discrimination apply only when an employer-employee relationship exists. Protection under employment-discrimination statutes provides a significant incentive for workers to claim that they are employees rather than independent contractors.

CASE EXAMPLE 16.1   A Puerto Rican television station, WIPR, contracted with a woman to co-host a television show profiling cities in Puerto Rico. The woman signed a new contract for each episode, each of which required her to work a certain number of days. She was under no other commitment to work for WIPR and was free to pursue other opportunities during the weeks between filming. WIPR did not withhold any taxes from the lump-sum amount it paid her for each contract. When the woman became pregnant, WIPR stopped contracting with her. She filed a lawsuit claiming that WIPR was discriminating against her in violation of federal employment-discrimination laws, but the court found in favor of WIPR. Because the parties had structured their relationship through the use of repeated fixed-length contracts and had described the woman as an independent contractor on tax documents, she could not maintain an employment-discrimination suit.[2] ●

Whether a worker is an employee or an independent contractor can also affect the employer's liability for the worker's actions. (See this chapter's *Management Perspective* feature below for more details on this topic.) In the following case, the court had to determine the status of a taxi driver whose passengers were injured in a collision.

---

2. *Alberty-Vélez v. Corporación de Puerto Rico para la Difusión Pública,* 361 F.3d 1 (1st Cir. 2004).

Management Perspective   Independent-Contractor Negligence

Management Faces a Legal Issue

Managers often hire independent contractors. They do so for a variety of reasons, such as reducing paperwork and avoiding certain tax liabilities. More important, business managers wish to avoid negligence lawsuits. As a general rule, employers are not liable for torts (wrongs) that an independent contractor commits against third parties. If an employer exercises significant control over the work activity of an independent contractor, however, that contractor may be considered an employee, and the employer may be held liable for the contractor's torts.

What the Courts Say

In one case, a trucking company that hired independent contractors to make deliveries was sued after a motorist was killed in a collision with one of the company's independent-contractor drivers. At trial, the trucking company prevailed. The plaintiff argued that the company had failed to investigate the background, qualifications, or experience of the driver. The appellate court, however, pointed out that an employer of an independent contractor has no control over the manner in which the work is done. The plaintiff failed to offer any proof as to why the company should have investigated the driver.[a]

In another case, a tenant whose hand was injured sued the building's owner. An independent contractor, hired by the owner to perform repair work on the outside of the building, had attempted to close the tenant's balcony door when the tenant's hand got caught,

causing her injury. The appellate court ultimately held that the building's owner and its managing agent could not be held liable for the independent contractor's alleged negligence. As in the previous case, the court noted that the employer (the building's owner) had no right to control the manner in which the independent contractor did his work. The tenant suffered harm because of the independent contractor's actions, not because the premises were in disrepair.[b]

Finally, another issue that sometimes arises is a business owner's liability for injuries to employees of independent contractors that the owner has hired. In one case, two employees of an independent subcontractor suffered electrical burns while working on a construction project. They sued the business owner of the project, among others. The defendants prevailed at trial, and on appeal, the court agreed.[c]

Implications for Managers

To minimize the possibility of being held liable for an independent contractor's negligence, managers should check the qualifications of all contractors before hiring them. A thorough investigation of a contractor's background is especially important when the work may present a danger to the public (as in delivering explosives). It is also wise to require a written contract in which the contractor assumes liability for any harm caused to third parties by the contractor's negligence. Managers should insist that independent contractors carry liability insurance and ensure that the liability insurance policy is current. Additionally, business managers should refrain from doing anything that would lead a third party to believe that an independent contractor is an employee. And, of course, they cannot maintain control over an independent contractor's actions.

---

a. *Stander v. Dispoz-O-Products, Inc.,* 973 So.2d 603 (Fla.App. 2008).

b. *Stagno v. 143-50 Hoover Owners Corp.,* 48 A.D.3d 548, 853 N.Y.S.2d 85 (2008).

c. *Dalton v. 933 Peachtree, LP,* 291 Ga.App. 123, 661 S.E.2d 156 (2008).

Case 16.1 Lopez v. El Palmar Taxi, Inc.

Court of Appeals of Georgia, 297 Ga.App. 121, 676 S.E.2d 460 (2009).

Is a taxi driver who is not subject to the control of the taxi company an independent contractor or an employee?

BACKGROUND AND FACTS

El Palmar Taxi, Inc., requires its drivers to supply their own cabs, which must display El Palmar's logo. The drivers pay gas, maintenance, and insurance costs, and a fee to El Palmar. They are expected to follow certain rules—dress neatly, for example—and to comply with the law, including licensing regulations, but they can work when they want for as long as they want. El Palmar might dispatch a driver to pick up a fare, or the driver can look for a fare. Mario Julaju drove a taxi under a contract with El Palmar that described him as an independent contractor. El Palmar sent Julaju to pick up Maria Lopez and her children. During the ride, Julaju's cab collided with a truck. To recover for their injuries, the Lopezes filed a suit in a Georgia state court against El Palmar. The employer argued that it was not liable because Julaju was an independent contractor. The court ruled in El Palmar's favor. The plaintiffs appealed.

IN THE WORDS OF THE COURT . . .
PHIPPS, Judge.

* * * *

In the complaint, Lopez alleged that she, accompanied by her children, hired El Palmar to transport them safely to their destination. * * * In its * * * answer, El Palmar denied this allegation and stated that Lopez had hired an independent contractor for transportation, not El Palmar.

* * * *

As a general rule, an employer is not responsible for [the actions of] its employee when the employee exercises an independent business and is not subject to the immediate direction and control of the employer. *To determine whether the relationship of the parties is that of employer and servant or that of employer and independent contractor, the primary test is whether the employer retains the right to control the time, manner and method of executing the work.* [Emphasis added.]

Here, Julaju executed an agreement with * * * El Palmar Taxi that he would work for El Palmar as an independent contractor. The only restrictions the contract imposed on him were to comply with all federal, state and local laws requiring business permits, certificates and licenses and to refrain from operating under the company's name in any jurisdiction where the vehicle could not legally be operated.

The evidence does not show that El Palmar assumed control over the time, manner or method of Julaju's work. He was free to work when and for as long as he wanted, he was not required to accept fares from El Palmar, he could obtain his own fares and he could work anywhere the taxi could legally be operated. The fact that the cars he drove displayed the El Palmar logo and the fact that he received calls from El Palmar are not sufficient to create an employer-employee relationship.

* * * The car [Julaju] drove the day of the collision was not owned by El Palmar. Thus, El Palmar cannot be held liable for Julaju's [actions] under the theory that Julaju was El Palmar's employee.

DECISION AND REMEDY

The state intermediate appellate court affirmed this part of the lower court's decision. A taxi driver who is not subject to the control of the taxi company is an independent contractor. But the appellate court reversed the judgment in El Palmar's favor on other grounds and remanded the case for trial.

WHAT IF THE FACTS WERE DIFFERENT?

Suppose that El Palmar had limited its driver to a set schedule in a specific area of the city and allowed him to pick up only certain passengers. Would these facts have established Julaju as an employee? Why or why not?

MANAGERIAL IMPLICATIONS

When an employment contract clearly designates one party as an independent contractor, the relationship between the parties is presumed to be that of employer and independent contractor. But this is only a presumption. Evidence can be introduced to show that the employer exercised sufficient control to establish the other party as an employee. The Internal Revenue Service is becoming increasingly aggressive in pursuing cases involving independent-contractor versus employee status. Thus, from a tax perspective, business managers need to ensure that all independent contractors fully control their own work.

CRITERIA USED BY THE IRS   The Internal Revenue Service (IRS) has established its own criteria for determining whether a worker is an independent contractor or an employee. Although the IRS once considered twenty factors in determining a worker's status, guidelines today encourage IRS examiners to focus on just one of those factors—the degree of control the business exercises over the worker.

The IRS tends to closely scrutinize a firm's classification of its workers because, as noted earlier, employers can avoid certain tax liabilities by hiring independent contractors instead of employees. Even when a firm classifies a worker as an independent contractor, the IRS may decide that the worker is actually an employee. In that situation, the employer will be responsible for paying any applicable Social Security, withholding, and unemployment taxes.

EMPLOYEE STATUS AND "WORKS FOR HIRE"   Under the Copyright Act of 1976, any copyrighted work created by an employee within the scope of her or his employment at the request of the employer is a "work for hire," and the *employer* owns the copyright to the work. When an employer hires an independent contractor—a freelance artist, writer, or computer programmer, for example—the independent contractor owns the copyright *unless* the parties agree in writing that the work is a "work for hire" and the work falls into one of nine specific categories, including audiovisual and other works.

CASE EXAMPLE 16.2   Artisan House, Inc., hired a professional photographer, Steven H. Lindner, owner of SHL Imaging, Inc., to take pictures of its products for the creation of color slides to be used by Artisan's sales force. Lindner controlled his own work and carefully chose the lighting and angles used in the photographs. When Lindner later discovered that Artisan had published the photographs in a catalogue and brochures without his permission, he had SHL register the photographs with the copyright office and file a lawsuit for copyright infringement. Artisan claimed that its publication of the photographs was authorized because they were works for hire. The court, however, decided that SHL was an independent contractor and owned the copyright to the photographs. SHL had only given Artisan permission (a license) to provide the photographs to its sales reps, not to reproduce them in other publications. Because Artisan had used the photographs in an unauthorized manner, the court ruled that Artisan was liable for copyright infringement.[3] ●

 How Agency Relationships Are Formed

Agency relationships normally are *consensual*—that is, they come about by voluntary consent and agreement between the parties. Generally, the agreement need not be in writing,[4] and consideration is not required.

A person must have contractual capacity to be a principal.[5] Those who cannot legally enter into contracts directly should not be allowed to do so indirectly through an agent. Any person can be an agent, though, regardless of whether he or she has the capacity to enter a contract (including minors).

An agency relationship can be created for any legal purpose. An agency relationship that is created for an illegal purpose or that is contrary to public policy is unenforceable. **EXAMPLE 16.3**   Sharp (as principal) contracts with McKenzie (as agent) to sell illegal narcotics. This agency relationship is unenforceable because selling illegal narcotics is a felony and is contrary to public policy. ● It is also illegal for physicians and other licensed professionals to employ unlicensed agents to perform professional actions.

---

3. *SHL Imaging, Inc. v. Artisan House, Inc.,* 117 F.Supp.2d 301 (S.D.N.Y. 2000).

4. The following are the two main exceptions to the statement that agency agreements need not be in writing: (1) Whenever agency authority empowers the agent to enter into a contract that the Statute of Frauds requires to be in writing, the agent's authority from the principal must likewise be in writing (this is called the *equal dignity rule,* to be discussed later in this chapter). (2) A power of attorney, which confers authority to an agent, must be in writing.

5. Note that some states allow a minor to be a principal, but any resulting contracts will be voidable by the minor.

A homeowner has asked a lawn-care specialist to contract with others for the care of the homeowner's lawn on a regular basis. What type of relationship is established between the homeowner and the lawn-care specialist?

Generally, an agency relationship can arise in four ways: by agreement of the parties, by ratification, by estoppel, or by operation of law.

Agency by Agreement

Most agency relationships are based on an express or implied agreement that the agent will act for the principal and that the principal agrees to have the agent so act. An agency agreement can take the form of an express written contract or be created by an oral agreement. **EXAMPLE 16.4** Reese asks Cary, a gardener, to contract with others for the care of his lawn on a regular basis. Cary agrees. An agency relationship is established between Reese and Cary for the lawn care. ●

An agency agreement can also be implied by conduct. **EXAMPLE 16.5** A hotel expressly allows only Boris Koontz to park cars, but Boris has no employment contract there. The hotel's manager tells Boris when to work, as well as where and how to park the cars. The hotel's conduct amounts to a manifestation of its willingness to have Boris park its customers' cars, and Boris can infer from the hotel's conduct that he has authority to act as a parking valet. It can be inferred that Boris is an agent-employee of the hotel, his purpose being to provide valet parking services for hotel guests. ●

In the following case, the court had to decide whether an agency relationship arose when a man who was being hospitalized asked his wife to sign the admissions papers for him.

Case 16.2 **Laurel Creek Health Care Center v. Bishop**

Court of Appeals of Kentucky, ___ S.W.3d ___ (2010).

Is an agency relationship formed when a person being hospitalized has his spouse sign the admissions papers?

BACKGROUND AND FACTS Gilbert Bishop was admitted to Laurel Creek Health Care Center suffering from various physical ailments. During an examination, Bishop told Laurel Creek staff that he could not use his hands well enough to write or hold a pencil, but he was otherwise found to be mentally competent. Bishop's sister, Rachel Combs, testified that when she arrived at the facility she offered to sign the admissions forms, but Laurel Creek employees told her that it was their policy to have a patient's spouse sign the admissions papers if the patient was unable to do so. Combs also testified that Bishop asked her to get his wife, Anna, so that she could sign his admissions papers. Combs then brought Anna to the hospital, and Anna signed the admissions paperwork, which contained a provision for mandatory arbitration.

Subsequently, Bishop went into cardiopulmonary arrest and died. Following his death, Bishop's family brought an action in a Kentucky state court against Laurel Creek for negligence. Laurel Creek requested that the trial court order the parties to proceed to arbitration in accordance with the mandatory arbitration provision contained in the admissions paperwork signed by Anna. The trial court denied the request on the ground that Anna was not Bishop's agent and had no legal authority to make decisions for him. Laurel Creek appealed.

IN THE WORDS OF THE COURT . . .
LAMBERT, Judge.
* * * *

Laurel Creek first argues that this is a case of actual agency and that Anna Bishop had actual authority as Gilbert's agent to sign the admissions paperwork and is therefore bound by the arbitration agreement therein.
* * * *

We agree with Laurel Creek that Gilbert created an actual agency relationship between him and his wife. According to his sister, Rachel,

Case 16.2–Continued

Gilbert specifically asked that his wife be brought to the nursing home so that she could sign the admissions documents for him, and Anna acted upon that delegation of authority and signed the admissions papers. This is consistent with the creation of actual authority as described in the *Restatement (Third) of Agency,* [Section] 2.01, Comment c (2006). The *Restatement* explains the rationale for the creation of actual agency in three steps. First, *"the principal manifests assent to be affected by the agent's action."* In the instant case, Gilbert asked that Anna come to the hospital to sign the papers for him. *Second, "the agent's actions establish the agent's consent to act on the principal's behalf."* Here, Anna signed all the admissions papers per her husband's request and therefore consented to act on Gilbert's behalf. *Third, by acting within such authority, the agent affects the principal's legal relations with third parties.* Clearly here, Anna's actions affected Gilbert's relations with Laurel Creek, a third party. [Emphasis added.]

* * * *

* * * The evidence indicates that Gilbert indicated to Laurel Creek that he was physically incapable of signing the documents but was of sound mental capacity and wanted his wife to sign the documents on his behalf. When Gilbert communicated this to his sister, and the sister brought Anna in to sign the documents, Gilbert created an agency relationship upon which Laurel Creek relied.

DECISION AND REMEDY   The Kentucky Court of Appeals reversed the trial court's judgment and remanded the case for further proceedings consistent with its opinion. An actual agency relationship between Bishop and his wife had been formed, and the trial court had erred when it found otherwise.

THE LEGAL ENVIRONMENT DIMENSION   *Laurel Creek argued that even if there was no actual agency relationship, an implied agency relationship existed. Is this argument valid? Why or why not?*

THE ECONOMIC DIMENSION   *Which party benefited from the court's ruling? Why?*

Agency by Ratification

On occasion, a person who is in fact not an agent (or who is an agent acting outside the scope of her or his authority) may make a contract on behalf of another (a principal). If the principal affirms that contract by word or by action, an agency relationship is created by **ratification.** Ratification involves a question of intent, and intent can be expressed by either words or conduct. The basic requirements for ratification will be discussed later in this chapter.

Ratification The act of accepting and giving legal force to an obligation that previously was not enforceable.

Agency by Estoppel

When a principal causes a third person to believe that another person is his or her agent, and the third person deals with the supposed agent, the principal is "estopped to deny" the agency relationship. In such a situation, the principal's actions create the *appearance* of an agency that does not in fact exist. The third person must prove that she or he *reasonably* believed that an agency relationship existed, though.[6] Facts and circumstances must show that an ordinary, prudent person familiar with business practice and custom would have been justified in concluding that the agent had authority.

"If God had an agent, the world wouldn't be built yet. It'd only be about Thursday."
Jerry Reynolds, 1940–present
(National Basketball Association executive)

CASE EXAMPLE 16.6   Marsha and Jerry Wiedmaier owned Wiedmaier, Inc., a corporation that operated a truck stop. Their son, Michael, did not own any interest in the corporation but had worked at the truck stop as a fuel operator. Michael decided to form his own business called Extreme Diecast, LLC. To obtain a line of credit with Motorsport Marketing, Inc., a company that sells racing memorabilia, Michael asked his mother to sign the credit application form. After Marsha had signed as "Secretary-Owner" of Wiedmaier, Inc., Michael added his name to the list of corporate owners and faxed it to Motorsport. Later, when Michael stopped making payments on the

---

6. These concepts also apply when a person who is in fact an agent undertakes an action that is beyond the scope of her or his authority, as will be discussed later in this chapter.

merchandise he had ordered, Motorsport sued Wiedmaier for the unpaid balance. The court ruled that Michael was an apparent agent of Wiedmaier, Inc., because the credit application had caused Motorsport to reasonably believe that Michael was acting as Wiedmaier's agent in ordering merchandise.[7] ●

Note that the acts or declarations of a purported *agent* in and of themselves do not create an agency by estoppel. Rather, it is the deeds or statements *of the principal* that create an agency by estoppel. In other words, in Case Example 16.6 above, if Marsha Wiedmaier had not signed the credit application on behalf of the principal-corporation, then Motorsport would not have been reasonable in believing that Michael was Wiedmaier's agent.

Agency by Operation of Law

The courts may find an agency relationship in the absence of a formal agreement in other situations as well. This can occur in family relationships, such as when one spouse purchases certain basic necessaries and charges them to the other spouse's charge account. The courts will often rule that a spouse is liable to pay for the necessaries, either because of a social policy of promoting the general welfare of the spouse or because of a legal duty to supply necessaries to family members.

Agency by operation of law may also occur in emergency situations, when the agent's failure to act outside the scope of his or her authority would cause the principal substantial loss. If the agent is unable to contact the principal, the courts will often grant this emergency power. For instance, a railroad engineer may contract on behalf of her or his employer for medical care for an injured motorist hit by the train.

Duties of Agents and Principals

Once the principal-agent relationship has been created, both parties have duties that govern their conduct. As discussed previously, an agency relationship is *fiduciary*—one of trust. In a fiduciary relationship, each party owes the other the duty to act with the utmost good faith. We now examine the various duties of agents and principals.

In general, for every duty of the principal, the agent has a corresponding right, and vice versa. When one party to the agency relationship violates his or her duty to the other party, the remedies available to the nonbreaching party arise out of contract and tort law. These remedies include monetary damages, termination of the agency relationship, an injunction, and required accountings.

Agent's Duties to the Principal

Generally, the agent owes the principal five duties—performance, notification, loyalty, obedience, and accounting.

PERFORMANCE   An implied condition in every agency contract is the agent's agreement to use reasonable diligence and skill in performing the work. When an agent fails entirely to perform her or his duties, liability for breach of contract normally will result. The degree of skill or care required of an agent is usually that expected of a reasonable person under similar circumstances. Generally, this is interpreted to mean ordinary care. If an agent has represented himself or herself as possessing special skills, however, the agent is expected to exercise the degree of skill or skills claimed. Failure to do so constitutes a breach of the agent's duty.

---

7. *Motorsport Marketing, Inc. v. Wiedmaier, Inc.*, 195 S.W.3d 492 (Mo.App. 2006).

(Yoon Hernandez/Creative Commons)

A real estate agent meets with clients in her office. Suppose that the agent knows a buyer who is willing to pay more than the asking price for a property. What duty would the agent breach if she bought the property from the seller and sold it at a profit to that buyer?

Not all agency relationships are based on contract. In some situations, an agent acts gratuitously—that is, not for monetary compensation. A gratuitous agent cannot be liable for breach of contract, as there is no contract—he or she is subject only to tort liability. Once a gratuitous agent has begun to act in an agency capacity, he or she has the duty to continue to perform in that capacity in an acceptable manner and is subject to the same standards of care and duty to perform as other agents.

NOTIFICATION   An agent is required to notify the principal of all matters that come to her or his attention concerning the subject matter of the agency. This is the duty of notification, or the duty to inform. **EXAMPLE 16.7** Lang, an artist, is about to negotiate a contract to sell a series of paintings to Barber's Art Gallery for $25,000. Lang's agent learns that Barber is insolvent and will be unable to pay for the paintings. The agent has a duty to inform Lang of this fact because it is relevant to the subject matter of the agency, which is the sale of Lang's paintings. ● Generally, the law assumes that the principal knows of any information acquired by the agent that is relevant to the agency—regardless of whether the agent actually passes on this information to the principal. It is a basic tenet of agency law that notice to the agent is notice to the principal.

LOYALTY   Loyalty is one of the most fundamental duties in a fiduciary relationship. Basically, the agent has the duty to act *solely for the benefit of his or her principal* and not in the interest of the agent or a third party. For example, an agent cannot represent two principals in the same transaction unless both know of the dual capacity and consent to it. The duty of loyalty also means that any information or knowledge acquired through the agency relationship is considered confidential. It would be a breach of loyalty to disclose such information either during the agency relationship or after its termination. Typical examples of confidential information are trade secrets and customer lists compiled by the principal.

BE AWARE   An agent's disclosure of confidential information could constitute the business tort of misappropriation of trade secrets.

In short, the agent's loyalty must be undivided. The agent's actions must be strictly for the benefit of the principal and must not result in any secret profit for the agent. **CASE EXAMPLE 16.8** Don Cousins contracts with Leo Hodgins, a real estate agent, to negotiate the purchase of an office building as an investment. While working for Cousins, Hodgins discovers that the property owner will sell the building only as a package deal with another parcel. If Hodgins then forms a new company with his brother to buy the two properties and resell the building to Cousins, he has breached his fiduciary duties. As a real estate agent, Hodgins has a duty to communicate all offers to his principal and may not secretly purchase the property and then resell it to his principal. Hodgins is required to act in Cousins's best interests and can become the purchaser in this situation only with Cousins's knowledge and approval.[8] ●

OBEDIENCE   When acting on behalf of a principal, an agent has a duty to follow all lawful and clearly stated instructions of the principal. Any deviation from such instructions is a violation of this duty. During emergency situations, however, when the principal cannot be consulted, the agent may deviate from the instructions without violating this duty. Whenever instructions are not clearly stated, the agent can fulfill the duty of obedience by acting in good faith and in a manner reasonable under the circumstances.

---

8. *Cousins v. Realty Ventures, Inc.*, 844 So.2d 860 (La.App. 5 Cir. 2003).

ACCOUNTING   Unless an agent and a principal agree otherwise, the agent has the duty to keep and make available to the principal an account of all property and funds received and paid out on behalf of the principal. This includes gifts from third parties in connection with the agency. For example, a gift from a customer to a salesperson for prompt deliveries made by the salesperson's firm, in the absence of a company policy to the contrary, belongs to the firm. The agent has a duty to maintain separate accounts for the principal's funds and for the agent's personal funds, and the agent must not intermingle these accounts.

Principal's Duties to the Agent

The principal also owes certain duties to the agent. These duties relate to compensation, reimbursement and indemnification, cooperation, and safe working conditions.

COMPENSATION   In general, when a principal requests certain services from an agent, the agent reasonably expects payment. The principal therefore has a duty to pay the agent for services rendered. For example, when an accountant or an attorney is asked to act as an agent, an agreement to compensate the agent for such service is implied. The principal also has a duty to pay that compensation in a timely manner. Except in a gratuitous agency relationship, in which an agent does not act for payment in return, the principal must pay the agreed-on value for an agent's services. If no amount has been expressly agreed on, the principal owes the agent the customary compensation for such services.

Preventing Legal Disputes

Many disputes arise because the principal and agent did not specify how much the agent would be paid. To avoid such disputes, always state in advance, and in writing, the amount or rate of compensation that you will pay your agents. Even when dealing with salespersons, such as real estate agents, who customarily are paid a percentage of the value of the sale, it is best to explicitly state the rate of compensation.

REMEMBER An agent who signs a check (or other negotiable instrument) on behalf of a principal may be personally liable on the instrument. Liability depends, in part, on whether the identity of the principal is disclosed and whether the parties intend the agent to be bound by her or his signature.

REIMBURSEMENT AND INDEMNIFICATION   Whenever an agent disburses funds to fulfill the request of the principal or to pay for necessary expenses in the course of reasonable performance of his or her agency duties, the principal has the duty to reimburse the agent for these payments. Agents cannot recover for expenses incurred through their own misconduct or negligence, though.

Subject to the terms of the agency agreement, the principal has the duty to compensate, or *indemnify,* an agent for liabilities incurred because of authorized and lawful acts and transactions. For instance, if the principal fails to perform a contract formed by the agent with a third party and the third party then sues the agent, the principal is obligated to compensate the agent for any costs incurred in defending against the lawsuit.

Additionally, the principal must indemnify (pay) the agent for the value of benefits that the agent confers on the principal. The amount of indemnification usually is specified in the agency contract. If it is not, the courts will look to the nature of the business and the type of loss to determine the amount. Note that this rule applies to acts by gratuitous agents as well. If the finder of a dog that becomes sick takes the dog to a veterinarian and pays the required fees for the veterinarian's services, the gratuitous agent is entitled to be reimbursed for those fees by the dog's owner.

COOPERATION   A principal has a duty to cooperate with the agent and to assist the agent in performing her or his duties. The principal must do nothing to prevent such performance.

When a principal grants an agent an exclusive territory, for example, the principal creates an *exclusive agency* and cannot compete with the agent or appoint or allow another agent to so compete. If the principal does so, she or he will be exposed to liability for the agent's lost sales or profits. **EXAMPLE 16.9** Akers (the principal) creates an exclusive agency by granting Johnson (the agent) an exclusive territory within which Johnson may sell Akers's products. If Akers begins to sell the products himself within Johnson's territory or permits another agent to do so, Akers has violated the exclusive agency and can be held liable for Johnson's lost sales or profits. ●

SAFE WORKING CONDITIONS   Under the common law, a principal is required to provide safe working premises, equipment, and conditions for all agents and employees. The principal has a duty to inspect the working conditions and to warn agents and employees about any unsafe areas. When the agent is an employee, the employer's liability is frequently covered by state workers' compensation insurance, and federal and state statutes often require the employer to meet certain safety standards (to be discussed in Chapter 17).

 Agent's Authority

An agent's authority to act can be either actual (express or implied) or apparent. If an agent contracts outside the scope of his or her authority, the principal may still become liable by ratifying the contract.

Actual Authority (Express or Implied)

As indicated, an agent's actual authority can be express or implied. *Express authority* is authority declared in clear, direct, and definite terms. Express authority can be given orally or in writing. In most states, the **equal dignity rule** requires that if the contract being executed is or must be in writing, then the agent's authority must also be in writing. Failure to comply with the equal dignity rule can make a contract voidable *at the option of the principal*. The law regards the contract at that point as a mere offer. If the principal decides to accept the offer, acceptance must be ratified, or affirmed, in writing.

EXAMPLE 16.10 Lee (the principal) orally asks Parkinson (the agent) to sell a ranch that Lee owns. Parkinson finds a buyer and signs a sales contract (a contract for an interest in realty must be in writing) on behalf of Lee to sell the ranch. The buyer cannot enforce the contract unless Lee subsequently ratifies Parkinson's agency status *in writing*. Once Parkinson's agency status is ratified, either party can enforce rights under the contract. ●

Modern business practice allows an exception to the equal dignity rule. An executive officer of a corporation normally is not required to obtain written authority from the corporation to conduct *ordinary* business transactions. The equal dignity rule does not apply when an agent acts in the presence of a principal or when the agent's act of signing is merely perfunctory (automatic). Thus, if Dickens (the principal) negotiates a contract but is called out of town the day it is to be signed and orally authorizes Santini to sign the contract, the oral authorization is sufficient.

Equal Dignity Rule   In most states, a rule stating that express authority given to an agent must be in writing if the contract to be made on behalf of the principal is required to be in writing.

Notary publics are authorized by a state to attest to the authenticity of signatures. In most states, there are few restrictions on who can become a notary public.

POWER OF ATTORNEY   Giving an agent a **power of attorney** confers express authority.[9] The power of attorney normally is a written document and is usually notarized. (A document is notarized when a **notary public**—a public official authorized to attest to the authenticity of signatures—signs and dates the document and imprints it with his or her seal of authority.) Most states have statutory provisions for creating a power of attorney.

A power of attorney can be special (permitting the agent to do specified acts only), or it can be general (permitting the agent to transact all business for the principal). Because a general power of attorney grants extensive authority to an agent to act on behalf of the principal in many ways, it should be used with great caution. Ordinarily, a power of attorney terminates on the incapacity or death of the person giving the power.[10]

Power of Attorney   A written document, which is usually notarized, authorizing another to act as one's agent; can be special (permitting the agent to do specified acts only) or general (permitting the agent to transact all business for the principal).

Notary Public   A public official authorized to attest to the authenticity of signatures.

IMPLIED AUTHORITY   Actual authority may also be implied. An agent has the *implied authority* to do what is reasonably necessary to carry out express authority and accomplish the objectives of the agency. Authority can also be implied by custom or inferred from the position the agent occupies. **EXAMPLE 16.11**   Mueller is employed by Al's Supermarket to manage one of its stores. Al's has not expressly stated that Mueller has authority to contract with third persons. In this situation, though, authority to manage a business implies authority to do what is reasonably required (as is customary or can be inferred from a manager's position) to operate the business. This includes forming contracts to hire employees, to buy merchandise and equipment, and to advertise the products sold in the store. ●

Apparent Authority

Apparent Authority   Authority that is only apparent, not real. In agency law, a person may be deemed to have had the power to act as an agent for another party if the other party's manifestations to a third party led the third party to believe that an agency existed when, in fact, it did not.

Actual authority (express or implied) arises from what the principal manifests *to the agent.* An agent has **apparent authority** when the principal, by either words or actions, causes a *third party* reasonably to believe that an agent has authority to act, even though the agent has no express or implied authority. If the third party changes her or his position in reliance on the principal's representations, the principal may be *estopped* (prevented) from denying that the agent had authority.

Apparent authority usually comes into existence through a principal's pattern of conduct over time. **CASE EXAMPLE 16.12**   Francis Azur was the president of ATM Corporation of America, and Michelle Vanek was his personal assistant. Vanek's responsibilities included opening Azur's personal bills, preparing and presenting checks for him to sign, balancing his checking and savings accounts, and reviewing his credit-card and bank statements. Vanek also had access to Azur's credit-card number so that she could make purchases for him. Over a period of seven years, Vanek withdrew unauthorized cash advances from Azur's credit-card account with Chase Bank, USA. The fraudulent charges were reflected on at least sixty-five monthly billing statements sent by Chase to Azur, and Vanek paid the bills by writing checks

---

9. An agent who holds the power of attorney is called an *attorney-in-fact* for the principal. The holder does not have to be an attorney-at-law (and often is not).

10. A *durable* power of attorney, however, continues to be effective despite the principal's incapacity. An elderly person, for example, might grant a durable power of attorney to provide for the handling of property and investments or specific health-care needs should she or he become incompetent.

and forging Azur's signature or by making online payments from Azur's checking account. In all, Vanek misappropriated more than $1 million from Azur. When Azur discovered Vanek's fraudulent scheme, he terminated her employment and closed the Chase account. Azur then sued Chase, seeking reimbursement of the fraudulent charges under the Truth-in-Lending Act, or TILA (which protects cardholders from liability for the fraudulent use of their credit cards—see Chapter 20). Because Vanek had apparent authority to use Azur's credit card, however, the court dismissed Azur's claim, and he was unable to recover for the loss.[11] ●

Ratification

BE AWARE An agent who exceeds his or her authority and enters into a contract that the principal does not ratify may be liable to the third party on the ground of misrepresentation.

As already mentioned, ratification occurs when the principal affirms an agent's *unauthorized* act. When ratification occurs, the principal is bound to the agent's act, and the act is treated as if it had been authorized by the principal *from the outset.* Ratification can be either express or implied.

If the principal does not ratify the contract, the principal is not bound, and the third party's agreement with the agent is viewed as merely an unaccepted offer. Because the third party's agreement is an unaccepted offer, the third party can revoke the offer at any time, without liability, before the principal ratifies the contract.

The requirements for ratification can be summarized as follows:

1. The agent must have acted on behalf of an identified principal who subsequently ratifies the action.
2. The principal must know of all material facts involved in the transaction. If a principal ratifies a contract without knowing all of the facts, the principal can rescind (cancel) the contract.
3. The principal must affirm the agent's act in its entirety.
4. The principal must have the legal capacity to authorize the transaction at the time the agent engages in the act and at the time the principal ratifies. The third party must also have the legal capacity to engage in the transaction.
5. The principal's affirmation must occur before the third party withdraws from the transaction.
6. The principal must observe the same formalities when approving the act done by the agent as would have been required to authorize it initially.

▶ Liability in Agency Relationships

Frequently, a question arises as to which party, the principal or the agent, should be held liable for contracts formed by the agent or for torts or crimes committed by the agent. We look here at these aspects of agency law.

Liability for Contracts

Disclosed Principal A principal whose identity is known to a third party at the time the agent makes a contract with the third party.

Partially Disclosed Principal A principal whose identity is unknown by a third party, but the third party knows that the agent is or may be acting for a principal at the time the agent and the third party form a contract.

Liability for contracts formed by an agent depends on how the principal is classified and on whether the actions of the agent were authorized or unauthorized. Principals are classified as disclosed, partially disclosed, or undisclosed.[12]

A **disclosed principal** is a principal whose identity is known by the third party at the time the contract is made by the agent. A **partially disclosed principal** is a principal whose identity is not known by the third party, but the third party knows

---

11. *Azur v. Chase Bank, USA,* 601 F.3d 212 (3d Cir. 2010).
12. *Restatement (Third) of Agency,* Section 1.04(2).

that the agent is or may be acting for a principal at the time the contract is made. **EXAMPLE 16.13** Sarah has contracted with a real estate agent to sell certain property. She wishes to keep her identity a secret, but the agent makes it perfectly clear to potential buyers of the property that the agent is acting in an agency capacity. In this situation, Sarah is a partially disclosed principal. • An **undisclosed principal** is a principal whose identity is totally unknown by the third party, and the third party has no knowledge that the agent is acting in an agency capacity at the time the contract is made.

Undisclosed Principal A principal whose identity is unknown by a third person, and the third person has no knowledge that the agent is acting for a principal at the time the agent and the third person form a contract.

AUTHORIZED ACTS If an agent acts within the scope of her or his authority, normally the principal is obligated to perform the contract regardless of whether the principal was disclosed, partially disclosed, or undisclosed. Whether the agent may also be held liable under the contract, however, depends on the disclosed, partially disclosed, or undisclosed status of the principal.

Disclosed or Partially Disclosed Principal. A disclosed or partially disclosed principal is liable to a third party for a contract made by an agent who is acting within the scope of her or his authority. If the principal is disclosed, an agent has no contractual liability for the nonperformance of the principal or the third party. If the principal is partially disclosed, in most states the agent is also treated as a party to the contract, and the third party can hold the agent liable for contractual nonperformance.[13]

CASE EXAMPLE 16.14 Walgreens leased commercial property at a mall owned by Kedzie Plaza Associates to operate a drugstore. A property management company, Taxman Corporation, signed the lease on behalf of the principal, Kedzie. The lease required the landlord to keep the sidewalks free of snow and ice, so Taxman, on behalf of Kedzie, contracted with another company to remove ice and snow from the sidewalks surrounding the Walgreens store. When a Walgreens employee slipped on ice outside the store and was injured, she sued Taxman, among others, for negligence. Because the principal's identity (Kedzie) was fully disclosed in the snow-removal contract, however, the court ruled that the agent, Taxman, could not be held liable. Taxman did not assume a contractual obligation to remove the snow but merely retained a contractor to do so on behalf of the owner.[14] •

Undisclosed Principal. When neither the fact of agency nor the identity of the principal is disclosed, the undisclosed principal is bound to perform just as if the principal had been fully disclosed at the time the contract was made. The agent is also liable as a party to the contract.

When a principal's identity is undisclosed and the agent is forced to pay the third party, the agent is entitled to be indemnified (compensated) by the principal. The principal had a duty to perform, even though his or her identity was undisclosed, and failure to do so will make the principal ultimately liable. Once the undisclosed principal's identity is revealed, the third party generally can elect to hold either the principal or the agent liable on the contract. Conversely, the undisclosed principal can require the third party to fulfill the contract, *unless* (1) the undisclosed principal was expressly excluded as a party in the contract; (2) the contract is a check (or other negotiable instrument) signed by the agent with no indication of signing in a

"Let every eye negotiate for itself and trust no agent."
William Shakespeare, 1564–1616
(English dramatist and poet)

---

13. *Restatement (Third) of Agency,* Section 6.02.
14. *McBride v. Taxman Corp.,* 327 Ill.App.3d 992, 765 N.E.2d 51 (2002).

representative capacity; or (3) the performance of the agent is personal to the contract, allowing the third party to refuse the principal's performance.

In the following case, three parties involved in an auto sales transaction were embroiled in a dispute over who was liable when the car's engine caught fire.

Case 16.3   Williams v. Pike

Court of Appeal of Louisiana, Second Circuit, 58 So.3d 525 (2011).
www.lacoa2.org[a]

BACKGROUND AND FACTS   Bobby Williams bought a car for $3,000 at Sherman Henderson's auto repair business in Monroe, Louisiana. Although the car's owner was Joe Pike, the owner of Justice Wrecker Service, Henderson negotiated the sale, accepted Williams's payment, and gave him two receipts. Williams drove the car to Memphis, Tennessee, where his daughter was a student. Three days after the sale, the car began to emit smoke and flames from under the hood. Williams extinguished the blaze and contacted Henderson. The next day, Williams's daughter had the vehicle towed at her expense to her apartment's parking lot, from which it was soon stolen. Williams filed a suit in a Louisiana state court against Pike and Henderson. The court awarded Williams $2,000, plus the costs of the suit, adding that if Williams had returned the car, it would have awarded him the entire price. Pike and Henderson appealed.

IN THE WORDS OF THE COURT . . .
DREW, J. [Judge]

* * * *

Pike, the owner of Justice Wrecker Service, obtained a permit to sell the car issued by the state. That permit shows Justice Wrecker to be the owner, not Henderson. The car was displayed for sale at Henderson's business and Henderson facilitated the sale, though he argues his lack of ownership * * * should protect him from a judgment.

The defendants [also] state that Williams did not prove the amount to which he was entitled as to a reduced price. They allege that this "small fire" should not have entitled Williams to a $2,000 reduction in the price.

Williams responds that the judgment should be affirmed because the car purchased from Pike did not serve the purpose for which it

a. In the left column, click on "Opinions/Docket/Calendar." In the menu, click on "Opinions/Dispositions." On the next page, in the "Select Year" row, click on "2011." In the result, scroll to the date "Mar 2, 2011" and click on the case number to access the opinion. The Court of Appeal of Louisiana for the Second Circuit maintains this Web site.

was intended. Plaintiff provided notice to both defendants because Henderson was acting as agent for Pike.

Henderson's agency relationship properly puts him in court as a defendant. Henderson negotiated and completed the sale to Williams and did not make abundantly clear to Williams that Henderson was acting for Pike. Williams testified at the time of purchase he was unaware of Pike, while Henderson testified he mentioned Pike to Williams at the time of sale. In Williams' view, he had a cause of action against Henderson for breach of the implied warranty of the vehicle, since Henderson held himself out as owner of the car and did not disclose to Williams this * * * relationship with Pike. [Emphasis added.]

Factors in calculating the reduction in purchase price include loss of use of the car, inconvenience caused by the seller's failure to correct the defect, and amount of payments made. Here, Williams paid $3,000 for a car which he used only three days. His daughter had to pay to have the car towed and had to travel to Louisiana for the trial. The $2,000 award was appropriate and within the trial court's great discretion. We cannot improve upon the trial court's decision here.

DECISION AND REMEDY   A state intermediate appellate court affirmed the ruling of the lower court, including its judgment and the assessment of costs against both defendants. The appellate court added the costs of the appeal to this amount. Both Pike and Henderson—the undisclosed principal and his agent—were liable to Williams.

WHAT IF THE FACTS WERE DIFFERENT?   *Suppose that Henderson had fully disclosed the fact of his agency relationship and the identity of his principal. Would the result have been different? Why or why not?*

THE LEGAL ENVIRONMENT DIMENSION
Is Henderson entitled to be compensated by Pike for any amount of the judgment that he pays to Williams? Explain.

UNAUTHORIZED ACTS   If an agent has no authority but nevertheless contracts with a third party, the principal cannot be held liable on the contract. It does not matter whether the principal was disclosed, partially disclosed, or undisclosed. The *agent* is liable, however. **EXAMPLE 16.15**   Scranton signs a contract for the purchase of a truck, purportedly acting as an agent under authority granted by Johnson. In fact,

Johnson has not given Scranton any such authority. Johnson refuses to pay for the truck, claiming that Scranton had no authority to purchase it. The seller of the truck is entitled to hold Scranton liable for payment. •

If the principal is disclosed or partially disclosed, the agent is liable to the third party as long as the third party relied on the agency status. The agent's liability here is based on the breach of an *implied warranty of authority* (an agent impliedly warrants that he or she has the authority to enter a contract on behalf of the principal), not on breach of the contract itself.[15] If the third party knows at the time the contract is made that the agent does not have authority—or if the agent expresses to the third party *uncertainty* as to the extent of her or his authority—then the agent is not personally liable.

E-Agent   A computer program that by electronic or other automated means can independently initiate an action or respond to electronic messages or data without review by an individual.

LIABILITY FOR E-AGENTS   Although in the past standard agency principles applied only to *human* agents, today these same principles are being applied to electronic agents. An electronic agent, or **e-agent**, is a semiautonomous computer program that is capable of executing specific tasks. E-agents used in e-commerce include software that can search through many databases and retrieve only information that is relevant for the user.

The Uniform Electronic Transactions Act (UETA), which was discussed in Chapter 9 and has been adopted by most states, contains several provisions relating to the principal's liability for the actions of e-agents. Section 15 of the UETA states that e-agents may enter into binding agreements on behalf of their principals. Presumably, then—at least in those states that have adopted the act—the principal will be bound by the terms in a contract entered into by an e-agent. Thus, when you place an order over the Internet, the company (principal) whose system took the order via an e-agent cannot claim that it did not receive your order.

The UETA also stipulates that if an e-agent does not provide an opportunity to prevent errors at the time of the transaction, the other party to the transaction can avoid the transaction. For instance, if an e-agent fails to provide an on-screen confirmation of a purchase or sale, the other party can avoid the effect of any errors.

Today, one can buy an array of products, including groceries, online. What act has taken steps to apply traditional agency principles to online transactions?

(Bill Stryker)

Liability for Torts and Crimes

Obviously, any person, including an agent, is liable for her or his own torts and crimes. Whether a principal can also be held liable for an agent's torts and crimes depends on several factors, which we examine here. In some situations, a principal may be held liable not only for the torts of an agent but also for the torts committed by an independent contractor.

PRINCIPAL'S TORTIOUS CONDUCT   A principal conducting an activity through an agent may be liable for harm resulting from the principal's own negligence or recklessness. Thus, a principal may be liable for giving improper instructions, authorizing the use of improper materials or

---

15. The agent is not liable on the contract because the agent was never intended personally to be a party to the contract.

tools, or establishing improper rules that resulted in the agent's committing a tort. **EXAMPLE 16.16** Jack knows that Suki cannot drive because her license has been suspended, but nevertheless, he tells her to use the company truck to deliver some equipment to a customer. If someone is injured as a result, Jack (the principal) will be liable for his own negligence in giving improper instructions to Suki. ●

PRINCIPAL'S AUTHORIZATION OF AGENT'S TORTIOUS CONDUCT   A principal who authorizes an agent to commit a tort may be liable to persons or property injured thereby, because the act is considered to be the principal's. **EXAMPLE 16.17** Selkow directs his agent, Warren, to cut the corn on specific acreage, which neither of them has the right to do. The harvest is therefore a trespass (a tort), and Selkow is liable to the owner of the corn. ●

Note also that an agent acting at the principal's direction can be liable as a *tortfeasor* (one who commits a wrong, or tort), along with the principal, for committing the tortious act even if the agent was unaware of the wrongfulness of the act. Assume in the above example that Warren, the agent, did not know that Selkow had no right to harvest the corn. Warren can be held liable to the owner of the field for damages, along with Selkow, the principal.

LIABILITY FOR AGENT'S MISREPRESENTATION   A principal is exposed to tort liability whenever a third person sustains a loss due to the agent's misrepresentation. The principal's liability depends on whether the agent was actually or apparently authorized to make representations and whether the representations were made within the scope of the agency. The principal is always directly responsible for an agent's misrepresentation made within the scope of the agent's authority. **EXAMPLE 16.18** Bassett is a demonstrator for Moore's products. Moore sends Bassett to a home show to demonstrate the products and to answer questions from consumers. Moore has given Bassett authority to make statements about the products. If Bassett makes only true representations, all is fine, but if he makes false claims, Moore will be liable for any injuries or damages sustained by third parties in reliance on Bassett's false representations. ●

LIABILITY FOR AGENT'S NEGLIGENCE   As mentioned, an agent is liable for his or her own torts. A principal may also be liable for harm an agent caused to a third party under the doctrine of ***respondeat superior***,[16] a Latin term meaning "let the master respond." It imposes **vicarious liability,** or indirect liability, on the employer—that is, liability without regard to the personal fault of the employer—for torts committed by an employee in the course or scope of employment.

Determining the Scope of Employment.   The key to determining whether a principal may be liable for the torts of an agent under the doctrine of *respondeat superior* is whether the torts are committed within the scope of the agency or employment. The factors that courts consider in determining whether a particular act occurred within the course and scope of employment are as follows:

1. Whether the employee's act was authorized by the employer.
2. The time, place, and purpose of the act.
3. Whether the act was one commonly performed by employees on behalf of their employers.

Respondeat Superior   Latin for "let the master respond." A doctrine under which a principal or an employer is held liable for the wrongful acts committed by agents or employees while acting within the course and scope of their agency or employment.

Vicarious Liability   Legal responsibility placed on one person for the acts of another; indirect liability imposed on a supervisory party (such as an employer) for the actions of a subordinate (such as an employee) because of the relationship between the two parties.

---

16. Pronounced ree-*spahn*-dee-uht soo-*peer*-ee-your.

4. The extent to which the employer's interest was advanced by the act.
5. The extent to which the private interests of the employee were involved.
6. Whether the employer furnished the means or instrumentality (for example, a truck or a machine) by which the injury was inflicted.
7. Whether the employer had reason to know that the employee would do the act in question and whether the employee had ever done it before.
8. Whether the act involved the commission of a serious crime.

(Evelynshere/Creative Commons)

Suppose that the driver of the bus in this photo caused a traffic accident that resulted in property damages and personal injuries. If the driver's employer (the principal) learns that the driver had been drinking alcohol during a break right before the incident, can the principal avoid liability? Why or why not?

The Distinction between a "Detour" and a "Frolic."   A useful insight into the "scope of employment" concept may be gained from the judge's classic distinction between a "detour" and a "frolic" in the case of *Joel v. Morison*.[17] In this case, an English court held that if a servant merely took a detour from his master's business, the master will be responsible. If, however, the servant was on a "frolic of his own" and not in any way "on his master's business," the master will not be liable.

EXAMPLE 16.19   Mandel, a traveling salesperson, while driving his employer's vehicle to call on a customer, decides to stop at the post office—which is one block off his route—to mail a personal letter. As Mandel approaches the post office, he negligently runs into a parked vehicle owned by Chan. In this situation, because Mandel's detour from the employer's business is not substantial, he is still acting within the scope of employment, and the employer is liable. The result would be different, though, if Mandel had decided to pick up a few friends for cocktails in another city and in the process had negligently run into Chan's vehicle. In that circumstance, the departure from the employer's business would be substantial, and the employer normally would not be liable to Chan for damages. Mandel would be considered to have been on a "frolic" of his own. •

NOTE   An agent-employee going to or from work or meals usually is not considered to be within the scope of employment. An agent-employee whose job requires travel, however, is considered to be within the scope of employment for the entire trip, including the return.

Employee Travel Time.   An employee going to and from work or to and from meals is usually considered outside the scope of employment. If travel is part of a person's position, however, such as a traveling salesperson or a regional representative of a company, then travel time is normally considered within the scope of employment. Thus, the duration of the business trip, including the return trip home, is within the scope of employment unless there is a significant departure from the employer's business.

Notice of Dangerous Conditions.   The employer is charged with knowledge of any dangerous conditions discovered by an employee and pertinent to the employment situation. **EXAMPLE 16.20**   Chad, a maintenance employee in Martin's apartment building, notices a lead pipe protruding from the ground in the building's courtyard. The employee neglects either to fix the pipe or to inform the employer of the danger. John falls on the pipe and is injured. The employer is charged with knowledge of the dangerous condition regardless of whether or not Chad actually informed the employer. That knowledge is imputed to the employer by virtue of the employment relationship. •

---

17. 6 Car. & P. 501, 172 Eng. Reprint 1338 (1834).

LIABILITY FOR AGENT'S INTENTIONAL TORTS   Most intentional torts that employees commit have no relation to their employment. Thus, their employers will not be held liable. Nevertheless, under the doctrine of *respondeat superior,* the employer can be liable for intentional torts of the employee that are committed within the course and scope of employment, just as the employer is liable for negligence. For instance, an employer is liable when an employee (such as a "bouncer" at a nightclub or a security guard at a department store) commits the tort of assault and battery or false imprisonment while acting within the scope of employment.

In addition, an employer who knows or should know that an employee has a propensity for committing tortious acts is liable for the employee's acts even if they would not ordinarily be considered within the scope of employment. For example, if the employer hires a bouncer knowing that he has a history of arrests for assault and battery, the employer may be liable if the employee viciously attacks a patron in the parking lot after hours.

An employer may also be liable for permitting an employee to engage in reckless actions that can injure others. **EXAMPLE 16.21**   An employer observes an employee smoking while filling containerized trucks with highly flammable liquids. Failure to stop the employee will cause the employer to be liable for any injuries that result if a truck explodes. ● (See this chapter's *Beyond Our Borders* feature below for a discussion of another approach to an employer's liability for an employee's acts.)

LIABILITY FOR INDEPENDENT CONTRACTOR'S TORTS   Generally, an employer is not liable for physical harm caused to a third person by the negligent act of an independent contractor in the performance of the contract. This is because the employer does not have the right to control the details of an independent contractor's performance. Exceptions to this rule are made in certain situations, though, such as when unusually hazardous activities are involved. Typical examples of such activities include blasting operations, the transportation of highly volatile chemicals, or the use of poisonous gases. In these situations, an employer cannot be shielded from liability merely by using an independent contractor. Strict liability is imposed on the employer-principal as a matter of law. Also, in some states, strict liability may be imposed by statute.

LIABILITY FOR AGENT'S CRIMES   An agent is liable for his or her own crimes. A principal or employer is not liable for an agent's crime even if the crime was

---

Beyond Our Borders   **Islamic Law and *Respondeat Superior***

The doctrine of *respondeat superior* is well established in the legal systems of the United States and in most Western countries. As you have already read, under this doctrine employers can be held liable for the acts of their agents, including employees. The doctrine of *respondeat superior* is not universal, however. Most Middle Eastern countries, for example,

do not follow this doctrine. Islamic law, as codified in the *sharia,* holds to a strict belief that responsibility for human actions lies with the individual and cannot be extended to others. This belief and other concepts of Islamic law are based on the writings of Muhammad, the seventh-century prophet whose revelations form the basis of the Islamic religion and, by extension,

the sharia. Muhammad's prophecies are documented in the Koran (Qur'an), which is the principal source of the *sharia.*

For Critical Analysis
How would U.S. society be affected if employers could not be held vicariously liable for their employees' torts?

committed within the scope of authority or employment—unless the principal participated by conspiracy or other action. In some jurisdictions, under specific statutes, a principal may be liable for an agent's violation, in the course and scope of employment, of regulations, such as those governing sanitation, prices, weights, and the sale of liquor.

How Agency Relationships Are Terminated

Agency law is similar to contract law in that both an agency and a contract can be terminated by an act of the parties or by operation of law. Once the relationship between the principal and the agent has ended, the agent no longer has the right (*actual* authority) to bind the principal. For an agent's *apparent* authority to be terminated, though, third persons may also need to be notified that the agency has been terminated.

Termination by Act of the Parties

An agency may be terminated by act of the parties in any of the following ways:

1. *Lapse of time.* When an agency agreement specifies the time period during which the agency relationship will exist, the agency ends when that time period expires. If no definite time is stated, then the agency continues for a reasonable time and can be terminated at will by either party. What constitutes a "reasonable time" depends, of course, on the circumstances and the nature of the agency relationship.

2. *Purpose achieved.* If an agent is employed to accomplish a particular objective, such as the purchase of breeding stock for a cattle rancher, the agency automatically ends after the cattle have been purchased. If more than one agent is employed to accomplish the same purpose, such as the sale of real estate, the first agent to complete the sale automatically terminates the agency relationship for all the others.

3. *Occurrence of a specific event.* When an agency relationship is to terminate on the happening of a certain event, the agency automatically ends when the event occurs. If Posner appoints Rubik to handle her business affairs while she is away, the agency terminates when Posner returns.

4. *Mutual agreement.* The parties to an agency can cancel (rescind) their contract by mutually agreeing to terminate the agency relationship, whether the agency contract is in writing or whether it is for a specific duration.

5. *Termination by one party.* As a general rule, either party can terminate the agency relationship (the act of termination is called *revocation* if done by the principal and *renunciation* if done by the agent). Although both parties have the *power* to terminate the agency, they may not possess the *right*. Wrongful termination can subject the canceling party to a suit for breach of contract. **EXAMPLE 16.22** Rawlins has a one-year employment contract with Munro to act as an agent in return for $65,000. Although Munro has the *power* to discharge Rawlins before the contract period expires, if he does so, he can be sued for breaching the contract because he had no *right* to terminate the agency. ●

When an agency has been terminated by act of the parties, it is the principal's duty to inform any third parties who know of the existence of the agency that it has been terminated (although notice of the termination may be given by others). Although an agent's actual authority ends when the agency is terminated, an agent's *apparent authority* continues until the third party receives notice (from any source) that such authority has been terminated. If the principal knows that a third party has dealt with the agent, the principal is expected to notify that person *directly*. For third parties who have heard about the agency but have not yet dealt with the agent, *constructive notice* is sufficient.[18]

No particular form is required for notice of agency termination to be effective. The principal can personally notify the agent, or the agent can learn of the termination through some other means. **EXAMPLE 16.23** Manning bids on a shipment of steel, and Stone is hired as an agent to arrange transportation of the shipment. When Stone learns that Manning has lost the bid, Stone's authority to make the transportation arrangement terminates. ● If the agent's authority is written, however, it normally must be revoked in writing.

Termination by Operation of Law

Termination of an agency by operation of law occurs in the circumstances discussed here. Note that when an agency terminates by operation of law, there is no duty to notify third persons.

1. *Death or insanity.* The general rule is that the death or mental incompetence of either the principal or the agent automatically and immediately terminates an ordinary agency relationship. Knowledge of the death is not required. **EXAMPLE 16.24** Geer sends Pyron to China to purchase a rare painting. Before Pyron makes the purchase, Geer dies. Pyron's agent status is terminated at the moment of Geer's death, even though Pyron does not know that Geer has died. ● Some states, however, have enacted statutes changing this common law rule to make knowledge of the principal's death a requirement for agency termination.

2. *Impossibility.* When the specific subject matter of an agency is destroyed or lost, the agency terminates. **EXAMPLE 16.25** Bullard employs Gonzalez to sell Bullard's house. Prior to any sale, the house is destroyed by fire. In this situation, Gonzalez's agency and authority to sell Bullard's house terminate. ● Similarly, when it is impossible for the agent to perform the agency lawfully because of a change in the law, the agency terminates.

3. *Changed circumstances.* When an event occurs that has such an unusual effect on the subject matter of the agency that the agent can reasonably infer that the principal will not want the agency to continue, the agency terminates. **EXAMPLE 16.26** Roberts hires Mullen to sell a tract of land for $20,000. Subsequently, Mullen learns that there is oil under the land and that the land is worth $1 million. The agency and Mullen's authority to sell the land for $20,000 are terminated. ●

4. *Bankruptcy.* If either the principal or the agent petitions for bankruptcy, the agency is *usually* terminated. In certain circumstances, as when the agent's financial status is irrelevant to the purpose of the agency, the agency relationship may continue. Insolvency—that is, the inability to pay debts when they become due or when the situation in which liabilities exceed assets—as distinguished from bankruptcy, does not necessarily terminate the relationship.

5. *War.* When the principal's country and the agent's country are at war with each other, the agency is terminated. In this situation, the agency is automatically suspended or terminated because there is no way to enforce the legal rights and obligations of the parties.

---

18. *Constructive notice* is information or knowledge of a fact imputed by law to a person if he or she could have discovered the fact by proper diligence. Constructive notice is often accomplished by newspaper publication.

Reviewing . . . Agency

Lynne Meyer, on her way to a business meeting and in a hurry, stopped at a Buy-Mart store for a new pair of nylons to wear to the meeting. There was a long line at one of the checkout counters, but a cashier, Valerie Watts, opened another counter and began loading the cash drawer. Meyer told Watts that she was in a hurry and asked Watts to work faster. Watts, however, slowed her pace. At this point, Meyer hit Watts. It is not clear from the record whether Meyer hit Watts intentionally or, in an attempt to retrieve the nylons, hit her inadvertently. In response, Watts grabbed Meyer by the hair and hit her repeatedly in the back of the head, while Meyer screamed for help. Management personnel separated the two women and questioned them about the incident. Watts was immediately fired for violating the store's no-fighting policy. Meyer subsequently sued Buy-Mart, alleging that the store was liable for the tort (assault and battery) committed by its employee. Using the information presented in the chapter, answer the following questions.

1. Under what doctrine discussed in this chapter might Buy-Mart be held liable for the tort committed by Watts?
2. What is the key factor in determining whether Buy-Mart is liable under this doctrine?
3. How is Buy-Mart's potential liability affected depending on whether Watts's behavior constituted an intentional tort or a tort of negligence?
4. Suppose that when Watts applied for the job at Buy-Mart, she disclosed in her application that she had previously been convicted of felony assault and battery. Nevertheless, Buy-Mart hired Watts as a cashier. How might this fact affect Buy-Mart's liability for Watts's actions?

 Key Terms

agency 472	fiduciary 473	ratification 479
apparent authority 484	independent contractor 473	*respondeat superior* 489
disclosed principal 485	notary public 484	undisclosed principal 486
e-agent 488	partially disclosed principal 485	vicarious liability 489
equal dignity rule 483	power of attorney 484	

 Chapter Summary: Agency

Agency Relationships (See pages 473–477.)	In a *principal-agent* relationship, an agent acts on behalf of and instead of the principal in dealing with third parties. An employee who deals with third parties is normally an agent. An independent contractor is not an employee, and the employer has no control over the details of physical performance. An independent contractor may or may not be an agent.
How Agency Relationships Are Formed (See pages 477–480.)	1. *Agreement*—The agency relationship is formed through express consent (oral or written) or implied by conduct. 2. *Ratification*—The principal either by act or by agreement ratifies the conduct of a person who is not in fact an agent. 3. *Estoppel*—The principal causes a third person to believe that another person is the principal's agent, and the third person acts to his or her detriment in reasonable reliance on that belief. 4. *Operation of law*—The agency relationship is based on a social duty (such as the need to support family members) or formed in emergency situations when the agent is unable to contact the principal and failure to act outside the scope of the agent's authority would cause the principal substantial loss.

Duties of Agents and Principals (See pages 480–483.)	1. *Duties of the agent*—
	  a. Performance—The agent must use reasonable diligence and skill in performing her or his duties or use the special skills that the agent has represented to the principal that the agent possesses.
	  b. Notification—The agent is required to notify the principal of all matters that come to his or her attention concerning the subject matter of the agency.

Chapter Summary: Agency, Continued

Duties of Agents and Principals–Continued	c. Loyalty–The agent has a duty to act solely for the benefit of the principal and not in the interest of the agent or a third party. d. Obedience–The agent must follow all lawful and clearly stated instructions of the principal. e. Accounting–The agent has a duty to make available to the principal records of all property and funds received and paid out on behalf of the principal. 2. *Duties of the principal–* a. Compensation–Except in a gratuitous agency relationship, the principal must pay the agreed-on value (or reasonable value) for an agent's services. b. Reimbursement and indemnification–The principal must reimburse the agent for all funds disbursed at the request of the principal and for all funds that the agent disburses for necessary expenses in the course of reasonable performance of his or her agency duties. c. Cooperation–A principal must cooperate with and assist an agent in performing her or his duties. d. Safe working conditions–A principal must provide safe working conditions for the agent-employee.
Agent's Authority (See pages 483–485.)	1. *Express authority*–Can be oral or in writing. Authorization must be in writing if the agent is to execute a contract that must be in writing. 2. *Implied authority*–Authority customarily associated with the position of the agent or authority that is deemed necessary for the agent to carry out expressly authorized tasks. 3. *Apparent authority*–Exists when the principal, by word or action, causes a third party reasonably to believe that an agent has authority to act, even though the agent has no express or implied authority. 4. *Ratification*–The affirmation by the principal of an agent's unauthorized action or promise. For the ratification to be effective, the principal must be aware of all material facts.
Liability in Agency Relationships (See pages 485–492.)	1. *Liability for contracts*–If the principal's identity is disclosed or partially disclosed at the time the agent forms a contract with a third party, the principal is liable to the third party under the contract if the agent acted within the scope of his or her authority. If the principal's identity is undisclosed at the time of contract formation, the agent is personally liable to the third party, but if the agent acted within the scope of his or her authority, the principal is also bound by the contract. 2. *Liability for agent's negligence*–Under the doctrine of *respondeat superior,* the principal is liable for any harm caused to another through the agent's torts if the agent was acting within the scope of her or his employment at the time the harmful act occurred. 3. *Liability for agent's intentional torts*–Usually, employers are not liable for the intentional torts that their agents commit, *unless:* a. The acts are committed within the scope of employment, and thus the doctrine of *respondeat superior* applies. b. The employer knows or should know that the employee has a propensity for committing tortious acts. c. The employer allowed an employee to engage in reckless acts that caused injury to another. 4. *Liability for independent contractor's torts*–A principal is not liable for harm caused by an independent contractor's negligence, unless hazardous activities are involved (in this situation, the principal is strictly liable for any resulting harm) or other exceptions apply. 5. *Liability for agent's crimes*–An agent is responsible for his or her own crimes, even if the crimes were committed while the agent was acting within the scope of authority or employment. A principal will be liable for an agent's crime only if the principal participated by conspiracy or other action or (in some jurisdictions) if the agent violated certain government regulations in the course of employment.
How Agency Relationships Are Terminated (See pages 492–493.)	1. *By act of the parties–* Notice to third parties is required when an agency is terminated by act of the parties. Direct notice is required for those who have previously dealt with the agency, but constructive notice will suffice for all other third parties. See page 492 for a list of the ways that an agency may be terminated by act of the parties. 2. *By operation of law–* Notice to third parties is not required when an agency is terminated by operation of law. See page 493 for a list of the ways that an agency can be terminated by operation of law.

ExamPrep

ISSUE SPOTTERS

1. Vivian, owner of Wonder Goods Company, employs Xena as an administrative assistant. In Vivian's absence, and without authority, Xena represents herself as Vivian and signs a promissory note in Vivian's name. In what circumstance is Vivian liable on the note?

2. Davis contracts with Estee to buy a certain horse on her behalf. Estee asks Davis not to reveal her identity. Davis makes a deal with Farmland Stables, the owner of the horse, and makes a down payment. Estee does not pay the rest of the price. Farmland Stables sues Davis for breach of contract. Can Davis hold Estee liable for whatever damages he has to pay? Why or why not?

—**Check your answers to these questions against the answers provided in Appendix G.**

BEFORE THE TEST

Go to **www.cengagebrain.com**, enter the ISBN number "9781111530617," and click on "Find" to locate this textbook's Web site. Then, click on "Access Now" under "Study Tools," and select "Chapter 16" at the top. There you will find an "Interactive Quiz" that you can take to assess your mastery of the concepts in this chapter, as well as "Flashcards" and a "Glossary" of important terms.

 For Review

1. What is the difference between an employee and an independent contractor?
2. How do agency relationships arise?
3. What duties do agents and principals owe to each other?
4. When is a principal liable for the agent's actions with respect to third parties? When is the agent liable?
5. What are some of the ways in which an agency relationship can be terminated?

 Questions and Case Problems

16–1. Ratification by Principal. Springer was a political candidate running for Congress. He was operating on a tight budget and instructed his campaign staff not to purchase any campaign materials without his explicit authorization. In spite of these instructions, one of his campaign workers ordered Dubychek Printing Co. to print some promotional materials for Springer's campaign. When the printed materials arrived, Springer did not return them but instead used them during his campaign. When Springer failed to pay for the materials, Dubychek sued for recovery of the price. Springer contended that he was not liable on the sales contract because he had not authorized his agent to purchase the printing services. Dubychek argued that the campaign worker was Springer's agent and that the worker had authority to make the printing contract. Additionally, Dubychek claimed that even if the purchase was unauthorized, Springer's use of the materials constituted ratification of his agent's unauthorized purchase. Is Dubychek correct? Explain.

16–2. Agency Formation. Adam Wade, Gett's friend, tells Timothy Brown that he is Gett's agent for the purchase of rare coins. Wade even shows Brown a local newspaper clipping mentioning Gett's interest in coin collecting. Brown, knowing of Wade's friendship with Gett, contracts with Wade to sell a rare coin valued at $25,000 to Gett. Wade takes the coin and disappears with it. On the payment due date, Brown seeks to collect from Gett, claiming that Wade's agency made Gett liable. Gett does not deny that Wade was a friend, but he claims that Wade was never his agent. Discuss fully whether an agency was in existence at the time the contract for the rare coin was made.

16–3. Employee versus Independent Contractor. Stephen Hemmerling was a driver for the Happy Cab Co. Hemmerling paid certain fixed expenses and abided by a variety of rules relating to the use of the cab, the hours that could be worked, and the solicitation of fares, among other things. Rates were set by the state. Happy Cab did not withhold taxes from Hemmerling's pay. While driving the cab, Hemmerling was injured in an accident and filed a claim against Happy Cab for workers' compensation benefits. Such benefits are not available to independent contractors. On what basis might the court hold that Hemmerling is an employee? Explain.

16–4. [icon] **Case Problem with Sample Answer. Undisclosed Principal.** Homeowners Jim and Lisa Criss hired Kevin and Cathie Pappas, doing business as Outside

Creations, to undertake a landscaping project. Kevin signed the parties' contract as "Outside Creations Rep." The Crisses' payments on the contract were by checks payable to Kevin, who deposited them in his personal account—there was no Outside Creations account. Later, alleging breach, the Crisses filed a suit in a Georgia state court against the Pappases. The defendants contended that they could not be liable because the contract was not with them personally. They claimed that they were the agents of Forever Green Landscaping and Irrigation, Inc., which had been operating under the name "Outside Creations" at the time of the contract and had since filed for bankruptcy. The Crisses pointed out that the name "Forever Green" was not in the contract. Can the Pappases be liable on this contract? Why or why not? [*Pappas v. Criss,* 296 Ga.App. 803, 676 S.E.2d 21 (2009)]

—**To view a sample answer for Case Problem 16–4, go to Appendix F at the end of this text.**

16–5. Agency by Ratification. Wesley Hall, an independent contractor managing property for Acree Investments, Ltd., lost control of a fire he had set to clear ten acres of Acree land. The runaway fire burned seventy-eight acres of Earl Barrs's property. Russell Acree, one of the owners of Acree Investments, had previously owned the ten acres, but he had put it into the company and he was no longer the principal owner. Hall had worked for Russell Acree in the past and had told the state forestry department that he was burning the land for Acree. Barrs sued Russell Acree for the acts of his agent, Hall. In his suit, Barrs noted that Hall had been an employee of Russell Acree, Hall had talked about burning the land "for Acree," Russell Acree had apologized to Barrs for the fire, and Acree Investments had not been identified as the principal property owner until Barrs had filed his lawsuit. Barrs argued that those facts were sufficient to create an agency by ratification to impose liability on Russell Acree. Was Barrs's agency by ratification claim valid? Why or why not? [*Barrs v. Acree,* 302 Ga.App. 521, 691 S.E.2d 575 (2010)]

16–6. Liability Based on Actual or Apparent Authority. Summerall Electric Co. and other subcontractors were hired by National Church Services, Inc. (NCS), which was the general contractor on a construction project for the Church of God at Southaven (the Church). As work progressed, payments from NCS to the subcontractors became later and later until they eventually stopped. The Church had paid NCS in full for the entire project beforehand, but apparently, NCS had mismanaged the project. When payments from NCS stopped, the subcontractors filed mechanic's liens (see Chapter 12) for the value of the work they had performed but for which they had not been paid. The subcontractors sued the Church, contending that NCS was its agent based on either actual authority or apparent authority, and thus the Church was liable for the payments. Was NCS an agent for the Church based on actual or apparent authority, thereby making the Church liable to the subcontractors? Discuss your reasons.

[*Summerall Electric Co. v. Church of God at Southaven,* 25 So.3d 1090 (App.Miss. 2010)]

16–7. Employment Relationships. William Moore owned and operated Moore Enterprises, a wholesale tire business, in Idaho. While in high school, William's son, Jonathan, worked as a Moore employee. Later, Jonathan started his own business, called Morecedes Tire. Morecedes regrooved tires and sold them to businesses, including Moore. Moore made payments for the tires not to Jonathan, but to Morecedes Tire, without tax withholding. A decade after Jonathan started Morecedes, William offered him work with Moore for $12 per hour. Jonathan accepted but retained Morecedes Tire. On the first day, William told Jonathan to load some tires on a trailer. While Jonathan was unhooking the trailer, a jack handle struck him. He suffered several broken bones in his face and a detached retina. He was never paid for the work. He filed a workers' compensation claim. Under Idaho's laws, an individual must be an employee—not an independent contractor—to obtain workers' compensation. What criteria do the courts use to determine employee status? How do they apply to Jonathan? Discuss. [*Moore v. Moore,* __ P.3d __ (Idaho 2011)]

16–8. Disclosed Principal. Mario Sclafani (doing business as Martinucci Desserts USA, Inc.), wanted to place small refrigeration units containing point-of-purchase imported Italian desserts in New York City restaurants. Felix Storch, Inc., makes commercial refrigeration units. Sclafani ordered custom units for $18,000. Felix faxed a credit application to Sclafani. The application was faxed back with Sclafani's business banking information, credit references, and a signature that appeared to be Sclafani's beneath a personal guaranty clause. Felix made and delivered the units. The imported dessert business failed, and the units were not paid for. Felix filed a suit in a New York state court against Sclafani to collect. Sclafani denied that he had seen the credit application or signed it and testified that he referred all credit questions to "the girls in the office." Among these parties, who is the principal? Who are the agents? Who is liable on the contract? Explain. [*Felix Storch, Inc. v. Martinucci Desserts USA, Inc.,* 30 Misc.3d 1217, 924 N.Y.S.2d 308 (2011)]

16–9. **A Question of Ethics. Agency Formation and Duties.** *Emergency One, Inc. (EO), makes fire and rescue vehicles. Western Fire Truck, Inc., contracted with EO to be its exclusive dealer in Colorado and Wyoming through December 2003. James Costello, a Western salesperson, was authorized to order EO vehicles for his customers. Without informing Western, Costello e-mailed EO about Western's difficulties in obtaining cash to fund its operations. He asked about the viability of Western's contract and his possible employment with EO. On EO's request, and in disregard of Western's instructions, Costello sent some payments for EO vehicles directly to EO. In addition, Costello, with EO's help, sent a competing bid to a potential Western customer. EO's representative e-mailed*

Costello, "You have my permission to kick [Western's] ass." In April 2002, EO terminated its contract with Western, which, after reviewing Costello's e-mail, fired Costello. Western filed a suit in a Colorado state court against Costello and EO, alleging, among other things, that Costello breached his duty as an agent and that EO aided and abetted the breach. [Western Fire Truck, Inc. v. Emergency One, Inc., 134 P.3d 570 (Colo.App. 2006)]

1. Was there an agency relationship between Western and Costello? Western required monthly reports from its sales staff, but Costello did not report regularly. Does this indicate that Costello was *not* Western's agent? In determining whether an agency relationship exists, is the *right* to control or the *fact* of control more important? Explain.

2. Did Costello owe Western a duty? If so, what was the duty? Did Costello breach it? How?

3. A Colorado state statute allows a court to award punitive damages in "circumstances of fraud, malice, or willful and wanton conduct." Did any of these circumstances exist in this case? Should punitive damages be assessed against either defendant? Why or why not?

16–10. **Critical-Thinking Legal Environment Question.** What policy is served by the law that employers do not have copyright ownership in works created by independent contractors (unless there is a written "work for hire" agreement)?

Chapter 17

Employment, Immigration, and Labor Law

"Show me the country in which there are no strikes, and I'll show you the country in which there is no liberty."

—Samuel Gompers, 1850–1924
(American labor leader)

Chapter Objectives

After reading this chapter, you should be able to answer the following questions:

1. What is the employment-at-will doctrine? When and why are exceptions to this doctrine made?

2. What federal statute governs working hours and wages?

3. Under the Family and Medical Leave Act of 1993, in what circumstances may an employee take family or medical leave?

4. What are the two most important federal statutes governing immigration and employment today?

5. What federal statute gave employees the right to organize unions and engage in collective bargaining?

(©Svetlana Larina, 2009. Used under license from Shutterstock.com)

Until the early 1900s, most employer-employee relationships were governed by the common law. Today, however, common law doctrines have to a large extent been displaced by statutory law. Although employers still generally are free to hire and fire workers at will under the common law *employment-at-will* doctrine, for example, an employer may not do so if the action would violate the employee's contractual or statutory rights. In many other ways as well, the workplace now is regulated by numerous statutes and administrative agency regulations.

Some of this statutory law originated during the Great Depression in the 1930s, when both state and federal governments began to regulate employment relationships. Legislation enacted during the 1930s and subsequent decades has established many protections for employees including the right to form labor unions and bargain with management for improved working conditions, salaries, and benefits. The ultimate weapon of labor is, of course, the strike, as the labor leader Samuel Gompers observed in the chapter-opening quotation. Strikes and lockouts (the employer's counterpart to the worker's right to strike) are still utilized by unions today. In 2011, for example, the owners of the National Football League (NFL) teams imposed a lockout during their dispute with NFL players over salaries and other issues (discussed on page 526).

In this chapter, we look at the most significant laws regulating employment relationships. We will deal with other important laws regulating the workplace—those that prohibit employment discrimination—in the next chapter.

 ## Employment at Will

> **Employment at Will**   A common law doctrine under which either party may terminate an employment relationship at any time for any reason, unless a contract specifies otherwise.

Traditionally, employment relationships have generally been governed by the common law doctrine of **employment at will**. Under the employment-at-will doctrine, either party may terminate the employment relationship at any time and for any reason, unless doing so would violate the provisions of an employment contract. The majority of U.S. workers continue to have the legal status of "employees at will." In other words, this common law doctrine is still in widespread use, and only one state (Montana) does not apply the doctrine.

Nonetheless, as mentioned in the chapter introduction, federal and state statutes governing employment relationships prevent this doctrine from being applied in a number of circumstances. Today, an employer is not permitted to fire an employee if doing so would violate a federal or state employment statute, such as one prohibiting employment termination for discriminatory reasons (see Chapter 18). Note that the distinction made under agency law (discussed in Chapter 16) between employee status and independent-contractor status is important here. The employment laws that are discussed in this chapter and in Chapter 18 apply only to the employer-employee relationship, not to independent contractors.

Exceptions to the Employment-at-Will Doctrine

Because of the harsh effects of the employment-at-will doctrine for employees, the courts have carved out various exceptions to the doctrine. These exceptions are based on contract theory, tort theory, and public policy.

> **REMEMBER**   An implied contract may exist if a party furnishes a service expecting to be paid, and the other party, who knows (or should know) of this expectation, has a chance to reject the service and does not.

EXCEPTIONS BASED ON CONTRACT THEORY   Some courts have held that an *implied* employment contract exists between an employer and an employee. If an employee is fired outside the terms of the implied contract, he or she may succeed in an action for breach of contract even though no written employment contract exists. **EXAMPLE 17.1**   BDI Enterprise's employment manual and personnel bulletin both state that, as a matter of policy, workers will be dismissed only for good cause. If an employee reasonably expects BDI to follow this policy, a court may find that there is an implied contract based on the terms stated in the manual and bulletin. ● Generally, in determining whether an employment manual created an implied contractual obligation, the courts focus on the employee's reasonable expectations.

An employer's oral promises to employees regarding discharge policy may also be considered part of an implied contract. If the employer fires a worker in a manner contrary to what was promised, a court may hold that the employer has violated the implied contract and is liable for damages. Most state courts will judge a claim of breach of an implied employment contract by traditional contract standards.

Courts in a few states have gone further and held that all employment contracts contain an implied covenant of good faith. This means that both sides promise to abide by the contract in good faith. If an employer fires an employee for an arbitrary or unjustified reason, the employee can claim that the covenant of good faith was breached and the contract violated.

EXCEPTIONS BASED ON TORT THEORY In a few situations, the discharge of an employee may give rise to an action for wrongful discharge under tort theories. Abusive discharge procedures may result in a suit for intentional infliction of emotional distress or defamation. In addition, some courts have permitted workers to sue their employers under the tort theory of fraud. **EXAMPLE 17.2** Goldfinch, Inc., induces a prospective employee to leave a lucrative job and move to another state by offering "a long-term job with a thriving business." In fact, Goldfinch is not only having significant financial problems but is also planning a merger that will result in the elimination of the position offered to the prospective employee. If the employee takes the job in reliance on Goldfinch's representations and is fired shortly thereafter, the employee may be able to bring an action against the employer for fraud. •

EXCEPTIONS BASED ON PUBLIC POLICY The most common exception to the employment-at-will doctrine is made on the basis of public policy. Courts may apply this exception when an employer fires a worker for reasons that violate a fundamental public policy of the jurisdiction. Generally, the public policy involved must be expressed clearly in the statutory law governing the jurisdiction.

An exception may also be made when an employee "blows the whistle" on an employer's wrongdoing. **Whistleblowing** occurs when an employee tells government authorities, upper-level managers, or the media that her or his employer is engaged in some unsafe or illegal activity. Whistleblowers on occasion have been protected from wrongful discharge for reasons of public policy. **CASE EXAMPLE 17.3** Rebecca Wendeln was the staff coordinator at a nursing home. One of the patients was wheelchair-bound and could be moved only by two persons using a special belt. When Wendeln discovered that the patient had been improperly moved and was injured as a result, she reported the incident to state authorities, as she was required to do by state law. Wendeln's supervisor angrily confronted her about the report, and she was fired shortly after that. Wendeln filed a lawsuit. The court held that although Wendeln was an employee at will, she was protected in this instance from retaliatory firing because a very clear mandate of public policy had been violated.[1] • Normally, however, whistleblowers seek protection from retaliatory discharge under federal and state statutory laws, such as the Whistleblower Protection Act of 1989.[2]

> **Whistleblowing** An employee's disclosure to government authorities, upper-level managers, or the media that the employer is engaged in unsafe or illegal activities.

Wrongful Discharge

Whenever an employer discharges an employee in violation of an employment contract or a statute protecting employees, the employee may bring an action for **wrongful discharge.** Even if an employer's actions do not violate any provisions in an employment contract or a statute, the employer may still be subject to liability under a common law doctrine, such as a tort theory or agency. Note that in today's business world, an employment contract may be established or modified via e-mail exchanges, as discussed in this chapter's *Management Perspective* feature on the following page.

> **Wrongful Discharge** An employer's termination of an employee's employment in violation of the law.

 Wage and Hour Laws

In the 1930s, Congress enacted several laws regulating the wages and working hours of employees. In 1931, Congress passed the Davis-Bacon Act,[3] which requires contractors and subcontractors working on federal government construction projects

> *"All I've ever wanted was an honest week's pay for an honest day's work."*
> Steve Martin, 1945–present
> (American actor and comedian)

---

1. *Wendeln v. The Beatrice Manor, Inc.,* 271 Neb. 373, 712 N.W.2d 226 (2006).
2. 5 U.S.C. Section 1201.
3. 40 U.S.C. Sections 276a–276a-5.

Management Perspective   Can Parties Create and Modify Employment Contracts via E-Mail?

Management Faces a Legal Issue

E-mail is used in nearly every aspect of the employment environment—from workplace communications to contracts with employees. Under the one-year rule of the Statute of Frauds, most employment contracts must be in writing. But electronic communications, including e-mail, instant messages, text messages, and even Twitter, can be used as evidence to show that a contract existed or that the parties modified their contract. A legal issue that managers are facing today involves how they negotiate and modify employment contracts. Specifically, what constitutes a signed writing has changed.

What the Courts Say

Consider an example. Robert Moroni negotiated a deal to provide consulting services for Medco Health Solutions, Inc., a third party administrator of prescription-drug plans. Medco's agent, Brian Griffin, sent Moroni an e-mail setting forth the details of the parties' agreement. Moroni e-mailed a counteroffer suggesting that he would work on Medco's projects two days a week for thirteen months, in exchange for $17,000 a month ($204,000 annually), plus travel expenses. Medco accepted via e-mail, and Moroni began performing the contract. When Medco refused to pay him, Moroni sued for breach of contract. Medco argued that no enforceable contract existed and that the e-mail showed only an agreement to agree. The court, however, ruled that the e-mail amounted to an agreement to the essential terms of an employment contract.[a]

In another case, Arthur Stevens sold his public relations firm in New York to Publicis, S.A.,[b] a French global communications company. The sale involved two contracts: a stock purchase agreement and an employment contract. The employment contract allowed Stevens to stay on as chief executive officer (CEO) of the new company for three years and contained an integration clause requiring any modification to be in a signed writing. Within six months of the sale, however, the new company had lost $900,000 and was not meeting revenue and profit targets. Stevens was removed as CEO and given the option of leaving the firm or staying to develop new business. An agent of Publicis, Bob Bloom, then e-mailed Stevens another option, giving him specific information on the responsibilities he could assume. Within a day, Stevens e-mailed a response, "I accept your proposal with total enthusiasm and excitement," and said that he was "psyched" about his new position. Nevertheless, Stevens later sued Publicis, claiming that it had breached the terms of his original employment contract by not keeping him on as CEO.

The court, however, held that in the e-mail exchanges with Bloom, Stevens had accepted the proposed modification of his employment contract in a signed writing. Because the e-mail modification was binding, Stevens could not sue Publicis.[c]

Implications for Managers

E-mail has become practically the only method of business communications today. Managers and business owners must now assume that any contract changes and decisions made via e-mail may be binding. Consequently, managers need to track and monitor their e-mails very carefully to ensure that they understand how their communications could potentially modify an employment contract or change the company's position within a business contract. Organizing e-mails into relevant files will help managers keep track of what was said and when. As communications technology continues to evolve online and through mobile devices, such as BlackBerrys, iPhones, and iPads, business managers will need to develop additional policies and strategies for their negotiations with prospective employees, suppliers, and partners.

---

a. *Moroni v. Medco Health Solutions, Inc.,* 2008 WL 3539476 (E.D.Mich. 2008).

b. *S.A.* are the initials for *Société Anonyme,* which is the French equivalent to a corporation in the United States.

c. *Stevens v. Publicis, S.A.,* 50 A.D.3d 253, 854 N.Y.S.2d 690 (1 Dept. 2008). See also *Naldi v. Grunberg,* 80 A.D.3d 1, 908 N.Y.S.2d 639 (1 Dept. 2010).

---

to pay "prevailing wages" to their employees. In 1936, the Walsh-Healey Act[4] was passed. This act requires that a minimum wage, as well as overtime pay at 1.5 times regular pay rates, be paid to employees of manufacturers or suppliers entering into contracts with agencies of the federal government.

In 1938, Congress passed the Fair Labor Standards Act (FLSA).[5] This act extended wage and hour requirements to cover all employers engaged in interstate commerce or in the production of goods for interstate commerce, plus selected types of other

---

4. 41 U.S.C. Sections 35–45.

5. 29 U.S.C. Sections 201–260.

businesses. More than 130 million American workers are protected (or covered) by the FLSA, which is enforced by the Wage and Hour Division of the U.S. Department of Labor. Here, we examine the FLSA's provisions in regard to child labor, minimum wages, and maximum hours.

Child Labor

The FLSA prohibits oppressive child labor. Children under fourteen years of age are allowed to do certain types of work, such as deliver newspapers, work for their parents, and work in the entertainment and (with some exceptions) agricultural areas. Children who are fourteen or fifteen years of age are allowed to work, but not in hazardous occupations. There are also numerous restrictions on how many hours per day (particularly on school days) and per week they can work.

Working times and hours are not restricted for persons between the ages of sixteen and eighteen, but they cannot be employed in hazardous jobs or in jobs detrimental to their health and well-being. None of these restrictions apply to persons over the age of eighteen.

Minimum Wage Requirements

Minimum Wage The lowest wage, either by government regulation or union contract, that an employer may pay an hourly worker.

The FLSA provides that a **minimum wage** of $7.25 per hour must be paid to employees in covered industries. Congress periodically revises this federal minimum wage. Additionally, many states have minimum wage laws. When the state minimum wage is greater than the federal minimum wage, the employee is entitled to the higher wage.

When an employee receives tips while on the job, an employer is required to pay only $2.13 an hour in direct wages—but only if that amount, plus the tips received, equals at least the federal minimum wage (because under the FLSA every covered employee is required to be paid $7.25 per hour). If an employee's tips combined with the employer's direct wages of at least $2.13 an hour do not equal the federal minimum hourly wage, the employer must make up the difference. The FLSA does not prevent employers, who are paying at least the federal minimum hourly wage, from taking employee tips and making another arrangement for tip distribution. Under the FLSA, employers who customarily furnish food or lodging to employees can deduct the reasonable cost of those services from the employees' wages.

Overtime Provisions and Exemptions

By working faithfully eight hours a day, you may eventually get to be a boss and work twelve hours a day."

Robert Frost, 1875–1963
(American poet)

Under the FLSA, employees who work more than forty hours per week normally must be paid 1.5 times their regular pay for all hours over forty. Note that the FLSA overtime provisions apply only after an employee has worked more than forty hours per *week*. Thus, employees who work for ten hours a day, four days per week, are not entitled to overtime pay because they do not work more than forty hours per week.

Certain employees—usually executive, administrative, and professional employees, as well as outside salespersons and computer programmers—are exempt from the FLSA's overtime provisions. Employers are not required to pay overtime wages to exempt employees. Employers can voluntarily pay overtime to ineligible employees but cannot waive or reduce the overtime requirements of the FLSA.

An executive employee is one whose primary duty is management. An employee's primary duty is determined by what he or she does that is of principal value to the employer, not by how much time the employee spends doing particular tasks.

CASE EXAMPLE 17.4 Kevin Keevican, a manager at a Starbucks store, worked seventy hours a week for $650 to $800, a 10 to 20 percent bonus, and paid sick leave. Keevican (and other former managers) filed a claim against Starbucks for unpaid overtime, claiming that he had spent 70 to 80 percent of his time waiting on customers and thus was not an executive employee. The court, however, found that Keevican was "the single highest-ranking employee" in his particular store and was responsible on site for that store's day-to-day overall operations. Because his primary duty was managerial, Starbucks was not required to pay overtime.[6] ●

In the following case, the issue before the court was whether an employee of a pharmaceutical company was exempt from the overtime requirements of the FLSA as an administrative employee.

---

6. *Mims v. Starbucks Corp.,* 2007 WL 10369 (S.D.Tex. 2007).

Case 17.1 Smith v. Johnson and Johnson

United States Court of Appeals, Third Circuit, 593 F.3d 280 (2010).
www.ca3.uscourts.gov[a]

Should certain Johnson & Johnson employees be exempt from overtime pay?

BACKGROUND AND FACTS Patty Lee Smith was a senior professional sales representative for McNeil Pediatrics, a wholly owned subsidiary of Johnson and Johnson (J&J). Smith's position required her to visit prescribing doctors to describe the benefits of J&J's pharmaceutical drug Concerta. Smith, however, did not sell Concerta (a controlled substance) directly to the doctors, as such sales are prohibited by law. J&J gave Smith a list of target doctors and told her to complete an average of ten visits per day, visiting every doctor on her target list at least once each quarter. To schedule visits with reluctant doctors, Smith had to be inventive and cultivate relationships with the doctor's staff—an endeavor in which she found that coffee and doughnuts were useful tools. J&J left the itinerary and order of Smith's visits to her discretion. J&J gave her a budget, and she could use the funds to take the doctors to lunch or to sponsor seminars. In Smith's deposition, she stated that she was unsupervised about 95 percent of the time. According to Smith, "It was really up to me to run the territory the way I wanted to." Smith earned a base salary of $66,000 but was not paid overtime. Smith filed a suit in a federal district court under the Fair Labor Standards Act (FLSA), seeking overtime pay. J&J moved for summary judgment in its favor,

arguing that Smith was exempt from the FLSA's overtime requirements because she was an administrative employee. The court granted the motion, and Smith appealed.

IN THE WORDS OF THE COURT . . .
GREENBERG, Circuit Judge.
* * * *

Under the administrative employee exemption, anyone employed in a bona fide administrative capacity is exempt from the FLSA's overtime requirements. The Secretary [of Labor] has defined an administrative employee as someone:

(1) Compensated on a salary or fee basis at a rate of not less than $455 per week * * * exclusive of board, lodging or other facilities;
(2) Whose primary duty is the performance of office or non-manual work directly related to the management or general business operations of the employer or the employer's customers; and
(3) Whose primary duty includes the exercise of discretion and independent judgment with respect to matters of significance. [Emphasis added.]

The parties agree that Smith's salary qualifies her for the administrative employee exemption, but dispute her qualification for that exemption under the remaining two sections.

We find that the administrative employee exemption applies to Smith. While testifying at her deposition Smith elaborated on the independent and managerial qualities that her position required. Her non-manual position required her to form a strategic plan designed to maximize sales in her territory. We think that this requirement satisfied the "directly related to the management or general business operations of the employer" provision of the administrative employee exemption because it involved a high level of planning and foresight, and the strategic plan that Smith developed guided the execution of her remaining duties.

---

a. In the "Opinions and Oral Arguments" box, select "Opinion Archives." When that page opens, select "February" in the listing under "2010 Decisions." Scroll down the list of "Precedential" cases in the left-hand column and click on the highlighted case title to access the opinion. The U.S. Court of Appeals for the Third Circuit maintains this Web site.

Case 17.1–Continued

When we turn to the "exercise of discretion and independent judgment with respect to matters of significance" requirement, we note that Smith executed nearly all of her duties without direct oversight. In fact, she described herself as the manager of her own business who could run her own territory as she saw fit. Given these descriptions, we conclude that Smith was subject to the administrative employee exemption.

DECISION AND REMEDY   The U.S. Court of Appeals for the Third Circuit affirmed the judgment of the district court. Smith qualified as an administrative employee and was thus exempt from the overtime requirements of the FLSA.

THE ETHICAL DIMENSION   *Is it unfair to exempt certain employees to deprive them of overtime wages? Why or why not?*

THE LEGAL ENVIRONMENT DIMENSION   *Johnson and Johnson argued that Smith was exempt under either the administrative employee exemption or the outside salesperson exemption. The district court found, though, that Smith did not qualify for the outside salesperson exemption. What single fact might have made Smith ineligible for the outside salesperson exemption?*

 Layoffs

During the latest economic recession in the United States, hundreds of thousands of workers lost their jobs as many businesses disappeared. Other companies struggling to keep afloat reduced costs by restructuring their operations and downsizing their workforces, which meant layoffs.

Mass layoffs of U.S. workers resulted in high unemployment rates. Later in this chapter, we will discuss unemployment insurance, which helps some workers manage financially until they can find another job. In this section, we discuss the laws pertaining to employee layoffs—an area that is increasingly the subject of litigation.

The Worker Adjustment and Retraining Notification (WARN) Act

Since 1988, federal law has required large employers to provide sixty days' notice before implementing a mass layoff or closing a plant that employs more than fifty full-time workers. The Worker Adjustment and Retraining Notification Act,[7] or WARN Act, applies to employers with at least one hundred full-time employees. It is intended to give workers advance notice so that they can start looking for a new job while they are still employed and to alert state agencies so that they can provide training and other resources for displaced workers.

The WARN Act defines the term *mass layoff* as a reduction in the workforce that, during any thirty-day period, results in an employment loss of either:

1. At least 33 percent of the full-time employees at a single job site and at least fifty employees; or
2. At least five hundred full-time employees.

An *employment loss* is defined as a layoff that exceeds six months or a reduction in hours of work of more than 50 percent during each month of any six-month period.

NOTIFICATION REQUIREMENTS   The WARN Act requires that advance notice of the layoff be sent to the affected workers *or* their representative (if the workers are members of a labor union), as well as to state and local government authorities. The state and local authorities are notified so that they can provide resources, such as job training, to displaced workers. Employers must also provide notice to part-time

---

7. 29 U.S.C. Sections 2101 *et seq.*

and seasonal employees who are being laid off, even though these workers do not count in determining whether the act's provisions are triggered. Note that even companies that anticipate filing for bankruptcy normally must provide notice under the WARN Act before implementing a mass layoff. Sometimes, however, employers can avoid the notice requirements by staggering layoffs over many months or at various locations.

REMEDIES FOR VIOLATIONS   If sued, an employer that orders a mass layoff or plant closing in violation of the WARN Act can be fined up to $500 for each day of the violation. Employees can recover back pay for each day of the violation (up to sixty days), plus reasonable attorneys' fees. An employee can also recover benefits under an employee benefit plan, including the cost of medical expenses that would have been covered and were not. Employees who are laid off may also claim that the layoff was in violation of employment-discrimination laws (see Chapter 18) if it disproportionately affects members of a protected class, such as minorities, older persons, or women.

State Laws May Also Require Layoff Notices

Many states also have statutes requiring employers to provide notice before initiating mass layoffs, and these laws may have different and even stricter requirements than the WARN Act. In New York, for instance, companies with fifty or more employees must provide ninety days' notice before any layoff that affects twenty-five or more full-time employees. The law in Illinois applies to companies with seventy-five or more employees and requires sixty days' advance notice of any layoff that affects twenty-five or more full-time employees at one plant or 250 employees.

"I stopped carrying a briefcase. I don't like to flaunt my employment."

(William Haefeli/ Conde Nast Publications/www.cartoonbank.com)

▶ Family and Medical Leave

In 1993, Congress passed the Family and Medical Leave Act (FMLA)[8] to allow employees to take time off from work for family or medical reasons. A majority of the states also have legislation allowing for a leave from employment for family or medical reasons, and many employers maintain private family-leave plans for their workers. FMLA regulations recently created new categories of leave for military caregivers and for qualifying exigencies that arise due to military service.

Coverage and Application of the FMLA

The FMLA requires employers that have fifty or more employees to provide employees with up to twelve weeks of unpaid family or medical leave during any twelve-month period. The FMLA expressly covers private and public (government) employees who have worked for their employers for at least a year.[9] An employee may take *family leave* to care for a newborn baby, an adopted child, or a foster child.[10]

---

8. 29 U.S.C. Sections 2601, 2611–2619, 2651–2654.

9. Note that changes to the FMLA rules allow employees who have taken a break from their employment to qualify for FMLA leave if they worked a total of twelve months during the previous seven years. See 29 C.F.R. Section 825.110(b)(1-2).

10. The foster care must be state sanctioned before such an arrangement falls within the coverage of the FMLA.

Working mothers face numerous challenges in attempting to balance family and income-earning activities. The federal Family and Medical Leave Act (FMLA) requires that employees be given up to twelve weeks of unpaid family medical leave per year. In some situations, employees are not covered by the FMLA. What is a major limitation on the FMLA's coverage?

An employee can take *medical leave* when the employee or the employee's spouse, child, or parent has a "serious health condition" requiring care.

In addition, an employee caring for a family member with a serious injury or illness incurred as a result of military duty can now take up to *twenty-six weeks of military caregiver leave* within a twelve-month period.[11] Also, an employee can take up to twelve weeks of *qualifying exigency* (emergency) *leave* to handle specified *nonmedical* emergencies when a spouse, parent, or child is on, or called to, active military duty.[12] For instance, when a spouse is deployed to Afghanistan, an employee may take exigency leave to arrange for child care or to deal with financial or legal matters.

When an employee takes FMLA leave, the employer must continue the worker's health-care coverage on the same terms as if the employee had continued to work. On returning from FMLA leave, most employees must be restored to their original position or to a comparable position (with nearly equivalent pay and benefits, for example). An important exception allows the employer to avoid reinstating a *key employee*—defined as an employee whose pay falls within the top 10 percent of the firm's workforce.

Violations of the FMLA

An employer that violates the FMLA can be required to provide various remedies, including the following:

1. Damages to compensate an employee for lost benefits, denied compensation, and actual monetary losses (such as the cost of providing for care of the family member) up to an amount equivalent to the employee's wages for twelve weeks (twenty-six weeks for military caregiver leave);
2. Job reinstatement; and
3. Promotion, if a promotion has been denied.

A successful plaintiff is entitled to court costs and attorneys' fees, and, if bad faith on the part of the employer is shown, can recover two times the amount of damages awarded by a judge or jury. Supervisors can also be held personally liable, as employers, for violations of the act. Employers generally are required to notify employees when an absence will be counted against leave authorized under the act. If an employer fails to provide such notice, and the employee consequently is damaged because he or she did not receive notice, the employer may be sanctioned.

▶ Worker Health and Safety

Under the common law, employees who were injured on the job had to file lawsuits against their employers to obtain recovery. Today, numerous state and federal statutes protect employees and their families from the risk of accidental injury, death, or disease resulting from their employment. This section discusses the primary federal statute governing health and safety in the workplace, along with state workers' compensation laws.

---

11. 29 C.F.R. Section 825.200.
12. 29 C.F.R. Section 825.126.

The Occupational Safety and Health Act

At the federal level, the primary legislation protecting employees' health and safety is the Occupational Safety and Health Act of 1970,[13] which is administered by the Occupational Safety and Health Administration (OSHA). The act imposes on employers a general duty to keep workplaces safe. To this end, OSHA has established specific safety standards that employers must follow depending on the industry. For instance, OSHA regulations require the use of safety guards on certain mechanical equipment and set maximum exposure levels to substances in the workplace that may be harmful to a worker's health.

The act also requires that employers post certain notices in the workplace, perform prescribed record keeping, and submit specific reports. For instance, employers with eleven or more employees are required to keep occupational injury and illness records for each employee. Each record must be made available for inspection when requested by an OSHA compliance officer. Whenever a work-related injury or disease occurs, employers must make reports directly to OSHA. If an employee dies or three or more employees are hospitalized because of a work-related incident, the employer must notify OSHA within eight hours. A company that fails to do so will be fined and may also be prosecuted under state law. Following the incident, a complete inspection of the premises is mandatory.

OSHA compliance officers may enter and inspect the facilities of any establishment covered by the Occupational Safety and Health Act. Employees may also file complaints of violations. Under the act, an employer cannot discharge an employee who files a complaint or who, in good faith, refuses to work in a high-risk area if bodily harm or death might result.

State Workers' Compensation Laws

Workers' Compensation Laws State statutes establishing an administrative procedure for compensating workers for injuries that arise out of—or in the course of—their employment, regardless of fault.

State **workers' compensation laws** establish an administrative procedure for compensating workers injured on the job. Instead of suing, an injured worker files a claim with the administrative agency or board that administers local workers' compensation claims.

This former employee of Quality Pork Processors filed a workers' compensation claim for a neurological illness contracted while working at the processing plant. Her claim was approved. What are the requirements for receiving workers' compensation benefits?

Most workers' compensation statutes are similar. No state covers all employees. Typically, domestic workers, agricultural workers, temporary employees, and employees of common carriers (companies that provide transportation services to the public) are excluded, but minors are covered. Usually, the statutes allow employers to purchase insurance from a private insurer or a state fund to pay workers' compensation benefits in the event of a claim. Most states also allow employers to be *self-insured*—that is, employers that show an ability to pay claims do not need to buy insurance.

In general, the only requirements to recover benefits under state workers' compensation laws are:

1. The existence of an employment relationship; and
2. An *accidental* injury that *occurred on the job or in the course of employment,* regardless of fault. (If an injury occurs while an employee is commuting to or from work, it usually will not be considered to have occurred on the job or in the course of employment and hence will not be covered.)

---

13. 29 U.S.C. Sections 553, 651–678.

An injured employee must notify her or his employer promptly (usually within thirty days of the accident). Generally, an employee must also file a workers' compensation claim with the appropriate state agency or board within a certain period (sixty days to two years) from the time the injury is first noticed, rather than from the time of the accident.

An employee's acceptance of workers' compensation benefits bars the employee from suing for injuries caused by the employer's negligence. By barring lawsuits for negligence, workers' compensation laws also prevent employers from raising common law defenses to negligence, such as contributory negligence, or assumption of risk. A worker may sue an employer who *intentionally* injures the worker, however.

Income Security

Federal and state governments participate in insurance programs designed to protect employees and their families by covering the financial impact of retirement, disability, death, hospitalization, and unemployment. The key federal law on this subject is the Social Security Act of 1935.[14]

This is the home page of the Social Security Administration. Who might wish to consult this Web site?

NOTE Social Security covers almost all jobs in the United States. Nine out of ten workers contribute to this protection for themselves and their families.

Social Security

The Social Security Act provides for old-age (retirement), survivors', and disability insurance. The act is therefore often referred to as OASDI. Both employers and employees must "contribute" under the Federal Insurance Contributions Act (FICA)[15] to help pay for benefits that will partially make up for the employees' loss of income on retirement.

The basis for the employee's and the employer's contributions is the employee's annual wage base—the maximum amount of the employee's wages that are subject to the tax. The employer withholds the employee's FICA contribution from the employee's wages and then matches this contribution. (In 2012, employers were required to withhold 6.2 percent of each employee's wages, up to a maximum wage base of $110,000, and to match this contribution.)[16]

Retired workers are then eligible to receive monthly payments from the Social Security Administration, which administers the Social Security Act. Social Security benefits are fixed by statute but increase automatically with increases in the cost of living.

Medicare

Medicare, a federal government health-insurance program, is administered by the Social Security Administration for people sixty-five years of age and older and for some under the age of sixty-five who are disabled. It originally had two parts, one

---

14. 42 U.S.C. Sections 301–1397e.
15. 26 U.S.C. Sections 3101–3125.
16. Under the Tax Relief, Unemployment Insurance Reauthorization, and Job Creation Act of 2010, the amount employees pay into Social Security was temporarily reduced from 6.2 percent to 4.2 percent in 2011 only.

pertaining to hospital costs and the other to nonhospital medical costs, such as visits to physicians' offices. Medicare now offers additional coverage options and a prescription-drug plan. People who have Medicare hospital insurance can also obtain additional federal medical insurance if they pay small monthly premiums, which increase as the cost of medical care increases.

As with Social Security contributions, both the employer and the employee "contribute" to Medicare, but unlike Social Security, there is no cap on the amount of wages subject to the Medicare tax. In 2012, both the employer and the employee were required to pay 1.45 percent of *all* wages and salaries to finance Medicare.[17] Thus, for Social Security and Medicare together, in 2012 the employer and the employee each paid 7.65 percent of the first $110,000 of income (6.2 percent for Social Security + 1.45 percent for Medicare) for a combined total of 15.3 percent. In addition, all wages and salaries above $110,000 were taxed at a combined (employer and employee) rate of 2.9 percent for Medicare. Self-employed persons pay both the employer and the employee portions of the Social Security and Medicare taxes (15.3 percent of income up to $110,000 and 2.9 percent of income above that amount in 2012). In addition, starting in 2013, a Medicare tax of 3.8 percent will be applied to all investment income for those making more than $200,000.

Private Pension Plans

The major federal act regulating employee retirement plans is the Employee Retirement Income Security Act (ERISA) of 1974.[18] This act empowers a branch of the U.S. Department of Labor to enforce its provisions governing employers that have private pension funds for their employees. ERISA created the Pension Benefit Guaranty Corporation (PBGC), an independent federal agency, to provide timely and uninterrupted payment of voluntary private pension benefits. The pension plans pay annual insurance premiums (at set rates adjusted for inflation) to the PBGC, which then pays benefits to participants in the event that a plan is unable to do so. Under the Pension Protection Act of 2006,[19] the director of the PBGC is appointed by the president and confirmed by the U.S. Senate.

ERISA does not require an employer to establish a pension plan. When a plan exists, however, ERISA specifies standards for its management. A key provision of ERISA concerns vesting. **Vesting** gives an employee a legal right to receive pension benefits at some future date when he or she stops working. Before ERISA was enacted, some employees who had worked for companies for as long as thirty years received no pension benefits when their employment terminated, because those benefits had not vested. ERISA establishes complex vesting rules. Generally, however, all employee contributions to pension plans vest immediately, and employee rights to employer contributions to a plan vest after five years of employment.

In an attempt to prevent mismanagement of pension funds, ERISA has established rules on how they must be invested. Pension managers must be cautious in choosing investments and must diversify the plan's investments to minimize the risk of large losses. ERISA also imposes detailed record-keeping and reporting requirements.

Vesting The creation of an absolute or unconditional right or power.

---

17. Note that as a result of the Health Care and Education Reconciliation Act of 2010, not only are Medicare tax rates expected to rise, but also the applicable compensation base will expand to include more than just wage and salary income.

18. 29 U.S.C. Sections 1001 *et seq.*

19. The Pension Protection Act amended 26 U.S.C. Sections 430–432, 436, 4966, 4967, 6039I, 6050U, 6050V, 6695A, 6720B, 7443B; and 29 U.S.C. Sections 1082–1085, 1202a.

Long lines of those searching for employment are often seen at job fairs throughout the country. When workers become unemployed, do they receive payments from the federal government or the state government?

Unemployment Compensation

To ease the financial impact of unemployment, the United States has a system of unemployment insurance. The Federal Unemployment Tax Act (FUTA) of 1935[20] created a state-administered system that provides unemployment compensation to eligible individuals. Under this system, employers pay into a fund, and the proceeds are paid out to qualified unemployed workers. The FUTA and state laws require employers that fall under the provisions of the act to pay unemployment taxes at regular intervals.

To be eligible for unemployment compensation, a worker must be willing and able to work. Workers who have been fired for misconduct or who have voluntarily left their jobs are not eligible for benefits. In the past, workers had to be actively seeking employment to continue receiving benefits. Due to the high unemployment rates after the Great Recession, however, President Barack Obama announced measures that allow jobless persons to retain their unemployment benefits while pursuing additional education and training (rather than seeking employment).

COBRA

For workers whose jobs have been terminated—and who are thus no longer eligible for group health-insurance plans—federal law also provides a right to continue their health-care coverage. The Consolidated Omnibus Budget Reconciliation Act (COBRA) of 1985[21] prohibits an employer from eliminating a worker's medical, optical, or dental insurance on the voluntary or involuntary termination of the worker's employment. Employers, with some exceptions, must provide information about COBRA's provisions to an employee who faces termination or a reduction of hours that would affect his or her eligibility for coverage under the plan. Only workers fired for gross misconduct are excluded from protection.

PROCEDURES   A worker has sixty days (beginning with the date that the group coverage would stop) to decide whether to continue with the employer's group insurance plan. If the worker chooses to discontinue the coverage, the employer has no further obligation. If the worker opts to continue coverage, though, the employer is obligated to keep the policy active for up to eighteen months (or twenty-nine months if the worker is disabled). The coverage provided must be the same as that enjoyed by the worker prior to the termination or reduction of work. If family members were originally included, for instance, COBRA prohibits their exclusion.

PAYMENT   The worker does not receive the insurance coverage for free. Generally, an employer can require the employee to pay all of the premiums, plus a 2 percent administrative charge. If the worker fails to pay the required amount (or if the employer completely eliminates its group benefit plan), the employer is relieved of

---

20. 26 U.S.C. Sections 3301–3310.
21. 29 U.S.C. Sections 1161–1169.

further responsibility. An employer that does not comply with COBRA risks substantial penalties, such as a tax of up to 10 percent of the annual cost of the group plan or $500,000, whichever is less.

Employer-Sponsored Group Health Plans

The Health Insurance Portability and Accountability Act (HIPAA),[22] which was discussed in Chapter 4 in the context of privacy protections, contains provisions that affect employer-sponsored group health plans. HIPAA does not require employers to provide health insurance, but it does establish requirements for those that do provide such coverage. For instance, HIPAA strictly limits an employer's ability to exclude coverage for *preexisting conditions,* except pregnancy.

In addition, HIPAA restricts the manner in which covered employers collect, use, and disclose the health information of employees and their families. Employers must train employees, designate privacy officials, and distribute privacy notices to ensure that employees' health information is not disclosed to unauthorized parties. Failure to comply with HIPAA regulations can result in civil penalties of up to $100 per person per violation (with a cap of $25,000 per year). The employer is also subject to criminal prosecution for certain types of HIPAA violations and can face up to $250,000 in criminal fines and imprisonment for up to ten years if convicted.

 ## Employee Privacy Rights

In the last thirty years, concerns about the privacy rights of employees have arisen in response to the sometimes invasive tactics used by employers to monitor and screen workers. Perhaps the greatest privacy concern in today's employment arena has to do with electronic performance monitoring.

Electronic Monitoring in the Workplace

According to a survey by the American Management Association, more than half of employers engage in some form of surveillance of their employees. Types of monitoring include reviewing employees' e-mail, blogs, instant messages, tweets, Internet use, and computer files; video recording of employee job performance; and recording and reviewing telephone conversations, voice mail, and text messages.

Various specially designed software products have made it easier for employers to track employees' Internet use, including the specific Web sites visited and the time spent surfing the Web. Indeed, inappropriate Web surfing seems to be a primary concern for employers. More than 75 percent of them are monitoring workers' Web connections. Filtering software, which was discussed in Chapter 4, is also being used to prevent employees from accessing certain Web sites, such as sites containing pornographic or sexually explicit images. Private employers generally are free to use filtering software to block access to certain Web sites because the First Amendment's protection of free speech prevents only *government employers* from restraining speech by blocking Web sites.

EMPLOYEE PRIVACY RIGHTS UNDER CONSTITUTIONAL AND TORT LAW   Recall from Chapter 4 that the U.S. Constitution does not explicitly guarantee a right to

---

22. 29 U.S.C.A. Sections 1181 *et seq.*

Employers are increasingly using sophisticated surveillance systems to monitor their employees' conduct in the workplace. What legitimate interests might employers have for using surveillance cameras?

("Redjar"/Creative Commons)

privacy. A personal right to privacy, however, has been inferred from other constitutional guarantees provided by the First, Third, Fourth, Fifth, and Ninth Amendments to the Constitution. Tort law (see Chapter 5), state constitutions, and a number of state and federal statutes also provide for privacy rights.

When determining whether an employer should be held liable for violating an employee's privacy rights, the courts generally weigh the employer's interests against the employee's reasonable expectation of privacy. Normally, if employees have been informed that their communications are being monitored, they cannot reasonably expect those interactions to be private. If employees are not informed that certain communications are being monitored, however, the employer may be held liable for invading their privacy. For this reason, most employers notify their employees about electronic monitoring. Nevertheless, establishing general policies or notifying employees about e-mail monitoring may not sufficiently protect an employer who monitors text messages or other forms of communications not specifically mentioned.

THE ELECTRONIC COMMUNICATIONS PRIVACY ACT Employers must comply with the Electronic Communications Privacy Act (ECPA) of 1986.[23] This act amended existing federal wiretapping law to cover electronic forms of communications, such as communications via cell phones or e-mail. The ECPA prohibits the intentional interception of any wire or electronic communication and the intentional disclosure or use of the information obtained by the interception. Excluded from coverage, however, are any electronic communications through devices that are "furnished to the subscriber or user by a provider of wire or electronic communication service" and that are being used by the subscriber or user, or by the provider of the service, "in the ordinary course of its business."

This "business-extension exception" to the ECPA permits employers to monitor employees' electronic communications made in the ordinary course of business. It does not, however, permit employers to monitor employees' personal communications. Under another exception to the ECPA, however, an employer may avoid liability under the act if the employees consent to having their electronic communications intercepted by the employer. Thus, an employer may be able to avoid liability under the ECPA by requiring employees to sign forms indicating that they consent to the monitoring of personal as well as business communications.

STORED COMMUNICATIONS Part of the ECPA is known as the Stored Communications Act (SCA).[24] The SCA prohibits intentional and unauthorized access to *stored* electronic communications and sets forth criminal and civil sanctions for violators. A person can violate the SCA by intentionally accessing a stored electronic communication or by intentionally exceeding the authorization given to access the communication. To prove a violation, however, an individual must show that the other party (for example, an employer) lacked the authority to access the stored communication. Proving this lack of authority may be difficult at times, especially when an employer provided the electronic communications device.

---

23. 18 U.S.C. Sections 2510–2521.
24. 18 U.S.C. Sections 2701–2711.

CASE EXAMPLE 17.5 Jeff Quon, a police sergeant for the city of Ontario, California, was issued a pager with wireless text-messaging services provided by Arch Wireless Operating Company. Although the city had a general policy that employees should not use work computers, Internet, and e-mail for personal matters, it did not expressly mention the pagers or text messaging. On several occasions, Quon paid the city over-age charges for exceeding the limit on text messages. Without Quon's knowledge, his supervisors then requested transcripts of his stored text messages from Arch Wireless and read them to determine whether the texts were work related or personal. When Quon learned that his supervisors had read his personal (and sexually explicit) texts to his wife, he filed a lawsuit against the city and Arch Wireless for violating his privacy rights. Ultimately, the United States Supreme Court held that the search of Quon's text messages was reasonable. Because the police department had a written policy, which Quon admitted that he understood applied to the pagers, he had no reasonable expectation of privacy.[25] ●

Preventing Legal Disputes

To avoid legal disputes, exercise caution when monitoring employees and make sure that any monitoring is conducted in a reasonable place and manner. Establish written policies that include all types of electronic devices used by your employees, and notify employees of how and when they may be monitored on these devices. Consider informing employees of the reasons for the monitoring. Explain what the concern is, what job repercussions could result, and what recourse employees have in the event that a negative action is taken against them. By providing more privacy protection to employees than is legally required, you can both avoid potential privacy complaints and give employees a sense that they retain some degree of privacy in their workplace, which can lead to greater job satisfaction.

Other Types of Monitoring

In addition to monitoring their employees' online activities, employers also engage in other types of employee screening and monitoring. These practices, which have included lie-detector tests, drug tests, genetic testing, and employment screening, have often been subject to challenge as violations of employee privacy rights.

LIE-DETECTOR TESTS At one time, many employers required employees or job applicants to take lie-detector (polygraph) tests in connection with their employment. In 1988, Congress passed the Employee Polygraph Protection Act,[26] which generally prohibits employers from requiring or causing employees or job applicants to take lie-detector tests or suggesting or requesting that they do so. The act also restricts employers' ability to use or ask about the results of any lie-detector test or to take any negative employment action based on the results.

Employers excepted from these prohibitions include federal, state, and local government employers; certain security service firms; and companies manufacturing and distributing controlled substances. Other employers may use lie-detector tests when investigating losses attributable to theft, including embezzlement and the theft of trade secrets.

DRUG TESTING In the interests of public safety, many employers, including government employers, require their employees to submit to drug testing. Government

"We are rapidly entering the age of no privacy, where everyone is open to surveillance at all times; where there are no secrets."
William O. Douglas, 1898–1980
(Associate justice of the United States Supreme Court, 1939–1975)

---

25. *City of Ontario, California v. Quon*, __ U.S. __, 130 S.Ct. 2619, 177 L.Ed.2d 216 (2010).
26. 29 U.S.C. Sections 2001 *et seq.*

Workers at a toxicology lab place employees' urine samples in barcoded test tubes before screening the samples for drugs. Many private employers today routinely require their employees to submit to drug testing. What recourse, if any, does an employee who does not consent to a drug test have against the employer?

(public) employers are constrained in drug testing by the Fourth Amendment to the U.S. Constitution, which prohibits unreasonable searches and seizures (see Chapter 6). Drug testing of public employees is allowed by statute for transportation workers and normally is upheld by the courts when drug use in a particular job may threaten public safety. Also, when there is a reasonable basis for suspecting government employees of using drugs, courts often find that drug testing does not violate the Fourth Amendment.

The Fourth Amendment does not apply to drug testing conducted by private employers. Hence, the privacy rights and drug testing of private-sector employees are governed by state law, which varies widely. Many states allow drug testing by private employers but place restrictions on when and how the testing may be performed. A collective bargaining agreement may also provide protection against drug testing (or authorize drug testing under certain conditions). The permissibility of a private employer's drug tests typically hinges on whether the testing was reasonable. Random drug tests and even "zero-tolerance" policies (that deny a "second chance" to employees who test positive for drugs) have been held to be reasonable.[27]

Federal government employees have long been required to submit to background checks as a condition of employment. Many workers who work at U.S. government facilities, however, are employees of private contractors, not of the government. They generally have not been subject to background checks. When new standards required background checks for all federal workers, including contract employees, several contract workers brought a lawsuit asserting that their privacy rights had been violated.

---

27. See, for example, *CITGO Asphalt Refining Co. v. Paper, Allied-Industrial, Chemical, and Energy Workers International Union Local No. 2-991*, 385 F.3d 809 (3d Cir. 2004).

Case 17.2 | National Aeronautics and Space Administration v. Nelson

Supreme Court of the United States, ___ U.S. ___, 131 S.Ct. 746, 178 L.Ed.2d 667 (2011).
www.supremecourt.gov[a]

COMPANY PROFILE *The National Aeronautics and Space Administration (NASA) is an independent federal agency charged with planning and conducting "space activities." One of NASA's facilities is the Jet Propulsion Laboratory (JPL) in Pasadena, California, which is NASA's primary center for deep-space robotics and communications. The JPL also develops and runs most U.S. unmanned space missions—from the Explorer 1 satellite in 1958 to the Mars rovers of this century. The JPL is owned by NASA but is operated by the California Institute of Technology (Cal Tech) and is staffed exclusively by contract employees.*

BACKGROUND AND FACTS In 2007, under newly implemented standards, contract employees with long-term access to federal facilities were ordered to complete a standard background check—the National Agency Check with Inquiries (NACI). The NACI is designed to obtain information on such issues as counseling and treatment, as well as mental and financial stability. Robert Nelson and other JPL employees filed a lawsuit in a federal district court against NASA, claiming that the NACI violated their privacy rights. The court denied the plaintiffs' request to prohibit use of the NACI, but the U.S. Court of Appeals for the Ninth Circuit reversed this decision. NASA appealed to the United States Supreme Court, arguing that the Privacy

---

a. In the "Supreme Court Documents" column, in the "Opinions" pull-down menu, select "Bound Volumes." On the next page, in the "For Search Term:" box, type "NASA v. Nelson" and click on "Search." In the result, click on the name of the case to access the opinion. The United States Supreme Court maintains this Web site.

Case 17.2–Continues next page ➥

Case 17.2—Continued

Act of 1974 provides sufficient protection for employees' privacy. This act allows the government to retain information only for "relevant and necessary" purposes, requires written consent before the information may be disclosed, and imposes criminal liability for violations.

IN THE WORDS OF THE COURT . . .
Justice *ALITO* delivered the opinion of the Court.

Respondents in this case, federal contract employees at a Government laboratory, claim that two parts of a standard employment background investigation violate their rights * * * . Respondents challenge a section of a form questionnaire that asks employees about treatment or counseling for recent illegal-drug use. They also object to certain open-ended questions on a form sent to employees' designated references.

* * * *

*We will assume for present purposes that the Government's challenged inquiries implicate a privacy interest of constitutional significance. We hold, however, that, whatever the scope of this interest, it does not prevent the Government from asking reasonable questions * * * in an employment background investigation that is subject to the Privacy Act's safeguards against public disclosure.* [Emphasis added.]

* * * *

* * * The questions challenged by respondents are part of a standard employment background check of the sort used by millions of private employers. The Government itself has been conducting employment investigations since the earliest days of the Republic. Since 1871, the President has enjoyed statutory authority to ascertain the fitness of applicants for the civil service as to age,

health, character, knowledge and ability for the employment sought and that [statute] appears to have been regarded as a codification of established practice. Standard background investigations similar to those at issue here became mandatory for all candidates for the federal civil service in 1953. And the particular investigations challenged in this case arose from a decision to extend that requirement to federal contract employees requiring long-term access to federal facilities.

As this long history suggests, the Government has an interest in conducting basic employment background checks. Reasonable investigations of applicants and employees aid the Government in ensuring the security of its facilities and in employing a competent, reliable workforce.

DECISION AND REMEDY   The United States Supreme Court reversed the judgment of the lower court and remanded the case. The NACI does not violate an individual's right to privacy because its inquiries are reasonable and the Privacy Act protects against the disclosure of private information.

WHAT IF THE FACTS WERE DIFFERENT?   *Suppose that after the decision in this case, a JPL employee refused to cooperate in an NACI background check. What would be the most likely consequences?*

THE LEGAL ENVIRONMENT DIMENSION   *The U.S. Constitution does not explicitly mention a general right to privacy. From what sources does the Court infer this right? (Hint: See the section on "Privacy Rights" in Chapter 4 on page 104.)*

GENETIC TESTING   A serious privacy issue arose when some employers began conducting genetic testing of employees or prospective employees in an effort to identify individuals who might develop significant health problems in the future. To date, however, only a few cases involving this issue have come before the courts.

To prevent the improper use of genetic information in employment and health insurance, in 2008 Congress passed the Genetic Information Nondiscrimination Act (GINA).[28] Under GINA, employers cannot make decisions about hiring, firing, job placement, or promotion based on the results of genetic testing. GINA also prohibits group health plans and insurers from denying coverage or charging higher premiums based solely on a genetic predisposition to developing a specific disease in the future.

SCREENING PROCEDURES   Preemployment screening procedures and background checks are another area of concern to potential employees. What kinds of questions are permissible on an employment application or a preemployment test? What kinds of questions go too far in invading the applicant's privacy? Is it an invasion of privacy, for example, to ask questions about the prospective employee's sexual orientation or religious convictions? Generally, questions on an employment application must have a reasonable nexus, or connection, with the job for which the person is applying.

---

28. 26 U.S.C. Section 9834; 42 U.S.C. Sections 300gg-53, 1320d-9, 2000ff-1 to 2000ff-11.

▶ Immigration Law

The United States had no laws restricting immigration until the late nineteenth century. Today, the most important laws governing immigration and employment are the Immigration Reform and Control Act (IRCA) of 1986[29] and the Immigration Act of 1990.[30] In recent years, immigration law has become an area of increasing concern for businesses as the number of immigrants—especially illegal immigrants—to the United States has grown. An estimated 12 million illegal immigrants now live in the United States. The great majority came to find jobs, but U.S. employers face serious penalties if they hire illegal immigrants. Thus, an understanding of immigration laws has become increasingly important for businesses.

(AP Photo/Elaine Thompson)

What to do about illegal immigrants is a controversial issue. Some believe that all illegal immigrants should be given amnesty and a chance to become citizens. Others believe that they should all be arrested and returned to their countries of origin. What are the roadblocks to the latter solution?

Immigration Reform and Control Act (IRCA)

When the IRCA was enacted in 1986, it provided amnesty to certain groups of illegal aliens living in the United States at the time. It also established a system that sanctions employers that hire illegal immigrants who lack work authorization. The IRCA makes it illegal to hire, recruit, or refer for a fee someone not authorized to work in this country. Through Immigration and Customs Enforcement officers, the federal government conducts random compliance audits and engages in enforcement actions against employers that hire illegal immigrants.

I-9 Verification A process that all employers in the United States must perform within three business days of hiring a new worker to verify the employment eligibility and identity of the worker by completing an I-9 Employment Eligibility Verification form.

I-9 EMPLOYMENT VERIFICATION To comply with current law (based on the 1986 act), an employer must perform **I-9 verifications** for new hires, including those hired as "contractors" or "day workers" if they work under the employer's direct supervision. Form I-9, Employment Eligibility Verification, which is available from U.S. Citizenship and Immigration Services,[31] must be completed within three days of a worker's commencement of employment. The three-day period is to allow the employer to check the form's accuracy and to review and verify documents establishing the prospective worker's identity and eligibility for employment in the United States.

The employer must attest, under penalty of perjury, that an employee produced documents establishing his or her identity and legal employability. Acceptable documents include a U.S. passport establishing the person's citizenship or a document authorizing a foreign citizen to work in the United States, such as a Permanent Resident Card or an Alien Registration Receipt (discussed on page 519).

---

29. 29 U.S.C. Section 1802.

30. This act amended various provisions of the Immigration and Nationality Act of 1952, 8 U.S.C. Sections 1101 *et seq.*

31. U.S. Citizenship and Immigration Services is a federal agency that is part of the U.S. Department of Homeland Security.

Note that most legal actions alleging violations of I-9 rules are brought against employees. An employee must state that she or he is a U.S. citizen or otherwise authorized to work in the United States. If the employee enters false information on an I-9 form or presents false documentation, the employer can fire the worker, who then may be subject to deportation.

The IRCA prohibits "knowing" violations, including situations in which an employer "should have known" that the worker was unauthorized. Good faith is a defense under the statute, and employers are legally entitled to rely on a document authorizing a person to work that reasonably appears on its face to be genuine, even if it is later established to be counterfeit.

ENFORCEMENT   U.S. Immigration and Customs Enforcement (ICE) is the largest investigative arm of the U.S. Department of Homeland Security. ICE has a general inspection program that conducts random compliance audits. Other audits may occur if the agency receives a written complaint alleging an employer's violations. Government inspections include a review of an employer's file of I-9 forms. The government does not need a subpoena or a warrant to conduct such an inspection.

If an investigation reveals a possible violation, ICE will bring an administrative action and issue a Notice of Intent to Fine, which sets out the charges against the employer. The employer has a right to a hearing on the enforcement action but must file a request within thirty days. This hearing is conducted before an *administrative law judge* (see Chapter 19), and the employer has a right to counsel and to *discovery* (see Chapter 3). The typical defense in such actions is good faith or substantial compliance with the documentation provisions.

PENALTIES   An employer who violates the law by hiring an unauthorized alien is subject to substantial penalties. The employer may be fined up to $2,200 for each unauthorized employee for a first offense, $5,000 per employee for a second offense, and up to $11,000 for subsequent offenses. Criminal penalties, including additional fines and imprisonment for up to ten years, apply to employers who have engaged in a "pattern or practice of violations." A company may also be barred from future government contracts for violations. In determining the penalty, ICE considers the seriousness of the violation (such as intentional falsification of documents) and the employer's past compliance. ICE regulations also provide for mitigation or aggravation of the penalty under certain circumstances, such as whether the employer cooperated in the investigation or is a small business.

The Immigration Act

Often, U.S. businesses find that they cannot hire sufficient domestic workers with specialized skills. For this reason, U.S. immigration laws have long made provisions for businesses to hire foreign workers with special qualification. The Immigration Act of 1990 placed caps on the number of visas (entry permits) that can be issued to immigrants each year.

Most temporary visas are set aside for workers who can be characterized as "persons of extraordinary ability," members of the professions holding advanced degrees, or other skilled workers and professionals. To hire these individuals, employers must submit a petition to U.S. Citizenship and Immigration Services, which determines whether the job candidate meets the legal standards. Each visa is for a specific job, and the law limits the employee's ability to change jobs once in the United States.

"Immigration is the sincerest form of flattery."

Jack Paar, 1918–2004
(American entertainer)

I-551 ALIEN REGISTRATION RECEIPTS   A company seeking to hire a noncitizen worker may do so if the worker is self-authorized. This means that the worker either is a lawful permanent resident or has a valid temporary Employment Authorization Document. A lawful permanent resident can prove his or her status to an employer by presenting an **I-551 Alien Registration Receipt**, known as a "green card," or a properly stamped foreign passport.

I-551 Alien Registration Receipt
A document, commonly known as a "green card," that shows that a foreign-born individual has been lawfully admitted for permanent residency in the United States. Persons seeking employment can prove to prospective employers that they are legally in the United States by showing this receipt.

Many immigrant workers are not already self-authorized, and employers may obtain labor certification, or green cards, for the immigrants they wish to hire. To gain authorization for hiring a foreign worker, the employer must show that no U.S. worker is qualified, willing, and able to take the job. The employer must also be able to show that the qualifications required for the job are a business necessity. Approximately fifty thousand new green cards are issued each year. A green card can be obtained only for a person who is being hired for a permanent, full-time position. (A separate authorization system provides for the temporary entry and hiring of non-immigrant visa workers.)

THE H-1B VISA PROGRAM   The most common and controversial visa program today is the H-1B visa system. To obtain an H-1B visa, the potential employee must be qualified in a "specialty occupation," meaning that the individual has highly specialized knowledge and has attained a bachelor's or higher degree or its equivalent. Individuals with H-1B visas can stay in the United States for three to six years and can work only for the sponsoring employer. The recipients of these visas include many high-tech workers, such as computer programmers and electronics specialists. A maximum of sixty-five thousand H-1B visas is set aside each year for new immigrants, and that limit is typically reached within the first few weeks of the year. Consequently, many businesses, such as Microsoft, continue to lobby Congress to expand the number of H-1B visas available to immigrants.

LABOR CERTIFICATION   A common criticism of the H-1B visa system is that it depresses the wages of U.S. workers because H-1B workers may be willing to work for less. The law addresses this complaint by requiring employers to pay H-1B workers the prevailing wage. Before an employer can submit an H-1B application, it must file a Labor Certification application on Form ETA 9035. The employer must agree to provide a wage level at least equal to the wages offered to other individuals with similar experience and qualifications and attest that the hiring will not adversely affect other workers similarly employed. The employer must also inform U.S. workers of the intent to hire a foreign worker by posting the form. The U.S. Department of Labor reviews the applications and may reject them for omissions or inaccuracies.

H-2, O, L, AND E VISAS   Other specialty temporary visas are available for other categories of employees. H-2 visas provide for workers performing agricultural labor of a seasonal nature. O visas provide entry for persons who have "extraordinary ability in the sciences, arts, education, business or athletics which has been demonstrated by sustained national or international acclaim." L visas allow a company's foreign managers or executives to work inside the United States. E visas permit the entry of certain foreign investors or entrepreneurs.

As the unemployment rate has remained stubbornly high since the recession, there has been growing public resentment toward illegal immigrants, who are perceived to be taking jobs away from U.S. citizens. Although immigration law has always been a federal matter, in 2010 the state of Arizona, which faces a large problem of unauthorized immigration along its border with Mexico, enacted its own immigration law (S.B. 1070). Essentially, S.B. 1070 requires a police officer who lawfully stops or detains someone and reasonably suspects that the person is an alien to make a reasonable attempt to determine the person's immigration status. The law would require immigrants to carry their alien registration documents at all times and would give police considerable discretion to question individuals regarding their immigration status.

Although fifteen other states proposed to enact legislation similar to Arizona's statute, the law immediately became highly controversial. Many contended that the law is unconstitutional because it would institutionalize racial profiling, which occurs when police target suspects because of their race or ethnicity. In this instance, the concern was that police would focus on stopping Hispanics, many of whom are U.S. citizens.

Before S.B. 1070 went into effect, the U.S. government filed a lawsuit in federal district court, seeking an injunction to block the implementation of the law. The government argued that the law violated the commerce clause and the supremacy clause and that it was preempted by the federal Immigration and Nationality Act.[32] (As discussed in Chapter 4, a valid federal statute takes precedence over, or preempts, a conflicting state law.) The district court agreed that the state law was preempted and granted the injunction, and the state of Arizona appealed.

In 2011, the U.S. Court of Appeals for the Ninth Circuit affirmed the district court's ruling.[33] Although the United States Supreme Court has not yet ruled on this issue, the appellate court's decision calls into question the legitimacy of state immigration laws. Nevertheless, Alabama and a few other states have passed legislation that uses slightly different language but is still aimed at stepping up enforcement against illegal immigrants in that state.

Labor Unions

In the 1930s, in addition to wage-hour laws, the government also enacted the first of several labor laws. These laws protect employees' rights to join labor unions, to bargain with management over the terms and conditions of employment, and to conduct strikes.

Federal Labor Laws

Federal labor laws governing union-employer relations have developed considerably since the first law was enacted in 1932. Initially, the laws were concerned with protecting the rights and interests of workers. Subsequent legislation placed some restraints on unions and granted rights to employers. Coverage of federal labor laws is broad and extends to all employers whose business activity either involves or affects interstate commerce.

Norris-LaGuardia Act   In 1932, Congress protected peaceful strikes, picketing, and boycotts in the Norris-LaGuardia Act.[34] The statute restricted the power of federal courts to issue injunctions against unions engaged in peaceful strikes. In effect, this act established a national policy permitting employees to organize.

---

32. 8 U.S.C. Sections 1101 *et seq.*

33. *United States v. Arizona,* 641 F.3d 339 (9th Cir. 2011).

34. 29 U.S.C. Sections 101–110, 113–115.

These aircraft mechanics are on strike in Enid, Oklahoma. They walked off the job after negotiators could not reach an agreement on a new contract. Under what circumstances does it make sense for union employees to go on strike? What are the costs of going on strike?

NATIONAL LABOR RELATIONS ACT   One of the foremost statutes regulating labor is the National Labor Relations Act (NLRA) of 1935.[35] This act established the rights of employees to engage in collective bargaining and to strike. The act also specifically defined a number of employer practices as unfair to labor:

1. Interference with the efforts of employees to form, join, or assist labor organizations or with the efforts of employees to engage in concerted activities for their mutual aid or protection.
2. An employer's domination of a labor organization or contribution of financial or other support to it.
3. Discrimination in the hiring or awarding of tenure to employees based on union affiliation.
4. Discrimination against employees for filing charges under the act or giving testimony under the act.
5. Refusal to bargain collectively with the duly designated representative of the employees.

The National Labor Relations Board. The NLRA also created the National Labor Relations Board (NLRB) to oversee union elections and to prevent employers from engaging in unfair and illegal union activities and unfair labor practices. When a union or employee believes that an employer has violated federal labor law (or vice versa), a charge is filed with a regional office of the NLRB. The NLRB has the authority to investigate employees' charges of unfair labor practices and to file complaints against employers in response to these charges.

When violations are found, the NLRB may issue a *cease-and-desist order* compelling the employer to stop engaging in the unfair practices. Cease-and-desist orders can be enforced by a federal appellate court if necessary. After the NLRB rules on claims of unfair labor practices, its decision may be appealed to a federal court. Under the NLRA, employers and unions have a duty to bargain in good faith. Bargaining over certain subjects is mandatory, and a party's refusal to bargain over these subjects is an unfair labor practice that can be reported to the NLRB.

Workers Protected by the NLRA. To be protected under the NLRA, an individual must be an *employee,* as that term is defined in the statute. Courts have long held that job applicants fall within the definition (otherwise, the NLRA's ban on discrimination in hiring would mean nothing). Additionally, the United States Supreme Court has held that individuals who are hired by a union to organize a company are to be considered employees of the company for NLRA purposes.[36] Some workers are specifically excluded from the NLRA. Railroad and airline workers are not covered by the NLRA but are covered by a separate act, the Railway Labor Act, which closely parallels the NLRA. Other types of workers, such as agricultural workers and domestic servants, are excluded from the NLRA and have no coverage under separate legislation.

LABOR-MANAGEMENT RELATIONS ACT   The Labor-Management Relations Act (LMRA) of 1947 (also called the Taft-Hartley Act)[37] was passed to proscribe certain

---

35. 20 U.S.C. Section 151.
36. *NLRB v. Town & Country Electric, Inc.,* 516 U.S. 85, 116 S.Ct. 450, 133 L.Ed.2d 371 (1995).
37. 29 U.S.C. Sections 141 *et seq.*

Closed Shop   A firm that requires union membership by its workers as a condition of employment. The closed shop was made illegal by the Labor-Management Relations Act of 1947.

Union Shop   A firm that requires all workers, once employed, to become union members within a specified period of time as a condition of their continued employment.

Right-to-Work Law   A state law providing that employees may not be required to join a union as a condition of retaining employment.

unfair union practices, such as the *closed shop*. A **closed shop** requires union membership by its workers as a condition of employment. Although the act made the closed shop illegal, it preserved the legality of the union shop. A **union shop** does not require membership as a prerequisite for employment but can, and usually does, require that workers join the union after a specified amount of time on the job.

The LMRA also prohibited unions from refusing to bargain with employers, engaging in certain types of picketing, and *featherbedding*—causing employers to hire more employees than necessary. The act also allowed individual states to pass their own **right-to-work laws,** which make it illegal for union membership to be required for *continued* employment in any establishment. Thus, union shops are technically illegal in the twenty-three states that have right-to-work laws.

LABOR-MANAGEMENT REPORTING AND DISCLOSURE ACT   In 1959, Congress enacted the Labor-Management Reporting and Disclosure Act (LMRDA).[38] The act established an employee bill of rights and reporting requirements for union activities. The act strictly regulates unions' internal business procedures, including union elections. For example, the LMRDA requires a union to hold regularly scheduled elections of officers using secret ballots. Ex-convicts are prohibited from holding union office. Moreover, union officials are accountable for union property and funds. Members have the right to attend and to participate in union meetings, to nominate officers, and to vote in most union proceedings. The act also outlawed **hot-cargo agreements,** in which employers voluntarily agree with unions not to handle, use, or deal in goods produced by nonunion employees working for other employers.

Hot-Cargo Agreement   An agreement in which an employer voluntarily agrees with a union not to handle, use, or deal in other employers' goods that were not produced by union employees; a type of secondary boycott explicitly prohibited by the Labor-Management Reporting and Disclosure Act of 1959.

Authorization Card   A card signed by an employee that gives a union permission to act on his or her behalf in negotiations with management.

Union Organization

Typically, the first step in organizing a union at a particular firm is to have the workers sign authorization cards. An **authorization card** usually states that the worker desires to have a certain union, such as the United Auto Workers, represent the workforce. If a majority of the workers sign authorization cards, the union organizers (unionizers) present the cards to the employer and ask for formal recognition of the union. The employer is not required to recognize the union at this point in the process, but it may do so voluntarily on a showing of majority support. (Under pro-labor legislation that has been proposed in the U.S. Congress, the employer would be required to recognize the union as soon as a majority of the workers had signed authorization cards—without holding an election, as described next.)[39]

UNION ELECTIONS   If the employer refuses to voluntarily recognize the union after a majority of the workers sign authorization cards—or if fewer than 50 percent of the workers sign authorization cards—the union organizers present the cards to the NLRB with a petition for an election. For an election to be held, the unionizers must demonstrate that at least 30 percent of the workers to be represented support a union or an election on unionization.

The proposed union must also represent an *appropriate bargaining unit*. Not every group of workers can form a single union. One key requirement of an appropriate bargaining unit is a *mutuality of interest* among all the workers to be represented by the union. Factors considered in determining whether there is a mutuality of interest

---

38. 29 U.S.C. Sections 401 *et seq.*

39. If the proposed Employee Free Choice Act becomes law, some of the information stated here may change.

include the *similarity of the jobs* of all the workers to be unionized and their physical location.

If all of these requirements are met, an election is held. The NLRB supervises the election and ensures secret voting and voter eligibility. If the proposed union receives majority support in a fair election, the NLRB certifies the union as the bargaining representative for the employees.

UNION ELECTION CAMPAIGNS   Many disputes between labor and management arise during union election campaigns. Generally, the employer has control over unionizing activities that take place on company property during working hours. Thus, an employer may limit the campaign activities of union supporters as long as the employer has a legitimate business reason for doing so. The employer may also reasonably limit the times and places that union solicitation occurs so long as the employer is not discriminating against the union.

EXAMPLE 17.6   A union is seeking to organize clerks at a department store owned by Amanti Enterprises. Amanti can prohibit all union solicitation in areas of the store open to the public because that activity could seriously interfere with the store's business. If Amanti allows solicitation for charitable causes in the workplace, however, it may not prohibit union solicitation. ●

An employer may campaign among its workers against the union, but the NLRB carefully monitors and regulates the tactics used by management. Otherwise, management might use its economic power to coerce the workers into voting against unionization. If the employer issued threats ("If the union wins, you'll all be fired") or engaged in other unfair labor practices, the NLRB may certify the union even though it lost the election. Alternatively, the NLRB may ask a court to order a new election.

In the following case, the question was whether managers' brief interruptions of unionizing activities constituted illegal surveillance in violation of the NLRA.

Case 17.3   **Local Joint Executive Board of Las Vegas v. National Labor Relations Board**

United States Court of Appeals, Ninth Circuit, 515 F.3d 942 (2008).

(Smneale/Creative Commons)

Were managers at the Aladdin casino engaged in illegal surveillance of union-organizing activities?

BACKGROUND AND FACTS   Aladdin Gaming, LLC, operates a hotel and casino in Las Vegas, Nevada. On May 30, 2003, Local Joint Executive Board of Las Vegas and two other unions (the unions) began an open campaign to organize Aladdin's housekeeping, food, and beverage departments. On two occasions during this campaign, human resources managers at Aladdin (Tracy Sapien and Stacey Briand) approached union organizers who were discussing unionization with employees in an employee dining room during a lunch break. Sapien and Briand interrupted the organizers while they were obtaining signatures on authorization cards and asked whether the employees were fully informed of the facts before signing. The unions filed a complaint with the National Labor Relations Board (NLRB) claiming that the managers' actions were illegal surveillance in violation of the National Labor Relations Act (NLRA). The NLRB ruled in favor of Aladdin, and the unions appealed.

IN THE WORDS OF THE COURT . . .
CALLAHAN, **Circuit Judge:**
* * * *

Section 8(a)(1) of the NLRA states that "it shall be an unfair labor practice for an employer (1) to interfere with, restrain, or coerce employees in the exercise of the rights guaranteed in section 157

Case 17.3—Continues next page ⇒

Case 17.3–Continued

of this title." The [NLRB] has interpreted Section 8(a)(1) to make observation of union activity unlawful, "if the observation goes beyond casual and becomes unduly intrusive." * * * *"The test for determining whether an employer engages in unlawful surveillance or whether it creates the impression of surveillance is an objective one and involves the determination of whether the employer's conduct, under the circumstances, was such as would tend to interfere with, restrain or coerce employees* in the exercise of the rights guaranteed under Section 7 of the [National Labor Relations] Act." [Emphasis added.]

    * * * *

There is no evidence that either Ms. Sapien or Ms. Briand used threats, force, or promises of benefits that would strip their speech of the protections of Section 8(c). Ms. Sapien attempted to give the buffet servers additional facts to consider before signing the union cards. Ms. Briand told Ms. Felix [an employee] that Ms. Bueno [another employee] should not sign a union card without fully understanding the consequences and provided her opinion that the union may not

be able to deliver on its promises. Ms. Felix voluntarily translated Ms. Briand's comments for Ms. Bueno [a Spanish speaker]. After Ms. Felix explained the translation, Ms. Briand left.

DECISION AND REMEDY The federal appellate court denied the unions' petition for review, concluding that the managers' brief interruptions of organizing activity did not constitute illegal surveillance.

WHAT IF THE FACTS WERE DIFFERENT?
If management employees had interrupted union-organizing activities twenty-five times rather than just twice, would the outcome of this case have been different? Why or why not?

THE LEGAL ENVIRONMENT DIMENSION
An administrative law judge (ALJ) originally ruled that the two brief verbal interruptions by Sapien and Briand violated the NLRA. Why might the ALJ have made this ruling?

Collective Bargaining

Collective Bargaining The process by which labor and management negotiate the terms and conditions of employment, including working hours and workplace conditions.

If the NLRB certifies the union, the union becomes the *exclusive bargaining representative* of the workers. The central legal right of a union is to engage in collective bargaining on the members' behalf. **Collective bargaining** is the process by which labor and management negotiate the terms and conditions of employment, including wages, benefits, working conditions, and other matters. Although management is not necessarily required to bargain over a decision to close or relocate a particular facility, it must bargain over the economic consequences of such decisions. Decisions whether to grant severance pay (compensation for the termination of employment), for example, are appropriate for bargaining.

When a union is officially recognized, it may demand to bargain with the employer and negotiate new terms or conditions of employment. In collective bargaining, as in most other business negotiations, each side uses its economic power to pressure or persuade the other side to grant concessions.

Bargaining does not mean that one side must give in to the other or that compromises must be made. It does mean that a demand to bargain with the employer must be taken seriously and that both sides must bargain in "good faith." Good faith bargaining means that management, for instance, must be willing to meet with union representatives and consider the union's wishes when negotiating a contract. Examples of bad faith bargaining on the part of management include engaging in a campaign to undermine the union among workers, constantly shifting positions on disputed contract terms, and sending bargainers who lack authority to commit the company to a contract. If an employer (or a union) refuses to bargain in good faith without justification, it has committed an unfair labor practice, and the other party may petition the NLRB for an order requiring good faith bargaining.

Strikes

Strike An action undertaken by unionized workers when collective bargaining fails. The workers leave their jobs, refuse to work, and (typically) picket the employer's workplace.

Even when labor and management have bargained in good faith, they may be unable to reach a final agreement. When extensive collective bargaining has been conducted and an impasse results, the union may call a strike against the employer to pressure it into making concessions. In a **strike,** the unionized workers leave their jobs and refuse to work. The workers also typically picket the workplace, walking or standing outside the facility with signs stating their complaints.

A strike is an extreme action. Striking workers lose their rights to be paid, and management loses production and may lose customers when orders cannot be filled. Labor law regulates the circumstances and conduct of strikes. Most strikes take the form of "economic strikes," which are initiated because the union wants a better contract. **EXAMPLE 17.7**   In 2010, the union representing workers at the Disneyland Hotel organized a hunger strike to draw attention to the prolonged contract dispute over health-care benefits and workloads. After two years of negotiations with the hotel, the workers still did not have a signed contract with health-care benefits. ●

THE RIGHT TO STRIKE   The right to strike is guaranteed by the NLRA, within limits, and strike activities, such as picketing, are protected by the free speech guarantee of the First Amendment to the U.S. Constitution. Persons who are not employees have a right to participate in picketing an employer. The NLRA also gives workers the right to refuse to cross a picket line of fellow workers who are engaged in a lawful strike. Employers are permitted to hire replacement workers (often called "scabs" by union supporters) to substitute for the workers who are on strike.

ILLEGAL STRIKES   An otherwise lawful strike may become illegal because of the conduct of the strikers. Violent strikes (including the threat of violence) are illegal. The use of violence against management employees or substitute workers is illegal. Certain forms of "massed picketing" are also illegal. If the strikers form a barrier and deny management or other nonunion workers access to the plant, the strike is illegal. Similarly, "sit-down" strikes, in which employees simply stay in the plant without working, are illegal.

> **Secondary Boycott**   A union's refusal to work for, purchase from, or handle the products of a secondary employer, with whom the union has no dispute, in order to force that employer to stop doing business with the primary employer, with whom the union has a labor dispute.

A **secondary boycott** is another type of illegal strike. It is a strike directed against someone other than the strikers' employer, such as the companies that sell materials to the employer. **EXAMPLE 17.8**   The unionized workers of SemiCo go out on strike. To increase their economic leverage, the workers picket the leading suppliers and customers of SemiCo in an attempt to hurt the company's business. SemiCo is considered the primary employer, and its suppliers and customers are considered secondary employers. Picketing of the suppliers or customers is a secondary boycott, which was made illegal by the Labor-Management Relations Act (Taft-Hartley Act). ●

> **Wildcat Strike**   This action occurs when a minority group of workers, perhaps dissatisfied with a labor union's representation, calls its own strike.

A **wildcat strike** occurs when a minority group of workers, perhaps dissatisfied with a union's representation, calls its own strike. The union is the exclusive bargaining representative of a group of workers, and only the union can call a strike. Therefore, a wildcat strike, unauthorized by the certified union, is illegal.

A strike may also be illegal if it contravenes a *no-strike clause*. The previous collective bargaining agreement between a union and an employer may have contained a clause in which the union agreed not to strike. The law permits the employer to enforce this no-strike clause and obtain an injunction against the strike in some circumstances.

THE RIGHTS OF STRIKERS AFTER A STRIKE ENDS   An important issue concerns the rights of strikers after the strike ends. In a typical economic strike over working conditions, the employer has a right to hire permanent replacements during the strike and need not terminate the replacement workers when the economic strikers seek to return to work. In other words, striking workers are not guaranteed the right to return to their jobs after the strike if satisfactory replacement workers have been found.

If the employer has not hired replacement workers to fill the strikers' positions, however, then the employer must rehire the economic strikers to fill any vacancies. Employers may not discriminate against former economic strikers, and those who are rehired retain their seniority rights. Different rules apply when a union strikes because the employer has engaged in unfair labor practices. In this situation, the employer may still hire replacements but must give the strikers back their jobs once the strike is over.

Lockouts

Lockout A lockout occurs when the employer shuts down the business to prevent employees from working. Lockouts are the employer's counterpart to the worker's right to strike and usually are used when a strike is imminent.

Lockouts are the employer's counterpart to the worker's right to strike. A **lockout** occurs when the employer shuts down to prevent employees from working. Lockouts usually are used when the employer believes that a strike is imminent. Lockouts may be a legal employer response.

CASE EXAMPLE 17.9   In a leading United States Supreme Court case on this issue, a union and an employer had reached a stalemate in collective bargaining. The employer feared that the union would delay a strike until the busy season and thereby cause the employer to suffer more greatly from the strike. The employer called a lockout before the busy season to deny the union this leverage, and the Court held that this action was legal.[40] ●

Some lockouts are illegal, however. An employer may not use a lockout as a tool to break the union and pressure employees into decertification. Consequently, an employer must show some economic justification for instituting a lockout.

EXAMPLE 17.10   In 2011, the owners of the National Football League (NFL) teams imposed a lockout on the National Football League Players Association, the players' union, after negotiations on a new collective bargaining agreement broke down. At issue was the owners' proposal to decrease players' salaries and extend the season by two games. The owners claimed that the salary decrease was necessary because their profits from ticket sales had declined due to the struggling economy. When the lockout was imposed, the union requested decertification, which cleared the way for a group of players to file an antitrust lawsuit (see Chapter 23). Meanwhile, retired NFL players filed a complaint against the league seeking more medical benefits and better pensions. A settlement was reached before the start of the 2011 football season. The players accepted 3 percent less of the revenue generated (47 percent rather than 50 percent) in exchange for better working conditions and more retirement benefits. The owners agreed to keep the same number of games per season. ●

Unfair Labor Practices

The preceding sections have discussed unfair labor practices involved in the significant acts of union elections, collective bargaining, and strikes. Many unfair labor practices may occur within the normal working relationship as well. The most important unfair practices are listed in Exhibit 17–1 below.

---

40.   *American Ship Building Co. v. NLRB,* 380 U.S. 300, 85 S.Ct. 955, 13 L.Ed.2d 855 (1965).

● *Exhibit* **17–1 Basic Unfair Labor Practices**

EMPLOYERS—IT IS UNFAIR TO . . .	UNIONS—IT IS UNFAIR TO . . .
1. Refuse to recognize a union and refuse to bargain in good faith.	1. Refuse to bargain in good faith.
2. Interfere with, restrain, or coerce employees in their efforts to form a union and bargain collectively.	2. Picket to coerce unionization without the support of a majority of the employees.
3. Dominate a union.	3. Demand the hiring of unnecessary excess workers.
4. Discriminate against union workers.	4. Discriminate against nonunion workers.
5. Punish employees for engaging in concerted activity.	5. Agree to participate in a secondary boycott.
	6. Engage in an illegal strike.
	7. Charge excessive membership fees.

Reviewing . . . Employment, Immigration, and Labor Law

Rick Saldona began working as a traveling salesperson for Aimer Winery in 1988. Sales constituted 90 percent of Saldona's work time. Saldona worked an average of fifty hours per week but received no overtime pay. In June 2011, Saldona's new supervisor, Caesar Braxton, claimed that Saldona had been inflating his reported sales calls and required Saldona to submit to a polygraph test. Saldona reported Braxton to the U.S. Department of Labor, which prohibited Aimer from requiring Saldona to take a polygraph test for this purpose. In August 2011, Saldona's wife, Venita, fell from a ladder and sustained a head injury while employed as a full-time agricultural harvester. Saldona delivered to Aimer's human resources department a letter from his wife's physician indicating that she would need daily care for several months, and Saldona took leave until December 2011. Aimer had sixty-three employees at that time. When Saldona returned to Aimer, he was informed that his position had been eliminated because his sales territory had been combined with an adjacent territory. Using the information presented in the chapter, answer the following questions.

1. Would Saldona have been legally entitled to receive overtime pay at a higher rate? Why or why not?
2. What is the maximum length of time Saldona would have been allowed to take leave to care for his injured spouse?
3. Under what circumstances would Aimer have been allowed to require an employee to take a lie-detector test?
4. Would Aimer likely be able to avoid reinstating Saldona under the key employee exception? Why or why not?

 ## Key Terms

authorization card 522	I-551 Alien Registration Receipt 519	union shop 522
closed shop 522	lockout 526	vesting 510
collective bargaining 524	minimum wage 503	whistleblowing 501
employment at will 500	right-to-work law 522	wildcat strike 525
hot-cargo agreement 522	secondary boycott 525	workers' compensation laws 508
I-9 verification 517	strike 524	wrongful discharge 501

 ## Chapter Summary: Employment, Immigration, and Labor Law

Employment at Will (See pages 500–501.)	1. *Employment-at-will doctrine*—Under this common law doctrine, either party may terminate the employment relationship at any time and for any reason ("at will"). This doctrine is still in widespread use throughout the United States, although federal and state statutes prevent it from being applied in certain circumstances. 2. *Exceptions to the employment-at-will doctrine*—To protect employees from some of the harsh results of the employment-at-will doctrine, courts have made exceptions to the doctrine on the basis of contract theory, tort theory, and public policy. Whistleblowers have occasionally received protection under the common law for reasons of public policy. 3. *Wrongful discharge*—Whenever an employer discharges an employee in violation of an employment contract or statutory law protecting employees, the employee may bring a suit for wrongful discharge.
Wage and Hour Laws (See pages 501–505.)	1. *Davis-Bacon Act (1931)*—Requires contractors and subcontractors working on federal government construction projects to pay their employees "prevailing wages." 2. *Walsh-Healey Act (1936)*—Requires firms that contract with federal agencies to pay their employees a minimum wage and overtime pay. 3. *Fair Labor Standards Act (1938)*—Extended wage and hour requirements to cover all employers whose activities affect interstate commerce plus certain other businesses. The act has specific requirements in regard to child labor, maximum hours, and minimum wages.

(Continued)

Chapter Summary: Employment, Immigration, and Labor Law, Continued

Layoffs (See pages 505–506.)	1. *The Worker Adjustment and Retraining Notification (WARN) Act*–Applies to employers with at least one hundred full-time employees and requires that sixty days' advance notice of mass layoffs (defined on page 505) be given to affected employees or their representative (if workers are in a labor union). Employers who violate the WARN Act can be fined up to $500 for each day of the violation and may also have to pay damages and attorneys' fees to the laid-off employees affected by the failure to warn. 2. *State layoff notice requirements*–Many states have statutes requiring employers to provide notice before initiating mass layoffs, and these laws may have different and even stricter requirements than the WARN Act.
Family and Medical Leave (See pages 506–507.)	The Family and Medical Leave Act (FMLA) requires employers with fifty or more employees to provide their employees with up to twelve weeks of unpaid leave (twenty-six weeks for military caregiver leave) during any twelve-month period. The FMLA authorizes leave for the following reasons: 1. *Family leave*–May be taken to care for a newborn baby, an adopted child, or a foster child. 2. *Medical leave*–May be taken when the employee or the employee's spouse, child, or parent has a serious health condition requiring care. 3. *Military caregiver leave*–May be taken when the employee is caring for a family member with a serious injury or illness incurred as a result of military duty. 4. *Qualifying exigency leave*–May be taken by an employee to handle specified nonmedical emergencies when a spouse, parent, or child is on, or is called to, active military duty.
Worker Health and Safety (See pages 507–509.)	1. *Occupational Safety and Health Act (1970)*–Requires employers to meet specific safety and health standards that are established and enforced by the Occupational Safety and Health Administration (OSHA). 2. *State workers' compensation laws*–Establish an administrative procedure for compensating workers who are injured in accidents that occur on the job, regardless of fault.
Income Security (See pages 509–512.)	1. *Social Security and Medicare*–The Social Security Act of 1935 provides for old-age (retirement), survivors', and disability insurance. Both employers and employees must make contributions under the Federal Insurance Contributions Act (FICA) to help pay for benefits that will partially make up for the employees' loss of income on retirement. The Social Security Administration also administers Medicare, a health-insurance program for older or disabled persons. 2. *Private pension plans*–The federal Employee Retirement Income Security Act (ERISA) of 1974 establishes standards for the management of employer-provided pension plans. 3. *Unemployment insurance*–The Federal Unemployment Tax Act of 1935 created a system that provides unemployment compensation to eligible individuals. Covered employers are taxed to help defray the costs of unemployment compensation. 4. *COBRA*–The Consolidated Omnibus Budget Reconciliation Act (COBRA) of 1985 requires employers to give employees, on termination of employment, the option of continuing their medical, optical, or dental insurance coverage for a certain period. 5. *HIPAA*–The Health Insurance Portability and Accountability Act (HIPAA) establishes certain requirements for employer-sponsored health insurance. Employers must comply with a number of administrative, technical, and procedural safeguards to ensure the privacy of employees' health information.
Employee Privacy Rights (See pages 512–516.)	A right to privacy has been inferred from guarantees provided by the First, Third, Fourth, Fifth, and Ninth Amendments to the U.S. Constitution. State laws may also provide for privacy rights. Employer practices that are often challenged by employees as invasive of their privacy rights include electronic performance monitoring, lie-detector tests, drug testing, genetic testing, and screening procedures.
Immigration Law (See pages 517–520.)	1. *Immigration Reform and Control Act (1986)*–Prohibits employers from hiring illegal immigrants; administered by U.S. Citizenship and Immigration Services. Compliance audits and enforcement actions are conducted by U.S. Immigration and Customs Enforcement. 2. *Immigration Act (1990)*–Limits the number of legal immigrants entering the United States by capping the number of visas (entry permits) that are issued each year.

Chapter Summary: Employment, Immigration, and Labor Law, Continued

Labor Unions
(See pages 520–526.)
	1. *Federal labor laws—*
	    a. Norris-LaGuardia Act (1932)—Protects peaceful strikes, picketing, and primary boycotts.
	    b. National Labor Relations Act (1935)—Established the rights of employees to engage in collective bargaining and to strike; also defined specific employer practices as unfair to labor. The National Labor Relations Board (NLRB) was created to administer and enforce the act.
	    c. Labor-Management Relations Act (1947)—Proscribes certain unfair union practices, such as the closed shop.
	    d. Labor-Management Reporting and Disclosure Act (1959)—Established an employee bill of rights and reporting requirements for union activities.
	2. *Union organization—*Union campaign activities and elections must comply with the requirements established by federal labor laws and the NLRB.
	3. *Collective bargaining—*The process by which labor and management negotiate the terms and conditions of employment (such as wages, benefits, and working conditions). The central legal right of a labor union is to engage in collective bargaining on the members' behalf.
	4. *Strikes—*When collective bargaining reaches an impasse, union members may use their ultimate weapon in labor-management struggles—the strike. A strike occurs when unionized workers leave their jobs and refuse to work.

ExamPrep

ISSUE SPOTTERS

1. Erin, an employee of Fine Print Shop, is injured on the job. For Erin to obtain workers' compensation, does her injury have to have been caused by Fine Print's negligence? Does it matter whether the action causing the injury was intentional? Explain.
2. Onyx applies for work with Precision Design Company, which tells her that it requires union membership as a condition of employment. She applies for work with Quality Engineering, Inc., which does not require union membership as a condition of employment but requires employees to join a union after six months on the job. Are these conditions legal? Why or why not?

—**Check your answers to these questions against the answers provided in Appendix G.**

BEFORE THE TEST

Go to **www.cengagebrain.com**, enter the ISBN number "9781111530617," and click on "Find" to locate this textbook's Web site. Then, click on "Access Now" under "Study Tools," and select "Chapter 17" at the top. There you will find an "Interactive Quiz" that you can take to assess your mastery of the concepts in this chapter, as well as "Flashcards" and a "Glossary" of important terms.

For Review

1. What is the employment-at-will doctrine? When and why are exceptions to this doctrine made?
2. What federal statute governs working hours and wages?
3. Under the Family and Medical Leave Act of 1993, in what circumstances may an employee take family or medical leave?
4. What are the two most important federal statutes governing immigration and employment today?
5. What federal statute gave employees the right to organize unions and engage in collective bargaining?

Questions and Case Problems

17–1. Wages and Hours. Calzoni Boating Co. is an interstate business engaged in manufacturing and selling boats. The company has five hundred nonunion employees. Representatives of these employees are requesting a four-day, ten-hours-per-day workweek, and Calzoni is concerned that this would require paying time and a half after eight hours per day. Which federal act is Calzoni thinking of that might require this? Will the act in fact require paying time and a half for all hours worked over eight hours per day if the employees' proposal is accepted? Explain.

17–2. Wrongful Discharge. Denton and Carlo were employed at an appliance plant. Their job required them to do occasional maintenance work while standing on a wire mesh twenty feet above the plant floor. Other employees had fallen through the mesh, and one was killed by the fall. When Denton and Carlo were asked by their supervisor to do work that would likely require them to walk on the mesh, they refused due to their fear of bodily harm or death. Because of their refusal to do the requested work, the two employees were fired from their jobs. Was their discharge wrongful? If so, under what federal employment law? To what federal agency or department should they turn for assistance?

17–3. Unfair Labor Practices. Consolidated Stores is undergoing a unionization campaign. Prior to the union election, management states that the union is unnecessary to protect workers. Management also provides bonuses and wage increases to the workers during this period. The employees reject the union. Union organizers protest that the wage increases during the election campaign unfairly prejudiced the vote. Should these wage increases be regarded as an unfair labor practice? Discuss.

17–4. Illegal Aliens. Nicole Tipton and Sadik Seferi owned and operated a restaurant in Iowa. Acting on a tip from the local police, agents of Immigration and Customs Enforcement executed search warrants at the restaurant and at an apartment where some restaurant workers lived. The agents discovered six undocumented aliens working at the restaurant and living together. When the I-9 forms for the restaurant's employees were reviewed, none were found for the six aliens. They were paid in cash while other employees were paid by check. The jury found Tipton and Seferi guilty of hiring and harboring illegal aliens. Both were given prison terms. The defendants challenged the conviction, contending that they did not violate the law because they did not know that the workers were unauthorized aliens. Was that argument credible? Why or why not? [*United States v. Tipton*, 518 F.3d 591 (8th Cir. 2008)]

17–5. Vesting. The United Auto Workers (UAW) represents workers at Caterpillar, Inc., and negotiates labor contracts on their behalf. A 1988 labor agreement provided lifetime no-cost medical benefits for retirees but did not state when the employees' rights to those benefits vested. This agreement expired in 1991. Caterpillar and the UAW did not reach a new agreement until 1998. Under the new agreement, retiree medical benefits were subject to certain limits, and retirees were to be responsible for paying some of the costs. Workers who retired during the period when no agreement was in force filed a suit in a federal district court to obtain benefits under the 1988 agreement. Review the Employee Retirement Income Security Act vesting rules for private pension plans on page 510. What is the most plausible application of those rules by analogy to these facts? Discuss. [*Winnett v. Caterpillar, Inc.*, 553 F.3d 1000 (6th Cir. 2009)]

17–6. Case Problem with Sample Answer. Minimum Wage. Misty Cumbie worked as a waitress at Vita Café in Portland, Oregon. The café was owned and operated by Woody Woo, Inc. Woody Woo paid its servers an hourly wage that was higher than the state's minimum wage, but the servers were required to contribute their tips into a "tip pool." Approximately one-third of the tip-pool funds went to the servers, and the rest was distributed to the kitchen staff that otherwise rarely received tips for their service. Cumbie sued Woody Woo, alleging that the tip-pooling arrangement violated the minimum wage provisions of the Fair Labor Standards Act (FLSA). The district court dismissed the suit for failure to state a claim. Cumbie appealed. Did Woody Woo's tip-pooling policy violate the FLSA rights of the servers? Explain your answer. [*Cumbie v. Woody Woo, Inc.*, 596 F.3d 577 (9th Cir. 2010)]

—To view a sample answer for Case Problem 17–6, go to Appendix F at the end of this text.

17–7. Unfair Labor Practices. The Laborers' International Union of North America, Local 578, and Shaw Stone & Webster Construction, Inc., were parties to a collective bargaining agreement that covered workers at the company. The agreement contained a union-security provision that required company employees (who were represented by the union) to join the union. If an employee failed to join or pay union dues, the union requested that the employee be fired. After Sebedeo Lopez went to work for Shaw Stone, he failed to pay his union initiation fee or monthly dues. Lopez's shop steward told him to pay these fees, although the amount owed was unclear. He was also told that the union was pressing the company to fire him. Lopez agreed to pay the fees and left a money order for $200 at the union's office, but the union claimed that it did not find the money order. Lopez promised to pay another $215 in a few days, but the union demanded his immediate dismissal. Shaw Stone fired him on the spot. Lopez complained to the National Labor Relations Board (NLRB), which brought unfair labor practice charges against the union. An administrative law judge ruled against the union, and the NLRB agreed. The union appealed. Was the union guilty of unfair labor practices under the National Labor Relations Act by having Lopez fired? Why or why not? [*Laborers' International Union of North America, Local 578 v. National Labor Relations Board,* 594 F.3d 732 (10th Cir. 2010)]

17–8. Workers' Compensation. As a safety measure, Dynea USA, Inc., required Tony Fairbanks, a millwright and company employee, to wear steel-toed boots. One afternoon, Fairbanks felt some discomfort on his left shin. At the end of the workday, he removed his boot, pulled his sock down, and saw a large red area below the top of the boot. Over the next two days, the red area became swollen and sore until Fairbanks had trouble walking. By the third day, the skin over the sore had broken. Within a week, Fairbanks was hospitalized with a methicillin-resistant *staphylococcus aureus* (MRSA) infection. Fairbanks notified Dynea and filed a workers' compensation claim. Dynea argued that the MRSA bacteria were on Fairbanks's skin before he came to work. What are the requirements to recover workers' compensation benefits? Does this claim qualify? Explain. [*In re Compensation of Fairbanks,* 241 Or.App. 311, 250 P.3d 389 (2011)]

17–9. A Question of Ethics. Workers' Compensation Law. *Beverly Tull had worked for Atchison Leather Products, Inc., in Kansas for ten years when, in 1999, she began to complain of hand, wrist, and shoulder pain. Atchison recommended that she contact a certain physician, who in April 2000 diagnosed the condition as carpal tunnel syndrome "severe enough" for surgery. In August, Tull filed a claim with the state workers' compensation board. Because Atchison changed workers' compensation insurance companies every year, a dispute arose as to which company should pay Tull's claim. Fearing liability, no insurer would authorize treatment, and Tull was forced to delay surgery until December. The board granted her temporary total disability benefits for the subsequent six weeks that she missed work. On April 23, 2002, Berger Co. bought Atchison. The new employer adjusted Tull's work to be less demanding and stressful, but she continued to suffer pain. In July, a physician diagnosed her condition as permanent. The board granted her permanent par-*

tial disability benefits. By May 2005, the bickering over the financial responsibility for Tull's claim involved five insurers—four of which had each covered Atchison for a single year and one of which covered Berger. [*Tull v. Atchison Leather Products, Inc.,* 37 Kan.App.2d 87, 150 P.3d 316 (2007)]

1. When an injured employee files a claim for workers' compensation, there is a proceeding to assess the injury and determine the amount of compensation. Should a dispute between insurers over the payment of the claim be resolved in the same proceeding? Why or why not?

2. The board designated April 23, 2002, as the date of Tull's injury. What is the reason for determining the date of a worker's injury? Should the board in this case have selected this date or a different date? Why?

3. How should the board assess liability for the payment of Tull's medical expenses and disability benefits? Would it be appropriate to impose joint and several liability on the insurers, or should the individual liability of each of them be determined? Explain.

17–10. **Video Question.** *Employment at Will.* Access the video using the instructions provided below to answer the following questions.

1. In the video, Laura asserts that she can fire Ray "for any reason. For no reason." Is this true? Explain your answer.

2. What exceptions to the employment-at-will doctrine are discussed in the chapter? Does Ray's situation fit into any of these exceptions?

3. Would Ray be protected from wrongful discharge under whistleblowing statutes? Why or why not?

4. Assume that you are the employer in this scenario. What arguments can you make that Ray should not be able to sue for wrongful discharge in this situation?

—To watch this video, go to **www.cengagebrain.com** and register the access code that came with your new book or log in to your existing account. Select the link for either the "Business Law Digital Video Library Online Access" or "Business Law CourseMate," and then click on "Complete Video List" to find the video for this chapter (Video 40).

Chapter 18

Employment Discrimination

> **"Equal rights for all, special privileges for none."**
>
> —**Thomas Jefferson, 1743–1826**
> (Third president of the United States, 1801–1809)

Contents

Chapter Objectives

After reading this chapter, you should be able to answer the following questions:

1. **Generally, what kind of conduct is prohibited by Title VII of the Civil Rights Act of 1964, as amended?**

2. **What is the difference between disparate-treatment discrimination and disparate-impact discrimination?**

3. **What remedies are available under Title VII of the 1964 Civil Rights Act, as amended?**

4. **What federal acts prohibit discrimination based on age and discrimination based on disability?**

5. **What are three defenses to claims of employment discrimination?**

Protected Class A group of persons protected by specific laws because of the group's defining characteristics. Under laws prohibiting employment discrimination, these characteristics include race, color, religion, national origin, gender, age, and disability.

Out of the 1960s civil rights movement to end racial and other forms of discrimination grew a body of law protecting employees against discrimination in the workplace. This protective legislation further eroded the employment-at-will doctrine, which was discussed in the previous chapter. In the past several decades, judicial decisions, administrative agency actions, and legislation have restricted the ability of both employers and unions to discriminate against workers on the basis of race, color, religion, national origin, gender, age, or disability. A class of persons defined by one or more of these criteria is known as a **protected class.** The laws designed to protect these individuals embody the sentiment expressed by Thomas Jefferson in the chapter-opening quotation.

One of the most talked-about cases in 2011 was the Wal-Mart gender discrimination case. A group of female employees sued Wal-Mart, the nation's largest private employer, alleging that store managers who had discretion over pay and promotions were biased against women and disproportionately favored men. The United States Supreme Court ruled in favor of Wal-Mart, effectively blocking the class action (a lawsuit in which a small group of plaintiffs sues on behalf of a larger group). The Court held that the women could not maintain a class action because they had failed to prove a company-wide policy of discrimination that had a common effect on all women covered by the class action.[1] This important decision may limit the rights of employees to sue their employers for job discrimination in a class action, but it does not change the rights of individuals to sue for employment discrimination.

Several federal statutes prohibit **employment discrimination** against members of protected classes. The most important statute is Title VII of the Civil Rights Act of 1964.[2] Title VII prohibits discrimination on the basis of race, color, religion, national origin, or gender at any stage of employment. The Age Discrimination in Employment Act of 1967[3] and the Americans with Disabilities Act of 1990[4] prohibit discrimination on the basis of age and disability, respectively.

This chapter focuses on the kinds of discrimination prohibited by these federal statutes. Note, though, that discrimination against employees on the basis of any of these criteria may also violate state human rights statutes or other state laws or public policies prohibiting discrimination.

Employment Discrimination Treating employees or job applicants unequally on the basis of race, color, national origin, religion, gender, age, or disability; prohibited by federal statutes.

▶ Title VII of the Civil Rights Act of 1964

Title VII of the Civil Rights Act of 1964 and its amendments prohibit job discrimination against employees, applicants, and union members on the basis of race, color, national origin, religion, or gender at any stage of employment. Title VII applies to employers with fifteen or more employees, labor unions with fifteen or more members, labor unions that operate hiring halls (to which members go regularly to be rationed jobs as they become available), employment agencies, and state and local governing units or agencies. A special section of the act prohibits discrimination in most federal government employment.

(Lyndon Baines Johnson Presidential Library and Museum)

President Lyndon B. Johnson signs the Civil Rights Act of 1964. Among the guests behind him is Martin Luther King, Jr.

The Equal Employment Opportunity Commission

Compliance with Title VII is monitored by the Equal Employment Opportunity Commission (EEOC). A victim of alleged discrimination must file a claim with the EEOC before bringing a suit against the employer. The EEOC may investigate the dispute and attempt to obtain the parties' voluntary consent to an out-of-court settlement. If a voluntary agreement cannot be reached, the EEOC may then file a suit against the employer on the employee's behalf. If the EEOC decides not to investigate the claim, the victim may bring her or his own lawsuit against the employer.

The EEOC does not investigate every claim of employment discrimination, regardless of the merits of the claim. Generally, it investigates only "priority cases," such as cases involving retaliatory discharge (firing an employee in retaliation for submitting a claim to the EEOC) and cases involving types of discrimination that are of particular concern to the EEOC.

---

1. *Wal-Mart Stores, Inc. v. Dukes,* ___ U.S. ___, 131 S.Ct. 2541, 180 L.Ed.2d 374 (2011).
2. 42 U.S.C. Sections 2000e–2000e-17.
3. 29 U.S.C. Sections 621–634.
4. 42 U.S.C. Sections 12102–12118.

Intentional and Unintentional Discrimination

Title VII prohibits both intentional and unintentional discrimination.

INTENTIONAL DISCRIMINATION   Intentional discrimination by an employer against an employee is known as **disparate-treatment discrimination.** Because intent may sometimes be difficult to prove, courts have established certain procedures for resolving disparate-treatment cases. Suppose that a woman applies for employment with a construction firm and is rejected. If she sues on the basis of disparate-treatment discrimination in hiring, she must show that (1) she is a member of a protected class, (2) she applied and was qualified for the job in question, (3) she was rejected by the employer, and (4) the employer continued to seek applicants for the position or filled the position with a person not in a protected class.

> **Disparate-Treatment Discrimination**
> A form of employment discrimination resulting when an employer intentionally discriminates against employees who are members of protected classes.

If the woman can meet these relatively easy requirements, she has made out a *prima facie* **case** of illegal discrimination. *Prima facie* is Latin for "at first sight." Legally, it refers to a fact that is presumed to be true unless contradicted by evidence. Making out a *prima facie* case of discrimination means that the plaintiff has met her initial burden of proof and will win in the absence of a legally acceptable employer defense. (Defenses will be discussed later in this chapter.) The burden then shifts to the employer-defendant, who must articulate a legal reason for not hiring the plaintiff. To prevail, the plaintiff must then show that the employer's reason is a *pretext* (not the true reason) and that discriminatory intent actually motivated the employer's decision.

> ***Prima Facie* Case**   A case in which the plaintiff has produced sufficient evidence of his or her claim that the case can go to a jury; a case in which the evidence compels a decision for the plaintiff if the defendant produces no affirmative defense or evidence to disprove the plaintiff's assertion.

UNINTENTIONAL DISCRIMINATION   Employers often use interviews and testing procedures to choose from among a large number of applicants for job openings. Minimum educational requirements are also common. These practices and procedures may have an unintended discriminatory impact on a protected class. (For tips on how human resources managers can prevent these types of discrimination claims, see the *Linking the Law to Management* feature on page 555.)

Disparate-impact discrimination occurs when a protected group of people is adversely affected by an employer's practices, procedures, or tests, even though they do not appear to be discriminatory. In a disparate-impact discrimination case, the complaining party must first show statistically that the employer's practices, procedures, or tests are discriminatory in effect. Once the plaintiff has made out a *prima facie* case, the burden of proof shifts to the employer to show that the practices or procedures in question were justified. There are two ways of proving that disparate-impact discrimination exists, as discussed next.

> **Disparate-Impact Discrimination**
> A form of employment discrimination that results from certain employer practices or procedures that, although not discriminatory on their face, have a discriminatory effect.

Pool of Applicants. A plaintiff can prove a disparate impact by comparing the employer's workforce with the pool of qualified individuals available in the local labor market. The plaintiff must show that as a result of educational or other job requirements or hiring procedures, the percentage of nonwhites, women, or members of other protected classes in the employer's workforce does not reflect the percentage of that group in the pool of qualified applicants. If a person challenging an employment practice can show a connection between the practice and the disparity, he or she has made out a *prima facie* case and need not provide evidence of discriminatory intent.

Rate of Hiring. A plaintiff can prove disparate-impact discrimination by comparing the selection rates of whites and nonwhites (or members of another protected class), regardless of the racial balance in the employer's workforce. When an educational or other job requirement or hiring procedure excludes members of a protected class from an employer's workforce at a substantially higher rate than nonmembers, discrimination exists.

The EEOC has devised a test, called the "four-fifths rule," to determine whether an employment examination is discriminatory on its face. Under this rule, a selection rate for protected classes that is less than four-fifths, or 80 percent, of the rate for the group with the highest rate will generally be regarded as evidence of disparate impact. **EXAMPLE 18.1** One hundred white applicants take an employment test, and fifty pass the test and are hired. One hundred minority applicants take the test, and twenty pass the test and are hired. Because twenty is less than four-fifths (80 percent) of fifty, the test would be considered discriminatory under the EEOC guidelines. •

Discrimination Based on Race, Color, and National Origin

Title VII prohibits employers from discriminating against employees or job applicants on the basis of race, color, or national origin. Although there has been some uncertainty in the federal courts about what constitutes race versus national origin discrimination, race is interpreted broadly to include the ancestry or ethnic characteristics of a group of persons, such as Native Americans. The national origin provisions make it unlawful to discriminate against persons based on their birth in another country, such as Iraq or the Philippines, or their ancestry or culture, such as Hispanic.

If an employer's standards or policies for selecting or promoting employees have a discriminatory effect on employees or job applicants in these protected classes, then a presumption of illegal discrimination arises. To avoid liability, the employer must then show that its standards or policies have a substantial, demonstrable relationship to realistic qualifications for the job in question.

CASE EXAMPLE 18.2 Jiann Min Chang was an instructor at Alabama Agricultural and Mechanical University (AAMU). When AAMU terminated his employment, Chang filed a lawsuit claiming discrimination based on national origin. Chang established a *prima facie* case because he (1) was a member of a protected class, (2) was qualified for the job, (3) suffered an adverse employment action, and (4) was replaced by someone outside his protected class (a non-Asian instructor). When the burden of proof shifted to the employer, however, AAMU showed that Chang had argued with a university vice president and refused to comply with her instructions. The court ruled that the university had not renewed Chang's contract for a legitimate reason—insubordination—and therefore was not liable for unlawful discrimination.[5] •

REVERSE DISCRIMINATION Note that discrimination based on race can also take the form of *reverse discrimination*, or discrimination against "majority group" individuals, such as white males. **CASE EXAMPLE 18.3** An African American woman fired four white men from their management positions at a school district. The men filed a lawsuit for racial discrimination, alleging that the woman was trying to eliminate white males from the department. The woman claimed that the terminations were part of a reorganization plan to cut costs in the department. The jury sided with the men and awarded them nearly $3 million in damages. The verdict was upheld on appeal (though the damages award was reduced slightly).[6] •

---

5. *Jiann Min Chang v. Alabama Agricultural and Mechanical University,* 2009 WL 3403180 (11th Cir. 2009).
6. *Johnston v. School District of Philadelphia,* ___ F.Supp.2d ___ (E.D.Pa. 2006).

In 2009, the United States Supreme Court issued a decision that will have a significant impact on disparate-impact and reverse discrimination litigation. Employers may find the application of the ruling somewhat confusing, however, because the Court found that an employer had engaged in reverse discrimination when it discarded test results in an attempt to avoid unlawful discrimination.

CASE EXAMPLE 18.4   The fire department in New Haven, Connecticut, administered a test to determine which firefighters were eligible for promotions. No African Americans and only two Hispanic firefighters passed the test. Fearing that it would be sued for racial discrimination if it used the test results for promotions, the city refused to certify (and basically discarded) the results. The white firefighters (and one Hispanic) who had passed the test then sued the city, claiming reverse discrimination. The lower courts found in favor of the city, but the United States Supreme Court reversed. The Court held that an employer can engage in intentional discrimination to remedy an unintentional disparate impact only if the employer has "a strong basis in evidence" to believe that it will be successfully sued for disparate-impact discrimination "if it fails to take the race-conscious, discriminatory action." Mere fear of litigation was not a sufficient reason for the city to discard its test results.[7] Subsequently, the city certified the test results and promoted the firefighters. ●

POTENTIAL "SECTION 1981" CLAIMS   Victims of racial or ethnic discrimination may also have a cause of action under 42 U.S.C. Section 1981. This section, which was enacted as part of the Civil Rights Act of 1866 to protect the rights of freed slaves, prohibits discrimination on the basis of race or ethnicity in the formation or enforcement of contracts. Because employment is often a contractual relationship, Section 1981 can provide an alternative basis for a plaintiff's action and is potentially advantageous because it does not place a cap on damages.

Discrimination Based on Religion

Title VII of the Civil Rights Act of 1964 also prohibits government employers, private employers, and unions from discriminating against persons because of their religion. Employers cannot treat their employees more or less favorably based on their religious beliefs or practices and cannot require employees to participate in any religious activity (or forbid them from participating in one). **EXAMPLE 18.5**   Three fifty-year-old men are dismissed from their jobs at a Florida car dealership. The men file a complaint with the EEOC alleging religious and age discrimination. They claim that the employer targeted them for not attending the weekly prayer meetings held at the dealership. If the men can show that the dealership required its employees to attend prayer gatherings and fired the men for not attending, they will have a valid case of religious discrimination. ●

An employer must "reasonably accommodate" the religious practices of its employees, unless to do so would cause undue hardship to the employer's business. If an employee's religion prohibits him or her from working on a certain day of the week or at a certain type of job, for instance, the employer must make a reasonable attempt to accommodate these religious requirements. Employers must reasonably accommodate an employee's religious belief even if the belief is not based on the doctrines of a traditionally recognized religion, such as Christianity or

Two Muslims perform religious prayers in Nashville, Tennessee. Under Title VII of the Civil Rights Act, do employers have to accommodate the religious practices of their employees?

(AP Photo/The Tennessean/Eric Parsons)

---

7. *Ricci v. DeStefano,* ___ U.S. ___, 129 S.Ct. 2658, 174 L.Ed.2d 490 (2009).

Judaism, or a denomination, such as Baptist. The only requirement is that the belief be sincerely held by the employee.

Discrimination Based on Gender

Under Title VII, as well as other federal acts (including the Equal Pay Act of 1963, which we also discuss here), employers are forbidden from discriminating against employees on the basis of gender. Employers are prohibited from classifying jobs as male or female and from advertising in help-wanted columns that are designated male or female unless the employer can prove that the gender of the applicant is essential to the job. Employers also cannot have separate male and female seniority lists or refuse to promote employees based on gender.

Generally, to succeed in a suit for gender discrimination, a plaintiff must demonstrate that gender was a determining factor in the employer's decision to fire or refuse to hire or promote her or him. Typically, this involves looking at all of the surrounding circumstances.

CASE EXAMPLE 18.6 Turner Industries Group contracted to provide maintenance services and labor at a fertilizer plant owned by Agrium Conda Phosphate Industries. Wanda Collier worked for Turner at the plant. In 2008, Collier informed both her supervisor at Turner and her supervisor at Agrium, David Eastridge, that Jack Daniell, Agrium's head of maintenance, had berated her and treated her unfairly. Eastridge told Collier that Daniell was "old school," had a problem with Collier's gender, and was harder on women. He spoke with Daniell about Collier's allegations, but concluded that the dispute was based on factors other than gender. A month later, Daniell confronted Collier again, pushed her up against a wall and berated her. Collier immediately reported this incident to her supervisors and filed formal complaints of gender discrimination at both Turner and Agrium. Turner offered to transfer her to another position, but she rejected the offer. A month later, Collier was fired. When she subsequently filed a gender discrimination suit in an Idaho district court, the court concluded that there was enough evidence that gender was a determining factor in Daniell's conduct to allow Collier's claims to go to a jury.[8] ●

PREGNANCY DISCRIMINATION The Pregnancy Discrimination Act of 1978,[9] which amended Title VII, expanded the definition of gender discrimination to include discrimination based on pregnancy. Women affected by pregnancy, childbirth, or related medical conditions must be treated—for all employment-related purposes, including the receipt of benefits under employee benefit programs—the same as other persons not so affected but similar in ability to work.

EQUAL PAY ACT The Equal Pay Act of 1963, which amended the Fair Labor Standards Act of 1938 (discussed in Chapter 17), prohibits employers from gender-based wage discrimination. For the act's equal pay requirements to apply, the male and female employees must work at the same establishment doing similar work (a barber and a beautician, for example). To determine whether the Equal Pay Act has been violated, a court will look to the primary duties of the two jobs. It is the job content rather than the job description that controls in all cases. If a court finds that the wage differential is due to any factor other than gender, such as a seniority or merit system, then it does not violate the Equal Pay Act.

> "A sign that says 'men only' looks very different on a bathroom door than a courthouse door."
>
> Thurgood Marshall, 1908–1993
> (Associate Justice of the United States Supreme Court, 1967–1991)

---

8. *Collier v. Turner Industries Group, LLC*, 2011 WL 2517020 (D. Idaho 2011).
9. 42 U.S.C. Section 2000e(k).

President Barack Obama signed the Lilly Ledbetter Fair Pay Act in 2009. Who benefits from this law?

Constructive Discharge   A termination of employment brought about by making the employee's working conditions so intolerable that the employee reasonably feels compelled to leave.

2009 EQUAL PAY LEGISLATION   Forty-five years after the Equal Pay Act was enacted, there was still a significant gap between the wages earned by male and female employees. Women in the United States typically earn about three-quarters of what men earn. This continuing disparity prompted Congress to pass the Paycheck Fairness Act of 2009, which closed some of the loopholes in the Equal Pay Act. Because the courts had interpreted the defense of "any factor other than gender" so broadly, employers had been able to justify alleged wage discrimination simply by not using the word *gender* or *sex*. The Paycheck Fairness Act clarified employers' defenses and prohibited the use of gender-based differentials in assessing an employee's education, training, or experience. The act also provided additional remedies for wage discrimination, including compensatory and punitive damages, which are available as remedies for discrimination based on race and national origin.

In 2009, Congress also overturned a 2007 decision by the United States Supreme Court, which had required a plaintiff alleging wage discrimination to file a complaint within 180 days of the decision that set the discriminatory pay.[10] Congress rejected this limit when it enacted the Lilly Ledbetter Fair Pay Act of 2009.[11] The act made discriminatory wages actionable under federal law regardless of when the discrimination began. Each time a person is paid discriminatory wages, benefits, or other compensation, a cause of action arises (and the plaintiff has 180 days from that date to file a complaint). In other words, if a plaintiff continues to work for the employer while receiving discriminatory wages, the time period for filing a complaint is basically unlimited.

Constructive Discharge

The majority of Title VII complaints involve unlawful discrimination in decisions to hire or fire employees. In some situations, however, employees who leave their jobs voluntarily can claim that they were "constructively discharged" by the employer. **Constructive discharge** occurs when the employer causes the employee's working conditions to be so intolerable that a reasonable person in the employee's position would feel compelled to quit.

PROVING CONSTRUCTIVE DISCHARGE   The plaintiff must present objective proof of intolerable working conditions, which the employer knew or had reason to know about yet failed to correct within a reasonable time period. Courts generally also require the employee to show causation—that the employer's unlawful discrimination caused the working conditions to be intolerable. Put a different way, the employee's resignation must be a foreseeable result of the employer's discriminatory action.

    EXAMPLE 18.7   Khalil's employer humiliates him in front of his co-workers by informing him that he is being demoted to an inferior position. Khalil's co-workers then continually insult and harass him about his national origin (he is from Iran). The employer is aware of this discriminatory treatment but does nothing to remedy the situation, despite repeated complaints from Khalil. After several months, Khalil quits his job and files a Title VII claim. In this situation, Khalil would likely have sufficient evidence to maintain an action for constructive discharge in violation of Title VII. ● Although courts weigh the facts on a case-by-case basis, employee demotion is one of the most frequently cited reasons for a finding of constructive discharge, particularly when the employee was subjected to humiliation.

---

10. *Ledbetter v. Goodyear Tire Co.,* 550 U.S. 618, 127 S.Ct. 2162, 167 L.Ed.2d 982 (2007).
11. Pub. L. No. 111-2, 123 Stat. 5 (January 5, 2009), amending 42 U.S.C. Section 2000e-5[e].

A federal jury decided that Madison Square Garden in New York City had to pay $11.6 million in damages for sexual harassment to fired executive Anucha Browne Sanders (center).

Sexual Harassment In the employment context, the demanding of sexual favors in return for job promotions or other benefits, or language or conduct that is so sexually offensive that it creates a hostile working environment.

APPLIES TO ALL TITLE VII DISCRIMINATION Note that constructive discharge is a theory that plaintiffs can use to establish any type of discrimination claims under Title VII, including race, color, national origin, religion, gender, pregnancy, and sexual harassment. Constructive discharge has also been successfully used in situations that involve discrimination based on age or disability (both of which will be discussed later in this chapter). Constructive discharge is most commonly asserted in cases involving sexual harassment, however.

When constructive discharge is claimed, the employee can pursue damages for loss of income, including back pay. These damages ordinarily are not available to an employee who left a job voluntarily.

Sexual Harassment

Title VII also protects employees against **sexual harassment** in the workplace. Sexual harassment can take two forms: *quid pro quo* harassment and hostile-environment harassment. *Quid pro quo* is a Latin phrase that is often translated to mean "something in exchange for something else." *Quid pro quo* harassment occurs when sexual favors are demanded in return for job opportunities, promotions, salary increases, and the like. According to the United States Supreme Court, hostile-environment harassment occurs when "the workplace is permeated with discriminatory intimidation, ridicule, and insult, that is sufficiently severe or pervasive to alter the conditions of the victim's employment and create an abusive working environment."[12]

The courts determine whether the sexually offensive conduct was sufficiently severe or pervasive as to create a hostile environment on a case-by-case basis. Typically, a single incident of sexually offensive conduct is not enough to create a hostile environment (although there have been exceptions when the conduct was particularly objectionable). Note also that if the employee who is alleging sexual harassment has signed an arbitration clause (see Chapter 3 on page 79), she or he will most likely be required to arbitrate the claim.[13]

Preventing Legal Disputes

To avoid sexual-harassment complaints, you should be proactive in preventing sexual harassment in the workplace. Establish written policies, distribute them to employees, and review them annually. Make it clear that the policies prohibiting harassment and discrimination apply to everyone at all levels of your organization. Provide training. Assure employees that no one will be punished for making a complaint. If you receive complaints, always take them seriously and investigate—no matter how trivial they might seem. Prompt remedial action is key, but it must not include any adverse action against the complainant (such as immediate termination). Also, never discourage employees from seeking the assistance of government agencies (such as the EEOC) or threaten or punish them for doing so. It is generally best to obtain the advice of counsel when you receive a serious sexual-harassment complaint.

HARASSMENT BY SUPERVISORS For an employer to be held liable for a supervisor's sexual harassment, the supervisor normally must have taken a tangible

---

12. *Harris v. Forklift Systems,* 510 U.S. 17, 114 S.Ct. 367, 126 L.Ed.2d 295 (1993). See also *Billings v. Town of Grafton,* 515 F.3d 39 (1st Cir. 2008).
13. See, for example, *EEOC v. Cheesecake Factory, Inc.,* 2009 WL 1259359 (D.Ariz. 2009).

Tangible Employment Action
A significant change in employment status, such as a change brought about by firing or failing to promote an employee; reassigning the employee to a position with significantly different responsibilities; or effecting a significant change in employment benefits.

employment action against the employee. A **tangible employment action** is a significant change in employment status or benefits, such as when an employee is fired, refused a promotion, demoted, or reassigned to a position with significantly different responsibilities. Only a supervisor, or another person acting with the authority of the employer, can cause this sort of injury. A constructive discharge also qualifies as a tangible employment action.[14]

THE *ELLERTH/FARAGHER* AFFIRMATIVE DEFENSE   In 1998, the United States Supreme Court issued several important rulings that have had a lasting impact on cases alleging sexual harassment by supervisors.[15] The Court held that an employer (a city) was liable for a supervisor's harassment of employees even though the employer was unaware of the behavior. Although the city had a written policy against sexual harassment, it had not distributed the policy to its employees and had not established any complaint procedures for employees who felt that they had been sexually harassed. In another case, the Court held that an employer can be liable for a supervisor's sexual harassment even though the employee does not suffer adverse job consequences.

The Court's decisions in these cases established what has become known as the "*Ellerth/Faragher* affirmative defense" to charges of sexual harassment. The defense has two elements:

1. That the employer has taken reasonable care to prevent and promptly correct any sexually harassing behavior (by establishing effective antiharassment policies and complaint procedures, for example).
2. That the plaintiff-employee unreasonably failed to take advantage of any preventive or corrective opportunities provided by the employer to avoid harm.

An employer that can prove both elements will not be liable for a supervisor's harassment.

RETALIATION BY EMPLOYERS   Employers sometimes retaliate against employees who complain about sexual harassment or other Title VII violations. Retaliation can take many forms. An employer might demote or fire the person, or otherwise change the terms, conditions, and benefits of his or her employment. Title VII prohibits retaliation, and employees can sue their employers. In a *retaliation claim,* an individual asserts that she or he has suffered a harm as a result of making a charge, testifying, or participating in a Title VII investigation or proceeding.

Plaintiffs do not have to prove that the challenged action adversely affected their workplace or employment.[16] Instead, to prove retaliation, plaintiffs must show that the challenged action was one that would likely have dissuaded a reasonable worker from making or supporting a charge of discrimination. In 2009, the United States Supreme Court ruled that Title VII's retaliation protection extends to an employee who speaks out about discrimination not on her or his own initiative, but in answering questions during an employer's internal investigation of another employee's complaint.[17]

---

14. See, for example, *Pennsylvania State Police v. Suders,* 542 U.S. 129, 124 S.Ct. 2342, 159 L.Ed.2d 204 (2004).
15. *Burlington Industries, Inc. v. Ellerth,* 524 U.S. 742, 118 S.Ct. 2257, 141 L.Ed.2d 633 (1998); and *Faragher v. City of Boca Raton,* 524 U.S. 775, 118 S.Ct. 2275, 141 L.Ed.2d 662 (1998).
16. *Burlington Northern and Santa Fe Railroad Co. v. White,* 548 U.S. 53, 126 S.Ct. 2405, 165 L.Ed.2d 345 (2006).
17. *Crawford v. Metropolitan Government of Nashville and Davidson County, Tennessee,* 555 U.S. 271, 129 S.Ct. 846, 172 L.Ed.2d 650 (2009).

In the following case, an employee was fired after his fiancée filed a gender discrimination claim against their employer. The United States Supreme Court had to decide whether the employer's firing of this employee constituted unlawful retaliation under Title VII.

Case 18.1 Thompson v. North American Stainless, LP

Supreme Court of the United States, ____ U.S. ____, 131 S.Ct. 863, 178 L.Ed.2d 694 (2011).
www.supremecourt.gov/opinions/10pdf/09-291.pdf [a]

BACKGROUND AND FACTS Eric Thompson and his fiancée, Miriam Regalado, were employees of North American Stainless, LP (NAS). In February 2003, Regalado filed a gender discrimination claim against NAS with the Equal Employment Opportunity Commission (EEOC). Three weeks later, NAS fired Thompson. Thompson then filed a claim with the EEOC. After conciliation efforts proved unsuccessful, he sued NAS in a U.S. district court, alleging violations of Title VII of the Civil Rights Act of 1964. Thompson claimed that NAS had fired him in retaliation for Regalado's complaint to the EEOC. The district court granted summary judgment for NAS, concluding that Title VII "does not permit third-party retaliation claims." Thompson appealed. The U.S. Court of Appeals for the Sixth Circuit affirmed the district court's decision. Thompson appealed again, and the United States Supreme Court granted *certiorari*.

IN THE WORDS OF THE COURT . . .
SCALIA, J. [Justice], delivered the opinion of the Court.
* * * *

* * * We have little difficulty concluding that if the facts alleged by Thompson are true, then NAS's firing of Thompson violated Title VII. In [a prior Supreme Court case] we held that Title VII's antiretaliation provision must be construed to cover a broad range of employer conduct. We reached that conclusion by contrasting the text of Title VII's antiretaliation provision with its substantive antidiscrimination provision. Title VII prohibits discrimination on the basis of race, color, religion, sex, and national origin "'with respect to . . . compensation, terms, conditions, or privileges of employment,'" and discriminatory practices that would "'deprive any individual of employment opportunities or otherwise adversely affect his status as an employee.'" In contrast, Title VII's antiretaliation provision prohibits an employer from "'discriminat[ing] against any of his employees'" for engaging in protected conduct, without specifying the employer acts that are prohibited. Based on this textual distinction and our understanding of the antiretaliation provision's purpose, we held that "the antiretaliation provision, unlike the substantive provision, is not limited to discriminatory actions that affect the terms and conditions of employment." Rather, *Title VII's antiretaliation provision prohibits any employer action that "well might have dissuaded a reasonable worker from making or supporting a charge of discrimination."* [Emphasis added.]

We think it obvious that a reasonable worker might be dissuaded from engaging in protected activity if she knew that her fiancé would be fired. Indeed, NAS does not dispute that Thompson's firing meets the standard set forth in [the Supreme Court precedent]. NAS raises the concern, however, that prohibiting reprisals against third parties will lead to difficult line-drawing problems concerning the types of relationships entitled to protection.

Although we acknowledge the force of this point, we do not think it justifies a categorical rule that third-party reprisals do not violate Title VII. As explained above, we adopted a broad standard in [the prior case] because Title VII's antiretaliation provision is worded broadly. *We think there is no textual basis for making an exception to it for third-party reprisals, and a preference for clear rules cannot justify departing from statutory text.* [Emphasis added.]
* * * *

The judgment of the Sixth Circuit is reversed, and the case is remanded for further proceedings consistent with this opinion.

DECISION AND REMEDY The United States Supreme Court ruled that Title VII's antiretaliation provision covers a broad range of employer conduct, including third party retaliation claims. The Court therefore remanded the case for a determination of the facts. If the facts were as Thompson alleged, then NAS's firing of Thompson had violated Title VII.

THE LEGAL ENVIRONMENT DIMENSION *Does it matter to Thompson's retaliation case whether his fiancée's claim of gender discrimination against NAS was successful? Explain.*

MANAGERIAL IMPLICATIONS *This case is important for business owners and managers because it illustrates the broad coverage of Title VII's antiretaliation provision. Any company that employs more than one member of a family must be very careful not to retaliate against one family member for legally protected actions taken by another family member. Many companies try to avoid potential problems by establishing a policy of not hiring relatives of employees. This may not always be feasible, however, particularly for employers in smaller cities, where many family members may work at the same local company. In addition, it may not be practical for large multinational corporations that employ thousands of workers. Furthermore, such a policy would not have avoided the problems that arose in this case because the employees were not married and thus were not "family." Business owners and managers therefore need to be aware of the potential for litigation if they retaliate against an employee based on another employee's conduct.*

---

a. The United States Supreme Court provides this URL, which goes directly to a PDF file of this case opinion.

HARASSMENT BY CO-WORKERS AND NONEMPLOYEES   When harassment by co-workers, rather than supervisors, creates a hostile working environment, an employee may still have a cause of action against the employer. Normally, though, the employer will be held liable only if the employer knew, or should have known, about the harassment and failed to take immediate remedial action.

Occasionally, a court may also hold an employer liable for harassment by *nonemployees* if the employer knew about the harassment and failed to take corrective action. **EXAMPLE 18.8**   Gordon, who owns and manages a Great Bites restaurant, knows that one of his regular customers, Dean, repeatedly harasses Sharon, a waitress. If Gordon does nothing and permits the harassment to continue, he may be liable under Title VII even though Dean is not an employee of the restaurant. •

SAME-GENDER HARASSMENT   In *Oncale v. Sundowner Offshore Services, Inc.,*[18] the United States Supreme Court held that Title VII protection extends to situations in which individuals are sexually harassed by members of the same gender. Proving that the harassment in same-gender cases is "based on sex" can be difficult, though. It is easier to establish a case of same-gender harassment when the harasser is homosexual.

CASE EXAMPLE 18.9   James Tepperwien was a security officer for three years at a nuclear power plant owned by Entergy Nuclear Operations. During that time, Tepperwien twice reported to his superiors that Vito Messina, another security officer who allegedly was gay, had sexually harassed him. After the first incident, Entergy made all the security officers read and sign its no-tolerance antiharassment policy. After the second incident, Messina was placed on administrative leave for ten weeks. After Messina returned to work, Tepperwien was disciplined for failing to report some missing equipment. He then filed another harassment complaint and quit his job, claiming that he had been constructively discharged and that Entergy had not taken sufficient steps to prevent further harassment.

The court noted that a male victim of same-gender harassment must show that he was harassed because he was male. The court found that Tepperwien had presented credible evidence that Messina was a homosexual and had made sexual advances toward other security officers. This evidence was sufficient to establish a *prima facie* case of hostile-environment sexual harassment, allowing the case to go to trial, but it was not enough to show the intolerable conditions required for a finding of constructive discharge.[19] •

Although federal law (Title VII) does not prohibit discrimination or harassment based on a person's sexual orientation, a growing number of states have enacted laws that prohibit sexual orientation discrimination in private employment. Also, many companies have voluntarily established nondiscrimination policies that include sexual orientation. (Workers in the United States often have more protection against sexual harassment in the workplace than workers in other countries, as this chapter's *Beyond Our Borders* feature on the facing page explains.)

Online Harassment

Employees' online activities can create a hostile working environment in many ways. Racial jokes, ethnic slurs, or other comments contained in e-mail, text or instant messages, and blog posts can become the basis for a claim of hostile-environment

> "*Sexual harassment at work: Is it a problem for the self-employed?*"
>
> Victoria Wood, 1953–present
> (English comedian and actor)

---

18. 523 U.S. 75, 118 S.Ct. 998, 140 L.Ed.2d 207 (1998).
19. *Tepperwien v. Entergy Nuclear Operations, Inc.,* 606 F.Supp.2d 427 (S.D.N.Y. 2009).

The problem of sexual harassment in the workplace is not confined to the United States. Indeed, it is a worldwide problem for female workers. In Argentina, Brazil, Egypt, Turkey, and many other countries, there is no legal protection against any form of employment discrimination.

Even in those countries that do have laws prohibiting discriminatory employment practices, including gender-based discrimination, those laws often do not specifically include sexual harassment as a discriminatory practice. Several countries have attempted to remedy this omission by passing new laws or amending others to specifically prohibit sexual harassment in the workplace. Japan, for example, has amended its Equal Employment Opportunity Law to include a provision making sexual harassment illegal.

Thailand has also passed its first sexual-harassment law.

The European Union has adopted a directive that specifically identifies sexual harassment as a form of discrimination. Nevertheless, women's groups throughout Europe contend that corporations in European countries tend to view sexual harassment with "quiet tolerance." They contrast this attitude with that of most U.S. corporations, which have implemented specific procedures to deal with harassment claims.

Sexual harassment continues to be a persistent problem, in part, because some people do not consider unwanted sexual advances toward women in the workplace to be sexual harassment. In addition, women who have been subjected to sexual advances by men in positions of power may

be reluctant to come forward with their claims. For example, in 2011 U.S. authorities arrested Dominique Strauss-Kahn, then the head of the International Monetary Fund and a prominent French politician, for allegedly assaulting an immigrant hotel maid in New York. Only after his arrest in New York did reports that Strauss-Kahn had been making unwanted sexual advances to female employees for years appear in France. Two French women who had worked for Strauss-Kahn between 2007 and 2010 filed sexual-harassment claims against him.

For Critical Analysis
Why do you think U.S. corporations are more aggressive than European companies in taking steps to prevent sexual harassment in the workplace?

harassment or other forms of discrimination. A worker who sees sexually explicit images on a co-worker's computer screen may find the images offensive and claim that they create a hostile working environment.

Nevertheless, employers may be able to avoid liability for online harassment by taking prompt remedial action. **CASE EXAMPLE 18.10** While working at WorldCom Corporation, Angela Daniels received racially harassing e-mailed jokes from another employee. Shortly afterward, the company issued a warning to the offending employee about the proper use of the e-mail system and held two meetings to discuss company policy on the use of the system. When Daniels sued WorldCom for racial discrimination, a federal district court concluded that the employer was not liable for its employee's racially harassing e-mails because the employer took prompt remedial action.[20] ●

Remedies under Title VII

Employer liability under Title VII may be extensive. If the plaintiff successfully proves that unlawful discrimination occurred, he or she may be awarded reinstatement, back pay, retroactive promotions, and damages. Compensatory damages are available only in cases of intentional discrimination. Punitive damages may be recovered against a private employer only if the employer acted with malice or reckless indifference to an individual's rights. The statute limits the total amount of compensatory and

---

20. *Daniels v. WorldCom Corp.*, 1998 WL 91261 (N.D.Tex. 1998). See also *Musgrove v. Mobil Oil Corp.*, 2003 WL 21653125 (N.D.Tex. 2003).

punitive damages that the plaintiff can recover from specific employers—ranging from $50,000 against employers with one hundred or fewer employees to $300,000 against employers with more than five hundred employees.

▶ Discrimination Based on Age

"Growing old is like being increasingly penalized for a crime you have not committed."

Anthony Powell, 1905–2000
(English novelist)

Age discrimination is potentially the most widespread form of discrimination, because anyone—regardless of race, color, national origin, or gender—could be a victim at some point in life. The Age Discrimination in Employment Act (ADEA) of 1967, as amended, prohibits employment discrimination on the basis of age against individuals forty years of age or older. The act also prohibits mandatory retirement for nonmanagerial workers. For the act to apply, an employer must have twenty or more employees, and the employer's business activities must affect interstate commerce. The EEOC administers the ADEA, but the act also permits private causes of action against employers for age discrimination.

The ADEA includes a provision that extends protections against age discrimination to federal government employees.[21] In 2008, the United States Supreme Court ruled that this provision encompasses not only claims of age discrimination, but also claims of retaliation for complaining about age discrimination, which are not specifically mentioned in the statute.[22] Thus, the ADEA protects federal and private-sector employees from retaliation based on age-related complaints.

Procedures under the ADEA

REMEMBER The Fourteenth Amendment prohibits any state from denying any person "the equal protection of the laws." This prohibition applies to the *federal* government through the due process clause of the Fifth Amendment.

The burden-shifting procedure under the ADEA differs from the procedure under Title VII as a result of a United States Supreme Court decision in 2009, which dramatically changed the burden of proof in age discrimination cases.[23] As explained earlier, if the plaintiff in a Title VII case can show that the employer was motivated, at least in part, by unlawful discrimination, the burden of proof shifts to the employer to articulate a legitimate nondiscriminatory reason. Thus, in cases in which the employer has a "mixed motive" for discharging an employee, the employer has the burden of proving its reason was legitimate.

Under the ADEA, in contrast, a plaintiff must show that the unlawful discrimination was not just a reason but *the* reason for the adverse employment action. In other words, the employee has the burden of establishing "but for" causation—that is, that age discrimination was the reason for the adverse decision. Thus, to establish a *prima facie* case, the plaintiff must show that he or she (1) was a member of the protected age group, (2) was qualified for the position from which he or she was discharged, and (3) was discharged because of age discrimination. Then the burden shifts to the employer. If the employer offers a legitimate reason for its action, then the plaintiff must show that the stated reason is only a pretext and that the plaintiff's age was the real reason for the employer's decision. The following case illustrates this procedure.

---

21. See 29 U.S.C. Section 632(a) (2000 ed., Supp. V).
22. *Gomez-Perez v. Potter,* 553 U.S. 474, 128 S.Ct. 1931, 170 L.Ed.2d 887 (2008).
23. *Gross v. FBL Financial Services,* ___ U.S. ___, 129 S.Ct. 2343, 174 L.Ed.2d 119 (2009).

Case 18.2   Mora v. Jackson Memorial Foundation, Inc.

United States Court of Appeals, Eleventh Circuit, 597 F.3d 1201 (2010).
www.ca11.uscourts.gov/opinions/search.php[a]

How can a company legally fire a sixty-two-year old employee because of her failing job performance without being accused of firing her because of her age?

BACKGROUND AND FACTS

Josephine Mora was sixty-two years old when she was fired from her job as a fund-raiser for Jackson Memorial Foundation, Inc. Mora's supervisor became dissatisfied with Mora's work and recommended that she be fired. The foundation's chief executive officer, Mr. Rodriguez, agreed. Later, however, Rodriguez decided to give Mora a different position in his office "where he could observe her more closely." Mora worked with Rodriguez for a month, and more errors and issues with professionalism supposedly arose. Mora contended that when Rodriguez fired her, he told her, "I need someone younger I can pay less." A former employee stated that she had heard this conversation, adding that she heard Rodriguez say to Mora, "You are very old; you are very inept. I need somebody younger that I can pay less and I can control." Another former employee stated that Rodriguez told her and another employee that Mora was "too old to be working here anyway." Rodriguez denied that he made these statements, and one of the employees substantiated Rodriguez's version of events. Mora sued the foundation in a federal district court for wrongful termination under the Age Discrimination in Employment Act (ADEA). The foundation moved for summary judgment, arguing that regardless of the discrimination issue, Mora still would have been terminated for poor job performance. The district court granted the motion, and Mora appealed.

IN THE WORDS OF THE COURT . . .
PER CURIAM [By the Whole Court].

* * * *

After Plaintiff [Mora] appealed, the Supreme Court, in *Gross v. FBL Financial Services,* clarified the nature of ADEA claims. The Supreme Court concluded that ADEA claims are not subject to the burden-shifting protocol set forth for Title VII suits in *Price Waterhouse v. Hopkins.*[b] The ADEA requires that "age [be] the reason that the employer decided to act." *Because an ADEA plaintiff must establish "but for" causality, no "same decision" affirmative defense [the argument that the same decision—to fire someone, for example— would have been made regardless of alleged discrimination] can*

exist: the employer either acted "because of" the plaintiff's age or it did not. [Emphasis added.]

Because the Supreme Court has excluded the whole idea of a "mixed motive" ADEA claim—and the corresponding "same decision" defense— we need not consider the district court's analysis of Defendant's [the foundation's] affirmative defense. Instead, * * * we look to determine whether a material factual question exists on this record about whether Defendant discriminated against her. We say "Yes."

* * * *

A plaintiff in an ADEA claim may "establish a claim of illegal age discrimination through either direct evidence or circumstantial evidence." Plaintiff's testimony that Rodriguez fired her because she was "too old" was substantiated by the affidavits of two other employees of Defendant. Rodriguez and [another employee] testified that no such comments were made * * *.

The resolution of this case depends on whose account of the pertinent conversations a jury would credit. We conclude that a reasonable juror could accept that Rodriguez made the discriminatory-sounding remarks and that the remarks are sufficient evidence of a discriminatory motive which was the "but for" cause of Plaintiff's dismissal. Summary judgment for Defendant was therefore incorrect.

We have considered cases factually similar to Plaintiff's. In [one case], we concluded that statements from a county official who "didn't want to hire any old pilots" were direct evidence of discrimination * * *. In [another case], we likewise concluded that an employer's statement that he wanted "aggressive, young men like himself to be promoted" was circumstantial evidence of discrimination.

While these cases were litigated under the now-defunct ADEA mixed motive theory, they remain instructive. Plaintiff's situation is similar. A reasonable juror could find that Rodriguez's statements should be taken at face value and that he fired Plaintiff because of her age.

DECISION AND REMEDY   The U.S. Court of Appeals for the Eleventh Circuit vacated (set aside) the decision of the trial court and remanded the case for further proceedings. Because there was a "disputed question of material fact" as to whether Mora had been fired because of her age, Jackson Memorial was not entitled to summary judgment.

THE ETHICAL DIMENSION   *Is the court's decision fair to employers? Why or why not?*

MANAGERIAL IMPLICATIONS   *Business owners and supervisory personnel should be careful to avoid statements regarding an employee's age that may sound discriminatory. If the employee later has to be dismissed due to poor performance, comments about his or her age may become the basis for an age discrimination lawsuit.*

---

a. In the "Search by Case Number or Docket Number:" box, enter "08-16113." In the search results, click on the File Name link to access the opinion. The U.S. Court of Appeals for the Eleventh Circuit maintains this Web site.

b. 490 U.S. 228, 109 S.Ct. 1775, 104 L.Ed.2d 268 (1989).

State Employees Not Covered by the ADEA

Generally, the states are immune from lawsuits brought by private individuals in federal court—unless a state consents to the suit. This immunity stems from the United States Supreme Court's interpretation of the Eleventh Amendment (the text of this amendment is included in Appendix B). **CASE EXAMPLE 18.11** In two Florida cases, professors and librarians contended that their employers—two Florida state universities—denied them salary increases and other benefits because they were getting old and their successors could be hired at lower cost. The universities claimed that as agencies of a sovereign state, they could not be sued in federal court without the state's consent. The cases ultimately reached the United States Supreme Court, which held that the Eleventh Amendment bars private parties from suing state employers for violations of the ADEA.[24] ●

State immunity under the Eleventh Amendment is not absolute, however, as the Supreme Court explained in 2004. In some situations, such as when fundamental rights are at stake, Congress has the power to abolish state immunity to private suits through legislation that unequivocally shows Congress's intent to subject states to private suits.[25] As a general rule, though, the Court has found that state employers are immune from private suits brought by employees under the ADEA (for age discrimination, as noted above), the Americans with Disabilities Act[26] (for disability discrimination), and the Fair Labor Standards Act[27] (which relates to wages and hours). In contrast, states are not immune from the requirements of the Family and Medical Leave Act.[28]

ⓞ Discrimination Based on Disability

The Americans with Disabilities Act (ADA) of 1990 was designed to eliminate discriminatory employment practices that prevent otherwise qualified workers with disabilities from fully participating in the national labor force. The ADA prohibits disability-based discrimination in workplaces with fifteen or more workers (with the exception of state government employers, who are generally immune under the Eleventh Amendment, as just discussed). Basically, the ADA requires that employers "reasonably accommodate" the needs of persons with disabilities unless to do so would cause the employer to suffer an "undue hardship." In 2008, Congress enacted the ADA Amendments Act,[29] which broadened the coverage of the ADA's protections, as will be discussed shortly.

Procedures under the ADA

To prevail on a claim under the ADA, a plaintiff must show that he or she (1) has a disability, (2) is otherwise qualified for the employment in question, and (3) was excluded from the employment solely because of the disability. As in Title VII cases, a plaintiff must pursue her or his claim through the EEOC before filing an action in

> *"Jobs are physically easier, but the worker now takes home worries instead of an aching back."*
>
> Homer Bigart, 1907–1991
> (American journalist)

---

24. *Kimel v. Florida Board of Regents,* 528 U.S. 62, 120 S.Ct. 631, 145 L.Ed.2d 522 (2000).

25. *Tennessee v. Lane,* 541 U.S. 509, 124 S.Ct. 1978, 158 L.Ed.2d 820 (2004).

26. *Board of Trustees of the University of Alabama v. Garrett,* 531 U.S. 356, 121 S.Ct. 955, 148 L.Ed.2d 866 (2001).

27. *Alden v. Maine,* 527 U.S. 706, 119 S.Ct. 2240, 144 L.Ed.2d 636 (1999).

28. *Nevada Department of Human Resources v. Hibbs,* 538 U.S. 721, 123 S.Ct. 1972, 155 L.Ed.2d 953 (2003).

29. 42 U.S.C. Sections 12103 and 12205a.

Co-workers discuss business matters. What is a disability under the Americans with Disabilities Act?

court for a violation of the ADA. The EEOC may decide to investigate and perhaps even sue the employer on behalf of the employee. If the EEOC decides not to sue, then the employee is entitled to sue in court.

Significantly, the United States Supreme Court held in 2002 that the EEOC could bring a suit against an employer for disability-based discrimination even though the employee had agreed to submit any job-related disputes to arbitration (see Chapter 3). The Court reasoned that because the EEOC was not a party to the arbitration agreement, the agreement was not binding on the EEOC.[30]

Plaintiffs in lawsuits brought under the ADA may obtain many of the same remedies available under Title VII. These include reinstatement, back pay, a limited amount of compensatory and punitive damages (for intentional discrimination), and certain other forms of relief. Repeat violators may be ordered to pay fines of up to $100,000.

What Is a Disability?

The ADA is broadly drafted to cover persons with a wide range of disabilities. Specifically, the ADA defines *disability* as "(1) a physical or mental impairment that substantially limits one or more of the major life activities of such individuals; (2) a record of such impairment; or (3) being regarded as having such an impairment." Health conditions that have been considered disabilities under the federal law include blindness, alcoholism, heart disease, cancer, muscular dystrophy, cerebral palsy, paraplegia, diabetes, acquired immune deficiency syndrome (AIDS), testing positive for the human immunodeficiency virus (HIV), and morbid obesity (defined as existing when an individual's weight is twice the normal weight for his or her height). The ADA excludes from coverage certain conditions, such as kleptomania (the obsessive desire to steal).

The Supreme Court Narrowly Interpreted the ADA   Although the ADA's definition of disability is broad, rulings by the United States Supreme Court from 1999 to 2007 interpreted that definition narrowly and made it harder for employees to establish a disability under the act. In 1999, the Court held that severe myopia, or nearsightedness, which can be corrected with lenses, does not qualify as a disability under the ADA.[31] In 2002, the Court held that repetitive-stress injuries (such as carpal tunnel syndrome) ordinarily do not constitute a disability under the ADA.[32] After that, the courts began focusing on how the person functioned when using corrective devices or taking medication, not on how the person functioned without these measures.[33]

2008 Amendments Reverse Prior Supreme Court Cases   In response to the Supreme Court's limiting decisions, Congress decided to amend the ADA in 2008. Basically, the amendments reverse the Court's restrictive interpretation of disability under the ADA and prohibit employers from considering mitigating measures

---

30. *EEOC v. Waffle House, Inc.,* 534 U.S. 279, 122 S.Ct. 754, 151 L.Ed.2d 755 (2002).

31. *Sutton v. United Airlines, Inc.,* 527 U.S. 471, 119 S.Ct. 2139, 144 L.Ed.2d 450 (1999).

32. *Toyota Motor Manufacturing, Kentucky, Inc. v. Williams,* 534 U.S. 184, 122 S.Ct. 681, 151 L.Ed.2d 615 (2002). This ruling was invalidated by the 2008 amendments to the ADA.

33. See, for example, *Orr v. Wal-Mart Stores, Inc.,* 297 F.3d 720 (8th Cir. 2002).

or medications when determining if an individual has a disability. In other words, disability is now determined on a case-by-case basis.

A condition may fit the definition of disability in one set of circumstances, but not in another. What makes the difference in an individual situation? The court in the following case answered that question.

Case 18.3   **Rohr v. Salt River Project Agricultural Improvement and Power District**

United States Court of Appeals, Ninth Circuit, 555 F.3d 850 (2009).
www.ca9.uscourts.gov[a]

Is diabetes a disability under the Americans with Disabilities Act?

HISTORICAL AND SOCIAL SETTING   *Diabetes is a chronic and incurable disease associated with an increased risk of heart disease, stroke, high blood pressure, blindness, kidney disease, nervous system disease, amputations, dental disease, complications of pregnancy, and sexual dysfunction. Type 1 diabetes, or juvenile diabetes, results from the body's failure to produce insulin—a hormone that is needed to convert food into energy. Type 2 results from the body's failure to properly use insulin. If left untreated, type 2 can cause seizures and a coma. In the United States, approximately 23.6 million children and adults, or 7.8 percent of the population, suffer from diabetes.*

BACKGROUND AND FACTS   Larry Rohr has type 2 diabetes. He tires quickly and suffers from high blood pressure, deteriorating vision, and loss of feeling in his hands and feet. Insulin injections, other medicine, blood tests, and a strict diet are fixtures of his daily life. If he fails to follow this regimen, his blood sugar rises to a level that aggravates his disease. At the time of his diagnosis, he was a welding metallurgy specialist for the Salt River Project Agricultural Improvement and Power District, which provides utility services to homes in Arizona. Due to the effort required to manage his diabetes, particularly his strict diet schedule, Rohr's physician forbade his assignment to tasks involving overnight, out-of-town travel. Salt River told Rohr that this would prevent him from performing the essential functions of his job, such as responding to power outages. Rohr was asked to transfer, apply for disability benefits, or take early retirement. He filed a suit in a federal district court against Salt River, alleging discrimination. The court issued a summary judgment in the employer's favor. Rohr appealed.

IN THE WORDS OF THE COURT . . .
BAER, Senior District Judge:
    * * * *

The ADA defines "disability," in pertinent part, as "a physical or mental impairment that substantially limits one or more of the major

life activities of such individual." Diabetes is a "physical impairment" because it affects the digestive, hemic [blood] and endocrine systems, and eating is a "major life activity." Whether Rohr's diabetes substantially limits his eating is an individualized inquiry. *Once an impairment is found, the issue is whether Rohr's diabetes substantially limits his activity of eating.* [Emphasis added.]
    * * * *

To determine whether an insulin-dependent type 2 diabetic like Rohr is substantially limited in his eating, we must compare the condition, manner or duration under which he can eat as compared to the condition, manner or duration under which the average person in the general population can eat.
    * * * *

Finally, we must consider not only whether the symptoms of Rohr's diabetes substantially limit one of his major life activities, but also whether his efforts to mitigate [diminish] the disease constitute a substantial limitation.
    * * * *

* * * For people like Rohr, who must treat their diabetes with insulin, the failure to take insulin will result in severe problems and eventually death. Insulin injections themselves can be dangerous. * * * It is difficult to determine how much insulin to take, as the necessary amount varies depending on the food and activity level. * * * To obtain the appropriate balance, Rohr must test his blood glucose levels * * * numerous times a day.

If daily insulin injections alone more or less stabilized Rohr's blood sugar levels, such that any limitation imposed on his diet would be minor, then Rohr's major life activity of eating might not be substantially limited. However, [there are] substantial limitations on his eating in spite of his medicine and insulin. He must snack regularly, plan his daily schedule around his diet, avoid skipping meals and eat immediately when he feels dizzy or light-headed. * * * Straying from a diet for more than one or two meals is not a cause for medical concern for most people, and skipping a meal, or eating a large one, does not expose them to the risk of fainting. * * * For Rohr, the effort required to control his diet is itself substantially limiting.

DECISION AND REMEDY   The U.S. Court of Appeals for the Ninth Circuit vacated the lower court's judgment and remanded the case for trial. Diabetes satisfies the ADA's definition of *disability* if it significantly restricts an individual's eating habits.

---

a. In the left-hand column, in the "Opinions" pull-down menu, click on "Published." On that page, click on "Advanced Search." In the "by Case No.:" box, type "06-16527" and click on "Search." In the result, click on the case title to access the opinion.

Case 18.3–Continued

THE E-COMMERCE DIMENSION   *If Rohr could have monitored his condition and regimen through a cell phone or other portable Internet connection, would the result in this case likely have been affected? Explain.*

THE LEGAL ENVIRONMENT DIMENSION   *Salt River argued that type 1 diabetes is harder to control than Rohr's type 2 diabetes. Assuming this is true, would it support a conclusion that Rohr does not suffer from a disability? Why or why not?*

Reasonable Accommodation

The ADA does not require that employers accommodate the needs of job applicants or employees with disabilities who are not otherwise qualified for the work. If a job applicant or an employee with a disability, with reasonable accommodation, can perform essential job functions, however, the employer must make the accommodation. Required modifications may include installing ramps for a wheelchair, establishing more flexible working hours, creating or modifying job assignments, and creating or improving training materials and procedures. Generally, employers should give primary consideration to employees' preferences in deciding what accommodations should be made.

UNDUE HARDSHIP   Employers who do not accommodate the needs of persons with disabilities must demonstrate that the accommodations would cause "undue hardship" in terms of being significantly difficult or expensive for the employer. Usually, the courts decide whether an accommodation constitutes an undue hardship on a case-by-case basis by looking at the employer's resources in relation to the specific accommodation.

EXAMPLE 18.12   Bryan Lockhart, who uses a wheelchair, works for a cell phone company that provides parking for its employees. Lockhart informs the company supervisors that the parking spaces are so narrow that he is unable to extend the ramp on his van that allows him to get in and out of the vehicle. Lockhart therefore requests that the company reasonably accommodate his needs by paying a monthly fee for him to use a larger parking space in an adjacent lot. In this situation, a court would likely find that it would not be an undue hardship for the employer to pay for additional parking for Lockhart. •

JOB APPLICATIONS AND PREEMPLOYMENT PHYSICAL EXAMS   Employers must modify their job-application process so that those with disabilities can compete for jobs with those who do not have disabilities. For instance, a job announcement might be modified to allow job applicants to respond by e-mail or letter, as well as by telephone, so that it does not discriminate against potential applicants with hearing impairments.

Employers are restricted in the kinds of questions they may ask on job-application forms and during preemployment interviews. Furthermore, they cannot require persons with disabilities to submit to preemployment physicals unless such exams are required of all other applicants. An employer can condition an offer of employment on the applicant's successfully passing a medical examination, but can disqualify the applicant only if the exam reveals medical problems that would render the applicant unable to perform the job.

CASE EXAMPLE 18.13   When filling the position of delivery truck driver, a company cannot screen out all applicants who are unable to meet the U.S. Department of Transportation's hearing standard. The company would first have to prove that

This paraplegic employee has a customized van that he parks in the handicap parking area outside his workplace. In general, providing such parking for employees who have a disability is considered a reasonable accommodation that employers must make.

(Paul Tople/MCT/Landov)

DON'T FORGET Preemployment screening procedures must be applied equally to all job applicants.

drivers who are deaf are not qualified to perform the essential job function of driving safely and pose a higher risk of accidents than drivers who are not deaf.[34] ● (For more on interviewing job applicants with disabilities, see the *Management Perspective* feature below.)

SUBSTANCE ABUSERS Drug addiction is a disability under the ADA because drug addiction is a substantially limiting impairment. Those who are actually using illegal drugs are not protected by the act, however. The ADA protects only persons with *former* drug addictions—those who have completed or are now in a supervised drug-rehabilitation program. Individuals who have used drugs casually in the past are not

---

34. *Bates v. United Parcel Service, Inc.*, 465 F.3d 1069 (9th Cir. 2006).

Management Perspective Interviewing Job Applicants with Disabilities

Management Faces a Legal Issue

Many employers have been held liable under the Americans with Disabilities Act because they have asked the wrong questions when interviewing job applicants with disabilities. The Equal Employment Opportunity Commission (EEOC) has issued guidelines about questions that employers may or may not ask job applicants with disabilities. For example, an interviewer may ask a job applicant whether he or she can meet the company's attendance requirements. In contrast, the interviewer cannot ask how many days a person was sick in the previous year. An employer can ask an applicant whether he or she can do the job, but not how he or she would do the job unless the disability is obvious, the applicant brings up the subject during the interview, or the employer asks the question of all applicants for that particular job. After a job offer is made, the employer is allowed to ask the applicant questions concerning her or his disability, including questions about previous workers' compensation claims or the extent of, say, a drinking or drug problem.

What the Courts Say

In one case, a job applicant suffered from a hearing impairment. He alleged that the potential employer discriminated against him because of his disability when he applied for a position as an information technology specialist. At trial, one of the key issues was how the interview was conducted. The interviewer claimed that he had no concerns about the applicant's deafness. But at one point during the interview, the interviewer passed a handwritten note asking the applicant, "How do you communicate in offices where no one can sign?" The applicant responded, "I have no problem with

writing as my basic communication." The court pointed out that the interviewer did not ask this question of any other applicant. Although the applicant ultimately did not prevail at trial, the court made it clear that the interviewer should not have asked the applicant any special questions.[a]

In another case, an applicant sued the federal government after applying for the position of bank examiner. He claimed that during an interview, there was an improper inquiry about his perceived disability. In fact, the applicant had previously suffered a stroke and slurred his words when he spoke. During the interview, he was asked what was wrong with his arm and whether his disability affected his mental coherence. Ultimately, the applicant lost his case because he had lied on his résumé. Nonetheless, the defendants would have had an easier time at trial had the interviewer followed the EEOC guidelines.[b]

Implications for Managers

When preparing for job interviews, most managers should consult with an attorney who specializes in employment issues. In particular, they should review the kinds of questions typically asked of job applicants during interviews or following employment offers. Any questions that increase the risk of a lawsuit from an applicant with disabilities must be altered. All questions should be consistent with EEOC guidelines. Anyone who interviews job applicants should be informed about what questions can and cannot be asked of candidates with disabilities. Note, however, that once a job has been offered, a manager is allowed to ask the candidate for his or her medical documents in order to verify the nature of the applicant's disability.

---

a. *Adeyemi v. District of Columbia*, 2007 WL 1020754 (D.C.Cir. 2007).
b. *Strong v. Paulson*, 2007 WL 2859789 (7th Cir. 2007). See also *Lorah v. Tetra Tech, Inc.*, 541 F.Supp.2d 629 (D.Del. 2008).

protected under the act. They are not considered addicts and therefore do not have a disability (addiction).

People suffering from alcoholism are protected by the ADA. Employers cannot legally discriminate against employees simply because they are suffering from alcoholism. Of course, employers have the right to prohibit the use of alcohol in the workplace and can require that employees not be under the influence of alcohol while working. Employers can also fire or refuse to hire a person who is an alcoholic if he or she poses a substantial risk of harm either to himself or herself or to others and the risk cannot be reduced by reasonable accommodation.

HEALTH INSURANCE PLANS　Workers with disabilities must be given equal access to any health insurance provided to other employees. Employers can exclude from coverage preexisting health conditions and certain types of diagnostic or surgical procedures, though. An employer can also put a limit, or cap, on health-care payments under its group health policy—as long as such caps are "applied equally to all insured employees" and do not "discriminate on the basis of disability." Whenever a group health-care plan makes a disability-based distinction in its benefits, the plan violates the ADA (unless the employer can justify its actions under the *business necessity* defense, which will be discussed shortly).

Association Discrimination

The ADA contains an "association provision" that protects qualified individuals from employment discrimination based on an identified disability of a person with whom the qualified individual is known to have a relationship or an association.[35] The purpose of this provision is to prevent employers from taking adverse employment actions based on stereotypes or assumptions about individuals who associate with people who have disabilities. An employer cannot, for instance, refuse to hire the parent of a child with a disability based on the assumption that the person will miss work too often or be unreliable.

To establish a *prima facie* case of association discrimination under the ADA, the plaintiff must show that she or he (1) was qualified for the job, (2) was subjected to an adverse employment action, and (3) was known by her or his employer to have a relative or an associate with a disability. In addition, the plaintiff must show that the adverse employment action occurred under circumstances raising a reasonable inference that the disability of the relative or associate was a determining factor in the employer's decision.

CASE EXAMPLE 18.14　Randall Francin had worked at Mosby, Inc., for twelve years before his wife was diagnosed with amyotrophic lateral sclerosis (Lou Gehrig's disease). He discussed his rights for leave under the Family and Medical Leave Act (see Chapter 17) with a company representative. Early in 2004, Francin received a "merit award increase" in salary and subsequently discussed his wife's illness with his supervisor. In September 2004, Francin was fired. Francin filed a lawsuit claiming that Mosby had discriminated against him because of his association with a person with a disability. Although the trial court granted a summary judgment for Mosby, the appellate court found that there was sufficient evidence that Francin's wife's illness was a contributing factor to his termination for the case to go to trial. Thus, summary judgment was inappropriate.[36] ●

---

35. 42 U.S.C. Section 12112(b)(4).

36. *Francin v. Mosby, Inc.*, 248 S.W.3d 619 (Mo. 2008).

Defenses to Employment Discrimination

The first line of defense for an employer charged with employment discrimination is, of course, to assert that the plaintiff has failed to meet his or her initial burden of proving that discrimination occurred. Once a plaintiff succeeds in proving that discrimination occurred, the burden shifts to the employer to justify the discriminatory practice. Often, employers attempt to justify the discrimination by claiming that it was the result of a business necessity, a bona fide occupational qualification, or a seniority system. In some cases, as noted earlier, an effective antiharassment policy and prompt remedial action when harassment occurs may shield employers from liability for sexual harassment under Title VII.

Business Necessity

Business Necessity   A defense to allegations of employment discrimination in which the employer demonstrates that an employment practice that discriminates against members of a protected class is related to job performance.

An employer may defend against a claim of disparate-impact (unintentional) discrimination by asserting that a practice that has a discriminatory effect is a **business necessity.** **EXAMPLE 18.15**   If requiring a high school diploma is shown to have a discriminatory effect, an employer might argue that a high school education is necessary for workers to perform the job at a required level of competence. If the employer can demonstrate to the court's satisfaction that a definite connection exists between a high school education and job performance, the employer normally will succeed in this business necessity defense. ●

Bona Fide Occupational Qualification

Bona Fide Occupational Qualification (BFOQ)   Identifiable characteristics reasonably necessary to the normal operation of a particular business. These characteristics can include gender, national origin, and religion, but not race.

Another defense applies when discrimination against a protected class is essential to a job—that is, when a particular trait is a **bona fide occupational qualification (BFOQ).** Race, however, can never be a BFOQ. Generally, courts have restricted the BFOQ defense to instances in which the employee's gender is essential to the job. **EXAMPLE 18.16**   A women's clothing store might legitimately hire only female sales attendants if part of an attendant's job involves assisting clients in the store's dressing rooms. Similarly, the Federal Aviation Administration can legitimately impose age limits for airline pilots— but an airline cannot impose weight limits only on female flight attendants. ●

Seniority Systems

Seniority System   In regard to employment relationships, a system in which those who have worked longest for the employer are first in line for promotions, salary increases, and other benefits. They are also the last to be laid off if the workforce must be reduced.

An employer with a history of discrimination might have no members of protected classes in upper-level positions. Even if the employer now seeks to be unbiased, it may face a lawsuit in which the plaintiff asks a court to order that minorities be promoted ahead of schedule to compensate for past discrimination. If no present intent to discriminate is shown, however, and if promotions or other job benefits are distributed according to a fair **seniority system** (in which workers with more years of service are promoted first or laid off last), the employer normally has a good defense against the suit.

According to the United States Supreme Court, this defense may also apply to alleged discrimination under the ADA. The case involved a baggage handler who had injured his back and requested an assignment to a different position at U.S. Airways, Inc. The airline refused to give the employee the position because another employee had seniority. The Court sided with U.S. Airways. If an employee with a disability requests an accommodation that conflicts with an employer's seniority system, the accommodation generally will not be considered "reasonable" under the act.[37]

---

37. *U.S. Airways, Inc. v. Barnett,* 535 U.S. 391, 122 S.Ct. 1516, 152 L.Ed.2d 589 (2002).

After-Acquired Evidence of Employee Misconduct

In some situations, employers have attempted to avoid liability for employment discrimination on the basis of "after-acquired evidence"—that is, evidence that the employer discovers after a lawsuit is filed—of an employee's misconduct. **EXAMPLE 18.17** An employer fires a worker who then sues the employer for employment discrimination. During pretrial investigation, the employer learns that the employee made material misrepresentations on his employment application—misrepresentations that, had the employer known about them, would have served as grounds to fire the individual. ●

According to the United States Supreme Court, after-acquired evidence of wrongdoing cannot be used to shield an employer entirely from liability for employment discrimination. It may, however, be used to limit the amount of damages for which the employer is liable.[38]

 ## Affirmative Action

Federal statutes and regulations providing for equal opportunity in the workplace were designed to reduce or eliminate discriminatory practices with respect to hiring, retaining, and promoting employees. **Affirmative action** programs go a step further and attempt to "make up" for past patterns of discrimination by giving members of protected classes preferential treatment in hiring or promotion. During the 1960s, all federal and state government agencies, private companies that contracted to do business with the federal government, and institutions that received federal funding were required to implement affirmative action policies.

Title VII of the Civil Rights Act of 1964 neither requires nor prohibits affirmative action. Thus, most private firms have not been required to implement affirmative action policies, though many have voluntarily done so. Affirmative action programs have been controversial, however, particularly when they have resulted in reverse discrimination (discussed on page 535).

Affirmative Action Job-hiring policies that give special consideration to members of protected classes in an effort to overcome present effects of past discrimination.

Constitutionality of Affirmative Action Programs

Because of their inherently discriminatory nature, affirmative action programs may violate the equal protection clause of the Fourteenth Amendment to the U.S. Constitution. The United States Supreme Court has held that any federal, state, or local affirmative action program that uses racial or ethnic classifications as the basis for making decisions is subject to strict scrutiny by the courts.[39] Recall from Chapter 4 that strict scrutiny is the highest standard, which means that most programs do not survive a court's analysis under this test.

Today, an affirmative action program normally is constitutional only if it attempts to remedy past discrimination and does not make use of quotas or preferences. Furthermore, once such a program has succeeded in the goal of remedying past discrimination, it must be changed or dropped.

---

38. *McKennon v. Nashville Banner Publishing Co.,* 513 U.S. 352, 115 S.Ct. 879, 130 L.Ed.2d 852 (1995).

39. See the landmark decision in *Adarand Constructors, Inc. v. Peña,* 515 U.S. 200, 115 S.Ct. 2097, 132 L.Ed.2d 158 (1995).

Some high schools in Seattle, Washington, make their student selections based on diversity criteria, rather than solely on past scholastic achievement. Under what circumstances is this constitutional?

Affirmative Action in Schools

Most of the affirmative action cases that have reached the United States Supreme Court in the last twenty years have been in the context of university admissions programs and schools, rather than employment. Generally, the Court has found that a school admissions policy that *automatically* awards minority applicants a specified number of points needed to guarantee admission violates the equal protection clause.[40] A school can, however, "consider race or ethnicity more flexibly as a 'plus' factor in the context of individualized consideration of each and every applicant."[41] In other words, it is unconstitutional for schools to apply a mechanical formula that gives "diversity bonuses" based on race or ethnicity.

CASE EXAMPLE 18.18   In 2007, the United States Supreme Court ruled on two cases involving the use of racial classifications in assigning students to schools in Seattle, Washington, and Jefferson County, Kentucky. Both school districts had adopted student assignment plans that relied on race to determine which schools certain children would attend. The Seattle school district plan classified children as "white" or "nonwhite" and used the racial classifications as a "tiebreaker" to determine which high school the students would attend. The school district in Jefferson County classified students as "black" or "other" to assign children to elementary schools. Parent groups from the relevant public schools filed lawsuits claiming that the racial preferences violated the equal protection clause. The Court held that the school districts failed to show that the use of racial classifications in their student assignment plans was necessary to achieve their stated goal of racial diversity. Hence, the Court found that the affirmative action programs of both school districts were unconstitutional.[42] ●

---

40. *Gratz v. Bollinger,* 539 U.S. 244, 123 S.Ct. 2411, 156 L.Ed.2d 257 (2003).
41. *Grutter v. Bollinger,* 539 U.S. 306, 123 S.Ct. 2325, 156 L.Ed.2d 304 (2003).
42. The Court consolidated the two cases and issued one opinion for both. See *Parents Involved in Community Schools v. Seattle School District No. 1,* 551 U.S. 701, 127 S.Ct. 2738, 168 L.Ed.2d 508 (2007).

 Reviewing . . . Employment Discrimination

Amaani Lyle, an African American woman, took a job as a scriptwriters' assistant at Warner Television Productions. She worked for the writers of *Weeds,* a popular, adult-oriented television series. One of her essential job duties was to type detailed notes for the scriptwriters during brainstorming sessions in which they discussed jokes, dialogue, and story lines. The writers then combed through Lyle's notes after the meetings for script material. During these meetings, the three male scriptwriters told lewd and vulgar jokes and made sexually explicit comments and gestures. They often talked about their personal sexual experiences and fantasies, and some of these conversations were then used in episodes of *Weeds.*

During the meetings, Lyle never complained that she found the writers' conduct offensive. After four months, she was fired because she could not type fast enough to keep up with the writers' conversations during the meetings. She filed a suit against Warner alleging sexual harassment and claiming that her termination was based on racial discrimination. Using the information presented in the chapter, answer the following questions.

1. Would Lyle's claim of racial discrimination be for intentional (disparate treatment) or unintentional (disparate impact) discrimination? Explain.
2. Can Lyle establish a *prima facie* case of racial discrimination? Why or why not?
3. Lyle was told when she was hired that typing speed was extremely important to her position. At the time, she

maintained that she could type eighty words per minute, so she was not given a typing test. It later turned out that Lyle could type only fifty words per minute. What impact might typing speed have on Lyle's lawsuit?

4. Lyle's sexual-harassment claim is based on the hostile work environment created by the writers' sexually offensive conduct at meetings that she was required to attend. The writers, however, argue that their behavior was essential to the "creative process" of writing *Weeds*, a show that routinely contained sexual innuendos and adult humor. Which defense discussed in the chapter might Warner assert using this argument?

Linking the Law *to Management*
Human Resource Management Comes to the Fore

In the good old days (at least according to company old-timers), the boss determined that the company needed additional workers. Then the boss would put an ad in the newspaper, interview job applicants, and pick the ones he or she liked. If the new hires did not work out, they would simply be fired, and the process would start over again. In big companies, a personnel officer would do the hiring and firing. In other words, for much of the business history of the United States, there were no rules, regulations, or laws that placed constraints on the hiring or firing process.

As you learned in this chapter, in today's business environment an ill-conceived hiring and firing process can result in a company facing a discrimination lawsuit in court. Moreover, managers today have to make sure that those who work under them do not engage in discriminatory behavior while on the job. Enter the human resource management specialist.

What Is Human Resource Management?

Human resource management (HRM) encompasses the activities required to acquire, maintain, and develop an organization's employees. HRM involves the design and application of formal systems in an organization to ensure the effective and efficient use of human talent to accomplish organizational goals.

Some of you reading this may eventually work in a human resources department. If so, you will need to be aware of the legal issues that you learned in this chapter (and in Chapters 16 and 17). In addition, all managers in large organizations have to be skilled in the basics of HRM. So-called flat organizations require that managers play an active role in recruiting and selecting the right personnel, as well as developing effective training programs.

The Acquisition Phase of HRM

Acquiring talented employees is the first step in an HRM system. All recruitment must be done without violating any of the laws and regulations outlined in this chapter. Obviously, recruitment must be color-blind, as well as indifferent to gender, religion, national origin, and age. A skilled HRM professional must devise recruitment methods that do not have even the slightest hint of discriminatory basis. Recruitment methods must also give an equal chance to people with disabilities. If a candidate with a disability must be rejected, the HRM professional must make sure that the rejection is based on the applicant's lack of training or ability, not on his or her disability.

On-the-Job HRM Issues

In addition, the HRM professional must monitor the on-the-job working environment. As you learned in this chapter, if some employees harass a co-worker, the courts could decide that such actions constituted constructive discharge. Sexual harassment is another major issue to consider. An HRM professional must work closely with an employment law specialist to develop a set of antiharassment rules and make sure that all employees are familiar with them. In addition, the HRM professional must create and supervise a grievance system so that any harassment can be stopped before it becomes actionable.

HRM Issues Concerning Employee Termination

In many states, employment is at will. In principle, a company can fire any employee for cause or no cause at any time. In reality, even in employment-at-will jurisdictions, lawsuits can arise for improper termination. An informed HRM specialist will develop a system to protect her or his company from termination lawsuits. There should be well-documented procedures that outline how the company will deal with an employee's improper or incompetent behavior. The company should also have an established policy about the amount of severance pay that terminated employees will receive. Sometimes, it is better to err on the side of generosity to maintain the goodwill of terminated employees.

FOR CRITICAL ANALYSIS

What are some types of actions that an HRM professional can take to reduce the probability of harassment lawsuits against her or his company?

Key Terms

affirmative action 553
bona fide occupational
  qualification (BFOQ) 552
business necessity 552
constructive discharge 538

disparate-impact discrimination 534
disparate-treatment discrimination 534
employment discrimination 533
prima facie case 534
protected class 532

seniority system 552
sexual harassment 539
tangible employment action 540

Chapter Summary: Employment Discrimination

Title VII of the Civil Rights Act of 1964 (See pages 533–544.)	Title VII prohibits employment discrimination based on race, color, national origin, religion, or gender. 1. *Procedures*—Employees must file a claim with the Equal Employment Opportunity Commission (EEOC). The EEOC may sue the employer on the employee's behalf. If it does not, the employee may sue the employer directly. 2. *Types of discrimination*—Title VII prohibits both intentional (disparate-treatment) and unintentional (disparate-impact) discrimination. Disparate-impact discrimination occurs when an employer's practice, such as hiring only persons with a certain level of education, has the effect of discriminating against a class of persons protected by Title VII. Title VII also extends to discriminatory practices, such as various forms of harassment, in the online environment. 3. *Remedies for discrimination under Title VII*—If a plaintiff proves that unlawful discrimination occurred, he or she may be awarded reinstatement, back pay, and retroactive promotions. Damages (both compensatory and punitive) may be awarded for intentional discrimination.
Discrimination Based on Age (See pages 544–546.)	The Age Discrimination in Employment Act (ADEA) of 1967 prohibits employment discrimination on the basis of age against individuals forty years of age or older. Procedures for bringing a case under the ADEA are similar to those for bringing a case under Title VII.
Discrimination Based on Disability (See pages 546–551.)	The Americans with Disabilities Act (ADA) of 1990 prohibits employment discrimination against persons with disabilities who are otherwise qualified to perform the essential functions of the jobs for which they apply. 1. *Procedures and remedies*—To prevail on a claim under the ADA, the plaintiff must show that she or he has a disability, is otherwise qualified for the employment in question, and was excluded from the employment solely because of the disability. Procedures under the ADA are similar to those required in Title VII cases. Remedies are also similar to those under Title VII. 2. *Definition of disability*—The ADA defines *disability* as a physical or mental impairment that substantially limits one or more major life activities, a record of such impairment, or being regarded as having such an impairment. 3. *Reasonable accommodation*—Employers are required to reasonably accommodate the needs of persons with disabilities. Reasonable accommodations may include altering job-application procedures, modifying the physical work environment, and permitting more flexible work schedules. Employers are not required to accommodate the needs of all workers with disabilities.
Defenses to Employment Discrimination (See pages 552–553.)	If a plaintiff proves that employment discrimination occurred, employers may avoid liability by successfully asserting certain defenses. Employers may assert that the discrimination was required for reasons of business necessity, to meet a bona fide occupational qualification, or to maintain a legitimate seniority system. Evidence of prior employee misconduct acquired after the employee has been fired is not a defense to discrimination.
Affirmative Action (See pages 553–554.)	Affirmative action programs attempt to "make up" for past patterns of discrimination by giving members of protected classes preferential treatment in hiring or promotion.

ExamPrep

ISSUE SPOTTERS

1. Ruth is a supervisor for Subs & Suds, a restaurant. Tim is a Subs & Suds employee. The owner announces that some employees will be discharged. Ruth tells Tim that if he has sex with her, he can keep his job. Is this sexual harassment? Why or why not?
2. Koko, a person with a disability, applies for a job at Lively Sales Corporation for which she is well qualified, but she is rejected. Lively continues to seek applicants and eventually fills the position with a person who does not have a disability. Could Koko succeed in a suit against Lively for discrimination? Explain.

—**Check your answers to these questions against the answers provided in Appendix G.**

BEFORE THE TEST

Go to **www.cengagebrain.com**, enter the ISBN number "9781111530617," and click on "Find" to locate this textbook's Web site. Then, click on "Access Now" under "Study Tools," and select "Chapter 18" at the top. There you will find an "Interactive Quiz" that you can take to assess your mastery of the concepts in this chapter, as well as "Flashcards" and a "Glossary" of important terms.

 For Review

1. Generally, what kind of conduct is prohibited by Title VII of the Civil Rights Act of 1964, as amended?
2. What is the difference between disparate-treatment discrimination and disparate-impact discrimination?
3. What remedies are available under Title VII of the 1964 Civil Rights Act, as amended?
4. What federal acts prohibit discrimination based on age and discrimination based on disability?
5. What are three defenses to claims of employment discrimination?

 Questions and Case Problems

18–1. Title VII Violations. Discuss fully whether either of the following actions would constitute a violation of Title VII of the 1964 Civil Rights Act, as amended.
1. Tennington, Inc., is a consulting firm and has ten employees. These employees travel on consulting jobs in seven states. Tennington has an employment record of hiring only white males.
2. Novo Films, Inc., is making a film about Africa and needs to employ approximately one hundred extras for this picture. To hire these extras, Novo advertises in all major newspapers in Southern California. The ad states that only African Americans need apply.

18–2. Religious Discrimination. When Kayla Caldwell got a job as a cashier at a Costco store, she wore multiple pierced earrings and had four tattoos, but she had no facial piercings. Over the next two years, Caldwell engaged in various forms of body modification, including facial piercing and cutting. Then Costco revised its dress code to prohibit all facial jewelry, except earrings. Caldwell was told that she would have to remove her facial jewelry. She asked for a complete exemption from the code, asserting that she was a member of the Church of Body Modification and that eyebrow piercing was part of her religion. She was told to remove the jewelry, cover it, or go home. She went home and was later discharged for her absence. Based on these facts, will Caldwell be successful in a lawsuit against Costco for religious discrimination in violation of Title VII? Does an employer have an obligation to accommodate its employees' religious practices? If so, to what extent?

18–3. Discrimination Based on Disability. Cerebral palsy limits Steven Bradley's use of his legs. He uses forearm crutches for short-distance walks and a wheelchair for longer distances. Standing for more than ten or fifteen minutes is difficult. With support, however, Bradley can climb stairs and get on and off a stool. His condition also restricts the use of his fourth finger to, for example, type, but it does not limit his ability to write—he completed two years of college. His grip strength is normal, and he can lift heavy objects. In 2001, Bradley applied for a "greeter" or "cashier" position at a Wal-Mart Stores, Inc., Supercenter in Richmond, Missouri. The job descriptions stated, "No experience or qualification is required." Bradley indicated that he was available for full- or part-time work from 4:00 P.M. to 10:00 P.M. any evening. His employment history showed that he was working as a proofreader and that he had previously worked as an administrator. His application was rejected, according to Janet Daugherty, the personnel manager, based on his "work history" and the "direct threat" that he posed to the safety of himself and others. Bradley claimed, however, that the store refused to hire him due to his disability. What steps must Bradley follow to pursue his claim? What does he need to show to prevail? Is he likely to meet these requirements? Discuss. [*EEOC v. Wal-Mart Stores, Inc.,* 477 F.3d 561 (8th Cir. 2007)]

18–4. Defenses to Employment Discrimination. The Milwaukee County Juvenile Detention Center established a new policy that required each unit of the facility to be staffed at all times by at least one officer of the same gender as the detainees housed at a unit. The purpose of the policy, administrators said, was to reduce the likelihood of sexual abuse of juveniles by officers of the other gender. Because there were many more male units in the center than female units, the policy had the effect of reducing the number of shifts available for women officers and increasing the number of shifts for men. Two female officers sued for gender discrimination. The district court held for the county, finding that the policy of assignment was based on a bona fide occupational qualification (BFOQ) and so was not illegal gender discrimination. The officers appealed. What would be evidence that the county had a valid BFOQ? [*Henry v. Milwaukee County,* 539 F.3d 573 (7th Cir. 2008)]

18–5. Sexual Harassment. The Metropolitan Government of Nashville and Davidson County, Tennessee (Metro), began looking into rumors of sexual harassment by the Metro School District's employee relations director, Gene Hughes. Veronica Frazier, a Metro human resources officer, asked Vicky Crawford, a Metro employee, whether she had witnessed "inappropriate behavior" by Hughes. Crawford described several instances of sexually harassing behavior. Two other employees also reported being sexually harassed by Hughes. Metro took no action against Hughes, but soon after completing the investigation, Metro accused Crawford of embezzlement and fired her. The two other employees were also fired. Crawford filed a suit in a federal district court against Metro, claiming retaliation under Title VII. What arguments can be made that Crawford's situation does or does not qualify as a retaliation claim under Title VII? Discuss. [*Crawford v. Metropolitan Government of Nashville and Davidson County, Tennessee,* 555 U.S. 271, 129 S.Ct. 846, 172 L.Ed.2d 650 (2009)]

18–6. Discrimination Based on Gender. Brenda Lewis worked for two years at Heartland Inns of America, LLC, and gradually worked her way up the management ladder. Lewis, who described herself as a tomboy, was commended for her good work. When she moved to a different Heartland hotel, the director of operations, Barbara Cullinan, told one of the owners that Lewis was not a "good fit" for the

front desk because she was not feminine enough. Cullinan told various people that the hotel wanted "pretty" girls at the front desk. Explaining to Lewis that her hiring had not been done properly, Cullinan said Lewis would need to perform another interview. Cullinan fired Lewis soon after the interview. The reason given in a letter was that Lewis was hostile during the interview process. Lewis sued Heartland for discrimination based on unlawful gender stereotyping. The district court dismissed the suit. Lewis appealed. Does her claim fall under Title VII's restriction on discrimination based on gender? Why or why not? [*Lewis v. Heartland Inns of America, LLC,* 591 F.3d 1033 (8th Cir. 2010)]

18–7. Case Problem with Sample Answer. Retaliation. Entek International, an Oregon-based company, hired Shane Dawson, a male homosexual, as a temporary production-line worker. Dawson worked with twenty-four other employees, all male. Certain individuals at work began making derogatory comments about Dawson's sexual orientation, calling him a "fag," a "homo," and a "worthless queer." Oregon law prohibits discrimination based on sexual orientation. Dawson asked his supervisor, Troy Guzon, to do something about the treatment he was receiving, but Guzon did not. In fact, Guzon also made derogatory comments about Dawson's sexual orientation. Dawson began to experience stress, and his work deteriorated. As a result of this situation, he went to the human resources department and filed a complaint. Two days later, he was fired. Dawson initiated a lawsuit, claiming that he had been fired in retaliation for filing a complaint, but the district court granted Entek a summary judgment. Dawson appealed. How should the federal appellate court rule? Has Dawson established a claim for retaliatory discharge? Should his case be allowed to go forward to a trial? Explain. [*Dawson v. Entek International,* 630 F.3d 928 (9th Cir. 2011)]

—To view a sample answer for Case Problem 18–7, go to Appendix F at the end of this text.

18–8. A Question of Ethics. Discrimination Based on Disability. *Titan Distribution, Inc., employed Quintak, Inc., to run its tire mounting and distribution operation in Des Moines, Iowa. Robert Chalfant worked for Quintak as a second-shift supervisor at Titan. He suffered a heart attack in 1992 and underwent heart bypass surgery in 1997. He also had arthritis. In July 2002, Titan decided to terminate Quintak. Chalfant applied to work at Titan. On his application, he described himself as having a disability. After a physical exam, Titan's doctor concluded that Chalfant could work in his current capacity, and he was notified that he would be hired. Despite the notice, Nadis Barucic, a Titan employee, wrote "not pass px" at the top of Chalfant's application, and he was not hired. He took a job with AMPCO Systems, a parking ramp management company. This work involved walking up to five miles a day and lifting more weight than he had at Titan. In September, Titan eliminated its second shift. Chalfant filed a suit in a federal district court against Titan, in part, under the Americans with Disabilities Act (ADA). Titan argued that the reason it had not hired Chalfant* *was not that he did not pass the physical, but no one—including Barucic—could explain why she had written "not pass px" on his application. Later, Titan claimed that Chalfant was not hired because the entire second shift was going to be eliminated. [Chalfant v. Titan Distribution, Inc., 475 F.3d 982 (8th Cir. 2007)]*

1. What must Chalfant establish to make his case under the ADA? Can he meet these requirements? Explain.

2. In employment-discrimination cases, punitive damages can be appropriate when an employer acts with malice or reckless indifference to an employee's protected rights. Would an award of punitive damages to Chalfant be appropriate in this case? Discuss.

18–9. **Critical-Thinking Legal Environment Question.** Why has the federal government limited the application of the statutes discussed in this chapter to firms with a specified number of employees, such as fifteen or twenty? Should these laws apply to all employers, regardless of size? Why or why not?

18–10. **Video Question. *Mary Tyler Moore.***
Access the video using the instructions provided below to answer the following questions.

1. In the video, Mr. Grant (Ed Asner) asks Mary (Mary Tyler Moore) some personal questions during a job interview, including why she is not married and what religion she practices. He also tells her that he "figured he'd hire a man." Can Mary make out a *prima facie* case of gender or religious discrimination based on these questions? Why or why not?

2. Can Mary prove a *prima facie* case of age discrimination because Mr. Grant asked her age during the interview and then implied that she was "hedging" about her age? What would she need to prove under the Age Discrimination in Employment Act?

3. How does the fact that Mr. Grant hired Mary as an associate producer affect her ability to establish a case of employment discrimination?

4. Mr. Grant says that he will hire Mary to see if it works out, but he will fire her if he does not like her or if she does not like him at the end of a trial period. Can he do that? Explain. If he fired Mary a few weeks later, would this affect her ability to sue for employment discrimination? Why or why not?

—To watch this video, go to **www.cengagebrain.com** and register the access code that came with your new book or log in to your existing account. Select the link for either the "Business Law Digital Video Library Online Access" or "Business Law CourseMate," and then click on "Complete Video List" to find the video for this chapter (Video 68).

UNIT THREE Cumulative Business Hypothetical

Two brothers, Ray and Paul Ashford, start a business manufacturing a new type of battery system for hybrid automobiles. They hit the market at the perfect time, and the batteries are in great demand.

1. When Ray and Paul started their business, they contributed equal amounts of capital but did not sign a formal agreement. What type of business entity would they be presumed to have formed, and how would any profits be divided? If they want to limit their liability but still remain a small business enterprise, what are their options? Which type of limited liability organization would you recommend, and why?

2. As their business becomes more successful, Ray and Paul seek to raise significant capital to build a manufacturing plant. They decide to form a corporation called Ashford Motors, Inc. Outline the steps that Ray and Paul need to follow to incorporate their business.

3. Loren, one of Ashford's salespersons, anxious to make a sale, intentionally quotes a price to a customer that is $500 lower than Ashford has authorized for that particular product. The customer purchases the product at the quoted price. When Ashford learns of the deal, it claims that it is not legally bound to the sales contract because it did not authorize Loren to sell the product at that price. Is Ashford bound by the contract? Discuss fully.

4. One day Gina, an Ashford employee, suffered a serious burn when she accidentally spilled some acid on her hand. The accident occurred because another employee, who was suspected of using illegal drugs, carelessly bumped into her. Gina's hand required a series of skin grafts before it healed sufficiently to allow Gina to return to work. Gina wants to obtain compensation for her lost wages and medical expenses. Can she do so? If so, how?

5. After Gina's injury, Ashford decides to conduct random drug tests on all of its employees. Several employees claim that the testing violates their privacy rights. If the employees bring a lawsuit, what factors will the court consider in deciding whether the random drug testing is legally permissible?

6. Ashford provides health insurance for its two hundred employees, including Dan. For personal medical reasons, Dan takes twelve weeks of leave. During this period, can Dan continue his coverage under Ashford's health-insurance plan? After Dan returns to work, Ashford closes Dan's division and terminates the employees, including Dan. Can Dan continue his coverage under Ashford's health-insurance plan? If so, at whose expense?

7. Aretha, another employee at Ashford, is disgusted by the sexually offensive behavior of several male employees. She has complained to her supervisor on several occasions about the offensive behavior, but the supervisor merely laughs at her concerns. Aretha decides to bring a legal action against the company for sexual harassment. Does Aretha's complaint concern *quid pro quo* harassment or hostile-environment harassment? What federal statute protects employees from sexual harassment? What remedies are available under that statute? What procedures must Aretha follow in pursuing her legal action?

Unit Four

The Regulatory Environment

(Moody 75/(Creative Commons)

Chapter 19

Powers and Functions of Administrative Agencies

> "Perhaps more values today are affected by [administrative] decisions than by those of all the courts."
>
> —Robert H. Jackson, 1892–1954
> (Associate justice of the United States Supreme Court, 1941–1954)

Chapter Objectives

After reading this chapter, you should be able to answer the following questions:

1. How are federal administrative agencies created?
2. What are the three basic functions of most administrative agencies?
3. What sequence of events must normally occur before an agency rule becomes law?
4. How do administrative agencies enforce their rules?
5. How do the three branches of government limit the power of administrative agencies?

(Moody75/Creative Commons)

As the chapter-opening quotation above suggests, government agencies established to administer the law have a significant impact on the day-to-day operation of the government and the economy. In its early years, the United States had a simple, non-industrial economy with little regulation. As the economy has grown and become more complex, the size of government has also increased, and so has the number of administrative agencies.

In some instances, new agencies have been created in response to a crisis. In the wake of the financial crisis that led to the Great Recession, for example, Congress enacted the Dodd-Frank Wall Street Reform and Consumer Protection Act of 2010. Among other things, this statute created the Financial Stability Oversight Council to identify and respond to emerging risks in the financial system. It also created the Consumer Financial Protection Bureau to protect consumers from abusive practices by financial institutions, including banks and nonbanks offering consumer financial products, mortgage lenders, and credit-card companies.

As the number of agencies has multiplied, so have the rules, orders, and decisions that they issue. Today, there are rules covering almost every aspect of a business's operations (see the *Linking the Law to Management* feature on pages 580 and 581). The regulations that administrative agencies issue make up the body of *administrative law,* which was mentioned in Chapter 1. In this chapter, we explain in greater detail the important principles of administrative law and their significant impact on businesses today.

▶ The Practical Significance of Administrative Law

Unlike statutory law, administrative law is created by administrative agencies, not by legislatures, but it is nevertheless of overriding significance for businesses. When Congress—or a state legislature—enacts legislation, it typically adopts a rather general statute and leaves the statute's implementation to an **administrative agency,** which then creates the detailed rules and regulations necessary to carry out the statute. The administrative agency, with its specialized personnel, has the time, resources, and expertise to make the detailed decisions required for regulation.

Administrative Agency   A federal or state government agency established to perform a specific function. Administrative agencies are authorized by legislative acts to make and enforce rules in order to administer and enforce the acts.

Administrative Agencies Exist at All Levels of Government

Administrative agencies are spread throughout the government. At the national level, numerous *executive agencies* exist within the cabinet departments of the executive branch. For example, the Food and Drug Administration is within the U.S. Department of Health and Human Services. Executive agencies are subject to the authority of the president, who has the power to appoint and remove officers of federal agencies. Exhibit 19–1 on the following page lists the cabinet departments and their most important subagencies.

There are also major *independent regulatory agencies* at the federal level, including the Federal Trade Commission, the Securities and Exchange Commission, and the Federal Communications Commission. The president's power is less pronounced in regard to independent agencies, whose officers serve for fixed terms and cannot be removed without just cause. Exhibit 19–2 on page 565 lists selected independent agencies and their principal functions.

There are administrative agencies at the state and local levels as well. Commonly, a state agency (such as a state pollution-control agency) is created as a parallel to a federal agency (such as the Environmental Protection Agency). Just as federal statutes take precedence over conflicting state statutes, so do federal agency regulations take precedence over conflicting state regulations. Because the rules of state and local agencies vary widely, we focus here exclusively on federal administrative law.

Agencies Provide a Comprehensive Regulatory Scheme

Often, administrative agencies at various levels of government work together and share the responsibility of creating and enforcing particular regulations. **EXAMPLE 19.1** When Congress enacted the Clean Air Act (see Chapter 21) in 1963, it provided only general directions for the prevention of air pollution. The specific pollution-control requirements imposed on business are almost entirely the product of decisions made by the Environmental Protection Agency (EPA), which was created in 1970. Moreover, the EPA works with parallel environmental agencies at the state level to analyze existing data and determine the appropriate pollution-control standards. ●

Legislation and regulations have benefits—in the example of the Clean Air Act, a cleaner environment than existed in decades past. At the same time, these benefits entail significant costs for business. The EPA has estimated the costs of compliance with the Clean Air Act at many tens of billions of dollars yearly. Although the agency has calculated that the overall benefits of its regulations often exceed their costs, the burden on business is substantial.

● *Exhibit* **19–1 Executive Departments and Important Subagencies**

DEPARTMENT AND DATE FORMED	SELECTED SUBAGENCIES
State (1789)	Passport Office; Bureau of Diplomatic Security; Foreign Service; Bureau of Human Rights and Humanitarian Affairs; Bureau of Consular Affairs; Bureau of Intelligence and Research
Treasury (1789)	Internal Revenue Service; U.S. Mint
Interior (1849)	U.S. Fish and Wildlife Service; National Park Service; Bureau of Indian Affairs; Bureau of Land Management
Justice (1870)[a]	Federal Bureau of Investigation; Drug Enforcement Administration; Bureau of Prisons; U.S. Marshals Service
Agriculture (1889)	Soil Conservation Service; Agricultural Research Service; Food Safety and Inspection Service; Forest Service
Commerce (1913)[b]	Bureau of the Census; Bureau of Economic Analysis; Minority Business Development Agency; U.S. Patent and Trademark Office; National Oceanic and Atmospheric Administration
Labor (1913)[b]	Occupational Safety and Health Administration; Bureau of Labor Statistics; Employment Standards Administration; Office of Labor-Management Standards; Employment and Training Administration
Defense (1949)[c]	National Security Agency; Joint Chiefs of Staff; Departments of the Air Force, Navy, Army; service academies
Housing and Urban Development (1965)	Office of Community Planning and Development; Government National Mortgage Association; Office of Fair Housing and Equal Opportunity
Transportation (1967)	Federal Aviation Administration; Federal Highway Administration; National Highway Traffic Safety Administration; Federal Transit Administration
Energy (1977)	Office of Civilian Radioactive Waste Management; Office of Nuclear Energy; Energy Information Administration
Health and Human Services (1980)[d]	Food and Drug Administration; Centers for Medicare and Medicaid Services; Centers for Disease Control and Prevention; National Institutes of Health
Education (1980)[d]	Office of Special Education and Rehabilitation Services; Office of Elementary and Secondary Education; Office of Postsecondary Education; Office of Vocational and Adult Education
Veterans Affairs (1989)	Veterans Health Administration; Veterans Benefits Administration; National Cemetery System
Homeland Security (2002)	U.S. Citizenship and Immigration Services; Directorate of Border and Transportation Services; U.S. Coast Guard; Federal Emergency Management Agency

a. Formed from the Office of the Attorney General (created in 1789).
b. Formed from the Department of Commerce and Labor (created in 1903).
c. Formed from the Department of War (created in 1789) and the Department of the Navy (created in 1798).
d. Formed from the Department of Health, Education, and Welfare (created in 1953).

 Agency Creation and Powers

Congress creates federal administrative agencies. By delegating some of its authority to make and implement laws, Congress can monitor indirectly a particular area in which it has passed legislation without becoming bogged down in the details relating to enforcement—details that are often best left to specialists.

Enabling Legislation A statute enacted by Congress that authorizes the creation of an administrative agency and specifies the name, composition, and powers of the agency being created.

To create an administrative agency, Congress passes **enabling legislation,** which specifies the name, purposes, functions, and powers of the agency being created. Federal administrative agencies can exercise only those powers that Congress has delegated to them in enabling legislation. Through similar enabling acts, state legislatures create state administrative agencies.

• *Exhibit* **19-2 Selected Independent Regulatory Agencies**

NAME AND DATE FORMED	PRINCIPAL DUTIES
Federal Reserve System Board of Governors (the Fed)—1913	Determines policy with respect to interest rates, credit availability, and the money supply. Starting in 2008, the Federal Reserve became involved in various "bailouts" in the financial sector, including a "conservatorship" of two large mortgage institutions (Fannie Mae and Freddie Mac) and control of the world's largest insurance company, AIG.
Federal Trade Commission (FTC)—1914	Prevents businesses from engaging in unfair trade practices; stops the formation of monopolies in the business sector; protects consumer rights.
Securities and Exchange Commission (SEC)—1934	Regulates the nation's stock exchanges, in which shares of stock are bought and sold; enforces the securities laws, which require full disclosure of the financial profiles of companies that wish to sell stock and bonds to the public.
Federal Communications Commission (FCC)—1934	Regulates all communications by telegraph, cable, telephone, radio, satellite, and television.
National Labor Relations Board (NLRB)—1935	Protects employees' rights to join unions and bargain collectively with employers; attempts to prevent unfair labor practices by both employers and unions.
Equal Employment Opportunity Commission (EEOC)—1964	Works to eliminate discrimination in employment based on religion, gender, race, color, disability, national origin, or age; investigates claims of discrimination.
Environmental Protection Agency (EPA)—1970	Undertakes programs aimed at reducing air and water pollution; works with state and local agencies to help fight environmental hazards. (It has recently been suggested that its status be elevated to that of a department.)
Nuclear Regulatory Commission (NRC)—1975	Ensures that electricity-generating nuclear reactors in the United States are built and operated safely; regularly inspects operations of such reactors.

Enabling Legislation—An Example

Congress created the Federal Trade Commission (FTC) in the Federal Trade Commission Act of 1914.[1] The act prohibits unfair and deceptive trade practices. It also describes the procedures that the agency must follow to charge persons or organizations with violations of the act, and it provides for judicial review of agency orders. The act grants the FTC the power to do the following:

1. Create "rules and regulations for the purpose of carrying out the Act."
2. Conduct investigations of business practices.
3. Obtain reports from interstate corporations concerning their business practices.
4. Investigate possible violations of federal antitrust statutes. (The FTC shares this task with the Antitrust Division of the U.S. Department of Justice.)
5. Publish findings of its investigations.
6. Recommend new legislation.
7. Hold trial-like hearings to resolve certain kinds of trade disputes that involve FTC regulations or federal antitrust laws.

The commission that heads the FTC is composed of five members, each of whom is appointed by the president, with the advice and consent of the Senate, for a term of seven years. The president designates one of the commissioners to be the chair.

---

1. 15 U.S.C. Sections 41–58.

Various offices and bureaus of the FTC undertake different administrative activities for the agency. The organization of the FTC is illustrated in Exhibit 19–3 below.

Agency Powers and the Constitution

Administrative agencies occupy an unusual niche in the U.S. governmental structure, because they exercise powers that are normally divided among the three branches of government. The constitutional principle of *checks and balances* allows each branch of government to act as a check on the actions of the other two branches. Furthermore, the U.S. Constitution authorizes only the legislative branch to create laws. Yet administrative agencies, to which the Constitution does not specifically refer, can make **legislative rules,** or *substantive rules,* that are as legally binding as laws that Congress passes.

Administrative agencies also issue **interpretive rules** that are not legally binding but simply indicate how an agency plans to interpret and enforce its statutory authority. **EXAMPLE 19.2** The Equal Employment Opportunity Commission periodically issues interpretive rules indicating how it plans to interpret the provisions of certain statutes, such as the Americans with Disabilities Act (see Chapter 18). These informal rules provide enforcement guidelines for agency officials. ●

Courts generally hold that Article I of the U.S. Constitution is the basis for all administrative law. Section 1 of that article grants all legislative powers to Congress and requires Congress to oversee the implementation of all laws. Article I, Section 8, gives Congress the power to make all laws necessary for executing its specified powers. Under what is known as the **delegation doctrine,** the courts interpret these passages as granting Congress the power to establish administrative agencies and delegate to them the power to create rules for implementing those laws.

The three branches of government exercise certain controls over agency powers and functions, as discussed next, but in many ways administrative agencies function independently. For this reason, administrative agencies, which constitute the **bureaucracy,** are sometimes referred to as the fourth branch of the U.S. government.

EXECUTIVE CONTROLS   The executive branch of government exercises control over agencies both through the president's power to appoint federal officers and

Legislative Rule An administrative agency rule that carries the same weight as a congressionally enacted statute.

Interpretive Rule An administrative agency rule that is simply a statement or opinion issued by the agency explaining how it interprets and intends to apply the statutes it enforces. Such rules are not binding on private individuals or organizations.

Delegation Doctrine A doctrine based on Article I, Section 8, of the U.S. Constitution, which has been construed to allow Congress to delegate some of its power to administrative agencies to make and implement laws.

Bureaucracy The organizational structure, consisting of government bureaus and agencies, through which the government implements and enforces the laws.

● *Exhibit* **19–3 Organization of the Federal Trade Commission**

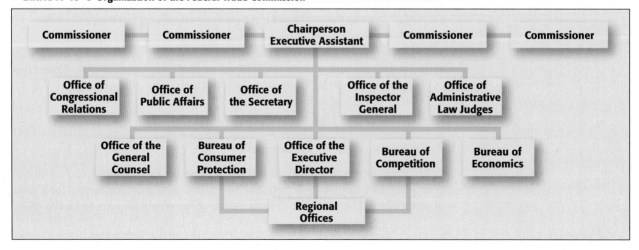

through the president's veto power. The president may veto enabling legislation presented by Congress or congressional attempts to modify an existing agency's authority.

LEGISLATIVE CONTROLS　Congress exercises authority over agency powers through legislation. Congress gives power to an agency through enabling legislation and can take power away—or even abolish an agency altogether—through subsequent legislation. Legislative authority is required to fund an agency, and enabling legislation usually sets certain time and monetary limits on the funding of particular programs. Congress can always revise these limits.

In addition to its power to create and fund agencies, Congress has the authority to investigate the implementation of its laws and the agencies that it has created. Congress also has the power to "freeze" the enforcement of most federal regulations before the regulations take effect.

JUDICIAL CONTROLS　The judicial branch exercises control over agency powers through the courts' review of agency actions. As you will read in the next section, the Administrative Procedure Act provides for judicial review of most agency decisions. Agency actions are not automatically subject to judicial review, however. The party seeking court review must first exhaust all administrative remedies under what is called the *exhaustion doctrine*.

In other words, the complaining party normally must have gone through the administrative process (from complaint to hearing to final agency order) before seeking court review. **EXAMPLE 19.3**　An employee who has a disability believes that she has suffered unlawful discrimination in the workplace (see Chapter 18). Before she can file a complaint in court, she must have filed a complaint with the Equal Employment Opportunity Commission (EEOC), and the EEOC must have issued its final ruling. ●

▶ The Administrative Procedure Act

All federal agencies must follow specific procedural requirements as they go about fulfilling their three basic functions: rulemaking, enforcement, and adjudication. In this section, we focus on agency *rulemaking* (enforcement and adjudication will be discussed later in this chapter). Sometimes, Congress specifies certain procedural requirements in an agency's enabling legislation. In the absence of any directives from Congress concerning a particular agency procedure, the Administrative Procedure Act (APA) of 1946[2] applies.

The Arbitrary and Capricious Test

One of Congress's goals in enacting the APA was to provide for more judicial control over administrative agencies. To that end, the APA provides that courts should "hold unlawful and set aside" agency actions found to be "arbitrary, capricious, an abuse of discretion, or otherwise not in accordance with law."[3] Under this standard, parties can challenge regulations as contrary to law or so irrational as to be arbitrary and capricious.

> *"Absolute discretion . . . is more destructive of freedom than any of man's other inventions."*
>
> —William O. Douglas, 1898–1980
> (Associate justice of the United States Supreme Court, 1939–1975)

---

2. 5 U.S.C. Sections 551–706.
3. 5 U.S.C. Section 706(2)(A).

The arbitrary and capricious standard does not have a precise definition, but in applying it, courts typically consider whether the agency has done any of the following:

1. Failed to provide a rational explanation for its decision.
2. Changed its prior policy without justification.
3. Considered legally inappropriate factors.
4. Failed to consider a relevant factor.
5. Rendered a decision plainly contrary to the evidence.

In the following case, a television network claimed that an agency's ruling was arbitrary and capricious.

Case 19.1   **Federal Communications Commission v. Fox Television Stations, Inc.**

Supreme Court of the United States, __ U.S. __, 129 S.Ct. 1800, 173 L.Ed.2d 738 (2009).
www.supremecourt.gov/opinions/opinions.aspx[a]

(Creative Commons/Gage Skidmore)

BACKGROUND AND FACTS   The Communications Act of 1934 established a system of limited-term broadcast licenses subject to various conditions. One condition was the indecency ban, which prohibits the uttering of "any obscene, indecent, or profane language by means of radio communication." The Federal Communications Commission (FCC) first invoked this ban on indecent broadcasts in 1975. At that time, the FCC defined indecent speech as "language that describes, in terms patently offensive as measured by contemporary community standards for the broadcast medium, sexual or excretory activities or organs, at times of the day when there is a reasonable risk that children may be in the audience." Before 2004, one of the factors used by the FCC in determining whether a broadcaster had violated the ban was whether the offensive language had been repeated, or "dwelled on," in the broadcast. If an offensive term was used just once in a broadcast, the FCC probably would not take any action. In 2004, however, the FCC changed this policy, declaring that an offensive term, such as the F-word, was actionably indecent even if it was used only once. In its 2004 ruling, the FCC specifically stated that previous FCC rulings allowing a "safe harbor" for a single utterance of an offensive term "were no longer good law." In 2006, the FCC applied this new rule to two Fox Television broadcasts, each of which contained a single use of the F-word. After the FCC ruled that these broadcasts were actionably indecent, Fox appealed to the U.S. Court of Appeals for the Second Circuit for a

review of the order. The appellate court reversed the agency's order, finding the FCC's reasoning inadequate under the Administrative Procedure Act. The FCC appealed to the United States Supreme Court.

IN THE WORDS OF THE COURT . . .
Justice *SCALIA* delivered the opinion of the Court.
   * * * *

The Administrative Procedure Act, which sets forth the full extent of judicial authority to review executive agency action for procedural correctness, permits (insofar as relevant here) the setting aside of agency action that is "arbitrary" or "capricious." * * * *We have made clear, however, that "a court is not to substitute its judgment for that of the agency," and should "uphold a decision of less than ideal clarity if the agency's path may reasonably be discerned."* [Emphasis added.]

In overturning the Commission's judgment, the Court of Appeals here relied in part on Circuit precedent requiring a more substantial explanation for agency action that changes prior policy. The Second Circuit has interpreted the Administrative Procedure Act and our opinion in [a previous case] as requiring agencies to make clear "why the original reasons for adopting the [displaced] rule or policy are no longer dispositive [a deciding factor]" as well as "why the new rule effectuates the statute as well as or better than the old rule."

We find no basis in the Administrative Procedure Act or in our opinions for a requirement that all agency change be subjected to more searching review. The Act mentions no such heightened standard.

To be sure, the requirement that an agency provide reasoned explanation for its action would ordinarily demand that it display awareness that it *is* changing position. * * * And of course the agency must show that there are good reasons for the new policy. *But it need not demonstrate to a court's satisfaction that the reasons for the new policy are <u>better</u> than the reasons for the old one; it suffices that the new policy is permissible under the statute, that there are good*

---

a. On the page that opens, under the heading "2008 Term" (which ended in June 2009), select "2008 Term Opinions of the Court." Then scroll down the list to "49" in the first column of the table and click on the case title to access this opinion. The Supreme Court of the United States maintains this Web site.

Case 19.1–Continued

reasons for it, and that the agency <u>believes</u> it to be better. [Emphasis on underscored words in original; other emphasis added.]

* * * *

Judged under the above described standards, the Commission's new enforcement policy and its order finding the broadcasts actionably indecent were neither arbitrary nor capricious. First, the Commission forthrightly acknowledged that its recent actions have broken new ground, taking account of inconsistent "prior Commission and staff action" and explicitly disavowing them as "no longer good law." * * * There is no doubt that the Commission knew it was making a change.

Moreover, the agency's reasons for expanding the scope of its enforcement activity were entirely rational. * * * It is surely rational (if not inescapable) to believe that a safe harbor for single words would "likely lead to more widespread use of the offensive language."

DECISION AND REMEDY The United States Supreme Court reversed the judgment of the U.S. Court of Appeals for the Second Circuit and remanded the case for further proceedings

consistent with this opinion.[b] The FCC's order declaring the Fox broadcasts actionably indecent was neither arbitrary nor capricious.

THE SOCIAL DIMENSION *Today, children are likely to be exposed to indecent language in various media far more often than they were in the 1970s, when the FCC first began to sanction indecent speech. How should this affect the government's regulation of broadcasts?*

THE TECHNOLOGICAL DIMENSION *Technological advances have made it easier for broadcasters to "bleep out" offending words in the programs that they air. Does this development support a more or less stringent enforcement policy by the FCC? Explain.*

---

b. On remand, the U.S. Court of Appeals for the Second Circuit ruled that the FCC's indecency policies were unconstitutionally vague and violated the broadcast network's First Amendment rights. See *Fox Television Stations, Inc. v. Federal Communications Commission,* 613 F.3d 317 (2d Cir. 2010). The FCC appealed the decision, and the Supreme Court granted *certiorari* but had not yet decided the case at the time this book was published.

Rulemaking

Rulemaking The actions undertaken by administrative agencies when formally adopting new regulations or amending old ones. Under the Administrative Procedure Act, rulemaking includes notifying the public of proposed rules or changes and receiving and considering the public's comments.

Notice-and-Comment Rulemaking A procedure in agency rulemaking that requires notice, opportunity for comment, and a published draft of the final rule.

The major function of an administrative agency is **rulemaking.** The APA defines a rule as "an agency statement of general or particular applicability and future effect designed to implement, interpret, or prescribe law and policy."[4] Regulations are sometimes said to be *legislative* because, like statutes, they have a binding effect. Thus, violators of agency rules may be punished. Because agency rules have such great legal force, the APA established procedures for agencies to follow in creating rules. Many rules must be adopted using the APA's *notice-and-comment rulemaking* procedure.

Notice-and-comment rulemaking involves three basic steps: notice of the proposed rulemaking, a comment period, and the final rule. The APA recognizes some limited exceptions to these procedural requirements, but they are seldom invoked. If the required procedures are violated, the resulting rule may be invalid. The impetus for rulemaking may come from various sources, including Congress, the agency itself, or private parties who may petition an agency to begin a rulemaking (or repeal a rule). For instance, environmental groups have petitioned for stricter air-pollution controls to combat global warming.

NOTICE OF THE PROPOSED RULEMAKING When a federal agency decides to create a new rule, the agency publishes a notice of the proposed rulemaking proceedings in the *Federal Register,* a daily publication of the executive branch that prints government orders, rules, and regulations. The notice states where and when the proceedings will be held, the agency's legal authority for making the rule (usually its enabling legislation), and the terms or subject matter of the proposed rule.

COMMENT PERIOD Following the publication of the notice of the proposed rulemaking proceedings, the agency must allow ample time for persons to comment on the proposed rule. The purpose of this comment period is to give interested parties

---

4. 5 U.S.C. Section 551(4).

the opportunity to express their views on the proposed rule in an effort to influence agency policy. The comments may be in writing or, if a hearing is held, may be given orally. The agency need not respond to all comments, but it must respond to any significant comments that bear directly on the proposed rule. The agency responds by either modifying its final rule or explaining, in a statement accompanying the final rule, why it did not make any changes. In some circumstances, particularly when the procedure being used in a specific instance is less formal, an agency may accept comments after the comment period is closed.

THE FINAL RULE   After the agency reviews the comments, it drafts the final rule and publishes it in the *Federal Register.* Such a final rule must contain a "concise general statement of . . . basis and purpose" that describes the reasoning behind the rule.[5] The final rule may change the terms of the proposed rule, in light of the public comments, but cannot change the proposal too radically, or a new proposal and a new opportunity for comment are required. The final rule is later compiled along with the rules and regulations of other federal administrative agencies in the *Code of Federal Regulations.*

The Dodd-Frank Act mentioned at the opening of this chapter provides recent examples of the rulemaking process. Although the statute contains hundreds of pages, its provisions are expressed only in general terms. The Financial Oversight Council, for example, was charged with ensuring that no more bailouts will be required to rescue financial institutions that are "too big to fail." Thus, one of the council's first tasks was to propose a rule establishing criteria for identifying a "financial market utility" that "is or is likely to become systemically important."

When the rule becomes final, the council will be able to establish more stringent requirements for institutions that fall into that category. The council is also preparing proposed rules for increasing capital requirements for financial institutions and requiring complex financial institutions to prepare so-called living wills—plans for their orderly shutdown in the event that they fail.

Final rules have binding legal effect unless the courts later overturn them. Because they are as binding as legislation, they are often referred to as legislative rules, as mentioned previously. If an agency failed to follow proper rulemaking procedures when it issued the final rule, however, the rule may not be binding.

CASE EXAMPLE 19.4   Members of the Hemp Industries Association (HIA) manufacture and sell food products made from hemp seed and oil. These products contain only trace amounts of tetrahydrocannabinols (THC, a component of marijuana) and are nonpsychoactive—that is, they do not affect a person's mind or behavior. In 2001, the U.S. Drug Enforcement Administration (DEA) published an interpretive rule declaring that "any product that contains any amount of THC is a Schedule I controlled substance [a drug whose availability is restricted by law]." Subsequently, without following formal rulemaking procedures, the DEA declared that two legislative rules relating to products containing natural THC were final. These rules effectively banned the possession and sale of the food products of the HIA's members. The HIA petitioned for court review, arguing that the DEA rules should not have been enforced. A federal appellate court agreed and ruled in favor of the HIA. The DEA should have held hearings on the record concerning the rules, invited public comment, and then issued formal rulings on each finding, conclusion, and exception. Because the DEA did not follow its formal rulemaking procedures, the rules were not enforceable.[6] •

---

5. 5 U.S.C. Section 555(c).

6. *Hemp Industries Association v. Drug Enforcement Administration,* 357 F.3d 1012 (9th Cir. 2004).

Informal Agency Actions

Rather than take the time to conduct notice-and-comment rulemaking, agencies have increasingly been using more informal methods of policymaking. These include issuing interpretive rules, which are specifically exempted from the APA's requirements. Such rules simply declare the agency's interpretation of its enabling statute's meaning and do not impose any direct and legally binding obligations on regulated parties. In addition, agencies issue various other materials, such as "guidance documents," that advise the public on the agencies' legal and policy positions.

Such informal actions are exempt from the APA's requirements because they do not establish legal rights—a party cannot be directly prosecuted for violating an interpretive rule or a guidance document. Nevertheless, an agency's informal action can be of practical importance because it warns regulated entities that the agency may engage in formal rulemaking if they fail to heed the positions taken informally by the agency.

Judicial Deference to Agency Decisions

When asked to review agency decisions, courts historically granted some deference (significant weight) to the agency's judgment, often citing the agency's expertise in the subject area of the regulation. This deference seems especially appropriate when applied to an agency's analysis of factual questions, but should it also extend to an agency's interpretation of its own legal authority? In *Chevron U.S.A., Inc. v. Natural Resources Defense Council, Inc.,*[7] the United States Supreme Court held that it should, thereby creating a standard of broadened deference to agencies on questions of legal interpretation.

The Holding of the *Chevron* Case

At issue in the *Chevron* case was whether the courts should defer to an agency's interpretation of a statute giving it authority to act. The Environmental Protection Agency (EPA) had interpreted the phrase "stationary source" in the Clean Air Act as referring to an entire manufacturing plant, and not to each facility within a plant. The agency's interpretation enabled it to adopt the so-called bubble policy, which allowed companies to offset increases in emissions in part of a plant with decreases elsewhere in the plant—an interpretation that reduced the pollution-control compliance costs faced by manufacturers. An environmental group challenged the legality of the EPA's interpretation.

The United States Supreme Court held that the courts should defer to an agency's interpretation of *law* as well as fact. The Court found that the agency's interpretation of the statute was reasonable and upheld the bubble policy. The Court's decision in the *Chevron* case created a new standard for courts to use when reviewing agency interpretations of law. The standard involves the following two questions:

1. Did Congress directly address the issue in dispute in the statute? If so, the statutory language prevails.
2. If the statute is silent or ambiguous, is the agency's interpretation "reasonable"? If it is, a court should uphold the agency's interpretation even if the court would have interpreted the law differently.

---

7. 467 U.S. 837, 104 S.Ct. 2778, 81 L.Ed.2d 694 (1984).

When Courts Will Give *Chevron* Deference to Agency Interpretation

The notion that courts should defer to agencies on matters of law was controversial. Under the holding of the *Chevron* case, when the meaning of a particular statute's language is unclear and an agency interprets it, the court must follow the agency's interpretation as long as it is reasonable. This led to considerable discussion and litigation to test the boundaries of the *Chevron* holding. For instance, are courts required to give deference to all agency interpretations or only to those that result from adjudication or formal rulemaking procedures? Are informal agency interpretations issued through opinion letters and internal memoranda also entitled to deference?

CASE EXAMPLE 19.5   The United States has a tariff (tax) schedule that authorizes the U.S. Customs Service to classify and fix the rate of duty on imports. "Ruling letters" set tariff classifications for particular imports. Mead Corporation imported "daily planners," which had been tariff-free for several years. The Customs Service issued a ruling letter reclassifying them as "bound diaries," which were subject to a tariff. Mead brought a lawsuit claiming that the ruling letter should not receive *Chevron* deference because it was not put into effect pursuant to notice-and-comment rulemaking. When the case reached the United States Supreme Court, the Court agreed that the ruling letter was *not* entitled to *Chevron* deference because ruling letters are interpretive and do not involve formal rulemaking procedures. Therefore, Mead was not required to pay an import tariff on the daily planners.[8] ●

In the following case, a medical educational foundation challenged an agency regulation that required it to deduct Social Security contributions from the wages of physicians who were going through its hospital residency program. The Supreme Court had to decide if the "full-time employee" rule enacted by the Treasury Department was entitled to *Chevron* deference.

---

8. *United States v. Mead Corp.*, 533 U.S. 218, 121 S.Ct. 2164, 150 L.Ed.2d 292 (2001).

Case 19.2   **Mayo Foundation for Medical Education and Research v. United States**

Supreme Court of the United States, ___ U.S. ___, 131 S.Ct. 704, 178 L.Ed.2d 588 (2011).

BACKGROUND AND FACTS   The Mayo Foundation for Medical Education and Research (Mayo) offers residency programs to physicians who have graduated from medical school and seek additional instruction in a chosen specialty. Although the resident physicians participate in some formal educational activities, they spend fifty to eighty hours a week caring for patients. As discussed in Chapter 17, the Federal Insurance Contributions Act (FICA) requires employees and employers to pay Social Security taxes on all wages employees receive. FICA, however, excludes from its definition of *employment* any "service performed in the employ of . . . a school, college, or university . . . if such service is performed by a student who is enrolled and regularly attending classes at [the school]."[a] From 1951 to 2004, the Treasury Department construed the student exception as exempting students who work for their schools "as an incident to and for the purpose of pursuing a course of study." In late 2004, the department issued new regulations providing that the services of an employee who is normally scheduled to work forty or more hours per week "are not incident to and for the purpose of pursuing a course of study." As an example, the rule stated that a medical resident whose normal schedule requires him or her to perform services forty or more hours per week is not a student. Mayo filed a suit in a federal district court, asserting that this rule was invalid. The district court agreed, but the U.S. Court of Appeals for the Eighth Circuit reversed the trial court's ruling, concluding that the department's regulation was a permissible interpretation of an ambiguous statute. Mayo appealed to the United States Supreme Court.

IN THE WORDS OF THE COURT . . .
Chief Justice *ROBERTS* delivered the opinion of the Court.
* * * *

* * * Mayo's residency programs, which usually last three to five years, train doctors primarily through hands-on experience. * * * In 2005, Mayo paid its residents annual "stipends" ranging between $41,000 and $56,000 and provided them with health insurance, malpractice insurance, and paid vacation time.

---

a. See U.S.C. Section 3121(b).

Case 19.2–Continued

Mayo residents also take part in "a formal and structured educational program." Residents are assigned textbooks and journal articles to read and are expected to attend weekly lectures and other conferences.

* * * *

On December 21, 2004, the [Treasury] Department adopted an amended rule prescribing that an employee's service is "incident" to his studies only when "[t]he educational aspect of the relationship between the employer and the employee, as compared to the service aspect of the relationship, [is] predominant." * * * The amended provision clarifies that the Department's analysis "is not affected by the fact that the services performed . . . may have an educational, instructional, or training aspect."

* * * *

We begin our analysis with the first step of the two-part framework announced in *Chevron,* and ask whether Congress has "directly addressed the precise question at issue." We agree with the Court of Appeals that Congress has not done so. The statute does not define the term "student," and does not otherwise attend to the precise question whether medical residents are subject to FICA.

* * * *

* * * Such an ambiguity would lead us inexorably [impossible to prevent] to *Chevron* step two, under which we may not disturb an agency rule unless it is " 'arbitrary or capricious in substance, or manifestly contrary to the statute.' "

* * * *

* * * The Department issued the full-time employee rule pursuant to the explicit authorization to "prescribe all needful rules and regulations for the enforcement" of the Internal Revenue Code. *The Department issued the full-time employee rule only after notice-and-comment procedures, again a consideration identified in our precedents as a "significant" sign that a rule merits* Chevron *deference.* [Emphasis added.]

* * * *

The full-time employee rule easily satisfies the second step of Chevron, *which asks whether the Department's rule is a "reasonable interpretation" of the enacted text.* To begin, Mayo accepts that "the 'educational aspect of the relationship between the employer and*

the employee, as compared to the service aspect of the relationship, [must] be predominant' " in order for an individual to qualify for the exemption. Mayo objects, however, to the Department's conclusion that residents who work more than 40 hours per week categorically cannot satisfy that requirement. Because residents' employment is itself educational, Mayo argues, the hours a resident spends working make him "more of a student, not less of one." [Emphasis added.]

We disagree. Regulation, like legislation, often requires drawing lines. Mayo does not dispute that the Treasury Department reasonably sought a way to distinguish between workers who study and students who work. Focusing on the hours an individual works and the hours [she or] he spends in studies is a perfectly sensible way of accomplishing that goal.

* * * The Department reasonably determined that taxing residents under FICA would further the purpose of the Social Security Act. * * * Although Mayo contends that medical residents have not yet begun their "working lives" because they are not "fully trained," the Department certainly did not act irrationally in concluding that these doctors * * * are the kind of workers that Congress intended to both contribute to and benefit from the Social Security system.

DECISION AND REMEDY   The United States Supreme Court affirmed the decision of the appellate court, holding that the Treasury Department's full-time employee rule was valid. The Court found that the number of hours worked was a reasonable way to distinguish between workers who studied and students who worked. Therefore, the rule easily satisfied the *Chevron* standard.

THE ETHICAL DIMENSION   *Many students have to work full time to pay for their education. Is it fair to require them to pay FICA taxes when they would not have to do so if they worked only thirty hours per week? Explain.*

THE LEGAL ENVIRONMENT DIMENSION   *Would the United States Supreme Court have deferred to the Treasury Department's full-time employee regulation even if it had disagreed with the rule? Why or why not?*

 ## Enforcement and Adjudication

Although rulemaking is the most prominent agency activity, enforcement of the rules is also critical. Often, an agency itself enforces its rules. It identifies alleged violators and pursues civil remedies against them in a proceeding held by the agency rather than in federal court, although the agency's determinations are reviewable in court.

Investigation

After final rules are issued, agencies conduct investigations to monitor compliance with those rules or the terms of the enabling statute. A typical agency investigation of this kind might begin when the agency receives a report of a possible violation. (See this chapter's *Insight into Ethics* feature on the next page for a discussion of how

Insight into Ethics   Should Pharmaceutical Companies Be Allowed to Tweet?

Where do Americans go when they need medical information? More than 60 percent turn to the Internet, and half of those go to social networks, such as Twitter and Facebook, to consult with others about diagnosis and treatments. According to pharmaceutical companies, however, much of the information that potential customers are finding online is incorrect.

Consumers Lack Complete Information on Drugs

Drug companies are, of course, in the business of selling prescription drugs, and they have an incentive to ensure that consumers have correct information about those drugs. Yet drug manufacturers spend less than 5 percent of their consumer advertising budgets on Internet advertising. (More than 95 percent of the $4 billion that these companies spend on direct consumer advertising goes to traditional outlets, such as newspapers, magazines, and television.)

Similarly, drug companies have little or no presence on sites such as Facebook and Twitter. Why not? They fear that the U.S. Food and Drug Administration (FDA) will retaliate if they do not list all of the potential side effects when they mention their drugs on the Web.

Web Ads and Tweets Have Size Limits

The FDA requires advertisements for prescription drugs to disclose all of the potential negative side effects. A magazine ad for a prescription drug, for example, typically includes a large block of small print that details potential side effects. Display ads on the Web are not amenable to such lists. So, to avoid violating the FDA's regulations, pharmaceutical companies run only general, disease-related search ads on the Web. Because the ads only rarely mention a drug's brand name, consumers looking for information about a particular drug rarely click on or find such ads.

As a result, consumers have less information about available prescription drugs. For the same reason, drug companies are reluctant to tweet about their drugs. How could they possibly describe all of the potential side effects in only 140 characters?

FOR CRITICAL ANALYSIS
Insight into the E-Commerce Environment

Do pharmaceutical companies have an ethical responsibility to correct erroneous information about their products on sites such as Wikipedia?

---

concern about violating regulations has made pharmaceutical companies reluctant to use Twitter and Facebook.)

Many agency rules also require considerable compliance reporting from regulated entities, and such a report may trigger an enforcement investigation. For example, environmental regulators often require reporting of emissions, and the U.S. Occupational Safety and Health Administration requires companies to report any work-related deaths.

INSPECTIONS AND TESTS   Many agencies gather information through on-site inspections. Sometimes, inspecting an office, a factory, or some other business facility is the only way to obtain the evidence needed to prove a regulatory violation. At other times, an inspection or test is used in place of a formal hearing to show the need to correct or prevent an undesirable condition. Administrative inspections and tests cover a wide range of activities, including safety inspections of underground coal mines, safety tests of commercial equipment and automobiles, and environmental monitoring of factory emissions. An agency may also ask a firm or individual to submit certain documents or records to the agency for examination. For instance, the Federal Trade Commission often asks to inspect corporate records for compliance.

Normally, business firms comply with agency requests to inspect facilities or business records because it is in any firm's interest to maintain a good relationship with regulatory bodies. In some instances, however, such as when a firm thinks an agency's request is unreasonable and may be detrimental to the firm's interest, the firm may refuse to comply with the request. In such situations, an agency may resort to the use of a subpoena or a search warrant.

SUBPOENAS   There are two basic types of subpoenas. The subpoena *ad testificandum* ("to testify") is an ordinary subpoena. It is a writ, or order, compelling a witness to appear at an agency hearing. The subpoena *duces tecum*[9] ("bring it with you") compels an individual or organization to hand over books, papers, records, or documents to the agency. An administrative agency may use either type of subpoena to obtain testimony or documents.

There are limits on what an agency can demand. To determine whether an agency is abusing its discretion in its pursuit of information as part of an investigation, a court may consider such factors as the following:

1. *The purpose of the investigation.* An investigation must have a legitimate purpose. Harassment is an example of an improper purpose. An agency may not issue an administrative subpoena to inspect business records if the motive is to harass or pressure the business into settling an unrelated matter.
2. *The relevance of the information being sought.* Information is relevant if it reveals that the law is being violated or if it assures the agency that the law is not being violated.
3. *The specificity of the demand for testimony or documents.* A subpoena must, for example, adequately describe the material being sought.
4. *The burden of the demand on the party from whom the information is sought.* In responding to a request for information, a party must bear the costs of, for example, copying the requested documents, but a business generally is protected from revealing information such as trade secrets.

SEARCH WARRANTS   The Fourth Amendment protects against unreasonable searches and seizures by requiring that in most instances a physical search for evidence must be conducted under the authority of a search warrant. An agency's search warrant is an order directing law enforcement officials to search a specific place for a specific item and seize it for the agency. Although it was once thought that administrative inspections were exempt from the warrant requirement, the United States Supreme Court held in *Marshall v. Barlow's, Inc.,*[10] that the requirement does apply to the administrative process.

Agencies can conduct warrantless searches in several situations. Warrants are not required to conduct searches in highly regulated industries. Firms that sell firearms or liquor, for example, are automatically subject to inspections without warrants. Sometimes, a statute permits warrantless searches of certain types of hazardous operations, such as coal mines. Also, a warrantless inspection in an emergency situation is normally considered reasonable.

Adjudication

After conducting an investigation of a suspected rule violation, an agency may initiate an administrative action against an individual or organization. Most administrative actions are resolved through negotiated settlements at their initial stages, without the need for formal **adjudication** (the resolution of the dispute through a hearing conducted by the agency).

Adjudication The act of rendering a judicial decision. In an administrative process, the proceeding in which an administrative law judge hears and decides issues that arise when an administrative agency charges a person or a firm with violating a law or regulation enforced by the agency.

NEGOTIATED SETTLEMENTS   Depending on the agency, negotiations may take the form of a simple conversation or a series of informal conferences. Whatever form the negotiations take, their purpose is to rectify the problem to the agency's satisfaction and eliminate the need for additional proceedings.

---

9. Pronounced *doo*-suhs *tee*-kum.
10. 436 U.S. 307, 98 S.Ct. 1816, 56 L.Ed.2d 305 (1978).

Settlement is an appealing option to firms for two reasons: to avoid appearing uncooperative and to avoid the expense involved in formal adjudication proceedings and in possible later appeals. Settlement is also an attractive option for agencies. To conserve their own resources and avoid formal actions, administrative agencies devote a great deal of effort to giving advice and negotiating solutions to problems.

FORMAL COMPLAINTS   If a settlement cannot be reached, the agency may issue a formal complaint against the suspected violator. **EXAMPLE 19.6** The Environmental Protection Agency (EPA) finds that Acme Manufacturing, Inc., is polluting groundwater in violation of federal pollution laws. The EPA issues a complaint against the violator in an effort to bring the plant into compliance with federal regulations. ● This complaint is a public document, and a press release may accompany it. The party charged in the complaint responds by filing an answer to the allegations. If the charged party and the agency cannot agree on a settlement, the case will be adjudicated.

Administrative Law Judge (ALJ) One who presides over an administrative agency hearing and has the power to administer oaths, take testimony, rule on questions of evidence, and make determinations of fact.

Agency adjudication involves a hearing before an **administrative law judge (ALJ).** Under the Administrative Procedure Act (APA), before the hearing takes place, the agency must issue a notice that includes the facts and law on which the complaint is based, the legal authority for the hearing, and its time and place. The administrative adjudication process is described next and illustrated graphically in Exhibit 19–4 below.

● *Exhibit* **19–4 The Process of Formal Administrative Adjudication**

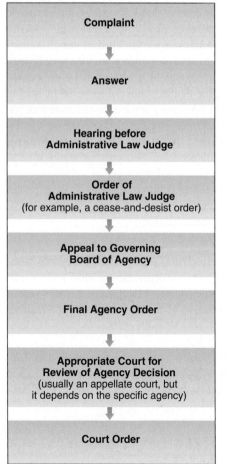

Complaint

↓

Answer

↓

Hearing before Administrative Law Judge

↓

Order of Administrative Law Judge (for example, a cease-and-desist order)

↓

Appeal to Governing Board of Agency

↓

Final Agency Order

↓

Appropriate Court for Review of Agency Decision (usually an appellate court, but it depends on the specific agency)

↓

Court Order

THE ROLE OF THE ADMINISTRATIVE LAW JUDGE   The ALJ presides over the hearing and has the power to administer oaths, take testimony, rule on questions of evidence, and make determinations of fact. Although technically the ALJ is not an independent judge and works for the agency prosecuting the case (in our example, the EPA), the law requires an ALJ to be an unbiased adjudicator (judge).

Certain safeguards prevent bias on the part of the ALJ and promote fairness in the proceedings. For example, the APA requires that the ALJ be separate from an agency's investigative and prosecutorial staff. The APA also prohibits *ex parte* (private) communications between the ALJ and any party to an agency proceeding, such as the EPA or the factory. Finally, provisions of the APA protect the ALJ from agency disciplinary actions unless the agency can show good cause for such an action.

HEARING PROCEDURES   Hearing procedures vary widely from agency to agency. Administrative agencies generally exercise substantial discretion over the type of procedure that will be used. Frequently, disputes are resolved through informal adjudication proceedings that resemble arbitration. **EXAMPLE 19.7** The Federal Trade Commission (FTC) charges Good Foods, Inc., with deceptive advertising. Representatives of Good Foods and of the FTC, their counsel, and the ALJ meet at a table in a conference room to resolve the dispute informally. ●

A formal adjudicatory hearing, in contrast, resembles a trial in many respects. Prior to the hearing, the parties are permitted to undertake discovery—involving depositions, interrogatories, and requests for documents or other information, as described in Chapter 3—although the discovery process is not quite as extensive as it would be in a court proceeding. The hearing itself must comply with the procedural requirements of the APA and must also meet the constitutional standards of due process. During the hearing, the parties may give testimony, present other evidence, and cross-examine adverse witnesses. A significant difference between a trial and an administrative agency hearing, though, is that normally much more information, including hearsay (second-hand information), can be introduced as evidence during an administrative hearing. The burden of proof in an enforcement proceeding is placed on the agency.

Initial Order In the context of administrative law, an agency's disposition in a matter other than a rulemaking. An administrative law judge's initial order becomes final unless it is appealed.

Final Order The final decision of an administrative agency on an issue. If no appeal is taken, or if the case is not reviewed or considered anew by the agency commission, the administrative law judge's initial order becomes the final order of the agency.

AGENCY ORDERS Following a hearing, the ALJ renders an **initial order,** or decision, on the case. Either party can appeal the ALJ's decision to the board or commission that governs the agency. If the factory in Example 19.6 on page 576 is dissatisfied with the ALJ's decision, it can appeal the decision to the EPA. If the factory is dissatisfied with the commission's decision, it can appeal the decision to a federal court of appeals. If no party appeals the case, the ALJ's decision becomes the **final order** of the agency. The ALJ's decision also becomes final if a party appeals and the commission and the court decline to review the case. If a party appeals and the case is reviewed, the final order comes from the commission's decision or (if that decision is appealed to a federal appellate court) that of the reviewing court.

 Public Accountability

As a result of growing public concern over the powers exercised by administrative agencies, Congress passed several laws to make agencies more accountable through public scrutiny. We discuss here the most significant of these laws.

Freedom of Information Act

Enacted in 1966, the Freedom of Information Act (FOIA)[11] requires the federal government to disclose certain records to any person on request, even if no reason is given for the request. The FOIA exempts certain types of records. For other records, though, a request that complies with the FOIA procedures need only contain a reasonable description of the information sought. An agency's failure to comply with such a request can be challenged in a federal district court. The media, industry trade associations, public-interest groups, and even companies seeking information about competitors rely on these FOIA provisions to obtain information from government agencies.

At issue in the following case was whether certain documents requested by members of the media were exempt under the FOIA and thus not available for release to the public.

---

11. 5 U.S.C. Section 552.

Case 19.3 | **United Technologies Corp. v. U.S. Department of Defense**

United States Court of Appeals, District of Columbia Circuit, 601 F.3d 557 (2010).
www.cadc.uscourts.gov/internet/home.nsf[a]

BACKGROUND AND FACTS Sikorsky Aircraft Corporation makes helicopters, and Pratt and Whitney produces aircraft engines. United Technologies Corporation wholly owns both companies, which have various foreign and domestic military and civilian customers. Both companies also sell their products to the United States. The Defense Contract Management Agency (DCMA), an agency within the U.S. Department of Defense (DOD) monitors defense contractors, including Sikorsky and Pratt, to ensure that they satisfy their contractual obligations when providing services and supplies to the United States. If the DCMA discovers a problem, it notifies the contractor and may issue a corrective action request (CAR) or an audit report to the contractor to remedy the problem. In 2004, a reporter submitted a Freedom of Information Act (FOIA) request to

---

a. Select "Opinions" from the options. On the page that opens, in the left column, click on "Browse by Date." At the top of the next page, choose "March" and "2010." Scroll down the list of search results to the case title and click on the link to the PDF to access the case. The U.S. Court of Appeals for the District of Columbia Circuit maintains this Web site.

Case 19.3–Continues next page ➡

Case 19.3–Continued

the regional DCMA office for copies of all CARs that had been issued to Sikorsky during the previous year concerning Sikorsky's Black Hawk helicopter. Another reporter requested information, including a CAR and audit-related documents, concerning Pratt's airplane engine center at Middletown, Connecticut. Sikorsky and Pratt argued that the documents were exempt from FOIA disclosure. The DCMA disagreed and ruled that the documents could be disclosed. Sikorsky and Pratt filed separate suits against the DOD in a federal district court, arguing that the decision to release the documents was arbitrary, capricious, and contrary to law under the Administrative Procedure Act. They sought declaratory and injunctive relief preventing the documents' disclosure. The district court granted summary judgment to the DOD in both cases, and Sikorsky and Pratt appealed.

IN THE WORDS OF THE COURT . . .
Karen LeCraft *HENDERSON*, Circuit Judge.
  * * * *

Exemption 4 covers "trade secrets and commercial or financial information obtained from a person and privileged or confidential." * * * *For the documents to be exempt from disclosure, their release must be likely to cause the contractors "substantial competitive harm" or "impair the Government's ability to obtain necessary information in the future."* [Emphasis added.]

To qualify [as a "substantial competitive harm"], an identified harm must "flow from the affirmative use of proprietary information by competitors."
  * * * *

* * * Sikorsky and Pratt maintain that the documents contain sensitive proprietary information about their quality control processes. Pratt's Director of Quality Military Engines attested that "a competitor with similar expertise could and would use the information to gain insights into the strengths and weaknesses of [Pratt's] quality control system as well as manufacturing techniques and use those insights to revise and improve its own quality control and manufacturing systems." Similarly, Sikorsky asserted that "proprietary information regarding Sikorsky's manufacturing process and procedures" is "inextricably intertwined with the quality control information"

included in the CARs and it asserted that "release of this proprietary information would substantially harm Sikorsky's competitive position because its competitors would use this information to their advantage * * * . In response, [the] DCMA simply stated that it had redacted [removed or obscured] all of the sensitive proprietary information and concluded that disclosure of the remaining information was not likely to cause the contractors substantial competitive harm.

We find [the] DCMA's response insufficient. The documents, even as redacted by [the] DCMA, appear to reveal details about Sikorsky's and Pratt's proprietary manufacturing and quality control processes. * * * The documents describe, in part, how the contractors build and inspect helicopters and/or engines. Once disclosed, competitors could, it appears, use the information to improve their own manufacturing and quality control systems, thus making "affirmative use of proprietary information" against which Exemption 4 is meant to guard.

DECISION AND REMEDY   The federal appellate court concluded that the DCMA had failed to provide a reasoned basis for its conclusion. The court remanded the case to the DCMA to examine the relevant data and give a satisfactory explanation for its decision, if it could, "including a rational connection between the facts found and the choice made."

THE ETHICAL DIMENSION   *Sikorsky and Pratt also argued that if the documents were released, their competitors would use the documents to discredit them in the eyes of current and potential customers. Would such actions amount to a "substantial competitive harm"? Explain.*

MANAGERIAL IMPLICATIONS   *Businesses that contract with government agencies to provide goods or services can expect to have their processes and procedures monitored by these agencies. This means that proprietary information, including trade secrets, may find its way into various government reports or other documents. To protect this information from competitors, managers in such businesses would be wise to seek counsel as to what types of documents are exempt from disclosure under the FOIA.*

Government in the Sunshine Act

Congress passed the Government in the Sunshine Act,[12] or open meeting law, in 1976. It requires that "every portion of every meeting of an agency" be open to "public observation." The act also requires procedures to ensure that the public is provided with adequate advance notice of the agency's scheduled meeting and agenda. Like the FOIA, the Sunshine Act contains certain exceptions. Closed meetings are permitted when (1) the subject of the meeting concerns accusing any person of a crime, (2) open meetings would frustrate implementation of future agency actions, or (3) the subject of the meeting involves matters relating to future litigation or rulemaking. Courts interpret these exceptions to allow open access whenever possible.

12. 5 U.S.C. Section 552b.

Regulatory Flexibility Act

Concern over the effects of regulation on the efficiency of businesses, particularly smaller ones, led Congress to pass the Regulatory Flexibility Act.[13] Under this act, whenever a new regulation will have a "significant impact upon a substantial number of small entities," the agency must conduct a regulatory flexibility analysis. The analysis must measure the cost that the rule would impose on small businesses and must consider less burdensome alternatives. The act also contains provisions to alert small businesses about forthcoming regulations. The act relieved small businesses of some record-keeping burdens, especially with regard to hazardous waste management.

Small Business Regulatory Enforcement Fairness Act

"Law . . . is a human institution, created by human agents to serve human ends."
—Harlan F. Stone, 1872–1946
(Chief justice of the United States Supreme Court, 1941–1946)

The Small Business Regulatory Enforcement Fairness Act (SBREFA) of 1996[14] allows Congress to review new federal regulations for at least sixty days before they take effect. This period gives opponents of the rules time to present their arguments to Congress.

The SBREFA also authorizes the courts to enforce the Regulatory Flexibility Act. This helps to ensure that federal agencies, such as the Internal Revenue Service, consider ways to reduce the economic impact of new regulations on small businesses. Federal agencies are required to prepare guides that explain in plain English how small businesses can comply with federal regulations.

The SBREFA set up the National Enforcement Ombudsman to receive comments from small businesses about their dealings with federal agencies. Based on these comments, Regional Small Business Fairness Boards rate the agencies and publicize their findings.

 ## State Administrative Agencies

Although much of this chapter deals with federal administrative agencies, state agencies also play a significant role in regulating activities within the states. Many of the factors that encouraged the proliferation of federal agencies also fostered the growing presence of state agencies. Reasons for the growth of administrative agencies at all levels of government include the inability of Congress and state legislatures to oversee the actual implementation of their laws and the greater technical competence of the agencies.

Commonly, a state creates an agency as a parallel to a federal agency to provide similar services on a more localized basis. For instance, a state department of public welfare shoulders some of the same responsibilities at the state level as the Social Security Administration does at the federal level. A state pollution-control agency follows the federal Environmental Protection Agency. Not all federal agencies have parallel state agencies, however. For instance, the Central Intelligence Agency has no parallel agency at the state level.

If the actions of parallel state and federal agencies conflict, the actions of the federal agency will prevail. **EXAMPLE 19.8** The Federal Aviation Administration (FAA) specifies the hours during which airplanes may land at and depart from airports. A California state agency issues inconsistent regulations governing the same activities. In a proceeding initiated by Interstate Distribution Corporation, an air transport company,

---

13. 5 U.S.C. Sections 601–612.
14. 5 U.S.C. Sections 801 *et seq.*

to challenge the state rules, the FAA regulations would be held to prevail. ● The priority of federal law over conflicting state laws is based on the supremacy clause of the U.S. Constitution. This clause, which is found in Article VI of the Constitution, states that the Constitution and "the Laws of the United States which shall be made in Pursuance thereof . . . shall be the supreme Law of the Land."

 ### Reviewing . . . Powers and Functions of Administrative Agencies

Assume that the Securities and Exchange Commission (SEC) has a rule under which it enforces statutory provisions prohibiting insider trading only when the insiders make monetary profits for themselves. Then the SEC makes a new rule, declaring that it has the statutory authority to bring enforcement actions against individuals even if they did not personally profit from the insider trading. The SEC simply announces the new rule without conducting a rulemaking proceeding. A stockbrokerage firm objects and says that the new rule was unlawfully developed without opportunity for public comment. The brokerage firm challenges the rule in an action that ultimately is reviewed by a federal appellate court. Using the information presented in the chapter, answer the following questions.

1. Is the SEC an executive agency or an independent regulatory agency? Does it matter to the outcome of this dispute? Explain.
2. Suppose that the SEC asserts that it has always had the statutory authority to pursue persons for insider trading regardless of whether they personally profited from the transaction. This is the only argument the SEC makes to justify changing its enforcement rules. Would a court be likely to find that the SEC's action was arbitrary and capricious under the Administrative Procedure Act (APA)? Why or why not?
3. Would a court be likely to give *Chevron* deference to the SEC's interpretation of the law on insider trading? Why or why not?
4. Now assume that a court finds that the new rule is merely "interpretive." What effect would this determination have on whether the SEC had to follow the APA's rulemaking procedures?

Linking the Law *to Management*
Dealing with Administrative Law

Whether you end up owning your own small business or working for a large corporation, you will be dealing with multiple aspects of administrative law. Recall that administrative law involves all of the rules, orders, and decisions of administrative agencies. At the federal level, these include the U.S. Food and Drug Administration, the Equal Employment Opportunity Commission, the National Labor Relations Board, and the U.S. Occupational Safety and Health Administration. All federal, state, and local government administrative agencies create rules that have the force of law. As a manager, you probably will have to pay more attention to administrative rules and regulations than to laws passed by local, state, and federal legislatures.

Federal versus State and Local Agency Regulations

The three levels of government create three levels of rules and regulations though their respective administrative agencies.

Typically, at least at the state level, there are agencies that govern business activities in a manner similar to federal agencies. You may face situations in which a state agency regulation and a federal agency regulation conflict. In general, federal agency regulations preempt, or take precedence over, conflicting state (or local) regulations.

As a manager, you will have to learn about agency regulations that pertain to your business activities. It will be up to you, as a manager or small-business owner, to ferret out those regulations that are most important and could potentially create the most liability if you violate them.

When Should You Participate in the Rulemaking Process?

All federal agencies and many state agencies invite public comments on proposed rules. For example, suppose that you manage a large construction company and your state occupational safety agency proposes a new rule requiring every employee on a construction site to wear hearing protection. You believe that the rule will lead to a less safe environment because your employees will not be able to communicate easily with one another.

Should you spend time offering comments to the agency? As an efficient manager, you make a trade-off calculation: First, you determine the value of the time that you would spend in attempting to prevent or at least alter the proposed rule. Then you compare this implicit cost with your estimate of the potential benefits your company would receive if the rule were not put into place.

Be Prepared for Investigations

All administrative agencies have investigatory powers. Agencies' investigators usually have the power to search business premises, although normally they first have to obtain a search warrant. As a manager, you have the choice of cooperating with agency investigators or providing the minimum amount of assistance. If you receive investigators regularly, you will often opt for cooperation. In contrast, if your business is rarely investigated, you may decide that the on-site proposed inspection is overreaching. Then you must contact your company's attorney for advice on how to proceed.

If an administrative agency cites you for a regulatory violation, you will probably negotiate a settlement with the agency rather than take your case before an administrative law judge. You will have to weigh the cost of the negotiated settlement with the potential cost of fighting the enforcement action.

Management Involves Flexibility

Throughout your business career, you will face hundreds of administrative rules and regulations, investigations, and perhaps enforcement proceedings for rule violations. You may sometimes be frustrated by seemingly meaningless regulations. You must accept that these are part of the legal environment in which you will work. The rational manager looks at administrative law as just another parameter that he or she cannot easily alter.

FOR CRITICAL ANALYSIS

Why are owner/operators of small businesses at a disadvantage relative to large corporations when they attempt to decipher complex regulations that apply to their businesses?

Key Terms

adjudication 575
administrative agency 563
administrative law judge (ALJ) 576
bureaucracy 566

delegation doctrine 566
enabling legislation 564
final order 577
initial order 577

interpretive rule 566
legislative rule 566
notice-and-comment rulemaking 569
rulemaking 569

Chapter Summary: Powers and Functions of Administrative Agencies

Agency Creation and Powers (See pages 564–567.)	1. Under the U.S. Constitution, Congress can delegate the implementation of its laws to government agencies. Congress can thus indirectly monitor an area in which it has passed laws without becoming bogged down in details relating to enforcement.
	2. Administrative agencies are created by enabling legislation, which usually specifies the name, composition, and powers of the agency.
	3. Agencies can create legislative rules, which are as binding as formal acts of Congress.
	4. The three branches of government exercise controls over agency powers and functions.
	a. Executive controls—The president can control agencies through appointments of federal officers and through vetoes of bills affecting agency powers.
	b. Legislative controls—Congress can give power to an agency, take it away, increase or decrease the agency's funding, or abolish the agency. The Administrative Procedure Act of 1946 also limits agencies.
	c. Judicial controls—Administrative agencies are subject to the judicial review of the courts.

(Continued)

Chapter Summary: Powers and Functions of Administrative Agencies, Continued

The Administrative Procedure Act (See pages 567–571.)	1. Administrative agencies exercise rulemaking, enforcement, and adjudicatory powers. 2. Agencies are authorized to create new regulations—their rulemaking function. This power is conferred on an agency in the enabling legislation. 3. Notice-and-comment rulemaking is the most common rulemaking procedure. It involves the publication of the proposed regulation in the *Federal Register,* followed by a comment period to allow private parties to comment on the proposed rule.
Judicial Deference to Agency Decisions (See pages 571–573.)	1. When reviewing agency decisions, courts typically grant deference (significant weight or consideration) to an agency's findings of fact and interpretations of law. 2. If Congress directly addressed the issue in dispute when enacting the statute, courts must follow the statutory language. 3. If the statute is silent or ambiguous, a court will uphold an agency's decision if the agency's interpretation of the statute was reasonable, even if the court would have interpreted the law differently. (This is known as *Chevron* deference.) 4. An agency must follow notice-and-comment rulemaking procedures before it is entitled to judicial deference in its interpretation of the law.

Enforcement and Adjudication (See pages 573–577.)	1. Administrative agencies investigate the entities that they regulate, both during the rulemaking process to obtain data and after rules are issued to monitor compliance.
	2. The most important investigative tools available to an agency are the following:
	  a. Inspections and tests—Used to gather information and to correct or prevent undesirable conditions.
	  b. Subpoenas—Orders that direct individuals to appear at a hearing or to hand over specified documents.
	3. Limits on administrative investigations include the following:
	  a. The investigation must be for a legitimate purpose.
	  b. The information sought must be relevant, and the investigative demands must be specific and not unreasonably burdensome.
	  c. The Fourth Amendment protects companies and individuals from unreasonable searches and seizures by requiring search warrants in most instances.
	4. After a preliminary investigation, an agency may initiate an administrative action against an individual or organization by filing a complaint. Most such actions are resolved at this stage before they go through the formal adjudicatory process.
	5. If there is no settlement, the case is presented to an administrative law judge (ALJ) in a proceeding similar to a trial.
	6. After a case is concluded, the ALJ renders an initial order, which can be appealed by either party to the board or commission that governs the agency and ultimately to a federal appeals court. If no appeal is taken or the case is not reviewed, then the order becomes the final order of the agency. The charged party may be ordered to pay damages or to stop carrying on some specified activity.

Public Accountability (See pages 577–579.)	Congress has passed several laws to make agencies more accountable through public scrutiny. These laws include the Freedom of Information Act, the Government in the Sunshine Act, the Regulatory Flexibility Act, and the Small Business Regulatory Enforcement Fairness Act.
State Administrative Agencies (See pages 579–580.)	States create agencies that parallel federal agencies to provide similar services on a more localized basis. If the actions of parallel state and federal agencies conflict, the actions of the federal agency will prevail.

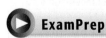 **ExamPrep**

ISSUE SPOTTERS

1. The U.S. Department of Transportation (DOT) sometimes hears an appeal from a party whose contract with the DOT has been canceled. An administrative law judge (ALJ), who works for the DOT, hears this appeal. What safeguards promote the ALJ's fairness?

2. Apples & Oranges Corporation learns that a federal administrative agency is considering a rule that will have a negative impact on the firm's ability to do business. Does the firm have any opportunity to express its opinion about the pending rule? Explain.

—**Check your answers to these questions against the answers provided in Appendix G.**

BEFORE THE TEST

Go to **www.cengagebrain.com**, enter the ISBN number "9781111530617," and click on "Find" to locate this textbook's Web site. Then, click on "Access Now" under "Study Tools," and select "Chapter 19" at the top. There you will find an "Interactive Quiz" that you can take to assess your mastery of the concepts in this chapter, as well as "Flashcards" and a "Glossary" of important terms.

 For Review

1. How are federal administrative agencies created?
2. What are the three basic functions of most administrative agencies?
3. What sequence of events must normally occur before an agency rule becomes law?
4. How do administrative agencies enforce their rules?
5. How do the three branches of government limit the power of administrative agencies?

 Questions and Case Problems

19–1. Rulemaking and Adjudication Powers. For decades, the Federal Trade Commission (FTC) resolved fair trade and advertising disputes through individual adjudications. In the 1960s, the FTC began promulgating rules that defined fair and unfair trade practices. In cases involving violations of these rules, the due process rights of participants were more limited and did not include cross-examination. This was because, although anyone found violating a rule would receive a full adjudication, the legitimacy of the rule itself could not be challenged in the adjudication. Any party charged with violating a rule was almost certain to lose the adjudication. Affected parties complained to a court, arguing that their rights before the FTC were unduly limited by the new rules. What will the court examine to determine whether to uphold the new rules?

19–2. **Question with Sample Answer. Informal Rulemaking.** Assume that the Food and Drug Administration (FDA), using proper procedures, adopts a rule describing its future investigations. This new rule covers all future circumstances in which the FDA wants to regulate food additives. Under the new rule, the FDA is not to regulate food additives without giving food companies an opportunity to cross-examine witnesses. At a subsequent time, the FDA wants to regulate methylisocyanate, a food additive. The FDA undertakes an informal rulemaking procedure, without cross-examination, and regulates methylisocyanate. Producers protest, saying that the FDA promised them the opportunity for cross-examination. The FDA responds that the Administrative Procedure Act does not require such cross-examination and that it is free to withdraw the promise made in its new rule.

If the producers challenge the FDA in court, on what basis would the court rule in their favor?

—**For a sample answer to Question 19–2, go to Appendix E at the end of this text.**

19–3. Judicial Controls. Under federal law, when accepting bids on a contract, an agency must hold "discussions" with all offerors. An agency may ask a single offeror for "clarification" of its proposal, however, without holding "discussions" with the others. Regulations define clarifications as "limited exchanges." In 2001, the U.S. Air Force asked for bids on a contract. The winning contractor would examine, assess, and develop means of integrating national intelligence assets with the U.S. Department of Defense space systems, to enhance the capabilities of the Air Force's Space Warfare Center. Among the bidders were Information Technology and Applications Corp. (ITAC) and RS Information Systems, Inc. (RSIS). The Air Force asked the parties for more information on their subcontractors but did not allow them to change their proposals. Determining that there were weaknesses in ITAC's bid, the Air Force awarded the contract to RSIS. ITAC filed a suit against the government, contending that the postproposal requests to RSIS, and its responses, were improper "discussions." Should the court rule in ITAC's favor? Why or why not? [*Information Technology & Applications Corp. v. United States,* 316 F.3d 1312 (Fed.Cir. 2003)].

19–4. Investigation. Riverdale Mills Corp. makes plastic-coated steel wire products in Massachusetts. Riverdale uses a water-based cleaning process that generates acidic and alkaline wastewater. To meet federal clean-water requirements, Riverdale has a system within its plant to treat the water. It then flows through a pipe that opens into a manhole-covered test pit outside the plant in full view of Riverdale's employees. Three hundred feet away, the pipe merges into the public sewer system. In October 1997, the U.S. Environmental Protection Agency (EPA) sent Justin Pimpare and Daniel Granz to inspect the plant. Without a search warrant and without Riverdale's express consent, the agents took samples from the test pit. Based on the samples, Riverdale and James Knott, the company's owner, were charged with criminal violations of the federal Clean Water Act. The defendants sued the EPA agents in a federal district court, alleging violations of the Fourth Amendment. What right does the Fourth Amendment provide in this context? This right is based on a "reasonable expectation of privacy." Should the agents be held liable? Why or why not? [*Riverdale Mills Corp. v. Pimpare,* 392 F.3d 55 (1st Cir. 2004)]

19–5. Rulemaking. The Investment Company Act prohibits a mutual fund from engaging in certain transactions in which there may be a conflict of interest between the manager of the fund and its shareholders. Under rules issued by the Securities and Exchange Commission (SEC), however, a fund that meets certain conditions may engage in an otherwise prohibited transaction. In 2004, the SEC added two new conditions. A year later, the SEC reconsidered the new conditions in terms of the costs that they would impose on the funds. Within eight days, and without asking for public input, the SEC readopted the conditions. The U.S. Chamber of Commerce—which is both a mutual fund shareholder and an association with mutual fund managers among its members—asked a federal appellate court to review the new rules. The Chamber charged that in readopting the rules, the SEC relied on materials not in the "rulemaking record" without providing an opportunity for public comment. The SEC countered that the information was otherwise "publicly available." In adopting a rule, should an agency consider information that is not part of the rulemaking record? Why or why not? [*Chamber of Commerce of the United States v. Securities and Exchange Commission,* 443 F.3d 890 (D.C.Cir. 2006)]

19–6. **Case Problem with Sample Answer. Agency Powers.** A well-documented rise in global temperatures has coincided with a significant increase in the concentration of carbon dioxide in the atmosphere. Many scientists believe that the two trends are related, because when carbon dioxide is released into the atmosphere, it produces a greenhouse effect, trapping solar heat. Under the Clean Air Act (CAA), the Environmental Protection Agency (EPA) is authorized to regulate "any" air pollutants "emitted into . . . the ambient air" that in its "judgment cause, or contribute to, air pollution." A group of private organizations asked the EPA to regulate carbon dioxide and other "greenhouse gas" emissions from new motor vehicles. The EPA refused, stating that Congress last amended the CAA in 1990 without authorizing new, binding auto-

emissions limits. The petitioners—nineteen states, including Massachusetts—asked a district court to review the EPA's denial. Did the EPA have the authority to regulate greenhouse gas emissions from new motor vehicles? If so, was its stated reason for refusing to do so consistent with that authority? Discuss. [*Massachusetts v. Environmental Protection Agency,* 549 U.S. 497, 127 S.Ct. 1438, 167 L. Ed.2d 248 (2007)]

—**To view a sample answer for Case Problem 19–6, go to Appendix F at the end of this text.**

19–7. Judicial Deference. Dave Conley, a longtime heavy smoker, was diagnosed with lung cancer and died two years later. His death certificate stated that the cause of death was cancer, but it also noted other significant conditions that had contributed to his death, including a history of cigarette smoking and coal mining. Conley's widow filed for benefits under the Black Lung Benefits Act, which provides for victims of black lung disease caused by coal mining. To qualify for benefits under the act, the exposure to coal dust must be a substantially contributing factor leading to the person's death. Under the statute, this meant to "hasten death." The U.S. Department of Labor collected Conley's work and medical records. An administrative law judge (ALJ) reviewed the record and took testimony from several physicians about the cause of Conley's death. Only one physician testified that the coal dust was a substantial factor in Conley's death, but he offered no evidence other than his testimony. Nevertheless, the ALJ ruled that the coal mining had been a substantial factor that had hastened Conley's death and awarded benefits to his widow. Conley's employer appealed to the Benefits Review Board (BRB), which reversed the ALJ's decision. The BRB found that there was insufficient evidence to hold that coal dust was a substantial factor in Conley's lung cancer. Conley's widow appealed. Should the court defer to the ALJ's decision on the cause of Conley's death? Which decision does the federal appellate court review, the ALJ's conclusions or the BRB's reversal? Explain your answers. [*Conley v. National Mines Corp.,* 595 F.3d 297 (6th Cir. 2010)]

19–8. Arbitrary and Capricious Test. Every year, Michael Manin, an airline pilot and flight instructor, had to renew his first-class airman medical certificate, which showed that he had met medical standards for aircraft operation. The application for renewal included questions regarding criminal history, including non-traffic misdemeanors. Manin had been convicted of disorderly conduct, a minor misdemeanor, in 1995 and again in 1997, but never disclosed these convictions on his yearly applications. The Federal Aviation Administration (FAA) discovered the two convictions in 2007 and issued an emergency order to revoke Manin's flight certificates in 2008. Manin filed an answer to this revocation order, as well as an administrative complaint. He claimed that he had not known he was required to report a conviction for a minor misdemeanor and also asserted that the complaint was stale (legally expired) under National

Transportation Safety Board (NTSB) regulations. At the hearing on Manin's complaint, the administrative law judge affirmed the emergency revocation order. Manin appealed to the full NTSB, which also affirmed. Manin then appealed to a federal appellate court, claiming that the NTSB had departed from its precedent in prior cases without explanation. The FAA conceded that the NTSB's statement of the rules pertaining to staleness was inaccurate, but it urged the court to affirm anyway. How should the court rule? Does an agency's departure from precedent without explanation mean that its decision was arbitrary and capricious? Explain. [*Manin v. National Transportation Safety Board,* 627 F.3d 1239 (D.C.Cir. 2011)]

19–9. 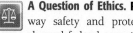 **A Question of Ethics. Rulemaking.** To ensure highway safety and protect driver health, Congress charged federal agencies with regulating the hours of service of commercial motor vehicle operators. Between 1940 and 2003, the regulations that applied to long-haul truck drivers were mostly unchanged. In 2003, the Federal Motor Carrier Safety Administration (FMCSA) revised the regulations significantly, increasing the number of daily and weekly hours that drivers could work. The agency had not considered the impact of the changes on the health of the drivers, however, and the revisions were overturned. The FMCSA then issued a notice that it would reconsider the revisions and opened them up for public comment. The agency analyzed the costs to the industry and the crash

risks due to driver fatigue under different options and concluded that the safety benefits of not increasing the hours did not outweigh the economic costs. In 2005, the agency issued a rule that was nearly identical to the 2003 version. Public Citizen, Inc., and others, including the Owner-Operator Independent Drivers Association, asked a district court to review the 2005 rule as it applied to long-haul drivers. [*Owner-Operator Independent Drivers Association, Inc. v. Federal Motor Carrier Safety Administration,* 494 F.3d 188 (D.C.Cir. 2007)]

1. The agency's cost-benefit analysis included new methods that were not disclosed to the public in time for comments. Was this unethical? Should the agency have disclosed the new methodology sooner? Why or why not?

2. The agency created a graph to show the risk of a crash as a function of the time a driver spent on the job. The graph plotted the first twelve hours of a day individually, but the rest of the time was depicted with an aggregate figure at the seventeenth hour. This made the risk at those hours appear to be lower. Is it unethical for an agency to manipulate data? Explain.

19–10.  **Critical-Thinking Legal Environment Question.** Does Congress delegate too much power to federal administrative agencies? Do the courts defer too much to Congress in its grant of power to those agencies? What are the alternatives to the agencies that we encounter in every facet of our lives?

Consumer Protection

Contents

Chapter Objectives

After reading this chapter, you should be able to answer the following questions:

1. **When will advertising be deemed deceptive?**

2. **What special rules apply to telephone solicitation?**

3. **What is Regulation Z, and to what type of transactions does it apply?**

4. **How does the Federal Food, Drug, and Cosmetic Act protect consumers?**

5. **What are the major federal statutes providing for consumer protection in credit transactions?**

(Moody75/Creative Commons)

During the heyday of the consumer movement in the 1960s and 1970s, Congress enacted a substantial amount of legislation to protect "the good of the people," to borrow a phrase from Marcus Tullius Cicero in the chapter-opening quotation above. All statutes, agency rules, and common law judicial decisions that serve to protect the interests of consumers are classified as *consumer law.*

Since the financial crisis of 2008, there has been a renewed interest in protecting consumers from abusive practices of credit-card companies, financial institutions, and insurance companies. Congress enacted new credit-card regulations that took effect in 2010, as well as various reforms to protect borrowers. Congress also enacted health-care reforms, including a law that requires chain restaurants to post the caloric content of foods on their menus.

Today, countless federal and state laws protect consumers from unfair trade practices, unsafe products, discriminatory or unreasonable credit requirements, and other problems related to consumer transactions. The Federal Trade Commission (FTC) plays a key role in the enforcement of the federal regulations, but many other administrative agencies are also involved in consumer protection. In fact, nearly every agency and department of the federal government has an office of consumer affairs, and most states have one or more such offices to help consumers.

• *Exhibit* **20–1** **Selected Areas of Consumer Law Regulated by Statutes**

Labeling and Packaging

Example—The Fair Packaging and Labeling Act of 1966

Advertising

Example—The Federal Trade Commission Act of 1914

Sales

Example—The FTC Mail-Order Rule of 1975

CONSUMER LAW

Food and Drugs

Example—The Federal Food, Drug, and Cosmetic Act of 1938

Product Safety

Example—The Consumer Product Safety Act of 1972

Credit Protection

Example—The Consumer Credit Protection Act of 1968

In this chapter, we examine some of the major laws and regulations protecting consumers. Because of the wide variation among state consumer protection laws, our primary focus is on federal legislation. Realize, though, that state laws often provide more sweeping and significant protections for the consumer than do federal laws. Exhibit 20–1 above indicates many of the areas of consumer law that are regulated by federal statutes.

 Deceptive Advertising

One of the earliest—and still one of the most important—federal consumer protection laws is the Federal Trade Commission Act of 1914 (mentioned in Chapter 19). The act created the FTC to carry out the broadly stated goal of preventing unfair and deceptive trade practices, including deceptive advertising, within the meaning of Section 5 of the act.

Deceptive Advertising Advertising that misleads consumers, either by making unjustified claims concerning a product's performance or by omitting a material fact concerning the product's composition or performance.

Generally, **deceptive advertising** occurs if a reasonable consumer would be misled by the advertising claim. Vague generalities and obvious exaggerations are permissible. These claims are known as puffery. Recall from the discussion of warranties in Chapter 11 that puffery consists of statements about a product that a reasonable person would not believe to be literally true. When a claim takes on the appearance of literal authenticity, however, it may create problems.

Advertising that *appears* to be based on factual evidence but that in fact cannot be scientifically supported will be deemed deceptive. **CASE EXAMPLE 20.1** MedLab, Inc., advertised that its weight-loss supplement (The New Skinny Pill) would cause users to lose substantial amounts of weight rapidly. The ads claimed that "clinical studies prove" the pill causes users to lose "as much as 15 to 18 pounds per week and as much as 50 percent of all excess weight in just 14 days, without dieting or exercising." The FTC sued MedLab for deceptive advertising. An expert hired by the FTC to evaluate the claim testified that to lose this much weight, "a 200-pound individual would need to run between 57 and 68 miles every day—the equivalent of more than two marathons per day. The court concluded that the advertisement was false and misleading, granted the FTC a summary judgment, and issued a permanent injunction to stop MedLab from running the ads.[1] •

1. *FTC v. MedLab, Inc.*,615 F.Supp.2d 1068 (N.D.Cal. 2009).

(Tamila/Creative Commons)

When Campbell's advertised that its soups helped fight heart disease, what important fact did the ads not include?

Bait-and-Switch Advertising   Advertising a product at a very attractive price (the bait) and then, once the consumer is in the store, saying that the advertised product either is not available or is of poor quality. The customer is then urged to purchase (switched to) a more expensive item.

Some advertisements contain "half-truths," meaning that the presented information is true but incomplete and, therefore, leads consumers to a false conclusion. **EXAMPLE 20.2** The maker of Campbell's soups advertised that "most" Campbell's soups were low in fat and cholesterol and thus were helpful in fighting heart disease. What the ad did not say was that Campbell's soups were also high in sodium and that high-sodium diets may increase the risk of heart disease. Hence, the FTC ruled that the company's claims were deceptive. ● Advertising featuring an endorsement by a celebrity may be deemed deceptive if the celebrity does not actually use the product.

Bait-and-Switch Advertising

The FTC has issued rules that govern specific advertising techniques. One of the more important rules is contained in the FTC's "Guides Against Bait Advertising."[2] The rule is designed to prevent **bait-and-switch advertising**—that is, advertising a very low price for a particular item that will likely be unavailable to the consumer and then encouraging him or her to purchase a more expensive item. The low price is the "bait" to lure the consumer into the store. The salesperson is instructed to "switch" the consumer to a different, more expensive item. According to the FTC guidelines, bait-and-switch advertising occurs if the seller refuses to show the advertised item, fails to have reasonable quantities of it available, fails to promise to deliver the advertised item within a reasonable time, or discourages employees from selling the item.

Online Deceptive Advertising

Deceptive advertising can occur in the online environment as well. The FTC actively monitors online advertising and has identified hundreds of Web sites that have made false or deceptive claims for products ranging from medical treatments for various diseases to exercise equipment and weight-loss aids.

The FTC has issued guidelines to help online businesses comply with existing laws prohibiting deceptive advertising.[3] These guidelines include the following three basic requirements:

1. All ads—both online and offline—must be truthful and not misleading.
2. The claims made in an ad must be substantiated, meaning that advertisers must have evidence to back up their claims.
3. Ads cannot be unfair, which the FTC defines as "likely to cause substantial consumer injury that consumers could not reasonably avoid and that is not outweighed by the benefit to consumers or competition."

"Ads are the cave art of the twentieth century."

Marshall McLuhan, 1911–1980
(Canadian academic and commentator)

The guidelines also call for "clear and conspicuous" disclosure of any qualifying or limiting information. The overall impression of the ad is important in meeting this requirement. The FTC suggests that advertisers should assume that consumers will not read an entire Web page. Therefore, to satisfy the "clear and conspicuous" requirement, advertisers should place the disclosure as close as possible to the claim being qualified or include the disclosure within the claim itself. If such placement is not feasible, the next-best location is on a section of the page to which a consumer

---

2. 16 C.F.R. Section 288.
3. "Advertising and Marketing on the Internet: Rules of the Road." *ftc.com.* September 2000. n.p. Web.

can easily scroll. Generally, hyperlinks to a disclosure are recommended only for lengthy disclosures or for disclosures that must be repeated in a variety of locations on the Web page.

As discussed in Chapter 6 on page 172, Congress passed the federal CAN-SPAM Act to combat the problems associated with unsolicited commercial e-mails, commonly referred to as spam. Many states have also passed consumer protection laws that regulate deceptive online advertising. In the following case, an e-mail service provider claimed that an online marketing company had violated a California statute that prohibited deceptive content in e-mail advertising. The court had to decide whether the CAN-SPAM Act preempted the state statute (preemption was discussed in Chapter 4).

Case 20.1   Hypertouch, Inc. v. ValueClick, Inc.

California Court of Appeal, Second District, 192 Cal.App.4th 805, 123 Cal.Rptr.3d 8 (2011).

BACKGROUND AND FACTS   Hypertouch, Inc., provides e-mail service to customers located inside and outside California. ValueClick, Inc., and its subsidiaries provide online marketing services to third party advertisers that promote retail products. ValueClick contracts with these third party advertisers to place offers on its Web sites. ValueClick also contracts with affiliates that send out commercial e-mail advertisements. The advertisements include links redirecting consumers to promotions on ValueClick's Web sites. If a consumer clicks through an e-mail advertisement and participates in a promotional offer, the affiliate that sent the initial e-mail is compensated for generating a customer "lead." The affiliate, rather than ValueClick, controls the content and headers of the e-mails. Hypertouch filed a complaint against ValueClick, its subsidiaries, and others for violating a California state statute that prohibits e-mail advertising that contains deceptive content and headings. The trial court held that the federal CAN-SPAM Act preempts the California statute and granted a summary judgment in favor of ValueClick. Hypertouch appealed.

IN THE WORDS OF THE COURT . . .
ZELON, J. [Judge]
    * * * *

A determination whether Hypertouch's claims are preempted by federal law requires an analysis of both section 17529.5 [the California statute] and the CAN-SPAM Act.
    * * * *

In 2003, the California Legislature passed Senate Bill 186, which imposed broad restrictions on advertising in unsolicited commercial e-mail advertisements sent from or to a computer within California. * * * The Legislature concluded that, to effectively regulate the abuses associated with spam, it was necessary to target not only the entities that send unsolicited commercial e-mail advertisements, but also the advertisers whose products and services are promoted in those e-mails[.]
    * * * *

Like several other California consumer protection statutes targeting deceptive advertising practices, section 17529.5 dispenses with many of the elements associated with common law fraud, which normally requires the plaintiff to prove "(a) [a] misrepresentation . . .; (b) knowledge of falsity (or *'scienter'*); (c) intent to defraud, [that is,] to induce reliance; (d) justifiable reliance; and (e) resulting damage."
    * * * *

The CAN-SPAM Act includes a provision that expressly preempts state statutes that regulate the use of commercial e-mail "except to the extent that any such statute . . . prohibits falsity or deception in any portion of a commercial [e-mail]." * * * [The legislative history indicates that the act] was intended "to implement 'one national standard' " regarding the content of commercial e-mail because "the patchwork of state laws had proven ineffective."

The legislative history also makes clear, however, that the Act's preemption provision was largely intended to target state statutes imposing content requirements on commercial e-mails, while leaving states free to regulate the use of deceptive practices in commercial e-mails in whatever manner they chose.
    * * * *

The [preemption] clause does not reference either fraud or the common law, but rather permits any state law that prohibits " 'falsity and deception in any portion of a commercial electronic mail message.' Congress "is certainly familiar with the word 'fraud' and choose[s] not to use it; the words 'falsity or deception' suggest broader application."

* * * [Furthermore,] at the time the CAN-SPAM Act was passed, Congress was aware that many states imposed liability for deceptive commercial e-mails without requiring reliance or other elements of common law fraud. Despite this knowledge, Congress chose not to use the word 'fraud' in the savings [preemption] provision, thereby suggesting that it intended the phrase "falsity or deception" to have a broader application.

Case 20.1–Continues next page ➡

Case 20.1–Continued

* * * *

Rather than broadening the scope of prohibited content in commercial e-mail, California's decision to dispense with the elements of common law fraud was intended to create a more effective mechanism for eradicating the use of deceptive commercial e-mails. Section 17529.5 seeks to accomplish this goal in two ways. *First, the statute permits a recipient of a deceptive commercial e-mail to bring suit regardless of whether they were actually misled or harmed by the deceptive message.* This ensures that the use of deceptive e-mail will not go unpunished merely because it failed to mislead its targets. Second, imposing strict liability on the advertisers who benefit from (and are the ultimate cause of) deceptive e-mails, forces those entities to take a more active role in supervising the complex web of affiliates who are promoting their products. [Emphasis added.]

* * * *

The numerous subject lines at issue in this suit contain a wide variety of different statements. Some simply state that the recipient of the e-mail can get a free gift ("Get a $300 gift card FREE" * * *), others suggest that the recipient can obtain something free for doing a particular task ("Let us know your opinion and win a free gift card") * * * [Emphasis added.]

[ValueClick has] made no effort to explain why a reasonable trier of fact could not conclude that many of the subject lines at issue here, such as those offering a free gift card with no qualifying language, would be likely to mislead a reasonable person. Instead, it targets isolated e-mails in the record, such as one e-mail with the subject line "GAP Promotion," and argues that those particular e-mails are,

as a matter of law, not deceptive. Regardless of whether Respondent is correct that the isolated e-mails it cites are not likely to mislead the recipient, that alone does not entitle it to summary judgment on [Hypertouch's claims.]

DECISION AND REMEDY The state appellate court held that California's anti-spam statute is not preempted by the federal CAN-SPAM Act, which exempts state laws that prohibit falsity or deception in commercial e-mail. The court therefore reversed the lower court's decision and remanded the case for trial.

THE SOCIAL DIMENSION *Describe some ways in which the heading of an e-mail advertisement might be deceptive.*

MANAGERIAL IMPLICATIONS *Business owners and managers who engage in e-mail advertising or contract with online marketing companies for that purpose need to be aware of and comply with the applicable state laws. The online marketing company in this case claimed that it was not responsible for the deceptive content of the advertising because it did not send or initiate the e-mails—that was done by the affiliates—and it did not know that the e-mails were deceptive. The state court rejected this argument, however, finding that California's law applies more broadly to any entity that advertises in deceptive e-mails. This holding will aid plaintiffs who sue under California's antispam statute. It may also persuade courts in other states to apply the same reasoning and broadly interpret their state laws against deceptive online advertising.*

Federal Trade Commission Actions

The FTC receives complaints from many sources, including competitors of alleged violators, consumers, consumer organizations, trade associations, Better Business Bureaus, government organizations, and state and local officials. If it receives numerous and widespread complaints about a problem, the FTC will investigate. If the FTC concludes that a given advertisement is unfair or deceptive, it sends a formal complaint to the alleged offender. The company may agree to settle the complaint without further proceedings. If no settlement is reached, the FTC can conduct a hearing before an administrative law judge (see page 576) at which the company can present its defense.

If the FTC succeeds in proving that an advertisement is unfair or deceptive, it usually issues a **cease-and-desist order** requiring the company to stop the challenged advertising. In some circumstances, it may also require **counteradvertising** in which the company advertises anew—in print, on the Internet, on radio, and on television—to inform the public about the earlier misinformation. The FTC sometimes institutes a **multiple product order,** which requires a firm to cease and desist from false advertising in regard to all of its products, not just the product that was the subject of the action.

When a company's deceptive ad involves wrongful charges to consumers, the FTC may seek other remedies, including restitution. **CASE EXAMPLE 20.3** Verity International, Ltd., billed phone-line subscribers who accessed certain online pornography sites at

Cease-and-Desist Order An administrative or judicial order prohibiting a person or business firm from conducting activities that an agency or court has deemed illegal.

Counteradvertising New advertising that is undertaken pursuant to a Federal Trade Commission order for the purpose of correcting earlier false claims that were made about a product.

Multiple Product Order An order issued by the Federal Trade Commission to a firm that has engaged in deceptive advertising by which the firm is required to cease and desist from false advertising not only in regard to the product that was the subject of the action but also in regard to all the firm's other products.

the rate for international calls to Madagascar. When consumers complained about the charges, Verity employees told them that the charges were valid and had to be paid, or the consumers would face further collection activity. A federal appellate court held that this representation of "uncontestability" was deceptive and a violation of the FTC Act and ordered Verity to pay nearly $18 million in restitution to consumers.[4] ●

 ## Telemarketing and Fax Advertising

The pervasive use of telemarketing led Congress to pass the Telephone Consumer Protection Act (TCPA) of 1991.[5] The act prohibits telephone solicitation using an automatic telephone dialing system or a prerecorded voice. Most states also have laws regulating telephone solicitation. The TCPA also makes it illegal to transmit ads via fax without first obtaining the recipient's permission.

The Federal Communications Commission (FCC) enforces the act. The FCC imposes substantial fines ($11,000 each day) on companies that violate the junk fax provisions of the TCPA and has fined one company as much as $5.4 million for violations.[6] The TCPA also gives consumers a right to sue for either the actual monetary loss resulting from a violation of the act or $500 in damages for each violation, whichever is greater. If a court finds that a defendant willfully or knowingly violated the act, the court has the discretion to triple the damages that are awarded.

REMEMBER Changes in technology often require changes in the law.

The Telemarketing and Consumer Fraud and Abuse Prevention Act of 1994[7] directed the FTC to establish rules governing telemarketing and to bring actions against fraudulent telemarketers. The FTC's Telemarketing Sales Rule of 1995[8] requires a telemarketer to identify the seller; describe the product being sold; and disclose all material facts related to the sale, including the total cost of the goods being sold, any restrictions on obtaining or using the goods, and whether a sale will be considered final and nonrefundable. The act makes it illegal for telemarketers to misrepresent information (including facts about their goods or services and earnings potential, for example). A telemarketer must also remove a consumer's name from its list of potential contacts if the consumer so requests. (For a discussion of how this rule applies to foreign telemarketers, see this chapter's *Beyond Our Borders* feature on the following page.) An amendment to the Telemarketing Sales Rule established the national Do Not Call Registry. Telemarketers must refrain from calling consumers who have placed their names on the list.

Advertising is essential to business. Before you advertise via faxes, however, you should know the applicable rules and be aware that the FCC aggressively enforces these rules. Make sure that all fax advertisements comply with the Telephone Consumer Protection Act and any state laws on faxes. Educate and train your employees about these laws. Do not send faxes without first obtaining the recipient's permission, and develop effective opt-out procedures so that anyone who no longer wants to receive faxes can notify you. Keep reliable records of the faxes you send and maintain these records for at least four years. Do not purchase lists of fax numbers from outsiders. Avoiding consumer complaints about unwanted faxes and phone calls is the best way to avoid potentially significant liability.

---

4. *Federal Trade Commission v. Verity International, Ltd.,* 443 F.3d 48 (2d Cir. 2006).

5. 47 U.S.C. Sections 227 *et seq.,* as modified by the Junk Fax Protection Act of 2005.

6. See *Missouri ex rel. Nixon v. American Blast Fax, Inc.,* 323 F.3d 649 (8th Cir. 2003); *cert.* denied, 540 U.S. 1104, 124 S.Ct. 1043, 157 L.Ed.2d 888 (2004). The term *ex rel.* in the case title means that the government brought this action on behalf of an individual (Nixon).

7. 15 U.S.C. Sections 6101–6108.

8. 16 C.F.R. Sections 310.1–310.8.

Beyond Our Borders   **Protecting U.S. Consumers from Cross-Border Telemarketers**

One of the problems that the Federal Trade Commission (FTC) faces in protecting consumers from scams is that the perpetrators frequently are located outside the United States. Nevertheless, the FTC has had some success in bringing cases under the Telemarketing Sales Rule (TSR) against telemarketers who violate the law from foreign locations.

As discussed in the text, the TSR requires telemarketers to disclose all material facts about the goods or services being offered and prohibits the telemarketers from misrepresenting information. Significantly, the TSR applies to any offer made to consumers in the United States—even if the offer comes from a foreign firm.

A Telemarketing Scam from Canada

Oleg Oks and Aleksandr Oks, along with several other residents of Canada, set up a number of sham corporations in Ontario. Through these businesses, they placed unsolicited outbound telephone calls to consumers in the United States. The telemarketers offered preapproved Visa or MasterCard credit cards to consumers who agreed to permit their bank accounts to be electronically debited for an advance fee of $319.

(©P. Vey/Conde Nast Publications/ www.cartoonbank.com)

"I just got home. Can you call back tomorrow when I'm still at work?"

The telemarketers frequently promised that the consumers would receive other items—such as a cell phone, satellite dish system, vacation package, or home security system—at no additional cost. In fact, *no consumers* who paid the advance fee received either a credit card or any of the promised gifts. Instead, consumers received a "member benefits" package that included items such as booklets on how to improve their creditworthiness or merchandise cards that could be used only to purchase goods from the catalogue provided.

Joint Cooperation to Prosecute the Telemarketers

The FTC, working in conjunction with the U.S. Postal Service and various Canadian

government and law enforcement agencies, conducted an investigation that lasted several years. Ultimately, in 2007 Oleg and Aleksandr Oks pleaded guilty in Canada to criminal charges for deceptive advertising. They were barred from telemarketing for ten years.[a]

In addition, the FTC filed a civil lawsuit against the Okses and other Canadian defendants in a federal court in Illinois. The court found that the defendants had violated the FTC Act and the TSR and ordered them to pay nearly $5 million in damages.[b]

For Critical Analysis

Suppose that this scam had originated in a country that was not as friendly and cooperative as Canada is with the United States. In that situation, how would the FTC obtain sufficient evidence to prosecute the foreign telemarketers? Is the testimony of U.S. consumers regarding the phone calls that they received sufficient proof? Why or why not?

---

a. Oleg was also sentenced to a year in jail and two years' probation.

b. *Federal Trade Commission v. Oks,* 2007 WL 3307009 (N.D.Ill. 2007). The court entered its final judgment on March 18, 2008.

 Labeling and Packaging

A number of federal and state laws deal specifically with the information given on labels and packages. In general, labels must be accurate, and they must use words that are understood by the ordinary consumer. In some instances, labels must specify the raw materials used in the product, such as the percentage of cotton, nylon, or other fibers used in a garment. In other instances, the products must carry a warning, such as those required on cigarette packages and advertising.[9]

Fuel Economy Labels on Automobiles

The Energy Policy and Conservation Act of 1975[10] requires automakers to attach an information label to every new car. This label must include the Environmental

---

9. 15 U.S.C. Sections 1331 *et seq.*
10. 49 U.S.C. Section 32908(b)(1).

Protection Agency's fuel economy estimate for the vehicle. In the following case, the buyer of a new car complained that the vehicle had failed to achieve the fuel economy estimate advertised in the automaker's brochure and listed on the label.

Case 20.2 | **Paduano v. American Honda Motor Co.**

California Court of Appeal, Fourth District, 169 Cal.App.4th 1453, 88 Cal.Rptr.3d 90 (2009).

Were the fuel economy estimates of the Honda Civic Hybrid exaggerated, and could an unhappy consumer get his money back?

BACKGROUND AND FACTS In 2004, Gaetano Paduano bought a new Honda Civic Hybrid in California. The information label on the car stated that the fuel economy estimates from the Environmental Protection Agency (EPA) were forty-seven miles per gallon (mpg) and forty-eight mpg for city and highway driving, respectively. Honda's sales brochure added, "Just drive the Hybrid like you would a conventional car and save on fuel bills." Paduano soon became frustrated with the car's fuel economy, which was less than half of the EPA's estimate. When American Honda Motor Company refused to repurchase the vehicle, Paduano filed a suit in a California state court against the automaker, alleging deceptive advertising in violation of the state's Consumer Legal Remedies Act and Unfair Competition Law. Honda argued that the federal Energy Policy and Conservation Act (EPCA), which prescribed the EPA's fuel economy estimate, preempted Paduano's claims. The court issued a summary judgment in Honda's favor. Paduano appealed to a state intermediate appellate court.

IN THE WORDS OF THE COURT . . .
AARON, J. [Judge]
* * * *

The basic rules of preemption are not in dispute: *Under the supremacy clause of the United States Constitution, Congress has the power to preempt state law concerning matters that lie within the authority of Congress. In determining whether federal law preempts state law, a court's task is to discern congressional intent.* Congress's express intent in this regard will be found when Congress explicitly states that it is preempting state authority. [Emphasis added.]
* * * *

Honda * * * argues that [the EPCA] prevents Paduano from pursuing his * * * claims. That provision states in pertinent part,

When a requirement under [the EPCA] is in effect, a State or a political subdivision of a State may adopt or enforce a law or regulation on disclosure of fuel economy or fuel operating costs for an automobile

covered by [the EPCA] only if the law or regulation is identical to that requirement.

* * * Honda goes on to assert that "Paduano's deceptive advertising and misrepresentation claims would impose *non* identical disclosure requirements."

Contrary to Honda's characterization * * * , Paduano's claims are based on statements Honda made in its advertising brochure to the effect that one may drive a Civic Hybrid in the same manner as one would a conventional car, and need not do anything "special," in order to achieve the beneficial fuel economy of the EPA estimates. * * * Paduano is challenging * * * Honda's * * * commentary in which it alludes to those estimates in a manner that may give consumers the misimpression that they will be able to achieve mileage close to the EPA estimates while driving a Honda hybrid in the same manner as they would a conventional vehicle. Paduano does not seek to require Honda to provide "additional alleged facts" regarding the Civic Hybrid's fuel economy, as Honda suggests, but rather, seeks to prevent Honda from making misleading claims about how easy it is to achieve better fuel economy. Contrary to Honda's assertions, if Paduano were to prevail on his claims, Honda would not have to do anything differently with regard to its disclosure of the EPA mileage estimates.
* * * *

* * * Allowing states to regulate false advertising and unfair business practices may further the goals of the EPCA, and we reject Honda's claim.

DECISION AND REMEDY The state intermediate appellate court concluded that federal law did not preempt Paduano's claims concerning Honda's advertising. The court reversed the judgment and remanded the case.

THE ETHICAL DIMENSION *Suppose that the defendant automaker had opposed this action solely to avoid paying for a car that had proved to be a "lemon." Would this have been unethical? Explain.*

THE LEGAL ENVIRONMENT DIMENSION *What does the interpretation of the law in this case suggest to businesspersons who sell products labeled with statements mandated by federal or state law?*

Food Labeling

Because the quality and safety of food are so important to consumers, several statutes deal specifically with food labeling. The Fair Packaging and Labeling Act requires that food product labels identify (1) the product; (2) the net quantity of the contents and, if the number of servings is stated, the size of a serving; (3) the manufacturer; and (4) the packager or distributor.[11] The act also provides for additional requirements concerning descriptions on packages, savings claims, components of nonfood products, and standards for the partial filling of packages.

The Nutrition Labeling and Education Act of 1990[12] requires food labels to provide standard nutrition facts (including the amount and type of fat that the food contains) and regulates the use of such terms as *fresh* and *low fat*. The U.S. Food and Drug Administration (FDA) and the U.S. Department of Agriculture (USDA) are the primary agencies that publish regulations on food labeling in the *Federal Register.* These rules are updated annually. For instance, rules that became effective in 2009 require the labels on fresh meats, vegetables, and fruits to indicate where the food originated so that consumers can know whether it was imported.

New Menu Labeling Regulations

Tucked into the health-care reform bill that President Obama signed into law in March 2010 was a provision aimed at combating the problem of obesity in the United States. The provision requires all restaurant chains with twenty or more locations to post the caloric content of the foods on their menus so that customers will know how many calories they are eating.[13] Foods offered through vending machines must also be labeled so that their caloric content is visible to would-be purchasers. The hope is that consumers, armed with this information, will consider the number of calories when they make their food choices. The new federal law supersedes all state and local laws already in existence.

The FDA is developing a national standard for menu labeling and establishing specific regulations supporting that standard. Any restaurant to which the law applies must post the caloric content of the foods listed on its standard menu, menu boards, or menu lists for drive-through windows. Signs must also be posted near salad bars and buffets to provide information on the foods offered there. Condiments, daily specials, and foods offered for only a limited period (less than sixty days) are exempt from the rules.

In addition, restaurants must post standard guidelines on the number of calories that an average person requires daily so that customers can determine what portion of a day's calories a particular food choice will provide. Many restaurant chains, including Dunkin' Donuts and KFC, are already trying to create lower-calorie foods that taste as good as their popular high-calorie items.

 ## Sales

A number of statutes protect consumers by requiring the disclosure of certain terms in sales transactions and providing rules governing home or door-to-door sales, mail-order transactions, referral sales, and unsolicited merchandise. The Federal Reserve Board of Governors, for example, has issued **Regulation Z,** which governs credit provisions associated with sales contracts (discussed later in this chapter). Many

Regulation Z   A set of rules issued by the Federal Reserve Board of Governors to implement the provisions of the Truth-in-Lending Act.

---

11. 15 U.S.C. Sections 4401–4408.

12. 21 U.S.C. Section 343.1.

13. See Section 4205 of the Patient Protection and Affordable Care Act, Pub. L. No.111-148, 124 Stat. 119 (March 23, 2010).

"Cooling-off" Laws Laws that allow buyers a period of time, such as three business days, in which to cancel door-to-door sales contracts.

states and the FTC have **"cooling-off" laws** that permit the buyers of goods sold door to door to cancel their contracts within three business days. The FTC rule further requires that consumers be notified in Spanish of this right if the oral negotiations for the sale were in that language.

Telephone and Mail-Order Sales

The FTC's Mail or Telephone Order Merchandise Rule of 1993 amended the FTC's Mail-Order Rule of 1975.[14] The rule provides specific protections for consumers who purchase goods over the phone, through the mail, or via a computer (Internet) or fax machine. For instance, merchants are required to ship orders within the time promised in their advertisements and to notify consumers when orders cannot be shipped on time. The rule also requires merchants to issue a refund within a specified period of time when a consumer cancels an order.

In addition, under the Postal Reorganization Act of 1970[15] a consumer who receives *unsolicited* merchandise sent by U.S. mail can keep it, throw it away, or dispose of it in any manner that she or he sees fit. The recipient will not be obligated to the sender.

Online Sales

The FTC and other federal agencies have brought numerous enforcement actions against those who perpetrate online fraud. Nonetheless, protecting consumers from fraudulent and deceptive sales practices conducted via the Internet has proved to be a challenging task. Faced with economic recession, job losses, mounting debt, and dwindling savings, many consumers are looking for any source of income. The number of consumers who have fallen prey to Internet fraud has actually grown in recent years. Complaints to the FTC about the sale of business opportunities, such as work-at-home offers, nearly doubled from 2008 to 2009 and tripled by 2012.

What are the FTC's Mail-Order Rule requirements with respect to when merchants must ship goods?

(©Stephen Coburn, 2009. Used under license from Shutterstock.com)

▶ Protection of Health and Safety

Although labeling and packaging laws (discussed earlier) promote consumer health and safety, there is a significant distinction between regulating the information dispensed about a product and regulating the actual content of the product. Tobacco products are the classic example. Producers of tobacco products are required to warn consumers about the hazards associated with the use of their products, but the sale of tobacco products has not been subjected to significant restrictions or banned outright despite the obvious dangers to health. We now examine various laws that regulate the actual products made available to consumers.

Food and Drugs

The first federal legislation regulating food and drugs was enacted in 1906 as the Pure Food and Drugs Act.[16] That law, as amended in 1938, exists now as the Federal Food, Drug, and Cosmetic Act (FDCA).[17] The act protects consumers against adulterated

---

14. 16 C.F.R. Sections 435.1–435.2.
15. 39 U.S.C. Section 3009.
16. 21 U.S.C. Sections 1–5, 7–15.
17. 21 U.S.C. Section 301.

and misbranded foods and drugs. As to foods, the act establishes food standards, specifies safe levels of potentially hazardous food additives, and sets classifications of food and food advertising. Most of these statutory requirements are monitored and enforced by the FDA.

The FDCA also charges the FDA with the responsibility of ensuring that drugs are safe before they are marketed to the public. Under an extensive set of procedures established by the FDA, drugs must be shown to be safe, as well as effective, before they may be marketed to the public. **CASE EXAMPLE 20.4** A group of terminally ill patients claimed that they were entitled, under the U.S. Constitution, to better access to experimental drugs before the FDA completed its clinical tests. The court, however, found that the FDA's policy of limiting access to drugs that were undergoing tests was rationally related to protecting patients from potentially unsafe drugs. Therefore, the court held that terminally ill patients do not have a fundamental constitutional right of access to experimental drugs.[18] ● A 1976 amendment to the FDCA[19] authorizes the FDA to regulate medical devices, such as pacemakers, and to withdraw from the market any such device that is mislabeled.

Consumer Product Safety

In 1972, Congress enacted the Consumer Product Safety Act,[20] which created the first comprehensive scheme of regulation over matters concerning consumer safety. The act also established the Consumer Product Safety Commission (CPSC) and gave it far-reaching authority over consumer safety.

The CPSC passed a rule stating that any product sold to children cannot contain lead. How could children be harmed if some lead was used in the manufacturing of dirt bikes?

THE CPSC'S AUTHORITY   The CPSC conducts research on the safety of individual products and maintains a clearinghouse on the risks associated with various products. The Consumer Product Safety Act authorizes the CPSC to do the following:

1. Set safety standards for consumer products.
2. Ban the manufacture and sale of any product that the commission believes poses an "unreasonable risk" to consumers. (Products banned by the CPSC have included various types of fireworks, cribs, and toys, as well as many products containing asbestos or vinyl chloride.)
3. Remove from the market any products it believes to be imminently hazardous. The CPSC frequently works with manufacturers to voluntarily recall defective products from stores. **EXAMPLE 20.5** In 2009, in cooperation with the CPSC, Kolcraft Enterprises, Inc., recalled one million infant play yards because of a defective latch that could cause a rail to fall, posing a risk to children. ●
4. Require manufacturers to report on any products already sold or intended for sale if the products have proved to be hazardous.
5. Administer other product-safety legislation, including the Child Protection and Toy Safety Act of 1969[21] and the Federal Hazardous Substances Act of 1960.[22]

NOTIFICATION REQUIREMENTS   The Consumer Product Safety Act imposes notification requirements on distributors of consumer products. Distributors must immediately notify the CPSC when they receive information that a product "contains

18. *Abigail Alliance for Better Access to Developmental Drugs v. von Eschenbach,* 495 F.3d 695 (D.C.Cir. 2007).
19. 21 U.S.C. Sections 352(o), 360(j), 360(k), and 360c–360k.
20. 15 U.S.C. Section 2051.
21. 15 U.S.C. Section 1262(e).
22. 15 U.S.C. Sections 1261–1273.

a defect which . . . creates a substantial risk to the public" or "an unreasonable risk of serious injury or death."

CASE EXAMPLE 20.6 A company that sold juicers received twenty-three letters from customers complaining that during operation the juicer suddenly exploded, sending pieces of glass and razor-sharp metal across the room. Nevertheless, the company waited more than six months before notifying the CPSC that the product posed a significant risk to the public. In a case filed by the federal government, the court held that when a company first receives information regarding a threat, the company is required to report the problem within twenty-four hours to the CPSC. Even if the company had to investigate the allegations, it should not have taken more than ten days to verify the information and report the problem. The court therefore found that the company had violated the law and ordered it to pay damages.[23] ●

Health-Care Reforms

In 2010, the health-care reforms enacted by Congress began to go into effect.[24] These laws gave Americans new rights and benefits with regard to health care and will eventually (in 2014) prohibit certain insurance company practices, such as denial of coverage for preexisting conditions and cancellation of coverage for technical mistakes.

The reforms protect consumers by helping more children get health coverage and allowing young adults (under the age of twenty-six) to be covered by their parents' health insurance. The act also ended lifetime limits and most annual limits on care, and it gave patients access to recommended preventive services (such as cancer screening, vaccinations, and well-baby checks) without cost. Medicare patients will get a 50-percent discount on name-brand drugs, and seniors who reached the gap in Medicare's prescription-drug coverage in 2010 received a one-time tax rebate of $250. The gap in Medicare's drug coverage is to be closed completely by 2020.

Up to 4 million small businesses are now eligible for tax credits to assist them in providing insurance benefits to workers. States can receive federal matching funds to cover health care for additional low-income individuals and families. The act also expanded coverage for early retirees and devoted funds to preventing Medicare and health-care fraud. Additional funding is allocated for construction of community health centers and to support public programs to keep Americans healthy.

The provisions also attempt to control the rising costs of insurance premiums. Currently, insurance companies must spend at least 85 percent of all premium dollars collected from large employers (80 percent of the premiums collected from individuals and small employers) on benefits and quality improvement. If an insurance company does not meet these goals, it must provide rebates to consumers. Additionally, states can require insurance companies to justify their premium increases to be eligible to participate in a new health-insurance exchange.

Credit Protection

Credit protection is one of the most important aspects of consumer protection legislation. Nearly 80 percent of U.S. consumers have credit cards, and most carry a balance on these cards, amounting to about $2.5 trillion of debt nationwide. In 2010,

---

23. *United States v. Mirama Enterprises, Inc.,* 185 F.Supp.2d 1148 (S.D.Cal. 2002).

24. Patient Protection and Affordable Care Act of 2010, Pub. L. No. 111-148, 124 Stat. 119 (March 23, 2010); and the Health Care and Education Reconciliation Act of 2010, Pub. L. No. 111-152, 124 Stat. 1029 (March 30, 2010).

Congress established a new agency, the Consumer Financial Protection Bureau, which is dedicated to overseeing the practices of banks, mortgage lenders, and credit-card companies.[25] We discuss significant consumer credit-protection legislation next.

Truth-in-Lending Act

A key statute regulating the credit and credit-card industries is the Truth-in-Lending Act (TILA), the name commonly given to Title 1 of the Consumer Credit Protection Act,[26] which was passed by Congress in 1968. (The TILA's role in regulating mortgage loans was discussed in Chapter 13.) The TILA has been amended several times, most recently in 2009, when Congress passed sweeping reforms to strengthen its consumer protections.[27]

The TILA is basically a *disclosure law*. It is administered by the Federal Reserve Board and requires sellers and lenders to disclose credit terms or loan terms so that individuals can shop around for the best financing arrangements. TILA requirements apply only to persons who, in the ordinary course of business, lend funds, sell on credit, or arrange for the extension of credit. Thus, sales or loans made between two consumers do not come under the protection of the act. Additionally, this law protects only debtors who are *natural* persons (as opposed to the artificial "person" of a corporation); it does not extend to other legal entities.

The disclosure requirements are found in Regulation Z. If the contracting parties are subject to the TILA, the requirements of Regulation Z apply to any transaction involving an installment sales contract that calls for payment to be made in more than four installments. Transactions subject to Regulation Z typically include installment loans, retail and installment sales, car loans, home-improvement loans, and certain real estate loans if the amount of financing is less than $25,000.

Under the provisions of the TILA, all of the terms of a credit instrument must be clearly and conspicuously disclosed. A lender must disclose the annual percentage rate (APR), finance charge, amount financed, and total payments (the sum of the amount loaned, plus any fees, finance charges, and interest at the end of the loan). The TILA provides for contract rescission (cancellation) if a creditor fails to follow the exact procedures required by the act.[28]

EQUAL CREDIT OPPORTUNITY   In 1974, Congress enacted, as an amendment to the TILA, the Equal Credit Opportunity Act (ECOA). The ECOA prohibits the denial of credit solely on the basis of race, religion, national origin, color, gender, marital status, or age. The act also prohibits credit discrimination on the basis of whether an individual receives certain forms of income, such as public-assistance benefits.

Under the ECOA, a creditor may not require the signature of an applicant's spouse, or a cosigner, on a credit instrument if the applicant qualifies under the creditor's standards of creditworthiness for the amount requested. **CASE EXAMPLE 20.7** Tonja, an African American, applied for financing with a used-car dealer. The dealer reviewed

> **NOTE** The Federal Reserve Board is part of the Federal Reserve System, which influences the lending and investing activities of commercial banks and the cost and availability of credit.

> *"Credit is a system whereby a person who can't pay gets another person who can't pay to guarantee that he can pay."*
>
> Charles Dickens, 1812–1870
> (English novelist)

---

25. This act was mentioned in Chapter 19.

26. 15 U.S.C. Sections 1601–1693r.

27. The TILA was amended in 1980 by the Truth-in-Lending Simplification and Reform Act; and significantly amended again in 2009 by the Credit Card Accountability Responsibility and Disclosure Act of 2009, Pub. L. No. 111-24, 123 Stat. 1734, enacting 15 U.S.C. Sections 1616, 1651, 1665c to 1665e, 1666i-1, 1666i-2, 1666b, and 1693l-1, and 16 U.S.C. Section 1a-7b, as well as amending many other provisions of the TILA.

28. Note, though, that amendments to the TILA enacted in 1995 prevent borrowers from rescinding loans because of minor clerical errors in the final documents that were signed [15 U.S.C. Sections 1605, 1631, 1635, 1640, and 1641].

Tonja's credit report and, without submitting the application to the lender, decided that she would not qualify. Instead of informing Tonja that she did not qualify, the dealer told her that she needed a cosigner on the loan to purchase the car. According to a federal appellate court, the dealership qualified as a creditor in this situation because it unilaterally denied credit. Thus, the dealer could be held liable under the ECOA.[29] •

Assume that your credit card is stolen, but you do not report the theft to the credit-card issuer. What is the maximum dollar liability you face?

CREDIT-CARD RULES   The TILA also contains provisions regarding credit cards. One provision limits the liability of a cardholder to $50 per card for unauthorized charges made before the creditor is notified that the card has been lost. If a consumer received an *unsolicited* credit card in the mail that is later stolen, the company that issued the card cannot charge the consumer for any unauthorized charges.

Another provision requires credit-card companies to disclose the balance computation method that is used to determine the outstanding balance, and to state when finance charges begin to accrue. Other provisions set forth procedures for resolving billing disputes with the credit-card company. These procedures may be used if, for example, a cardholder thinks that an error has occurred in billing or wishes to withhold payment for a faulty product purchased by credit card.

In 2009, President Barack Obama signed into law amendments to the credit-card protections of the TILA that became effective in 2010. The most significant provisions of the new rules are as follows:

1. Protect consumers from retroactive increases in interest rates on existing card balances unless the account is sixty days delinquent.
2. Require companies to provide forty-five days' advance notice to consumers before making changes to the credit-card terms.
3. Require companies to send out monthly bills to cardholders twenty-one days before the due date.
4. Prevent companies from increasing the interest rate charged on a customer's credit-card balance except in specific situations, such as when a promotional rate ends.
5. Prevent companies from charging over-limit fees except in specified situations.
6. Require companies to apply payments in excess of the minimum amount due to the customer's higher-interest balances first when the borrower has balances with different rates (such as the higher interest rates commonly charged for cash advances).
7. Prevent companies from computing finance charges based on the previous billing cycle (known as double-cycle billing, which hurts consumers because they are charged interest for the previous cycle even though they have paid the bill in full).

CONSUMER LEASES   The Consumer Leasing Act (CLA) of 1988[30] amended the TILA to provide protection for consumers who lease automobiles and other goods. The CLA applies to those who lease or arrange to lease consumer goods in the ordinary

---

29. *Treadway v. Gateway Chevrolet Oldsmobile, Inc.,* 362 F.3d 971 (7th Cir. 2004).
30. 15 U.S.C. Sections 1667–1667e.

course of their business. The act applies only if the goods are priced at $25,000 or less and if the lease term exceeds four months. The CLA and its implementing regulation, Regulation M,[31] require lessors to disclose in writing all of the material terms of the lease.

Fair Credit Reporting Act

Congress enacted the Fair Credit Reporting Act (FCRA) to protect consumers against inaccurate credit reporting.[32] The act provides that consumer credit reporting agencies may issue credit reports to users only for specified purposes, including the extension of credit, the issuance of insurance policies, compliance with a court order, and compliance with a consumer's request for a copy of her or his own credit report. Any time a consumer is denied credit or insurance on the basis of his or her credit report, the consumer must be notified of that fact and of the name and address of the credit reporting agency that issued the report. The same notice must be sent to consumers who are charged more than others ordinarily would be for credit or insurance because of their credit reports.

Under the FCRA, consumers can request the source of any information used by the credit agency, as well as the identity of anyone who has received an agency's report. Consumers are also permitted to have access to the information contained about them in a credit reporting agency's files. If a consumer discovers that the agency's files contain inaccurate information about his or her credit standing, the agency, on the consumer's written request, must investigate the disputed information. Any unverifiable or erroneous information must be deleted within a reasonable period of time.

An agency that fails to comply with the act is liable for actual damages, plus additional damages not to exceed $1,000 and attorneys' fees. The FCRA also allows a court to award punitive damages for a "willful" violation.

CASE EXAMPLE 20.8 Branch Banking & Trust Company of Virginia (BB&T) gave Rex Saunders an auto loan but failed to provide him with a payment coupon book and rebuffed his attempts to make payments on the loan. In fact, BB&T told Saunders that it had not extended a loan to him. Eventually, BB&T discovered its mistake and demanded full payment, plus interest and penalties. When payment was not immediately forthcoming, BB&T declared that Saunders was in default. It then repossessed the car and forwarded adverse credit information about Saunders to credit reporting agencies, without noting that Saunders disputed the information. Saunders filed a lawsuit alleging violations of the FCRA and was awarded $80,000 in punitive damages. An appellate court found that the damages award was reasonable, given BB&T's willful violation.[33] ●

Fair and Accurate Credit Transactions Act

In an effort to combat rampant identity theft (discussed in Chapter 6), Congress passed the Fair and Accurate Credit Transactions (FACT) Act of 2003.[34] The act established a national fraud alert system so that consumers who suspect that they have been or may be victimized by identity theft can place an alert in their credit files. The FACT Act also requires the major credit reporting agencies to provide consumers

> "*A consumer is a shopper who is sore about something.*"
> Harold Coffin, 1905–1981
> (American humorist)

---

31. 12 C.F.R. Part 213.
32. 15 U.S.C. Sections 1681 *et seq.*
33. *Saunders v. Branch Banking & Trust Co. of Virginia,* 526 F.3d 142 (4th Cir. 2008).
34. Pub. L. No. 108-159, 117 Stat. 1952 (December 4, 2003).

with a free copy of their credit reports every twelve months. Another provision requires account numbers on credit-card receipts to be truncated (shortened) so that merchants, employees, and others who have access to the receipts cannot obtain a consumer's name and full credit-card number. The act also mandates that financial institutions work with the FTC to identify "red flag" indicators of identity theft and to develop rules for disposing of sensitive credit information.

The FACT Act also gives consumers who have been victimized by identity theft some assistance in rebuilding their credit reputations. For example, credit reporting agencies must stop reporting allegedly fraudulent account information once the consumer establishes that identify theft has occurred. Business owners and creditors are required to provide a consumer with copies of any records that can help the consumer prove that a particular account or transaction is fraudulent (records showing that an account was created with a fraudulent signature, for example). In addition, to help prevent the spread of erroneous credit information, the act allows consumers to report the accounts affected by identity theft directly to the creditors.

Fair Debt Collection Practices Act

In 1977, Congress enacted the Fair Debt Collection Practices Act (FDCPA)[35] in an attempt to curb what were perceived to be abuses by collection agencies. The act applies only to specialized debt-collection agencies and attorneys who regularly attempt to collect debts on behalf of someone else, usually for a percentage of the amount owed. Creditors attempting to collect debts are not covered by the act unless, by misrepresenting themselves, they cause the debtors to believe that they are collection agencies.

PROHIBITED DEBT-COLLECTION TACTICS   The FDCPA explicitly prohibits a collection agency from doing any of the following:

1. Contacting the debtor at the debtor's place of employment if the debtor's employer objects.
2. Contacting the debtor during inconvenient or unusual times (for example, calling the debtor at three o'clock in the morning) or at any time if the debtor is being represented by an attorney.
3. Contacting third parties other than the debtor's parents, spouse, or financial adviser about payment of a debt unless a court authorizes such action.
4. Using harassment or intimidation (for example, using abusive language or threatening violence) or employing false or misleading information (for example, posing as a police officer).
5. Communicating with the debtor at any time after receiving notice that the debtor is refusing to pay the debt, except to advise the debtor of further action to be taken by the collection agency.

NOTIFICATION AND BONA FIDE ERRORS   The FDCPA also requires a collection agency to include a **validation notice** whenever it initially contacts a debtor for payment of a debt or within five days of that initial contact. The notice must state that the debtor has thirty days in which to dispute the debt and to request a written verification of the debt from the collection agency. The debtor's request for debt validation must be in writing. (See the discussion in this chapter's *Management Perspective* feature on the next page for more on FDCPA requirements.)

Validation Notice   An initial notice to a debtor from a collection agency, required by federal law, informing the debtor that he or she has thirty days to challenge the debt and request verification.

---

35. 15 U.S.C. Section 1692.

Management Perspective   Dealing with the Fair Debt Collection Practices Act's Requirements

Management Faces a Legal Issue

How closely must collection agencies follow the strict requirements of the Fair Debt Collection Practices Act (FDCPA)? Does a collection agency have to cease all contact with a defaulting debtor once that debtor has hired an attorney or a mediation service? Can a collection agency leave a voice message for a defaulting consumer? These are just some of the issues that face owners and managers of collection agencies.

What the Courts Say

In one case, Paul Schmitt owed a debt to First Bank USA. He retained an attorney, who told the bank that Schmitt was unable to pay the debt. The attorney further advised that if the account was turned over to a collection agency, the bank should inform the agency of the attorney's representation. The bank transferred the account to a collection agency without informing it of the debtor's legal representation. When that collection agency sent a letter directly to Schmitt, he brought suit for violation of the FDCPA. Ultimately, an appellate court ruled in favor of the collection agency, stating that it had not violated the FDCPA because it did not have knowledge of the debtor's legal representation.[a]

What constitutes incomplete notice in a collection letter? That was the issue in a case involving Collectors Training Institute of Illinois, a debt collector, which stated in a demand letter that "[u]nless you notify this office within 30 (thirty) days after the receipt of this notice that you dispute the validity of this debt, or any portion thereof,

this debt will be assumed to be valid." The debtor sued the debt collector arguing that such a statement did not accurately provide the validation notice required by the FDCPA. The debtor claimed that the statement was misleading because it did not include the phrase "by the debt collector" at the end—the phrasing set forth as the legal standard by the FDCPA. A Pennsylvania court sided with the debtor. It ruled that without the phrase "by the debt collector," an unsophisticated debtor could have been misled into thinking that the debt would be assumed valid by another entity, such as a court or a credit reporting agency.[b]

Debt-collection practices have also raised privacy concerns. There have been many lawsuits against collection agencies over voice messages or voicemails left by debt collectors. The FDCPA prohibits third party disclosure. Does leaving a voice message regarding a debt collection on an answering machine constitute such a disclosure? That depends on the jurisdiction and the situation. For example, a Florida court ruled in favor of the debtor. It stated that if a collection agency leaves a voice message for a consumer on an answering machine—even at home—other people (third parties) could hear the message.[c]

Implications for Managers

Managers of debt-collection agencies or business accounting departments face a dilemma at all times—the more they try to avoid possible lawsuits under the FDCPA, the less effective they will be in collecting past-due debts. Hence, it is usually worthwhile to seek more specific information on the Web site of the American Collectors Association regarding what language should be used for debt collection.

---

a. *Schmitt v. FMA Alliance*, 398 F.3d 995 (8th Cir. 2005).

b. *Galuska v. Collectors Training Institute of Illinois, Inc.*, 2008 WL 2050809 (M.D.Pa. 2008).

c. *Berg v. Merchants Association Collection Division, Inc.*, 586 F.Supp.2d 1336 (S.D.Fla. 2009).

The enforcement of the FDCPA is primarily the responsibility of the Federal Trade Commission. The act provides that a debt collector who fails to comply with the act is liable for actual damages, plus additional damages not to exceed $1,000 and attorneys' fees.

Debt collectors who violate the act are exempt from liability if they can show that the violation was not intentional and resulted from a bona fide error—regardless of existing procedures that were adopted to avoid such an error. The "bona fide error" defense typically has been applied to mistakes of fact or clerical errors, but should the defense also apply to mistakes of law? In other words, if a violation occurs because a debt collector misinterpreted the legal requirements of the FDCPA, can the debt collector avoid liability under the act? That was the issue in the following case.

Case 20.3 Jerman v. Carlisle, McNellie, Rini, Kramer & Ulrich, LPA

Supreme Court of the United States, ___ U.S. ___, 130 S.Ct. 1605, 176 L.Ed.2d 519 (2010).
www.supremecourt.gov/opinions/opinions.aspx[a]

(©Stephen Van Horn, 2010.
Used under license from Shutterstock.com)

BACKGROUND AND FACTS The law firm Carlisle, McNellie, Rini, Kramer & Ulrich, LPA (Legal Professional Association), represented Countrywide Home Loans, Inc. Carlisle filed a complaint in an Ohio state court on behalf of Countrywide against Karen L. Jerman. Carlisle sought foreclosure of a mortgage held by Countrywide on real property that Jerman owned. Carlisle served a notice on Jerman stating that the mortgage debt would be assumed valid unless Jerman disputed it in writing. Jerman's lawyer sent a letter disputing the debt. Carlisle sought verification from its client, Countrywide. When Countrywide acknowledged that Jerman had already paid the debt in full, Carlisle withdrew the foreclosure lawsuit. Jerman then filed a lawsuit against Carlisle for violation of the Fair Debt Collection Practices Act (FDCPA). Specifically, Jerman claimed that Carlisle had violated the FDCPA by requiring her to dispute the debt in writing. Although the trial court agreed that Carlisle had violated the act, it nonetheless concluded that the act shielded Carlisle from liability because the violation was not intentional and resulted from a bona fide error. The U.S. Court of Appeals for the Sixth Circuit affirmed. That court, while acknowledging that a bona fide error defense normally is available only for clerical and factual errors, extended it to "mistakes of law." Jerman appealed to the United States Supreme Court.

IN THE WORDS OF THE COURT . . .
Justice *SOTOMAYOR* delivered the opinion of the Court.
* * * *

We granted *certiorari* to resolve the conflict of authority as to the scope of the FDCPA's bona fide error defense * * * .
* * * *

The parties disagree about whether a "violation" resulting from a debt collector's misinterpretation of the legal requirements of the FDCPA can ever be "not intentional" under 1692k(c). Jerman contends that when a debt collector intentionally commits the act giving rise to the violation (here, sending a notice that included the "in writing" language), a misunderstanding about what the Act requires cannot render the violation "not intentional," given the general rule that

mistake or ignorance of law is no defense. Carlisle * * * , in contrast, argue[s] that nothing in the statutory text excludes legal errors from the category of "bona fide error[s]" covered by 1692k(c) * * * . Carlisle urges us, therefore, to read 1692k(c) to encompass "all types of error," including mistakes of law.

We decline to adopt the expansive reading of Section 1692k(c) that Carlisle proposes. *We have long recognized the "common maxim, familiar to all minds, that ignorance of the law will not excuse any person, either civilly or criminally." Our law is therefore no stranger to the possibility that an act may be "intentional" for purposes of civil liability, even if the actor lacked actual knowledge that her conduct violated the law.* [Emphasis added.]

* * * When Congress has intended to provide a mistake-of-law defense to civil liability, it has often done so more explicitly than here.
* * * *

We draw additional support for the conclusion that bona fide errors in Section 1692k(c) do not include mistaken interpretations of the FDCPA from the requirement that a debt collector maintain "procedures reasonably adapted to avoid any such error." The dictionary defines "procedure" as "a series of steps followed in a regular orderly definite way." In that light, the statutory phrase is more naturally read to apply to processes that have mechanical or other such "regular orderly" steps to avoid mistakes–for instance, the kind of internal controls a debt collector might adopt to ensure its employees do not communicate with consumers at the wrong time of day or make false representations as to the amount of a debt. * * * We do not dispute that some entities may maintain procedures to avoid legal errors. But legal reasoning is not a mechanical or strictly linear process. For this reason, we find * * * that the broad statutory requirement of procedures reasonably designed to avoid "any" bona fide error indicates that the relevant procedures are ones that help to avoid errors like clerical or factual mistakes. Such procedures are more likely to avoid error than those applicable to legal reasoning, particularly in the context of a comprehensive and complex federal statute such as the FDCPA that imposes open-ended prohibitions on, *inter alia* [among other things], "false, deceptive," or "unfair" practices.

DECISION AND REMEDY The United States Supreme Court reversed the judgment of the U.S. Court of Appeals for the Sixth Circuit and remanded the case for further proceedings consistent with its opinion. The FDCPA bona fide error exemption applies to processes that include mechanical or other regular, orderly steps intended to avoid mistakes, but not to mistakes of law.

---

a. Under the heading "2009 Term," select "2009 Term Opinions of the Court." On the page that opens, scroll down the list of cases to "4/21/10" in the "Date" column and click on the link with the case title to access the opinion. The United States Supreme Court maintains this Web site.

Case 20.3–Continues next page ➡

Case 20.3–Continued

THE LEGAL ENVIRONMENT DIMENSION   *One of the concerns raised by Carlisle was that if attorneys could be held liable for their reasonable misinterpretations of the FDCPA's requirements, there would be a "flood of lawsuits" against creditors' attorneys by plaintiffs seeking damages and attorneys' fees. Should this concern have any bearing on the outcome of this case? Why or why not?*

THE ECONOMIC DIMENSION   *Jerman's attorneys contended that if the Court agreed with Carlisle's argument (that the bona fide error defense included errors in legal interpretation), ethical debt collectors would be placed at a disadvantage. Why would this be?*

Reviewing . . . Consumer Protection

Leota Sage saw a local motorcycle dealer's advertisement in a newspaper offering a MetroRider EZ electric scooter for $1,699. When she went to the dealership, however, she learned that the EZ model was sold out. The salesperson told Sage that he still had the higher-end MetroRider FX model in stock for $2,199 and would sell her one for $1,999. Sage was disappointed but decided to purchase the FX model. Sage told the sales representative that she wished to purchase the scooter on credit and was directed to the dealer's credit department. As she filled out the credit forms, the clerk told Sage, an African American, that she would need a cosigner. Sage could not understand why she would need a cosigner and asked to speak to the manager. The manager apologized, told her that the clerk was mistaken, and said that he would "speak to" the clerk. The manager completed Sage's credit application, and Sage then rode the scooter home. Seven months later, Sage received a letter from the Federal Trade Commission (FTC) asking questions about her transaction with the motorcycle dealer and indicating that it had received complaints from other consumers. Using the information presented in the chapter, answer the following questions.

1. Did the dealer engage in deceptive advertising? Why or why not?
2. Suppose that Sage had ordered the scooter through the dealer's Web site but the dealer had been unable to deliver it by the date promised. What would the FTC have required the merchant to do in that situation?
3. Assuming that the clerk required a cosigner based on Sage's race or gender, what act prohibits such credit discrimination?
4. What organization has the authority to ban the sale of scooters based on safety concerns?

Key Terms

bait-and-switch advertising **588**	counteradvertising **590**	Regulation Z **594**
cease-and-desist order **590**	deceptive advertising **587**	validation notice **601**
"cooling-off" laws **595**	multiple product order **590**	

Chapter Summary: Consumer Protection

Deceptive Advertising (See pages 587–591.)	1. *Definition of deceptive advertising*—Generally, an advertising claim will be deemed deceptive if it would mislead a reasonable consumer.
	2. *Bait-and-switch advertising*—Advertising a lower-priced product (the bait) when the intention is not to sell the advertised product but to lure consumers into the store and convince them to buy a higher-priced product (the switch) is prohibited by the FTC.
	3. *Online deceptive advertising*—The FTC has issued guidelines to help online businesses comply with existing laws prohibiting deceptive advertising.
	4. *FTC actions against deceptive advertising*—
	  a. Cease-and-desist order—Requiring the advertiser to stop the challenged advertising.
	  b. Counteradvertising—Requiring the advertiser to advertise and correct the earlier misinformation.
	  c. Multiple product order—Requiring the advertiser to stop false advertising in regard to *all* of its products.

Chapter Summary: Consumer Protection, Continued

Telemarketing and Fax Advertising (See page 591.)	The Telephone Consumer Protection Act of 1991 prohibits telephone solicitation using an automatic telephone dialing system or a prerecorded voice, as well as the transmission of advertising materials via fax without first obtaining the recipient's permission.
Labeling and Packaging (See pages 592–594.)	Manufacturers must comply with the labeling or packaging requirements for their specific products. In general, all labels must be accurate and not misleading.
Sales (See pages 594–595.)	1. *Telephone and mail-order sales*—Federal and state statutes and regulations govern certain practices of sellers who solicit over the telephone or through the mails and prohibit the use of the mails to defraud individuals. 2. *Online sales*—Both state and federal laws protect consumers to some extent against fraudulent and deceptive online sales practices.
Protection of Health and Safety (See pages 595–597.)	1. *Food and drugs*—The Federal Food, Drug, and Cosmetic Act of 1916, as amended in 1938, protects consumers against adulterated and misbranded foods and drugs. The act establishes food standards, specifies safe levels of potentially hazardous food additives, and sets classifications of food and food advertising. 2. *Consumer product safety*—The Consumer Product Safety Act of 1972 seeks to protect consumers from risk of injury from hazardous products. The Consumer Product Safety Commission has the power to remove products that are deemed imminently hazardous from the market and to ban the manufacture and sale of hazardous products. 3. *Health-care reforms*—In 2010, Congress enacted health-care reforms that gave Americans new rights and benefits regarding their health care and insurance coverage.

Credit Protection (See pages 597–604.)	1. *Truth-in-Lending Act, or TILA*—A disclosure law that requires sellers and lenders to disclose credit terms or loan terms in certain transactions, including retail and installment sales and loans, car loans, home-improvement loans, and certain real estate loans. Additionally, the TILA provides for the following:
	  a. Equal credit opportunity—Creditors are prohibited from discriminating on the basis of race, religion, marital status, gender, national origin, color, or age.
	  b. Credit-card protection—Liability of cardholders for unauthorized charges is limited to $50, providing notice requirements are met. Consumers are not liable for unauthorized charges made on unsolicited credit cards. The act also sets out procedures to be used in settling disputes between credit-card companies and their cardholders.
	  c. Consumer leases—The Consumer Leasing Act (CLA) of 1988 protects consumers who lease automobiles and other goods priced at $25,000 or less if the lease term exceeds four months.
	2. *Fair Credit Reporting Act*—Entitles consumers to request verification of the accuracy of a credit report and to have unverified or false information removed from their files.
	3. *Fair and Accurate Credit Transactions Act*—Attempts to combat identity theft by establishing a national fraud alert system. Requires account numbers to be truncated and credit reporting agencies to provide one free credit report per year to consumers. Assists victims of identity theft in rebuilding their credit.
	4. *Fair Debt Collection Practices Act*—Prohibits debt collectors from using unfair debt-collection practices, such as contacting the debtor at his or her place of employment if the employer objects or at unreasonable times, contacting third parties about the debt, and harassing the debtor.

 ExamPrep

ISSUE SPOTTERS

1. Gert buys a notebook computer from EZ Electronics. She pays for it with her credit card. When the computer proves defective, she asks EZ to repair or replace it, but EZ refuses. What can Gert do?
2. United Pharmaceuticals, Inc., believes that it has developed a new drug that will be effective in the treatment of patients with AIDS. The drug has had only limited testing, but United wants to make the drug widely available as soon as possible. To market the drug, what must United show the U.S. Food and Drug Administration?

—**Check your answers to these questions against the answers provided in Appendix G.**

BEFORE THE TEST

Go to **www.cengagebrain.com**, enter the ISBN number "9781111530617," and click on "Find" to locate this textbook's Web site. Then, click on "Access Now" under "Study Tools," and select "Chapter 20" at the top. There you will find an "Interactive Quiz" that you can take to assess your mastery of the concepts in this chapter, as well as "Flashcards" and a "Glossary" of important terms.

 ## For Review

1. When will advertising be deemed deceptive?
2. What special rules apply to telephone solicitation?
3. What is Regulation Z, and to what type of transactions does it apply?
4. How does the Federal Food, Drug, and Cosmetic Act protect consumers?
5. What are the major federal statutes providing for consumer protection in credit transactions?

 ## Questions and Case Problems

20–1. Unsolicited Merchandise. Andrew, a resident of California, received an advertising circular in the U.S. mail announcing a new line of regional cookbooks distributed by the Every-Kind Cookbook Co. Andrew didn't want any books and threw the circular away. Two days later, Andrew received in the mail an introductory cookbook entitled *Lower Mongolian Regional Cookbook,* as announced in the circular, on a "trial basis" from Every-Kind. Andrew did not go to the trouble to return the cookbook. Every-Kind demanded payment of $20.95 for the *Lower Mongolian Regional Cookbook.* Discuss whether Andrew can be required to pay for the book.

20–2. Credit-Card Rules. Maria Ochoa receives two new credit cards on May 1. She had solicited one of them from Midtown Department Store, and the other arrived unsolicited from High-Flying Airlines. During the month of May, Ochoa makes numerous credit-card purchases from Midtown Department Store, but she does not use the High-Flying Airlines card. On May 31, a burglar breaks into Ochoa's home and steals both credit cards, along with other items. Ochoa notifies Midtown Department Store of the theft on June 2, but she fails to notify High-Flying Airlines. Using the Midtown credit card, the burglar makes a $500 purchase on June 1 and a $200 purchase on June 3. The burglar then charges a vacation flight on the High-Flying Airlines card for $1,000 on June 5. Ochoa receives the bills for these charges and refuses to pay them. Discuss Ochoa's liability in these situations.

20–3. Sales. On June 28, a salesperson for Renowned Books called on the Gonchars at their home. After a very persuasive sales pitch by the agent, the Gonchars agreed in writing to purchase a twenty-volume set of historical encyclopedias from Renowned Books for a total of $299. A down payment of $35 was required, with the remainder of the cost to be paid in monthly payments over a one-year period. Two days later, the Gonchars, having second thoughts, contacted the book company and stated that they had decided to rescind

the contract. Renowned Books said this would be impossible. Has Renowned Books violated any consumer law by not allowing the Gonchars to rescind their contract? Explain.

20–4. Debt Collection. 55th Management Corp. in New York City owns residential property that it leases to various tenants. In June 2000, claiming that one of the tenants, Leslie Goldman, owed more than $13,000 in back rent, 55th retained Jeffrey Cohen, an attorney, to initiate nonpayment proceedings. Cohen filed a petition in a New York state court against Goldman, seeking recovery of the unpaid rent and at least $3,000 in attorneys' fees. After receiving notice of the petition, Goldman filed a suit in a federal district court against Cohen. Goldman contended that the notice of the petition constituted an initial contact that, under the Fair Debt Collection Practices Act (FDCPA), required a validation notice. Because Cohen did not give Goldman a validation notice at the time, or within five days, of the notice of the petition, Goldman argued that Cohen was in violation of the FDCPA. Should the filing of a suit in a state court be considered "communication," requiring a debt collector to provide a validation notice under the FDCPA? Why or why not? [*Goldman v. Cohen*, 445 F.3d 152 (2d Cir. 2006)]

20–5. Case Problem with Sample Answer. Food Labeling. The Nutrition Labeling and Education Act (NLEA) requires packaged food to have a "Nutrition Facts" panel that sets out "nutrition information," including "the total number of calories" per serving. Before the new menu labeling requirements enacted in 2010 (discussed on page 594), restaurants were exempt from the NLEA's requirements. The NLEA also regulates nutrition-content claims, such as "low sodium," that a purveyor might choose to add to a label. The NLEA permits a state or local law to require restaurants to disclose nutrition information about the food they serve, but expressly preempts state or local attempts to regulate nutrition-content claims. New York City Health Code Section 81.50 requires 10 percent of the restaurants in the city, including McDonald's, Burger King, and Kentucky Fried Chicken, to post calorie content information on their menus. The New York State Restaurant Association (NYSRA) filed a suit in a federal district court, contending that the NLEA preempts Section 81.50. (Under the U.S. Constitution, state or local laws that conflict with existing federal laws are preempted.) Is the NYSRA correct? Explain. [*New York State Restaurant Association v. New York City Board of Health*, 556 F.3d 114 (2d Cir. 2009)]

—**To view a sample answer for Case Problem 20–5, go to Appendix F at the end of this text.**

20–6. Deceptive Advertising. Brian Cleary and Rita Burke filed a suit against the major cigarette maker Philip Morris USA, Inc., seeking class-action status for a claim of deceptive advertising. They claimed that "light" cigarettes, such as Marlboro Lights, were advertised as safer than regular cigarettes, even though the health effects are the same. They contended that the tobacco companies concealed the true nature of light cigarettes. Philip Morris correctly claimed that it was authorized by the government to advertise cigarettes, including light cigarettes. Assuming that is true, should Cleary and Burke still be able to bring a deceptive advertising claim against the tobacco company? Why or why not? [*Cleary v. Philip Morris USA, Inc.*, 683 F.Supp.2d 730 (N.D.Ill. 2010)]

20–7. Credit-Card Protection. James A. McCoy held a credit card issued by Chase Bank USA, N.A. McCoy's cardholder agreement with Chase stated that he would receive preferred rates (lower interest rates) if he met certain conditions, such as making at least the required minimum payments when due. Without informing McCoy in advance of the increase, Chase raised the rates on McCoy's card when he defaulted on a payment. McCoy filed a complaint in a California state court against Chase for increasing the interest rate and applying that increase retroactively. Chase removed the action to the federal district court. McCoy claimed that Chase had violated Regulation Z by failing to notify him of the increase until after it had taken effect. He argued that he was entitled to notice from Chase before it raised the interest rate on his credit card due to his delinquency or default. In 2009, Congress enacted credit-card rules that amended the Truth-in-Lending Act (TILA) to require forty-five days' advance notice of most increases in credit-card annual percentage rates. Chase, however, had increased McCoy's interest rate before the new rules were enacted. Before the 2009 amendments to TILA's credit-card rules took effect, did Regulation Z require a lender to provide a cardholder with a change-in-terms notice before raising the cardholder's interest rate following delinquency or default? Explain. How did the amendments change the law? [*Chase Bank USA, N.A. v. McCoy*, ___U.S. ___, 131 S.Ct. 871, 178 L.Ed.2d 716 (2011)]

20–8. A Question of Ethics. Debt-Collection Practices. *After graduating from law school—and serving time in prison for attempting to collect debts by posing as an FBI agent—Barry Sussman theorized that if a debt-collection business collected only debts that it owned as a result of buying*

checks written on accounts with insufficient funds (NSF checks), it would not be subject to the Federal Debt Collection Practices Act (FDCPA). Sussman formed Check Investors, Inc., to act on his theory. Check Investors bought more than 2.2 million NSF checks, with an estimated face value of about $348 million, for pennies on the dollar. Check Investors added a fee of $125 or $130 (more than the legal limit in most states) to the face amount of each check and aggressively pursued its drawer to collect. The firm's employees were told to accuse drawers of being criminals and to threaten them with arrest and prosecution. The threats were false. Check Investors never took steps to initiate a prosecution. The employees contacted the drawers' family members and used "saturation phoning"—phoning a drawer numerous times in a short period. They used abusive language, referring to drawers as "deadbeats," "retards," "thieves," and "idiots." Between January 2000 and January 2003, Check Investors netted more than $10.2 million from its efforts. [*Federal Trade Commission v. Check Investors, Inc.*, 502 F.3d 159 (3d Cir. 2007)]

1. The Federal Trade Commission filed a suit in a federal district court against Check Investors and others, alleging, in part, violations of the FDCPA. Was Check Investors a "debt collector," collecting "debts," within the meaning of the FDCPA? If so, did its methods violate the FDCPA? Were its practices unethical? What might Check Investors argue in its defense? Discuss.

2. Are "deadbeats" the primary beneficiaries of laws such as the FDCPA? If not, how would you characterize debtors who default on their obligations?

20–9. **Critical-Thinking Legal Environment Question.** Many states have enacted laws that go even further than federal law to protect consumers. These laws vary tremendously from state to state. Generally, is having different laws fair to sellers who may be prohibited from engaging in a practice in one state that is legal in another? How might these different laws affect a business? Is it fair that residents of one state have more protection than residents of another?

20–10. **Video Question.** *Advertising Communication Law: Bait and Switch.*
Access the video using the instructions provided below to answer the following questions.

1. Is the auto dealership's advertisement for the truck in the video deceptive? Why or why not?

2. Is the advertisement for the truck an offer to which the dealership is bound? Does it matter if Betty detrimentally relied on the advertisement?

3. Is Tony committed to buying Betty's trade-in truck for $3,000 because that is what he told her over the phone?

—To watch this video, go to **www.cengagebrain.com** and register the access code that came with your new book or log in to your existing account. Select the link for either the "Business Law Digital Video Library Online Access" or "Business Law CourseMate," and then click on "Complete Video List" to find the video for this chapter (Video 48).

Chapter 21

Protecting the Environment

> "Man, however, much he may like to pretend the contrary, is part of nature."
>
> —Rachel Carson, 1907–1964
> (American writer and conservationist)

Contents

- Common Law Actions
- Federal, State, and Local Regulations
- Air Pollution
- Water Pollution
- Toxic Chemicals
- Hazardous Waste Disposal

Chapter Objectives

After reading this chapter, you should be able to answer the following questions:

1. Under what common law theories can polluters be held liable?
2. What is an environmental impact statement, and who must file one?
3. What does the Environmental Protection Agency do?
4. What major federal statutes regulate air and water pollution?
5. What is Superfund? What categories of persons are liable under Superfund?

(Moody75/Creative Commons)

As the chapter-opening quotation above observes, we are all "part of nature." Consequently, concern over the degradation of the environment has increased over time in response to the environmental effects of population growth, urbanization, and industrialization. Environmental protection is not without a price, however. For many businesses, the costs of complying with environmental regulations are high, and for some they may seem too high. A constant tension exists between the desirability of increasing profits and productivity and the need to protect the environment.

To a great extent, environmental law consists of statutes passed by federal, state, or local governments and regulations issued by administrative agencies. Before examining statutory and regulatory environmental laws, however, we look at the remedies against environmental pollution that are available under the common law.

Common Law Actions

Common law remedies against environmental pollution originated centuries ago in England. Those responsible for operations that created dirt, smoke, noxious odors, noise, or toxic substances were sometimes held liable under common law theories of nuisance or negligence. Today, injured individuals continue to rely on the common law to obtain damages and injunctions against business polluters.

Nuisance

Nuisance A common law doctrine under which persons may be held liable for using their property in a manner that unreasonably interferes with others' rights to use or enjoy their own property.

Under the common law doctrine of **nuisance,** persons may be held liable if they use their property in a manner that unreasonably interferes with others' rights to use or enjoy their own property. In these situations, the courts commonly balance the harm caused by the pollution against the costs of stopping it.

Courts have often refused to issue an injunction prohibiting the pollution altogether on the ground that the hardships that would be imposed on the polluter and on the community are relatively greater than the hardships suffered by the plaintiff. **EXAMPLE 21.1** A factory that causes neighboring landowners to suffer from smoke, soot, and vibrations may be left in operation if it is the core of the local economy. The injured parties may be awarded only monetary damages, which may include compensation for the decrease in the value of their property caused by the factory's operation. •

Under the common law, individuals were denied *standing* (access to the courts—see Chapter 3) unless they suffered a harm distinct from the harm suffered by the public at large. In some states, a property owner still may not bring a nuisance action unless she or he can identify a "private nuisance"—a distinct harm separate from that affecting the general public. A public authority (such as a state's attorney general), though, can sue to abate a "public" nuisance.

Negligence and Strict Liability

An injured party may sue a business polluter in tort under the negligence and strict liability theories discussed in Chapter 5. The basis for a negligence action is the business's alleged failure to use reasonable care toward the party whose injury was foreseeable and was caused by the lack of reasonable care. For instance, employees might sue an employer whose failure to use proper pollution controls contaminated the air and caused the employees to suffer respiratory illnesses. Lawsuits for personal injuries caused by exposure to a toxic substance, such as asbestos, radiation, or hazardous waste, have given rise to a growing body of tort law known as **toxic torts.**

Toxic Tort A civil wrong arising from exposure to a toxic substance, such as asbestos, radiation, or hazardous waste.

Businesses that engage in ultrahazardous activities—such as the transportation of radioactive materials—are strictly liable for any injuries the activities cause. In a strict liability action, the injured party does not need to prove that the business failed to exercise reasonable care.

 Federal, State, and Local Regulations

All levels of government in the United States regulate some aspect of the environment. In this section, we look at some of the ways in which the federal, state, and local governments control business activities and land use in the interests of environmental preservation and protection.

Federal Regulations

Congress has enacted a number of statutes to control the impact of human activities on the environment. Exhibit 21–1 on page 611 lists and summarizes some major federal environmental statutes. Some of these laws have been passed in an attempt to improve the quality of air and water. Other laws specifically regulate toxic chemicals, including pesticides, herbicides, and hazardous wastes.

ENVIRONMENTAL REGULATORY AGENCIES The primary agency regulating environmental law is, of course, the Environmental Protection Agency (EPA), which was created in 1970 to coordinate federal environmental responsibilities. Other federal agencies with authority to regulate specific environmental matters include the Department of the Interior, the Department of Defense, the Department of Labor, the Food and Drug Administration, and the Nuclear Regulatory Commission. All agencies of the federal government must take environmental factors into consideration when making significant decisions. In addition, as mentioned, state and local agencies play an important role in enforcing federal environmental legislation.

Most federal environmental laws provide that private parties can sue to enforce environmental regulations if government agencies fail to do so—or if agencies go too far in their enforcement actions. Typically, a threshold hurdle in such suits is meeting the requirements for standing to sue.

ENVIRONMENTAL IMPACT STATEMENTS   The National Environmental Policy Act (NEPA) of 1969[1] requires that an **environmental impact statement (EIS)** be prepared for every major federal action that significantly affects the quality of the environment. An EIS must analyze (1) the impact on the environment that the action will have, (2) any adverse effects on the environment and alternative actions that might be taken, and (3) irreversible effects the action might generate.

> **Environmental Impact Statement (EIS)**
> A statement required by the National Environmental Policy Act for any major federal action that will significantly affect the quality of the environment. The statement must analyze the action's impact on the environment and explore alternative actions that might be taken.

An action qualifies as "major" if it involves a substantial commitment of resources (monetary or otherwise). An action is "federal" if a federal agency has the power to control it. If a private developer wishes to construct a ski resort on federal land, for example, an EIS may be needed. The construction or operation of a nuclear plant, which requires a federal permit, requires an EIS. If an agency decides that an EIS is unnecessary, it must issue a statement supporting this conclusion. Private individuals, consumer interest groups, businesses, and others who believe that a federal agency's actions threaten the environment often use EISs as a means of challenging those actions.

State and Local Regulations

In addition to the federal regulations, many states have enacted laws to protect the environment. State laws may restrict a business's discharge of chemicals into the air or water or regulate its disposal of toxic wastes. States may also regulate the disposal or recycling of other wastes, including glass, metal, plastic containers, and paper. Additionally, states may restrict emissions from motor vehicles.

City, county, and other local governments also regulate some aspects of the environment. For instance, local zoning laws may be designed to inhibit or regulate the growth of cities and suburbs or to protect the natural environment. In the interest of safeguarding the environment, such laws may prohibit certain land uses. Even when zoning laws permit a business's proposed development, the proposal may have to be altered to lessen the development's impact on the environment. In addition, cities and counties may impose rules regulating methods of waste removal, the appearance of buildings, the maximum noise level, and other aspects of the local environment.

State and local regulatory agencies also play a significant role in implementing federal environmental legislation. Typically, the federal government relies on state and local governments to enforce federal environmental statutes and regulations such as those regulating air quality.

---

1. 42 U.S.C. Sections 4321–4370d.

• *Exhibit* **21–1** **Major Federal Environmental Statutes**

POPULAR NAME	PURPOSE	STATUTE REFERENCE
Rivers and Harbors Appropriations Act (1899)	To prohibit ships and manufacturers from discharging and depositing refuse in navigable waterways.	33 U.S.C. Sections 401–418.
Federal Insecticide, Fungicide, and Rodenticide Act (1947)	To control the use of pesticides and herbicides.	7 U.S.C. Sections 136–136y.
Federal Water Pollution Control Act (1948)	To eliminate the discharge of pollutants from major sources into navigable waters.	33 U.S.C. Sections 1251–1387.
Clean Air Act (1963, 1970)	To control air pollution from mobile and stationary sources.	42 U.S.C. Sections 7401–7671q.
National Environmental Policy Act (1969)	To limit environmental harm from federal government activities.	42 U.S.C. Sections 4321–4370d.
Ocean Dumping Act (1972)	To prohibit the dumping of radiological, chemical, and biological warfare agents and high-level radioactive waste into the ocean.	16 U.S.C. Sections 1401–1445.
Endangered Species Act (1973)	To protect species that are threatened with extinction.	16 U.S.C. Sections 1531–1544.
Safe Drinking Water Act (1974)	To regulate pollutants in public drinking water systems.	42 U.S.C. Sections 300f–300j-25.
Resource Conservation and Recovery Act (1976)	To establish standards for hazardous waste disposal.	42 U.S.C. Sections 6901–6986.
Toxic Substances Control Act (1976)	To regulate toxic chemicals and chemical compounds.	15 U.S.C. Sections 2601–2692.
Comprehensive Environmental Response, Compensation, and Liability Act (1980)	To regulate the clean-up of hazardous waste–disposal sites.	42 U.S.C. Sections 9601–9675.
Oil Pollution Act (1990)	To establish liability for the clean-up of navigable waters after oil spills.	33 U.S.C. Sections 2701–2761.
Small Business Liability Relief and Brownfields Revitalization Act (2002)	To allow developers who comply with state voluntary clean-up programs to avoid federal liability for the properties that they decontaminate and develop.	42 U.S.C. Section 9628.

▶ Air Pollution

Federal involvement with air pollution goes back to the 1950s and 1960s, when Congress authorized funds for air-pollution research and enacted the Clean Air Act to address multistate air pollution.[2] The Clean Air Act provides the basis for issuing regulations to control pollution coming both from mobile sources (such as automobiles and other vehicles) and from stationary sources (such as electric utilities and industrial plants).

Mobile Sources

Regulations governing air pollution from automobiles and other mobile sources specify pollution standards and establish time schedules for meeting the standards. For example, 1990 amendments to the Clean Air Act required automobile manufacturers to cut new automobiles' exhaust emissions of nitrogen oxide by 60 percent and emissions of hydrocarbons and carbon monoxide by 35 percent by 1998. Beginning with

> *"There's so much pollution in the air now that if it weren't for our lungs, there'd be no place to put it all."*
>
> Robert Orben, 1927–present
> (American comedian)

---

2. 42 U.S.C. Sections 7401–7671.

2004 models, the rules also applied to sport-utility vehicles (SUVs) and light trucks. The EPA periodically updates the pollution standards in light of new developments and data, reducing the amount of emissions allowed.

In 2009, the Obama administration announced a long-term goal of reducing emissions, including those from cars and SUVs, by 80 percent by 2050. In 2010, the administration ordered the EPA to develop national standards regulating fuel economy and emissions for medium- and heavy-duty trucks starting with 2014 models.

A growing concern among many scientists and others around the world is that greenhouse gases, such as carbon dioxide (CO_2), are contributing to global warming. The Clean Air Act, as amended, however, does not specifically mention CO_2 emissions. Therefore, until 2009, the EPA did not regulate CO_2 emissions from motor vehicles.

CASE EXAMPLE 21.2   Environmental groups and several states sued the EPA in an effort to force the agency to regulate CO_2 emissions. When the case reached the United States Supreme Court, the EPA argued that the plaintiffs lacked standing because global warming has widespread effects and thus an individual plaintiff could not show the particularized harm required for standing. Furthermore, the agency maintained, it did not have authority under the Clean Air Act to address global climate change and regulate CO_2. The Court, however, ruled that Massachusetts had standing because its coastline, including state-owned lands, faced an imminent threat from rising sea levels caused by global warming. The Court also held that the Clean Air Act's broad definition of air pollutant gives the EPA authority to regulate CO_2 and requires the EPA to regulate any air pollutants that might "endanger public health or welfare." Accordingly, the Court ordered the EPA to determine whether CO_2 was a pollutant that endangered public health.[3] ●
In 2009, the EPA concluded that greenhouse gases, including CO_2 emissions, do constitute a public danger.

Stationary Sources

The Clean Air Act authorizes the EPA to establish air-quality standards for stationary sources (such as manufacturing plants) but recognizes that the primary responsibility for preventing and controlling air pollution rests with state and local governments. The EPA sets primary and secondary levels of ambient standards— that is, the maximum permissible levels of certain pollutants—and the states formulate plans to achieve those standards. Different standards apply depending on whether the sources of pollution are located in clean areas or polluted areas and whether they are existing sources or major new sources.

The standards are aimed at controlling hazardous air pollutants—those likely to cause death or serious irreversible or incapacitating illness such as cancer or neurological and reproductive damage. The Clean Air Act requires the EPA to list all regulated hazardous air pollutants on a prioritized schedule. In all, nearly two hundred substances, including asbestos, benzene, beryllium, cadmium, and vinyl chloride, have been classified as hazardous. They are emitted from stationary sources by a variety of business activities, including smelting (melting ore to produce metal), dry cleaning, house painting, and commercial baking. Instead of establishing specific emissions standards for each hazardous air pollutant, the 1990 amendments to the Clean Air Act require major sources of pollutants to use pollution-control equipment that represents the *maximum achievable control*

The most common stationary sources of air pollution are factories and electricity-generating facilities. For the application of the EPA's ambient standards, does it matter where the factory or electricity-generating facility is located? Why or why not?

©Klaus Kaulitzki, 2009. Used under license from Shutterstock.com)

---

3. *Massachusetts v. Environmental Protection Agency,* 549 U.S. 497, 127 S.Ct. 1438, 167 L.Ed.2d 248 (2007).

technology, or MACT, to reduce emissions. The EPA issues guidelines as to what equipment meets these standards.[4]

Mercury is one of the listed hazardous substances. The EPA attempted nonetheless to remove mercury from its list of hazardous substances emitted from electric utility steam-generating units. In the following case, New Jersey and others challenged this delisting.

---

4. The EPA has also issued rules to regulate hazardous air pollutants emitted by landfills. See 40 C.F.R. Sections 60.750–60.759.

Case 21.1 | New Jersey v. Environmental Protection Agency

United States Court of Appeals, District of Columbia Circuit, 517 F.3d 574 (2008).
www.cadc.uscourts.gov/bin/opinions/allopinions.asp[a]

(©Yuriy Chaban, 2010.
Used under license from Shutterstock.com)

Can the EPA arbitrarily delist an emission formerly deemed dangerous?

BACKGROUND AND FACTS The Environmental Protection Agency (EPA) published a rule—the Delisting Rule—that had the effect of removing from its regulation the emissions of mercury from steam-generating electricity plants that used coal or oil as their energy sources. This Delisting Rule ran counter to the EPA's own conclusions at the end of 2000 that it was "appropriate and necessary" to regulate mercury emissions. At that time, it placed mercury on its list of hazardous air pollutants (HAPs) to be monitored at electricity-generating sites. New Jersey and fourteen additional states, as well as various state agencies, challenged the EPA's action.

IN THE WORDS OF THE COURT . . .
ROGERS, Circuit Judge.
* * * *

First, Congress required EPA to regulate more than one hundred specific HAPs, including mercury and nickel compounds. Further, EPA was required to list and to regulate, on a prioritized schedule, "all categories and subcategories of major sources and areas sources" that emit one or more HAPs. *In seeking to ensure that regulation of HAPs reflects the "maximum reduction in emissions which can be achieved by application of [the] best available control technology," Congress imposed specific, strict pollution control requirements on both new and existing sources of HAPs.* [Emphasis added.]

---

a. Click on the "Opinions" box in the center of the page. In the left column, in the "Quick Search" box, type "05-1097a" and click on "Search." In the result, click on the link to access the opinion. The Court of Appeals for the District of Columbia Circuit maintains this Web site.

Second, Congress restricted the opportunities for EPA and others to intervene in the regulation of HAP sources. For HAPs that result in health effects other than cancer, as is true of mercury, Congress directed that the Administrator "may delete any source category" from the section 112(c)(1) list only after determining that "emissions from no source in the category or subcategory concerned . . . exceed a level which is adequate to protect public health with an ample margin of safety and no adverse environmental effect will result from emissions from any source."
* * * *

EPA maintains that it possesses authority to remove EGUs [electrical generating units] from * * * [the] list under the "fundamental principle of administrative law that an agency has inherent authority to reverse an earlier administrative determination or ruling where an agency has a principled basis for doing so."

EPA states in its brief that it has previously removed sources listed * * * without satisfying the requirements of [the statute]. But previous statutory violations cannot excuse the one now before the court. "We do not see how merely applying an unreasonable statutory interpretation for several years can transform it into a reasonable interpretation."

DECISION AND REMEDY The U.S. Court of Appeals for the District of Columbia Circuit ruled in favor of New Jersey and the other plaintiffs. The EPA was required to rescind its delisting of mercury.

WHAT IF THE FACTS WERE DIFFERENT? *Suppose that the EPA had carried out scientific tests that showed mercury was relatively harmless as a by-product of electricity generation. How might this have affected the court's ruling?*

THE GLOBAL DIMENSION *Because air pollution knows no borders, how did this ruling affect our neighboring countries?*

Violations of the Clean Air Act

For violations of emission limits under the Clean Air Act, the EPA can assess civil penalties of up to $25,000 per day. Additional fines of up to $5,000 per day can be assessed for other violations, such as failing to maintain the required records. To penalize those who find it more cost-effective to violate the act than to comply with it, the EPA is authorized to obtain a penalty equal to the violator's economic benefits from noncompliance. Persons who provide information about violators may be paid up to $10,000. Private individuals can also sue violators.

Those who knowingly violate the act may be subject to criminal penalties, including fines of up to $1 million and imprisonment for up to two years (for false statements or failures to report violations). Corporate officers are among those who may be subject to these penalties.

▶ Water Pollution

Water pollution stems mostly from industrial, municipal, and agricultural sources. Pollutants entering streams, lakes, and oceans include organic wastes, heated water, sediments from soil runoff, nutrients (including fertilizers and human and animal wastes), and toxic chemicals and other hazardous substances. We look here at laws and regulations governing water pollution.

Federal regulations governing the pollution of water can be traced back to the Rivers and Harbors Appropriations Act of 1899.[5] These regulations prohibited ships and manufacturers from discharging or depositing refuse in navigable waterways without a permit. In 1948, Congress passed the Federal Water Pollution Control Act (FWPCA),[6] but its regulatory system and enforcement powers proved to be inadequate.

> "Among the treasures of our land is water—fast becoming our most valuable, most prized, most critical resource."
>
> Dwight D. Eisenhower, 1890–1969
> (Thirty-fourth president of the United States, 1953–1961)

The Clean Water Act

In 1972, amendments to the FWPCA—known as the Clean Water Act (CWA)—established the following goals: (1) make waters safe for swimming, (2) protect fish and wildlife, and (3) eliminate the discharge of pollutants into the water. The amendments set specific time schedules, which were extended by amendment in 1977 and by the Water Quality Act of 1987.[7] Under these schedules, the EPA limits the discharge of various types of pollutants based on the technology available for controlling them.

FOCUS ON POINT-SOURCE EMISSIONS   The CWA established a permit system, called the National Pollutant Discharge Elimination System (NPDES), for regulating discharges from "point sources" of pollution that include industrial, municipal (such as pipes and sewage treatment plants), and agricultural facilities.[8] Under this system, any point source emitting pollutants into water must have a permit. Pollution not from point sources, such as runoff from small farms, is not subject to much regulation. NPDES permits can be issued by the EPA and authorized state agencies and Indian tribes, but only if the discharge will not violate water-quality standards.

---

5. 33 U.S.C. Sections 401–418.
6. 33 U.S.C. Sections 1251–1387.
7. This act amended 33 U.S.C. Section 1251.
8. 33 U.S.C. Section 1342.

NPDES permits must be reissued every five years. Although initially the NPDES system focused mainly on industrial wastewater, it was later expanded to cover storm water discharges.

In practice, the permit system under the CWA includes the following elements:

1. National effluent (pollution) standards set by the EPA for each industry.
2. Water-quality standards set by the states under EPA supervision.
3. A *discharge permit* program that sets water-quality standards to limit pollution.
4. Special provisions for toxic chemicals and for oil spills.
5. Construction grants and loans from the federal government for *publicly owned treatment works,* primarily sewage treatment plants.

When water from rainstorms flows over streets, parking lots, commercial sites, and other developed areas, the water collects sediments, trash, used motor oil, raw sewage, pesticides, and other toxic contaminants. This polluted runoff flows into urban storm sewers, which often empty into rivers or oceans. In the following case, the plaintiffs claimed that Los Angeles County, California, was responsible for heavily polluted stormwater runoff flowing into navigable rivers in the surrounding area.

Case 21.2   **Natural Resources Defense Council, Inc. v. County of Los Angeles**

United States Court of Appeals, Ninth Circuit, ___ F.3d ___ (2011).

Did Los Angeles County discharge urban storm water into navigable waters of the Los Angeles River in violation of the Clean Water Act?

BACKGROUND AND FACTS

Two environmental organizations—the Natural Resources Defense Council (NRDC) and the Santa Monica Baykeeper—brought a lawsuit against the county of Los Angeles and the Los Angeles County Flood Control District, which included eighty-four cities and some unincorporated areas. The NRDC and Santa Monica alleged that the county and the district were discharging urban stormwater runoff into navigable waters in violation of the Clean Water Act. The levels of pollutants detected in four rivers—the Santa Clara River, the Los Angeles River, the San Gabriel River, and Malibu Creek—exceeded the limits allowed in the National Pollutant Discharge Elimination System (NPDES) permit that governs municipal stormwater discharges in Los Angeles County. All parties agreed that the rivers did not meet water-quality standards. The issue was whether the NRDC and Santa Monica had proved that the county and the district were responsible. The defendants claimed that there was no evidence establishing their responsibility for discharging stormwater carrying pollutants into the rivers. The federal district court held in favor of the defendants (the county and district agencies), and the NRDC and Santa Monica appealed.

IN THE WORDS OF THE COURT . . .
M. *SMITH*, Circuit Judge:
* * * *

This case concerns high levels of pollutants, particularly heavy metals and fecal bacteria, identified by mass-emissions monitoring stations for the four Watershed Rivers (the Monitoring Stations). * * * The purpose of mass-emissions monitoring is to * * * estimate the mass emissions from the MS4 [the main municipal storm sewer system in Los Angeles County], * * * [and] determine if the MS4 is contributing to exceedances of Water Quality Standards. The [NPDES] Permit requires that mass-emission readings be taken five times per year for the Watershed Rivers.

The Los Angeles River and San Gabriel River Monitoring Stations are located in a channelized portion of the MS4 [where the water flows through a concrete-lined structure] that is owned and operated by the District.

The Malibu Creek Monitoring Station is not located within a channelized portion of the MS4 but at an "existing stream gage station" near Malibu Canyon Road. * * * The Santa Clara River Monitoring Station is located in the City of Santa Clara and [is also not in the channelized portion of the MS4].
* * * *

"The Clean Water Act regulates the discharge of pollutants into navigable waters, prohibiting their discharge unless certain statutory

Case 21.2–Continues next page ➡

Case 21.2–Continued

exceptions apply." One such exception is for discharges by entities or individuals who hold NPDES permits. The NPDES permitting program is the "centerpiece" of the Clean Water Act and the primary method for enforcing the effluent and water-quality standards established by the EPA and state governments.

* * * Since the inception of the NPDES, Congress has expanded NPDES permitting to bring municipal dischargers within the Clean Water Act's coverage.

* * * *

Section 402(p)(3)(iii) of the CWA [Clean Water Act] mandates that permits for discharges from municipal separate storm sewers *shall require controls to reduce the discharge of pollutants* to the maximum extent practicable (MEP), including management practices, control techniques and systems, design and engineering methods, and such other provisions as the Director determines appropriate for the control of such pollutants. [Emphasis in original.]

* * * *

Our prior case law emphasizes that NPDES permit enforcement is not scattershot—each permit term is simply enforced as written.

* * * *

[This] Permit's provisions plainly specify that the mass-emissions monitoring is intended to measure compliance and that "[a]ny violation of this Order" is a Clean Water Act violation. The Permit is available for public inspection to aid this purpose. Accordingly, we agree with the district court's determination that an exceedance detected through mass-emissions monitoring is a Permit violation that gives rise to liability for contributing dischargers.

* * * *

* * * There is evidence in the record showing that polluted stormwater from the MS4 was added to two of the Watershed Rivers: the Los Angeles River and San Gabriel River. Because the mass-emissions stations, as the appropriate locations to measure compliance, for these two rivers are located in a section of the MS4 owned and operated by the District, when pollutants were detected, they had not yet exited the point source into navigable waters. As such, there is no question over who controlled the polluted stormwater at the time it was measured or who caused or contributed to the exceedances when that water was again discharged to the rivers—in both cases, the District. As a matter of law and fact, the MS4 is distinct from the two navigable rivers; the MS4 is an intra-state man-made construction—not a naturally occurring Watershed River.

DECISION AND REMEDY The federal appellate court concluded that the plaintiffs were entitled to summary judgment on the district's liability for discharges into the Los Angeles River and San Gabriel River. Accordingly, the court reversed the lower court's decision on these claims but affirmed it as to the Santa Clara River and Malibu Creek, because those monitoring stations were not located within the channelized portion of the MS4.

WHAT IF THE FACTS WERE DIFFERENT? *Suppose that Los Angeles County had moved all of its monitoring stations outside the "channelized portion of the MS4." How might that have changed the outcome?*

THE ETHICAL DIMENSION *The court rejected the district's argument that it should not be held liable for merely channeling pollutants that were generated by others. Under the Clean Water Act, does it matter who created the pollution? If so, should it matter? Explain.*

STANDARDS FOR EQUIPMENT Regulations generally specify that the *best available control technology*, or BACT, be installed. The EPA issues guidelines as to what equipment meets this standard. Essentially, the guidelines require the most effective pollution-control equipment available. New sources must install BACT equipment before beginning operations. Existing sources are subject to timetables for the installation of BACT equipment and must immediately install equipment that utilizes the *best practical control technology*, or BPCT. The EPA also issues guidelines as to what equipment meets this standard.

The EPA must take into account many factors when issuing and updating the rules that impose standards to attain the goals of the CWA. Some provisions of the act instruct the EPA to weigh the cost of the technology applied against the benefits achieved. The statute that covers power plants, however, neither requires nor prohibits a comparison of the economic costs and benefits. The question in the following case was whether the EPA could make this comparison anyway.

Case 21.3 **Entergy Corp. v. Riverkeeper, Inc.**

Supreme Court of the United States, 566 U.S. 208, 129 S.Ct. 1498, 173 L.Ed.2d 369 (2009).
www.findlaw.com/casecode/supreme.html[a]

Can the EPA use cost-benefit analyses to determine whether power plants are implementing the best technological method for minimal environmental impact when cooling water?

HISTORICAL AND ENVIRONMENTAL SETTING

In generating electricity, a power plant produces heat. To cool the operating machinery, the plant can use water pulled from a nearby source through a cooling water intake structure. The structure affects the environment by squashing aquatic organisms against intake screens or sucking the organisms into the cooling system. The Clean Water Act mandates that "cooling water intake structures reflect the best technology available for minimizing adverse environmental impact." For more than thirty years, the Environmental Protection Agency (EPA) made the "best technology available" determination on a case-by-case basis. In 2001 and 2004, the EPA adopted "Phase I" and "Phase II" rules for power plants.

BACKGROUND AND FACTS Phase I rules require new power plants to restrict their inflow of water "to a level commensurate with that which can be attained by a closed-cycle recirculating cooling water system." Phase II rules apply "national performance standards" to more than five hundred existing plants but do not require closed-cycle cooling systems. The EPA found that converting these facilities to closed-cycle operations would cost $3.5 billion per year. The facilities would then produce less power while burning the same amount of coal. Moreover, other technologies can attain nearly the same results as closed-cycle systems. Phase II rules also allow a variance from the national performance standards if a facility's cost of compliance "would be significantly greater than the benefits." Environmental organizations, including Riverkeeper, Inc., challenged the Phase II regulations, arguing that existing plants should be required to convert to closed-cycle systems. The U.S. Court of Appeals for the Second Circuit issued a ruling in the plaintiffs' favor. Power-generating companies, including Entergy Corporation, appealed.

IN THE WORDS OF THE COURT . . .
Justice *SCALIA* delivered the opinion of the Court.
 * * * *

In setting the Phase II national performance standards and providing for site-specific cost-benefit variances, the EPA relied on its view that [the] "best technology available" standard permits

consideration of the technology's costs and of the relationship between those costs and the environmental benefits produced.

 * * * The "best" technology–that which is "most advantageous"–may well be the one that produces the most of some good, here a reduction in adverse environmental impact. But "best technology" may also describe the technology that most efficiently produces some good. *In common parlance one could certainly use the phrase "best technology" to refer to that which produces a good at the lowest per-unit cost, even if it produces a lesser quantity of that good than other available technologies.* [Emphasis added.]

 * * * This latter reading is [not] precluded by the statute's use of the phrase "for minimizing adverse environmental impact." *Minimizing * * * is a term that admits of degree and is not necessarily used to refer exclusively to the "greatest possible reduction."* [Emphasis added.]

Other provisions in the Clean Water Act also suggest the agency's interpretation. When Congress wished to mandate the greatest feasible reduction in water pollution, it did so in plain language: The provision governing the discharge of toxic pollutants into the Nation's waters requires the EPA to set "effluent limitations which shall require the elimination of discharges of all pollutants * * * ." The less ambitious goal of "minimizing adverse environmental impact" suggests, we think, that the agency retains some discretion to determine the extent of reduction that is warranted under the circumstances. That determination could plausibly involve a consideration of the benefits derived from reductions and the costs of achieving them.

 * * * [Under other Clean Water Act provisions that impose standards on sources of pollution discharges] the EPA is instructed to consider, among other factors, "the total cost of application of technology in relation to the * * * benefits to be achieved."
 * * * *

This * * * comparison of * * * statutory factors * * * leads us to the conclusion that it was well within the bounds of reasonable interpretation for the EPA to conclude that cost-benefit analysis is not categorically forbidden.
 * * * *

While not conclusive, it surely tends to show that the EPA's current practice is a reasonable and hence legitimate exercise of its discretion to weigh benefits against costs that the agency has been proceeding in essentially this fashion for over 30 years.

DECISION AND REMEDY The United States Supreme Court concluded that the EPA permissibly relied on a cost-benefit analysis to set national performance standards and to allow for variances from those standards as part of the Phase II regulations.

---

a. In the "Browse Supreme Court Opinions" section, click on "2009." On that page, scroll to the name of the case and click on it to access the opinion.

Case 21.3–Continues next page ➡

Case 21.3–Continued

The Court reversed the lower court's judgment and remanded the case.

THE ETHICAL DIMENSION   *In this case, aquatic organisms were most directly at risk. Is it acceptable to apply cost-benefit analyses to situations in which the lives of people are directly affected? Explain.*

THE GLOBAL DIMENSION   *In analyzing the costs and benefits of an action that affects the environment, should a line be drawn at a nation's borders? Why or why not?*

VIOLATIONS OF THE CLEAN WATER ACT   Under the CWA, violators are subject to a variety of civil and criminal penalties. Depending on the violation, civil penalties range from $10,000 per day to $25,000 per day, but not more than $25,000 per violation. Criminal penalties, which apply only if a violation was intentional, range from a fine of $2,500 per day and imprisonment for up to one year to a fine of $1 million and fifteen years' imprisonment. An injunction and damages can also be imposed. The polluting party can be required to clean up the pollution or pay for the cost of doing so.

Wetlands

Wetlands   Water-saturated areas of land that are designated by a government agency as protected areas that support wildlife and therefore cannot be filled in or dredged by private contractors or parties without a permit.

The Clean Water Act prohibits the filling or dredging of **wetlands** unless a permit is obtained from the Army Corps of Engineers. The EPA defines *wetlands* as "those areas that are inundated or saturated by surface or ground water at a frequency and duration sufficient to support . . . vegetation typically adapted for life in saturated soil conditions." Wetlands are thought to be vital to the ecosystem because they filter streams and rivers and provide habitat for wildlife. Although in the past the EPA's broad interpretation of what constitutes a wetland generated substantial controversy, the courts have considerably scaled back the CWA's protection of wetlands in recent years.[9]

Drinking Water

The Safe Drinking Water Act of 1974[10] requires the EPA to set maximum levels for pollutants in public water systems. Public water system operators must come as close as possible to meeting the EPA's standards by using the best available technology that is economically and technologically feasible. The EPA is particularly concerned about contamination from underground sources, such as pesticides and wastes leaked from landfills or disposed of in underground injection wells. Many of these substances are associated with cancer and may cause damage to the central nervous system, liver, and kidneys.

The act was amended in 1996 to give the EPA more flexibility in setting regulatory standards. These amendments also imposed requirements on suppliers of drinking water. Each supplier must send to every household it supplies with water an annual statement describing the source of its water, the level of any contaminants contained in the water, and any possible health concerns associated with the contaminants.

Although some evidence suggests that trace amounts of pharmaceuticals may be entering the nation's drinking water, the law does not yet require suppliers to test for these substances. The drugs come from prescription medications taken by humans and antibiotics and other medications given to livestock. Although the body absorbs some

---

9. See, for example, *Rapanos v. United States,* 547 U.S. 715, 126 S.Ct. 2208, 165 L.Ed.2d 159 (2006).
10. 42 U.S.C. Sections 300f to 300j-25.

of these drugs, a portion is not metabolized and enters the public water supply. Most tap water is not treated to remove these chemical compounds. Tests have shown that the drinking water of at least 41 million Americans contains very small amounts of medications, including antibiotics, anticonvulsants, mood stabilizers, and hormones. Scientists have not yet determined whether such small quantities (measured in parts per billion) will have long-term health consequences, and the EPA has not issued regulations.

Ocean Dumping

The Marine Protection, Research, and Sanctuaries Act of 1972[11] (popularly known as the Ocean Dumping Act), as amended in 1983, regulates the transportation and dumping of material into ocean waters. It prohibits entirely the ocean dumping of radiological, chemical, and biological warfare agents and high-level radioactive waste. The act also established a permit program for transporting and dumping other materials, and designated certain areas as marine sanctuaries. Each violation of any provision in the Ocean Dumping Act may result in a civil penalty of up to $50,000. A knowing violation is a criminal offense that may result in a $50,000 fine, imprisonment for not more than a year, or both. A court may also grant an injunction to prevent an imminent or continuing violation of the Ocean Dumping Act.

Oil Pollution

After more than 10 million gallons of oil leaked into Alaska's Prince William Sound from the *Exxon Valdez* supertanker in 1989, Congress responded by passing the Oil Pollution Act of 1990.[12] (At that time, the *Exxon Valdez* disaster was the worst oil spill in U.S. history, but the BP oil spill in the Gulf of Mexico in 2010 surpassed it.) Under this act, any onshore or offshore oil facility, oil shipper, vessel owner, or vessel operator that discharges oil into navigable waters or onto an adjoining shore can be liable for clean-up costs, as well as damages.

Under the act, damage to natural resources, private property, and the local economy, including the increased cost of providing public services, is compensable. The penalties range from $2 million to $350 million, depending on the size of the vessel and on whether the oil spill came from a vessel or an offshore facility. The party held responsible for the clean-up costs can bring a civil suit for contribution from other potentially liable parties. Oil tankers using U.S. ports must now be double hulled to limit the severity of accidental spills.

Toxic Chemicals

Originally, most environmental clean-up efforts were directed toward reducing smog and making water safe for fishing and swimming. Today, the control of toxic chemicals used in agriculture and in industry has become increasingly important.

Pesticides and Herbicides

The Federal Insecticide, Fungicide, and Rodenticide Act (FIFRA) of 1947[13] regulates pesticides and herbicides. Under FIFRA, pesticides and herbicides must be (1) registered before they can be sold, (2) certified and used only for approved applications,

---

11. 16 U.S.C. Sections 1401–1445.
12. 33 U.S.C. Sections 2701–2761.
13. 7 U.S.C. Sections 135–136y.

and (3) used in limited quantities when applied to food crops. The EPA can cancel or suspend registration of substances that are identified as harmful and may also inspect factories where the chemicals are made. Under 1996 amendments to FIFRA, there must be no more than a one-in-a-million risk to people of developing cancer from any kind of exposure to the substance, including eating food that contains pesticide residues.[14]

It is a violation of FIFRA to sell a pesticide or herbicide that is either unregistered or has had its registration canceled or suspended. It is also a violation to sell a pesticide or herbicide with a false or misleading label or to destroy or deface any labeling required under the act. Penalties for commercial dealers include imprisonment for up to one year and a fine of no more than $25,000. Farmers and other private users of pesticides or herbicides who violate the act are subject to a $1,000 fine and incarceration for up to thirty days.

Note that a state can also regulate the sale and use of federally registered pesticides. **CASE EXAMPLE 21.3**   After the EPA conditionally registered Strongarm, a weed-killing pesticide, Dow Agrosciences, LLC, sold Strongarm to Texas peanut farmers. When the farmers applied it, however, Strongarm damaged their crops and failed to control the growth of weeds. The farmers sued Dow, but the lower courts ruled that FIFRA preempted their claims. The farmers appealed to the United States Supreme Court. The Supreme Court held that under a specific provision of FIFRA, a state can regulate the sale and use of federally registered pesticides so long as the regulation does not permit anything that FIFRA prohibits.[15] ●

Toxic Substances

The first comprehensive law covering toxic substances was the Toxic Substances Control Act of 1976.[16] The act was passed to regulate chemicals and chemical compounds that are known to be toxic—such as asbestos and polychlorinated biphenyls, popularly known as PCBs—and to institute investigation of any possible harmful effects from new chemical compounds. The regulations authorize the EPA to require that manufacturers, processors, and other organizations planning to use chemicals first determine their effects on human health and the environment. The EPA can regulate substances that potentially pose an imminent hazard or an unreasonable risk of injury to health or the environment. The EPA may require special labeling, limit the use of a substance, set production quotas, or prohibit the use of a substance altogether.

Hazardous Waste Disposal

Some industrial, agricultural, and household wastes pose more serious threats than others. If not properly disposed of, these toxic chemicals may present a substantial danger to human health and the environment. If released into the environment, they may contaminate public drinking water resources.

Resource Conservation and Recovery Act

In 1976, Congress passed the Resource Conservation and Recovery Act (RCRA)[17] in reaction to concern over the effects of hazardous waste materials on the environment. The RCRA required the EPA to determine which forms of solid waste should be

---

14. 21 U.S.C. Section 346a.

15. *Bates v. Dow Agrosciences, LLC,* 544 U.S. 431, 125 S.Ct. 1788, 161 L.Ed.2d 687 (2005).

16. 15 U.S.C. Sections 2601–2692.

17. 42 U.S.C. Sections 6901–6986.

considered hazardous and to establish regulations to monitor and control hazardous waste disposal. The act also requires all producers of hazardous waste materials to label and package properly any hazardous waste to be transported. The RCRA was amended in 1984 and 1986 to decrease the use of land containment in the disposal of hazardous waste and to require smaller generators of hazardous waste to comply with the act.

Under the RCRA, a company may be assessed a civil penalty of up to $25,000 for each violation. Penalties are based on the seriousness of the violation, the probability of harm, and the extent to which the violation deviates from RCRA requirements. Criminal penalties include fines of up to $50,000 for each day of violation, imprisonment for up to two years (in most instances), or both. Criminal fines and the period of imprisonment can be doubled for certain repeat offenders.

Superfund

In 1980, Congress passed the Comprehensive Environmental Response, Compensation, and Liability Act (CERCLA),[18] commonly known as Superfund, to regulate the clean-up of leaking hazardous waste–disposal sites. A special federal fund was created for that purpose.

CERCLA, as amended in 1986, has four primary elements:

1. It established an information-gathering and analysis system that enables the government to identify chemical dump sites and determine the appropriate action.
2. It authorized the EPA to respond to hazardous substance emergencies and to arrange for the clean-up of a leaking site directly if the persons responsible for the problem fail to clean up the site.
3. It created a Hazardous Substance Response Trust Fund (also known as Superfund) to pay for the clean-up of hazardous sites using funds obtained through taxes on certain businesses.
4. It allowed the government to recover the cost of clean-up from the persons who were (even remotely) responsible for hazardous substance releases.

POTENTIALLY RESPONSIBLE PARTIES   Superfund provides that when a release or a threatened release of hazardous chemicals from a site occurs, the EPA can clean up the site and recover the cost of the clean-up from the following persons: (1) the person who generated the wastes disposed of at the site, (2) the person who transported the wastes to the site, (3) the person who owned or operated the site at the time of the disposal, or (4) the current owner or operator. A person falling within one of these categories is referred to as a **potentially responsible party.**

JOINT AND SEVERAL LIABILITY   Liability under Superfund is usually joint and several—that is, a person who generated *only a fraction of the hazardous waste* disposed of at the site may nevertheless be liable for *all* of the clean-up costs. CERCLA authorizes a party who has incurred clean-up costs to bring a "contribution action" against any other person who is liable or potentially liable for a percentage of the costs.

MINIMIZING LIABILITY   One way for a business to minimize its potential liability under Superfund is to conduct environmental compliance audits of its own

Potentially Responsible Party A party liable for the costs of cleaning up a hazardous waste–disposal site. Any person who generated the hazardous waste, transported it, owned or operated the waste site at the time of disposal, or owns or operates the site at the present time may be responsible for some or all of the clean-up costs.

---

18. 42 U.S.C. Sections 9601–9675.

operations regularly. A business can perform internal investigations of its own operations and lands to determine whether any environmental hazards exist.

The EPA encourages companies to conduct self-audits and promptly detect, disclose, and correct wrongdoing. Companies that do so are subject to lighter penalties (fines may be reduced as much as 75 percent) for violations of environmental laws. Under EPA guidelines, the EPA will waive all fines if a small company corrects environmental violations within 180 days after being notified of the violations (or 360 days if pollution-prevention techniques are involved). The policy does not apply to criminal violations of environmental laws, though, or to actions that pose a significant threat to public health, safety, or the environment.

DEFENSES   There are a few defenses to liability under CERCLA. The most important is the innocent landowner defense.[19] Under this defense, an innocent property owner may be able to avoid liability by showing that he or she had no contractual or employment relationship with the person who released the hazardous substance on the land. Thus, if the property was transferred by contract from the third party who disposed of the substances to the current owner, the defense normally will not be available.

To assert the defense, the landowner must be able to show that at the time the property was acquired, she or he had no reason to know that hazardous substances had been disposed of on it. The landowner must also show that at the time of the purchase, she or he undertook all appropriate investigation into the previous ownership and uses of the property to determine whether there was reason to be concerned about hazardous substances. In effect, this defense protects only property owners who took precautions and investigated the possibility of environmental hazards at the time they bought the property.

---

19. 42 U.S.C. Section 9601(35)(B).

 Reviewing . . . Protecting the Environment

Early in the 2000s, residents of Lake Caliopa, Minnesota, began noticing an unusually high number of lung ailments among their population. A group of concerned local citizens pooled their resources and commissioned a study of the frequency of these health conditions per capita compared to national averages. The study concluded that residents of Lake Caliopa experienced four to seven times the frequency of asthma, bronchitis, and emphysema as the population nationwide. During the study period, citizens began expressing concerns about the large volume of smog emitted by the Cotton Design apparel manufacturing plant on the outskirts of town. The plant had opened its production facility two miles east of town beside the Tawakoni River in 1999 and employed seventy full-time workers by 2009.

Just downstream on the Tawakoni River, the city of Lake Caliopa operated a public waterworks facility, which supplied all city residents with water. In August 2010, the Minnesota Pollution Control Agency required Cotton Design to install new equipment to control air and water pollution. In May 2011, citizens brought a class-action lawsuit in a Minnesota state court against Cotton Design for various respiratory ailments allegedly caused or compounded by smog from Cotton Design's factory. Using the information presented in the chapter, answer the following questions.

1. Under the common law, what would each plaintiff be required to identify in order to be given relief by the court?
2. Are air-quality regulations typically overseen by the federal, state, or local government?
3. What standard for limiting emissions into the air does Cotton Design's pollution-control equipment have to meet?
4. What information must Lake Caliopa send to every household that the city supplies with water?

Key Terms

environmental impact statement (EIS) 610   potentially responsible party 621   wetlands 618
nuisance 609   toxic tort 609

Chapter Summary: Protecting the Environment

Common Law Actions (See pages 608–609.)	1. *Nuisance*—A common law doctrine under which actions against pollution-causing activities may be brought. In some states, an action is permissible only if an individual suffers a harm separate and distinct from that of the general public. 2. *Negligence and strict liability*—Parties may recover damages for injuries sustained as a result of a firm's pollution-causing activities if they can demonstrate that the harm was a foreseeable result of the firm's failure to exercise reasonable care (negligence). Businesses engaging in ultrahazardous activities are liable for whatever injuries the activities cause, regardless of whether the firms exercise reasonable care.
Federal, State, and Local Regulations (See pages 609–610.)	1. *Federal regulations*—See Exhibit 21–1 on page 611 for a list of major federal environmental legislation. a. Environmental protection agencies—The primary agency regulating environmental law is the federal Environmental Protection Agency (EPA), which was created in 1970 to coordinate federal environmental programs. The EPA administers most federal environmental policies and statutes. b. Assessing environmental impact—The National Environmental Policy Act of 1969 imposes environmental responsibilities on all federal agencies and requires the preparation of an environmental impact statement (EIS) for every major federal action. An EIS must analyze the action's impact on the environment, its adverse effects and possible alternatives, and its irreversible effects on environmental quality. 2. *State and local regulations*—Activities affecting the environment are controlled at the local and state levels through regulations relating to land use, the disposal and recycling of garbage and waste, and pollution-causing activities in general.
Air Pollution (See pages 611–614.)	1. *Mobile sources*—Automobiles and other vehicles are mobile sources of air pollution, and the EPA establishes pollution-control standards and time schedules for meeting these standards. 2. *Stationary sources*—The Clean Air Act requires the EPA to list all regulated hazardous air pollutants that are emitted from stationary sources on a prioritized schedule. These include substances such as asbestos, mercury, and vinyl chloride that are known to cause harm to humans. Major sources of air pollution are required to use the *maximum achievable control technology* to reduce emissions.
Water Pollution (See pages 614–619.)	1. *Clean Water Act*—This 1972 act amended an earlier federal law by setting specific time schedules to improve water quality. The act also requires cities and businesses to obtain a permit before discharging waste into navigable waters. The EPA limits discharges of various pollutants based on the technology available for controlling them. 2. *Wetlands*—Certain water-saturated areas are designated wetlands and protected from dredging or filling without a permit. This is intended to provide natural habitat to support wildlife, such as migratory birds. 3. *Drinking water*—Federal law requires the EPA to set maximum levels for pollutants in public water systems and requires public systems to use the best available technology to prevent contamination from underground sources. Each supplier of public water must send to every household it supplies with water an annual statement describing the water's source, the level of any contaminants, and any possible health concerns associated with these contaminants. 4. *Ocean dumping*—Federal law prohibits the dumping of radiological, chemical, and biological warfare agents and high-level radioactive waste into the ocean. 5. *Oil pollution*—Federal law provides that any offshore or onshore oil facility, oil shipper, vessel owner, or vessel operator that discharges oil into navigable waters or onto a shoreline is liable for clean-up costs and damages.

(Continued)

Chapter Summary: Protecting the Environment, Continued

Toxic Chemicals (See pages 619–620.)	The federal government regulates the pesticides and herbicides that can be used in agriculture, as well as the use and transportation of chemical compounds known to be toxic.
Hazardous Waste Disposal (See pages 620–622.)	Federal laws regulate the disposal of certain types of industrial, agricultural, and household wastes that present serious dangers to human health and the environment. These hazardous wastes must be properly labeled and packaged before they can be transported. Moreover, under Superfund, when a hazardous substance is released into the environment, the EPA can clean up the site and recover the costs from a broad array of potentially responsible parties.

 ExamPrep

ISSUE SPOTTERS

1. ChemCorp generates hazardous wastes from its operations. Disposal Trucking Company transports those wastes to Eliminators, Inc., which owns a hazardous waste–disposal site. Eliminators sells the property on which the disposal site is located to Fluid Properties, Inc. If the Environmental Protection Agency cleans up the site, from whom can it recover the cost?

2. Resource Refining Company's plant emits smoke and fumes. Resource's operation includes a short railway system, and trucks enter and exit the grounds continuously. Constant vibrations from the trains and trucks rattle nearby residential neighborhoods. The residents sue Resource. Are there any reasons why the court might refuse to issue an injunction against Resource's operation? Explain.

—**Check your answers to these questions against the answers provided in Appendix G.**

BEFORE THE TEST

Go to **www.cengagebrain.com**, enter the ISBN number "9781111530617," and click on "Find" to locate this textbook's Web site. Then, click on "Access Now" under "Study Tools," and select "Chapter 21" at the top. There you will find an "Interactive Quiz" that you can take to assess your mastery of the concepts in this chapter, as well as "Flashcards" and a "Glossary" of important terms.

 For Review

1. Under what common law theories can polluters be held liable?
2. What is an environmental impact statement, and who must file one?
3. What does the Environmental Protection Agency do?
4. What major federal statutes regulate air and water pollution?
5. What is Superfund? What categories of persons are liable under Superfund?

 Questions and Case Problems

21–1. Clean Air Act. Current scientific knowledge indicates that there is no safe level of exposure to a cancer-causing agent. In theory, even one molecule of such a substance has the potential for causing cancer. Section 112 of the Clean Air Act requires that all cancer-causing substances be regulated to ensure a margin of safety. Some environmental groups have argued that all emissions of such substances must be eliminated if a margin of safety is to be reached. Such total elimination would likely shut down many major U.S. industries. Should the Environmental Protection Agency totally eliminate all emissions of cancer-causing chemicals? Discuss.

21–2. Environmental Laws. Fruitade, Inc., is a processor of a soft drink called Freshen Up. Fruitade uses returnable bottles, which it cleans with a special acid to allow for further beverage processing. The acid is diluted with water and then allowed to pass into a navigable stream. Fruitade crushes its broken bottles and throws the crushed glass into the stream. Discuss fully any environmental laws that Fruitade has violated.

21–3. Clean Water Act. The Anacostia River, which flows through Washington, D.C., is one of the ten most polluted rivers in the country. For bodies of water such as the Anacostia, the Clean Water Act requires states (which, under the act, include the District of Columbia) to set a "total maximum daily load" (TMDL) for pollutants. A TMDL is to be set "at a level necessary to implement the applicable water-quality standards with seasonal variations." The Anacostia contains biochemical pollutants that consume oxygen, putting the river's aquatic life at risk for suffocation. In addition, the river is murky, stunting the growth of plants that rely on sunlight and impairing recreational use. The Environmental Protection Agency (EPA) approved one TMDL limiting the *annual* discharge of oxygen-depleting pollutants and a second limiting the *seasonal* discharge of pollutants contributing to turbidity. Neither TMDL limited daily discharges. Friends of the Earth, Inc. (FoE), asked a federal district court to review the TMDLs. What is FoE's best argument in this dispute? What is the EPA's likely response? What should the court rule, and why? [*Friends of the Earth, Inc. v. Environmental Protection Agency,* 446 F.3d 140 (D.C.Cir. 2006)]

21–4. Environmental Impact Statement. The fourth largest crop in the United States is alfalfa, of which 5 percent is exported to Japan. RoundUp Ready alfalfa is genetically engineered to resist glyphosate, the active ingredient in the herbicide RoundUp. The U.S. Department of Agriculture (USDA) regulates genetically engineered agricultural products through the Animal and Plant Health Inspection Service (APHIS). APHIS concluded that RoundUp Ready alfalfa does not have any harmful effects on the health of humans or livestock and deregulated it. Geertson Seed Farms and others filed a suit in a federal district court against Mike Johanns (the secretary of the USDA) and others, asserting that APHIS's decision required the preparation of an environmental impact statement (EIS). The plaintiffs argued, among other things, that the introduction of RoundUp Ready alfalfa might significantly decrease the availability of, or even eliminate, all nongenetically engineered varieties. The plaintiffs were concerned that the RoundUp Ready alfalfa might contaminate standard alfalfa because alfalfa is pollinated by bees, which can travel as far as two miles from a pollen source. If contamination occurred, farmers would not be able to market "contaminated" varieties as "organic," which would affect the sales of "organic" livestock and exports to Japan, which does not allow the import of glyphosate-resistant alfalfa. Should an EIS be prepared in this case? Why or why not? [*Geertson Seed Farms v. Johanns,* __ F.Supp.2d __ (N.D.Cal. 2007)]

21–5. **Case Problem with Sample Answer. Environmental Impact Statement.** The U.S. National Park Service (NPS) manages the Grand Canyon National Park in Arizona under a management plan that is subject to periodic review. In 2006, after nine years of background work and the completion of a comprehensive environmental impact statement, the NPS issued a new management plan for the park. One part of the plan allowed for the continued use of rafts on the Colorado River, which runs through the Grand Canyon. The number of the rafts was limited, however. Several environmental groups criticized the plan because they felt that it still allowed too many rafts on the river. The groups requested that a federal appellate court overturn the plan, claiming that it violated the wilderness status of the national park. When can a federal court overturn a determination by an agency such as the NPS? Explain. [*River Runners for Wilderness v. Martin,* 593 F.3d 1064 (9th Cir. 2010)]

—To view a sample answer for Case Problem 21–5, go to Appendix F at the end of this text.

21–6. **A Question of Ethics.** *In the Clean Air Act, Congress allowed California, which has particular problems with clean air, to adopt its own standard for emissions from cars and trucks, subject to the approval of the Environmental Protection Agency (EPA) according to certain criteria. Congress also allowed other states to adopt California's standard after the EPA's approval. In 2004, in an effort to address global warming, the California Air Resources Board amended the state's standard to attain "the maximum feasible and cost-effective reduction of GHG [greenhouse gas] emissions from motor vehicles." The regulation, which applies to new passenger vehicles and light-duty trucks for 2009 and later, imposes decreasing limits on emissions of carbon dioxide through 2016. While EPA approval was pending, Vermont and other states adopted similar standards. Green Mountain Chrysler Plymouth Dodge Jeep and other auto dealers, automakers, and associations of automakers filed a suit in a federal district court against George Crombie (secretary of the Vermont Agency of Natural Resources) and others, seeking relief from the state regulations. [Green Mountain Chrysler Plymouth Dodge Jeep v. Crombie, __ F.Supp.2d __ (D.Vt. 2007)]*

1. Under the Environmental Policy and Conservation Act (EPCA) of 1975, the National Highway Traffic Safety Administration sets fuel economy standards for new cars. The plaintiffs argued, among other things, that the EPCA, which prohibits states from adopting fuel economy standards, preempts Vermont's GHG regulation. Do the GHG rules equate to the fuel economy standards? Discuss.

2. Do Vermont's rules tread on the efforts of the federal government to address global warming internationally? Who should regulate GHG emissions? The federal government? The state governments? Both? Neither? Why?

3. The plaintiffs claimed that they would go bankrupt if they were forced to adhere to the state's GHG standards. Should they be granted relief on this basis? Does history support their claim? Explain.

21–7. **Critical-Thinking Legal Environment Question.** It has been estimated that for every dollar spent cleaning up hazardous waste sites, administrative agencies spend seven dollars in overhead. Can you think of any way to trim these administrative costs? Explain.

Chapter 22

Real Property and Land-Use Control

> "The right of property is the most sacred of all the rights of citizenship."
>
> —Jean-Jacques Rousseau, 1712–1778
> (French writer and philosopher)

Contents

Chapter Objectives

After reading this chapter, you should be able to answer the following questions:

1. What can a person who holds property in fee simple absolute do with the property?
2. What are the requirements for acquiring property by adverse possession?
3. What limitations may be imposed on the rights of property owners?
4. What are the respective duties of the landlord and the tenant concerning the use and maintenance of leased property?
5. What is the purpose of zoning laws?

(Moody75/Creative Commons)

From earliest times, property has provided a means for survival. Primitive peoples lived off the fruits of the land, eating the vegetation and wildlife. Later, as the vegetation was cultivated and the wildlife domesticated, property provided farmland and pasture. Throughout history, property has continued to be an indicator of family wealth and social position. Indeed, an individual's right to his or her property has become, in the words of Jean-Jacques Rousseau above, one of the "most sacred of all the rights of citizenship."

In this chapter, we first examine the nature of real property. We then look at the various ways in which real property can be owned and how ownership rights in real property are transferred from one person to another. We also discuss leased property and landlord-tenant relationships. The chapter concludes with an examination of land-use control.

The Nature of Real Property

Real property consists of land and the buildings, plants, and trees that are on it. Real property also includes subsurface and airspace rights, as well as personal property that has become permanently attached to real property. Whereas personal property is movable, real property—also called *real estate* or *realty*—is immovable.

Land

Land includes the soil on the surface of the earth and the natural or artificial structures that are attached to it. It further includes all the waters contained on or under the surface and much, but not necessarily all, of the airspace above it. The exterior boundaries of land extend down to the center of the earth and up to the farthest reaches of the atmosphere (subject to certain qualifications).

Airspace and Subsurface Rights

The owner of real property has rights to the airspace above the land, as well as to the soil and minerals underneath it. Limitations on either airspace rights or subsurface rights normally must be indicated on the document that transfers title at the time of purchase. When no such limitations, or *encumbrances,* are noted, a purchaser generally can expect to have an unlimited right to possession of the property.

AIRSPACE RIGHTS   Disputes concerning airspace rights may involve the right of commercial and private planes to fly over property and the right of individuals and governments to seed clouds and produce rain artificially. Flights over private land normally do not violate property rights unless the flights are so low and so frequent that they directly interfere with the owner's enjoyment and use of the land.[1] Leaning walls or buildings and projecting eave spouts or roofs may also violate the airspace rights of an adjoining property owner.

SUBSURFACE RIGHTS   In many states, land ownership may be separated, in that the surface of a piece of land and the subsurface may have different owners. Subsurface rights can be extremely valuable, as these rights include the ownership of minerals, oil, and natural gas. Subsurface rights would be of little value, however, if the owner could not use the surface to exercise those rights. Hence, a subsurface owner has a right (called a *profit*—see page 630) to go onto the surface of the land to, for example, discover and mine minerals.

When ownership is separated into surface and subsurface rights, each owner can pass title to what she or he owns without the consent of the other owner. Of course, conflicts can arise between the surface owner's use of the property and the subsurface owner's need to extract minerals, oil, or natural gas. In that situation, one party's interest may become subservient (secondary) to the other party's interest either by statute or by case law. If the owners of the subsurface rights excavate (dig), they are absolutely liable if their excavation causes the surface to collapse. Many states have statutes that also make the excavators liable for any damage to structures on the land. Typically, these statutes provide precise requirements for excavations of various depths.

Plant Life and Vegetation

Plant life, both natural and cultivated, is also considered to be real property. In many instances, the natural vegetation, such as trees, adds greatly to the value of the realty. When a parcel of land is sold and the land has growing crops on it, the sale includes the crops, unless otherwise specified in the sales contract. When crops are sold by themselves, however, they are considered to be personal property or goods. Consequently, the sale of crops is a sale of goods and thus is governed by the Uniform Commercial Code (UCC) rather than by real property law.[2]

> *"The meek shall inherit the earth, but not the mineral rights."*
>
> J. Paul Getty, 1892–1976
> (American entrepreneur and industrialist)

---

1. *United States v. Causby,* 328 U.S. 256, 66 S.Ct. 1062, 90 L.Ed. 1206 (1946).
2. See UCC 2–107(2), discussed in Chapter 11.

Fixtures

Fixture An item that was once personal property but has become attached to real property in such a way that it takes on the characteristics of real property and becomes part of that real property.

Certain personal property can become so closely associated with the real property to which it is attached that the law views it as real property. Such property is known as a **fixture**—an item *affixed* to realty, meaning that it is attached to the real property by roots; embedded in it; permanently situated on it; or permanently attached by means of cement, plaster, bolts, nails, or screws. The fixture can be physically attached to real property, be attached to another fixture, or even be without any actual physical attachment to the land (such as a statue). As long as the owner intends the property to be a fixture, normally it will be a fixture.

Fixtures are included in the sale of land if the sales contract does not provide otherwise. The sale of a house includes the land and the house and the garage on the land, as well as the cabinets, plumbing, and windows. Because these are permanently affixed to the property, they are considered to be a part of it. Certain items, such as drapes and window-unit air conditioners, are difficult to classify. Thus, a contract for the sale of a house or commercial realty should indicate which items of this sort are included in the sale.

The following case illustrates the importance of intent in determining whether property is a fixture.

Case 22.1 APL Limited v. State of Washington Department of Revenue

Court of Appeals of Washington, 154 Wash.App. 1020 (2010).

(Dennis Hamilton/Orcmid/Creative Commons)

Are loading-dock cranes considered a fixture?

BACKGROUND AND FACTS   The Port of Seattle entered into a thirty-year lease with APL Limited and others (collectively, APL) for premises at Terminal 5 for loading and unloading shipping-container ships. The Port had substantially rebuilt Terminal 5 and had constructed and installed loading cranes. These cranes run on steel crane rails that are set one hundred feet apart, embedded in a concrete apron, and supported by specially designed steel-reinforced concrete piers engineered specifically to support the cranes. The cranes themselves are steel structures 198 feet tall, 85 feet wide, and more than 370 feet long—each weighing more than eight hundred tons. They are hard-wired to a dedicated high-voltage electrical system that includes a power substation built specifically for Terminal 5 to power the cranes. The cranes are attached to the power substation by cables that are more than two inches thick. The cranes have been in use continuously on Terminal 5 since their construction more than twenty years ago. APL sued the state for a refund of sales tax paid on the rent for the cranes, claiming that the cranes were fixtures. The state argued that the cranes were personal property and, as such, subject to sales tax. The trial court granted the state's motion for summary judgment, and APL appealed.

IN THE WORDS OF THE COURT . . .
GROSSE, J. [Judge]
* * * *

Case law dictates that to determine whether the cranes are personal property or real property, [that is,] fixtures, we apply the common law test. Under this test, we must consider the following three prongs:

(1) Actual annexation to the realty, or something appurtenant thereto; (2) application to the use or purpose to which that part of the realty with which it is connected is appropriated; and (3) the intention of the party making the annexation to make a permanent accession to the freehold.

All three prongs must be met for a chattel to become a fixture. Both parties agree that the second prong is met in this instance but dispute the first and third prongs. [Emphasis added.]

Applying a confusing factual scenario, the trial court decided that the first prong, annexation, was not met and therefore it need not consider any of the other facts presented. This was error because the determinative factor for whether a chattel [movable property] annexed to real property becomes part of the real property or retains its character as personal property is the third prong: the intent with which the chattel was annexed to the land. *Intent can be determined from the nature of the chattel attached and its relation or necessity to the activity conducted on the land and the manner in which it is annexed. When the owner and the person that annexes the chattel are one and the same, a rebuttable presumption arises that the owner's intention was for the chattel to become part of the realty.* [Emphasis added.]

Case 22.1–Continued

* * * *

In its oral ruling, the trial court itself recognized that it had not examined the facts regarding the Port's intent to annex these cranes. Because annexation is so intertwined with the intent to annex, one cannot be examined without the other. * * * The factual inferences that can be drawn from the evidence presented should be permitted to be argued to the trial court. Because the trial court did not consider these inferences, summary judgment was inappropriate.

DECISION AND REMEDY   The state appellate court reversed the trial court's ruling. Because the trial court did not give sufficient scrutiny to the role of intent in determining whether the

cranes were personal or real property, summary judgment was inappropriate.

WHAT IF THE FACTS WERE DIFFERENT?   *Suppose that the cranes in this case had been much smaller and could have been moved to other locations with little cost or trouble. Would the result have been different? Why or why not?*

THE ECONOMIC DIMENSION   *Did the fact that the appellate court reversed the judgment of the trial court mean that the cranes were fixtures? Explain.*

When real property is being sold, transferred, or subjected to a security interest, make sure that any contract specifically lists which fixtures are to be included. Without such a list, the parties may have very different ideas as to what is being transferred with the real property (or included as collateral for a loan). It is much simpler and less expensive to itemize fixtures in a contract than to engage in litigation.

Ownership Interests in Real Property

> *"Few ... men own their property. The property owns them."*
>
> Robert G. Ingersoll, 1833–1899
> (American politician and lecturer)

Ownership of property is an abstract concept that cannot exist independently of the legal system. No one can actually possess or *hold* a piece of land, the airspace above it, the earth below it, and all the water contained on it. The legal system therefore recognizes certain rights and duties that constitute ownership interests in real property.

Property ownership is often viewed as a bundle of rights. One who possesses the entire bundle of rights is said to hold the property in *fee simple,* which is the most complete form of ownership. When only some of the rights in the bundle are transferred to another person, the effect is to limit the ownership rights of both the transferor of the rights and the recipient.

Ownership in Fee Simple

Fee Simple Absolute   An ownership interest in land in which the owner has the greatest possible aggregation of rights, privileges, and power. Ownership in fee simple absolute is assigned forever to a person and her or his heirs without limitation.

In a **fee simple absolute,** the owner has the greatest aggregation of rights, privileges, and power possible. The owner can give the property away or dispose of the property by *deed* (the instrument used to transfer property, as will be discussed later in this chapter) or by will. When there is no will, the fee simple ownership interest passes to the owner's legal heirs on her or his death. A fee simple is potentially infinite in duration and is assigned forever to a person and her or his heirs without limitation or condition. The owner has the rights of *exclusive* possession and use of the property.

The rights that accompany a fee simple include the right to use the land for whatever purpose the owner sees fit. Of course, other laws, including applicable zoning, noise, and environmental laws, may limit the owner's ability to use the property in certain ways. A person who uses his or her property in a manner that unreasonably interferes with others' right to use or enjoy their own property can be liable for the tort of *nuisance* (see page 609).

CASE EXAMPLE 22.1   Nancy and James Biglane owned and lived in a building in Natchez, Mississippi. Next door to the Biglanes' property was a popular bar called the Under the Hill Saloon that featured live music. During the summer, the Saloon, which had no air-conditioning, opened its windows and doors, and live music echoed up and down the street. Although the Biglanes installed extra insulation, thicker windows, and air-conditioning units in their building, the noise from the Saloon kept them awake at night. Eventually, the Biglanes sued the owners of the Saloon for nuisance. The court held that the noise from the bar unreasonably interfered with the Biglanes' right to enjoy their property and enjoined (prevented) the Saloon from opening its windows and doors while playing music.[3] ●

Life Estates

Life Estate An interest in land that exists only for the duration of the life of some person, usually the holder of the estate.

Conveyance The transfer of title to land from one person to another by deed; a document (such as a deed) by which an interest in land is transferred from one person to another.

A **life estate** is an estate that lasts for the life of some specified individual. A **conveyance,** or transfer of real property, "to A for his life" creates a life estate. In a life estate, the life tenant's ownership rights cease to exist on the life tenant's death.[4] The life tenant has the right to use the land, provided that he or she commits no waste (injury to the land). In other words, the life tenant cannot use the land in a manner that would adversely affect its value. The life tenant is entitled to any rents generated by the land and can harvest crops from the land. If mines and oil wells are already on the land, the life tenant can extract minerals and oil and is entitled to the royalties, but he or she cannot exploit the land by creating new wells or mines.

The life tenant can create liens, *easements* (discussed below), and leases, but none can extend beyond the life of the tenant. In addition, with few exceptions, the owner of a life estate has an exclusive right to possession during her or his life.

Along with these rights, the life tenant also has some duties—to keep the property in repair and to pay property taxes. In short, the owner of the life estate has the same rights as a fee simple owner except that the life tenant must maintain the value of the property during her or his tenancy.

Nonpossessory Interests

Nonpossessory Interest In the context of real property, an interest in land that does not include any right to possess the property.

Easement A nonpossessory right to use another's property in a manner established by either express or implied agreement.

Profit In real property law, the right to enter onto and remove something of value from the property of another.

In contrast to the types of property interests just described, some interests in land do not include any rights to possess the property. These interests are therefore known as **nonpossessory interests.** They include easements, profits, and licenses.

An **easement** is the right of a person to make limited use of another person's real property without taking anything from the property. An easement, for instance, can be the right to walk or drive across another's property. In contrast, a **profit**[5] is the right to go onto land owned by another and take away some part of the land itself or some product of the land. **EXAMPLE 22.2** Akmed owns Sandy View. Akmed gives Carmen the right to go there to remove all the sand and gravel that she needs for her cement business. Carmen has a profit. ●

Easements and profits can be classified as either *appurtenant* or *in gross*. Because easements and profits are similar and the same rules apply to both, we discuss them together.

---

3. *Biglane v. Under the Hill Corp.,* 949 So.2d 9 (Miss.Sup.Ct. 2007).

4. Because a life tenant's rights in the property cease at death, life estates frequently are used to avoid probate proceedings that would be necessary to transfer the property under a will. The person who owns the property deeds it to the person who would eventually inherit the property and reserves a life estate for herself or himself. That way, the property owner can live there until death, and the property then passes to the intended heir without the need for legal proceedings.

5. The term *profit,* as used here, does not refer to the profits made by a business firm. Rather, it means a gain or an advantage.

CONTRAST   An easement appurtenant requires two adjacent pieces of land owned by two different persons, but an easement in gross involves only one piece of land owned by someone other than the owner of the easement.

EASEMENT OR PROFIT APPURTENANT   An easement or profit *appurtenant* arises when the owner of one piece of land has a right to go onto (or remove something from) an adjacent piece of land owned by another. The land that is benefited by the easement is called the *dominant estate,* and the land that is burdened is called the *servient estate.* Because easements appurtenant are intended to *benefit the land,* they run (are conveyed) with the land when it is transferred. **EXAMPLE 22.3**   Acosta has a right to drive his car across Green's land, which is adjacent to Acosta's land. This right-of-way over Green's property is an easement appurtenant to Acosta's property and can be used only by Acosta. If Acosta sells his land, the easement runs with the land to benefit the new owner. •

EASEMENT OR PROFIT IN GROSS   In an easement or profit *in gross,* the person who has a right to use or take things from another's land does not own an adjacent tract of land. These easements are intended to *benefit a particular person or business,* not a particular piece of land, and cannot be transferred. **EXAMPLE 22.4**   Avery owns a parcel of land with a marble quarry. Avery conveys (transfers) to Classic Stone Corporation the right to come onto her land and remove up to five hundred pounds of marble per day. Classic Stone owns a profit in gross and cannot transfer this right to another. •
Similarly, when a utility company is granted an easement to run its power lines across another's property, it obtains an easement in gross.

CREATION OF AN EASEMENT OR PROFIT   Most easements and profits are created by an express grant in a contract, deed (see page 634), or will. This allows the parties to include terms defining the extent and length of time of use. In some situations, an easement or profit can also be created without an express agreement.
    An easement or profit may arise by *implication* when the circumstances surrounding the division of a parcel of property imply its existence. **EXAMPLE 22.5**   Barrow divides a parcel of land that has only one well for drinking water. If Barrow conveys the half without a well to Jarad, a profit by implication arises because Jarad needs drinking water. •
    An easement may also be created by *necessity.* An easement by necessity does not require a division of property for its existence. A person who rents an apartment, for example, has an easement by necessity in the private road leading up to it.
    An easement arises by *prescription* when one person exercises an easement, such as a right-of-way, on another person's land without the landowner's consent, and the use is apparent and continues for the length of time required by the applicable statute of limitations. (In much the same way, title to property may be obtained by *adverse possession*—discussed on page 635.)

TERMINATION OF AN EASEMENT OR PROFIT   An easement or profit can be terminated or extinguished in several ways. The simplest way is to deed it back to the owner of the land that is burdened by it. Another way is to abandon it and create evidence of intent to relinquish the right to use it. Mere nonuse will not extinguish an easement or profit *unless the nonuse is accompanied by an overt act showing the intent to abandon.* Also, if the owner of an easement or profit becomes the owner of the property burdened by it, then it is merged into the property.

License   In the context of real property, a revocable right or privilege of a person to come onto another person's land.

LICENSE   In the context of real property, a **license** is the revocable right of a person to come onto another person's land. It is a personal privilege that arises from the consent of the owner of the land and can be revoked by the owner. A ticket to attend a movie at a theater is an example of a license. **EXAMPLE 22.6** The owner of a Broadway theater issues Alena a ticket to see a play. If Alena is refused entry into the theater because she is improperly dressed, she has no right to force her way into the theater. The ticket is only a revocable license and not a conveyance of an interest in property. ●

In essence, a license grants a person the authority to enter the land of another and perform a specified act or series of acts without obtaining any permanent interest in the land. When a person with a license exceeds the authority granted and undertakes some action on the property that is not permitted, the property owner can sue that person for trespass (discussed in Chapter 5).

CASE EXAMPLE 22.7 A Catholic church granted Prince Realty Management, LLC, a three-month license to use a three-foot strip of its property adjacent to Prince's property. The license authorized Prince to "put up plywood panels," creating a temporary fence to protect Prince's property during the construction of a new building, and then restore the boundary line between the properties with a new brick fence. During the license's term, Prince installed steel piles and beams on the licensed property. When Prince ignored the church's demands that these structures be removed, the church sued Prince for trespass. The court held that because the license allowed only temporary structures and Prince had exceeded its authority by installing steel piles and beams, the church was entitled to damages.[6] ●

Transfer of Ownership

Ownership interests in real property are frequently transferred (conveyed) by sale, and the terms of the transfer are specified in a real estate sales contract. Often, real estate brokers or agents who are licensed by the state assist the buyers and sellers during the sales transaction. Real property ownership can also be transferred by gift, by will or inheritance, by possession, or by *eminent domain*. When ownership rights in real property are transferred, the type of interest being transferred and the conditions of the transfer normally are set forth in a *deed* executed by the person who is conveying the property.

Real Estate Sales Contracts

In some ways, a sale of real estate is similar to a sale of goods because it involves a transfer of ownership, often with specific warranties. A sale of real estate, however, is generally a more complicated transaction that involves certain formalities that are not required in a sale of goods. Usually, after lengthy negotiations (involving offers, counteroffers, and responses), the parties enter into a detailed contract setting forth their agreement. A contract for a sale of land includes such terms as the purchase price, the type of deed the buyer will receive, the condition of the premises, and any items that will be included.

Unless the buyer pays cash for the property, he or she must obtain financing through a mortgage loan. (As discussed in Chapter 13, a *mortgage* is a loan made by an individual or institution, such as a banking institution or trust company, for which the property is given as security.) Real estate sales contracts are often contingent on the buyer's ability to obtain financing at or below a specified rate of interest. The contract may also be contingent on the buyer's sale of other real property, the seller's

---

6. *Roman Catholic Church of Our Lady of Sorrows v. Prince Realty Management, LLC,* 47 A.D.3d 909, 850 N.Y.S.2d 569 (2008).

acquisition of title insurance, or the completion of a survey of the property and its passing one or more inspections. Normally, the buyer is responsible for having the premises inspected for physical or mechanical defects and for insect infestation.

CLOSING DATE AND ESCROW   The contract usually fixes a date for performance, or **closing,** which is frequently four to twelve weeks after the contract is signed. On this day, the seller conveys the property to the buyer by delivering the deed to the buyer in exchange for payment of the purchase price. Deposits toward the purchase price normally are held in a special account, called an **escrow account,** until all of the conditions of sale have been met. Once the closing takes place, the funds remaining in the escrow account (after payments have been made to the escrow agency, title insurance company, and any lien holders) are transferred to the seller. The *escrow agent,* which may be a title company, bank, or special escrow company, acts as a neutral party in the sales transaction and facilitates the sale by allowing the buyer and seller to close the transaction without having to exchange documents and funds.

IMPLIED WARRANTIES IN THE SALE OF NEW HOMES   Most states recognize a warranty—the **implied warranty of habitability** (see also page 642)—in the sale of new homes. The seller of a new house warrants that it will be fit for human habitation even if the deed or contract of sale does not include such a warranty.

Essentially, the seller is warranting that the house is in reasonable working order and is of reasonably sound construction. Thus, under this warranty, the seller of a new home is in effect a guarantor of its fitness. In some states, the warranty protects not only the first purchaser but any subsequent purchaser as well.

SELLER'S DUTY TO DISCLOSE HIDDEN DEFECTS   In most jurisdictions, courts impose on sellers a duty to disclose any known defect that materially affects the value of the property and that the buyer could not reasonably discover. Failure to disclose such a material defect gives the buyer a right to rescind the contract and to sue for damages based on fraud or misrepresentation.

A dispute may arise over whether the seller knew of the defect before the sale, and there is normally a limit to the time within which the buyer can bring a suit against the seller based on the defect. For instance, in Louisiana, the prescribed limit for a suit against a seller who knew, or can be presumed to have known, of the defect is one year from the day that the buyer discovered it. If the seller did not know of the defect, the limit is one year from the date of the sale.

CASE EXAMPLE 22.8   Matthew Humphrey paid $44,000 for a house in Louisiana and partially renovated it. He then sold the house to Terry and Tabitha Whitehead for $67,000. A few months after the Whiteheads moved in, they discovered rotten wood behind the tile in the bathroom and experienced problems with the fireplace and the plumbing. Two years later, the Whiteheads filed a suit against Humphrey seeking to rescind the sale. They argued that the plumbing problems were a latent defect that the seller had failed to disclose. Evidence revealed that prior to the sale, the parties were made aware of issues regarding the sewer system and that corrective actions were taken. At the time of the sale, the toilets flushed, and neither side realized that the latent defects had not been resolved. The court ruled that rescission was not warranted for the sewer problems because the Whiteheads had waited too long after their discovery to file a claim against Humphrey. The court did order Humphrey to pay damages for the repairs to the fireplace and for replacing some

---

Closing   The final step in the sale of real estate; also called *settlement* or *closing escrow.* The escrow agent coordinates the closing with the recording of deeds, the obtaining of title insurance, and other closing activities. A number of costs must be paid, in cash, at the time of closing.

Escrow Account   An account, generally held in the name of the depositor and the escrow agent, containing funds to be paid to a third person on fulfillment of the escrow condition.

Implied Warranty of Habitability   An implied promise by a seller of a new house that the house is fit for human habitation, meaning in a condition that is safe and suitable for people to live there.

of the rotten wood, however, because Humphrey knew about these defects at the time of the sale.[7] ●

Deeds

Deed A document by which title to property (usually real property) is passed.

Possession and title to land are passed from person to person by means of a **deed**—the instrument of conveyance of real property. A deed is a writing signed by an owner of real property that transfers title to another. Deeds must meet certain requirements, but unlike a contract, a deed does not have to be supported by legally sufficient consideration. Gifts of real property are common, and they require deeds even though there is no consideration for the gift. To be valid, a deed must be delivered and include the following:

1. The names of the *grantor* (the giver or seller) and the *grantee* (the donee or buyer).
2. Words evidencing an intent to convey the property (for example, "I hereby bargain, sell, grant, or give").
3. A legally sufficient description of the land.
4. The grantor's (and usually her or his spouse's) signature.

WARRANTY DEEDS   Different types of deeds provide different degrees of protection against defects of title. A **warranty deed** makes the greatest number of warranties and thus provides the greatest protection against defects of title. In most states, special language is required to create a general warranty deed.

Warranty Deed A deed in which the grantor assures (warrants to) the grantee that the grantor has title to the property conveyed in the deed. A deed provides the greatest amount of protection for the grantee.

Warranty deeds commonly include a number of *covenants,* or promises, that the grantor makes to the grantee. These covenants include a covenant that the grantor has the title to, and the power to convey, the property; a covenant of quiet enjoyment (a warranty that the buyer will not be disturbed in her or his possession of the land); and a covenant that transfer of the property is made without knowledge of adverse claims of third parties. Generally, the warranty deed makes the grantor liable for all defects of title by the grantor and previous titleholders.

EXAMPLE 22.9   Julio sells a two-acre lot and office building by warranty deed. Subsequently, a third person shows up who has better title than Julio had and forces the buyer off the property. Here, the covenant of quiet enjoyment has been breached. The buyer can sue Julio to recover the purchase price of the land, plus any other damages incurred as a result. ●

Special Warranty Deed A deed in which the grantor warrants only that the grantor or seller held good title during his or her ownership of the property and does not warrant that there were no defects of title when the property was held by previous owners.

SPECIAL WARRANTY DEEDS   In contrast to a warranty deed, a **special warranty deed,** which is also referred to as a *limited warranty deed,* warrants only that the grantor or seller held good title during his or her ownership of the property. In other words, the grantor is not warranting that there were no defects of title when the property was held by previous owners.

If the special warranty deed discloses all liens or other encumbrances, the seller will not be liable to the buyer if a third person subsequently interferes with the buyer's ownership. If the third person's claim arises out of, or is related to, some act of the seller, however, the seller will be liable to the buyer for damages.

Quitclaim Deed A deed intended to pass any title, interest, or claim that the grantor may have in the property without warranting that such title is valid. A quitclaim deed offers the least amount of protection against defects of title.

QUITCLAIM DEEDS   A **quitclaim deed** offers the least amount of protection against defects of title. Basically, a quitclaim deed conveys to the grantee whatever interest the grantor had. So, if the grantor had no interest, then the grantee receives no interest. Naturally, if the grantor had a defective title or no title at all, a conveyance

---

7. *Whitehead v. Humphrey,* 954 So.2d 859 (La.App. 2007).

by warranty deed or special warranty deed would not cure the defects. Such deeds, however, will give the buyer a cause of action to sue the seller.

A quitclaim deed can and often does serve as a release of the grantor's interest in a particular parcel of property. **EXAMPLE 22.10** After ten years of marriage, Sandi and Jim are getting a divorce. During the marriage, Sandi purchased a parcel of waterfront property next to her grandparents' home in Louisiana. Jim helped make some improvements to the property, but he is not sure what ownership interests, if any, he has in the property because Sandi used her own funds (acquired before the marriage) to purchase the lot. Jim agrees to quitclaim the property to Sandi as part of the divorce settlement, releasing any interest he might have in that piece of property. ●

RECORDING STATUTES Every jurisdiction has **recording statutes,** which allow deeds to be recorded for a fee. The grantee normally pays this fee because he or she is the one who will be protected by recording the deed.

Recording a deed gives notice to the public that a certain person is now the owner of a particular parcel of real estate. Thus, prospective buyers can check the public records to see whether there have been earlier transactions creating interests or rights in specific parcels of real property. Putting everyone on notice as to the identity of the true owner is intended to prevent the previous owners from fraudulently conveying the land to other purchasers. Deeds are recorded in the county where the property is located. Many state statutes require that the grantor sign the deed in the presence of two witnesses before it can be recorded.

Recording Statutes Statutes that allow deeds, mortgages, and other real property transactions to be recorded so as to provide notice to future purchasers or creditors of an existing claim on the property.

Will or Inheritance

Property that is transferred on an owner's death is passed either by will or by state inheritance laws. If the owner of land dies with a will, the land passes in accordance with the terms of the will. If the owner dies without a will, state inheritance statutes prescribe how and to whom the property will pass.

Adverse Possession

Adverse possession is a means of obtaining title to land without delivery of a deed. Essentially, when one person possesses the property of another for a certain statutory period of time (three to thirty years, with ten years being most common), that person, called the *adverse possessor,* acquires title to the land and cannot be removed from it by the original owner. The adverse possessor may ultimately obtain a perfect title just as if there had been a conveyance by deed.

Adverse Possession The acquisition of title to real property by occupying it openly, without the consent of the owner, for a period of time specified by a state statute. The occupation must be actual, open, continuous, exclusive, and in opposition to all others, including the owner.

REQUIREMENTS FOR ADVERSE POSSESSION For property to be held adversely, four elements must be satisfied:

1. Possession must be *actual and exclusive,* meaning that the possessor must take sole physical occupancy of the property.
2. The possession must be *open, visible, and notorious,* not secret or clandestine. The possessor must occupy the land for all the world to see.
3. Possession must be *continuous and peaceable for the required period of time.* This requirement means that the possessor must not be interrupted in the occupancy by the true owner or by the courts.
4. Possession must be *hostile and adverse.* In other words, the possessor must claim the property as against the whole world. He or she cannot be living on the property with the permission of the owner.

PURPOSE OF THE DOCTRINE   Additionally, some states have other requirements for adverse possession. The adverse possession doctrine is justified by several public-policy concerns, including society's interest in resolving boundary disputes, in determining title when title to property is in question, and in ensuring that real property remains in the stream of commerce. More fundamentally, the doctrine punishes owners who do not take action when they see adverse possession and rewards possessors for putting land to productive use.

In the following case, the question before the court was whether a landowner had obtained title to a portion of adjacent land by adverse possession.

Case 22.2   Scarborough v. Rollins

Court of Appeals of Mississippi, 44 So.3d 381 (2010).
www.mssc.state.ms.us[a]

(Ingvar Parmmate/Wikimedia Commons)

Who owned the gravel road that ran between two properties?

BACKGROUND AND FACTS   Charles Scarborough and Mildred Rollins were adjoining landowners, sharing one common boundary. Based on Rollins's survey of the property, Rollins believed that she owned a portion of a gravel road located to the south of the apartment buildings she owned. In contrast, Scarborough believed that the gravel road was located totally on his property and that he owned some property north of the gravel road toward Rollins's apartment buildings. In July 2006, Scarborough filed a complaint seeking to quiet and confirm his title to the property. Rollins filed a counterclaim seeking to quiet and confirm her title. The court entered judgment for Rollins. Scarborough appealed.

IN THE WORDS OF THE COURT . . .
ISHEE, J. [Judge]
     * * * *

Scarborough asserts that the trial court erred in finding that Rollins proved that she owned the property in dispute by adverse possession. Scarborough claims that Rollins failed to prove by clear and convincing evidence that her possession of the disputed grassy area down to the northern edge of the gravel road has been hostile, open, notorious, visible, continuing, exclusive, and peaceful. Scarborough also claims that Rollins's paying taxes and mowing the grass north of the gravel

road by her and her predecessors in title, as well as [a prior owner's] installation of a gas line are not such adverse actions that gave him sufficient notice that he would know that Rollins was claiming the disputed area and that she was attempting to deny him ownership thereof and exclude him therefrom. Scarborough asserts that both he and Rollins used the disputed land, thus exercising joint use of the land; therefore, a claim of adverse possession is not supported. Scarborough also asserts that Rollins paid taxes only on the land situated north of her monumented south boundary line while he paid taxes on all of the land called for in his deed, including the gravel road and the land north of the gravel road up to Rollins's south boundary.

To succeed on a claim of adverse possession, the claimant has the burden to prove each element by clear and convincing evidence. * * * *Adverse possession requires the claimant to prove that her possession or occupancy was: (1) under claim of ownership; (2) actual or hostile; (3) open, notorious, and visible; (4) continuous and uninterrupted for a period of ten years; (5) exclusive; and (6) peaceful. [Emphasis added.]*
1. Under Claim of Ownership
The deed to Rollins's property presented to the chancery court indicated that she owned the property at or near the disputed property. Evidence was provided to show that Rollins and her predecessors-in-title paid the taxes on all of the property north of the gravel road. However, Scarborough only paid taxes on the property that was south of the gravel road.
2. Actual or Hostile
Evidence was provided to the chancery court that for more than thirty-five years, no one other than Rollins and her predecessors-in-title, the Blacks, used this property.
3. Open, Notorious, and Visible
[One witness] testified at trial that his family's ownership of that land was open and obvious. He stated that everyone in Starkville, who was around the apartments, knew that the apartment complex owned the yard up to the edge of the gravel road.
4. Continuous and Uninterrupted for a Period of Ten Years
Testimony at trial from [three witnesses] all provided that Rollins and her predecessors-in-title used the property for more than thirty-five years.

---

a. Under "Quick Links" on the right-hand side of the page, click on "Decisions Search" in the "Court of Appeals" section. On the next page, click on "Natural Language." When that page opens, type "2008-CA-01579-COA" in the box, click on the square for "Entire Site," and then click on "Search." In the result, click on the item in the list for "03 MAR 2010." The Mississippi Judiciary maintains this Web site.

Case 22.2—Continued

5. Exclusive

Testimony at trial * * * indicated that no one, until Scarborough, claimed to have used any part of the property in dispute.

6. Peaceful

Rollins testified that until September 2007, she and her predecessors-in-title enjoyed peaceful possession of the property.

We find that Rollins satisfied the elements required for adverse possession.

* * * *

The chancery court properly held that the gravel road which is to the north of Scarborough's property and to the south of Rollins's property was the boundary between the parties and that Rollins was entitled to an award of actual and punitive damages and attorney's fees due to the conversion of her property by Scarborough.

DECISION AND REMEDY The Court of Appeals of Mississippi affirmed the lower court's judgment and assessed all costs of the appeal to Scarborough. Rollins had proved title to the land by adverse possession.

WHAT IF THE FACTS WERE DIFFERENT? *Suppose that Rollins had not paid any taxes on the disputed land and that Scarborough had done so. Would the result have been different? Explain.*

THE E-COMMERCE DIMENSION *How might the Internet have facilitated either party's claim to the disputed property?*

Limitations on the Rights of Property Owners

No ownership rights in real property can ever really be absolute—that is, an owner of real property cannot always do whatever she or he wishes on or with the property. Nuisance and environmental laws, for example, restrict certain types of activities. Holding the property is also conditional on the payment of property taxes. Zoning laws and building permits frequently restrict one's use of the realty.

In addition, if a property owner fails to pay debts, the property may be seized to satisfy judgment creditors. In short, the rights of every property owner are subject to certain conditions and limitations. We look here at some of the important ways in which owners' rights in real property can be limited.

Eminent Domain

Even ownership in fee simple absolute is limited by a superior ownership. Just as the king was the ultimate landowner in medieval England, today the government has an ultimate ownership right in all land in the United States. This right, known as **eminent domain,** is sometimes referred to as the *condemnation power* of government to take land for public use. It gives the government the right to acquire possession of real property in the manner directed by the U.S. Constitution and the laws of the state whenever the public interest requires it.

Property may be taken only for public use, not for private benefit. **EXAMPLE 22.11** When a new public highway is to be built, the government decides where to build it and how much land to condemn. After the government determines that a particular parcel of land is necessary for public use, it will first offer to buy the property. If the owner refuses the offer, the government brings a judicial (**condemnation**) proceeding to obtain title to the land. Then, in another proceeding, the court determines the *fair value* of the land, which usually is approximately equal to its market value. ● (For more on eminent domain, read this chapter's *Linking the Law to Economics* feature on page 647.)

When the government uses its power of eminent domain to acquire land owned by a private party, a **taking** occurs. Under the takings clause of the Fifth Amendment to the U.S. Constitution, the government must pay "just compensation" to the owner. State constitutions contain similar provisions.

Eminent Domain The power of a government to take land from private citizens for public use on the payment of just compensation.

Condemnation The process of taking private property for public use through the government's power of eminent domain.

Taking The taking of private property by the government for public use. The government may not take private property for public use without "just compensation."

In 2005, the United States Supreme Court ruled that the power of eminent domain may be used to further economic development.[8] Since that decision, a number of state legislatures have passed laws limiting the power of the government to use eminent domain, particularly for urban redevelopment projects that benefit private developers.

The following case involved condemnation actions brought by a town to acquire rights-of-way for a natural gas pipeline to be constructed through the town. The issue was whether the pipeline was for public use, even though it was not built to furnish natural gas to the residents of that town.

---

8. *Kelo v. City of New London, Connecticut*, 545 U.S. 528, 125 S.Ct. 2655, 162 L.Ed.2d 439 (2005).

Case 22.3   Town of Midland v. Morris

Court of Appeals of North Carolina, 704 S.E.2d 329 (2011).

BACKGROUND AND FACTS   The Transcontinental Pipeline transports and distributes natural gas from the Gulf of Mexico to the northeastern United States. The city of Monroe, North Carolina, decided to supply its citizens and the surrounding area with natural gas by constructing a direct connection between its natural gas distribution system and the Transcontinental Pipeline. To construct the connecting pipeline, Monroe needed to acquire the rights to property along a forty-two-mile route. To do this, Monroe entered into an agreement with the town of Midland under which Midland would acquire the property (either by voluntary transfer or by eminent domain) and grant an easement to Monroe. In exchange, Midland would have the right to install a tap on the pipeline and receive discounted natural gas services. In 2008, Midland began the process of acquiring the property necessary for construction of the pipeline. When negotiations for voluntary acquisitions of the rights-of-way failed, Midland exercised its eminent domain authority to condemn the needed property. Midland filed fifteen condemnation actions, which the property owners (including Harry Morris) challenged. The trial court ruled in favor of Midland, and the property owners appealed. The property owners claimed, among other things, that Midland's condemnation of the property was not for public use or benefit because Midland had no concrete plans to furnish natural gas services from the pipeline to the city and its citizens.

IN THE WORDS OF THE COURT . . .
STEPHENS, Judge.
    * * * *

Property Owners first argue that because Midland neither currently provides natural gas services to its citizens, nor currently has any plans to provide natural gas to its citizens in the future, the condemnations were undertaken in violation of the statutes governing eminent domain. We disagree.
    * * * *

    * * * *We find it manifest *[obvious] that Midland may acquire property by condemnation to establish a gas transmission and distribution system, even in the absence of a concrete, immediate plan to furnish gas services to its citizens.* [Emphasis added.]

While we acknowledge the existence of the requirement that the public enterprise be established and conducted for the city and its citizens, we conclude that this requirement is satisfied by Midland's placement of a tap on the Pipeline and by Midland's acquisition of the right to low-cost natural gas. Further, * * * *there is nothing in the record to indicate that Midland will never offer natural gas services to its citizens. In fact, Midland's contracted-for right to install a tap on the Pipeline "from which to operate and supply its own natural gas distribution utility for the benefit of Midland's utility customers" indicates just the opposite:* that Midland will, eventually, furnish natural gas services to its citizens. [Emphasis added.]
    * * * *

Property Owners further argue that Midland's condemnations violate [the state's statute] because the condemnations are not "for the public use or benefit."
    * * * *

Despite the disjunctive language of this statutory requirement, our courts have determined the propriety of a condemnation under [the statute] based on the condemnation's satisfaction of both a "public use test" and a "public benefit test."

The first approach—the public use test—asks whether the public has a right to a definite use of the condemned property. The second approach—the public benefit test—asks whether some benefit accrues to the public as a result of the desired condemnation.

Under the public use test, "the principal and dispositive determination is whether the general public has a right to a definite use of the property sought to be condemned." * * * Applying this test to the present case in the appropriate context, there is nothing to indicate that gas services—were they to be provided by Midland—would be available to anything less than the entire population. Accordingly, there can be no doubt that the Midland condemnations would pass the public use test * * * .
    * * * *

Under the public benefit test, *"a given condemnor's desired use of the condemned property in question is for 'the public use or benefit' if that use would contribute to the general welfare and prosperity*

Case 22.3–Continued

of the public at large." In this case, we must take care in defining Midland's "desired use" of the property. Midland is condemning the property to run the Pipeline and to control a tap on the Pipeline, not to immediately provide gas to the citizens of Midland. Accordingly, it is the *availability* of natural gas that must contribute to the general welfare and prosperity of the public at large. [Emphasis added.]

As noted by our Courts, the construction and extension of public utilities, and especially the concomitant commercial and residential growth, provide a clear public benefit to local citizens. * * * Midland's tap on the Pipeline, and its potential to provide natural gas service, likely will spur growth, as well as provide Midland with an advantage in industrial recruitment. These opportunities must be seen as public benefits accruing to the citizens of Midland, such that Midland's condemnations are for the public benefit.

DECISION AND REMEDY The appellate court affirmed the lower court's decision that Midland had lawfully exercised its

eminent domain power. Even though Midland might never tap into the pipeline, the condemnation satisfied the public use test because it gave the citizens of Midland a right to a definite use of the condemned property. Furthermore, the availability of natural gas benefited the public at large because it would likely contribute to growth and enhance the general prosperity of Midland.

THE ETHICAL DIMENSION *Is it fair that a city can exercise its eminent domain power to take property even though the property will not be used immediately to benefit the city's residents? Why or why not?*

THE ECONOMIC DIMENSION *The town of Midland—and its taxpaying citizens—had to pay fair value to fifteen property owners for the property it acquired through eminent domain. Is it right to make the citizens of one town pay for a pipeline constructed primarily to benefit another town? Discuss.*

Restrictive Covenants

Restrictive Covenant A private restriction on the use of land that is binding on the party that purchases the property originally as well as on subsequent purchasers. If its benefit or obligation passes with the land's ownership, it is said to "run with the land."

A private restriction on the use of land is known as a **restrictive covenant.** If the restriction is binding on the party who purchases the property originally and on subsequent purchasers as well, it is said to "run with the land." A covenant running with the land must be in writing (usually it is in the deed), and subsequent purchasers must have reason to know about it.

EXAMPLE 22.12 In the course of developing a fifty-lot suburban subdivision, Levitt records a declaration of restrictions that effectively limits construction on each lot to one single-family house. Each lot's deed includes a reference to the declaration with a provision that the purchaser and her or his successors are bound to those restrictions. Thus, each purchaser assumes ownership with notice of the restrictions. If an owner attempts to build a duplex (or any structure that does not comply with the restrictions) on a lot, the other owners may obtain a court order enjoining the construction. Alternatively, Levitt might simply have included the restrictions on the subdivision's map, filed the map in the appropriate public office, and included a reference to the map in each deed. In this way, each owner would also have been held to have constructive notice of the restrictions. •

Inverse Condemnation

Inverse Condemnation The taking of private property by the government without payment of just compensation as required by the U.S. Constitution. The owner must sue the government to recover just compensation.

Typically, a government agency exercises the power of eminent domain in order to seize private property through litigation or negotiation. If the agency obtains the private land through agreement or judgment, it then pays compensation to the landowner. **Inverse condemnation,** in contrast, occurs when a government simply takes private property from a landowner without paying any compensation at all. In this situation, the landowner is forced to sue the government for compensation for the lost value of the land. The taking can be accomplished physically, as when a government agency simply uses or occupies the land. Regulations issued by a government agency may also result in a property losing much of its market value.

CASE EXAMPLE 22.13 In Walton County, Florida, water flows through a ditch from Oyster Lake to the Gulf of Mexico. When Hurricane Opal caused the water to rise in Oyster Lake, Walton County reconfigured the drainage to divert the overflow onto the nearby property of William and Patricia Hemby. The flow was eventually restored to pre-Opal conditions, but during a later emergency, water was diverted onto the Hembys' property again. This diversion was not restored. The Hembys filed a suit against the county. After their deaths, their daughter Cozette Drake pursued the claim. The court found that by allowing the water diversion, created during emergency conditions, to remain on Drake's property long after the emergency had passed, the county had engaged in a permanent or continuous physical invasion. This invasion rendered Drake's property useless and deprived her of its beneficial enjoyment. Drake was therefore entitled to receive compensation from the county.[9] ●

▶ Leasehold Estates

Leasehold Estate An interest in real property that is held by a tenant for only a limited time under a lease. In every leasehold estate, the tenant has a qualified right to possess and/or use the land.

A **leasehold estate** is created when a real property owner or lessor (landlord) agrees to convey the right to possess and use the property to a lessee (tenant) for a certain period of time. In every leasehold estate, the tenant has a *qualified* right to exclusive possession (qualified by the right of the landlord to enter on the premises to ensure that waste is not being committed). The *temporary* nature of possession, under a lease, is what distinguishes a tenant from a purchaser, who acquires title to the property. The tenant can use the land—for example, by harvesting crops—but cannot injure it by such activities as cutting down timber for sale or extracting oil.

Fixed-Term Tenancy

Fixed-Term Tenancy A type of tenancy under which property is leased for a specified period of time, such as a month, a year, or a period of years; also called a *tenancy for years.*

A **fixed-term tenancy,** also called a *tenancy for years,* is created by an express contract by which property is leased for a specified period of time, such as a day, a month, a year, or a period of years. Signing a one-year lease to occupy an apartment, for instance, creates a fixed-term tenancy. Note that the term need not be specified by date and can be conditioned on the occurrence of an event, such as leasing a cabin for the summer or an apartment during Mardi Gras. At the end of the period specified in the lease, the lease ends (without notice), and possession of the property returns to the lessor. If the tenant dies during the period of the lease, the lease interest passes to the tenant's heirs as personal property. Often, leases include renewal or extension provisions.

Periodic Tenancy

Periodic Tenancy A lease interest in land for an indefinite period involving payment of rent at fixed intervals, such as week to week, month to month, or year to year.

A **periodic tenancy** is created by a lease that does not specify how long it is to last but does specify that rent is to be paid at certain intervals. This type of tenancy is automatically renewed for another rental period unless properly terminated. **EXAMPLE 22.14** Kayla enters into a lease with Capital Properties. The lease states, "Rent is due on the tenth day of every month." This provision creates a periodic tenancy from month to month. ● This type of tenancy can also extend from week to week or from year to year.

Under the common law, to terminate a periodic tenancy, the landlord or tenant must give at least one period's notice to the other party. If the tenancy extends from month to month, for example, one month's notice must be given prior to the last

Does a periodic tenancy terminate at a specific date by contract?

(©M. Salerno, 2009. Used under license from Shutterstock.com)

---

9. *Drake v. Walton County,* 6 So.3d 717 (Fla.App. 2009).

month's rent payment. State statutes may require a different period of notice before termination of a periodic tenancy, however.

Tenancy at Will

Tenancy at Will A type of tenancy that either party can terminate without notice; can arise when a landowner allows a person to live on the premises without paying rent.

With a **tenancy at will,** either party can terminate the tenancy without notice. This type of tenancy can arise if a landlord rents property to a tenant "for as long as both agree" or allows a person to live on the premises without paying rent. Tenancies at will are rare today because most state statutes require a landlord to provide some period of notice to terminate a tenancy (as previously noted). States may also require a landowner to have sufficient cause (reason) to end a residential tenancy. Certain events, such as the death of either party or the voluntary commission of waste by the tenant, automatically terminate a tenancy at will.

Tenancy at Sufferance

Tenancy at Sufferance A type of tenancy under which a tenant who, after rightfully being in possession of leased premises, continues (wrongfully) to occupy the property after the lease has terminated. The tenant has no right to possess the property and occupies it only because the person entitled to evict the tenant has not done so.

The mere possession of land without right is called a **tenancy at sufferance.** A tenancy at sufferance is not a true tenancy because it is created when a tenant *wrongfully* retains possession of property. Whenever a tenancy for years or a periodic tenancy ends and the tenant continues to retain possession of the premises without the owner's permission, a tenancy at sufferance is created.

When a commercial or residential tenant wrongfully retains possession, the landlord is entitled to damages. Typically, the damages are based on the fair market rental value of the premises after the expiration of the lease. If the landlord has increased the rent for the premises, and the tenant does not agree to pay the higher rent and does not vacate the premises, then the proper standard of damages may be an issue. A court has to determine whether another tenant was willing to pay the higher rent during the time the existing tenant retained possession. If the landlord cannot show that another tenant was ready to rent the property at the higher rent, the proper standard of damages is the existing rental rate (rather than the higher rate).

▶ Landlord-Tenant Relationships

A lease contract establishes a landlord-tenant relationship. As mentioned, a lease contract arises when a property owner (landlord) agrees to give another party (the tenant) the exclusive right to possess the property—usually for a price and for a specified term. In most states, statutes require leases for terms exceeding one year to be in writing. The lease should describe the property and indicate the length of the term, the amount of the rent, and how and when it is to be paid.

NOTE Sound business practice dictates that a lease for commercial property should be written carefully and should clearly define the parties' rights and obligations.

State or local law often dictates permissible lease terms. For example, a statute or ordinance might prohibit the leasing of a structure that is in poor physical condition or is not in compliance with local building codes. In 1972, in an effort to create more uniformity in the law governing landlord-tenant relationships, the National Conference of Commissioners on Uniform State Laws issued the Uniform Residential Landlord and Tenant Act (URLTA). Twenty-one states have adopted variations of the URLTA.

In the past forty years, landlord-tenant relationships, which were traditionally governed by contract law, have become much more complex, as has the law governing them. We look now at the respective rights and duties of landlords and tenants.

Rights and Duties

The rights and duties of landlords and tenants generally pertain to four broad areas of concern—the possession, use, maintenance, and, of course, rent of leased property.

POSSESSION   A landlord is obligated to give a tenant possession of the property that the tenant has agreed to lease. After obtaining possession, the tenant retains the property exclusively until the lease expires, unless the lease states otherwise.

The covenant of quiet enjoyment mentioned previously also applies to leased premises. Under this covenant, the landlord promises that during the lease term, neither the landlord nor anyone having a superior title to the property will disturb the tenant's use and enjoyment of the property. This covenant forms the essence of the landlord-tenant relationship, and if it is breached, the tenant can terminate the lease and sue for damages.

If the landlord deprives the tenant of possession of the leased property or interferes with the tenant's use or enjoyment of it, an eviction occurs. An **eviction** arises, for instance, when the landlord changes the lock and refuses to give the tenant a new key. A **constructive eviction** occurs when the landlord wrongfully performs or fails to perform any of the duties the lease requires, thereby making the tenant's further use and enjoyment of the property exceedingly difficult or impossible. Examples of constructive eviction include a landlord's failure to provide heat in the winter, electricity, or other essential utilities.

USE AND MAINTENANCE OF THE PREMISES   If the parties do not limit by agreement the uses to which the property may be put, the tenant may make any use of it, as long as the use is legal and reasonably relates to the purpose for which the property is adapted or ordinarily used and does not injure the landlord's interest.

The tenant is responsible for any damage to the premises that he or she causes, intentionally or negligently, and may be held liable for the cost of returning the property to the physical condition it was in at the lease's inception. Also, the tenant is not entitled to create a *nuisance* by substantially interfering with others' quiet enjoyment of their property rights. Unless the parties have agreed otherwise, the tenant is not responsible for ordinary wear and tear and the property's consequent depreciation in value.

In some jurisdictions, landlords of residential property are required by statute to maintain the premises in good repair. Landlords must also comply with any applicable state statutes and city ordinances regarding maintenance and repair of buildings.

IMPLIED WARRANTY OF HABITABILITY   The implied warranty of habitability, which was discussed earlier in the context of the sale of new homes, also applies to residential leases. It requires a landlord who leases residential property to ensure that the premises are habitable—that is, safe and suitable for people to live in. Also, the landlord must make repairs to maintain the premises in that condition for the lease's duration. Generally, this warranty applies to major, or *substantial*, physical defects that the landlord knows or should know about and has had a reasonable time to repair—for example, a large hole in the roof.

RENT   Rent is the tenant's payment to the landlord for the tenant's occupancy or use of the landlord's real property. Usually, the tenant must pay the rent even if she or he refuses to occupy the property or moves out, as long as the refusal or the move is unjustified and the lease is in force. Under the common law, if the

---

"Give a landlord an inch and he'll build an apartment house."

Saul Antin, 1949–present
(American businessman)

Eviction   A landlord's act of depriving a tenant of possession of the leased premises.

Constructive Eviction   A form of eviction that occurs when a landlord fails to perform adequately any of the duties required by the lease, thereby making the tenant's further use and enjoyment of the property exceedingly difficult or impossible.

NOTE   Options that may be available to a tenant on a landlord's breach of the implied warranty of habitability include repairing the defect and deducting the cost from the rent, canceling the lease, and suing for damages.

leased premises were destroyed by fire or flood, the tenant still had to pay rent. Today, however, if an apartment building burns down, most state's laws do not require tenants to continue to pay rent.

In some situations, such as when a landlord breaches the implied warranty of habitability, a tenant may be allowed to withhold rent as a remedy. When rent withholding is authorized under a statute, the tenant must usually put the amount withheld into an *escrow account.* The funds are held in the name of the tenant and an *escrow agent* (usually the court or a government agency) and are returnable to the tenant if the landlord fails to make the premises habitable.

Transferring Rights to Leased Property

Either the landlord or the tenant may wish to transfer her or his rights to the leased property during the term of the lease. If a landlord transfers complete title to the leased property to another, the tenant becomes the tenant of the new owner. The new owner may then collect the rent but must abide by the terms of the existing lease.

ASSIGNMENT   The tenant's transfer of his or her entire interest in the leased property to a third person is an *assignment of the lease.* Many leases require that an assignment have the landlord's written consent. An assignment that lacks consent can be avoided (nullified) by the landlord. State statutes may specify that the landlord may not unreasonably withhold consent, though. Also, a landlord who knowingly accepts rent from the assignee may be held to have waived the consent requirement.

When an assignment is valid, the assignee acquires all of the tenant's rights under the lease. An assignment, however, does not release the original tenant (the assignor) from the obligation to pay rent should the assignee default. Also, if the assignee exercises an option under the original lease to extend the term, the assigning tenant remains liable for the rent during the extension, unless the landlord agrees otherwise.

SUBLEASES   The tenant's transfer of all or part of the premises for a period shorter than the lease term is a **sublease.** Many leases also require the landlord's written consent for a sublease. If the landlord's consent is required, a sublease without such permission is ineffective. Also, like an assignment, a sublease does not release the tenant from her or his obligations under the lease.

EXAMPLE 22.15   Derek, a student, leases an apartment for a two-year period. Although Derek had planned on attending summer school, he decides to accept a job offer in Europe for the summer months instead. Derek therefore obtains his landlord's consent to sublease the apartment to Ava. Ava is bound by the same terms of the lease as Derek, and the landlord can hold Derek liable if Ava violates the lease terms. ●

 ## Land-Use Control

Each state regulates the use of the land within its political boundaries. Most states delegate control over land use to various planning boards and zoning authorities at the city or county level. The federal government normally does not engage in land-use control except with respect to federally owned land and environmental regulations (see page 610). The federal government does influence state and local regulations, however, through the allocation of federal funds. Stipulations on land use may be a condition to a state's receipt of such funds.

"Even in hell the peasant will have to serve the landlord, for, while the landlord is boiling in a cauldron, the peasant will have to put wood under it."

Russian Proverb

Sublease   A lease executed by the lessee of real estate to a third person, conveying the same interest that the lessee enjoys but for a shorter term than that held by the lessee.

Zoning Laws

Zoning Laws Laws that divide a municipality into districts and prescribe the use to which property within each district may be put.

The rules and regulations that collectively manage the development and use of land are known as **zoning laws.** Zoning laws were first used in the United States to segregate slaughterhouses, distilleries, kilns, and other businesses that might pose a nuisance to nearby residences. As modern urban areas have grown, so has the need to organize uses of land. Today, zoning laws enable the government of a municipality—a town, city, or county—to control the speed and type of development within its borders by creating different zones and regulating the use of property allowed in each zone.

The United States Supreme Court has held that zoning is a constitutional exercise of a government's police powers.[10] Therefore, as long as its zoning ordinances are rationally related to the health, safety, or welfare of the community, a municipal government has broad discretion to carry out zoning as it sees fit. Here, we look first at the scope of zoning laws and then at some common exceptions to these laws.

Purpose and Scope of Zoning Laws

The purpose of zoning laws is to manage the land within a community in a way that encourages sustainable and organized development while controlling growth in a manner that serves the interests of the community. One of the basic elements of zoning is the classification of land by permissible use as part of a comprehensive municipal plan, but zoning extends to other aspects of land use as well.

PERMISSIBLE USES OF LAND Municipalities generally divide their available land into districts according to the land's present and potential future uses. Typically, land is classified into three types of permissible uses: residential, commercial or business, and industrial. Conservation districts are also found in some municipalities. These districts are areas dedicated to carrying out local soil and water conservation efforts—for example, wetlands might be designated as a conservation district.

Residential Use Use of land for construction of buildings for human habitation only.

Commercial Use Use of land for business activities only. Also called *business use.*

In areas dedicated for **residential use,** landowners can construct buildings for human habitation. Land assigned for business activities is designated as being for **commercial use,** sometimes called business use. **EXAMPLE 22.16** An area with a number of retail stores, offices, supermarkets, and hotels might be designated as a commercial or business district. Land used for entertainment purposes, such as movie theaters and sports stadiums, also falls into this category, as does land used for government activities. ●

Industrial Use Use of land for light or heavy manufacturing, shipping, or heavy transportation.

The third major category is **industrial use,** which typically encompasses light and heavy manufacturing, shipping, and heavy transportation. **EXAMPLE 22.17** Undeveloped land with easy access to highways and railroads might be classified as suitable for future use by industry. A city might then permit heavy activity, such as the operation of a factory in that area. ● Although industrial uses can be profitable for a city seeking to raise tax revenue, such uses can also result in noise, smoke, or vibrations that interfere with others' enjoyment of their property. Consequently, areas zoned for industrial use generally are kept as far as possible from residential districts and some commercial districts.

A city's residential, commercial, and industrial districts may be divided, in turn, into subdistricts. For example, zoning ordinances regulate the type, density, size, and approved uses of structures within a given district. Thus, a residential district may be

---

10. *Village of Euclid v. Ambler Realty Co.,* 272 U.S. 365, 47 S.Ct. 114, 71 L.Ed. 303 (1926).

divided into low-density (single-family homes with large lots), high-density (single- and multiple-family homes with small lots), and planned-unit (condominiums or apartments) subdistricts.

OTHER ZONING RESTRICTIONS   Zoning rules extend to much more than the permissible use of land. In residential districts, for example, an ordinance may require a house or garage to be set back a specific number of feet from a neighbor's property line. In commercial districts, zoning rules may attempt to maintain a certain visual aesthetic. Therefore, businesses may be required to construct buildings of a certain height and width so that they conform to the style of other commercial buildings in the area.

Businesses may also be required to provide parking for patrons or take other measures to manage traffic. In some instances, municipalities limit construction of new businesses to prevent traffic congestion. Zoning laws may even attempt to regulate the public morals of the community. For example, cities commonly impose severe restrictions on the location and operation of adult businesses.

Exceptions to Zoning Laws

Zoning restrictions are not absolute. It is impossible for zoning laws to account for every contingency. The purpose of zoning is to enable the municipality to control development but not to prevent it altogether or limit the government's ability to adapt to changing circumstances or unforeseen needs. Hence, legal processes have been developed to allow for exceptions to zoning laws. Here, we look at these exceptions, known as *variances* and *special-use permits,* as well as at the *special incentives* that governments may offer to encourage certain kinds of development.

VARIANCES   When a property owner wants to use his or her land in a manner not permitted by zoning rules, she or he can request a **variance,** which allows an exception to the rules. Property owners normally request variances in hardship situations.

EXAMPLE 22.18   Lin Wang, a homeowner, wants to replace her single-car garage with a two-car garage, but if she does so, the garage will be closer to her neighbor's property than is permitted by the zoning rules. Hence, she may ask for a variance. Similarly, a church might request a variance from height restrictions in order to erect a new steeple, or a furniture retail store might ask for a variance from footprint limitations so that it can expand its showroom (a building's *footprint* is the area of ground that it covers). ● Note that the hardship may not be self-created—that is, a person usually cannot buy property with zoning regulations in effect and then argue that a variance is needed for the property to be used for the owner's intended purpose.

In almost all instances, before a variance is granted, there must be a public hearing with adequate notice to neighbors who may object to the exception. The property owner requesting the variance must demonstrate that it is necessary for reasonable development, is the least intrusive solution to the problem, and will not alter the essential character of the neighborhood. After the public hearing, a hearing examiner appointed by the municipality (or the local zoning board or commission) determines whether to grant the exception. When a variance is granted, it applies only to the specific parcel of land for which it was requested and does not create a regulation-free zone.

SPECIAL-USE PERMITS   Sometimes, zoning laws permit a use, but only if the property owner complies with specific requirements to ensure that the proposed use does not harm the immediate neighborhood. In such instances, the zoning board will issue **special-use permits,** also called *conditional-use permits.*

Variance   A form of relief from zoning laws that is granted to a property owner to allow the property to be used in a manner not permitted by zoning regulations.

Special-Use Permit   A permit that allows an exemption to zoning regulations for a particular piece of property as long as the property owner complies with specific requirements to ensure that the proposed use does not affect the characteristics of the area.

EXAMPLE 22.19 An area is designated as a residential district, but small businesses are permitted to operate there so long as they do not affect the characteristics of the neighborhood. A bank asks the zoning board for a special-use permit to open a branch in the area. At the public hearing, the bank's managers demonstrate that the branch will be housed in a building that conforms to the style of other structures in the area, that adequate parking will be available, and that landscaping will shield the parking lot from public view. Unless there are strong objections from the branch's prospective neighbors, the board will likely grant the permit. ●

SPECIAL INCENTIVES In addition to granting exceptions to zoning regulations, municipalities may also wish to encourage certain kinds of development. To do so, they offer incentives, often in the form of lower tax rates or tax credits. For instance, to attract new businesses that will provide jobs for local citizens and increase the tax base, a city may offer incentives in the form of lower property tax rates for a period of years. Similarly, homeowners may receive tax credits for historical preservation if they renovate and maintain older homes.

Municipalities also offer incentives to further environmental goals. For example, tax incentives are used to encourage property owners to replace aging buildings with new ones that minimize energy use, reduce resource consumption, and promote green transportation choices—such as by providing outlets for plugging in electric cars.

Tax credits provided by cities and towns also encourage construction firms to participate actively in "green" construction, which involves using processes and materials that are environmentally responsible and resource-efficient. Between 5 and 10 percent of the buildings started in 2010 incorporated green building techniques. Firms that "build green" may obtain the LEED™ certification from the U.S. Green Building Council. (LEED stands for Leadership in Energy and Environmental Design. LEED certification is the recognized standard in the United States and elsewhere for measuring building sustainability.) To receive the certification, a building or real estate development must use resources sustainably, reduce energy use, conserve water, limit carbon dioxide emissions, and achieve other environmentally friendly goals.

Reviewing . . . Real Property and Land-Use Control

Vern Shoepke purchased a two-story home from Walter and Eliza Bruster in the town of Roche, Maine. The warranty deed did not specify what covenants would be included in the conveyance. The property was adjacent to a public park that included a popular Frisbee golf course. (Frisbee golf is a sport similar to golf but using Frisbees.) Wayakichi Creek ran along the north end of the park and along Shoepke's property. The deed allowed Roche citizens the right to walk across a five-foot-wide section of the lot beside Wayakichi Creek as part of a two-mile public trail system. Teenagers regularly threw Frisbee golf discs from the walking path behind Shoepke's property over his yard to the adjacent park. Shoepke habitually shouted and cursed at the teenagers, demanding that they not throw the discs over his yard. Two months after moving into his Roche home, Shoepke leased the second floor to Lauren Slater for nine months. (The lease agreement did not specify that Shoepke's consent would be required to sublease the second floor.) After three months of tenancy, Slater sublet the second floor to a local artist, Javier Indalecio. Over the remaining six months, Indalecio's use of oil paints damaged the carpeting in Shoepke's home. Using the information presented in the chapter, answer the following questions.

1. What is the term for the right of Roche citizens to walk across Shoepke's land on the trail?
2. What covenants would most courts infer were included in the warranty deed that was used in the property transfer from the Brusters to Shoepke?
3. Can Shoepke hold Slater financially responsible for the damage to the carpeting caused by Indalecio? Why or why not?
4. Suppose that Slater—to offset her liability for the carpet damage caused by Indalecio—files a counterclaim against Shoepke for breach of the covenant of quiet enjoyment. Could the fact that teenagers continually throw Frisbees over the leased property arguably be a breach of the covenant of quiet enjoyment? Why or why not?

Linking the Law *to Economics*
Eminent Domain

As you learned in this chapter, private ownership of land is always limited by the government's power to take private property for public use through eminent domain. The U.S. Constitution allows private property to be condemned so that it can used for public benefit.

You may have already learned in an economics course that when an exchange is voluntary, both parties by definition are better off—otherwise, they would not engage in the exchange. In contrast, an involuntary exchange occurs when, for example, a robber puts a gun to your head and says, "Your wallet or your life." Voluntary exchange is the basis of all market economic systems. Indeed, some economists argue that the only way a nation can experience economic growth is through voluntary exchange because both parties to such exchanges always benefit.

In this country, much real property is privately owned and is transferred through voluntary exchange. The owner exchanges property for a payment that the purchaser agrees to make. If the owner thinks that the offered payment is not sufficient, then the sale does not occur.

The Government Can Force Involuntary Transfers

When a government exercises its right to obtain private property through eminent domain, however, the exchange is not voluntary. The government is forcing the property owner to sell his or her property. When property is sold involuntarily, though, the seller is worse off. The justification for allowing the government to take property through involuntary transfers is that the government will put the property to a use that will benefit the community more than the transaction will hurt the previous property owner. For example, the property owners whose homes are condemned so that land can be used for a new school will suffer less than the community will benefit from having well-educated children.

When Government Does Not Use Eminent Domain for a Public Purpose

In recent years, some local governments have used the power of eminent domain to obtain private property in order to resell it to another private party. In addition to raising ethical questions, such transactions have economic consequences.

Consider, for example, how private real estate developers operate. If an area of town appears undervalued, the developers will calculate the costs of buying the land, including the houses from the homeowners, tearing the houses down, and building a shopping mall on the site. In making these financial projections, the developers have to determine whether, when all costs are included, the projected revenues will yield a profit.

Now suppose that the municipal government forces those same homeowners to sell their land to the government, which then resells it to the developers. Obviously, the developers obtain the land at a lower cost than they would have had to pay if they had acquired it directly from the homeowners. In essence, the local government is forcing current homeowners to subsidize private developers so that they can put up a shopping mall.

Although some people argue that the local government is providing the subsidy, that is not the situation. The subsidy is coming from those homeowners who were forced to sell because the government condemned their property. As this example illustrates, any use of eminent domain to take private property to be sold to other private companies has adverse consequences that may not be completely justified on any grounds.

FOR CRITICAL ANALYSIS

Under what circumstances is it cheaper for private developers to obtain formerly private property through the government's use of eminent domain?

 **Key Terms**

Chapter Summary: Real Property and Land-Use Control

The Nature of Real Property (See pages 626–629.)	Real property (also called real estate or realty) is immovable. It includes land, subsurface and airspace rights, plant life and vegetation, and fixtures.
Ownership Interests in Real Property (See pages 629–632.)	1. *Fee simple absolute*—The most complete form of ownership. 2. *Life estate*—An estate that lasts for the life of a specified individual, during which time the individual is entitled to possess, use, and benefit from the estate. The life tenant's ownership rights in the life estate cease to exist on her or his death. 3. *Nonpossessory interest*—An interest that involves the right to use real property but not to possess it. Easements, profits, and licenses are nonpossessory interests.
Transfer of Ownership (See pages 632–637.)	1. *By deed*—When real property is sold or transferred as a gift, title to the property is conveyed by means of a deed. A deed must meet specific legal requirements. A *warranty deed* provides the most extensive protection against defects of title. A *quitclaim deed* conveys to the grantee only whatever interest the grantor had in the property. A deed may be recorded in the manner prescribed by *recording statutes* in the appropriate jurisdiction to give third parties notice of the owner's interest. 2. *By will or inheritance*—If the owner dies after having made a valid will, the land passes as specified in the will. If the owner dies without having made a will, the heirs inherit according to state inheritance statutes. 3. *By adverse possession*—When a person possesses the property of another for a statutory period of time (ten years is the most common), that person acquires title to the property, provided the possession is actual and exclusive, open and visible, continuous and peaceable, and hostile and adverse (without the permission of the owner).
Limitations on the Rights of Property Owners (See pages 637–640.)	1. *Eminent domain*—The government's power to take land for public use, with just compensation, when the public interest requires the taking. 2. *Restrictive covenant*—A private restriction on the use of land (often included in a deed). 3. *Inverse condemnation*—A government's taking of private property without paying compensation to the property owner, as when an agency restricts the use of private property, thereby lowering its value.
Leasehold Estates (See pages 640–641.)	A leasehold estate is an interest in real property that is held for only a limited period of time, as specified in the lease agreement. Types of tenancies include the following: 1. *Fixed-term tenancy*—Tenancy for a period of time stated by express contract. 2. *Periodic tenancy*—Tenancy for a period determined by the frequency of rent payments; automatically renewed unless proper notice is given. 3. *Tenancy at will*—Tenancy for as long as both parties agree; no notice of termination is required. 4. *Tenancy at sufferance*—Possession of land without legal right.
Landlord-Tenant Relationships (See pages 641–643.)	1. *Lease agreement*—The landlord-tenant relationship is created by a lease agreement. State or local laws may dictate whether the lease must be in writing and what lease terms are permissible. 2. *Rights and duties*—The rights and duties that arise under a lease agreement generally pertain to the following areas: a. Possession—The tenant has an exclusive right to possess the leased premises. Under the covenant of quiet enjoyment, the landlord promises that during the lease term neither the landlord nor anyone having superior title to the property will disturb the tenant's use and enjoyment of the property.

Chapter Summary: Real Property and Land-Use Control, Continued

Landlord-Tenant Relationships—Continued	b. Use and maintenance of the premises—Unless the parties agree otherwise, the tenant may make any legal use of the property. The tenant is responsible for any damage that he or she causes. The landlord must comply with laws that set specific standards for the maintenance of real property. The implied warranty of habitability requires that a landlord furnish and maintain residential premises in a habitable condition (that is, in a condition safe and suitable for human life). c. Rent—The tenant must pay the rent as long as the lease is in force, unless the tenant justifiably refuses to occupy the property or withholds the rent because of the landlord's failure to maintain the premises properly. 3. *Transferring rights to leased property—* a. If the landlord transfers complete title to the leased property, the tenant becomes the tenant of the new owner. The new owner may then collect the rent but must abide by the existing lease. b. Generally, in the absence of an agreement to the contrary, tenants may assign their rights (but not their duties) under a lease contract to a third person. Tenants may also sublease leased property to a third person, but the original tenant is not relieved of any obligations to the landlord under the lease. In either situation, the landlord's consent may be required, but statutes may prohibit the landlord from unreasonably withholding consent.
Land-Use Control (See pages 643–646.)	Each state regulates land use within its boundaries, typically through municipal planning boards and zoning authorities. Zoning laws divide an area into districts to which specific land-use regulations apply. Certain areas are designated for residential use, commercial use, or industrial use. A property owner who wants an exception from zoning regulations can seek a variance or a special-use permit.

ExamPrep

ISSUE SPOTTERS

1. Bernie sells his house to Consuela under a warranty deed. Later, Delmira appears, holding a better title to the house than Consuela has. Delmira wants Consuela off the property. What can Consuela do?
2. Grey owns a commercial building in fee simple. Grey transfers temporary possession of the building to Haven Corporation. Can Haven transfer possession for an even shorter time to Idyll Company? Explain.

—**Check your answers to these questions against the answers provided in Appendix G.**

BEFORE THE TEST

Go to **www.cengagebrain.com**, enter the ISBN number "9781111530617," and click on "Find" to locate this textbook's Web site. Then, click on "Access Now" under "Study Tools," and select "Chapter 22" at the top. There you will find an "Interactive Quiz" that you can take to assess your mastery of the concepts in this chapter, as well as "Flashcards" and a "Glossary" of important terms.

For Review

1. What can a person who holds property in fee simple absolute do with the property?
2. What are the requirements for acquiring property by adverse possession?
3. What limitations may be imposed on the rights of property owners?
4. What are the respective duties of the landlord and the tenant concerning the use and maintenance of leased property?
5. What is the purpose of zoning laws?

Questions and Case Problems

22–1. Property Ownership. Twenty-two years ago, Lorenz was a wanderer. At that time, he decided to settle down on an unoccupied, three-acre parcel of land that he did not own. People in the area told him that they had no idea who owned the property. Lorenz built a house on the land, got married, and raised three children while living there. He fenced in the land, installed a gate with a sign above it that read "Lorenz's Homestead," and removed trespassers. Lorenz is now confronted by Joe Reese, who has a deed in his name as owner of the property. Reese, claiming ownership of the land, orders Lorenz and his family off the property. Discuss who has the better "title" to the property.

22–2. Deeds. Wiley and Gemma are neighbors. Wiley's lot is extremely large, and his present and future use of it will not involve the entire area. Gemma wants to build a single-car garage and driveway along the present lot boundary. Because the placement of her existing structures makes it impossible for her to comply with an ordinance requiring buildings to be set back fifteen feet from an adjoining property line, Gemma cannot build the garage. Gemma contracts to purchase ten feet of Wiley's property along their boundary line for $3,000. Wiley is willing to sell but will give Gemma only a quitclaim deed, whereas Gemma wants a warranty deed. Discuss the differences between these deeds as they would affect the rights of the parties if the title to this ten feet of land later proves to be defective.

22–3. Eviction. James owns a three-story building. He leases the ground floor to Juan's Mexican restaurant. The lease is to run for a five-year period and contains an express covenant of quiet enjoyment. One year later, James leases the top two stories to the Upbeat Club, a discotheque. The club's hours run from 5:00 P.M. to 1:00 A.M. The noise from the Upbeat Club is so loud that it is driving customers away from Juan's restaurant. Juan has notified James of the interference and has called the police on a number of occasions. James refuses to talk to the owners of the Upbeat Club or to do anything to remedy the situation. Juan abandons the premises. James files suit for breach of the lease agreement and for the rental payments still due under the lease. Juan claims that he was constructively evicted and files a countersuit for damages. Discuss who will be held liable.

22–4. Ownership in Fee Simple. Thomas and Teresa Cline built a house on a 76-acre parcel of real estate next to Roy Berg's home and property in Augusta County, Virginia. The homes were about 1,800 feet apart but in view of each other. After several disagreements between the parties, Berg equipped an 11-foot tripod with motion sensors and floodlights that intermittently illuminated the Clines' home. Berg also installed surveillance cameras that tracked some of the movement on the Clines' property. The cameras transmitted on an open frequency, which could be received by any television within range. The Clines asked

Berg to turn off, or at least redirect, the lights. When he refused, they erected a fence for 200 feet along the parties' common property line. The 32-foot-high fence consisted of 20 utility poles spaced 10 feet apart with plastic wrap stretched between the poles. This effectively blocked the lights and cameras. Berg filed a suit against the Clines in a Virginia state court, complaining that the fence interfered unreasonably with his use and enjoyment of his property. He asked the court to order the Clines to take the fence down. What are the limits on an owner's use of property? How should the court rule in this case? Why? [*Cline v. Berg*, 273 Va. 142, 639 S.E.2d 231 (2007)]

22–5. Commercial Lease Terms. Gi Hwa Park entered into a lease with Landmark HHH, LLC, for retail space in the Plaza at Landmark, a shopping center in Virginia. The lease required that the landlord keep the roof "in good repair" and that the tenant obtain insurance on her inventory and absolve the landlord from any losses to the extent of the insurance proceeds. Park opened a store—The Four Seasons—in the space, specializing in imported men's suits and accessories. Within a month of the opening and continuing for nearly eight years, water intermittently leaked through the roof, causing damage. Landmark eventually had a new roof installed, but water continued to leak into The Four Seasons. On a night of record rainfall, the store suffered substantial water damage, and Park was forced to close the store. On what basis might Park seek to recover from Landmark? What might Landmark assert in response? Which party's argument is more likely to succeed, and why? [*Landmark HHH, LLC v. Gi Hwa Park*, 277 Va. 50, 671 S.E.2d 143 (2009)]

22–6. **Case Problem with Sample Answer. Adverse Possession.** In 1974, Alana Mansell built a large shed, which she used as a three-car garage, on the back of her property. This building encroached on a neighbor's property by fourteen feet; however, the neighbor knew of the encroachment and informally approved it. But the neighbor did not transfer ownership of the property to Mansell. In 2001, Betty Hunter bought Mansell's neighbor's property. The survey done at that time indicated the encroachment. In 2003, Hunter's attorney notified Mansell about the encroachment, but nothing was done. In 2006, Mansell installed a concrete foundation under the garage, which had previously been dirt. Mansell also sought a declaratory judgment that she was the fee simple owner of the area under the garage that encroached on Hunter's property, arguing that the possession of the property from 1974 to 2001 gave her ownership by adverse possession. Hunter filed a counterclaim, demanding removal of the encroaching structure. The trial court held that the property belonged to Hunter, but did not order removal of the garage. Hunter and Mansell appealed. Would the open occupation of the property for nearly thirty years give Mansell title by adverse possession? Explain your answer. [*Hunter v. Mansell,* 240 P.3d 469 (Colo.App. 2010)]

—**For a sample answer for Case Problem 22–6, go to Appendix F at the end of this text.**

22–7. Zoning and Variances. Joseph and Lois Ryan hired a contractor to build a home in Weston, Connecticut. The contractor submitted plans to the town that included a roof height of thirty-eight feet for the proposed dwelling. This exceeded the town's roof-height restriction of thirty-five feet. The contractor and the architect revised the plans to meet the restriction, and the town approved the plans and issued a zoning permit and a building permit. After the roof was constructed, a code enforcement officer discovered that it measured thirty-seven feet, seven inches high. The officer issued a cease-and-desist order requiring the Ryans to "remove the height violation and bring the structure into compliance." The Ryans appealed to the zoning board, claiming that the error was not theirs but that of their general contractor and architect. The zoning board upheld the cease-and-desist order but later granted the Ryans a variance because "the roof height was out of compliance by approximately two feet, . . . the home [was] perched high on the land and [was] not a detriment to the neighborhood, and . . . the hardship was created by the contractor's error." Neighbors (including Curtis Morikawa) appealed to a court. They argued that the hardship claimed was solely economic. In addition, they argued that even though it was unintended, the hardship was self-created. The trial court ruled in favor of the neighbors, and the Ryans appealed. How should the court rule? Were there legitimate grounds for granting a variance? Discuss. [*Morikawa v. Zoning Board of Appeals of Town of Weston,* 126 Conn.App. 400, 11 A.3d 735 (2011)]

22–8. [icon] **A Question of Ethics. Seller's Duty to Disclose.** *In 1999, Stephen and Linda Kailin bought the Monona Center, a mall in Madison, Wisconsin, from Perry Armstrong for $760,000. The contract provided, "Seller represents to Buyer that as of the date of acceptance Seller had no notice or knowledge of conditions affecting the Property or transaction" other than certain items disclosed at the time of the offer. Armstrong told the Kailins of the Center's eight tenants, their lease expiration dates, and the monthly and annual rent due under each lease. One of the lessees, Ring's All-American Karate, occupied about a third of the Center's space under a five-year lease. Because of Ring's financial difficulties, Armstrong had agreed to reduce its rent for nine months in 1997. By the time of the sale to the Kailins, Ring owed $13,910 in unpaid rent, but Armstrong did not tell the Kailins, who did not ask. Ring continued to fail to pay rent and finally vacated the Center. The Kailins filed a suit in a Wisconsin state court against Armstrong and others, alleging, among other things, misrepresentation. [Kailin v. Armstrong, 2002 WI App. 70, 252 Wis.2d 676, 643 N.W.2d 132 (2002)]*

1. Did Armstrong have a duty to disclose Ring's delinquency and default to the Kailins? Explain.

2. What obligation, if any, did Ring have to the Kailins or Armstrong after failing to pay the rent and eventually defaulting on the lease? Why?

22–9. [icon] **Critical-Thinking Legal Environment Question.** Garza Construction Co. erects a silo (a grain storage facility) on Reeve's ranch. Garza also lends Reeve funds to pay for the silo under an agreement providing that the silo is not to become part of the land until Reeve completes the loan payments. Before the silo is paid for, Metropolitan State Bank, the mortgage holder on Reeve's land, forecloses on the property. Metropolitan contends that the silo is a fixture to the realty and that the bank is therefore entitled to the proceeds from its sale. Garza argues that the silo is personal property and that the proceeds should therefore go to Garza. Is the silo a fixture? Why or why not?

Chapter 23

Antitrust Law and Promoting Competition

> "Competition is not only the basis of protection to the consumer but is the incentive to progress."
>
> —Herbert Hoover, 1874–1964
> (Thirty-first president of the United States, 1929–1933)

(Moody75/Creative Commons)

Contents

- **The Sherman Antitrust Act**
- **Section 1 of the Sherman Act**
- **Section 2 of the Sherman Act**
- **The Clayton Act**
- **Enforcement and Exemptions**
- **U.S. Antitrust Laws in the Global Context**

Chapter Objectives

After reading this chapter, you should be able to answer the following questions:

1. **What is a monopoly? What is market power? How do these concepts relate to each other?**

2. **What type of activity is prohibited by Section 1 of the Sherman Act? What type of activity is prohibited by Section 2 of the Sherman Act?**

3. **What are the four major provisions of the Clayton Act, and what types of activities do these provisions prohibit?**

4. **What agencies of the federal government enforce the federal antitrust laws?**

5. **What are four activities that are exempt from the antitrust laws?**

Today's antitrust laws are the direct descendants of common law actions intended to limit *restraints of trade* (agreements between firms that have the effect of reducing competition in the marketplace). Such actions originated in fifteenth-century England. In the United States, concern over monopolistic practices arose after the Civil War with the growth of large business enterprises and their attempts to reduce competition. To thwart competition, they legally tied themselves together in business trusts. A business trust is a form of business organization in which trustees hold title to property for the benefit of others. The most powerful of these trusts, the Standard Oil trust, is examined in this chapter's *Landmark in the Legal Environment* feature on page 654.

Many states tried to curb such monopolistic behavior by enacting statutes outlawing the use of trusts. That is why all the laws regulating economic competition in the United States today are referred to as **antitrust laws.** At the national level, Congress passed the Sherman Antitrust Act in 1890.[1] In 1914, Congress passed the Clayton Act[2] and the Federal Trade Commission Act[3] to further curb anticompetitive or unfair business practices. Congress later amended the 1914 acts to broaden and strengthen their coverage.

Antitrust Law Laws protecting commerce from unlawful restraints.

---

[1] 15 U.S.C. Sections 1–7.
[2] 15 U.S.C. Sections 12–27.
[3] 15 U.S.C. Sections 41–58.

This chapter examines these major antitrust statutes, focusing particularly on the Sherman Act and the Clayton Act, as amended, and the types of activities they prohibit. Remember in reading this chapter that the basis of antitrust legislation is the desire to foster competition. Antitrust legislation was initially created—and continues to be enforced—because of our society's belief that competition leads to lower prices, generates more product information, and results in a more equitable distribution of wealth between consumers and producers. As President Herbert Hoover indicated in the chapter-opening quotation, competition not only protects the consumer, but also provides "the incentive to progress." Consumers and society as a whole benefit when producers compete to develop better products that they can sell at lower prices.

▶ The Sherman Antitrust Act

In 1890, Congress passed "An Act to Protect Trade and Commerce against Unlawful Restraints and Monopolies"—commonly known as the Sherman Antitrust Act or, more simply, as the Sherman Act. The Sherman Act was and remains one of the government's more powerful weapons in the effort to maintain a competitive economy.

Major Provisions of the Sherman Act

> *"I don't know what a monopoly is until somebody tells me."*
>
> Steve Ballmer, 1956–present
> (Chief executive officer of Microsoft Corporation)

Sections 1 and 2 contain the main provisions of the Sherman Act:

1. Every contract, combination in the form of trust or otherwise, or conspiracy, in restraint of trade or commerce among the several States, or with foreign nations, is hereby declared to be illegal [and is a felony punishable by a fine and/or imprisonment].

2. Every person who shall monopolize, or attempt to monopolize, or combine or conspire with any other person or persons, to monopolize any part of the trade or commerce among the several States, or with foreign nations, shall be deemed guilty of a felony [and is similarly punishable].

Differences between Section 1 and Section 2

These two sections of the Sherman Act are quite different. Violation of Section 1 requires two or more persons, as a person cannot contract or combine or conspire alone. Thus, the essence of the illegal activity is *the act of joining together*. Section 2, though, can apply either to one person or to two or more persons because it refers to "every person." Thus, unilateral conduct can result in a violation of Section 2.

The cases brought to court under Section 1 of the Sherman Act differ from those brought under Section 2. Section 1 cases are often concerned with finding an agreement (written or oral) that leads to a restraint of trade. Section 2 cases deal with the structure of a monopoly that already exists in the marketplace. The term **monopoly** generally is used to describe a market in which there is a single seller or a very limited

Monopoly   A term generally used to describe a market in which there is a single seller or a very limited number of sellers.

One of Standard Oil's refineries in Richmond, California, around 1900.

(Library of Congress)

Landmark in the Legal Environment   The Sherman Antitrust Act of 1890

The author of the Sherman Antitrust Act of 1890, Senator John Sherman, was the brother of the famous Civil War general William Tecumseh Sherman and a recognized financial authority. Sherman had been concerned for years about what he saw as diminishing competition within U.S. industry and the emergence of monopolies, such as the Standard Oil trust.

The Standard Oil Trust   By 1890, the Standard Oil trust had become the foremost petroleum refining and marketing combination in the United States. Streamlined, integrated, and centrally controlled, Standard Oil maintained an indisputable monopoly over the industry. The trust controlled 90 percent of the U.S. market for refined petroleum products, making it impossible for small producers to compete with such a leviathan.

The increasing consolidation in U.S. industry, and particularly the Standard Oil trust, came to the attention of the public in March 1881. Henry Demarest Lloyd, a young journalist from Chicago, published an article in the *Atlantic Monthly* entitled "The Story of a Great Monopoly." The article attempted to demonstrate that the U.S. petroleum industry was dominated by one firm—Standard Oil. Lloyd's article was so popular that the issue was reprinted six times. It marked the beginning of the U.S. public's growing concern over the rise of monopolies.

The Passage of the Sherman Antitrust Act   The common law regarding trade regulation was not always consistent. Certainly, it was not very familiar to the members of Congress.

The public concern over large business integrations and trusts was familiar, however. In 1888, 1889, and again in 1890, Senator Sherman introduced in Congress bills designed to destroy the large combinations of capital that, he felt, were creating a lack of balance within the nation's economy. Sherman told Congress that the Sherman Act "does not announce a new principle of law, but applies old and well-recognized principles of the common law."[a] In 1890, the Fifty-First Congress enacted the bill into law. Generally, the act prohibits business combinations and conspiracies that restrain trade and commerce, as well as certain monopolistic practices.

• **Application to Today's Legal Environment**   *The Sherman Antitrust Act remains very relevant to today's world. Since the widely publicized monopolization case against Microsoft Corporation in 2001,[b] the U.S. Department of Justice and state attorneys general have brought numerous Sherman Act cases against other corporations, including eBay, Intel, and Philip Morris.[c]*

---

a. 21 *Congressional Record* 2456 (1890).

b. *United States v. Microsoft Corp.,* 253 F.3d 34 (D.C.Cir. 2001). This case will be discussed in Case Example 23.7 on page 662. See also *New York v. Microsoft Corp.,* 531 F.Supp.2d 141 (D.D.C. 2008); and *Massachusetts v. Microsoft Corp.,* 379 F.3d 1199 (D.C.Cir. 2004).

c. See, for example, *United States v. Philip Morris USA, Inc.,* 566 F.3d 1095 (D.C.Cir. 2009); *In re eBay Seller Antitrust Litigation,* 545 F.Supp.2d 1027 (N.D.Cal. 2008); and *In re Intel Corp. Microprocessor Antitrust Litigation,* 2007 WL 137152 (D.Del. 2007).

Monopoly Power   The ability of a monopoly to dictate what takes place in a given market.

Market Power   The power of a firm to control the market price of its product. A monopoly has the greatest degree of market power.

number of sellers. Whereas Section 1 focuses on agreements that are restrictive—that is, agreements that have a wrongful purpose—Section 2 looks at the so-called misuse of **monopoly power** in the marketplace.

Monopoly power exists when a firm has an extreme amount of **market power**— the power to affect the market price of its product. Both Section 1 and Section 2 seek to curtail market practices that result in undesired monopoly pricing and output behavior. For a case to be brought under Section 2, however, the "threshold" or "necessary" amount of monopoly power must already exist. We will return to a discussion of these two sections of the Sherman Act after we look at the act's jurisdictional requirements.

Jurisdictional Requirements

The Sherman Act applies only to restraints that have a substantial impact on interstate commerce. Courts generally have held that any activity that substantially affects interstate commerce falls within the scope of the Sherman Act. As will be discussed later in this chapter, the Sherman Act also extends to U.S. nationals abroad that are engaged in activities that have an effect on U.S. foreign commerce. State laws regulate local restraints on competition.

▶ Section 1 of the Sherman Act

The underlying assumption of Section 1 of the Sherman Act is that society's welfare is harmed if rival firms are permitted to join in an agreement that consolidates their market power or otherwise restrains competition. The types of trade restraints that Section 1 of the Sherman Act prohibits generally fall into two broad categories: *horizontal restraints* and *vertical restraints,* both of which will be discussed shortly. First, though, we look at the rules that the courts may apply when assessing the anticompetitive impact of alleged restraints on trade.

Per Se Violations versus the Rule of Reason

Per Se **Violation**   A type of anticompetitive agreement that is considered to be so injurious to the public that there is no need to determine whether it actually injures market competition. Rather, it is in itself *(per se)* a violation of the Sherman Act.

Rule of Reason   A test by which a court balances the positive effects (such as economic efficiency) of an agreement against its potentially anticompetitive effects. In antitrust litigation, many practices are analyzed under the rule of reason.

Some restraints are so blatantly and substantially anticompetitive that they are deemed *per se* **violations**—illegal *per se* (on their face, or inherently)—under Section 1. Other agreements, however, even though they result in enhanced market power, do not *unreasonably* restrain trade. Using what is called the **rule of reason,** the courts analyze anticompetitive agreements that allegedly violate Section 1 of the Sherman Act to determine whether they may, in fact, constitute reasonable restraints on trade.

The need for a rule-of-reason analysis of some agreements in restraint of trade is obvious—if the rule of reason had not been developed, almost any business agreement could conceivably be held to violate the Sherman Act. Justice Louis Brandeis effectively phrased this sentiment in *Chicago Board of Trade v. United States*:

> Every agreement concerning trade, every regulation of trade, restrains. To bind, to restrain, is of their very essence. The true test of legality is whether the restraint imposed is such as merely regulates and perhaps thereby promotes competition or whether it is such as may suppress or even destroy competition.[4]

When analyzing an alleged Section 1 violation under the rule of reason, a court will consider several factors. These factors include the purpose of the agreement, the parties' market ability to implement the agreement to achieve that purpose, and the effect or potential effect of the agreement on competition. Another factor that a court might consider is whether the parties could have relied on less restrictive means to achieve their purpose.

In the following case, the United States Supreme Court had to decide if a Section 1 violation had occurred. In addition, the Court had to determine whether the violation should have been considered a *per se* violation or analyzed under the rule of reason.

---

4. 246 U.S. 231, 38 S.Ct. 242, 62 L.Ed. 683 (1918).

Case 23.1   **American Needle, Inc. v. National Football League**

Supreme Court of the United States, ___ U.S. ___, 130 S.Ct. 2201, 176 L.Ed.2d 947 (2010).
www.supremecourt.gov/opinions/opinions.aspx[a]

BACKGROUND AND FACTS   The National Football League (NFL) includes thirty-two separately owned professional football teams. Each team has its own name, colors, and logo,

---

a. Under "2009 Term," click on "2009 Term Opinions of the Court." In the results, scroll down the list of cases to "5/24/10" and click on the highlighted case title to access the opinion. The United States Supreme Court maintains this Web site.

and owns related intellectual property. In 1963, the teams formed National Football League Properties (NFLP) to develop, license, and market their trademarked items, such as caps and jerseys. Until 2000, the NFLP granted nonexclusive licenses to a number of vendors, permitting them to manufacture and sell apparel bearing NFL team insignias. American Needle, Inc., was one of those licensees. In late 2000, the teams authorized the NFLP to grant exclusive licenses, and

Case 23.1–Continues next page ⇨

Case 23.1–Continued

(Photo by Christian Petersen/Getty Images for Reebok)

Can the National Football League (NFL) designate Reebok as its exclusive provider of branded headgear without violating antitrust law?

the NFLP granted Reebok International, Ltd., an exclusive ten-year license to manufacture and sell trademarked headwear for all thirty-two teams. It then declined to renew American Needle's nonexclusive license. American Needle brought an action in a federal district court alleging that the NFL agreements, its teams, the NFLP, and Reebok violated Section 1 of the Sherman Act. In response, the defendants argued that they were not capable of conspiring within the meaning of Section 1 because they are a single economic enterprise as far as the marketing of trademarked goods is concerned. The district court granted summary judgment in favor of the defendants. The U.S. Court of Appeals for the Seventh Circuit affirmed the trial court's decision, and American Needle appealed to the United States Supreme Court.

IN THE WORDS OF THE COURT . . .
Justice *STEVENS* delivered the opinion of the Court.
* * * *

As the case comes to us, we have only a narrow issue to decide: whether the NFL respondents are capable of engaging in a "contract, combination * * * or conspiracy," as defined by Section 1 of the Sherman Act, or * * * whether the alleged activity by the NFL respondents "must be viewed as that of a single enterprise for purposes of Section 1."
* * * *

* * * The question is whether the agreement [among the teams with respect to the marketing of its intellectual property] joins together "independent centers of decision-making." If it does, the entities are capable of conspiring under Section 1, and the court must decide whether the restraint of trade is an unreasonable and therefore illegal one.

* * * Each of the [NFL] teams is a substantial, independently owned, and independently managed business. "Their general corporate actions are guided or determined" by "separate corporate consciousnesses," and "their objectives are" not "common." The teams compete with one another, not only on the playing field, but to attract fans, for gate receipts and for contracts with managerial and playing personnel.

Directly relevant to this case, the teams compete in the market for intellectual property. To a firm making hats, the Saints and the Colts are two potentially competing suppliers of valuable trademarks. When each NFL team licenses its intellectual property, it is not pursuing the "common interests of the whole" league but is instead pursuing interests of each "corporation itself"; teams are acting as "separate economic actors pursuing separate economic interests," and each team therefore is a potential "independent center of decision-making."

Decisions by NFL teams to license their separately owned trademarks collectively and to only one vendor are decisions that "depriv[e] the marketplace of independent centers of decision-making," and therefore of actual or potential competition.
* * * *

Respondents argue that * * * they constitute a single entity because without their cooperation, there would be no NFL football. * * * But the Court of Appeals' reasoning is unpersuasive.

The justification for cooperation is not relevant to whether that cooperation is concerted or independent action. *A "contract, combination * * * or conspiracy" that is necessary or useful to a joint venture is still a "contract, combination * * * or conspiracy" if it "deprives the marketplace of independent centers of decision-making."* Any joint venture involves multiple sources of economic power cooperating to produce a product. And for many such ventures, the participation of others is necessary. But that does not mean that necessity of cooperation transforms concerted action into independent action; a nut and a bolt can only operate together, but an agreement between nut and bolt manufacturers is still subject to Section 1 analysis. [Emphasis added.]
* * * *

Football teams that need to cooperate are not trapped by antitrust law. * * * The fact that NFL teams share an interest in making the entire league successful and profitable, and that they must cooperate in the production and scheduling of games, provides a perfectly sensible justification for making a host of collective decisions. But the conduct at issue in this case is still concerted activity under the Sherman Act that is subject to Section 1 analysis.

When "restraints on competition are essential if the product is to be available at all," *per se* rules of illegality are inapplicable, and instead the restraint must be judged according to the flexible Rule of Reason. In such instances, the agreement is likely to survive the Rule of Reason. And depending upon the concerted activity in question, the Rule of Reason may not require a detailed analysis; it "can sometimes be applied in the twinkling of an eye."

DECISION AND REMEDY   The United States Supreme Court reversed the judgment of the appellate court and remanded the case for further proceedings consistent with this opinion. The agreement among the NFL teams to license their intellectual property exclusively through the NFLP to Reebok constituted concerted activity subject to Section 1 analysis.

THE LEGAL ENVIRONMENT DIMENSION   *The Court observed that when restraints on competition are judged under the rule of reason, "the agreement is likely to survive." What did the Court mean by this statement?*

THE ECONOMIC DIMENSION   *Does the Court's ruling mean that the NFL teams' activities with respect to the marketing of their intellectual property through the NFLP were illegal? Explain.*

(Yoshikazu Tsuno/AFP/Getty Images)

Asian LCD flat-screen makers were fined $600 million by the U.S. Department of Justice for price fixing.

Horizontal Restraint Any agreement that in some way restrains competition between rival firms competing in the same market.

Price-Fixing Agreement An agreement between competitors to fix the prices of products or services at a certain level.

Group Boycott The refusal by a group of competitors to deal with a particular person or firm; prohibited by the Sherman Act.

Horizontal Restraints

The term **horizontal restraint** is encountered frequently in antitrust law. A horizontal restraint is any agreement that in some way restrains competition between rival firms competing in the same market.

PRICE FIXING Any **price-fixing agreement**—an agreement among competitors to fix prices—constitutes a *per se* violation of Section 1. Perhaps the definitive case regarding price-fixing agreements is still the 1940 case of *United States v. Socony-Vacuum Oil Co.*[5] In that case, a group of independent oil producers in Texas and Louisiana were caught between falling demand due to the Great Depression of the 1930s and increasing supply from newly discovered oil fields in the region. In response to these conditions, a group of major refining companies agreed to buy "distress" gasoline (excess supplies) from the independents so as to dispose of it in an "orderly manner." Although there was no explicit agreement as to price, it was clear that the purpose of the agreement was to limit the supply of gasoline on the market and thereby raise prices.

There may have been good business reasons for the agreement. Nonetheless, the United States Supreme Court recognized the dangerous effects that such an agreement could have on open and free competition. The Court held that the reasonableness of a price-fixing agreement is never a defense. Any agreement that restricts output or artificially fixes price is a *per se* violation of Section 1. The rationale of the *per se* rule was best stated in what is now the most famous portion of the Court's opinion—footnote 59. In that footnote, Justice William O. Douglas compared a freely functioning price system to a body's central nervous system, condemning price-fixing agreements as threats to "the central nervous system of the economy."

CASE EXAMPLE 23.1 The manufacturer of the prescription drug Cardizem CD, which can help prevent heart attacks, was about to lose its patent on the drug. Another company developed a generic version in anticipation of the patent's expiration. After the two firms became involved in litigation over the patent, the first company agreed to pay the second company $40 million per year not to market the generic version until their dispute was resolved. This agreement was held to be a *per se* violation of the Sherman Act because it restrained competition between rival firms and delayed the entry of generic versions of Cardizem into the market.[6] •

GROUP BOYCOTTS A **group boycott** is an agreement by two or more sellers to refuse to deal with (boycott) a particular person or firm. Such group boycotts have been held to constitute *per se* violations of Section 1 of the Sherman Act. Section 1 has been violated if it can be demonstrated that the boycott or joint refusal to deal was undertaken with the intention of eliminating competition or preventing entry into a given market. Some boycotts, such as group boycotts against a supplier for political reasons, may be protected under the First Amendment right to freedom of expression, however.

HORIZONTAL MARKET DIVISION It is a *per se* violation of Section 1 of the Sherman Act for competitors to divide up territories or customers. **EXAMPLE 23.2**

---

5. 310 U.S. 150, 60 S.Ct. 811, 84 L.Ed. 1129 (1940).
6. *In re Cardizem CD Antitrust Litigation,* 332 F.3d 896 (6th Cir. 2003).

Manufacturers A, B, and C compete against each other in the states of Kansas, Nebraska, and Oklahoma. By agreement, A sells products only in Kansas, B sells only in Nebraska, and C sells only in Oklahoma. This concerted action not only reduces marketing costs but also allows all three (assuming there is no other competition) to raise the price of the goods sold in their respective states. The same violation would take place if A, B, and C agreed that A would sell only to institutional purchasers (such as school districts, universities, state agencies and departments, and cities) in all three states, B only to wholesalers, and C only to retailers. ●

TRADE ASSOCIATIONS   Businesses in the same general industry or profession frequently organize trade associations to pursue common interests. A trade association may engage in various joint activities such as exchanging information, representing the members' business interests before governmental bodies, conducting advertising campaigns, and setting regulatory standards to govern the industry or profession. Generally, the rule of reason is applied to many of these horizontal actions. If a court finds that a trade association practice or agreement that restrains trade is sufficiently beneficial both to the association and to the public, it may deem the restraint reasonable.

Concentrated Industry   An industry in which a large percentage of market sales is controlled by either a single firm or a small number of firms.

A **concentrated industry** is one in which either a single firm or a small number of firms control a large percentage of market sales. In concentrated industries, trade associations can be, and have been, used as a means to facilitate anticompetitive actions, such as fixing prices or allocating markets. When trade association agreements have substantially anticompetitive effects, a court will consider them to be in violation of Section 1 of the Sherman Act.

Vertical Restraints

Vertical Restraint   Any restraint of trade created by agreements between firms at different levels in the manufacturing and distribution process.

A **vertical restraint** of trade results from an agreement between firms at different levels in the manufacturing and distribution process. In contrast to horizontal relationships, which occur at the same level of operation, vertical relationships encompass the entire chain of production. The chain of production normally includes the purchase of inventory, basic manufacturing, distribution to wholesalers, and eventual sale of a product at the retail level. For some products, these distinct phases may be carried out by different firms. In other instances, a single firm carries out two or more of the separate functional phases. Such enterprises are considered to be **vertically integrated firms.**

Vertically Integrated Firm   A firm that carries out two or more functional phases (manufacture, distribution, and retailing, for example) of the chain of production.

Even though firms operating at different functional levels are not in direct competition with one another, they are in competition with other firms. Thus, agreements between firms standing in a vertical relationship may affect competition. Some vertical restraints are *per se* violations of Section 1, whereas others are judged under the rule of reason.

TERRITORIAL OR CUSTOMER RESTRICTIONS   In arranging for the distribution of its products, a manufacturing firm often wishes to insulate dealers from direct competition with other dealers selling the product. To this end, it may institute territorial restrictions or attempt to prohibit wholesalers or retailers from reselling the product to certain classes of buyers, such as competing retailers.

A firm may have legitimate reasons for imposing such territorial or customer restrictions. **EXAMPLE 23.3**   A computer manufacturer may wish to prevent a dealer from cutting costs and undercutting rivals by selling computers without promotion or customer service, while relying on nearby dealers to provide these services. In this situation, the cost-cutting dealer reaps the benefits (sales of the product) paid for by other dealers who undertake promotion and arrange for customer service. By not providing customer service, the cost-cutting dealer may also harm the manufacturer's reputation. ●

Territorial and customer restrictions were once considered *per se* violations of Section 1 of the Sherman Act.[7] In 1977, however, the United States Supreme Court reconsidered the treatment accorded to such vertical restrictions and held that they should be judged under the rule of reason.

CASE EXAMPLE 23.4 GTE Sylvania, Inc., a manufacturer of television sets, limited the number of retail franchises that it granted in any given geographic area. It also required each franchisee to sell only Sylvania products from the location at which it was franchised. Sylvania retained sole discretion to increase the number of retailers in an area. When Sylvania decided to open a new franchise, it terminated the franchise of Continental T.V., Inc., an existing franchisee in that area that would have been in competition with the new franchise. Continental filed a lawsuit claiming that Sylvania's vertically restrictive franchise system violated Section 1 of the Sherman Act. The United States Supreme Court found that "vertical restrictions promote interbrand competition by allowing the manufacturer to achieve certain efficiencies in the distribution of his products." Therefore, Sylvania's vertical system, which was not price restrictive, did not constitute a *per se* violation of Section 1 of the Sherman Act.[8] ●

The decision in the *Continental* case marked a definite shift from rigid characterization of territorial and customer restrictions to a more flexible economic analysis of these vertical restraints under the rule of reason. This rule is still applied in most vertical restraint cases.[9]

RESALE PRICE MAINTENANCE AGREEMENTS An agreement between a manufacturer and a distributor or retailer in which the manufacturer specifies what the retail prices of its products must be is referred to as a **resale price maintenance agreement.** Such agreements were once considered to be *per se* violations of Section 1, but in 1997 the United States Supreme Court ruled that *maximum* resale price maintenance agreements should be judged under the rule of reason.[10] The setting of a maximum price that retailers and distributors can charge for a manufacturer's products may sometimes increase competition and benefit consumers.

Resale Price Maintenance Agreement
An agreement between a manufacturer and a retailer in which the manufacturer specifies what the retail prices of its products must be.

 ## Section 2 of the Sherman Act

Section 1 of the Sherman Act prohibits certain concerted, or joint, activities that restrain trade. In contrast, Section 2 condemns "every person who shall monopolize, or attempt to monopolize." Thus, two distinct types of behavior are subject to sanction under Section 2: *monopolization* and *attempts to monopolize*. One tactic that may be involved in either offense is **predatory pricing.** Predatory pricing involves an attempt by one firm to drive its competitors from the market by selling its product at prices substantially *below* the normal costs of production. Once the competitors are eliminated, the firm (predator) presumably will attempt to recapture its losses and go on to earn higher profits by driving prices up far above their competitive levels.

Predatory Pricing The pricing of a product below cost with the intent to drive competitors out of the market.

---

7. See *United States v. Arnold, Schwinn & Co.,* 388 U.S. 365, 87 S.Ct. 1856, 18 L.Ed.2d 1249 (1967).

8. *Continental T.V., Inc. v. GTE Sylvania, Inc.,* 433 U.S. 36, 97 S.Ct. 2549, 53 L.Ed.2d 568 (1977).

9. Note that there is some disagreement in the case law on when a vertical restraint should be considered unreasonable. See, for example, *State of New York by Abrams v. Anheuser-Busch,* 811 F.Supp. 848 (E.D.N.Y. 1993), which calls into doubt one of the holdings of the *Continental* case.

10. *State Oil Co. v. Khan,* 522 U.S. 3, 118 S.Ct. 275, 139 L.Ed.2d 199 (1997).

Monopolization

Monopolization The possession of monopoly power in the relevant market and the willful acquisition or maintenance of that power, as distinguished from growth or development as a consequence of a superior product, business acumen, or historic accident.

The United States Supreme Court has defined the offense of **monopolization** as involving the following two elements: "(1) the possession of monopoly power in the relevant market and (2) the willful acquisition or maintenance of [that] power as distinguished from growth or development as a consequence of a superior product, business acumen, or historic accident."[11] A violation of Section 2 requires that both these elements—monopoly power and an intent to monopolize—be established.

MONOPOLY POWER   The Sherman Act does not define *monopoly*. In economic theory, monopoly refers to control of a single market by a single entity. It is well established in antitrust law, however, that a firm may be deemed a monopolist even though it is not the sole seller in a market. Additionally, size alone does not determine whether a firm is a monopoly. **EXAMPLE 23.5**   A "mom and pop" grocery located in the isolated town of Happy Camp, Idaho, is a monopolist if it is the only grocery serving that particular market. Size in relation to the market is what matters because monopoly involves the power to affect prices. ●

Monopoly power may be proved by direct evidence that the firm used its power to control prices and restrict output.[12] Usually, however, there is not enough evidence to show that the firm was intentionally controlling prices, so the plaintiff has to offer indirect, or circumstantial, evidence of monopoly power. To prove monopoly power indirectly, the plaintiff must show that the firm has a dominant share of the relevant market and that there are significant barriers for new competitors entering that market.

In the following case, the court had to decide whether there was sufficient evidence to show that a company possessed monopoly power in the relevant market.

---

11. *United States v. Grinnell Corp.,* 384 U.S. 563, 86 S.Ct. 1698, 16 L.Ed.2d 778 (1966).

12. See, for example, *Broadcom Corp. v. Qualcomm, Inc.,* 501 F.3d 297 (3d Cir. 2007).

Case 23.2   **E. I. DuPont de Nemours and Co. v. Kolon Industries, Inc.**

United States Court of Appeals, Fourth Circuit, 637 F.3d 435 (2011).

COMPANY PROFILE   *DuPont was founded in 1802 as a gunpowder manufacturer. Today, it operates in ninety countries in the fields of agriculture, apparel, communications, electronics, home construction, nutrition, and transportation. A recent major investment was in a biodegradable ingredient used in cosmetics, liquid detergents, and antifreeze.*

BACKGROUND AND FACTS   DuPont manufactures and sells para-aramid fiber, which is a complex synthetic fiber used to make body armor, fiber-optic cables, and tires, among other things. Although several companies around the world manufacture this fiber, only three sell into the U.S. market—DuPont (based in the United States), Teijin (based in the Netherlands), and Kolon Industries, Inc. (based in Korea). DuPont is the industry leader, producing more than 70 percent of all para-aramid fibers purchased in the United States. In February 2009, DuPont brought a lawsuit against Kolon for misappropriation of trade secrets. Kolon counterclaimed that DuPont had monopolized and attempted to monopolize the para-aramid

market in violation of Section 2 of the Sherman Act. Kolon claimed that DuPont had illegally used multiyear supply agreements for all of its high-volume para-aramid fiber customers. Under the agreements, the customers were required to purchase between 80 and 100 percent of their para-aramid needs from DuPont. Kolon alleged that those agreements removed substantial commercial opportunities from competition and limited other para-aramid fiber producers' ability to compete. DuPont moved to dismiss the counterclaim, arguing that Kolon had failed to sufficiently plead (demonstrate) unlawful exclusionary conduct, among other things. A federal district court agreed and dismissed Kolon's counterclaim. Kolon appealed to the U.S. Court of Appeals for the Fourth Circuit.

IN THE WORDS OF THE COURT . . .
James WYNN, United States Circuit Judge.
      * * * *

      * * * *To prove a Section 2 monopolization offense, a plaintiff must establish two elements: (1) the possession of monopoly power; and

Case 23.2–Continued

(2) willful acquisition or maintenance of that power—as opposed to simply superior products or historic accidents. An attempted monopolization offense consists of: (1) the use of anticompetitive conduct; (2) with specific intent to monopolize; and (3) a dangerous probability of success. [Emphasis added.]

* * * *

* * * To run afoul of Section 2, a defendant must be guilty of illegal conduct "to foreclose competition, to gain a competitive advantage, or to destroy a competitor." Conduct that might otherwise be lawful may be impermissibly exclusionary under antitrust law when practiced by a monopolist. Indeed, "a monopolist is not free to take certain actions that a company in a competitive * * * market may take, because there is no market constraint on a monopolist's behavior." And although not per se illegal, exclusive dealing arrangements can constitute an improper means of acquiring or maintaining a monopoly.

* * * *

Here, the district court assumed that Kolon adequately pled possession of monopoly power. That assumption was correct, given that Kolon pled, among other things, that: numerous barriers to entry into the U.S. para-aramid fiber market exist and supply is low; DuPont has long dominated the U.S. para-aramid fiber market; and DuPont currently controls over 70 percent of that market, i.e., that "DuPont's market share remains greater than 70% of all sales by purchase volume of para-aramid fiber in the United States."

* * * *

* * * Kolon complained that "because DuPont's supply contracts severely restricted access to customers and preclude effective competition, DuPont's conduct has had a direct, substantial, and adverse effect on competition. And DuPont's anticompetitive conduct has allowed it to control output and increase prices for para-aramid fiber in the United States." And "[b]y precluding Kolon from competition for these customers when demand for para-aramid fibers has significantly increased and supply is low, DuPont's conduct has constrained the only potential entrant to the United States in decades from effectively entering the market, reducing if not practically eliminating additional competition, as well as preserving and growing DuPont's monopoly position." These allegations are sufficient to withstand a motion to dismiss.

DECISION AND REMEDY   The federal appellate court reversed the district court's decision, finding that Kolon had alleged sufficient facts to show that DuPont's behavior violated the prohibition against monopolization and attempted monopolization in Section 2 of the Sherman Act.

WHAT IF THE FACTS WERE DIFFERENT?   *Suppose that DuPont had 45 percent of the market and Kolon and numerous other competitors had the remaining 55 percent. Would the appellate court have ruled the same way? Why or why not?*

MANAGERIAL IMPLICATIONS   *Kolon's success in raising antitrust issues against a major supplier of a particular product in the United States can give some hope to other companies that are attempting to expand their market share against a dominant competitor. In other words, managers who see competitive opportunities, even though their companies have only a very small market share, may be able to resort to the courts to prevent the dominant company or companies from acting in anticompetitive ways.*

RELEVANT MARKET   Before a court can determine whether a firm has a dominant market share, it must define the relevant market. The relevant market consists of two elements: a relevant product market and a relevant geographic market.

Relevant Product Market.   The relevant product market includes all products that, although produced by different firms, have identical attributes, such as sugar. It also includes products that are reasonably interchangeable for the purpose for which they are produced. Products will be considered reasonably interchangeable if consumers treat them as acceptable substitutes.[13]

What should the relevant product market include? This is often a key issue in monopolization cases because the way the market is defined may determine whether a firm has monopoly power. In defining the relevant product market, the key issue is the degree of interchangeability between products. By defining the product market narrowly, the degree of a firm's market power is enhanced.

CASE EXAMPLE 23.6   Whole Foods Market, Inc., wished to acquire Wild Oats Markets, Inc., its main competitor in nationwide high-end organic food supermarkets. The Federal Trade Commission (FTC) filed a Section 2 claim against Whole Foods to prevent the merger. The FTC argued that the relevant product market consisted of only "premium natural and organic supermarkets" rather than all supermarkets, as Whole

---

13. See, for example, *HDC Medical, Inc. v. Minntech Corp.*, 474 F.3d 543 (8th Cir. 2007).

(Kari Sullivan/Creative Commons)

The Federal Trade Commission fought Whole Foods Market's merger with competitor Wild Oats Markets, Inc., claiming that the merger would lessen competition in the organic food market. Should the many supermarket chains that now offer high-end organic foods be considered competitors of Whole Foods?

KEEP IN MIND   Section 2 of the Sherman Act essentially condemns the act of monopolizing, not the possession of monopoly power.

Foods maintained. An appellate court accepted the FTC's narrow definition of the relevant market and remanded the case to the lower court to decide what remedies were appropriate, as the merger had already taken place. Whole Foods later entered into a settlement with the FTC under which it was required to divest (sell or give up control over) thirteen stores, most of which were formerly Wild Oats outlets.[14] ●

Relevant Geographic Market.   The second component of the relevant market is the geographic boundaries of the market. For products that are sold nationwide, the geographic boundaries of the market encompass the entire United States. If transportation costs are significant or a producer and its competitors sell in only a limited area (one in which customers have no access to other sources of the product), the geographic market is limited to that area. A national firm may thus compete in several distinct areas and have monopoly power in one area but not in another.

Generally, the geographic market is that section of the country within which a firm can increase its price a bit without attracting new sellers or without losing many customers to alternative suppliers outside that area. Of course, the Internet and e-commerce are changing the notion of the size and limits of a geographic market. It may become difficult to perceive any geographic market as local, except for products that are not easily transported, such as concrete.

THE INTENT REQUIREMENT   Monopoly power, in and of itself, does not constitute the offense of monopolization under Section 2 of the Sherman Act. The offense also requires an *intent* to monopolize. A dominant market share may be the result of business acumen or the development of a superior product. It may simply be the result of a historic accident. In these situations, the acquisition of monopoly power is not an antitrust violation. Indeed, it would be contrary to society's interest to condemn every firm that acquired a position of power because it was well managed and efficient and marketed a product desired by consumers.

If a firm possesses market power as a result of carrying out some purposeful act to acquire or maintain that power through anticompetitive means, then it is in violation of Section 2. In most monopolization cases, intent may be inferred from evidence that the firm had monopoly power and engaged in anticompetitive behavior.

CASE EXAMPLE 23.7   Navigator, the first popular graphical Internet browser, used Java technology that was able to run on a variety of platforms. When Navigator was introduced, Microsoft perceived a threat to its dominance of the operating-system market. Microsoft developed a competing browser, Internet Explorer, and then began to require computer makers that wanted to install the Windows operating system to also install Explorer and exclude Navigator. In addition, Microsoft included codes in Windows that would cripple the operating system if Explorer was deleted, and it also paid Internet service providers to distribute Explorer and exclude Navigator. Because of this pattern of exclusionary conduct, a court found that Microsoft was guilty of monopolization in violation of Section 2 of the Sherman Act. The court reasoned that Microsoft's pattern of conduct could be rational only if the firm knew that it possessed monopoly power.[15] ●

---

14. *FTC v. Whole Foods Market, Inc.,* 548 F.3d 1028 (D.C.Cir. 2008); and 592 F.Supp.2d 107 (D.D.C. 2009).
15. *United States v. Microsoft Corp.,* 253 F.3d 34 (D.C.Cir. 2001). Microsoft has faced numerous antitrust claims and has settled a number of lawsuits in which it was accused of antitrust violations and anti-competitive tactics.

Preventing Legal Disputes

Because exclusionary conduct can have legitimate efficiency-enhancing effects, it can be difficult to determine when conduct will be viewed as anticompetitive and a violation of Section 2 of the Sherman Act. Thus, a business that possesses monopoly power must be careful that its actions cannot be inferred to be evidence of intent to monopolize. Even if your business does not have a dominant market share, you would be wise to take precautions. Make sure that you can articulate clear, legitimate reasons for the particular conduct or contract and that you do not provide any direct evidence (damaging e-mails, for example) of an intent to exclude competitors. A court will be less likely to infer the intent to monopolize if the specific conduct was aimed at increasing output and lowering per-unit costs, improving product quality, or protecting a patented technology or innovation. Exclusionary conduct and agreements that have no redeeming qualities are much more likely to be deemed illegal.

UNILATERAL REFUSALS TO DEAL As discussed previously, joint refusals to deal (group boycotts) are subject to close scrutiny under Section 1 of the Sherman Act. A single manufacturer acting unilaterally, though, normally is free to deal, or not to deal, with whomever it wishes.[16]

Nevertheless, in limited circumstances, a unilateral refusal to deal will violate antitrust laws. These instances involve offenses proscribed under Section 2 of the Sherman Act and occur only if (1) the firm refusing to deal has—or is likely to acquire—monopoly power and (2) the refusal is likely to have an anticompetitive effect on a particular market. **CASE EXAMPLE 23.8** The owner of three of the four major downhill ski areas in Aspen, Colorado, refused to continue participating in a jointly offered six-day "all Aspen" lift ticket. The Supreme Court ruled that the owner's refusal to cooperate with its smaller competitor was a violation of Section 2 of the Sherman Act. Because the company owned three-fourths of the local ski areas, it had monopoly power, and thus its unilateral refusal had an anticompetitive effect on the market.[17] ●

Attempts to Monopolize

Attempted Monopolization Any action by a firm to eliminate competition and gain monopoly power.

Section 2 also prohibits **attempted monopolization** of a market. Any action challenged as an attempt to monopolize must have been specifically intended to exclude competitors and garner monopoly power. The attempt must also have had a "dangerous" probability of success—only *serious* threats of monopolization are condemned as violations. The probability cannot be dangerous unless the alleged offender possesses some degree of market power.

As mentioned earlier, predatory pricing is a form of anticompetitive conduct that, in theory, could be used by firms that are attempting to monopolize. (Predatory pricing may also lead to claims of price discrimination, to be discussed shortly.) Predatory bidding involves the acquisition and use of *monopsony power*, which is market power on the *buy* side of a market. This may occur when a buyer bids up the price of an input too high for its competitors to pay, causing them to leave the market. The predatory bidder may then attempt to drive down input prices to reap above-competitive profits and recoup any losses it suffered in bidding up the prices.

The question in the following case was whether a claim of predatory bidding is sufficiently similar to a claim of predatory pricing that the same test should apply to both.

---

16. See, for example, *Pacific Bell Telephone Co. v. Linkline Communications, Inc.,* 555 U.S. 438, 129 S.Ct. 1109, 172 L.Ed.2d 836 (2009).

17. *Aspen Skiing Co. v. Aspen Highlands Skiing Corp.,* 472 U.S. 585, 105 S.Ct. 2847, 86 L.Ed.2d 467 (1985). See also *America Channel, LLC v. Time Warner Cable, Inc.,* 2007 WL 142173 (D.Minn. 2007).

Case 23.3   Weyerhaeuser Co. v. Ross-Simmons Hardwood Lumber Co.

Supreme Court of the United States, 549 U.S. 312, 127 S.Ct. 1069, 166 L.Ed.2d 911 (2007).

Was predatory bidding on the price of alder logs tantamount to predatory pricing and therefore illegal?

BACKGROUND AND FACTS   Weyerhaeuser Company entered the Pacific Northwest's hardwood lumber market in 1980. By 2000, Weyerhaeuser owned six mills processing 65 percent of the red alder logs in the region. Meanwhile, Ross-Simmons Hardwood Lumber Company operated a single competing mill. When the prices of logs rose and those for lumber fell, Ross-Simmons suffered heavy losses. Several million dollars in debt, the mill closed in 2001. Ross-Simmons filed a suit in a federal district court against Weyerhaeuser, alleging attempted monopolization under Section 2 of the Sherman Act. Ross-Simmons claimed that Weyerhaeuser used its dominant position in the market to bid up the prices of logs and prevent its competitors from being profitable. Weyerhaeuser argued that the antitrust test for predatory pricing applies to a claim of predatory bidding and that Ross-Simmons had not met this standard. The district court ruled in favor of the plaintiff, a federal appellate court affirmed, and Weyerhaeuser appealed.

IN THE WORDS OF THE COURT . . .
Justice *THOMAS* delivered the opinion of the Court.
      * * * *

Predatory-pricing and predatory-bidding claims are analytically similar. This similarity results from the close theoretical connection between monopoly and monopsony. The kinship between monopoly and monopsony suggests that similar legal standards should apply to claims of monopolization and to claims of monopsonization.

* * * Both claims involve the deliberate use of unilateral pricing measures for anticompetitive purposes. And both claims logically require firms to incur short-term losses on the chance that they might reap supracompetitive [above-competitive] profits in the future.
      * * * *

* * * *"Predatory pricing schemes are rarely tried, and even more rarely successful." Predatory pricing requires a firm to suffer certain losses in the short term on the chance of reaping supracompetitive profits in the future. A rational business will rarely make this sacrifice. The same reasoning applies to predatory bidding. [Emphasis added.]
      * * * *

* * * A failed predatory-pricing scheme may benefit consumers.
* * * Failed predatory-bidding schemes can also * * * benefit consumers.

In addition, predatory bidding presents less of a direct threat of consumer harm than predatory pricing. A predatory-pricing scheme ultimately achieves success by charging higher prices to consumers. By contrast, a predatory-bidding scheme could succeed with little or no effect on consumer prices because a predatory bidder does not necessarily rely on raising prices in the output market to recoup its losses.
      * * * *

* * * [Thus] our two-pronged [predatory pricing] test should apply to predatory-bidding claims.

* * * * A plaintiff must prove that the alleged predatory bidding led to below-cost pricing of the predator's outputs. That is, the predator's bidding on the buy side must have caused the cost of the relevant output to rise above the revenues generated in the sale of those outputs. * * * Given the multitude of procompetitive ends served by higher bidding for inputs, the risk of chilling procompetitive behavior with too lax a liability standard is * * * serious * * *. Consequently, only higher bidding that leads to below-cost pricing in the relevant output market will suffice as a basis for liability for predatory bidding.

A predatory-bidding plaintiff also must prove that the defendant has a dangerous probability of recouping the losses incurred in bidding up input prices through the exercise of monopsony power. Absent proof of likely recoupment, a strategy of predatory bidding makes no economic sense because it would involve short-term losses with no likelihood of offsetting long-term gains.

Ross-Simmons has conceded that it has not satisfied [this] standard. Therefore, its predatory-bidding theory of liability cannot support the jury's verdict.

DECISION AND REMEDY   The United States Supreme Court held that the antitrust test that applies to claims of predatory pricing also applies to claims of predatory bidding. Because Ross-Simmons conceded that it had not met this standard, the Court vacated the lower court's judgment and remanded the case.

WHAT IF THE FACTS WERE DIFFERENT?   *Logs represent up to 75 percent of a mill's total costs. Efficient equipment can increase both the speed at which lumber can be recovered from a log and the amount of lumber recovered. The Court noted that "Ross-Simmons appears to have engaged in little efficiency-enhancing investment." If Ross-Simmons had invested in state-of-the-art technology, how might the circumstances in this case have been different?*

THE ECONOMIC DIMENSION   *Why does a plaintiff alleging predatory bidding have to prove that the defendant's "bidding on the buy side caused the cost of the relevant output to rise above the revenues generated in the sale of those outputs"?*

▶ The Clayton Act

In 1914, Congress attempted to strengthen federal antitrust laws by enacting the Clayton Act. The Clayton Act was aimed at specific anticompetitive or monopolistic practices that the Sherman Act did not cover. The substantive provisions of the act deal with four distinct forms of business behavior, which are declared illegal but not criminal. In each instance, the act states that the behavior is illegal only if it tends to substantially lessen competition or to create monopoly power. The major offenses under the Clayton Act are set out in Sections 2, 3, 7, and 8 of the act.

Section 2 (The Robinson-Patman Act)—Price Discrimination

Price Discrimination Setting prices in such a way that two competing buyers pay two different prices for an identical product or service.

Section 2 of the Clayton Act prohibits **price discrimination,** which occurs when a seller charges different prices to competing buyers for identical goods or services. Congress strengthened this section by amending it with the passage of the Robinson-Patman Act in 1936. As amended, Section 2 prohibits price discrimination that cannot be justified by differences in production costs, transportation costs, or cost differences due to other reasons. In short, a seller is prohibited from charging a lower price to one buyer than is charged to that buyer's competitor.

REQUIREMENTS   To violate Section 2, the seller must be engaged in interstate commerce, the goods must be of like grade and quality, and goods must have been sold to two or more purchasers. In addition, the effect of the price discrimination must be to substantially lessen competition, tend to create a monopoly, or otherwise injure competition. Without proof of an actual injury resulting from the price discrimination, the plaintiff cannot recover damages.

Note that price discrimination claims can arise from discounts, offsets, rebates, or allowances given to one buyer over another. Moreover, giving favorable credit terms, delivery, or freight charges to some buyers but not others can also lead to allegations of price discrimination. For example, offering goods to different customers at the same price but including free delivery for certain buyers may violate Section 2 in some circumstances.

"Becoming number one is easier than remaining number one."

Bill Bradley, 1943–present
(American politician and athlete)

DEFENSES   There are several statutory defenses to liability for price discrimination.

1. *Cost justification.* If the seller can justify the price reduction by demonstrating that a particular buyer's purchases saved the seller costs in producing and selling the goods, the seller will not be liable for price discrimination.
2. *Meeting the price of competition.* If the seller charged the lower price in a good faith attempt to meet an equally low price of a competitor, the seller will not be liable for price discrimination. **CASE EXAMPLE 23.9** Water Craft was a retail dealership of Mercury Marine outboard motors in Baton Rouge, Louisiana. Mercury Marine also sold its motors to other dealers in the Baton Rouge area. When Water Craft discovered that Mercury was selling its outboard motors at a substantial discount to Water Craft's largest competitor, it filed a price discrimination lawsuit against Mercury. In this situation, the court held that Mercury Marine had shown that the discounts given to Water Craft's competitor were made in good faith to meet the low price charged by another manufacturer of marine motors.[18] ●
3. *Changing market conditions.* A seller may lower its price on an item in response to changing conditions affecting the market for or the marketability of the goods

---

18. *Water Craft Management, LLC v. Mercury Marine,* 457 F.3d 484 (5th Cir. 2006).

concerned. Sellers are allowed to readjust their prices to meet the realities of the market without liability for price discrimination. Thus, if an advance in technology makes a particular product less marketable than it was previously, a seller can lower the product's price.

Section 3—Exclusionary Practices

Under Section 3 of the Clayton Act, sellers or lessors cannot sell or lease goods "on the condition, agreement or understanding that the . . . purchaser or lessee thereof shall not use or deal in the goods . . . of a competitor or competitors of the seller." In effect, this section prohibits two types of vertical agreements involving exclusionary practices—exclusive-dealing contracts and tying arrangements.

Exclusive-Dealing Contract
An agreement under which a seller forbids a buyer to purchase products from the seller's competitors.

EXCLUSIVE-DEALING CONTRACTS   A contract under which a seller forbids a buyer to purchase products from the seller's competitors is called an **exclusive-dealing contract.** A seller is prohibited from making an exclusive-dealing contract under Section 3 if the effect of the contract is "to substantially lessen competition or tend to create a monopoly."

CASE EXAMPLE 23.10 Standard Oil Company, the largest gasoline seller in the nation in the late 1940s, made exclusive-dealing contracts with independent stations in seven western states. The contracts involved 16 percent of all retail outlets, with sales amounting to approximately 7 percent of all retail sales in that market. In a case decided in 1949, the United States Supreme Court said that the market was substantially concentrated because the seven largest gasoline suppliers all used exclusive-dealing contracts with their independent retailers. Together, these suppliers controlled 65 percent of the market. Looking at market conditions after the arrangements were instituted, the Court found that market shares were extremely stable and that entry into the market was apparently restricted. Thus, the Court held that Section 3 of the Clayton Act had been violated because competition was "foreclosed in a substantial share" of the relevant market.[19] ●

Note that since the Supreme Court's 1949 decision, a number of subsequent decisions have called the holding in this case into doubt. Today, it is clear that to violate antitrust law, an exclusive-dealing agreement (or *tying arrangement,* discussed next) must qualitatively and substantially harm competition. To prevail, a plaintiff must present affirmative evidence that the performance of the agreement will foreclose competition and harm consumers.

Tying Arrangement   An agreement between a buyer and a seller in which the buyer of a specific product or service becomes obligated to purchase additional products or services from the seller.

TYING ARRANGEMENTS   In a **tying arrangement,** or *tie-in sales agreement,* a seller conditions the sale of a product (the tying product) on the buyer's agreement to purchase another product (the tied product) produced or distributed by the same seller. The legality of a tie-in agreement depends on many factors, particularly the purpose of the agreement and its likely effect on competition in the relevant markets (the market for the tying product and the market for the tied product).

Section 3 of the Clayton Act has been held to apply only to commodities, not to services. Tying arrangements, however, can also be considered agreements that restrain trade in violation of Section 1 of the Sherman Act. Thus, cases involving tying arrangements of services have been brought under Section 1 of the Sherman Act. Although earlier cases condemned tying arrangements as illegal *per se,* courts now evaluate tying agreements under the rule of reason.

---

19. *Standard Oil Co. of California v. United States,* 337 U.S. 293, 69 S.Ct. 1051, 93 L.Ed. 1371 (1949).

CASE EXAMPLE 23.11 Illinois Tool Works, Inc., made printing systems that included various patented components and used a specially designed, but unpatented, ink. It sold the systems to original equipment manufacturers (OEMs) that incorporated the systems into printers that were used in printing bar codes. As part of each deal, the OEMs agreed to buy ink exclusively from Illinois and not to refill the patented ink containers with ink of any other kind. Independent Ink, Inc., sold ink with the same chemical composition as Illinois's product at lower prices. Independent filed a suit against Illinois, alleging, among other things, that it was engaged in illegal tying in violation of the Sherman Act. Independent argued that because Illinois owned patents in the other components of the printing systems, market power could be presumed. The United States Supreme Court, however, ruled that a plaintiff that alleges an illegal tying arrangement involving a patented product must prove that the defendant has market power in the tying product. The Court therefore remanded the case to the trial court to give Independent an opportunity to offer such evidence.[20] ●

Section 7—Mergers

Under Section 7 of the Clayton Act, a person or business organization cannot hold stock and/or assets in another entity "where the effect . . . may be to substantially lessen competition." Section 7 is the statutory authority for preventing mergers or acquisitions that could result in monopoly power or a substantial lessening of competition in the marketplace. Section 7 applies to horizontal mergers and vertical mergers, both of which we discuss in the following subsections.

Market Concentration The degree to which a small number of firms control a large percentage share of a relevant market; determined by calculating the percentages held by the largest firms in that market.

A crucial consideration in most merger cases is the **market concentration** of a product or business. Determining market concentration involves allocating percentage market shares among the various companies in the relevant market. When a small number of companies control a large share of the market, the market is concentrated. If the four largest grocery stores in Chicago accounted for 80 percent of all retail food sales, for example, the market clearly would be concentrated in those four firms.

Competition, however, is not necessarily diminished solely as a result of market concentration, and courts will consider other factors in determining whether a merger will violate Section 7. One factor of particular importance in evaluating the effects of a merger is whether the merger will make it more difficult for *potential* competitors to enter the relevant market.

Horizontal Merger A merger between two firms that are competing in the same marketplace.

HORIZONTAL MERGERS Mergers between firms that compete with each other in the same market are called **horizontal mergers.** If a horizontal merger creates an entity with a significant market share, the merger will be presumed illegal because it increases market concentration. When analyzing the legality of a horizontal merger, the courts also consider three other factors: the overall concentration of the relevant product market, the relevant market's history of tending toward concentration, and whether the apparent design of the merger is to establish market power or to restrict competition.

Herfindahl-Hirschman Index (HHI) An index of market power used to calculate whether a merger of two businesses will result in sufficient monopoly power to violate antitrust laws.

The Federal Trade Commission (FTC) and the U.S. Department of Justice (DOJ) have established guidelines indicating which mergers will be challenged. Under the guidelines, the first factor to be considered is the degree of concentration in the relevant market. In determining market concentration, the FTC and the DOJ employ the **Herfindahl-Hirschman Index (HHI).** The HHI is computed by summing the

---

20. *Illinois Tool Works, Inc. v. Independent Ink, Inc.,* 547 U.S. 28, 126 S.Ct. 1281, 164 L.Ed.2d 26 (2006).

squares of the percentage market shares of the firms in the relevant market. If there are four firms with shares of 30 percent, 30 percent, 20 percent, and 20 percent, respectively, then the HHI equals 2,600 (900 + 900 + 400 + 400 = 2,600).

If the premerger HHI is less than 1,000, then the market is unconcentrated, and the merger is unlikely to be challenged. If the premerger HHI is between 1,000 and 1,800, the industry is moderately concentrated, and the merger will be challenged only if it increases the HHI by 100 points or more. If the HHI is greater than 1,800, the market is highly concentrated. In a highly concentrated market, a merger that produces an increase in the HHI of between 50 and 100 points raises "significant" competitive concerns. Mergers that produce an increase in the HHI of more than 100 points in a highly concentrated market are deemed likely to enhance market power.[21]

Vertical Merger The acquisition by a company at one level in a marketing chain of a company at a higher or lower level in the chain (such as a company merging with one of its suppliers or retailers).

VERTICAL MERGERS A **vertical merger** occurs when a company at one stage of production acquires a company at a higher or lower stage of production. An example of a vertical merger is a company merging with one of its suppliers or retailers. In the past, courts focused almost exclusively on "foreclosure" in assessing vertical mergers. Foreclosure may occur because competitors of the merging firms lose opportunities to sell to, or buy products from, the merging firms.

Today, whether a vertical merger will be deemed illegal generally depends on several factors, such as whether the merger would produce a firm controlling an undue percentage share of the relevant market. The courts also analyze whether the merger would result in a significant increase in the concentration of firms in that market, the barriers to entry into the market, and the apparent intent of the merging parties. Mergers that do not prevent competitors of either merging firm from competing in a segment of the market will not be condemned as "foreclosing" competition and are legal.

Section 8—Interlocking Directorates

Section 8 of the Clayton Act deals with *interlocking directorates*—that is, the practice of having individuals serve as directors on the boards of two or more competing companies simultaneously. Specifically, no person may be a director in two or more competing corporations at the same time if either of the corporations has capital, surplus, or undivided profits aggregating more than $26,867,000 or competitive sales of $2,686,700 or more. The FTC adjusts the threshold amounts each year. (The amounts given here are those announced by the FTC in 2011.)

 Enforcement and Exemptions

The federal agencies that enforce the federal antitrust laws are the U.S. Department of Justice (DOJ) and the Federal Trade Commission (FTC). The FTC was established by the Federal Trade Commission Act of 1914. Section 5 of that act condemns all forms of anticompetitive behavior that are not covered under other federal antitrust laws.

Agency Actions

Divestiture The act of selling one or more of a company's divisions or parts, such as a subsidiary or plant; often mandated by the courts in merger or monopolization cases.

Only the DOJ can prosecute violations of the Sherman Act, which can be either criminal or civil offenses. Either the DOJ or the FTC can enforce the Clayton Act, but violations of that statute are not crimes and can be pursued only through civil proceedings. The DOJ or the FTC may ask the courts to impose various remedies, including **divestiture**

---

21. *Chicago Bridge & Iron Co. v. Federal Trade Commission,* 534 F.3d 410 (5th Cir. 2008).

(making a company give up one or more of its operating functions) and dissolution. A meatpacking firm, for example, might be forced to divest itself of control or ownership of butcher shops.

The FTC has the sole authority to enforce violations of Section 5 of the Federal Trade Commission Act. FTC actions are effected through administrative orders, but if a firm violates an FTC order, the FTC can seek court sanctions for the violation.

The president, of course, plays a role in establishing enforcement policies at the agencies. The Obama administration has taken a more active antitrust stance than the George W. Bush administration did. The Obama administration is vigorously enforcing antitrust regulations—similar to the approach that the European Union has taken in recent years.

Private Actions

CONTRAST Section 5 of the Federal Trade Commission Act is broader than the other antitrust laws. It covers nearly all anticompetitive behavior, including conduct that does not violate either the Sherman Act or the Clayton Act.

A private party who has been injured as a result of a violation of the Sherman Act or the Clayton Act can sue for damages and attorneys' fees. In some instances, private parties may also seek injunctive relief to prevent antitrust violations. The courts have determined that the ability to sue depends on the directness of the injury suffered by the would-be plaintiff.

Thus, a person wishing to sue under the Sherman Act must prove (1) that the antitrust violation either caused or was a substantial factor in causing the injury that was suffered and (2) that the unlawful actions of the accused party affected business activities of the plaintiff that were protected by the antitrust laws.

In 2007, the United States Supreme Court limited the ability of private parties to pursue antitrust lawsuits without presenting some evidence of facts that suggest that an illegal agreement was made. **CASE EXAMPLE 23.12** A group of subscribers to local telephone and high-speed Internet services filed a class-action lawsuit against several regional telecommunication companies (including Bell Atlantic). The plaintiffs claimed that the companies had conspired with one another and engaged in *parallel conduct*—offering similar services and pricing—over a period of years to prevent other companies from entering the market and competing. The Supreme Court dismissed the case, finding that "without more, parallel conduct does not suggest conspiracy." A bare assertion of conspiracy is not enough to allow an antitrust lawsuit to go forward. The Court noted that more specificity is necessary to avoid potentially "massive" discovery costs, which are especially likely to occur when the suit is brought by a large class of plaintiffs.[22] ●

Treble Damages

Treble Damages Damages that, by statute, are three times the amount that the fact finder determines is owed.

In recent years, more than 90 percent of all antitrust actions have been brought by private plaintiffs. One reason for this is that successful plaintiffs may recover **treble damages**—three times the damages that they have suffered as a result of the violation. In a situation involving a price-fixing agreement, normally each competitor is jointly and severally liable for the total amount of any damages, including treble damages if they are imposed.

Exemptions from Antitrust Laws

There are many legislative and constitutional limitations on antitrust enforcement. Most of the statutory or judicially created exemptions to antitrust laws apply in such areas as labor, insurance, and foreign trade (see Exhibit 23–1 on the following page).

---

22. *Bell Atlantic Corp. v. Twombly*, 550 U.S. 544, 127 S.Ct. 1955, 167 L.Ed.2d 929 (2007).

● *Exhibit* **23–1 Exemptions to Antitrust Enforcement**

EXEMPTION	SOURCE AND SCOPE
Labor	Clayton Act—Permits unions to organize and bargain without violating antitrust laws and specifies that strikes and other labor activities normally do not violate any federal law.
Agricultural associations	Clayton Act and Capper-Volstead Act of 1922—Allow agricultural cooperatives to set prices.
Fisheries	Fisheries Cooperative Marketing Act of 1976—Allows the fishing industry to set prices.
Insurance companies	McCarran-Ferguson Act of 1945—Exempts the insurance business in states in which the industry is regulated.
Exporters	Webb-Pomerene Act of 1918—Allows U.S. exporters to engage in cooperative activity to compete with similar foreign associations. Export Trading Company Act of 1982—Permits the U.S. Department of Justice to exempt certain exporters.
Professional baseball	The United States Supreme Court has held that professional baseball is exempt because it is not "interstate commerce."[a]
Oil marketing	Interstate Oil Compact of 1935—Allows states to set quotas on oil to be marketed in interstate commerce.
Defense activities	Defense Production Act of 1950—Allows the president to approve, and thereby exempt, certain activities to further the military defense of the United States.
Small businesses' cooperative research	Small Business Administration Act of 1958—Allows small firms to undertake cooperative research.
State actions	The United States Supreme Court has held that actions by a state are exempt if the state clearly articulates and actively supervises the policy behind its action.[b]
Regulated industries	Industries (such as airlines) are exempt when a federal administrative agency (such as the Federal Aviation Administration) has primary regulatory authority.
Businesspersons' joint efforts to seek government action	Cooperative efforts by businesspersons to obtain legislative, judicial, or executive action are exempt unless it is clear that an effort is "objectively baseless" and is an attempt to make anticompetitive use of government processes.[c]

a. *Federal Baseball Club of Baltimore, Inc. v. National League of Professional Baseball Clubs,* 259 U.S. 200, 42 S.Ct. 465, 66 L.Ed. 898 (1922). A federal district court has held that this exemption applies only to the game's reserve system. (Under the reserve system, teams hold players' contracts for the players' entire careers. The reserve system generally is being replaced by the free agency system.) See *Piazza v. Major League Baseball,* 831 F.Supp. 420 (E.D.Pa. 1993).

b. See *Parker v. Brown,* 317 U.S. 341, 63 S.Ct. 307, 87 L.Ed. 315 (1943).

c. *Eastern Railroad Presidents Conference v. Noerr Motor Freight, Inc.,* 365 U.S. 127, 81 S.Ct. 523, 5 L.Ed.2d 464 (1961); and *United Mine Workers of America v. Pennington,* 381 U.S. 657, 89 S.Ct. 1585, 14 L.Ed.2d 626 (1965). These two cases established the exception often referred to as the *Noerr-Pennington* doctrine.

One of the most significant exemptions covers joint efforts by businesspersons to obtain legislative, judicial, or executive action. Under this exemption, for example, Blu-ray producers can jointly lobby Congress to change the copyright laws without being held liable for attempting to restrain trade. Another exemption covers professional baseball teams.

 ## U.S. Antitrust Laws in the Global Context

U.S. antitrust laws have a broad application. Not only may persons in foreign nations be subject to their provisions, but the laws may also be applied to protect foreign consumers and competitors from violations committed by U.S. business firms. Consequently, *foreign persons,* a term that by definition includes foreign governments, may sue under U.S. antitrust laws in U.S. courts.

The Extraterritorial Application of U.S. Antitrust Laws

Section 1 of the Sherman Act provides for the extraterritorial effect of the U.S. antitrust laws. The United States is a major proponent of free competition in the global economy, and thus any conspiracy that has a *substantial effect* on U.S. commerce is within the reach of the Sherman Act. The violation may even occur outside the United States, and foreign governments as well as persons can be sued for violation of U.S. antitrust laws. Before U.S. courts will exercise jurisdiction and apply antitrust laws, it must be shown that the alleged violation had a substantial effect on U.S. commerce. U.S. jurisdiction is automatically invoked, however, when a *per se* violation occurs.

If a domestic firm, for example, joins a foreign cartel to control the production, price, or distribution of goods, and this cartel has a *substantial effect* on U.S. commerce, a *per se* violation may exist. Hence, both the domestic firm and the foreign cartel could be sued for violation of the U.S. antitrust laws. Likewise, if a foreign firm doing business in the United States enters into a price-fixing or other anticompetitive agreement to control a portion of U.S. markets, a *per se* violation may exist.

The Application of Foreign Antitrust Laws

Large U.S. companies increasingly need to worry about the application of foreign antitrust laws as well. The European Union, in particular, has stepped up its enforcement actions against antitrust violators, as discussed in this chapter's *Beyond Our Borders* feature below.

Many other nations also have laws that promote competition and prohibit trade restraints. For instance, Japanese antitrust laws forbid unfair trade practices,

Beyond Our Borders The European Union's Expanding Role in Antitrust Litigation

The European Union (EU) has laws promoting competition that are stricter in many respects than those of the United States. Although the EU's laws provide only for civil, rather than criminal, penalties, the rules exhibit a different philosophy and define more conduct as anticompetitive than U.S. laws do. The EU has issued strict enforcement guidelines that define what it means for a dominant company to harm competition by abusing its market power. The guidelines also include detailed provisions to prohibit dominant companies from requiring their customers to buy products solely from them or requiring customers to buy bundles of products.

The EU actively pursues antitrust violators, especially individual companies and cartels that engage in monopolistic conduct. For example, in 2009, the EU fined Intel, Inc., $1.44 billion in an antitrust case. According to European regulators, Intel offered computer manufacturers and retailers price discounts and marketing subsidies if they agreed to buy Intel's semiconductor chips rather than the chips produced by Intel's main competitor in Europe. The EU has also fined Microsoft Corporation more than $2 billion in the last ten years for anticompetitive conduct.

The EU is investigating Google, Inc., for potentially violating European antitrust laws by thwarting competition in Internet search engines. Ironically, in 2011, Microsoft—which has paid substantial fines to the EU for its own anticompetitive conduct—filed its own complaint with the EU against Google. Among other things, Microsoft claims that Google has unlawfully restricted competing search engines from accessing YouTube, content from book publishers, advertiser data, and more. (Note that an advertiser filed a similar case against Google in the United States, alleging that Google had monopolized or attempted to monopolize Internet search engines. A federal appellate court dismissed that case in 2011.[a])

For Critical Analysis
Some commentators argue that EU regulators are too focused on reining in powerful U.S. technology companies, such as Microsoft and Intel. How might the large fines imposed by the EU on successful U.S. technology firms affect competition in the United States?

---

a. See *TradeComet.com, LLC v. Google, Inc.,* 647 F.3d 472 (2d Cir. 2011).

monopolization, and restrictions that unreasonably restrain trade. In 2008, China enacted its first antitrust rules, which restrict monopolization and price fixing (although China has claimed that the government may set prices on exported goods without violating these rules). Indonesia, Malaysia, South Korea, and Vietnam all have statutes protecting competition. Argentina, Brazil, Chile, Peru, and several other Latin American countries have adopted modern antitrust laws as well.

Most of these antitrust laws apply extraterritorially, as U.S. antitrust laws do. This means that a U.S. company may be subject to another nation's antitrust laws if the company's conduct has a substantial effect on that nation's commerce. For instance, in 2008 South Korea fined Intel, Inc., the world's largest semiconductor chip maker, $25 million for antitrust violations. In 2005, Intel settled an antitrust case brought by Japan.

 ## Reviewing . . . Antitrust Law and Promoting Competition

The Internet Corporation for Assigned Names and Numbers (ICANN) is a nonprofit entity that organizes Internet domain names. It is governed by a board of directors elected by various groups with commercial interests in the Internet. One of ICANN's functions is to authorize an entity to serve as a registrar for certain "top level domains" (TLDs). ICANN entered into an agreement with VeriSign to provide registry services for the ".com" TLD in accordance with ICANN's specifications. VeriSign complained that ICANN was restricting the services that it could make available as a registrar and was blocking new services, imposing unnecessary conditions on those services, and setting prices at which the services were offered. VeriSign claimed that ICANN's control of the registry services for domain names violated Section 1 of the Sherman Act. Using the information presented in the chapter, answer the following questions.

1. Should ICANN's actions be judged under the rule of reason or be deemed a *per se* violation of Section 1 of the Sherman Act?
2. Should ICANN's action be viewed as a horizontal or a vertical restraint of trade?
3. Does it matter that ICANN's directors are chosen by groups with a commercial interest in the Internet? Why or why not?
4. If the dispute is judged under the rule of reason, what might be ICANN's defense for having a standardized set of registry services that must be used?

 ## Key Terms

antitrust law 652	market concentration 667	resale price maintenance agreement 659
attempted monopolization 663	market power 654	rule of reason 655
concentrated industry 658	monopolization 660	treble damages 669
divestiture 668	monopoly 653	tying arrangement 666
exclusive-dealing contract 666	monopoly power 654	vertical merger 668
group boycott 657	*per se* violation 655	vertical restraint 658
Herfindahl-Hirschman Index (HHI) 667	predatory pricing 659	vertically integrated firm 658
horizontal merger 667	price discrimination 665	
horizontal restraint 657	price-fixing agreement 657	

 ## Chapter Summary: Antitrust Law and Promoting Competition

The Sherman Antitrust Act (1890) (See pages 653–664.)	1. *Major provisions–*
	a. Section 1–Prohibits contracts, combinations, and conspiracies in restraint of trade.
	   (1) Horizontal restraints subject to Section 1 include price-fixing agreements, group boycotts (joint refusals to deal), horizontal market divisions, and trade association agreements.
	   (2) Vertical restraints subject to Section 1 include territorial or customer restrictions and resale price maintenance agreements.
	b. Section 2–Prohibits monopolies and attempts to monopolize.

Chapter Summary: Antitrust Law and Promoting Competition, Continued

The Sherman Antitrust Act (1890)–Continued	2. *Jurisdictional requirements*–The Sherman Act applies only to activities that have a significant impact on interstate commerce.
	3. *Interpretive rules*–
	  a. *Per se* rule–Applied to restraints on trade that are so inherently anticompetitive that they cannot be justified and are deemed illegal as a matter of law.
	  b. Rule of reason–Applied when an anticompetitive agreement may be justified by legitimate benefits. Under the rule of reason, the lawfulness of a trade restraint will be determined by the purpose and effects of the restraint.

The Clayton Act (1914)
(See pages 665–668.)
	The major provisions are as follows:
	1. *Section 2*–As amended in 1936 by the Robinson-Patman Act, prohibits price discrimination that substantially lessens competition and prohibits a seller engaged in interstate commerce from selling to two or more buyers goods of similar grade and quality at different prices when the result is a substantial lessening of competition or the creation of a competitive injury.
	2. *Section 3*–Prohibits exclusionary practices, such as exclusive-dealing contracts and tying arrangements, when the effect may be to substantially lessen competition.
	3. *Section 7*–Prohibits mergers when the effect may be to substantially lessen competition or to tend to create a monopoly.
	  a. Horizontal merger–The acquisition by merger or consolidation of a competing firm engaged in the same relevant market. Will be presumed unlawful if the entity created by the merger will have more than a small percentage market share.
	  b. Vertical merger–The acquisition by a seller of one of its buyers or vice versa. Will be unlawful if the merger prevents competitors of either merging firm from competing in a segment of the market that otherwise would be open to them, resulting in a substantial lessening of competition.
	4. *Section 8*–Prohibits interlocking directorates.

Enforcement and Exemptions (See pages 668–670.)	1. *Enforcement*–Federal agencies that enforce antitrust laws are the U.S. Department of Justice and the Federal Trade Commission. The latter was established by the Federal Trade Commission Act of 1914. Private parties who have been injured as a result of violations of the Sherman Act or Clayton Act may also bring civil suits. In recent years, many private parties have filed such suits largely because, if successful, they may be awarded treble damages and attorneys' fees. 2. *Exemptions*–Numerous exemptions from antitrust enforcement have been created. See Exhibit 23–1 on page 670 for a list of significant exemptions.
U.S. Antitrust Laws in the Global Context (See pages 670–672.)	1. *Application of U.S. laws*–U.S. antitrust laws are broad and can be applied in foreign nations to protect foreign consumers and competitors. Foreign governments and persons can also bring actions under U.S. antitrust laws. Section 1 of the Sherman Act applies to any conspiracy that has a substantial effect on U.S. commerce. 2. *Application of foreign laws*–Many other nations also have laws that promote competition and prohibit trade restraints, and some are more restrictive than U.S. laws. These foreign antitrust laws are increasingly being applied to U.S. firms.

ExamPrep

ISSUE SPOTTERS

1 Under what circumstances would Pop's Market, a small store in a small, isolated town, be considered a monopolist? If Pop's is a monopolist, is it in violation of Section 2 of the Sherman Act? Why or why not?

2 Maple Corporation conditions the sale of its syrup on the buyer's agreement to buy Maple's pancake mix. What factors would a court consider in deciding whether this arrangement violates the Clayton Act?

—**Check your answers to these questions against the answers provided in Appendix G.**

BEFORE THE TEST

Go to **www.cengagebrain.com**, enter the ISBN number "9781111530617," and click on "Find" to locate this textbook's Web site. Then, click on "Access Now" under "Study Tools," and select "Chapter 23" at the top. There you will find an "Interactive Quiz" that you can take to assess your mastery of the concepts in this chapter, as well as "Flashcards" and a "Glossary" of important terms.

For Review

1. What is a monopoly? What is market power? How do these concepts relate to each other?
2. What type of activity is prohibited by Section 1 of the Sherman Act? What type of activity is prohibited by Section 2 of the Sherman Act?
3. What are the four major provisions of the Clayton Act, and what types of activities do these provisions prohibit?
4. What agencies of the federal government enforce the federal antitrust laws?
5. What are four activities that are exempt from the antitrust laws?

Questions and Case Problems

23–1. Sherman Act. An agreement that is blatantly and substantially anticompetitive is deemed a *per se* violation of Section 1 of the Sherman Act. Under what rule is an agreement analyzed if it appears to be anticompetitive but is not a *per se* violation? In making this analysis, what factors will a court consider?

23–2. Antitrust Laws. Allitron, Inc., and Donovan, Ltd., are interstate competitors selling similar appliances, principally in the states of Illinois, Indiana, Kentucky, and Ohio. Allitron and Donovan agree that Allitron will no longer sell in Indiana and Ohio and that Donovan will no longer sell in Illinois and Kentucky. Have Allitron and Donovan violated any antitrust laws? If so, which law? Explain.

23–3. Group Boycott. Jorge's Appliance Corp. was a new retail seller of appliances in Sunrise City. Because of its innovative sales techniques and financing, Jorge's caused the appliance department of No-Glow Department Store, a large chain store with a great deal of buying power, to lose a substantial amount of sales. No-Glow told a number of appliance manufacturers from whom it made large-volume purchases that if they continued to sell to Jorge's, No-Glow would stop buying from them. The manufacturers immediately stopped selling appliances to Jorge's. Jorge's filed a suit against No-Glow and the manufacturers, claiming that their actions constituted an antitrust violation. No-Glow and the manufacturers were able to prove that Jorge's was a small retailer with a small market share. They claimed that because the relevant market was not substantially affected, they were not guilty of restraint of trade. Discuss fully whether there was an antitrust violation.

23–4. Price Fixing. Texaco, Inc., and Shell Oil Co. are competitors in the national and international oil and gasoline markets. They refine crude oil into gasoline and sell it to service station owners and others. Between 1998 and 2002, Texaco and Shell engaged in a joint venture, Equilon Enterprises, to consolidate their operations in the western United States and a separate venture, Motiva Enterprises, for the same purpose in the eastern United States. This ended their competition in the domestic refining and marketing of gasoline. As part of the ventures, Texaco and Shell agreed to pool their resources and share the risks and profits of their joint activities. The Federal Trade Commission and several states approved the formation of these entities without restricting the pricing of their gasoline, which the ventures began to sell at a single price under the original Texaco and Shell brand names. Fouad Dagher and other station owners filed a suit in a federal district court against Texaco and Shell, alleging that the defendants were engaged in illegal price fixing. Do the circumstances in this case fit the definition of a price-fixing agreement? Explain. [*Texaco Inc. v. Dagher,* 547 U.S. 1, 126 S.Ct. 1276, 164 L.Ed.2d 1 (2006)]

23–5. Restraint of Trade. In 1999, residents of the city of Madison, Wisconsin, became concerned that excessive consumption of liquor seemed to be increasing near the campus of the University of Wisconsin–Madison (UW), leading to more frequent use of detoxification facilities and calls for police services in the campus area. Under pressure from UW, which shared these concerns, the city initiated a new policy, imposing conditions on area taverns to discourage price reduction "specials" believed to encourage high-volume and dangerous drinking. In 2002, the city began to draft an ordinance to ban all drink specials. Tavern owners responded by announcing that they had "voluntarily" agreed to discontinue drink specials on Friday and Saturday nights after 8 P.M. The city put its ordinance on hold. UW student Nic Eichenseer and others filed a suit in a Wisconsin state court against the Madison–Dane County Tavern League, Inc. (an association of local tavern owners), and others, alleging violations of antitrust law. On what might the plaintiffs base a claim for relief? Are the defendants in this case exempt from the antitrust laws? What should the court rule? Why? [*Eichenseer v. Madison–Dane County Tavern League, Inc.,* 2006 WI App. 226, 725 N.W.2d 274 (2006)]

23–6. Tying Arrangement. John Sheridan owned a Marathon gas station franchise. He sued Marathon Petroleum Co. under Section 1 of the Sherman Act and Section 3 of the Clayton Act, charging it with illegally tying the processing of credit-card sales to the gas station. As a condition of obtaining a Marathon dealership, dealers had to agree to let the franchisor process credit cards. They could not shop around to see if credit-card processing could be obtained at a lower price from another source. The district court dismissed the case for failure to state a claim. Sheridan appealed. Is there a tying arrangement? If so, does it violate the law? Explain. [*Sheridan v. Marathon Petroleum Co.,* 530 F.3d 590 (7th Cir. 2008)]

23–7. Case Problem with Sample Answer. Section 2 of the Sherman Act. When Deer Valley Resort Co. (DVRC) was developing its ski resort in the Wasatch Mountains near Park City, Utah, it sold parcels of land in the resort village to third parties. Each sales contract reserved the right of approval over the conduct of certain businesses on the property, including ski rentals. For fifteen years, DVRC permitted Christy Sports, LLC, to rent skis in competition with DVRC's ski rental outlet. When DVRC opened a new midmountain ski rental outlet, it revoked Christy's permission to rent skis. This meant that most skiers who flew into Salt Lake City and shuttled to Deer Valley had few choices: they could carry their ski equipment onto their flights, take a shuttle into Park City and look for cheaper ski rentals there, or rent from DVRC. Christy filed a suit in a federal district court against DVRC. Was DVRC's action an attempt to monopolize in violation of Section 2 of the Sherman Act? Why or why not? [*Christy Sports, LLC v. Deer Valley Resort Co.,* 555 F.3d 1188 (10th Cir. 2009)]

—To view a sample answer for Case Problem 23–7, go to Appendix F at the end of this text.

23–8. Price Fixing. A group of consumers, including Keven Starr, sued several companies that produce, license, and distribute music sold as digital files over the Internet or on CDs. These companies controlled 80 percent of the digital music sold in the United States. They formed joint ventures called MusicNet and Duet to sell music to consumers. Through these ventures, the music sellers could communicate about pricing, terms, and use restrictions. Because the prices were so high, most consumers avoided them. Instead, song-by-song distribution over the Internet became more common.

As a result, the music companies were forced to lower prices, but most sales were still done through MusicNet as the distributor. Eventually, the music companies agreed to a price of 70 cents wholesale for songs distributed on the Internet, but they refused to sell through another distributor, eMusic, which charged 25 cents per song. Consumers alleged that the music companies engaged in a conspiracy to restrain the distribution of Internet music and to fix and maintain artificially high prices. Do the consumers have a credible antitrust case to pursue in this situation? Discuss. [*Starr v. Sony BMG Music Entertainment,* 592 F.3d 314 (2d Cir. 2010)]

23–9. A Question of Ethics. Section 1 of the Sherman Act. In the 1990s, DuCoa, LP, made choline chloride, a B-complex vitamin essential for the growth and development of animals. The U.S. market for choline chloride was divided into thirds among DuCoa, Bioproducts, Inc., and Chinook Group, Ltd. To stabilize the market and keep the price of the vitamin higher than it would otherwise be, the companies agreed to fix the price and allocate market share by deciding which of them would offer the lowest price to each customer. At times, however, the companies dis-regarded the agreement. During an increase in competitive activity in August 1997, Daniel Rose became president of DuCoa. The next month, a subordinate advised him of the conspiracy. By February 1998, Rose had begun to implement a strategy to persuade DuCoa's competitors to rejoin the conspiracy. By April, the three companies had reallocated their market shares and increased their prices. In June, the U.S. Department of Justice began to investigate allegations of price fixing in the vitamin market. Ultimately, a federal district court convicted Rose of conspiracy to violate Section 1 of the Sherman Act. [*United States v. Rose,* 449 F.3d 627 (5th Cir. 2006)]

1. The court "enhanced" Rose's sentence to thirty months' imprisonment, one year of supervised release, and a $20,000 fine based on, among other things, his role as "a manager or supervisor" in the conspiracy. Rose appealed this enhancement to the U.S. Court of Appeals for the Fifth Circuit. Was it fair to increase Rose's sentence on this ground? Why or why not?

2. Was Rose's participation in the conspiracy unethical? If so, how might Rose have behaved ethically instead? If not, could any of the participants' conduct be considered unethical? Explain.

23–10. Critical-Thinking Legal Environment Question. Critics of antitrust law claim that in the long run, competitive market forces will eliminate private monopolies unless they are fostered by government regulation. Can you think of any examples of monopolies that continue to be fostered by government in the United States?

Chapter 24

Investor Protection and Corporate Governance

> "You are remembered
> for the rules you break."
>
> —Douglas MacArthur, 1880–1964
> (U.S. Army general)

Contents

- **The Securities Act of 1933**
- **The Securities Exchange Act of 1934**
- **State Securities Laws**
- **Corporate Governance**
- **Online Securities Fraud and Ponzi Schemes**

Chapter Objectives

After reading this chapter, you should be able to answer the following questions:

1. **What is meant by the term *securities*?**
2. **What are the two major statutes regulating the securities industry?**
3. **What is insider trading? Why is it prohibited?**
4. **What are some of the features of state securities laws?**
5. **What certification requirements does the Sarbanes-Oxley Act impose on corporate executives?**

Security Generally, a stock certificate, bond, note, debenture, warrant, or other document or record evidencing an ownership interest in a corporation or a promise of repayment of debt by a corporation.

After the stock market crash of 1929, Congress enacted legislation to regulate securities markets. **Securities** generally are defined as any documents or records evidencing corporate ownership (stock) or debts (bonds). The goal of regulation was to provide investors with more information to help them make buying and selling decisions about securities and to prohibit deceptive, unfair, and manipulative practices.

Today, the sale and transfer of securities are heavily regulated by federal and state statutes and by government agencies, and even more regulations have been enacted since the Great Recession. For example, the Dodd-Frank Act, which Congress passed in 2010 (see page 562), requires significant changes to the financial regulatory environment to reform Wall Street. As a result, the Securities and Exchange Commission (SEC) developed rules to implement the provisions of that act. Despite all of these efforts to regulate the securities markets, people continue to break the rules—and be remembered for it, as the chapter-opening quotation above indicates. Billionaire hedge-fund manager, Raj Rajaratnam, for example, who was sentenced to prison in 2011, perpetrated one of the largest and most lucrative insider-trading schemes in history.

This chapter discusses the nature of federal securities regulation and its effect on the business world. We first examine the major traditional laws governing securities offerings and trading. We then discuss corporate governance and the

Sarbanes-Oxley Act of 2002,[1] which affects certain types of securities transactions. Finally, we look at the problem of online securities fraud and Ponzi schemes. Before we begin, though, the important role played by the SEC in the regulation of federal securities laws requires some attention. We examine the origin and functions of the SEC in this chapter's *Landmark in the Legal Environment* feature on the following page.

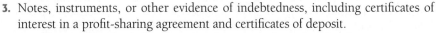

The Securities Act of 1933

The Securities Act of 1933[2] governs initial sales of stock by businesses. The act was designed to prohibit various forms of fraud and to stabilize the securities industry by requiring that all essential information concerning the issuance of securities be made available to the investing public. Basically, the purpose of this act is to require disclosure. The 1933 act provides that all securities transactions must be registered with the SEC, unless they are exempt from registration requirements.

During the stock market crash of 1929, hordes of investors crowded Wall Street to learn the latest news. How did the crash affect stock trading thereafter?

(National Archives)

What Is a Security?

Section 2(1) of the Securities Act of 1933 contains a broad definition of securities, which generally include the following:[3]

1. Instruments and interests commonly known as securities, such as preferred and common stocks, treasury stocks, bonds, debentures, and stock warrants.
2. Any interests in securities, such as stock options, puts, calls, or other types of privilege on a security or on the right to purchase a security or a group of securities in a national security exchange.
3. Notes, instruments, or other evidence of indebtedness, including certificates of interest in a profit-sharing agreement and certificates of deposit.
4. Any fractional undivided interest in oil, gas, or other mineral rights.
5. Investment contracts, which include interests in limited partnerships and other investment schemes.

In interpreting the act, the United States Supreme Court has held that an **investment contract** is any transaction in which a person (1) invests (2) in a common enterprise (3) reasonably expecting profits (4) derived *primarily* or *substantially* from others' managerial or entrepreneurial efforts. Known as the *Howey* test, this definition continues to guide the determination of what types of contracts can be considered securities.[4]

For our purposes, it is probably convenient to think of securities in their most common forms—stocks and bonds issued by corporations. Bear in mind, though, that securities can take many forms, including interests in whiskey, cosmetics, worms, beavers, boats, vacuum cleaners, muskrats, and cemetery lots. Almost any stake in the ownership or debt of a company can be considered a security. Investment contracts in condominiums, franchises, limited partnerships in real estate, and oil or gas

Investment Contract In securities law, a transaction in which a person invests in a common enterprise reasonably expecting profits that are derived primarily from the efforts of others.

---

1. 15 U.S.C. Sections 7201 *et seq.*
2. 15 U.S.C. Sections 77–77aa.
3. 15 U.S.C. Section 77b(1). Amendments in 1982 added stock options.
4. *SEC v. W. J. Howey Co.*, 328 U.S. 293, 66 S.Ct. 1100, 90 L.Ed. 1244 (1946).

Landmark in the Legal Environment   The Securities and Exchange Commission

In 1931, the U.S. Senate passed a resolution calling for an extensive investigation of securities trading. The investigation led, ultimately, to the passage by Congress of the Securities Act of 1933, which is also known as the *truth-in-securities* bill. In the following year, Congress passed the Securities Exchange Act. This 1934 act created the Securities and Exchange Commission (SEC).

Major Responsibilities of the SEC   The SEC was created as an independent regulatory agency with the function of administering the 1933 and 1934 acts. Its major responsibilities in this respect are as follows:

1. Interprets federal securities laws and investigates securities law violations.
2. Issues new rules and amends existing rules.
3. Oversees the inspection of securities firms, brokers, investment advisers, and ratings agencies.
4. Oversees private regulatory organizations in the securities, accounting, and auditing fields.
5. Coordinates U.S. securities regulation with federal, state, and foreign authorities.

The SEC's Expanding Regulatory Powers   Since its creation, the SEC's regulatory functions have gradually been increased by legislation granting it authority in different areas. For example, to curb further securities fraud, the Securities Enforcement Remedies and Penny Stock Reform Act of 1990[a] was enacted to expand the SEC's enforcement options and allow SEC administrative law judges to hear cases involving more types of alleged securities law violations. In addition, the act provides that courts can prevent persons who have engaged in securities fraud from serving as officers and directors of publicly held corporations. The Securities Acts Amendments of 1990 authorized the SEC to seek sanctions against those who violate foreign securities laws.[b]

The National Securities Markets Improvement Act of 1996 expanded the power of the SEC to exempt persons, securities, and transactions from the requirements of the securities laws.[c]

IN TODAY'S MARKET NEWS, GREED ROARED BACK.

©Harley Schwadron

SCHWADRon

(This part of the act is also known as the Capital Markets Efficiency Act.) The act also limited the authority of the states to regulate certain securities transactions and particular investment advisory firms.[d] The Sarbanes-Oxley Act of 2002, which will be discussed later in this chapter, further expanded the authority of the SEC by directing the agency to issue new rules relating to corporate disclosure requirements and by creating an oversight board to regulate public accounting firms.

The SEC requires companies to disclose the potential financial impacts of future events such as increased competition, changes in regulatory rules, and pending lawsuits. Recently, at the urging of environmental groups and large institutional investors, the SEC added the potential impact of climate change related to global warming to the list of information that publicly held companies should disclose. Companies must note in their quarterly and annual reports to shareholders any significant developments in federal and state regulations regarding climate change. For example, companies should disclose estimates for any material capital expenditures for pollution-control facilities and any risk factors related to existing or pending environmental legislation.

• Application to Today's Legal Environment   *The SEC is working to make the regulatory process more efficient and more relevant to today's securities trading practices. To this end, the SEC has embraced modern technology and communications methods, especially the Internet, more completely than many other federal agencies have. For example, the agency now requires—not just allows—companies to file certain information electronically so that it can be posted on the SEC's EDGAR (Electronic Data Gathering, Analysis, and Retrieval) database.*

---

a. 15 U.S.C. Section 77g.
b. 15 U.S.C. Section 78a.
c. 15 U.S.C. Sections 77z-3, 78mm.

---

d. 15 U.S.C. Section 80b-3a.

---

or other mineral rights have qualified as securities. **CASE EXAMPLE 24.1** Alpha Telcom sold, installed, and maintained pay-phone systems. As part of its pay-phone program, Alpha guaranteed buyers a 14 percent return on the amount of their purchase. Alpha was operating at a net loss, however, and continually borrowed funds to pay investors the fixed rate of return it had promised. Eventually, the company filed for bankruptcy, and the SEC brought an action alleging that Alpha had violated the Securities Act of

1933. In this situation, a federal court concluded that the pay-phone program was a security because it involved an investment contract.[5] •

Preventing Legal Disputes

Securities are not limited to stocks and bonds but can encompass a wide variety of legal claims. The analysis hinges on the nature of the transaction rather than on the particular instrument or rights involved. Because Congress enacted securities laws to regulate investments, in whatever form and by whatever name they are called, almost any type of security that might be sold as an investment can be subject to securities laws. When in doubt about whether an investment transaction involves securities, seek the advice of a specialized attorney.

Registration Statement

Section 5 of the Securities Act of 1933 broadly provides that a security must be *registered* before being offered to the public unless it qualifies for an exemption. The issuing corporation must file a *registration statement* with the SEC and must provide all investors with a *prospectus*. A **prospectus** is a written disclosure document that describes the security being sold, the financial operations of the issuing corporation, and the investment or risk attaching to the security. The prospectus also serves as a selling tool for the issuing corporation. The SEC now allows an issuer to deliver its prospectus to investors electronically via the Internet.[6] In principle, the registration statement and the prospectus supply sufficient information to enable unsophisticated investors to evaluate the financial risk involved.

Prospectus A written document, required by securities laws, that describes the security being sold, the financial operations of the issuing corporation, and the investment or risk attaching to the security.

CONTENTS OF THE REGISTRATION STATEMENT The registration statement must be written in plain English and fully describe the following:

1. The securities being offered for sale, including their relationship to the registrant's other capital securities.
2. The corporation's properties and business (including a financial statement certified by an independent public accounting firm).
3. The management of the corporation, including managerial compensation, stock options, pensions, and other benefits. Any interests of directors or officers in any material transactions with the corporation must be disclosed.
4. How the corporation intends to use the proceeds of the sale.
5. Any pending lawsuits or special risk factors.

DON'T FORGET The purpose of the Securities Act of 1933 is disclosure—the SEC does not consider whether a security is worth the investment price.

All companies, both domestic and foreign, must file their registration statements electronically so that they can be posted on the SEC's EDGAR (Electronic Data Gathering, Analysis, and Retrieval) database. The EDGAR database includes material on initial public offerings, proxy statements, corporations' annual reports, registration statements, and other documents that have been filed with the SEC. Investors can access the database via the Internet (www.sec.gov/edgar.shtml) to obtain information that can be used to make investment decisions.

---

5. *SEC v. Alpha Telcom, Inc.,* 187 F.Supp.2d 1250 (2002). See also *SEC v. Edwards,* 540 U.S. 389, 124 S.Ct. 892, 157 L.Ed.2d 813 (2004), in which the United States Supreme Court held that an investment scheme offering contractual entitlement to a fixed rate of return can be an investment contract and therefore can be considered a security under federal law.
6. Basically, an electronic prospectus must meet the same requirements as a printed prospectus. The SEC has special rules that address situations in which the graphics, images, or audio files in a printed prospectus cannot be reproduced in an electronic form. 17 C.F.R. Section 232.304.

REGISTRATION PROCESS   The registration statement does not become effective until it has been reviewed and approved by the SEC (unless it is filed by a *well-known seasoned issuer,* as discussed below). The 1933 act restricted the types of activities that an issuer can engage in at each stage in the registration process. During the *prefiling period* (before the registration statement is filed), the issuer normally cannot sell or offer to sell the securities. Once the registration statement has been filed, a waiting period begins while the SEC reviews the registration statement for completeness.[7]

During the *waiting period,* the securities can be offered for sale but cannot be sold by the issuing corporation. Only certain types of offers are allowed. All issuers can distribute a *preliminary prospectus,* which contains most of the information that will be included in the final prospectus but often does not include a price. Most issuers can also use a *free-writing prospectus* during this period (although some inexperienced issuers will need to file a preliminary prospectus first).[8] A **free-writing prospectus** is any type of written, electronic, or graphic offer that describes the issuer or its securities and includes a legend indicating that the investor may obtain the prospectus at the SEC's Web site.

Once the SEC has reviewed and approved the registration statement and the waiting period is over, the registration is effective, and the *posteffective period* begins. The issuer can now offer and sell the securities without restrictions. If the company issued a preliminary or free-writing prospectus to investors, it must provide those investors with a final prospectus either before or at the time they purchase the securities. The issuer can require investors to download the final prospectus from a Web site if it notifies them of the appropriate Internet address.

RESTRICTIONS RELAXED FOR WELL-KNOWN SEASONED ISSUERS   In 2005, the SEC revised the registration process and loosened some of the restrictions on large experienced issuers.[9] The rules created new categories of issuers depending on their size and presence in the market and provided a simplified registration process for these issuers. The large, well-known securities firms that issue most securities have the greatest flexibility. A *well-known seasoned issuer* (WKSI) is a firm that has issued at least $1 billion in securities in the previous three years or has at least $700 million of value of outstanding stock in the hands of the public. WKSIs can file registration statements the day they announce a new offering and are not required to wait for SEC review and approval. They can also use a free-writing prospectus at any time, even during the prefiling period.

Exempt Securities and Transactions

Certain types of securities are exempt from the registration requirements of the Securities Act of 1933. These securities—which generally can also be resold without being registered—are summarized in Exhibit 24–1 on the facing page under the "Exempt Securities" heading.[10] The exhibit also lists and describes certain transactions that are exempt from registration requirements under various SEC regulations.

The transaction exemptions are the most important because they are very broad and can enable an issuer to avoid the high cost and complicated procedures associated

Free-Writing Prospectus   Any type of written, electronic, or graphic offer that describes the issuing corporation or its securities and includes a legend indicating that the investor may obtain the prospectus at the Securities and Exchange Commission's Web site.

---

7. The waiting period must last at least twenty days but always extends much longer because the SEC inevitably requires numerous changes and additions to the registration statement.

8. See SEC Rules 164 and 433.

9. Securities Offering Reform, codified at 17 C.F.R. Sections 200, 228, 229, 230, 239, 240, 243, 249, and 274.

10. 15 U.S.C. Section 77c.

• *Exhibit* 24–1 **Exemptions for Securities Offerings under the 1933 Securities Act**

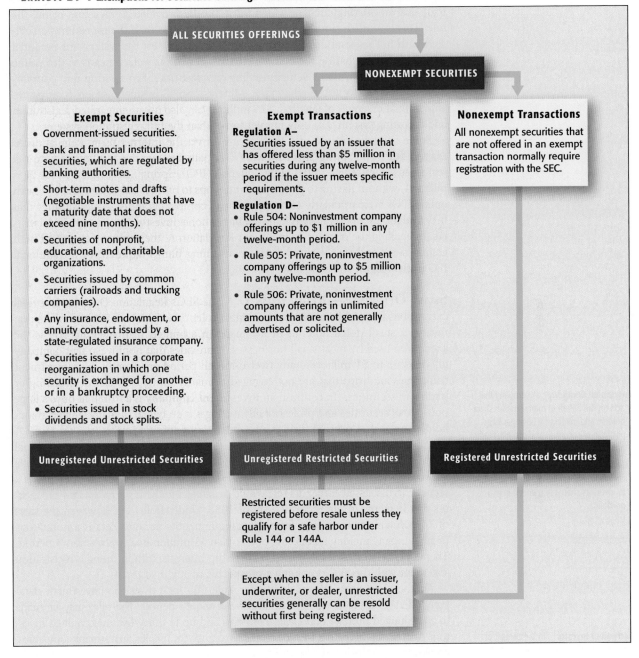

ALL SECURITIES OFFERINGS

NONEXEMPT SECURITIES

Exempt Securities
- Government-issued securities.
- Bank and financial institution securities, which are regulated by banking authorities.
- Short-term notes and drafts (negotiable instruments that have a maturity date that does not exceed nine months).
- Securities of nonprofit, educational, and charitable organizations.
- Securities issued by common carriers (railroads and trucking companies).
- Any insurance, endowment, or annuity contract issued by a state-regulated insurance company.
- Securities issued in a corporate reorganization in which one security is exchanged for another or in a bankruptcy proceeding.
- Securities issued in stock dividends and stock splits.

Exempt Transactions

Regulation A–
Securities issued by an issuer that has offered less than $5 million in securities during any twelve-month period if the issuer meets specific requirements.

Regulation D–
- Rule 504: Noninvestment company offerings up to $1 million in any twelve-month period.
- Rule 505: Private, noninvestment company offerings up to $5 million in any twelve-month period.
- Rule 506: Private, noninvestment company offerings in unlimited amounts that are not generally advertised or solicited.

Nonexempt Transactions

All nonexempt securities that are not offered in an exempt transaction normally require registration with the SEC.

Unregistered Unrestricted Securities

Unregistered Restricted Securities

Registered Unrestricted Securities

Restricted securities must be registered before resale unless they qualify for a safe harbor under Rule 144 or 144A.

Except when the seller is an issuer, underwriter, or dealer, unrestricted securities generally can be resold without first being registered.

BE AWARE The issuer of an exempt security does not have to disclose the same information that other issuers do.

with registration. Because the exemptions overlap somewhat, an offering may qualify for more than one. Hence, many sales of securities occur without registration. Even when a transaction is exempt from the registration requirements, the offering is still subject to the antifraud provisions of the 1933 act (as well as those of the 1934 act discussed later in this chapter).

REGULATION A OFFERINGS Securities issued by an issuer that has offered less than $5 million in securities during any twelve-month period are exempt from registration.[11] Under Regulation A,[12] the issuer must file with the SEC a notice of the issue and an offering circular, which must also be provided to investors before the sale. This is a much simpler and less expensive process than the procedures associated with full registration. Companies are allowed to "test the waters" for potential interest before preparing the offering circular. To *test the waters* means to determine potential interest without actually selling any securities or requiring any commitment on the part of those who express interest. Small-business issuers (companies with annual revenues of less than $25 million) can also use an integrated registration and reporting system that uses simpler forms than the full registration system.

Some companies have sold their securities via the Internet using Regulation A. **EXAMPLE 24.2**   The Spring Street Brewing Company became the first company to sell securities via an online initial public offering (IPO). Spring Street raised about $1.6 million—without having to pay any commissions to brokers or underwriters. • Such online IPOs are particularly attractive to small companies and start-up ventures that may find it difficult to raise capital from institutional investors or through underwriters. By making the offering online under Regulation A, the company can avoid both commissions and the costly and time-consuming filings required for a traditional IPO under federal and state law.

SMALL OFFERINGS—REGULATION D   The SEC's Regulation D contains several exemptions from registration requirements (Rules 504, 505, and 506) for offers that involve a small dollar amount or are made in a limited manner. Rule 504 is the exemption used by most small businesses. It provides that noninvestment company offerings up to $1 million in any twelve-month period are exempt. Noninvestment companies are firms that are not engaged primarily in the business of investing or trading in securities. (In contrast, an **investment company** is a firm that buys a large portfolio of securities and professionally manages it on behalf of many smaller shareholders/owners. A **mutual fund** is a type of investment company.)

EXAMPLE 24.3   Zeta Enterprises is a limited partnership that develops commercial property. Zeta intends to offer $600,000 of its limited partnership interests for sale between June 1 and next May 31. Because an interest in a limited partnership is a security, as discussed earlier, its sale would be subject to the registration and prospectus requirements of the Securities Act of 1933. Under Rule 504, however, the sales of Zeta's interests are exempt from these requirements because Zeta is a noninvestment company making an offering of less than $1 million in a twelve-month period. Therefore, Zeta can sell its limited partnership interests without filing a registration statement with the SEC or issuing a prospectus to any investor. •

Another exemption is available under Rule 505 for private, noninvestment company offerings up to $5 million in any twelve-month period. The offer may be made to an unlimited number of *accredited investors* and up to thirty-five unaccredited investors. **Accredited investors** include banks, insurance companies, investment companies, employee benefit plans, the issuer's executive officers and directors, and persons whose income or net worth exceeds a certain threshold. The SEC must be notified of the sales, and precautions must be taken because these restricted securities may be resold only by registration or in an exempt transaction. No general solicitation or advertising is allowed. The issuer must provide any unaccredited investors with disclosure documents that generally are the same as those used in registered offerings.

Investment Company   A company that acts on the behalf of many smaller shareholders and owners by buying a large portfolio of securities and professionally managing that portfolio.

Mutual Fund   A specific type of investment company that continually buys or sells to investors shares of ownership in a portfolio.

Accredited Investor   In the context of securities offerings, a "sophisticated" investor, such as a bank, an insurance company, an investment company, the issuer's executive officers and directors, and any person whose income or net worth exceeds certain limits.

---

11. 15 U.S.C. Section 77c(b).
12. 17 C.F.R. Sections 230.251–230.263.

KEEP IN MIND   An investor can be "sophisticated" by virtue of his or her education and experience or by investing through a knowledgeable, experienced representative.

PRIVATE PLACEMENT EXEMPTION   Private, noninvestment company offerings in unlimited amounts that are not generally solicited or advertised are exempt under Rule 506. This exemption is often referred to as the *private placement* exemption because it exempts "transactions not involving any public offering."[13] To qualify for the exemption, the issuer must believe that each unaccredited investor has sufficient knowledge or experience in financial matters to be capable of evaluating the investment's merits and risks.[14]

The private placement exemption is perhaps most important to firms that want to raise funds through the sale of securities without registering them. **EXAMPLE 24.4**   To raise capital to expand its operations, Citco Corporation decides to make a private $10 million offering of its common stock directly to two hundred accredited investors and thirty highly sophisticated, but unaccredited, investors. Citco provides all of these investors with a prospectus and material information about the firm, including its most recent financial statements. As long as Citco notifies the SEC of the sale, this offering will likely qualify for the private placement exemption. The offering is nonpublic and not generally advertised. There are fewer than thirty-five unaccredited investors, and each of them possesses sufficient knowledge and experience to evaluate the risks involved. The issuer has provided all purchasers with the material information. Thus, Citco will *not* be required to comply with the registration requirements of the Securities Act of 1933. •

RESALES   Most securities can be resold without registration. The Securities Act of 1933 provides exemptions for resales by most persons other than issuers or underwriters. The average investor who sells shares of stock does not have to file a registration statement with the SEC. Resales of restricted securities, however, trigger the registration requirements unless the party selling them complies with Rule 144 or Rule 144A. These rules are sometimes referred to as "safe harbors."

Rule 144.   Rule 144 exempts restricted securities from registration on resale if all of the following conditions are met:

1. There is adequate current public information about the issuer. ("Adequate current public information" refers to the reports that certain companies are required to file under the Securities Exchange Act of 1934.)
2. The person selling the securities has owned them for at least six months if the issuer is subject to the reporting requirements of the 1934 act.[15] If the issuer is not subject to the 1934 act's reporting requirements, the seller must have owned the securities for at least one year.
3. The securities are sold in certain limited amounts in unsolicited brokers' transactions.
4. The SEC is notified of the resale.[16]

Rule 144A.   Securities that at the time of issue are not of the same class as securities listed on a national securities exchange or quoted in a U.S. automated interdealer

---

13. 15 U.S.C. Section 77d(2).
14. 7 C.F.R. Section 230.506.
15. Before 2008, when amendments to Rule 144 became effective, the holding period was one year if the issuer was subject to the reporting requirements of the 1934 act. See the revised SEC Rules and Regulations at 72 Federal Rules 71546-01, 2007 WL 4368599, Release No. 33-8869. This reduced holding period allows non-public issuers to raise capital electronically from private and overseas sources more quickly.
16. 17 C.F.R. Section 230.144.

CONTRAST Securities do not have to be held for a specific period (six months or one year) to be exempt from registration on a resale under Rule 144A, as they do under Rule 144.

quotation system may be resold under Rule 144A.[17] They may be sold only to a qualified institutional buyer (an institution, such as an insurance company or a bank that owns and invests at least $100 million in securities). The seller must take reasonable steps to ensure that the buyer knows that the seller is relying on the exemption under Rule 144A.

Violations of the 1933 Act

It is a violation of the Securities Act of 1933 to intentionally defraud investors by misrepresenting or omitting facts in a registration statement or prospectus. Liability is also imposed on those who are negligent for not discovering the fraud. Selling securities before the effective date of the registration statement or under an exemption for which the securities do not qualify results in liability.

REMEDIES   Criminal violations are prosecuted by the U.S. Department of Justice. Violators may be fined up to $10,000, imprisoned for up to five years, or both. The SEC is authorized to seek civil sanctions against those who willfully violate the 1933 act. It can request an injunction to prevent further sales of the securities involved or ask the court to grant other relief, such as an order to a violator to refund profits. Parties who purchase securities and suffer harm as a result of false or omitted statements may also bring suits in a federal court to recover their losses and other damages.

> "The way to stop financial 'joy-riding' is to arrest the chauffeur, not the automobile."
>
> Woodrow Wilson, 1856–1924
> (Twenty-eighth president of the United States, 1913–1921)

DEFENSES   There are three basic defenses to charges of violations under the 1933 act. A defendant can avoid liability by proving that (1) the statement or omission was not material, (2) the plaintiff knew about the misrepresentation at the time of purchasing the securities, or (3) the defendant exercised *due diligence* in preparing the registration and reasonably believed at the time that the statements were true and that there were no omissions of material facts. The due diligence defense is the most important because it can be asserted by any defendant except the issuer of the securities.

The following case involved allegations of omissions of material information from an issuing company's registration statement. The defendants contended that the omissions were not material.

---

17. 17 C.F.R. Section 230.144A.

Case 24.1   **Litwin v. Blackstone Group, LP**

United States Court of Appeals, Second Circuit, 634 F.3d 706 (2011).
www.ca2.uscourts.gov[a]

BACKGROUND AND FACTS   Blackstone Group, LP, manages investments. Its corporate private equity division accounts

---

a. In the left column, click on "Decisions." On the next page, in the "Enter Docket #, Date, Party Name or find decisions that contain:" box, type "09-4426-cv" and click on "Search." In the result, click on the docket number to access the opinion (the case name is shown as *Landmen Partners, Inc. v. Blackstone Group, LP*). The U.S. Court of Appeals for the Second Circuit maintains this Web site.

for nearly 40 percent of the assets under the company's management. In preparation for an initial public offering (IPO), Blackstone filed a registration statement with the Securities and Exchange Commission (SEC). At the time, corporate private equity's investments included FGIC Corporation and Freescale Semiconductor, Inc. FGIC insured investments in subprime mortgages. Before the IPO, FGIC's customers began to suffer large losses. By the time of the IPO, this situation was generating substantial losses for FGIC and, in turn, for Blackstone. Meanwhile, Freescale had recently lost an exclusive contract to

Case 24.1–Continued

make wireless 3G chipsets for Motorola, Inc. (its largest customer). Blackstone's registration statement did not mention the impact on its revenue of the investments in FGIC and Freescale. Martin Litwin and others who invested in the IPO filed a suit in a federal district court against Blackstone and its officers, alleging material omissions from the statement. Blackstone filed a motion to dismiss, which the court granted. The plaintiffs appealed.

IN THE WORDS OF THE COURT . . .
STRAUB, Circuit Judge:
　＊＊＊＊

　Materiality is an inherently fact-specific finding that is satisfied when a plaintiff alleges a statement or omission that a reasonable investor would have considered significant in making investment decisions. ＊＊＊ However, it is not necessary to assert that the investor would have acted differently if an accurate disclosure was made. Rather, when a district court is presented with a motion [to dismiss] a complaint may not properly be dismissed on the ground that the alleged misstatements or omissions are not material unless they are so obviously unimportant to a reasonable investor that reasonable minds could not differ on the question of their importance. [Emphasis added.]
　＊＊＊＊

　In this case, the key information that plaintiffs assert should have been disclosed is whether, and to what extent, the particular known trend, event, or uncertainty might have been reasonably expected to materially affect Blackstone's investments. ＊＊＊ Plaintiffs are not seeking the disclosure of the mere fact of Blackstone's investment in FGIC, of the downward trend in the real estate market, or of Freescale's loss of its exclusive contract with Motorola. Rather, plaintiffs claim that Blackstone was required to disclose the manner in which those then-known trends, events, or uncertainties might

reasonably be expected to materially impact Blackstone's future revenues.

　＊＊＊ The question, of course, is not whether a loss in a particular investment's value will merely affect revenues, because ＊＊＊ it will almost certainly have some effect. *The relevant question is whether Blackstone reasonably expects the impact to be material.* [Emphasis added.]

　＊＊＊ Because Blackstone's Corporate Private Equity segment plays such an important role in Blackstone's business and provides value to all of its other asset management and financial advisory services, a reasonable investor would almost certainly want to know information related to that segment that Blackstone reasonably expects will have a material adverse effect on its future revenues. Therefore, the alleged ＊＊＊ omissions relating to FGIC and Freescale were plausibly material.

DECISION AND REMEDY　The U.S. Court of Appeals for the Second Circuit vacated the lower court's dismissal and remanded the case. The plaintiffs had provided sufficient allegations that Blackstone had omitted material information that it was required to disclose under the securities laws for the case to go to trial.

THE LEGAL ENVIRONMENT DIMENSION　*Litwin alleged that Blackstone had negligently omitted material information from the registration statement. What will he and the others have to show to prove their case?*

THE ECONOMIC DIMENSION　*Blackstone's IPO raised more than $4.5 billion, and the company's officers received nearly all of the net proceeds. If Blackstone had disclosed the omitted information in its registration statement, how might these results have been different?*

 ## The Securities Exchange Act of 1934

The Securities Exchange Act of 1934 provides for the regulation and registration of securities exchanges, brokers, dealers, and national securities associations, such as the National Association of Securities Dealers (NASD). Unlike the 1933 act, which is a one-time disclosure law, the 1934 act provides for continuous periodic disclosures by publicly held corporations to enable the SEC to regulate subsequent trading. For a discussion of how the Securities Exchange Act applies in the online context, see the *Online Developments* feature on the next page.

　The Securities Exchange Act of 1934 applies to companies that have assets in excess of $10 million and five hundred or more shareholders. These corporations are referred to as Section 12 companies because they are required to register their securities under Section 12 of the 1934 act. Section 12 companies are required to file reports with the SEC annually and quarterly, and sometimes even monthly if specified events occur (such as a merger). Other provisions in the 1934 act require all securities brokers and dealers to be registered, keep detailed records of their activities, and file annual reports with the SEC.

Online Developments

Corporate Blogs and Tweets Must Comply with the Securities Exchange Act

In the fast-paced world of securities trading, there is great demand for the latest information about companies, earnings, and market conditions. Corporations are meeting this demand by establishing Web sites and blogs, and using other interactive online media, such as Twitter and online shareholder forums. Nearly 20 percent of Fortune 500 companies now sponsor blogs. Corporations that use the Internet to distribute information to investors, however, must make sure that they comply with SEC regulations. For purposes of federal securities laws, the SEC treats statements by employees on online media, such as blogs and Twitter, the same as other company statements.

Beware of Tweets Containing Financial Information

Some corporate blogs include links to corporate employees' accounts on Twitter, LinkedIn, Tumblr, and similar sites so that readers can communicate directly with, and get updates from, the individual who posted the information. For example, eBay, Inc., launched its corporate blog in 2008. A few months later, Richard Brewer-Hay, a seasoned blogger whom eBay hired to report online about the company, began *tweeting* (posting updates on Twitter) about eBay's quarterly earnings and what took place at Silicon Valley technology conferences. Brewer-Hay's tweets gained him a following, but then eBay's lawyers required him to include a regulatory disclaimer with certain posts to avoid problems with the SEC. Many members of his audience were disappointed by the company's supervision, which curbed his spontaneity. Brewer-Hay is now much more reserved in his tweets on financial matters and often simply repeats eBay executives' statements verbatim.[a]

A 2008 SEC Release Provides Guidance

The reaction of eBay's lawyers to Brewer-Hay's tweets was prompted, in part, by an interpretive release issued by the SEC in

August 2008. As noted earlier, the SEC generally embraces new technology and encourages companies to use it. In the release, the SEC noted that, in some circumstances, posting information on a company's Web site may be a "sufficient method of public disclosure."

The release also acknowledged that company-sponsored blogs, shareholders' electronic forums, and other interactive Web features can be a useful means of ongoing communications between companies and their shareholders and other stakeholders. The SEC cautioned, though, that all communications made by or on behalf of a company are subject to the antifraud provisions of federal securities laws. "While blogs or forums can be informal and conversational in nature, statements made there . . . will not be treated differently from other company statements." In addition, the release stated that companies cannot require investors to waive protections under federal securities laws as a condition of participating in a blog or forum. The release also warned companies that, in some situations, they can be liable for providing hyperlinks to third party information or inaccurate summaries of financial information on their Web sites.[b]

In July 2011, an attorney for the SEC announced that the agency was going to allow disclosure of financial information through corporate blogs. The SEC will provide guidance to companies on when they can use their Web sites and blogs to disclose material information.

FOR CRITICAL ANALYSIS

Would Brewer-Hay's tweets about what had transpired at technology conferences require SEC disclosures? Why or why not?

---

a. Cari Tuna, "Corporate Blogs and 'Tweets' Must Keep SEC in Mind," *Wall Street Journal Online,* April 27, 2009: n.p. Web.

b. SEC Release Nos. 34–58288, IC–28351, File No. S7–23–08, Commission Guidance on the Use of Company Web Sites.

The act also authorizes the SEC to engage in market surveillance to deter undesirable market practices such as fraud, market manipulation (attempts at illegally influencing stock prices), and misrepresentation. In addition, the act provides for the SEC's regulation of proxy solicitations for voting (discussed in Chapter 15).

Section 10(b), SEC Rule 10b-5, and Insider Trading

SEC Rule 10b-5 A rule of the Securities and Exchange Commission that makes it unlawful, in connection with the purchase or sale of any security, to make any untrue statement of a material fact or to omit a material fact if such omission causes the statement to be misleading.

Section 10(b) is one of the more important sections of the Securities Exchange Act of 1934. This section prohibits the use of any manipulative or deceptive mechanism in violation of SEC rules and regulations. Among the rules that the SEC has promulgated pursuant to the 1934 act is **SEC Rule 10b-5,** which prohibits the commission of fraud in connection with the purchase or sale of any security.

FBI agents escort Joseph Contorinis from FBI headquarters in New York in 2009. He was accused of making several million dollars from insider tips provided by an investment banker.

(AP Photo/Louis Lanzano)

Insider Trading   The purchase or sale of securities on the basis of inside information—that is, information that has not been made available to the public.

APPLICABILITY OF SEC RULE 10B-5   SEC Rule 10b-5 applies to almost all trading of securities, whether on organized exchanges, in over-the-counter markets, or in private transactions. Generally, the rule covers just about any form of security, including, among other things, notes, bonds, agreements to form a corporation, and joint-venture agreements. The securities need not be registered under the 1933 act for the 1934 act to apply.

SEC Rule 10b-5 applies only when the requisites of federal jurisdiction—such as the use of stock exchange facilities or any means of interstate commerce—are present, but this requirement is easily met because almost every commercial transaction involves interstate contacts. In addition, the states have corporate securities laws, many of which include provisions similar to SEC Rule 10b-5.

INSIDER TRADING   One of the major goals of Section 10(b) and SEC Rule 10b-5 is to prevent so-called **insider trading,** which occurs when persons buy or sell securities on the basis of *inside information* (information that is not available to the public). Corporate directors, officers, and others such as majority shareholders, for instance, often have advance inside information that can affect the future market value of the corporate stock. Obviously, if they act on this information, their positions give them a trading advantage over the general public and other shareholders.

The 1934 Securities Exchange Act defines inside information and extends liability to those who take advantage of such information in their personal transactions when they know that the information is unavailable to those with whom they are dealing. Section 10(b) of the 1934 act and SEC Rule 10b-5 apply to anyone who has access to or receives information of a nonpublic nature on which trading is based—not just to corporate "insiders."

DISCLOSURE UNDER SEC RULE 10B-5   Any material omission or misrepresentation of material facts in connection with the purchase or sale of a security may violate not only the Securities Act of 1933 but also the antifraud provisions of Section 10(b) of the 1934 act and SEC Rule 10b-5. The key to liability (which can be civil or criminal) under Section 10(b) and SEC Rule 10b-5 is whether the insider's information is *material*.

The following are some examples of material facts calling for disclosure under SEC Rule 10b-5:

1. Fraudulent trading in the company stock by a broker-dealer.
2. A dividend change (whether up or down).
3. A contract for the sale of corporate assets.
4. A new discovery, a new process, or a new product.
5. A significant change in the firm's financial condition.
6. Potential litigation against the company.

Note that any one of these facts, by itself, is not *automatically* considered a material fact. Rather, it will be regarded as a material fact if it is significant enough that it would likely affect an investor's decision as to whether to purchase or sell the company's securities. **EXAMPLE 24.5**   Sheen, Inc., is the defendant in a class-action product liability suit that its attorney, Paula Frasier, believes that the company will lose. Frasier has advised Sheen's directors, officers, and accountants that the company will likely have to pay a substantial damages award. Sheen plans to make a $5 million offering of newly issued stock before the date when the trial is expected to end. Sheen's potential liability and the financial consequences to the firm are material facts that must be disclosed because they are significant enough to affect an investor's decision as to whether to purchase the stock. ●

The following is one of the classic cases interpreting materiality under SEC Rule 10b-5.

Classic Case 24.2   Securities and Exchange Commission v. Texas Gulf Sulphur Co.

United States Court of Appeals, Second Circuit, 401 F.2d 833 (1968).

HISTORICAL AND ENVIRONMENTAL SETTING

In 1957, the Texas Gulf Sulphur Company (TGS) began exploring for minerals in eastern Canada. In March 1959, aerial geophysical surveys were conducted over more than fifteen thousand square miles of the area. The operations revealed numerous variations in the conductivity of the rock, which indicated a remarkable concentration of commercially exploitable minerals. One site of such variations was near Timmins, Ontario. On October 29 and 30, 1963, a ground survey of the site near Timmins indicated a need to drill for further evaluation.

After sample drilling revealed potential mineral deposits, company executives made substantial stock purchases. Did they violate insider-trading laws?

BACKGROUND AND FACTS

In 1963, the Texas Gulf Sulphur Company drilled a hole that appeared to yield a core with an exceedingly high mineral content, although further drilling would be necessary to establish whether there was enough ore to be mined commercially. TGS kept secret the results of the core sample. After learning of the ore discovery, officers and employees of the company made substantial purchases of TGS's stock or accepted stock options (rights to purchase stock). On April 11, 1964, an unauthorized report of the mineral find appeared in the newspapers. On the following day, April 12, TGS issued a press release that played down the discovery and stated that it was too early to tell whether the ore find would be significant. Later on, TGS announced a strike of at least 25 million tons of ore. The news led to a substantial increase in the price of TGS stock. The Securities and Exchange Commission (SEC) brought a suit in a federal district court against the officers and employees of TGS for violating the insider-trading prohibition of SEC Rule 10b-5. The officers and employees argued that the prohibition did not apply. They reasoned that the information on which they had traded was not material, as the find had not been commercially proved. The trial court held that most of the defendants had not violated SEC Rule 10b-5, and the SEC appealed.

IN THE WORDS OF THE COURT . . .
WATERMAN, Circuit Judge.

* * * *

* * * Whether facts are material within Rule 10b-5 when the facts relate to a particular event and are undisclosed by those persons who are knowledgeable thereof *will depend at any given time upon a balancing of both the indicated probability that the event will occur and the anticipated magnitude of the event in light of the totality of the company activity. Here, * * * knowledge of the possibility, which surely was more than marginal, of the existence of a mine of the vast magnitude indicated by the remarkably rich drill core located rather close to the surface (suggesting mineability by the less expensive openpit method) within the confines of a large anomaly (suggesting an extensive region of mineralization) might well have affected the price of TGS stock and would certainly have been an important fact to a reasonable, if speculative, investor in deciding whether he should buy, sell, or hold.* [Emphasis added.]

* * * *

* * * A major factor in determining whether the * * * discovery was a material fact is the importance attached to the drilling results by those who knew about it. * * * The timing by those who knew of it of their stock purchases * * * –purchases in some cases by individuals who had never before purchased * * * TGS stock– virtually compels the inference that the insiders were influenced by the drilling results.

DECISION AND REMEDY

The appellate court ruled in favor of the SEC. All of the trading by insiders who knew of the mineral find before its true extent had been publicly announced had violated SEC Rule 10b-5.

WHAT IF THE FACTS WERE DIFFERENT?

Suppose that further drilling revealed that this site did not contain enough ore for it to be mined commercially. Would the defendants still have been liable for violating SEC Rule 10b-5? Why or why not?

IMPACT OF THIS CASE ON TODAY'S LAW

This classic case affirmed the principle that the test of whether information is "material," for SEC Rule 10b-5 purposes, is whether it would affect the judgment of reasonable investors. The corporate insiders' purchases of stock and stock options indicated that they were influenced by the results and that the information about the results was material. The courts continue to cite this case when applying SEC Rule 10b-5 to other cases of alleged insider trading.

THE PRIVATE SECURITIES LITIGATION REFORM ACT OF 1995 One of the unintended effects of SEC Rule 10b-5 was to deter the disclosure of forward-looking information. To understand why, consider an example. **EXAMPLE 24.6** QT Company announces that its projected earnings in a future time period will be a certain amount, but the forecast turns out to be wrong. The earnings are in fact much lower, and the price of QT's stock is affected—negatively. The shareholders then bring a class-action suit against the company, alleging that the directors violated SEC Rule 10b-5 by disclosing misleading financial information. ●

In an attempt to rectify this problem and promote disclosure, Congress passed the Private Securities Litigation Reform Act of 1995. The act provides a "safe harbor" for publicly held companies that make forward-looking statements, such as financial forecasts. Those who make such statements are protected against liability for securities fraud as long as the statements are accompanied by "meaningful cautionary statements identifying important factors that could cause actual results to differ materially from those in the forward-looking statement."[18]

After the 1995 act was passed, a number of securities class-action suits were filed in state courts to skirt the requirements of the 1995 federal act. In response, Congress passed the Securities Litigation Uniform Standards Act of 1998 (SLUSA).[19] The act placed stringent limits on the ability of plaintiffs to bring class-action suits in state courts against firms whose securities are traded on national stock exchanges. SLUSA not only prevents the purchasers and sellers of securities from bringing class-action fraud claims under state securities laws, but also applies to investors who are fraudulently induced to hold on to their securities.[20]

OUTSIDERS AND SEC RULE 10B-5 The traditional insider-trading case involves true insiders—corporate officers, directors, and majority shareholders who have access to (and trade on) inside information. Increasingly, however, liability under Section 10(b) of the 1934 act and SEC Rule 10b-5 has been extended to certain "outsiders"—those persons who trade on inside information acquired indirectly. Two theories have been developed under which outsiders may be held liable for insider trading: the *tipper/tippee theory* and the *misappropriation theory*.

Tipper/Tippee Theory. Anyone who acquires inside information as a result of a corporate insider's breach of his or her fiduciary duty can be liable under SEC Rule 10b-5. This liability extends to **tippees** (those who receive "tips" from insiders) and even remote tippees (tippees of tippees). At the trial of Raj Rajaratnam (mentioned at the opening of this chapter), for instance, government prosecutors presented extensive wiretap evidence that Rajaratnam had received numerous tips from corporate insiders about such matters as company earnings and pending mergers.

The key to liability under this theory is that the inside information must be obtained as a result of someone's breach of a fiduciary duty to the corporation whose shares are involved in the trading. The tippee is liable under this theory only if (1) there is a breach of a duty not to disclose inside information, (2) the disclosure is in exchange for personal benefit, and (3) the tippee knows (or should know) of this breach and benefits from it.

Tippee A person who receives inside information.

---

18. 15 U.S.C. Sections 77z-2, 78u-5.
19. Pub. L. No. 105-353. This act amended many sections of Title 15 of the *United States Code*.
20. *Merrill Lynch, Pierce, Fenner & Smith, Inc. v. Dabit,* 547 U.S. 71, 126 S.Ct. 1503, 164 L.Ed.2d 179 (2006).

Misappropriation Theory.   Liability for insider trading may also be established under the misappropriation theory. This theory holds that an individual who wrongfully obtains (misappropriates) inside information and trades on it for her or his personal gain should be held liable because, in essence, she or he stole information rightfully belonging to another.

The misappropriation theory has been controversial because it significantly extends the reach of SEC Rule 10b-5 to outsiders who ordinarily would *not* be deemed fiduciaries of the corporations in whose stock they trade. The United States Supreme Court, however, has held that liability under SEC Rule 10b-5 can be based on the misappropriation theory. It is not always wrong to disclose material, non-public information about a company to another person. Nevertheless, a person who obtains the information and trades securities on it can be liable.

CASE EXAMPLE 24.7   Patricia Rocklage was the wife of Scott Rocklage, the chair and chief executive officer of Cubist Pharmaceuticals, Inc. Scott had sometimes disclosed material, nonpublic information about Cubist to Patricia, and she had always kept the information confidential. In December 2001, however, when Scott told Patricia that one of Cubist's key drugs had failed its clinical trial and reminded her not to tell anyone, Patricia refused to keep the information secret. She then warned her brother, William Beaver, who owned Cubist stock. William sold his 5,583 Cubist shares and tipped off his friend David Jones, who sold his 7,500 shares. On January 16, 2002, Cubist publicly announced the trial results, and the price of its stock dropped. William and David had avoided losses of $99,527 and $133,222, respectively, by selling when they did. The SEC filed a lawsuit against Patricia, William, and David, alleging insider trading. The defendants claimed that because Patricia had told Scott that she was going to tell William about the failed trial, they had not "misappropriated" the information. The court, however, determined that Patricia had "engaged in deceptive devices," because she "tricked her husband into revealing confidential information to her so that she could, and did, assist her brother with the sale of his Cubist stock." The court therefore found all three defendants guilty of insider trading under the misappropriation theory.[21] ●

INSIDER REPORTING AND TRADING—SECTION 16(B)

Section 16(b) of the 1934 act provides for the recapture by the corporation of all profits realized by an insider on any purchase and sale or sale and purchase of the corporation's stock within any six-month period.[22] It is irrelevant whether the insider actually uses inside information. *All such* **short-swing profits** *must be returned to the corporation.* In this context, *insiders* means officers, directors, and large stockholders of Section 12 corporations (those owning at least 10 percent of the class of equity securities registered under Section 12 of the 1934 act). To discourage such insiders from using nonpublic information about their companies for their personal benefit in the stock market, they must file reports with the SEC concerning their ownership and trading of the corporation's securities.

Section 16(b) applies not only to stock but also to warrants, options, and securities convertible into stock. In addition, the courts have fashioned complex rules for determining profits. Note that the SEC exempts a number of transactions under Rule 16b-3.[23] For all of these reasons, corporate insiders are wise to seek specialized

Short-Swing Profits   Profits earned by a purchase and sale, or sale and purchase, of the same security within a six-month period. Under Section 16(b) of the 1934 Securities Exchange Act, these profits must be returned to the corporation if earned by company insiders from transactions in the company's stock.

---

21. *SEC v. Rocklage,* 470 F.3d 1 (1st Cir. 2006).

22. A person who expects the price of a particular stock to decline can realize profits by "selling short"—selling at a high price and repurchasing later at a lower price to cover the "short sale."

23. 17 C.F.R. Section 240.16b-3.

counsel before trading in the corporation's stock. Exhibit 24–2 below compares the effects of SEC Rule 10b-5 and Section 16(b).

Regulation of Proxy Statements

Section 14(a) of the Securities Exchange Act of 1934 regulates the solicitation of proxies (see Chapter 15) from shareholders of Section 12 companies. The SEC regulates the content of proxy statements. Whoever solicits a proxy must fully and accurately disclose in the proxy statement all of the facts that are pertinent to the matter on which the shareholders are to vote. SEC Rule 14a-9 is similar to the antifraud provisions of SEC Rule 10b-5. Remedies for violations are extensive, ranging from injunctions to prevent a vote from being taken to monetary damages.

Violations of the 1934 Act

As mentioned earlier, violations of Section 10(b) of the Securities Exchange Act of 1934 and SEC Rule 10b-5, including insider trading, may be subject to criminal or civil liability. For either criminal or civil sanctions to be imposed, however, *scienter* must exist—that is, the violator must have had an intent to defraud or knowledge of her or his misconduct (see Chapter 10). *Scienter* can be proved by showing that the defendant made false statements or wrongfully failed to disclose material facts.

Violations of Section 16(b) include the sale by insiders of stock acquired less than six months before the sale (or less than six months after the sale if selling short). These violations are subject to civil sanctions. Liability under Section 16(b) is strict liability. Neither *scienter* nor negligence is required.

• *Exhibit* **24–2** **Comparison of SEC Rule 10b-5 and Section 16(b)**

AREA OF COMPARISON	SEC RULE 10b-5	SECTION 16(b)
What is the subject matter of the transaction?	Any security (does not have to be registered).	Any security (does not have to be registered).
What transactions are covered?	Purchase or sale.	Short-swing purchase and sale or short-swing sale and purchase.
Who is subject to liability?	Almost anyone with inside information under a duty to disclose—including officers, directors, controlling shareholders, and tippees.	Officers, directors, and certain shareholders who own 10 percent or more.
Is omission or misrepresentation necessary for liability?	Yes.	No.
Are there any exempt transactions?	No.	Yes, there are a number of exemptions.
Who may bring an action?	A person transacting with an insider, the SEC, or a purchaser or seller damaged by a wrongful act.	A corporation or a shareholder by derivative action.

In the following case, the defendants were accused of securities fraud in violation of Section 10(b) and SEC Rule 10b-5. At issue was whether they had acted with *scienter*.

Case 24.3 | Gebhart v. Securities and Exchange Commission

United States Court of Appeals, Ninth Circuit, 595 F.3d 1034 (2010).
www.ca9.uscourts.gov/opinions[a]

Can the Securities and Exchange Commission successfully prosecute financial advisers who do not investigate investments fully?

BACKGROUND AND FACTS

Alvin Gebhart worked at Mutual of New York (MONY), where he sold annuities and mutual funds. Jack Archer, a fellow MONY salesperson, told Gebhart about Community Service Group (CSG)—a business venture that purchased mobile home parks, converted them to resident ownership, and assisted residents in purchasing them. MHP Conversions, LLC, which was created to facilitate the conversion process, issued promissory notes that were sold to individual investors to raise funds for CSG's purchase of the parks. Each note stated that it would "ultimately be secured by a deed of trust" on the particular park to be purchased with the funds. In 1996, Gebhart moved from MONY to Mutual Service Corporation (MSC), a broker-dealer and member of the National Association of Securities Dealers (NASD). His wife, Donna Gebhart, joined him at MSC. Over the next several years, the Gebharts, on Archer's recommendation, sold nearly $2.4 million in MHP promissory notes to forty-five of their clients, who bought the notes based on the Gebharts' positive statements about the investment. It became obvious later that these statements were false. The Gebharts had failed to disclose that their statements were based on information provided by Archer rather than their own, independent investigation. At the time of MHP's collapse, the Gebharts' clients had more than $1.5 million invested in outstanding MHP notes. The Gebharts were fired, and in 2002, the NASD filed a complaint against them for securities fraud. A NASD hearing panel found that the Gebharts had acted in good faith and rejected the fraud charges, but the NASD National Adjudicatory Council (NAC) reversed. The NAC found that the Gebharts had committed fraud, imposed a lifetime bar on Alvin Gebhart, and imposed a one-year suspension and a $15,000 fine on Donna Gebhart. The Securities and Exchange Commission (SEC) upheld the NAC's

ruling, and the Gebharts petitioned a federal appellate court to review the SEC's decision.

IN THE WORDS OF THE COURT . . .
FISHER, Circuit Judge.
* * * *

To establish a violation of Section 10(b) and Rule 10b-5, the SEC is required to "show that there has been a misstatement or omission of material fact, made with *scienter*." "The plaintiffs may establish scienter by proving either actual knowledge or recklessness."
* * * *

Scienter * * * *is a subjective inquiry. It turns on the defendant's actual state of mind. Thus, although we may consider the objective unreasonableness of the defendant's conduct to raise an inference of scienter, the ultimate question is whether the defendant knew his or her statements were false, or was consciously reckless as to their truth or falsity.* [Emphasis added.]
* * * *

The Gebharts contend that the SEC applied an erroneous *scienter* standard in this case by focusing exclusively on * * * objective inquiry and disregarding evidence of subjective good faith. We disagree. The SEC considered all of the evidence bearing on the Gebharts' actual state of mind, including the Gebharts' extreme departure from ordinary standards of care, and found that the Gebharts were consciously aware of the risk that their statements were false. There was no error.

The SEC certainly considered the objective unreasonableness of the Gebharts' actions as *part* of its analysis. The SEC found that the Gebharts failed to perform any meaningful investigation into the MHP promissory notes—an extreme departure from ordinary standards of care that "created the substantial [and obvious] risk * * * that their representations were not true." The SEC found that the Gebharts "made no effort to investigate or understand why their clients were being sold second (and not first) deeds of trust; no effort to identify the first trust deed holders or the amounts of those outstanding trust deeds; and no effort to ensure their clients' investments were actually being secured by recorded trust deeds." The Gebharts made "no effort" to corroborate Archer's representations that the parks were not overly encumbered.

The SEC properly considered the objective unreasonableness of the Gebharts' actions as some evidence supporting the inference that the Gebharts acted with *scienter,* but did not treat it as dispositive [a deciding factor]. The * * * [SEC] evaluated "the evidence the Gebharts put forward to demonstrate their good faith beliefs" as "part of the

---

a. On the page that opens, select the "Advanced Search" mode and enter "08-74943" in the "by Case No.:" box. Then click on "Search." In the search results, click on the case title to access the opinion. The U.S. Court of Appeals for the Ninth Circuit maintains this Web site.

Case 24.3–Continued

complete mix of facts bearing on an evaluation of their [actual] state of mind" and concluded that the "evidence from the Gebharts about their subjective belief was not sufficient to overcome" the inference of *scienter* created by the evidence as a whole. The Gebharts' assertions of good faith were "not plausible" and lacked "credibility." Based on the evidence as a whole, the SEC determined that the Gebharts "knew they had no direct knowledge of the truth or falsity" of their statements, and made their statements "despite not knowing whether they were true or false." The SEC correctly applied the appropriate *scienter* standard.

DECISION AND REMEDY   The U.S. Court of Appeals for the Ninth Circuit upheld the SEC's decision. The Gebharts had acted

with *scienter* and had thus committed securities fraud in violation of Section 10(b) and Rule 10b-5.

THE LEGAL ENVIRONMENT DIMENSION   *At one point in the opinion, the court noted that "there is no evidence in the record that the Gebharts ever intended to defraud anyone." Why, then, did the court conclude that the Gebharts had acted with* scienter?

THE POLITICAL DIMENSION   *According to the court, if the evidence before an agency is "susceptible to more than one rational interpretation," the court "may not substitute its judgment for that of the agency." Why do the courts show such deference to agency rulings?*

CRIMINAL PENALTIES   For violations of Section 10(b) and Rule 10b-5, an individual may be fined up to $5 million, imprisoned for up to twenty years, or both. A partnership or a corporation may be fined up to $25 million. Under Section 807 of the Sarbanes-Oxley Act of 2002, for a *willful* violation of the 1934 act the violator may be imprisoned for up to twenty-five years in addition to being subject to a fine.

For a defendant to be convicted in a criminal prosecution under the securities laws, there can be no reasonable doubt that the defendant knew he or she was acting wrongfully—a jury is not allowed merely to speculate that the defendant may have acted willfully.

CASE EXAMPLE 24.8   Martha Stewart, founder of a well-known media and homemaking empire, was charged with intentionally deceiving investors based on public statements she made. In 2001, Stewart's stockbroker allegedly had informed Stewart that the head of ImClone Systems, Inc., was selling his shares in that company. Stewart then sold her ImClone shares. The next day, ImClone announced that the U.S. Food and Drug Administration had failed to approve Erbitux, the company's greatly anticipated medication. After the government began investigating Stewart's ImClone trades, she publicly stated that she had previously instructed her stockbroker to sell her ImClone stock if the price fell to $60 per share. The government then filed a lawsuit, claiming that Stewart's statement showed she had the intent to deceive investors. The court, however, acquitted Stewart on this charge because "to find the essential element of criminal intent beyond a reasonable doubt, a rational juror would have to speculate."[24] ●

CIVIL SANCTIONS   The SEC can also bring suit in a federal district court against anyone violating or aiding in a violation of the 1934 act or SEC rules by purchasing or selling a security while in the possession of material nonpublic information.[25] The violation must occur on or through the facilities of a national securities exchange or from or through a broker or dealer. The court may assess a penalty for as much as triple the profits gained or the loss avoided by the guilty party. The Insider Trading and Securities Fraud Enforcement Act of 1988 enlarged the class of persons who

---

24. *United States v. Stewart,* 305 F.Supp.2d 368 (S.D.N.Y. 2004).
25. The Insider Trading Sanctions Act of 1984, 15 U.S.C. Section 78u(d)(2)(A), (C).

may be subject to civil liability for insider trading and gave the SEC authority to give monetary rewards to informants.[26]

Private parties may also sue violators of Section 10(b) and Rule 10b-5. A private party may obtain rescission (cancellation) of a contract to buy securities or damages to the extent of the violator's illegal profits. Those found liable have a right to seek contribution from those who share responsibility for the violations, including accountants, attorneys, and corporations. For violations of Section 16(b), a corporation can bring an action to recover the short-swing profits.

▶ State Securities Laws

BE AWARE   Federal securities laws do not take priority over state securities laws.

Today, every state has its own corporate securities laws, or blue sky laws, that regulate the offer and sale of securities within its borders. The phrase *blue sky laws* dates to a 1917 decision by the United States Supreme Court in which the Court declared that the purpose of such laws was to prevent "speculative schemes which have no more basis than so many feet of 'blue sky.'"[27] Article 8 of the Uniform Commercial Code, which has been adopted by all of the states, also imposes various requirements relating to the purchase and sale of securities.

Requirements under State Securities Laws

Typically, state laws have disclosure requirements and antifraud provisions, many of which are patterned after Section 10(b) of the Securities Exchange Act of 1934 and SEC Rule 10b-5. State laws also provide for the registration of securities offered or issued for sale within the state and impose disclosure requirements. Methods of registration, required disclosures, and exemptions from registration vary among states. Unless an exemption from registration is applicable, issuers must register or qualify their stock with the appropriate state official, often called a *corporations commissioner.* Additionally, most state securities laws regulate securities brokers and dealers.

Concurrent Regulation

State securities laws apply mainly to intrastate transactions. Since the adoption of the 1933 and 1934 federal securities acts, the state and federal governments have regulated securities concurrently. Issuers must comply with both federal and state securities laws, and exemptions from federal law are not exemptions from state laws.

The dual federal and state system has not always worked well, particularly during the early 1990s, when the securities markets underwent considerable expansion. In response, Congress passed the National Securities Markets Improvement Act of 1996, which eliminated some of the duplicate regulations and gave the SEC exclusive power to regulate most national securities activities. The National Conference of Commissioners on Uniform State Laws then substantially revised the Uniform Securities Act to coordinate state and federal securities regulation and enforcement efforts. The new version was offered to the states for adoption in 2002. Seventeen states have adopted the Uniform Securities Act, and other states are considering its adoption.[28]

---

26. 15 U.S.C. Section 78u-1.

27. *Hall v. Geiger-Jones Co.,* 242 U.S. 539, 37 S.Ct. 217, 61 L.Ed. 480 (1917).

28. At the time this book went to press, the Uniform Securities Act had been adopted in Georgia, Hawaii, Idaho, Indiana, Iowa, Kansas, Maine, Michigan, Minnesota, Mississippi, Missouri, New Mexico, Oklahoma, South Carolina, South Dakota, Vermont, and Wisconsin, as well as in the U.S. Virgin Islands. You can find current information on state adoptions at www.nccusl.com.

Beyond Our Borders | Corporate Governance in Other Nations

Corporate governance has become an issue of concern not only for U.S. corporations, but also for corporate entities around the world. With the globalization of business, a corporation's bad acts (or lack of control systems) can have far-reaching consequences. Different models of corporate governance exist, often depending on the degree of capitalism in the particular nation. In the United States,

corporate governance tends to give priority to shareholders' interests. This approach encourages significant innovation and cost and quality competition.

In contrast, the coordinated model of governance that prevails in continental Europe and Japan considers the interests of so-called stakeholders—employees, managers, suppliers, customers, and the community—to be a priority. The

coordinated model still encourages innovation and cost and quality competition, but not to the same extent as the U.S. model.

For Critical Analysis
Why does the presence of a capitalist system affect a nation's perspective on corporate governance?

▶ Corporate Governance

Corporate Governance A set of policies or procedures affecting the way a corporation is directed or controlled.

Corporate governance can be narrowly defined as the relationship between a corporation and its shareholders. Some argue for a broader definition—that corporate governance specifies the rights and responsibilities among different participants in the corporation, such as the board of directors, managers, shareholders, and other stakeholders, and spells out the rules and procedures for making decisions on corporate affairs. Regardless of the way it is defined, effective corporate governance requires more than just compliance with laws and regulations. (For a discussion of corporate governance in other nations, see this chapter's *Beyond Our Borders* feature above.)

Effective corporate governance is essential in large corporations because corporate ownership (by shareholders) is separated from corporate control (by officers and managers). Under these circumstances, officers and managers may attempt to advance their own interests at the expense of the shareholders. The well-publicized corporate scandals in the early 2000s clearly illustrate the reasons for concern about managerial opportunism.

Attempts at Aligning the Interests of Officers with Those of Shareholders

Stock Option A right to buy a given number of shares of stock at a set price, usually within a specified time period.

These protesters were demonstrating against benefits and stock options granted to Toll Brothers, Inc., founding chairman and chief executive Robert Toll.

Some corporations have sought to align the financial interests of their officers with those of the company's shareholders by providing the officers with **stock options,** which enable them to purchase shares of the corporation's stock at a set price. When the market price rises above that level, the officers can sell their shares for a profit. Because a stock's market price generally increases as the corporation prospers, the options give the officers a financial stake in the corporation's well-being and supposedly encourage them to work hard for the benefit of the shareholders.

Options have turned out to be an imperfect device for providing effective governance, however. Executives in some companies have been tempted to "cook" the company's books in order to keep share prices higher so that they could sell their stock for a profit. Executives in other corporations have experienced no losses when share prices dropped. Instead, their options were

(AP Photo/Matt Rourke)

"repriced" so that they did not suffer from the share price decline and could still profit from future increases above the lowered share price. Thus, although stock options theoretically can motivate officers to protect shareholder interests, stock option plans have often become a way for officers to take advantage of shareholders.

With stock options generally failing to work as planned and numerous headline-making scandals occurring within major corporations, there has been an outcry for more "outside" directors (those with no formal employment affiliation with the company). The theory is that independent directors will more closely monitor the actions of corporate officers. Hence, today we see more boards with outside directors. Note, though, that outside directors may not be truly independent of corporate officers—they may be friends or business associates of the leading officers.

The Goal Is to Promote Accountability

Effective corporate governance standards are designed to address problems (such as those briefly discussed above) and to motivate officers to make decisions that promote the financial interests of the company's shareholders. Generally, corporate governance entails corporate decision-making structures that monitor employees (particularly officers) to ensure that they are acting for the benefit of the shareholders. Thus, corporate governance involves, at a minimum:

1. The audited reporting of financial progress at the corporation, so managers can be evaluated.
2. Legal protections for shareholders, so violators of the law, who attempt to take advantage of shareholders, can be punished for misbehavior and victims may recover damages for any associated losses.

Effective corporate governance can have considerable practical significance because corporate decision makers necessarily become more accountable for their actions to shareholders. Firms that are more accountable to shareholders typically report higher profits, higher sales growth, higher firm value, and other economic advantages. Thus, a corporation with better corporate governance and greater accountability to investors may also have a higher valuation than a corporation that is less concerned about governance.

Governance and Corporate Law

State corporation statutes set up the legal framework for corporate governance. Under the corporate law of Delaware, where most major companies incorporate, all corporations must have certain structures of corporate governance in place. The most important structure, of course, is the board of directors because the board makes the major decisions about the future of the corporation.

Some argue that shareholder democracy is the key to improving corporate governance. If shareholders could have more say on major corporate decisions, they presumably could have more control over the corporation. Essential to shareholder democracy is the election of the board of directors, usually at the corporation's annual meeting.

Although shareholders vote for directors, they often find it difficult to elect their nominees because organizing enough shareholders to sway an election can be very costly. In 2010, the SEC announced that it would work to modernize shareholder voting and proxy rules to reduce these costs and give shareholders direct access to other shareholders through the company's facilities for communicating with shareholders. The SEC's goal is to make the contest more even between the shareholders' candidates and the company's nominees.

"Honesty is the single most important factor having a direct bearing on the final success of an individual, a corporation, or a product."

Ed McMahon, 1923–2009
(American entertainer)

THE BOARD OF DIRECTORS   Under corporate law, a corporation must have a board of directors elected by the shareholders. Almost anyone can become a director, though some organizations, such as the New York Stock Exchange, require certain standards of service for directors of their listed corporations.

Directors are responsible for ensuring that the corporation's officers are operating wisely and in the exclusive interest of shareholders. The directors receive reports from the officers and give them managerial directions. In reality, though, corporate directors devote a relatively small amount of time to monitoring officers.

Ideally, shareholders would monitor the directors' supervision of the officers. In practice, however, it can be difficult for shareholders to monitor directors and hold them responsible for corporate failings. Although the directors can be sued for failing to do their jobs effectively, directors are rarely held personally liable.

THE AUDIT COMMITTEE   A crucial committee of the board of directors is the *audit committee,* which oversees the corporation's accounting and financial reporting processes, including both internal and outside auditors. Unless the committee members have sufficient expertise and are willing to spend the time to carefully examine the corporation's accounts, however, the audit committee may be ineffective.

The audit committee also oversees the corporation's "internal controls," which are the measures taken to ensure that reported results are accurate. They are carried out largely by the company's internal auditing staff. As an example, these controls help to determine whether a corporation's debts are collectible. If the debts are not collectible, it is up to the audit committee to make sure that the corporation's financial officers do not simply pretend that payment will eventually be made. (The *Linking the Law to Taxation* feature on page 702 discusses how corporations, at least during the next few years, might benefit from *deleveraging,* or repurchasing, their debts.)

THE COMPENSATION COMMITTEE   Another important committee of the board of directors is the *compensation committee.* This committee monitors and determines the compensation the company's officers are paid. As part of this process, the committee is responsible for assessing the officers' performance and for designing a compensation system that will better align the officers' interests with those of shareholders.

The Sarbanes-Oxley Act of 2002

As discussed in Chapter 2, in 2002 following a series of corporate scandals, Congress passed the Sarbanes-Oxley Act. The act separately addresses certain issues relating to corporate governance. Generally, the act attempts to increase corporate accountability by imposing strict disclosure requirements and harsh penalties for violations of securities laws. Among other things, the act requires chief corporate executives to take responsibility for the accuracy of financial statements and reports that are filed with the SEC.

Additionally, the act requires that certain financial and stock-transaction reports be filed with the SEC earlier than was required under the previous rules. The act also created a new entity, called the Public Company Accounting Oversight Board, which regulates and oversees public accounting firms. Other provisions of the act establish private civil actions and expand the SEC's remedies in administrative and civil actions.

Michael Oxley is a former member of the U.S. House of Representatives and vice president of the NASDAQ, the over-the-counter stock exchange. When in Congress, he cosponsored legislation that imposed large compliance costs on publicly held companies. What is the name of that legislation?

(Fred Prouser/Reuters/Landov)

Because of the importance of this act for corporate leaders and for those dealing with securities transactions, we present excerpts and explanatory comments in Appendix D at the end of this text. We also highlight some of its key provisions relating to corporate accountability in Exhibit 24–3 below.

MORE INTERNAL CONTROLS AND ACCOUNTABILITY The Sarbanes-Oxley Act includes some traditional securities law provisions but also introduces direct *federal* corporate governance requirements for public companies (companies whose shares are traded in the public securities markets). The law addresses many of the corporate governance procedures just discussed and creates new requirements in an attempt to make the system work more effectively. The requirements deal with independent monitoring of company officers by both the board of directors and auditors.

Sections 302 and 404 of Sarbanes-Oxley require high-level managers (the most senior officers) to establish and maintain an effective system of internal controls. Moreover, senior management must reassess the system's effectiveness annually. Some companies already had strong and effective internal control systems in place

---

● *Exhibit* 24–3 **Some Key Provisions of the Sarbanes-Oxley Act of 2002 Relating to Corporate Accountability**

Certification Requirements—Under Section 906 of the Sarbanes-Oxley Act, the chief executive officers (CEOs) and chief financial officers (CFOs) of most major companies listed on public stock exchanges must certify financial statements that are filed with the SEC. CEOs and CFOs have to certify that filed financial reports "fully comply" with SEC requirements and that all of the information reported "fairly represents in all material respects, the financial conditions and results of operations of the issuer."

Under Section 302 of the act, CEOs and CFOs of reporting companies are required to certify that a signing officer reviewed each quarterly and annual filing with the SEC and that it contains no untrue statements of material fact. Also, the signing officer or officers must certify that they have established an internal control system to identify all material information and that any deficiencies in the system were disclosed to the auditors.

Effectiveness of Internal Controls on Financial Reporting—Under Section 404(a), all public companies are required to assess the effectiveness of their internal control over financial reporting. Section 404(b) requires independent auditors to report on management's assessment of internal controls, but companies with a public float of less than $75 million are exempted from this requirement.

Loans to Directors and Officers—Section 402 prohibits any reporting company, as well as any private company that is filing an initial public offering, from making personal loans to directors and executive officers (with a few limited exceptions, such as for certain consumer and housing loans).

Protection for Whistleblowers—Section 806 protects "whistleblowers"—employees who report ("blow the whistle" on) securities violations by their employers—from being fired or in any way discriminated against by their employers.

Blackout Periods—Section 306 prohibits certain types of securities transactions during "blackout periods"—periods during which the issuer's ability to purchase, sell, or otherwise transfer funds in individual account plans (such as pension funds) is suspended.

Enhanced Penalties for—

- *Violations of Section 906 Certification Requirements*—A CEO or CFO who certifies a financial report or statement filed with the SEC knowing that the report or statement does not fulfill all of the requirements of Section 906 will be subject to criminal penalties of up to $1 million in fines, ten years in prison, or both. *Willful* violators of the certification requirements may be subject to $5 million in fines, twenty years in prison, or both.

- *Violations of the Securities Exchange Act of 1934*—Penalties for securities fraud under the 1934 act were also increased (as discussed earlier in this chapter). Individual violators may be fined up to $5 million, imprisoned for up to twenty years, or both. *Willful* violators may be imprisoned for up to twenty-five years in addition to being fined.

- *Destruction or Alteration of Documents*—Anyone who alters, destroys, or conceals documents or otherwise obstructs any official proceeding will be subject to fines, imprisonment for up to twenty years, or both.

- *Other Forms of White-Collar Crime*—The act stiffened the penalties for certain criminal violations, such as federal mail and wire fraud, and ordered the U.S. Sentencing Commission to revise the sentencing guidelines for white-collar crimes (see Chapter 6).

Statute of Limitations for Securities Fraud—Section 804 provides that a private right of action for securities fraud may be brought no later than two years after the discovery of the violation or five years after the violation, whichever is earlier.

before the passage of the act, but others had to take expensive steps to bring their internal controls up to the new federal standard. These include "disclosure controls and procedures" to ensure that company financial reports are accurate and timely. Assessment must include the documenting of financial results and accounting policies before reporting the results. After the act was passed, hundreds of companies reported that they had identified and corrected shortcomings in their internal control systems.

The 2002 act initially required all public companies to have an independent auditor file a report with the SEC on management's assessment of internal controls. Congress, however, enacted an exemption for smaller companies in 2010 in an effort to reduce compliance costs. Public companies with a market capitalization, or public float, of less than $75 million no longer need to have an auditor report on management's assessment of internal controls.

CERTIFICATION AND MONITORING REQUIREMENTS   Section 906 requires that chief executive officers and chief financial officers certify that the information in the corporate financial statements "fairly represents in all material respects, the financial conditions and results of operations of the issuer." These corporate officers are subject to both civil and criminal penalties for violation of this section. This requirement makes officers directly accountable for the accuracy of their financial reporting and avoids any "ignorance defense" if shortcomings are later discovered.

Sarbanes-Oxley also includes requirements to improve directors' monitoring of officers' activities. All members of the corporate audit committee for public companies must be outside directors. The New York Stock Exchange (NYSE) has a similar rule that also extends to the board's compensation committee. The audit committee must have a written charter that sets out its duties and provides for performance appraisal. At least one "financial expert" must serve on the audit committee, which must hold executive meetings without company officers being present. The audit committee must establish procedures to encourage "whistleblowers" to report violations. In addition to reviewing the internal controls, the committee also monitors the actions of the outside auditor.

> "*Make money your God and it will plague you like the devil.*"
> Henry Fielding, 1707–1754
> (English author)

▶ Online Securities Fraud and Ponzi Schemes

A major problem facing the SEC today is how to enforce the antifraud provisions of the securities laws in the online environment. In 1999, in the first cases involving illegal online securities offerings, the SEC filed suit against three individuals for illegally offering securities on an Internet auction site. In essence, all three indicated that their companies would go public soon and attempted to sell unregistered securities via the Web auction site. All of these actions were in violation of Sections 5, 17(a)(1), and 17(a)(3) of the 1933 Securities Act. Since then, the SEC has brought a variety of Internet-related fraud cases and regularly issues interpretive releases to explain how securities laws apply in the online environment.

Online Investment Scams

An ongoing problem is how to curb online investment scams. As discussed in Chapter 6, the Internet has created a new vehicle for criminals to use to commit fraud and has provided them with new ways of targeting innocent investors. The criminally inclined can use spam, online newsletters and bulletin boards, chat rooms, blogs, and tweets to spread false information and perpetrate fraud. For a relatively small cost, criminals can even build sophisticated Web pages to facilitate their investment scams.

FRAUDULENT E-MAILS   There are countless variations of online investment scams, most of which promise spectacular returns for small investments. A person might receive spam e-mail, for example, that falsely claims a home business can "turn $5 into $60,000 in just three to six weeks." Another popular investment scam claims "your stimulus package has arrived" and promises you can make $100,000 a year using your home computer. Although most people today are dubious of the bogus claims made in spam messages, such offers can be more attractive during times of economic recession. Often, investment scams are simply the electronic version of pyramid schemes in which the participants attempt to profit solely by recruiting new participants.

ONLINE INVESTMENT NEWSLETTERS AND FORUMS   Hundreds of online investment newsletters provide free information on stocks. Legitimate online newsletters can help investors gather valuable information, but some of these newsletters are used for fraud. The law allows companies to pay people who write these newsletters to tout their securities, but the newsletters are required to disclose who paid for the advertising. Many fraudsters either fail to disclose or lie about who paid them. Thus, an investor reading an online newsletter may believe that the information is unbiased, when in fact the fraudsters will directly profit by convincing investors to buy or sell particular stocks.

The same deceptive tactics can be used on online bulletin boards (such as newsgroups and usenet groups), blogs, and social networking sites, including Twitter. While hiding their true identity, fraudsters may falsely pump up a company or reveal some "inside" information about a new product or lucrative contract to convince people to invest. By using multiple aliases on an online forum, a single person can easily create the illusion of widespread interest in a small stock.

Hacking into Online Stock Accounts

Millions of people now buy and sell investments online through online brokerage companies such as E*Trade and TD Ameritrade. Sophisticated hackers have learned to use online investing to their advantage. By installing keystroke-monitoring software on computer terminals in public places, such as hotels, libraries, and airports, hackers can gain access to online account information. All they have to do is wait for a person to access an online trading account and then monitor the next several dozen keystrokes to determine the customer's account number and password. Once they have the log-in information, they can access the customer's account and liquidate her or his existing stock holdings.

The hackers then use the customer's funds to purchase thinly traded, microcap securities, also known as penny stocks. The goal is to boost the price of a stock that the hacker has already purchased at a lower price. Then, when the stock price goes up, the hacker sells all the stock and wires the funds to either an offshore account or a dummy corporation, making it difficult for the SEC to trace the transactions and prosecute the offender.

EXAMPLE 24.9   Aleksey Kamardin, a twenty-one-year-old Florida college student, purchased 55,000 shares of stock in Fuego Entertainment using an E*Trade account in his own name. Kamardin then hacked into other customers' accounts at E*Trade and other brokerage companies, and used their funds to purchase a total of 458,000 shares of Fuego stock. When the stock price rose from $0.88 per share to $1.28 per share, Kamardin sold all of his shares, making a profit of $9,164.28 in about three hours. Kamardin did this with other thinly traded stocks as well, allegedly making $82,960 in about five weeks. The SEC filed charges against him, and he was later ordered to return the profits, plus interest. ●

Ponzi Schemes

In recent years, the SEC has filed an increasing number of enforcement actions against perpetrators of *Ponzi schemes* (see page 31). In these scams, the fraudster promises high returns to investors and then uses their funds to pay previous investors. In 2009, Bernie Madoff was convicted of bilking investors out of more than $65 billion in the largest Ponzi scheme to date.

OFFSHORE FRAUD   Ponzi schemes sometimes target U.S. residents and convince them to invest in offshore companies or banks. **EXAMPLE 24.10** Texas billionaire R. Allen Stanford, of the Stanford Financial Group, was indicted for allegedly orchestrating a $7 billion scheme to defraud more than five thousand investors. For about ten years, Stanford advised clients to buy certificates of deposit with improbably high interest rates from his Antigua-based Stanford International Bank. Some early investors were paid returns from the funds provided by later investors, but Stanford allegedly used $1.6 billion of the funds for personal expenditures. He also falsified financial statements that were filed with the SEC and reportedly paid more than $100,000 in bribes to an Antigua official to ensure that the bank would not be audited. ●

"RISK-FREE" FRAUD   Another type of fraud scheme offers risk-free or low-risk investments to lure investors. **EXAMPLE 24.11** For several years, Michael C. Regan used his firm to fraudulently obtain at least $15.9 million from dozens of investors by selling securities in his River Stream Fund. Regan told investors that he had a proven track record of successful securities trading and showed them falsified financial documents with artificially high account balances. In reality, Regan was not a registered investment adviser and had suffered substantial investment losses. Regan promised investors returns averaging 20 percent with minimal risk to their principal and claimed to be using an investment strategy based on "short-term price trends." He used less than half of the funds entrusted to him for trading purposes and personally spent at least $2.4 million. In 2009, the SEC filed a complaint and Regan agreed to settle the case and return more than $8.7 million of the wrongfully acquired funds. ●

 Reviewing . . . Investor Protection and Corporate Governance

Dale Emerson served as the chief financial officer for Reliant Electric Company, a distributor of electricity serving portions of Montana and North Dakota. Reliant was in the final stages of planning a takeover of Dakota Gasworks, Inc., a natural gas distributor that operated solely within North Dakota. Emerson went on a weekend fishing trip with his uncle, Ernest Wallace. Emerson mentioned to Wallace that he had been putting in a lot of extra hours at the office planning a takeover of Dakota Gasworks. When he returned from the fishing trip, Wallace purchased $20,000 worth of Reliant stock. Three weeks later, Reliant made a tender offer to Dakota Gasworks stockholders and purchased 57 percent of Dakota Gasworks stock. Over the next two weeks, the price of Reliant stock rose 72 percent before leveling out. Wallace then sold his Reliant stock for a gross profit of $14,400. Using the information presented in the chapter, answer the following questions.

(Continued)

1. Would registration with the SEC be required for Dakota Gasworks securities? Why or why not?
2. Did Emerson violate Section 10(b) of the Securities Exchange Act of 1934 and SEC Rule 10b-5? Why or why not?
3. What theory or theories might a court use to hold Wallace liable for insider trading?
4. Under the Sarbanes-Oxley Act of 2002, who would be required to certify the accuracy of financial statements filed with the SEC?

Linking the Law *to Taxation*

The Tax Consequences of Deleveraging during an Economic Crisis

Part of corporate governance involves making sure that the corporation effectively examines trade-offs involved in any future action. When corporate boards or upper management makes decisions, those decisions affect employees, customers, and shareholders. In a time of economic crisis, *deleveraging,* or repurchasing debt, is one possible action that a corporation may take to reduce its debt.

Why Companies Leverage

Corporations engage in leveraging—borrowing on a large scale in order to make additional investments—particularly in boom times. Leverage in capital structure is neither good nor bad. Companies in volatile industries avoid taking on too much debt, but other companies have found that debt is an important part of their capital structure. In any event, corporations have to be flexible in their ratio of debt to equity as market conditions change.

Recessions, such as the one that began in 2008, create uncertainty. Uncertainty is the enemy of capital markets. Formerly routine credit transactions become unavailable, even to solvent firms, and companies that have leveraged—have large debt loads—may find that credit has disappeared altogether. Suppliers may refuse to ship goods to such corporations unless they agree to pay cash on delivery. This pessimism ripples through the economy. Today, not only have auto manufacturers suffered, but so too have community hospitals, restaurants, hotels, and a host of firms in other industries.

The Downside of Deleveraging

Many corporations' publicly traded debt instruments have been selling at very deep discounts. One way for a company to improve its balance sheet and to reassure suppliers that it will be able to pay its bills is to retire that debt (at deep discounts). Some corporations could do this by issuing additional shares of stock to obtain the financing for such debt retirement. Moreover, repurchasing corporate debt may be a beneficial use of cash for corporations

when consumer demand slows and alternative capital investments do not offer immediate returns.

Until 2009, however, corporate finance officers faced a daunting cost for such debt retirement plans. Under tax code and regulatory changes made in the 1980s, the difference between the original issue price of debt and the lower price for which it was repurchased was treated as taxable income. Finance managers call this a tax liability on "phantom income" (calculated as the difference between the issued price and the repurchase price of corporate debt). Such tax liabilities have prevented many corporations from necessary capital restructuring. Additionally, the tax liability on phantom income helped to create a perverse preference for bankruptcy. To avoid the tax liability, a heavily leveraged firm might choose bankruptcy over debt retirement even though bankruptcy destroys asset values, customer relations, and, most of all, jobs.

A New Tax Incentive for Finance Managers to Consider

In 2009, as part of the economic stimulus bill, the Obama administration created a new tax break that applies to the retirement of heavily discounted debt instruments by corporations. Under this provision, tax liabilities on phantom income will not trigger corporate income taxes until 2014. At that time, corporations that have retired discounted debt will be able to spread out their tax liabilities over a five-year period.

Soon after, homebuilder Hovnanian Enterprises paid $105 million to repurchase $315 million of its unsecured debt. That $210 million of phantom income will not be taxable until 2014. At about the same time, GE Capital, a unit of General Electric, offered to buy back $1.46 billion of its bonds.

FOR CRITICAL ANALYSIS

If you were a finance manager in a large corporation, under what circumstances might you argue that the corporation should deleverage?

Key Terms

accredited investor 682
corporate governance 695
free-writing prospectus 680
insider trading 687
investment company 682

investment contract 677
mutual fund 682
prospectus 679
SEC Rule 10b-5 686
security 676

short-swing profits 690
stock option 695
tippee 689

 Chapter Summary: Investor Protection and Corporate Governance

The Securities Act of 1933 (See pages 677–685.)	Prohibits fraud and stabilizes the securities industry by requiring disclosure of all essential information relating to the issuance of securities to the investing public. 1. *Prospectus*—The issuer must provide investors with a *prospectus* that describes the security being sold, the issuing corporation, and the risk attaching to the security. 2. *Registration requirements*—Securities, unless exempt, must be registered with the SEC before being offered to the public. The *registration statement* must include detailed financial information about the issuing corporation; the intended use of the proceeds of the securities being issued; and certain disclosures, such as interests of directors or officers and pending lawsuits. 3. *Exemptions*—The SEC has exempted certain offerings from the requirements of the Securities Act of 1933. Exemptions may be based on the size of the issue, whether the offering is private or public, and whether advertising is involved. Exemptions are summarized in Exhibit 24–1 on page 681. 4. *Violations*—Intentionally defrauding investors by misrepresenting or omitting facts in the registration statement or prospectus is a violation of the 1933 act.

The Securities Exchange Act of 1934 (See pages 685–694.)	Provides for the regulation and registration of securities exchanges, brokers, dealers, and national securities associations (such as the NASD). Maintains a continuous disclosure system for all corporations with securities on the securities exchanges and for those companies that have assets in excess of $10 million and five hundred or more shareholders (Section 12 companies).
	 1. *SEC Rule 10b-5 [under Section 10(b) of the 1934 act]*–
	   a. Applies to almost all trading of securities—a firm's securities do not have to be registered under the 1933 act for the 1934 act to apply.
	   b. Applies only when the requisites of federal jurisdiction (such as use of the mails, stock exchange facilities, or any facility of interstate commerce) are present.
	   c. Applies to insider trading by corporate officers, directors, majority shareholders, and any persons receiving inside information (information not available to the public) who base their trading on this information.
	   d. Liability for violations can be civil or criminal.
	   e. May be violated by failing to disclose "material facts" that must be disclosed under this rule.
	   f. Liability may be based on the tipper/tippee or the misappropriation theory.
	 2. *Insider trading [under Section 16(b) of the 1934 act]*—To prevent corporate insiders from taking advantage of inside information, the 1934 act requires officers, directors, and shareholders owning 10 percent or more of the issued stock of a corporation to turn over to the corporation all short-term profits (called *short-swing profits*) realized from the purchase and sale or sale and purchase of corporate stock within any six-month period.
	 3. *Regulation of proxies*—The SEC regulates the content of proxy statements sent to shareholders of Section 12 companies. Section 14(a) is essentially a disclosure law, with provisions similar to the antifraud provisions of SEC Rule 10b-5.
	 4. *Violations*—Violations of the 1934 act may be subject to criminal or civil liability.

(Continued)

Chapter Summary: Investor Protection and Corporate Governance, Continued

State Securities Laws (See page 694.)	All states have corporate securities laws *(blue sky laws)* that regulate the offer and sale of securities within state borders. These laws are designed to prevent "speculative schemes which have no more basis than so many feet of 'blue sky.'" States regulate securities concurrently with the federal government. The Uniform Securities Act of 2002, which has been adopted by seventeen states and is being considered by several others, is designed to promote coordination and reduce duplication between state and federal securities regulation.
Corporate Governance (See pages 695–699.)	1. *Definition*—Corporate governance is the system by which business corporations are governed, including policies and procedures for making decisions on corporate affairs. 2. *The need for corporate governance*—Corporate governance is necessary in large corporations because corporate ownership (by the shareholders) is separated from corporate control (by officers and managers). This separation of corporate ownership and control can often result in conflicting interests. Corporate governance standards address such issues. 3. *Sarbanes-Oxley Act of 2002*—This act attempts to increase corporate accountability by imposing strict disclosure requirements and harsh penalties for violations of securities laws.
Online Securities Fraud and Ponzi Schemes (See pages 699–701.)	A major problem facing the SEC today is how to enforce the antifraud provisions of the securities laws in the online environment. Internet-related forms of securities fraud include numerous types of investment scams and hacking into online trading accounts. Ponzi schemes also pose a significant problem for the SEC.

ExamPrep

ISSUE SPOTTERS

1. When a corporation wishes to issue certain securities, it must provide sufficient information for an unsophisticated investor to evaluate the financial risk involved. Specifically, the law imposes liability for making a false statement or omission that is "material." What sort of information would an investor consider material?
2. Lee is an officer of Magma Oil, Inc. Lee knows that a Magma geologist has just discovered a new deposit of oil. Can Lee take advantage of this information to buy and sell Magma stock? Why or why not?

—**Check your answers to these questions against the answers provided in Appendix G.**

BEFORE THE TEST

Go to **www.cengagebrain.com**, enter the ISBN number "9781111530617," and click on "Find" to locate this textbook's Web site. Then, click on "Access Now" under "Study Tools," and select "Chapter 24" at the top. There you will find an "Interactive Quiz" that you can take to assess your mastery of the concepts in this chapter, as well as "Flashcards" and a "Glossary" of important terms.

For Review

1. What is meant by the term *securities?*
2. What are the two major statutes regulating the securities industry?
3. What is insider trading? Why is it prohibited?
4. What are some of the features of state securities laws?
5. What certification requirements does the Sarbanes-Oxley Act impose on corporate executives?

Questions and Case Problems

24–1. Registration Requirements. Langley Brothers, Inc., a corporation incorporated and doing business in Kansas, decides to sell common stock worth $1 million to the public. The stock will be sold only within the state of Kansas. Joseph Langley, the chairman of the board, says the offering need not be registered with the Securities and Exchange Commission. His brother, Harry, disagrees. Who is right? Explain.

24–2. Registration Requirements. Huron Corp. has 300,000 common shares outstanding. The owners of these outstanding shares live in several different states. Huron has decided to split the 300,000 shares two for one. Will Huron Corp. have to file a registration statement and prospectus on the 300,000 new shares to be issued as a result of the split? Explain.

24–3. Insider Trading. David Gain was chief executive officer (CEO) of Forest Media Corp., which became interested in acquiring RS Communications, Inc., in 2011. To initiate negotiations, Gain met with RS's CEO, Gill Raz, on Friday, July 12. Two days later, Gain phoned his brother Mark, who, on Monday, bought 3,800 shares of RS stock. Mark discussed the deal with their father, Jordan, who bought 20,000 RS shares on Thursday. On July 25, the day before the RS bid was due, Gain phoned his parents' home, and Mark bought another 3,200 RS shares. The same routine was followed over the next few days, with Gain periodically phoning Mark or Jordan, both of whom continued to buy RS shares. Forest's bid was refused, but on August 5, RS announced its merger with another company. The price of RS stock rose 30 percent, increasing the value of Mark and Jordan's shares by $664,024 and $412,875, respectively. Did Gain engage in insider trading? What is required to impose sanctions for this offense? Could a court hold Gain liable? Why or why not?

24–4. Securities Violations. In 1997, WTS Transnational, Inc., required financing to develop a prototype of an unpatented fingerprint-verification system. At the time, WTS had no revenue, $655,000 in liabilities, and only $10,000 in assets. Thomas Cavanagh and Frank Nicolois, who operated an investment banking company called U.S. Milestone (USM), arranged the financing using Curbstone Acquisition Corp. Curbstone had no assets but had registered approximately 3.5 million shares of stock with the Securities and Exchange Commission (SEC). Under the terms of the deal, Curbstone acquired WTS, and the resulting entity was named Electro-Optical Systems Corp. (EOSC). New EOSC shares were issued to all of the WTS shareholders. Only Cavanagh and others affiliated with USM could sell EOSC stock to the public, however. Over the next few months, these individuals issued false press releases, made small deceptive purchases of EOSC shares at high prices, distributed hundreds of thousands of shares to friends and relatives, and sold their own shares at inflated prices through third party companies they owned. When the SEC began to investigate, the share price fell to its actual value, and innocent investors lost more than $15 million. Were any securities laws violated in this case? If so, what might be an appropriate remedy? [*SEC v. Cavanagh,* 445 F.3d 105 (2d Cir. 2006)]

24–5. Case Problem with Sample Answer. Duty to Disclose. Orphan Medical, Inc., was a pharmaceutical company that focused on central nervous system disorders. Its major product was the drug Xyrem. In June 2004, Orphan merged with Jazz, and Orphan shareholders received $10.75 per share for their stock. Before the merger was final, Orphan completed a phase of testing of Xyrem that indicated that the U.S. Food and Drug Administration (FDA) would allow the drug to go to the next stage of testing, which was necessary for the drug to be widely marketed. If that happened, the value of the drug and Orphan would go up, and the stock would have been worth more than $10.75. Little Gem Life Sciences, LLC, was an Orphan shareholder that received $10.75 a share. It sued, claiming violations of federal securities laws because shareholders were not told, during the merger process, that the current stage of FDA tests had been successful. Little Gem claimed that if the information had been public, the stock price would have been higher. The district court dismissed the suit, holding that it did not meet the standards required by the Private Securities Litigation Reform Act. Little Gem appealed. Did Orphan's directors have a duty to reveal all relevant drug-testing information to shareholders? Why or why not? [*Little Gem Life Sciences, LLC v. Orphan Medical, Inc.,* 537 F.3d 913 (8th Cir. 2008)]

—To view a sample answer for Case Problem 24–5, go to Appendix F at the end of this text.

24–6. Violations of the 1934 Act. To comply with accounting principles, a company that engages in software development must either "expense" the cost (record it immediately on the company's financial statement) or "capitalize" it (record it as a cost incurred in increments over time). If the project is in the pre- or post-development stage, the cost must be expensed. Otherwise it may be capitalized. Capitalizing a cost makes a company look more profitable in the short term. Digimarc Corp., which provides secure personal identification documents such as drivers' licenses using digital watermark technology, announced that it had improperly capitalized software development costs over at least the previous eighteen months. The errors resulted in $2.7 million in overstated earnings, requiring a restatement of prior financial statements. Zucco Partners, LLC, which had bought Digimarc stock within the relevant period, filed a suit in a federal district court against the firm. Zucco claimed that it could show that there had been disagreements within Digimarc over its accounting. Is this sufficient to establish a violation of SEC Rule 10b-5? Why or why not? [*Zucco Partners, LLC v. Digimarc Corp.*, 552 F.3d 981 (9th Cir. 2009)]

24–7. Insider Trading. Jabil Circuit, Inc., is a publicly traded electronics and technology company headquartered in St. Petersburg, Florida. In 2008, a group of shareholders who owned Jabil stock from 2001 to 2007 sued the company and its auditors, directors, and officers for insider trading. Stock options were a part of Jabil's compensation for executives. In some situations, stock options were backdated to a point in time when the stock price was lower, so that the options were worth more to certain company executives. Backdating is not illegal so long as it is reported, but Jabil did not report the fact that backdating had occurred. Thus, expenses were under-reported, and net income was overstated by millions of dollars. The shareholders claimed that by rigging the stock price by backdating, the executives had engaged in insider trading and could pick favorable purchase prices and that there was a general practice of selling stock before unfavorable news about the company was reported to the public. The shareholders, however, had no specific information about these stock trades or when (or even if) a particular executive was aware of any accounting errors during the time of any backdating purchases. Were the shareholders' allegations sufficient to assert that insider trading had occurred under Rule 10b-5? Why or why not? [*Edward J. Goodman Life Income Trust v. Jabil Circuit, Inc.*, 594 F.3d 783 (11th Cir. 2010)]

24–8. Violations of the 1934 Act. Matrixx Initiatives, Inc., makes and sells over-the-counter pharmaceutical products. Its core brand is Zicam, which accounts for 70 percent of its sales. Matrixx received reports that some consumers had lost their sense of smell (a condition called *anosmia*) after using Zicam Cold Remedy. Four product liability suits were filed against Matrixx, seeking damages for anosmia. In public statements relating to revenues and product safety, however, Matrixx did not reveal this information. James Siracusano and other Matrixx investors filed a suit in a federal district court against the company and its executives under Section 10(b) of the Securities Exchange Act of 1934 and SEC Rule 10b-5, claiming that the statements were misleading because they did not disclose the information regarding the product liability suits. Matrixx argued that to be material, information must consist of a statistically significant number of adverse events that require disclosure. Because Siracusano's claim did not allege that Matrixx knew of a statistically significant number of adverse events, the company contended that the claim should be dismissed. What is the standard for materiality in this context? Should Siracusano's claim be dismissed? Explain. [*Matrixx Initiatives, Inc. v. Siracusano*, ___ U.S. ___, 131 S.Ct. 1309, 179 L.Ed.2d 398 (2011)]

24–9. **A Question of Ethics. Violations of the 1934 Act.** Melvin Lyttle told John Montana and Paul Knight about a "Trading Program" that purportedly would buy and sell securities in deals that were fully insured, as well as monitored and controlled by the Federal Reserve Board. Without checking the details or even verifying whether the Program existed, Montana and Knight, with Lyttle's help, began to sell interests in the Program to investors. For a minimum investment of $1 million, the investors were promised extraordinary rates of return—from 10 percent to as much as 100 percent per week—without risk. They were told, among other things, that the Program would "utilize banks that can ensure full bank integrity of The Transaction whose undertaking[s] are in complete harmony with international banking rules and protocol and who [sic] guarantee maximum security of a Funder's Capital Placement Amount." Nothing was required but the investors' funds and their silence—the Program was to be kept secret. Over a four-month period in 1999, Montana raised approximately $23 million from twenty-two investors. The promised gains did not accrue, however. Instead, Montana, Lyttle, and Knight depleted the investors' funds in high-risk trades or spent the funds on themselves. [*SEC v. Montana*, 464 F.Supp.2d 772 (S.D.Ind. 2006)]

1. The Securities and Exchange Commission (SEC) filed a suit in a federal district court against Montana and the others, seeking an injunction, civil penalties, and disgorgement (giving up) of profits with interest. The SEC alleged, among other things, violations of Section 10(b) of the Securities Exchange Act of 1934 and SEC Rule 10b-5. What is required to establish a violation of these laws? Explain how and why the facts in this case meet, or fail to meet, these requirements.

2. It is often remarked, "There's a sucker born every minute!" Does that phrase describe the Program's investors? Ultimately, about half of the investors recouped the amount they invested. Should the others be considered at least partly responsible for their own losses? Why or why not?

24–10. **Video Question. *Jack's Restaurant, Scene 1.*** Access the video using the instructions provided below to answer the following questions.

1. Assuming that the companies involved in the merger are Section 12 companies, what statutory provisions prohibit Susan from trading company stock based on her inside knowledge of the merger with GTS?

2. Did Susan breach a fiduciary duty to the corporation by telling the bartender about the proposed merger? Does the fact that she may be laid off by the company after the merger affect her duties? Explain.

3. Under what legal theory might it be illegal for the bartender to buy shares in the company based on the information that he got from Susan? Analyze the owner's potential liability. Is there enough evidence of *scienter* in this scenario for the Securities and Exchange Commission to file criminal charges against Susan if the bartender buys the stock? Discuss.

—To watch this video, go to **www.cengagebrain.com** and register the access code that came with your new book or log in to your existing account. Select the link for either the "Business Law Digital Video Library Online Access" or "Business Law CourseMate," and then click on "Complete Video List" to find the video for this chapter (Video 76).

UNIT FOUR Cumulative Business Hypothetical

Falwell Motors, Inc., is a large corporation that manufactures automobile batteries.

1. The Federal Trade Commission (FTC) learns that one of the retail stores that sells Falwell's batteries engages in deceptive advertising practices. What actions can the FTC take against the retailer?

2. For years, Falwell has shipped the toxic waste created by its manufacturing process to a waste-disposal site in the next county. The waste site has become contaminated by leakage from toxic waste containers delivered to the site by other manufacturers. Can Falwell be held liable for clean-up costs, even though its containers were not the ones that leaked? If so, what is the extent of its liability?

3. Falwell faces stiff competition from Alchem, Inc., another battery manufacturer. To acquire control over Alchem, Falwell makes a tender offer to Alchem's shareholders. If Falwell succeeds in its attempt and Alchem is merged into Falwell, will the merger violate any antitrust laws? Suppose that the merger falls through. The vice president of Falwell's battery division and the president of Alchem agree to divide up the market between them, so they will not have to compete for customers. Is this agreement legal? Explain.

4. One of Falwell's employees learns that Falwell is contemplating a takeover of a rival. The employee tells her husband about the possibility. The husband calls their broker, who purchases shares in the target corporation for the employee and her husband, as well as for himself. Has the employee violated any securities law? Has her husband? Has the broker? Explain.

Appendix A

How to Brief Cases and Analyze Case Problems

How to Brief Cases

To fully understand the law with respect to business, you need to be able to read and understand court decisions. To make this task easier, you can use a method of case analysis that is called *briefing*. There is a fairly standard procedure that you can follow when you "brief" any court case. You must first read the case opinion carefully. When you feel you understand the case, you can prepare a brief of it.

Although the format of the brief may vary, typically it will present the essentials of the case under headings such as the following:

1. **Citation.** Give the full citation for the case, including the name of the case, the date it was decided, and the court that decided it.
2. **Facts.** Briefly indicate (a) the reasons for the lawsuit; (b) the identity and arguments of the plaintiff(s) and defendant(s), respectively; and (c) the lower court's decision—if appropriate.
3. **Issue.** Concisely phrase, in the form of a question, the essential issue before the court. (If more than one issue is involved, you may have two—or even more—questions here.)
4. **Decision.** Indicate here—with a "yes" or "no," if possible—the court's answer to the question (or questions) in the *Issue* section above.
5. **Reason.** Summarize as briefly as possible the reasons given by the court for its decision (or decisions) and the case or statutory law relied on by the court in arriving at its decision.

An Example of a Briefed Sample Court Case

As an example of the format used in briefing cases, we present here a briefed version of the sample court case that was presented in the Appendix to Chapter 1 in Exhibit 1A–3 on pages 28–30.

FEHR v. ALGARD
Superior Court of New Jersey, Appellate Division,
__ A.3d __, 2011 WL 13670 (2011).

FACTS Cathy Algard owns Sterling Harbor Motel & Marina, Inc. (SHM). SHM sponsored the Sterling Harbor Duke of Fluke Tournament in Wildwood, New Jersey. Prizes included the "single heaviest fluke prize" for the contestant who caught the heaviest live flounder and the "five heaviest fluke prize" for the boat catching the five flounder with the greatest combined weight. On behalf of Edward Fehr's boat, the *Gina Ariella,* Jack Aydelotte presented the heaviest live flounder. He also submitted five other fish for the five-fluke award. The judges ruled that two of the five flounder had not been caught during the contest and disqualified the *Gina Ariella.* Fehr filed a suit in a New Jersey state court against Algard, alleging breach of contract. The court issued a summary judgment in Fehr's favor, crowned him the "Duke of Fluke," and awarded him damages. Algard appealed.

ISSUE Can a contestant's award be withheld if that person did not comply with all of the contest's rules?

DECISION Yes. A state appellate court reversed the judgment of the lower court and remanded the case to give Algard an opportunity to prove that Aydelotte's deception warranted disqualification of the *Gina Ariella.*

REASON The state appellate court explained that the tournament—like the offer of a prize in any contest—becomes a binding contract in favor of a contestant who complies with the rules. The question was whether Fehr complied and was therefore entitled to the award. Fehr argued that he presented the heaviest live flounder and Algard's failure to award him the prize was a breach of contract. Algard pointed out that Aydelotte signed an entry form that proclaimed "anyone who is found to have provided false information is subject to immediate disqualification."

The court stated, "The order of plaintiff's submissions for prizes should not allow the first fish to be considered for an award, if, in fact, he then tried to weigh-in day old fish." The court added, however, that "if the judges are found to have acted in bad faith and exceeded the rules in making a decision, plaintiff may prevail."

Review of Sample Court Case

Next, we provide a review of the briefed version to indicate the kind of information that is contained in each section.

CITATION The name of the case is *Fehr v. Algard*. Fehr is the plaintiff, and Algard is the defendant. The Superior Court of New Jersey, Appellate Division, decided this case in 2011. The citation states that this case can be found in the online Westlaw database at 2011 WL 13670.

FACTS The *Facts* section identifies the plaintiff and the defendant, describes the events leading up to this suit, the allegations made by the plaintiff in the initial suit, and (because this case is a decision of a state intermediate appellate court) the lower court's ruling and the party appealing. The appellant's contention on appeal is also sometimes included here.

ISSUE The *Issue* section presents the central issue (or issues) decided by the court. In this case, the Superior Court of New Jersey, Appellate Division, considers whether a contestant who may not have complied with all of the rules of the contest can still receive an award.

DECISION The *Decision* section includes the court's ruling on the issues before it. The decision reflects the opinion of the judge or justice hearing the case. Decisions by appellate courts are frequently phrased in reference to the lower court's decision. That is, the appellate court may "affirm" the lower court's ruling or "reverse" it. Here, the court determined that a contestant should not be considered for an award if he did not comply with all of the rules. The rules stated that a contestant would be disqualified for providing false information. On that basis, the contest judges could legitimately reject a contestant's submission for an award. The appellate court reversed the ruling of the lower court, which had been in the contestant's favor.

REASON The *Reason* section includes references to the relevant laws and legal principles that were applied in arriving at the conclusion in the case before the court. This section also explains the court's application of the law to the facts in the case. In this case, the court applied the principles of contract law to the contract between the contest's sponsors and the contestants.

Analyzing Case Problems

In addition to learning how to brief cases, students of business law and the legal environment also find it helpful to know how to analyze case problems. Part of the study of business law and the legal environment usually involves analyzing case problems, such as those included in selected chapters of this text.

For each case problem in this book, we provide the relevant background and facts of the lawsuit and the issue before the court. When you are assigned one of these problems, your job will be to determine how the court should decide the issue, and why. In other words, you will need to engage in legal analysis and reasoning. Here, we offer some suggestions on how to make this task less daunting. We begin by presenting a sample problem:

> While Janet Lawson, a famous pianist, was shopping in Quality Market, she slipped and fell on a wet floor in one of the aisles. The floor had recently been mopped by one of the store's employees, but there were no signs warning customers that the floor in that area was wet. As a result of the fall, Lawson injured her right arm and was unable to perform piano concerts for the next six months. Had she been able to perform the scheduled concerts, she would have earned approximately $60,000 over that period of time. Lawson sued Quality Market for this amount, plus another $10,000 in medical expenses. She claimed that the store's failure to warn customers of the wet floor constituted negligence and therefore the market was liable for her injuries. Will the court agree with Lawson? Discuss.

Understand the Facts

This may sound obvious, but before you can analyze or apply the relevant law to a specific set of facts, you must have a clear understanding of those facts. In other words, you should read through the case problem carefully—more than once, if necessary—to make sure you understand the identity of the plaintiff(s) and defendant(s) and the progression of events that led to the lawsuit.

In the sample case problem just given, the identity of the parties is fairly obvious. Janet Lawson is the one bringing the suit—therefore, she is the plaintiff. She is bringing the suit against Quality Market, so it is the defendant. Some of the case problems you may work on have multiple plaintiffs or defendants. Often, it is helpful to use abbreviations for the parties. A plaintiff, for example, may be denoted by a *pi* symbol (π), and a defendant by a *delta* (Δ) or triangle.

The events leading to the lawsuit are also fairly straightforward. Lawson slipped and fell on a wet floor, and she contends that Quality Market should be liable for her injuries because it was negligent in not posting a sign warning customers of the wet floor.

When you are working on case problems, realize that the facts should be accepted as they are given. For example, in our sample problem, it should be accepted that the floor was wet and that there was no sign. In other words, avoid making conjectures, such as "Maybe the floor wasn't too wet," or "Maybe an employee was getting a sign to put up," or "Maybe someone stole the sign." Questioning the facts as they are presented will only create confusion in your analysis.

Legal Analysis and Reasoning

Once you understand the facts given in the case problem, you can begin to analyze the case. The IRAC method is a helpful tool to use in the legal analysis and reasoning process. IRAC is an acronym for Issue, Rule, Application, Conclusion. Applying this method to our sample problem would involve the following steps:

1. First, you need to decide what legal **issue** is involved in the case. In our sample case, the basic issue is whether Quality Market's failure to warn customers of the wet floor constituted negligence. As discussed in Chapter 5, negligence is a *tort*—a civil wrong. In a tort lawsuit, the plaintiff seeks to be compensated for another's wrongful act. A defendant will be deemed negligent if he or she breached a duty of care owed to the plaintiff and the breach of that duty caused the plaintiff to suffer harm.

2. Once you have identified the issue, the next step is to determine what **rule of law** applies to the issue. To make this determination, carefully review the text of the chapter in which the relevant rule of law for the problem appears. Our sample case problem involves the tort of negligence, which is covered in Chapter 5. The applicable rule of law is the tort law principle that business owners owe a duty to exercise reasonable care to protect their customers ("business invitees"). Reasonable care, in this context, includes either removing— or warning customers of—*foreseeable* risks about which the owner *knew* or *should have known*. Business owners need not warn customers of "open and obvious" risks, however. If a business owner breaches this duty of care (fails to exercise the appropriate degree of care toward customers), and the breach of duty causes a customer to be injured, the business owner will be liable to the customer for the customer's injuries.

3. The next—and usually the most difficult—step in analyzing case problems is the **application** of the relevant rule of law to the specific facts of the case you are studying. In our sample problem, applying the tort law principle just discussed presents few difficulties. An employee of the store had mopped the floor in the aisle where Lawson slipped and fell, but no sign was present indicating that the floor was wet. That a customer might fall on a wet floor is clearly a foreseeable risk. Therefore, the failure to warn customers about the wet floor was a breach of the duty of care owed by the business owner to the store's customers.

4. Once you have completed Step 3 in the IRAC method, you should be ready to draw your **conclusion.** In our sample problem, Quality Market is liable to Lawson for her injuries because the market's breach of its duty of care caused Lawson's injuries.

The fact patterns in the case problems presented in this text are not always as simple as those in our sample problem. Often, for example, a case has more than one plaintiff or defendant. A case may also involve more than one issue and have more than one applicable rule of law. Furthermore, in some case problems the facts may indicate that the general rule of law should not apply. For example, suppose that a store employee advised Lawson not to walk on the floor in the aisle because it was wet, but Lawson decided to walk on it anyway. This fact could alter the outcome of the case because the store could then raise the defense of assumption of risk (see Chapter 5). Nonetheless, a careful review of the chapter should always provide you with the knowledge you need to analyze the problem thoroughly and arrive at accurate conclusions.

The Constitution of the United States

PREAMBLE

We the People of the United States, in Order to form a more perfect Union, establish Justice, insure domestic Tranquility, provide for the common defence, promote the general Welfare, and secure the Blessings of Liberty to ourselves and our Posterity, do ordain and establish this Constitution for the United States of America.

ARTICLE I

Section 1. All legislative Powers herein granted shall be vested in a Congress of the United States, which shall consist of a Senate and House of Representatives.

Section 2. The House of Representatives shall be composed of Members chosen every second Year by the People of the several States, and the Electors in each State shall have the Qualifications requisite for Electors of the most numerous Branch of the State Legislature.

No Person shall be a Representative who shall not have attained to the Age of twenty five Years, and been seven Years a Citizen of the United States, and who shall not, when elected, be an Inhabitant of that State in which he shall be chosen.

Representatives and direct Taxes shall be apportioned among the several States which may be included within this Union, according to their respective Numbers, which shall be determined by adding to the whole Number of free Persons, including those bound to Service for a Term of Years, and excluding Indians not taxed, three fifths of all other Persons. The actual Enumeration shall be made within three Years after the first Meeting of the Congress of the United States, and within every subsequent Term of ten Years, in such Manner as they shall by Law direct. The Number of Representatives shall not exceed one for every thirty Thousand, but each State shall have at Least one Representative; and until such enumeration shall be made, the State of New Hampshire shall be entitled to chuse three, Massachusetts eight, Rhode Island and Providence Plantations one, Connecticut five, New York six, New Jersey four, Pennsylvania eight, Delaware one, Maryland six, Virginia ten, North Carolina five, South Carolina five, and Georgia three.

When vacancies happen in the Representation from any State, the Executive Authority thereof shall issue Writs of Election to fill such Vacancies.

The House of Representatives shall chuse their Speaker and other Officers; and shall have the sole Power of Impeachment.

Section 3. The Senate of the United States shall be composed of two Senators from each State, chosen by the Legislature thereof, for six Years; and each Senator shall have one Vote.

Immediately after they shall be assembled in Consequence of the first Election, they shall be divided as equally as may be into three Classes. The Seats of the Senators of the first Class shall be vacated at the Expiration of the second Year, of the second Class at the Expiration of the fourth Year, and of the third Class at the Expiration of the sixth Year, so that one third may be chosen every second Year; and if Vacancies happen by Resignation, or otherwise, during the Recess of the Legislature of any State, the Executive thereof may make temporary Appointments until the next Meeting of the Legislature, which shall then fill such Vacancies.

No Person shall be a Senator who shall not have attained to the Age of thirty Years, and been nine Years a Citizen of the United States, and who shall not, when elected, be an Inhabitant of that State for which he shall be chosen.

The Vice President of the United States shall be President of the Senate, but shall have no Vote, unless they be equally divided.

The Senate shall chuse their other Officers, and also a President pro tempore, in the Absence of the Vice President, or when he shall exercise the Office of President of the United States.

The Senate shall have the sole Power to try all Impeachments. When sitting for that Purpose, they shall be on Oath or Affirmation. When the President of the United States is tried, the Chief Justice shall preside: And no Person shall be convicted without the Concurrence of two thirds of the Members present.

Judgment in Cases of Impeachment shall not extend further than to removal from Office, and disqualification to hold and enjoy any Office of honor, Trust, or Profit under the United States: but the Party convicted shall nevertheless be liable and subject to Indictment, Trial, Judgment, and Punishment, according to Law.

Section 4. The Times, Places and Manner of holding Elections for Senators and Representatives, shall be prescribed in each State by the Legislature thereof; but the Congress may at any time by Law make or alter such Regulations, except as to the Places of chusing Senators.

The Congress shall assemble at least once in every Year, and such Meeting shall be on the first Monday in December, unless they shall by Law appoint a different Day.

Section 5. Each House shall be the Judge of the Elections, Returns, and Qualifications of its own Members, and a Majority of each shall constitute a Quorum to do Business; but a smaller Number may adjourn from day to day, and may be authorized to compel the Attendance of absent Members, in such Manner, and under such Penalties as each House may provide.

Each House may determine the Rules of its Proceedings, punish its Members for disorderly Behavior, and, with the Concurrence of two thirds, expel a Member.

Each House shall keep a Journal of its Proceedings, and from time to time publish the same, excepting such Parts as may in their Judgment require Secrecy; and the Yeas and Nays of the Members of either House on any question shall, at the Desire of one fifth of those Present, be entered on the Journal.

Neither House, during the Session of Congress, shall, without the Consent of the other, adjourn for more than three days, nor to any other Place than that in which the two Houses shall be sitting.

Section 6. The Senators and Representatives shall receive a Compensation for their Services, to be ascertained by Law, and paid out of the Treasury of the United States. They shall in all Cases, except Treason, Felony and Breach of the Peace, be privileged from Arrest during their Attendance at the Session of their respective Houses, and in going to and returning from the same; and for any Speech or Debate in either House, they shall not be questioned in any other Place.

No Senator or Representative shall, during the Time for which he was elected, be appointed to any civil Office under the Authority of the United States, which shall have been created, or the Emoluments whereof shall have been increased during such time; and no Person holding any Office under the United States, shall be a Member of either House during his Continuance in Office.

Section 7. All Bills for raising Revenue shall originate in the House of Representatives; but the Senate may propose or concur with Amendments as on other Bills.

Every Bill which shall have passed the House of Representatives and the Senate, shall, before it become a Law, be presented to the President of the United States; If he approve he shall sign it, but if not he shall return it, with his Objections to the House in which it shall have originated, who shall enter the Objections at large on their Journal, and proceed to reconsider it. If after such Reconsideration two thirds of that House shall agree to pass the Bill, it shall be sent together with the Objections, to the other House, by which it shall likewise be reconsidered, and if approved by two thirds of that House, it shall become a Law. But in all such Cases the Votes of both Houses shall be determined by Yeas and Nays, and the Names of the Persons voting for and against the Bill shall be entered on the Journal of each House respectively. If any Bill shall not be returned by the President within ten Days (Sundays excepted) after it shall have been presented to him, the Same shall be a Law, in like Manner as if he had signed it, unless the Congress by their Adjournment prevent its Return in which Case it shall not be a Law.

Every Order, Resolution, or Vote, to which the Concurrence of the Senate and House of Representatives may be necessary (except on a question of Adjournment) shall be presented to the President of the United States; and before the Same shall take Effect, shall be approved by him, or being disapproved by him, shall be repassed by two thirds of the Senate and House of Representatives, according to the Rules and Limitations prescribed in the Case of a Bill.

Section 8. The Congress shall have Power To lay and collect Taxes, Duties, Imposts and Excises, to pay the Debts and provide for the common Defence and general Welfare of the United States; but all Duties, Imposts and Excises shall be uniform throughout the United States;

To borrow Money on the credit of the United States;

To regulate Commerce with foreign Nations, and among the several States, and with the Indian Tribes;

To establish an uniform Rule of Naturalization, and uniform Laws on the subject of Bankruptcies throughout the United States;

To coin Money, regulate the Value thereof, and of foreign Coin, and fix the Standard of Weights and Measures;

To provide for the Punishment of counterfeiting the Securities and current Coin of the United States;

To establish Post Offices and post Roads;

To promote the Progress of Science and useful Arts, by securing for limited Times to Authors and Inventors the exclusive Right to their respective Writings and Discoveries;

To constitute Tribunals inferior to the supreme Court;

To define and punish Piracies and Felonies committed on the high Seas, and Offenses against the Law of Nations;

To declare War, grant Letters of Marque and Reprisal, and make Rules concerning Captures on Land and Water;

To raise and support Armies, but no Appropriation of Money to that Use shall be for a longer Term than two Years;

To provide and maintain a Navy;

To make Rules for the Government and Regulation of the land and naval Forces;

To provide for calling forth the Militia to execute the Laws of the Union, suppress Insurrections and repel Invasions;

To provide for organizing, arming, and disciplining, the Militia, and for governing such Part of them as may be employed in the Service of the United States, reserving to the States respectively, the Appointment of the Officers, and the Authority of training the Militia according to the discipline prescribed by Congress;

To exercise exclusive Legislation in all Cases whatsoever, over such District (not exceeding ten Miles square) as may, by Cession of particular States, and the Acceptance of Congress, become the Seat of the Government of the United States, and to exercise like Authority over all Places purchased by the Consent of the Legislature of the State in which the Same shall be, for the Erection of Forts, Magazines, Arsenals, dock-Yards, and other needful Buildings;—And

To make all Laws which shall be necessary and proper for carrying into Execution the foregoing Powers, and all other Powers vested by this Constitution in the Government of the United States, or in any Department or Officer thereof.

Section 9. The Migration or Importation of such Persons as any of the States now existing shall think proper to admit, shall not be prohibited by the Congress prior to the Year one thousand eight hundred and eight, but a Tax or duty may be imposed on such Importation, not exceeding ten dollars for each Person.

The privilege of the Writ of Habeas Corpus shall not be suspended, unless when in Cases of Rebellion or Invasion the public Safety may require it.

No Bill of Attainder or ex post facto Law shall be passed.

No Capitation, or other direct, Tax shall be laid, unless in Proportion to the Census or Enumeration herein before directed to be taken.

No Tax or Duty shall be laid on Articles exported from any State.

No Preference shall be given by any Regulation of Commerce or Revenue to the Ports of one State over those of another: nor shall Vessels bound to, or from, one State be obliged to enter, clear, or pay Duties in another.

No Money shall be drawn from the Treasury, but in Consequence of Appropriations made by Law; and a regular Statement and Account of the Receipts and Expenditures of all public Money shall be published from time to time.

No Title of Nobility shall be granted by the United States: And no Person holding any Office of Profit or Trust under them, shall, without the Consent of the Congress, accept of any present, Emolument, Office, or Title, of any kind whatever, from any King, Prince, or foreign State.

Section 10. No State shall enter into any Treaty, Alliance, or Confederation; grant Letters of Marque and Reprisal; coin Money; emit Bills of Credit; make any Thing but gold and silver Coin a Tender in Payment of Debts; pass any Bill of Attainder, ex post facto Law, or Law impairing the Obligation of Contracts, or grant any Title of Nobility.

No State shall, without the Consent of the Congress, lay any Imposts or Duties on Imports or Exports, except what may be absolutely necessary for executing its inspection Laws: and the net Produce of all Duties and Imposts, laid by any State on Imports or Exports, shall be for the Use of the Treasury of the United States; and all such Laws shall be subject to the Revision and Controul of the Congress.

No State shall, without the Consent of Congress, lay any Duty of Tonnage, keep Troops, or Ships of War in time of Peace, enter into any Agreement or Compact with another State, or with a foreign Power, or engage in War, unless actually invaded, or in such imminent Danger as will not admit of delay.

ARTICLE II

Section 1. The executive Power shall be vested in a President of the United States of America. He shall hold his Office during the Term of four Years, and, together with the Vice President, chosen for the same Term, be elected, as follows:

Each State shall appoint, in such Manner as the Legislature thereof may direct, a Number of Electors, equal to the whole Number of Senators and Representatives to which the State may be entitled in the Congress; but no Senator or Representative, or Person holding an Office of Trust or Profit under the United States, shall be appointed an Elector.

The Electors shall meet in their respective States, and vote by Ballot for two Persons, of whom one at least shall not be an Inhabitant of the same State with themselves. And they shall make a List of all the Persons voted for, and of the Number of Votes for each; which List they shall sign and certify, and transmit sealed to the Seat of the Government of the United States, directed to the President of the Senate. The President of the Senate shall, in the Presence of the Senate and House of Representatives, open all the Certificates, and the Votes shall then be counted. The Person having the greatest Number of Votes shall be the President, if such Number be a Majority of the whole Number of Electors appointed; and if there be more than one who have such Majority, and have an equal Number of Votes, then the House of Representatives shall immediately chuse by Ballot one of them for President; and if no Person have a Majority, then from the five highest on the List the said House shall in like Manner chuse the President. But in chusing the President, the Votes shall be taken by States, the Representation from each State having one Vote; A quorum for this Purpose shall consist of a Member or Members from two thirds of the States, and a Majority of all the States shall be necessary to a Choice. In every Case, after the Choice of the President, the Person having the greater Number of Votes of the Electors shall be the Vice President. But if there should remain two or more who have equal Votes, the Senate shall chuse from them by Ballot the Vice President.

The Congress may determine the Time of chusing the Electors, and the Day on which they shall give their Votes; which Day shall be the same throughout the United States.

No person except a natural born Citizen, or a Citizen of the United States, at the time of the Adoption of this Constitution, shall be eligible to the Office of President; neither shall any Person be eligible to that Office who shall not have attained to the Age of thirty five Years, and been fourteen Years a Resident within the United States.

In Case of the Removal of the President from Office, or of his Death, Resignation or Inability to discharge the Powers and Duties of the said Office, the same shall devolve on the Vice President, and the Congress may by Law provide for the Case of Removal, Death, Resignation or Inability, both of the President and Vice President, declaring what Officer shall then act as President, and such Officer shall act accordingly, until the Disability be removed, or a President shall be elected.

The President shall, at stated Times, receive for his Services, a Compensation, which shall neither be increased nor diminished during the Period for which he shall have been elected, and he shall not receive within that Period any other Emolument from the United States, or any of them.

Before he enter on the Execution of his Office, he shall take the following Oath or Affirmation: "I do solemnly swear (or affirm) that I will faithfully execute the Office of President of the United States, and will to the best of my Ability, preserve, protect and defend the Constitution of the United States."

Section 2. The President shall be Commander in Chief of the Army and Navy of the United States, and of the Militia of the several States, when called into the actual Service of the United States; he may require the Opinion, in writing, of the principal Officer in each of the executive Departments, upon any Subject relating to the Duties of their respective Offices, and he shall have Power to grant Reprieves and Pardons for Offenses against the United States, except in Cases of Impeachment.

He shall have Power, by and with the Advice and Consent of the Senate to make Treaties, provided two thirds of the Senators present concur; and he shall nominate, and by and with the Advice and Consent of the Senate, shall appoint Ambassadors, other public Ministers and Consuls, Judges of the supreme Court, and all other Officers of the United States, whose Appointments are not herein otherwise provided for, and which shall be established by Law; but the Congress may by Law vest the Appointment of such inferior Officers, as they think proper, in the President alone, in the Courts of Law, or in the Heads of Departments.

The President shall have Power to fill up all Vacancies that may happen during the Recess of the Senate, by granting Commissions which shall expire at the End of their next Session.

Section 3. He shall from time to time give to the Congress Information of the State of the Union, and recommend to their Consideration such Measures as he shall judge necessary and expedient; he may, on extraordinary Occasions, convene both Houses, or either of them, and in Case of Disagreement between them, with Respect to the Time of Adjournment, he may adjourn them to such Time as he shall think proper; he shall receive Ambassadors and other public Ministers; he shall take Care that the Laws be faithfully executed, and shall Commission all the Officers of the United States.

Section 4. The President, Vice President and all civil Officers of the United States, shall be removed from Office on Impeachment for, and Conviction of, Treason, Bribery, or other high Crimes and Misdemeanors.

ARTICLE III

Section 1. The judicial Power of the United States, shall be vested in one supreme Court, and in such inferior Courts as the Congress may from time to time ordain and establish. The Judges, both of the supreme and inferior Courts, shall hold their Offices during good Behaviour, and shall, at stated Times, receive for their Services a Compensation, which shall not be diminished during their Continuance in Office.

Section 2. The judicial Power shall extend to all Cases, in Law and Equity, arising under this Constitution, the Laws of the

United States, and Treaties made, or which shall be made, under their Authority;—to all Cases affecting Ambassadors, other public Ministers and Consuls;—to all Cases of admiralty and maritime Jurisdiction;—to Controversies to which the United States shall be a Party;—to Controversies between two or more States;—between a State and Citizens of another State;—between Citizens of different States;—between Citizens of the same State claiming Lands under Grants of different States, and between a State, or the Citizens thereof, and foreign States, Citizens or Subjects.

In all Cases affecting Ambassadors, other public Ministers and Consuls, and those in which a State shall be a Party, the supreme Court shall have original Jurisdiction. In all the other Cases before mentioned, the supreme Court shall have appellate Jurisdiction, both as to Law and Fact, with such Exceptions, and under such Regulations as the Congress shall make.

The Trial of all Crimes, except in Cases of Impeachment, shall be by Jury; and such Trial shall be held in the State where the said Crimes shall have been committed; but when not committed within any State, the Trial shall be at such Place or Places as the Congress may by Law have directed.

Section 3. Treason against the United States, shall consist only in levying War against them, or, in adhering to their Enemies, giving them Aid and Comfort. No Person shall be convicted of Treason unless on the Testimony of two Witnesses to the same overt Act, or on Confession in open Court.

The Congress shall have Power to declare the Punishment of Treason, but no Attainder of Treason shall work Corruption of Blood, or Forfeiture except during the Life of the Person attainted.

ARTICLE IV

Section 1. Full Faith and Credit shall be given in each State to the public Acts, Records, and judicial Proceedings of every other State. And the Congress may by general Laws prescribe the Manner in which such Acts, Records and Proceedings shall be proved, and the Effect thereof.

Section 2. The Citizens of each State shall be entitled to all Privileges and Immunities of Citizens in the several States.

A Person charged in any State with Treason, Felony, or other Crime, who shall flee from Justice, and be found in another State, shall on Demand of the executive Authority of the State from which he fled, be delivered up, to be removed to the State having Jurisdiction of the Crime.

No Person held to Service or Labour in one State, under the Laws thereof, escaping into another, shall, in Consequence of any Law or Regulation therein, be discharged from such Service or Labour, but shall be delivered up on Claim of the Party to whom such Service or Labour may be due.

Section 3. New States may be admitted by the Congress into this Union; but no new State shall be formed or erected within the Jurisdiction of any other State; nor any State be formed by the Junction of two or more States, or Parts of States, without the Consent of the Legislatures of the States concerned as well as of the Congress.

The Congress shall have Power to dispose of and make all needful Rules and Regulations respecting the Territory or other Property belonging to the United States; and nothing in this Constitution shall be so construed as to Prejudice any Claims of the United States, or of any particular State.

Section 4. The United States shall guarantee to every State in this Union a Republican Form of Government, and shall protect each of them against Invasion; and on Application of the Legislature, or of the Executive (when the Legislature cannot be convened) against domestic Violence.

ARTICLE V

The Congress, whenever two thirds of both Houses shall deem it necessary, shall propose Amendments to this Constitution, or, on the Application of the Legislatures of two thirds of the several States, shall call a Convention for proposing Amendments, which, in either Case, shall be valid to all Intents and Purposes, as part of this Constitution, when ratified by the Legislatures of three fourths of the several States, or by Conventions in three fourths thereof, as the one or the other Mode of Ratification may be proposed by the Congress; Provided that no Amendment which may be made prior to the Year One thousand eight hundred and eight shall in any Manner affect the first and fourth Clauses in the Ninth Section of the first Article; and that no State, without its Consent, shall be deprived of its equal Suffrage in the Senate.

ARTICLE VI

All Debts contracted and Engagements entered into, before the Adoption of this Constitution shall be as valid against the United States under this Constitution, as under the Confederation.

This Constitution, and the Laws of the United States which shall be made in Pursuance thereof; and all Treaties made, or which shall be made, under the Authority of the United States, shall be the supreme Law of the Land; and the Judges in every State shall be bound thereby, any Thing in the Constitution or Laws of any State to the Contrary notwithstanding.

The Senators and Representatives before mentioned, and the Members of the several State Legislatures, and all executive and judicial Officers, both of the United States and of the several States, shall be bound by Oath or Affirmation, to support this Constitution; but no religious Test shall ever be required as a Qualification to any Office or public Trust under the United States.

ARTICLE VII

The Ratification of the Conventions of nine States shall be sufficient for the Establishment of this Constitution between the States so ratifying the Same.

AMENDMENT I [1791]

Congress shall make no law respecting an establishment of religion, or prohibiting the free exercise thereof; or abridging the freedom of speech, or of the press; or the right of the people peaceably to assembly, and to petition the Government for a redress of grievances.

AMENDMENT II [1791]

A well regulated Militia, being necessary to the security of a free State, the right of the people to keep and bear Arms, shall not be infringed.

AMENDMENT III [1791]

No Soldier shall, in time of peace be quartered in any house, without the consent of the Owner, nor in time of war, but in a manner to be prescribed by law.

AMENDMENT IV [1791]

The right of the people to be secure in their persons, houses, papers, and effects, against unreasonable searches and seizures, shall not be violated, and no Warrants shall issue, but upon probable cause, supported by Oath or affirmation, and particularly describing the place to be searched, and the persons or things to be seized.

AMENDMENT V [1791]

No person shall be held to answer for a capital, or otherwise infamous crime, unless on a presentment or indictment of a Grand Jury, except in cases arising in the land or naval forces, or in the Militia, when in actual service in time of War or public danger; nor shall any person be subject for the same offence to be twice put in jeopardy of life or limb; nor shall be compelled in any criminal case to be a witness against himself, nor be deprived of life, liberty, or property, without due process of law; nor shall private property be taken for public use, without just compensation.

AMENDMENT VI [1791]

In all criminal prosecutions, the accused shall enjoy the right to a speedy and public trial, by an impartial jury of the State and district wherein the crime shall have been committed, which district shall have been previously ascertained by law, and to be informed of the nature and cause of the accusation; to be confronted with the witnesses against him; to have compulsory process for obtaining witnesses in his favor, and to have the Assistance of Counsel for his defence.

AMENDMENT VII [1791]

In Suits at common law, where the value in controversy shall exceed twenty dollars, the right of trial by jury shall be preserved, and no fact tried by jury, shall be otherwise re-examined in any Court of the United States, than according to the rules of the common law.

AMENDMENT VIII [1791]

Excessive bail shall not be required, nor excessive fines imposed, nor cruel and unusual punishments inflicted.

AMENDMENT IX [1791]

The enumeration in the Constitution, of certain rights, shall not be construed to deny or disparage others retained by the people.

AMENDMENT X [1791]

The powers not delegated to the United States by the Constitution, nor prohibited by it to the States, are reserved to the States respectively, or to the people.

AMENDMENT XI [1798]

The Judicial power of the United States shall not be construed to extend to any suit in law or equity, commenced or prosecuted against one of the United States by Citizens of another State, or by Citizens or Subjects of any Foreign State.

AMENDMENT XII [1804]

The Electors shall meet in their respective states, and vote by ballot for President and Vice-President, one of whom, at least, shall not be an inhabitant of the same state with themselves; they shall name in their ballots the person voted for as President, and in distinct ballots the person voted for as Vice-President, and they shall make distinct lists of all persons voted for as President, and of all persons voted for as Vice-President, and of the number of votes for each, which lists they shall sign and certify, and transmit sealed to the seat of the government of the United States, directed to the President of the Senate;—The President of the Senate shall, in the presence of the Senate and House of Representatives, open all the certificates and the votes shall then be counted;—The person having the greatest number of votes for President, shall be the President, if such number be a majority of the whole number of Electors appointed; and if no person have such majority, then from the persons having the highest numbers not exceeding three on the list of those voted for as President, the House of Representatives shall choose immediately, by ballot, the President. But in choosing the President, the votes shall be taken by states, the representation from each state having one vote; a quorum for this purpose shall consist of a member or members from two-thirds of the states, and a majority of all states shall be necessary to a choice. And if the House of Representatives shall not choose a President whenever the right of choice shall devolve upon them, before the fourth day of March next following, then the Vice-President shall act as President, as in the case of the death or other constitutional disability of the President.—The person having the greatest number of votes as Vice-President, shall be the Vice-President, if such number be a majority of the whole number of Electors appointed, and if no person have a majority, then from the two highest numbers on the list, the Senate shall choose the Vice-President; a quorum for the purpose shall consist of two-thirds of the whole number of Senators, and a majority of the whole number shall be necessary to a choice. But no person constitutionally ineligible to the office of President shall be eligible to that of Vice-President of the United States.

AMENDMENT XIII [1865]

Section 1. Neither slavery nor involuntary servitude, except as a punishment for crime whereof the party shall have been duly convicted, shall exist within the United States, or any place subject to their jurisdiction.

Section 2. Congress shall have power to enforce this article by appropriate legislation.

AMENDMENT XIV [1868]

Section 1. All persons born or naturalized in the United States, and subject to the jurisdiction thereof, are citizens of the United States and of the State wherein they reside. No State shall make or enforce any law which shall abridge the privileges or immunities of citizens of the United States; nor shall any State deprive any person of life, liberty, or property, without due process of law; nor deny to any person within its jurisdiction the equal protection of the laws.

Section 2. Representatives shall be apportioned among the several States according to their respective numbers, counting the whole number of persons in each State, excluding Indians not taxed. But when the right to vote at any election for the choice of electors for President and Vice President of the United States, Representatives in Congress, the Executive and Judicial officers of a State, or the members of the Legislature thereof, is denied to any of the male inhabitants of such State, being twenty-one years of age, and citizens of the United States, or in any way abridged, except for participation in rebellion, or other crime, the basis of representation therein shall be reduced in the proportion which the number of such male citizens shall bear to the whole number of male citizens twenty-one years of age in such State.

Section 3. No person shall be a Senator or Representative in Congress, or elector of President and Vice President, or hold any office, civil or military, under the United States, or under any State, who having previously taken an oath, as a member of Congress, or as an officer of the United States, or as a member of any State legislature, or as an executive or judicial officer of any State, to support the Constitution of the United States, shall have engaged in insurrection or rebellion against the same, or given aid or comfort to the enemies thereof. But Congress may by a vote of two-thirds of each House, remove such disability.

Section 4. The validity of the public debt of the United States, authorized by law, including debts incurred for payment of pensions and bounties for services in suppressing insurrection or rebellion, shall not be questioned. But neither the United States nor any State shall assume or pay any debt or obligation incurred in aid of insurrection or rebellion against the United States, or any claim for the loss or emancipation of any slave; but all such debts, obligations and claims shall be held illegal and void.

Section 5. The Congress shall have power to enforce, by appropriate legislation, the provisions of this article.

AMENDMENT XV [1870]

Section 1. The right of citizens of the United States to vote shall not be denied or abridged by the United States or by any State on account of race, color, or previous condition of servitude.

Section 2. The Congress shall have power to enforce this article by appropriate legislation.

AMENDMENT XVI [1913]

The Congress shall have power to lay and collect taxes on incomes, from whatever source derived, without apportionment among the several States, and without regard to any census or enumeration.

AMENDMENT XVII [1913]

Section 1. The Senate of the United States shall be composed of two Senators from each State, elected by the people thereof, for six years; and each Senator shall have one vote. The electors in each State shall have the qualifications requisite for electors of the most numerous branch of the State legislatures.

Section 2. When vacancies happen in the representation of any State in the Senate, the executive authority of such State shall issue writs of election to fill such vacancies: Provided, That the legislature of any State may empower the executive thereof to make temporary appointments until the people fill the vacancies by election as the legislature may direct.

Section 3. This amendment shall not be so construed as to affect the election or term of any Senator chosen before it becomes valid as part of the Constitution.

AMENDMENT XVIII [1919]

Section 1. After one year from the ratification of this article the manufacture, sale, or transportation of intoxicating liquors within, the importation thereof into, or the exportation thereof from the United States and all territory subject to the jurisdiction thereof for beverage purposes is hereby prohibited.

Section 2. The Congress and the several States shall have concurrent power to enforce this article by appropriate legislation.

Section 3. This article shall be inoperative unless it shall have been ratified as an amendment to the Constitution by the legislatures of the several States, as provided in the Constitution, within seven years from the date of the submission hereof to the States by the Congress.

AMENDMENT XIX [1920]

Section 1. The right of citizens of the United States to vote shall not be denied or abridged by the United States or by any State on account of sex.

Section 2. Congress shall have power to enforce this article by appropriate legislation.

AMENDMENT XX [1933]

Section 1. The terms of the President and Vice President shall end at noon on the 20th day of January, and the terms of Senators and Representatives at noon on the 3d day of January, of the years in which such terms would have ended if this article had not been ratified; and the terms of their successors shall then begin.

Section 2. The Congress shall assemble at least once in every year, and such meeting shall begin at noon on the 3d day of January, unless they shall by law appoint a different day.

Section 3. If, at the time fixed for the beginning of the term of the President, the President elect shall have died, the Vice President elect shall become President. If the President shall not have been chosen before the time fixed for the beginning of his term, or if the President elect shall have failed to qualify, then the Vice President elect shall act as President until a President shall have qualified; and the Congress may by law provide for the case wherein neither a President elect nor a Vice President elect shall have qualified, declaring who shall then act as President, or the manner in which one who is to act shall be selected, and such person shall act accordingly until a President or Vice President shall have qualified.

Section 4. The Congress may by law provide for the case of the death of any of the persons from whom the House of Representatives may choose a President whenever the right of choice shall have devolved upon them, and for the case of the death of any of the persons from whom the Senate may choose a Vice President whenever the right of choice shall have devolved upon them.

Section 5. Sections 1 and 2 shall take effect on the 15th day of October following the ratification of this article.

Section 6. This article shall be inoperative unless it shall have been ratified as an amendment to the Constitution by the legislatures of three-fourths of the several States within seven years from the date of its submission.

AMENDMENT XXI [1933]

Section 1. The eighteenth article of amendment to the Constitution of the United States is hereby repealed.

Section 2. The transportation or importation into any State, Territory, or possession of the United States for delivery or use therein of intoxicating liquors, in violation of the laws thereof, is hereby prohibited.

Section 3. This article shall be inoperative unless it shall have been ratified as an amendment to the Constitution by conventions in the several States, as provided in the Constitution, within seven years from the date of the submission hereof to the States by the Congress.

AMENDMENT XXII [1951]

Section 1. No person shall be elected to the office of the President more than twice, and no person who has held the office of President, or acted as President, for more than two years of a term to which some other person was elected President shall be elected to the office of President more than once. But this Article shall not apply to any person holding the office of President when this Article was proposed by the Congress, and shall not prevent any person who may be holding the office of President, or acting as President, during the term within which this Article becomes operative from holding the office of President or acting as President during the remainder of such term.

Section 2. This article shall be inoperative unless it shall have been ratified as an amendment to the Constitution by the legislatures of three-fourths of the several States within seven years from the date of its submission to the States by the Congress.

AMENDMENT XXIII [1961]

Section 1. The District constituting the seat of Government of the United States shall appoint in such manner as the Congress may direct:

A number of electors of President and Vice President equal to the whole number of Senators and Representatives in Congress to which the District would be entitled if it were a State, but in no event more than the least populous state; they shall be in addition to those appointed by the states, but they shall be considered, for the purposes of the election of President and Vice President, to be electors appointed by a state; and they shall meet in the District and perform such duties as provided by the twelfth article of amendment.

Section 2. The Congress shall have power to enforce this article by appropriate legislation.

AMENDMENT XXIV [1964]

Section 1. The right of citizens of the United States to vote in any primary or other election for President or Vice President, for electors for President or Vice President, or for Senator or Representative in Congress, shall not be denied or abridged by the United States, or any State by reason of failure to pay any poll tax or other tax.

Section 2. The Congress shall have power to enforce this article by appropriate legislation.

AMENDMENT XXV [1967]

Section 1. In case of the removal of the President from office or of his death or resignation, the Vice President shall become President.

Section 2. Whenever there is a vacancy in the office of the Vice President, the President shall nominate a Vice President who shall take office upon confirmation by a majority vote of both Houses of Congress.

Section 3. Whenever the President transmits to the President pro tempore of the Senate and the Speaker of the House of Representatives his written declaration that he is unable to discharge the powers and duties of his office, and until he transmits to them a written declaration to the contrary, such powers and duties shall be discharged by the Vice President as Acting President.

Section 4. Whenever the Vice President and a majority of either the principal officers of the executive departments or of such other body as Congress may by law provide, transmit to the President pro tempore of the Senate and the Speaker of the House of Representatives their written declaration that the President is unable to discharge the powers and duties of his office, the Vice President shall immediately assume the powers and duties of the office as Acting President.

Thereafter, when the President transmits to the President pro tempore of the Senate and the Speaker of the House of Representatives his written declaration that no inability exists, he shall resume the powers and duties of his office unless the Vice President and a majority of either the principal officers of the executive department or of such other body as Congress may by law provide, transmit within four days to the President pro tempore of the Senate and the Speaker of the House of Representatives their written declaration that the President is unable to discharge the powers and duties of his office. Thereupon Congress shall decide the issue, assembling within forty-eight hours for that purpose if not in session. If the Congress, within twenty-one days after receipt of the latter written declaration, or, if Congress is not in session, within twenty-one days after Congress is required to assemble, determines by two-thirds vote of both Houses that the President is unable to discharge the powers and duties of his office, the Vice President shall continue to discharge the same as Acting President; otherwise, the President shall resume the powers and duties of his office.

AMENDMENT XXVI [1971]

Section 1. The right of citizens of the United States, who are eighteen years of age or older, to vote shall not be denied or abridged by the United States or by any State on account of age.

Section 2. The Congress shall have power to enforce this article by appropriate legislation.

AMENDMENT XXVII [1992]

No law, varying the compensation for the services of the Senators and Representatives, shall take effect, until an election of Representatives shall have intervened.

Article 2 of the Uniform Commercial Code

ARTICLE 2
SALES

Part 1 Short Title, General Construction and Subject Matter

§ 2–101. Short Title.

This Article shall be known and may be cited as Uniform Commercial Code—Sales.

§ 2–102. Scope; Certain Security and Other Transactions Excluded from This Article.

Unless the context otherwise requires, this Article applies to transactions in goods; it does not apply to any transaction which although in the form of an unconditional contract to sell or present sale is intended to operate only as a security transaction nor does this Article impair or repeal any statute regulating sales to consumers, farmers or other specified classes of buyers.

§ 2–103. Definitions and Index of Definitions.

(1) In this Article unless the context otherwise requires
(a) "Buyer" means a person who buys or contracts to buy goods.
(b) "Good faith" in the case of a merchant means honesty in fact and the observance of reasonable commercial standards of fair dealing in the trade.
(c) "Receipt" of goods means taking physical possession of them.
(d) "Seller" means a person who sells or contracts to sell goods.

(2) Other definitions applying to this Article or to specified Parts thereof, and the sections in which they appear are:

"Acceptance". Section 2–606.
"Banker's credit". Section 2–325.
"Between merchants". Section 2–104.
"Cancellation". Section 2–106(4).
"Commercial unit". Section 2–105.
"Confirmed credit". Section 2–325.
"Conforming to contract". Section 2–106.
"Contract for sale". Section 2–106.
"Cover". Section 2–712.
"Entrusting". Section 2–403.
"Financing agency". Section 2–104.
"Future goods". Section 2–105.
"Goods". Section 2–105.
"Identification". Section 2–501.
"Installment contract". Section 2–612.
"Letter of Credit". Section 2–325.

"Lot". Section 2–105.
"Merchant". Section 2–104.
"Overseas". Section 2–323.
"Person in position of seller". Section 2–707.
"Present sale". Section 2–106.
"Sale". Section 2–106.
"Sale on approval". Section 2–326.
"Sale or return". Section 2–326.
"Termination". Section 2–106.

(3) The following definitions in other Articles apply to this Article:
"Check". Section 3–104.
"Consignee". Section 7–102.
"Consignor". Section 7–102.
"Consumer goods". Section 9–109.
"Dishonor". Section 3–507.
"Draft". Section 3–104.

(4) In addition Article 1 contains general definitions and principles of construction and interpretation applicable throughout this Article.

As amended in 1994 and 1999.

§ 2–104. Definitions: "Merchant"; "Between Merchants"; "Financing Agency".

(1) "Merchant" means a person who deals in goods of the kind or otherwise by his occupation holds himself out as having knowledge or skill peculiar to the practices or goods involved in the transaction or to whom such knowledge or skill may be attributed by his employment of an agent or broker or other intermediary who by his occupation holds himself out as having such knowledge or skill.

(2) "Financing agency" means a bank, finance company or other person who in the ordinary course of business makes advances against goods or documents of title or who by arrangement with either the seller or the buyer intervenes in ordinary course to make or collect payment due or claimed under the contract for sale, as by purchasing or paying the seller's draft or making advances against it or by merely taking it for collection whether or not documents of title accompany the draft. "Financing agency" includes also a bank or other person who similarly intervenes between persons who are in the position of seller and buyer in respect to the goods (Section 2–707).

(3) "Between merchants" means in any transaction with respect to which both parties are chargeable with the knowledge or skill of merchants.

§ 2–105. Definitions: Transferability; "Goods"; "Future" Goods; "Lot"; "Commercial Unit".

(1) "Goods" means all things (including specially manufactured goods) which are movable at the time of identification to the contract for sale other than the money in which the price is to be paid, investment securities (Article 8) and things in action. "Goods" also includes the unborn young of animals and growing crops and

other identified things attached to realty as described in the section on goods to be severed from realty (Section 2–107).

(2) Goods must be both existing and identified before any interest in them can pass. Goods which are not both existing and identified are "future" goods. A purported present sale of future goods or of any interest therein operates as a contract to sell.

(3) There may be a sale of a part interest in existing identified goods.

(4) An undivided share in an identified bulk of fungible goods is sufficiently identified to be sold although the quantity of the bulk is not determined. Any agreed proportion of such a bulk or any quantity thereof agreed upon by number, weight or other measure may to the extent of the seller's interest in the bulk be sold to the buyer who then becomes an owner in common.

(5) "Lot" means a parcel or a single article which is the subject matter of a separate sale or delivery, whether or not it is sufficient to perform the contract.

(6) "Commercial unit" means such a unit of goods as by commercial usage is a single whole for purposes of sale and division of which materially impairs its character or value on the market or in use. A commercial unit may be a single article (as a machine) or a set of articles (as a suite of furniture or an assortment of sizes) or a quantity (as a bale, gross, or carload) or any other unit treated in use or in the relevant market as a single whole.

§ 2–106. Definitions: "Contract"; "Agreement"; "Contract for Sale"; "Sale"; "Present Sale"; "Conforming" to Contract; "Termination"; "Cancellation".

(1) In this Article unless the context otherwise requires "contract" and "agreement" are limited to those relating to the present or future sale of goods. "Contract for sale" includes both a present sale of goods and a contract to sell goods at a future time. A "sale" consists in the passing of title from the seller to the buyer for a price (Section 2–401). A "present sale" means a sale which is accomplished by the making of the contract.

(2) Goods or conduct including any part of a performance are "conforming" or conform to the contract when they are in accordance with the obligations under the contract.

(3) "Termination" occurs when either party pursuant to a power created by agreement or law puts an end to the contract otherwise than for its breach. On "termination" all obligations which are still executory on both sides are discharged but any right based on prior breach or performance survives.

(4) "Cancellation" occurs when either party puts an end to the contract for breach by the other and its effect is the same as that of "termination" except that the cancelling party also retains any remedy for breach of the whole contract or any unperformed balance.

§ 2–107. Goods to Be Severed from Realty: Recording.

(1) A contract for the sale of minerals or the like (including oil and gas) or a structure or its materials to be removed from realty is a contract for the sale of goods within this Article if they are to be severed by the seller but until severance a purported present sale thereof which is not effective as a transfer of an interest in land is effective only as a contract to sell.

(2) A contract for the sale apart from the land of growing crops or other things attached to realty and capable of severance without material harm thereto but not described in subsection (1) or of timber to be cut is a contract for the sale of goods within this Article whether the subject matter is to be severed by the buyer or by the seller even though it forms part of the realty at the time of contracting, and the parties can by identification effect a present sale before severance.

(3) The provisions of this section are subject to any third party rights provided by the law relating to realty records, and the contract for sale may be executed and recorded as a document transferring an interest in land and shall then constitute notice to third parties of the buyer's rights under the contract for sale.
As amended in 1972.

Part 2 Form, Formation and Readjustment of Contract
§ 2–201. Formal Requirements; Statute of Frauds.

(1) Except as otherwise provided in this section a contract for the sale of goods for the price of $500 or more is not enforceable by way of action or defense unless there is some writing sufficient to indicate that a contract for sale has been made between the parties and signed by the party against whom enforcement is sought or by his authorized agent or broker. A writing is not insufficient because it omits or incorrectly states a term agreed upon but the contract is not enforceable under this paragraph beyond the quantity of goods shown in such writing.

(2) Between merchants if within a reasonable time a writing in confirmation of the contract and sufficient against the sender is received and the party receiving it has reason to know its contents, its satisfies the requirements of subsection (1) against such party unless written notice of objection to its contents is given within ten days after it is received.

(3) A contract which does not satisfy the requirements of subsection (1) but which is valid in other respects is enforceable

(a) if the goods are to be specially manufactured for the buyer and are not suitable for sale to others in the ordinary course of the seller's business and the seller, before notice of repudiation is received and under circumstances which reasonably indicate that the goods are for the buyer, has made either a substantial beginning of their manufacture or commitments for their procurement; or

(b) if the party against whom enforcement is sought admits in his pleading, testimony or otherwise in court that a contract for sale was made, but the contract is not enforceable under this provision beyond the quantity of goods admitted; or

(c) with respect to goods for which payment has been made and accepted or which have been received and accepted (Sec. 2–606).

§ 2–202. Final Written Expression: Parol or Extrinsic Evidence.

Terms with respect to which the confirmatory memoranda of the parties agree or which are otherwise set forth in a writing intended by the parties as a final expression of their agreement with respect to such terms as are included therein may not be contradicted by evidence of any prior agreement or or of a contemporaneous oral agreement but may be explained or supplemented

(a) by course of dealing or usage of trade (Section 1–205) or by course of performance (Section 2–208); and

(b) by evidence of consistent additional terms unless the court finds the writing to have been intended also as a complete and exclusive statement of the terms of the agreement.

§ 2–203. Seals Inoperative.

The affixing of a seal to a writing evidencing a contract for sale or an offer to buy or sell goods does not constitute the writing a sealed instrument and the law with respect to sealed instruments does not apply to such a contract or offer.

§ 2–204. Formation in General.

(1) A contract for sale of goods may be made in any manner sufficient to show agreement, including conduct by both parties which recognizes the existence of such a contract.

(2) An agreement sufficient to constitute a contract for sale may be found even though the moment of its making is undetermined.

(3) Even though one or more terms are left open a contract for sale does not fail for indefiniteness if the parties have intended to make a contract and there is a reasonably certain basis for giving an appropriate remedy.

§ 2–205. Firm Offers.

An offer by a merchant to buy or sell goods in a signed writing which by its terms gives assurance that it will be held open is not revocable, for lack of consideration, during the time stated or if no time is stated for a reasonable time, but in no event may such period of irrevocability exceed three months; but any such term of assurance on a form supplied by the offeree must be separately signed by the offeror.

§ 2–206. Offer and Acceptance in Formation of Contract.

(1) Unless other unambiguously indicated by the language or circumstances

    (a) an offer to make a contract shall be construed as inviting acceptance in any manner and by any medium reasonable in the circumstances;

    (b) an order or other offer to buy goods for prompt or current shipment shall be construed as inviting acceptance either by a prompt promise to ship or by the prompt or current shipment of conforming or nonconforming goods, but such a shipment of non-conforming goods does not constitute an acceptance if the seller seasonably notifies the buyer that the shipment is offered only as an accommodation to the buyer.

(2) Where the beginning of a requested performance is a reasonable mode of acceptance an offeror who is not notified of acceptance within a reasonable time may treat the offer as having lapsed before acceptance.

§ 2–207. Additional Terms in Acceptance or Confirmation.

(1) A definite and seasonable expression of acceptance or a written confirmation which is sent within a reasonable time operates as an acceptance even though it states terms additional to or different from those offered or agreed upon, unless acceptance is expressly made conditional on assent to the additional or different terms.

(2) The additional terms are to be construed as proposals for addition to the contract. Between merchants such terms become part of the contract unless:

    (a) the offer expressly limits acceptance to the terms of the offer;

    (b) they materially alter it; or

    (c) notification of objection to them has already been given or is given within a reasonable time after notice of them is received.

(3) Conduct by both parties which recognizes the existence of a contract is sufficient to establish a contract for sale although the writings of the parties do not otherwise establish a contract. In such case the terms of the particular contract consist of those terms on which the writings of the parties agree, together with any supplementary terms incorporated under any other provisions of this Act.

§ 2–208. Course of Performance or Practical Construction.

(1) Where the contract for sale involves repeated occasions for performance by either party with knowledge of the nature of the performance and opportunity for objection to it by the other, any course of performance accepted or acquiesced in without objection shall be relevant to determine the meaning of the agreement.

(2) The express terms of the agreement and any such course of performance, as well as any course of dealing and usage of trade, shall be construed whenever reasonable as consistent with each other; but when such construction is unreasonable, express terms shall control course of performance and course of performance shall control both course of dealing and usage of trade (Section 1–205).

(3) Subject to the provisions of the next section on modification and waiver, such course of performance shall be relevant to show a waiver or modification of any term inconsistent with such course of performance.

§ 2–209. Modification, Rescission and Waiver.

(1) An agreement modifying a contract within this Article needs no consideration to be binding.

(2) A signed agreement which excludes modification or rescission except by a signed writing cannot be otherwise modified or rescinded, but except as between merchants such a requirement on a form supplied by the merchant must be separately signed by the other party.

(3) The requirements of the statute of frauds section of this Article (Section 2–201) must be satisfied if the contract as modified is within its provisions.

(4) Although an attempt at modification or rescission does not satisfy the requirements of subsection (2) or (3) it can operate as a waiver.

(5) A party who has made a waiver affecting an executory portion of the contract may retract the waiver by reasonable notification received by the other party that strict performance will be required of any term waived, unless the retraction would be unjust in view of a material change of position in reliance on the waiver.

§ 2–210. Delegation of Performance; Assignment of Rights.

(1) A party may perform his duty through a delegate unless otherwise agreed or unless the other party has a substantial interest in having his original promisor perform or control the acts required by the contract. No delegation of performance relieves the party delegating of any duty to perform or any liability for breach.

(2) Except as otherwise provided in Section 9–406, unless otherwise agreed, all rights of either seller or buyer can be assigned except where the assignment would materially change the duty of the other party, or increase materially the burden or risk imposed on him by his contract, or impair materially his chance of obtaining return performance. A right to damages for breach of the whole contract or a right arising out of the assignor's due performance of his entire obligation can be assigned despite agreement otherwise.

(3) The creation, attachment, perfection, or enforcement of a security interest in the seller's interest under a contract is not a

transfer that materially changes the duty of or increases materially the burden or risk imposed on the buyer or impairs materially the buyer's chance of obtaining return performance within the purview of subsection (2) unless, and then only to the extent that, enforcement actually results in a delegation of material performance of the seller. Even in that event, the creation, attachment, perfection, and enforcement of the security interest remain effective, but (i) the seller is liable to the buyer for damages caused by the delegation to the extent that the damages could not reasonably by prevented by the buyer, and (ii) a court having jurisdiction may grant other appropriate relief, including cancellation of the contract for sale or an injunction against enforcement of the security interest or consummation of the enforcement.

(4) Unless the circumstances indicate the contrary a prohibition of assignment of "the contract" is to be construed as barring only the delegation to the assignee of the assignor's performance.

(5) An assignment of "the contract" or of "all my rights under the contract" or an assignment in similar general terms is an assignment of rights and unless the language or the circumstances (as in an assignment for security) indicate the contrary, it is a delegation of performance of the duties of the assignor and its acceptance by the assignee constitutes a promise by him to perform those duties. This promise is enforceable by either the assignor or the other party to the original contract.

(6) The other party may treat any assignment which delegates performance as creating reasonable grounds for insecurity and may without prejudice to his rights against the assignor demand assurances from the assignee (Section 2–609).

As amended in 1999.

Part 3 General Obligation and Construction of Contract

§ 2–301. General Obligations of Parties.

The obligation of the seller is to transfer and deliver and that of the buyer is to accept and pay in accordance with the contract.

§ 2–302. Unconscionable Contract or Clause.

(1) If the court as a matter of law finds the contract or any clause of the contract to have been unconscionable at the time it was made the court may refuse to enforce the contract, or it may enforce the remainder of the contract without the unconscionable clause, or it may so limit the application of any unconscionable clause as to avoid any unconscionable result.

(2) When it is claimed or appears to the court that the contract or any clause thereof may be unconscionable the parties shall be afforded a reasonable opportunity to present evidence as to its commercial setting, purpose and effect to aid the court in making the determination.

§ 2–303. Allocations or Division of Risks.

Where this Article allocates a risk or a burden as between the parties "unless otherwise agreed", the agreement may not only shift the allocation but may also divide the risk or burden.

§ 2–304. Price Payable in Money, Goods, Realty, or Otherwise.

(1) The price can be made payable in money or otherwise. If it is payable in whole or in part in goods each party is a seller of the goods which he is to transfer.

(2) Even though all or part of the price is payable in an interest in realty the transfer of the goods and the seller's obligations with

reference to them are subject to this Article, but not the transfer of the interest in realty or the transferor's obligations in connection therewith.

§ 2–305. Open Price Term.

(1) The parties if they so intend can conclude a contract for sale even though the price is not settled. In such a case the price is a reasonable price at the time for delivery if

(a) nothing is said as to price; or

(b) the price is left to be agreed by the parties and they fail to agree; or

(c) the price is to be fixed in terms of some agreed market or other standard as set or recorded by a third person or agency and it is not so set or recorded.

(2) A price to be fixed by the seller or by the buyer means a price for him to fix in good faith.

(3) When a price left to be fixed otherwise than by agreement of the parties fails to be fixed through fault of one party the other may at his option treat the contract as cancelled or himself fix a reasonable price.

(4) Where, however, the parties intend not to be bound unless the price be fixed or agreed and it is not fixed or agreed there is no contract. In such a case the buyer must return any goods already received or if unable so to do must pay their reasonable value at the time of delivery and the seller must return any portion of the price paid on account.

§ 2–306. Output, Requirements and Exclusive Dealings.

(1) A term which measures the quantity by the output of the seller or the requirements of the buyer means such actual output or requirements as may occur in good faith, except that no quantity unreasonably disproportionate to any stated estimate or in the absence of a stated estimate to any normal or otherwise comparable prior output or requirements may be tendered or demanded.

(2) A lawful agreement by either the seller or the buyer for exclusive dealing in the kind of goods concerned imposes unless otherwise agreed an obligation by the seller to use best efforts to supply the goods and by the buyer to use best efforts to promote their sale.

§ 2–307. Delivery in Single Lot or Several Lots.

Unless otherwise agreed all goods called for by a contract for sale must be tendered in a single delivery and payment is due only on such tender but where the circumstances give either party the right to make or demand delivery in lots the price if it can be apportioned may be demanded for each lot.

§ 2–308. Absence of Specified Place for Delivery.

Unless otherwise agreed

(a) the place for delivery of goods is the seller's place of business or if he has none his residence; but

(b) in a contract for sale of identified goods which to the knowledge of the parties at the time of contracting are in some other place, that place is the place for their delivery; and

(c) documents of title may be delivered through customary banking channels.

§ 2–309. Absence of Specific Time Provisions; Notice of Termination.

(1) The time for shipment or delivery or any other action under a contract if not provided in this Article or agreed upon shall be a reasonable time.

(2) Where the contract provides for successive performances but is indefinite in duration it is valid for a reasonable time but unless otherwise agreed may be terminated at any time by either party.

(3) Termination of a contract by one party except on the happening of an agreed event requires that reasonable notification be received by the other party and an agreement dispensing with notification is invalid if its operation would be unconscionable.

§ 2–310. Open Time for Payment or Running of Credit; Authority to Ship Under Reservation.

Unless otherwise agreed

(a) payment is due at the time and place at which the buyer is to receive the goods even though the place of shipment is the place of delivery; and

(b) if the seller is authorized to send the goods he may ship them under reservation, and may tender the documents of title, but the buyer may inspect the goods after their arrival before payment is due unless such inspection is inconsistent with the terms of the contract (Section 2–513); and

(c) if delivery is authorized and made by way of documents of title otherwise than by subsection (b) then payment is due at the time and place at which the buyer is to receive the documents regardless of where the goods are to be received; and

(d) where the seller is required or authorized to ship the goods on credit the credit period runs from the time of shipment but post-dating the invoice or delaying its dispatch will correspondingly delay the starting of the credit period.

§ 2–311. Options and Cooperation Respecting Performance.

(1) An agreement for sale which is otherwise sufficiently definite (subsection (3) of Section 2–204) to be a contract is not made invalid by the fact that it leaves particulars of performance to be specified by one of the parties. Any such specification must be made in good faith and within limits set by commercial reasonableness.

(2) Unless otherwise agreed specifications relating to assortment of the goods are at the buyer's option and except as otherwise provided in subsections (1)(c) and (3) of Section 2–319 specifications or arrangements relating to shipment are at the seller's option.

(3) Where such specification would materially affect the other party's performance but is not seasonably made or where one party's cooperation is necessary to the agreed performance of the other but is not seasonably forthcoming, the other party in addition to all other remedies

(a) is excused for any resulting delay in his own performance; and

(b) may also either proceed to perform in any reasonable manner or after the time for a material part of his own performance treat the failure to specify or to cooperate as a breach by failure to deliver or accept the goods.

§ 2–312. Warranty of Title and Against Infringement; Buyer's Obligation Against Infringement.

(1) Subject to subsection (2) there is in a contract for sale a warranty by the seller that

(a) the title conveyed shall be good, and its transfer rightful; and

(b) the goods shall be delivered free from any security interest or other lien or encumbrance of which the buyer at the time of contracting has no knowledge.

(2) A warranty under subsection (1) will be excluded or modified only by specific language or by circumstances which give the buyer reason to know that the person selling does not claim title in himself or that he is purporting to sell only such right or title as he or a third person may have.

(3) Unless otherwise agreed a seller who is a merchant regularly dealing in goods of the kind warrants that the goods shall be delivered free of the rightful claim of any third person by way of infringement or the like but a buyer who furnishes specifications to the seller must hold the seller harmless against any such claim which arises out of compliance with the specifications.

§ 2–313. Express Warranties by Affirmation, Promise, Description, Sample.

(1) Express warranties by the seller are created as follows:

(a) Any affirmation of fact or promise made by the seller to the buyer which relates to the goods and becomes part of the basis of the bargain creates an express warranty that the goods shall conform to the affirmation or promise.

(b) Any description of the goods which is made part of the basis of the bargain creates an express warranty that the goods shall conform to the description.

(c) Any sample or model which is made part of the basis of the bargain creates an express warranty that the whole of the goods shall conform to the sample or model.

(2) It is not necessary to the creation of an express warranty that the seller use formal words such as "warrant" or "guarantee" or that he have a specific intention to make a warranty, but an affirmation merely of the value of the goods or a statement purporting to be merely the seller's opinion or commendation of the goods does not create a warranty.

§ 2–314. Implied Warranty: Merchantability; Usage of Trade.

(1) Unless excluded or modified (Section 2–316), a warranty that the goods shall be merchantable is implied in a contract for their sale if the seller is a merchant with respect to goods of that kind. Under this section the serving for value of food or drink to be consumed either on the premises or elsewhere is a sale.

(2) Goods to be merchantable must be at least such as

(a) pass without objection in the trade under the contract description; and

(b) in the case of fungible goods, are of fair average quality within the description; and

(c) are fit for the ordinary purposes for which such goods are used; and

(d) run, within the variations permitted by the agreement, of even kind, quality and quantity within each unit and among all units involved; and

(e) are adequately contained, packaged, and labeled as the agreement may require; and

(f) conform to the promises or affirmations of fact made on the container or label if any.

(3) Unless excluded or modified (Section 2–316) other implied warranties may arise from course of dealing or usage of trade.

§ 2–315. Implied Warranty: Fitness for Particular Purpose.

Where the seller at the time of contracting has reason to know any particular purpose for which the goods are required and that the buyer is relying on the seller's skill or judgment to select or furnish suitable goods, there is unless excluded or modified under the next section an implied warranty that the goods shall be fit for such purpose.

§ 2–316. Exclusion or Modification of Warranties.

(1) Words or conduct relevant to the creation of an express warranty and words or conduct tending to negate or limit warranty shall be construed wherever reasonable as consistent with each other; but subject to the provisions of this Article on parol or extrinsic evidence (Section 2–202) negation or limitation is inoperative to the extent that such construction is unreasonable.

(2) Subject to subsection (3), to exclude or modify the implied warranty of merchantability or any part of it the language must mention merchantability and in case of a writing must be conspicuous, and to exclude or modify any implied warranty of fitness the exclusion must be by a writing and conspicuous. Language to exclude all implied warranties of fitness is sufficient if it states, for example, that "There are no warranties which extend beyond the description on the face hereof."

(3) Notwithstanding subsection (2)

(a) unless the circumstances indicate otherwise, all implied warranties are excluded by expressions like "as is", "with all faults" or other language which in common understanding calls the buyer's attention to the exclusion of warranties and makes plain that there is no implied warranty; and

(b) when the buyer before entering into the contract has examined the goods or the sample or model as fully as he desired or has refused to examine the goods there is no implied warranty with regard to defects which an examination ought in the circumstances to have revealed to him; and

(c) an implied warranty can also be excluded or modified by course of dealing or course of performance or usage of trade.

(4) Remedies for breach of warranty can be limited in accordance with the provisions of this Article on liquidation or limitation of damages and on contractual modification of remedy (Sections 2–718 and 2–719).

§ 2–317. Cumulation and Conflict of Warranties Express or Implied.

Warranties whether express or implied shall be construed as consistent with each other and as cumulative, but if such construction is unreasonable the intention of the parties shall determine which warranty is dominant. In ascertaining that intention the following rules apply:

(a) Exact or technical specifications displace an inconsistent sample or model or general language of description.

(b) A sample from an existing bulk displaces inconsistent general language of description.

(c) Express warranties displace inconsistent implied warranties other than an implied warranty of fitness for a particular purpose.

§ 2–318. Third Party Beneficiaries of Warranties Express or Implied.

Note: If this Act is introduced in the Congress of the United States this section should be omitted. (States to select one alternative.)

Alternative A

A seller's warranty whether express or implied extends to any natural person who is in the family or household of his buyer or who

is a guest in his home if it is reasonable to expect that such person may use, consume or be affected by the goods and who is injured in person by breach of the warranty. A seller may not exclude or limit the operation of this section.

Alternative B

A seller's warranty whether express or implied extends to any natural person who may reasonably be expected to use, consume or be affected by the goods and who is injured in person by breach of the warranty. A seller may not exclude or limit the operation of this section.

Alternative C

A seller's warranty whether express or implied extends to any person who may reasonably be expected to use, consume or be affected by the goods and who is injured by breach of the warranty. A seller may not exclude or limit the operation of this section with respect to injury to the person of an individual to whom the warranty extends.

As amended 1966.

§ 2–319. F.O.B. and F.A.S. Terms.

(1) Unless otherwise agreed the term F.O.B. (which means "free on board") at a named place, even though used only in connection with the stated price, is a delivery term under which

(a) when the term is F.O.B. the place of shipment, the seller must at that place ship the goods in the manner provided in this Article (Section 2–504) and bear the expense and risk of putting them into the possession of the carrier; or

(b) when the term is F.O.B. the place of destination, the seller must at his own expense and risk transport the goods to that place and there tender delivery of them in the manner provided in this Article (Section 2–503);

(c) when under either (a) or (b) the term is also F.O.B. vessel, car or other vehicle, the seller must in addition at his own expense and risk load the goods on board. If the term is F.O.B. vessel the buyer must name the vessel and in an appropriate case the seller must comply with the provisions of this Article on the form of bill of lading (Section 2–323).

(2) Unless otherwise agreed the term F.A.S. vessel (which means "free alongside") at a named port, even though used only in connection with the stated price, is a delivery term under which the seller must

(a) at his own expense and risk deliver the goods alongside the vessel in the manner usual in that port or on a dock designated and provided by the buyer; and

(b) obtain and tender a receipt for the goods in exchange for which the carrier is under a duty to issue a bill of lading.

(3) Unless otherwise agreed in any case falling within subsection (1)(a) or (c) or subsection (2) the buyer must seasonably give any needed instructions for making delivery, including when the term is F.A.S. or F.O.B. the loading berth of the vessel and in an appropriate case its name and sailing date. The seller may treat the failure of needed instructions as a failure of cooperation under this Article (Section 2–311). He may also at his option move the goods in any reasonable manner preparatory to delivery or shipment.

(4) Under the term F.O.B. vessel or F.A.S. unless otherwise agreed the buyer must make payment against tender of the required documents and the seller may not tender nor the buyer demand delivery of the goods in substitution for the documents.

§ 2–320. C.I.F. and C. & F. Terms.

(1) The term C.I.F. means that the price includes in a lump sum the cost of the goods and the insurance and freight to the named destination. The term C. & F. or C.F. means that the price so includes cost and freight to the named destination.

(2) Unless otherwise agreed and even though used only in connection with the stated price and destination, the term C.I.F. destination or its equivalent requires the seller at his own expense and risk to

(a) put the goods into the possession of a carrier at the port for shipment and obtain a negotiable bill or bills of lading covering the entire transportation to the named destination; and

(b) load the goods and obtain a receipt from the carrier (which may be contained in the bill of lading) showing that the freight has been paid or provided for; and

(c) obtain a policy or certificate of insurance, including any war risk insurance, of a kind and on terms then current at the port of shipment in the usual amount, in the currency of the contract, shown to cover the same goods covered by the bill of lading and providing for payment of loss to the order of the buyer or for the account of whom it may concern; but the seller may add to the price the amount of the premium for any such war risk insurance; and

(d) prepare an invoice of the goods and procure any other documents required to effect shipment or to comply with the contract; and

(e) forward and tender with commercial promptness all the documents in due form and with any indorsement necessary to perfect the buyer's rights.

(3) Unless otherwise agreed the term C. & F. or its equivalent has the same effect and imposes upon the seller the same obligations and risks as a C.I.F. term except the obligation as to insurance.

(4) Under the term C.I.F. or C. & F. unless otherwise agreed the buyer must make payment against tender of the required documents and the seller may not tender nor the buyer demand delivery of the goods in substitution for the documents.

§ 2–321. C.I.F. or C. & F.: "Net Landed Weights"; "Payment on Arrival"; Warranty of Condition on Arrival.

Under a contract containing a term C.I.F. or C. & F.

(1) Where the price is based on or is to be adjusted according to "net landed weights", "delivered weights", "out turn" quantity or quality or the like, unless otherwise agreed the seller must reasonably estimate the price. The payment due on tender of the documents called for by the contract is the amount so estimated, but after final adjustment of the price a settlement must be made with commercial promptness.

(2) An agreement described in subsection (1) or any warranty of quality or condition of the goods on arrival places upon the seller the risk of ordinary deterioration, shrinkage and the like in transportation but has no effect on the place or time of identification to the contract for sale or delivery or on the passing of the risk of loss.

(3) Unless otherwise agreed where the contract provides for payment on or after arrival of the goods the seller must before payment allow such preliminary inspection as is feasible; but if the goods are lost delivery of the documents and payment are due when the goods should have arrived.

§ 2–322. Delivery "Ex-Ship".

(1) Unless otherwise agreed a term for delivery of goods "ex-ship" (which means from the carrying vessel) or in equivalent language

is not restricted to a particular ship and requires delivery from a ship which has reached a place at the named port of destination where goods of the kind are usually discharged.

(2) Under such a term unless otherwise agreed

(a) the seller must discharge all liens arising out of the carriage and furnish the buyer with a direction which puts the carrier under a duty to deliver the goods; and

(b) the risk of loss does not pass to the buyer until the goods leave the ship's tackle or are otherwise properly unloaded.

§ 2–323. Form of Bill of Lading Required in Overseas Shipment; "Overseas".

(1) Where the contract contemplates overseas shipment and contains a term C.I.F. or C. & F. or F.O.B. vessel, the seller unless otherwise agreed must obtain a negotiable bill of lading stating that the goods have been loaded on board or, in the case of a term C.I.F. or C. & F., received for shipment.

(2) Where in a case within subsection (1) a bill of lading has been issued in a set of parts, unless otherwise agreed if the documents are not to be sent from abroad the buyer may demand tender of the full set; otherwise only one part of the bill of lading need be tendered. Even if the agreement expressly requires a full set

(a) due tender of a single part is acceptable within the provisions of this Article on cure of improper delivery (subsection (1) of Section 2–508); and

(b) even though the full set is demanded, if the documents are sent from abroad the person tendering an incomplete set may nevertheless require payment upon furnishing an indemnity which the buyer in good faith deems adequate.

(3) A shipment by water or by air or a contract contemplating such shipment is "overseas" insofar as by usage of trade or agreement it is subject to the commercial, financing or shipping practices characteristic of international deep water commerce.

§ 2–324. "No Arrival, No Sale" Term.

Under a term "no arrival, no sale" or terms of like meaning, unless otherwise agreed,

(a) the seller must properly ship conforming goods and if they arrive by any means he must tender them on arrival but he assumes no obligation that the goods will arrive unless he has caused the non-arrival; and

(b) where without fault of the seller the goods are in part lost or have so deteriorated as no longer to conform to the contract or arrive after the contract time, the buyer may proceed as if there had been casualty to identified goods (Section 2–613).

§ 2–325. "Letter of Credit" Term; "Confirmed Credit".

(1) Failure of the buyer seasonably to furnish an agreed letter of credit is a breach of the contract for sale.

(2) The delivery to seller of a proper letter of credit suspends the buyer's obligation to pay. If the letter of credit is dishonored, the seller may on seasonable notification to the buyer require payment directly from him.

(3) Unless otherwise agreed the term "letter of credit" or "banker's credit" in a contract for sale means an irrevocable credit issued by a financing agency of good repute and, where the shipment is overseas, of good international repute. The term "confirmed credit" means that the credit must also carry the direct obligation of such an agency which does business in the seller's financial market.

§ 2–326. Sale on Approval and Sale or Return; Rights of Creditors.

(1) Unless otherwise agreed, if delivered goods may be returned by the buyer even though they conform to the contract, the transaction is

(a) a "sale on approval" if the goods are delivered primarily for use, and

(b) a "sale or return" if the goods are delivered primarily for resale.

(2) Goods held on approval are not subject to the claims of the buyer's creditors until acceptance; goods held on sale or return are subject to such claims while in the buyer's possession.

(3) Any "or return" term of a contract for sale is to be treated as a separate contract for sale within the statute of frauds section of this Article (Section 2–201) and as contradicting the sale aspect of the contract within the provisions of this Article or on parol or extrinsic evidence (Section 2–202).

As amended in 1999.

§ 2–327. Special Incidents of Sale on Approval and Sale or Return.

(1) Under a sale on approval unless otherwise agreed

(a) although the goods are identified to the contract the risk of loss and the title do not pass to the buyer until acceptance; and

(b) use of the goods consistent with the purpose of trial is not acceptance but failure seasonably to notify the seller of election to return the goods is acceptance, and if the goods conform to the contract acceptance of any part is accep-tance of the whole; and

(c) after due notification of election to return, the return is at the seller's risk and expense but a merchant buyer must follow any reasonable instructions.

(2) Under a sale or return unless otherwise agreed

(a) the option to return extends to the whole or any commercial unit of the goods while in substantially their original condition, but must be exercised seasonably; and

(b) the return is at the buyer's risk and expense.

§ 2–328. Sale by Auction.

(1) In a sale by auction if goods are put up in lots each lot is the subject of a separate sale.

(2) A sale by auction is complete when the auctioneer so announces by the fall of the hammer or in other customary manner. Where a bid is made while the hammer is falling in acceptance of a prior bid the auctioneer may in his discretion reopen the bidding or declare the goods sold under the bid on which the hammer was falling.

(3) Such a sale is with reserve unless the goods are in explicit terms put up without reserve. In an auction with reserve the auctioneer may withdraw the goods at any time until he announces completion of the sale. In an auction without reserve, after the auctioneer calls for bids on an article or lot, that article or lot cannot be withdrawn unless no bid is made within a reasonable time. In either case a bidder may retract his bid until the auctioneer's announcement of completion of the sale, but a bidder's retraction does not revive any previous bid.

(4) If the auctioneer knowingly receives a bid on the seller's behalf or the seller makes or procures such as bid, and notice has not been given that liberty for such bidding is reserved, the buyer may at his option avoid the sale or take the goods at the price of the last good faith bid prior to the completion of the sale. This subsection shall not apply to any bid at a forced sale.

Part 4 Title, Creditors and Good Faith Purchasers

§ 2–401. Passing of Title; Reservation for Security; Limited Application of This Section.

Each provision of this Article with regard to the rights, obligations and remedies of the seller, the buyer, purchasers or other third parties applies irrespective of title to the goods except where the provision refers to such title. Insofar as situations are not covered by the other provisions of this Article and matters concerning title became material the following rules apply:

(1) Title to goods cannot pass under a contract for sale prior to their identification to the contract (Section 2–501), and unless otherwise explicitly agreed the buyer acquires by their identification a special property as limited by this Act. Any retention or reservation by the seller of the title (property) in goods shipped or delivered to the buyer is limited in effect to a reservation of a security interest. Subject to these provisions and to the provisions of the Article on Secured Transactions (Article 9), title to goods passes from the seller to the buyer in any manner and on any conditions explicitly agreed on by the parties.

(2) Unless otherwise explicitly agreed title passes to the buyer at the time and place at which the seller completes his performance with reference to the physical delivery of the goods, despite any reservation of a security interest and even though a document of title is to be delivered at a different time or place; and in particular and despite any reservation of a security interest by the bill of lading

(a) if the contract requires or authorizes the seller to send the goods to the buyer but does not require him to deliver them at destination, title passes to the buyer at the time and place of shipment; but

(b) if the contract requires delivery at destination, title passes on tender there.

(3) Unless otherwise explicitly agreed where delivery is to be made without moving the goods,

(a) if the seller is to deliver a document of title, title passes at the time when and the place where he delivers such documents; or

(b) if the goods are at the time of contracting already identified and no documents are to be delivered, title passes at the time and place of contracting.

(4) A rejection or other refusal by the buyer to receive or retain the goods, whether or not justified, or a justified revocation of acceptance revests title to the goods in the seller. Such revesting occurs by operation of law and is not a "sale".

§ 2–402. Rights of Seller's Creditors Against Sold Goods.

(1) Except as provided in subsections (2) and (3), rights of unsecured creditors of the seller with respect to goods which have been identified to a contract for sale are subject to the buyer's rights to recover the goods under this Article (Sections 2–502 and 2–716).

(2) A creditor of the seller may treat a sale or an identification of goods to a contract for sale as void if as against him a retention of possession by the seller is fraudulent under any rule of law of the state where the goods are situated, except that retention of possession in good faith and current course of trade by a merchant-seller

for a commercially reasonable time after a sale or identification is not fraudulent.

(3) Nothing in this Article shall be deemed to impair the rights of creditors of the seller

(a) under the provisions of the Article on Secured Transactions (Article 9); or

(b) where identification to the contract or delivery is made not in current course of trade but in satisfaction of or as security for a pre-existing claim for money, security or the like and is made under circumstances which under any rule of law of the state where the goods are situated would apart from this Article constitute the transaction a fraudulent transfer or voidable preference.

§ 2–403. Power to Transfer; Good Faith Purchase of Goods; "Entrusting".

(1) A purchaser of goods acquires all title which his transferor had or had power to transfer except that a purchaser of a limited interest acquires rights only to the extent of the interest purchased. A person with voidable title has power to transfer a good title to a good faith purchaser for value. When goods have been delivered under a transaction of purchase the purchaser has such power even though

(a) the transferor was deceived as to the identity of the purchaser, or

(b) the delivery was in exchange for a check which is later dishonored, or

(c) it was agreed that the transaction was to be a "cash sale", or

(d) the delivery was procured through fraud punishable as larcenous under the criminal law.

(2) Any entrusting of possession of goods to a merchant who deals in goods of that kind gives him power to transfer all rights of the entruster to a buyer in ordinary course of business.

(3) "Entrusting" includes any delivery and any acquiescence in retention of possession regardless of any condition expressed between the parties to the delivery or acquiescence and regardless of whether the procurement of the entrusting or the possessor's disposition of the goods have been such as to be larcenous under the criminal law.

(4) The rights of other purchasers of goods and of lien creditors are governed by the Articles on Secured Transactions (Article 9), Bulk Transfers (Article 6) and Documents of Title (Article 7).

As amended in 1988.

Part 5 Performance

§ 2–501. Insurable Interest in Goods; Manner of Identification of Goods.

(1) The buyer obtains a special property and an insurable interest in goods by identification of existing goods as goods to which the contract refers even though the goods so identified are nonconforming and he has an option to return or reject them. Such identification can be made at any time and in any manner explicitly agreed to by the parties. In the absence of explicit agreement identification occurs

(a) when the contract is made if it is for the sale of goods already existing and identified;

(b) if the contract is for the sale of future goods other than those described in paragraph (c), when goods are shipped, marked or otherwise designated by the seller as goods to which the contract refers;

(c) when the crops are planted or otherwise become growing crops or the young are conceived if the contract is for the sale of unborn young to be born within twelve months after contracting or for the sale of crops to be harvested within twelve months or the next normal harvest season after contracting whichever is longer.

(2) The seller retains an insurable interest in goods so long as title to or any security interest in the goods remains in him and where the identification is by the seller alone he may until default or insolvency or notification to the buyer that the identification is final substitute other goods for those identified.

(3) Nothing in this section impairs any insurable interest recognized under any other statute or rule of law.

§ 2–502. Buyer's Right to Goods on Seller's Insolvency.

(1) Subject to subsections (2) and (3) and even though the goods have not been shipped a buyer who has paid a part or all of the price of goods in which he has a special property under the provisions of the immediately preceding section may on making and keeping good a tender of any unpaid portion of their price recover them from the seller if:

(a) in the case of goods bought for personal, family, or household purposes, the seller repudiates or fails to deliver as required by the contract; or

(b) in all cases, the seller becomes insolvent within ten days after receipt of the first installment on their price.

(2) The buyer's right to recover the goods under subsection (1)(a) vests upon acquisition of a special property, even if the seller had not then repudiated or failed to deliver.

(3) If the identification creating his special property has been made by the buyer he acquires the right to recover the goods only if they conform to the contract for sale.

As amended in 1999.

§ 2–503. Manner of Seller's Tender of Delivery.

(1) Tender of delivery requires that the seller put and hold conforming goods at the buyer's disposition and give the buyer any notification reasonably necessary to enable him to take delivery. The manner, time and place for tender are determined by the agreement and this Article, and in particular

(a) tender must be at a reasonable hour, and if it is of goods they must be kept available for the period reasonably necessary to enable the buyer to take possession; but

(b) unless otherwise agreed the buyer must furnish facilities reasonably suited to the receipt of the goods.

(2) Where the case is within the next section respecting shipment tender requires that the seller comply with its provisions.

(3) Where the seller is required to deliver at a particular destination tender requires that he comply with subsection (1) and also in any appropriate case tender documents as described in subsections (4) and (5) of this section.

(4) Where goods are in the possession of a bailee and are to be delivered without being moved

(a) tender requires that the seller either tender a negotiable document of title covering such goods or procure acknowledgment by the bailee of the buyer's right to possession of the goods; but

(b) tender to the buyer of a non-negotiable document of title or of a written direction to the bailee to deliver is sufficient tender unless the buyer seasonably objects, and receipt by the bailee of notification of the buyer's rights fixes those rights as against the bailee and all third persons; but risk of loss of the goods and of any failure by the bailee to honor the non-negotiable document of title or to obey the direction remains on the seller until the buyer has had a reasonable time to present the document or direction, and a refusal by the bailee to honor the document or to obey the direction defeats the tender.

(5) Where the contract requires the seller to deliver documents

(a) he must tender all such documents in correct form, except as provided in this Article with respect to bills of lading in a set (subsection (2) of Section 2–323); and

(b) tender through customary banking channels is sufficient and dishonor of a draft accompanying the documents constitutes non-acceptance or rejection.

§ 2–504. Shipment by Seller.

Where the seller is required or authorized to send the goods to the buyer and the contract does not require him to deliver them at a particular destination, then unless otherwise agreed he must

(a) put the goods in the possession of such a carrier and make such a contract for their transportation as may be reasonable having regard to the nature of the goods and other circumstances of the case; and

(b) obtain and promptly deliver or tender in due form any document necessary to enable the buyer to obtain possession of the goods or otherwise required by the agreement or by usage of trade; and

(c) promptly notify the buyer of the shipment.

Failure to notify the buyer under paragraph (c) or to make a proper contract under paragraph (a) is a ground for rejection only if material delay or loss ensues.

§ 2–505. Seller's Shipment under Reservation.

(1) Where the seller has identified goods to the contract by or before shipment:

(a) his procurement of a negotiable bill of lading to his own order or otherwise reserves in him a security interest in the goods. His procurement of the bill to the order of a financing agency or of the buyer indicates in addition only the seller's expectation of transferring that interest to the person named.

(b) a non-negotiable bill of lading to himself or his nominee reserves possession of the goods as security but except in a case of conditional delivery (subsection (2) of Section 2–507) a non-negotiable bill of lading naming the buyer as consignee reserves no security interest even though the seller retains possession of the bill of lading.

(2) When shipment by the seller with reservation of a security interest is in violation of the contract for sale it constitutes an improper contract for transportation within the preceding section but impairs neither the rights given to the buyer by shipment and identification of the goods to the contract nor the seller's powers as a holder of a negotiable document.

§ 2–506. Rights of Financing Agency.

(1) A financing agency by paying or purchasing for value a draft which relates to a shipment of goods acquires to the extent of the payment or purchase and in addition to its own rights under the draft and any document of title securing it any rights of the shipper in the goods including the right to stop delivery and the shipper's right to have the draft honored by the buyer.

(2) The right to reimbursement of a financing agency which has in good faith honored or purchased the draft under commitment to or authority from the buyer is not impaired by subsequent discovery of defects with reference to any relevant document which was apparently regular on its face.

§ 2–507. Effect of Seller's Tender; Delivery on Condition.

(1) Tender of delivery is a condition to the buyer's duty to accept the goods and, unless otherwise agreed, to his duty to pay for them. Tender entitles the seller to acceptance of the goods and to payment according to the contract.

(2) Where payment is due and demanded on the delivery to the buyer of goods or documents of title, his right as against the seller to retain or dispose of them is conditional upon his making the payment due.

§ 2–508. Cure by Seller of Improper Tender or Delivery; Replacement.

(1) Where any tender or delivery by the seller is rejected because non-conforming and the time for performance has not yet expired, the seller may seasonably notify the buyer of his intention to cure and may then within the contract time make a conforming delivery.

(2) Where the buyer rejects a non-conforming tender which the seller had reasonable grounds to believe would be acceptable with or without money allowance the seller may if he seasonably notifies the buyer have a further reasonable time to substitute a conforming tender.

§ 2–509. Risk of Loss in the Absence of Breach.

(1) Where the contract requires or authorizes the seller to ship the goods by carrier

(a) if it does not require him to deliver them at a particular destination, the risk of loss passes to the buyer when the goods are duly delivered to the carrier even though the shipment is under reservation (Section 2–505); but

(b) if it does require him to deliver them at a particular destination and the goods are there duly tendered while in the possession of the carrier, the risk of loss passes to the buyer when the goods are there duly so tendered as to enable the buyer to take delivery.

(2) Where the goods are held by a bailee to be delivered without being moved, the risk of loss passes to the buyer

(a) on his receipt of a negotiable document of title covering the goods; or

(b) on acknowledgment by the bailee of the buyer's right to possession of the goods; or

(c) after his receipt of a non-negotiable document of title or other written direction to deliver, as provided in subsection (4)(b) of Section 2–503.

(3) In any case not within subsection (1) or (2), the risk of loss passes to the buyer on his receipt of the goods if the seller is a merchant; otherwise the risk passes to the buyer on tender of delivery.

(4) The provisions of this section are subject to contrary agreement of the parties and to the provisions of this Article on sale on approval (Section 2–327) and on effect of breach on risk of loss (Section 2–510).

§ 2–510. Effect of Breach on Risk of Loss.

(1) Where a tender or delivery of goods so fails to conform to the contract as to give a right of rejection the risk of their loss remains on the seller until cure or acceptance.

(2) Where the buyer rightfully revokes acceptance he may to the extent of any deficiency in his effective insurance coverage treat the risk of loss as having rested on the seller from the beginning.

(3) Where the buyer as to conforming goods already identified to the contract for sale repudiates or is otherwise in breach before risk of their loss has passed to him, the seller may to the extent of any deficiency in his effective insurance coverage treat the risk of loss as resting on the buyer for a commercially reasonable time.

§ 2–511. Tender of Payment by Buyer; Payment by Check.

(1) Unless otherwise agreed tender of payment is a condition to the seller's duty to tender and complete any delivery.

(2) Tender of payment is sufficient when made by any means or in any manner current in the ordinary course of business unless the seller demands payment in legal tender and gives any extension of time reasonably necessary to procure it.

(3) Subject to the provisions of this Act on the effect of an instrument on an obligation (Section 3–310), payment by check is conditional and is defeated as between the parties by dishonor of the check on due presentment.

As amended in 1994.

§ 2–512. Payment by Buyer Before Inspection.

(1) Where the contract requires payment before inspection nonconformity of the goods does not excuse the buyer from so making payment unless

   (a) the non-conformity appears without inspection; or

   (b) despite tender of the required documents the circumstances would justify injunction against honor under this Act (Section 5–109(b)).

(2) Payment pursuant to subsection (1) does not constitute an acceptance of goods or impair the buyer's right to inspect or any of his remedies.

As amended in 1995.

§ 2–513. Buyer's Right to Inspection of Goods.

(1) Unless otherwise agreed and subject to subsection (3), where goods are tendered or delivered or identified to the contract for sale, the buyer has a right before payment or acceptance to inspect them at any reasonable place and time and in any reasonable manner. When the seller is required or authorized to send the goods to the buyer, the inspection may be after their arrival.

(2) Expenses of inspection must be borne by the buyer but may be recovered from the seller if the goods do not conform and are rejected.

(3) Unless otherwise agreed and subject to the provisions of this Article on C.I.F. contracts (subsection (3) of Section 2–321), the buyer is not entitled to inspect the goods before payment of the price when the contract provides

   (a) for delivery "C.O.D." or on other like terms; or

   (b) for payment against documents of title, except where such payment is due only after the goods are to become available for inspection.

(4) A place or method of inspection fixed by the parties is presumed to be exclusive but unless otherwise expressly agreed it does not postpone identification or shift the place for delivery or for passing the risk of loss. If compliance becomes impossible, inspection shall be as provided in this section unless the place or method fixed was clearly intended as an indispensable condition failure of which avoids the contract.

§ 2–514. When Documents Deliverable on Acceptance; When on Payment.

Unless otherwise agreed documents against which a draft is drawn are to be delivered to the drawee on acceptance of the draft if it is payable more than three days after presentment; otherwise, only on payment.

§ 2–515. Preserving Evidence of Goods in Dispute.

In furtherance of the adjustment of any claim or dispute

   (a) either party on reasonable notification to the other and for the purpose of ascertaining the facts and preserving evidence has the right to inspect, test and sample the goods including such of them as may be in the possession or control of the other; and

   (b) the parties may agree to a third party inspection or survey to determine the conformity or condition of the goods and may agree that the findings shall be binding upon them in any subsequent litigation or adjustment.

Part 6 Breach, Repudiation and Excuse

§ 2–601. Buyer's Rights on Improper Delivery.

Subject to the provisions of this Article on breach in installment contracts (Section 2–612) and unless otherwise agreed under the sections on contractual limitations of remedy (Sections 2–718 and 2–719), if the goods or the tender of delivery fail in any respect to conform to the contract, the buyer may

   (a) reject the whole; or

   (b) accept the whole; or

   (c) accept any commercial unit or units and reject the rest.

§ 2–602. Manner and Effect of Rightful Rejection.

(1) Rejection of goods must be within a reasonable time after their delivery or tender. It is ineffective unless the buyer seasonably notifies the seller.

(2) Subject to the provisions of the two following sections on rejected goods (Sections 2–603 and 2–604),

   (a) after rejection any exercise of ownership by the buyer with respect to any commercial unit is wrongful as against the seller; and

   (b) if the buyer has before rejection taken physical possession of goods in which he does not have a security interest under the provisions of this Article (subsection (3) of Section 2–711), he is under a duty after rejection to hold them with reasonable care at the seller's disposition for a time sufficient to permit the seller to remove them; but

   (c) the buyer has no further obligations with regard to goods rightfully rejected.

(3) The seller's rights with respect to goods wrongfully rejected are governed by the provisions of this Article on Seller's remedies in general (Section 2–703).

§ 2–603. Merchant Buyer's Duties as to Rightfully Rejected Goods.

(1) Subject to any security interest in the buyer (subsection (3) of Section 2–711), when the seller has no agent or place of business

at the market of rejection a merchant buyer is under a duty after rejection of goods in his possession or control to follow any reasonable instructions received from the seller with respect to the goods and in the absence of such instructions to make reasonable efforts to sell them for the seller's account if they are perishable or threaten to decline in value speedily. Instructions are not reasonable if on demand indemnity for expenses is not forthcoming.

(2) When the buyer sells goods under subsection (1), he is entitled to reimbursement from the seller or out of the proceeds for reasonable expenses of caring for and selling them, and if the expenses include no selling commission then to such commission as is usual in the trade or if there is none to a reasonable sum not exceeding ten per cent on the gross proceeds.

(3) In complying with this section the buyer is held only to good faith and good faith conduct hereunder is neither acceptance nor conversion nor the basis of an action for damages.

§ 2–604. Buyer's Options as to Salvage of Rightfully Rejected Goods.

Subject to the provisions of the immediately preceding section on perishables if the seller gives no instructions within a reasonable time after notification of rejection the buyer may store the rejected goods for the seller's account or reship them to him or resell them for the seller's account with reimbursement as provided in the preceding section. Such action is not accep-tance or conversion.

§ 2–605. Waiver of Buyer's Objections by Failure to Particularize.

(1) The buyer's failure to state in connection with rejection a particular defect which is ascertainable by reasonable inspection precludes him from relying on the unstated defect to justify rejection or to establish breach

(a) where the seller could have cured it if stated seasonably; or

(b) between merchants when the seller has after rejection made a request in writing for a full and final written statement of all defects on which the buyer proposes to rely.

(2) Payment against documents made without reservation of rights precludes recovery of the payment for defects apparent on the face of the documents.

§ 2–606. What Constitutes Acceptance of Goods.

(1) Acceptance of goods occurs when the buyer

(a) after a reasonable opportunity to inspect the goods signifies to the seller that the goods are conforming or that he will take or retain them in spite of their nonconformity; or

(b) fails to make an effective rejection (subsection (1) of Section 2–602), but such acceptance does not occur until the buyer has had a reasonable opportunity to inspect them; or

(c) does any act inconsistent with the seller's ownership; but if such act is wrongful as against the seller it is an acceptance only if ratified by him.

(2) Acceptance of a part of any commercial unit is acceptance of that entire unit.

§ 2–607. Effect of Acceptance; Notice of Breach; Burden of Establishing Breach After Acceptance; Notice of Claim or Litigation to Person Answerable Over.

(1) The buyer must pay at the contract rate for any goods accepted.

(2) Acceptance of goods by the buyer precludes rejection of the goods accepted and if made with knowledge of a non-conformity cannot be revoked because of it unless the acceptance was on the reasonable assumption that the non-conformity would be seasonably cured but acceptance does not of itself impair any other remedy provided by this Article for non-conformity.

(3) Where a tender has been accepted

(a) the buyer must within a reasonable time after he discovers or should have discovered any breach notify the seller of breach or be barred from any remedy; and

(b) if the claim is one for infringement or the like (subsection (3) of Section 2–312) and the buyer is sued as a result of such a breach he must so notify the seller within a reasonable time after he receives notice of the litigation or be barred from any remedy over for liability established by the litigation.

(4) The burden is on the buyer to establish any breach with respect to the goods accepted.

(5) Where the buyer is sued for breach of a warranty or other obligation for which his seller is answerable over

(a) he may give his seller written notice of the litigation. If the notice states that the seller may come in and defend and that if the seller does not do so he will be bound in any action against him by his buyer by any determination of fact common to the two litigations, then unless the seller after seasonable receipt of the notice does come in and defend he is so bound.

(b) if the claim is one for infringement or the like (subsection (3) of Section 2–312) the original seller may demand in writing that his buyer turn over to him control of the litigation including settlement or else be barred from any remedy over and if he also agrees to bear all expense and to satisfy any adverse judgment, then unless the buyer after seasonable receipt of the demand does turn over control the buyer is so barred.

(6) The provisions of subsections (3), (4) and (5) apply to any obligation of a buyer to hold the seller harmless against infringement or the like (subsection (3) of Section 2–312).

§ 2–608. Revocation of Acceptance in Whole or in Part.

(1) The buyer may revoke his acceptance of a lot or commercial unit whose non-conformity substantially impairs its value to him if he has accepted it

(a) on the reasonable assumption that its nonconformity would be cured and it has not been seasonably cured; or

(b) without discovery of such non-conformity if his acceptance was reasonably induced either by the difficulty of discovery before acceptance or by the seller's assurances.

(2) Revocation of acceptance must occur within a reasonable time after the buyer discovers or should have discovered the ground for it and before any substantial change in condition of the goods which is not caused by their own defects. It is not effective until the buyer notifies the seller of it.

(3) A buyer who so revokes has the same rights and duties with regard to the goods involved as if he had rejected them.

§ 2–609. Right to Adequate Assurance of Performance.

(1) A contract for sale imposes an obligation on each party that the other's expectation of receiving due performance will not be impaired. When reasonable grounds for insecurity arise with respect to the performance of either party the other may in writing demand adequate assurance of due performance and until he receives such assurance may if commercially reasonable suspend any performance for which he has not already received the agreed return.

(2) Between merchants the reasonableness of grounds for insecurity and the adequacy of any assurance offered shall be determined according to commercial standards.

(3) Acceptance of any improper delivery or payment does not prejudice the party's right to demand adequate assurance of future performance.

(4) After receipt of a justified demand failure to provide within a reasonable time not exceeding thirty days such assurance of due performance as is adequate under the circumstances of the particular case is a repudiation of the contract.

§ 2–610. Anticipatory Repudiation.

When either party repudiates the contract with respect to a performance not yet due the loss of which will substantially impair the value of the contract to the other, the aggrieved party may

    (a) for a commercially reasonable time await performance by the repudiating party; or

    (b) resort to any remedy for breach (Section 2–703 or Section 2–711), even though he has notified the repudiating party that he would await the latter's performance and has urged retraction; and

    (c) in either case suspend his own performance or proceed in accordance with the provisions of this Article on the seller's right to identify goods to the contract notwithstanding breach or to salvage unfinished goods (Section 2–704).

§ 2–611. Retraction of Anticipatory Repudiation.

(1) Until the repudiating party's next performance is due he can retract his repudiation unless the aggrieved party has since the repudiation cancelled or materially changed his position or otherwise indicated that he considers the repudiation final.

(2) Retraction may be by any method which clearly indicates to the aggrieved party that the repudiating party intends to perform, but must include any assurance justifiably demanded under the provisions of this Article (Section 2–609).

(3) Retraction reinstates the repudiating party's rights under the contract with due excuse and allowance to the aggrieved party for any delay occasioned by the repudiation.

§ 2–612. "Installment Contract"; Breach.

(1) An "installment contract" is one which requires or authorizes the delivery of goods in separate lots to be separately accepted, even though the contract contains a clause "each delivery is a separate contract" or its equivalent.

(2) The buyer may reject any installment which is non-conforming if the non-conformity substantially impairs the value of that installment and cannot be cured or if the non-conformity is a defect in the required documents; but if the non-conformity does not fall within subsection (3) and the seller gives adequate assurance of its cure the buyer must accept that installment.

(3) Whenever non-conformity or default with respect to one or more installments substantially impairs the value of the whole contract there is a breach of the whole. But the aggrieved party reinstates the contract if he accepts a non-conforming installment without seasonably notifying of cancellation or if he brings an action with respect only to past installments or demands performance as to future installments.

§ 2–613. Casualty to Identified Goods.

Where the contract requires for its performance goods identified when the contract is made, and the goods suffer casualty without fault of either party before the risk of loss passes to the buyer, or in a proper case under a "no arrival, no sale" term (Section 2–324) then

    (a) if the loss is total the contract is avoided; and

    (b) if the loss is partial or the goods have so deteriorated as no longer to conform to the contract the buyer may nevertheless demand inspection and at his option either treat the contract as voided or accept the goods with due allowance from the contract price for the deterioration or the deficiency in quantity but without further right against the seller.

§ 2–614. Substituted Performance.

(1) Where without fault of either party the agreed berthing, loading, or unloading facilities fail or an agreed type of carrier becomes unavailable or the agreed manner of delivery otherwise becomes commercially impracticable but a commercially reasonable substitute is available, such substitute performance must be tendered and accepted.

(2) If the agreed means or manner of payment fails because of domestic or foreign governmental regulation, the seller may withhold or stop delivery unless the buyer provides a means or manner of payment which is commercially a substantial equivalent. If delivery has already been taken, payment by the means or in the manner provided by the regulation discharges the buyer's obligation unless the regulation is discriminatory, oppressive or predatory.

§ 2–615. Excuse by Failure of Presupposed Conditions.

Except so far as a seller may have assumed a greater obligation and subject to the preceding section on substituted performance:

    (a) Delay in delivery or non-delivery in whole or in part by a seller who complies with paragraphs (b) and (c) is not a breach of his duty under a contract for sale if performance as agreed has been made impracticable by the occurrence of a contingency the nonoccurrence of which was a basic assumption on which the contract was made or by compliance in good faith with any applicable foreign or domestic governmental regulation or order whether or not it later proves to be invalid.

    (b) Where the causes mentioned in paragraph (a) affect only a part of the seller's capacity to perform, he must allocate production and deliveries among his customers but may at his option include regular customers not then under contract as well as his own requirements for further manufacture. He may so allocate in any manner which is fair and reasonable.

    (c) The seller must notify the buyer seasonably that there will be delay or non-delivery and, when allocation is required under paragraph (b), of the estimated quota thus made available for the buyer.

§ 2–616. Procedure on Notice Claiming Excuse.

(1) Where the buyer receives notification of a material or indefinite delay or an allocation justified under the preceding section he may by written notification to the seller as to any delivery concerned, and where the prospective deficiency substantially impairs the value of the whole contract under the provisions of this Article relating to breach of installment contracts (Section 2–612), then also as to the whole,

    (a) terminate and thereby discharge any unexecuted portion of the contract; or

    (b) modify the contract by agreeing to take his available quota in substitution.

(2) If after receipt of such notification from the seller the buyer fails so to modify the contract within a reasonable time not exceeding thirty days the contract lapses with respect to any deliveries affected.

(3) The provisions of this section may not be negated by agreement except in so far as the seller has assumed a greater obligation under the preceding section.

Part 7 Remedies

§ 2–701. Remedies for Breach of Collateral Contracts Not Impaired.

Remedies for breach of any obligation or promise collateral or ancillary to a contract for sale are not impaired by the provisions of this Article.

§ 2–702. Seller's Remedies on Discovery of Buyer's Insolvency.

(1) Where the seller discovers the buyer to be insolvent he may refuse delivery except for cash including payment for all goods theretofore delivered under the contract, and stop delivery under this Article (Section 2–705).

(2) Where the seller discovers that the buyer has received goods on credit while insolvent he may reclaim the goods upon demand made within ten days after the receipt, but if misrepresentation of solvency has been made to the particular seller in writing within three months before delivery the ten day limitation does not apply. Except as provided in this subsection the seller may not base a right to reclaim goods on the buyer's fraudulent or innocent misrepresentation of solvency or of intent to pay.

(3) The seller's right to reclaim under subsection (2) is subject to the rights of a buyer in ordinary course or other good faith purchaser under this Article (Section 2–403). Successful reclamation of goods excludes all other remedies with respect to them.

§ 2–703. Seller's Remedies in General.

Where the buyer wrongfully rejects or revokes acceptance of goods or fails to make a payment due on or before delivery or repudiates with respect to a part or the whole, then with respect to any goods directly affected and, if the breach is of the whole contract (Section 2–612), then also with respect to the whole undelivered balance, the aggrieved seller may

(a) withhold delivery of such goods;

(b) stop delivery by any bailee as hereafter provided (Section 2–705);

(c) proceed under the next section respecting goods still unidentified to the contract;

(d) resell and recover damages as hereafter provided (Section 2–706);

(e) recover damages for non-acceptance (Section 2–708) or in a proper case the price (Section 2–709);

(f) cancel.

§ 2–704. Seller's Right to Identify Goods to the Contract Notwithstanding Breach or to Salvage Unfinished Goods.

(1) An aggrieved seller under the preceding section may

(a) identify to the contract conforming goods not already identified if at the time he learned of the breach they are in his possession or control;

(b) treat as the subject of resale goods which have demonstrably been intended for the particular contract even though those goods are unfinished.

(2) Where the goods are unfinished an aggrieved seller may in the exercise of reasonable commercial judgment for the purposes of avoiding loss and of effective realization either complete the manufacture and wholly identify the goods to the contract or cease manufacture and resell for scrap or salvage value or proceed in any other reasonable manner.

§ 2–705. Seller's Stoppage of Delivery in Transit or Otherwise.

(1) The seller may stop delivery of goods in the possession of a carrier or other bailee when he discovers the buyer to be insolvent (Section 2–702) and may stop delivery of carload, truckload, planeload or larger shipments of express or freight when the buyer repudiates or fails to make a payment due before delivery or if for any other reason the seller has a right to withhold or reclaim the goods.

(2) As against such buyer the seller may stop delivery until

(a) receipt of the goods by the buyer; or

(b) acknowledgment to the buyer by any bailee of the goods except a carrier that the bailee holds the goods for the buyer; or

(c) such acknowledgment to the buyer by a carrier by reshipment or as warehouseman; or

(d) negotiation to the buyer of any negotiable document of title covering the goods.

(3) (a) To stop delivery the seller must so notify as to enable the bailee by reasonable diligence to prevent delivery of the goods.

(b) After such notification the bailee must hold and deliver the goods according to the directions of the seller but the seller is liable to the bailee for any ensuing charges or damages.

(c) If a negotiable document of title has been issued for goods the bailee is not obliged to obey a notification to stop until surrender of the document.

(d) A carrier who has issued a non-negotiable bill of lading is not obliged to obey a notification to stop received from a person other than the consignor.

§ 2–706. Seller's Resale Including Contract for Resale.

(1) Under the conditions stated in Section 2–703 on seller's remedies, the seller may resell the goods concerned or the undelivered balance thereof. Where the resale is made in good faith and in a commercially reasonable manner the seller may recover the difference between the resale price and the contract price together with any incidental damages allowed under the provisions of this Article (Section 2–710), but less expenses saved in consequence of the buyer's breach.

(2) Except as otherwise provided in subsection (3) or unless otherwise agreed resale may be at public or private sale including sale by way of one or more contracts to sell or of identification to an existing contract of the seller. Sale may be as a unit or in parcels and at any time and place and on any terms but every aspect of the sale including the method, manner, time, place and terms must be commercially reasonable. The resale must be reasonably identified as referring to the broken contract, but it is not necessary that the goods be in existence or that any or all of them have been identified to the contract before the breach.

(3) Where the resale is at private sale the seller must give the buyer reasonable notification of his intention to resell.

(4) Where the resale is at public sale

(a) only identified goods can be sold except where there is a recognized market for a public sale of futures in goods of the kind; and

(b) it must be made at a usual place or market for public sale if one is reasonably available and except in the case of goods which are perishable or threaten to decline in value speedily the seller must give the buyer reasonable notice of the time and place of the resale; and

(c) if the goods are not to be within the view of those attending the sale the notification of sale must state the place where the goods are located and provide for their reasonable inspection by prospective bidders; and

(d) the seller may buy.

(5) A purchaser who buys in good faith at a resale takes the goods free of any rights of the original buyer even though the seller fails to comply with one or more of the requirements of this section.

(6) The seller is not accountable to the buyer for any profit made on any resale. A person in the position of a seller (Section 2–707) or a buyer who has rightfully rejected or justifiably revoked acceptance must account for any excess over the amount of his security interest, as hereinafter defined (subsection (3) of Section 2–711).

§ 2–707. "Person in the Position of a Seller".

(1) A "person in the position of a seller" includes as against a principal an agent who has paid or become responsible for the price of goods on behalf of his principal or anyone who otherwise holds a security interest or other right in goods similar to that of a seller.

(2) A person in the position of a seller may as provided in this Article withhold or stop delivery (Section 2–705) and resell (Section 2–706) and recover incidental damages (Section 2–710).

§ 2–708. Seller's Damages for Non-Acceptance or Repudiation.

(1) Subject to subsection (2) and to the provisions of this Article with respect to proof of market price (Section 2–723), the measure of damages for non-acceptance or repudiation by the buyer is the difference between the market price at the time and place for tender and the unpaid contract price together with any incidental damages provided in this Article (Section 2–710), but less expenses saved in consequence of the buyer's breach.

(2) If the measure of damages provided in subsection (1) is inadequate to put the seller in as good a position as performance would have done then the measure of damages is the profit (including reasonable overhead) which the seller would have made from full performance by the buyer, together with any incidental damages provided in this Article (Section 2–710), due allowance for costs reasonably incurred and due credit for payments or proceeds of resale.

§ 2–709. Action for the Price.

(1) When the buyer fails to pay the price as it becomes due the seller may recover, together with any incidental damages under the next section, the price

(a) of goods accepted or of conforming goods lost or damaged within a commercially reasonable time after risk of their loss has passed to the buyer; and

(b) of goods identified to the contract if the seller is unable after reasonable effort to resell them at a reasonable price or the circumstances reasonably indicate that such effort will be unavailing.

(2) Where the seller sues for the price he must hold for the buyer any goods which have been identified to the contract and are still in his control except that if resale becomes possible he may resell them at any time prior to the collection of the judgment. The net proceeds of any such resale must be credited to the buyer and payment of the judgment entitles him to any goods not resold.

(3) After the buyer has wrongfully rejected or revoked acceptance of the goods or has failed to make a payment due or has repudiated (Section 2–610), a seller who is held not entitled to the price under this section shall nevertheless be awarded damages for non-acceptance under the preceding section.

§ 2–710. Seller's Incidental Damages.

Incidental damages to an aggrieved seller include any commercially reasonable charges, expenses or commissions incurred in stopping delivery, in the transportation, care and custody of goods after the buyer's breach, in connection with return or resale of the goods or otherwise resulting from the breach.

§ 2–711. Buyer's Remedies in General; Buyer's Security Interest in Rejected Goods.

(1) Where the seller fails to make delivery or repudiates or the buyer rightfully rejects or justifiably revokes acceptance then with respect to any goods involved, and with respect to the whole if the breach goes to the whole contract (Section 2–612), the buyer may cancel and whether or not he has done so may in addition to recovering so much of the price as has been paid

(a) "cover" and have damages under the next section as to all the goods affected whether or not they have been identified to the contract; or

(b) recover damages for non-delivery as provided in this Article (Section 2–713).

(2) Where the seller fails to deliver or repudiates the buyer may also

(a) if the goods have been identified recover them as provided in this Article (Section 2–502); or

(b) in a proper case obtain specific performance or replevy the goods as provided in this Article (Section 2–716).

(3) On rightful rejection or justifiable revocation of acceptance a buyer has a security interest in goods in his possession or control for any payments made on their price and any expenses reasonably incurred in their inspection, receipt, transportation, care and custody and may hold such goods and resell them in like manner as an aggrieved seller (Section 2–706).

§ 2–712. "Cover"; Buyer's Procurement of Substitute Goods.

(1) After a breach within the preceding section the buyer may "cover" by making in good faith and without unreasonable delay any reasonable purchase of or contract to purchase goods in substitution for those due from the seller.

(2) The buyer may recover from the seller as damages the difference between the cost of cover and the contract price together with any incidental or consequential damages as hereinafter defined (Section 2–715), but less expenses saved in consequence of the seller's breach.

(3) Failure of the buyer to effect cover within this section does not bar him from any other remedy.

§ 2–713. Buyer's Damages for Non-Delivery or Repudiation.

(1) Subject to the provisions of this Article with respect to proof of market price (Section 2–723), the measure of damages for

non-delivery or repudiation by the seller is the difference between the market price at the time when the buyer learned of the breach and the contract price together with any incidental and consequential damages provided in this Article (Section 2–715), but less expenses saved in consequence of the seller's breach.

(2) Market price is to be determined as of the place for tender or, in cases of rejection after arrival or revocation of acceptance, as of the place of arrival.

§ 2–714. Buyer's Damages for Breach in Regard to Accepted Goods.

(1) Where the buyer has accepted goods and given notification (subsection (3) of Section 2–607) he may recover as damages for any non-conformity of tender the loss resulting in the ordinary course of events from the seller's breach as determined in any manner which is reasonable.

(2) The measure of damages for breach of warranty is the difference at the time and place of acceptance between the value of the goods accepted and the value they would have had if they had been as warranted, unless special circumstances show proximate damages of a different amount.

(3) In a proper case any incidental and consequential damages under the next section may also be recovered.

§ 2–715. Buyer's Incidental and Consequential Damages.

(1) Incidental damages resulting from the seller's breach include expenses reasonably incurred in inspection, receipt, transportation and care and custody of goods rightfully rejected, any commercially reasonable charges, expenses or commissions in connection with effecting cover and any other reasonable expense incident to the delay or other breach.

(2) Consequential damages resulting from the seller's breach include

   (a) any loss resulting from general or particular requirements and needs of which the seller at the time of contracting had reason to know and which could not reasonably be prevented by cover or otherwise; and

   (b) injury to person or property proximately resulting from any breach of warranty.

§ 2–716. Buyer's Right to Specific Performance or Replevin.

(1) Specific performance may be decreed where the goods are unique or in other proper circumstances.

(2) The decree for specific performance may include such terms and conditions as to payment of the price, damages, or other relief as the court may deem just.

(3) The buyer has a right of replevin for goods identified to the contract if after reasonable effort he is unable to effect cover for such goods or the circumstances reasonably indicate that such effort will be unavailing or if the goods have been shipped under reservation and satisfaction of the security interest in them has been made or tendered. In the case of goods bought for personal, family, or household purposes, the buyer's right of replevin vests upon acquisition of a special property, even if the seller had not then repudiated or failed to deliver.

As amended in 1999.

§ 2–717. Deduction of Damages From the Price.

The buyer on notifying the seller of his intention to do so may deduct all or any part of the damages resulting from any breach of the contract from any part of the price still due under the same contract.

§ 2–718. Liquidation or Limitation of Damages; Deposits.

(1) Damages for breach by either party may be liquidated in the agreement but only at an amount which is reasonable in the light of the anticipated or actual harm caused by the breach, the difficulties of proof of loss, and the inconvenience or nonfeasibility of otherwise obtaining an adequate remedy. A term fixing unreasonably large liquidated damages is void as a penalty.

(2) Where the seller justifiably withholds delivery of goods because of the buyer's breach, the buyer is entitled to restitution of any amount by which the sum of his payments exceeds

   (a) the amount to which the seller is entitled by virtue of terms liquidating the seller's damages in accordance with subsection (1), or

   (b) in the absence of such terms, twenty per cent of the value of the total performance for which the buyer is obligated under the contract or $500, whichever is smaller.

(3) The buyer's right to restitution under subsection (2) is subject to offset to the extent that the seller establishes

   (a) a right to recover damages under the provisions of this Article other than subsection (1), and

   (b) the amount or value of any benefits received by the buyer directly or indirectly by reason of the contract.

(4) Where a seller has received payment in goods their reasonable value or the proceeds of their resale shall be treated as payments for the purposes of subsection (2); but if the seller has notice of the buyer's breach before reselling goods received in part performance, his resale is subject to the conditions laid down in this Article on resale by an aggrieved seller (Section 2–706).

§ 2–719. Contractual Modification or Limitation of Remedy.

(1) Subject to the provisions of subsections (2) and (3) of this section and of the preceding section on liquidation and limitation of damages,

   (a) the agreement may provide for remedies in addition to or in substitution for those provided in this Article and may limit or alter the measure of damages recoverable under this Article, as by limiting the buyer's remedies to return of the goods and repayment of the price or to repair and replacement of non-conforming goods or parts; and

   (b) resort to a remedy as provided is optional unless the remedy is expressly agreed to be exclusive, in which case it is the sole remedy.

(2) Where circumstances cause an exclusive or limited remedy to fail of its essential purpose, remedy may be had as provided in this Act.

(3) Consequential damages may be limited or excluded unless the limitation or exclusion is unconscionable. Limitation of consequential damages for injury to the person in the case of consumer goods is prima facie unconscionable but limitation of damages where the loss is commercial is not.

§ 2–720. Effect of "Cancellation" or "Rescission" on Claims for Antecedent Breach.

Unless the contrary intention clearly appears, expressions of "cancellation" or "rescission" of the contract or the like shall not be construed as a renunciation or discharge of any claim in damages for an antecedent breach.

§ 2–721. Remedies for Fraud.

Remedies for material misrepresentation or fraud include all remedies available under this Article for non-fraudulent breach. Neither rescission or a claim for rescission of the contract for sale nor rejection or return of the goods shall bar or be deemed inconsistent with a claim for damages or other remedy.

§ 2–722. Who Can Sue Third Parties for Injury to Goods.

Where a third party so deals with goods which have been identified to a contract for sale as to cause actionable injury to a party to that contract

(a) a right of action against the third party is in either party to the contract for sale who has title to or a security interest or a special property or an insurable interest in the goods; and if the goods have been destroyed or converted a right of action is also in the party who either bore the risk of loss under the contract for sale or has since the injury assumed that risk as against the other;

(b) if at the time of the injury the party plaintiff did not bear the risk of loss as against the other party to the contract for sale and there is no arrangement between them for disposition of the recovery, his suit or settlement is, subject to his own interest, as a fiduciary for the other party to the contract;

(c) either party may with the consent of the other sue for the benefit of whom it may concern.

§ 2–723. Proof of Market Price: Time and Place.

(1) If an action based on anticipatory repudiation comes to trial before the time for performance with respect to some or all of the goods, any damages based on market price (Section 2–708 or Section 2–713) shall be determined according to the price of such goods prevailing at the time when the aggrieved party learned of the repudiation.

(2) If evidence of a price prevailing at the times or places described in this Article is not readily available the price prevailing within any reasonable time before or after the time described or at any other place which in commercial judgment or under usage of trade would serve as a reasonable substitute for the one described may be used, making any proper allowance for the cost of transporting the goods to or from such other place.

(3) Evidence of a relevant price prevailing at a time or place other than the one described in this Article offered by one party is not admissible unless and until he has given the other party such notice as the court finds sufficient to prevent unfair surprise.

§ 2–724. Admissibility of Market Quotations.

Whenever the prevailing price or value of any goods regularly bought and sold in any established commodity market is in issue, reports in official publications or trade journals or in newspapers or periodicals of general circulation published as the reports of such market shall be admissible in evidence. The circumstances of the preparation of such a report may be shown to affect its weight but not its admissibility.

§ 2–725. Statute of Limitations in Contracts for Sale.

(1) An action for breach of any contract for sale must be commenced within four years after the cause of action has accrued. By the original agreement the parties may reduce the period of limitation to not less than one year but may not extend it.

(2) A cause of action accrues when the breach occurs, regardless of the aggrieved party's lack of knowledge of the breach. A breach of warranty occurs when tender of delivery is made, except that where a warranty explicitly extends to future performance of the goods and discovery of the breach must await the time of such performance the cause of action accrues when the breach is or should have been discovered.

(3) Where an action commenced within the time limited by subsection (1) is so terminated as to leave available a remedy by another action for the same breach such other action may be commenced after the expiration of the time limited and within six months after the termination of the first action unless the termination resulted from voluntary discontinuance or from dismissal for failure or neglect to prosecute.

(4) This section does not alter the law on tolling of the statute of limitations nor does it apply to causes of action which have accrued before this Act becomes effective.

ARTICLE 2A
LEASES

Part 1 General Provisions

§ 2A–101. Short Title.

This Article shall be known and may be cited as the Uniform Commercial Code—Leases.

§ 2A–102. Scope.

This Article applies to any transaction, regardless of form, that creates a lease.

§ 2A–103. Definitions and Index of Definitions.

(1) In this Article unless the context otherwise requires:

(a) "Buyer in ordinary course of business" means a person who in good faith and without knowledge that the sale to him [or her] is in violation of the ownership rights or security interest or leasehold interest of a third party in the goods buys in ordinary course from a person in the business of selling goods of that kind but does not include a pawnbroker. "Buying" may be for cash or by exchange of other property or on secured or unsecured credit and includes receiving goods or documents of title under a pre-existing contract for sale but does not include a transfer in bulk or as security for or in total or partial satisfaction of a money debt.

(b) "Cancellation" occurs when either party puts an end to the lease contract for default by the other party.

(c) "Commercial unit" means such a unit of goods as by commercial usage is a single whole for purposes of lease and division of which materially impairs its character or value on the market or in use. A commercial unit may be a single article, as a machine, or a set of articles, as a suite of furniture or a line of machinery, or a quantity, as a gross or carload, or any other unit treated in use or in the relevant market as a single whole.

(d) "Conforming" goods or performance under a lease contract means goods or performance that are in accordance with the obligations under the lease contract.

(e) "Consumer lease" means a lease that a lessor regularly engaged in the business of leasing or selling makes to a lessee who is an individual and who takes under the lease primarily for a personal, family, or household purpose [, if the total payments to be made under the lease contract, excluding payments for options to renew or buy, do not exceed $_____].

(f) "Fault" means wrongful act, omission, breach, or default.

(g) "Finance lease" means a lease with respect to which:

(i) the lessor does not select, manufacture or supply the goods;

(ii) the lessor acquires the goods or the right to possession and use of the goods in connection with the lease; and

(iii) one of the following occurs:

(A) the lessee receives a copy of the contract by which the lessor acquired the goods or the right to possession and use of the goods before signing the lease contract;

(B) the lessee's approval of the contract by which the lessor acquired the goods or the right to possession and use of the goods is a condition to effectiveness of the lease contract;

(C) the lessee, before signing the lease contract, receives an accurate and complete statement designating the promises and warranties, and any disclaimers of warranties, limitations or modifications of remedies, or liquidated damages, including those of a third party, such as the manufacturer of the goods, provided to the lessor by the person supplying the goods in connection with or as part of the contract by which the lessor acquired the goods or the right to possession and use of the goods; or

(D) if the lease is not a consumer lease, the lessor, before the lessee signs the lease contract, informs the lessee in writing (a) of the identity of the person supplying the goods to the lessor, unless the lessee has selected that person and directed the lessor to acquire the goods or the right to possession and use of the goods from that person, (b) that the lessee is entitled under this Article to any promises and warranties, including those of any third party, provided to the lessor by the person supplying the goods in connection with or as part of the contract by which the lessor acquired the goods or the right to possession and use of the goods, and (c) that the lessee may communicate with the person supplying the goods to the lessor and receive an accurate and complete statement of those promises and warranties, including any disclaimers and limitations of them or of remedies.

(h) "Goods" means all things that are movable at the time of identification to the lease contract, or are fixtures (Section 2A–309), but the term does not include money, documents, instruments, accounts, chattel paper, general intangibles, or minerals or the like, including oil and gas, before extraction. The term also includes the unborn young of animals.

(i) "Installment lease contract" means a lease contract that authorizes or requires the delivery of goods in separate lots to be separately accepted, even though the lease contract contains a clause "each delivery is a separate lease" or its equivalent.

(j) "Lease" means a transfer of the right to possession and use of goods for a term in return for consideration, but a sale, including a sale on approval or a sale or return, or retention or creation of a security interest is not a lease. Unless the context clearly indicates otherwise, the term includes a sublease.

(k) "Lease agreement" means the bargain, with respect to the lease, of the lessor and the lessee in fact as found in their language or by implication from other circumstances including course of dealing or usage of trade or course of performance as provided in this Article. Unless the context clearly indicates otherwise, the term includes a sublease agreement.

(l) "Lease contract" means the total legal obligation that results from the lease agreement as affected by this Article and any other applicable rules of law. Unless the context clearly indicates otherwise, the term includes a sublease contract.

(m) "Leasehold interest" means the interest of the lessor or the lessee under a lease contract.

(n) "Lessee" means a person who acquires the right to possession and use of goods under a lease. Unless the context clearly indicates otherwise, the term includes a sublessee.

(o) "Lessee in ordinary course of business" means a person who in good faith and without knowledge that the lease to him [or her] is in violation of the ownership rights or security interest or leasehold interest of a third party in the goods, leases in ordinary course from a person in the business of selling or leasing goods of that kind but does not include a pawnbroker. "Leasing" may be for cash or by exchange of other property or on secured or unsecured credit and includes receiving goods or documents of title under a pre-existing lease contract but does not include a transfer in bulk or as security for or in total or partial satisfaction of a money debt.

(p) "Lessor" means a person who transfers the right to possession and use of goods under a lease. Unless the context clearly indicates otherwise, the term includes a sublessor.

(q) "Lessor's residual interest" means the lessor's interest in the goods after expiration, termination, or cancellation of the lease contract.

(r) "Lien" means a charge against or interest in goods to secure payment of a debt or performance of an obligation, but the term does not include a security interest.

(s) "Lot" means a parcel or a single article that is the subject matter of a separate lease or delivery, whether or not it is sufficient to perform the lease contract.

(t) "Merchant lessee" means a lessee that is a merchant with respect to goods of the kind subject to the lease.

(u) "Present value" means the amount as of a date certain of one or more sums payable in the future, discounted to the date certain. The discount is determined by the interest rate specified by the parties if the rate was not manifestly unreasonable at the time the transaction was entered into; otherwise, the discount is determined by a commercially reasonable rate that takes into account the facts and circumstances of each case at the time the transaction was entered into.

(v) "Purchase" includes taking by sale, lease, mortgage, security interest, pledge, gift, or any other voluntary transaction creating an interest in goods.

(w) "Sublease" means a lease of goods the right to possession and use of which was acquired by the lessor as a lessee under an existing lease.

(x) "Supplier" means a person from whom a lessor buys or leases goods to be leased under a finance lease.

(y) "Supply contract" means a contract under which a lessor buys or leases goods to be leased.

(z) "Termination" occurs when either party pursuant to a power created by agreement or law puts an end to the lease contract otherwise than for default.

(2) Other definitions applying to this Article and the sections in which they appear are:

"Accessions". Section 2A–310(1).

"Construction mortgage". Section 2A–309(1)(d).

"Encumbrance". Section 2A–309(1)(e).

"Fixtures". Section 2A–309(1)(a).

"Fixture filing". Section 2A–309(1)(b).

"Purchase money lease". Section 2A–309(1)(c).

(3) The following definitions in other Articles apply to this Article:

"Accounts". Section 9–106.

"Between merchants". Section 2–104(3).

"Buyer". Section 2–103(1)(a).

"Chattel paper". Section 9–105(1)(b).

"Consumer goods". Section 9–109(1).

"Document". Section 9–105(1)(f).

"Entrusting". Section 2–403(3).

"General intangibles". Section 9–106.

"Good faith". Section 2–103(1)(b).

"Instrument". Section 9–105(1)(i).

"Merchant". Section 2–104(1).

"Mortgage". Section 9–105(1)(j).

"Pursuant to commitment". Section 9–105(1)(k).

"Receipt". Section 2–103(1)(c).

"Sale". Section 2–106(1).

"Sale on approval". Section 2–326.

"Sale or return". Section 2–326.

"Seller". Section 2–103(1)(d).

(4) In addition Article 1 contains general definitions and principles of construction and interpretation applicable throughout this Article.

As amended in 1990 and 1999.

§ 2A–104. Leases Subject to Other Law.

(1) A lease, although subject to this Article, is also subject to any applicable:

> (a) certificate of title statute of this State: (list any certificate of title statutes covering automobiles, trailers, mobile homes, boats, farm tractors, and the like);

> (b) certificate of title statute of another jurisdiction (Section 2A–105); or

> (c) consumer protection statute of this State, or final consumer protection decision of a court of this State existing on the effective date of this Article.

(2) In case of conflict between this Article, other than Sections 2A–105, 2A–304(3), and 2A–305(3), and a statute or decision referred to in subsection (1), the statute or decision controls.

(3) Failure to comply with an applicable law has only the effect specified therein.

As amended in 1990.

§ 2A–105. Territorial Application of Article to Goods Covered by Certificate of Title.

Subject to the provisions of Sections 2A–304(3) and 2A–305(3), with respect to goods covered by a certificate of title issued under a statute of this State or of another jurisdiction, compliance and the effect of compliance or noncompliance with a certificate of title statute are governed by the law (including the conflict of laws rules) of the jurisdiction issuing the certificate until the earlier of

(a) surrender of the certificate, or (b) four months after the goods are removed from that jurisdiction and thereafter until a new certificate of title is issued by another jurisdiction.

§ 2A–106. Limitation on Power of Parties to Consumer Lease to Choose Applicable Law and Judicial Forum.

(1) If the law chosen by the parties to a consumer lease is that of a jurisdiction other than a jurisdiction in which the lessee resides at the time the lease agreement becomes enforceable or within 30 days thereafter or in which the goods are to be used, the choice is not enforceable.

(2) If the judicial forum chosen by the parties to a consumer lease is a forum that would not otherwise have jurisdiction over the lessee, the choice is not enforceable.

§ 2A–107. Waiver or Renunciation of Claim or Right After Default.

Any claim or right arising out of an alleged default or breach of warranty may be discharged in whole or in part without consideration by a written waiver or renunciation signed and delivered by the aggrieved party.

§ 2A–108. Unconscionability.

(1) If the court as a matter of law finds a lease contract or any clause of a lease contract to have been unconscionable at the time it was made the court may refuse to enforce the lease contract, or it may enforce the remainder of the lease contract without the unconscionable clause, or it may so limit the application of any unconscionable clause as to avoid any unconscionable result.

(2) With respect to a consumer lease, if the court as a matter of law finds that a lease contract or any clause of a lease contract has been induced by unconscionable conduct or that unconscionable conduct has occurred in the collection of a claim arising from a lease contract, the court may grant appropriate relief.

(3) Before making a finding of unconscionability under subsection (1) or (2), the court, on its own motion or that of a party, shall afford the parties a reasonable opportunity to pre-sent evidence as to the setting, purpose, and effect of the lease contract or clause thereof, or of the conduct.

(4) In an action in which the lessee claims unconscionability with respect to a consumer lease:

> (a) If the court finds unconscionability under subsection (1) or (2), the court shall award reasonable attorney's fees to the lessee.

> (b) If the court does not find unconscionability and the lessee claiming unconscionability has brought or maintained an action he [or she] knew to be groundless, the court shall award reasonable attorney's fees to the party against whom the claim is made.

> (c) In determining attorney's fees, the amount of the recovery on behalf of the claimant under subsections (1) and (2) is not controlling.

§ 2A–109. Option to Accelerate at Will.

(1) A term providing that one party or his [or her] successor in interest may accelerate payment or performance or require collateral or additional collateral "at will" or "when he [or she] deems himself [or herself] insecure" or in words of similar import must be construed to mean that he [or she] has power to do so only if he [or she] in good faith believes that the prospect of payment or performance is impaired.

(2) With respect to a consumer lease, the burden of establishing good faith under subsection (1) is on the party who exercised the power; otherwise the burden of establishing lack of good faith is on the party against whom the power has been exercised.

Part 2 Formation and Construction of Lease Contract

§ 2A–201. Statute of Frauds.

(1) A lease contract is not enforceable by way of action or defense unless:

(a) the total payments to be made under the lease contract, excluding payments for options to renew or buy, are less than $1,000; or

(b) there is a writing, signed by the party against whom enforcement is sought or by that party's authorized agent, sufficient to indicate that a lease contract has been made between the parties and to describe the goods leased and the lease term.

(2) Any description of leased goods or of the lease term is sufficient and satisfies subsection (1)(b), whether or not it is specific, if it reasonably identifies what is described.

(3) A writing is not insufficient because it omits or incorrectly states a term agreed upon, but the lease contract is not enforceable under subsection (1)(b) beyond the lease term and the quantity of goods shown in the writing.

(4) A lease contract that does not satisfy the requirements of subsection (1), but which is valid in other respects, is enforceable:

(a) if the goods are to be specially manufactured or obtained for the lessee and are not suitable for lease or sale to others in the ordinary course of the lessor's business, and the lessor, before notice of repudiation is received and under circumstances that reasonably indicate that the goods are for the lessee, has made either a substantial beginning of their manufacture or commitments for their procurement;

(b) if the party against whom enforcement is sought admits in that party's pleading, testimony or otherwise in court that a lease contract was made, but the lease contract is not enforceable under this provision beyond the quantity of goods admitted; or

(c) with respect to goods that have been received and accepted by the lessee.

(5) The lease term under a lease contract referred to in subsection (4) is:

(a) if there is a writing signed by the party against whom enforcement is sought or by that party's authorized agent specifying the lease term, the term so specified;

(b) if the party against whom enforcement is sought admits in that party's pleading, testimony, or otherwise in court a lease term, the term so admitted; or

(c) a reasonable lease term.

§ 2A–202. Final Written Expression: Parol or Extrinsic Evidence.

Terms with respect to which the confirmatory memoranda of the parties agree or which are otherwise set forth in a writing intended by the parties as a final expression of their agreement with respect to such terms as are included therein may not be contradicted by evidence of any prior agreement or of a contemporaneous oral agreement but may be explained or supplemented:

(a) by course of dealing or usage of trade or by course of performance; and

(b) by evidence of consistent additional terms unless the court finds the writing to have been intended also as a complete and exclusive statement of the terms of the agreement.

§ 2A–203. Seals Inoperative.

The affixing of a seal to a writing evidencing a lease contract or an offer to enter into a lease contract does not render the writing a sealed instrument and the law with respect to sealed instruments does not apply to the lease contract or offer.

§ 2A–204. Formation in General.

(1) A lease contract may be made in any manner sufficient to show agreement, including conduct by both parties which recognizes the existence of a lease contract.

(2) An agreement sufficient to constitute a lease contract may be found although the moment of its making is undetermined.

(3) Although one or more terms are left open, a lease contract does not fail for indefiniteness if the parties have intended to make a lease contract and there is a reasonably certain basis for giving an appropriate remedy.

§ 2A–205. Firm Offers.

An offer by a merchant to lease goods to or from another person in a signed writing that by its terms gives assurance it will be held open is not revocable, for lack of consideration, during the time stated or, if no time is stated, for a reasonable time, but in no event may the period of irrevocability exceed 3 months. Any such term of assurance on a form supplied by the offeree must be separately signed by the offeror.

§ 2A–206. Offer and Acceptance in Formation of Lease Contract.

(1) Unless otherwise unambiguously indicated by the language or circumstances, an offer to make a lease contract must be construed as inviting acceptance in any manner and by any medium reasonable in the circumstances.

(2) If the beginning of a requested performance is a reasonable mode of acceptance, an offeror who is not notified of acceptance within a reasonable time may treat the offer as having lapsed before acceptance.

§ 2A–207. Course of Performance or Practical Construction.

(1) If a lease contract involves repeated occasions for performance by either party with knowledge of the nature of the performance and opportunity for objection to it by the other, any course of performance accepted or acquiesced in without objection is relevant to determine the meaning of the lease agreement.

(2) The express terms of a lease agreement and any course of performance, as well as any course of dealing and usage of trade, must be construed whenever reasonable as consistent with each other; but if that construction is unreasonable, express terms control course of performance, course of performance controls both course of dealing and usage of trade, and course of dealing controls usage of trade.

(3) Subject to the provisions of Section 2A–208 on modification and waiver, course of performance is relevant to show a waiver or modification of any term inconsistent with the course of performance.

§ 2A–208. Modification, Rescission and Waiver.

(1) An agreement modifying a lease contract needs no consideration to be binding.

(2) A signed lease agreement that excludes modification or rescission except by a signed writing may not be otherwise modified or rescinded, but, except as between merchants, such a requirement on a form supplied by a merchant must be separately signed by the other party.

(3) Although an attempt at modification or rescission does not satisfy the requirements of subsection (2), it may operate as a waiver.

(4) A party who has made a waiver affecting an executory portion of a lease contract may retract the waiver by reasonable notification received by the other party that strict performance will be required of any term waived, unless the retraction would be unjust in view of a material change of position in reliance on the waiver.

§ 2A–209. Lessee under Finance Lease as Beneficiary of Supply Contract.

(1) The benefit of the supplier's promises to the lessor under the supply contract and of all warranties, whether express or implied, including those of any third party provided in connection with or as part of the supply contract, extends to the lessee to the extent of the lessee's leasehold interest under a finance lease related to the supply contract, but is subject to the terms warranty and of the supply contract and all defenses or claims arising therefrom.

(2) The extension of the benefit of supplier's promises and of warranties to the lessee (Section 2A–209(1)) does not: (i) modify the rights and obligations of the parties to the supply contract, whether arising therefrom or otherwise, or (ii) impose any duty or liability under the supply contract on the lessee.

(3) Any modification or rescission of the supply contract by the supplier and the lessor is effective between the supplier and the lessee unless, before the modification or rescission, the supplier has received notice that the lessee has entered into a finance lease related to the supply contract. If the modification or rescission is effective between the supplier and the lessee, the lessor is deemed to have assumed, in addition to the obligations of the lessor to the lessee under the lease contract, promises of the supplier to the lessor and warranties that were so modified or rescinded as they existed and were available to the lessee before modification or rescission.

(4) In addition to the extension of the benefit of the supplier's promises and of warranties to the lessee under subsection (1), the lessee retains all rights that the lessee may have against the supplier which arise from an agreement between the lessee and the supplier or under other law.

As amended in 1990.

§ 2A–210. Express Warranties.

(1) Express warranties by the lessor are created as follows:

(a) Any affirmation of fact or promise made by the lessor to the lessee which relates to the goods and becomes part of the basis of the bargain creates an express warranty that the goods will conform to the affirmation or promise.

(b) Any description of the goods which is made part of the basis of the bargain creates an express warranty that the goods will conform to the description.

(c) Any sample or model that is made part of the basis of the bargain creates an express warranty that the whole of the goods will conform to the sample or model.

(2) It is not necessary to the creation of an express warranty that the lessor use formal words, such as "warrant" or "guarantee," or

that the lessor have a specific intention to make a warranty, but an affirmation merely of the value of the goods or a statement purporting to be merely the lessor's opinion or commendation of the goods does not create a warranty.

§ 2A–211. Warranties Against Interference and Against Infringement; Lessee's Obligation Against Infringement.

(1) There is in a lease contract a warranty that for the lease term no person holds a claim to or interest in the goods that arose from an act or omission of the lessor, other than a claim by way of infringement or the like, which will interfere with the lessee's enjoyment of its leasehold interest.

(2) Except in a finance lease there is in a lease contract by a lessor who is a merchant regularly dealing in goods of the kind a warranty that the goods are delivered free of the rightful claim of any person by way of infringement or the like.

(3) A lessee who furnishes specifications to a lessor or a supplier shall hold the lessor and the supplier harmless against any claim by way of infringement or the like that arises out of compliance with the specifications.

§ 2A–212. Implied Warranty of Merchantability.

(1) Except in a finance lease, a warranty that the goods will be merchantable is implied in a lease contract if the lessor is a merchant with respect to goods of that kind.

(2) Goods to be merchantable must be at least such as

(a) pass without objection in the trade under the description in the lease agreement;

(b) in the case of fungible goods, are of fair average quality within the description;

(c) are fit for the ordinary purposes for which goods of that type are used;

(d) run, within the variation permitted by the lease agreement, of even kind, quality, and quantity within each unit and among all units involved;

(e) are adequately contained, packaged, and labeled as the lease agreement may require; and

(f) conform to any promises or affirmations of fact made on the container or label.

(3) Other implied warranties may arise from course of dealing or usage of trade.

§ 2A–213. Implied Warranty of Fitness for Particular Purpose.

Except in a finance of lease, if the lessor at the time the lease contract is made has reason to know of any particular purpose for which the goods are required and that the lessee is relying on the lessor's skill or judgment to select or furnish suitable goods, there is in the lease contract an implied warranty that the goods will be fit for that purpose.

§ 2A–214. Exclusion or Modification of Warranties.

(1) Words or conduct relevant to the creation of an express warranty and words or conduct tending to negate or limit a warranty must be construed wherever reasonable as consistent with each other; but, subject to the provisions of Section 2A–202 on parol or extrinsic evidence, negation or limitation is inoperative to the extent that the construction is unreasonable.

(2) Subject to subsection (3), to exclude or modify the implied warranty of merchantability or any part of it the language must mention "merchantability", be by a writing, and be conspicuous.

Subject to subsection (3), to exclude or modify any implied warranty of fitness the exclusion must be by a writing and be conspicuous. Language to exclude all implied warranties of fitness is sufficient if it is in writing, is conspicuous and states, for example, "There is no warranty that the goods will be fit for a particular purpose".

(3) Notwithstanding subsection (2), but subject to subsection (4),

(a) unless the circumstances indicate otherwise, all implied warranties are excluded by expressions like "as is" or "with all faults" or by other language that in common understanding calls the lessee's attention to the exclusion of warranties and makes plain that there is no implied warranty, if in writing and conspicuous;

(b) if the lessee before entering into the lease contract has examined the goods or the sample or model as fully as desired or has refused to examine the goods, there is no implied warranty with regard to defects that an examination ought in the circumstances to have revealed; and

(c) an implied warranty may also be excluded or modified by course of dealing, course of performance, or usage of trade.

(4) To exclude or modify a warranty against interference or against infringement (Section 2A–211) or any part of it, the language must be specific, be by a writing, and be conspicuous, unless the circumstances, including course of performance, course of dealing, or usage of trade, give the lessee reason to know that the goods are being leased subject to a claim or interest of any person.

§ 2A–215. Cumulation and Conflict of Warranties Express or Implied.

Warranties, whether express or implied, must be construed as consistent with each other and as cumulative, but if that construction is unreasonable, the intention of the parties determines which warranty is dominant. In ascertaining that intention the following rules apply:

(a) Exact or technical specifications displace an inconsistent sample or model or general language of description.

(b) A sample from an existing bulk displaces inconsistent general language of description.

(c) Express warranties displace inconsistent implied warranties other than an implied warranty of fitness for a particular purpose.

§ 2A–216. Third-Party Beneficiaries of Express and Implied Warranties.

Alternative A

A warranty to or for the benefit of a lessee under this Article, whether express or implied, extends to any natural person who is in the family or household of the lessee or who is a guest in the lessee's home if it is reasonable to expect that such person may use, consume, or be affected by the goods and who is injured in person by breach of the warranty. This section does not displace principles of law and equity that extend a warranty to or for the benefit of a lessee to other persons. The operation of this section may not be excluded, modified, or limited, but an exclusion, modification, or limitation of the warranty, including any with respect to rights and remedies, effective against the lessee is also effective against any beneficiary designated under this section.

Alternative B

A warranty to or for the benefit of a lessee under this Article, whether express or implied, extends to any natural person who may reasonably be expected to use, consume, or be affected by the goods and who is injured in person by breach of the warranty. This section does not displace principles of law and equity that extend a warranty to or for the benefit of a lessee to other persons. The operation of this section may not be excluded, modified, or limited, but an exclusion, modification, or limitation of the warranty, including any with respect to rights and remedies, effective against the lessee is also effective against the beneficiary designated under this section.

Alternative C

A warranty to or for the benefit of a lessee under this Article, whether express or implied, extends to any person who may reasonably be expected to use, consume, or be affected by the goods and who is injured by breach of the warranty. The operation of this section may not be excluded, modified, or limited with respect to injury to the person of an individual to whom the warranty extends, but an exclusion, modification, or limitation of the warranty, including any with respect to rights and remedies, effective against the lessee is also effective against the beneficiary designated under this section.

§ 2A–217. Identification.

Identification of goods as goods to which a lease contract refers may be made at any time and in any manner explicitly agreed to by the parties. In the absence of explicit agreement, identification occurs:

(a) when the lease contract is made if the lease contract is for a lease of goods that are existing and identified;

(b) when the goods are shipped, marked, or otherwise designated by the lessor as goods to which the lease contract refers, if the lease contract is for a lease of goods that are not existing and identified; or

(c) when the young are conceived, if the lease contract is for a lease of unborn young of animals.

§ 2A–218. Insurance and Proceeds.

(1) A lessee obtains an insurable interest when existing goods are identified to the lease contract even though the goods identified are nonconforming and the lessee has an option to reject them.

(2) If a lessee has an insurable interest only by reason of the lessor's identification of the goods, the lessor, until default or insolvency or notification to the lessee that identification is final, may substitute other goods for those identified.

(3) Notwithstanding a lessee's insurable interest under subsections (1) and (2), the lessor retains an insurable interest until an option to buy has been exercised by the lessee and risk of loss has passed to the lessee.

(4) Nothing in this section impairs any insurable interest recognized under any other statute or rule of law.

(5) The parties by agreement may determine that one or more parties have an obligation to obtain and pay for insurance covering the goods and by agreement may determine the beneficiary of the proceeds of the insurance.

§ 2A–219. Risk of Loss.

(1) Except in the case of a finance lease, risk of loss is retained by the lessor and does not pass to the lessee. In the case of a finance lease, risk of loss passes to the lessee.

(2) Subject to the provisions of this Article on the effect of default on risk of loss (Section 2A–220), if risk of loss is to pass to the lessee and the time of passage is not stated, the following rules apply:

(a) If the lease contract requires or authorizes the goods to be shipped by carrier

(i) and it does not require delivery at a particular destination, the risk of loss passes to the lessee when the goods are duly delivered to the carrier; but

(ii) if it does require delivery at a particular destination and the goods are there duly tendered while in the possession of the carrier, the risk of loss passes to the lessee when the goods are there duly so tendered as to enable the lessee to take delivery.

(b) If the goods are held by a bailee to be delivered without being moved, the risk of loss passes to the lessee on acknowledgment by the bailee of the lessee's right to possession of the goods.

(c) In any case not within subsection (a) or (b), the risk of loss passes to the lessee on the lessee's receipt of the goods if the lessor, or, in the case of a finance lease, the supplier, is a merchant; otherwise the risk passes to the lessee on tender of delivery.

§ 2A–220. Effect of Default on Risk of Loss.

(1) Where risk of loss is to pass to the lessee and the time of passage is not stated:

(a) If a tender or delivery of goods so fails to conform to the lease contract as to give a right of rejection, the risk of their loss remains with the lessor, or, in the case of a finance lease, the supplier, until cure or acceptance.

(b) If the lessee rightfully revokes acceptance, he [or she], to the extent of any deficiency in his [or her] effective insurance coverage, may treat the risk of loss as having remained with the lessor from the beginning.

(2) Whether or not risk of loss is to pass to the lessee, if the lessee as to conforming goods already identified to a lease contract repudiates or is otherwise in default under the lease contract, the lessor, or, in the case of a finance lease, the supplier, to the extent of any deficiency in his [or her] effective insurance coverage may treat the risk of loss as resting on the lessee for a commercially reasonable time.

§ 2A–221. Casualty to Identified Goods.

If a lease contract requires goods identified when the lease contract is made, and the goods suffer casualty without fault of the lessee, the lessor or the supplier before delivery, or the goods suffer casualty before risk of loss passes to the lessee pursuant to the lease agreement or Section 2A–219, then:

(a) if the loss is total, the lease contract is avoided; and

(b) if the loss is partial or the goods have so deteriorated as to no longer conform to the lease contract, the lessee may nevertheless demand inspection and at his [or her] option either treat the lease contract as avoided or, except in a finance lease that is not a consumer lease, accept the goods with due allowance from the rent payable for the balance of the lease term for the deterioration or the deficiency in quantity but without further right against the lessor.

Part 3 Effect of Lease Contract

§ 2A–301. Enforceability of Lease Contract.

Except as otherwise provided in this Article, a lease contract is effective and enforceable according to its terms between the parties, against purchasers of the goods and against creditors of the parties.

§ 2A–302. Title to and Possession of Goods.

Except as otherwise provided in this Article, each provision of this Article applies whether the lessor or a third party has title to the goods, and whether the lessor, the lessee, or a third party has possession of the goods, notwithstanding any statute or rule of law that possession or the absence of possession is fraudulent.

§ 2A–303. Alienability of Party's Interest Under Lease Contract or of Lessor's Residual Interest in Goods; Delegation of Performance; Transfer of Rights.

(1) As used in this section, "creation of a security interest" includes the sale of a lease contract that is subject to Article 9, Secured Transactions, by reason of Section 9–109(a)(3).

(2) Except as provided in subsections (3) and Section 9–407, a provision in a lease agreement which (i) prohibits the voluntary or involuntary transfer, including a transfer by sale, sublease, creation or enforcement of a security interest, or attachment, levy, or other judicial process, of an interest of a party under the lease contract or of the lessor's residual interest in the goods, or (ii) makes such a transfer an event of default, gives rise to the rights and remedies provided in subsection (4), but a transfer that is prohibited or is an event of default under the lease agreement is otherwise effective.

(3) A provision in a lease agreement which (i) prohibits a transfer of a right to damages for default with respect to the whole lease contract or of a right to payment arising out of the transferor's due performance of the transferor's entire obligation, or (ii) makes such a transfer an event of default, is not enforceable, and such a transfer is not a transfer that materially impairs the propsect of obtaining return performance by, materially changes the duty of, or materially increases the burden or risk imposed on, the other party to the lease contract within the purview of subsection (4).

(4) Subject to subsection (3) and Section 9–407:

(a) if a transfer is made which is made an event of default under a lease agreement, the party to the lease contract not making the transfer, unless that party waives the default or otherwise agrees, has the rights and remedies described in Section 2A–501(2);

(b) if paragraph (a) is not applicable and if a transfer is made that (i) is prohibited under a lease agreement or (ii) materially impairs the prospect of obtaining return performance by, materially changes the duty of, or materially increases the burden or risk imposed on, the other party to the lease contract, unless the party not making the transfer agrees at any time to the transfer in the lease contract or otherwise, then, except as limited by contract, (i) the transferor is liable to the party not making the transfer for damages caused by the transfer to the extent that the damages could not reasonably be prevented by the party not making the transfer and (ii) a court having jurisdiction may grant other appropriate relief, including cancellation of the lease contract or an injunction against the transfer.

(5) A transfer of "the lease" or of "all my rights under the lease", or a transfer in similar general terms, is a transfer of rights and, unless the language or the circumstances, as in a transfer for security, indicate the contrary, the transfer is a delegation of duties by the transferor to the transferee. Acceptance by the transferee constitutes a promise by the transferee to perform those duties. The promise is enforceable by either the transferor or the other party to the lease contract.

(6) Unless otherwise agreed by the lessor and the lessee, a delegation of performance does not relieve the transferor as against the other party of any duty to perform or of any liability for default.

(7) In a consumer lease, to prohibit the transfer of an interest of a party under the lease contract or to make a transfer an event of default, the language must be specific, by a writing, and conspicuous. As amended in 1990 and 1999.

§ 2A–304. Subsequent Lease of Goods by Lessor.

(1) Subject to Section 2A–303, a subsequent lessee from a lessor of goods under an existing lease contract obtains, to the extent of the leasehold interest transferred, the leasehold interest in the goods that the lessor had or had power to transfer, and except as provided in subsection (2) and Section 2A–527(4), takes subject to the existing lease contract. A lessor with voidable title has power to transfer a good leasehold interest to a good faith subsequent lessee for value, but only to the extent set forth in the preceding sentence. If goods have been delivered under a transaction of purchase the lessor has that power even though:

(a) the lessor's transferor was deceived as to the identity of the lessor;

(b) the delivery was in exchange for a check which is later dishonored;

(c) it was agreed that the transaction was to be a "cash sale"; or

(d) the delivery was procured through fraud punishable as larcenous under the criminal law.

(2) A subsequent lessee in the ordinary course of business from a lessor who is a merchant dealing in goods of that kind to whom the goods were entrusted by the existing lessee of that lessor before the interest of the subsequent lessee became enforceable against that lessor obtains, to the extent of the leasehold interest transferred, all of that lessor's and the existing lessee's rights to the goods, and takes free of the existing lease contract.

(3) A subsequent lessee from the lessor of goods that are subject to an existing lease contract and are covered by a certificate of title issued under a statute of this State or of another jurisdiction takes no greater rights than those provided both by this section and by the certificate of title statute.

As amended in 1990.

§ 2A–305. Sale or Sublease of Goods by Lessee.

(1) Subject to the provisions of Section 2A–303, a buyer or sublessee from the lessee of goods under an existing lease contract obtains, to the extent of the interest transferred, the leasehold interest in the goods that the lessee had or had power to transfer, and except as provided in subsection (2) and Section 2A–511(4), takes subject to the existing lease contract. A lessee with a voidable leasehold interest has power to transfer a good leasehold interest to a good faith buyer for value or a good faith sublessee for value, but only to the extent set forth in the preceding sentence. When goods have been delivered under a transaction of lease the lessee has that power even though:

(a) the lessor was deceived as to the identity of the lessee;

(b) the delivery was in exchange for a check which is later dishonored; or

(c) the delivery was procured through fraud punishable as larcenous under the criminal law.

(2) A buyer in the ordinary course of business or a sublessee in the ordinary course of business from a lessee who is a merchant dealing in goods of that kind to whom the goods were entrusted by the lessor obtains, to the extent of the interest transferred, all of the lessor's and lessee's rights to the goods, and takes free of the existing lease contract.

(3) A buyer or sublessee from the lessee of goods that are subject to an existing lease contract and are covered by a certificate of title issued under a statute of this State or of another jurisdiction takes no greater rights than those provided both by this section and by the certificate of title statute.

§ 2A–306. Priority of Certain Liens Arising by Operation of Law.

If a person in the ordinary course of his [or her] business furnishes services or materials with respect to goods subject to a lease contract, a lien upon those goods in the possession of that person given by statute or rule of law for those materials or services takes priority over any interest of the lessor or lessee under the lease contract or this Article unless the lien is created by statute and the statute provides otherwise or unless the lien is created by rule of law and the rule of law provides otherwise.

§ 2A–307. Priority of Liens Arising by Attachment or Levy on, Security Interests in, and Other Claims to Goods.

(1) Except as otherwise provided in Section 2A–306, a creditor of a lessee takes subject to the lease contract.

(2) Except as otherwise provided in subsection (3) and in Sections 2A–306 and 2A–308, a creditor of a lessor takes subject to the lease contract unless the creditor holds a lien that attached to the goods before the lease contract became enforceable.

(3) Except as otherwise provided in Sections 9–317, 9–321, and 9–323, a lessee takes a leasehold interest subject to a security interest held by a creditor of the lessor.

As amended in 1990 and 1999.

§ 2A–308. Special Rights of Creditors.

(1) A creditor of a lessor in possession of goods subject to a lease contract may treat the lease contract as void if as against the creditor retention of possession by the lessor is fraudulent under any statute or rule of law, but retention of possession in good faith and current course of trade by the lessor for a commercially reasonable time after the lease contract becomes enforceable is not fraudulent.

(2) Nothing in this Article impairs the rights of creditors of a lessor if the lease contract (a) becomes enforceable, not in current course of trade but in satisfaction of or as security for a pre-existing claim for money, security, or the like, and (b) is made under circumstances which under any statute or rule of law apart from this Article would constitute the transaction a fraudulent transfer or voidable preference.

(3) A creditor of a seller may treat a sale or an identification of goods to a contract for sale as void if as against the creditor retention of possession by the seller is fraudulent under any statute or rule of law, but retention of possession of the goods pursuant to a lease contract entered into by the seller as lessee and the buyer as lessor in connection with the sale or identification of the goods is not fraudulent if the buyer bought for value and in good faith.

§ 2A–309. Lessor's and Lessee's Rights When Goods Become Fixtures.

(1) In this section:

(a) goods are "fixtures" when they become so related to particular real estate that an interest in them arises under real estate law;

(b) a "fixture filing" is the filing, in the office where a mortgage on the real estate would be filed or recorded, of a financing statement covering goods that are or are to become fixtures and conforming to the requirements of Section 9–502(a) and (b);

(c) a lease is a "purchase money lease" unless the lessee has possession or use of the goods or the right to possession or use of the goods before the lease agreement is enforceable;

(d) a mortgage is a "construction mortgage" to the extent it secures an obligation incurred for the construction of an improvement on land including the acquisition cost of the land, if the recorded writing so indicates; and

(e) "encumbrance" includes real estate mortgages and other liens on real estate and all other rights in real estate that are not ownership interests.

(2) Under this Article a lease may be of goods that are fixtures or may continue in goods that become fixtures, but no lease exists under this Article of ordinary building materials incorporated into an improvement on land.

(3) This Article does not prevent creation of a lease of fixtures pursuant to real estate law.

(4) The perfected interest of a lessor of fixtures has priority over a conflicting interest of an encumbrancer or owner of the real estate if:

(a) the lease is a purchase money lease, the conflicting interest of the encumbrancer or owner arises before the goods become fixtures, the interest of the lessor is perfected by a fixture filing before the goods become fixtures or within ten days thereafter, and the lessee has an interest of record in the real estate or is in possession of the real estate; or

(b) the interest of the lessor is perfected by a fixture filing before the interest of the encumbrancer or owner is of record, the lessor's interest has priority over any conflicting interest of a predecessor in title of the encumbrancer or owner, and the lessee has an interest of record in the real estate or is in possession of the real estate.

(5) The interest of a lessor of fixtures, whether or not perfected, has priority over the conflicting interest of an encumbrancer or owner of the real estate if:

(a) the fixtures are readily removable factory or office machines, readily removable equipment that is not primarily used or leased for use in the operation of the real estate, or readily removable replacements of domestic appliances that are goods subject to a consumer lease, and before the goods become fixtures the lease contract is enforceable; or

(b) the conflicting interest is a lien on the real estate obtained by legal or equitable proceedings after the lease contract is enforceable; or

(c) the encumbrancer or owner has consented in writing to the lease or has disclaimed an interest in the goods as fixtures; or

(d) the lessee has a right to remove the goods as against the encumbrancer or owner. If the lessee's right to remove terminates, the priority of the interest of the lessor continues for a reasonable time.

(6) Notwithstanding paragraph (4)(a) but otherwise subject to subsections (4) and (5), the interest of a lessor of fixtures, including the lessor's residual interest, is subordinate to the conflicting interest of an encumbrancer of the real estate under a construction mortgage recorded before the goods become fixtures if the goods become fixtures before the completion of the construction. To the extent given to refinance a construction mortgage, the conflicting interest of an encumbrancer of the real estate under a mortgage has this priority to the same extent as the encumbrancer of the real estate under the construction mortgage.

(7) In cases not within the preceding subsections, priority between the interest of a lessor of fixtures, including the lessor's residual interest, and the conflicting interest of an encumbrancer or owner of the real estate who is not the lessee is determined by the priority rules governing conflicting interests in real estate.

(8) If the interest of a lessor of fixtures, including the lessor's residual interest, has priority over all conflicting interests of all owners and encumbrancers of the real estate, the lessor or the lessee may (i) on default, expiration, termination, or cancellation of the lease agreement but subject to the agreement and this Article, or (ii) if necessary to enforce other rights and remedies of the lessor or lessee under this Article, remove the goods from the real estate, free and clear of all conflicting interests of all owners and encumbrancers of the real estate, but the lessor or lessee must reimburse any encumbrancer or owner of the real estate who is not the lessee and who has not otherwise agreed for the cost of repair of any physical injury, but not for any diminution in value of the real estate caused by the absence of the goods removed or by any necessity of replacing them. A person entitled to reimbursement may refuse permission to remove until the party seeking removal gives adequate security for the performance of this obligation.

(9) Even though the lease agreement does not create a security interest, the interest of a lessor of fixtures, including the lessor's residual interest, is perfected by filing a financing statement as a fixture filing for leased goods that are or are to become fixtures in accordance with the relevant provisions of the Article on Secured Transactions (Article 9).

As amended in 1990 and 1999.

§ 2A-310. Lessor's and Lessee's Rights When Goods Become Accessions.

(1) Goods are "accessions" when they are installed in or affixed to other goods.

(2) The interest of a lessor or a lessee under a lease contract entered into before the goods became accessions is superior to all interests in the whole except as stated in subsection (4).

(3) The interest of a lessor or a lessee under a lease contract entered into at the time or after the goods became accessions is superior to all subsequently acquired interests in the whole except as stated in subsection (4) but is subordinate to interests in the whole existing at the time the lease contract was made unless the holders of such interests in the whole have in writing consented to the lease or disclaimed an interest in the goods as part of the whole.

(4) The interest of a lessor or a lessee under a lease contract described in subsection (2) or (3) is subordinate to the interest of

(a) a buyer in the ordinary course of business or a lessee in the ordinary course of business of any interest in the whole acquired after the goods became accessions; or

(b) a creditor with a security interest in the whole perfected before the lease contract was made to the extent that the creditor makes subsequent advances without knowledge of the lease contract.

(5) When under subsections (2) or (3) and (4) a lessor or a lessee of accessions holds an interest that is superior to all interests in the whole, the lessor or the lessee may (a) on default, expiration, termination, or cancellation of the lease contract by the other party but subject to the provisions of the lease contract and this Article, or (b) if necessary to enforce his [or her] other rights and remedies under this Article, remove the goods from the whole, free and clear of all interests in the whole, but he [or she] must reimburse

any holder of an interest in the whole who is not the lessee and who has not otherwise agreed for the cost of repair of any physical injury but not for any diminution in value of the whole caused by the absence of the goods removed or by any necessity for replacing them. A person entitled to reimbursement may refuse permission to remove until the party seeking removal gives adequate security for the performance of this obligation.

§ 2A–311. Priority Subject to Subordination.

Nothing in this Article prevents subordination by agreement by any person entitled to priority.

As added in 1990.

Part 4 Performance of Lease Contract: Repudiated, Substituted and Excused

§ 2A–401. Insecurity: Adequate Assurance of Performance.

(1) A lease contract imposes an obligation on each party that the other's expectation of receiving due performance will not be impaired.

(2) If reasonable grounds for insecurity arise with respect to the performance of either party, the insecure party may demand in writing adequate assurance of due performance. Until the insecure party receives that assurance, if commercially reasonable the insecure party may suspend any performance for which he [or she] has not already received the agreed return.

(3) A repudiation of the lease contract occurs if assurance of due performance adequate under the circumstances of the particular case is not provided to the insecure party within a reasonable time, not to exceed 30 days after receipt of a demand by the other party.

(4) Between merchants, the reasonableness of grounds for insecurity and the adequacy of any assurance offered must be determined according to commercial standards.

(5) Acceptance of any nonconforming delivery or payment does not prejudice the aggrieved party's right to demand adequate assurance of future performance.

§ 2A–402. Anticipatory Repudiation.

If either party repudiates a lease contract with respect to a performance not yet due under the lease contract, the loss of which performance will substantially impair the value of the lease contract to the other, the aggrieved party may:

(a) for a commercially reasonable time, await retraction of repudiation and performance by the repudiating party;

(b) make demand pursuant to Section 2A–401 and await assurance of future performance adequate under the circumstances of the particular case; or

(c) resort to any right or remedy upon default under the lease contract or this Article, even though the aggrieved party has notified the repudiating party that the aggrieved party would await the repudiating party's performance and assurance and has urged retraction. In addition, whether or not the aggrieved party is pursuing one of the foregoing remedies, the aggrieved party may suspend performance or, if the aggrieved party is the lessor, proceed in accordance with the provisions of this Article on the lessor's right to identify goods to the lease contract notwithstanding default or to salvage unfinished goods (Section 2A–524).

§ 2A–403. Retraction of Anticipatory Repudiation.

(1) Until the repudiating party's next performance is due, the repudiating party can retract the repudiation unless, since the repudiation, the aggrieved party has cancelled the lease contract or materially changed the aggrieved party's position or otherwise indicated that the aggrieved party considers the repudiation final.

(2) Retraction may be by any method that clearly indicates to the aggrieved party that the repudiating party intends to perform under the lease contract and includes any assurance demanded under Section 2A–401.

(3) Retraction reinstates a repudiating party's rights under a lease contract with due excuse and allowance to the aggrieved party for any delay occasioned by the repudiation.

§ 2A–404. Substituted Performance.

(1) If without fault of the lessee, the lessor and the supplier, the agreed berthing, loading, or unloading facilities fail or the agreed type of carrier becomes unavailable or the agreed manner of delivery otherwise becomes commercially impracticable, but a commercially reasonable substitute is available, the substitute performance must be tendered and accepted.

(2) If the agreed means or manner of payment fails because of domestic or foreign governmental regulation:

(a) the lessor may withhold or stop delivery or cause the supplier to withhold or stop delivery unless the lessee provides a means or manner of payment that is commercially a substantial equivalent; and

(b) if delivery has already been taken, payment by the means or in the manner provided by the regulation discharges the lessee's obligation unless the regulation is discriminatory, oppressive, or predatory.

§ 2A–405. Excused Performance.

Subject to Section 2A–404 on substituted performance, the following rules apply:

(a) Delay in delivery or nondelivery in whole or in part by a lessor or a supplier who complies with paragraphs (b) and (c) is not a default under the lease contract if performance as agreed has been made impracticable by the occurrence of a contingency the nonoccurrence of which was a basic assumption on which the lease contract was made or by compliance in good faith with any applicable foreign or domestic governmental regulation or order, whether or not the regulation or order later proves to be invalid.

(b) If the causes mentioned in paragraph (a) affect only part of the lessor's or the supplier's capacity to perform, he [or she] shall allocate production and deliveries among his [or her] customers but at his [or her] option may include regular customers not then under contract for sale or lease as well as his [or her] own requirements for further manufacture. He [or she] may so allocate in any manner that is fair and reasonable.

(c) The lessor seasonably shall notify the lessee and in the case of a finance lease the supplier seasonably shall notify the lessor and the lessee, if known, that there will be delay or nondelivery and, if allocation is required under paragraph (b), of the estimated quota thus made available for the lessee.

§ 2A–406. Procedure on Excused Performance.

(1) If the lessee receives notification of a material or indefinite delay or an allocation justified under Section 2A–405, the lessee

may by written notification to the lessor as to any goods involved, and with respect to all of the goods if under an installment lease contract the value of the whole lease contract is substantially impaired (Section 2A–510):

(a) terminate the lease contract (Section 2A–505(2)); or

(b) except in a finance lease that is not a consumer lease, modify the lease contract by accepting the available quota in substitution, with due allowance from the rent payable for the balance of the lease term for the deficiency but without further right against the lessor.

(2) If, after receipt of a notification from the lessor under Section 2A–405, the lessee fails so to modify the lease agreement within a reasonable time not exceeding 30 days, the lease contract lapses with respect to any deliveries affected.

§ 2A–407. Irrevocable Promises: Finance Leases.

(1) In the case of a finance lease that is not a consumer lease the lessee's promises under the lease contract become irrevocable and independent upon the lessee's acceptance of the goods.

(2) A promise that has become irrevocable and independent under subsection (1):

(a) is effective and enforceable between the parties, and by or against third parties including assignees of the parties, and

(b) is not subject to cancellation, termination, modification, repudiation, excuse, or substitution without the consent of the party to whom the promise runs.

(3) This section does not affect the validity under any other law of a covenant in any lease contract making the lessee's promises irrevocable and independent upon the lessee's acceptance of the goods.

As amended in 1990.

Part 5 Default

A. In General

§ 2A–501. Default: Procedure.

(1) Whether the lessor or the lessee is in default under a lease contract is determined by the lease agreement and this Article.

(2) If the lessor or the lessee is in default under the lease contract, the party seeking enforcement has rights and remedies as provided in this Article and, except as limited by this Article, as provided in the lease agreement.

(3) If the lessor or the lessee is in default under the lease contract, the party seeking enforcement may reduce the party's claim to judgment, or otherwise enforce the lease contract by self-help or any available judicial procedure or nonjudicial procedure, including administrative proceeding, arbitration, or the like, in accordance with this Article.

(4) Except as otherwise provided in Section 1–106(1) or this Article or the lease agreement, the rights and remedies referred to in subsections (2) and (3) are cumulative.

(5) If the lease agreement covers both real property and goods, the party seeking enforcement may proceed under this Part as to the goods, or under other applicable law as to both the real property and the goods in accordance with that party's rights and remedies in respect of the real property, in which case this Part does not apply.

As amended in 1990.

§ 2A–502. Notice After Default.

Except as otherwise provided in this Article or the lease agreement, the lessor or lessee in default under the lease contract is not entitled to notice of default or notice of enforcement from the other party to the lease agreement.

§ 2A–503. Modification or Impairment of Rights and Remedies.

(1) Except as otherwise provided in this Article, the lease agreement may include rights and remedies for default in addition to or in substitution for those provided in this Article and may limit or alter the measure of damages recoverable under this Article.

(2) Resort to a remedy provided under this Article or in the lease agreement is optional unless the remedy is expressly agreed to be exclusive. If circumstances cause an exclusive or limited remedy to fail of its essential purpose, or provision for an exclusive remedy is unconscionable, remedy may be had as provided in this Article.

(3) Consequential damages may be liquidated under Section 2A–504, or may otherwise be limited, altered, or excluded unless the limitation, alteration, or exclusion is unconscionable. Limitation, alteration, or exclusion of consequential damages for injury to the person in the case of consumer goods is prima facie unconscionable but limitation, alteration, or exclusion of damages where the loss is commercial is not prima facie unconscionable.

(4) Rights and remedies on default by the lessor or the lessee with respect to any obligation or promise collateral or ancillary to the lease contract are not impaired by this Article.

As amended in 1990.

§ 2A–504. Liquidation of Damages.

(1) Damages payable by either party for default, or any other act or omission, including indemnity for loss or diminution of anticipated tax benefits or loss or damage to lessor's residual interest, may be liquidated in the lease agreement but only at an amount or by a formula that is reasonable in light of the then anticipated harm caused by the default or other act or omission.

(2) If the lease agreement provides for liquidation of damages, and such provision does not comply with subsection (1), or such provision is an exclusive or limited remedy that circumstances cause to fail of its essential purpose, remedy may be had as provided in this Article.

(3) If the lessor justifiably withholds or stops delivery of goods because of the lessee's default or insolvency (Section 2A–525 or 2A–526), the lessee is entitled to restitution of any amount by which the sum of his [or her] payments exceeds:

(a) the amount to which the lessor is entitled by virtue of terms liquidating the lessor's damages in accordance with subsection (1); or

(b) in the absence of those terms, 20 percent of the then present value of the total rent the lessee was obligated to pay for the balance of the lease term, or, in the case of a consumer lease, the lesser of such amount or $500.

(4) A lessee's right to restitution under subsection (3) is subject to offset to the extent the lessor establishes:

(a) a right to recover damages under the provisions of this Article other than subsection (1); and

(b) the amount or value of any benefits received by the lessee directly or indirectly by reason of the lease contract.

§ 2A–505. Cancellation and Termination and Effect of Cancellation, Termination, Rescission, or Fraud on Rights and Remedies.

(1) On cancellation of the lease contract, all obligations that are still executory on both sides are discharged, but any right based

on prior default or performance survives, and the cancelling party also retains any remedy for default of the whole lease contract or any unperformed balance.

(2) On termination of the lease contract, all obligations that are still executory on both sides are discharged but any right based on prior default or performance survives.

(3) Unless the contrary intention clearly appears, expressions of "cancellation," "rescission," or the like of the lease contract may not be construed as a renunciation or discharge of any claim in damages for an antecedent default.

(4) Rights and remedies for material misrepresentation or fraud include all rights and remedies available under this Article for default.

(5) Neither rescission nor a claim for rescission of the lease contract nor rejection or return of the goods may bar or be deemed inconsistent with a claim for damages or other right or remedy.

§ 2A–506. Statute of Limitations.

(1) An action for default under a lease contract, including breach of warranty or indemnity, must be commenced within 4 years after the cause of action accrued. By the original lease contract the parties may reduce the period of limitation to not less than one year.

(2) A cause of action for default accrues when the act or omission on which the default or breach of warranty is based is or should have been discovered by the aggrieved party, or when the default occurs, whichever is later. A cause of action for indemnity accrues when the act or omission on which the claim for indemnity is based is or should have been discovered by the indemnified party, whichever is later.

(3) If an action commenced within the time limited by subsection (1) is so terminated as to leave available a remedy by another action for the same default or breach of warranty or indemnity, the other action may be commenced after the expiration of the time limited and within 6 months after the termination of the first action unless the termination resulted from voluntary discontinuance or from dismissal for failure or neglect to prosecute.

(4) This section does not alter the law on tolling of the statute of limitations nor does it apply to causes of action that have accrued before this Article becomes effective.

§ 2A–507. Proof of Market Rent: Time and Place.

(1) Damages based on market rent (Section 2A–519 or 2A–528) are determined according to the rent for the use of the goods concerned for a lease term identical to the remaining lease term of the original lease agreement and prevailing at the times specified in Sections 2A–519 and 2A–528.

(2) If evidence of rent for the use of the goods concerned for a lease term identical to the remaining lease term of the original lease agreement and prevailing at the times or places described in this Article is not readily available, the rent prevailing within any reasonable time before or after the time described or at any other place or for a different lease term which in commercial judgment or under usage of trade would serve as a reasonable substitute for the one described may be used, making any proper allowance for the difference, including the cost of transporting the goods to or from the other place.

(3) Evidence of a relevant rent prevailing at a time or place or for a lease term other than the one described in this Article offered by one party is not admissible unless and until he [or she] has given the other party notice the court finds sufficient to prevent unfair surprise.

(4) If the prevailing rent or value of any goods regularly leased in any established market is in issue, reports in official publications or trade journals or in newspapers or periodicals of general circulation published as the reports of that market are admissible in evidence. The circumstances of the preparation of the report may be shown to affect its weight but not its admissibility.

As amended in 1990.

B. Default by Lessor

§ 2A–508. Lessee's Remedies.

(1) If a lessor fails to deliver the goods in conformity to the lease contract (Section 2A–509) or repudiates the lease contract (Section 2A–402), or a lessee rightfully rejects the goods (Section 2A–509) or justifiably revokes acceptance of the goods (Section 2A–517), then with respect to any goods involved, and with respect to all of the goods if under an installment lease contract the value of the whole lease contract is substantially impaired (Section 2A–510), the lessor is in default under the lease contract and the lessee may:

   (a) cancel the lease contract (Section 2A–505(1));

   (b) recover so much of the rent and security as has been paid and is just under the circumstances;

   (c) cover and recover damages as to all goods affected whether or not they have been identified to the lease contract (Sections 2A–518 and 2A–520), or recover damages for nondelivery (Sections 2A–519 and 2A–520);

   (d) exercise any other rights or pursue any other remedies provided in the lease contract.

(2) If a lessor fails to deliver the goods in conformity to the lease contract or repudiates the lease contract, the lessee may also:

   (a) if the goods have been identified, recover them (Section 2A–522); or

   (b) in a proper case, obtain specific performance or replevy the goods (Section 2A–521).

(3) If a lessor is otherwise in default under a lease contract, the lessee may exercise the rights and pursue the remedies provided in the lease contract, which may include a right to cancel the lease, and in Section 2A–519(3).

(4) If a lessor has breached a warranty, whether express or implied, the lessee may recover damages (Section 2A–519(4)).

(5) On rightful rejection or justifiable revocation of acceptance, a lessee has a security interest in goods in the lessee's possession or control for any rent and security that has been paid and any expenses reasonably incurred in their inspection, receipt, transportation, and care and custody and may hold those goods and dispose of them in good faith and in a commercially reasonable manner, subject to Section 2A–527(5).

(6) Subject to the provisions of Section 2A–407, a lessee, on notifying the lessor of the lessee's intention to do so, may deduct all or any part of the damages resulting from any default under the lease contract from any part of the rent still due under the same lease contract.

As amended in 1990.

§ 2A–509. Lessee's Rights on Improper Delivery; Rightful Rejection.

(1) Subject to the provisions of Section 2A–510 on default in installment lease contracts, if the goods or the tender or delivery fail in any respect to conform to the lease contract, the lessee may reject or accept the goods or accept any commercial unit or units and reject the rest of the goods.

(2) Rejection of goods is ineffective unless it is within a reasonable time after tender or delivery of the goods and the lessee seasonably notifies the lessor.

§ 2A-510. Installment Lease Contracts: Rejection and Default.

(1) Under an installment lease contract a lessee may reject any delivery that is nonconforming if the nonconformity substantially impairs the value of that delivery and cannot be cured or the nonconformity is a defect in the required documents; but if the nonconformity does not fall within subsection (2) and the lessor or the supplier gives adequate assurance of its cure, the lessee must accept that delivery.

(2) Whenever nonconformity or default with respect to one or more deliveries substantially impairs the value of the installment lease contract as a whole there is a default with respect to the whole. But, the aggrieved party reinstates the installment lease contract as a whole if the aggrieved party accepts a nonconforming delivery without seasonably notifying of cancellation or brings an action with respect only to past deliveries or demands performance as to future deliveries.

§ 2A-511. Merchant Lessee's Duties as to Rightfully Rejected Goods.

(1) Subject to any security interest of a lessee (Section 2A-508(5)), if a lessor or a supplier has no agent or place of business at the market of rejection, a merchant lessee, after rejection of goods in his [or her] possession or control, shall follow any reasonable instructions received from the lessor or the supplier with respect to the goods. In the absence of those instructions, a merchant lessee shall make reasonable efforts to sell, lease, or otherwise dispose of the goods for the lessor's account if they threaten to decline in value speedily. Instructions are not reasonable if on demand indemnity for expenses is not forthcoming.

(2) If a merchant lessee (subsection (1)) or any other lessee (Section 2A-512) disposes of goods, he [or she] is entitled to reimbursement either from the lessor or the supplier or out of the proceeds for reasonable expenses of caring for and disposing of the goods and, if the expenses include no disposition commission, to such commission as is usual in the trade, or if there is none, to a reasonable sum not exceeding 10 percent of the gross proceeds.

(3) In complying with this section or Section 2A-512, the lessee is held only to good faith. Good faith conduct hereunder is neither acceptance or conversion nor the basis of an action for damages.

(4) A purchaser who purchases in good faith from a lessee pursuant to this section or Section 2A-512 takes the goods free of any rights of the lessor and the supplier even though the lessee fails to comply with one or more of the requirements of this Article.

§ 2A-512. Lessee's Duties as to Rightfully Rejected Goods.

(1) Except as otherwise provided with respect to goods that threaten to decline in value speedily (Section 2A-511) and subject to any security interest of a lessee (Section 2A-508(5)):

(a) the lessee, after rejection of goods in the lessee's possession, shall hold them with reasonable care at the lessor's or the supplier's disposition for a reasonable time after the lessee's seasonable notification of rejection;

(b) if the lessor or the supplier gives no instructions within a reasonable time after notification of rejection, the lessee may store the rejected goods for the lessor's or the supplier's account or ship them to the lessor or the supplier or dispose of them for the lessor's or the supplier's account with reimbursement in the manner provided in Section 2A-511; but

(c) the lessee has no further obligations with regard to goods rightfully rejected.

(2) Action by the lessee pursuant to subsection (1) is not acceptance or conversion.

§ 2A-513. Cure by Lessor of Improper Tender or Delivery; Replacement.

(1) If any tender or delivery by the lessor or the supplier is rejected because nonconforming and the time for performance has not yet expired, the lessor or the supplier may seasonably notify the lessee of the lessor's or the supplier's intention to cure and may then make a conforming delivery within the time provided in the lease contract.

(2) If the lessee rejects a nonconforming tender that the lessor or the supplier had reasonable grounds to believe would be acceptable with or without money allowance, the lessor or the supplier may have a further reasonable time to substitute a conforming tender if he [or she] seasonably notifies the lessee.

§ 2A-514. Waiver of Lessee's Objections.

(1) In rejecting goods, a lessee's failure to state a particular defect that is ascertainable by reasonable inspection precludes the lessee from relying on the defect to justify rejection or to establish default:

(a) if, stated seasonably, the lessor or the supplier could have cured it (Section 2A-513); or

(b) between merchants if the lessor or the supplier after rejection has made a request in writing for a full and final written statement of all defects on which the lessee proposes to rely.

(2) A lessee's failure to reserve rights when paying rent or other consideration against documents precludes recovery of the payment for defects apparent on the face of the documents.

§ 2A-515. Acceptance of Goods.

(1) Acceptance of goods occurs after the lessee has had a reasonable opportunity to inspect the goods and

(a) the lessee signifies or acts with respect to the goods in a manner that signifies to the lessor or the supplier that the goods are conforming or that the lessee will take or retain them in spite of their nonconformity; or

(b) the lessee fails to make an effective rejection of the goods (Section 2A-509(2)).

(2) Acceptance of a part of any commercial unit is acceptance of that entire unit.

§ 2A-516. Effect of Acceptance of Goods; Notice of Default; Burden of Establishing Default after Acceptance; Notice of Claim or Litigation to Person Answerable Over.

(1) A lessee must pay rent for any goods accepted in accordance with the lease contract, with due allowance for goods rightfully rejected or not delivered.

(2) A lessee's acceptance of goods precludes rejection of the goods accepted. In the case of a finance lease, if made with knowledge of a nonconformity, acceptance cannot be revoked because of it. In any other case, if made with knowledge of a nonconformity, acceptance cannot be revoked because of it unless the acceptance was on the reasonable assumption that the nonconformity would be seasonably cured. Acceptance does not of itself impair any other remedy provided by this Article or the lease agreement for nonconformity.

(3) If a tender has been accepted:

(a) within a reasonable time after the lessee discovers or should have discovered any default, the lessee shall notify the lessor and the supplier, if any, or be barred from any remedy against the party notified;

(b) except in the case of a consumer lease, within a reasonable time after the lessee receives notice of litigation for infringement or the like (Section 2A–211) the lessee shall notify the lessor or be barred from any remedy over for liability established by the litigation; and

(c) the burden is on the lessee to establish any default.

(4) If a lessee is sued for breach of a warranty or other obligation for which a lessor or a supplier is answerable over the following apply:

(a) The lessee may give the lessor or the supplier, or both, written notice of the litigation. If the notice states that the person notified may come in and defend and that if the person notified does not do so that person will be bound in any action against that person by the lessee by any determination of fact common to the two litigations, then unless the person notified after seasonable receipt of the notice does come in and defend that person is so bound.

(b) The lessor or the supplier may demand in writing that the lessee turn over control of the litigation including settlement if the claim is one for infringement or the like (Section 2A–211) or else be barred from any remedy over. If the demand states that the lessor or the supplier agrees to bear all expense and to satisfy any adverse judgment, then unless the lessee after seasonable receipt of the demand does turn over control the lessee is so barred.

(5) Subsections (3) and (4) apply to any obligation of a lessee to hold the lessor or the supplier harmless against infringement or the like (Section 2A–211).

As amended in 1990.

§ 2A–517. Revocation of Acceptance of Goods.

(1) A lessee may revoke acceptance of a lot or commercial unit whose nonconformity substantially impairs its value to the lessee if the lessee has accepted it:

(a) except in the case of a finance lease, on the reasonable assumption that its nonconformity would be cured and it has not been seasonably cured; or

(b) without discovery of the nonconformity if the lessee's acceptance was reasonably induced either by the lessor's assurances or, except in the case of a finance lease, by the difficulty of discovery before acceptance.

(2) Except in the case of a finance lease that is not a consumer lease, a lessee may revoke acceptance of a lot or commercial unit if the lessor defaults under the lease contract and the default substantially impairs the value of that lot or commercial unit to the lessee.

(3) If the lease agreement so provides, the lessee may revoke acceptance of a lot or commercial unit because of other defaults by the lessor.

(4) Revocation of acceptance must occur within a reasonable time after the lessee discovers or should have discovered the ground for it and before any substantial change in condition of the goods which is not caused by the nonconformity. Revocation is not effective until the lessee notifies the lessor.

(5) A lessee who so revokes has the same rights and duties with regard to the goods involved as if the lessee had rejected them.

As amended in 1990.

§ 2A–518. Cover; Substitute Goods.

(1) After a default by a lessor under the lease contract of the type described in Section 2A–508(1), or, if agreed, after other default by the lessor, the lessee may cover by making any purchase or lease of or contract to purchase or lease goods in substitution for those due from the lessor.

(2) Except as otherwise provided with respect to damages liquidated in the lease agreement (Section 2A–504) or otherwise determined pursuant to agreement of the parties (Sections 1–102(3) and 2A–503), if a lessee's cover is by lease agreement substantially similar to the original lease agreement and the new lease agreement is made in good faith and in a commercially reasonable manner, the lessee may recover from the lessor as damages (i) the present value, as of the date of the commencement of the term of the new lease agreement, of the rent under the new lease agreement applicable to that period of the new lease term which is comparable to the then remaining term of the original lease agreement minus the present value as of the same date of the total rent for the then remaining lease term of the original lease agreement, and (ii) any incidental or consequential damages, less expenses saved in consequence of the lessor's default.

(3) If a lessee's cover is by lease agreement that for any reason does not qualify for treatment under subsection (2), or is by purchase or otherwise, the lessee may recover from the lessor as if the lessee had elected not to cover and Section 2A–519 governs.

As amended in 1990.

§ 2A–519. Lessee's Damages for Non-Delivery, Repudiation, Default, and Breach of Warranty in Regard to Accepted Goods.

(1) Except as otherwise provided with respect to damages liquidated in the lease agreement (Section 2A–504) or otherwise determined pursuant to agreement of the parties (Sections 1–102(3) and 2A–503), if a lessee elects not to cover or a lessee elects to cover and the cover is by lease agreement that for any reason does not qualify for treatment under Section 2A–518(2), or is by purchase or otherwise, the measure of damages for non-delivery or repudiation by the lessor or for rejection or revocation of acceptance by the lessee is the present value, as of the date of the default, of the then market rent minus the present value as of the same date of the original rent, computed for the remaining lease term of the original lease agreement, together with incidental and consequential damages, less expenses saved in consequence of the lessor's default.

(2) Market rent is to be determined as of the place for tender or, in cases of rejection after arrival or revocation of acceptance, as of the place of arrival.

(3) Except as otherwise agreed, if the lessee has accepted goods and given notification (Section 2A–516(3)), the measure of damages for non-conforming tender or delivery or other default by a lessor is the loss resulting in the ordinary course of events from the lessor's default as determined in any manner that is reasonable together with incidental and consequential damages, less expenses saved in consequence of the lessor's default.

(4) Except as otherwise agreed, the measure of damages for breach of warranty is the present value at the time and place of acceptance of the difference between the value of the use of the goods accepted and the value if they had been as warranted for the lease

term, unless special circumstances show proximate damages of a different amount, together with incidental and consequential damages, less expenses saved in consequence of the lessor's default or breach of warranty.

As amended in 1990.

§ 2A–520. Lessee's Incidental and Consequential Damages.

(1) Incidental damages resulting from a lessor's default include expenses reasonably incurred in inspection, receipt, transportation, and care and custody of goods rightfully rejected or goods the acceptance of which is justifiably revoked, any commercially reasonable charges, expenses or commissions in connection with effecting cover, and any other reasonable expense incident to the default.

(2) Consequential damages resulting from a lessor's default include:

(a) any loss resulting from general or particular requirements and needs of which the lessor at the time of contracting had reason to know and which could not reasonably be prevented by cover or otherwise; and

(b) injury to person or property proximately resulting from any breach of warranty.

§ 2A–521. Lessee's Right to Specific Performance or Replevin.

(1) Specific performance may be decreed if the goods are unique or in other proper circumstances.

(2) A decree for specific performance may include any terms and conditions as to payment of the rent, damages, or other relief that the court deems just.

(3) A lessee has a right of replevin, detinue, sequestration, claim and delivery, or the like for goods identified to the lease contract if after reasonable effort the lessee is unable to effect cover for those goods or the circumstances reasonably indicate that the effort will be unavailing.

§ 2A–522. Lessee's Right to Goods on Lessor's Insolvency.

(1) Subject to subsection (2) and even though the goods have not been shipped, a lessee who has paid a part or all of the rent and security for goods identified to a lease contract (Section 2A–217) on making and keeping good a tender of any unpaid portion of the rent and security due under the lease contract may recover the goods identified from the lessor if the lessor becomes insolvent within 10 days after receipt of the first installment of rent and security.

(2) A lessee acquires the right to recover goods identified to a lease contract only if they conform to the lease contract.

C. Default by Lessee

§ 2A–523. Lessor's Remedies.

(1) If a lessee wrongfully rejects or revokes acceptance of goods or fails to make a payment when due or repudiates with respect to a part or the whole, then, with respect to any goods involved, and with respect to all of the goods if under an installment lease contract the value of the whole lease contract is substantially impaired (Section 2A–510), the lessee is in default under the lease contract and the lessor may:

(a) cancel the lease contract (Section 2A–505(1));

(b) proceed respecting goods not identified to the lease contract (Section 2A–524);

(c) withhold delivery of the goods and take possession of goods previously delivered (Section 2A–525);

(d) stop delivery of the goods by any bailee (Section 2A–526);

(e) dispose of the goods and recover damages (Section 2A–527), or retain the goods and recover damages (Section 2A–528), or in a proper case recover rent (Section 2A–529)

(f) exercise any other rights or pursue any other remedies provided in the lease contract.

(2) If a lessor does not fully exercise a right or obtain a remedy to which the lessor is entitled under subsection (1), the lessor may recover the loss resulting in the ordinary course of events from the lessee's default as determined in any reasonable manner, together with incidental damages, less expenses saved in consequence of the lessee's default.

(3) If a lessee is otherwise in default under a lease contract, the lessor may exercise the rights and pursue the remedies provided in the lease contract, which may include a right to cancel the lease. In addition, unless otherwise provided in the lease contract:

(a) if the default substantially impairs the value of the lease contract to the lessor, the lessor may exercise the rights and pursue the remedies provided in subsections (1) or (2); or

(b) if the default does not substantially impair the value of the lease contract to the lessor, the lessor may recover as provided in subsection (2).

As amended in 1990.

§ 2A–524. Lessor's Right to Identify Goods to Lease Contract.

(1) After default by the lessee under the lease contract of the type described in Section 2A–523(1) or 2A–523(3)(a) or, if agreed, after other default by the lessee, the lessor may:

(a) identify to the lease contract conforming goods not already identified if at the time the lessor learned of the default they were in the lessor's or the supplier's possession or control; and

(b) dispose of goods (Section 2A–527(1)) that demonstrably have been intended for the particular lease contract even though those goods are unfinished.

(2) If the goods are unfinished, in the exercise of reasonable commercial judgment for the purposes of avoiding loss and of effective realization, an aggrieved lessor or the supplier may either complete manufacture and wholly identify the goods to the lease contract or cease manufacture and lease, sell, or otherwise dispose of the goods for scrap or salvage value or proceed in any other reasonable manner.

As amended in 1990.

§ 2A–525. Lessor's Right to Possession of Goods.

(1) If a lessor discovers the lessee to be insolvent, the lessor may refuse to deliver the goods.

(2) After a default by the lessee under the lease contract of the type described in Section 2A–523(1) or 2A–523(3)(a) or, if agreed, after other default by the lessee, the lessor has the right to take possession of the goods. If the lease contract so provides, the lessor may require the lessee to assemble the goods and make them available to the lessor at a place to be designated by the lessor which is reasonably convenient to both parties. Without removal, the lessor may render unusable any goods employed in trade or business, and may dispose of goods on the lessee's premises (Section 2A–527).

(3) The lessor may proceed under subsection (2) without judicial process if that can be done without breach of the peace or the lessor may proceed by action.

As amended in 1990.

§ 2A–526. Lessor's Stoppage of Delivery in Transit or Otherwise.

(1) A lessor may stop delivery of goods in the possession of a carrier or other bailee if the lessor discovers the lessee to be insolvent and may stop delivery of carload, truckload, planeload, or larger shipments of express or freight if the lessee repudiates or fails to make a payment due before delivery, whether for rent, security or otherwise under the lease contract, or for any other reason the lessor has a right to withhold or take possession of the goods.

(2) In pursuing its remedies under subsection (1), the lessor may stop delivery until

(a) receipt of the goods by the lessee;

(b) acknowledgment to the lessee by any bailee of the goods, except a carrier, that the bailee holds the goods for the lessee; or

(c) such an acknowledgment to the lessee by a carrier via reshipment or as warehouseman.

(3) (a) To stop delivery, a lessor shall so notify as to enable the bailee by reasonable diligence to prevent delivery of the goods.

(b) After notification, the bailee shall hold and deliver the goods according to the directions of the lessor, but the lessor is liable to the bailee for any ensuing charges or damages.

(c) A carrier who has issued a nonnegotiable bill of lading is not obliged to obey a notification to stop received from a person other than the consignor.

§ 2A–527. Lessor's Rights to Dispose of Goods.

(1) After a default by a lessee under the lease contract of the type described in Section 2A–523(1) or 2A–523(3)(a) or after the lessor refuses to deliver or takes possession of goods (Section 2A–525 or 2A–526), or, if agreed, after other default by a lessee, the lessor may dispose of the goods concerned or the undelivered balance thereof by lease, sale, or otherwise.

(2) Except as otherwise provided with respect to damages liquidated in the lease agreement (Section 2A–504) or otherwise determined pursuant to agreement of the parties (Sections 1–102(3) and 2A–503), if the disposition is by lease agreement substantially similar to the original lease agreement and the new lease agreement is made in good faith and in a commercially reasonable manner, the lessor may recover from the lessee as damages (i) accrued and unpaid rent as of the date of the commencement of the term of the new lease agreement, (ii) the present value, as of the same date, of the total rent for the then remaining lease term of the original lease agreement minus the present value, as of the same date, of the rent under the new lease agreement applicable to that period of the new lease term which is comparable to the then remaining term of the original lease agreement, and (iii) any incidental damages allowed under Section 2A–530, less expenses saved in consequence of the lessee's default.

(3) If the lessor's disposition is by lease agreement that for any reason does not qualify for treatment under subsection (2), or is by sale or otherwise, the lessor may recover from the lessee as if the lessor had elected not to dispose of the goods and Section 2A–528 governs.

(4) A subsequent buyer or lessee who buys or leases from the lessor in good faith for value as a result of a disposition under this section takes the goods free of the original lease contract and any rights of the original lessee even though the lessor fails to comply with one or more of the requirements of this Article.

(5) The lessor is not accountable to the lessee for any profit made on any disposition. A lessee who has rightfully rejected or justifiably revoked acceptance shall account to the lessor for any excess over the amount of the lessee's security interest (Section 2A–508(5)).

As amended in 1990.

§ 2A–528. Lessor's Damages for Non-acceptance, Failure to Pay, Repudiation, or Other Default.

(1) Except as otherwise provided with respect to damages liquidated in the lease agreement (Section 2A–504) or otherwise determined pursuant to agreement of the parties (Section 1–102(3) and 2A–503), if a lessor elects to retain the goods or a lessor elects to dispose of the goods and the disposition is by lease agreement that for any reason does not qualify for treatment under Section 2A–527(2), or is by sale or otherwise, the lessor may recover from the lessee as damages for a default of the type described in Section 2A–523(1) or 2A–523(3)(a), or if agreed, for other default of the lessee, (i) accrued and unpaid rent as of the date of the default if the lessee has never taken possession of the goods, or, if the lessee has taken possession of the goods, as of the date the lessor repossesses the goods or an earlier date on which the lessee makes a tender of the goods to the lessor, (ii) the present value as of the date determined under clause (i) of the total rent for the then remaining lease term of the original lease agreement minus the present value as of the same date of the market rent as the place where the goods are located computed for the same lease term, and (iii) any incidental damages allowed under Section 2A–530, less expenses saved in consequence of the lessee's default.

(2) If the measure of damages provided in subsection (1) is inadequate to put a lessor in as good a position as performance would have, the measure of damages is the present value of the profit, including reasonable overhead, the lessor would have made from full performance by the lessee, together with any incidental damages allowed under Section 2A–530, due allowance for costs reasonably incurred and due credit for payments or proceeds of disposition.

As amended in 1990.

§ 2A–529. Lessor's Action for the Rent.

(1) After default by the lessee under the lease contract of the type described in Section 2A–523(1) or 2A–523(3)(a) or, if agreed, after other default by the lessee, if the lessor complies with subsection (2), the lessor may recover from the lessee as damages:

(a) for goods accepted by the lessee and not repossessed by or tendered to the lessor, and for conforming goods lost or damaged within a commercially reasonable time after risk of loss passes to the lessee (Section 2A–219), (i) accrued and unpaid rent as of the date of entry of judgment in favor of the lessor (ii) the present value as of the same date of the rent for the then remaining lease term of the lease agreement, and (iii) any incidental damages allowed under Section 2A–530, less expenses saved in consequence of the lessee's default; and

(b) for goods identified to the lease contract if the lessor is unable after reasonable effort to dispose of them at a reasonable price or the circumstances reasonably indicate that effort will be unavailing, (i) accrued and unpaid rent as of the date of entry of judgment in favor of the lessor, (ii) the present value as of the same date of the rent for the then remaining lease term of the lease agreement, and (iii) any incidental damages allowed under Section 2A–530, less expenses saved in consequence of the lessee's default.

(2) Except as provided in subsection (3), the lessor shall hold for the lessee for the remaining lease term of the lease agreement any goods that have been identified to the lease contract and are in the lessor's control.

(3) The lessor may dispose of the goods at any time before collection of the judgment for damages obtained pursuant to subsection (1). If the disposition is before the end of the remaining lease term of the lease agreement, the lessor's recovery against the lessee for damages is governed by Section 2A–527 or Section 2A–528, and the lessor will cause an appropriate credit to be provided against a judgment for damages to the extent that the amount of the judgment exceeds the recovery available pursuant to Section 2A–527 or 2A–528.

(4) Payment of the judgment for damages obtained pursuant to subsection (1) entitles the lessee to the use and possession of the goods not then disposed of for the remaining lease term of and in accordance with the lease agreement.

(5) After default by the lessee under the lease contract of the type described in Section 2A–523(1) or Section 2A–523(3)(a) or, if agreed, after other default by the lessee, a lessor who is held not entitled to rent under this section must nevertheless be awarded damages for non-acceptance under Sections 2A–527 and 2A–528.

As amended in 1990.

§ 2A–530. Lessor's Incidental Damages.

Incidental damages to an aggrieved lessor include any commercially reasonable charges, expenses, or commissions incurred in stopping delivery, in the transportation, care and custody of goods after the lessee's default, in connection with return or disposition of the goods, or otherwise resulting from the default.

§ 2A–531. Standing to Sue Third Parties for Injury to Goods.

(1) If a third party so deals with goods that have been identified to a lease contract as to cause actionable injury to a party to the lease contract (a) the lessor has a right of action against the third party, and (b) the lessee also has a right of action against the third party if the lessee:

> (i) has a security interest in the goods;

> (ii) has an insurable interest in the goods; or

> (iii) bears the risk of loss under the lease contract or has since the injury assumed that risk as against the lessor and the goods have been converted or destroyed.

(2) If at the time of the injury the party plaintiff did not bear the risk of loss as against the other party to the lease contract and there is no arrangement between them for disposition of the recovery, his [or her] suit or settlement, subject to his [or her] own interest, is as a fiduciary for the other party to the lease contract.

(3) Either party with the consent of the other may sue for the benefit of whom it may concern.

§ 2A–532. Lessor's Rights to Residual Interest.

In addition to any other recovery permitted by this Article or other law, the lessor may recover from the lessee an amount that will fully compensate the lessor for any loss of or damage to the lessor's residual interest in the goods caused by the default of the lessee.

As added in 1990.

Appendix D

The Sarbanes-Oxley Act of 2002 (Excerpts and Explanatory Comments)

Note: The authors' explanatory comments appear in italics following the excerpt from each section.

SECTION 302

Corporate responsibility for financial reports[1]

(a) Regulations required

The Commission shall, by rule, require, for each company filing periodic reports under section 13(a) or 15(d) of the Securities Exchange Act of 1934 (15 U.S.C. 78m, 78o(d)), that the principal executive officer or officers and the principal financial officer or officers, or persons performing similar functions, certify in each annual or quarterly report filed or submitted under either such section of such Act that—

(1) the signing officer has reviewed the report;

(2) based on the officer's knowledge, the report does not contain any untrue statement of a material fact or omit to state a material fact necessary in order to make the statements made, in light of the circumstances under which such statements were made, not misleading;

(3) based on such officer's knowledge, the financial statements, and other financial information included in the report, fairly present in all material respects the financial condition and results of operations of the issuer as of, and for, the periods presented in the report;

(4) the signing officers—

(A) are responsible for establishing and maintaining internal controls;

(B) have designed such internal controls to ensure that material information relating to the issuer and its consolidated subsidiaries is made known to such officers by others within those entities, particularly during the period in which the periodic reports are being prepared;

(C) have evaluated the effectiveness of the issuer's internal controls as of a date within 90 days prior to the report; and

(D) have presented in the report their conclusions about the effectiveness of their internal controls based on their evaluation as of that date;

(5) the signing officers have disclosed to the issuer's auditors and the audit committee of the board of directors (or persons fulfilling the equivalent function)—

(A) all significant deficiencies in the design or operation of internal controls which could adversely affect the issuer's ability to record, process, summarize, and report financial data and have identified for the issuer's auditors any material weaknesses in internal controls; and

(B) any fraud, whether or not material, that involves management or other employees who have a significant role in the issuer's internal controls; and

(6) the signing officers have indicated in the report whether or not there were significant changes in internal controls or in other factors that could significantly affect internal controls subsequent to the date of their evaluation, including any corrective actions with regard to significant deficiencies and material weaknesses.

(b) Foreign reincorporations have no effect

Nothing in this section shall be interpreted or applied in any way to allow any issuer to lessen the legal force of the statement required under this section, by an issuer having reincorporated or having engaged in any other transaction that resulted in the transfer of the corporate domicile or offices of the issuer from inside the United States to outside of the United States.

(c) Deadline

The rules required by subsection (a) of this section shall be effective not later than 30 days after July 30, 2002.

EXPLANATORY COMMENTS: *Section 302 requires the chief executive officer (CEO) and chief financial officer (CFO) of each public company to certify that they have reviewed the company's quarterly and annual reports to be filed with the Securities and Exchange Commission (SEC). The CEO and CFO must certify that, based on their knowledge, the reports do not contain any untrue statement of a material fact or any half-truth that would make the report misleading, and that the information contained in the reports fairly presents the company's financial condition.*

In addition, this section also requires the CEO and CFO to certify that they have created and designed an internal control system for their company and have recently evaluated that system to ensure that it is effectively providing them with relevant and accurate financial information. If the signing officers have found any significant deficiencies or weaknesses in the company's system or have discovered

---

1. This section of the Sarbanes-Oxley Act is codified at 15 U.S.C. Section 7241.

any evidence of fraud, they must have reported the situation, and any corrective actions they have taken, to the auditors and the audit committee.

Section 306

Insider trades during pension fund blackout periods[2]

(a) Prohibition of insider trading during pension fund blackout periods

(1) In general

Except to the extent otherwise provided by rule of the Commission pursuant to paragraph (3), it shall be unlawful for any director or executive officer of an issuer of any equity security (other than an exempted security), directly or indirectly, to purchase, sell, or otherwise acquire or transfer any equity security of the issuer (other than an exempted security) during any blackout period with respect to such equity security if such director or officer acquires such equity security in connection with his or her service or employment as a director or executive officer.

(2) Remedy

(A) In general

Any profit realized by a director or executive officer referred to in paragraph (1) from any purchase, sale, or other acquisition or transfer in violation of this subsection shall inure to and be recoverable by the issuer, irrespective of any intention on the part of such director or executive officer in entering into the transaction.

(B) Actions to recover profits

An action to recover profits in accordance with this subsection may be instituted at law or in equity in any court of competent jurisdiction by the issuer, or by the owner of any security of the issuer in the name and in behalf of the issuer if the issuer fails or refuses to bring such action within 60 days after the date of request, or fails diligently to prosecute the action thereafter, except that no such suit shall be brought more than 2 years after the date on which such profit was realized.

(3) Rulemaking authorized

The Commission shall, in consultation with the Secretary of Labor, issue rules to clarify the application of this subsection and to prevent evasion thereof. Such rules shall provide for the application of the requirements of paragraph (1) with respect to entities treated as a single employer with respect to an issuer under section 414(b), (c), (m), or (o) of Title 26 to the extent necessary to clarify the application of such requirements and to prevent evasion thereof. Such rules may also provide for appropriate exceptions from the requirements of this subsection, including exceptions for purchases pursuant to an automatic dividend reinvestment program or purchases or sales made pursuant to an advance election.

---

2. Codified at 15 U.S.C. Section 7244.

(4) Blackout period

For purposes of this subsection, the term "blackout period", with respect to the equity securities of any issuer—

(A) means any period of more than 3 consecutive business days during which the ability of not fewer than 50 percent of the participants or beneficiaries under all individual account plans maintained by the issuer to purchase, sell, or otherwise acquire or transfer an interest in any equity of such issuer held in such an individual account plan is temporarily suspended by the issuer or by a fiduciary of the plan; and

(B) does not include, under regulations which shall be prescribed by the Commission—

(i) a regularly scheduled period in which the participants and beneficiaries may not purchase, sell, or otherwise acquire or transfer an interest in any equity of such issuer, if such period is—

(I) incorporated into the individual account plan; and

(II) timely disclosed to employees before becoming participants under the individual account plan or as a subsequent amendment to the plan; or

(ii) any suspension described in subparagraph (A) that is imposed solely in connection with persons becoming participants or beneficiaries, or ceasing to be participants or beneficiaries, in an individual account plan by reason of a corporate merger, acquisition, divestiture, or similar transaction involving the plan or plan sponsor.

(5) Individual account plan

For purposes of this subsection, the term "individual account plan" has the meaning provided in section 1002(34) of Title 29, except that such term shall not include a one-participant retirement plan (within the meaning of section 1021(i)(8)(B) of Title 29).

(6) Notice to directors, executive officers, and the Commission

In any case in which a director or executive officer is subject to the requirements of this subsection in connection with a blackout period (as defined in paragraph (4)) with respect to any equity securities, the issuer of such equity securities shall timely notify such director or officer and the Securities and Exchange Commission of such blackout period.

* * * *

EXPLANATORY COMMENTS: *Corporate pension funds typically prohibit employees from trading shares of the corporation during periods when the pension fund is undergoing significant change. Prior to 2002, however, these blackout periods did not affect the corporation's executives, who frequently received shares of the corporate stock as part of their compensation. Section 306 was Congress's solution to the basic unfairness of this situation. This section of the act required the SEC to issue rules that prohibit any director or executive officer from trading during pension fund blackout periods. (The SEC later issued these rules, entitled Regulation Blackout Trading*

Restriction, or Reg BTR.) Section 306 also provided shareholders with a right to file a shareholder's derivative suit against officers and directors who have profited from trading during these blackout periods (provided that the corporation has failed to bring a suit). The officer or director can be forced to return to the corporation any profits received, regardless of whether the director or officer acted with bad intent.

Section 402

Periodical and other reports[3]

* * * *

(i) Accuracy of financial reports

Each financial report that contains financial statements, and that is required to be prepared in accordance with (or reconciled to) generally accepted accounting principles under this chapter and filed with the Commission shall reflect all material correcting adjustments that have been identified by a registered public accounting firm in accordance with generally accepted accounting principles and the rules and regulations of the Commission.

(j) Off-balance sheet transactions

Not later than 180 days after July 30, 2002, the Commission shall issue final rules providing that each annual and quarterly financial report required to be filed with the Commission shall disclose all material off-balance sheet transactions, arrangements, obligations (including contingent obligations), and other relationships of the issuer with unconsolidated entities or other persons, that may have a material current or future effect on financial condition, changes in financial condition, results of operations, liquidity, capital expenditures, capital resources, or significant components of revenues or expenses.

(k) Prohibition on personal loans to executives

(1) In general

It shall be unlawful for any issuer (as defined in section 7201 of this title), directly or indirectly, including through any subsidiary, to extend or maintain credit, to arrange for the extension of credit, or to renew an extension of credit, in the form of a personal loan to or for any director or executive officer (or equivalent thereof) of that issuer. An extension of credit maintained by the issuer on July 30, 2002, shall not be subject to the provisions of this subsection, provided that there is no material modification to any term of any such extension of credit or any renewal of any such extension of credit on or after July 30, 2002.

(2) Limitation

Paragraph (1) does not preclude any home improvement and manufactured home loans (as that term is defined in section 1464 of Title 12), consumer credit (as defined in section 1602 of this title), or any extension of credit under an open end credit plan (as defined in section 1602 of this title), or a charge card (as defined in section 1637(c)(4)(e) of this title), or any extension of credit by a broker or dealer registered under section 78o of this title to an employee of that broker or dealer to buy, trade, or carry securities, that is permitted under rules or regulations of the Board of Governors of the Federal Reserve System pursuant to section 78g of this title (other than an extension of credit that would be used to purchase the stock of that issuer), that is—

(A) made or provided in the ordinary course of the consumer credit business of such issuer;

(B) of a type that is generally made available by such issuer to the public; and

(C) made by such issuer on market terms, or terms that are no more favorable than those offered by the issuer to the general public for such extensions of credit.

(3) Rule of construction for certain loans

Paragraph (1) does not apply to any loan made or maintained by an insured depository institution (as defined in section 1813 of Title 12), if the loan is subject to the insider lending restrictions of section 375b of Title 12.

(l) Real time issuer disclosures

Each issuer reporting under subsection (a) of this section or section 78o(d) of this title shall disclose to the public on a rapid and current basis such additional information concerning material changes in the financial condition or operations of the issuer, in plain English, which may include trend and qualitative information and graphic presentations, as the Commission determines, by rule, is necessary or useful for the protection of investors and in the public interest.

EXPLANATORY COMMENTS: *Before this act, many corporate executives typically received extremely large salaries, significant bonuses, and abundant stock options, even when the companies for which they worked were suffering. Executives were also routinely given personal loans from corporate funds, many of which were never paid back. The average large company during that period loaned almost $1 million a year to top executives, and some companies loaned hundreds of millions of dollars to their executives every year. Section 402 amended the 1934 Securities Exchange Act to prohibit public companies from making personal loans to executive officers and directors. There are a few exceptions to this prohibition, such as home-improvement loans made in the ordinary course of business. Note also that while loans are forbidden, outright gifts are not. A corporation is free to give gifts to its executives, including cash, provided that these gifts are disclosed on its financial reports. The idea is that corporate directors will be deterred from making substantial gifts to their executives by the disclosure requirement—particularly if the corporation's financial condition is questionable—because making such gifts could be perceived as abusing their authority.*

Section 403

Directors, officers, and principal stockholders[4]

(a) Disclosures required

(1) Directors, officers, and principal stockholders required to file

---

3. This section of the Sarbanes-Oxley Act amended some of the provisions of the 1934 Securities Exchange Act and added the paragraphs reproduced here at 15 U.S.C. Section 78m.

4. This section of the Sarbanes-Oxley Act amended the disclosure provisions of the 1934 Securities Exchange Act, at 15 U.S.C. Section 78p.

Every person who is directly or indirectly the beneficial owner of more than 10 percent of any class of any equity security (other than an exempted security) which is registered pursuant to section 78l of this title, or who is a director or an officer of the issuer of such security, shall file the statements required by this subsection with the Commission (and, if such security is registered on a national securities exchange, also with the exchange).

(2) Time of filing

The statements required by this subsection shall be filed—

(A) at the time of the registration of such security on a national securities exchange or by the effective date of a registration statement filed pursuant to section 78l(g) of this title;

(B) within 10 days after he or she becomes such beneficial owner, director, or officer;

(C) if there has been a change in such ownership, or if such person shall have purchased or sold a security-based swap agreement (as defined in section 206(b) of the Gramm-Leach-Bliley Act (15 U.S.C. 78c note)) involving such equity security, before the end of the second business day following the day on which the subject transaction has been executed, or at such other time as the Commission shall establish, by rule, in any case in which the Commission determines that such 2-day period is not feasible.

(3) Contents of statements

A statement filed—

(A) under subparagraph (A) or (B) of paragraph (2) shall contain a statement of the amount of all equity securities of such issuer of which the filing person is the beneficial owner; and

(B) under subparagraph (C) of such paragraph shall indicate ownership by the filing person at the date of filing, any such changes in such ownership, and such purchases and sales of the security-based swap agreements as have occurred since the most recent such filing under such subparagraph.

(4) Electronic filing and availability

Beginning not later than 1 year after July 30, 2002—

(A) a statement filed under subparagraph (C) of paragraph (2) shall be filed electronically;

(B) the Commission shall provide each such statement on a publicly accessible Internet site not later than the end of the business day following that filing; and

(C) the issuer (if the issuer maintains a corporate website) shall provide that statement on that corporate website, not later than the end of the business day following that filing.

* * * *

EXPLANATORY COMMENTS: *This section dramatically shortens the time period provided in the Securities Exchange Act of 1934 for disclosing transactions by insiders. The prior law stated that most*

transactions had to be reported within ten days of the beginning of the following month, although certain transactions did not have to be reported until the following fiscal year (within the first forty-five days). In several instances, some insider trading was not disclosed (and was therefore not discovered) until long after the transactions. So Congress added this section to reduce the time period for making disclosures. Under Section 403, most transactions by insiders must be electronically filed with the SEC within two business days. Also, any company that maintains a Web site must post these SEC filings on its site by the end of the next business day. Congress enacted this section in the belief that if insiders are required to file reports of their transactions promptly with the SEC, companies will do more to police themselves and prevent insider trading.

Section 404

Management assessment of internal controls[5]

(a) Rules required

The Commission shall prescribe rules requiring each annual report required by section 78m(a) or 78o(d) of this title to contain an internal control report, which shall—

(1) state the responsibility of management for establishing and maintaining an adequate internal control structure and procedures for financial reporting; and

(2) contain an assessment, as of the end of the most recent fiscal year of the issuer, of the effectiveness of the internal control structure and procedures of the issuer for financial reporting.

(b) Internal control evaluation and reporting

With respect to the internal control assessment required by subsection (a) of this section, each registered public accounting firm that prepares or issues the audit report for the issuer shall attest to, and report on, the assessment made by the management of the issuer. An attestation made under this subsection shall be made in accordance with standards for attestation engagements issued or adopted by the Board. Any such attestation shall not be the subject of a separate engagement.

EXPLANATORY COMMENTS: *This section was enacted to prevent corporate executives from claiming they were ignorant of significant errors in their companies' financial reports. For instance, several CEOs testified before Congress that they simply had no idea that the corporations' financial statements were off by billions of dollars. Congress therefore passed Section 404, which requires each annual report to contain a description and assessment of the company's internal control structure and financial reporting procedures. The section also requires that an audit be conducted of the internal control assessment, as well as the financial statements contained in the report. This section goes hand in hand with Section 302 (which, as discussed previously, requires various certifications attesting to the accuracy of the information in financial reports).*

Section 404 has been one of the more controversial and expensive provisions in the Sarbanes-Oxley Act because it requires companies to assess their own internal financial controls to make sure that their financial statements are reliable and accurate. A corporation might

---

5. Codified at 15 U.S.C. Section 7262.

need to set up a disclosure committee and a coordinator, establish codes of conduct for accounting and financial personnel, create documentation procedures, provide training, and outline the individuals who are responsible for performing each of the procedures. Companies that were already well managed have not experienced substantial difficulty complying with this section. Other companies, however, have spent millions of dollars setting up, documenting, and evaluating their internal financial control systems. Although initially creating the internal financial control system is a one-time-only expense, the costs of maintaining and evaluating it are ongoing. Some corporations that spent considerable sums complying with Section 404 have been able to offset these costs by discovering and correcting inefficiencies or frauds within their systems. Nevertheless, it is unlikely that any corporation will find compliance with this section to be inexpensive.

Section 802 (a)

Destruction, alteration, or falsification of records in Federal investigations and bankruptcy[6]

Whoever knowingly alters, destroys, mutilates, conceals, covers up, falsifies, or makes a false entry in any record, document, or tangible object with the intent to impede, obstruct, or influence the investigation or proper administration of any matter within the jurisdiction of any department or agency of the United States or any case filed under title 11, or in relation to or contemplation of any such matter or case, shall be fined under this title, imprisoned not more than 20 years, or both.

Destruction of corporate audit records[7]

(a) (1) Any accountant who conducts an audit of an issuer of securities to which section 10A(a) of the Securities Exchange Act of 1934 (15 U.S.C. 78j-1(a)) applies, shall maintain all audit or review workpapers for a period of 5 years from the end of the fiscal period in which the audit or review was concluded.

(2) The Securities and Exchange Commission shall promulgate, within 180 days, after adequate notice and an opportunity for comment, such rules and regulations, as are reasonably necessary, relating to the retention of relevant records such as workpapers, documents that form the basis of an audit or review, memoranda, correspondence, communications, other documents, and records (including electronic records) which are created, sent, or received in connection with an audit or review and contain conclusions, opinions, analyses, or financial data relating to such an audit or review, which is conducted by any accountant who conducts an audit of an issuer of securities to which section 10A(a) of the Securities Exchange Act of 1934 (15 U.S.C. 78j-1(a)) applies. The Commission may, from time to time, amend or supplement the rules and regulations that it is required to promulgate under this section, after adequate notice and an opportunity for comment, in order to ensure that such rules and regulations adequately comport with the purposes of this section.

(b) Whoever knowingly and willfully violates subsection (a)(1), or any rule or regulation promulgated by the Securities and Exchange Commission under subsection (a)(2), shall be fined under this title, imprisoned not more than 10 years, or both.

(c) Nothing in this section shall be deemed to diminish or relieve any person of any other duty or obligation imposed by Federal or State law or regulation to maintain, or refrain from destroying, any document.

EXPLANATORY COMMENTS: *Section 802(a) enacted two new statutes that punish those who alter or destroy documents. The first statute is not specifically limited to securities fraud cases. It provides that anyone who alters, destroys, or falsifies records in federal investigations or bankruptcy may be criminally prosecuted and sentenced to a fine or to up to twenty years in prison, or both. The second statute requires auditors of public companies to keep all audit or review working papers for five years but expressly allows the SEC to amend or supplement these requirements as it sees fit. The SEC has, in fact, amended this section by issuing a rule that requires auditors who audit reporting companies to retain working papers for seven years from the conclusion of the review. Section 802(a) further provides that anyone who knowingly and willfully violates this statute is subject to criminal prosecution and can be sentenced to a fine, imprisoned for up to ten years, or both.*

This portion of the Sarbanes-Oxley Act implicitly recognizes that persons who are under investigation often are tempted to respond by destroying or falsifying documents that might prove their complicity in wrongdoing. The severity of the punishment should provide a strong incentive for these individuals to resist the temptation.

SECTION 804

Time limitations on the commencement of civil actions arising under Acts of Congress[8]

(a) Except as otherwise provided by law, a civil action arising under an Act of Congress enacted after the date of the enactment of this section may not be commenced later than 4 years after the cause of action accrues.

(b) Notwithstanding subsection (a), a private right of action that involves a claim of fraud, deceit, manipulation, or contrivance in contravention of a regulatory requirement concerning the securities laws, as defined in section 3(a)(47) of the Securities Exchange Act of 1934 (15 U.S.C. 78c(a)(47)), may be brought not later than the earlier of—

   (1) 2 years after the discovery of the facts constituting the violation; or

   (2) 5 years after such violation.

EXPLANATORY COMMENTS: *Prior to the enactment of this section, Section 10(b) of the Securities Exchange Act of 1934 had no express statute of limitations. The courts generally required plaintiffs to have filed suit within one year from the date that they should (using due diligence) have discovered that a fraud had been committed but no later than three years after the fraud occurred. Section 804 extends this period by specifying that plaintiffs must file a lawsuit within two years after they discover (or should have discovered) a fraud but no later than five years after the fraud's occurrence. This*

---

6. Codified at 15 U.S.C. Section 1519.
7. Codified at 15 U.S.C. Section 1520.

8. Codified at 28 U.S.C. Section 1658.

provision has prevented the courts from dismissing numerous securities fraud lawsuits.

SECTION 806

Civil action to protect against retaliation in fraud cases[9]

(a) Whistleblower protection for employees of publicly traded companies.—

No company with a class of securities registered under section 12 of the Securities Exchange Act of 1934 (15 U.S.C. 78l), or that is required to file reports under section 15(d) of the Securities Exchange Act of 1934 (15 U.S.C. 78o(d)), or any officer, employee, contractor, subcontractor, or agent of such company, may discharge, demote, suspend, threaten, harass, or in any other manner discriminate against an employee in the terms and conditions of employment because of any lawful act done by the employee—

(1) to provide information, cause information to be provided, or otherwise assist in an investigation regarding any conduct which the employee reasonably believes constitutes a violation of section 1341, 1343, 1344, or 1348, any rule or regulation of the Securities and Exchange Commission, or any provision of Federal law relating to fraud against shareholders, when the information or assistance is provided to or the investigation is conducted by—

(A) a Federal regulatory or law enforcement agency;

(B) any Member of Congress or any committee of Congress; or

(C) a person with supervisory authority over the employee (or such other person working for the employer who has the authority to investigate, discover, or terminate misconduct); or

(2) to file, cause to be filed, testify, participate in, or otherwise assist in a proceeding filed or about to be filed (with any knowledge of the employer) relating to an alleged violation of section 1341, 1343, 1344, or 1348, any rule or regulation of the Securities and Exchange Commission, or any provision of Federal law relating to fraud against shareholders.

(b) Enforcement action.—

(1) In general.—A person who alleges discharge or other discrimination by any person in violation of subsection (a) may seek relief under subsection (c), by—

(A) filing a complaint with the Secretary of Labor; or

(B) if the Secretary has not issued a final decision within 180 days of the filing of the complaint and there is no showing that such delay is due to the bad faith of the claimant, bringing an action at law or equity for de novo review in the appropriate district court of the United States, which shall have jurisdiction over such an action without regard to the amount in controversy.

(2) Procedure.—

(A) In general.—An action under paragraph (1)(A) shall be governed under the rules and procedures set forth in section 42121(b) of title 49, United States Code.

(B) Exception.—Notification made under section 42121(b)(1) of title 49, United States Code, shall be made to the person named in the complaint and to the employer.

(C) Burdens of proof.—An action brought under paragraph (1)(B) shall be governed by the legal burdens of proof set forth in section 42121(b) of title 49, United States Code.

(D) Statute of limitations.—An action under paragraph (1) shall be commenced not later than 90 days after the date on which the violation occurs.

(c) Remedies.—

(1) In general.—An employee prevailing in any action under subsection (b)(1) shall be entitled to all relief necessary to make the employee whole.

(2) Compensatory damages.—Relief for any action under paragraph (1) shall include—

(A) reinstatement with the same seniority status that the employee would have had, but for the discrimination;

(B) the amount of back pay, with interest; and

(C) compensation for any special damages sustained as a result of the discrimination, including litigation costs, expert witness fees, and reasonable attorney fees.

(D) Rights retained by employee.—Nothing in this section shall be deemed to diminish the rights, privileges, or remedies of any employee under any Federal or State law, or under any collective bargaining agreement.

EXPLANATORY COMMENTS: *Section 806 is one of several provisions that were included in the Sarbanes-Oxley Act to encourage and protect whistleblowers—that is, employees who report their employer's alleged violations of securities law to the authorities. This section applies to employees, agents, and independent contractors who work for publicly traded companies or testify about such a company during an investigation. It sets up an administrative procedure at the U.S. Department of Labor for individuals who claim that their employer retaliated against them (fired or demoted them, for example) for blowing the whistle on the employer's wrongful conduct. It also allows the award of civil damages—including back pay, reinstatement, special damages, attorneys' fees, and court costs—to employees who prove that they suffered retaliation. Since this provision was enacted, whistleblowers have filed numerous complaints with the Department of Labor under this section.*

SECTION 807

Securities fraud[10]

Whoever knowingly executes, or attempts to execute, a scheme or artifice—

(1) to defraud any person in connection with any security of an issuer with a class of securities registered

---

9. Codified at 18 U.S.C. Section 1514A.

10. Codified at 18 U.S.C. Section 1348.

under section 12 of the Securities Exchange Act of 1934 (15 U.S.C. 78l) or that is required to file reports under section 15(d) of the Securities Exchange Act of 1934 (15 U.S.C. 78o(d)); or

(2) to obtain, by means of false or fraudulent pretenses, representations, or promises, any money or property in connection with the purchase or sale of any security of an issuer with a class of securities registered under section 12 of the Securities Exchange Act of 1934 (15 U.S.C. 78l) or that is required to file reports under section 15(d) of the Securities Exchange Act of 1934 (15 U.S.C. 78o(d)); shall be fined under this title, or imprisoned not more than 25 years, or both.

EXPLANATORY COMMENTS: *Section 807 adds a new provision to the federal criminal code that addresses securities fraud. Prior to 2002, federal securities law had already made it a crime—under Section 10(b) of the Securities Exchange Act of 1934 and SEC Rule 10b-5, both of which are discussed in Chapter 24—to intentionally defraud someone in connection with a purchase or sale of securities, but the offense was not listed in the federal criminal code. Also, paragraph 2 of Section 807 goes beyond what is prohibited under securities law by making it a crime to obtain by means of false or fraudulent pretenses any money or property from the purchase or sale of securities. This new provision allows violators to be punished by up to twenty-five years in prison, a fine, or both.*

SECTION 906

Failure of corporate officers to certify financial reports[11]

(a) Certification of periodic financial reports.—Each periodic report containing financial statements filed by an issuer with the Securities Exchange Commission pursuant to section 13(a) or 15(d) of the Securities Exchange Act of 1934 (15 U.S.C. 78m(a) or 78o(d)) shall be accompanied by a written statement

---

11. Codified at 18 U.S.C. Section 1350.

by the chief executive officer and chief financial officer (or equivalent thereof) of the issuer.

(b) Content.—The statement required under subsection (a) shall certify that the periodic report containing the financial statements fully complies with the requirements of section 13(a) or 15(d) of the Securities Exchange Act of 1934 (15 U.S.C. 78m or 78o(d)) and that information contained in the periodic report fairly presents, in all material respects, the financial condition and results of operations of the issuer.

(c) Criminal penalties.—Whoever—

(1) certifies any statement as set forth in subsections (a) and (b) of this section knowing that the periodic report accompanying the statement does not comport with all the requirements set forth in this section shall be fined not more than $1,000,000 or imprisoned not more than 10 years, or both; or

(2) willfully certifies any statement as set forth in subsections (a) and (b) of this section knowing that the periodic report accompanying the statement does not comport with all the requirements set forth in this section shall be fined not more than $5,000,000, or imprisoned not more than 20 years, or both.

EXPLANATORY COMMENTS: *As previously discussed, under Section 302 a corporation's CEO and CFO are required to certify that they believe the quarterly and annual reports their company files with the SEC are accurate and fairly present the company's financial condition. Section 906 adds "teeth" to these requirements by authorizing criminal penalties for those officers who intentionally certify inaccurate SEC filings. Knowing violations of the requirements are punishable by a fine of up to $1 million, ten years in prison, or both. Willful violators may be fined up to $5 million, sentenced to up to twenty years in prison, or both. Although the difference between a knowing and a willful violation is not entirely clear, the section is obviously intended to remind corporate officers of the serious consequences of certifying inaccurate reports to the SEC.*

Sample Answers for Selected Questions with Sample Answer

1–4A QUESTION WITH SAMPLE ANSWER.
Sources of Law.

1. The U.S. Constitution—The U.S. Constitution is the supreme law of the land. A law in violation of the Constitution, no matter what its source, will be declared unconstitutional and will not be enforced.

2. The federal statute—Under the U.S. Constitution, when there is a conflict between federal law and state law, federal law prevails.

3. The state statute—State statutes are enacted by state legislatures. Areas not covered by state statutory law are governed by state case law.

4. The U.S. Constitution—State constitutions are supreme within their respective borders unless they conflict with the U.S. Constitution, which is the supreme law of the land.

5. The federal administrative regulation—Under the U.S. Constitution, when there is a conflict between federal law and state law, federal law prevails.

2–2A QUESTION WITH SAMPLE ANSWER.
Ethical Duties.

Factors for the firm to consider in making its decision include the appropriate ethical standard. Under the utilitarian standard, an action is correct, or "right," when, among the people it affects, it produces the greatest amount of good for the greatest number. When an action affects the majority adversely, it is morally wrong. Applying the utilitarian standard requires the following:

(a) A determination of which individuals will be affected by the action in question;

(b) An assessment, or cost-benefit analysis, of the negative and positive effects of alternative actions on these individuals; and

(c) The choice of the alternative that will produce maximum societal utility.

Ethical standards may also be based on a concept of duty, which postulates that the end can never justify the means and that human beings should not be treated as mere means to an end. But ethical decision making in a business context is not always simple, particularly when an action will have different effects on different groups of people: shareholders, employees, society, and other stakeholders, such as the local community. Thus, another factor to consider is to whom the firm believes it owes a duty.

3–2A QUESTION WITH SAMPLE ANSWER.
Jurisdiction.

Marya can bring suit in all three courts. The trucking firm did business in Florida, and the accident occurred there. Thus, the state of Florida would have jurisdiction over the defendant. Because the firm was headquartered in Georgia and had its principal place of business in that state, Marya could also sue in a Georgia court. Finally, because the amount in controversy exceeds $75,000, the suit could be brought in federal court on the basis of diversity of citizenship. In deciding whether to file her case in a federal court or in a Georgia state court, Marya may be influenced by several factors including the distance to the respective courthouses, the reputation of the particular judges, and availability of different remedies in state versus federal court.

4–2A QUESTION WITH SAMPLE ANSWER.
Free Exercise Clause.

As the text points out, Thomas has a constitutionally protected right to his religion and the free exercise of it. In denying his unemployment benefits, the state violated these rights. Employers are obligated to make reasonable accommodations for their employees' beliefs, right or wrong, that are openly and sincerely held. Thomas's beliefs were openly and sincerely held. By placing him in a department that made military goods, his employer effectively put him in a position of having to choose between his job and his religious principles. This unilateral decision on the part of the employer was the reason Thomas left his job and why the company was required to compensate Thomas for his resulting unemployment.

5–2A QUESTION WITH SAMPLE ANSWER.
Wrongful Interference.

To answer this question, you must first decide if there is a legal theory under which Harley may be able to recover. A possibility is the intentional tort of wrongful interference with a contractual relationship. To recover damages under this theory, Harley would need to show:

(a) That he and Martha had a valid contract,

(b) That Lothar knew of this contractual relationship, and

(c) That Lothar intentionally convinced Martha to break her contract with Harley.

Even though Lothar hoped that his advertisements would persuade Martha to break her contract with Harley, the question states that Martha's decision to change bakers was based solely on the advertising and not on anything else that Lothar did. Lothar's advertisements did not constitute a tort. Note, though, that although Harley cannot collect from Lothar for Martha's actions, he does have a cause of action against Martha for her breach of their contract.

6–2A QUESTION WITH SAMPLE ANSWER.
Cyber Scam.

This is fraud committed in an e-mail sent via the Internet. The elements of fraud are as follows:

(a) The misrepresentation of material facts or conditions made with knowledge that they are false or with reckless disregard for the truth;

(b) The intent to induce another to rely on the misrepresentation;

(c) Justifiable reliance on the misrepresentation by the deceived party;

(d) Damages suffered as a result of the reliance; and

(e) A causal connection between the misrepresentation and the injury.

If any of this e-mailer's recipients reply to her false plea with money, it is likely that all of the requirements for fraud will have been met. The scam described in this question is similar to the "Nigerian letter fraud scam" mentioned in the text. In this type of scam, an individual sends an e-mail promising the recipient a percentage of money held in a bank account or payable from a government agency or other source if he or she will send funds to help a fictitious official transfer the amount in the account to another bank. The details of the scam are often adjusted to reflect current events, such as news-making conflicts, tax refunds or payments, or natural disasters.

7–2A QUESTION WITH SAMPLE ANSWER.
Dumping.

Yes, it is a reasonable approach to rely on the producers' financial records. The records reflect the producers' costs reasonably well because the producers have used the same allocation methodologies for a number of years. Historically, such records are relied on to present important financial information to shareholders, lenders, tax authorities, auditors, and other third parties. Provided that the producers' records and books comply with generally accepted accounting principles and were verified by independent auditors, it is reasonable to use them to determine the production costs and fair market value of canned pineapple in the United States.

8–2A QUESTION WITH SAMPLE ANSWER.
Copyright Infringement.

1. Making a photocopy of an article in a scholarly journal "for purposes such as . . . scholarship, or research, is not an infringement of copyright" under Section 107 of the Copyright Act (the fair use exception).

2. This is an example of trademark infringement rather than copyright infringement. Whenever a trademark is copied to a substantial degree or used in its entirety by one who is not entitled to its use, the trademark has been infringed.

3. Recording a television program "for purposes such as . . . teaching . . . is not an infringement of copyright" under Section 107 of the Copyright Act.

14–2A QUESTION WITH SAMPLE ANSWER.
Dissolution of a Limited Partnership.

1. A limited partner's interest is assignable. In fact, assignment allows the assignee to become a substituted limited partner with the consent of the remaining partners. The assignment, however, does not dissolve the limited partnership.

2. Bankruptcy of the limited partnership itself causes dissolution, but bankruptcy of one of the limited partners does not dissolve the partnership unless it causes the bankruptcy of the firm.

3. The retirement, death, or insanity of a general partner dissolves the partnership unless the business can be continued by the remaining general partners. Because Dorinda was the only general partner, her death dissolves the limited partnership.

19–2A QUESTION WITH SAMPLE ANSWER.
Informal Rulemaking.

The court will first consider whether the agency followed the procedures prescribed in the Administrative Procedure Act (APA). Ordinarily, courts will not require agencies to use procedures beyond those of the APA. Courts will, however, compel agencies to follow their own rules. If an agency has adopted a rule granting extra procedures, the agency must provide those extra procedures, at least until the rule is formally rescinded. Ultimately, in this case, the court will most likely rule for the food producers.

Appendix F

Sample Answers for *Case Problems with Sample Answer*

2–6A CASE PROBLEM WITH SAMPLE ANSWER.
Violation of Internal Ethical Codes.

A firm may have acted unethically but still not be held legally accountable unless the party that was wronged can establish some basis of liability. This makes sense because rules of law are designed to require plaintiffs to prove certain elements that establish a defendant's liability in order recover for injuries or loss. Internal ethical codes are a firm's policy statements rather than rules of law, and the violation of internal codes is not a basis for liability. In this case, even though Prudential's conduct was clearly wrongful—and may even have been illegal because of the hidden broker fee—Havensure had the burden of proving liability. Havensure did not establish that it has a valid cause of action against Prudential for violating its ethical code. The appellate court stated that, "Although violations of 'recognized ethical codes' or 'established customs or practices' may be significant in evaluating the nature of an actor's conduct, Havensure has identified no authority suggesting that a violation of internal policies has . . . significance." Furthermore, even if Prudential had violated state law by including hidden broker fees, such a violation would be a matter of concern for insurance regulators, but does not, in itself, create an obligation to Havensure, according to the court.

3–5A CASE PROBLEM WITH SAMPLE ANSWER.
Arbitration Clause.

Based on a recent holding by the Washington State supreme court, the federal appellate court held that the arbitration provision was unconscionable and thus invalid. Because it was invalid, the restriction on class-action lawsuits was also invalid. The state court held that for consumers to be offered a contract that restricted class actions and required individual arbitration improperly stripped consumers of rights they would normally have to attack certain industry practices. Class-action suits are often brought when the losses suffered by an individual consumer as a result of deceptive or unfair industry practices are too small to warrant the consumer bringing suit. In other words, the alleged added cell phone fees are so small that no one consumer would be likely to litigate or arbitrate the matter due to the expenses involved. Eliminating that cause of action by the arbitration clause violates public policy, so that provision is void and unenforceable.

4–5A CASE PROBLEM WITH SAMPLE ANSWER.
Freedom of Speech.

Yes, the court should issue an injunction to prevent the enforcement of the rules because they suppress free speech and are not reasonable restrictions. To be reasonable, the rules must further "an important or substantial governmental interest," be content neutral, and be unrelated to the suppression of free expression. In addition, as the court hearing the case pointed out, any "incidental restriction on alleged First Amendment freedoms [must be] no greater than is essential to the furtherance of that interest." The means chosen must not "burden substantially more speech than is necessary to further the government's legitimate interests. . . . For example, a city has a legitimate aesthetic interest in forbidding the littering of its public areas with paper, but that could not justify a prohibition against the public distribution of handbills, even though the recipients might well toss them on the street." Such a ban would not be upheld because "a free society prefers to punish the few who abuse rights of speech after they break the law than to throttle them and all others beforehand."

Here, the rules hindered young adults' access to the materials they need for lawful artistic expression. The "prohibition against young adults' possession of spray paint and markers in public places—because it applies even where the individuals have a legitimate purpose for their use—imposes a substantial burden on innocent expression." Because the regulations "burdened substantially more speech than is necessary to achieve the City's legitimate interest in preventing illegal graffiti," they were unenforceable.

5–6A CASE PROBLEM WITH SAMPLE ANSWER.
Libel and Invasion of Privacy.

Eubanks could not make a case for either libel or invasion of privacy. The paper had a privilege to publish the information in a public record, and it acted in good faith (the mistake was inadvertent). The trial court awarded the newspaper summary judgment, and the appellate court affirmed. On appeal, the plaintiff claimed that the trial court erred in applying the fair-report privilege, which Section 611 of the Restatement (Second) of Torts defines as follows: The publication of defamatory matter concerning another in a report of an official action or proceeding . . . is privileged if the report is accurate and complete or a fair abridgement [shortening] of the occurrence reported."

Eubanks argued that the publication was not an accurate and complete report because the second e-mail made clear that the first was not correct. Nevertheless, the court found that the original newspaper article "was a complete and accurate summary of an official report from the Lake in the Hills police department . . . that stated the plaintiff was charged with the crimes of theft and attempted obstruction of justice. The fair-report privilege applied to the publication of this information because it was an official report from a police department."

The paper had a privilege to print the information. That privilege was not abused. No information was changed, and there was no "actual malice" in the publication. There was no evidence that the later e-mail had been seen before the paper went to publication. Hence, there was no basis for a suit for libel or invasion of privacy.

6–6A CASE PROBLEM WITH SAMPLE ANSWER.
Fourth Amendment.

Under the Fourth Amendment, a police officer must obtain a search warrant to search private property. In a traffic stop, however, it seems unreasonable to require an officer to obtain a warrant to search one of the vehicle's occupants. Yet it also seems reasonable to apply some standard to prevent police misconduct. An officer might be held to a standard of probable cause, which consists of reasonable grounds to believe that a person should be searched. In some situations, however, an officer may have a reasonable suspicion short of probable cause to believe that a person poses a risk of violence. In a traffic stop, the normal reaction of a person stopped for a driving infraction would not present such a risk, but it might arise from the possibility that evidence of a more serious crime might be discovered. A criminal's motivation to use violence to prevent such a discovery could be great. And because the vehicle would already be stopped, the additional intrusion would be minimal. Under these circumstances, a limited search of the person for weapons would protect the officer, the individual, and the public. Thus, an officer who conducts a routine traffic stop can perform a patdown search of a passenger on a reasonable suspicion that the person may be armed and dangerous. In this case, a jury convicted Johnson of the charge, but a state appellate court reversed the conviction. The United States Supreme Court reversed the appellate court's judgment and remanded the case.

7–5A CASE PROBLEM WITH SAMPLE ANSWER.
Sovereign Immunity.

The key international legal principles at play here are comity and sovereign immunity. Comity requires one nation to give effect to the laws and judicial decrees of another. Sovereign immunity prevents the U.S. courts from exercising jurisdiction over foreign nations unless certain conditions are met. In this case, the United States Supreme Court reversed the decision of the U.S. Court of Appeals for the Ninth Circuit and remanded the case. The Court found that lower courts gave insufficient weight to the sovereign status of the Republic of the Philippines and its Commission in considering whether the interests of those parties would be prejudiced if the case proceeded. Giving full effect to sovereign immunity promotes the comity and dignity interest that contributed to the development of the immunity doctrine. The claims here arise from historically and politically significant events for the Republic and its people. They have a unique interest in resolving matters related to Arelma's assets. A foreign state has a comity interest in using its courts for a dispute if it has a right to do so. Other nations should not bypass the courts of the Philippines without good cause. To seize assets of the Philippines would be a specific affront. The lower courts erred in ruling on the merits of the case. The Pimentel class has interests, but the courts did not accord proper weight to the compelling sovereign immunity claim.

8–5A CASE PROBLEM WITH SAMPLE ANSWER.
Copyright.

A license is created when one party gives his or her property to another, without a transfer of ownership, and allows the other party to copy and distribute it. A copyright owner waives the right to sue for copyright infringement while the license is in effect. In this case, the parties' conduct established that Wilchcombe gave LJESB and the other defendants a license to use his song. He created the song at Lil Jon's request. He knew that it would be used on LJESB's album and that it would be widely distributed. Through Lil Jon and LJESB's contracts with TeeVee Toons, Inc., that defendant acquired whatever rights the other defendants had to the song. Wilchcombe never indicated to any of the defendants that their use of the song would constitute copyright infringement. Thus, the license constitutes a valid defense to Wilchcombe's claim of copyright infringement, and the defendants are entitled to a judgment in their favor on that claim. The court issued a summary judgment in the defendants' favor, and on Wilchcombe's appeal, the U.S. Court of Appeals for the Eleventh Circuit affirmed this judgment.

9–7A CASE PROBLEM WITH SAMPLE ANSWER.
Licensing Statutes.

Whether a contract with an unlicensed person is legal and enforceable depends on the purpose of the statute. If the purpose is to protect the public from unauthorized practitioners, then a contract involving an unlicensed practitioner is generally illegal and unenforceable. Here, the applicable licensing statute was presumably intended to protect the public from unauthorized, unlicensed practitioners. PEMS did not have a broker's license. Thus, if PEMS was acting as a broker, the unlicensed firm forfeited its right to collect a commission for its services. The statutory definition of a broker includes any person who deals with the sale of a business. It seems clear that this definition encompasses PEMS—the firm analyzed Rupp's operational and financial condition, paid legal fees, carefully managed Rupp's confidential data, and screened more than a dozen potential buyers. PEMS also provided key data to RIA to enable it to make a successful purchase of Rupp. Therefore, PEMS is barred from maintaining a suit to collect an unpaid commission. In the actual case on which this problem is based, the court dismissed PEMS's claim on the ground that the unlicensed firm was acting as a broker. A state intermediate appellate court affirmed the decision, agreeing that PEMS was acting as a "broker" in the sale of the business and that, having no broker's license, it was barred from maintaining a suit to collect a broker's commission.

10–6A CASE PROBLEM WITH SAMPLE ANSWER.
Liquidated Damages and Penalties.

The prepayment penalty is not improper. The word *penalty* is used in many contracts when in fact liquidated damages are being assessed. "Where there is a breach of a contract, liquidated damages provisions must be 'reasonable in the light of the anticipated or actual loss caused by the breach and the difficulties of proof of loss.' A liquidated damages provision must not be 'unreasonably large for the expected loss from a breach of contract,' or 'unreasonably disproportionate to the expected loss on the very breach that did occur and was sued upon.' In an action for breach of contract, a liquidated damages provision that fails the above tests amounts to an unenforceable penalty."

Planned Pethood had the right to prepay the loan principal, but doing so triggered the prepayment penalty that was clearly stated in the contract. The alternative was for Pethood to pay the loan annually, year by year, for ten years as the note called for. When Pethood took advantage of the prepayment alternative, the prepayment penalty was not unreasonable. Many loan agreements include such a provision, and the sum required does not violate some notion of equity and is not unconscionable.

11–7A CASE PROBLEM WITH SAMPLE ANSWER.
Remedies of the Buyer.

Under Section 2–714(1) of the Uniform Commercial Code (UCC), a buyer who has accepted nonconforming goods may keep the goods and recover for any loss "resulting in the ordinary course of events" according to "any manner which is reasonable." But the buyer must notify the seller of the breach within a reasonable time after the defect is discovered. Under UCC 2–607(3), failure to give notice of the defect to the seller bars the buyer from pursuing any remedy. When the goods delivered are not as promised, the measure of damages equals the difference between the value of the goods as accepted and their value if they had been delivered as warranted, unless special circumstances indicate damages of a different amount, under UCC 2–714(2). The buyer may also be entitled to incidental and consequential damages under UCC 2–714(3).

In this problem, Woodridge bought eighty-seven trailers from STM through McCarty, an independent sales agent. McCarty showed Woodridge title documents that Woodridge later claimed were defective, presumably because the documents did not indicate Woodridge was the buyer. Instead of notifying STM that Woodridge considered the purported defects to be a breach of their contract, however, Woodridge told McCarty to keep the documents and sell the trailers for Woodridge. Woodridge did not tender the trailers or the documents to STM to give the seller the opportunity to cure the alleged breach. By undertaking to sell the trailers, Woodridge acted inconsistently with STM's ownership. This meant that Woodridge accepted the trailers. Much later, after the trailers had been resold and their proceeds were unaccounted for, Woodridge demanded that STM refund the contract price. But Woodridge did not notify STM about the alleged defect in the title documents until the suit was filed three months later. This is not a reasonable time under the circumstances. Thus, Woodridge does not have a right to recover damages for accepted goods.

In the case on which this problem is based, the court issued a judgment in favor of STM. On Woodridge's appeal, the U.S. Court of Appeals for the Eleventh Circuit affirmed the judgment, according to the reasoning set out here.

12–7A CASE PROBLEM WITH SAMPLE ANSWER.
Protection for Debtors.

As in this problem, certain property of a debtor is exempt under state law from creditors' actions. In most states, certain types of real and personal property are exempt from execution. Each state permits a debtor to retain the family home, either in its entirety or up to a specified dollar amount, free from the claims of unsecured creditors. In a few states, statutes allow the homestead exemption only if the judgment debtor has a family. In this problem, state law allows a $100,000 homestead exemption if the debtor or spouse lives in the home. A greater exemption of $175,000 is allowed if either the debtor or the spouse who lives in the home is disabled and "unable to engage in gainful employment."

Here, the Mas own half of a two-unit residential building. Betty and her mother live in one of the units. Her husband Bill lives in China. The Mas assert that they are entitled to the greater exemption of $175,000 because Bill cannot work as a waiter or a driver due to "gout and dizziness." But state law requires that to obtain the greater exemption, the disabled spouse must live in the home. Bill does not live on the property—he lives in China. Thus, the Mas are entitled only to an exemption of $100,000, not to the $175,000 exemption.

On the sale of the residence, most likely by public auction, the amount of the proceeds that represents the Mas' interest in the property would be distributed as follows:

1. The Mas would be given $100,000 as Bill's homestead exemption.
2. Zhang and the other plaintiffs would be paid the remainder toward the judgment debt, presumably leaving a deficiency,

which would be subject to a deficiency judgment ("leftover debt") that could be satisfied from any other nonexempt property (personal or real) that Bill or the other defendants may own, as permitted by state law.

In the actual case on which this problem is based, on the reasoning set out above, the court issued a judgment in the plaintiffs' favor.

13–7A CASE PROBLEM WITH SAMPLE ANSWER.
Wrongful Foreclosure.

The plaintiffs argued that the foreclosure was void and that they were entitled to damages because the $33,500 amount paid by the defendant-mortgagee for the property so shocked the conscience that it could be considered a wrongful foreclosure or a breach of fiduciary duty. The fair market value of the property at the time of the foreclosure was the key fact in deciding this issue. The defendant contended that the fair market value of the property at the time of the foreclosure was the price bid at the foreclosure sale—that is, $33,500. The plaintiffs contended that the fair market value of the property was $65,000.

The evidence is overwhelming that the value of the property at the time of the foreclosure was the same as the price paid at the foreclosure sale—that is, $33,500. The only direct evidence that did not agree that the fair market value of the property was $33,500 was Mr. Sharpe's testimony. Mr. Sharpe testified that the fair market value was $65,000. Although a property owner may give an opinion about the value of his or her property, the owner must be able to support that opinion with fact. As the U.S. Court of Appeals for the Eleventh Circuit recognized, any testimony by an owner may be "self-serving and unsupported by other evidence." Mr. Sharpe based his opinion on an appraisal and the local tax assessor's yearly valuation of the property. On cross-examination, he could not support his testimony. He did not produce the appraisal he mentioned, and he did not produce the appraiser, the only one who could have testified about the appraisal. Therefore, based on the legal standard applicable under Alabama law, the court held, as a conclusion of law, that the price the defendant bid at the foreclosure sale was not inadequate. The defendant bid the value of the property. Consequently, the defendant does not have any liability under wrongful foreclosure.

14–7A CASE PROBLEM WITH SAMPLE ANSWER.
LLC Management.

In a member-managed limited liability company (LLC), all of the members participate in management, and decisions are made by majority vote. The managers of an LLC—whether member or manager managed—owe fiduciary duties to the company and its members. These duties include the duty of loyalty and the duty of care. An LLC's operating agreement can include provisions governing decision-making procedures. For example, the agreement can set forth procedures for choosing or removing members or managers.

Here, Bluewater is a member-managed LLC. Under the applicable state law, every member of a member-managed LLC is entitled to participate in managing the business. The Bluewater operating agreements provide for a "super-majority" vote to remove and buy out a member—if the "member has either committed a felony or under any other circumstances that would jeopardize the company status" as a contractor. Without giving a reason, however, three of the four members of Bluewater "fired" the fourth member.

Under these facts and principles, Smith, Mosser, and Floyd breached their fiduciary duties, the Bluewater operating agreements, and the state LLC statute. The Bluewater members breached their fiduciary duties by their treatment of Williford. The defendants also breached the Bluewater operating agreements. A supermajority ouster was allowed only when the member to be ousted had committed a felony or had jeopardized the company's status as an approved contractor—the defendants' ouster notice alleged neither. And by attempting to oust Williford, the defendants violated Mississippi's LLC statute, which provides that every member of a member-managed LLC is entitled to participate in managing the business. As a member of both Bluewater LLCs, Williford was entitled to participate in the management of both, and he could not be "fired."

In the actual case on which this problem is based, the court issued a judgment in Williford's favor with a damages award of nearly $350,000. A state intermediate appellate court reversed the judgment, but the Mississippi Supreme Court reversed the appellate court's ruling and affirmed the trial court's judgment, based, in part, on the reasoning stated above.

15–5A CASE PROBLEM WITH SAMPLE ANSWER.
Rights of Shareholders.

Shareholders in a corporation have common law and statutory inspection rights. Under the Revised Model Business Corporation Act, every shareholder is entitled to examine specified corporate records. A shareholder can inspect the books in person or through an agent such as an attorney, accountant, or other authorized assistant. A request to inspect must be made in advance. The right of inspection is limited to the inspection and copying of corporate books and records for a proper purpose. This limitation is imposed because the power of inspection is fraught with potential for abuse—for example, it can result in the disclosure of trade secrets and other confidential information. Thus, a corporation is allowed to protect itself. But a shareholder who is denied the right of inspection can seek a court order to compel the inspection.

Here, Woods, through Hair Ventures, has the right to inspect Biolustre's books and records. She made the request in advance and had a proper purpose for the inspection—to obtain information about Biolustre's financial situation. Woods, and other shareholders, had not received notice of shareholders' meetings or corporate financial reports for years, or notice of Biolustre's plan to issue additional stock. Hair Ventures had a substantial investment in the company. Davila's conduct should not prevent Hair Ventures from exercising its right as a shareholder to inspect Biolustre's books and records. Even if Woods shared the information she obtained during the inspection with Davila, his intent to communicate it to the other shareholders would not be a proper reason for denying Woods the right to inspect the books.

In the actual case on which this problem is based, the court ordered Biolustre to produce its books and records for Hair Ventures' inspection. A state intermediate appellate court affirmed the trial court's decision.

16–5A CASE PROBLEM WITH SAMPLE ANSWER.
Undisclosed Principal.

The disclosure of a principal by an agent who is acting within the scope of his or her authority when entering into a contract with a third party absolves the agent of liability for the nonperformance of the contract. This is the principle that the Pappases cited in their defense to the Crisses' suit. If a principal is partially disclosed or undisclosed, the principal and the agent may both be liable for nonperformance. These are the principles that the Crisses might cite to make their case. Even if Kevin Pappas might arguably

have disclosed that he was acting on behalf of a principal named Outside Creations, there is no indication that he was acting on behalf of an entity named Forever Green. He signed the contract as Outside Creations' "rep," but the payments on the contract were by checks payable to him personally, which he deposited in his personal account. There was no Outside Creations account. The contract did not mention Forever Green, the Pappases did not mention Forever Green, the Crisses knew nothing about Forever Green, and there was no Forever Green account.

In the actual case on which this problem is based, the court issued a summary judgment in the homeowners' favor, finding that the contract was between the homeowners and the Pappases personally, not Kevin Pappas as the agent of Forever Green. A state intermediate appellate court affirmed.

17–6A CASE PROBLEM WITH SAMPLE ANSWER.
Minimum Wage.

No. The federal appellate court affirmed the dismissal by the district court. When tipping is a customary part of a business as it is in the restaurant industry, the tips—in the absence of an explicit agreement to the contrary—belong to the recipient (Cumbie). When another arrangement is made (as Woody Woo did with its tip-pooling arrangement), however, it is likely valid unless there is a statutory limitation. The Fair Labor Standards Act (FLSA) does not prevent employers who are paying at least the minimum wage from taking employee tips and making another arrangement for tip distributions. A tip-pool arrangement is fine so long as it does not reduce the servers' hourly wages to less than the state's minimum wage. Thus, Woody Woo, which pays its servers over and above the state's minimum wage before tips, is complying with the law.

18–7A CASE PROBLEM WITH SAMPLE ANSWER.
Retaliation.

Yes, Dawson has established a claim for retaliatory discharge, according to the U.S. Court of Appeals for the Ninth Circuit. Under Oregon law, it is an unlawful employment practice for an employer to discriminate against an individual based on sexual orientation. It is also unlawful for an employer to discharge an individual because that person has filed a complaint. To establish a *prima facie* case of retaliatory discharge, a plaintiff must prove that (1) the defendant intentionally retaliated against the employee because he or she filed a discrimination complaint, (2) the defendant did so with the intent of forcing the employee to leave the employment, and (3) the employee left the employment as a result of the retaliation. Dawson engaged in a protected activity when he went to the human resources department and filed a complaint. "The protected activity occurred at most two days before the discharge and the treatment of Dawson was a topic during both the protected activity and the discharge." Therefore, Dawson has offered enough evidence that "a reasonable trier of fact could find in favor of Dawson on his retaliation claim." The federal appellate court held that the district court had erred in granting a summary judgment for the employer. The court reversed the decision and remanded the case for trial.

19–6A CASE PROBLEM WITH SAMPLE ANSWER.
Agency Powers.

The United States Supreme Court held that greenhouse gases fit within the Clean Air Act's (CAA's) definition of "air pollutant." Thus, the Environmental Protection Agency (EPA) has the authority under that statute to regulate the emission of such gases from new motor vehicles. According to the Court, the definition, which includes "any" air pollutant, embraces all airborne compounds "of whatever stripe." The EPA's focus on Congress's 1990 amendments (or their lack) indicates nothing about the original intent behind the statute (and its amendments before 1990). Nothing in the statute suggests that Congress meant to curtail the agency's power to treat greenhouse gases as air pollutants. In other words, the agency has a preexisting mandate to regulate "any air pollutant" that may endanger the public welfare.

The EPA also argued that, even if it had the authority to regulate greenhouse gases, the agency would not exercise that authority because any regulation would conflict with other administration priorities. The Court acknowledged that the CAA conditions EPA action on the agency's formation of a "judgment," but explained that judgment must relate to whether a pollutant "cause[s], or contribute[s] to, air pollution which may reasonably be anticipated to endanger public health or welfare." Thus, the EPA can avoid issuing regulations only if the agency determines that greenhouse gases do not contribute to climate change (or if the agency reasonably explains why it cannot or will not determine whether they do). The EPA's refusal to regulate was thus "arbitrary, capricious, or otherwise not in accordance with law." The Court remanded the case for the EPA to "ground its reasons for action or inaction in the statute."

20–5A CASE PROBLEM WITH SAMPLE ANSWER.
Food Labeling.

Before the new menu-labeling requirements were enacted in 2010, the Nutrition Labeling and Education Act (NLEA) did not regulate nutrition information labeling for restaurant foods, and states and local governments could adopt their own rules. The NLEA does regulate nutrition content claims on restaurant food, however, and states' and local governments' attempts to regulate those claims are expressly preempted. The issue in this case is whether the calorie disclosures mandated for chain restaurants' menus and menu boards under New York City Health Code Section 81.50 are "information" or "claims." The types of information that fall under the provision covering "nutrition information" include "total number of calories." The calorie-content information required by Section 81.50 is of the type that falls under this provision. In requiring restaurants to post calorie information on their menus, Section 81.50 thus falls within the area that the NLEA left open to state and local governments. In other words, the NLEA permits the information required by Section 81.50. At the time this case was decided, federal law did not preempt this local regulation.

In the actual case on which this problem is based, the court issued a summary judgment in the defendants' favor, and based on the reasoning stated above, the U.S. Court of Appeals for the Second Circuit affirmed. (Note that if the case had been decided after 2010, the court would likely have found that the federal law preempted the regulations involved here.)

21–5A CASE PROBLEM WITH SAMPLE ANSWER.
Environmental Impact Statement.

The appeals court found that the plaintiffs failed to establish that the National Park Service (NPS) acted in an arbitrary and capricious manner when it adopted the plan. When an agency acts in an arbitrary and capricious manner, the court has grounds for intervention. Otherwise, it defers to the expertise of the agency, as revealed in the record. Here, the court found that the environmental impact statement was comprehensive and that the NPS had credible reason to believe that the use of rafts on the river did not damage the wilderness status of portions of the park. Since the NPS acted within its statutory guidelines and followed proper procedure in its decision making, the court would not intervene in the agency's decision.

22–7A CASE PROBLEM WITH SAMPLE ANSWER.
Adverse Possession.

No. The appeals court affirmed that the property belonged to Hunter and ordered the encroaching structure removed because it was a continuing trespass. Since Mansell initially occupied the property under an informal agreement with the original owner of the property, adverse possession never started. Mansell was a lessee. When Hunter bought the property, the free lease of the property under the garage ended. Mansell never notified the previous owner or Hunter that she was claiming adverse possession so that the hostile possession time would begin. Hunter had objected to the possession in 2003. So Mansell's garage was trespassing on Hunter's property. Hunter may agree to sell Mansell the property, but she need not do so. In that event, the garage must be removed to end the continuing trespass.

23–7A CASE PROBLEM WITH SAMPLE ANSWER.
Monopolization.

No. DVRC's action does not represent an attempt to monopolize in violation of the Sherman Act. DVRC merely returned to a position that it had a right to occupy from the beginning. In their contract, DVRC had expressly informed Christy that their relationship could change at any time. Thus, Christy knew from the beginning that its ski rental business could operate only with DVRC's permission, subject to DVRC's business judgment. If DVRC had terminated a profitable relationship without any economic justification, it might have shown a willingness to forgo short-term profits to achieve an anticompetitive end. But there is no indication that DVRC terminated a profitable business relationship or that DVRC was motivated by anything other than a desire to make more profits. Rather than forgoing short-term profits, DVRC can expect to increase its short-term profits by operating its own ski rental facility. The court in the case on which this problem is based dismissed Christy's suit, and the U.S. Court of Appeals for the Tenth Circuit affirmed that decision.

24–7A CASE PROBLEM WITH SAMPLE ANSWER.
Duty to Disclose.

No. The appeals court affirmed that there was no negligence by the officers of Orphan. There was no duty to disclose early drug trial data, nor was there a duty to give shareholders access to such data. There was no evidence of an intent to mislead investors in Orphan. Federal drug procedure is technical and lengthy. The fact that one stage of testing was successful was no guarantee that further testing would be successful or that the U.S. Food and Drug Administration would allow the drug to be widely marketed. Hence, officers had good reason to be careful not to set off speculation by releasing good news that might, in the long run, turn out not to be favorable.

Answers to *Issue Spotters*

Chapter 1:

1A No. The U.S. Constitution is the supreme law of the land and applies to all jurisdictions. A law in violation of the Constitution (in this question, the First Amendment to the Constitution) will be declared unconstitutional.

2A Case law includes courts' interpretations of statutes, as well as constitutional provisions and administrative rules. Statutes often codify common law rules. For these reasons, a judge might rely on the common law as a guide to the intent and purpose of a statute.

Chapter 2:

1A Maybe. On the one hand, it is not the company's "fault" when a product is misused. Also, keeping the product on the market is not a violation of the law, and stopping sales would hurt profits. On the other hand, suspending sales could reduce suffering and could prevent negative publicity that might result if sales continued.

2A When a corporation decides to respond to what it sees as a moral obligation to correct for past discrimination by adjusting pay differences among its employees, an ethical conflict is raised between the firm and its employees and between the firm and its shareholders (not between the employees). This dilemma arises directly out of the effect of such a decision on the firm's profits. With respect to the employees and the shareholders, the firm arguably has an obligation to stay in business. If adjusting pay differences among employees increases profitability, then staying in business is not an issue, and the dilemma is easily resolved in favor of "doing the right thing."

Chapter 3:

1A Yes. Submission of the dispute to mediation or nonbinding arbitration is mandatory, but compliance with a decision of the mediator or arbitrator is voluntary.

2A Tom could file a motion for a directed verdict. This motion asks the judge to direct a verdict for Tom on the ground that Sue presented no evidence that would justify granting her relief. The judge grants the motion if there is insufficient evidence to raise an issue of fact.

Chapter 4:

1A No. Even if commercial speech is not related to illegal activities and is not misleading, it may be restricted if a state has a substantial interest that cannot be achieved by less restrictive means. In this case, the interest in energy conservation is substantial, but it could be achieved by less restrictive means. That would be the utilities' defense against the enforcement of this state law.

2A Yes. The tax would limit the liberty of some persons (out-of-state businesses), so it is subject to review under the equal protection clause. Protecting local businesses from out-of-state competition is not a legitimate government objective. Thus, such a tax would violate the equal protection clause.

Chapter 5:

1A Probably. To recover on the basis of negligence, the injured party as a plaintiff must show that the truck's owner owed the plaintiff a duty of care, that the owner breached that duty, that the plaintiff was injured, and that the breach caused the injury. In this problem, the owner's actions breached the duty of reasonable care. The direct cause of the injury was the billboard falling on the plaintiff, not the plaintiff's own negligence. Thus, liability turns on whether the plaintiff can connect the breach of duty to the injury. This involves the test of proximate cause—the question of foreseeability. The consequences to the injured party must have been a foreseeable result of the owner's carelessness.

2A The company might defend against the electrician's claim by asserting that it had no duty to warn of a dangerous risk that the electrician should have recognized. According to the problem, the danger is common knowledge in the electrician's field and should have been clear to this electrician, given his years of training and experience. The firm could also raise the defense of comparative negligence. Both parties' negligence, if any, could be weighed and the liability distributed proportionately. The defendant could also assert assumption of risk, claiming that the electrician voluntarily entered into a dangerous situation knowing the risk involved.

Chapter 6:

1A Yes. With respect to the gas station, Daisy has obtained goods by false pretenses. She might also be charged with larceny and forgery, and most states have special statutes covering illegal use of credit cards.

2A Yes. The National Information Infrastructure Protection Act of 1996 amended the Counterfeit Access Device and Computer Fraud and Abuse Act of 1984. The statute provides that a person who accesses a computer online, without permission, to obtain classified data (such as consumer credit files in a credit agency's database) is subject to criminal prosecution. The crime has two elements: accessing the computer without permission and taking data. It is a felony if done for private financial gain. Penalties include fines and imprisonment for up to twenty years. The victim of the theft can also bring a civil suit against the criminal to obtain damages and other relief.

Chapter 7:

1A Under the principle of comity, a U.S. court would defer to and give effect to foreign laws and judicial decrees that are consistent with U.S. law and public policy.

2A The practice described is known as dumping. Dumping is the sale of imported goods at "less than fair value" and is regarded as an unfair international trade practice. Based on the price of those goods in the exporting country, an extra tariff, known as an anti-dumping duty, can be imposed on the imports.

Chapter 8:

1A This is patent infringement. A software maker in this situation might best protect its product, save litigation costs, and profit from its patent by the use of a license. In the context of this problem, a license would grant permission to sell a patented item. (A license can be limited to certain purposes and to the licensee only.)

2A Yes. This may be an instance of trademark dilution. Dilution occurs when a trademark is used, without permission, in a way that diminishes the distinctive quality of the mark. Dilution does not require proof that consumers are likely to be confused by a connection between the unauthorized use and the mark. The products involved do not have to be similar. Dilution does require, however, that a mark be famous when the dilution occurs.

Chapter 9:

1A Yes. An offer must be communicated to the offeree so that the offeree knows about it. For example, the offer of a reward must be communicated to offerees. An offeree who knows of the offer and performs the required act can then claim the reward.

2A First, it might be noted that the Uniform Electronic Transactions Act (UETA) does not apply unless the parties to a contract agree to use e-commerce in their transaction. In this deal, of course, the parties used e-commerce. The UETA removes barriers to e-commerce by giving the same legal effect to e-records and e-signatures as to paper documents and signatures. The UETA does not include rules for those transactions, however.

Chapter 10:

1A No. When parties base their contract on a common assumption about a material fact that proves false, the transaction can be avoided if, because of the mistake, the exchange of values is different from what the parties contemplated. In other words, what the buyer actually found on the property was not part of the bargain between the buyer and the seller.

2A Contracts that are executory on both sides—contracts on which neither party has performed—can be rescinded solely by agreement. Contracts that are executed on one side—contracts on which one party has performed—can be rescinded only if the party who has performed receives consideration for the promise to call off the deal.

Chapter 11:

1A A shipment of nonconforming goods constitutes an acceptance and a breach, unless the seller seasonably notifies the buyer that the nonconforming shipment does not constitute an acceptance and is offered only as an accommodation. Without the notification, the shipment is an acceptance and a breach. Thus, here the shipment was both an acceptance and a breach.

2A Yes. The manufacturer is liable for the injuries to the user of the product. A manufacturer is liable for its failure to exercise due care to any person who sustains an injury proximately caused by a negligently made (defective) product. In this problem, the failure to inspect is a failure to use due care.

Chapter 12:

1A Each of the parties can place a mechanic's lien on the debtor's property. If the debtor does not pay what is owed, the property can be sold to satisfy the debt. The only requirements are that the lien be filed within a specific time from the time of the work, depending on the state statute, and that notice of the foreclosure and sale be given to the debtor in advance.

2A Yes. A debtor's payment to a creditor for a preexisting debt, made within ninety days of a bankruptcy filing (one year in the case of an insider or fraud), can be recovered if the payment gives the creditor more than he or she would have received in the bankruptcy proceedings. A trustee can recover this preference using his or her specific avoidance powers.

Chapter 13:

1A The major terms that must be disclosed under the Truth in Lending Act include the loan principal, the interest rate at which the loan is made, the annual percentage rate (APR) (the actual cost of the loan on a yearly basis), and all fees and costs associated with the loan. These disclosures must be made on standardized forms and based on uniform formulas of calculation. Certain types of loans have special disclosure requirements.

2A Foreclosure is the process that allows a lender to repossess and auction off property that is securing a loan. The two most common types of foreclosure are judicial foreclosure and power of sale foreclosure. In the former—available in all states—a court supervises the process. This is the most common method of foreclosure. In the latter—available in only a few states—a lender forecloses on and sells the property without court supervision.

If the sale proceeds cover the mortgage debt and foreclosure costs, the debtor receives any surplus. If the proceeds do not cover the debt and costs, the mortgagee can seek to recover the difference through a deficiency judgment, which is obtained in a separate action. A deficiency judgment entitles the creditor to recover this difference from a sale of the debtor's other nonexempt property. Before a foreclosure sale, a mortgagor can redeem the property by paying the debt, plus any interest and costs. This right is known as the equity of redemption. In some states, a mortgagor may redeem property within a certain time—called a statutory period of redemption—after the sale.

Chapter 14:

1A The members of a limited liability company (LLC) may designate a group to run their firm—then, the firm is considered a manager-managed LLC. The group may include only members, only nonmembers, or members and nonmembers. If, instead, all members participate in management, the firm is a member-managed LLC. In fact, unless the members agree otherwise, all members are considered to participate in the management of the firm.

2A Yes. Failing to meet a specified sales quota can constitute a breach of a franchise agreement. If the franchisor is acting in good faith, "cause" may also include the death or disability of the franchisee, the insolvency of the franchisee, and a breach of another term of the franchise agreement.

Chapter 15:

1A Yes. Small businesses that meet certain requirements can qualify as S corporations, created specifically to permit small businesses to avoid double taxation. The six requirements of an S corporation are (1) the firm must be a domestic corporation; (2) the firm must not be a member of an affiliated group of corporations; (3) the firm must have fewer than a certain number of shareholders; (4) the shareholders must be individuals, estates, or qualified trusts (or corporations in some instances); (5) there can be only one class of stock; and (6) no shareholder can be a nonresident alien.

2A Yes. A shareholder can bring a derivative suit on behalf of a corporation, if some wrong is done to the corporation. Normally, any damages recovered go into the corporate treasury.

Chapter 16:

1A When a person enters into a contract on another's behalf without the authority to do so, the other may be liable on the contract if he or she approves or affirms that contract. In other words, the employer-principal would be liable on the note in this problem on ratifying it. Whether the employer-principal ratifies the note or not, the unauthorized agent is most likely also liable on it.

2A Yes. A principal has a duty to indemnify an agent for liabilities incurred because of authorized and lawful acts and transactions and for losses suffered because of the principal's failure to perform his or her duties.

Chapter 17:

1A To obtain workers' compensation benefits, Erin does not need to show that her injury was caused by Fine Print's negligence or intentional conduct. If she was injured on the job, she can file a workers' compensation claim. Workers' compensation laws establish a procedure for compensating workers who are injured on the job. Instead of suing to collect benefits, an injured worker notifies the employer of an injury and files a claim with the appropriate state agency. The right to recover is normally determined without regard to negligence or fault, but intentionally inflicted injuries are not covered. Unlike the potential for recovery in a lawsuit based on negligence or fault, recovery under a workers' compensation statute is limited to the specific amount designated in the statute for the employee's injury.

2A No. A closed shop (a company that requires union membership as a condition of employment) is illegal. A union shop (a company that does not require union membership as a condition of employment but requires workers to join the union after a certain amount of time on the job) is illegal in a state with a right-to-work law, which makes it illegal to require union membership for continued employment.

Chapter 18:

1A Yes. One type of sexual harassment occurs when a request for sexual favors is a condition of employment, and the person making the request is a supervisor or acts with the authority of the employer. A tangible employment action, such as continued employment, may also lead to the employer's liability for the supervisor's conduct. That the injured employee is a male and the supervisor a female, instead of the other way around, would not affect the outcome. Same-gender harassment is also actionable.

2A Yes, if she can show that she was not hired solely because of her disability. The other elements for a discrimination suit based on a disability are that the plaintiff (1) has a disability and (2) is otherwise qualified for the job. Both of these elements appear to be satisfied in this problem.

Chapter 19:

1A Under the Administrative Procedure Act (APA), the administrative law judge (ALJ) must be separate from the agency's investigative and prosecutorial staff. *Ex parte* communications between the ALJ and a party to a proceeding are prohibited. Under the APA, an ALJ is exempt from agency discipline except on a showing of good cause.

2A Yes. Administrative rulemaking starts with the publication of a notice of the rulemaking in the *Federal Register*. A public hearing is held at which proponents and opponents can offer evidence and question witnesses. After the hearing, the agency considers what was presented at the hearing and drafts the final rule.

Chapter 20:

1A Under the Truth-in-Lending Act, a buyer who wishes to withhold payment for a faulty product purchased with a credit card must follow specific procedures to settle the dispute. The credit-card issuer then must intervene and attempt to settle the dispute.

2A Under an extensive set of procedures established by the U.S. Food and Drug Administration, which administers the federal Food, Drug, and Cosmetic Act, drugs must be shown to be effective as well as safe before they may be marketed to the public. In general, manufacturers are responsible for ensuring that the drugs they offer for sale are free of any substances that could injure consumers.

Chapter 21:

1A The Comprehensive Environmental Response, Compensation, and Liability Act of 1980 regulates the clean-up of hazardous waste disposal sites. Any potentially responsible party can be charged with the entire cost of cleaning up a site. Potentially responsible parties include the person that generated the waste (ChemCorp), the person that transported the waste to the site (Disposal), the person that owned or operated the site at the time of the disposal (Eliminators), and the current owner or operator of the site (Fluid). A party held responsible for the entire cost may be able to recoup some of it in a lawsuit against other potentially responsible parties.

2A Yes. On the ground that the hardships that would be imposed on the polluter and on the community are greater than the hardships suffered by the residents, the court might deny an injunction. If the plant is the core of the local economy, for instance, the residents may be awarded only damages.

Chapter 22:

1A This is a breach of the warranty deed's covenant of quiet enjoyment. The buyer can sue the seller and recover the purchase price of the house, plus any damages.

2A Yes. An owner of a fee simple has the most rights possible—he or she can give the property away, sell it, transfer it by will, use it for almost any purpose, possess it to the exclusion of all the world, or (as in this case) transfer possession for any period of time. The party to whom possession is transferred can also transfer her or his interest (usually only with the owner's permission) for any lesser period of time.

Chapter 23:

1A Size alone does not determine whether a firm is a monopoly—size in relation to the market is what matters. A small store in a small, isolated town is a monopolist if it is the only store serving that market. Monopoly involves the power to affect prices and output. If a firm has sufficient market power to control prices and exclude competition, that firm has monopoly power. Monopoly power in itself is not a violation of Section 2 of the Sherman Act. The offense also requires an intent to acquire or maintain that power through anticompetitive means. In other words, Pop's is a monopolist, but it is not in violation of Section 2 of the Sherman Act.

2A This agreement is a tying arrangement. The legality of a tying arrangement depends on a number of factors, including the purpose of the agreement and the agreement's likely effect on competition in the relevant markets (the market for the tying product and the market for the tied product). Tying arrangements for commodities are subject to Section 3 of the Clayton Act. The court would consider the above factors to determine if the agreement violated the Clayton Act. Tying arrangements for services can also be agreements in restraint of trade in violation of Section 1 of the Sherman Act.

Chapter 24:

1A The average investor is not concerned with minor inaccuracies but with facts that, if disclosed, would tend to deter him or her from buying the securities. These would include facts that have an important bearing on the condition of the issuer and its business—liabilities, loans to officers and directors, customer delinquencies, and pending lawsuits.

2A No. The Securities Exchange Act of 1934 extends liability to officers and directors in their personal transactions for taking advantage of inside information when they know it is unavailable to the persons with whom they are dealing.

Glossary

A

Acceleration Clause • A clause in a mortgage loan contract that makes the entire loan balance become due if the borrower misses or is late in making only one monthly mortgage payment.

Acceptance • A voluntary act by the offeree that shows assent, or agreement, to the terms of an offer; may consist of words or conduct.

Accredited Investor • In the context of securities offerings, a "sophisticated" investor, such as a bank, an insurance company, an investment company, the issuer's executive officers and directors, and any person whose income or net worth exceeds certain limits.

Actionable • Capable of serving as the basis of a lawsuit. An actionable claim can be pursued in a lawsuit or other court action.

Act of State Doctrine • A doctrine providing that the judicial branch of one country will not examine the validity of public acts committed by a recognized foreign government within its own territory.

Actual Malice • The deliberate intent to cause harm, which exists when a person makes a statement either knowing that it is false or showing a reckless disregard for whether it is true. In a defamation suit, a statement made about a public figure normally must be made with actual malice for the plaintiff to recover damages.

Actus Reus • A guilty (prohibited) act. The commission of a prohibited act is one of the two essential elements required for criminal liability, the other element being the intent to commit a crime.

Adjudication • The act of rendering a judicial decision. In an administrative process, the proceeding in which an administrative law judge hears and decides issues that arise when an administrative agency charges a person or a firm with violating a law or regulation enforced by the agency.

Adjustable-Rate Mortgage (ARM) • A mortgage in which the rate of interest paid by the borrower changes periodically, often with reference to a predetermined government interest rate (the index).

Administrative Agency • A federal or state government agency established to perform a specific function. Administrative agencies are authorized by legislative acts to make and enforce rules in order to administer and enforce the acts.

Administrative Law • The body of law created by administrative agencies (in the form of rules, regulations, orders, and decisions) in order to carry out their duties and responsibilities.

Administrative Law Judge (ALJ) • One who presides over an administrative agency hearing and has the power to administer oaths, take testimony, rule on questions of evidence, and make determinations of fact.

Adverse Possession • The acquisition of title to real property by occupying it openly, without the consent of the owner, for a period of time specified by a state statute. The occupation must be actual, open, continuous, exclusive, and in opposition to all others, including the owner.

Affirmative Action • Job-hiring policies that give special consideration to members of protected classes in an effort to overcome present effects of past discrimination.

Agency • A relationship between two parties in which one party (the agent) agrees to represent or act for the other (the principal).

Agreement • A meeting of two or more minds in regard to the terms of a contract; usually broken down into two events—an offer by one party to form a contract and an acceptance of the offer by the person to whom the offer is made.

Alien Corporation • A designation in the United States for a corporation formed in another country but doing business in the United States.

Alternative Dispute Resolution (ADR) • The resolution of disputes in ways other than those involved in the traditional judicial process. Negotiation, mediation, and arbitration are forms of ADR.

Annual Percentage Rate (APR) • The cost of credit on a yearly basis, typically expressed as an annual percentage.

Answer • Procedurally, a defendant's response to the plaintiff's complaint.

Anticipatory Repudiation • An assertion or action by a party indicating that he or she will not perform an obligation that the party is contractually obligated to perform at a future time.

Antitrust Law • Laws protecting commerce from unlawful restraints.

Apparent Authority • Authority that is only apparent, not real. In agency law, a person may be deemed to have had the power to act as an agent for another party if the other party's manifestations to a third party led the third party to believe that an agency existed when, in fact, it did not.

Appraiser • An individual who specializes in determining the value of certain real or personal property.

Appropriation • In tort law, the use by one person of another person's name, likeness, or other identifying characteristic without permission and for the benefit of the user.

Arbitration • The settling of a dispute by submitting it to a disinterested third party (other than a court), who renders a decision that is (most often) legally binding.

Arbitration Clause • A clause in a contract that provides that, in the event of a dispute, the parties will submit the dispute to arbitration rather than litigate the dispute in court.

Arson • The intentional burning of another's building. Some statutes have expanded this to include any real property regardless of ownership and the destruction of property by other means—for example, by explosion.

Articles of Incorporation • The document filed with the appropriate governmental agency, usually the secretary of state, when a business is incorporated. State statutes usually prescribe what kind of information must be contained in the articles of incorporation.

Articles of Organization • The document filed with a designated state official by which a limited liability company is formed.

Articles of Partnership • A written agreement that sets forth each partner's rights and obligations with respect to the partnership.

Artisan's Lien • A possessory lien given to a person who has made improvements and added value to another person's personal property as security for payment for services performed.

Assault • Any word or action intended to make another person fearful of immediate physical harm; a reasonably believable threat.

Assignment • The act of transferring to another all or part of one's rights arising under a contract.

Assumption of Risk • A doctrine under which a plaintiff may not recover for injuries or damage suffered from risks he or she knows of and has voluntarily assumed.

Attachment • In the context of judicial liens, a court-ordered seizure and taking into custody of property prior to the securing of a judgment for a past-due debt.

Attempted Monopolization • Any action by a firm to eliminate competition and gain monopoly power.

Authorization Card • A card signed by an employee that gives a union permission to act on his or her behalf in negotiations with management.

Automatic Stay • In bankruptcy proceedings, the suspension of virtually all litigation and other action by creditors against the debtor or the debtor's property; the stay is effective the moment the debtor files a petition in bankruptcy.

Average Prime Offer Rate • The mortgage rate offered to the best-qualified borrowers as established by a survey of lenders.

Award • In litigation, the amount of monetary compensation awarded to a plaintiff in a civil lawsuit as damages. In the context of alternative dispute resolution, the decision rendered by an arbitrator.

B

Bait-and-Switch Advertising • Advertising a product at a very attractive price (the bait) and then, once the consumer is in the store, saying that the advertised product either is not available or is of poor quality. The customer is then urged to purchase (switched to) a more expensive item.

Balloon Mortgage • A loan that allows the debtor to make small monthly payments for an initial period, such as eight years, but then requires a large balloon payment for the entire remaining balance of the mortgage loan at the end of that period.

Bankruptcy Court • A federal court of limited jurisdiction that handles only bankruptcy proceedings, which are governed by federal bankruptcy law.

Battery • The unexcused, harmful or offensive, intentional touching of another.

Beyond a Reasonable Doubt • The standard of proof used in criminal cases. If there is any reasonable doubt that a criminal defendant committed the crime with which she or he has been charged, then the verdict must be "not guilty."

Bilateral Contract • A type of contract that arises when a promise is given in exchange for a return promise.

Bilateral Mistake • A mistake that occurs when both parties to a contract are mistaken about the same material fact.

Bill of Rights • The first ten amendments to the U.S. Constitution.

Binding Authority • Any source of law that a court must follow when deciding a case. Binding authorities include constitutions, statutes, and regulations that govern the issue being decided, as well as court decisions that are controlling precedents within the jurisdiction.

Bona Fide Occupational Qualification (BFOQ) • Identifiable characteristics reasonably necessary to the normal operation of a particular business. These characteristics can include gender, national origin, and religion, but not race.

Botnet • A network of computers that have been appropriated without the knowledge of their owners and used to spread harmful programs via the Internet; short for robot network.

Breach • The failure to perform a legal obligation.

Breach of Contract • The failure, without legal excuse, of a promisor to perform the obligations of a contract.

Bridge Loan • A short-term loan that allows a buyer to make a down payment on a new home before selling her or his current home. The current home is used as collateral.

Brief • A formal legal document prepared by a party's attorney for the appellant or the appellee (in answer to the appellant's brief) and submitted to an appellate court when a case is appealed. The appellant's brief outlines the facts and issues of the case, the judge's rulings or jury's findings that should be reversed or modified, the applicable law, and the arguments on the client's behalf.

Browse-Wrap Term • A term or condition of use that is presented to an Internet user at the time certain products, such as software, are being downloaded but that need not be agreed to (by clicking "I agree," for example) before the user is able to install or use the product.

Bureaucracy • The organizational structure, consisting of government bureaus and agencies, through which the government implements and enforces the laws.

Burglary • The unlawful entry or breaking into a building with the intent to commit a felony. (Some state statutes expand this to include the intent to commit any crime.)

Business Ethics • Ethics in a business context; a consensus as to what constitutes right or wrong behavior in the world of business and the application of moral principles to situations that arise in a business setting.

Business Invitee • A person, such as a customer or a client, who is invited onto business premises by the owner of those premises for business purposes.

Business Judgment Rule • A rule that immunizes corporate management from liability for actions that result in corporate losses or damages if the actions are undertaken in good faith and are within both the power of the corporation and the authority of management to make.

Business Necessity • A defense to allegations of employment discrimination in which the employer demonstrates that an employment practice that discriminates against members of a protected class is related to job performance.

Business Tort • Wrongful interference with another's business rights.

Buyout Price • The amount payable to a partner on his or her dissociation from a partnership, based on the amount distributable to that partner if the firm were wound up on that date, and offset by any damages for wrongful dissociation.

Bylaws • A set of governing rules adopted by a corporation or other association.

C

Case Law • The rules of law announced in court decisions. Case law includes the aggregate of reported cases that interpret judicial precedents, statutes, regulations, and constitutional provisions.

Categorical Imperative • A concept developed by the philosopher Immanuel Kant as an ethical guideline for behavior. In deciding whether an action is right or wrong, or desirable or undesirable, a person should evaluate the action in terms of what would happen if everybody else in the same situation, or category, acted the same way.

Causation in Fact • An act or omission without which an event would not have occurred.

Cease-and-Desist Order • An administrative or judicial order prohibiting a person or business firm from conducting activities that an agency or court has deemed illegal.

Certificate of Limited Partnership • The basic document filed with a designated state official by which a limited partnership is formed.

Certification Mark • A mark used by one or more persons, other than the owner, to certify the region, materials, mode of manufacture, quality, or other characteristic of specific goods or services.

Checks and Balances • The principle under which the powers of the national government are divided among three separate branches—the executive, legislative, and judicial branches—each of which exercises a check on the actions of the others.

Choice-of-Language Clause • A clause in a contract designating the official language by which the contract will be interpreted in the event of a future disagreement over the contract's terms.

Choice-of-Law Clause • A clause in a contract designating the law (such as the law of a particular state or nation) that will govern the contract.

Citation • A reference to a publication in which a legal authority—such as a statute or a court decision—or other source can be found.

Civil Law • The branch of law dealing with the definition and enforcement of all private or public rights, as opposed to criminal matters.

Civil Law System • A system of law derived from that of the Roman Empire and based on a code rather than case law; the predominant system of law in the nations of continental Europe and the nations that were once their colonies.

Click-on Agreement • An agreement that arises when a buyer, engaging in a transaction on a computer, indicates assent to be bound by the terms of an offer by clicking on a button that says, for example, "I agree."

Close Corporation • A corporation whose shareholders are limited to a small group of persons, often only family members. In a close corporation, the shareholders' rights to transfer shares to others are usually restricted.

Closed Shop • A firm that requires union membership by its workers as a condition of employment. The closed shop was made illegal by the Labor-Management Relations Act of 1947.

Closing • The final step in the sale of real estate; also called settlement or closing escrow. The escrow agent coordinates the closing with the recording of deeds, the obtaining of title insurance, and other closing activities. A number of costs must be paid, in cash, at the time of closing.

Cloud Computing • A subscription-based or pay-per-use service that, in real time over the Internet, extends a computer's software or storage capabilities. By using the services of large companies with excess storage and computing capacity, a company can increase its information technology capabilities without investing in new infrastructure, training new personnel, or licensing new software.

Collective Bargaining • The process by which labor and management negotiate the terms and conditions of employment, including working hours and workplace conditions.

Collective Mark • A mark used by members of a cooperative, association, union, or other organization to certify the region, materials, mode of manufacture, quality, or other characteristic of specific goods or services.

Comity • The principle by which one nation defers to and gives effect to the laws and judicial decrees of another nation. This recognition is based primarily on respect.

Commerce Clause • The provision in Article I, Section 8, of the U.S. Constitution that gives Congress the power to regulate interstate commerce.

Commercial Impracticability • A doctrine under which a court may excuse the parties from performing a contract when the performance becomes much more difficult or costly due to an event that the parties did not foresee or anticipate at the time the contract was made.

Commercial Use • Use of land for business activities only. Also called business use.

Commingle • To put funds or goods together into one mass so that they are mixed to such a degree that they no longer have separate identities. In corporate law, if personal and corporate interests are commingled to the extent that the corporation has no separate identity, a court may "pierce the corporate veil" and expose the shareholders to personal liability.

Common Law • The body of law developed from custom or judicial decisions in English and U.S. courts, not attributable to a legislature.

Comparative Negligence • A rule in tort law that reduces the plaintiff's recovery in proportion to the plaintiff's degree of fault, rather than barring recovery completely; used in the majority of states.

Compensatory Damages • A monetary award equivalent to the actual value of injuries or damage sustained by the aggrieved party.

Complaint • The pleading made by a plaintiff alleging wrongdoing on the part of the defendant; the document that, when filed with a court, initiates a lawsuit.

Computer Crime • Any wrongful act that is directed against computers and computer parts or that involves the wrongful use or abuse of computers or software.

Concentrated Industry • An industry in which a large percentage of market sales is controlled by either a single firm or a small number of firms.

Concurrent Jurisdiction • Jurisdiction that exists when two different courts have the power to hear a case. For example, some cases can be heard in a federal or a state court.

Condemnation • The process of taking private property for public use through the government's power of eminent domain.

Condition • A qualification, provision, or clause in a contractual agreement, the occurrence or nonoccurrence of which creates, suspends, or terminates the obligations of the contracting parties.

Condition Precedent • In a contractual agreement, a condition that must be met before a party's promise becomes absolute.

Confiscation • A government's taking of a privately owned business or personal property without a proper public purpose or an award of just compensation.

Conforming Goods • Goods that conform to contract specifications.

Consequential Damages • Special damages that compensate for a loss that does not directly or immediately result from the breach (for example, lost profits). For the plaintiff to collect consequential damages, they must have been reasonably foreseeable at the time the breach or injury occurred.

Consideration • Generally, the value given in return for a promise or a performance. The consideration, which must be present to make the contract legally binding, must be something of legally sufficient value and bargained for.

Constitutional Law • The body of law derived from the U.S. Constitution and the constitutions of the various states.

Construction Loan • A loan obtained by a borrower to finance the building of a new home. Construction loans are often set up to release funds at particular stages of the project.

Constructive Discharge • A termination of employment brought about by making the employee's working conditions so intolerable that the employee reasonably feels compelled to leave.

Constructive Eviction • A form of eviction that occurs when a landlord fails to perform adequately any of the duties required by the lease, thereby making the tenant's further use and enjoyment of the property exceedingly difficult or impossible.

Consumer-Debtor • An individual whose debts are primarily consumer debts (debts for purchases made primarily for personal or household use).

Contract • An agreement that can be enforced in court; formed by two or more competent parties who agree, for consideration, to perform or to refrain from performing some legal act now or in the future.

Contractual Capacity • The threshold mental capacity required by the law for a party who enters into a contract to be bound by that contract.

Contributory Negligence • A rule in tort law that completely bars the plaintiff from recovering any damages if the damage suffered is partly the plaintiff's own fault; used in a minority of states.

Conversion • Wrongfully taking or retaining possession of an individual's personal property and placing it in the service of another.

Conveyance • The transfer of title to land from one person to another by deed; a document (such as a deed) by which an interest in land is transferred from one person to another.

"Cooling-off" Laws • Laws that allow buyers a period of time, such as three business days, in which to cancel door-to-door sales contracts.

Copyright • The exclusive right of an author or originator of a literary or artistic production to publish, print, or sell that production for a statutory period of time. A copyright has the same monopolistic nature as a patent or trademark, but it differs in that it applies exclusively to works of art, literature, and other works of authorship (including computer programs).

Corporate Governance • A set of policies or procedures affecting the way a corporation is directed or controlled.

Corporate Social Responsibility • The idea that corporations can and should act ethically and be accountable to society for their actions.

Corporation • A legal entity formed in compliance with statutory requirements that is distinct from its shareholder-owners.

Correspondent Bank • A bank in which another bank has an account (and vice versa) for the purpose of facilitating fund transfers.

Cost-Benefit Analysis • A decision-making technique that involves weighing the costs of a given action against the benefits of that action.

Co-Surety • A joint surety; a person who assumes liability jointly with another surety for the payment of an obligation.

Counteradvertising • New advertising that is undertaken pursuant to a Federal Trade Commission order for the purpose of correcting earlier false claims that were made about a product.

Counterclaim • A claim made by a defendant in a civil lawsuit against the plaintiff. In effect, the defendant is suing the plaintiff.

Counteroffer • An offeree's response to an offer in which the offeree rejects the original offer and at the same time makes a new offer.

Course of Dealing • Prior conduct between parties to a contract that establishes a common basis for their understanding.

Covenant Not to Compete • A contractual promise of one party to refrain from competing with another party for a certain period of time and within a certain geographic area.

Cover • Under the UCC, a remedy that allows the buyer or lessee, on the seller's or lessor's breach, to obtain the goods, in good faith and within a reasonable time, from another seller or lessor and substitute them for the goods due under the contract.

Cram-Down Provision • A provision of the Bankruptcy Code that allows a court to confirm a debtor's Chapter 11 reorganization plan even though only one class of creditors has accepted it. To use this provision, the court must demonstrate that the plan does not discriminate unfairly against any creditors and is fair and equitable.

Creditors' Composition Agreement • An agreement formed between a debtor and his or her creditors in which the creditors agree to accept a lesser sum than that owed by the debtor in full satisfaction of the debt.

Crime • A wrong against society set forth in a statute and, if committed, punishable by society through fines and/or imprisonment—and, in some cases, death.

Criminal Law • Law that defines and governs actions that constitute crimes. Generally, criminal law has to do with wrongful actions committed against society for which society demands redress.

Cure • The right of a party who tenders nonconforming performance to correct that performance within the contract period.

Cyber Crime • A crime that occurs online, in the virtual community of the Internet, as opposed to the physical world.

Cyber Fraud • Any misrepresentation knowingly made over the Internet with the intention of deceiving another and on which a reasonable person would and does rely to his or her detriment.

Cyber Mark • A trademark in cyberspace.

Cyber Tort • A tort committed in cyberspace.

Cyberlaw • An informal term used to refer to all laws governing electronic communications and transactions, particularly those conducted via the Internet.

Cybernotary • A legally recognized authority that can certify the validity of digital signatures.

Cybersquatting • The act of registering a domain name that is the same as, or confusingly similar to, the trademark of another and then offering to sell that domain name back to the trademark owner.

Cyberterrorist • A person who uses the Internet to attack or sabotage businesses and government agencies with the purpose of disrupting infrastructure systems.

D

Damages • Money sought as a remedy for a breach of contract or a tortious action.

Debtor in Possession (DIP) • In Chapter 11 bankruptcy proceedings, a debtor who is allowed to continue in possession of the estate in property (the business) and to continue business operations.

Deceptive Advertising • Advertising that misleads consumers, either by making unjustified claims concerning a product's performance or by omitting a material fact concerning the product's composition or performance.

Deed • A document by which title to property (usually real property) is passed.

Deed in Lieu of Foreclosure • An alternative to foreclosure in which the mortgagor voluntarily conveys the property to the lender in satisfaction of the mortgage.

Defamation • Anything published or publicly spoken that causes injury to another's good name, reputation, or character.

Default • The act of failing to pay a debt, perform an obligation, or appear in court when legally required to do so. A court can enter a default judgment against a defendant who fails to appear in court to answer or defend against a plaintiff's claim.

Default Judgment • A judgment entered by a court against a defendant who has failed to appear in court to answer or defend against the plaintiff's claim.

Defendant • One against whom a lawsuit is brought; the accused person in a criminal proceeding.

Deficiency Judgment • A judgment against the borrower for the amount of debt remaining unpaid after the collateral is sold.

Delegation • The transfer of a contractual duty to a third party. The party delegating the duty (the delegator) to the third party (the delegatee) is still obliged to perform on the contract should the delegatee fail to perform.

Delegation Doctrine • A doctrine based on Article I, Section 8, of the U.S. Constitution, which has been construed to allow Congress to delegate some of its power to administrative agencies to make and implement laws.

Deposition • The testimony of a party to a lawsuit or a witness taken under oath before a trial.

Discharge • The termination of an obligation. In contract law, discharge occurs when the parties have fully performed their contractual obligations or when events, conduct of the parties, or operation of law releases the parties from performance. In bankruptcy, the release of a debtor from all debts that are provable, except those specifically excepted from discharge by statute.

Disclosed Principal • A principal whose identity is known to a third party at the time the agent makes a contract with the third party.

Discovery • A phase in the litigation process during which the opposing parties may obtain information from each other and from third parties prior to trial.

Disparagement of Property • An economically injurious falsehood made about another's product or property; a general term for torts that are more specifically referred to as slander of quality or slander of title.

Disparate-Impact Discrimination • A form of employment discrimination that results from certain employer practices or procedures that, although not discriminatory on their face, have a discriminatory effect.

Disparate-Treatment Discrimination • A form of employment discrimination resulting when an employer intentionally discriminates against employees who are members of protected classes.

Dissociation • The severance of the relationship between a partner and a partnership when the partner ceases to be associated with the carrying on of the partnership business.

Dissolution • The formal disbanding of a partnership or a corporation.

Distributed Network • A network that can be used by persons located (distributed) around the country or the globe to share computer files.

Distribution Agreement • A contract between a seller and a distributor of the seller's products setting out the terms and conditions of the distributorship.

Diversity of Citizenship • Under Article III, Section 2, of the U.S. Constitution, a basis for federal district court jurisdiction over a lawsuit between (1) citizens of different states, (2) a foreign country and citizens of a state or of different states, or (3) citizens of a state and citizens or subjects of a foreign country. The amount in controversy must be more than $75,000 before a federal district court can take jurisdiction in such cases.

Divestiture • The act of selling one or more of a company's divisions or parts, such as a subsidiary or plant; often mandated by the courts in merger or monopolization cases.

Dividend • A distribution to corporate shareholders of corporate profits or income, disbursed in proportion to the number of shares held.

Docket • The list of cases entered on a court's calendar and thus scheduled to be heard by the court.

Domain Name • The last part of an Internet address, such as "westlaw.com." The top level (the part of the name to the right of the period) indicates the type of entity that operates the site (com is an abbreviation for "commercial"). The second level (the part of the name to the left of the period) is chosen by the entity.

Domestic Corporation • In a given state, a corporation that does business in, and is organized under the law of, that state.

Double Jeopardy • A situation occurring when a person is tried twice for the same criminal offense; prohibited by the Fifth Amendment to the U.S. Constitution.

Down Payment • The part of the purchase price of real property that is paid up front, reducing the amount of the loan or mortgage.

Dram Shop Act • A state statute that imposes liability on the owners of bars and taverns, as well as those who serve alcoholic drinks to the public, for injuries resulting from accidents caused by intoxicated persons when the sellers or servers of alcoholic drinks contributed to the intoxication.

Due Process Clause • The provisions in the Fifth and Fourteenth Amendments to the U.S. Constitution that guarantee that no person shall be deprived of life, liberty, or property without due process of law. Similar clauses are found in most state constitutions.

Dumping • The selling of goods in a foreign country at a price below the price charged for the same goods in the domestic market.

Duress • Unlawful pressure brought to bear on a person, causing the person to perform an act that she or he would not otherwise have performed.

Duty of Care • The duty of all persons, as established by tort law, to exercise a reasonable amount of care in their dealings with others. Failure to exercise due care, which is normally determined by the reasonable person standard, constitutes the tort of negligence.

E

E-Agent • A computer program that by electronic or other automated means can independently initiate an action or respond to electronic messages or data without review by an individual.

Easement • A nonpossessory right to use another's property in a manner established by either express or implied agreement.

E-Contract • A contract that is formed electronically.

E-Evidence • Evidence that consists of computer-generated or electronically recorded information, including e-mail, voice mail, spreadsheets, document preparation systems, and other data.

Embezzlement • The fraudulent appropriation of funds or other property by a person to whom the funds or property has been entrusted.

Eminent Domain • The power of a government to take land from private citizens for public use on the payment of just compensation.

Employment at Will • A common law doctrine under which either party may terminate an employment relationship at any time for any reason, unless a contract specifies otherwise.

Employment Discrimination • Treating employees or job applicants unequally on the basis of race, color, national origin, religion, gender, age, or disability; prohibited by federal statutes.

Enabling Legislation • A statute enacted by Congress that authorizes the creation of an administrative agency and specifies the name, composition, and powers of the agency being created.

Entrapment • In criminal law, a defense in which the defendant claims that he or she was induced by a public official—usually an undercover agent or police officer—to commit a crime that he or she would not otherwise have committed.

Entrepreneur • One who initiates and assumes the financial risk of a new business enterprise and undertakes to provide or control its management.

Environmental Impact Statement (EIS) • A statement required by the National Environmental Policy Act for any major federal action that will significantly affect the quality of the environment. The statement must analyze the action's impact on the environment and explore alternative actions that might be taken.

Equal Dignity Rule • In most states, a rule stating that express authority given to an agent must be in writing if the contract to be made on behalf of the principal is required to be in writing.

Equal Protection Clause • The provision in the Fourteenth Amendment to the U.S. Constitution that guarantees that a state may not "deny to any person within its jurisdiction the equal protection of the laws." This clause mandates that the state governments must treat similarly situated individuals in a similar manner.

Equitable Principles and Maxims • General propositions or principles of law that have to do with fairness (equity).

Equitable Right of Redemption • The right of a borrower who is in default on a mortgage loan to redeem or purchase the property prior to foreclosure proceedings.

Escrow Account • An account, generally held in the name of the depositor and the escrow agent, containing funds to be paid to a third person on fulfillment of the escrow condition.

E-Signature • As defined by the Uniform Electronic Transactions Act, "an electronic sound, symbol, or process attached to or logically associated with a record and executed or adopted by a person with the intent to sign the record."

Establishment Clause • The provision in the First Amendment to the U.S. Constitution that prohibits the government from establishing any state-sponsored religion or enacting any law that promotes religion or favors one religion over another.

Ethical Reasoning • A reasoning process in which an individual links his or her moral convictions or ethical standards to the particular situation at hand.

Ethics • Moral principles and values applied to social behavior.

Eviction • A landlord's act of depriving a tenant of possession of the leased premises.

Exclusionary Rule • In criminal procedure, a rule under which any evidence that is obtained in violation of the accused's rights guaranteed by the Fourth, Fifth, and Sixth Amendments to the U.S. Constitution, as well as any evidence derived from illegally obtained evidence, will not be admissible in court.

Exclusive-Dealing Contract • An agreement under which a seller forbids a buyer to purchase products from the seller's competitors.

Exclusive Jurisdiction • Jurisdiction that exists when a case can be heard only in a particular court or type of court.

Exculpatory Clause • A clause that releases a contractual party from liability in the event of monetary or physical injury, no matter who is at fault.

Executed Contract • A contract that has been completely performed by both parties.

Executory Contract • A contract that has not yet been fully performed.

Export • The sale of goods and services by domestic firms to buyers located in other countries.

Express Contract • A contract in which the terms of the agreement are stated in words, oral or written.

Express Warranty • A seller's or lessor's oral or written promise, ancillary to an underlying sales or lease agreement, as to the quality, description, or performance of the goods being sold or leased.

Expropriation • The seizure by a government of a privately owned business or personal property for a proper public purpose and with just compensation.

F

Federal Form of Government • A system of government in which the states form a union and the sovereign power is divided between the central government and the member states.

Federal Question • A question that pertains to the U.S. Constitution, acts of Congress, or treaties. A federal question provides a basis for federal jurisdiction.

Fee Simple Absolute • An ownership interest in land in which the owner has the greatest possible aggregation of rights, privileges, and power. Ownership in fee simple absolute is assigned forever to a person and her or his heirs without limitation.

Felony • A crime—such as arson, murder, rape, or robbery—that carries the most severe sanctions, ranging from one year in a state or federal prison to the death penalty.

Fiduciary • As a noun, a person having a duty created by his or her undertaking to act primarily for another's benefit in matters connected with the undertaking. As an adjective, a relationship founded on trust and confidence.

Filtering Software • A computer program that is designed to block access to certain Web sites, based on their content. The software blocks the retrieval of a site whose URL or key words are on a list within the program.

Final Order • The final decision of an administrative agency on an issue. If no appeal is taken, or if the case is not reviewed or considered anew by the agency commission, the administrative law judge's initial order becomes the final order of the agency.

Firm Offer • An offer (by a merchant) that is irrevocable without the necessity of consideration for a stated period of time or, if no definite period is stated, for a reasonable time (neither period to exceed three months). A firm offer by a merchant must be in writing and must be signed by the offeror.

Fixed-Rate Mortgage • A standard mortgage with a fixed, or unchanging, rate of interest. The loan payments on these mortgages remain the same for the duration of the loan.

Fixed-Term Tenancy • A type of tenancy under which property is leased for a specified period of time, such as a month, a year, or a period of years; also called a tenancy for years.

Fixture • An item that was once personal property but has become attached to real property in such a way that it takes on the characteristics of real property and becomes part of that real property.

Forbearance • An agreement between a lender and a borrower in which the lender agrees to temporarily cease requiring mortgage payments, delay foreclosure, or accept smaller payments than previously scheduled.

Force Majeure Clause • A provision in a contract stipulating that certain unforeseen events—such as war, political upheavals, or acts of God—will excuse a party from liability for nonperformance of contractual obligations.

Foreclosure • A proceeding in which a mortgagee either takes title to or forces the sale of the mortgagor's property in satisfaction of a debt.

Foreign Corporation • In a given state, a corporation that does business in the state without being incorporated therein.

Foreign Exchange Market • A worldwide system in which foreign currencies are bought and sold.

Forgery • The fraudulent making or altering of any writing in a way that changes the legal rights and liabilities of another.

Formal Contract • A contract that by law requires a specific form for its validity.

Forum-Selection Clause • A provision in a contract designating the court, jurisdiction, or tribunal that will decide any disputes arising under the contract.

Franchise • Any arrangement in which the owner of a trademark, trade name, or copyright licenses another to use that trademark, trade name, or copyright in the selling of goods or services.

Franchisee • One receiving a license to use another's (the franchisor's) trademark, trade name, or copyright in the sale of goods and services.

Franchisor • One licensing another (the franchisee) to use the owner's trademark, trade name, or copyright in the selling of goods or services.

Fraudulent Misrepresentation • Any misrepresentation, either by misstatement or by omission of a material fact, knowingly made with the intention of deceiving another and on which a reasonable person would and does rely to his or her detriment.

Free Exercise Clause • The provision in the First Amendment to the U.S. Constitution that prohibits the government from interfering with people's religious practices or forms of worship.

Free-Writing Prospectus • Any type of written, electronic, or graphic offer that describes the issuing corporation or its securities and includes a legend indicating that the investor may obtain the prospectus at the Securities and Exchange Commission's Web site.

Frustration of Purpose • A court-created doctrine under which a party to a contract will be relieved of his or her duty to perform when the objective purpose for performance no longer exists due to reasons beyond that party's control.

G

Garnishment • A legal process used by a creditor to collect a debt by seizing property of the debtor (such as wages) that is being held by a third party (such as the debtor's employer).

General Partner • In a limited partnership, a partner who assumes responsibility for the management of the partnership and liability for all partnership debts.

Good Samaritan Statute • A state statute stipulating that persons who provide emergency services to, or rescue, someone in peril cannot be sued for negligence, unless they act recklessly, thereby causing further harm.

Grand Jury • A group of citizens called to decide, after hearing the state's evidence, whether a reasonable basis (probable cause) exists for believing that a crime has been committed and that a trial ought to be held.

Group Boycott • The refusal by a group of competitors to deal with a particular person or firm; prohibited by the Sherman Act.

Guarantor • A person who agrees to satisfy the debt of another (the debtor) only after the principal debtor defaults. Thus, a guarantor's liability is secondary.

H

Hacker • A person who uses one computer to break into another.

Herfindahl-Hirschman Index (HHI) • An index of market power used to calculate whether a merger of two businesses will result in sufficient monopoly power to violate antitrust laws.

Historical School • A school of legal thought that emphasizes the evolutionary process of law and looks to the past to discover what the principles of contemporary law should be.

Home Equity Loan • A loan in which the lender accepts a person's home equity (the portion of the home's value that is paid off) as collateral, which can be seized if the loan is not repaid on time.

Homeowners' Insurance • Insurance that protects a homeowner's property against damage from storms, fire, and other hazards. Lenders may require that a borrower carry homeowners' insurance on mortgaged property.

Homestead Exemption • A law permitting a debtor to retain the family home, either in its entirety or up to a specified dollar amount, free from the claims of unsecured creditors or trustees in bankruptcy.

Horizontal Merger • A merger between two firms that are competing in the same marketplace.

Horizontal Restraint • Any agreement that in some way restrains competition between rival firms competing in the same market.

Hot-Cargo Agreement • An agreement in which an employer voluntarily agrees with a union not to handle, use, or deal in other employers' goods that were not produced by union employees; a type of secondary boycott explicitly prohibited by the Labor-Management Reporting and Disclosure Act of 1959.

Hybrid Mortgage • A mortgage that starts as a fixed-rate mortgage and then converts to an adjustable-rate mortgage.

I

I-9 Verification • A process that all employers in the United States must perform within three business days of hiring a new worker to verify the employment eligibility and identity of the worker by completing an I-9 Employment Eligibility Verification form.

I-551 Alien Registration Receipt • A document, commonly known as a "green card," that shows that a foreign-born individual has been lawfully admitted for permanent residency in the United States. Persons seeking employment can prove to prospective employers that they are legally in the United States by showing this receipt.

Identity Theft • The theft of identity information, such as a person's name, driver's license number, or Social Security number. The information is then usually used to access the victim's financial resources.

Implied Contract • A contract formed in whole or in part from the conduct of the parties (as opposed to an express contract).

Implied Warranty • A warranty that the law derives by implication or inference from the nature of the transaction or the relative situation or circumstances of the parties.

Implied Warranty of Fitness for a Particular Purpose • A warranty that goods sold or leased are fit for a particular purpose. The warranty arises when any seller or lessor knows the particular purpose for which a buyer or lessee will use the goods and knows that the buyer or lessee is relying on the skill and judgment of the seller or lessor to select suitable goods.

Implied Warranty of Habitability • An implied promise by a seller of a new house that the house is fit for human habitation, meaning in a condition that is safe and suitable for people to live there.

Implied Warranty of Merchantability • A warranty that goods being sold or leased are reasonably fit for the ordinary purpose for which they are sold or leased, are properly packaged and labeled, and are of fair quality. The warranty automatically arises in every sale or lease of goods made by a merchant who deals in goods of the kind sold or leased.

Impossibility of Performance • A doctrine under which a party to a contract is relieved of his or her duty to perform when performance becomes objectively impossible or totally impracticable (through no fault of either party).

Incidental Beneficiary • A third party who incidentally benefits from a contract but whose benefit was not the reason the contract was formed. An incidental beneficiary has no rights in a contract and cannot sue to have the contract enforced.

Independent Contractor • One who works for, and receives payment from, an employer but whose working conditions and methods are not controlled by the employer. An independent contractor is not an employee but may be an agent.

Indictment • A charge by a grand jury that a named person has committed a crime.

Industrial Use • Use of land for light or heavy manufacturing, shipping, or heavy transportation.

Informal Contract • A contract that does not require a specified form or formality to be valid.

Information • A formal accusation or complaint (without an indictment) issued in certain types of actions (usually criminal actions involving lesser crimes) by a government prosecutor.

Information Return • A tax return submitted by a partnership that only reports the income and losses earned by the business. The partnership as an entity does not pay taxes on the income received by the partnership.

Initial Order • In the context of administrative law, an agency's disposition in a matter other than a rulemaking. An administrative law judge's initial order becomes final unless it is appealed.

Inside Director • A member of the board of directors who is also an officer of the corporation.

Insider Trading • The purchase or sale of securities on the basis of inside information—that is, information that has not been made available to the public.

Intangible Property • Property that cannot be seen or touched but exists only conceptually, such as corporate stocks and bonds. Article 2 of the UCC does not govern intangible property.

Intellectual Property • Property resulting from intellectual, creative processes.

Intended Beneficiary • A third party for whose benefit a contract is formed. An intended beneficiary can sue the promisor if such a contract is breached.

Intentional Tort • A wrongful act knowingly committed.

Interest-Only (IO) Mortgage • A mortgage that gives the borrower the option of paying only the interest portion of the monthly payment and forgoing the payment of principal for a specified period of time. After the IO payment option is exhausted, the borrower's payment increases to include payments on the principal.

International Law • The law that governs relations among nations. International customs, treaties, and organizations are important sources of international law.

International Organization • Any membership group that operates across national borders. These organizations can be governmental organizations, such as the United Nations, or nongovernmental organizations, such as the Red Cross.

Interpretive Rule • An administrative agency rule that is simply a statement or opinion issued by the agency explaining how it interprets and intends to apply the statutes it enforces. Such rules are not binding on private individuals or organizations.

Interrogatories • A series of written questions for which written answers are prepared by a party to a lawsuit, usually with the assistance of the party's attorney, and then signed under oath.

Inverse Condemnation • The taking of private property by the government without payment of just compensation as required by the

U.S. Constitution. The owner must sue the government to recover just compensation.

Investment Company • A company that acts on the behalf of many smaller shareholders and owners by buying a large portfolio of securities and professionally managing that portfolio.

Investment Contract • In securities law, a transaction in which a person invests in a common enterprise reasonably expecting profits that are derived primarily from the efforts of others.

J

Joint and Several Liability • In partnership law, a doctrine under which a plaintiff can file a lawsuit against all of the partners together (jointly) or one or more of the partners separately (severally, or individually). All partners in a partnership can be held liable regardless of whether the partner participated in, knew about, or ratified the conduct that gave rise to the lawsuit.

Joint Liability • In partnership law, partners share liability for partnership obligations and debts. Thus, if a third party sues a partner on a partnership debt, the partner has the right to insist that the other partners be sued with him or her.

Judicial Foreclosure • A court-supervised foreclosure proceeding in which the court determines the validity of the debt and, if the borrower is in default, issues a judgment for the lender.

Judicial Review • The process by which a court decides on the constitutionality of legislative enactments and actions of the executive branch.

Jurisdiction • The authority of a court to hear and decide a specific case.

Jurisprudence • The science or philosophy of law.

Justiciable Controversy • A controversy that is not hypothetical or academic but real and substantial; a requirement that must be satisfied before a court will hear a case.

L

Larceny • The wrongful taking and carrying away of another person's personal property with the intent to permanently deprive the owner of the property. Some states classify larceny as either grand or petit, depending on the property's value.

Law • A body of enforceable rules governing relationships among individuals and between individuals and their society.

Lease • Under Article 2A of the UCC, a transfer of the right to possess and use goods for a period of time in exchange for payment.

Lease Agreement • In regard to the lease of goods, an agreement in which one person (the lessor) agrees to transfer the right to the possession and use of property to another person (the lessee) in exchange for rental payments.

Leasehold Estate • An interest in real property that is held by a tenant for only a limited time under a lease. In every leasehold estate, the tenant has a qualified right to possess and/or use the land.

Legal Positivism • A school of legal thought centered on the assumption that there is no law higher than the laws created by a national government. Laws must be obeyed, even if they are unjust, to prevent anarchy.

Legal Realism • A school of legal thought of the 1920s and 1930s that generally advocated a less abstract and more realistic approach to the law, an approach that takes into account customary practices and the circumstances in which transactions take place. This school left a lasting imprint on American jurisprudence.

Legislative Rule • An administrative agency rule that carries the same weight as a congressionally enacted statute.

Lessee • A person who acquires the right to the possession and use of another's goods in exchange for rental payments.

Lessor • A person who transfers the right to the possession and use of goods to another in exchange for rental payments.

Letter of Credit • A written instrument, usually issued by a bank on behalf of a customer or other person, in which the issuer promises to honor drafts or other demands for payment by third parties in accordance with the terms of the instrument.

Libel • Defamation in writing or other form having the quality of permanence (such as a digital recording).

License • In the context of intellectual property law, an agreement permitting the use of a trademark, copyright, patent, or trade secret for certain limited purposes. In the context of real property, a revocable right or privilege of a person to come onto another person's land.

Lien • A claim against specific property to satisfy a debt.

Life Estate • An interest in land that exists only for the duration of the life of some person, usually the holder of the estate.

Limited Liability Company (LLC) • A hybrid form of business enterprise that offers the limited liability of the corporation but the tax advantages of a partnership.

Limited Liability Partnership (LLP) • A hybrid form of business organization that is used mainly by professionals who normally do business in a partnership. Like a partnership, an LLP is a pass-through entity for tax purposes, but the personal liability of the partners is limited.

Limited Partner • In a limited partnership, a partner who contributes capital to the partnership but has no right to participate in the management and operation of the business. The limited partner assumes no liability for partnership debts beyond the capital contributed.

Limited Partnership (LP) • A partnership consisting of one or more general partners (who manage the business and are liable to the full extent of their personal assets for debts of the partnership) and one or more limited partners (who contribute only assets and are liable only up to the extent of their contributions).

Liquidated Damages • An amount, stipulated in a contract, that the parties to the contract believe to be a reasonable estimate of the damages that will occur in the event of a breach.

Liquidation • The sale of all of the nonexempt assets of a debtor and the distribution of the proceeds to the debtor's creditors.

Litigation • The process of resolving a dispute through the court system.

Lockout • A lockout occurs when the employer shuts down the business to prevent employees from working. Lockouts are the employer's counterpart to the worker's right to strike and usually are used when a strike is imminent.

Long Arm Statute • A state statute that permits a state to obtain personal jurisdiction over nonresident defendants. A defendant must have certain "minimum contacts" with that state for the statute to apply.

M

Mailbox Rule • A rule providing that an acceptance of an offer becomes effective on dispatch (on being placed in an official mailbox), if mail is, expressly or impliedly, an authorized means of communication of acceptance to the offeror.

Malpractice • Professional misconduct or the lack of the requisite degree of skill as a professional. Negligence—the failure to exercise due care—on the part of a professional, such as a physician, is commonly referred to as malpractice.

Malware • Any program that is harmful to a computer or a computer user; for example, worms and viruses.

Market Concentration • The degree to which a small number of firms control a large percentage share of a relevant market; determined by calculating the percentages held by the largest firms in that market.

Market Power • The power of a firm to control the market price of its product. A monopoly has the greatest degree of market power.

Market-Share Liability • A theory under which liability is shared among all firms that manufactured and distributed a particular product during a certain period of time. This form of liability sharing is used only when the true source of the harmful product is unidentifiable.

Mechanic's Lien • A statutory lien on the real property of another to ensure payment for work performed and materials furnished for the repair or improvement of real property, such as a building.

Mediation • A method of settling disputes outside the courts by using the services of a neutral third party, who acts as a communicating agent between the parties and assists them in negotiating a settlement.

Member • A person who has an ownership interest in a limited liability company.

Mens Rea • Mental state, or intent. Normally, a wrongful mental state is as necessary as a wrongful act to establish criminal liability. What constitutes such a mental state varies according to the wrongful action. Thus, for murder, the mens rea is the intent to take a life.

Merchant • A person who is engaged in the purchase and sale of goods. Under the UCC, a person who deals in goods of the kind involved in the sales contract or who holds herself or himself out as having skill or knowledge peculiar to the practices or goods being purchased or sold.

Meta Tag • A key word in a document that can serve as an index reference to the document. On the Web, search engines return results based, in part, on these tags in Web documents.

Minimum Wage • The lowest wage, either by government regulation or union contract, that an employer may pay an hourly worker.

Mirror Image Rule • A common law rule that requires that the terms of the offeree's acceptance adhere exactly to the terms of the offeror's offer for a valid contract to be formed.

Misdemeanor • A lesser crime than a felony, punishable by a fine or incarceration in jail for up to one year.

Mitigation of Damages • A rule requiring a plaintiff to do whatever is reasonable to minimize the damages caused by the defendant.

Money Laundering • Engaging in financial transactions to conceal the identity, source, or destination of illegally gained funds.

Monopolization • The possession of monopoly power in the relevant market and the willful acquisition or maintenance of that power, as distinguished from growth or development as a consequence of a superior product, business acumen, or historic accident.

Monopoly • A term generally used to describe a market in which there is a single seller or a very limited number of sellers.

Monopoly Power • The ability of a monopoly to dictate what takes place in a given market.

Moral Minimum • The minimum degree of ethical behavior expected of a business firm, which is usually defined as compliance with the law.

Mortgage • A written document that gives a creditor (the mortgagee) an interest in, or lien on, the debtor's (mortgagor's) real property as security for a debt.

Motion for a Directed Verdict • In a jury trial, a motion for the judge to take the decision out of the hands of the jury and to direct a verdict for the party who filed the motion on the ground that the other party has not produced sufficient evidence to support her or his claim.

Motion for a New Trial • A motion asserting that the trial was so fundamentally flawed (because of error, newly discovered evidence, prejudice, or another reason) that a new trial is necessary to prevent a miscarriage of justice.

Motion for Judgment _n.o.v._ • A motion requesting the court to grant judgment in favor of the party making the motion on the ground that the jury's verdict against him or her was unreasonable and erroneous.

Motion for Judgment on the Pleadings • A motion by either party to a lawsuit at the close of the pleadings requesting the court to decide the issue solely on the pleadings without proceeding to trial. The motion will be granted only if no facts are in dispute.

Motion for Summary Judgment • A motion requesting the court to enter a judgment without proceeding to trial. The motion can be based on evidence outside the pleadings and will be granted only if no facts are in dispute.

Motion to Dismiss • A pleading in which a defendant asserts that the plaintiff's claim fails to state a cause of action (that is, has no basis in law) or that there are other grounds on which the suit should be dismissed. Although the defendant normally is the party requesting a dismissal, either the plaintiff or the court can also make a motion to dismiss the case.

Multiple Product Order • An order issued by the Federal Trade Commission to a firm that has engaged in deceptive advertising by which the firm is required to cease and desist from false advertising not only in regard to the product that was the subject of the action but also in regard to all the firm's other products.

Mutual Fund • A specific type of investment company that continually buys or sells to investors shares of ownership in a portfolio.

Mutual Rescission • An agreement between the parties to cancel their contract, releasing the parties from further obligations under the contract. The object of the agreement is to restore the parties to the positions they would have occupied had no contract ever been formed.

N

National Law • Law that pertains to a particular nation (as opposed to international law).

Natural Law • The belief that government and the legal system should reflect universal moral and ethical principles that are inherent in human nature. The natural law school is the oldest and one of the more significant schools of legal thought.

Negative Amortization • This occurs when the payment made by the borrower is less than the interest due on the loan and the difference is added to the principal. As a result, the balance owed on the loan increases rather than decreases over time.

Negligence • The failure to exercise the standard of care that a reasonable person would exercise in similar circumstances.

Negligence _Per Se_ • An action or failure to act in violation of a statutory requirement.

Negotiation • A process in which parties attempt to settle their dispute informally, with or without attorneys to represent them.

Nonpossessory Interest • In the context of real property, an interest in land that does not include any right to possess the property.

Normal Trade Relations (NTR) Status • A status granted by each member country of the World Trade Organization to other member countries. Each member is required to treat other members at least as well as it treats the country that receives its most favorable treatment with respect to trade.

Notary Public • A public official authorized to attest to the authenticity of signatures.

Notice-and-Comment Rulemaking • A procedure in agency rulemaking that requires notice, opportunity for comment, and a published draft of the final rule.

Notice of Default • A formal notice to a borrower that he or she is in default on mortgage payments and may face foreclosure if the payments are not brought up to date. The notice is filed by the lender in the county where the property is located.

Notice of Sale • A formal notice to a borrower who is in default on a mortgage that the mortgaged property will be sold in a foreclosure proceeding. The notice is sent to the borrower and is typically recorded with the county, posted on the property, and published in a newspaper.

Novation • The substitution, by agreement, of a new contract for an old one, with the rights under the old one being terminated. Typically, novation involves the substitution of a new party for one of the original parties to the contract.

Nuisance • A common law doctrine under which persons may be held liable for using their property in a manner that unreasonably interferes with others' rights to use or enjoy their own property.

O

Objective Theory of Contracts • A theory under which the intent to form a contract will be judged by outward, objective facts (what the party said when entering into the contract, how the party acted or appeared, and the circumstances surrounding the transaction) as interpreted by a reasonable person, rather than by the party's own secret, subjective intentions.

Offer • A promise or commitment to perform or refrain from performing some specified act in the future.

Offeree • A person to whom an offer is made.

Offeror • A person who makes an offer.

Online Dispute Resolution (ODR) • The resolution of disputes with the assistance of organizations that offer dispute-resolution services via the Internet.

Operating Agreement • In a limited liability company, an agreement in which the members set forth the details of how the business will be managed and operated. State statutes typically give the members wide latitude in deciding for themselves the rules that will govern their organization.

Option Contract • A contract under which the offeror cannot revoke the offer for a stipulated time period.

Order for Relief • A court's grant of assistance to a complainant. In bankruptcy proceedings, the order relieves the debtor of the immediate obligation to pay the debts listed in the bankruptcy petition.

Ordinance • A regulation enacted by a city or county legislative body that becomes part of that state's statutory law.

Outside Director • A member of the board of directors who does not hold a management position at the corporation.

P

Partially Disclosed Principal • A principal whose identity is unknown by a third party, but the third party knows that the agent is or may be acting for a principal at the time the agent and the third party form a contract.

Partnering Agreement • An agreement between a seller and a buyer who frequently do business with each other concerning the terms and conditions that will apply to all subsequently formed electronic contracts.

Partnership • An agreement by two or more persons to carry on, as co-owners, a business for profit.

Pass-Through Entity • A business entity that has no tax liability. The entity's income is passed through to the owners, and the owners pay taxes on the income.

Patent • A government grant that gives an inventor the exclusive right or privilege to make, use, or sell his or her invention for a limited time period.

Peer-to-Peer (P2P) Networking • The sharing of resources (such as files, hard drives, and processing styles) among multiple computers without the need for a central network server.

Penalty • A contractual clause that states that a certain amount of monetary damages will be paid in the event of a future default or breach of contract. The damages are a punishment for a default and not an accurate measure of compensation for the contract's breach. The agreement as to the penalty amount will not be enforced, and recovery will be limited to actual damages.

Perfect Tender Rule • A rule under which a seller or lessor is required to deliver goods that conform perfectly to the requirements of the contract. A tender of nonconforming goods automatically constitutes a breach of contract.

Performance • In contract law, the fulfillment of one's duties arising under a contract with another; the normal way of discharging one's contractual obligations.

Periodic Tenancy • A lease interest in land for an indefinite period involving payment of rent at fixed intervals, such as week to week, month to month, or year to year.

***Per Se* Violation** • A type of anticompetitive agreement that is considered to be so injurious to the public that there is no need to determine whether it actually injures market competition. Rather, it is in itself (*per se*) a violation of the Sherman Act.

Persuasive Authority • Any legal authority or source of law that a court may look to for guidance but on which it need not rely in making its decision. Persuasive authorities include cases from other jurisdictions and secondary sources of law.

Petition in Bankruptcy • The document that is filed with a bankruptcy court to initiate bankruptcy proceedings. The official forms required for a petition in bankruptcy must be completed accurately, sworn to under oath, and signed by the debtor.

Petty Offense • In criminal law, the least serious kind of criminal offense, such as a traffic or building-code violation.

Phishing • The attempt to acquire financial data, passwords, or other personal information from consumers by sending e-mail messages that purport to be from a legitimate business, such as a bank or a credit-card company.

Piercing the Corporate Veil • An action in which a court disregards the corporate entity and holds the shareholders personally liable for corporate debts and obligations.

Plaintiff • One who initiates a lawsuit.

Plea Bargaining • The process by which a criminal defendant and the prosecutor in a criminal case work out a mutually satisfactory disposition of the case, subject to court approval; usually involves the defendant's pleading guilty to a lesser offense in return for a lighter sentence.

Pleadings • Statements made by the plaintiff and the defendant in a lawsuit that detail the facts, charges, and defenses involved in the litigation. The complaint and answer are part of the pleadings.

Police Powers • Powers possessed by the states as part of their inherent sovereignty. These powers may be exercised to protect or promote the public order, health, safety, morals, and general welfare.

Potentially Responsible Party • A party liable for the costs of cleaning up a hazardous waste—disposal site. Any person who generated the hazardous waste, transported it, owned or operated the waste site at the time of disposal, or owns or operates the site at the present time may be responsible for some or all of the clean-up costs.

Power of Attorney • A written document, which is usually notarized, authorizing another to act as one's agent; can be special (permitting the agent to do specified acts only) or general (permitting the agent to transact all business for the principal).

Power of Sale Foreclosure • A foreclosure procedure that is not court supervised and is available only in some states.

Precedent • A court decision that furnishes an example or authority for deciding subsequent cases involving identical or similar facts.

Predatory Pricing • The pricing of a product below cost with the intent to drive competitors out of the market.

Predominant-Factor Test • A test courts use to determine whether a contract is primarily for the sale of goods or for the sale of services.

Preemption • A doctrine under which certain federal laws preempt, or take precedence over, conflicting state or local laws.

Preemptive Rights • Rights held by shareholders that entitle them to purchase newly issued shares of a corporation's stock, equal in percentage to shares already held, before the stock is offered to any outside buyers. Preemptive rights enable shareholders to maintain their proportionate ownership and voice in the corporation.

Preference • In bankruptcy proceedings, property transfers or payments made by the debtor that favor (give preference to) one creditor over others. The bankruptcy trustee is allowed to recover payments made both voluntarily and involuntarily to one creditor in preference over another.

Preferred Creditor • One who has received a preferential transfer from a debtor.

Prepayment Penalty Clause • A clause in a mortgage loan contract that requires the borrower to pay a penalty if the mortgage is repaid in full within a certain period. A prepayment penalty helps to protect the lender if the borrower refinances within a short time after obtaining a mortgage.

Price Discrimination • Setting prices in such a way that two competing buyers pay two different prices for an identical product or service.

Price-Fixing Agreement • An agreement between competitors to fix the prices of products or services at a certain level.

***Prima Facie* Case** • A case in which the plaintiff has produced sufficient evidence of his or her claim that the case can go to a jury; a case in which the evidence compels a decision for the plaintiff if the defendant produces no affirmative defense or evidence to disprove the plaintiff's assertion.

Primary Source of Law • A document that establishes the law on a particular issue, such as a constitution, a statute, an administrative rule, or a court decision.

Principle of Rights • The principle that human beings have certain fundamental rights (to life, liberty, and the pursuit of happiness, for example). Those who adhere to this "rights theory" believe that a key factor in determining whether a business decision is ethical is how that decision affects the rights of various groups, including employees, customers, and suppliers.

Privilege • A legal right, exemption, or immunity granted to a person or a class of persons. In the context of defamation, an absolute privilege immunizes the person making the statements from a lawsuit, regardless of whether the statements were malicious.

Probable Cause • Reasonable grounds for believing that a person should be arrested or searched.

Probate Court • A state court of limited jurisdiction that conducts proceedings relating to the settlement of a deceased person's estate.

Procedural Law • Law that establishes the methods of enforcing the rights established by substantive law.

Product Liability • The legal liability of manufacturers, sellers, and lessors of goods to consumers, users, and bystanders for injuries or damage that are caused by the goods.

Profit • In real property law, the right to enter onto and remove something of value from the property of another.

Promise • An assertion that something either will or will not happen in the future.

Promisee • A person to whom a promise is made.

Promisor • A person who makes a promise.

Promissory Estoppel • A doctrine that applies when a promisor makes a clear and definite promise on which the promisee justifiably relies; such a promise is binding if justice will be better served by the enforcement of the promise.

Prospectus • A written document, required by securities laws, that describes the security being sold, the financial operations of the issuing corporation, and the investment or risk attaching to the security.

Protected Class • A group of persons protected by specific laws because of the group's defining characteristics. Under laws prohibiting employment discrimination, these characteristics include race, color, religion, national origin, gender, age, and disability.

Proximate Cause • Legal cause, which exists when the connection between an act and an injury is strong enough to justify imposing liability.

Proxy • In corporate law, a written agreement between a stockholder and another party in which the stockholder authorizes the other party to vote the stockholder's shares in a certain manner.

Puffery • A seller's or lessor's exaggerated claims concerning the quality of goods. Such claims involve opinions rather than facts and are not considered to be legally binding promises or warranties.

Punitive Damages • Monetary damages that may be awarded to a plaintiff to punish the defendant and deter similar conduct in the future.

Q

Quasi Contract • A fictional contract imposed on parties by a court in the interests of fairness and justice; usually imposed to avoid the unjust enrichment of one party at the expense of another.

Question of Fact • In a lawsuit, an issue that involves only disputed facts, and not what the law is on a given point. Questions of fact are decided by the jury in a jury trial (by the judge if there is no jury).

Question of Law • In a lawsuit, an issue involving the application or interpretation of a law. Only a judge, not a jury, can rule on questions of law.

Quitclaim Deed • A deed intended to pass any title, interest, or claim that the grantor may have in the property without warranting that such title is valid. A quitclaim deed offers the least amount of protection against defects of title.

Quorum • The number of members of a decision-making body that must be present before business may be transacted.

Quota • A set limit on the amount of goods that can be imported.

R

Ratification • The act of accepting and giving legal force to an obligation that previously was not enforceable.

Reaffirmation Agreement • An agreement between a debtor and a creditor in which the debtor reaffirms, or promises to pay, a debt dischargeable in bankruptcy. To be enforceable, the agreement must be made prior to the discharge of the debt by the bankruptcy court.

Reamortize • Restart the amortization schedule (a table of the periodic payments the borrower makes to pay off a debt), changing the way the payments are configured.

Reasonable Person Standard • The standard of behavior expected of a hypothetical "reasonable person"; the standard against which negligence is measured and that must be observed to avoid liability for negligence.

Record • According to the Uniform Electronic Transactions Act, information that is either inscribed on a tangible medium or stored in an electronic or other medium and is retrievable.

Recording Statutes • Statutes that allow deeds, mortgages, and other real property transactions to be recorded so as to provide notice to future purchasers or creditors of an existing claim on the property.

Reformation • A court-ordered correction of a written contract so that it reflects the true intentions of the parties.

Regulation Z • A set of rules issued by the Federal Reserve Board of Governors to implement the provisions of the Truth-in-Lending Act.

Remedy • The relief given to an innocent party to enforce a right or compensate for the violation of a right.

Replevin • An action to recover identified goods in the hands of a party who is wrongfully withholding them from the other party.

Reply • Procedurally, a plaintiff's response to a defendant's answer.

Resale Price Maintenance Agreement • An agreement between a manufacturer and a retailer in which the manufacturer specifies what the retail prices of its products must be.

Rescission • A remedy whereby a contract is canceled and the parties are returned to the positions they occupied before the contract was made; may be effected through the mutual consent of the parties, by their conduct, or by court decree.

Residential Use • Use of land for construction of buildings for human habitation only.

Res Ipsa Loquitur • A doctrine under which negligence may be inferred simply because an event occurred, if it is the type of event that would not occur in the absence of negligence. Literally, the term means "the facts speak for themselves."

Respondeat Superior • Latin for "let the master respond." A doctrine under which a principal or an employer is held liable for the wrongful acts committed by agents or employees while acting within the course and scope of their agency or employment.

Restitution • An equitable remedy under which a person is restored to his or her original position prior to loss or injury, or placed in the position he or she would have been in had the breach not occurred.

Restrictive Covenant • A private restriction on the use of land that is binding on the party that purchases the property originally as well as on subsequent purchasers. If its benefit or obligation passes with the land's ownership, it is said to "run with the land."

Retained Earnings • The portion of a corporation's profits that has not been paid out as dividends to shareholders.

Reverse Mortgage • A loan product typically provided to older homeowners that allows them to extract funds (in either a lump sum or multiple payments) for the equity in their home. The mortgage does not need to be repaid until the home is sold or the owner leaves or dies.

Revocation • In contract law, the withdrawal of an offer by the offeror. Unless the offer is irrevocable, it can be revoked at any time prior to acceptance without liability.

Right of Contribution • The right of a co-surety who pays more than her or his proportionate share on a debtor's default to recover the excess paid from other co-sureties.

Right of Reimbursement • The legal right of a person to be restored, repaid, or indemnified for costs, expenses, or losses incurred or expended on behalf of another.

Right of Subrogation • The right of a person to stand in the place of (be substituted for) another, giving the substituted party the same legal rights that the original party had.

Right-to-Work Law • A state law providing that employees may not be required to join a union as a condition of retaining employment.

Robbery • The act of forcefully and unlawfully taking personal property of any value from another. Force or intimidation is usually necessary for an act of theft to be considered a robbery.

Rulemaking • The actions undertaken by administrative agencies when formally adopting new regulations or amending old ones. Under the Administrative Procedure Act, rulemaking includes notifying the public of proposed rules or changes and receiving and considering the public's comments.

Rule of Four • A rule of the United States Supreme Court under which the Court will not issue a writ of certiorari unless at least four justices approve of the decision to issue the writ.

Rule of Reason • A test by which a court balances the positive effects (such as economic efficiency) of an agreement against its potentially anticompetitive effects. In antitrust litigation, many practices are analyzed under the rule of reason.

S

Sale • The passing of title to property from the seller to the buyer for a price.

Sales Contract • A contract for the sale of goods under which the ownership of goods is transferred from a seller to a buyer for a price.

Scienter • Knowledge on the part of the misrepresenting party that material facts have been falsely represented or omitted with an intent to deceive.

S Corporation • A close business corporation that has met certain requirements set out in the Internal Revenue Code and thus qualifies for special income tax treatment. Essentially, an S corporation is taxed the same as a partnership, but its owners enjoy the privilege of limited liability.

Search Warrant • An order granted by a public authority, such as a judge, that authorizes law enforcement personnel to search particular premises or property.

Seasonably • Within a specified time period or, if no period is specified, within a reasonable time.

Secondary Boycott • A union's refusal to work for, purchase from, or handle the products of a secondary employer, with whom the union has no dispute, in order to force that employer to stop doing business with the primary employer, with whom the union has a labor dispute.

Secondary Source of Law • A publication that summarizes or interprets the law, such as a legal encyclopedia, a legal treatise, or an article in a law review.

SEC Rule 10b-5 • A rule of the Securities and Exchange Commission that makes it unlawful, in connection with the purchase or sale of any security, to make any untrue statement of a material fact or to omit a material fact if such omission causes the statement to be misleading.

Security • Generally, a stock certificate, bond, note, debenture, warrant, or other document or record evidencing an ownership interest in a corporation or a promise of repayment of debt by a corporation.

Self-Defense • The legally recognized privilege to protect oneself or one's property against injury by another. The privilege of self-defense usually applies only to acts that are reasonably necessary to protect oneself, one's property, or another person.

Self-Incrimination • The giving of testimony that may subject the testifier to criminal prosecution. The Fifth Amendment to the U.S. Constitution protects against self-incrimination by providing that no person "shall be compelled in any criminal case to be a witness against himself."

Seniority System • In regard to employment relationships, a system in which those who have worked longest for the employer are first in line for promotions, salary increases, and other benefits. They are also the last to be laid off if the workforce must be reduced.

Service Mark • A mark used in the sale or advertising of services to distinguish the services of one person from those of others. Titles, character names, and other distinctive features of radio and television programs may be registered as service marks.

Sexual Harassment • In the employment context, the demanding of sexual favors in return for job promotions or other benefits, or language or conduct that is so sexually offensive that it creates a hostile working environment.

Shareholder's Derivative Suit • A suit brought by a shareholder to enforce a corporate cause of action against a third party.

Short Sale • A sale of real property by a borrower for an amount that is less than the balance owed on the mortgage loan. The lender must consent to the sale, and the borrower usually must show some financial hardship.

Short-Swing Profits • Profits earned by a purchase and sale, or sale and purchase, of the same security within a six-month period. Under Section 16(b) of the 1934 Securities Exchange Act, these profits must be returned to the corporation if earned by company insiders from transactions in the company's stock.

Shrink-Wrap Agreement • An agreement whose terms are expressed in a document located inside a box in which goods (usually software) are packaged.

Slander • Defamation in oral form.

Slander of Quality (Trade Libel) • The publication of false information about another's product, alleging that it is not what its seller claims.

Slander of Title • The publication of a statement that denies or casts doubt on another's legal ownership of any property, causing financial loss to that property's owner.

Small Claims Court • A special court in which parties may litigate small claims (such as $5,000 or less). Attorneys are not required in small claims courts and, in some states, are not allowed to represent the parties.

Sociological School • A school of legal thought that views the law as a tool for promoting justice in society.

Sole Proprietorship • The simplest form of business organization, in which the owner is the business. The owner reports business income on his or her personal income tax return and is legally responsible for all debts and obligations incurred by the business.

Sovereign Immunity • A doctrine that immunizes foreign nations from the jurisdiction of U.S. courts when certain conditions are satisfied.

Spam • Bulk e-mails, particularly of commercial advertising, sent in large quantities without the consent of the recipients.

Special-Use Permit • A permit that allows an exemption to zoning regulations for a particular piece of property as long as the property owner complies with specific requirements to ensure that the proposed use does not affect the characteristics of the area.

Special Warranty Deed • A deed in which the grantor warrants only that the grantor or seller held good title during his or her ownership of the property and does not warrant that there were no defects of title when the property was held by previous owners.

Specific Performance • An equitable remedy requiring exactly the performance that was specified in a contract; usually granted only when money damages would be an inadequate remedy and the subject matter of the contract is unique (for example, real property).

Standing to Sue • The requirement that an individual must have a sufficient stake in a controversy before he or she can bring a lawsuit. The plaintiff must demonstrate that he or she has been either injured or threatened with injury.

Stare Decisis • A common law doctrine under which judges are obligated to follow the precedents established in prior decisions.

Statute of Frauds • A state statute under which certain types of contracts must be in writing to be enforceable.

Statute of Limitations • A federal or state statute setting the maximum time period during which a certain action can be brought or certain rights enforced.

Statutory Law • The body of law enacted by legislative bodies (as opposed to constitutional law, administrative law, or case law).

Statutory Right of Redemption • A right provided by statute in some states that allows borrowers to redeem or repurchase their property after a judicial foreclosure for a limited period of time.

Stock Buyback • A company's purchase of shares of its own stock on the open market.

Stock Certificate • A certificate issued by a corporation evidencing the ownership of a specified number of shares in the corporation.

Stock Option • A right to buy a given number of shares of stock at a set price, usually within a specified time period.

Stock Warrant • A certificate that grants the owner the option to buy a given number of shares of stock, usually within a set time period.

Strict Liability • Liability regardless of fault. In tort law, strict liability is imposed on those engaged in abnormally dangerous activities, on persons who keep dangerous animals, and on manufacturers or sellers that introduce into commerce goods that are unreasonably dangerous when in a defective condition.

Strike • An action undertaken by unionized workers when collective bargaining fails. The workers leave their jobs, refuse to work, and (typically) picket the employer's workplace.

Sublease • A lease executed by the lessee of real estate to a third person, conveying the same interest that the lessee enjoys but for a shorter term than that held by the lessee.

Subprime Mortgage • A high-risk loan made to a borrower who does not qualify for a standard mortgage because of his or her poor credit rating or high debt-to-income ratio. Lenders typically charge a higher interest rate on subprime mortgages.

Substantive Law • Law that defines, describes, regulates, and creates legal rights and obligations.

Summons • A document informing a defendant that a legal action has been commenced against her or him and that the defendant must appear in court on a certain date to answer the plaintiff's complaint.

Supremacy Clause • The requirement in Article VI of the U.S. Constitution that provides that the Constitution, laws, and treaties of the United States are "the supreme Law of the Land." Under this clause, state and local laws that directly conflict with federal law will be rendered invalid.

Surety • A person, such as a cosigner on a note, who agrees to be primarily responsible for the debt of another.

Suretyship • An express contract in which a third party to a debtor-creditor relationship (the surety) promises to be primarily responsible for the debtor's obligation.

Symbolic Speech • Nonverbal expressions of beliefs. Symbolic speech, which includes gestures, movements, and articles of clothing, is given substantial protection by the courts.

T

Taking • The taking of private property by the government for public use. The government may not take private property for public use without "just compensation."

Tangible Employment Action • A significant change in employment status, such as a change brought about by firing or failing to promote an employee; reassigning the employee to a position with significantly different responsibilities; or effecting a significant change in employment benefits.

Tangible Property • Property that has physical existence and can be distinguished by the senses of touch and sight.

Tariff • A tax on imported goods.

Tenancy at Sufferance • A type of tenancy under which a tenant who, after rightfully being in possession of leased premises, continues (wrongfully) to occupy the property after the lease has terminated. The tenant has no right to possess the property and occupies it only because the person entitled to evict the tenant has not done so.

Tenancy at Will • A type of tenancy that either party can terminate without notice; can arise when a landowner allows a person to live on the premises without paying rent.

Tender • An unconditional offer to perform an obligation by a person who is ready, willing, and able to do so.

Tender of Delivery • Under the Uniform Commercial Code, a seller's or lessor's act of placing conforming goods at the disposal of the buyer or lessee and giving the buyer or lessee whatever notification is reasonably necessary to enable the buyer or lessee to take delivery.

Third Party Beneficiary • One for whose benefit a promise is made in a contract but who is not a party to the contract.

Tippee • A person who receives inside information.

Tort • A civil wrong not arising from a breach of contract; a breach of a legal duty that proximately causes harm or injury to another.

Tortfeasor • One who commits a tort.

Toxic Tort • A civil wrong arising from exposure to a toxic substance, such as asbestos, radiation, or hazardous waste.

Trade Dress • The image and overall appearance of a product—for example, the distinctive decor, menu, layout, and style of service of a particular restaurant. Basically, trade dress is subject to the same protection as trademarks.

Trade Name • A term that is used to indicate part or all of a business's name and that is directly related to the business's reputation and goodwill. Trade names are protected under the common law (and under trademark law, if the name is the same as the firm's trademarked product).

Trade Secret • Information or a process that gives a business an advantage over competitors that do not know the information or process.

Trademark • A distinctive mark, motto, device, or emblem that a manufacturer stamps, prints, or otherwise affixes to the goods it produces so that they may be identified on the market and their origins made known. Once a trademark is established (under the common law or through registration), the owner is entitled to its exclusive use.

Treasury Securities • Government debt issued by the U.S. Department of the Treasury. The interest rate on Treasury securities is often used as a baseline for measuring the rate on loan products with higher interest rates.

Treaty • In international law, a formal written agreement negotiated between two nations or among several nations. In the United States, all treaties must be approved by the Senate.

Treble Damages • Damages that, by statute, are three times the amount that the fact finder determines is owed.

Trespass to Land • The entry onto, above, or below the surface of land owned by another without the owner's permission or legal authorization.

Trespass to Personal Property • The unlawful taking or harming of another's personal property; interference with another's right to the exclusive possession of his or her personal property.

Tying Arrangement • An agreement between a buyer and a seller in which the buyer of a specific product or service becomes obligated to purchase additional products or services from the seller.

U

Ultra Vires • A Latin term meaning "beyond the powers"; in corporate law, acts of a corporation that are beyond its express and implied powers to undertake.

Unconscionable • A contract or clause that is void on the basis of public policy because one party, as a result of his or her disproportionate bargaining power, is forced to accept terms that are unfairly burdensome and that unfairly benefit the dominating party.

Undisclosed Principal • A principal whose identity is unknown by a third person, and the third person has no knowledge that the agent is acting for a principal at the time the agent and the third person form a contract.

Unenforceable Contract • A valid contract rendered unenforceable by some statute or law.

Uniform Law • A model law created by the National Conference of Commissioners on Uniform State Laws and/or the American Law Institute for the states to consider adopting. Each state has the option of adopting or rejecting all or part of a uniform law. If a state adopts the law, it becomes statutory law in that state.

Unilateral Contract • A contract that results when an offer can be accepted only by the offeree's performance.

Unilateral Mistake • A mistake that occurs when one party to a contract is mistaken as to a material fact.

Union Shop • A firm that requires all workers, once employed, to become union members within a specified period of time as a condition of their continued employment.

Unreasonably Dangerous Product • In product liability law, a product that is defective to the point of threatening a consumer's health and safety. A product will be considered unreasonably dangerous if it is dangerous beyond the expectation of the ordinary consumer or if a less dangerous alternative was economically feasible for the manufacturer, but the manufacturer failed to produce it.

Usage of Trade • Any practice or method of dealing having such regularity of observance in a place, vocation, or trade as to justify an expectation that it will be observed with respect to the transaction in question.

U.S. Trustee • A government official who performs certain administrative tasks that a bankruptcy judge would otherwise have to perform.

Utilitarianism • An approach to ethical reasoning that evaluates behavior in light of the consequences of that behavior for those who will be affected by it, rather than on the basis of any absolute ethical or moral values. In utilitarian reasoning, a "good" decision is one that results in the greatest good for the greatest number of people affected by the decision.

V

Validation Notice • An initial notice to a debtor from a collection agency, required by federal law, informing the debtor that he or she has thirty days to challenge the debt and request verification.

Valid Contract • A contract that results when the elements necessary for contract formation are present.

Variance • A form of relief from zoning laws that is granted to a property owner to allow the property to be used in a manner not permitted by zoning regulations.

Venue • The geographic district in which a legal action is tried and from which the jury is selected.

Vertical Merger • The acquisition by a company at one level in a marketing chain of a company at a higher or lower level in the chain (such as a company merging with one of its suppliers or retailers).

Vertical Restraint • Any restraint of trade created by agreements between firms at different levels in the manufacturing and distribution process.

Vertically Integrated Firm • A firm that carries out two or more functional phases (manufacture, distribution, and retailing, for example) of the chain of production.

Vesting • The creation of an absolute or unconditional right or power.

Vicarious Liability • Legal responsibility placed on one person for the acts of another; indirect liability imposed on a supervisory party (such as an employer) for the actions of a subordinate (such as an employee) because of the relationship between the two parties.

Virus • A computer program that can replicate itself over a network, such as the Internet, and interfere with the normal use of a computer. A virus cannot exist as a separate entity and must attach itself to another program to move through a network.

Vishing • A variation of phishing that involves some form of voice communication. The consumer receives either an e-mail or a phone call from someone claiming to be from a legitimate business and asking for personal information. Instead of being asked to respond by e-mail as in phishing, the consumer is asked to call a phone number.

Void Contract • A contract having no legal force or binding effect.

Voidable Contract • A contract that may be legally avoided (canceled) at the option of one or both of the parties.

Voir Dire • An Old French phrase meaning "to speak the truth." In legal language, the process in which the attorneys question prospective jurors to learn about their backgrounds, attitudes, biases, and other characteristics that may affect their ability to serve as impartial jurors.

Voluntary Consent • The knowing and voluntary agreement to the terms of a contract. If a contract is formed as a result of a mistake, misrepresentation, undue influence, or duress, voluntary consent is lacking, and the contract will be voidable.

W

Warranty Deed • A deed in which the grantor assures (warrants to) the grantee that the grantor has title to the property conveyed in the deed. A deed provides the greatest amount of protection for the grantee.

Watered Stock • Shares of stock issued by a corporation for which the corporation receives, as payment, less than the stated value of the shares.

Wetlands • Water-saturated areas of land that are designated by a government agency as protected areas that support wildlife and therefore cannot be filled in or dredged by private contractors or parties without a permit.

Whistleblowing • An employee's disclosure to government authorities, upper-level managers, or the media that the employer is engaged in unsafe or illegal activities.

White-Collar Crime • Nonviolent crime committed by individuals or corporations to obtain a personal or business advantage.

Wildcat Strike • This action occurs when a minority group of workers, perhaps dissatisfied with a labor union's representation, calls its own strike.

Winding Up • The second of two stages in the termination of a partnership or corporation. Once the firm is dissolved, it continues to exist legally until the process of winding up all business affairs is complete.

Workers' Compensation Laws • State statutes establishing an administrative procedure for compensating workers for injuries that arise out of—or in the course of—their employment, regardless of fault.

Workout • An out-of-court agreement between a debtor and creditors in which the parties work out a payment plan or schedule under which the debtor's debts can be discharged.

Workout Agreement • A formal contract in which a debtor and his or her creditors agree to negotiate a payment plan for the amount due on the loan instead of proceeding to foreclosure.

Worm • A computer program that can automatically replicate itself over a network such as the Internet and interfere with the normal use of a computer. A worm does not need to be attached to an existing file to move from one network to another.

Writ of Attachment • A court's order, issued prior to a trial to collect a debt, directing the sheriff or another public officer to seize nonexempt property of the debtor. If the creditor prevails at trial, the seized property can be sold to satisfy the judgment.

Writ of *Certiorari* • A writ from a higher court asking a lower court for the record of a case.

Writ of Execution • A court's order, issued after a judgment has been entered against a debtor, directing the sheriff to seize and sell any of the debtor's nonexempt real or personal property.

Wrongful Discharge • An employer's termination of an employee's employment in violation of the law.

Z

Zoning Laws • Laws that divide a municipality into districts and prescribe the use to which property within each district may be put.

Table of Cases

Index